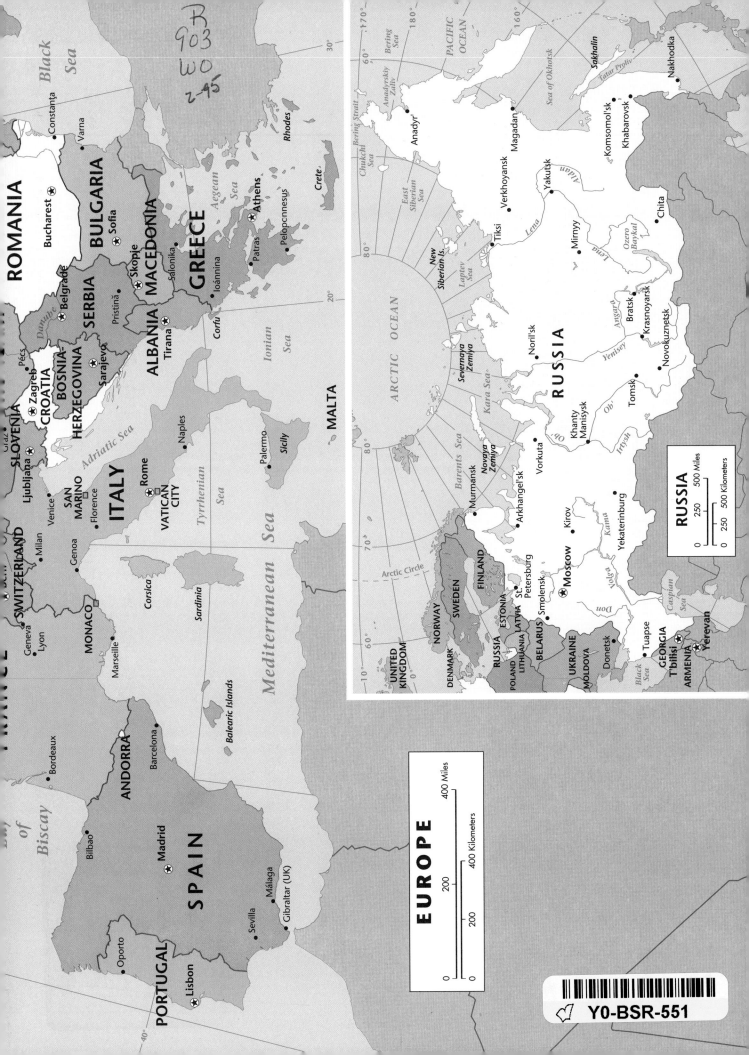

WORLDMARK ENCYCLOPEDIA OF THE NATIONS

Volume 5

WORLDMARK
ENCYCLOPEDIA OF THE NATIONS

EUROPE

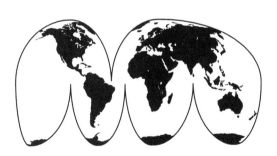

Formerly published by Worldmark Press, Ltd.

Gale Research Inc.

An International Thomson Publishing Company

I(T)P

NEW YORK • LONDON • BONN • BOSTON • DETROIT • MADRID
MELBOURNE • MEXICO CITY • PARIS • SINGAPORE • TOKYO
TORONTO • WASHINGTON • ALBANY NY • BELMONT CA • CINCINNATI OH

Gale Research Inc. Staff

Jane Hoehner, *Developmental Editor*
Allison McNeill, Rebecca Nelson, and Kelle S. Sisung, *Contributing Developmental Editors*
Marie Ellavich, Jolen Gedridge, and Camille Killens, *Associate Developmental Editors*
Lawrence W. Baker, *Senior Developmental Editor*

Mary Beth Trimper, *Production Director*
Evi Seoud, *Assistant Production Manager*
Mary Kelley, *Production Associate*

Cynthia Baldwin, *Product Design Manager*
Barbara J. Yarrow, *Graphic Services Supervisor*
Todd Nessell, *Macintosh Artist*

Library of Congress Cataloging-in-Publication Data

Worldmark encyclopedia of the nations. — 8th ed.
    5 v.
    Includes bibliographical references and index.
    Contents: v. 1. United Nations — v. 2. Africa — v. 3. Americas —
v. 4. Asia & Oceania — v. 5. Europe.
    ISBN 0-8103-9878-8 (set). — ISBN 0-8103-9893-1 (v. 1). — ISBN
0-8103-9880-x (v. 2)
      1. Geography—Encyclopedias. 2. History—Encyclopedias.
    3. Economics—Encyclopedias. 4. Political science—Encyclopedias.
    5. United Nations—Encyclopedias.
    G63.W67   1995
    903—dc20   94–38556
                                                                 CIP

This book is printed on acid-free paper that meets the minimum requirements of American National Standard for Information Sciences—Permanence Paper for Printed Library Materials, ANSI Z39.48-1984. ∞™

ISBN 0-8103-9883-4

Printed in the United States of America by Gale Research Inc.
Published simultaneously in the United Kingdom
by Gale Research International Limited
(An affiliated company of Gale Research Inc.)

10 9 8 7 6 5 4 3 2 1

CONTENTS

For Conversion Tables, Abbreviations and Acronyms, Glossaries, World Tables, Notes to the Eighth Edition, and other supplementary materials, see Volume 1.

GUIDE TO COUNTRY ARTICLES

All information contained within a country article is uniformly keyed by means of small superior numerals to the left of the subject headings. A heading such as "Population," for example, carries the same key numeral (6) in every article. Thus, to find information about the population of Albania, consult the table of contents for the page number where the Albania article begins and look for section 6 thereunder. Introductory matter for each nation includes coat of arms, capital, flag (descriptions given from hoist to fly or from top to bottom), anthem, monetary unit, weights and measures, holidays, and time zone.

FLAG COLOR SYMBOLS

 Yellow   Red   Green   Blue   Orange   Brown   White   Black

SECTION HEADINGS IN NUMERICAL ORDER

1 Location, size, and extent
2 Topography
3 Climate
4 Flora and fauna
5 Environment
6 Population
7 Migration
8 Ethnic groups
9 Languages
10 Religions
11 Transportation
12 History
13 Government
14 Political parties
15 Local government
16 Judicial system
17 Armed forces
18 International cooperation
19 Economy
20 Income
21 Labor
22 Agriculture
23 Animal husbandry
24 Fishing
25 Forestry
26 Mining

27 Energy and power
28 Industry
29 Science and technology
30 Domestic trade
31 Foreign trade
32 Balance of payments
33 Banking and securities
34 Insurance
35 Public finance
36 Taxation
37 Customs and duties
38 Foreign investment
39 Economic development
40 Social development
41 Health
42 Housing
43 Education
44 Libraries and museums
45 Media
46 Organizations
47 Tourism, travel, and
   recreation
48 Famous persons
49 Dependencies
50 Bibliography

SECTION HEADINGS IN ALPHABETICAL ORDER

Agriculture	22
Animal husbandry	23
Armed forces	17
Balance of payments	32
Banking and securities	33
Bibliography	50
Climate	3
Customs and duties	37
Dependencies	49
Domestic trade	30
Economic development	39
Economy	19
Education	43
Energy and power	27
Environment	5
Ethnic groups	8
Famous persons	48
Fishing	24
Flora and fauna	4
Foreign investment	38
Foreign trade	31
Forestry	25
Government	13
Health	41
History	12
Housing	42

Income	20
Industry	28
Insurance	34
International cooperation	18
Judical system	16
Labor	21
Languages	9
Libraries and museums	44
Local government	15
Location, size, and extent	1
Media	45
Migration	7
Mining	26
Organizations	46
Political parties	14
Population	6
Public finance	35
Religions	10
Science and technology	29
Social development	40
Taxation	36
Topography	2
Tourism, travel, and recreation	47
Transportation	11

FREQUENTLY USED ABBREVIATIONS AND ACRONYMS

ad—Anno Domini
am—before noon
b.—born
bc—Before Christ
c—Celsius
c.—circa (about)
cm—centimeter(s)
Co.—company
Corp.—corporation
cu ft—cubic foot, feet
cu m—cubic meter(s)
d.—died
e—east
e—evening
e.g.—exempli gratia
   (for example)
ed.—edition, editor
est.—estimated
et al.—et alii (and others)

etc.—et cetera (and so on)
f—Fahrenheit
fl.—flourished
FRG—Federal Republic of
   Germany
ft—foot, feet
ft³—cubic foot, feet
GATT—General Agreement on
   Tariffs and Trade
GDP—gross domestic products
gm—gram
GMT—Greenwich Mean Time
GNP—gross national product
GRT—gross registered tons
ha—hectares
i.e.—id est (that is)
in—inch(es)
kg—kilogram(s)
km—kilometer(s)

kw—kilowatt(s)
kwh—kilowatt-hour(s)
lb—pound(s)
m—meter(s); morning
m³—cubic meter(s)
mi—mile(s)
Mt.—mount
Mw—megawatt(s)
n—north
n.d.—no date
NA—not available
oz—ounce(s)

pm—after noon
r.—reigned
rev. ed.—revised edition
s—south
sq—square
St.—saint
UK—United Kingdom
UN—United Nations
US—United States
USSR—Union of Soviet
   Socialist Republics
w—west

A fiscal split year is indicated by a stroke (e.g. 1987/88).
For acronyms of UN agencies and ther intergovernmental organizations, as well as other abbreviations used in text, see the United Nations volume.
A dollar sign ($) stands for us$ unless otherwise indicated.
Note that 1 billion = 1,000 million = 10^9.

ALBANIA

Republic of Albania
Republika é e Shqipërisë

CAPITAL: Tiranë (Tirana).

FLAG: The flag consists of a red standard at the center of which is a black double-headed eagle.

ANTHEM: *Hymni i Flamúrit (Anthem of the Flag)* begins "Rreth flamúrit të për bashkuar" ("The flag that united us in the struggle").

MONETARY UNIT: The lek (L) of 100 qindarka is a convertible paper currency. There are coins of 5, 10, 20, 50 qindarka, and 1 lek, and notes of 1, 3, 5, 10, 25, 50, 100, and 500 leks. L1 = $0.1483 (or $1 = L6.743).

WEIGHTS AND MEASURES: The metric system is the legal standard.

HOLIDAYS: New Year's Day, 1 January; Small Bayram, end of Ramadan, 3 March*; International Women's Day, 8 March; Catholic Easter, 14–17 April; Orthodox Easter, 23 April; Great Bayram, Feast of the Sacrifice, 10 May*; Independence Day, 28 November; Christmas Day, 25 December.

*These holidays are dependent on the Islamic lunar calendar and may vary by one or two days from the dates given.

TIME: 1 PM = noon GMT.

¹LOCATION, SIZE, AND EXTENT

Albania is situated on the west coast of the Balkan Peninsula opposite the "heel" of the Italian "boot," from which it is separated on the SW and W by the Strait of Otranto and the Adriatic Sea. It is bordered on the N and E by Serbia and Macedonia, and on the SE by Greece, with a total boundary length of 1,082 km (672 mi). Comparatively, Albania is slightly larger than the state of Maryland, with a total area of 28,750 sq km (11,100 sq mi) and extends 340 km (211 mi) N–S and 148 km (92 mi) E–W. Albania's capital city, Tiranë, is located in the west central part of the country.

²TOPOGRAPHY

Albania is predominantly mountainous, with 70% of the territory at elevations of more than 300 m (1,000 ft). The rest of the country consists of a coastal lowland and the lower reaches of river valleys opening onto the coastal plain. The Albanian mountains, representing a southern continuation of the Dinaric system, rise abruptly from the plains and are especially rugged along the country's borders. The highest peak, Korab (2,751 m/9,026 ft) lies in eastern Albania on the Yugoslav border. The most important rivers—the Drin, the Buna, the Mat, the Shkumbin, the Seman, and the Vijosë—empty into the Adriatic. Albania shares Lake Shkodër with Montenegro, Lake Ohrid with Macedonia, and Lake Prespë with Yugoslavia and Greece.

³CLIMATE

Albania has a variety of climatic conditions, being situated in the transition zone between the typical Mediterranean climate in the west and the moderate continental in the east. The average annual temperature is 15°C (59°F). Rainy winters (with frequent cyclones) and dry, hot summers are typical of the coastal plain. Summer rainfall is more frequent and winters colder in the mountainous interior. Annual precipitation ranges from about 100 cm (40 in) on the coast to more than 250 cm (100 in) in the mountains.

⁴FLORA AND FAUNA

The mountainous topography produces a zonation of flora and fauna. The dry lowlands are occupied by a bush-shrub association known as maquis, in which hairy, leathery leaves reduce transpiration to a minimum. There are some woods in the low-lying regions, and larger forests of oak, beech, and other deciduous species begin at 910 m (2,986 ft). Black pines and other conifers are found at higher elevations in the northern part of the country. There are few wild animals, even in the mountains, but wild birds still abound in the lowland forests.

⁵ENVIRONMENT

As of 1987, the Mediterranean monk seal was an endangered species in Albania. Deforestation remains Albania's principal environmental problem, despite government afforestation programs.

While Albania has a comparatively small amount of water at 2.4 cu mi, 100% of its urban population and 95% of its rural population have access to pure water.

A total of 1.9% of Albania's lands, amounting to 210 sq mi, is protected by environmental laws.

Albania produces 3,895 metric tons of carbon dioxide emissions from solid sources, 4,679 metric tons of emissions from liquid sources and 762 metric tons from gaseous sources.

By 1994, of the 3,100 to 3,300 plant species on Albania, 76 were endangered. Two mammal species and 14 bird species are also threatened.

⁶POPULATION

A census in April 1989 showed a population of 3,182,417; 64% of the population was rural and 36% urban in 1990 (only about 20% of the population had been urban in 1950). Albania's population in mid 1994 was estimated at 3,514,140; the projection for the year 2000 was 3,589,000, assuming a crude birthrate of 20 per 1,000 population and a death rate of 5.2 for 1995–2000. Average population density in 1994 was 122 per sq km (317 per sq mi). Tiranë, the capital and principal city, had a population of 251,000 in 1991. Other important towns were Durrës, 86,900; Shkodër, 83,700; Elbasan, 83,200; and Vlorë, 76,000.

Population increase has been exceptionally rapid by European standards. The birthrate, despite a decline from over 40 births per 1,000 of population in the 1950s to 25 in 1992, remains among the highest in Europe. Death rates, meanwhile, fell from 14 per 1,000 in 1950 to 6 in 1992, yielding a net natural increase of 19 per 1,000.

[7]MIGRATION

In the 19th century, Albanians emigrated to other Balkan countries (Romania, Bulgaria, Turkey, Greece), and to Egypt and Russia. During the first decades of the 20th century, emigration—for economic reasons—was primarily to the US (largely to Massachusetts), Argentina, Australia, and France. Emigration following World War II has occurred on a very limited scale, mainly for political reasons. Between 1945 and 1990, Albania has remained virtually isolated from the rest of Europe. In the early 1990s, about 2 million Albanians lived in Yugoslavia. Many ethnic Albanians live in Greece, Italy, and Macedonia.

[8]ETHNIC GROUPS

Generally regarded as descendants of the ancient Illyrians, the Albanians make up about 98% of the population, according to the 1989 census. This count had 58,758 Greeks. However, Western estimates give credence to Greek claims that there are more than 300,000 ethnic Greeks in Albania. There were also 4,697 Macedonians tabulated, and there are small numbers of Gypsies, Vlachs, Bulgarians, and Serbs. The Albanians themselves fall into two major groups: the Ghegs in the north and the Tosks in the south, divided by the Shkumbin River.

[9]LANGUAGES

Albanian (Shqip), an independent member of the Indo-European family of languages derived from both ancient Illyrian and ancient Thracian, has been greatly modified by Latin, Slavonic, Greek, and Turkish influences. It was not until 1908 that a common Latin alphabet was established for Albanian. In addition to letters of the English alphabet, Albanian uses the diacritics ç (representing the sound of *ch* in *church*) and ë (the sound of *i* in *dirt*). Other unusual letter values are *c* (the sound of *ts* in *gets*), *x* (the sound of *ds* in *woods*), *xh* (the sound of *j* in *jaw*), *j* (the sound of *y* in *yet*), *q* (the sound of *ky* in *stockyard*), and *y* (the sound of the German *ü*). There are two distinct dialects—Gheg, spoken in the north, and Tosk, spoken in the south. During the period between World Wars I and II, Gheg was officially favored as standard Albanian; after World War II, because the principal leaders of the regime were southerners, Tosk became the standard. Greek is spoken by a minority in the southeast border area.

[10]RELIGIONS

Historically, as many as 70% of Albanians were Muslims. In 1967, the government closed more than 2,100 mosques, churches, monasteries, and other places of worship and declared the country an atheist state. Subsequent complaints in the official press about the survival of religious customs (refusal to eat pork on the part of Muslims, failure to work at Easter on the part of Christians) suggest that the official abolition of public religion had by no means ended private observance. In 1990 and 1991, official opposition to religious activities came to an end and churches and mosques were selectively allowed to reopen. Albania is now a self-proposed secular state that allows freedom of religion and the exercise of it. In the total population, the percentage of Muslims remains stable at 65%; Eastern Orthodox, 20%; and Roman Catholic, 13%.

[11]TRANSPORTATION

Many roads are unsuitable for motor transport; bicycles and donkeys are common. There had been virtually no private cars in the country, but they were becoming more common with the opening of the borders. In 1991, there were 16,700 km (10,377 mi) of roads, of which 6,700 km (4,163 mi) were paved highways and roads, the rest being forest and agricultural roads. One of the many new infrastructural projects was the construction of a 241 km (150 mi) four-land highway linking Durrës with Greece, via Pogradec and Kapshtica.

Railroad construction began in 1947, and lines in 1991 had a total length of 509 km (316 mi) of standard gauge track, and 34 km (21 mi) of narrow gauge rail, including the Durrës-Tiranë, Durrës-Elbasan, Ballsh Rrogozhinë, Vorë-Shkodër, and Selenicë-Vlorë lines. In 1979, Albania signed an agreement with Yugoslavia to construct a rail link between Shkodër and Titograd; the link was opened to international freight traffic in September 1986.

Albania's rivers are not navigable, but there is some local shipping on lakes Shkodër, Ohrid, and Prespë. Coastwise vessels link the ports of Durrës, Vlorë, Sarandë, and Shëngjin. Durrës is the principal port for foreign trade. The merchant fleet of Albania in 1991 consisted of 11 vessels totaling about 55,000 GRT. A freight ferry service between Durrës and Trieste was inaugurated in 1983.

Flights from Tiranë's international airport connect the Albanian capital with Athens, Belgrade, and Switzerland (the latter route opened in June 1986).

[12]HISTORY

Origins and the Middle Ages

The Albanians are considered descendants of ancient Illyrian or Thracian tribes of Indo-European origin that may have come to the Balkan Peninsula even before the Greeks. Although several Greek colonies were established along the coast, the hinterland remained independent. An Illyrian kingdom was formed in the 3d century BC and even after it was conquered by Rome in 167 BC, some mountain tribes were never subdued. Among them were the Albani or Albanoi, whose city Albanopolis was mentioned in the 2d century BC by Ptolemy in his *Geography*. Later, while nominally under Byzantine rule, Albania was raided by Slav invaders in the 6th century and was annexed to Bulgaria in the 9th century. Temporary inroads were made by Venice, which established coastal colonies, and by the Normans, who seized Durrës in 1082–85. Albanian expansion took place under the Angevin kings of Naples in the 13th century, and again under the Serbs in the 14th century. Short-lived independent principalities flourished during the second half of the 14th century.

From the Ottomans to Independence

Turkish advances, which began in 1388, were resisted from 1443 to 1468 by Gjerj Kastrioti, better known as Scanderbeg, the Albanian national hero, but by 1479 the Turks attained complete control of the area. Over the succeeding centuries, Islam spread throughout most of the country. Turkish rule continued through the 19th century, which saw an intensification of nationalistic feeling, often erupting into open rebellion. In November 1912, during the First Balkan War, the National Assembly convened in Vlorë under the chairmanship of Ismail Kemali and proclaimed Albania's independence. The proclamation was supported by Austria-Hungary but opposed by Russia, Serbia, Greece, and Turkey. At a conference in London in 1913, Albania's national boundaries were established—they have remained virtually unchanged since that time—and the nation was placed under the tutelage of the great powers. Albania then became a principal battleground during World War I. By the time the war ended, portions of Albania were under Italian, French, and Yugoslav control.

Albania again asserted its independence in 1920, and a provisional government was established, as the Italians and French withdrew. Following a period of unstable parliamentary government (1921–24), Ahmet Zogu, the chief of the Mat district, seized power with Yugoslav support. He proclaimed Albania a republic in 1925, with himself as president, and a kingdom in 1928, with himself as King Zog I. A series of concessions to Italy made Albania a virtual Italian protectorate, and after Zog was forced into exile in April 1939, Italy occupied Albania, uniting it with the Italian crown. During World War II, Communist-led guerrillas under Enver Hoxha resisted Italian and German forces. The Congress of Permeti (24 May 1944) formed Albania's provisional government, naming Hoxha as premier; the congress banned the return of former King Zog, and called for a constituent assembly to meet after the complete liberation of the country. In November 1944, the Hoxha government was established in Tiranë.

Under Communist Rule

The constitution of 1946 declared Albania a people's republic. Early close relations with Yugoslavia were abruptly severed when the Soviet-Yugoslav break occurred in 1948. Partly because of fundamental differences with Yugoslavia, whose borders include about 1.7 million Albanians, and partly because of ideological divergences, Albanian-Soviet relations worsened at the 22d Communist Party Congress, and the USSR severed diplomatic relations with Albania in December 1961 and evacuated its naval and submarine bases at Vlorë.

Relations with Communist countries other than China worsened during the 1960s, as Albania ceased to participate in the activities of the Warsaw Treaty Organization by September 1968 following the Soviet invasion of Czechoslovakia. With Yugoslavia, however, there were signs of rapprochement; an Albanian-Yugoslav trade pact was signed in 1970, and trade between the two nations consequently flourished. Gestures were also made to improve relations with Albania's other neighbor, Greece.

Albania's relations with China, its ally and supporter since 1961, seemed to cool somewhat after 1971. China's détente with the US ran counter to Albania's policy of opposition to the USSR and the US. China's assistance to Albania ceased when the US denounced the overthrow of China's "Gang of Four" in October of 1976.

On 28 December 1976, Albania adopted a new constitution which formally established Marxism-Leninism as the dominant ideology and proclaimed the principle of self-reliance. The following year, Albania broke off most of its links with China and accused it of "social imperialist" policies, and in 1978 trade relations were also suspended. In 1983, however, Albania received a Chinese delegation to discuss the resumption of trade relations. Meanwhile, relations with Yugoslavia worsened following the riots by ethnic Albanians in Yugoslavia's Kosovo province in March 1981; Yugoslavia charged that Albania had instigated the protests, and Albania accused Yugoslavia of ethnic discrimination. (Nevertheless, as of 1987 Yugoslavia was Albania's main trading partner, and Albania's first rail connection with the outside world, the Shköder-Titograd link, was opened in 1986.)

Internally, Albania seemed to be locked in bitter political conflict as the 1980s began. Prime Minister Mehmet Shehu, relieved of his defense portfolio in April 1980, died in December 1981, an alleged suicide. A year later, Hoxha charged that Shehu had been working for the US, Soviet, and Yugoslav secret services and that Shehu even had orders from Yugoslavia to kill him. Western and Yugoslav press accounts speculated that Shehu had favored an opening to the West and had been executed in the course of a power struggle. Throughout 1981–83, an extensive purge of those even remotely connected with Shehu was conducted. This

LOCATION: 39°38′ to 42°39′N; 19°16′ to 21°4′E. **BOUNDARY LENGTHS:** Yugoslavia, 476 km (296 mi); Greece, 256 km (159 mi); coastline, 472 km (293 mi).
TERRITORIAL SEA LIMIT: 15 mi.

was in keeping with previous purges in the 1950s of those sympathizing with Yugoslavia, in the 1960s of pro-Soviet officials, and in the late 1970s of pro-West and pro-China policymakers. On 25 September 1982, according to Albanian reports, a group of armed Albanian exiles landed on the coast and was promptly liquidated. Hoxha alleged that they had been sent by Yugoslavia.

Hoxha died on 11 April 1985 and was succeeded as first secretary of the Workers Party by Ramiz Alia, who had been chairman of the presidium of the People's Assembly since 1982.

In the mid-1980s, Albania took steps to end its isolation. In 1987, it established diplomatic relations with Canada, Spain, Bolivia, and the Federal Republic of Germany. In August 1987, Albania signed a treaty with Greece formally ending the state of war that had existed between the two countries since World War II.

Democracy and Free Market

As unrest spread in the late 1980s through Central and Eastern Europe in opposition to long lasting Communist dictatorships, economic hardships in Albania grew ever deeper. Albania's political leadership had to open up more diplomatic and trade relationships with Western nations as the only available source of potential assistance. At the same time, internal unrest and a search for alternative democratic political solutions led by 1990 to mass protests and calls for the Government's resignation. Thousands of Albanians wanted to emigrate in spite of imposed restrictions and became refugees housed in foreign embassies waiting for ships to take them abroad, particularly to Italy. President Ramiz Alia initiated the process for reestablishing diplomatic relations with the US, discontinued since the 1939 annexation of Albania by Italy. Restrictions on travel abroad were eased and religious practices allowed for the first time since their prohibition in 1944.

The Communist Party Government still intended to maintain both its control and its socialist system while allowing for some democracy. But it was not to be and by December 1990 the opposition Democratic Party was formed. On 7 February 1991, some 8,000 students went on strike in Tiranë demanding economic changes and the Government's resignation. In the face of persistent unrest President Alia scheduled multiparty elections for 31 March 1991. Even with the Communist Party still in control, the Democratic Party managed to win 75 of the 250 People's Assembly seats (mostly in urban areas) with 160 seats won by the Communist Party. Ramiz Alia was reelected President and a still all-Communist Council of Ministers was appointed under Prime Minister Fatos Nano. By June 1991, continuous unrest forced Alia to agree to a first coalition government between its Communist (renamed Socialist) Party and the new Democratic Party. The latter withdrew from the coalition government in December 1991 charging the majority Socialists with preventing any reforms. President Alia then called for new general elections on 22 March 1992, that gave the Democratic Party a majority of seats (92 of 140). Sali Berisha was elected president with Alexsander Meksi his prime minister.

President Berisha and his Democratic Party pushed hard for radical reforms to create a market economy and democratic institutions internally, while bringing Albania back into the international mainstream after half a century of isolation. By the end of 1993 barriers to foreign trade had been removed, the Albanian lek made fully convertible, inflation brought under control, the serious productivity decrease halted, and an anti-corruption drive mounted. The privatization of the economy had been successfully initiated, particularly in the agricultural sector, with 90% of land distributed to private farmers. Most subsidies were ended except to large industrial enterprises, who still wait for foreign investments that are not yet coming to the unstable Balkan area.

In foreign relations, Albania, under Berisha's leadership, is trying to balance the internal pressure to assist both the repressed Albanian majority in the Kosovo region of Serbia towards its independence, and the sizable Albanian minority in Macedonia to obtain human and political rights. The need to preserve Albania's own stability remains yet they must avoid any action that might trigger a wider Balkan conflagration. Albania's Western trade partners realize its internal economic and humanitarian needs and have been generous with their assistance that, between mid-1991 and 1993, has amounted to $1 billion, mostly from European Union countries led by Italy. The US and Albania have developed very close relations and Albania hopes for US support to upgrade its weak armed forces. Albania has also requested membership in NATO and, even though rejected, continues its cooperation with NATO. Because of its own border problems with Greece, Albania supports the independence of Macedonia and was one of the first nations to recognize Macedonia in spite of Greece's refusal to do so. Albania, a majority (70%) Moslem country, has joined the Organization of the Islamic Conference mainly to gain some economic support. Albania also hosted Pope John Paul II's visit in April 1993, having established diplomatic relations with the Vatican in September 1991, and has been intensifying its traditional good relationship with Italy, whose annexation of Albania in 1939 is by now only a faint memory. Assuming that Albania continues on its present course of serious reforms and the Democratic Party maintains its unity, the country has a very good chance to experience a period of successful development, both political and economic. These gains would make Albania both an active participant on the European scene and a potentially beneficial link to the Islamic nations.

[13]GOVERNMENT

Under the 1976 constitution, Albania was a socialist republic. Legislative authority was vested in the unicameral People's Assembly, elected every four years from a single list of candidates. In elections held 2 February 1987, 250 deputies were elected by 1,830,653 voters, with no votes cast against and one vote invalid. Voter participation was allegedly 100%. Suffrage is extended to men and women from the age of 18 and is compulsory. The 1976 constitution specifies that "the rights of citizens are indivisible from the fulfillment of their duties and cannot be exercised in opposition to the socialist order."

The delays in the drafting of a new constitution caused a severe political crisis in the summer of 1993. As of the spring of 1994, Albania's government is still based on the 29 April 1991 Law on Constitutional Provisions that established the principle of separation of powers, the protection of private property and human rights a multi-party parliament, and a president of the republic with broad powers. President Sali Berisha (Democratic Party) was elected 9 April 1992 and Prime Minister Gabriel Meksi (Democratic Party) has held office since 10 April 1992.

[14]POLITICAL PARTIES

Before the 1990s, the only political party was the Communist Party, which was founded in 1941 and has been known officially as the Workers Party (Partija e Punes) since 1948. As of November 1986, it had about 147,000 members, as compared with 45,382 in 1948. The Albanian Democratic Front was the party's major subsidiary organization; other subsidiary groups included the Union of Albanian Working Youth and the Women's Union of Albania.

Under the 1976 constitution, the first secretary of the Workers Party was commander-in-chief of the armed forces. The constitution described the Workers Party as the "sole directing political power in state and society."

The 45-year hold over Albania by its Communist Party dictatorship was broken in December 1990 with the formation of the opposition Democratic Party. In the 31 March 1991 elections the Communist Party obtained 160 of the 250 People's Assembly seats. While the Democratic Party received only 75 seats, it did gain control of all the six major urban areas. In the elections held on 22 March 1992 some 18 parties participated, but only five of them received enough votes to gain a share of the 140 seats in the unicameral assembly: Democratic Party (92), Socialist Party (former Communist) (38), Social Democratic Party (7), Unity for Human Rights (Greek Minority) Party (2), Republican Party (1).

The Democratic Party (Edvard Selami, Chairman) advocates a pluralistic democracy and a free market economy, separation of powers, human rights and private property protection, and privatization of farms, retailing, transportation, housing, and large industrial concerns. The Socialist Party (Fatos Nano, First Secretary) consists mainly of former Communist Party members clinging to the memory of their past in power and opposes most measures advocated or implemented by the majority Democratic Party. The Socialists also strongly vent their anti-capitalist positions taking advantage of the difficulties generated by the transition to a democratic system and a free market economy. The Social Democratic Party (Skender Gjinushi) is mostly allied to the Democratic Party but is also free to oppose it in some areas, such as the delays in the adoption of a new constitution. The Republican Party (Sabri Godo) also supports the Democratic Party in most cases but has not yet worked out a clear program of its own. The old constitution made voting universal and compulsory at age 18.

15LOCAL GOVERNMENT

As of 1987, Albania was divided into 26 districts (rrethe), including the city of Tiranë; subdivisions as of 1982 included 65 cities and towns and 438 united villages comprising 2,664 villages. All these subdivisions are governed by people's councils, elected for three-year terms by eligible voters. The councils direct economic, social, cultural, and administrative activity in their jurisdictional areas; they appoint executive committees to administer day-to-day activities.

Following the introduction of a multi-party system since December 1990 and the elections of 1991 and 1992, local governments are no longer dominated by a single (Communist) party and party competition is an important element at the local level.

16JUDICIAL SYSTEM

The judicial system includes district courts, a court of appeals and a Court of Cassation. The district courts are trial level courts from which appeal can be taken to the court of appeals and then to the Court of Cassation. At each of the three levels, the courts are divided into civil, criminal and military chambers.

There is also a Constitutional Court (also known as the High Court or Supreme Court) with jurisdiction to resolve questions of constitutional interpretation which arise during the course of any case on appeal. In a 1993 decision, the Constitutional Court invalidated a law which would have disbarred lawyers who were active during the communist era, and ordered the lawyers reinstated.

Parliament appoints the nine judges on the Constitutional Court and the seven members of the Court of Cassation. A Supreme Judicial Council appoints all other judges. Judges are appointed for life and may be dismissed by the body which appointed them in the event of conviction for serious crime. In 1992, the Supreme Judicial Council began to remove judges who had served under the former Communist regime.

17ARMED FORCES

Men of 19 to 35 years of age are liable for 18 months of compulsory service in the army or for three years in the air force, navy, or paramilitary units. Men from 35 to 55 are subject to obligatory military service in the reserves. As of 1993, the estimated strength of the Albanian armed forces was 42,000 including 27,000 in the army, 2,000 in the navy, and 11,000 in the air force. The navy had 2 submarines and 64 patrol and coastal combat vessels, including 30 hydrofoils supplied by China. The air force had 112 combat aircraft, 18 transports, and 28 unarmed helicopters. In addition to the regular armed forces under the Ministry of Defense, Albania has around 16,000 border guards and internal security forces. Defense appropriations for 1990 were estimated at L28.1 billion. Defense spending has declined because of high inflation.

18INTERNATIONAL COOPERATION

Albania, a UN member since 14 December 1955, belongs to the following specialized agencies: ECE, FAO, IAEA, ITU, UNESCO, UPU, WHO, and WMO. Albania was originally also a member of the CMEA and the Warsaw Pact, but in 1968 it formally announced its withdrawal from both (it had ended participation in CMEA in 1961). It was the only European country that declined to participate in the Helsinki Conference on Security and Cooperation in Europe in 1974–75. The constitution of 1976 reasserted the principle of self-reliance.

In 1986 and 1987, Albania began to abandon its strict isolationism and was establishing contacts and diplomatic relations with numerous countries, including Iceland, Sweden, Spain, Portugal, France, Greece, Turkey, Mexico, Ecuador, Singapore, Cambodia, Viet Nam, Canada, and Bolivia.

19ECONOMY

Albania has always been an underdeveloped country. Before World War II, there were only a few small-scale industrial plants and only a few of the larger towns had electricity. Subsoil resources were potentially rich, but only coal, bitumen and oil were extracted—by Italian companies. Transportation was poorly developed. Stockbreeding contributed about half of the agricultural output; by 1938, tilled area represented only 23% of the agricultural land. Forests were exploited and reforestation neglected.

After the war, the Communist regime pursued an industrialization program with a centrally planned economy. Development projects received priority, especially mining, industry, power, and transportation. Consumer goods, agriculture, livestock, and housing were relatively neglected. By 1950, Albania had its first standard-gauge railways, a textile combine, a hydroelectric power plant, a tobacco fermentation plant, and a sugar refinery. Mineral extraction, especially of oil, chrome ore (the main export product) and iron-nickel, was increased. Land cultivated under crops or orchards expanded from 406,000 hectares (1,003,000 acres) in 1955 to 709,800 hectares (1,753,944 acres) in 1983. Although collectivized, farmland was again privatized in 1992 and distributed to peasants. But despite significant progress, living standards in Albania were still among the lowest in Europe. When central planning was abandoned, there was no mechanism to take its place, and GDP fell 45% during 1990-92. It rose by at least 10% in 1993, however. After prices were freed, the inflation rate shot up to 226% in 1992, but dropped to 86% in 1993. Unemployment mounted rapidly and was estimated at 30% in 1993.

20INCOME

In 1992, Albania's GNP was $2.5 billion at current prices, or $760 per capita.

21LABOR

Employment had risen steadily under the aegis of the state when the Communist regime began its industrialization program, with the number of wage and salary earners increasing from about 65,000 in 1947 to 462,900 in 1973 and 697,800 in 1983. Since communism was abandoned in favor of a free market economy in 1991, a transitional dislocation of workers and resources has taken place, resulting in an estimated unemployment rate of 40% in 1992. The work force was distributed as follows in 1991: manufacturing and mining, 35%; agriculture (excluding collective farmers), 24%; construction, 9%; trade, 7%; business support services, 4%; transport and communications, 5%; and community, social, and personal services, 16%. Over 40% of all workers are female.

In 1991, workers were granted the legal right to create independent trade unions. The Independent Confederation of Trade Unions of Albania (BSPSH) was formed as the umbrella organization for several smaller unions. In 1992, several conflicts and schisms within the BSPSH occurred. That same year, civilians in the defense industry as well as teachers organized unions. The rival Confederation of Unions, closely tied to the Socialist party, operates mostly as a continuation of the state-sponsored federation of the Communist era.

All citizens have the right to organize and bargain collectively, except the military and civilian employees of the military. Currently, unions deal directly with the government since all large enterprises are still state owned, and little privatization has occurred outside the retail and agricultural sectors. The minimum work age is 14. As of 1992, working conditions had not been legally addressed, although there may be some qualification included in the new constitution.

22AGRICULTURE

In the late 1980s, about 55% of the economically active population was engaged in agriculture (compared with 85% before World War II). Although Albania's mountainous terrain limits the amount of land available for agriculture, the cultivated and arable area was about 26% of the total (700,000 hectares/1.7 million acres) in 1991. Albania claims to be 95% self-sufficient in food. Nearly two thirds of the population is rural, and agriculture provides one-half of value added.

The first collective farm was created in 1946, but collectivization did not move forward on a large scale until 1955. By early 1962, 1,263 collectives included about 2,000 villages and covered almost 80% of the cultivated area. Consolidation reduced the collectives to 1,064 by December 1964. State farms, meanwhile, had expanded and by 1960 they accounted for about 12% of the cultivated area. By 1964, only 10% of the cultivated area was privately farmed, and by 1973, 100% of the agricultural land was reported as socialized, either in collective or state farms. Collective farm consolidations and mergers reduced their number to 420 in April 1983, including "advanced type" cooperatives. The cooperatives accounted for 74% of total agricultural production. By the mid-1980s, the number of collective farmers was about 800,000.

After the government abandoned central planning, the economy collapsed from the void. The decline saw the agricultural sector shrink by 21% in 1991, but agricultural production rebounded in 1992 in response to the privatization of cooperative farms and the elimination of fixed pricing. The number of tractors increased from 359 in 1950 to 4,500 in 1960 and to 12,500 in 1991. In 1991, irrigation systems covered 60% of the arable land. Artificial fertilizers supplied to farms rose from 8,000 tons of active substance in 1960 to 99,900 tons in 1978.

Wheat is the principal crop; corn, oats, sorghum, and potatoes are also important. Greater emphasis is being placed on the production of cash crops—cotton, tobacco, rice, sugar beets, vegetables, sunflowers, and fruits and nuts. FAO estimates of crop output in 1992 (in tons) included wheat, 330,000; corn, 200,000; sugar beets, 140,000; vegetables and melons, 248,000; potatoes, 60,000; grapes, 66,000; sorghum, 15,000; and oats 8,000.

23ANIMAL HUSBANDRY

The major problem of Albanian animal husbandry has been a shortage of fodder. As a result, livestock numbers remained virtually constant or increased very slowly in the postwar decades. When central planning was abandoned, uncertain monetary and credit policies caused inflation to soar, which eroded export earnings. Albania, which had been a net exporter of food products, became heavily dependent on food aid. Sheep, originally the most important stock, dropped from 1.84 million in 1946 to 1 million in 1992. The following table shows the estimated status of livestock for 1970, 1985, and 1992:

	1970	1985	1992
Sheep	1,610,000	1,204,000	1,000,000
Poultry	1,790,000	5,000,000	5,000,000
Goats	1,330,000	703,000	800,000
Cattle	435,000	614,000	500,000
Hogs	150,000	210,000	170,000
Horses	42,000	43,000	100,000

Estimates of livestock products in 1992 include 338,000 tons of cows' milk, 38,000 tons of sheep's milk, 47,000 tons of goats' milk, 17,000 tons of beef and veal, 12,000 tons of pork, 8,000 tons of mutton and lamb, and 11,000 tons of eggs.

24FISHING

Fishing is an important occupation along the Adriatic coast. In 1958, a development program for inland fisheries was begun, and the results were improved exploitation and conservation as well as increased fish reserves and catches. Annual fish production was estimated at 12,000 tons in 1991.

25FORESTRY

In 1991, forests covered 1.05 million hectares (2.59 million acres), or about 38% of the total land area. As a result of exploitation, erosion, and neglect, about 70% of the forested area consists of little more than shoots and wild shrubs, and exploitation of the remaining accessible forests exceeds optimum annual limits. The average annual output of sawn wood had been 200,000 cu m during the communist era, but climbed to 382,000 cu m in 1991. Between 1971 and 1978, 65,310 hectares (161,380 acres) were afforested, compared with a total of 61,900 hectares (153,000 acres) for 1961–70.

26MINING

In 1991, Albania remained an important mineral producer, in spite of frequent work stoppages at mining and metallurgical plant sites (which reportedly account for 47% of the GNP). Nearly a half century of self-imposed isolation during the Communist era crippled Albania's mineral industry with a shortage of capital, aging and inadequate machinery, overstaffing, and environmental damage. Albania is the principal chrome-producing country in Europe (and the third largest in the world). The most important chrome mines are at Katjel and Mëmlisht and at Bulqize in the upper reaches of the Drin River. Chrome ore production rose from 7,000 tons in 1938 to 1.08 million tons in 1987, but then fell to 500,000 tons in 1991. A new chromium-ore enrichment plant was put into operation at Bulqize in 1972. Copper is mined at Pukë and at Rrubig, where the ore is concentrated and smelted. The deposits near Kukës are the richest in Albania. Copper ore production decreased by 51% between 1987 and 1991; in the latter year, production was estimated at 6,100 tons (metal content). Mine output of nickel in 1991 was 7,500 tons.

In 1969, sizable coal deposits were discovered near Tiranë; lignite output in 1991 was 1.1 million tons. Albania is one of the few countries producing natural asphalt, mined at Selenicë.

27ENERGY AND POWER

Albania has both thermal and hydroelectric power stations to generate electricity, but the latter are more significant and have the greater potential. Total power production increased from 85 million kwh in 1955 to 578 million kwh in 1967, and to 4,900 million kwh in 1985, before falling to 2,800 million kwh in 1991. Hydroelectric sources accounted for over 90% of the total production in 1991. The net installed capacity was estimated at 720,000 kw in 1991. Rural electrification was achieved in 1970.

The third five-year plan (1961–65) emphasized hydroelectric power, which contributed most of the envisaged 87% increase in electricity generation. The 24,000-kw Shkopet plant and the 27,000-kw Bistricë plant became operational in 1962. A 100,000-kw thermal plant at Fier went into operation in 1968, and the Mao Tse-tung hydroelectric plant was completed in 1971. The "Light of the Party" hydroelectric plant on the Drin River, with a total installed capacity of 500,000 kw, began operations in 1978. The seventh five-year plan (1981–85) provided for construction of a hydropower station at Koman, also on the Drin, with a capacity of 600,000 kw; the first two turbines were installed there by early 1986. A new hydroelectric and irrigation complex at Bënjë was to be built under the 1986–90 development plan. With the end of central planning and subsequent opening of the borders, the demands for energy are expected to significantly increase.

Petroleum production has become significant. Crude oil output rose from 108,000 tons in 1938 to 870,000 tons in 1967, and 3.5 million tons in 1985. Production fell to 700,000 tons in 1991 from 1.07 million tons in 1990. Four oil refineries are located at Ballsh, Stalin, Fier, and Çerrik. In 1991, Albania also produced 170 million cu m of natural gas.

²⁸INDUSTRY

Before World War II, industry was confined to a cement plant at Shkoder and to small-scale flour-milling, food-processing, cigarette-making, and fellmongery. In 1937–39, industry's contribution to the GNP was only 10%, by far the lowest in Eastern Europe. There was virtually no export of industrial products. After the war, the government emphasized industrial development, primarily development projects. Gross industrial output increased annually by 20% during 1951–60, by 12% during 1961–70, by 9% during 1971–80, by 5% during 1981–85, and by 3% during 1986–90. The socialized sector accounted for over 95% of gross output by the late 1950s and 100% by the 1970s. The industrial labor force, which virtually tripled between 1946 and 1960, continued to increase rapidly during the 1960s and, in 1990, 23% of all wage and salary earners were employed in industry (including mining).

Among the major plants constructed since 1946 are the Stalin textile combine at Tiranë, cotton gins at Fier and Rrogozhine, a tobacco fermentation plant at Shkoder, a sugar refinery at Maliq, oil refineries at Cerrik and Stalin, an iron and steel plant at Elbasan, and a copper-smelting plant at Lac. Production of major items in 1991 included cement, 193,000 tons; residual fuel oil, 290,000 tons; gasoline, 80,000 tons; kerosene, 10,000 tons; phosphate fertilizers, 30,000 tons; and cigarettes, 1.1 billion. These figures were radically lower than those for 1990. Industrial production fell a further 44% in 1992 and 10% in 1993. Privatization was proceeding slowly, with joint state-private ventures planned or sale of state enterprises at auction.

²⁹SCIENCE AND TECHNOLOGY

In 1993, there were 29 scientific and technological institutes in Albania, 19 of them concerned with agricultural research. The main scientific organization, the Academy of Sciences (founded in 1972), has a scientific library and six scientific institutes dealing with hydrometeorology, computer mathematics, biology, seismology, hydraulic research, and nuclear physics. The Geologists' Association of Albania, founded in 1989, has 870 members.

The Natural Science Museum has exhibits relating to zoology, botany, geology, and mineralogy.

Luigj Gurakugi University of Shkoder, founded in 1991, has a faculty in natural sciences. The Agricultural University of Tiranë, founded in 1971, has 5,100 students. The University of Tiranë, founded in 1957, has faculties in natural science, medicine, and mechanics and electronics.

The Higher Agricultural Institute, founded in 1971, has a library of 12,000 volumes.

³⁰DOMESTIC TRADE

Wholesale trade became a state monopoly in 1946. Initially, private retail trade played an important role, but by 1970 trade was fully socialized. By December 1990, retail units had been privatized again. All price controls were eliminated except on a few consumer items and monopoly-controlled products.

Shops in Albania are generally small, but department stores have been established in Tiranë, Durres, Korce, and other larger cities. Consumer cooperatives conduct trade in the rural areas.

Shop hours are Mondays and Tuesdays, 7 AM to 2 PM and 5 to 8 PM, and other weekdays, 7 AM to 2 PM. Before 1 January 1959, all sales were for cash, but after that date limited consumer credit was sanctioned.

³¹FOREIGN TRADE

Before World War II, about 50% of the exports consisted of the entire production of chrome ore and crude oil and some timber; the balance consisted of agricultural goods and fish. Good grains, sugar, and coffee made up about 20% of the imports; textiles, about 24%; and paper, machinery, chemicals, leather, metals, and oil products, about 53%. As the value of imports almost tripled that of exports, the deficit was met largely by Italian loans. Italy received two-thirds of Albanian exports and supplied Albania with up to half its imports. Under the Communist government, foreign trade became a state monopoly. The volume of turnover increased substantially and the structure and orientation changed radically.

Between 1950 and 1967, trade volume increased sixfold, to L1,043 million in 1967. Total trade volume (imports plus exports) rose 49% between 1966 and 1970. In 1960, trade with the socialist states accounted for about 90% of total trade; the Soviet share of this was half. Political and economic differences between Albania and the USSR resulted in suspension of aid to and trade with Albania. In 1961, 54% of total foreign trade was with the USSR and 7% with China; by 1964, trade with the former had ceased entirely, while trade with China had risen to 55%. After the Albanian-Chinese split in the late 1970s, economic contacts with China ceased. Talks aimed at renewing trade between the two nations were held in 1983, resulting in trade agreements worth about $5–7 million.

In the early 1990s, Albania exported chromium ore and concentrate, ferro-nickel ore, copper wires, electric power, food products, tobacco products, and handicrafts. Imports included raw materials, machinery, fuel, minerals, metals, and foodstuffs.

In 1990, exports totaled L2,288.5 million, and imports came to L3,796.6 million. Of exports, fuels and electricity constituted 47%, processed foodstuffs 20%, and raw materials of plant or animal origins, 18%. Of imports, machinery and equipment constituted 25%, and fuels, minerals, and metals, 25%. Raw materials of plant or animal origin came to 16%; foodstuffs, 10%; chemical and rubber products, 9 %; and spare parts and bearings, 6%.

Czechoslovakia took 15% of Albania's exports in 1990. Other major destinations were Germany, Italy, Bulgaria, Yugoslavia, Switzerland, and Hungary. The chief sources of Albania's imports were Germany (18%), Italy, Czechoslovakia, Bulgaria, China, and Austria.

³²BALANCE OF PAYMENTS

After four decades of communism, Albania privatized collective farms in 1992, which caused agricultural production to recover. This growing agricultural supply, (along with fiscal consolidation) is expected to reduce the current account deficit from 70% of GDP in 1992 to 40% of GDP by 1996.

In 1992, merchandise exports totaled $70 million and imports $523 million. The merchandise trade balance was $–453 million. The following table summarizes Albania's balance of payments for 1991 and 1992 (in millions of dollars):

	1991	1992
CURRENT ACCOUNT		
Goods, services, and income	–257.3	–555.3
Unrequited transfers	89.3	523.7
TOTALS	–168.0	–31.6
CAPITAL ACCOUNT		
Direct investment	—	20.0
Other long-term capital	21.4	36.3
Other short-term capital	–202.6	–25.6
Exceptional financing	196.0	—
Reserves	28.0	–13.5
TOTALS	42.8	17.2
Errors and omissions	125.2	14.4
Total change in reserves	28.0	–14.0

33BANKING AND SECURITIES

The Communist regime nationalized all banking and financial institutions in 1945 and established the Bank of the Albanian State, which is the bank of issue. The bank also controlled foreign transactions, helped prepare financial plans for the economy, accepted savings deposits, financed economic activities, and performed other banking functions. An agricultural bank was created in 1970 to provide credit facilities for agricultural cooperatives.

On 10 August 1949, the Directorate of Savings was established to grant loans and to accept savings deposits in branches throughout the country; the system has grown steadily ever since. The number of branches increased from 1,538 in 1960 to 3,600 in 1984. An annual interest of 2–3% was paid to depositors.

When the Soviet Union collapsed in 1991, Albania decided to become an independent country and develop a market economy. The banking system has changed to meet the demands of a free-market economy, The country has a two-tier system with a central bank, the National Bank of Albania, that issues currency and regulates the commercial banks. The other government banks are: the Agricultural Banks, the Albanian State Bank, Commercial Bank, Savings Bank of Albania. Foreign banks include the Swiss-Albania Iliria Bank. In 1990 there were 107 savings banks with 3,800 branches and agencies.

34INSURANCE

Insurance was nationalized by the Communist government after World War II. Under the jurisdiction of the Ministry of Finance, the program is administered by the Institute for Insurance, created in 1950. Half the profits are earmarked for the state budget, the other half for a reserve fund.

35PUBLIC FINANCE

After launching ambitious reforms in 1991, Albania became a member of the World Bank, IMF, and EBRD, enabling it to receive multilevel financial assistance to jump-start its economy. The EBRD in particular will provide technical assistance to develop telecommunications and tourism infrastructures, as well as assist in banking reform and privatization. Revenues in 1991 amounted to $1.1 billion, while expenditures came to $1.4 billion, including capital expenditures of $70 million. The external debt in 1991 stood at $500 million.

36TAXATION

Personal income is taxed at rates of 10–30%, and the corporate rates vary from 30–50%. Withholding taxes range from 5–20%, and the payroll/social security tax rate is 27%. The turnover tax, levied at a standard rate of 15%, is a differentiated sales tax on all commodities.

37CUSTOMS AND DUTIES

Under the jurisdiction of the Ministry of Trade, the General Directorate of Customs and Duties administers customs regulations. With certain specified exemptions, all goods are subject to duties ranging from 5% for raw materials, intermediate goods, and foodstuffs to 30% for industrial and capital goods. As of 2 December 1991, customs duties apply equally to public and private sector imports.

38FOREIGN INVESTMENT

Prior to 1990, no foreign capital was invested in postwar Albania, but various Communist states aided the Albanian industrialization program, supplying credit, machinery and equipment, and technicians. Prior to 1961, assistance by Soviet-bloc technicians in geologic surveys, construction, and operation of factories was vital to Albanian economic growth. Following the Soviet suspension of credits, withdrawal of technicians, and elimination of trade, China increased its activity in all these areas. In 1978, China terminated all its economic and military cooperation with Albania, and the following year Albania was for the first time without any foreign assistance. In the 1980s, some economic assistance was provided by the FRG. After the fall of communism, foreign investment was encouraged, and 149 joint ventures were agreed upon. Foreign investment in 1993 totaled $205 million. Incentives include free transfer of profits and four-year tax holidays.

39ECONOMIC DEVELOPMENT

Albania formerly had a state-controlled, centrally-planned economy, with emphasis on industrial development and socialized agriculture. Under Workers Party directives, short-term and long-range plans were formulated by the Economic Planning Commission, a government agency. By the mid-1980s, the economy was virtually under complete state control; enterprises were either directly owned by the state or managed through cooperatives.

From 1951, Albanian economic development was directed by five-year plans, most of which stressed heavy industry. The target growth rates of the seventh five-year plan (1981–85) were not achieved; in net material product, the actual increase was only 44% of the planned figure; in industrial production, the corresponding number was 72%; in agriculture, 41%; and in exports, 49%. The eighth five-year plan (1986–90) stressed energy and mineral resources development. The net material product was to rise by 35–37%, industrial production, by 29–31%, agricultural output by 35–37%, and the volume of foreign trade by 34–36%. In fact, economic growth in these years came to only 6%. Agricultural output grew 2% and industrial production, 13%. A sweeping economic reform program was announced in 1992. It called for widespread private ownership of farmland, state-owned companies and housing, and the removal of trade restrictions and price controls.

Albania's chief foreign aid donor, the EU, had issued grants worth $2.4 billion by early 1994. Albania received $335.3 million in economic aid during 1991.

40SOCIAL DEVELOPMENT

The Act on State Social Insurance, which came into force in January 1959, provided benefits for disability, old age, survivors, retirement, and meritorious service. The program, administered by the trade unions, covers all workers and salaried state employees, cooperative craftsmen, students (up to 24 years of age), and those performing compulsory military service. Collective farmers became subject to social insurance in 1972. Career military personnel are covered by a special social insurance scheme. Contributions are paid by employers, and additional sums are provided in the state budget.

An old age pension is granted when the insured reaches a certain age, depending upon class of work and length of service. The range is from 50 years for men and 45 years for women with 20 and 15 years of service, respectively, in arduous jobs—such as underground mining and foundry work—to 55 or 60 years for men (50–55 years for women) with 25 (for women, 20) years of employment in other categories of work. The amount of the pension is normally 70% of average monthly pay before retirement.

Disabled workers are divided into three classes and, if older than 20 years of age, must meet length-of-employment requirements. The amount of the pension varies between 85% and 40%, and provisions are made for small supplements. The pay for sick leave in the mid-1980s ranged from 70–85% of a worker's wages. Survivors' pensions varied between 40% of the insured's wage for one and 65% of wage for three or more members in the family. Pensions for meritorious service are given to professional personnel; the amount is the same as for old age pensioners.

Albanian's constitution prohibits discrimination based on sex, and women make up roughly half the labor force. In 1993, the country's first nonpolitical women's group, Reflexione, was formed to expand women's legal rights. The group plans to establish Albania's first shelter and counseling service for battered women.

⁴¹HEALTH

Insured persons, and pensioners and members of their families are entitled to free medical care, as provided for in the State Social Insurance Act. Total health expenditures for 1990 were $84 million. Albania's population in 1993 was 3.34 million. In 1990, there were 4,467 doctors and 1,099 dentists. From 1988 to 1992, there were 1.4 doctors per 1,000 people, and from 1985 to 1990, there 4.1 hospital beds per 1,000 people. There is a medical school in Tiranë (part of the Enver Hoxha University), and some Albanians receive medical training abroad.

The general improvement of health conditions in the country is reflected in the lower mortality rate, down to 5.3 deaths per 1,000 in 1993, as compared with 17.8 per 1,000 in 1938. In 1992, average life expectancy was estimated at 73 years (70 years for men and 76 years for women), compared to 38 years at the end of World War II. Albania's infant mortality rate, estimated at 28 per 1,000 live births in 1992, has also declined over the years. There were 76,000 births in 1992, and the birth rate in 1993 was 22.7 per 1,000. In addition, from 1990 to 1992, Albania had high immunization rates for children up to one year old: tuberculosis (94%); diphtheria, pertussis, and tetanus (96%); and measles (87%). In 1990, the incidence of tuberculosis was 40 in 100,000 people. In 1990, 72% of the population had access to safe water, and 92% of the population had access to health care.

⁴²HOUSING

During World II, about 61,000 buildings of all types were destroyed, including 35,400 dwellings. Housing was generally primitive in rural areas and poor elsewhere. After the war, housing continued to be a problem for a variety of reasons: primary emphasis on industrial construction, shortages of materials and skilled labor, and lack of or inadequate assistance for private building. Moreover, the increase of urban population worsened an already desperate situation. Consequently, new housing construction has been concentrated in Tiranë, Vlorë, Elbasan, Shkodër, Durrës, and Korçë, as well as in other industrial and mining sites.

Investments for housing construction by state enterprises increased from L163 million (at 1977 prices) in 1951–55 to L402 million in 1976–78. Between 1951 and 1978, peasants built 163,478 new but mostly small and simple houses; during the same period, 11,781 housing units were built by other private persons, and 110,883 units were built by the state. During the first half of the 1980s, about 12,000 new dwelling units were constructed annually, half of them built by the state and half by individuals. Some 85,000 new units were to be built during the eighth five-year plan (1986–90). In 1986, 72% of Albania's housing units had a water supply, 67% had a bath or shower, 40% had central heating, and 60% had toilet facilities. The total housing stock in 1991 numbered 756,000.

⁴³EDUCATION

Before and during World War II, about three-fourths of the population was illiterate. Great strides have been made since then, and today the regime claims that complete literacy has been achieved; however, Western estimates put the literacy rate at 80%.

The basic compulsory school program, extending for eight years (ages 7 to 15), combines practical work with study. Preschool training is general but not obligatory.

In 1990, there were 1,726 primary level schools with a teaching staff of 28,798. Students attending them were 551,294. At the secondary level, there were 9,708 teachers and 205,774 students. Of these, 2,250 attended teacher training and 135,935 were in vocational programs in 1990. Government expenditure on education amounted to 11.1% of the total governmental expenditure for 1988.

In 1957, the Institute of Sciences was elevated to university rank, and Tiranë State University became the first and only institution of university status in Albania. It was later renamed Enver Hoxha University of Tiranë. In 1971, two more universities were founded—Universiteti I Koree and Universiteti Bujguesor I Tiranes. In 1991, the University of Shkodër was established.

There were also other institutes of higher learning including two agricultural schools, one institute for fine arts, one institute of physical culture, and three teacher-training institutes.

⁴⁴LIBRARIES AND MUSEUMS

The largest library in Albania is the National Library in Tiranë with over 1 million volumes. Public libraries exist in many communities with notable ones in Elbasan (284,000 volumes), Shkoder (250,000 volumes), Durrës (180,000 volumes) and Korçë (139,000 volumes).

The principal museums are the Albanian National Culture Museum, the Museum of Archaeology, the Natural Science Museum, and the National Historical Museum, all located in Tiranë. In the early 1980s there were 33 provincial museums, among them the Berat Museum, known for its collection of historic documents. The Museum of the Struggle for National Liberation was founded in 1977 in Korge. The cities of Berat and Gjirokastër, the first dating from antiquity and the second from the Middle Ages, have been designated "museum-cities."

⁴⁵MEDIA

Communications are owned and operated by the state and are administered by the Ministry of Communications. In 1990, there were 6,000 telephones. Fourteen radio stations operated by Radiotelevizioni Shqiptar, are located at Kashar, a suburb of Tiranë, and at Shkodër, Stalin, Vlorë, Gjirokastër, Korçë, and several other towns. Television was introduced in 1961, color broadcasts in 1981. There were 9 television stations in 1991. In the same year, there were about 285,000 television sets and 577,000 radios.

All newspapers and periodicals were published either directly by the Workers Party or by its mass organizations. As of 1992, there were four daily newspapers published in Tiranë. The two major ones were *Zëri i Popullit*, the Workers Party central organ, with an estimated daily circulation of 105,000 and *Bashkimi*

Kombetar, the Democratic Front's central organ, with a circulation of 30,000. Other important publications are *Zëri i Rinisë,* published by the Union of Working Youth, and *Shqiptarja e Rë,* published by the women's organizations. In 1988 there were 74 periodicals. In the same year there were 28 theaters and 106 cinemas. ATA (Albanian Telegraphic Agency) is the official news agency.

[46]ORGANIZATIONS

Trade unions in Albania were prohibited until 1991. Before 1991 the official trade unions of the country were responsible for promoting the production goals of the country's Communist government. In 1991, independent trade unions were established to promote the rights of workers. The Union of Independent Trade Unions is the most important umbrella trade organization. Other trade unions operate in the defense, agriculture, food processing, and mining sectors of the economy. Albania has three chambers of commerce. The Chamber of Commerce of the republic of Albania promotes the economic and business activities of the country in world markets. Other chambers of commerce are located in Shkodei, Durrës and Gjirokastër.

[47]TOURISM, TRAVEL, AND RECREATION

Albania has been the most inaccessible country in Eastern Europe; relatively few Westerners have visited the country. About 6,000 people visited Albania annually in the 1970s. In the early 1980s, persons explicitly forbidden to visit the country were US citizens, Soviet citizens, and full-bearded men.

Since the advent of democracy, Albania has slowly become accessible to the outside world. Tourists can now obtain visas within 2 weeks. During the visit, they are escorted by guides from Albturist, the official tourist agency. In promoting travel to Albania, the agency cites the Adriatic beaches, especially at Durrës, Vlorë, and Sarandë, and the picturesque lakes. In 1990, 30,000 foreign tourists visited Albania.

The most popular sports are soccer, gymnastics, volleyball, and basketball. In 1959, 1969, 1974, 1979, and 1984, Albania organized National Spartakiads, or nationwide sports competitions; some 760,000 Albanians took part in the 1984 Spartakiad.

[48]FAMOUS ALBANIANS

Much Albanian popular lore is based on the exploits of the national hero Gjergj Kastrioti (known as Scanderbeg, 1405–68), who led his people against the Turks.

Ahmet Bey Zogu (1895–1961), shepherd, military commander, minister of the interior, and premier, was elected first president of the new republic in 1925; in 1928, when Albania became a kingdom, he ascended the throne as Zog I. After Italian forces occupied Albania in April 1939, he fled the country, dying in exile in southern France. Two major political leaders were Enver Hoxha (1908–85), postwar Albania's first premier, minister of foreign affairs, and defense minister; and Mahmet Shehu (1913–81), who replaced Hoxha as premier in 1954, when Hoxha became first secretary of the Workers Party's Central Committee. Since Hoxha's death, the first secretary of the Workers Party and head of state has been Ramiz Alia (b.1925).

Albania's written literature of a nationalist character first developed among Italo-Albanians in Calabria in the mid-19th century and among the Albanian intellectuals in Constantinople in the second half of the 19th century. Naim Erashëri (1846–1900), Albania's national poet, belonged to the Constantinople group. His most highly regarded works are *Bagëti e Bujqësi (Cattle and Land), Histori e Skenderbeut (History of Scanderbeg),* and a collection of short poems, *Lulet e Verës (Spring Flowers).* Kostandin Kristoforidhi (K. Nelko, 1827–95) translated the Old and New Testaments into Albanian and compiled a standard Albanian-Greek dictionary. Faik Konitza (1875–1942), prewar Albanian minister to Washington, edited a literary review, *Albania,* which became the focal publication of Albanian writers living abroad. Gjergj Fishta (1871–1940), a Franciscan friar who was active in the nationalist movement, wrote a long epic poem, *Lahuta e Malcís (The Lute of the Mountains),* which is regarded as a masterpiece of Albanian literature. Bishop Fan Stylian Noli (1882–1965), a political leader in the early 1920s, was Albania's foremost translator of Shakespeare, Ibsen, Cervantes, and other world classics. Lasgush Poradeci (1899–1987) was a highly regarded lyric poet.

[49]DEPENDENCIES

Albania has no territories or colonies.

[50]BIBLIOGRAPHY

Amery, Julian. *Sons of the Eagle: A Study in Guerrilla War.* New York: Macmillan, 1949.

Bland, William B. *Albania.* Oxford; Santa Barbara, Calif.: Clio, 1988.

Griffith, William E. *Albania and the Sino-Soviet Rift.* Cambridge, Mass.: MIT Press, 1963.

Hall, Derek R. *Albania and the Albanians.* New York: St. Martin's Press, 1994.

Halliday, Jon (ed.). *The Artful Albanian: Memoirs of Enver Hoxha.* Topsfield, Mass.: Salem House, 1987.

Logoreci, Anton. *The Albanians: Europe's Forgotten Survivors.* Boulder, Colo.: Westview, 1978.

Marmullaku, Ramadan. *Albania and the Albanians.* Hamden, Conn.: Archon, 1975.

Myrdal, Jan, and Gun Kessle. *Albania Defiant.* New York: Monthly Review, 1976.

Pano, Nicholas C. *Albania: Politics, Economics, and Society.* Boulder, Colo.: Lynne Rienner, 1986.

Perspectives on Albania. New York: St. Martin's Press, 1992.

Pipa, Arshi. *Albanian Stalinism: Ideo-political Aspects.* Boulder, Colo.: East European, 1990.

Pollo, Stefanay, and Arben Puto. *The History of Albania.* London: Routledge & Kegan Paul, 1981.

Prifti, Peter R. *Socialist Albania Since 1944.* Cambridge, Mass.: MIT Press, 1978.

Robinson, Vandeleur. *Albania's Road to Freedom.* London: Allen & Unwin, 1941.

Schnytzer, Adi. *Stalinist Economic Strategy in Practice: The Case of Albania.* New York: Oxford University Press, 1982.

Sjoberg, Orjan. *Rural Change and Development in Albania.* Boulder, Colo.: Westview Press, 1991.

Skendi, Stavro. *The Albanian National Awakening, 1878–1912.* Princeton, N.J.: Princeton University Press, 1967.

Thirty-Five Years of Socialist Albania: Statistical Data on the Development of the Economy and Culture. Tiranë: "8 Nëntori" Publishing House, 1981.

ANDORRA

Principality of Andorra
Principat d'Andorra

CAPITAL: Andorra la Vella.

FLAG: The national flag is a tricolor of blue, yellow, and red vertical stripes. On the state flag the yellow stripe bears the coat of arms (shown in the French version on the flag and in the Spanish version above it).

ANTHEM: The *Himne Andorra* begins "El gran Carlemany mon pare" ("Great Charlemagne my father").

MONETARY UNIT: Andorra has no currency of its own; both the Spanish peseta (P) and the French franc (Fr) are used. P1 = $0.0073 (or $1 = P137.38); Fr1 = $0.1751 (or $1 = Fr5.71).

WEIGHTS AND MEASURES: The metric system and some old local standards are used.

HOLIDAYS: New Year's Day, 1 January; National Festival, 8 September; Christmas, 25 December. Movable religious holidays include Good Friday and Easter Monday.

TIME: 1 PM = noon GMT.

¹LOCATION, SIZE, AND EXTENT

Landlocked Andorra lies on the southern slopes of the Pyrenees Mountains between the French departments of Ariège and Pyrénées-Orientales to the N and the Spanish provinces of Gerona and Lérida to the S, with a total boundary length of 125 km (77.7 mi).

Andorra is slightly more than 2.5 times the size of Washington, D.C., with a total area of 450 sq km (174 sq mi), extending 30.1 km (18.7 mi) E–W and 25.4 km (15.8 mi) N–S.

Andorra's capital city, Andorra la Vella, is located in the southwestern part of the country.

²TOPOGRAPHY

Andorra is situated in a single drainage basin, but its main stream, the Riu Valira, has two distinct branches and six open basins; hence the term "Valleys" (Les Valls) was traditionally employed as part of the name of the principality. The section of the river flowing through El Serrat by way of Ordino and La Massana is the Valira d'Ordino, while that flowing through Canillo, Encamp, and Les Escaldes is the Valira d'Orient. Most of the country is rough and mountainous, and there is little level surface. All the valleys are at least 900 m (3,000 ft) high, and the mean altitude is over 1,800 m (6,000 ft). There are lofty peaks, of which the highest is Coma Pedrosa (2,946 m/9,665 ft).

³CLIMATE

Because of its high elevation, Andorra has severe winters. The northern valleys are completely snowed up for several months. Most rain falls in April and October. Humidity is very low. Summers are warm or mild, depending on the altitude. There are considerable variations between maximum day and night temperatures.

⁴FLORA AND FAUNA

The plant and animal life is similar to that found in the neighboring areas of France and Spain. Chestnut and walnut trees grow only in the area around Sant Julía de Lòria, the lowest village. Elsewhere, evergreen oaks still are common. Higher regions and many valleys have pines, firs, and various forms of subalpine and alpine plant life. At the highest altitudes there are no trees, but grass is plentiful during the summer. There are carnations, violets, bellflowers, and daisies, as well as blackberries, wild strawberries, and moss. Bears, wolves, foxes, martens, Pyrenean chamois, rabbits, hares, eagles, vultures, wild ducks, and geese may be found in isolated areas. The mountain streams contain trout, brochet, and crayfish.

⁵ENVIRONMENT

Andorra was once heavily forested, and one explanation for the name of the country is that it came from the Moorish word *aldarra*, meaning "place thick with trees." Andorra's mountainous environment attracts 12 million tourists each year. In recent decades, however, the forested area has been decreasing steadily. Overgrazing of mountain meadows by sheep, with consequent soil erosion, is another environmental problem.

⁶POPULATION

The population in 1990 was 54,507, with a density of 117 persons per sq km (302 per sq mi). The population increased at an annual rate of 4% from 1986, mostly because of immigration. The population is concentrated in the seven urbanized valleys that form Andorra's political districts. Andorran citizens are outnumbered three-to-one by other ethnic groups, the majority of whom are of Spanish descent.

The capital is Andorra la Vella, which had a population of 20,437 in 1990. Other leading towns are Les Escaldes, Sant Julía de Lòria, Encamp, and La Massana.

⁷MIGRATION

Immigration consists mainly of Spanish, Portuguese, and French nationals who intend to work in Andorra. Living in Andorra in 1990 were 27,066 Spanish and 4,130 French immigrants, who together constituted 57% of the resident population.

⁸ETHNIC GROUPS

Andorrans numbered 15,616 in 1990 and made up 29% of the population; they are of Catalan stock. The remainder were mostly Spanish (53.6% of the population) and French (6.5%), but also included 7,695 others, of which at least half were Portuguese.

9LANGUAGES

The official language is Catalan. French and Spanish are also spoken.

10RELIGIONS

Over 92% of all Andorans are Roman Catholic, and Roman Catholicism, introduced to the area at an early date, is the official religion of the state. Small populations of Protestant denominations are also represented (0.5%), and there is a smaller Jewish community as well (0.4%).

11TRANSPORTATION

A north-south highway links Andorra la Vella with the Spanish and French borders. Secondary roads and trails also cross the border but are sometimes closed in winter because of deep snows. There are over 100 km (60 mi) of surfaced roads and 41,321 (in 1992) motor vehicles.

Buses, the principal means of mass transit, provide regular service to Seo de Urgel and Barcelona in Spain, and to Perpignan in France. Among several cable cars, the most important operates between Encamp and Engolasters Lake. Most merchandise is transported by vehicles from neighboring countries.

Andorra does not have railways or commercial airports, but the airport at Seo de Urgel is only 20 km (12.5 mi) from Andorra la Vella. The nearest international airports are at Barcelona, Spain, located 215 km (134 mi) from Andorra, and at Toulouse, France, 165 km (103 mi) away. There is daily bus service from the Barcelona and Toulouse airports to Andorra.

12HISTORY

According to one tradition, Charlemagne gave the region the name Andorra for its supposed likeness to the biblical town of Endor. Tradition also asserts that Charlemagne granted the Andorran people a charter in return for their help in fighting the Moors, and that Charlemagne's son Louis I, king of France, confirmed the charter.

It is generally agreed that Charles the Bald, the son of Louis, appointed the count of Urgel (now Seo de Urgel) overlord of Andorra and gave him the right to collect the imperial tribute. The bishop of Urgel, however, also claimed Andorra as part of the endowment of his cathedral. In 1226, the lords of the countship of Foix, in present-day south-central France, by marriage became heirs to the counts of Urgel. The quarrels between the Spanish bishop and the French counts over rights in Andorra led in 1278 to their adoption of a paréage, a feudal institution recognizing equal rights of two lords to a seigniorage.

In 1505, Germaine of Foix married Ferdinand V of Castile, thereby bringing the lordship of Andorra under Spanish rule. On taking over the kingdom in 1519, Emperor Charles V granted the lordship of Les Valls, as it was then known, to Germaine of Foix's line in perpetuity. Henry III of Navarre, who was also count of Foix, in 1589 ascended the French throne as Henry IV, and by an edict of 1607 established the head of the French state, along with the bishop of Urgel, as co-princes of Andorra.

In 1793, the French revolutionary government refused the traditional Andorran tribute as smacking of feudalism and renounced its suzerainty, despite the wish of the Andorrans to enjoy French protection and avoid being under exclusively Spanish influence.

Andorra remained neutral in the Napoleonic wars with Spain. Napoleon restored the co-principality in 1806 after the Andorrans petitioned him to do so. French title to the principality subsequently passed from the kings to the president of France.

Long an impoverished land having little contact with any nations other than adjoining France and Spain, Andorra after World War II achieved considerable prosperity through a developing tourist industry. This development, abetted by improvements in transport and communications, has tended to break down Andorra's isolation and to bring Andorrans into the mainstream of European history. Public demands for democratic reforms led to the extension of the franchise to women in the 1970s and to the creation of new and more fully autonomous organs of government in the early 1980s.

Andorra formally became a parliamentary democracy in May 1993 following approval of a new constitution by a popular referendum in March 1993. The new constitution retained the French and Spanish co-princes although with reduced, and narrowly defined, powers. Civil rights were greatly expanded including the legalization of political parties and trade unions, and provision was made for an independent judiciary. Andorra acceded to the European communities custom union in 1991 and was admitted to the UN on 28 July 1993.

13GOVERNMENT

The governmental system of Andorra is unique. Authority is shared equally by the president of France and the bishop of Urgel as co-princes. Andorra pays a nominal biennial tribute of Fr960 to the president of France and P460 to the bishop. Each year the bishop receives from Andorra 12 cheeses, 12 capons, 12 partridges, and 6 hams. The co-princes are represented by Permanent Delegates and veguers.

The French delegate is the prefect of the department of Pyrénées-Orientales and resides at Perpignan; the other delegate is one of the vicars-general of Urgel diocese. The veguers reside in Andorra. Both the delegates and veguers acquire Andorran nationality ex officio, but are not usually native Andorrans.

Legislation is enacted by the General Council, consisting of 28 members, 4 councillors from each of the 7 parishes, elected at the same time for a four-year term since December 1981. Of the 28 seats, 14 are based on a national list and 14 are elected. As the result of institutional reform, the council appointed an Executive Council in January 1982; in October 1986, the council had six members.

The current President of the Council is Oscar Ribas Reig (the first elected head of government of Andorra) and who was appointed in January 1994 following the December 1993 general election. The General Council designates as its head a first syndic (syndic procureur général) and a second syndic for the conduct of administration; upon election to their three-year terms, these syndics cease to be members of the council.

The franchise, which at one time was limited to third-generation Andorran males of 25 years of age or over, by 1981 had been extended to include all native Andorrans of Andorran parentage (at age 21) and first-generation Andorrans of foreign parentage (at age 28).

In October 1985, the voting age was lowered to 18 years. In October 1992, the suffrage was broadened to include spouses of Andorran citizens and long-term residents.

Following a general election in December 1993, a new government was formed in February 1994 led by Oscar Ribas Reig of the National Democratic Grouping (AND).

14POLITICAL PARTIES

Prior to 1993, political parties had been illegal in Andorra, though the Democratic Party of Andorra (formed in 1979) was tolerated. There have been two main factions in organized political life—conservatives and liberals.

The general election of December 1993 was the first under Andorra's new constitution. Five parties gained representation in the 28-seat General Council as follows: National Democratic Grouping (AND)—8 seats; Liberal Union (UL)—5 seats; New Democracy (ND)—5 seats; and 10 seats divided between the National Andorran Coalition (CNA) and the National Democratic Initiative (IDN).

[15]LOCAL GOVERNMENT

Andorra is divided into seven parishes or districts: Canillo, Ordino, Encamp, La Massana, Sant Julía de Lória, and Andorra la Vella and Les Escaldes, which became a separate district in 1978. Eligible voters in each of the districts elect members of its parish council (comú).

Local affairs are administered by parish councils and quarts. Each council generally consists of 8 to 14 members elected by universal suffrage for four-year terms at the same time as general councillors. Councils elect a senior consul and a junior consul. Each quart functions as a submunicipality, administering communal property within a village.

[16]JUDICIAL SYSTEM

The 1993 constitution guarantees an independent judiciary and the judiciary has in fact been independent. A Superior Council of Justice oversees and administers the judicial system. The new constitution also calls for respect for the promotion of liberty, equality, justice, tolerance, defense of human rights, dignity of the person, and privacy, and guarantees against arbitrary arrest and detention. Appeals from lower courts, including appeals of constitutional issues, will be decided by a separate Supreme Court. Other details of the new court system have not yet been established.

Under the current system, civil cases in the first instance are heard by four judges (batlles). Appeals are heard in the Court of Appeal. Final appeals in civil cases are brought before the Supreme Court of Andorra at Perpignan, France, or the ecclesiastical court of the bishop.

Criminal cases are heard in Andorra la Vella by the Tribunal des Quarts, consisting of the veguers, and the judge of appeal, two batlless, and two members of the General Council. Few criminal trials are held, and the principality's jail is used only for persons awaiting sentencing. Sentenced criminals have the choice of French or Spanish jails. The courts apply the customary law of Andorra, supplementing it where necessary with Roman law and customary Catalan law. Traditional laws are compiled in the Manual Digest of 1748 and the Politar of 1763; legal standards are found in the Instructions to Bailiffs of 1740.

[17]ARMED FORCES

Andorra has no defense force, and the police force is small. The sole military expenses are for ammunition used in salutes at official ceremonies, the lone responsibility of Andorra's small army. France and Spain are pledged to defend Andorra.

[18]INTERNATIONAL COOPERATION

Aside from France and Spain, Andorra has no full diplomatic relations with the rest of the world. Although not a UN member, it does participate in some UNESCO activities.

[19]ECONOMY

The Andorran economy is primarily based on trade and tourism, with the traffic between France and Spain providing most of the revenue. With more than 240 hotels and 50 restaurants, the tourist trade is an important component of the economy.

The Andorran banking system is of some importance as a tax haven for foreign financial transactions and investments. Andorra also is a tax haven because there are no direct taxes.

There is also active trade in consumer goods because they are duty-free in Andorra. Because imported manufactured items are duty-free and thus less expensive than in countries where they are dutiable, smuggling of these goods from Andorra to such countries has long been a thriving enterprise.

[20]INCOME

In 1992, Andorra's GNP was $760 million at current prices, or $14,000 per capita. The principal component is tourism.

LOCATION: 42°25′ to 42°40′N; 1°25′E. BOUNDARY LENGTHS: France, 60 km (37.3 mi); Spain, 65 km (40.4 mi).

[21]LABOR

Commerce engages about 24% of the economically active population (estimated at around 20,000 in the early 1990s); restaurants and hotels, 19%; manufacturing, 11%; construction, 12%; public administration, 10%; business services, 5%; agriculture, 1%, and other sectors, 18%. Trade unions are not permitted.

With no business regulation or registration requirements, smuggling goods between France and Spain is a leading source of informal employment.

[22]AGRICULTURE

Because of Andorra's mountainous character, only about 2% of the land is suitable for crops. However, until the tourism sector in Andorra experienced an upsurge, agriculture had been the mainstay of the economy. Hay, tobacco, and vegetables must be irrigated; cereals, mainly rye and barley, are dry-cropped. Most of the cropped land is devoted to hay production for animal feed. Since there is insufficient sunlight on northward-facing slopes and the lands in shadow are too cold for most crops, some southward-facing fields high in the mountains must be used even though they are a considerable distance from the farmers' homes.

Tobacco, the most distinctive Andorran crop, is grown on the best lands. Andorran tobacco is usually mixed with eastern tobaccos, because of its strong quality. Other farm products include cereals, potatoes, and garden vegetables. Grapes are used mainly for raisins and for the making of anisette. The lack of modern methods on Andorra's family farms is causing the agricultural sector to decrease in importance. Most food is now imported.

23 ANIMAL HUSBANDRY

For many centuries, until eclipsed by tourism and other service industries, sheep raising was the basis of Andorra's economy. Andorran mules are still greatly prized. Cattle, sheep, and goats are raised both in the valleys and in some of the higher areas. Cattle are raised mainly for their meat, and there are few dairy cows. When the cattle move upward in the spring, entire families move to temporary villages in the mountains to herd, mow, and plant. Large droves of sheep and goats from France and Spain feed in Andorra in the summer, and the Spanish-owned animals in particular are looked after by Andorran shepherds. On their way back to their native land, many of the animals are sold at annual fairs; the Spanish fairs are usually held in Andorra in September and the French in November. Andorra's own animal fairs are also held in the fall.

Livestock includes an estimated 9,000 sheep, 1,100 cattle, and 200 horses. Meat production has increased in recent years, but imports account for about 90% of total meat consumption. The milk produced is sufficient for domestic consumption, and some milk has been exported to Spain.

24 FISHING

The streams are full of trout and other freshwater fish, but Andorra imports most fish for domestic consumption from Spain.

25 FORESTRY

Less than one-fourth of the total area is forested. Fuel wood may be freely gathered by anyone, but it may not be bought or sold. Wood needed for building purposes is cut in rotation from a different district each year. For centuries logs have been shipped to Spain. Most reforestation is in pines.

26 MINING

For hundreds of years, Andorran forges were famous in northern Spain. There are still iron ore deposits in the valley of Ordino and in many of the mountain areas, but access to them is difficult.

In addition to iron, small amounts of lead are still mined, and alum and building stones are extracted. The sulfurous waters of Les Escaldes are used in washing wool.

27 ENERGY AND POWER

The largest hydroelectric plant, at Encamp, has a capacity of 26.5 ms and provides about 40% of Andorra's electric power needs, with most of the remainder being imported from Spain. The total installed capacity in 1991 was 35,000 kw and energy production totaled 140 million kwh.

There are four gas companies, with Andor Gas supplying propane and the others butane.

28 INDUSTRY

Andorra produces cigars, cigarettes, textiles, leather, building materials, and furniture, both for local use and for export. Woolen blankets and scarves are made at Les Escaldes.

Many enterprises produce frozen foods, pastry, and other commodities. There are distilleries for the production of anisette, vermouth, liqueurs, and brandy.

Several firms manufacture woolen goods. There are a number of construction companies, the largest producing building materials from iron.

29 SCIENCE AND TECHNOLOGY

There are no advanced research facilities. Students wishing to

pursue scientific and technical careers usually receive their training in France or Spain.

30 DOMESTIC TRADE

Andorra la Vella has many stores where commodities of all kinds and origins may be purchased. The larger villages have small general stores. The French, Spanish, and Andorran animal fairs that take place at Andorra la Vella, Encamp, Ordino, and elsewhere are attended by most Andorrans and by many French and Spanish farmers.

There is a high level of competition between the large department stores and the small shops. There are some 600 retail establishments in the country, of which the department and jewelry stores are the most numerous, followed by food and clothing outlets.

There are over 240 hotels and 50 restaurants catering to the thriving tourist trade.

31 FOREIGN TRADE

Owing to the large traffic of unaccounted goods across Andorra's borders, official statistics do not reflect the true volume of transactions. Of recorded trade, close to half is with France and one-third with Spain. The majority of imports consist of consumer goods sold to visitors. Reported imports exceed recorded exports by more than 30:1.

A customs union with the EC (now the EU) took effect in 1991, allowing industrial goods to pass between Andorra and EC members under a uniform customs tariff. The EU's external tariffs are to be applied by Andorra to its trade with non-EU members.

32 BALANCE OF PAYMENTS

Tourism is an important source of foreign earnings, especially during the skiing season. With the creation of the EC Unified Market, Andorra has lost its privileged status as a duty-free haven within the EC, thus severely diminishing foreign currency inflows.

33 BANKING AND SECURITIES

An unofficial Convention of Banks and Bankers periodically attends to financial affairs. The banking system attracts foreign financial transactions and investments because there are no direct taxes in Andorra.

There were six private banks in 1994. About half of all deposits are made in pesetas, with one-fourth in francs and the balance in other currencies. There is no stock exchange, and therefore, stocks and bonds are not traded in Andorra.

34 INSURANCE

The principal firm is the Andorra Insurance Co., established in 1951, which provides coverage that includes life, fire, accident, and plate glass. There are several other insurance companies.

35 PUBLIC FINANCE

The central government budget in 1987 included expenditures of P11,000 million. The treasury deficit fell from 12.7% of GDP in 1988 to a surplus of 1% in 1991 because of fiscal structural changes. The government has introduced exchange and trade restrictions in order to minimize imports and lower external debts. In 1992, budget revenues came to $14.6 billion, while expenditures amounted to $14.6 billion, including $3.5 billion in capital expenditures. The external debt in 1992 was estimated at $26 billion.

36 TAXATION

There is no income tax on the individual or corporate level. Employees pay social security taxes at rates of 5–9%; employers pay 13%. As of October 1991, a value-added type tax had been enacted and was expected to impose charges of 1–7% on the production and import of goods. Also scheduled for implementation under the

1992 budget law are a registration tax on certain activities, expected to provide 8.6% of government revenues, and a tax on electricity consumption and telephone services expected to contribute 1.6% of state revenues.

³⁷CUSTOMS AND DUTIES
Since 1 July 1991, a customs duty has been levied ad valorem on agricultural imports from the EC at rates of 2–60%.

³⁸FOREIGN INVESTMENT
No recent information is available.

³⁹ECONOMIC DEVELOPMENT
Government policy is to encourage local industries and to promote private investment. In addition to handicrafts, manufacturing includes cigars, cigarettes, and furniture. There is a plan to make Andorra a major financial center.

⁴⁰SOCIAL DEVELOPMENT
There is a social welfare system, introduced in 1966 for functionaries and expanded in 1968 to cover the entire population.

There is no legal discrimination against women, although they have only enjoyed full suffrage since 1970 and play only a very minimal role in the country's government.

⁴¹HEALTH
In 1981, there were 42 doctors and 113 hospital beds. Infant mortality was estimated at 8 per 1,000 births in 1992; life expectancy was estimated at 77 years.

⁴²HOUSING
Most Andorran houses are made of stone. Since the flat land is used for farm crops, the rural houses are frequently backed against the mountainsides. The high villages (cortals) are situated on a line between the highest fields and the lowest limits of high-level pastures. Isolated houses (bordes) are found at higher elevations. Many families maintain temporary dwellings in the highest pasture areas.

⁴³EDUCATION
By law, students must attend school until age 16. Education is provided by both French- and Spanish-language schools. The French government partially subsidizes education in Andorra's French-language schools; schools in the southern section, near Spain, are supported by the church. The local language, Catalan, recently has been introduced at a school under the control of the Roman Catholic Church. A total of 9,024 students attended the 18 schools in Andorra in 1991. In the 1990/91 academic year, 1,861 students were enrolled at infant schools, 5,584 at primary schools and 1,579 at secondary, technical and special schools.

About 50% of Andorran children attend French primary schools, and the rest attend Spanish or Andorran school. In general, Andorran schools follow the Spanish curriculum, and their diplomas are recognized by Spain.

While there are no schools of higher education; secondary graduates who continue their education attend schools in France or Spain. Virtually the entire adult population is literate.

⁴⁴LIBRARIES AND MUSEUMS
There is a small library in Andorra la Vella. The National Library and National Archives founded in 1974 and 1975 respectively are located in Andorra la Vella. Several museums have been founded since 1975.

⁴⁵MEDIA
Automatic telephone service was begun in 1967; in 1990, there were 17,700 telephones. Postal and telegraph services are handled by the Spanish and French administrations; a telex system was installed in 1970.

Radio programming was broadcast over two private stations, Spanish-owned Radio Andorra and French-owned Sud-Radio, until their contracts expired in 1981. The government then established new stations operated by Andorrans and supervised by the General Council.

In 1990, there was one AM station. Television transmission is provided through technical accords with the Spanish and French government networks. In 1991 there were an estimated 10,000 radios and 7,000 television sets.

Andorra's main newspaper, the weekly *Poble Andorra*, had a circulation of 3,000 in 1992. Other newspapers, with smaller circulations, are the dailies *Diari D'Anderra, Independent,* and *Informacions Diari,* and the weeklies *Cerreu Andorra* and *Informacions.* French and Spanish newspapers are also widely available.

⁴⁶ORGANIZATIONS
There are no cultural or business organizations of major importance. Two international music festivals are organized by special organizations. Religious festivals are staged periodically in the larger villages, and are organized by local groups.

⁴⁷TOURISM, TRAVEL, AND RECREATION
Tourism has brought considerable prosperity to Andorra, and now constitutes the principal source of income. Visitors, mostly from France and Spain, come to Andorra each summer to attend the fairs and festivals, to buy consumer items at lower prices than are obtainable in the neighboring countries, and to enjoy the pleasant weather and beautiful scenery. There is skiing at Pas de la Casa and Soldeu in winter.

Shrines and festivals are both key attractions to tourists. Romanesque churches and old houses of interest are located in Ordino, Encamp, Sant Julía de Lória, Les Escaldes, Santa Coloma, and other villages. The best known is the shrine of Our Lady of Meritxell, Andorra's patroness, between Canillo and Encamp.

Pilgrims come from France and Spain to pay homage on 8 September, the festival day of Andorra's patroness. Each of the larger villages has its own festival during which the sardana, Andorra's national dance, is performed.

There is an International Music Festival each June and July, and an International Jazz Festival at Escaldes-Engordany in July.

An estimated 12 million tourists visit Andorra each year. Over 250 hotels (a majority located in Andorra la Vella and Les Escaldes) cater to their needs.

⁴⁸FAMOUS ANDORRANS
There are no internationally famous Andorrans.

⁴⁹DEPENDENCIES
Andorra has no territories or colonies.

⁵⁰BIBLIOGRAPHY
Carter, Youngman. *On to Andorra.* New York: Norton, 1964.
Deane, Shirley. *The Road to Andorra.* New York: Morrow, 1961.
Frisch, Max. *Andorra* (a play). London: Methuen, 1964.
Guildera, Josep Maria. *Una História d'Andorra.* Barcelona: Aedos, 1960.
Morgan, Bryan. *Andorra, the Country in Between.* Nottingham: Palmer, 1964.
National Accounts Statistics: Main Aggregates and Detailed Tables, 1991: Part I. New York: United Nations, 1993.
Stockholm International Peace Research Institute. *SIPRI Yearbook 1993: World Armaments and Disarmament.* Oxford,

England: Oxford University Press, 1993.

Taylor, Barry. *Andorra*. Oxford, England, and Santa Barbara, Calif.: Clio Press, 1993.

United Nations Conference on Trade and Development. *Handbook of International Trade and Development Statistics*. New York: United Nations, 1993.

World Bank. *World Tables 1994*. Baltimore and London, England: Johns Hopkins University Press, 1994.

ARMENIA

Republic of Armenia
Hayastani Hanrapetut 'Yun

CAPITAL: Yerevan.

FLAG: Three horizontal bands of red (top), blue and gold.

ANTHEM: *Mer Hayrenik.*

MONETARY UNIT: The dram (introduced 22 November 1993) is a paper currency in denominations of 10, 25, 50, 100, 200, and 500 drams. The dram (D) is intended to replace the Armenian ruble and the Russian ruble (R). Currently 1 dram = 200 Armenian rubles or R84. D1 =$0.07 (or $1 = D14.3)

WEIGHTS AND MEASURES: The metric system is in force.

HOLIDAYS: New Year, 1–2 January; Christmas, 6 January; Easter, 1–4 April; Day of Remembrance of the Victims of the Genocide, 24 April; Peace Day, 9 May; Anniversary of Declaration of First Armenian Republic, 1918, 28 May; Public Holiday, 21 September; Day of Remembrance of the Victims of the Earthquake, 7 December, New Year, 31 December.

TIME: 4 PM = noon GMT.

¹LOCATION, SIZE, AND EXTENT

Armenia is a landlocked nation located in southeastern Europe. Comparatively, the area occupied by Armenia is slightly larger than the state of Maryland with a total area of 29,800 sq km (11,506 sq mi). Armenia shares boundaries with Georgia on the N, Azerbaijan on the E, Iran on the S, and Turkey on the W and has a total boundary length of 1,254 km (779 mi). Armenia's capital city, Yerevan, is located near its southeast boundary.

²TOPOGRAPHY

The topography of Armenia features the high Armenian Plateau, with mountains (many peaks are above 10,000 feet), little forest land, fast flowing rivers, and the Aras River Valley, which contains good soil.

³CLIMATE

Armenia's climate ranges from subtropical to alpine-like in the mountains. The mean temperature in August is 25°C (77°F). In January, the mean temperature is –3°C (27°F). Rainfall is infrequent. The capital city receives 33 cm of rain annually (13 in), though more rainfall occurs in the mountains.

⁴FLORA AND FAUNA

Armenia is located in what geographers call the Aral Caspian Lowland. The country has broad sandy deserts and low grassy plateaus. The region is home to European bison, snow leopards, cheetahs, and porcupines.

⁵ENVIRONMENT

In 1994, Armenia's chief environmental problems were the result of natural disasters, pollution, and warfare. A strong earthquake in 1988 resulted in 55,000 casualties. Radiation from the meltdown of the nuclear reactor facility at Chernobyl in the former Soviet Union also polluted the environment in Armenia. The war between Armenia and Azerbaijan has added more strain to the country's economy and limited the amount of resources aimed at preserving the environment. Environmental issues have been kept alive by a movement that began in 1988 over the problem of air pollution.

⁶POPULATION

The population of Armenia was 3,278,677 in 1989. It was estimated at 3,415,566 in mid-1992. A population of 3,608,000 was estimated for 2000, assuming a crude birth rate of 15.6 per 1,000 population and a crude death rate of 6.3, for a natural increase of 9.3 for 1995–2000. The estimated population density in 1992 was 115 per sq km (297 per sq mi). Yerevan, the capital, had an estimated population of 1,202,000 at the beginning of 1990.

⁷MIGRATION

Independent Armenia is only a portion of historic Armenia, which at its greatest extent also included lands now in Turkey, Iran, and Azerbaijan. There are Armenian communities in these countries and also in Russia, Georgia, Lebanon, Syria, and the US. According to unofficial accounts, more than 500,000 people fled Armenia between 1991 and 1994.

⁸ETHNIC GROUPS

Armenians comprised 93% of the population in 1989. Another 2.6% were Azerbaijans, 1.7% were Kurds, and 1.6% were Russians.

⁹LANGUAGES

Armenian belongs to an independent branch of the Indo-European linguistic family. It is a highly inflective language, with a complicated system of declensions. It is agglutinative, rich in consonants, and has no grammatical gender. The vocabulary includes many Persian loan words. There are two main dialects: East Armenian, the official language of Armenia, and West, or Turkish, Armenian. The alphabet, patterned after Persian and Greek letters, has 38 characters. Armenian literature dates from the early 5th century AD.

¹⁰RELIGIONS

In September 1991, Armenia declared its independence from the Soviet Union, of which it had been a member since 1920. Armenia was a Christian country since the 4th century and witnessed a resurgence of the Armenian Apostolic Church after independence.

In 1992, 94% of the population was Armenian Orthodox, with smaller representations of Russian Orthodox and Roman Catholic.

11 TRANSPORTATION

As of 1990, there were 840 km (522 mi) of 1-meter-gauge railroad, not including industrial lines. Supplies that arrive from Turkey by rail must be reloaded, due to a difference in rail gauges. Goods which cross Georgia or Azerbaijan are subject to travel delay from strikes and blockages, and may be interdicted.

The highway system includes 10,500 km (6,525 mi) of surfaced roads; four-lane highways connect the major cities.

The airport at Yerevan is fairly well maintained and receives scheduled flights from Moscow, Paris, New York, and Sofia.

Cargo shipments to landlocked Armenia are routed through ports in Georgia and Turkey.

12 HISTORY

Armenia existed as an independent kingdom long before the birth of Christ. In the 1st century BC, Armenian rule extended into what is now Syria and Iraq. Defeated by the Roman general Pompey, Armenia became a client state of the Roman Empire. Armenia adopted Christianity at the beginning of the 4th century AD.

Although there were periods of relative autonomy (notably from 809 to 1045), over the centuries Armenia came under the sway of several empires, including the Roman, Byzantine, Persian, Arab, and Ottoman. In 1639, Armenia was divided between the Ottoman and Persian empires. In 1828, Russia seized what had been Persian Armenia.

With the collapse of the Russian and Ottoman empires, Armenia declared its independence on 28 May 1918. The August 1920 Treaty of Sevres accorded international recognition of Armenian independence, but shortly thereafter both Turkey and Soviet Russia invaded. The Soviet Republic of Armenia was declared on 29 November 1920. During the 1920s, Moscow drew internal borders in the Caucasus which resulted in Nagorno-Karabakh, a predominantly Armenian region, being separated from the rest of Soviet Armenia by a few miles of territory in Soviet Azerbaijan, in which Nagorno-Karabakh had the status of an "autonomous republic."

Armenia declared its independence from the Soviet Union on 23 August 1990. Armenia and Azerbaijan began fighting over which would control Nagorno-Karabakh in February 1988. The war has continued ever since. Armenian forces have captured the entire Nagorno-Karabakh region plus a significant portion of Azerbaijan proper. Despite Armenian military success, the war has resulted in a prolonged economic crisis for the new republic.

13 GOVERNMENT

Armenia still operates under its Soviet-era constitution. Free elections to the Supreme Soviet (since renamed the National Assembly) were held in 1990. Although the legislature consists of 259 seats, only 195 deputies were actually elected after three rounds of voting (20 May, 3 June, and 15 July) by the time parliament actually convened on 20 July 1990. The parliament elected Levon Ter-Petrossyan of the Armenian Pan-National Movement (APNM) as its chairman on 3 August 1990. He has served as Armenia's chief executive ever since.

A new post-Soviet constitution was supposed to be formulated, but this has been the subject of heated disagreement between the Ter-Petrossyan government and the opposition parties. The Ter-Petrossyan draft constitution has proposed a government with a strong presidency while the opposition parties' draft has proposed a government with a strong legislature. There has also been disagreement over whether there should be an elected constituent assembly to formulate the new constitution or whether a referendum should be held on the existing drafts.

During the parliamentary debate on this issue held in April 1994, neither position could muster the two-thirds majority required for amending the constitution.

14 POLITICAL PARTIES

The president belongs to the APNM. In 1990, this party was strongly nationalist and anti-Communist. It strongly supported the Armenians in Nagorno-Karabakh. Since being in power, Ter-Petrossyan's positions have moderated to a certain extent. Despite Armenia's support for it, he refuses to recognize the self-declared Nagorno-Karabakh Republic. He has also sought improved relations with Turkey—Armenia's historical enemy. In the summer of 1992, the APNM lost its parliamentary majority as a result of defections.

There are seven opposition parties represented in parliament. Most of them are ultra-nationalist, calling for recognition of the Nagorno-Karabakh Republic. They are divided, however, over economic issues.

15 LOCAL GOVERNMENT

Armenia is divided into over two dozen administrative regions which are directly managed by the federal government.

16 JUDICIAL SYSTEM

The court system consists of district courts of first instance, a Supreme Court and military tribunals. The Supreme Court consists of three sections: (1) a section which hears the more serious crimes such as murder, rape, and egregious official misconduct; (2) a civil and commercial section; and (3) an appellate section which reviews district court verdicts. A Presidium of the Supreme Court reviews cases tried in the first section of the Supreme Court.

The Ministry of Justice nominates, a panel of judicial peers reviews and comments, and the Parliament approves Supreme Court judges. District Court judges are elected to 5-year terms and their terms extended till a new constitution can be adopted. The military tribunal is modeled on the old Soviet-era military procurator system.

The judiciary is not quite fully independent, judges remaining susceptible to political pressures.

The courts currently apply the Soviet Criminal Code. The applicable criminal procedure includes the right to an attorney, right to a public trial and to confrontation of witnesses, and the right to appeal. There is currently no bail and no trial by jury. New laws on judicial reform are currently being considered.

17 ARMED FORCES

The armed forces may number 50,000 regular soldiers and 30,000 militiamen, reinforced with 23,000 Russian soldiers in four divisions. No reliable estimates are available regarding military expenditures, but they probably total no more than $200 million.

18 INTERNATIONAL COOPERATION

Armenia was admitted to the UN on 2 March 1992. The country is also a member of the CSCE, IMF, UNCTAD, UNESCO, and WHO. Armenia is applying for membership in other international organizations, and is a member of the CIS. The US recognized Armenia's independence from the former Soviet Union 25 December 1991. President George Bush stated that day the country meets the US's criteria regarding democracy, respect for human rights, and stability. A US embassy opened in the capital in February 1992.

19 ECONOMY

The Armenian economy is primarily agricultural, with crops of grain, sugar beets, potatoes, and other vegetables, as well as grapes and other fruit.

In December 1988, a severe earthquake destroyed a substantial proportion of Armenia's productive capacity, resulting in a continuing regional trade deficit. The Armenian economy has also been severely disrupted by the break-up of the former Soviet Union. Trade with the other former Soviet republics, on which Armenia relies heavily, has been jeopardized by political instability in Georgia and Azerbaijan.

In the first quarter of 1992, Armenia's national income had fallen 50% from the same period in the previous year.

[20] INCOME

In 1992, the GNP was $2,719 million at current prices, or $780 per capita. For the period 1985–92 the average inflation rate was 33.6%, resulting in a real growth rate in per capita GNP of –8.2%.

[21] LABOR

In 1990, of the total labor force of 1,630,000, 42% were involved in industry and construction; 18% in forestry and agriculture, and 40% in other sectors.

As of 1992, the lack of a new constitution severely discouraged any advancement of legal guarantees concerning workers' rights to voluntarily form and join unions. The unions in place are remnants of the Soviet period and were not freely organized by the workers.

Almost all factories, enterprises, and organizations were still under state control in 1992 despite the passage of a law privatizing state enterprises; unions and employers must still therefore negotiate with the participation of the government. Minimum wages are set by decree rather than legislation, and do not provide a decent standard of living for a worker and family.

[22] AGRICULTURE

Before the collapse of the Soviet Union, about 16% of Armenia's land was cultivated. Agriculture accounts for about 26% of employment. The 15% surge in agricultural output in 1991 mildly helped an otherwise declining economy cope with its legacy of problems inherited from the former Soviet economy.

Production for 1992 included vegetables and melons, 472,000 tons; potatoes, 343,000 tons; wheat, 160,000 tons; grapes, 160,000 tons; and tobacco, 1,000 tons. In 1990, there were some 13,600 tractors and 1,400 harvester-threshers in service.

[23] ANIMAL HUSBANDRY

Over one-fifth of the total land area is permanent pastureland. In 1992, the livestock population included: sheep, 980,000; cattle, 550,000; pigs, 200,000; and chickens, 9,000. In 1992, some 56,000 tons of meat were produced, including 20,000 tons of beef and veal, 6,000 tons of mutton and lamb, 17,000 tons of poultry, and 13,000 tons of pork. In 1992, 300,000 tons of milk, 22,000 tons of eggs, and 2,000 tons of greasy wool were also produced. Meat, milk, and butter are the chief agricultural imports.

[24] FISHING

Fishing is limited to the Arpa River and Lake Sevan. Commercial fishing is not a significant part of the economy.

[25] FORESTRY

Forests and woodlands cover about 12% of Armenia. Soviet mismanagement, the 1988 earthquake, hostilities with Azerbaijan, and fuel shortages have impaired development. Available timber is used for firewood during the harsh winters.

[26] MINING

Mineral resources in Armenia are concentrated in the southern region, near Azerbaijan and Iran, where there are several copper

LOCATION: 40°0′N to 45°0′E BOUNDARY LENGTHS: Total boundary lengths, 1,254 km (780 mi); Azerbaijan (east), 566 km (352 mi); Azerbaijan (south), 221 km (137 mi); Georgia, 164 km (102 mi); Iran, 35 km (22 mi); Turkey, 268 km (167 mi).

and molybdenum mines operating. Infrastructural problems, however, currently inhibit the ability of Armenia's mineral sector to compete on the world market, although the nation is not too distant from rail and port facilities which supply European markets. Perlite is mined southeast of Yerevan, and a gold mine is located near Zod.

[27] ENERGY AND POWER

With only negligible reserves of oil, natural gas, and coal, and with no production, Armenia is heavily reliant on foreign imports. Consumption in 1992 included oil, 37,000 barrels per day; natural gas, 70 billion cu ft (1.98 billion cu m); and coal, 181,000 tons. Total electrical consumption in 1992 was 7,300 million kwh.

Electricity production in 1992 totaled 6,800 million kwh, primarily from the now-disabled Yerevan nuclear plant (815,000 kw capacity), the Hrazdan (near Akhta) oil/natural gas plant (1,210,000 kw capacity), and the Yerevan heat/power plant (550,000 kw capacity).

The December 1988 earthquake disrupted the Yerevan nuclear power plant, which had supplied 40% of Armenia's power needs, creating almost total dependence on imported oil and natural gas for power. When ethnic hostilities with Azerbaijan again resurfaced in 1992, Azerbaijan discontinued service of its pipeline to Armenia (with natural gas from Turkmenistan). The only other supply routes passed either through Turkey (which was sympathetic to Azerbaijan) or through Georgia (which was dealing with its own civil chaos). The ongoing energy shortage has stimulated an interest in restarting the damaged Yerevan nuclear plant, which includes an agreement of assistance by Russia.

[28]INDUSTRY

The main industries are mechanical engineering, chemicals, textiles, and food processing. Since the collapse of the former Soviet Union, industrial production has been severely disrupted by political instability and shortages of power.

Armenia is moving to privatize its predominant industries. The privatization targets include: building materials, footwear, mining, textiles (carpet weaving and knitted wear), foodstuffs and beverages (wine, brandy), chemical (rubber, synthetic and plastic materials, fertilizers) and mechanical engineering (machine tools, presses, foundries). Armenia has the highest number of cooperatives (per capita) in the Commonwealth of Independent States. Experts estimate that most small enterprises (in the full range of sectors) have been privatized. The privatization of large-scale enterprises, however, will take place much more slowly.

Armenia produced 7.7% of the A.C. electric motors and 5.5% of metal cutting machines in the former Soviet Union. It also produced 4.7% of knitted garments, 3.2% of grapes, 2.8% of sugar, 2.3% of hosiery, 2.2% of shoes, 2.0% of other fruits and berries, 1.9% of canned goods, 1.9% of vegetables and 1.5% of vegetable oil.

Before the earthquake in 1988, Armenia exported trucks, tires, electronics and instruments to other republics. A number of plants in these industries were destroyed by the earthquake. Before the earthquake, Armenia produced about 25% of all Soviet elevators. Although this elevator factory was destroyed in the earthquake, it is scheduled for reconstruction. Armenia was also a major producer of chemical products; some 59% of the chemicals produced in Armenia were exported to other republics. The Narit plant, before its closing in December 1989, was the sole producer of one grade of synthetic rubber and of certain chemicals essential to Soviet manufacturing industries. One of two national plants producing aluminum foil for food packaging is located in Armenia. Armenia has the highest number of specialists with higher education and second highest number of scientists of all the former republics.

[29]SCIENCE AND TECHNOLOGY

The Armenian Academy of Sciences, founded in 1943, has departments of mathematical, physico-technical, chemical, earth, and biological sciences with 23 institutes. Armenia has nine institutes conducting research in medicine, agriculture, physics, and engineering. Yerevan State University, founded in 1920, has faculties of mathematics, physics, radiophysics, chemistry, biology, and geology.

[30]DOMESTIC TRADE

Consumer prices are deregulated in all areas except bread, public utilities, and transport, where there have been substantive increases. As of 1993, bread was rationed, with a daily quota of 250 grams per person. The price was R60 rubles in May 1994.

Over 300 small enterprises have been privatized.

[31]FOREIGN TRADE

Imports and exports accounted for over 50% of Armenia's GDP in the 1980s. In 1988, exports (in world market prices) were valued at R2,200 million, and imports at R3,600. Inter-republic trade, which has suffered due to political instability and border hostilities, is of particular importance. In 1988, it represented 82% of Armenia's imports and 98% of its exports. Oil from Russia accounts for two-thirds of Armenia's imports.

[32]BALANCE OF PAYMENTS

Armenian enterprises have had difficulties financing any importation of industrial inputs, especially since Moscow froze Armenia's foreign exchange reserves at the end of 1991. Payment agreements between the former Soviet republics have also been largely ignored. Consequently, production losses have reduced exports and exacerbated a trade deficit. Since 1991/92, Azerbaijan has also imposed a blockade against Armenia, further worsening the disruption in trade and payments. In 1994, Armenia's current account deficit was projected to increase by $150 million.

[33]BANKING AND SECURITIES

The National Bank of the Republic of Armenia is the central bank of Armenia, charged with regulating the money supply, circulating currency, and regulating the commercial banks of the country. Commercial banks in Armenia include the Agricultural Bank of Armenia (1991), 42 branches; Bank for Industry and Construction (1991), State Commercial Bank of the Republic of Armenia (1991), 18 branches; and Veneshekekonombank of Armenia (1974).

[34]INSURANCE

Insurance is largely controlled by government organizations inherited from the Soviet system, although private insurance companies are not unknown. Civil violence continues to stifle the development of the insurance industry.

[35]PUBLIC FINANCE

The decline of economic activity and the abandonment of payment agreements between the former Soviet republics has caused fiscal revenues to drop since independence. From 1989 to 1992, government revenue declined from over 50% of GDP to 18% of GDP. Expenditures, however, amounted to 32% of GDP in 1992. In order to control the fiscal deficit, the government has terminated virtually all subsidies and diminished private investment. The fiscal deficit in 1992 was equivalent to 14% of GDP and was largely financed through arrears and credit from the banking sector. The external debt stood at $650 million at the end of 1991.

[36]TAXATION

Taxation in Armenia takes several forms. The enterprise profit tax is progressive, with tax rates ranging from 12% to 25%. State and private banks and other financial institutions are obliged to pay a 45% profit tax rate. Taxable profits are determined as the difference between revenues and the sum of wages, amortization payments, raw and intermediate purchases, social security contributions, insurance fees, and interest expenses. Newly-formed enterprises are exempt from taxes for the first two years, but there is no provision for carrying forward losses.

Individual income taxes are withheld by enterprises and are paid to the Ministry of Finance monthly. Income taxes are progressive and consist of four steps: 12%, 30%, 40%, and 45%. A tax on fixed assets of state-owned enterprises is expected to be introduced in order to raise revenue, induce privatization, and discourage rapid wage growth. Tax rates will be applied sectorally.

The 1992 draft budget assumed the introduction of a value-added tax with a unified rate of 28% (same as in the other former Soviet republics). Exports to countries other than the CIS would be zero-rated, as would goods whose prices are fixed.

Excise taxes are planned to be levied on a wide variety of

goods. These goods include spirits, wine, cognac, tobacco, caviar, and "delectables," jewelry, fur, coffee and tea, carpets, cars, electronic goods, china and crystal. The possibility of levying such a tax on oil is now being discussed.

37CUSTOMS AND DUTIES

Most goods are imported duty-free. Imports of machinery and equipment for use in manufacturing by enterprises with foreign investment are exempt from all customs duties.

38FOREIGN INVESTMENT

As of August 1993, Armenia was in the process of drawing up legislation to govern the establishment of joint ventures and joint stock companies with foreign entities. Many business activities are still regulated by the government.

39ECONOMIC DEVELOPMENT

The government's economic reform program was launched by its privatization of agricultural land in 1991, which boosted crop output 30% and resulted in a 15% increase in agricultural production. Privatization of input supplies, distribution, and marketing is also planned.

The republic has substantial deposits of gold, copper, zinc, bauxite, and other minerals, which could be developed with Western capital. The government is currently exploring alternative trade routes, and seeking export orders from the West to aid production and earn foreign exchange.

40SOCIAL DEVELOPMENT

Women in Armenia largely occupy traditional roles circumscribed by their families. A 1992 employment law does formally prohibit discrimination based on sex.

41HEALTH

There were 79,000 births in 1992, with an infant mortality rate of 29 per 1,000 live births that year. Life expectancy in 1991 averaged 72 years (75 years for females and 68 years for males). The 1993 death rate was 6 per 1,000 people, with 7,000 war-related deaths from 1989 to 1992. In 1990, the incidence of tuberculosis was 127 per 100,000 people, and between 1985 and 1990, the mortality rate was broken down as follows: communicable diseases, maternal/perinatal causes, 60 per 100,000; non-communicable diseases, 580 per 100,000; and injuries, 66 per 100,000.

From 1988 to 1992, there were 4.28 physicians per 1,000 inhabitants, and from 1985 to 1990, there were 9 hospital beds per 1,000. The country spent a total of $506 million on health care in 1990.

42HOUSING

In 1990, Armenia had 15 square meters of housing space per capita. As of 1 January 1991, there were 142,000 households on waiting lists for housing in urban areas, or 34.6% of all households. Of privately owned urban housing in 1989, 94% had running water, 79.8% had sewer lines, 50.7% had central heating, 42.5% had hot water, 61.7% had bathtubs, and 96.9% had gas.

43EDUCATION

The official language is Armenian. Adult literacy was estimated at 98.8% in 1990 (males, 99.4%, and females, 98.1%). Education is compulsory and free at the primary and secondary levels. The education system is based on the old Soviet system; however, since the early 1990s, more emphasis has been placed on Armenian history and culture. There are two universities in Yerevan: the Yerevan State University (founded in 1919) and the State Engineering University of Armenia. Seven other educational institutions are located in the capital.

In 1990, a total of 68,400 students were enrolled in all higher level institutions.

44LIBRARIES AND MUSEUMS

The National Library is in Yerevan; several towns and villages have public libraries as well. The Armenian Academy of Sciences and the universities each have research libraries. Yerevan's museums include the National Gallery of Arts, the Museum of Modern Art, and the Museum of Ancient Manuscripts.

45MEDIA

There are approximately 260,000 telephones, or 8 per 100 persons. Communications links to other former Soviet republics are by land line or microwave, and to other countries by satellite and through Moscow. Armenian and Russian radio and television stations broadcast throughout the country.

In 1989, there were 85 newspapers in Armenia, of which 79 were published in Armenian. These had a combined 1989 circulation of 1.5 million; those published in other languages had a total circulation of 103,000.

46ORGANIZATIONS

Important political movements in Armenia include the Armenian National Movement and the National Self-Determination Association. Armenian trade unions belong to the umbrella organization Council of Armenia Trade Unions. The Chamber of Commerce and Industry of the Republic of Armenia promotes the economic and business activities of the country in world markets.

47TOURISM, TRAVEL, AND RECREATION

Circumstances in recent years—including the 1988 earthquake and ethnic conflict over the Nagarno-Karabakh region—have been unfavorable for tourism.

48FAMOUS ARMENIANS

Levon Ter-Petrossyan has been president of Armenia since November 1991. Gagik G. Haroutunian has been prime minister, vice president, and chairman of the Council of Ministers since November 1991. Gregory Nare Katzi, who lived in the 10th century, was Armenia's first great poet. Nineteenth-century novelists include Hakob Maliq-Hakobian whose pen name is "Raffi" and the playwright Gabriel Sundukian.

49DEPENDENCIES

Armenia has no territories or colonies.

50BIBLIOGRAPHY

Armenia at the Crossroads: Democracy and Nationhood in the Post-Soviet Era: Essays, Interviews, and Speeches by the Leaders of the National Democratic Movement in Armenia. Watertown, Mass.: Blue Crane Books, 1991.

Bournoutian, George A. *A History of the Armenian People.* Costa Mesa, Calif.: Mazda Publishers, 1993.

Brook, Stephen. *Claws of the Crab: Georgia and Armenia in Crisis.* London, England: Sinclair-Stevenson, 1992.

Chahin, M. *The Kingdom of Armenia.* London, and New York: Croom Helm, 1987.

Garsoian, Nina G. *Armenia Between Byzantium and the Sasanians.* London: Variorum Reprints, 1985.

Hovannisian, Richard G. *The Armenian Genocide: History, Politics, Ethics.* New York: St. Martin's Press, 1992.

Lang, David Marshall. *Armenia, Cradle of Civilization,* 3rd ed. London, and Boston: Allen & Unwin, 1980.

Nassibian, Akaby. *Britain and the Armenian Question, 1915–1923.* New York: St. Martin's Press; London: Croom Helm, 1984.

Nersessian, Vrej. *Armenia*. Oxford, England, and Santa Barbara, Calif.: Clio, 1993.

Suny, Ronald Grigor. *Armenia in the Twentieth Century*. Chico, Calif.: Scholars Press, 1983.

Suny, Ronald Grigor. *Looking Toward Ararat: Armenia in Modern History*. Bloomington: Indiana University Press, 1993.

Walker, Christopher J. *Armenia: the Survival of a Nation,* Rev. 2nd ed. New York: St. Martin's Press, 1990.

AUSTRIA

Republic of Austria
Republik Österreich

CAPITAL: Vienna (Wien).

FLAG: The flag consists of a white horizontal stripe between two red stripes.

ANTHEM: *Land der Berge, Land am Ströme (Land of Mountains, Land on the River).*

MONETARY UNIT: The schilling (s) is a paper currency of 100 groschen. There are coins of 1, 2, 5, 10, and 50 groschen and 1, 5, 10, 20, 25, 50, 100, 500, 1,000, and 2,000 schillings, and notes of 20, 50, 100, 500, 1,000, and 5,000 schillings. s1 = $0.0851 (or $1 = s11.757).

WEIGHTS AND MEASURES: The metric system is in use.

HOLIDAYS: New Year's Day, 1 January; Epiphany, 6 January; May Day, 1 May; Assumption, 15 August; National Day, 26 October; All Saints' Day, 1 November; Immaculate Conception, 8 December; Christmas, 25 December; St. Stephen's Day, 26 December. Movable religious holidays include Easter Monday, Ascension, Whitmonday, and Corpus Christi. In addition, there are provincial holidays.

TIME: 1 PM = noon GMT.

¹LOCATION, SIZE, AND EXTENT

Austria, with an area of 83,850 sq km (32,375 sq mi), is a landlocked country in Central Europe, extending 573 km (356 mi) E–W and 294 km (183 mi) N–S. Comparatively, Austria is slightly smaller than the state of Maine. Bounded on the N by Germany and the Czech Republic, on the E by Hungary, on the S by Slovenia and Italy, and on the W by Liechtenstein and Switzerland, Austria has a total boundary length of 2,496 km (1,551 mi).

While not making any territorial claims, Austria oversees the treatment of German speakers in the South Tyrol (now part of the autonomous province of Trentino-Alto Adige), which was ceded to Italy under the Treaty of St.-Germain-en-Laye in 1919.

Austria's capital city, Vienna, is located in the northeastern part of the country.

²TOPOGRAPHY

Most of western and central Austria is mountainous, and much of the flatter area to the east is hilly, but a series of passes and valleys permits travel within the country and has made Austria an important bridge between various sections of Europe. The principal topographic regions are the Eastern Alps, constituting 62.8% of Austria's land area; the Alpine and Carpathian foothills (11.3%); the Pannonian lowlands of the east (11.3%); the granite and gneiss highlands of the Bohemian Massif (10.1%); and the Vienna Basin (4.4%). The highest point of the Austrian Alps is the Grossglockner, 3,797 m (12,457 ft). The Danube (Donau) River, fully navigable along its 350-km (217-mi) course through northeastern Austria, is the chief waterway, and several important streams—the Inn, Enns, Drava (Drau), and Mur—are tributaries to it. Included within Austria are many Alpine lakes, most of the Neusiedler See (the lowest point in Austria, 115 m/377 ft above sea level), and part of Lake Constance (Bodensee).

³CLIMATE

Climatic conditions depend on location and altitude. Temperatures range from an average of about –2°C (28°F) in January to about 19°C (66°F) in July. Rainfall ranges from more than 200 cm (80 in) annually in the hills bordering the Alps to less than 60 cm (24 in) in the driest region, east of the Neusiedler See.

⁴FLORA AND FAUNA

Plants and animals are those typical of Central Europe. Austria is one of Europe's most heavily wooded countries, with 44% of its area under forests. Deciduous trees (particularly beech, birch, and oak) and conifers (fir) cover the mountains up to about 1,200 m (4,000 ft); above that point fir predominates and then gives way to larch and stone pine. There is a large variety of wildlife. Although chamois are now rare, deer, hare, fox, badger, marten, Alpine chough, grouse, marmot, partridge, and pheasant are still plentiful. The birds of the reed beds around the Neusiedler See include purple heron, spoonbill, and avocet. The ibex, once threatened, has begun breeding again. Hunting is strictly regulated.

⁵ENVIRONMENT

The Ministry of Health and Environmental Protection, established in 1972, is responsible for the coordination at the national level of all environmental protection efforts. Together with the Austrian Federal Health Institute, founded in 1973, the ministry has produced studies aimed at establishing a national waste disposal plan as well as standards for tolerable noise, sulfur dioxide, and carbon monoxide levels, and for the emissions of the iron and steel and ceramics industries. A toxic waste law enacted in 1984 established strict regulations for the collection, transport, and disposal of dangerous substances. As of 1994, the main environmental problems facing Austria are air, water, and land pollution. One major source of the problem is industrial and power facilities which use coal and oil. The Austrian government has imposed strict regulations on gas emissions, which helped to reduce sulphur dioxide by two-thirds over an eight-year period beginning in 1980. Austria contributes 0.2% of the world's total gas emissions.

The same chemical agents that pollute the air eventually reach the land and water supplies. Austrians continue to fight the problem of acid rain which has damaged 25% of the country's forests. In general, environmental legislation is based on the "polluter pays" principle. The water resources fund of the Ministry for Buildings and Technology distributed more than s20 billion for canalization and waste-water purification plants between 1959 and the early 1980s; the Danube and the Mur have been the special focus of efforts to improve water quality. In 1985, Austria spent 1.7% of its GDP on environmental protection, and the percentage was expected to reach 2% by 1990. Endangered species in 1987 included Freya's damselfly and the dusky large blue butterfly. Of the country's 85 species of mammals, two are threatened. Thirteen of Austria's 201 bird species are endangered. There are 25 endangered plant species in a total of 2,900 as of 1994.

6POPULATION

According to the 1991 census, Austria's population was 7,795,786. The nation's crude birth rate was 12.1 per 1,000 population and the death rate 10.5. The population density in 1991 was 93 per sq km (241 per sq mi). About 21.5% of the population live in communities of 2,000 or fewer inhabitants, 50% in towns or cities of 2,000–100,000 persons. The remaining 28.5% reside in the five cities that, as of the 1991 census, had 100,000 or more inhabitants: Vienna (Wien), the capital, 1,539,848; Graz, 237,810; Linz, 203,044; Salzburg, 143,978; and Innsbruck, 118,112.

7MIGRATION

Every Austrian has the constitutional right to migrate. For several years after the end of World War II, fairly large numbers of Austrians emigrated, mostly to Australia, Canada, and the US, but as the economy recovered from war damage, emigration became insignificant. Austria retains the principle of the right of asylum, and the benefits of Austrian social legislation are granted to refugees and displaced persons. Between 1945 and 1983, 1,942,782 refugees from more than 30 countries came to Austria, of whom about 590,000 became Austrian citizens (including some 302,000 German-speaking expatriates from Czechoslovakia, Romania, and Yugoslavia). Following the political upheavals in Hungary in 1956, Czechoslovakia in 1968, and Poland in 1981, Austria received large numbers of refugees from these countries: 180,432 Hungarians, about 100,000 Czechs and Slovaks, and 33,142 Poles. Between 1968 and 1986, 261,857 Jewish emigrants from the Soviet Union passed through Austria, about one-third of them going to Israel and the rest to other countries, primarily the US. Of Austrians living abroad, some 186,900 were residents of Germany in 1991.

As of 1992 there were 273,884 foreign workers in Austria, of whom 133,576 were Yugoslavs and 55,637 Turks. That year there were 16,238 applications for asylum and 11,920 foreigners naturalized. The total number of foreigners was about 413,400 in 1990. At the end of 1992 Austria was harboring 60,900 refugees, including 42,100 from the former Yugoslavia.

8ETHNIC GROUPS

Austrians are a people of mixed Dinaric, Nordic, Alpine, and East Baltic origin. Aside from resident foreigners, ethnic minorities include about 20,000 Slovenes in southern Carinthia and 25,000 Croatians in the Burgenland. About 2% of the Burgenland population is Hungarian. There are also some Czechs, Slovaks, Serbians, and Italians.

9LANGUAGES

The official language is German, and nearly 99% of the inhabitants speak it as their mother tongue. People in Vorarlberg Province speak German with an Alemannic accent, similar to that in Switzerland. In other provinces, Austrians speak various Bavarian dialects. There are also Croatian-, Slovene-, and Hungarian-speaking minorities, and small groups of Czech, Slovak, and Polish speakers in Vienna.

10RELIGIONS

Freedom of worship is guaranteed. Up to 84% of the people are Roman Catholic; 6% are Protestant, and 2% belong to other religious groups, including Muslims (1%). Some 6% of Austrians profess no religion. Austria's Jewish population was more than 200,000 in 1938; by the end of World War II it stood at no more than 4,000. Mainly because of immigration from the former USSR and Eastern Europe, the number of Jews increased to an estimated 7,000 in 1990.

11TRANSPORTATION

Austria has a dense transportation network. The Federal Railway Administration controlled 90% of Austria's 6,028 km (3,746 mi) of railways in 1991. About half of the railroad network has been electrified. In 1991, the public railroads carried 173 million passengers and 64.7 million tons of goods. That year, Austria also had 526 funiculars and chair lifts.

In 1991, highways totaled 95,412 km (59,289 mi), of which paved roads accounted for 34,612 km (21,508 mi). In 1991 there were 3,100,014 passenger cars, and 259,308 trucks.

Austria has 446 km (277 mi) of inland waterways, over 80% of which are navigable by engine-powered vessels. Most of Austria's overseas trade passes through the Italian port of Trieste; the rest is shipped from German ports. In 1991, the oceangoing merchant fleet of Austria consisted of 32 ships with a capacity of 137,000 GRT.

Of the six major airports in Austria—Schwechat (near Vienna), Graz, Innsbruck, Klagenfurt, Linz, and Salzburg—Schwechat is by far the most important. In 1992, Austrian airports performed 4,867 million passenger-km (3,024 million passenger-mi) and 101 million freight ton-km (62.8 million freight ton-mi) of service. In 1991, a total of 52 airlines, including Austrian Airlines (est. in 1957), Austrian Air Services, Lauda Air, and Tyrolean Airways provided flights for 3,722,567 arriving and 3,722,535 departing passengers.

12HISTORY

Human settlements have existed in what is now Austria since prehistoric times. In 15–14 BC, the region, already overrun by various tribes, including the Celts, was conquered by the Romans, who divided it among the provinces of Noricum, Pannonia, and Illyria. The Romans founded several towns that survive today: Vindobona (Vienna), Juvavum (Salzburg), Valdidena (Innsbruck), and Brigantium (Bregenz). After the fall of the Roman Empire, Austria became (about AD 800) a border province of Charlemagne's empire until the 10th century, when it was joined to the Holy Roman Empire as Österreich ("Kingdom of the East").

From the late 13th to the early 20th century, the history of Austria is tied to that of the Habsburg family. In 1282, Rudolf von Habsburg (Rudolf I, newly elected German emperor) gave Austria (Upper and Lower Austria, Carinthia, Styria, and Carniola) to his sons, Albrecht and Rudolf, thus inaugurating the male Habsburg succession that would continue unbroken until 1740. The highest point of Habsburg rule came in the 1500s when Emperor Maximilian I (r.1493–1519) arranged a marriage between his son and the daughter of King Ferdinand and Queen Isabella of Spain. Maximilian's grandson became King Charles I of Spain in 1516 and, three years later, was elected Holy Roman emperor, as Charles V. Until Charles gave up his throne in 1556, he ruled over Austria, Spain, the Netherlands, and much of Italy, as well as over large possessions in the Americas. Charles gave Austria to his brother Ferdinand, who had already been elected king of Hungary and Bohemia in 1526; the Habsburgs maintained their reign over Austria, Bohemia, and Hungary until 1918.

When the last Habsburg king of Spain died in 1700, France as well as Austria laid claim to the throne. The dispute between the

LOCATION: 46°22′ to 49°1′N; 9°22′ to 17°10′E **BOUNDARY LENGTHS:** Germany, 819 km (509 mi); Czech and Slovak Republics, 571 km (355 mi); Hungary, 354 km (220 mi); the former Yugoslavia, 330 km (205 mi); Italy, 430 km (267 mi); Liechtenstein, 35 km (22 mi); Switzerland, 168 km (104 mi).

continental powers erupted into the War of the Spanish Succession (1701–14) and drew in other European countries in alliance with the respective claimants. At the end of the war, Austria was given control of the Spanish Netherlands (Belgium), Naples, Milan, and Sardinia. (It later lost Naples, together with Sicily, in the War of the Polish Succession, 1733–35.) In 1740, after the death of Charles VI, several German princes refused to acknowledge his daughter and only child, Maria Theresa, as the legitimate ruler of Austria, thus provoking the War of the Austrian Succession (1740–48). Maria Theresa lost Silesia to Prussia but held on to her throne, from which she proceeded to institute a series of major internal reforms as ruler of Austria, Hungary, and Bohemia. After 1765, she ruled jointly with her son, Holy Roman Emperor Joseph II (r.1765–90). Following his mother's death in 1780, Joseph, an enlightened despot, sought to abolish serfdom and introduce religious freedom, but he succeeded only in creating considerable unrest. Despite the political turmoil, Austria's cultural life flourished during this period, which spanned the careers of the composers Haydn and Mozart.

During the French Revolutionary and Napoleonic wars, Austria suffered a further diminution of territory. In 1797, it gave up Belgium and Milan to France, receiving Venice, however, in recompense. In 1805, Austria lost Venice, as well as the Tyrol and part of Dalmatia, to Napoleon. Some restitution was made by the Congress of Vienna (1814–15), convened after Napoleon's defeat;

it awarded Lombardy, Venetia, and Istria and restored all of Dalmatia to Austria, but it denied the Habsburgs the return of former possessions in Baden and the Netherlands.

From 1815 to 1848, Austria, under the ministry of Prince Klemens von Metternich, dominated European politics as the leading power of both the German Confederation and the Holy Alliance (Austria, Russia, and Prussia). Unchallenged abroad, the reactionary Metternich achieved peace at home through ruthless suppression of all liberal or nationalist movements among the people in the Habsburg empire. In 1848, however, revolutions broke out in Hungary and Bohemia and in Vienna itself; Metternich resigned and fled to London. Although the revolutions were crushed, Emperor Ferdinand I abdicated in December. He was succeeded by his 18-year-old nephew, Franz Josef I, who was destined to occupy the Austrian throne for 68 years, until his death in 1916. During his reign, Austria attempted to set up a strong central government that would unify all the Habsburg possessions under its leadership. But nationalist tensions persisted, exacerbated by outside interference. In 1859, in a war over Habsburg-controlled Lombardy, French and Sardinian troops defeated the Austrians, ending Austrian preeminence in Italian politics; and in 1866, Prussia forced Austria out of the political affairs of Germany after the Seven Weeks' War. In 1867, Hungarian nationalists, taking advantage of Austria's weakened state, compelled Franz Josef to sign an agreement giving Hungary equal rights with Austria. In the ensuing Dual Monarchy, the Austrian Empire and the Kingdom of Hungary were united under one ruler. Each country had its own national government, but both shared responsibility for foreign affairs, defense, and finance. Self-government for the empire's Magyar (Hungarian) population was balanced by continued suppression of the Slavs.

On 28 June 1914, at Sarajevo, Serbian patriots, members of the Slavic movement, assassinated Archduke Francis Ferdinand, nephew of the emperor and heir to the Austrian throne. Their act set off World War I, in which Austria-Hungary was joined by Germany (an ally since 1879), Italy (a member, with the first two, of the Triple Alliance of 1882), and Turkey. They became known as the Central Powers. In 1915, Italy defected to the side of the Allies—France, Russia, the UK, and (from 1917) the US. After the defeat of the Central Powers and the collapse of their empires in 1918, Austria, now reduced to its German-speaking sections, was proclaimed a republic. The Treaty of St.-Germain-en-Laye (1919) fixed the borders of the new state and forbade it any kind of political or economic union with Germany without League of Nations approval.

During the next decade, Austria was plagued by inflation, food shortages, unemployment, financial scandals, and, as a consequence, growing political unrest. The country's two major political groupings, the Christian Socialist Party and the Social Democratic Party, were almost equal in strength, with their own private paramilitary movements. A small Austrian Nazi party, advocating union with Germany, constituted a third group. In March 1933, Chancellor Engelbert Dollfuss, leader of the Christian Socialists, dissolved the Austrian parliament, suspended the democratic constitution of 1920, and ruled by decree, hoping to control the unrest. In February 1934, civil strife erupted; government forces broke up the opposition Social Democratic Party, executing or imprisoning many persons. Dollfuss thereupon established an authoritarian corporate state along Fascist lines. On 25 July, the Nazis, emboldened by Adolf Hitler's rise in Germany, assassinated Dollfuss in an abortive coup. Kurt von Schuschnigg, who had served under Dollfuss as minister of justice and education, then became chancellor. For the next four years, Schuschnigg struggled to keep Austria independent amid growing German pressure for annexation (Anschluss). On 11 March 1938, however, German troops entered the country, and two days later Austria was proclaimed a part of the German Reich. In 1939, Austria, now known as Ostmark, entered World War II as part of the Axis powers.

Allied troops entered Austria in April 1945, and the country was divided into US, British, French, and Soviet zones of occupation. Declaring the 1920 constitution in force, the occupying powers permitted Austrians to set up a provisional government but limited Austrian sovereignty under an agreement of 1946. Austria made effective use of foreign economic aid during the early postwar years. The US and the UK supplied $379 million worth of goods between 1945 and 1948; another $110 million was provided by private organizations; and Marshall Plan aid amounted to $962 million. Inflation was checked by the early 1950s, and for most of the remainder of that decade the economy sustained one of the world's highest growth rates.

On 15 May 1955, after more than eight years of negotiations, representatives of Austria and the four powers signed, at Vienna, the Austrian State Treaty, reestablishing an independent and democratic Austria, and in October all occupation forces withdrew from the country. Under the treaty, Austria agreed to become permanently neutral.

As a neutral nation, Austria has remained outside the political and military alliances into which postwar Europe is divided. Economically, however, it has developed close links with Western Europe, joining EFTA in 1960 and concluding free-trade agreements with the EEC in 1972. Because of its location, Austria

serves as an entrepôt between the Western trade blocs and the CMEA, with which it also has trade relations. Austria has twice been the site of US-USSR summit meetings. In June 1961, President John F. Kennedy and Premier Nikita S. Khrushchev conferred in Vienna, and in June 1979, Presidents Jimmy Carter and Leonid I. Brezhnev signed a strategic arms limitation agreement in the Austrian capital.

On 8 July 1986, following elections in May and June, former UN Secretary-General Kurt Waldheim was sworn in as president of Austria. During the presidential campaign, Waldheim was accused of having belonged to Nazi organizations during World War II and of having taken part in war crimes while stationed in Greece and Yugoslavia with the German army from 1942 to 1945; he denied the charges. After his inauguration, diplomats of many nations made a point of avoiding public contact with the new president, and on 27 April 1987, the US Justice Department barred him from entering the US. To the dismay of many leaders, Pope John Paul II granted Waldheim an audience at the Vatican on 25 June.

Waldheim declined to run for a second term and in July 1992, Thomas Klentel was elected federal president. Relations with Israel, which had been strained under Waldheim's presidency, returned to normal.

Immigration and the economy remain the most important political issues. Several measures to tighten asylum and immigration requests were considered and annual quotas were adopted. Efforts to contain immigration have sparked violence including a letter bomb to Vienna Mayor Helmut Zilk.

The recession in Germany led to an economic decline in 1992–93. Austria has sought to broaden its trade ties not only with Europe but also with the East. A referendum in 1994 approved Austria's application for membership in the EC.

13 GOVERNMENT

The second Austrian republic was established on 19 December 1945. According to the constitution of 1920, as amended in 1929, Austria is a federal republic with a democratically elected parliament. The president, elected by popular vote for a six-year term, appoints a federal chancellor (Bundeskanzler), usually the leader of the largest party in parliament, for a term not exceeding that of parliament (four years); upon the chancellor's proposal, the president nominates ministers (who should not serve in parliament at the same time) to head the administrative departments of government. The ministers make up the cabinet, which formulates and directs national policy. Cabinet ministers serve out their terms subject to the confidence of a parliamentary majority. The president is limited to two terms of office.

The parliament, known as the Federal Assembly (Bundesversammlung), consists of the National Council (Nationalrat) and Federal Council (Bundesrat). The Bundesrat has 63 members, elected by the country's unicameral provincial legislatures (Landtage) in proportion to the population of each province. The Nationalrat has 183 members (prior to 1970, 165 members), elected directly in nine election districts for four-year terms by secret ballot on the basis of proportional representation. All citizens 25 years of age or older are eligible to serve in parliament; all citizens 19 years of age or older may vote. Voting is compulsory for presidential elections. The electoral law was amended in February 1990 to extend the franchise to Austrians living permanently or temporarily abroad. All legislation originates in the Nationalrat; the Bundesrat exercises only a suspensory veto.

14 POLITICAL PARTIES

The restoration of the republic in 1945 revived political activity in Austria. In general elections that November, the Austrian People's Party (Österreichische Volkspartei—ÖVP), successor to the prewar Christian Socialists, emerged as the strongest party, with the reborn Socialist Party of Austria (Sozialistische Partei Österreichs—SPÖ) trailing slightly. The ÖVP and SPÖ, controlling 161 of the 165 seats in the Nationalrat, formed a coalition government and worked closely with the Allies to construct an independent and democratic Austria. This coalition held until after the elections of 1966, when the ÖVP, with a majority of 11 seats, formed a one-party government headed by Chancellor Josef Klaus. In 1970, the SPÖ won a plurality in the Nationalrat and was able to put together a minority Socialist government under its leader, Bruno Kreisky. Kreisky remained in power until 1983—longer than any other non-Communist European head of government. The Socialist Party was renamed the Social Democratic Party in 1991, and began to advocate free-market oriented policies. It has also supported Austria's entry into the EC.

The ÖVP, also referred to as Austria's Christian Democratic Party, favors free enterprise, competition, and the reduction of class differences. Organized in three sections—businessmen, farmers, and employees—it advocates provincial rights and strongly supports the Catholic Church. The SPÖ, also known as the Social Democratic Party, advocates moderate reforms through democratic processes. It favors continued nationalization of key industries, economic planning, and widespread social welfare benefits. It is closely allied with the Austrian Trade Union Federation and its constituent unions. While the two parties differ on economic policy, they have concurred in Austria's course of neutrality and on many specific issues of foreign policy.

A third political group, the Union of Independents (Verband der Unabhängigen—VdU), appeared in 1949. Strongly antisocialist, with anticlerical, pan-German elements, it challenged the coalition in the elections of that year, winning 16 seats. By the mid-1950s, however, the VdU, consistently denied a voice in government by the two major parties, had begun to disintegrate. In 1955, it was reorganized, under new leadership, as the Freedom Party of Austria (Freiheitliche Partei Österreichs—FPÖ). In 1970, with six seats in the Nationalrat, the FPÖ was accepted as a negotiating partner by the SPÖ. The party favors individual initiative over collective security. In June 1992, FPO dissidents founded the Free Democratic Party.

The Communist Party of Austria (Kommunistische Partei Österreichs—KPÖ) has declined steadily in strength since the end of World War II. It has had no parliamentary representation, for example, since 1959, when it lost the three seats won in 1956. The KPÖ was the first party in the Nationalrat to propose, in 1953, that Austria become a neutral nation.

In the elections of 24 April 1983, dominated by economic issues, the SPÖ (with 47.8% of the vote) won 90 seats, down from 95 in 1979; the ÖVP (with 43.21%) 81; and the FPÖ (with 4.97%) 12. The KPÖ polled 0.66% of the vote but won no seats. Two new environmentalist groups, the United Greens of Austria (Vereinten Grünen Österreichs) and the Alternative List–Austria (Alternative Liste Österreichs), likewise failed to gain representation in the Nationalrat, although they collectively polled more than 3% of the total vote. In May, Kreisky, having failed to win a clear majority, resigned. He was succeeded as party leader and chancellor by Fred Sinowatz, who proceeded to form a coalition government with the FPÖ.

Following the election of Kurt Waldheim to the presidency in June 1986, Sinowatz resigned and was succeeded by Franz Vranitzky, a former finance minister. The SPÖ-FPÖ coalition broke down in September 1986. Following parliamentary elections on 23 November 1986, a new government was sworn in on 21 January 1987, with Vranitzky from the SPÖ as chancellor and Alois Mock, FPÖ chairman, as vice-chancellor and prime minister.

In the general election of 7 October 1990, the "grand coalition" continued. The 183 seats in the Nationalrat were distributed as follows: SPO (80), OVP (60), FPO (33), and the Green Alternative (10).

15 LOCAL GOVERNMENT

Austria is divided into nine provinces (Länder): Vienna (Wien), Lower Austria (Niederösterreich), Upper Austria (Oberösterreich), Styria (Steiermark), Carinthia (Kärnten), Tyrol (Tirol), Salzburg, Burgenland, and Vorarlberg. The relationship between the provinces and the central government is defined by the constitution. Most administrative, legislative, and judicial authority—including taxation, welfare, and police—is granted to the central government. The Länder, which enjoy all residual powers, act as executors of federal authority.

Each province has its own unicameral legislature, elected on the basis of proportional representation. All legislation must be submitted through the provincial governor (Landeshauptmann) to the competent federal ministry for concurrence. If such concurrence is not obtained, the provincial legislature can reinstate the bill by majority vote. In case of prolonged conflict between the federal authorities and the provincial legislatures, the Constitutional Court may be appealed to for settlement.

The provincial governor, elected by the provincial legislature (Landtag), is assisted by a cabinet (Landesrat) consisting of ministries analogous to those at the federal level. Each province is divided into several administrative districts (Bezirke), each of which is under a district commissioner (Bezirkshauptmann). Local self-government is vested in popularly elected communal councils which, in turn, elect various local officers, including the mayor (Bürgermeister) and his deputies. There are some 2,300 communities in Austria, as well as 14 cities that have independent charters and fall directly under provincial authority rather than that of the districts. Vienna is both a municipality and a province.

16 JUDICIAL SYSTEM

As of 1985, Austria had about 200 local courts (Bezirksgerichte) with civil jurisdiction. There were also 20 provincial and district courts (Landesgerichte and Kreisgerichte) with civil and criminal jurisdiction and 4 higher provincial courts (Oberlandesgerichte) with criminal jurisdiction, located in Vienna, Graz, Innsbruck, and Linz. The Supreme Court (Oberster Gerichtshof), in Vienna, acts as the final appellate court for criminal and civil cases. The Constitutional Court (Verfassungsgerichtshof) has supreme jurisdiction over constitutional and civil rights issues. The Administrative Court (Verwaltungsgerichtshof) ensures the legal functioning of public administration. A central auditing authority controls financial administration. Judges are appointed by the federal government and cannot be removed or transferred. Trial by jury was reintroduced in 1951. There is no capital punishment.

The judiciary is independent of the other branches. Judges are appointed for life and cannot be removed.

Until recently, the law allowed for detention of suspects for 48 hours without judicial review and up to two years of detention during the course of a criminal investigation. Amendments to the law in 1994 require more stringent judicial review of pretrial and investigative detention. Criminal defendants are afforded a presumption of innocence, public trials, and jury trial for major offenses, as well as a number of other procedural rights.

17 ARMED FORCES

Universal conscription has been in effect continuously since 1918. The Federal Constitutional Law on the Neutrality of Austria, enacted 26 October 1955, provides for a federal army and air force and conscription for all males between the ages of 19 and 50. A law passed on 15 July 1971 reduced compulsory military service from nine to six months. In 1993, the Austrian armed forces of 52,000 included 22,400 conscripts.

The Austrian army had 46,000 members, and the air service 6,000 with 54 combat aircraft. Active reserve strength is 200,000 with 66,000 receiving annual training. Another 960,000 have had military training.

The president of the republic is the supreme commander of the Austrian armed forces. Important issues affecting national defense are handled by the National Defense Council, presided over by the federal chancellor and consisting of members of the government, the inspector-general of the armed forces, and representatives of the political parties. The 1992 defense budget was s19.86 billion or $1.7 billion, which is 1% of gross domestic product.

Austria provides more than 1,000 service personnel to six different peacekeeping operations, five under UN auspices.

[18]INTERNATIONAL COOPERATION

The Federal Constitutional Law on the Neutrality of Austria, adopted on 26 October 1955, binds the nation to perpetual neutrality and bans it from joining any military alliances or permitting the establishment of foreign military bases on its territory.

Austria became a member of the UN on 14 December 1955. It is a member of ECE and all the nonregional specialized agencies, and is a party to GATT and the Law of the Sea. Since 1960, Austrian troops have been part of the UN peacekeeping force in the Congo (now Zaire), on Cyprus, and in the Middle East. By 1985, 21,914 Austrian soldiers had been involved in these missions. Austria belongs to the Council of Europe, EFTA, and OECD, and on 22 July 1972 signed a free-trade accord with the EEC. Many long-standing trade agreements have also been in force with CMEA countries. Austria's interest in the third world is exemplified by membership in the Asian and Inter-American development banks and by its permanent observer status with the OAS.

Vienna has served an important role as a meeting place and headquarters site for a variety of international activities. The headquarters of OPEC, IAEA, UNIDO, and the International Institute for Applied Systems Analysis are located in Vienna, which has also been the site of past USSR-US strategic-arms limitation talks (SALT) and talks on arms reductions in Europe.

[19]ECONOMY

The state maintains a strong presence in the Austrian economy, although private enterprise continues to occupy a central position. Basic industries, including mineral production, heavy industry, rail and water transport, and utilities, were nationalized during 1946–47 and in 1970 were reorganized under a state-owned holding company, the Austrian Industrial Administration.

Austria's period of unparalleled prosperity lasted from the 1950s through the early 1970s; the economy was characterized by a high rate of growth, modest price increases, and a favorable climate in industrial relations. By 1975, Austrian industry, the single most important sector of the economy, had more than quadrupled in value over 1945. But the general economic slowdown that followed the oil price hike of late 1973 affected Austria as it did other European countries. During 1978–81, annual real growth averaged 2.6%, about standard for the OECD countries, but there was no real growth in 1981 and only 1.1% growth in 1982, as Austria endured its most prolonged recession since World War II. The following years saw an improvement. Between 1984 and 1991, annual real GDP growth averaged 2.8%. In 1992, it was 1.7%. Unemployment, historically low in post-World War II Austria, reached 6.8% in 1993. Inflation was moderate, the cost of living rising 17.7% between 1986 and 1992.

[20]INCOME

In 1992, Austria's GNP was $174,767 million at current prices, or $22,110 per capita. For the period 1985–92 the average inflation rate was 2.8%, resulting in a real growth rate in per capita GNP of 2.4%.

The US CIA reports that in 1992 the GDP was $143.3 billion US dollars. The UN estimates that in 1991 agriculture, hunting,

forestry, and fishing contributed 3% to GDP; mining and quarrying, less than 1%; manufacturing, 26%; electricity, gas, and water, 3%; construction, 7%; wholesale and retail trade, 16%; transport, storage, and communication, 6%; finance, insurance, real estate, and business services, 17%; community, social, and personal services, 4%; and other sources, 17%.

[21]LABOR

In 1991 there were 3,481,700 employed persons, of whom 1,283,700 were employed in industry. Foreign laborers, mainly from the former Yugoslavia and Turkey, constitute about 5% of the total work force (140,206 in 1985). The unemployment rate was only 3.1% in 1989, but increased to 3.5% by 1991. At the beginning of 1993, 1,633,480 workers were organized into the 14 trade unions affiliated in the Austrian Trade Union Federation (Österreichische Gewerkschaftsbund—OGB), which negotiates collective bargaining agreements with the Federal Economic Chamber (Bundeskammer der gewerblichen Wirtschaft), representing employers. In 1992, 58% of the work force was unionized.

Since 1975, the workweek has been set at a maximum of 40 hours, although the OGB has pushed for a 35-hour workweek with full wage compensation. Most Austrian workers put in 38–38.5 hours per week. A 50% differential is generally paid for overtime on weekdays, 100% on Sundays and holidays. Every employee is entitled to a paid vacation of 30–36 workdays annually, depending on length of employment. In addition, since 1977 every employee has had the right to one week of paid leave each year to look after a close relative in case of sickness. Two bonuses, each equivalent to one month's salary, are payable yearly, usually in June and December. By law, firms with a staff of more than 5 must have elected workers' representatives; firms with 20 or more must have elected workers' councils. These groups participate in the setting of personnel policy, management decisions, and working conditions. Disputes over wages, working hours, working conditions, and vacations are settled by a labor court or an arbitration board. Division of work, transfer, dismissal, and other matters ordinarily are settled by joint decisions of employers and workers' councils. Special legislation regulates the work hours and conditions of minors and women. Austria has had very few strikes in recent years; there were only three in 1992, involving 7,562 persons.

[22]AGRICULTURE

Although small, the agricultural sector is highly diversified and efficient. Most production is oriented toward local consumption.

Of Austria's total area, about 18% was arable in 1991; meadows and pasturelands constituted another 23.8%. The best cropland is in the east, which has the most level terrain. Farms are almost exclusively family-owned. Most holdings are small or medium-sized and, in many cases, scattered. As of March 1993, agriculture employed 6% of the labor force.

The use of farm machinery has been increasing steadily; 351,444 tractors were in operation in 1991, up from 78,748 in 1957. Austria today uses less land and manpower and produces more food than it did before World War II. Better seeding and more intensive and efficient application of fertilizers have helped raise farm yields and have enhanced self-sufficiency in foodstuffs. Agriculture is highly protected by the government; overproduction, especially evidenced by recurring grain surpluses, requires a hefty subsidy to be paid by the government in order to sell abroad at market prices. Nevertheless, the Austrian government has been able to maintain farm income, although Austria has some of the highest food costs in Europe.

Chief crops, in terms of sown area and yield, are wheat, rye, oats, barley, potatoes, and sugar beets. Austria is near self-sufficiency in wheat, oats, rye, fruits, vegetables, sugar, and a number of other items. Major crop yields in 1992 included (in tons) sugar beets, 2,843,000; barley, 1,210,000; wheat, 1,200,000; potatoes, 780,000; rye, 270,000; and oats, 200,000. Vineyards yielded 258,000 tons of grapes crushed for wine.

23ANIMAL HUSBANDRY

Dairy and livestock breeding, traditionally the major agricultural activities, account for about three-fifths of gross agricultural income.

Milk, butter, cheese, and meat are excellent, and Austria is self-sufficient in dairy products and in most meats. In 1992, livestock included 3,629,000 hogs, 323,000 sheep, 44,900 horses, and 14 million poultry. Meat and poultry production in 1992 totaled 824,000 tons. During the same year, Austrian dairy farms also produced 3,300,000 tons of milk, 112,500 tons of cheese, and 42,000 tons of butter. In 1992, some 93,000 tons of eggs were produced, which satisfied over 90% of domestic demand. By specializing in quality strains of cattle, hogs, and horses, Austrian breeders have gained wide international recognition. In 1992, exports of live animals, primarily cattle, were valued at almost $90.8 million.

24FISHING

Fishing is not important commercially, and fish do not constitute a large part of the Austrian diet. Commercial catches consist mainly of carp and trout. A sizable segment of the population engages in sport fishing.

25FORESTRY

About 46% of Austria's total area is forested, mostly in the foothills and mountains. About four-fifths of the trees are coniferous, primarily spruce; beech is the most important broadleaf type.

Overcutting during World War II and in the postwar period resulted in a decline in timber production from 9.5 million m^3 in 1936 to a low of about 7.1 million m^3, but annual yield rose to 16.7 million m^3 by 1991. Austria is the world's sixth-largest exporter of coniferous sawn timber, about 85% of which is exported within the EC area. To prevent overcutting, export restrictions have been introduced, and reforestation is widely promoted. Exports of raw timber and cork are supplemented by exports of such forestry products as paper, cardboard boxes, prefabricated houses, toys, matches, turpentine, and volatile oils. In 1970, forestry accounted for 1.8% of GDP, but had fallen to 0.9% by 1990.

26MINING

After a period of expansion following World War II, mineral production has generally stagnated in recent decades. The iron ore production (2,130,000 tons of iron and ore produced in 1991, mainly from Styrian surface mines) is insufficient for domestic needs; in 1990, 3,892,000 tons of iron ore were imported. Production of bituminous coal declined steadily after World War II and in 1968 ceased altogether. Lignite production has been declining since 1963, when output was 6,053,000 tons; in 1991, an estimated 2,081,000 tons were produced, a steady decrease from the 2,786,000 of 1987. In 1990, 3,596,000 tons of coal, mostly bituminous, were imported, principally from Poland and the former Czechoslovakia. Crude magnesite production totaled 1,179,000 tons during the same year. Austria is also a leading European producer of graphite, with an estimated output of 19,750 tons in 1991. Other minerals, with their 1991 output (in tons), include talc, 161,425 (up 17% from 1990); gypsum, 654,594; aluminum, 140,400; sulfur, 42,000; crude kaolin, 352,344; and common salt, 660,000.

27ENERGY AND POWER

Austria is one of the foremost producers of hydroelectric power in Europe. The most important power facilities are publicly owned; 50% of the shares of the large private producers are owned by provincial governments.

In 1991, total power production amounted to 51,484 million kwh, of which 32,728 million kwh (64%) were produced by hydroelectric plants and 18,756 million kwh (36%) by thermal plants. Total domestic consumption during that year was 52,209 million kwh; exports of 7,738 million kwh went to neighboring European countries, while power totaling 8,503 million kwh was imported. During the winter, when there is less flowing water for hydroelectric power, domestic electricity demands must be supplemented by imports from neighboring countries.

The electric power industry's share of Austria's total energy requirement was 12.3% in 1991. Liquid fuels accounted for 45.2%, gaseous fuels 21%, and other sources (chiefly coal and lignite) 21.5%. Oil, first produced in 1863, is found both in Upper Austria, near Wolfsegg am Hausruck, and in Lower Austria, in the vicinity of Vienna. After reaching a peak of about 3,700,000 tons in 1955, oil production gradually declined to 1,214,000 tons in 1991. Petroleum reserves at the start of 1991 were estimated at 15 million tons. In 1990, Austria imported nearly 6.9 million tons of crude oil, mainly from Algeria, Libya, and Nigeria. Natural gas production was 1,329 million m^3 in 1991, far short of domestic needs; consumption amounted to 6,285 million m^3 in that year. In 1991, 53.6 million tons of oil and natural gas were transported within, into, and through Austria via 3,336 km (2,073 mi) of pipelines.

28INDUSTRY

Industrial output has increased vastly since the beginning of World War II and contributed 28% of the GDP (including mining) in 1992. In 1946, the federal parliament nationalized basic industries. Major parts of the electric and electronics, chemical, iron and steel, and machinery industries are state controlled. However, privatization of many state companies was being planned during 1993–94.

Iron and steel production (98% of which is nationalized), has greatly expanded its output since 1937. In 1992, 3,953,107 tons of crude steel and 3,435,180 tons of rolled steel were produced. A total of 20,026 automobiles, buses, trucks and tractors, 8,203 motorcycles, 8,149 mopeds, and 105,041 bicycles were manufactured in 1989.

The most important sectors of the textile industry (which in 1992 employed 28,641 workers) are embroidery, spinning, weaving, and knitting. The value of textile production in 1992 was s33,097 million. Some 19,241 tons of cotton yarn were produced in 1992.

The chemical industry, which was relatively unimportant before World War II, now ranks third in value of production. In 1992, it produced 182,595 tons of fertilizers, 115,050 tons of rubber and asbestos products, 105,379 tons of paints and coating compounds, 178,035 tons of soaps and scouring agents, and more than s12 billion worth of pharmaceuticals. Petroleum refinery products (in tons) included fuel oil, 1,821,275; diesel oil, 3,242,282; gasoline, 2,458,365; and kerosene, 391,334.

Other leading industries, in terms of production value and employment, are electrical and electronic machinery and equipment, pulp and paper, ceramics, and especially foodstuffs and allied products. Austria has always been famous for its skilled craftsmen, such as glassblowers, goldsmiths, jewelers, lacemakers, potters, stonecutters, and wood-carvers.

29SCIENCE AND TECHNOLOGY

Scientific institutes in Austria play an important role in conducting and coordinating advanced research. Among the important institutes located in Vienna are the Austrian Academy of Sciences (founded in 1847) and the Institute of Radium Research and

Nuclear Physics (1910), one of the world's first centers for atomic research. The Austrian Research Center has an experimental nuclear reactor at Seibersdorf, near Vienna. In 1973, Laxenberg Castle, just south of Vienna, became the home of the International Institute for Applied Systems Analysis. The Ludwig Boltzmann Society had 72 research institutes in 1986; their fields of interest ranged from acupuncture to petroleum. One of the most important scientific organizations is the Association of Austrian Scientific Societies, which comprises more than 130 scientific associations. The Austrian Research Council supports and coordinates scientific research. Austria has 11 universities offering training in basic and applied sciences and 13 federal colleges of technology.

³⁰DOMESTIC TRADE

Vienna is the commercial, banking, and industrial center, and railroad lines passing through it connect Austria with all neighboring countries. Vienna is the major, but not the only, distribution center; every large provincial city is the hub of marketing and distribution for the surrounding area. Most items are sold in privately owned general or special stores, but consumer cooperatives are also active. In 1988 there were 18,509 wholesale trade establishments. There were 40,929 retail establishments that year. The Consumers' Cooperative, with 1,058 branches, was active in retail trade.

Normal business hours are from 8 or 9 AM to 5 or 6 PM, Mondays through Fridays. Banks usually stay open from 8 AM to 12:30 PM and from 1:30 to 3 PM (5:30 PM on Thursday). Advertising is displayed in newspapers, periodicals, and trade journals, and on posters on public conveyances, public stands, and billboards. Considerable advertising is done in cinemas. International fairs are held every spring and autumn in Vienna, and specialized fairs are held regularly in Dornbirn, Graz, Innsbruck, Klagenfurt, Ried im Innkreis, and Wels.

³¹FOREIGN TRADE

Austria depends heavily on foreign trade, and the government consistently maintains strong ties with the West while being careful to preserve the country's neutrality. In 1972, Austria achieved association with the EEC without encountering much Soviet opposition. Austria formerly had long-term bilateral trade agreements with CMEA nations, and has also played an important role as a mediator in East-West trade dealings. It applied for membership in 1989.

Austria's commodity trade pattern has changed importantly since the 1930s. Because of its increasing self-sufficiency in agricultural production, expansion in output of certain basic industries, and development of new industries, Austria is no longer as dependent as in pre–World War II years on imports of food and raw materials.

The rise in industrial capacity has resulted in an extensive rise in export volume, with finished and semifinished goods accounting for well over 80% of the total export value.

Principal exports in 1992 (in millions of schillings) were:

Machinery and transportation equipment	189,622
of which transportation equipment	(36,386)
Chemical products	42,171
Iron and steel	25,629
Paper and cardboard products	28,615
Raw materials, less fuels	19,871
Textiles	22,498
Foodstuffs	13,126
Metalware	25,388
Other exports	120,636
	———
TOTAL	487,556

Principal imports in 1992 (in millions of schillings) were:

Machinery and transportation equipment	234,771
of which transportation equipment	(82,126)
Mineral fuels and energy	30,430
Clothing	28,780
Chemical products	58,321
Foodstuffs	26,850
Textiles	21,034
Other imports	22,498
	———
TOTAL	593,924

In 1937, Germany was Austria's chief customer, accounting for 15% of its exports and 16% of its imports. In 1992, 39.8% of Austria's exports and 42.9% of its imports were accounted for by Germany. Other important trading partners are Italy, accounting for 8.8% of total exports and 8.6% of total imports; France, 4.4% of both exports and imports; and Switzerland, 5.9% of exports, 4% of imports. Austria's exchanges with EC countries represented 66.1% of its total exports and 67.9% of imports; with EFTA countries, 8.6% of exports, 6.8% of imports; and with Eastern Europe, 11.6% of exports, 7.3% of imports. Principal trade partners in 1992 (in millions of schillings) were:

	EXPORTS	IMPORTS	BALANCE
Germany	194,136	254,644	–60,508
Italy	42,919	51,232	–8,313
Switzerland	28,920	23,782	5,138
Belgium	16,934	9,028	7,906
US	12,853	23,392	–10,539
France	21,368	26,372	–5,004
UK	17,406	16,160	1,246
Netherlands	14,221	16,045	–1,824
Hungary	15,558	11,959	3,599
Japan	7,492	28,067	–20,575
Other countries	115,749	133,243	–17,494
	———	———	———
TOTALS	487,556	593,924	–106,368

³²BALANCE OF PAYMENTS

Austria's habitual trade deficits are partly offset by surpluses in services, particularly from tourism. Large credits on capital accounts, including portfolio investment and short-term transactions, also counterbalance the shortfall in commodity trade. In 1992, stronger growth in exports than in imports caused a drop in the trade deficit, which was largely offset by service revenues, mainly from tourism.

In 1992 merchandise exports totaled $43,386 million and imports $52,228 million. The merchandise trade balance was $–8,841 million. The following table summarizes Austria's balance of payments for 1991 and 1992 (in millions of US dollars):

	1991	1992
CURRENT ACCOUNT		
Goods, services, and income	192	238
Unrequited transfers	–76	–940
	———	———
TOTALS	116	–703
CAPITAL ACCOUNT		
Direct investment	–933	–1,056
Portfolio investment	1,180	1,970
Other long-term capital	–2,339	–1,462
Other short-term capital	2,080	1,592
Reserves	–836	–2,593
	———	———
TOTALS	–848	–1,550
Errors and omissions	730	2,253
Total change in reserves	–892	–2,034

33 BANKING AND SECURITIES

The Austrian National Bank (Österreichische Nationalbank), originally opened on 2 January 1923 but taken over by the German Reichsbank in 1938, was reestablished on 3 July 1945. The bank is a corporation with capital shares fixed by law at s150 million; 50% of the shares are, by law, owned by the government. The central bank and the bank of issue, it preserves the domestic purchasing power of the Austrian currency and its value in terms of stable foreign currencies, and controls external transactions affecting the balance of payments. It also sets reserve requirements for credit institutions.

The Austrian banking system also includes joint-stock banks, banking houses, and private banks, as well as postal savings banks, private savings banks, mortgage banks, building societies, and specialized cooperative credit institutions. The most important credit institutions are the joint-stock commercial banks, the two largest of which, the Creditanstalt-Bankverein and the Österreichische Länderbank, were nationalized in 1946; shares representing 40% of the nominal capital of the two were sold to the public in 1957. At the end of 1993, savings deposits of all credit institutions amounted to s1,643 billion. At the end of 1993, the total money supply in circulation, as measured by M2, was s1,952 billion.

A special decree of Empress Maria Theresa (1 August 1771) provided for the establishment of a stock exchange in Vienna. The exchange also deals in five Austrian and seven foreign investment certificates.

34 INSURANCE

Insurance in Austria is regulated by the Ministry of Finance under legislation effective 1 January 1979. Motor-vehicle third-party liability, aviation accident and third-party liability, and nuclear-risk liability coverages are compulsory. Armed sportsmen, accountants, pipeline operators, and notaries are also required to carry liability insurance. In 1989 Austria had 70 insurance companies, and the following year premiums totaled $1075.4 per capita, or 5% of the GDP. At the end of 1992, s769 billion worth of life insurance was in force.

35 PUBLIC FINANCE

The government's proposed annual budget is submitted to the Nationalrat before the beginning of each calendar year (which coincides with the fiscal year). Within certain limits, the Finance Minister can subsequently permit the maximum expenditure levels to be exceeded, but any other excess spending must receive the approval of the Nationalrat in the form of a supplementary appropriations bill or an amendment to the budgetary legislation. Annual expenditures, which in the early 1960s rose markedly owing to increases in defense expenditures, social services, federal operations, and capital expenditures, were less expansionary in 1965–70. During the 1970s, the annual budget again began to rise, expenditures increasing at a faster rate than revenues, but by the mid-1980s, both expenditures and revenues were increasing at about the same rate. In 1992, total budget expenditures amounted to s635.9 billion, while revenues came to s573.9, for a deficit of s62 billion (3% of GDP). As a result of a mini-recession in 1993, the budget deficit widened to s98.2 billion, which was equivalent to 4.7% of GDP. The increase in the budget deficit was mainly due to the government's decision to let automatic stabilizers work, when it became apparent that business activity was slowing down. Allocations in 1992 included: education, science, and research, s86.4 billion; social welfare, health, and housing, s186.3 billion; and roads and transport, s128.6 billion.

After the German occupation of Austria in 1938, the German authorities refused to respect Austria's external debt liabilities, and the service of such debt ceased. Since 1945, however, Austria has paid the service of all its indebtedness and all amounts payable under its postwar agreements for settlement of its prewar external debt. In 1991, the federal public debt amounted to s937.7 billion, of which s147 billion was foreign debt. The following table shows actual expenditures for 1990 and 1991 in billions of schillings.

REVENUE AND GRANTS	1990	1991
Tax revenue	570.01	616.13
Non-tax revenue	54.66	58.89
Capital revenue	1.54	1.23
Grants	3.19	4.36
TOTAL	629.40	680.61

EXPENDITURES & LENDING MINUS REPAYMENTS		
General public services	34.35	40.89
Defense	17.67	18.05
Public order and safety	16.77	18.36
Education	64.10	71.04
Health	89.07	97.54
Social Security and welfare	313.83	336.74
Housing and community amenities	18.79	20.84
Recreation, cultural and religious affairs	4.59	5.24
Economic affairs and services	67.95	69.67
Other expenditures	64.61	73.39
Adjustments	—	—
Lending minus repayments	18.56	20.54
TOTAL	710.29	772.30
Deficit/Surplus	−80.89	−91.69

In 1991 Austria's total public debt stood at 945.61 billion shillings.

36 TAXATION

The income tax for individuals ranged in 1992 from 10% on annual taxable income of up to s50,000 to 50% on taxable income of s700,000 or more, with tax relief available for individuals. Payroll withholding tax is in effect. Taxes are levied on corporations (30% of profits, less deductions and credits), trade income, real estate, inheritance, dividends, gifts, and several miscellaneous services and properties. A value-added tax was introduced 1 January 1973 at a basic rate of 16%; the standard rate in 1992 was 20%. A reduced rate of 10% applied to basic foodstuffs, farm products, horticultural and fishery products, books and newspapers, rental of immovable property, tourism, and some professional services. There was also an augmented rate of 32% on automobiles, airplanes, and ships.

37 CUSTOMS AND DUTIES

Austria is committed to a program of progressive trade liberalization. Virtually all imports from EFTA and EC countries are duty-free. The tariff schedule is moderately protective (for example, 17–25% for machinery and 20–35% for textiles), although essential foodstuffs and some raw materials either are free or have a low rate. In addition, certain finished goods not manufactured in Austria are duty-free.

Import licenses are not required, except for goods that appear on the restrictive lists, such as tobacco and tobacco products, salt, war materials, and poisons. An automatic licensing procedure is applied to certain products. Free-trade zones are located at Graz, Linz, Innsbruck, and Vienna.

38 FOREIGN INVESTMENT

Between 1948 and 1954, an estimated $4 billion was invested in the Austrian economy. Austria has raised foreign capital largely through loans rather than as direct investment. Many post–World War II projects were financed by US aid; US grants and loans in the postwar period totaled about $1.3 billion, before they began to taper off in 1952. To stimulate domestic and foreign investment, especially in underdeveloped areas of Austria, two specialized investment credit institutions were founded in the late 1950s.

Cumulative direct foreign investment in Austria rose from $600 million in 1967 to $1.3 billion in 1973 and $3.2 billion in 1980; in 1992, it reached $14.2 billion. Austrian investment abroad was s16.3 billion ($1.4 billion) in 1993.

Foreign investment is concentrated in vehicles and parts, metals, electrical engineering, petroleum, and chemicals. The Austrian government welcomes productive foreign investment, offering a wide range of assistance and incentives at all levels, ranging from indirect tax incentives to direct investment grants. Of particular interest are investments in industries seeking to create new employment, in high technology, engaged in using local products, and not competing in sectors already in excess capacity. Full foreign ownership is permitted, except in nationalized sectors, and such enterprises have the same rights and obligations as domestic companies.

39ECONOMIC DEVELOPMENT

The federal government has a majority share in two of the three largest commercial banks and all or most of the nation's electricity, coal and metal mining, and iron and steel production, as well as part of Austria's chemical, electrical, machine, and vehicle industries. The republic's share in the nationalized industries was handed over on 1 January 1970 to the Austrian Industrial Administration Co. (Österreichische Industrieverwaltungs-Aktiengesellschaft—ÖIAG), of which the government is the sole shareholder. The ÖIAG, in line with the government's industrialization program, regrouped the nationalized industries into six sectors: iron and steel, nonferrous metals, shipbuilding and engineering, electrical engineering, oil and chemicals, and coal. This was later regrouped into five sections: steel; metals; machinery and turnkey operations; electronics, petroleum, petrochemicals and plastics; and chemicals, pharmaceuticals, and fertilizers.

The nationalized establishments operate according to free-enterprise principles and do not receive tax concessions. Private investors are now allowed to buy shares in them. The government, however, maintains voting control in these transactions. The legislation providing for ÖIAG's reorganization of the iron and steel industry included co-determination provisions granting employees the right to fill one-third of the seats on the board of directors. The postal, telephone, and telegraph services and radio and television transmission are state monopolies, as is the trade in tobacco, alcohol, salt, and explosives.

During the 1970s, the Kreisky government placed new emphasis on centralized economic planning. Key elements in the new policy were the planning of public investment, selective promotion of private sector investment, coordinated expansion of the energy sector and state-owned industry, and assistance for the structural improvement of agriculture. Special emphasis was given to the reform of the handicrafts industry.

Austria's official development assistance to developing countries and multilateral agencies amounted to $548 million, or 0.34% of GNP in 1991.

40SOCIAL DEVELOPMENT

Austria has one of the most advanced and comprehensive systems of social legislation in the world. The General Social Insurance Bill of 1955 unified all social security legislation and greatly increased the scope of benefits and number of insured. All wage and salary earners must carry sickness, disability, accident, old age, and unemployment insurance, with varying contribution levels by employer and employee for each type of insurance. Employers must contribute 4.5% of payroll earnings to a family allowance fund. Health insurance is available to industrial and agricultural workers, federal and professional employees, and members of various other occupational groups. For those without insurance or adequate means, treatment is paid for by public welfare funds.

Unemployment benefits mostly range from 40–50% of previous normal earnings. After three years' service, regular benefits are paid up to between 20 and 30 weeks; thereafter, for an indefinite period, a worker, subject to a means test, may receive emergency relief amounting to 92–95% of the regular benefit. Citizens are eligible for old age pensions after age 65 if they have 750 weeks of contributions paid or credited.

Family allowances are paid monthly, depending on the number of dependent children, with the amount doubled for any child who is severely handicapped. The state provides school lunches for more than 100,000 children annually. In addition, it administers the organization of children's holiday programs and provides for the care of crippled children, for whom there is a state training school. The state also grants a special birth allowance and a payment for newlyweds setting up their first home; unmarried people establishing a common household may apply for tax remission. The government provides maternity benefits, takes care of destitute old people, and provides for war victims and disabled veterans. Administration of social insurance is carried out in the provinces by autonomous bodies in which both employers and employees are represented. Payment is also made to victims of political persecution during the Nazi era and to victims of violent crime.

Although women make up an increasing percentage of the work force, they are still underrepresented in business and the professions, and not allowed in the military. While the number of women in government is low in relation to the overall population, there are female members of parliament, cabinet ministers, state secretaries, town councilors, and mayors. A 1975 federal law provides for complete equality between husband and wife in maintaining the household and raising children. Abortion is available on request during the first three months of pregnancy. The fertility rate for 1985–90 was estimated at 1.5.

41HEALTH

Austria's federal government formulates health policy directive, and public hygiene standards are high. The country spent $13,193 million on health care in 1990, and, in recent years, has expanded its public health facilities. Virtually every Austrian has benefits of health insurance. In principle, anyone is entitled to use the facilities provided by Austria's health service. The costs are borne by the social insurance plan, or, in cases of hardship, by the social welfare program.

In 1992, Austria had 27,370 physicians—1 per every 286 patients. In addition, there were approximately 5,000 specialists and 1,099 dentists. In 1989, there were 1,099 midwives. In 1992, there were 326 hospitals with 78,945 beds (from 1985 to 1990—10.8 hospital beds per 1,000 people). Life expectancy at birth in 1991 was 80 years for women and 73 years for men. The infant mortality rate in 1992 was 7 per 1,000 live births, with 91,000 births in the same year. Between the years of 1980 and 1993, 71% of married women (ages 15–49) used contraceptives. Mandatory maternity leave (during which employment is prohibited by law) amounts to 8 weeks before and 8 weeks after birth. Mothers or fathers can take one year off work, in which case they receive maternity pay from the unemployment insurance plan. They can split the two years or one parent can take both years.

Between 1990 and 1992, Austria immunized its 1-year-old children as follows: tuberculosis (97%); diphtheria, pertussis, and tetanus (90%); polio (90%); and measles (60%). The overall death rate in 1993 was 11.2 per 1,000 people, and there were 20 cases of tuberculosis per 100,000 people in 1990. Mortality from 1985 to 1990 was broken down as follows: (1) communicable diseases, maternal/perinatal causes—30 per 100,000 people; (2) noncommunicable diseases—437 per 100,000 people; and (3) injuries—55 per 100,000. Vienna's medical school and research institutes are world famous; spas (with thermal springs), health resorts, and sanatoriums are popular among Austrians as well as foreigners.

42HOUSING

During the First Republic (1919–38), Vienna and several other Austrian municipalities supported a progressive housing policy and built model apartment houses for workers. From the end of World War II until 1967, 157,386 small homes were built under the Federal Accommodation Fund, and 75,663 damaged homes were repaired under the Housing Reconstruction Fund. A system of subsidies for public housing has since been decentralized, and control turned over to local authorities. The Housing Improvement Act of 1969 provides for state support for modernization of outdated housing. In 1985, 41,153 new units were built, bringing the number of all dwellings in the country to 3,217,389. In 1990, 25% of Austria's housing stock had been built before 1919; 19% between 1971 and 1980; 18% between 1961 and 1970; 15% between 1945 and 1960; 13% after 1981; and 10% between 1919 and 1944. About 61% of all dwellings had a private bath and central heating. The most common heating fuels used in housing units were oil (27%), wood (22%), gas (20%), coal (14%), and electricity (9%).

43EDUCATION

The Austrian educational system has its roots in the medieval monastic schools that flourished toward the end of the 11th century. The present state education system goes back to the school reforms introduced by Maria Theresa in 1774. In 1869, the Imperial Education Law unified the entire system of compulsory education.

In 1962, Austria's education system was completely reorganized into a comprehensive education law, and compulsory education was extended from eight to nine years. Since 1975, all schools are coeducational and education at state school is free of charge. Financial support is provided for postsecondary schooling.

Primary education lasts for four years after which students can choose between two systems: the extended elementary school or secondary school. This lasts for four years, after which they may either attend a one-year polytechnical course followed by vocational training, or join the upper classes of secondary school, which runs for four years.

Students may also attend an intermediate or higher vocational school for a period of five years. Those who complete their studies at secondary or higher vocational school are qualified to attend the universities. In the school year 1991–92, 1,133,144 pupils were educated in 6,629 schools. At the primary level in 1991, 378,676 pupils and 34,902 teachers were registered with 3,716 schools. At the secondary level, there were 78,069 teachers and 736,385 pupils enrolled. Of this student body, 10,785 were in teacher training programs and 303,604 were in vocational courses.

Austria maintains a vigorous adult education system. Almost all adult education bodies owe their existence to private initiative. The Ministry of Education, under the auspices of the Development Planning for a Cooperative System of Adult Education in Austria, has joined private bodies in setting up projects for enhancing the quality of adult education programs.

There are 12 university-level institutions and six fine-art colleges offering 430 subjects and about 600 possible degrees.

In 1991–92, about 216,529 students enrolled full time in universities and all higher level institutions. The teaching staff numbered 15,201. In 1992, nearly s22.7 billion was allocated for expenditure on universities and fine-art colleges.

44LIBRARIES AND MUSEUMS

Austria ia rich in its availability to large library collections and is filled with strong unique collections. The largest and most important of Austria's 2,400 libraries is the Austrian National Library, which contains more than 6.1 million items. It includes eight main collections: printed books, manuscripts, music, maps, papyri, portrait and picture archives, literature archives, and a theater collection. The National Library serves as a center for the training of professional librarians, prepares the Austrian national bibliography, and provides a reference service for Austrian libraries. The largest university libraries are: Graz University (2.2 million volumes), followed by the University of Vienna (2.1 million), and Innsbruck University (800,000). Austria also has several hundred private libraries, such as the renowned libraries in the monasteries at Melk and Admont.

The Haus-, Hof-, und Staatsarchiv, founded in Vienna in 1749, was combined in 1945 with the Allgemeine Verwaltungsarchiv to form the Austrian State Archives. The Archives' collection ranks as one of the most important in the world, with more than 100,000 manuscripts and documents, some dating as far back as the year 816. Most notable are the state documents of the Holy Roman Empire—including those of the Imperial Court Council (from 1555), the Imperial Court Chancellery (from 1495), and the Mainz Imperial Chancellery (from 1300); documents of the subsequent Austrian State Chancellery; and those of the Austro-Hungarian Foreign Ministry.

The most important museums had their origins in the private collections of the House of Habsburg. The Museum of Fine Arts (Kunsthistorisches Museum) in Vienna contains a vast collection of Flemish, Italian, and German paintings by old masters. It also houses distinguished collections of Egyptian and Oriental objects, classical art, sculpture and applied art, tapestries, coins, and old musical instruments. The Albertina Museum houses the world's largest graphic art collection, including the most extensive collection in existence of the works of Albrecht Dürer. The Secular Treasury (Schatzkammer) houses the jewels and insignia of the Holy Roman Empire and of all the Austrian emperors. The numerous collections formerly in the possession of the imperial court have in large part been brought together for display in the Natural History Museum, the Museum of Fine Arts, and the Hofburg (Innsbruck). Vienna's Schönbrunn Palace contains a collection of imperial coaches from the Habsburg court. The Austrian Gallery in Belvedere Castle (Vienna), formerly the summer palace of Prince Eugene of Savoy, houses unique examples of medieval Austrian art as well as works of 19th- and 20th-century Austrian artists. The Museum of Modern Art was opened in Vienna's Palais Liechtenstein in 1979; incorporated into it was the Museum of the 20th Century, founded in 1962.

There are also other castles, manor houses, monasteries, and convents, many of which date from the Middle Ages and which are of interest for their architecture as well as for their contents. Important scientific collections are housed in the Natural History Museum, the Museums of Anthropology and Folklore, and the Technical Museum, all in Vienna; the Joanneum, in Graz; the Ferdinandeum, in Innsbruck; the Carolino Augusteum and the House of Nature, in Salzburg; and the Folk Museum, in Hallstatt, Upper Austria, which contains local prehistoric discoveries dating from the 4th and 3d centuries BC.

45MEDIA

The Austrian Post and Telegraph Administration operates all telephone, telegraph, teletype, and postal services. In 1991, 4,309,564 telephones were in use. The Austrian Broadcasting Corp., a joint company organized in 1957 and reformed in 1967 and 1974 to ensure its political and financial autonomy, administers the nation's broadcasting system. It broadcasts nationally over three radio and two television networks, and also provides a short-wave news service in German, English, French, and Spanish. At the beginning of 1991 there were 2,500,000 licensed television sets and 2,636,000 licensed radios.

As of 1991, Austria had 34 daily papers. Vienna accounts for about half of total readership. Many dailies are affiliated with political parties. Freedom of the press is constitutionally guaranteed, and there is no state censorship; the Austrian Press Council is largely concerned with self-regulatory controls and the effective application of a code of ethics. The Austrian Press Agency is independent of the government and operates on a nonprofit basis; most major newspapers share in its financing.

The leading newspapers (with their average midweek daily circulations for 1991) are:

	ORIENTATION	CIRCULATION
VIENNA		
Neue Kronen Zeitung	Independent	978,500
Kurier	Independent	426,100
Die Presse	Independent	78,600
Der Standard	NA	73,900
PROVINCES		
Kleine Zeitung (Graz)	Independent	260,600
Oberösterreichische Nachrichten (Linz)	Independent	107,900
Tiroler-Tageszeitung (Innsbruck)	Independent	97,400
Neue Zeit (Graz)	Social Democrat	73,000
Salzburger Nachrichten (Salzburg)	Independent	72,300

The leading periodicals include the weekly's Wochenpresse—Wirtschaftswoche with a circulation of 51,427, and Profil with a circulation of 110,000, and the monthly Trend which had a circulation of 90,000 in 1991.

46ORGANIZATIONS

The Federal Economic Chamber, including representatives of commerce, industry, trade, and transport, has official representatives in most countries. Every province has an economic chamber organized in the same way as the federal chamber. District chambers of agriculture are combined into provincial chambers, which are further consolidated in a national confederation. Provincial chambers of labor are combined in a national chamber. The Federation of Austrian Industrialists, with an organizational membership of almost 5,000, is subdivided into departments for trade, industry, finance, social policies, and communications, with sections for press relations and organization. There are associations of bankers, insurance companies, and publishers, as well as other commercial and professional groups.

Approximately 10,000 sports clubs are affiliated with the Austrian Federal Sports Organization, which comprises the Federal Sports Council and the Federal Specialist Sports Council which represents Austria's 49 recognized specialist sports associations.

47TOURISM, TRAVEL, AND RECREATION

Austria ranks high among European tourist countries. It has a year-round tourist season: in winter, tourists come to the famous skiing resorts and attend outstanding musical events in Vienna; in summer, visitors are attracted by scenery, sports, and cultural festivals, notably in Vienna and Salzburg. Of the 4,000 communities in Austria, nearly half are considered tourist centers.

Foreign tourist traffic is the leading single source of foreign exchange, and tourism is a major contributor to the Austrian economy. Of an estimated 19,092,000 foreign tourists in 1991, travelers from Germany accounted for 64.5%, followed by Dutch travelers, representing 9.3%. In the same year, receipts from tourism amounted to US$13.9 billion. There were 315,141 rooms in hotels, inns, and pensions with 654,127 beds and a 33.9% occupancy rate.

Visitors entering Austria for a short stay need only a valid

passport if from the US or Western European countries, but an Austrian visa is required for visits exceeding three months.

Tourist attractions in the capital include 15 state theaters and the Vienna State Opera (which also houses the Vienna Philharmonic); the Vienna Boys' Choir; St. Stephen's Cathedral; the Schönbrunn and Belvedere palaces; and the Spanish Riding Academy, with its famous Lippizaner stallions. Just beyond the city boundary are the Vienna Woods, with their picturesque wine taverns.

About 40 or 50 towns and villages qualify as major resorts for Alpine skiing, and Innsbruck has been the site of two Winter Olympics, in 1964 and 1976. Mountaineering is another Austrian specialty, with Austrian climbers having scaled high peaks all over the world. Austrians have frequently taken titles in world canoeing championships. Soccer is a very popular sport. Austria also puts on a number of prominent annual events for cyclists. Probably the most challenging tour on the amateurs' program is the "Tour d'Autriche", which has been held every year since 1949. This race through Austria's mountains covers a total distance of almost 1,500 kilometers. Motor racing, motorcycle racing and speedway racing are also extremely popular sports in Austria.

48FAMOUS AUSTRIANS

Political Figures

Monarchs who played a leading role in Austrian and world history include Rudolf I of Habsburg (1218–91), founder of the Habsburg dynasty and Holy Roman emperor from 1273; Maria Theresa (1717–80), who succeeded to the Habsburg dominions by means of the Pragmatic Sanction of 1740; her son Joseph II (1741–90), the "benevolent despot" who became Holy Roman emperor in 1765; Franz Josef (1830–1916), emperor of Austria at the outbreak of World War I; and his brother Maximilian (Ferdinand Maximilian Josef, 1832–1867), who became emperor of Mexico in 1864, ruling on behalf of Emperor Napoleon III of France, and was deposed and executed. Prince Klemens Wenzel Nepomuk Lothar von Metternich (1773–1859), Austrian foreign minister from 1809 to 1848, was the architect of the European balance of power established at the Congress of Vienna in 1815. Adolf Hitler (1889–1945), born in Braunau, was dictator of Germany from 1933 until his death. Leading Austrian statesmen since World War II are Bruno Kreisky (b.1911), Socialist Party chairman and chancellor of Austria from 1970 to 1983; and Kurt Waldheim (b.1918), Austrian diplomat and foreign minister, who was UN secretary-general from 1971 to 1981 and was elected to the presidency in June 1986.

Artists, Writers, and Scientists

Austria has produced many excellent artists, writers, and scientists but is probably most famous for its outstanding composers. Beginning in the 18th century and for 200 years, Vienna was the center of European musical culture. Among its great masters were Franz Joseph Haydn (1732–1809), Wolfgang Amadeus Mozart (1756–91), Franz Schubert (1797–1828), Anton Bruckner (1824–96), Gustav Mahler (1860–1911), Hugo Wolf (1860–1903), Arnold Schönberg (1874–1951), Anton von Webern (1883–1945), and Alban Berg (1885–1935). Although born in northwestern Germany, Ludwig van Beethoven (1770–1827) and Johannes Brahms (1833–97) settled in Vienna and spent the rest of their lives there. Composers of light music, typical of Austria, are Johann Strauss, Sr. (1804–49), Johann Strauss, Jr. (1825–99), Dalmatian-born Franz von Suppé (Francesco Ezechiele Ermenegildo Cavaliere Suppe-Demelli, 1819–95), Hungarian-born Franz Lehár (1870–1948), and Oskar Straus (1870–1954). Outstanding musicians are the conductors Clemens Krauss (1893–1954), Karl Böhm (1894–1981), and Herbert von Karajan (b.1908); the pianists Artur Schnabel (1882–1951) and Alfred Brendel (b.1931); and the violinist Fritz Kreisler (1875–1962).

Leading dramatists and poets include Franz Grillparzer (1791–1872), Nikolaus Lenau (1802–50), Ludwig Anzengruber (1839–81), and Hugo von Hofmannsthal (1874–1929). Novelists and short-story writers of interest are Adalbert Stifter (1805–68), Marie von Ebner-Eschenbach (1830–1916), Arthur Schnitzler (1862–1931), Hermann Bahr (1863–1934), Stefan Zweig (1881–1942), Robert Musil (1880–1942), Hermann Broch (1886–1952), Yakov Lind (b.1927), and Peter Handke (b.1942). Although born in Czechoslovakia, the satiric polemicist Karl Kraus (1874–1936), the poet Rainer Maria Rilke (1875–1926), the novelist and short-story writer Franz Kafka (1883–1924), and the poet and novelist Franz Werfel (1890–1946) are usually identified with Austrian literary life. Film directors of Austrian birth include Max Reinhardt (Maximilian Goldman, 1873–1943), Erich von Stroheim (Erich Oswald Stroheim, 1885–1957), Fritz Lang (1890–1976), Josef von Sternberg (1894–1969), Otto Preminger (1905–86), and Billy Wilder (b.1906). Internationally known performers born in Austria include Lotte Lenya (Karoline Blamauer, 1900–81) and Maximilian Schell (b.1930).

Architects and Artists

Two great architects of the Baroque period were Johann Bernhard Fischer von Erlach (1656–1723) and Johann Lucas von Hildebrandt (1668–1745). Three prominent 20th-century painters were Gustav Klimt (1862–1918), Oskar Kokoschka (1886–1980), and Egon Schiele (1890–1918).

Physicians

Psychoanalysis was founded in Vienna by Sigmund Freud (1856–1939) and extended by his Austrian colleagues Alfred Adler (1870–1937), Otto Rank (1884–1939), Theodor Reik (1888–1969), and Wilhelm Reich (1897–1957). Eugen Böhm-Bawerk (1851–1914) and Joseph Alois Schumpeter (1883–1950) were outstanding economists. A renowned geneticist was Gregor Johann Mendel (1822–84). Christian Johann Doppler (1803–53), a physicist and mathematician, described the wave phenomenon known today as the Doppler shift. Lise Meitner (1878–1968) was the physicist who first identified nuclear fission. Austrian Nobel Prize winners in physics are Erwin Schrödinger (1887–1961), in 1933; Victor Franz Hess (1883–1964), authority on cosmic radiation, in 1936; and atomic theorist Wolfgang Pauli (1900–1958), discoverer of the exclusion principle, in 1945. Winners of the Nobel Prize in chemistry are Fritz Pregl (1869–1930), who developed microanalysis, in 1923; Richard Zsigmondy (1865–1929), inventor of the ultramicroscope, in 1925; biochemist Richard Kuhn (1900–1967), a pioneer in vitamin research, in 1938; and biochemist Max Ferdinand Perutz (b.1914) for research in blood chemistry, in 1962. Winners of the Nobel Prize in physiology or medicine are otologist Robert Bárány (1876–1936), in 1914; psychiatrist Julius Wagner-Jauregg (1857–1940), for developing a treatment for general paresis, in 1927; Karl Landsteiner (1868–1943), discoverer of blood groups, in 1930; German-born pharmacologist Otto Loewi (1873–1961), for his study of nerve impulse transmission, in 1936; Carl Ferdinand Cori (b.1896) and his wife, Gerti Theresa Radnitz Cori (1896–1957), whose work with enzymes led to new ways of fighting diabetes, in 1947; and Konrad Lorenz (b.1903), discoverer of the "imprinting" process of learning, in 1973. In 1974, Friedrich August von Hayek (b.1899), a noted monetary theorist, was awarded the Nobel Prize in economics.

Humanitarians

The Nobel Peace Prize was awarded to Baroness Berta Kinsky von Suttner (b.Prague, 1843–1914), founder of the Austrian Society of Peace Lovers and author of *Lay Down Your Arms!*, in 1905; and to Alfred Hermann Fried (1864–1921), a prolific publicist for the cause of international peace, in 1911. One of the most influential philosophers of the contemporary age was Ludwig Josef Johann Wittgenstein (1889–1951). Rudolf Steiner (1861–1925), the founder of anthroposophy, was an Austrian. Theodor Herzl (b.Budapest, 1860–1904), founder of the Zionist movement, was an early advocate of the establishment of a Jewish state in Palestine. Simon Wiesenthal (b.Poland, 1908), a Nazi concentration-camp survivor, has searched for Nazi war criminals around the world.

Athletes

Austrians have excelled in international Alpine skiing competition. In 1956, Toni Sailer (b.1935) won all three Olympic gold medals in men's Alpine skiing events. Annemarie Moser-Pröll (b.1953) retired in 1980 after winning a record six women's World Cups, a record 62 World Cup races in all, and the 1980 women's downhill skiing Olympic championship. Franz Klammer (b.1953), who won the 1976 men's downhill Olympic title, excited spectators with his aggressive style. Arnold Schwarzenegger (b.1947) is the foremost bodybuilder in the world.

[49] DEPENDENCIES

Austria has no territories or colonies.

[50] BIBLIOGRAPHY

American University. *Area Handbook for Austria*. Washington, D.C.: Government Printing Office, 1976.

Bader, William B. *Austria Between East and West, 1945–1955*. Stanford, Calif.: Stanford University Press, 1966.

Barker, Elisabeth. *Austria, 1918–72*. Coral Gables, Fla.: University of Miami Press, 1973.

Bauer, Robert A. *The Austrian Solution: International Conflict and Cooperation*. Charlottesville: University of Virginia Press, 1982.

Bischof, Gunter and Anton Pelinka (eds.) *Austria in the New Europe*. New Brunswick, N.J.: Transaction, 1993.

Cohen, Bernard. *Waldheim*. New York: Adama Books, 1987.

Federal Press Service. *Austria: Facts and Figures*. Vienna: Federal Press Service, 1992.

Fitzmaurice, John. *Austrian Politics and Society Today: in Defence of Austria*. Foreword by Bruno Kreisky. New York: St. Martin's Press, 1990.

Gulick, Charles Adams. *Austria from Habsburg to Hitler*. Berkeley: University of California Press, 1948.

Hankel, Wilhelm. *Prosperity Amidst Crisis: Austria's Economic Policy and the Energy Crunch*. Boulder, Colo.: Westview, 1981.

Jelavich, Barbara. *Modern Austria: Empire and Republic, 1815–1986*. Cambridge, and New York: Cambridge University Press, 1987.

Johnston, William M. *The Austrian Mind: An Intellectual and Social History*. Berkeley: University of California Press, 1976.

Kann, Robert Adolf. *A History of the Habsburg Empire, 1526–1918*. Berkeley: University of California Press, 1974.

Kurzer, Paulette. *Business and Banking: Political Change and Economic Integration in Western Europe*. Ithaca, N.Y.: Cornell University Press, 1993.

Leeper, Alexander Wigram Allen. *A History of Medieval Austria*. London: Oxford University Press, 1941.

Maass, Walter B. *Country Without a Name: Austria Under Nazi Rule, 1938–1945*. New York: Ungar, 1979.

Musulin, Stella. *Austria and the Austrians*. New York: Praeger, 1972.

Prawy, Marcel. *The Vienna Opera*. New York: Praeger, 1970.

Salt, Denys. *Austria*. Santa Barbara, Calif.: ABC-Clio, 1986.

Siegler, Heinrich. *Austria—Problems and Achievements, 1945–1964*. Vienna: Siegler, 1965.

Steiner, Kurt (ed.). *Modern Austria*. Palo Alto, Calif.: Society for the Promotion of Science and Scholarship, 1981.

———. *Tradition and Innovation in Contemporary Austria*. Palo Alto, Calif.: Society for the Promotion of Science and Scholarship, 1982.

———. *Politics in Austria*. Boston: Little, Brown, 1972.

Sully, Melanie. *Political Parties and Elections in Austria*. New York: St. Martin's, 1981.

Sweeney, Jim and Josef Weidenholzer (eds.) *Austria: a Study in Modern Achievement*. Brookfield, Vt.: Avebury, 1988.

———. *Austria and Its Political and Social Issues*. Brookfield, Vt.: Gower, 1987.

BELARUS

Republic of Belarus
Respublika Belarus

CAPITAL: Minsk.

FLAG: Three horizontal bands of white (top), red, and white.

ANTHEM: *Maladaya Belarus.*

MONETARY UNIT: The Belarus ruble circulates along with the Russian rouble (R). The government has a varying exchange rate for trade between Belarus and Russia.

WEIGHTS AND MEASURES: The metric system is in force.

HOLIDAYS: New Year's Day, 1 January; Orthodox Christmas, 7 January; International Women's Day, 8 March; Labor Day, 1 May; Victory Day, 9 May; Independence Day, 27 July; Day of Commemoration, 2 November; Christmas, 25 December.

TIME: 2 PM = noon GMT.

[1]LOCATION, SIZE, AND EXTENT

Belarus is a landlocked nation located in eastern Europe, between Poland and Russia. Comparatively the area occupied by Belarus is slightly smaller than the state of Kansas, with a total area of 207,600 sq km (80,154 sq mi). Belarus shares boundaries with Latvia on the N, Russia on the N and E, Ukraine on the S, Poland on the S, and Lithuania on the NW. The boundary length of Belarus totals 3,098 km (1,925 mi).

The capital city of Belarus, Minsk, is located near the center of the country.

[2]TOPOGRAPHY

The topography of Belarus is generally flat and contains much marshland.

[3]CLIMATE

The country's climate is transitional between continental and maritime. July's mean temperature is 19.4°C (67°F). January's mean temperature is -5°C (23°F). Rainfall averages between 57 cm (22.5 in) and 61 cm (26.5 in) annually.

[4]FLORA AND FAUNA

One-third of the country is forest. Some of the mammals in the forest include deer, brown bears, rabbits, and squirrels. The southern region is a swampy expanse. The marshes are home to ducks, frogs, turtles, raccoons, and muskrats.

[5]ENVIRONMENT

As part of the legacy of the former Soviet Union, Belarus' main environmental problems are chemical and nuclear pollution. Belarus was the republic most affected by the accident at the Chernobyl nuclear power plant in April 1986. Northerly winds prevailed at the time of the accident; therefore, most of the fallout occurred over farmland in the southeastern section of the country (primarily in the Gomel and Mogilev oblasts). Most experts estimate that 25–30% of Belarus' farmland was irradiated and should not be used for agricultural production or to collect wild berries and mushrooms although it continues to be used for these and other purposes.

In addition, Belarus has significant air and water pollution from industrial sources. The most common pollutants are formaldehyde, carbon emissions, and petroleum-related chemicals. The soils also contain unsafe levels of lead, zinc, copper and the agricultural chemical DDT.

As of 1994, Belarus had 214 species of plants and 178 animal species.

[6]POPULATION

The population of Belarus was 10,199,709 in 1989. It was estimated at 10,271,000 in 1991 and at 10,437,418 in 1995 by the US Bureau of the Census. The UN projects a population of 10,811,000 in 2000, based on a crude birth rate of 14.1 per 1,000 people, a crude death rate of 9.2, and a net natural increase of 4.9. The estimated population density in 1995 is about 50 per sq km (130 per sq mi). At the start of 1990 Minsk, the capital, had an estimated population of 1,613,000. The estimated population of other cities included Homyel, 506,000; Mahilyow, 363,000; Hrodna, 277,000, and Brest (formerly Brest–Litovsk), 209,000.

[7]MIGRATION

Immigration from other Soviet republics exceeded emigration by 10,300 in 1989. In 1990, emigration to other Soviet republics exceeded immigration by 32,000.

[8]ETHNIC GROUPS

In 1989, Belarussians formed 78% of the population. Russians compromised 13%, Poles, 4%, Ukrainians, 3%, and Jews, 1%.

[9]LANGUAGES

Belarussian belongs to the eastern group of Slavic languages and is very similar to Russian. It did not become a separate language until the 15th century, when it was the official language of the grand duchy of Lithuania. It is written in the Cyrillic alphabet but has two letters not in Russian and a number of distinctive sounds. The vocabulary has borrowings from Polish, Lithuanian, German, Latin, and Turkic.

[10]RELIGIONS

The Eastern Orthodox Church predominates, and there is a Roman Catholic population, one quarter of whom are of Polish ethnicity, of 14%. Baptist missionaries from the US have been

37

active in Belarus since independence. As of 1990, there was a small but significant Jewish population of 75,000.

[11]TRANSPORTATION

About 5,570 km (3,460 mi) of railways traverse Belarus, connecting it to Russia, Ukraine, Lithuania, Poland, and Latvia. Of the 98,200 km (61,000 mi) of highways in 1990, 66,100 km (41,100 mi) were hard-surfaced.

The European Bank for Reconstruction and Development (EBRD) initiated a study of railways and roads in 1993 to help determine locational advantages for future development in Belarus. The focus of the EBRD study will also include the development of the trucking industry.

Because Belarus is landlocked, there are no ports or merchant fleet.

[12]HISTORY

The Belarussians are the descendants of Slavic tribes that migrated into the region in the 9th century. They trace their distinct identity from the 13th century when the Mongols conquered Russia and parts of Ukraine. During this period, Belarus managed to maintain its identity as part of the Grand Duchy of Lithuania. The merger of the Grand Duchy with Poland in 1569 put the territory of Belarus under Polish rule. After the division of Poland in the late 18th century, Belarus fell to the Russian Empire.

In March 1918, at the time of the Soviet-German Treaty of Brest-Litovsk in which Moscow agreed to relinquish claim to a substantial amount of territory which Germany had captured in exchange for peace with Germany, the Belarussian National Republic was formed with German military assistance. However, after the German government collapsed in November 1918 and German forces were withdrawn from the region, Bolshevik troops moved in and set up the Byelorussian Soviet Socialist Republic in January 1919. In 1922 the Belarus SSR became one of the 15 socialist republics to form the Union of Soviet Socialist Republics.

Stalin, as part of the 1939 Molotov-Ribbentrop pact, annexed parts of eastern Poland to Belarus. In general, Belarus was devastated by World War II.

Throughout the early 1990s the Belarussian leadership supported keeping the Soviet Union intact. In March 1991, 83% of the population voted against disbanding it. However, shortly after the abortive August 1991 coup attempt against Mikhail Gorbachev, the independence of Belarus was declared on 26 August 1991.

Since disbanding the USSR, Belarus has made very little progress toward economic and political reform. The economy is failing and the political environment is characterized by a vigorous effort on the part of the Soviet-era apparatchiks to retain power.

[13]GOVERNMENT

In May 1993, a draft constitution was presented to the twelfth session of parliament, which adopted 88 of the new constitution's 153 articles. The Belarussian legislature is still known as the Supreme Soviet.

Until mid-1994, Belarus was the only former Soviet republic not to have a president. The chairman of the Supreme Soviet was considered the chief of state, but power remained in the hands of the Council of Ministers headed by a prime minister.

On 19 July 1994, elections for president were held in Belarus. Alyaksandr Lukashenka received 80.1% of the vote. He was elected on a platform of clearing out the Communist establishment ruling Belarus. Lukashenka, however, is not a democrat but a Communist populist who appears to have no plans for implementing political or economic reform. Lukashenka's primary opponent was Vyacheslau Kebich, the prime minister and favorite of the apparatchiks, who garnered only 14.1% of the vote.

[14]POLITICAL PARTIES

The Belarus Supreme Soviet was elected in 1990 and is dominated by Communist Party and government bureaucrats. The Communist Party was declared illegal after the abortive August 1991 coup attempt, but was re-legalized in February 1993. It and two other pro-Communist parties merged into one political party called the People's Movement of Belarus in May 1993.

The primary opposition party, the Belarussian Popular Front, holds only 10% of the seats in parliament. They have made repeated calls for elections because the current parliament is still left over from the Soviet system. These elections have not yet been held.

On the whole, political parties have not gathered the momentum evident in other former Soviet republics. None of the parties have a large public following. Public opinion polls show that roughly 70% of the electorate do not support any of the current political parties.

[15]LOCAL GOVERNMENT

Under the Soviet-era constitution, Belarus is divided into six oblasts (provinces), 120 raions (regions), and hundreds of village soviets (councils). Established during the Soviet era, these continue to be dominated by Communist apparatchiks. The oblasts are roughly parallel to counties in the United States. Each has a capital city, and the name of the oblast is typically also the name of this city. The oblasts (and capital cities) in Belarus are:

OBLAST	POPULATION
Minsk	3.1 million
Gomel	1.7 million
Brest	1.4 million
Vitebsk	1.4 million
Mogilev	1.3 million
Grono	1.2 million

[16]JUDICIAL SYSTEM

Although changes are expected to be implemented soon under the revised constitution, the government continues to operate under the judicial system which was put in place under the former Soviet Union. The courts system consists of district courts, city or province courts, and republic courts. Higher courts serve as appellate courts but also serve as courts of first instance. Trials are generally public unless closed on grounds of national security. Litigants have a right to counsel and, in cases of need, to appointment of counsel at state expense.

[17]ARMED FORCES

An offshoot of the Soviet armed forces, the armed forces of Belarus number 125,000 and will shrink with further reorganization to 90,000, organized as an army, air force, and air defense force. Belarus has pledged to transfer its 80 mobile ICBMs (SS–25) to Russia for destruction under US supervision. Its conventional forces are a 95,000-man army of 10 divisions and 23 brigades of combined arms and modern Soviet equipment, including 1,850 tanks, 5,000 other combat vehicles, and 1,400 artillery pieces. The air force (20,000 personnel and 502 aircraft) supports the army while the air defense force mans 115 interceptors and 650 anti-aircraft missiles with 10,000 personnel.

[18]INTERNATIONAL COOPERATION

Belarus was admitted to the UN on 22 October 1945. The country is also a member of the CSCE, IMF, UNESCO, and the World Bank.

Belarus is applying for membership in other international organizations, and it is a member of the CIS. The country has signed the Nuclear Non-proliferation Treaty. The country has many formal diplomatic ties with many nations. The US recognized Belarus' sovereignty 25 December 1991. US diplomatic relations with Belarus were established two days later. The US Embassy is located in Minsk, the capital.

19ECONOMY
Belarus' economy is geared toward industrial production, which accounts for about 40% of GDP, mostly in machinery and metallurgy with a significant military component. Forestry and agriculture, notably potatoes, grain, peat, and cattle, are also important. Belarus' economy is closely integrated with those of Eastern Europe and the other republics of the former Soviet Union, and the break-up of the Soviet Union was highly disruptive to it. The demand for military products was cut sharply, and supplies of imported energy and raw materials were curtailed.

20INCOME
In 1992, the GNP was $30,127 million at current prices, or $2,910 per capita. For the period 1985–92 the average inflation rate was 41.6%.

21LABOR
Of the 4,887,400 persons employed in 1992, 21% were engaged in agriculture, 30% in mining, 23% in services, 10% in construction, and 16% in other sectors.

An independent trade union movement is still developing in Belarus. The Federation of Trade Unions of Belarus, a remnant of the Soviet Union, boasts a membership of 5 million and follows government orders. Independent trade unions include the Free Trade Union of Belarus (with about 10,000 members), the Confederation of Labor of Belarus (4,000 members), the Independent Miners Union (3,000), and the Union of Air Traffic Controllers.

Several strikes occurred in 1992, most importantly one beginning in March by the Independent Miners Union of Belarus at the potassium mines in Salihorsk which lasted several months. The right to organize and bargain collectively is guaranteed by existing legislation. Unions deal with the government since the economy is still largely controlled by the state. The statutory minimum employment age is 16, and the workweek is set at 41 hours. Safety and health standards in the working place are often ignored.

22AGRICULTURE
Belarus had about 6,158,000 hectares (15,215,000 acres) of arable land (29.7% of the total) before the fragmentation and dismantling of the Soviet Union began. In 1991, agriculture contributed 17.7% to GDP, down from 22.8% in 1990. Production levels (in 1,000 tons) for 1992 include: potatoes, 8,000; rye, 2,700; sugar beets, 1,350; oats, 800; wheat, 400; and corn, 25. In 1990, 127,000 and 31,000 tractors and combines, respectively, were in service.

23ANIMAL HUSBANDRY
About 15% of the total land area is devoted to pastureland. In 1992, there were some 6,600,000 cattle, 4,700,000 pigs, 400,000 sheep, and 50 million chickens. Of the 970,000 tons of meat produced in 1992, beef and veal accounted for 49%; poultry, 13%; pork, 36%, and other meats, 2%. Belarus produces more dairy products than any other former Soviet republic except Russia. In 1992, 5.8 million tons of milk, 189,800 tons of eggs, 130,000 tons of butter and ghee, and 700 tons of greasy wool were produced.

In 1991, exports of animal skins and leather accounted for 2% of total exports.

24FISHING
As a landlocked nation, fishing is confined to the system of rivers (Pripyat, Byarezina, Nyoman, Zach Dvina, Sozh, Dnieper) that crosses Belarus.

LOCATION: 53°53′N; 28°0′E **BOUNDARY LENGTHS:** Total boundary lengths, 3,098 km (1,925 mi); Latvia 141 km (88 mi); Lithuania 502 km (312 mi); Poland, 605 km (376 mi); Russia 959 km (596 mi); Ukraine, 891 km (554 mi).

25FORESTRY
About one-third of the total land area is covered by forests and woodlands. Radioactive contamination of some forestland from the 1986 Chernobyl disaster has severely restricted output. Exports of wood and paper products accounted for 1.8% of total exports in 1990.

26MINING
Peat is found throughout the country and is processed by 37 fuel briquetting plants. Potash is mined in the Salihorsk region.

27ENERGY AND POWER
Domestic electricity is produced by four thermal plants. Belarus also imports electricity generated by nuclear and hydroelectric plants. In 1991, consumption of electricity totaled 49 billion kwh.

Only a small portion of Belarus' energy requirement is met by local production. About 40,000 barrels of oil are produced per day, along with a nominal amount of peat and natural gas. There are two major oil refineries: Mazyr, with a capacity of 300,000 barrels per day, and Polatsk, which can process 500,000 barrels per day. Belarus is an important transit route for Russian oil and natural gas exports to Eastern Europe, via pipelines which can carry up to 1,030,000 barrels per day of oil and 800 billion cu ft per year of natural gas. In March 1993, Poland and Russia entered into an agreement to build a 2,500-mile natural gas pipe-line from Russia's northern Yamal Peninsula, through Belarus and Poland, to Germany. When completed by 2010, the new pipeline will have a capacity of more than 2 trillion cu ft (56.6 billion cu m) per year. To maintain stable supplies of oil and natural gas, Belarus has entered an EBRD-sponsored joint project with Russia to develop 60 million tons of oil from idle wells in Russia's Tymen region, in exchange for guaranteed Russian oil supplies.

28INDUSTRY

Belarus does not have an extensively developed industrial base. There is some manufacturing and industry as well as agricultural processing. Many residents are involved in agriculture. Belarus' main industries are engineering, machine tools, agricultural equipment, chemicals, motor vehicles, and some consumer dura-bles, such as watches, televisions, and radios.

29SCIENCE AND TECHNOLOGY

The Belarussian Academy of Sciences, with over 30 institutes spread throughout the republic, is the most prominent science institution. Belarus also has nearly 140 technical colleges.

30DOMESTIC TRADE

In 1992, retail prices rose more than 1,000%, and a parallel national currency (also called the ruble) was introduced and declared the only legal tender for purchasing goods such as food, alcohol, and tobacco.

31FOREIGN TRADE

Before the collapse of the Soviet Union, Belarus exported about 40% of its industrial output to other Soviet republics and imported 90% of its primary energy and 70% of its raw materials from them.

In 1988, total exports were valued at R16,400 million, and imports at R47,400 million. In the same year, 91% of Belarus' total exports went to other Soviet republics, and 79% of its total imports came from them.

32BALANCE OF PAYMENTS

Belarus recorded a mild trade surplus in 1992, in spite of regula-tory constraints. As trade with the former Soviet republics increases at world market prices, however, the balance of pay-ments will probably become negative due to higher import bills for inputs and energy.

33BANKING AND SECURITIES

The National Bank of Belarus is the central bank of Belarus, charged with regulating the money supply, circulating currency, and regulating the commercial banks of the country. The currency unit is the ruble.

The country had a total of 26 commercial banks with 363 branches in 1992. The commercial banks included: the Agroin-dustrial Bank, Foreign Trade Bank, and the Bank of Industry and Construction, Belarus has a savings bank with 151 branches.

34INSURANCE

The insurance system is still largely under the aegis of the govern-ment, as a legacy of the Soviet era.

35PUBLIC FINANCE

Since the breakup of the Soviet Union, Belarus has maintained an extensive system of subsidies and profit restrictions, which are maintained by fiscal revenues approaching 40% of GDP.

The following table shows actual revenues and expenditures for 1992 in millions of rubles.

REVENUE AND GRANTS	
Tax revenue	281,219
Non-tax revenue	5,800
Capital revenue	5,232
Grants	8,947
TOTAL	301,198

EXPENDITURES & LENDING MINUS REPAYMENTS	
General public service	9,890
Defense	14,224
Public order and safety	7,463
Education	60,727
Health	8,563
Social security and welfare	125,759
Housing and community amenities	4,233
Recreation, cultural, and religious affairs	3,134
Economic affairs and services	80,653
Other expenditures	29,648
Adjustments	—
Lending minus repayments	3,480
TOTAL	347,774
Deficit/Surplus	–47,076

In 1992, Belarus' total public debt stood at R236,989 million, of which R123,549 million was financed abroad. Belarus' public debt thus far has been low, due to Russia's agreement in 1992 to assume its share of debt from the former USSR.

36TAXATION

The personal income tax rate ranges from 4.7–30%, and the cor-porate rate varies from 15%–60% with a standard rate of 30%. Also levied are a 3% turnover tax; a value-added tax ranging from 10% to a standard rate of 20%; a 10–75% excise tax; and a 64.8% employer payroll tax.

37CUSTOMS AND DUTIES

Although most imports are officially unrestricted, they are effec-tively limited by the foreign exchange shortage. Imports are sub-ject to a general tariff rate of 15%.

38FOREIGN INVESTMENT

In 1993, the government inaugurated a three-year privatization program to attract foreign capital.

39ECONOMIC DEVELOPMENT

In 1992, external financing from non-former Soviet Union sources is estimated at about US$160 million, while financing from within that bloc is expected to total some R87 billion. Indus-trial reform will call for substantial private and public investment in infrastructure. Privatization and anti-monopoly laws have been implemented to revitalize the industrial sector, and new private commercial banks have been established.

40SOCIAL DEVELOPMENT

The government has subsidized food and other basic goods to preserve social stability. Many factories have given workers man-datory unpaid vacations and four-day workweeks to avoid clos-ing down.

No effective central mechanism exists to enforce workplace safety standards, and the minimum wage is insufficient to provide a decent standard of living.

While there are no legal restrictions on women's participation in public life, social barriers remain substantial. Women do not hold any ministerial positions and occupy fewer than five parlia-mentary seats.

[41]HEALTH

Between 1988 and 1992, the country had 4.05 doctors per 1,000 people, and between 1985 and 1990, there were 879 hospitals with 13.2 hospitals beds per 1,000 people. There were also 1,434 clinics. In 1990, there were 36,365 physicians and 5,035 dentists. In addition to hospitals and medical personnel, the medical infrastructure comprises pharmacies and other retail outlets from which people and institutions acquire medicines and other basic medical supplies. There are approximately 1,130 pharmacies and "sanitary-hygiene" stores in Belarus. In terms of locale (and assuming even distribution), an average of 5.4 pharmacies exist per thousand square kilometers. This figure is higher in the urban areas than in the rural areas. Total health care expenditures in 1990 were $1,613 million.

The incident with the most wide-ranging effects on the health of the Belorussian population is the accident at the Chernobyl nuclear power plant in April 1986. An estimated 2.2 million Belorussians were directly affected by radioactive fallout. As a result of the disaster, the population is constantly subject to increased amounts of background radiation that weakens the immune systems of individuals in contaminated areas; many are said to suffer from "Chernobyl AIDS."

The 1993 birth rate was 16 per 1,000 inhabitants, with 136,000 births in 1992. Life expectancy in 1992 was 71 years (76 for females and 66 for males). Between 1990 and 1992, children one year of age were immunized against the following: tuberculosis (94%); diphtheria, pertussis, and tetanus (90%); polio (90%); and measles (94%).

The infant mortality rate in 1992 was 20 per 1,000 live births, and the overall death rate for the country was 10 per 1,000 in 1993. Mortality between 1985 and 1990 was broken down as follows: communicable diseases, maternal/perinatal causes, 28 per 100,000 people; noncommunicable diseases, 625 per 100,000; and injuries, 90 per 100,000. In 1990, there were 50 cases of tuberculosis per 100,000 people.

[42]HOUSING

In 1989, 24.5% of all privately owned urban housing had running water, 22% had sewer lines, 40.9% had central heating, and 9% had hot water. In 1990, Belarus had 17.9 square meters of housing space per capita and, as of 1 January 1991, 635,000 households (or 28.8%) were on waiting lists for housing in urban areas.

[43]EDUCATION

The official language is Belarussian, which is written in the Cyrillic script. In 1990, the literacy rate was 97.9% (99.4% for males and 96.6% for females). Education is compulsory for children between the ages of 7 and 17. Secondary education lasts for five years, beginning at age 12. The government is now putting more emphasis on replacing Russian with Belarussian. In 1991, there were 5,100 primary level schools with 113,100 teachers and 897,000 students. Secondary level schools had 691,300 students.

There are three universities in Belarus. The largest is the Belarussian State University, which is located in Minsk and was founded in 1921. Along with these universities, there are four polytechnic institutes and 19 educational institutes. All higher level institutions had 187,400 students and 17,000 teaching staff in 1991.

[44]LIBRARIES AND MUSEUMS

Libraries and cultural institutions are concentrated in Minsk.

[45]MEDIA

As of 1993, freedom of the press is restricted through the Government's virtual monopoly over forms of mass communication and its desire to limit media criticism of its actions. It controls the editorial content and policy of the largest circulation daily newspapers and of radio and television broadcasts. However, the Government does give its political opposition air time on television and radio.

There was approximately one telephone for every 17 people as of early 1990. The government operates one radio station and one television station in Minsk. In 1991, there were 3,170,000 radios and 2,760,000 television sets. There are 28 daily newspapers, with a combined circulation (in 1991) of 2,738,000. The most widely read (with 1991 circulation figures) are *Sovetskaya Belorussiya* (645,500); *Narodnaya Gazeta* (387,000); *Belorusskaya Niva* (130,000); and *Zarya* (107,500). In 1989, almost 3,000 books and pamphlets were published.

[46]ORGANIZATIONS

Belarus's important organizations include the Chamber of Commerce and Industry of the Republic of Belarus. Important agricultural and industrial organizations include the Belarussian Peasants' Union, the Union of Entrepreneurs and Farmers, and the Union of Small Ventures.

[47]TOURISM, TRAVEL, AND RECREATION

The difficult transition to democratic rule and a free market economy have delayed the development of the tourism sector.

[48]FAMOUS BELARUSSIANS

Frantsky Sharyna, who lived in the first quarter of the 16th century, translated the Bible into Belarussian. Symeon of Polatsk was a 17th-century poet who wrote in Belarussian. Naksim Bahdanovich was an important 19th-century poet. Modern writers include Vladzimir Dubouka and Yazep Pushcha, both poets. Kuzma Chorny and Kandrat Krapiva were writers of fiction during the outpouring of Belarussian poetry and literature during the 1920s. Famous modern composers from Belarus included Dzmitry Lukas, Ryhor Pukst, and Yauhen Hlebau.

[49]DEPENDENCIES

Belarus has no territories or colonies.

[50]BIBLIOGRAPHY

Buckley, Mary. *Redefining Russian Society and Polity*. Boulder, Colo.: Westview Press, 1993.

Durgo, A.S. (ed.). *Russia Changes: The Events of August 1991 and the Russian Constitution*. Commack, N.Y.: Nova Science, 1992.

Khasbulatov, R.I. *The Struggle for Russia: Power and Change in the Democratic Revolution*. New York: Routledge, 1993.

Kuznetsov, A.P. *Foreign Investment in Contemporary Russia: Managing Capital Entry*. New York: St. Martin's, 1994.

Lubachko, Ivan S. *Belorussia under Soviet Rule, 1917–1957*. Lexington: University Press of Kentucky, 1972.

McFaul, Michael. *The Troubled Birth of Russian Democracy: Parties, Personalities, and Programs*. Stanford, Calif.: Hoover Institution Press, Stanford University, 1993.

Mesbahi, Mohiaddin (ed.). *Russia and the Third World in the Post-Soviet Era*. Gainesville, Fla.: University Press of Florida, 1994.

Odling-Smee, John et al. (eds.) *Belarus*. Washington, D.C.: International Monetary Fund, 1992.

Schulz-Torge, Ulrich-Joachim (ed.). *Who's Who in Russia Today: A Biographical Dictionary of More than 2,100 Individuals from the Russian Federation Including the other Fourteen USSR Republics*. New Providence: K.G. Saur, 1994.

Sword, Keith, (ed.) *The Soviet Takeover of the Polish Eastern Provinces, 1939–41*. New York: St. Martin's Press, 1991.

The Modern Encyclopedia of Russian, Soviet and Eurasian History. Gulf Breeze, Fla.: Academic International Press, 1994.

Tec, Nechama. *Defiance: The Bielski Partisans*. New York:

Oxford University Press, 1993.

Vakar, Nicholas P. *Belorussia: The Making of a Nation, a Case Study.* Cambridge, Mass.: Harvard University Press, 1956.

——. *A Bibliographical Guide to Belorussia.* Cambridge, Mass.: Harvard University Press, 1956.

Williamson, John. *Economic Consequences of Soviet Disintegration.* Washington, DC: Institute for International Economics, 1993.

Zaprudnik, I.A. *Belarus: At a Crossroads in History.* Boulder, Colo.: Westview Press, 1993.

BELGIUM

Kingdom of Belgium

[Dutch:] *Koninkrijk België* [French:] *Royaume de Belgique*

CAPITAL: Brussels (Brussel, Bruxelles).

FLAG: The flag, adopted in 1831, is a tricolor of black, yellow, and red vertical stripes.

ANTHEM: *La Brabançonne (The Song of Brabant),* named after the Duchy of Brabant.

MONETARY UNIT: The Belgian franc (BFr) is a paper currency of 100 centimes. There are coins of 50 centimes and 1, 5, 20, 50, and 500 francs, and notes of 100, 500, 1,000, and 5,000 francs. BFr1 = $0.0291 (or $1 = BFr34.375).

WEIGHTS AND MEASURES: The metric system is the legal standard.

HOLIDAYS: New Year's Day, 1 January; Labor Day, 1 May; Independence Day, 21 July; Assumption Day, 15 August; All Saints' Day, 1 November; Armistice Day, 11 November; Dynasty Day, 15 November; and Christmas, 25 December. Movable holidays are Easter Monday, Ascension, and Whitmonday.

TIME: 1 PM = noon GMT.

¹LOCATION, SIZE, AND EXTENT

Situated in northwestern Europe, Belgium has an area of 30,510 sq km (11,780 sq mi) and extends 280 km (174 mi) SE–NW and 222 km (137 mi) NE–SW. Comparatively, the area occupied by Belgium is slightly larger than the state of Maryland. Belgium borders on the Netherlands to the N, Germany and Luxembourg to the E, France to the S and SW, and the North Sea to the NW, with a total boundary length of 1,449 km (900 mi).

Belgium's capital city, Brussels, is located in the north central part of the country.

²TOPOGRAPHY

The coastal region, extending about 16–48 km (10–30 mi) inland, consists of sand dunes, flat pastureland, and polders (land reclaimed from the sea and protected by dikes), and attains a maximum of 15 m (50 ft) above sea level. Eastward, this region gradually gives way to a gently rolling central plain, whose many fertile valleys are irrigated by an extensive network of canals and waterways. Altitudes in this region are about 60–180 m (200–600 ft). The Ardennes, a heavily wooded plateau, is located in southeast Belgium and continues into France. It has an average altitude of about 460 m (1,500 ft) and reaches a maximum of 694 m (2,276 ft) at the Signal de Botrange, the country's highest point. Chief rivers are the Scheldt (Schelde, Escaut) and the Meuse (Maas), both of which rise in France, flow through Belgium, pass through the Netherlands, and empty into the North Sea.

³CLIMATE

In the coastal region, the climate is mild and humid. There are marked temperature changes farther inland. In the high southeasterly districts, hot summers alternate with very cold winters. Except in the highlands, rainfall is seldom heavy. The average annual temperature is 8°C (46°F); in Brussels, the mean temperature is 10°C (50°F), ranging from 3°C (37°F) in January to 18°C (64°F) in July. Average annual rainfall is 70 cm (28 in).

⁴FLORA AND FAUNA

The digitalis, wild arum, hyacinth, strawberry, goldenrod, lily of the valley, and other plants common to temperate zones grow in abundance. Beech and oak are the predominant trees. Among mammals still found in Belgium are the boar, fox, badger, squirrel, weasel, marten, and hedgehog. The many varieties of aquatic life include pike, carp, trout, eel, barbel, perch, smelt, chub, roach, bream, shad, sole, mussels, crayfish, and shrimp.

⁵ENVIRONMENT

About 520 sq km (200 sq mi) of reclaimed coastal land is protected from the sea by concrete dikes. In 1994, Belgium's most significant environmental problems were air, land and water pollution due to the heavy concentration of industrial facilities in the country. The sources of pollution range from nuclear radiation to mercury from industry and pesticides from agricultural activity. The country's water supply is threatened by hazardous levels of heavy metals, mercury, and phosphorous. It has a renewable water supply of 20 cu mi. Pollution of rivers and canals was considered the worst in Europe as of 1970, when strict water-protection laws were enacted. A toxic waste disposal law was introduced in 1974, but by the mid-1980s, little had been done to implement it. Air pollution reaches dangerous levels due to high concentrations of lead and hydrocarbons. Belgium's problems with air pollution have also affected neighboring countries through its contribution to the conditions which cause acid rain. Belgium contributes .4% of the world's total for gas emissions. The Ministry of Public Health and Environment is Belgium's principal environmental agency, and there is also a Secretary of State for Public Health and Environment. The Belgian government has created several environmental policies to eliminate the country's pollution problems: the 1990–95 plan on Mature Development, an Environmental Policy Plan, and the Waste Plan.

As of 1987, the Mediterranean mouflon was listed as endangered. By 1994, there were two species of mammals, and 13 species of birds that were endangered. Nine plant species were also threatened.

⁶POPULATION

One of the most densely populated countries in the world, Belgium had a population of 9,978,681 in 31 March 1991, with a density of 327 persons per sq km (847 per sq mi). By 1995, an estimated 97% of the population was urban, with the major areas located within 100 km (60 mi) of Brussels. The largest cities, with their 1989 populations, are Brussels (including suburbs), 964,385; Antwerp (Antwerpen, Anvers), 470,349; Gent (Ghent, Gand), 230,543; Charleroi, 206,779; Liège (Luik), 196,825; Brugge (Bruges), 117,460; and Namur (Namen), 103,466.

The UN population projection for the year 2000 was 10,084,000, assuming a crude birth rate of 11.9 per 1,000 population, a crude death rate of 10.9, and a net natural increase of 1 during 1995–2000.

[7]MIGRATION

At the end of 1991, 922,502 persons of foreign nationality were living in Belgium. The major nationalities, in order of ranking, were Italians, French, Moroccans, Dutch, and Spanish. In 1989 there were 59,169 immigrants and 33,458 emigrants. Internal migration came to 386,359.

[8]ETHNIC GROUPS

Two thousand years ago the population of Belgium, as mentioned by Julius Caesar in his book on the Gallic wars, was of Celtic stock. This population was displaced or lost its identity, however, during the great invasions that brought down the Roman Empire. The Salian Franks, who settled there during the 4th century AD, are considered the ancestors of Belgium's present population.The origin of the language frontier in Belgium has never been satisfactorily explained. In the indigenous population, the ratio of Flemings (Dutch speakers) to Walloons (French speakers) is about 5 to 3. In 1991, the Flemish region had a population of 5,767,856, the Walloon region 3,258,795, and the bilingual Brussels region 960,324. A German-speaking region had 67,584 people.

[9]LANGUAGES

According to a 1970 constitutional revision, there are three official languages in Belgium—French, Dutch (also called Flemish), and German. Dutch is the language of the four provinces of Antwerp, Limburg, East Flanders (Oost-Vlaanderen), and West Flanders (West-Vlaanderen), which form the northern half of the country. French is the language of the four southern Walloon provinces of Hainaut, Liège, Luxembourg, and Namur. The central province of Brabant is divided into three districts—one French-speaking (Nivelles, Nijvel), one Dutch-speaking (Leuven, Louvain), and one bilingual (composed of the 19 boroughs of the capital city, Brussels). The majority of people in the Brussels metropolitan area are French-speaking.

The relationship between the two major language groups has been tense at times. For many years, French was the only official language. A series of laws enacted in the 1930s established equality between the two languages. Dutch became the language of the administration, the schools, and the courts in the Flemish region (Flanders), while French continued to be the language of Wallonia. The use of German is regulated in the same way in the German-speaking municipalities in the province of Liège. As a rule, French is studied in all secondary schools in the Flemish region, while Dutch is a required secondary-school subject in Wallonia.

In 1963, a set of laws created four linguistic regions (with bilingual status for Brussels), a decision incorporated into the constitution in 1970. Subsequent legislation in 1971–74 provided for cultural autonomy, regional economic power, and linguistic equality in the central government. Disagreement over the future status of bilingual Brussels intensified during the late 1970s. In 1980, after a political crisis, the Flemish and Walloon regions were given greater autonomy, but the issue of Brussels, a predominantly French-speaking territory surrounded by a Dutch-speaking region, remained intractable and was deferred.

[10]RELIGIONS

Religious liberty is guaranteed by the constitution, and no inquiries regarding religion are made by census takers. According to 1993 estimates, about 86% of the population is Roman Catholic and less than 1% is Protestant; most of the remainder are nonreligious. In 1993 there were also an estimated 250,000 Muslims living in Belgium, and more than 32,000 Jews. Part of the stipend of the clergy of the Roman Catholic, Protestant, Muslim, and Jewish faiths is paid by the state.

[11]TRANSPORTATION

The railway network, the densest in the world, comprises 3,667 km (2,279 mi) of track operated by the government-controlled Belgian National Railway Co. In addition, Belgium has a regional railway network of 27,950 km (17,367 mi). The road network comprised 103,396 km (64,250 mi), of which 11,717 km (7,281 mi) was national highway. Motor vehicles in 1991 included 3,928,906 passenger cars and 363,850 trucks. That year, Belgian manufacturers produced 1,153,515 vehicles.

Inland waterways comprise 2,043 km (1,270 mi) of rivers and canals, and are linked with those of France, Germany, and the Netherlands. The chief port, Antwerp, on the Scheldt River, about 84 km (52 mi) from the sea, handles three-fourths of the country's foreign cargo. Other leading ports are Gent and Zeebrugge. Liège is the third-largest inland river port in Western Europe, after Duisburg, Germany and Paris. At the end of 1985, the Belgian merchant fleet comprised six vessels, with a total of 10,000 GRT. The Belgian merchant fleet had numbered 101 ships (2.2 million GRT) in 1985, but offshore registry programs and so-called "flags of convenience" enticed shipowners to foreign registry.

The Belgian national airline, Sabena, formed in 1923, is the third-oldest international airline. In 1992, Sabena flew 6,207 million passenger-km and over 386 million ton-km of freight. Brussels' National Airport, an important international terminus, is served by more than 30 major airlines.

In addition, Belgium has 4,628 km (2,876 mi) of petroleum and natural gas pipelines.

[12]HISTORY

Belgium is named after the Belgae, a Celtic people whose territory was conquered in 57 BC by Julius Caesar and was organized by him as Gallia Belgica. In 15 BC, Augustus made Gallia Belgica (which at that time included much of present-day France) a province of the Roman Empire. In the 5th century AD, it was overrun by the Franks, and in the 8th century, it became part of the empire of Charlemagne. But this empire soon fell apart, and in the 10th century there emerged several feudal units that later would become provinces of Belgium. These included the counties of Flanders, Hainaut, and Namur, the duchy of Brabant, and the prince-bishopric of Liège. During the three following centuries, trade flourished in the towns of the county of Flanders. Antwerp, Bruges, Ypres (Ieper), and Ghent in particular became very prosperous. In the 15th century, most of the territory that currently forms Belgium, the Netherlands, and Luxembourg—formerly called the Low Countries and now called the Benelux countries—came under the rule of the dukes of Burgundy as the result of a shrewd policy of intermarriage. Through the marriage of Mary of Burgundy with Archduke Maximilian of Austria, those same provinces, then collectively known as the Netherlands, became part of the Habsburg empire in the early 1500s. When Maximilian's grandson Emperor Charles V divided his empire, the Netherlands was united with Spain (1555) under Philip II, who dedicated himself to the repression of Protestantism. His policies resulted in a revolt led by the Protestants.

Thus began a long war which, after a 12-year truce (1609–21), became intermingled with the Thirty Years' War. Under the

LOCATION: 49°29′52″ to 51°30′21″N; 2°32′48″ to 6°25′38″E. **BOUNDARY LENGTHS:** Netherlands, 450 km (280 mi); Germany, 162 km (101 mi); Luxembourg, 148 km (92 mi); France, 620 km (385 mi); North Sea, 66 km (41 mi). **TERRITORIAL SEA LIMIT:** 12 mi.

Treaty of Westphalia (1648), which ended the Thirty Years' War, independence was granted to the northern Protestant provinces. The southern half remained Roman Catholic and under Spanish rule. By this time, the southern Low Countries (the territory now known as Belgium) had become embroiled in Franco-Spanish power politics. Belgium was invaded on several occasions, and part of its territory was lost to France.

Under the Peace of Utrecht (1713), which concluded the War of the Spanish Succession, Belgium became part of the Austrian Empire. The country was occupied by the French during the War of the Austrian Succession (1744) but was restored to Austria by the Treaty of Aix-la-Chapelle (1748). Belgium entered a period of recovery and material progress under Maria Theresa and her son Joseph II. The latter's administrative reforms created widespread discontent, however, which culminated in the Révolution Brabançonne of 1789. Leopold II, successor to Joseph II, defeated the Belgians and reoccupied the country, but his regime won little popular support. In 1792, the French army invaded the Belgian provinces, which were formally ceded to France by the Treaty of Campo Formio (1797). This French regime was defeated by the anti-Napoleonic coalition at Waterloo in 1815.

Belgium was united with the Netherlands by the Congress of Vienna in 1815. This action caused widespread discontent, culminating in a series of uprisings. The Dutch were compelled to retreat, and on 4 October 1830, Belgium was declared independent by a provisional government. The powers of the Congress of Vienna met again at London in June 1831 and accepted the separation of Belgium and the Netherlands. However, William I, king

of the United Netherlands, refused to recognize the validity of this action. On 2 August 1831, he invaded Belgium, but the Dutch force was repulsed by a French army. In 1839, he was forced to accept the Treaty of the XXIV Articles, by which Belgian independence was formally recognized. The European powers guaranteed Belgium's status as "an independent and perpetually neutral state."

In 1831, the Belgian Parliament had chosen Prince Leopold of Saxe-Coburg-Gotha as ruler of the new kingdom, which was already in the process of industrialization. In 1865, Leopold I was succeeded by Leopold II (r.1865–1909), who financed exploration and settlement in the Congo River Basin of Africa, thereby laying the foundations of Belgium's colonial empire. Leopold's nephew, Albert I, came to the throne in 1909. At the outbreak of World War I, German troops invaded Belgium (4 August 1914). The Belgian army offered fierce resistance, but by the end of November 1914, the only Belgian towns not occupied by the Germans were Nieuport (Nieuwpoort), Furnes (Veurne), and Ypres. Belgium, on the side of the Allies, continued to struggle to liberate the kingdom. Ypres, in particular, was the scene of fierce fighting: nearly 100,000 men lost their lives at a battle near there in April and May 1915 (during which the Germans used chlorine gas), and at least 300,000 Allied troops lost their lives in this region during an offensive that lasted from late July to mid-November 1917.

Under the Treaty of Versailles (1919), Germany ceded to Belgium the German-speaking districts of Eupen, Malmédy, St. Vith, and Moresnet. The country made a remarkable recovery from the war, and by 1923, manufacturing industries were nearly back to normal. After a heated controversy with Germany over reparations payments, Belgium joined France in the occupation of the Ruhr in 1923. In 1934, Leopold III succeeded Albert.

Belgium was again attacked on 10 May 1940, when, without warning, the German air force bombed Belgian airports, railroad stations, and communications centers, and Belgian soil was invaded. Antwerp fell on 18 May and Namur on 23 May. By the end of the month, British, French, and Belgian forces were trapped in northwestern Belgium. King Leopold III surrendered unconditionally on 28 May and was taken prisoner of war. The Belgian government-in-exile, in London, continued the war on the side of the Allies. With the country's liberation from the Germans by the Allies and the well-organized Belgian underground, the Belgian government returned to Brussels in September 1944. During the Allied landings in Normandy, King Leopold III had been deported to Germany. In his absence, his brother Prince Charles was designated by Parliament as regent of the kingdom.

The country was economically better off after World War II than after World War I. However, a tense political situation resulted from the split that had developed during the war years between Leopold III and the exiled government in London, which had repudiated the king's surrender. After his liberation by the US 7th Army, the king chose to reside in Switzerland. On 12 March 1950, 57.7% of the Belgian electorate declared itself in favor of allowing Leopold III to return as sovereign. The general elections of 4 June 1950 gave an absolute majority to the Christian Social Party, which favored his return, and on 22 July 1950, Leopold came back from exile. But the Socialists and Liberals continued to oppose his resumption of royal prerogatives, and strikes, riots, and demonstrations ensued. On 1 August 1950, Leopold agreed to abdicate, and on 17 July 1951, one day after Leopold actually gave up his throne, his son Baudouin I was formally proclaimed king.

In 1960, the Belgian Congo (now Zaire), a major vestige of Belgium's colonial empire, became independent. The event was followed by two years of brutal civil war, involving mercenaries from Belgium and other countries. Another Belgian territory in Africa, Ruanda-Urundi, became independent as the two states of Rwanda and Burundi in 1962.

As a participant in the Marshall Plan, a member of NATO, and a leader in the movement for European integration, Belgium shared fully in the European prosperity of the first three postwar decades. Domestic political conflict during this period centered on the unequal distribution of wealth and power between Flemings and Walloons. The Flemings generally contended that they were not given equal opportunity with the Walloons in government and business and that the Dutch language was regarded as inferior to French. The Walloons, in turn, complained of their minority status and the economic neglect of their region. In response to these conflicts, and after a series of cabinet crises, a revised constitution adopted in 1970 created the framework for complete regional autonomy in economic and cultural spheres. In July 1974, legislation provided for the granting of autonomy to Flanders, Wallonia, and Brussels upon a two-thirds vote in Parliament. However, the necessary consensus could not be realized. In 1977, a Christian Social–Socialist coalition proposed to establish a federal administration representing the three regions, but could not obtain parliamentary approval for the proposal. In 1980, however, following several acts of violence as a result of the dispute, Parliament allowed the establishment in stages of regional executive and legislative bodies for Flanders and Wallonia, with administrative control over cultural affairs, public health, roads, and urban projects.

Belgium was transferred into a federal state in July 1993. The country is divided into three regions (Flanders, Wallonia, and Brussels) and three linguistic communities (Flemish, French, and German). Regional parliaments in the future will be directly elected along with regional governments.

Labor unrest and political violence have erupted in recent years. In 1982, as a result of an industrial recession, worsened by rising petroleum prices and debt servicing costs, the government imposed an austerity program; an intensification of the austerity program, announced in May 1986, aimed to cut public-sector spending, restrain wages, and simplify the taxation system. Vigorous trade-union protests have taken place to protest the freezing of wages and cuts in social security payments. Belgium has one of the largest national debts in Western Europe.

A riot in May 1985, at a soccer match between English and Italian clubs, caused the death of 39 spectators, and precipitated a political crisis. The government coalition collapsed over charges of inefficient policing, and a general election returned the Christian Social–Liberal alliance to power in November 1985. This in turn accelerated terrorist attacks on public places as well as NATO facilities, responsibility for which was claimed by an extreme left-wing group, Cellules Combattantes Communistes (CCC). Security was tightened in 1986. Linguistic disputes between the French- and Dutch-speaking sections have continued to break out. Extremist parties have sought to capitalize on anti-immigrant feeling among the general population.

Economic performance has continued to lag, contributing to an unemployment rate over 12% and a worsening of the government deficit. In 1994, the government instituted an environment tax on a range of goods based on the amount of pollution caused in their production.

King Baudouin died on 31 July 1993 suddenly while vacationing in Spain. He was 62 years old. Since he had no children, he was succeeded by his brother, Prince Albert (59) of Liège. King Baudouin had abdicated for a day in April 1990 to avoid having to sign legislation legalizing abortion.

13GOVERNMENT

Belgium is a hereditary monarchy governed under the constitution of 1831. This document has been frequently amended in recent years to grant recognition and autonomy to the Dutch- and French-speaking communities. Executive power is vested in the king, who appoints and removes ministers, civil servants, judges, and officers. In June 1991, Parliament approved a constitutional amendment to allow female members of the royal family to succeed to the throne. The monarch, however, would continue to be known as king regardless of gender.

With approval of Parliament, the king has the power to declare war and conclude treaties; he is commander-in-chief of the armed forces. According to the constitution, the king's rights include conferring titles of nobility, granting pardons, and administering the coinage of money. However, none of the king's acts becomes effective unless countersigned by a minister, who assumes responsibility for such acts before Parliament. Therefore, the king must choose ministers who represent the majority in Parliament. Each ministry is created in response to necessity, and there is no fixed number of ministers.

Legislative power is vested in the king and in the two-chamber Parliament. The Chamber of Representatives has 212 members, who are elected for a four-year term by direct suffrage and through a system of proportional representation. The Senate has 185 members elected for a four-year term. These numbers will be reduced to 150 and 71 for general elections after 1994. All persons 18 years of age and older are entitled to vote in parliamentary elections, and those who fail to vote are subject to fines. In time of emergency, the king may convoke extraordinary sessions. The government and both chambers may introduce legislation, and both chambers have equal rights. When a bill is introduced, a committee examines it and appoints a rapporteur, who reports on it before the full assembly. The king may dissolve the chambers either simultaneously or separately, but an election must be provided for within 40 days and a session of the new Parliament must meet within two months.

In accordance with the constitutional reform of 1980, there are three communities: the Dutch-, the French-, and the German-speaking communities. They have, in a wholly autonomous manner, responsibility for cultural affairs and for matters concerning the individual. There are also three regions (Flanders, Wallonia, and Brussels), which are responsible for the regional aspects of a broad range of concerns, including the economy, energy, housing, and environmental policy. The institutions of the communities and regions are based on the same principles as those of the national political structure: each entity has a "regional parliament" (the council), whose decisions are implemented by a "regional government" (the executive). The council and the executive are directly elected and can only be brought down by a vote of no confidence.

14POLITICAL PARTIES

Political parties in Belgium are organized along ethnolinguistic lines, with each group in Flanders having its Walloon counterpart. The three major political alliances are the Christian Social parties, consisting of the Parti Social Chrétien (PSC) and the Christelijke Volkspartij (CVP); the Socialist parties, the Parti Socialiste (PS) and Socialistische Partij (SP); and the Liberal parties, Parti Réformateur et Liberal (PRL) and Partij voor Vrijheid en Vooruitgang (PVV). The People's Union (Volksunie, or VU) is the Flemish nationalistic party, while the French-speaking Democratic Front (Front Démocratique des Francophones—FDF) affirms the rights of the French-speaking population of Brussels. The Communist Party has never received more than a small majority of the votes in Belgium.

Following the November 1991 election, Jean-Luc Dehaene was appointed prime minister in 1992, replacing Wilfried Martens, who had held this position since 1979. Dehaene headed the same governing coalition composed of the two Christian Social parties (CVP and PSC) and the two Socialist parties (PS and SP).

Ecology parties (ECOCO/AGALEV) have become important political actors by gaining seats in the Chamber and Senate. The environment tax passed in 1993 was a key demand in return for their support of constitutional reforms.

Several minor parties have obtained parliamentary representation as a result of the proportional election rules.

Party strength in the Chamber of Representatives after the November 1991 election was as follows: CVP, 16.7% (39 seats); PS, 13.6% (35 seats); SP, 12% (28 seats); VLD (formerly PVV), 11.9% (26 seats); PRL, 8.2% (20 seats); PSC, 7.8% (18 seats); VB, 6.7% (12 seats); VU, 5.9% (10 seats); ECOCO, 5.1% (10 seats); AGALEV, 4.9% (7 seats); and others 7.3% (7 seats).

15LOCAL GOVERNMENT

Belgium is divided into nine provinces: Antwerp, East Flanders, West Flanders, and Limburg in the north, Hainaut, Liège, Luxembourg, and Namur in the south, and Brabant in the center. Each of the provinces has a council of 50 to 90 members elected for four-year terms by direct suffrage and empowered to legislate in matters of local concern. A governor, appointed by the king, is the highest executive officer in each province.

Each municipality has a town council elected for a six-year term. The council elects an executive body called the board of aldermen. The head of the municipality is the burgomaster, who is appointed by the sovereign upon nomination by the town council. Recently, the number of municipalities has been greatly reduced through consolidation.

In 1971, Brussels was established as a separate bilingual area, presided over by a proportionally elected metropolitan council. Linguistic parity was stipulated for the council's executive committee.

16JUDICIAL SYSTEM

Belgian law is modeled on the French legal system. The judiciary is an independent branch of government on an equal footing with the legislative and the executive branches. Minor offenses are dealt with by justices of the peace and police tribunals. More serious offenses and civil lawsuits are brought before district courts of first instance. Other district courts are commerce and labor tribunals. Verdicts rendered by these courts may be appealed before 5 regional courts of appeal or the 5 regional labor courts in Antwerp, Brussels, Ghent, Mons, and Liège. All offenses punishable by prison sentences of more than five years must be dealt with by the 9 courts of assize, the only jury courts in Belgium. The highest courts are 5 civil and criminal courts of appeal and the supreme Court of Cassation. The latter's function is to verify that the law has been properly applied and interpreted. The constitutionality of legislation is the province of the Council of State, an advisory legal group.

When an error of procedure is found, the decision of the lower court is overruled and the case must be tried again. Although capital punishment is still part of the criminal code, the death penalty is traditionally commuted. The last execution for a civil crime in Belgium occurred in 1918.

A system of military tribunals, including appellate courts, handle both military and common law offenses involving military personnel. The government is considering narrowing the jurisdiction of these court to military offenses.

Detainees must be brought before a judge within 24 hours of arrest. Although there are provisions for bail, it is rarely granted.

17ARMED FORCES

Belgium's active armed forces in 1993 numbered 80,700, including 32,300 conscripts and 2,950 women. Combat forces include one armored brigade, two mechanized infantry brigades, and a parachute–commando regiment, which together form an integral part of NATO forces in Western Europe. A task force of 19,000 is in Germany. Belgium also maintains an immediate intervention land force, to be airlifted by the Belgian air force and readily available for deployment in any emergency. The armed forces were recruited by an annual conscription that supplements voluntary enlistmented until 1994, when Belgium abolished the draft.

Army personnel numbered 54,000 in 1993. The air force, with 17,300 personnel, has six F–16 A/B squadrons and a Mirage-equipped reconnaissance squadron. The navy is small, with 4,400 personnel in 1993, and mans 4 frigates and 16 mine warfare craft; its mission is limited to the protection of the North Sea and the English Channel. Army reserves numbered 139,000 in 1993. The all-forces medical service has 5,000 on active duty and 36,800 reserves. A national gendarmerie numbers about 16,000.

In 1991 Belgium spent $4.7 billion on defense or 2.7% of gross domestic product, but almost half of the budget comes from NATO allies. Belgium imports $200 million in arms (aircraft and ships) from its allies and exports $30 million, mostly small arms.

18INTERNATIONAL COOPERATION

Belgium is a charter member of the UN, having joined on 27 December 1945, and participates in ECE and all the nonregional specialized agencies. Paul-Henri Spaak of Belgium served as the UN General Assembly's first president (1946–47); from 1957 to 1961, he served as the secretary-general of NATO, of which Belgium is also a member. The country has been partnered with Luxembourg in the Belgium-Luxembourg Economic Union (BLEU) since 1922. In 1958, Belgium signed a treaty forming the Benelux (Belgium-Netherlands-Luxembourg) Economic Union, following a 10-year period in which a customs union of the three countries was in effect. Belgium is also a member of the Asian Development Bank, Council of Europe, EC, IDB, and OECD, is a permanent observer of the OAS, and is a signatory to GATT and the Law of the Sea.

Brussels, the seat of EC institutions, has become an important regional center for Western Europe. In 1967, the Supreme Headquarters Allied Powers Europe (SHAPE) were transferred from Rocquencourt, near Paris, to a site near Mons. On 16 October 1967, the NATO Council's headquarters were moved from Paris to Brussels. As of 1986, Belgium was home to 986 headquarters of international organizations.

[19]ECONOMY

In relation to its size and population, Belgium is among the most highly industrialized countries in Europe. Poor in natural resources, it imports raw materials in great quantity and processes them largely for export. Exports came to 70% of Belgium's GDP in 1992.

For a century and a half, Belgium has maintained its status as an industrial country, not only by virtue of its geographical position and transport facilities but also because of its ability for most of this period to shape production to meet the changing requirements of world commerce. Since the 1950s, the Belgian Parliament has enacted economic expansion laws to enable long-established industries to modernize obsolete plant equipment. Belgium's highly developed transportation systems are closely linked with those of its neighbors. Its chief port, Antwerp, is one of the world's busiest. Real growth averaged 5.4% annually during 1967–73 but, like that of other OECD countries, slumped to 2.5% during 1973–80, and 0.7% during 1981–85. It averaged 2.6% during 1984–91 and was 0.9% in 1992. It fell by about 1.3% in 1993.

Public debt was 127% of GDP in 1993, the highest in the EC; however, Belgium has had the highest rate of private savings in the EC. Consumer prices rose only 15.8% between 1988 and 1993. The unemployment rate was 9.4% in 1993.

[20]INCOME

In 1992, Belgium's GNP was $209,594 million at current prices, or $20,880 per capita. For the period 1985–92 the average inflation rate was 3.0%, resulting in a real growth rate in per capita GNP of 208.0%.

In 1992 the GDP was $177.9 billion in current US dollars. It is estimated that in 1990 agriculture, hunting, forestry, and fishing contributed 2% to GDP; mining, quarrying, and manufacturing, 22%; electricity, gas, and water, 2%; construction, 5%; wholesale and retail trade, 17%; transport, storage, and communication, 8%; finance, insurance, real estate, and business services, 5%; community, social, and personal services, 19%; and other sources, 18%.

[21]LABOR

As of 1991, the Belgian work force totaled 4,100,000. Of the 1991 total, 3,700,000 persons were employed, of whom 1,000,000 were in industry and 2,600,000 in services. The number of compensated full-time unemployed was 472,900 as of January 1992; the overall rate for 1991 was 8.1%. Unemployment is expected to increase to 9.3% by 1996.

The leading central labor organizations are the General Federation of Labor, affiliated with ICFTU, with 1,124,072 members (1982); the Central Union, with 260,000 members; and the Federation of Christian Trade Unions, which has some 1,210,000 members in 14 affiliated unions. The General Federation of Liberal Trade Unions has about 120,000 members.

Labor unrest flared in Wallonia in 1982 when Socialist-led unions struck to protest the government's austerity program. The government's plan to restructure the steel industry led to violent clashes between steelworkers and police in February and March. However, in early 1983, government workers agreed to accept pay cuts of 2.5% in order to ease unemployment. After rising an annual average of 7.7% during 1970–73 and 3.2% during 1973–80, real wages increased only by an annual average of 1.2%

during 1980–85. In 1992 there were 35 strikes involving 25,626 workers resulting in 119,757 lost work days, occurring predominantly in the health care, transportation, metal, teaching, and shipyard sectors.

Belgium has a five-day, 40-hour workweek. Workers enjoy unemployment insurance, medical insurance, paid holidays, four weeks' annual vacation (for which a bonus is paid from the social security fund), family benefits, severance pay, and workers' compensation. The insurance system is financed by taxes from employers and employees, as well as by government funds. Because of the 1988–90 economic boom, financing of the social security system fell from 37.3% of total revenue in 1983 to 16% in 1992.

[22]AGRICULTURE

Agriculture's role in the economy continues to decrease. In 1990, 2.4% of the employed population worked on farms, compared with 3.7% in 1973. Agriculture's share in the GNP fell from 3.8% in 1973 to 2% in 1992. Agriculture (including forestry and fishing) grew by 6.3% in 1991 and an estimated 7.3% in 1992, due to increased vegetable production. Many marginal farms have disappeared; the remaining farms are small but intensively cultivated. About 80% of the country's food needs are covered domestically. The richest farm areas are in Flanders and Brabant. As of 1990, about 1,290,000 hectares (3,187,600 acres), or 45.5% of Belgium's total area, were under cultivation. Over half the land cultivated was used for pasture land or green fodder; one-quarter was used for the production of cereals.

Government price policy encourages increased production of wheat and barley with decreasing production of rye and oats. Increased emphasis is being placed on horticulture, and nearly all fruits found in temperate climates are grown in Belgium. Chief among these are apples, pears, and cherries. Producers of tomatoes and apples were obliged to refrain from marketing part of their 1992 harvests in order to hold up prices.

Belgium imports considerable quantities of bread and feed grains, fodder concentrates, and fruits. Its only agricultural exports are processed foods and a few specialty items such as endive, chicory, flower bulbs, sugar, and chocolates.

[23]ANIMAL HUSBANDRY

Livestock raising is the most important single sector of Belgian agriculture. In 1992 there were about 3.1 million head of cattle, 6.5 million hogs, 133,000 sheep, and 18,000 horses. Belgian farmers breed some of the finest draft horses in the world, including the famous Percherons.

The country is self-sufficient in butter, milk, meat, and eggs. Some cheese is imported, mainly from the Netherlands. Milk production amounted to 3.5 million tons in 1992.

[24]FISHING

The chief fishing ports are Zeebrugge and Ostend (Oostende, Ostende), from which 197 boats sail the North Atlantic from the North Sea to Iceland. The total catch in 1991 was 40,226 tons, whose exports were valued at $227.5 million. Principal species caught are herring, sole, cod, haddock, shrimp, sprat, plaice, and ray.

[25]FORESTRY

Forests cover 21% of the area of Belgium. Commercial production of timber is limited; the combined output for Belgium and Luxembourg was 5 million cu m in 1991. Most common trees are beech and oak, but considerable plantings of conifers have been made in recent years. Belgium serves as a large transhipment center for temperate hardwood logs, softwood lumber, and softwood plywood. Large quantities of timber for the woodworking industry are imported from Zaire. Belgium's wood processing industry consists of 2,210 enterprises, over half of which are furniture manufacturers.

26 MINING

The Belgian coal mining industry has been in operation since the 12th century. Metallic mining was in its heyday from 1850–70, after which mining activity decreased until the last iron ore operations at Musson and Halanzy were closed in 1978. Coal, the only mineral resource of major importance, is now mined in the Sambre–Meuse Valley. The shift to alternate sources of energy, as well as foreign competition in coal, has led to a steady decline in output. Production fell from 8.8 million tons during 1973 to 4.3 million in 1987 to 634,000 in 1991.

The refining of copper, zinc, and minor metals and the production of steel (all from imported materials), were the most developed mineral industries in Belgium. Most base metal raw materials are imported from Africa. With a per capita steel production exceeding 1.1 metric ton per inhabitant, Belgium was second only to Luxembourg in per capita steel production in 1991. Belgium is also an important producer of several industrial minerals, including limestone, dolomite, whiting, soda ash, sodium sulfate, silica sand, and marble.

27 ENERGY AND POWER

In 1991 there were 118 power stations operating in Belgium, with an installed capacity of 14,097,000 kw. Of a total power output of 71,945 million kwh that year, 39% was conventional thermal, 60% was nuclear (25% in 1981), and 1% was hydroelectric. The principal sources of primary energy for conventional power production are low-grade coal and by-products of the oil industry. Belgium is heavily dependent on imports of crude oil, but it exports refined oil products. Power rates in Belgium are regulated through a voluntary agreement between labor, industry, and private power interests. As of 1992, the last two operating coal mines, at Beringen and Zolder, were to be closed. Belgium obtains most of its coal from South Africa.

28 INDUSTRY

Industry, highly developed in Belgium, is devoted mainly to the processing of imported raw materials into semifinished and finished products, most of which are then exported. Steel production is the single most important sector of industry, with Belgium ranking high among world producers of iron and steel. However, it must import all its iron ore, which comes principally from Brazil, West Africa, and Venezuela. About four-fifths of Belgium's steel products and more than three-quarters of its crude steel output are exported. In recent years, Belgian industry has been hampered by high labor costs, aging plant facilities, and a shrinking market for its products. Nevertheless, industrial production rose by nearly 11% between 1987 and 1991, as a result of falling energy costs (after 1985) and financial costs, and only a moderate rise in wage costs. High-technology industries have been slow to develop.

Production of crude steel declined from 16.2 million tons in 1974 to 11.3 million tons in 1991, while the output of finished steel dropped from 12.2 million tons to 8.98 million. By 1981, 60% of all Belgian steel production and 80% of all Wallonian steel (concentrated in Charleroi and Liège) came under the control of a single company, the government-owned Cockerill-Sambre. Plans for this firm, whose government subsidies ended (in conformity with EC policy) in 1985, called for heavy investment in plant modernization, coupled with cutbacks in employment and plant capacity.

In 1991, Belgium produced 477,972 tons of crude copper, 383,053 tons of crude zinc, and 110,684 tons of crude lead. The bulk of metal manufactures consists of heavy machinery, structural steelwork, and industrial equipment. The railroad equipment industry supplies one of the most extensive railroad systems in Europe. An important shipbuilding industry is centered in Temse, south of Antwerp. Belgian engineering and construction firms have built steel plants, chemical works, power stations, port facilities, and office buildings throughout the world.

The textile industry, dating from the Middle Ages, produces cottons, woolens, linens, and synthetic fibers. In 1991, spinning industry production (including cotton, wool, linen, and jute) totaled 172,329 tons of yarn, and the weaving industry produced 520,616 tons of fabric. With the exception of flax, all raw materials are imported. Centers of the textile industry are Bruges, Brussels, Verviers, Ghent, Courtrai (Kortrijk), and Malines (Mechelen). Carpets are made in large quantities at Saint-Nicolas (Sint-Niklaas). Brussels and Bruges are noted for fine linen and lace.

The chemical industry manufactures a wide range of products, from heavy chemicals and explosives to pharmaceuticals and photographic supplies. Production in 1991 included sulfuric acid, 1,935,921 tons; nitric acid, 1,439,533 tons; synthetic ammonia, 505,380 tons; and crude tar, 177,230 tons. The diamond-cutting industry in Antwerp supplies most of the US industrial diamond requirements. Belgium has one of the largest glass industries in the world. Val St. Lambert is especially known for its fine crystal glassware. Belgian refineries (chiefly in Antwerp) turn out oil products.

29 SCIENCE AND TECHNOLOGY

The Royal Academy of Sciences, Letters, and Fine Arts, founded in Brussels in 1772 and since divided into French and Flemish counterparts, has sections for mathematics and physical sciences and the natural sciences. The National Scientific Research Fund (inaugurated in 1928), in Brussels, promotes scientific research by providing subsidies and grants to scientists and students. The Royal Institute of Natural Sciences (founded 1846), also in Brussels, provides general scientific services in the areas of biology, mineralogy, paleontology, and zoology. In 1988, total research and development expenditures amounted to BFr913 billion; 20,124 technicians and 16,646 scientists and engineers were engaged in research and development.

Among the nation's distinguished scientific institutions are the Center for the Study of Nuclear Energy (founded 1952), with a staff of 850, which has conducted research and development work on fast-breeder reactors, fusion reactors, and the nuclear fuel cycle; the Royal Observatory of Belgium (founded 1826), specializing in radioastronomy and geodynamics; the Royal Meteorological Institute (reorganized in 1913); and the Von Karman Institute for Fluid Dynamics (1956), supported by NATO. There are, in addition, societies for the study of tropical medicine, archaeology, biology, zoology, anthropology, astronomy, chemistry, mathematics, geography, and inventions. Belgium has 18 universities and colleges offering degrees in basic and applied sciences.

30 DOMESTIC TRADE

Brussels is the main center for commerce and for the distribution of manufactured goods. Other important centers include Antwerp, Liège, and Ghent. Most large wholesale firms engage in import and export. Customary terms of sale are payment within 30–90 days after delivery, depending upon the commodity and the credit rating of the purchaser. Domestic trade volume increased in value by 124% between 1980 and 1993; turnover in department and chain stores increased by 121% and in supermarkets by 104%. Of the total trade value, food accounts for 37.5%, household furnishings 16.6%, clothing and textiles 14.9%, and other goods 31%. The cooperative movement is relatively unimportant in Belgium, as compared with other European countries; turnover by consumer cooperatives diminished by 88% between 1980 and 1993.

Business hours are mainly from 8 or 9 AM to noon, and from 2 to 5:30 PM, Monday through Friday. Banks are open from 9 AM to between 3:30 and 5:30 PM, Monday–Friday. Important international trade fairs are held annually in Brussels and Ghent. Advertising techniques are well developed, and the chief medium is the press. Advertising is prohibited on the national radio and television networks.

31 FOREIGN TRADE

Foreign trade plays a greater role in the Belgian economy than in any other EU country except Luxembourg. Exports constituted 70% of GDP in 1992 and imports, 67%. Belgium's chief exports are iron and steel (semifinished and manufactured), foodstuffs, textiles, machinery, road vehicles and parts, nonferrous metals, diamonds, and chemicals. Its imports are general manufactures, foodstuffs, diamonds, metals and metal ores, petroleum and petroleum products, chemicals, clothing, machinery, electrical equipment, and motor vehicles. Partnered with Luxembourg in the BLEU, Belgium does not issue separate statistics on foreign trade.

Principal exports of Belgium-Luxembourg in 1992 (in billions of Belgian francs) were as follows:

Machinery and transport equipment	1,072.5
Manufactured goods	1,481.9
Raw materials	105.4
Chemicals	582.3
Food and live animals	384.4
Mineral fuels	137.2
Beverages and tobacco	28.1
Other exports	176.1
TOTAL	3,967.9

Principal imports of Belgium-Luxembourg in 1992 (in billions of Belgian francs) were as follows:

Manufactured goods	1,340.6
Machinery and transport equipment	1,029.6
Mineral fuels	305.2
Food and live animals	349.5
Chemicals	478.9
Raw materials, excluding fuels	216.0
Beverages and tobacco	49.7
Other imports	254.2
TOTALS	4,023.7

In 1992, more than 87% of Belgium-Luxembourg's foreign trade was carried on with OECD countries, chiefly members of the EEC. Germany was the leading customer in 1992, followed by France and the Netherlands. Germany has been the chief supplier since 1953, replacing the US, which in the years immediately after World War II had surpassed France. Trade with Eastern European countries accounted for 1.6% of exports and 1.8% of imports in 1985; trade with OPEC members, 2.1% of exports and 2.6% of imports.

Principal trade partners in 1992 (in billions of Belgian francs) were as follows:

	EXPORTS	IMPORTS	BALANCE
Germany	906.6	962.5	−55.9
France	764.0	662.6	101.4
Netherlands	541.9	704.5	−162.6
UK	311.4	309.7	1.7
US	153.1	176.7	−23.6
Italy	233.8	180.8	53
Other countries	1,057.1	1,026.9	30.2
TOTALS	3,967.9	4,023.7	−55.8

32 BALANCE OF PAYMENTS

Belgium-Luxembourg ran deficits on current accounts each year from 1976 through 1984. Trade deficits, incurred consistently in the late 1970s and early 1980s, were only partly counterbalanced by invisible exports, such as tourism and services, and capital transfers. Foreign exchange reserves stood at an estimated $10.7 billion in 1993.

In 1992, the Belgian franc was strong due to both current and long-term capital account surpluses. The Belgian franc is equivalent at par with the Luxembourg franc; the two nations formed the Belgian–Luxembourg Economic Union (BLEU) in 1921. In 1992, imports exceeded exports by BFr55.8 billion, representing decreases of 1.4% in exports and 2.2% in imports from 1991. The BLEU trade deficit is due in large part to reliance on imported energy; the trade balance in 1992 excluding energy products amounted to a surplus of BFr115 billion. In 1992, the current account surplus for BLEU came to BFr160 billion, while the overall BLEU balance of payments (including errors and omissions) amounted to a surplus of BFr518 billion.

33 BANKING AND SECURITIES

The National Bank of Belgium (Banque Nationale de Belgique—BNB, founded in 1850), the sole bank of issue, originally was a joint-stock institution. The Belgian government took over 50% of its shares in 1948. Its directors are appointed by the government, but the bank retains a large degree of autonomy. In Belgium, most regulatory powers are vested in the Banking Commission, an autonomous administrative body that monitors compliance of all banks with national banking laws. In order to restrain inflation and maintain monetary stability, the BNB varied its official discount rate from 2.75% in 1953 to a peak of 8.75% in December 1974; by 1978, the rate was reduced to 6%, but it rose steadily to a high of 15% in 1981 before declining to 11.5% at the end of 1982 and 9.75% by December 1985. As of 1993 the discount rate was 5.25%. As of 31 December 1992, the BNB had total foreign assets of BFr731.9 billion. Money supply, as measured by M2, amounted to BFr3,117.2 billion.

By law, the name "bank" in Belgium may be used only by institutions engaged mainly in deposit bank activities and short-term operations. Commercial banks are not authorized to invest long-term capital in industrial or business enterprises. The largest commercial bank, the General Banking Society, came into being in 1965 through a merger of three large banks. Demand deposits of the commercial banking sector totaled BFr584.8 billion at the end of 1990. The National Society for Industrial Credit provides medium-term loans to industrial firms and exporters. Other institutions supply credit to small business and to farmers. The leading savings institute is the General Savings and Retirement Fund, which operates mainly through post office branches.

The principal stock exchange is in Brussels, with a smaller exchange in Antwerp. They deal in national, provincial, and municipal government bonds, government lottery bonds, and company shares. The issuance of shares and bonds to the public is subject to the control of the Banking Commission in Brussels. There are also a number of special industrial exchanges; the most prominent one is the Diamond Exchange in Antwerp.

34 INSURANCE

Insurance transactions are regulated by the Insurance Control Office of the Ministry of Economic Affairs. There were 267 insurance companies in Belgium in 1989, including 33 life insurance firms, 29 non-life insurance companies, and 59 composite companies. In 1990, insurance premiums totaled US$868.3 per capita or 4.1% of the GDP. Compulsory classes of insurance in Belgium are workers' compensation, automobile liability, and inland marine liabilities. Life insurance in force at the end of 1991 totaled BFr7,957 billion. Life and disability insurance needs are to a large extent met by Belgium's extensive social security system.

35 PUBLIC FINANCE

The government's budgetary year coincides with the calendar year. In the final months of the year, the minister of finance places before Parliament a budget containing estimated revenues and expenditures for the following year, and a finance law authorizing the collection of taxes is passed before 1 January. Inasmuch as expenditure budgets generally are not all passed by then, "provisional twelfths" enable the government to meet expenditures month by month, until all expenditure budgets are passed. Current expenditures, supposedly covered by the usual revenues (including all tax and other government receipts), relate to the normal functioning of government services and to pension and public debt charges. Capital expenditures consist mainly of public projects and are normally covered by borrowings.

In 1991 Belgium's total public debt stood at BFr7,469.1 billion, of which BFr1,086.1 billion was financed abroad. Improvements in fiscal and external balances in the early 1990s and a slowdown in external debt growth enables the Belgian government to easily obtain loans on the local credit market. As a member of the G-10 group of leading financial nations, Belgium actively participates in the IMF, World Bank, and the Paris Club. Belgium is a leading donor nation, and it closely follows development and debt issues, particularly with respect to Zaire and other African nations.

[36]TAXATION

The most important direct tax is the income tax. Since enactment of the tax law of 20 November 1962, this tax has been levied on the total amount of each taxpayer's income from all sources. The tax in 1993 had a top marginal rate of 55%, with an additional 6–8% municipal tax surcharge. Taxes are not paid in one lump sum, but rather by a series of prepayments on the various sources of income. There is a withholding tax on salaries that is turned over directly to the revenue officer. Self-employed persons send a prepayment to the revenue officer during the first half of July. Banks and stockbrokers who offer dividends must first deduct a prepayment of 25%. Taxes on real estate are based on the assessed rental value.

The corporate income tax, which is levied on all distributed profits, was lowered from 48% to 45% in 1982, to 43% in 1987, and stood at 38% in 1993. Nondistributed profits are taxed at progressive rates ranging from 28% to 41%. In some instances, local government bodies are entitled to impose additional levies. Numerous tax exemptions are granted to promote investments in Belgium.

In 1971, a value-added tax system was introduced, replacing sales and excise taxes. A general rate of 19.5% was applied as of 1993 to industrial goods, with a reduced rate of 6% applying to basic necessities and an interim rate of 12% to certain other products.

[37]CUSTOMS AND DUTIES

Customs duties are levied at the time of importation and are generally ad valorem. Rates are determined by the customs convention between the three Benelux countries, and are the same in the three countries. Industrial raw materials and foodstuffs are generally free of tax. As of mid-1977, customs barriers between Belgium and the other EC countries ceased to exist. However, value-added taxes are levied on the importation of tobacco, alcohol, beer, mineral water, and fuel oils. There are no export duties.

[38]FOREIGN INVESTMENT

Foreign investment in Belgium generally takes the form of establishing subsidiaries of foreign firms in the country. As of 1991, foreign investments in Belgium totaled $36.7 billion. Countries with large investments include the US, Germany, UK, Netherlands, France, and Switzerland. In 1987, more than 900 US companies had operations in Belgium; nearly 400 of these operations were regional headquarters. Total US investment was $10.7 billion in 1992.

The Belgian government actively promotes foreign investment. In recent years, the government has given special encouragement to industries that will create new skills and increase export earnings. In 1982, a new system of tax exemptions encouraging investment in corporate stocks took effect. The government grants equal treatment under the law, as well as special tax inducements and assistance, to foreign firms that establish enterprises in the country. There is no regulation prescribing the proportion of foreign to domestic capital that may be invested in an enterprise. The foreign investor can repatriate all capital profits, and long-term credit is available. Local authorities sometimes offer special assistance and concessions to new foreign enterprises in their area.

Belgian investment abroad is substantial in the fields of transport (particularly in Latin American countries), nonferrous metals, metalworking, and photographic materials.

[39]ECONOMIC DEVELOPMENT

Belgian economic policy is based upon the encouragement of private enterprise, with very little government intervention in the economy. Also, as a country heavily dependent upon foreign trade, Belgium has traditionally favored the freest exchange of goods, without tariffs or other limitations. Restrictions on free enterprise and free trade have always been due to external pressure and abnormal circumstances, as in time of war or economic decline.

To meet increased competition in world markets and to furnish relief for areas of the country suffering from chronic unemployment, the government has taken measures to promote the modernization of plants and the creation of new industries. Organizations have been established to provide financial aid and advice, marketing and scientific research, studies on methods of increasing productivity, and nuclear research for economic utilization. Government policy aims at helping industry to hold costs down and to engage in greater production of finished (rather than semifinished) goods. Results have been mixed, with greater success in chemicals and light manufacturing than in the critical iron and steel industry.

To promote industrial expansion, the government encourages the private sector through incentives. There are two concurrent incentive schemes in operation. The first scheme, in effect since 1959, offers incentives to firms that invest in specified development areas or promote vital industrial activities. The second program, launched in 1966, provides exceptional assistance to companies setting up or expanding plants (or creating research and development centers or trading ventures in connection with manufacturing investments) in declining mining areas or regions suffering from acute economic difficulties. Under both schemes the most important methods of assistance are interest-rate rebates on loans to finance capital investment and outright grants extended to finance new projects (interest rebates and grants are larger if the new investment is in one of the more depressed areas). A 1970 law consolidated Belgium's existing incentives legislation and added new capital and fiscal incentives for research-oriented companies. In 1993, the government modified its policy of forbidding more than 49% private ownership in government banks, insurance companies, and the national telecommunications company.

A 1993–96 plan calls for raising employment by reducing the burden of high social security contributions, encouraging work-share arrangements, and freezing real wages and salaries in 1995–96 to make Belgian goods more competitive. Indirect taxes were raised in 1994 to offset the loss in revenue from social security.

Official development assistance extended to other countries by Belgium amounted to 0.42% of the GNP, or about $824 million, in 1991. The chief recipients are Belgium's former African colonies of Zaire, Rwanda, and Burundi.

[40]SOCIAL DEVELOPMENT

Belgium has a highly developed social security system dating back to mutual benefit societies begun in 1894. The central coordinating organ for welfare is the National Social Security Office. It collects all workers' and employers' contributions for old age pensions and life insurance, as well as management's payments for family allowances, paid vacations, and other benefits. It is not a policymaking and disbursing organization, but rather serves as a bookkeeping center, clearinghouse, and supervising organ, turning over the funds it collects to specific social welfare agencies. It is administered by a board made up of representatives of the leading employers' organizations and labor union federations, and has an impartial chairman.

The fertility rate was 1.6 in 1985–90. Abortion is legal only in cases of medical necessity. Some 81% of married Belgian women surveyed between 1980 and 1993, were using contraception. The government actively promotes women's rights and provided for a National Women's Center in its 1994 budget. In 1992, a royal decree was issued barring sexual harassment in both the public and private sectors.

[41]HEALTH

Every city or town in Belgium has a public assistance committee (elected by the city or town council), which is in charge of health and hospital services in its community. These committees organize clinics and visiting nurse services, run public hospitals, and pay for relief patients in private hospitals. There is a national health insurance plan, membership of which covers practically the whole population. A number of private hospitals are run by local communities or mutual aid societies attached to religious organizations. A school health program includes annual medical examinations for all school children. Private and public mental institutions include observation centers, asylums, and colonies where mental patients live in groups and enjoy a limited amount of liberty.

A number of health organizations, begun by private initiative and run under their own charters, now enjoy semiofficial status and receive government subsidies. Among them are the Belgian Red Cross, the National Tuberculosis Society, the League for Mental Hygiene, and the National Children's Fund. The last of these, working through its own facilities and through cooperating agencies, provides prenatal and postnatal consultation clinics for mothers, a visiting nurse service, and other health services. Belgium's total health care expenditures for 1990 were $14,428 million.

From 1988 to 1992, Belgium had 3.21 doctors per 1,000 people (in 1990, 34,300 physicians); in 1989, there were 12,014 pharmacists and 6,592 dentists. From 1985 to 1990, there were approximately 9 hospital beds per 1,000 people. In 1988, there were nearly 400 hospitals (just over half of these classed as acute hospitals), with a total bed capacity of nearly 10,000.

In 1992, Belgium had 122,000 births. Between 1990 and 1992, the country immunized 1 year-old children as follows: diphtheria, pertussis, and tetanus (87%); polio (99%); and measles (75%). The incidence of tuberculosis was 16 in 100,000 in 1990 and, in that same year, 95% of the population had access to safe drinking water. The infant mortality rate in 1992 was 9 per 1,000 live births, and the overall death rate was 11 per 1,000 people in 1993. Between 1985 and 1990, mortality was categorized as follows: (1) communicable diseases, maternal/perinatal causes—52 per 100,000 people; (2) noncommunicable diseases— 459 per 100,000; and (3) injuries—68 per 100,000. Average life expectancy in 1992 was 76 years (80 years for females and 73 years for males).

[42]HOUSING

Belgium no longer has a housing shortage. In the mid-1970s, an average of over 60,000 new dwellings were built every year; by the early 1980s, however, the government sought by reducing the value-added tax on residential construction to revitalize the depressed housing market. Public funds have been made available in increasing amounts to support the construction of low-cost housing, with low-interest mortgages granted by the General Savings and Retirement Fund. As of 1981, 67% of all housing units were one-family houses and 24% were apartments. Owners occupied 60% of all dwellings and 35% were rented. Housing starts totaled 46,645 in 1992, up from 44,484 in 1991. The total number of dwellings in 1991 was 4,198,000.

[43]EDUCATION

Adult illiteracy is virtually nonexistent. Education is free and compulsory for children between the ages of 6 and 16; education in secondary schools is also free. The teaching language is that of the region, i.e., French, Dutch, or German.

Belgium has two complete school systems operating side by side. One is organized by the state or by local authorities and is known as the official school system. The other, the private school system, is largely Roman Catholic. Somewhat more than half the school population is in private schools. For a long time, the rivalry between the two systems and the question of subsidies to private schools were the main issues in Belgian politics. The controversy was settled in 1958, and both systems are presently financed with government funds along more or less identical lines. Since 1971, new constitutional guidelines have strengthened the autonomy of Wallonia and Flanders in educational administration and policymaking.

In 1991, Belgium had 4,158 primary schools with 72,589 teachers and 711,521 students. Secondary level schools had 765,672 students and 110,599 teachers the same year. Of the total, 374,335 students were in vocational programs. Higher education centers on the eight main universities: the state universities of Ghent, Liège, Antwerp, and Mons; the two branches of the Free University of Brussels, which in 1970 became separate private institutions, one Dutch (Vrije Universiteit Brussel) and the other French (Université Libre de Bruxelles); the Catholic University of Brussels; and the Catholic University of Louvain, which also split in 1970 into the Katholicke Universiteit Leuven (Dutch) and the Université Catholique de Louvain (French). The higher level institutions had 271,007 students in 1989.

Government expenditure for education rose rapidly after the school agreement of 1958, and accounted for about 15.1% of the government's budget in 1989.

[44]LIBRARIES AND MUSEUMS

There are large libraries, general and specialized, in the principal cities. Brussels has the kingdom's main reference collections, the Royal Library (founded in 1837), with about 3 million volumes, as well as the Library of Parliament (4 million volumes), the Library of the Royal Institute of Natural Sciences (710,000 volumes), and the General Archives of the Kingdom, founded in 1794, with 350,000 documents from the 11th to the 20th centuries. Antwerp is the seat of the Archives and the Museum of Flemish Culture, which has an open library of 55,000 volumes. The university libraries of Louvain (3.3 million volumes), Ghent (3 million volumes), and Liège (2 million volumes) date back to 1425, 1797, and 1817, respectively. The library of the Free University of Brussels (1846) has 1.5 million volumes. Also in Brussels is the library of Commission of the European Communities. In addition, there are several hundred private, special, and business libraries, especially in Antwerp and Brussels, and more than 2,500 public libraries throughout the country.

Belgium's 200 or more museums, many of them with art and historical treasures dating back to the Middle Ages and earlier, are found in cities and towns throughout the country. Among Antwerp's outstanding institutions are the Royal Museum of Fine

Arts, which includes works of old masters and moderns; the Open-Air Museum of Sculpture in Middelheim Park, displaying works by Rodin, Maillol, Marini, Moore, and others; and the Rubens House, containing 17th-century furnishings and paintings by Peter Paul Rubens. Brussels' museums include the Royal Museum of Fine Arts (founded 1795), which has medieval, Renaissance, and modern collections; the Royal Museum of Central Africa (1897), which has rich collections of African arts and crafts, natural history, ethnography, and prehistory; and the Royal Museum of Art and History (1835), with its special collections of Chinese porcelain and furniture, Flemish tapestries, and of 18th- and 19th-century applied and decorative art. Museums in Bruges, Liège, Ghent, Malines, and Verviers have important general or local collections.

45MEDIA

International and domestic telegraph and telephone service, operated by a government agency, is well developed. Postal service is frequent and reliable. There were 5,138,282 telephones in 1991.

National radio and television service is organized into Dutch and French branches. Commercial broadcasting is permitted, hence costs are defrayed through annual license fees on radio and television receivers. There are two national medium-wave stations, one broadcasting in French, the other in Dutch. In addition, there are five Dutch-language and three French-language regional stations. Three short-wave transmitters are used for overseas broadcasts. Belgium has four national television stations, two in each language. Cable television subscribers can receive up to 13 additional stations, from the UK and Belgium's continental neighbors. In 1991 there were 4,500,000 television sets and 7,675,000 radio sets in use.

The Belgian press has full freedom of expression as guaranteed by the constitution of 1831. Newspapers are published in French and Dutch, and generally reflect the views of one of the major parties. Agence Belga is the official news agency. In 1991 there were 23 daily newspapers. There were also several newspapers dealing with economic and financial matters. The total circulation of Belgian dailies in 1991 was estimated at 2.2 million copies. Principal Belgian dailies with their 1991 circulations were as follows:

	LANGUAGE	ORIENTATION	CIRCULATION
BRUSSELS			
De Standaard			
(and affiliated papers)	Dutch	Flemish-Catholic	377,900
Het Laatste Nieuws	Dutch	Independent	301,300
Le Soir	French	Independent	213,000
La Lanterne	French	Socialist	133,000
La Libre Belgique	French	Catholic-Independent	80,800
ANTWERP			
De Gazet van Antwerpen	Dutch	Christian Democrat	189,900
CHARLEROI			
La Nouvelle Gazette	French	Liberal	83,900
GHENT			
Het Volk	Dutch	Catholic-Labor	192,500
Nieuwe Gids			

About 500 weeklies appear in Belgium, most of them in French or Dutch and a few in German or English. Their overall weekly circulation is estimated to exceed 6.5 million copies.

46ORGANIZATIONS

Among Belgium's numerous learned societies are the French and Dutch organizations each bearing the names of the Royal Academy of Sciences, Letters, and Fine Arts and the Royal Academy of Medicine; in addition, there are the Royal Academy of French

Language and Literature and the Royal Academy of Dutch Language and Literature.

Business and industry are organized in the Belgium Business Federation (1885), the Chambers of Commerce, and the American Chamber of Commerce in Brussels, as well as on the basis of industrial sectors and in local bodies. Among the latter, the Flemish and Walloon economic councils and the nine provincial economic councils are the most important.

Architects, painters, and sculptors are organized in the Association of Professional Artists of Belgium. Among the other occupational groups are the Belgian Medical Federation, the Association of Women Chief Executives, and the Belgian Students' Federation. There is a cultural council for each of the three official languages. The many sports societies include the Royal Belgian Athletic League and soccer, cycling, archery, homing pigeon, tennis, hunting, boating, camping, and riding clubs. Veterans' and disabled veterans' associations, the Red Cross, Boy Scouts, Girl Scouts, voluntary associations to combat the major diseases, and philanthropic societies are all active in Belgium.

47TOURISM, TRAVEL, AND RECREATION

Belgium has three major tourist regions: the seacoast, the old Flemish cities, and the Ardennes Forest in the southeast. Ostend is the largest North Sea resort; others are Blankenberge and Knokke. Among Flemish cities, Bruges, Gent, and Ypres stand out, while Antwerp also has many sightseeing attractions, including the busy port, exhibitions of the diamond industry, and the Antwerp Zoo, an oasis of green in the city center. The European Community designated Antwerp Cultural Capital of Europe for 1993, with festivities that ran from March to the end of the year. Brussels, home of the European Community headquarters, is a modern city whose most famous landmark is the Grand'Place. The capital is the site of the Palais des Beaux-Arts, with its varied concert and dance programs, and of the Théâtre Royal de la Monnaie, home of the internationally famous Ballet of the 20th Century. St. Michael's Cathedral and Notre Dame du Sablon are the city's best-known churches. The Erasmus House in the suburb of Anderlecht and the Royal Palace and Gardens at nearby Laeken are popular tourist centers. Louvain possesses an architecturally splendid city hall and a renowned university. Malines, seat of the Belgian primate, has a handsome cathedral. Liège, in the eastern industrial heartland, boasts one of the finest Renaissance buildings, the palace of its prince-bishops. Tournai is famous for its Romanesque cathedral. Spa, in the Ardennes, is one of Europe's oldest resorts and gave its name to mineral spring resorts in general. Namur, Dinant, and Huy have impressive fortresses overlooking one of the most important strategic crossroads in Western Europe, the Meuse Valley.

Receipts from tourism amounted to $3.4 million in 1991, when Belgium had 91,696 hotel beds with a 22% occupancy rate. Tourists that year spent an estimated 12,170,000 nights in Belgian accommodations. The $450-million expansion of Brussels national airport was completed in 1993.

For temporary visits, not exceeding three consecutive months each season, travelers should be in possession of a valid passport. No visa is required for citizens of the US, Canada, Australia, New Zealand, Japan, or most countries of Western Europe or Latin America.

48FAMOUS BELGIANS

Belgium has produced many famous figures in the arts. In the 15th century, one of the great periods of European painting culminated in the work of Jan van Eyck (1390?–1441) and Hans Memling (1430?–94). They were followed by Hugo van der Goes (1440?–82), and Pieter Brueghel the Elder (1525?–69), the ancestor of a long line of painters. Generally considered the greatest of Flemish painters are Peter Paul Rubens (1577–1640) and

Anthony Van Dyck (1599–1641). In the 19th century, Henri Evenepoel (1872–99) continued this tradition. The 20th century boasts such names as James Ensor (1860–1949), Paul Delvaux (b.1897), and René Magritte (1898–1967). Modern Belgian architecture was represented by Victor Horta (1861–1947) and Henry van de Velde (1863–1957).

Belgium made substantial contributions to the development of music through the works of such outstanding 15th- and 16th-century composers as Johannes Ockeghem (1430?–95), Josquin des Prés (1450?–1521), Heinrich Isaac (1450?–1517), Adrian Willaert (1480?–1562), Nicolas Gombert (1490?–1556), Cipriano de Rore (1516–65), Philippe de Monte (1521–1603), and Roland de Lassus (known originally as Roland de Latre and later called Orlando di Lasso, 1532–94), the "Prince of Music." Later Belgian composers of renown include François-Joseph Gossec (1734–1829), Peter Van Maldere (1729–68), André Ernest Modeste Grétry (1741–1813), César Franck (1822–90), and Joseph Jongen (1873–1953). Among famous interpreters are the violinists Eugène Ysaye (1858–1931) and Arthur Grumiaux (1921–86). André Cluytens (1905–67) was the conductor of the National Orchestra of Belgium. Maurice Béjart (Maurice Berger, b.1927), an internationally famous choreographer, has been director of the Ballet of the 20th Century since 1959.

Outstanding Belgian names in French historical literature are Jean Froissart (1333?–1405?) and Philippe de Commynes (1447?–1511?), whereas early Dutch literature boasts the mystical writing of Jan van Ruysbroeck (1293–1381). The 19th century was marked by such important writers as Charles de Coster (1827–79), Camille Lemonnier (1844–1913), Georges Eeckhoud (1854–1927), and Emile Verhaeren (1855–1916) in French; and by Hendrik Conscience (1812–83) and Guido Gezelle (1830–99) in Flemish. Among contemporary authors writing in French, Michel de Ghelderode (1898–1962), Suzanne Lilar (b.1901), Georges Simenon (b.1903-1989), and Françoise Mallet-Joris (b.1930) have been translated into English. Translations of Belgian authors writing in Dutch include works by Johan Daisne (b.1912) and Hugo Claus (b.1929).

Eight Belgians have won the Nobel Prize in various fields. The poet and playwright Maurice Maeterlinck (1862–1949), whose symbolist dramas have been performed in many countries, received the prize for literature in 1911. Jules Bordet (1870–1961) received the physiology or medicine award in 1919 for his contributions to immunology. The same award went to Corneille J. F. Heymans (1892–1968) in 1938 and was shared by Albert Claude (1898–1983) and Christian de Duve (b.1917) in 1974. Russian-born Ilya Prigogine (b.1917) won the chemistry prize in 1977. Three Belgians have won the Nobel Peace Prize: Auguste Beernaert (1829–1912) in 1909, Henri Lafontaine (1854–1943) in 1913, and Father Dominique Pire (1910–69) in 1958.

Belgium's chief of state since 1951 had been King Baudouin I (1930–93), the son of Leopold III (1901–83), who reigned from 1934 until his abdication in 1951.

49DEPENDENCIES
Belgium has no territories or colonies.

50BIBLIOGRAPHY

American University. *Area Handbook for Belgium.* 2d ed. Washington, D.C.: Government Printing Office, 1984.

Baudhuin, Fernand. *Belgique 1900–1960.* Louvain: Institut de Recherches Économiques et Sociales, 1961.

Bond, Brian. *Britain, France, and Belgium, 1939–1940,* 2nd ed. London and Washington, D.C.: Brassey's, 1990.

Cowie, Donald. *Belgium: The Land and the People.* Cranbury, N.J.: A.S. Barnes, 1977.

De Banat, Jean-Pierre. *Business Guide to Belgium.* Chicago:

Commerce Clearing House, 1978.

De Meeüs, Adrien. *History of the Belgians.* New York: Praeger, 1961.

Dumont, Georges H. *Histoire des Belges.* Brussels: Dessart, 1954–56.

Dutt, Ashok K. and Frank J. Costa (eds.) *Perspectives on Planning and Urban Development in Belgium.* Boston: Kluwer Academic Publishers, 1992.

Fitzmaurice, John. *The Politics of Belgium: Crisis and Compromise in a Plural Society.* New York: St. Martin's, 1983.

Gamblin, André. *Géographie Économique et Humaine de la Belgique.* Paris: Centre de documentation universitaire, 1960.

Gerson, Horst, and Engelbert H. ter Kuile. *Art and Architecture in Belgium, 1600–1800.* Baltimore: Penguin Books, 1960.

Geyl, Pieter. *Holland and Belgium: Their Common History and Their Relations.* Leiden: Sijthoff, 1920.

Gutman, Myron P. *War and Rural Life in the Early Modern Low Countries.* Princeton, N.J.: Princeton University Press, 1980.

Helmreich, Jonathan E. *Belgium and Europe: A Study in Small Power Diplomacy.* Hawthorne, N.Y.: Mouton, 1976.

Herremans, Maurice-Pierre. *La Question Flamande.* Brussels: Librarie Meurice, 1948.

———. *La Wallonie, ses Griefs, ses Aspirations.* Brussels: Éditions Marie-Julienne, 1952.

Hooghe, Liesbet. *A Leap in the Dark: Nationalist Conflict and Federal Reform in Belgium.* Ithaca, N.Y.: Cornell University Press, 1991.

Huggett, Frank E. *Modern Belgium.* New York: Praeger, 1969.

Krewson, Margrit B. (Margrit Beran). *The Netherlands and Northern Belgium, a Selective Bibliography of Reference Works,* Rev. ed. Washington, D.C.: Government Printing Office, 1989.

Lanier, Alison R. *Update—Belgium.* Chicago: Intercultural Press, 1980.

Lijphart, Arend (ed.). *Conflict and Coexistence in Belgium: The Dynamics of a Culturally Divided Society.* Berkeley: University of California, Institute of International Studies, 1981.

Loder, Dorothy. *Land and People of Belgium.* Rev. ed. Philadelphia: Lippincott, 1977.

Luykx, Theo. *Politieke geschiedenis van België van 1789 tot heden.* Brussels: Elsevier, 1964.

Murphy, Alexander B. *The Regional Dynamics of Language Differentiation in Belgium: A Study in Cultural-political Geography.* Chicago: University of Chicago, Committee on Geographical Studies, 1988.

OECD. *Belgium-Luxembourg.* OECD Economic Surveys. Paris (annual).

Picard, Leo. *Geschiedenis van de Vlaamsche en Groot-Nederlandsche Beweging.* 2 vols. Antwerp: De Sikkel, 1942–59.

Pierson, Marc-Antoine. *Histoire du Socialisme en Belgique.* Brussels: Institut Emile Vandervelde, 1953.

Pirenne, Henri. *Belgian Democracy: Its Early History.* London: Longmans, Green, 1915.

———. *Histoire de Belgique.* 7 vols. Brussels: Lamertin, 1902–32.

Riley, R. C., and Gregory Ashworth. *Benelux: An Economic Geography of Belgium, the Netherlands, and Luxembourg.* New York: Holmes & Meier, 1975.

Van Houtte, J. A. *An Economic History of the Low Countries, 800–1800.* New York: St. Martin's, 1977.

Van Kalken, Frans. *La Belgique Contemporaine (1780–1949): Histoire d'une Évolution Politique.* Paris: Colin, 1950.

Wee, Herman van der. *The Low Countries in Early Modern Times.* Brookfield, Vt.: Variorum, 1993.

Wilenski, Reginald H. *Flemish Painters, 1430–1830.* New York: Viking Press, 1960.

BOSNIA AND HERZEGOVINA

Republic of Bosnia and Herzegovina
Republika Bosnia i Herzegovina

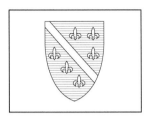

CAPITAL: Sarajevo.

FLAG: White with a large blue shield; the shield contains white Roman crosses with a white diagonal band.

ANTHEM: A new national anthem was being prepared in late fall 1994.

MONETARY UNIT: The dinar was introduced October 1994. No exchange rate was available at the time of publication.

WEIGHTS AND MEASURES: The metric system is the legal standard.

HOLIDAYS: New Year's Day, 1–2 January; Labor Days, 1–2 May; 27 July; 25 November.

TIME: 1 PM = noon GMT.

¹LOCATION, SIZE, AND EXTENT

Bosnia and Herzegovina is located in southeastern Europe on the Balkan Peninsula, between Croatia and Serbia and Montenegro. Comparatively, Bosnia and Herzegovina is slightly larger than the state of Tennessee, with a total area of 51,233 sq km (19,781 sq mi). Bosnia and Herzegovina shares boundaries with Croatia on the N, W, and S, Serbia on the E, and the Adriatic Sea on the S, with a total boundary length of 1,389 km (863 mi). Bosnia and Herzegovina's capital city, Sarajevo, is located near the center of the country.

²TOPOGRAPHY

The topography of Bosnia and Herzegovina features hills, mountains, and valleys. Approximately 50% of the land is forested. The climate in Bosnia and Herzegovina is characterized by hot summers and cold winters. Areas of high elevation have short, cool summers and long, severe winters. Mild rainy winters occur along the coast. Approximately 20% of the land in Bosnia and Herzegovina is arable. Bosnia and Herzegovina's natural resources include coal, iron, bauxite, manganese, timber, wood products, copper, chromium, lead, and zinc. Bosnia and Herzegovina is subject to frequent and destructive earthquakes.

³CLIMATE

The climate features hot summers and cold winters. In higher elevations of the country, summers tend to be short and cold while winters tend to be long and severe. Along the coast, winters tend to be short and rainy. In July, the mean temperature is 22.5°C (72.5°F). January's mean temperature is 0°C (32°F). Annual rainfall averages roughly 62.5 cm (24.6 in).

⁴FLORA AND FAUNA

The region's climate has given Bosnia and Herzegovina a wealth of diverse flora and fauna. Ferns, flowers, mosses, and common trees populate the landscape. Wild animals include deer, brown bears, rabbits, fox, and wild boars.

⁵ENVIRONMENT

Metallurgical plants contribute to air pollution. Water is scarce, as are landfill sites.

⁶POPULATION

The population of Bosnia and Herzegovina was 4,365,639 in 1991 and was estimated to be 4,618,804 in July 1993 by the US government's Central Intelligence Agency. It was projected by the World Bank at 4,400,000 in 2010, based on a crude birthrate of 14 per 1,000 people, a crude death rate of 6, and a net natural increase of 8. The population density in 1991 was 85 per sq km (221 per sq mi). The population was 34% urban in 1991. Sarajevo, the capital, had a population of 415,631, and Banja Luka, 142,644.

⁷MIGRATION

Many people living in Bosnia and Herzegovina fled the war that followed independence. In other countries, their numbers were lumped together with other refugees from "Yugoslavia" or "former Yugoslavia." In 1994, there were over 800,000 refugees outside of Bosnia and Herzegovina. In addition, the US government estimates that as many as 1.2 million persons have been displaced within the country due to the ongoing conflict.

⁸ETHNIC GROUPS

In 1991, 43.7% of the people were Muslims—indigenous South Slavs of the Islamic faith. Serbs comprised 31.4%, and Croats, 17.3%. Some 239,845 (5.5%) declared themselves as Yugoslavs.

⁹LANGUAGES

The native language of all the major ethnic groups is Serbo–Croatian, which belongs to the southern Slavic group.

¹⁰RELIGIONS

Historically, part of the Turkish Empire from the 15th century, the provinces of Bosnia and Herzegovina passed into the control of the Austro-Hungarian Empire in 1878. Following World War II, they were incorporated into the Yugoslavian federation.

Throughout its history, ethnicity and religion have served as flashpoints for conflict and changes in government. Predominantly, Sunni Muslims comprise over 40% of the population, Serbian Orthodox 31%, and Roman Catholics some 19%. A small Baha'i community is present as well.

¹¹TRANSPORTATION

The main railway is a 1-m gauge track which connects the Croatian port at Dubrovnik to Sarajevo and crosses the Sava before returning into Croatia at the northern border. In 1991, there were 21,168 km (13,154 mi) of highways, 54% of which were paved.

¹²HISTORY

Origins

Bosnia and Herzegovina occupies the area between historical Croatia/Slavonia to the north, Dalmatia to the south, and Serbia/Montenegro to the east/south-east. Populated in ancient times by Thracians, Illyrians, Celts, with Greek colonies since 400 BC, the area was taken over by the Romans around 168 BC. However, it took the Romans some one hundred and fifty years to gain control of the entire area, which they called Dalmatia Province. The most difficult aspect of their occupation was getting past the coastal cities to build roads to rich mining sites in the interior, which still maintained its native, Illyrian character in resistance to pressures to Romanize. Eventually, many Romanized Illyrians became important leaders in the Roman armies and administration and some even became emperors. The division of the Roman Empire into the western and eastern halves in AD 395 found Bosnia as the frontier land of the western half, since the dividing line ran south from Sirmium on the Sava river along the Drina River to Skadar Lake by the Adriatic coast.

Slavic tribes have been raiding and settling in the Balkan area in large numbers since the 5th century AD, moving in slowly from their original lands east of the Carpathian Mountains. These early Slavic settlers were joined in the 7th century AD by Croatian and Serbian tribes invited by Byzantine Emperor Heraclius to help him fight the Avars. The area of Bosnia and Herzegovina became the meeting ground of Croats (western area) and Serbs (eastern area). As medieval Bulgarians, Croatians, and Serbians developed their first states, Bosnia became a battleground among them and the Byzantine Empire. Christianization of the area was completed by the ninth century, when most of the Bosnian area came under the influence of Rome and Croats became Catholic, while most Serbs fell under the influence of the Byzantine Empire and became Eastern Orthodox.

The Bosnian area between the 9th and 11th centuries was essentially under Croatian influence when not conquered by Bulgarians, Serbs, or Byzantium. After Hungary and Croatia effected their royal union in AD 1102, Hungary took over Bosnia and the Dalmatian cities in 1136. Bosnia was then ruled by Croatian "Bans" under joint Hungarian-Croatian sovereignty. When the soldiers supplied by Ban Borić (r.1150–1167) to the Hungarian Army were defeated by Byzantium in 1167 at Zemun, Bosnia came under Byzantine rule. Hungary renewed its claim to Bosnia in 1185, during Ban Kulin's reign (1180–1204), which was marked by his independence from Hungary, partly due to the inaccessibility of its mountainous terrain.

Geography itself was an incentive to the local autonomy of Bosnia's individual regions of Podrina, Central Bosnia, Lower Bosnia, and Hum (today's Herzegovina). Each region had its own local hereditary nobility and customs, and was divided into districts ("župas"). The typical Bosnian family of this period had possession of its land without dependence on a feudal relationship to prince or king, as was the case in much of Europe. Bosnia was nominally Catholic under the jurisdiction of the Archbishop of Dubrovnik, who would consecrate a Bishop of Bosnia, usually from local Bosnian priests. These Bosnian Catholics used a Slavic liturgy and a modified cyrillic alphabet called "Bosanča" and had no knowledge of Latin. The region of Hum, on the other hand, was settled by Serbs in the interior, was mixed Orthodox and Catholic in the coastal area and mostly ruled by princes of the Serbian dynasty (Nemanja) until 1326.

The Catholic Church in Bosnia was isolated from the coastal areas and had developed its own Slavic liturgy and practices. These customs were suspect to the Latin hierarchy in both Hungary and the coastal cities. Ignorance of the language and customs of simple people and poor communications generated rumors and accusations of heresy against the Bosnian Church and Ban Kulin, its supposed protector. Kulin called a Church Council in 1203 at Bolino Polje that declared its loyalty to the Pope and renounced errors in its practices. Reports of heresy in Bosnia persisted, possibly fanned by Hungary, and caused visits by Papal legates in the 1220s. By 1225 the Pope was calling on the Hungarians to launch a crusade against the Bosnia heretics. In 1233, the native Bishop of Bosnia was removed and a German Dominican appointed to replace him. In spite of Ban Ninoslav's (1233–1250) renunciation of the "heresy," the Hungarians undertook a crusade in 1235–41, accompanied by Dominicans who were already erecting a cathedral in Vrhbosna (today's Sarajevo) in 1238. The Hungarians used the crusade to take control of most of Bosnia, but had to retreat in 1241 because of the Tartars attack on Hungary. This allowed the Bosnians to regain their independence and in 1248 the Pope sent a neutral team (a Franciscan and a Bishop from the coastal town of Senj) to investigate the situation but no report is extant.

The Hungarians insisted that the Bosnian Church, which they suspected of practicing dualist, Manichaeic beliefs tied to the Bogomils of Bulgaria and the French Cathars, be subjected to the Archbishop of Kalocsa in Hungary, who it was thought would intervene to end these heretical practices. In 1252, the Pope obliged. However, no Bishop was sent to Bosnia itself—only to Djakovo in Slavonia—so this act had no impact on the Bosnian Church. The crusades against the Bosnian Church caused a deep animosity towards the Hungarians that in the long run weakened Bosnian's determination to resist the invasion of the Islamic Turks. Thus the Bosnian Church that professed to be loyal to Catholicism, even though it continued in its practice of ascetic and rather primitive rituals by its Catholic monastic order, was pushed into separation from Rome.

Around 1288, Stjepan Kotroman became Ban of the Northern Bosnia area. In his quest to consolidate all of Bosnia under his rule, though, he was challenged by the Šubić family of Croatia, who had taken over Western Bosnia. Paul I Šubić then expanded his family's area of control, becoming Ban of Bosnia and later, in 1305, Ban of All Bosnia. However, the power of the Šubić family declined in subsequent years, and Kotroman's son Stjepan Kotromanić was able to take control of Central Bosnia by 1318, serving as a vassal of the Croatian Ban of Bosnia, Mladen Šubić. Kotromanić then allied himself with Charles Robert, King of Hungary, to defeat Mladen Šubić, helping Kotromanić to consolidate his control over Bosnia, the Neretva River Delta, and over Hum, which he took in 1326 but lost in 1350 to Dušan the Great of Serbia. In recognition of the role the Hungarians had played in his consolidation of power in Bosnia, Ban Kotromanić gave his daughter Elizabeth into marriage to King Louis of Hungary in 1353, the year of his death.

Raised in the Orthodox faith, Kotromanić was converted to Catholicism by Franciscan fathers, an order he had allowed into Bosnia in 1342. The Franciscans concentrated their efforts at conversion on the members of the Bosnian Church (or "Bogomili") and, by 1385, had built some 35 monasteries, four in Bosnia itself. Since most Franciscans were Italian and did not know the Slavic language, their effectiveness was not as great as it could have been and it was concentrated in the towns where numerous non-Bosnians had settled to ply their trades. During

LOCATION: 44°17′N; 17°30′E. **BOUNDARY LENGTHS:** Total boundary lengths, 1,389 km (863 mi); Croatia (northern), 751 km (467 mi); Croatia (south), 91 km (57 mi); Serbia, 312 km (194 mi); Montenegro, 215 km (134 mi).

this period silver and other mines were opened which were administered by the townspeople of Dubrovnik. This influx of commerce helped in the development of prosperous towns in key locations and customs duties from increased trade enriched Bosnian nobles. A whole new class of native craftsmen developed in towns where foreign colonies also prospered and interacted with the native population, thus raising Bosnia's overall cultural level.

Kotromanić's heir was his nephew Tvrtko (r.1353–1391) who would become the greatest ruler of Bosnia. Tvrtko could not command the loyalty of the nobles at first, however, and he soon lost the western part of Hum (1357) to Hungary as the dowry promised to King Louis of Hungary when he married Elizabeth, Kotromanić's daughter. But by 1363, Tvrtko had grown powerful enough to repel Hungarian attacks into Northern Bosnia. In 1366 Tvrtko fled to the Hungarian Court, having been unable to repress a revolt by his own nobles, and with Hungarian help regained his lands in 1367. In 1373 he obtained the upper Drina and Lim Rivers region. In 1377 he was crowned King of Bosnia and Serbia (his grandmother was a Nemanja) at the Mileševo monastery where Saint Sava, the founder of the Serbian Orthodox Church, was buried. Between 1378 and 1385, Tvrtko also gained control of the coastal territory of Trebinje and Konavli near Dubrovnik, along with the port city of Kotor. In 1389, Tvrtko sent his troops to support the Serbian armies of Prince Lazar and Vuk Branković at the legendary Battle of Kosovo Polje. The battle itself was a draw but it exhausted the Serbs' capability to resist the further Turkish invasions. The Turks retreated, having suffered the death of Sultan Murad I, assassinated by a Serbian military leader, and Tvrtko's commander at Kosovo claimed victory. Having sent such a message to Italy, Tvrtko was hailed as a savior of Christendom. He had made a first step towards a possible unification of Bosnia and Serbian lands, but the Turks, and then his own death in 1391, made it impossible.

Bosnia did not disintegrate after Tvrtko's death, but was held together through a Council of the key nobles. The Council elected weak kings to maintain their own power and privileges. Tvrtko had no legitimate descendants so his cousin Dabiša (r.1391–1395) was elected, followed by his widow Helen of Hum (r.1395–1398), and then Stjepan Ostoja (r.1398–1404), opposed by Tvrtko II (r.1404–1409), probably Tvrtko I's illegitimate son. Between 1404 and 1443, Bosnia witnessed civil wars between factions of the nobles taking opposite sides in the Hungarian wars of succession. Thus Stjepan Ostoja was returned to the throne from 1409 to 1418, followed by Stjepan Ostojić (r.1418–1421), then Tvrtko II again (r.1421–1443). During this period the Turks participated in Bosnian affairs as paid mercenaries, through their own raids, and by taking sides in the struggles for the Bosnian throne. The Turks supported Tvrtko II, who managed to rule for over twenty years by recognizing the sovereignty of both the Hungarians and Turks, and playing one against the other. After the Turks' conquest of Serbia in 1439 made them direct neighbors of Bosnia along the Drina River, Turkish raids into Bosnia increased. The Ottomans assumed a key role in internal Bosnian affairs and became the mediator for Bosnian nobles' quarrels. The Bosnian nobles and their Council clung to their opposition to a centralized royal authority, even though it could have mounted a stronger defense against Hungarians and Turks. Thus Bosnia grew ever weaker with the skillful maneuvering of the Turks. Twenty years after Tvrtko II's death, in 1443, the Turks conquered an exhausted Bosnia with a surprise campaign.

Herzegovina (named after the ruler of Hum, Stefan Vukčić who called himself Herzeg/Duke) was occupied by the Turks gradually by 1482, and the two regions were subject to the Ottoman Empire for the next 400 years until the 1878 takeover by Austria.

Under Ottoman Rule

The mass conversion of Bosnian Christians to Islam, a rather unique phenomenon in European history, is explained by two schools of thought. The traditional view recognizes the existence of a strong "Bogomil" heresy of dualism and social protest. These Bosnian Christians, having been persecuted by both Catholic and Orthodox Churches and rulers, welcomed the Ottomans and easily converted in order to preserve their land holdings. In doing so, they became trusted Ottoman soldiers and administrators. The other school of thought denies the existence of a strong and influential "Bogomil" heresy, but defines the Bosnian Christian church as a nativistic, anti-Hungarian, loosely organized religion with a Catholic theological background and simple, peasant-based prac-

tices supported by its monastic order. The rulers/kings of Bosnia were Catholic (with the single exception of Ostoja) and very tolerant of the Orthodox and so-called Bosnian religions. However, these religious organizations had very few priests and monks, and therefore were not very strong. The Bosnian Church was practically eliminated in 1459 through conversions to official Catholicism, or the forced exile of its leadership. Thus, by the time of the Turkish conquest, the Bosnian Church had ceased to exist and the allure of privileged status under the Ottomans was too strong for many to resist.

The Ottomans introduced in Bosnia and Herzegovina their administration, property concepts, and customs. The adherents to Islam were the ruling class, regardless of their national or ethnic backgrounds. Christian peasants practically became serfs to Muslim landlords while in the towns civil and military administrators had control over an increasingly Muslim population. Large numbers of Bosnians fled the Turkish takeover and settled in Venetian-occupied coastal areas where many continued the fight against the Turks as "Uskoki" raiders. Others emigrated north or west into Slavonia and Croatia and were organized as lifetime soldiers along military regions ("Krajina") in exchange for freemen status, land, and other privileges. On the Bosnian side, Christians were not required to enter military service, but the so-called "blood tax" took a heavy toll by turning boys forcibly into Muslim "Janissaries"—professional soldiers converted to Islam who would generally forget their origins and become oppressors of the Sultan's subjects. Girls were sent to harems. Taxation became more and more oppressive, leading to revolts by the Christian peasantry that elicited bloody repressions.

Bosnia and Herzegovina was ruled by a "Pasha" or "Vizier" appointed by the Sultan and assisted by a Chancellor, supreme justice, and treasurer, each heading his own bureaucracy, both central and spread into eight districts ("Sandžaks"). Justice was administered by a "Khadi" who was both prosecutor and judge using the Koran for legal guidance, thus favoring Muslim subjects. Catholics, who were outside the established Orthodox and Jewish communities represented by the Greek Orthodox Patriarch and Chief Rabbi in Constantinople, were particularly exposed to arbitrary persecutions. In spite of all this, communities of followers of the Orthodox (Serbian) Church and Catholic (Croatian) Church survived into the late 19th century when in 1878 Austria obtained the authority to occupy Bosnia and Herzegovina, putting an end to four centuries of Ottoman rule.

Under Austro-Hungarian Rule

Historically both Croats and Serbs have competed for control over Bosnia. The Croats, who had included Bosnia in their medieval kingdom, could not effectively continue their rule once joined with the more powerful Hungarians in their royal union. The Serbs, on the other hand, were assisted by Hungary in their expansion at the expense of the Byzantine Empire. Later, they also received Hungarian support in their resistance to Turkish inroads and therefore could not invest their energies in Bosnia, in their view a "Hungarian" territory. Thus Bosnia was able to assert its own autonomy and individuality, but did not evolve into a separate nation. With the Austrian occupation, however, a new period began marked by a search for a Bosnian identity, supported by Austria who had an interest in countering the national unification ambitions of both Croats and Serbs.

The population of Bosnia and Herzegovina was divided into three major religious-ethnic groups: Croatian Catholics, Serbian Orthodox, and Bosnian Muslims. With the disappearance of the Bosnian Church just before the Ottoman occupation in 1463, most Bosnians were Croatian and Catholic, with a Serbian Orthodox population concentrated in Eastern Herzegovina and along the Drina River frontier with Serbia. The Serbs were mostly peasants, many of whom became serfs to Muslim landlords. Their priests, who were generally poorly educated, lived as peasants among them. Serbian urban dwellers, insignificant in number at first, grew to be an important factor by the late Ottoman period and developed their own churches and schools in the 19th century. Crafts and commerce were the main occupations of the new Serbian middle class.

Croats were also mostly peasants and, like the Serbs, became serfs to Muslim landlords. Members of the Franciscan order lived among the peasants, even though they also had built several monasteries in urban centers. There was almost no Croat middle class at the start of the Austrian period and the Catholic clergy was generally its advocate.

The Muslim group consisted of three social subgroups: the elites, the peasants, and urban lower classes. Most Muslims were peasants, but they were free peasants with a standard of living not better than that of the Christian serf-peasants. The Muslim "Hodžas" (priests) lived among the peasants as peasants themselves. The second subgroup consisted of merchants, craftsmen and artisans and were mostly concentrated in towns. Together with the urban lower classes, these two groups made up the Muslim majorities in most towns by 1878. The members of the Muslim elites were mostly religious functionaries, landowners, and commercial entrepreneurs, all favored by Islamic laws and traditions. Following the 1878 occupation, Austria recognized the right of Turkish functionaries to keep their posts, the right of Muslims to be in communication with their religious leaders in the Ottoman Empire, the right of Turkish currency to circulate in Bosnia, and also promised to respect all traditions and customs of the Bosnian Muslims. The Austrian approach to the administration of Bosnia and Herzegovina was close to the British colonial model that retained the existing elites and cultural individuality while gradually introducing Western administrative and education models.

Bosnia and Herzegovina was divided by the Turks into six administrative regions that were confirmed by Austria: Sarajevo, Travnik, Bihać, Donja Tuzla, Banja Luka, and Mostar (Herzegovina). Each was headed by a regional supervisor. Participation in cultural and religious organizations was encouraged, while engaging in politics was prohibited. The Austrians promoted a policy of equality between Christians and Muslims, banned organizations of an open political purpose, and prohibited the use of national names (Serb and Croat) for public institutions. At the same time, educational institutions designed to promote loyalty to Bosnia (and Austria) as such were encouraged. Censorship and other means were used to insulate Bosnians from the influence of their Croatian and Serbian co-nationals across the borders. By terminating the earlier Muslim secular/religious unity, many administrative and judicial functions were no longer carried out by the Muslim elites, but were instead presided over by the Austrian bureaucracy and judiciary, though a separate Muslim Judiciary was continued. The Muslim landowners lost some privileges but were able to retain their land and the system of serfdom was allowed to continue.

A widespread and important institution supporting Muslim cultural life was the "Vakif" (Vakuf in Serbian/Croatian). The Vakuf was a revenue-producing property set up and administered as a family foundation for the support of specified causes. Once set up, a Vakuf could not be sold, bequeathed, or divided and was exempt from normal taxes. In 1878 it was estimated that one-fourth to one-third of usable land in Bosnia was tied to Vakufs. The administration of Vakufs was lax and open to much manipulation and abuse. The Austrian administration was able to establish effective controls over the Vakuf system by 1894 through a centralized commission and the involvement of prominent Muslims in the administration of Vakuf revenues in support of Islamic institutions.

The continuation of serfdom by the Austrian authorities was a deep disappointment for the peasants that were eagerly expecting emancipation. Abuses led to peasant revolts until the Austrians introduced cash payments of the tithe (one tenth of harvest due to the state) and the appraising of harvest value as basis for payment in kind (one third) to the landlord. A land-registry system was instituted in 1884, and land owners that could not prove legal ownership lost title to some properties. This policy generated wide discontent among Muslim landowners. Another cause of frequent disorders were cases of religious conversions. Under Muslim law, a Muslim convert to another faith was to be executed (this penalty was later eased to banishment). The Austrian policy of confessional equality required a freedom of religious conversion without any penalty and a conversion statute was issued in 1891.

The general aim of the Austrian administration was to guide the development of a co-equal confessional society that would focus its efforts on cultural and economic progress without political and national assertiveness. Benjamin von Kallay, the first Austrian Chief Administrator for Bosnia and Herzegovina wanted to avoid anything that could lead to the creation of a separate Muslim nation in Bosnia. On the other hand, he was determined to insulate Bosnians from external developments in the South Slavic areas. Such a position was unrealistic, however, since all of the main groups—Serbs, Croats, and Muslims—identified themselves with their own national/religious groups in the neighboring areas and had developed intense cultural/political relationships with them. Serbs looked at Serbia's successes and hoped for unification with their motherland. Croats followed closely the Croatian-Hungarian tensions and hoped likewise for their unification. The Muslim community, meanwhile, struggled for its own cultural/religious autonomy within a Bosnia that still recognized the Ottoman Sultan's sovereignty and looked to him for assistance.

The unilateral annexation of Bosnia and Herzegovina to Austria in 1908 exacerbated Austria's relations with Serbia (and almost caused a war) and with the Hungarian half of the Hapsburg Crown that opposed the enlargement of the Slavic population of Austro-Hungary. Serbia's victories in the Balkan wars added fuel to the "Yugoslav" movement among the South Slavs of Austria, including Bosnia and Herzegovina. Here the Austrian administration countered the growing "Yugoslav" assertiveness with a "divide and rule" initiative of developing a separate "Bosnian" national consciousness which they hoped would tie together Serbs, Croats, and Muslims. All nationalist movements use elements of history to develop their own mythology to unite their members. Thus, the medieval Bosnian kingdom was the basis for development of a Bosnian national consciousness. It was opposed by most Serbs and Croats, who awaited unification with Serbia or Croatia, but gave some sense of security to the more isolated Muslim Bosnian community. Already by the beginning of the 20th century, separate ethnic organizations and related political associations had to be allowed. The 1908 annexation led to the promulgation of a constitution, legal recognition of political parties, and a Bosnian Parliament in 1910. The internal political liberalization then allowed the Austrian administration to concentrate on the repression of student radicals, internal and external terrorists, and other such perceived threats to their rule.

The Muslim community was split internally, with a leadership dominated by landowners and weakened by the forced emigration to Turkey of its top leaders. It finally came together in 1906 and formed the Muslim National Organization ("Muslimanska Narodna Organizacija") as its political party, with the blessing of its emigre leaders in Istanbul. Intense negotiations with the Austrian administration produced agreements on religious and cultural autonomy as well as landowners' rights. The latter were a pre-eminent concern, and landowners were able to preserve their ownership rights based on Ottoman law and the peasants' payments of compulsory dues. The religious autonomy of the Muslim faith was assured by having the nominees for the top offices confirmed by the Sultan's religious head upon request by the Austrian Embassy in Istanbul. The same process was also used in matters of religious dogma and law.

Cultural autonomy for Muslims was affirmed through the streamlining of the preexisting "vakuf" system into local, regional, and central assemblies responsible for the operation of the "vakufs" and the related educational system. Overall, the Muslims of Bosnia had achieved their objectives: preserving their large landholdings with peasants still in a quasi-serfdom condition; assuring their cultural autonomy; and retaining access to the Sultan, head of a foreign country, in matters of their religious hierarchies. Politically, the Muslim National Organization participated in the first parliament as part of the majority supportive of the Austrian government.

Serbs and Croats had also formed political organizations, the nature of which reflected Bosnia's peculiar ethnic and socio-political conditions. The Serbian National Organization ("Srpska Narodna Organizacija") was founded in 1907 as a coalition of three factions. The Croatian National Community ("Hrvatska Narodna Zajednica") was formed in 1908 by liberal Croat intellectuals, followed in 1910 by the Croatian Catholic Association ("Hrvatska Katolička Udruga"). A cross-ethnic Social Democratic party, formed in 1909, failed to win any seats in the Parliament. A Muslim Progressive Party, formed in 1908, found hardly any support even after changing its name to the Muslim Independent Party. The Muslims were more conservative and were opposed to the agrarian reform demanded by the Serbs and Croats, who each continued to favor an association or unification with their respective "Mother Country." Croats asserted the Croatian character of Bosnia based on its Croatian past, while Serbs just as adamantly claimed its Serbian character and supported Serbia's "Greater Serbia" policies.

Given the demographics of Bosnia and Herzegovina (1910 census: Serbian Orthodox, 43%; Croat Catholics, 23%; Muslims, 32%) each side needed the support of the Muslims who, though pressured to declare themselves Serbs or Croats, very seldom would do so and would rather keep their own separate identity. Up until the Balkan wars, Muslims and Serbs would support one another hoping for some kind of political autonomy. Croats advocated unification with Croatia and a trialist reorganization of the Hapsburg Monarchy, giving the united South Slavs a coequal status with Austrians and Hungarians. Any cooperation by the Muslims was predicated on support for the continuation of serfdom. This stance prevented cooperation with the Croatian Catholic Association, which insisted on agrarian reform and the termination of serfdom.

With the Serbian victories and Ottoman defeat in the Balkan wars, Serbs became more assertive and Croats more willing to cooperate with them in the growing enthusiasm generated by the idea of "Yugoslavism." A parliamentary majority of Serbs and Croats could have effected the liberation of the peasants in 1913 but the Hungarians opposed it. The assassination of Archduke Ferdinand on 28 June 1914, and World War I, combined to make the issue moot when the Parliament was adjourned. The assassination of the Archduke was apparently the work of members of the "Young Bosnia" students association supported (unofficially) by Serbia through its extremist conspiratorial associations, the "Black Hand" and the "Serbian National Defense." The Austrian ultimatum to Serbia was extremely harsh but Serbia met all the conditions that did not violate its sovereignty. Austria nevertheless declared war and immediately attacked Serbia. The Serbian community of Bosnia and Herzegovina was subjected to a regime of terror and indiscriminate executions by the Austrian authorities. Serbian leaders were subjected to trials, court martial proceedings, and infamous concentrations camps where internees died of epidemics and starvation.

First (Royal) Yugoslavia

Throughout World War I, Bosnians fought in Austrian units, particularly on the Italian front until Austria's surrender. Then the Bosnian National Council decided to unite with the Kingdom of Serbia, as Vojvodina had done and the Montenegrin assembly did on 24 November 1918. On 27 November 1918 the delegation from the Zagreb-based National Council of the Slovenes, Croats, and Serbs also requested unification with Serbia of the Slovene, Croat, and Serbian lands of Austro-Hungary. Following the Declaration of Union on 1 December 1918, a provisional government was set made up of representatives of Serbia and the National Council, with other groups added later. A provisional Assembly was also convened consisting of members of the Serbian Parliament, nominees from the National Council and other regional Assemblies such as Bosnia and Herzegovina and Vojvodina. In November 1920 a Constituent Assembly was elected and functioned as both the legislature and constitutional convention. Bosnian Serbs supported the Serbian Agrarian Party, while two Muslim parties, the National Muslim Organization from Bosnia and Herzegovina and the Džemijet Party of the Kosovo and Macedonia Muslims had seats in the assembly. Croats, on the other hand, joined the mainstream parties of Croatia.

By joining the Kingdom of Serbs, Croats, and Slovenes in 1918, Bosnia and Herzegovina ceased to exist as a distinct political/historical unit, particularly since the heads of local governments were appointed by and directly accountable to the central government in Belgrade. After ten years of a tumultuous parliamentary history culminating in the assassination of Croatian deputies, King Alexander dissolved parliament and disbanded all political parties, establishing a royal dictatorship in 1929. He then reorganized the country into a "Yugoslavia" made up of nine administrative regions ("Banovine") named after rivers. What once was Bosnia and Herzegovina was split among four of the new units (Vrbaska, Drinska, Primorska, and Zetska). Serb and Croat peasants were finally freed from their feudal obligations to Muslim landlords through the agrarian reforms decreed in 1919 and slowly implemented over the next twenty years. Except for Bosnia and Herzegovina and Dalmatia, land held by ex-enemies (Austrians, Hungarians, Turks) were expropriated without compensation and redistributed to the peasants—1.75 million of them plus 2.8 million dependents. As a result, the average size of agricultural holdings fell to 15 acres, causing inefficiencies and very low yields per acre. Peasants were forced to borrow even to buy food and necessities. They fell deeply in debt, both to local shopkeepers who charged 100–200% interest and to banks that charged exorbitant rates up to 50%. In comparison, peasant cooperatives in Slovenia used single digit interest rates.

Politically, the Muslim Organization, as a small party, allied itself mostly with the Slovene People's Party and either the Serbian Democratic or Radical parties in order to participate in a series of governments before the 1929 royal dictatorship was implemented. The Muslim Organization's main goals were to obtain the best possible compensation for land expropriated from Bosnia's Muslim landowners and to preserve the Muslims' cultural identity. In 1932, Muslim leaders joined the Croats, Slovenes, and some Liberal Serbs in issuing the Zagreb manifesto calling for an end to the King's dictatorship and for democratization and regional autonomies. For this the centralist regime interned and imprisoned several of the leaders and instituted wider repressions. Following the assassination of King Alexander in 1934 in Marseilles, France, the Croat Peasants Party was joined by the Muslims, Serbian Agrarians, and Serbian Democrats in opposition to the Centralists, winning 38% of the votes in spite of the Government's intimidating tactics. With the opposition refusing to take part in the Parliament a new government was formed by the Serbian Radicals with the inclusion of the Muslims and the Slovene People's Party.

This new coalition government lasted until 1939, but was never able to resolve the "Croatian" autonomy issue. In addition, while under the leadership of Milan Stojadinović, Yugoslavia's foreign policy moved the country closer to Italy and Germany. Meanwhile a growing consensus had developed that the "Croatian" question had to be solved, particularly in view of the aggressive ambitions of Yugoslavia's neighbors. Thus, the Regent Prince Paul and Dr. Vladimir Maček, leader of the Croatian Peasant Party, worked with the Minister of Social Policy, Dragiša Cvetković, on an agreement establishing a Croatian "Banovina" made up of the historical regions of Croatia-Slavonia and Dalmatia along with parts of Vojvodina, Srem, and Bosnia. The president of the senate, Monsignor Anton Korošec (also leader of the Slovene People's Party), engineered the resignation of five ministers, two Slovenes, two Muslim, and Dragiša Cvetković. Regent Paul then called on Cvetković to form a new government. Dr. Maček became Vice-Premier and Ivan Subašić was named "Ban" of the autonomous Croatian "Banovina," which was given its own "Sabor" (Parliament). The Croatian parties considered this development as a positive first phase towards their goal of an independent Croatia that would incorporate all of Bosnia and Herzegovina. The Serbian centralists, on the other hand, saw this phase as a threat to their own designs of incorporating Bosnia and Herzegovina (and Serb populated areas of Croatia) into a "Greater Serbia" unit of Yugoslavia. Thus, on the eve of World War II, the stage was set for a direct confrontation between the independent minded Croatians and centralistic Serbs. The Muslims of Bosnia were caught in their crossfire.

World War II

Germany, Italy, and their allies Hungary, Romania, and Bulgaria, attacked Yugoslavia on 6 April 1941 and divided the country among themselves. The Croatian terrorist Ustaša organization collaborated with the aggressors and was allowed to proclaim an Independent State of Croatia on 10 April 1941. This new state incorporated the old Croatian "Banovina" in addition to all of Bosnia and Herzegovina. Of its total population of 6.3 million, one third were Serbian and 750,000 were Muslim. Once entrenched in power, the Ustaša troops began implementing their plan for "cleansing" their Greater Croatia of the Serbian population by the use of terror, mass deportations, and genocidal massacres later condemned by the Nürnberg Court.

The Serbian population responded in kind with its Cetnik formations and by joining the Partisan resistance movement led by Josip Broz-Tito, head of the Yugoslav Communist Party. Bosnia and Herzegovina suffered terrible losses in several German-led offensives against Bosnian resistance, and in the internecine civil war among Communist dominated Partisans, nationalist Cetniks (mostly Serbs) and Croatian Ustaše and homeguard units. The Muslim population in particular was caught in the middle between the Ustaše and the Serbian Cetniks. The Ustaše considered the Muslims of Croatian origin and expected them to collaborate with the Ustaša regime. The Serbian Cetniks, on the other hand, viewed most Muslims as the hated Turks and Ustaša col-

laborators, and therefore engaged in slaughters of Muslims, particularly in Eastern Bosnia around the cities of Foča and Goražde.

The political programs of the Cetniks and Partisans were a reflection of the old centralist (Serbian) hegemony and the Federalist positions of the pre-war opposition parties. Thus the Partisan resistance, though aiming at a revolutionary power grab, offered a federated Yugoslavia made up of individual republics for each national group—Serbs, Croats, Slovenes, newly recognized Macedonians and Montenegrins. To avoid a battle over a Serbian-Croatian border issue, Bosnia and Herzegovina was resurrected as a buffer area between Serbia and Croatia. It would also allow (again) for the cultural autonomy of the Muslim population. The Allied and Soviet support the Partisans received enabled them to prevail, and they organized Socialist Yugoslavia as a Federative People's Republic with Bosnia and Herzegovina as one of the constituent republics approximately within the boundaries of the former Austrian province.

When Soviet armies entered Yugoslavia from Romania and Bulgaria in the fall of 1944—Marshal Tito with them—military units and civilians that had opposed the partisans had no choice but retreat to Austria or Italy to save themselves. Among them were the "Cetnik" units of Draža Mihajlović, and "Homeguards" from Serbia, Croatia, and Slovenia that had been under German control but were pro-Allies in their convictions and hopes. Also in retreat were the units of the Croatian "Ustaša" that had collaborated with Italy and Germany in order to achieve (and control) an "independent" greater Croatia, and in the process had committed terrible and large scale massacres of Serbs, Jews, Gypsies, and others who opposed them. Of course, Serbs and Partisans counteracted and a fratricidal civil war raged over Yugoslavia, pitting Croats against Serbs, Communists against Nationalists. These skirmishes not only wasted countless lives, they used up the energy and property that could have been used instead against the occupiers. After the end of the war, the Communist led forces took control of all of Yugoslavia and instituted a violent dictatorship that committed systematic crimes and human rights violations on an unexpectedly large scale. Thousands upon thousands of their former opponents were returned from Austria by British military authorities only to be tortured and massacred by Partisan executioners.

Second (Communist) Yugoslavia

Such was the background for the formation of the second Yugoslavia as a Federative People's Republic of five nations—Slovenes, Croats, Serbs, Macedonians, and Montenegrins—and Bosnia and Herzegovina as a buffer area with its mix of Serb, Muslim, and Croat populations. The problem of large Hungarian and Muslim Albanian populations in Serbia was solved by creating the autonomous region of Vojvodina (Hungarian minority) and Kosovo (Muslim Albanian majority) to assure their political and cultural development. Tito attempted a balancing act to satisfy most of the nationality issues that were carried over unresolved from the first Yugoslavia, but failed to satisfy anyone.

Compared to pre-1941 Yugoslavia where Serbs enjoyed their controlling role, the numerically stronger Serbs in the new Yugoslavia had "lost" the Macedonian area they considered "Southern Serbia"; they had lost the opportunity to incorporate Montenegro into Serbia; they had lost direct control over the Hungarian minority in Vojvodina and Muslim Albanians of Kosovo (viewed as the cradle of the Serbian nation since the Middle Ages); they could not longer incorporate into Serbia the large Serbian populated areas of Bosnia; and they had not obtained an autonomous region for the large minority Serbian population within the Croatian Republic. The Croats, while gaining back from Hungary the Medjumurje area and from Italy the cities of Rijeka

(Fiume), Zadar (Zara), some Dalmatian islands, and the Istrian Peninsula, had "lost" the Srem area to Serbia and Bosnia and Herzegovina, which had been part of the World War II "independent" Croatian state under the Ustaša leadership. In addition, the Croats were confronted with a deeply resentful Serbian minority that became ever more pervasive in public administrative and security positions. The Slovenes had obtained back from Hungary the Prekmurje enclave and from Italy most of the Slovenian lands taken over by Italy following World War I (Julian Region and Northern Istria). Italy retained control over the "Venetian Slovenia" area, the Gorizia area, and the port city of Trieste. (Trieste was initially part of the UN protected "Free Territory of Trieste," split in 1954 between Italy and Yugoslavia, with Trieste itself given to Italy.) Nor were the Slovenian claims to the southern Carinthia area of Austria satisfied. The "loss" of Trieste was a bitter pill for the Slovenes and many blamed it on the fact that Tito's Yugoslavia was, initially, Stalin's advance threat to Western Europe, thus making Western Europe and the United States more supportive of Italy.

The official position of the Marxist Yugoslav regime was that national rivalries and conflicting interests would gradually diminish through their sublimation into a new Socialist order. Without capitalism, nationalism was supposed to wither away. Therefore, in the name of their "unity and brotherhood" motto, any "nationalistic" expression of concern was prohibited and repressed by the dictatorial and centralized regime of the "League of Yugoslav Communists" acting through the "Socialist Alliance" as its mass front organization. As a constituent Republic of the Federal Yugoslavia, Bosnia and Herzegovina shared in the history of the second experiment in "Yugoslavism."

After a short post-war "coalition" government period, the elections of 11 November 1945, boycotted by the non-communist "coalition" parties, gave the Communist-led People's Front 90% of the vote. A Constituent Assembly met on November 29 and abolished the monarchy, establishing the Federative People's Republic of Yugoslavia. In January 1946, a new constitution was adopted, based on the 1936 Soviet constitution. The Stalin-engineered expulsion of Yugoslavia from the Soviet-dominated Cominform Group in 1948 was actually a blessing for Yugoslavia after its leadership was able to survive Stalin's pressures. Survival had to be justified, both practically and in theory, by developing a "road to Socialism" based on Yugoslavia's own circumstances. This new "road map" evolved rather quickly in response to some of Stalin's accusations and Yugoslavia's need to perform a balancing act between the NATO alliance and the Soviet bloc. Having taken over all power after World War II, the Communist dictatorship under Tito pushed the nationalization of the economy through a policy of forced industrialization, to be supported by the collectivization of agriculture.

The agricultural reform of 1945–46 (limited private ownership of a maximum of 35 hectares [85 acres] and a limited free market after the initial forced delivery of quotas to the state at very low prices) had to be abandoned because of the strong passive, but at times active, resistance by the peasants. The actual collectivization efforts were initiated in 1949 using welfare benefits and lower taxes as incentives along with direct coercion. But collectivization had to be abandoned by 1958 simply because its inefficiency and low productivity could not support the concentrated effort of industrial development.

By the 1950s, Yugoslavia had initiated the development of its internal trademark: self-management of enterprises through workers councils and local decision-making as the road to Marx's "withering away of the state." Following the failure of the first five-year plan (1947–51), the second five-year plan (1957–61) was completed in four years by relying on the well-established self-management system. Economic targets were set from the local to the republic level and then coordinated by a Federal Planning Institute to meet an overall national economic strategy. This system supported a period of very rapid industrial growth in the 1950s. But a high consumption rate encouraged a volume of imports, largely financed by foreign loans, far in excess of exports,. In addition, inefficient and low-productivity industries were kept in place through public subsidies, cheap credit, and other artificial protective measures that led to a serious crisis by 1961.

Reforms were necessary and, by 1965, "market socialism" was introduced with laws that abolished most price controls and halved import duties while withdrawing export subsidies. After necessary amounts were left with the earning enterprise, the rest of the earned foreign currencies were deposited with the national bank and used by the state, other enterprises, or were used to assist less developed areas. Councils were given more decision-making power on investing their earnings. They also tended to vote for higher salaries in order to meet steep increases in the cost of living. Unemployment grew rapidly even though "political factories" were still subsidized. The government thus relaxed its restrictions to allow labor migration particularly to West Germany where workers were needed for its thriving economy. Foreign investment was encouraged up to 49% in joint enterprises, and barriers to the movement of people and exchange of ideas were largely removed. The role of trade unions continued to be one of transmission of instructions from government to workers, allocation of perks along with the education/training of workers, monitoring legislation, and overall protection of the self-management system. Strikes were legally neither allowed nor forbidden but—until the 1958 miners strike in Trbovlje, Slovenia—were not publicly acknowledged and were suppressed. After 1958, strikes were tolerated as an indication of problems to be resolved. Unions, however, did not initiate strikes but were expected to convince workers to go back to work.

Having survived its expulsion from the Cominform in 1948 and Stalin's attempts to take control, Yugoslavia began to develop a foreign policy independent of the Soviet Union. By mid-1949 Yugoslavia ceased its support of the Greek Communists in their civil war against the then Royalist government of Greece. In October 1949, Yugoslavia was elected to one of the non-permanent seats on the UN Security Council and openly condemned North Korea's aggression toward South Korea. Following the "rapprochement" opening with the Soviet Union initiated by Nikita Khrushchev and his 1956 denunciation of Stalin, Tito intensified his work on developing the movement of non-aligned "third world" nations. This would become Yugoslavia's external trademark, in cooperation with Nehru of India, Nasser of Egypt, and others. With the September 1961 Belgrade summit conference of non-aligned nations, Tito became the recognized leader of the movement. The non-aligned position served Tito's Yugoslavia well by allowing Tito to draw on economic and political support from the Western powers while neutralizing any aggressiveness from the Soviet bloc. While Tito had acquiesced, reluctantly, to the 1956 Soviet invasion of Hungary for fear of chaos and its liberalizing impact on Yugoslavia, he condemned the Soviet invasion of Dubček's Czechoslovakia in 1968, as did Romania's Ceausescu, both fearing their countries might be the next in line for "corrective" action by the Red Army and the Warsaw Pact. Just before his death on 4 May 1980, Tito also condemned the Soviet invasion of Afghanistan. Yugoslavia actively participated in the 1975 Helsinki Conference and agreements and the first 1977–78 review conference that took place in Belgrade, even though Yugoslavia's one-party communist regime perpetrated and condoned numerous human rights violations. Overall, in the 1970s and 1980s, Yugoslavia maintained fairly good relations with its neighboring states by playing down or solving pending disputes—such as the Trieste issue with Italy in 1975—and by developing cooperative projects and increased trade.

Ravaged by the war, occupation, resistance, and civil war losses and preoccupied with carrying out the elimination of all actual and potential opposition, the Communist government faced the double task of building its Socialist economy while rebuilding the country. As an integral part of the Yugoslav federation, Bosnia and Herzegovina was, naturally, impacted by Yugoslavia's internal and external political developments. The main problems facing communist Yugoslavia and Bosnia and Herzegovina were essentially the same as the unresolved ones under Royalist Yugoslavia. As the "Royal Yugoslavism" had failed in its assimilative efforts, so did the "Socialist Yugoslavism" fail to overcome the forces of nationalism. Bosnia and Herzegovina differs from the other republics because its area has been the meeting ground of Serbian and Croatian nationalist claims, with the Muslims as a third party, pulled to both sides. Centuries of coexistence of the three major national groups had made Bosnia and Herzegovina into a territorial maze where no boundaries could be drawn to clearly separate Serbs, Croats, and Muslims without resorting to violence and forced movements of people. The inability to negotiate a peaceful partition of Bosnia and Herzegovina between Serbia and Croatia doomed the first interwar Yugoslavia to failure. The Socialist experiment with "Yugoslavism" in post–World War II Yugoslavia was particularly relevant to the situation in Bosnia and Herzegovina where the increasing incidence of intermarriage, particularly between Serbs and Croats, caused the introduction of the "Yugoslav" category with the 1961 census. By 1981 the "Yugoslav" category was selected by 1.2 million citizens, (5.4% of the total population), a large increase over the 273,077 number in 1971. Muslims, not impacted much by intermarriage, have also been recognized since 1971 as a separate "people" and numbered two million in 1981 in Yugoslavia. The 1991 census showed the population of Bosnia and Herzegovina consisting mainly of Muslims (43.7%), Serbs (31.4%), and Croats (17.3%) with 6% "Yugoslavs" out of a total population of 4,364,000.

Bosnia as a political unit has existed since at least 1150. Headed by a "Ban" in the Croatian tradition, Bosnia lasted for over 300 years with an increasing degree of independence from Hungary through King Tvrtko I and his successors until the occupation by the Ottoman Turks in 1463 (1482 for Herzegovina). Bosnia and Herzegovina was then ruled by the Turks for 415 years until 1878, and by Austria-Hungary for forty years until 1918. Bosnia and Herzegovina ceased to be a separate political unit only for the 27 years of the first Yugoslavia (1918–1945) and became again a separate unit for 47 years as one of the republics of the Federal Socialist Yugoslavia until 1992. Yet, in spite of an 800-year history of common development, the Serbs, Croats, and Muslims of Bosnia and Herzegovina never assimilated into a single nation. Bosnia was initially settled by Croats who became Catholic and then by Orthodox Serbs escaping from the Turks. Under the Turks, large numbers converted to Islam and, in spite of a common language, their religious and cultural differences kept the Serbs, Croats, and Muslims apart through history so that Bosnia and Herzegovina has been more a geographic-political notion than a unified nation.

Consequently, while the resurgent nationalism was galvanizing Croatia into an intensifying confrontation with Serbia, the Bosnian leadership had to keep an internal balance by joining one or the other side depending on its own interests. Bosnia and Herzegovina was torn between the two opposing "liberal" and "conservative/centralist" coalitions. In terms of widening civil and political liberties, Bosnia and Herzegovina usually supported in

most cases the liberal group. Its own economic needs as a less developed area, however, pulled it into the conservative coalition with Serbia in order to keep the source of development funds flowing to itself, Montenegro, Macedonia, and Serbia (for the Kosovo region). Also, the "Yugoslav" framework was for Bosnia and Herzegovina an assurance against its possible, and very likely bloody, partitioning between Serbia and Croatia.

The liberal group, centered in Slovenia and Croatia, grew stronger on the basis of the deepening resentment against forced subsidizing of less-developed areas of the federation and build-up of the Yugoslav army. Finally, the increased political and economic autonomy enjoyed by the Republics after the 1974 Constitution and particularly following Tito's death in 1980, assisted in turning Tito's motto of "unity and brotherhood" into "freedom and democracy" to be achieved through either a confederative rearrangement of Yugoslavia or by complete independence of the Republics. The debate over the reforms of the 1960s had led to a closer scrutiny—not only of the economic system, but also of the decision-making process at the republic and federal levels, particularly the investment of funds to less developed areas that Slovenia and Croatia felt were very poorly managed, if not squandered. Other issues of direct impact on Bosnia and Herzegovina fueled acrimony between individual nations, such as the 1967 Declaration in Zagreb claiming a Croatian linguistic and literary tradition separate from the Serbian one, thus undermining the validity of the "Serbo-Croatian" language. Also, Kosovo Albanians and Montenegrins, along with Slovenes and Croats began to assert their national rights as superior to their rights as Yugoslav nationals.

The Eighth Congress of the League of Communists of Yugoslavia (LCY) in December 1964 acknowledged that ethnic prejudice and antagonisms existed in socialist Yugoslavia. The Congress went on record against the position that Yugoslavia's nations had become obsolete and were disintegrating into a socialist "Yugoslavism." Thus the republics, based on individual nations, became bastions of a strong Federalism that advocated the devolution and decentralization of authority from the federal to the republic level. "Yugoslav Socialist Patriotism" was at times defined as a deep feeling for one's own national identity within the socialist self-management of Yugoslavia.

Economic reforms were the other focus of the Eighth LCY Congress led by Croatia and Slovenia, with emphasis on efficiencies and local economic development decisions with profit criteria as their basis. The liberal bloc (Slovenia, Croatia, Macedonia, Vojvodina) prevailed over the Conservative group and the reforms of 1965 did away with central investment planning and political factories. The positions of the two blocks hardened into a national-liberal coalition that viewed the conservative, centralist group led by Serbia as the Greater Serbian attempt at majority domination.

The devolution of power in economic decision-making spearheaded by the Slovenes assisted in the "federalization" of the League of Communists of Yugoslavia. This resulted in a league of quasi-sovereign republican parties. Under strong prodding from the Croats, the party agreed in 1970 to the principle of unanimity for decision making that, in practice, meant a veto power for each republic. However, the concentration of economic resources in Serbian hands continued with Belgrade banks controlling half of total credits and some 80% of foreign credits. This was also combined with the fear of Serbian political and cultural domination. The Croats were particularly sensitive regarding language, alarmed by the use of the Serbian version of Serbo-Croatian as the norm with the Croatian version as a deviation. The language controversy thus exacerbated the economic and political tensions, leading to easily inflamed ethnic confrontations.

To the conservative centralists the devolution of power to the republic level meant the subordination of the broad "Yugoslav" and "Socialist" interests to the narrower "nationalist" interest of republic national majorities. With the Croat League of Communists taking the liberal position in 1970, nationalism was rehabilitated as long as it didn't slide into chauvinism. Thus the "Croatian Spring" bloomed and impacted all the other republics of Yugoslavia. Meanwhile, as the result of a series of 1967–68 constitutional amendments that limited federal power in favor of the republics and autonomous provinces, the Federal Government was seen by liberals more as an inter-republican problem-solving mechanism bordering on a confederative arrangement. A network of inter-republican committees established by mid-1971 proved to be very efficient at resolving a large number of difficult issues in a short time. The coalition of liberals and nationalists in Croatia generated sharp condemnation in Serbia, where its own brand of nationalism grew stronger, but as part of a conservative-centralist alliance. Thus the liberal/federalist versus conservative/centralist opposition became entangled in the rising nationalism within each opposing bloc.

Particularly difficult was the situation in Croatia and Serbia because of issues relating to their ethnic minorities—Serbian in Croatia and Hungarian/Albanian in Serbia. Serbs in Croatia sided with the Croat conservatives and sought a constitutional amendment guaranteeing their own national identity and rights and, in the process, they challenged the "sovereignty" of the Croatian nation and state, as well as its right to self-determination, including the right to secession. The conservatives won and the amendment declared that "the Socialist Republic of Croatia [was] the national state of the Croatian nation, the state of the Serbian nation in Croatia, and the state of the nationalities inhabiting it."

Meanwhile Slovenia, not burdened by large minorities, developed a similar liberal and nationalist direction along with Croatia. This fostered an incipient separatist sentiment opposed by both the liberal and conservative party wings. Led by Stane Kavčič, head of the Slovenian government, the liberal wing gained as much political local latitude from the Federal level as possible during "Slovenian Spring" of the early 1970s. By the summer of 1971, the Serbian party leadership was pressuring President Tito to put an end to the "dangerous" development of Croatian nationalism. While Tito wavered because of his support for the balancing system of autonomous republic units, the situation quickly reached critical proportions also in terms of the direct interests of Bosnia and Herzegovina. Croat nationalists, complaining about discrimination against Croats in Bosnia and Herzegovina, demanded the incorporation of Western Herzegovina into Croatia. Serbia countered by claiming Southeastern Herzegovina for itself. Croats also advanced many economic and political claims: to a larger share of their foreign currency earnings, to the issuance of their own currency, to establishment of their own national bank to negotiate foreign loans, to the printing of Croatian postage stamps, to a Croatian army and to recognition of the Croatian *Sabor* (Assembly) as the highest Croatian political body and, finally, to Croatian secession and complete independence.

Confronted with such intensive agitation, the liberal Croatian party leadership could not back down and did not try to restrain the public demands nor the widespread university students' strike of November 1971. This situation caused the loss of support from the liberal party wings of Slovenia and even Macedonia. At this point Tito intervened, condemned the Croatian liberal leadership on 1 December 1971 and supported the conservative wing. The liberal leadership group resigned on 12 December 1971. When Croatian students demonstrated and demanded an independent Croatia, the Yugoslav army was ready to move in if necessary. A wholesale purge of the party liberals followed, with tens of thousands expelled from the party. Key functionaries lost their positions, while several thousands were imprisoned (including Franjo Tudjman who later became president in independent Croatia). Leading Croatian nationalist organizations and their publications were closed. On 8 May 1972 the Croatian party also expelled its liberal wing leaders and the purge of nationalists continued through 1973 in Croatia, as well as in Slovenia and Macedonia. However, the issues and sentiments raised during the "Slovene and Croat Springs" of 1969–71 did not disappear. Tito and the conservatives were forced to satisfy nominally some demands and the 1974 Constitution was an attempt to resolve the strained inter-republican relations as each republic pursued its own interests over and above a conceivable overall "Yugoslav" interest. The repression of liberal-nationalist Croats was accompanied by a growing influence of the Serbian element in the Croatian Party (24% in 1980) and police force (majority), contributing to the continued persecution and imprisonment of Croatian nationalists into the 1980s.

Beginning in 1986, work began on amendments to the 1974 Constitution. When these were submitted in 1987, they created a furor, particularly in Slovenia. Opposition was strongest to the amendments that proposed creation of a unified legal system, central control of transportation and communication, centralizing the economy into a unified market, and granting more control to Serbia over its autonomous provinces of Kosovo and Vojvodina. These changes were seen as being accomplished at the expense of the individual republics. A recentralization of the League of Communists was also recommended but opposed by liberal/nationalist groups. Serbia also proposed changes to the bicameral Federal Skupština (Assembly)—replacing it with a tricameral one where deputies would no longer be elected by their republican assemblies but through a "one person, one vote" national system. Slovenia, Croatia, and Bosnia strongly opposed the change; they also opposed the additional Chamber of Associated Labor that would have increased the Federal role in the economy. The debates over the recentralizing amendments caused an even greater focus in Slovenia and Croatia on the concept of a confederative structure based on self-determination of sovereign states, and a multiparty democratic system as the only one that could maintain some semblance of a "Yugoslav" state.

By 1989, the relations between Slovenia and Serbia reached a crisis point, especially following the Serbian assumption of control in the Kosovo and Vojvodina provinces (as well as in Montenegro). Their leadership groups refused even to meet and Serbs began a boycott of Slovenian products, withdrew savings from Slovenian banks, and terminated economic cooperation and trade with Slovenia. Serbian President Milošević's tactics were extremely distasteful to the Slovenians and the use of force against the Albanian population of the Kosovo province worried the Slovenes (and Croats) about the possible use of force by Serbia against Slovenia itself. The tensions with Serbia convinced the Slovenian leadership of the need to take protective measures and, in September 1989, draft amendments to the Constitution of Slovenia were published. These included the right to secession, the sole right of the Slovenian legislature to introduce martial law and to control the deployment of armed forces in Slovenia. The latter was particularly needed, since the Yugoslav Army, largely controlled by a mostly Serbian/Montenegrin officer corps dedicated to the preservation of a communist system, had a self-interest in preserving the source of their own budgetary allocations of some 51% of the Yugoslav federal budget.

A last attempt at salvaging Yugoslavia was to be made as the extraordinary Congress of the League of Communists of Yugoslavia convened in January 1990 to review proposed reforms such as free multiparty elections and freedom of speech. The Slovenian delegation attempted to broaden the spectrum of reforms but was rebuffed and walked out on 23 January 1990, pulling out of the Yugoslav League. The Slovenian Communists then renamed their party the Party for Democratic Renewal. The political debate in Slovenia intensified and some nineteen parties were formed by early 1990. On 10 April 1990 the first free elections since before World War II were held in Slovenia where there still was a three-chamber Assembly: political affairs, associated labor, and territorial communities. A coalition of six newly formed democratic parties, called Demos, won 55% of the votes, with the remainder going to the Party for Democratic Renewal, the former Communists, 17%; the Socialist Party, 5%; and the Liberal Democratic Party (heir to the Slovenia Youth Organization), 15%. The Demos coalition organized the first freely elected Slovenian Government of the post-Communist era with Dr. Lojze Peterle as the Prime Minister.

Milan Kučan, former head of the League of Communists of Slovenia was elected President with 54% of the vote. His election was seen as recognition of his efforts to effect a bloodless transfer of power from a monopoly by the Communist party to a free multiparty system and his standing up to the recentralizing attempts by Serbia.

All of these developments had also a deep impact on Bosnia and Herzegovina. When the Antifascist Council of the National Liberation of Yugoslavia (AVNOJ) proclaimed the federal principle on 29 November 1943, Bosnia and Herzegovina was included as one of the constituent republics of post-World War II Yugoslavia. Muslims made up 30.9% of the population by 1948, with 45% for the Serbs and 24% for the Croats. Muslims, however, were not considered a "nation" yet, since Alexsander Ranković, Tito's close friend and chief of security, had favored an unofficial "Serbianization" policy vis-à-vis the Muslim population. Only after Ranković's dismissal in 1966 and a subsequent purge of his secret police was a real debate opened on the issue of a Muslim "nation." Serbs claimed that Muslims were islamicized Serbs, and Croats claimed that Muslims were descendants of the Croatian Bosnian Church (Bogomils) that had converted to Islam. The Muslims themselves, meanwhile, claimed their own separate identity and were recognized as equal to Serbs and Croats. They entered the 1971 census as "Muslims, in the ethnic sense."

The sense of Muslim identity grew stronger and incorporated demands for Muslim institutions parallel to the Serbian and Croatian ones. Muslims sought to define themselves as the only "true" Bosnians and thus a call to define Bosnia and Herzegovina as a "Muslim" Republic. Muslim activist groups multiplied during the 1970s and 1980s, and one such group was put on trial in April 1983 for illegally plotting the creation of a Muslim Republic. Members were sentenced to long jail terms, but given amnesty in 1988. One of the group was the 1994 president of Bosnia and Herzegovina, Alija Izetbegović.

Since the 1970s and into the late 1980s the Muslims' self-assertiveness as an ethnic community grew ever stronger and was viewed as a balancing element between Serbs and Croats. As the winds of change away from communism swept the western republics of Slovenia and Croatia in 1989 and 1990, Bosnia and Herzegovina also was preparing for multiparty elections to be held on 18 November 1990. Meanwhile, across Bosnia and Herzegovina's borders with Croatia, the Serbian population was clamoring for its own cultural and political autonomy. Serbs perceived threats from the Croatian Democratic Union, the winner in the April 1990 elections in Croatia with 205 out of 356 seats in the tricameral Croatian parliament.

By July 1990, a Bosnia and Herzegovina branch of the Croatia-based Serbian Democratic Party had become very active in the 18 Bosnian communes with Serbian majorities adjacent to the Croatia "Krajina" (border area). By the fall of 1990, the program of the Serbian Democratic Party in Croatia had advanced a plan to include the Bosnian Serbs into a joint "Krajina" state which would have a federal arrangement with Serbia proper. This arrangement, it was hoped, would undercut any thoughts of a confederation of Slovenia, Croatia, and Bosnia and Herzegovina. Such a confederation, however, was favored by the Party of Democratic Action (Muslim) and the Croatian Democratic Union. In spite of their differences in long term goals, the three nationalist parties were committed to the continuation of Bosnia and Herzegovina and to the termination of Communist rule. On 1 August 1990, Bosnia and Herzegovina declared itself a "sovereign and democratic state." The former Communist Party became the Party of Democratic Change, while Yugoslavia's Prime Minister Marković formed the Alliance of Reform Forces that advocated his economic reforms.

The electoral results gave 87 seats in the parliament to the Muslim Party, 71 to the Serbian Party, 44 to the Croatian Democratic Union with 18 to the former Communists and 13 to the Alliance of Reform Forces. The three ethnic parties then formed a coalition government with Alija Izetbegović of the Muslim Party as President of Bosnia and Herzegovina.

Independence and War

Meanwhile, Slovenia and Croatia had published a joint proposal in October 1990 for a confederation of Yugoslavia as a last attempt at a negotiated solution, but to no avail. The Slovenian legislature also adopted a draft constitution in October proclaiming that "Slovenia will become an independent state." On 23 December 1990, a plebiscite was held on Slovenia's "disassociation" from Yugoslavia if a confederal solution could not be negotiated within a six month period. An overwhelming majority of 89% of voters approved the secession provision and on 26 December 1990, a Declaration of Sovereignty was also adopted. All federal laws were declared void in Slovenia as of 20 February 1991, and, since no negotiated agreement was possible, Slovenia declared its independence on 25 June 1991. On 27 June 1991, the Yugoslav Army tried to seize control of Slovenia and its borders with Italy, Austria, and Hungary under the pretext that it was its constitutional duty to assure the integrity of Socialist Yugoslavia. The Yugoslav Army units were surprised by the resistance they encountered from the Slovenian "territorial guards" which surrounded Yugoslav Army tank units, isolated them, and engaged in close combat, mostly along border checkpoints. These battles ended in most cases with Yugoslav units surrendering to the Slovenian forces. Fortunately, casualties were limited on both sides, but over 3,200 Yugoslav Army soldiers surrendered and were taken prisoner. They were well treated by the Slovenes, who in a public relations coup, had the prisoners call their parents all over Yugoslavia to come to Slovenia and take their sons back home. The war in Slovenia was ended in ten days due to the intervention of the European Community, which, with the Brioni agreements of 7 July 1991, established a cease fire, and a three-month moratorium of Slovenia's and Croatia's implementation of independence. This gave time to the Yugoslav Army to retreat from Slovenia with all its hardware and supplies by the end of October 1991.

The coalition government of Bosnia and Herzegovina had a very difficult time maintaining the spirit of ethnic cooperation won in its elections, while the situation in Slovenia and Croatia was moving to the point of no return with their declaration of independence of 25 June 1991 and the wars that followed. Particularly worrisome were the clashes in Croatia between Serbian paramilitary forces and Croatian police and the intervention of the Yugoslav Army in order to "keep the peace." Another element that worried the Bosnian government was the concentration of Yugoslav Army units in Bosnia and Herzegovina following their retreat first from Slovenia and then from Croatia. On 15 October 1991 the parliament of Bosnia and Herzegovina, minus its Serbian delegation (they had walked out before the vote), approved documents providing the legal basis for the republic's eventual independence. In response to it, the Serbian Democratic Party held a plebiscite in the two-thirds of Bosnian territory under Serbian control and announced the establishment of a Serbian Republic inside Bosnia and Herzegovina.

In December 1991, the Bosnian Parliament passed a Declaration of Sovereignty and President Izetbegović submitted to the European Community an application for international recognition of Bosnia and Herzegovina as an independent nation. As required by the European Community, a referendum on independence was held on 29 February 1992. With the Serbs abstaining in opposition to the secession from Yugoslavia, Muslims and Croats approved an independent Bosnia and Herzegovina by a vote of 99.7%. In reaction to the referendum, Serbs proceeded to prepare for war in close cooperation with the Yugoslav army.

A last attempt at reaching a compromise was made at a conference in Lisbon in late February 1992, when a provisional consensus of the three parties was obtained on a draft constitutional agreement to partition Bosnia and Herzegovina into three ethnic-based "cantons." But President Izetbegović, trusting the US would not allow a Balkan war and hoping for a better deal than the proposed 44% of Bosnian territory with over 80% of the Muslim population, rejected the provisional Lisbon agreement.

On 1 March 1992 in Sarajevo a Serbian wedding party was fired upon. This was the spark that ignited armed confrontations in Sarajevo and other areas of Bosnia and Herzegovina. The breakdown of the Lisbon agreements infuriated the Bosnian Serbs who, by late March of 1992, formally established their own "Serbian Republic of Bosnia and Herzegovina." The international recognition of Bosnia and Herzegovina by the European Community and the US (along with the recognition of Slovenia and Croatia) was issued on 6 April 1992, the anniversary of the 1941 Nazi invasion of Yugoslavia. This action was viewed as another affront to the Serbs, and gave more impetus to Serbian determination to oppose the further splitting of Yugoslavia that would cause the final separation of Serbs in Croatia and Bosnia and Herzegovina from Serbia proper. The bond among the Serbs of Croatia and Bosnia with the Serbian government controlled by Slobodan Milošević, and with the Yugoslav Army was firmly cemented. The decision of Serbia, along with the Serbs of Bosnia and Croatia, to take advantage of Yugoslavia's demise and try to unite Serbian territories in Croatia and Bosnia and Herzegovina with Serbia proper precipitated the wars in Croatia first and then in Bosnia and Herzegovina. Desperate acts by desperate Serbs engaged in "ethnic cleansing" (torching, and systematic rape and executions in imitation of the World War II Ustaša tactics) revolted the whole world and elicited retaliation by the initially allied Croats and Muslims.

War spread in Bosnia in mid-1992 with the relentless bombardment of Sarajevo by Serbs and the brutal use of "ethnic cleansing," primarily by Serbs intent on freeing the areas along the Drina River of Muslim inhabitants. Croats and Muslims retaliated in kind, if not in degree, while Serbs took over control of some 70% of the country and used concentration camps and raping of women as systematic terror tactics to achieve their "cleansing" goals. Croats kept control of western Herzegovina, while their Muslim allies tried to resist Serbian attacks on mostly Muslim cities and towns full of refugees exposed to shelling and starvation while the world watched in horror. The European Community, the US, the UN, and NATO coordinated peacekeep-

ing efforts, dangerous air deliveries to Sarajevo, air drops of food and medicinal supplies to keep the people of Sarajevo from dying of starvation and sicknesses.

The various plans proposing the division of Bosnia and Herzegovina into ethnic "cantons" were not acceptable to the winning Serbian side. They were well supplied with weapons by the departed Yugoslav Army and had their own armament factories. Meanwhile, an international arms embargo was imposed on all former Yugoslav Republics, preventing the Bosnian government from acquiring needed weapons, except through illegal smuggling mostly from Islamic countries. The "cantonization" plans were also a partial cause for the breakdown of the Muslim-Croatian alliance when the two sides began fighting over areas of mixed Croat and Muslim populations. One such area was the city of Mostar in Herzegovina, where the Croats had established the Croatian union of "Herzeg-Bosnia," later (August 1993) named the state of Herzeg-Bosnia. Finally, under the threat of air strikes from NATO, the Serbs agreed to stop the shelling of Sarajevo and hand over (or remove) their heavy artillery by February 1994, so Sarajevo could get a respite from its bloody siege of several years. A truce was implemented by mid-February 1994 and was barely holding while continuing negotiations were taking place that, on US initiative, brought Croats and Muslims back together on a confederation plan accepted by the two sides and signed in Washington on 18 March 1994.

In July 1994, the EC, the US, and Russia agreed on a partition plan giving the Croat-Muslim side 51% of the land, with 49% offered to the Bosnian Serbs who, holding 70%, would need to give up a large area under their control. As of the end of July 1994, the Bosnian Serbs' parliament had rejected the plan and had resumed occasional sniping and mortar shelling of Sarajevo, shooting at UN peacekeepers and supply airplanes, and blocking of the single access road to Sarajevo. After almost two-and-a-half years of war, destruction, and terrible suffering imposed on the people of Bosnia and Herzegovina, the efforts of the international community and its very cumbersome decision-making process had brought Bosnia and Herzegovina back to the partitioning plan originally agreed on at the Lisbon meeting of February 1992.

The legacy of centuries of confrontations by the Austro-Hungarian, Russian, and Turkish Empires in the Balkans continues to haunt the area and a further broadening of the conflict including most of the Balkan nations appears possible. As of fall 1994, President Milošević of Serbia had closed the borders between Serbia and Bosnia and Herzegovina in order to stop any further assistance to the "Republika Srpska" that he himself helped establish. Serbia desperately needed the lifting of the economic sanctions imposed against it by the UN in May 1992 in order to survive and, apparently, Serbia's own interests have prevailed for the time being over the direct drive towards a "Greater Serbia." This change of heart is due in large part to the strong support by Russia for the latest 51% (Muslim-Croat) to 49% (Serbs) partitioning plan. President Milošević agreed to "extricate" Serbia from its direct support for the Bosnian Serbs in the hope that a compromise partitioning plan that would allow each side to "confederate" with Croatia and Serbia respectively and would offer both sides the opportunity to turn their energies to positive efforts of physical and psychological reconstruction. In this way, Milošević would reach the Greater Serbia goal indirectly and at the same time disengage Serbia and himself from sanctions and possible war crimes prosecutions.

The stakes in the Bosnia and Herzegovina conflict are very high, including the future stability of Europe, the future of European integration, the viability of the UN, NATO, and the Helsinki principles and their implementation along with a more workable collective security system. Even more pressing is the hope of avoiding a much wider conflagration in the Balkans that might turn NATO members against one another and tear apart the entire Western alliance.

13GOVERNMENT

The outcome of the December 1990 parliamentary elections gave almost 34% of the votes to the Muslim Party of Democratic Action (SDA) for 87 of the 240 seats in the Bicameral legislature. Alija Izetbegović, head of the SDA, became president of the seven-member Presidency of Bosnia and Herzegovina, with a Croat as Prime Minister and a Serb presiding over the legislature.

The war being waged in Bosnia and Herzegovina since April 1992 has prevented the working out of a constitution agreeable to the three main groups, and so far none of the constitutional plans submitted for terminating the hostilities has been accepted by all three parties to the conflict.

The February 1992 Lisbon proposal about the partitioning of Bosnia and Herzegovina into "ethnic cantons" was rejected by the Muslim side. The Vance-Owen proposal of early January 1993 dividing Bosnia and Herzegovina, still a unified state, into nine "ethnic majority" provinces with Sarajevo as a central weak government district was accepted by Croats and Muslims on 7 January 1993 and ratified on 20 January 1993 by the Bosnian Serbs' Parliament with a 55-to-15 vote in spite of deep misgivings. However, two key events delayed the necessary detailed implementation discussions: Croat forces' attacks on Muslims in Bosnia and Herzegovina and on Serbs in Croatia, and the new administration of President Bill Clinton, from whom the Bosnian Muslims hoped to obtain stronger support, even military intervention. Thus by mid-March 1993, only the Croats had agreed to the three essential points of the Vance-Owen proposal, namely the Constitutional Principles (ten provinces), the Military Arrangements, and the detailed map of the ten provinces. On 25 March 1993 the Bosnian Muslims agreed to all the terms, but the Bosnian Serb legislature on 2 April 1993 rejected the revised ten-province map and the Vance-Owen plan was scuttled.

The Owen-Stoltenberg plan was based on a June 1993 proposal in Geneva by Presidents Tudjman and Milošević about partitioning Bosnia and Herzegovina into three ethnic-based "states." Owen-Stoltenberg announced the new plan in August 1993 indicating that the three ethnic states were realistically based on the acceptance of Serbian and Croatian territorial "conquests." At the same time the Croat Bosnian "Parliament" announced the establishment of the "State of Herzeg-Bosnia" and the Croatian Democratic Alliance withdrew its members from the Bosnian Parliament. The Bosnian Parliament then rejected the Owen-Stoltenberg Plan while seeking further negotiations on the Muslim state's territory and clarifications on the international status of Bosnia and Herzegovina.

The next (current) plan, developed with the more proactive participation of the United States and bringing together again the Croats and Muslims into a federation of their own, was signed in Washington on 18 March 1994 following the Sarajevo cease fire of 17 March. On 31 March 1994 the Bosnian assembly in Sarajevo approved the new constitutional provisions establishing a Federation of Muslims and Croats with the Presidency to alternate between Croats and Muslims. A joint interim government is to be formed until new elections are held, and final boundaries of the federation are to be defined following agreements with the Bosnian Serbs. The Muslim-Croat federation would share the responsibility for defense, commerce, and foreign affairs while divided into 15 smaller regions with either Muslim or Croat majority populations. The Geneva contact group (US, UK, France, Germany, Russia) agreed on a new partition plan in July 1994 that divides Bosnia and Herzegovina 51% to the joint Muslim-Croat federation and 49% to the Serbs currently holding

70% of the lands. A two-week deadline for acceptance was given the Serbs in July 1994. The plan was approved by the Muslims and Croats on 18 July 1994 while declared absolutely unacceptable by the Serbs, demanding access to the Adriatic Sea, share in the Sarajevo-based government, end to the economic sanctions against Serbia, recognition of sovereignty, and freedom for their "Republika Srpska" to merge with Serbia at a later date as the Muslim-Croat federation would be allowed into a confederation with Croatia.

As of fall 1994, the President was Alija Izetbegović, and the Prime Minister was Haris Silajdžić.

14POLITICAL PARTIES

The two-tier elections of November–December 1990 for the parliament of Bosnia and Herzegovina had the following results:

Muslim Party of Democratic Action (SDA)	
President Alija Izetbegović	87 seats
Serbian Democratic Party (SDS)	
President Radovan Karadžić	71 seats
Croatian Democratic Union (HDZ)	
President Stjepan Kljuić	44 seats
League of Communist-Party of Democratic Change	18 seats
Alliance of Reform Forces	13 seats

The Serbian and Croatian parties opposed a unitary Bosnia and Herzegovina (favored by the Muslim Party) in favor of a temporary confederation as a transition to unification with their "mother state" of Serbia or Croatia. Serbs wanted a strongly centralized Federal Yugoslavia, the Muslims a decentralized federal Yugoslavia, while the Croats favored a weak confederation structure.

15LOCAL GOVERNMENT

The reorganization of local government in Bosnia and Herzegovina cannot be accomplished until the end of hostilities and development of a new constitution.

16JUDICIAL SYSTEM

The Bosnian conflict has disrupted the ordinary functioning of courts in most areas.

17ARMED FORCES

There is no national force, although the nominal Muslim government controls 30,000–50,000 militiamen, who face 50,000 Croats and 67,000 Serbs. The Serbs control most of the Russian materiel abandoned by the defunct Yugoslavian army. A major portion of the UN Protection Force (about 10,000 personnel from 29 nations) is deployed to Bosnia and Herzegovina.

18INTERNATIONAL COOPERATION

Bosnia and Herzegovina was admitted to the UN on 22 May 1992. Bosnia and Herzegovina is also a member of the CSCE and UNESO. The country is applying for membership in other international organizations. The US and EC countries have recognized Bosnia and Herzegovina. The UN sent peacekeeping troops to the region in the spring of 1992 to mediate an ongoing civil war in the region

19ECONOMY

Bosnia and Herzegovina ranked next to Macedonia as the poorest republic of the former Yugoslav SFR. Although industry accounts for over 50% of GDP, Bosnia and Herzegovina is primarily agricultural. Farms have been small and inefficient, thus necessitating food imports. Industry has been greatly overstaffed, with Bosnia and Herzegovina accounting for much of the former Yugoslav SFR's metallic ore and coal production. Timber production and textiles also have been important.

[20]INCOME

In 1991, Bosnia and Herzegovina's GDP was an estimated $1,400 million at current prices, or $3,200 per capita. In 1991, the average inflation rate was 80% per month, resulting in a real growth rate in GDP of –37%.

[21]LABOR

Before the civil war, the labor force in 1991 amounted to 1,026,254, with 2% engaged in agriculture, 45% in industry and mining, and the remainder in other sectors. In February 1992, unemployment was estimated at 28%.

Until the outbreak of war in 1992, all workers were legally entitled to form or join unions. Several Bosnian trade unions and professional organizations advocated peace during the chaotic early months of 1992. The majority of Bosnian union members probably belonged to the quasi-official Council of Independent Trade Unions of Bosnia and Herzegovina. Ethnically motivated dismissals and squelching of union activities escalated in the context of the war.

The minimum employment age before the war was 16, but many younger children often assisted with family agricultural work. Many children have been exploited because of the war, particularly for military functions like reconnaissance and running messages.

[22]AGRICULTURE

About 19.8% (1,015,000 hectares/2,508,000 acres) of the total area was considered as arable land in 1991; another 27.6% (1,400,000 hectares/3,459,000 acres) was estimated to be used as permanent pasture land. Since the disintegration of the Yugoslav SFR, civil fighting in the major agricultural areas has often interrupted harvests and caused considerable crop loss, as indicated by the following table of production (in 1,000 tons):

	1991	1992
Corn	1,267	873
Wheat	474	352
Potatoes	395	296
Fruit	255	168
Vegetables and melons	248	153
Onions, dry	60	40

[23]ANIMAL HUSBANDRY

As of 1991, there were some 1.4 million hectares (3.5 million acres) of permanent pastureland, representing about 27% of the total area. Because of the breakup of the Yugoslav SFR and subsequent civil war, the livestock population has significantly fallen since 1990 as shown in the following table (in 1,000s):

	1990	1991	1992
Sheep	1,319	1,317	1,287
Cattle	874	853	826
Pigs	614	617	590
Horses	100	96	70
Chickens	9,000	10,000	8,000

Production of meat fell from 158,000 tons in 1990 to 142,000 tons in 1991 to 126,000 tons in 1992. From 1990 to 1992, milk production has declined by 22% to only 705,000 tons in 1992; egg production similarly fell by 31% to 20,000 tons during that time.

[24]FISHING

With no ports on its 20 km (12 mi) of Adriatic coastline, marine fishing is not commercially significant. Inland fishing occurs on the Sava, Una, and Drina Rivers.

[25]FORESTRY

In 1991, about 2.3 million hectares (5.7 million acres) were forested, accounting for nearly 46% of the total area. Much of the output has been used for fuel since civil unrest erupted.

[26]MINING

Nonfuel mineral resources include copper, lead, zinc, gold, and iron ore. Iron ore is mined at Vareš, Ljubija, and Radovan. Bauxite is also mined by Energoinvest at Vlasenica, Jajce, Bosanska, Krupa, Posusje, Listica, and Citluk. Energoinvest also operated a lead-zinc mine at Srebrenica and a manganese mine at Buzim in 1991. Salt is produced from brine at Tuzla, and mined at Tušanj.

[27]ENERGY AND POWER

As of 1991, total installed electrical capacity was 14,400 million kw. Electrical generation has been irregular since the onslaught of civil conflict. Brown coal and lignite mines are located around Tuzla. In 1991, the annual capacity for the brown coal mines totaled 12 million tons; lignite mine capacity was 7 million tons. A petroleum refinery at Bosanski Brod had an annual capacity of 100 million tons in 1991. Domestic mineral fuel production has been erratic since the beginning of the civil war.

[28]INDUSTRY

Mining and mining-related activities make up the bulk of Bosnia and Herzegovina's industry. Steel production, vehicle assembly, textiles, tobacco products, wooden furniture, and domestic appliances are also important industries. Industrial production has plummeted since 1990 because of the civil war.

[29]SCIENCE AND TECHNOLOGY

Under Tito, Bosnia and Herzegovina became the research center for the former Yugoslav SFR's military and defense-related industrial plants.

[30]DOMESTIC TRADE

Commerce has been severely restricted by the ongoing interethnic civil strife.

[31]FOREIGN TRADE

In 1990, exports amounted to over $2.0 billion, of which manufactured goods accounted for 31%; machinery and transport equipment, 20.8%; raw materials, 18%; other manufactured products, 17.3%; chemicals, 9.4%; fuel and lubricants, 1.2%; and food and live animals, 1.2%. Imports in 1990 totaled almost $1.9 billion, of which fuels and lubricants made up 32%; machinery and transport equipment, 23.3%; other manufactured items, 21.3%; chemicals, 10%; raw materials, 6.7%; food and live animals, 5.5%; and beverages and tobacco, 1.9%.

International trade with Bosnia and Herzegovina has been limited since the beginning of the civil war. The UN and EC are continuing to try to mediate a peace plan.

[32]BALANCE OF PAYMENTS

No reliable economic statistics for 1992 were available because of the civil war.

[33]BANKING AND SECURITIES

The central bank of Bosnia and Herzegovina is the National Bank of Bosnia and Herzegovina. In June 1992 Yugoslavia's central bank refused to issue Yugoslavian dinars in Bosnia and Herzegovina. Commercial banks in the country include Privredna Banka Sarajevo (December 1989).

[34]INSURANCE

No recent information is available.

35 PUBLIC FINANCE

The breakup of the Yugoslav SFR and the ongoing civil war have severely disrupted the government's ability to account for revenues and expenditures.

36 TAXATION

Current information is unavailable due to civil unrest.

37 CUSTOMS AND DUTIES

Current information is unavailable due to civil unrest.

38 FOREIGN INVESTMENT

Private investment has plummeted because of the bitter interethnic war.

39 ECONOMIC DEVELOPMENT

Once the interethnic and interrepublic civil war is concluded, Bosnia and Herzegovina will likely require substantial foreign aid to rebuild the collapsed economy.

40 SOCIAL DEVELOPMENT

Bosnia's economy and social fabric have been devastated by the war. In spite of minimum wage guarantees, delays and partial payments are widespread. Serbia has imposed an embargo on food deliveries. Enforcement of sick leave and other benefit programs, as well as occupational health and safety measures, has been lax. By October 1993, over 800,000 Bosnian refugees had fled the country, while another 1.2 million were displaced within its borders. In 1993, the war inflicted rape and other forms of physical abuse on women, including the strip-searching of Muslim women in Mostar.

41 HEALTH

There have been over 200,000 war-related deaths. In 1992 alone, Bosnia suffered 120,000 war-related deaths. Figures for 1993 and 1994 were not available at the time of publishing in late 1994.

42 HOUSING

No recent information is available.

43 EDUCATION

Education at the elementary level is free and compulsory for eight years. At the secondary level, children have the option to take up general education (gymnasium), vocational, or technical. General secondary lasts for four years and qualifies the students for university education.

There are four main universities: the University of Banjaluka (founded in 1975); University of Mostar (founded in 1977); and University of Tuzla (founded in 1976). The fourth, University of Sarajevo (founded in 1949), is the oldest and offers social sciences, humanities, sciences, medicine, law, and engineering.

44 LIBRARIES AND MUSEUMS

Before the dissolution of the Yugoslav SFR, Sarajevo, as the capital, was an important center of cultural activity. Numerous historic sites have been damaged from the war.

45 MEDIA

Communications facilities in Sarajevo and other Bosnian cities have been nearly destroyed by the ongoing civil war. Radio-Television Sarajevo administers radio and television broadcasts. In 1991, Sarajevo had four radio and two television stations, all broadcasting in Serbo-Croatian.

In Sarajevo, the daily newspaper *Oslobodjenje* has managed to publish continuously throughout the siege of that city despite power and phone line outages, newsprint shortages, and direct attacks on its offices. Founded in 1943 as a Nazi resistance publication, *Oslobodjenje*, which is published in Serbo-Croatian, had a circulation of 69,368 in 1986. In 1993, two of its editors received international recognition from the *World Press Review*.

46 ORGANIZATIONS

The Chamber of Economy of Bosnia and Herzegovina promotes trade and commerce in world markets. There are 17 learned societies in Bosnia and Herzegovina. Research institutions in the country are concentrated in the areas of nuclear technology, meteorology, historical monument preservation, and language.

47 TOURISM, TRAVEL, AND RECREATION

The civil war has prevented the development of a tourist industry in Bosnia and Herzegovina. Sarajevo, the capital city, was the site of the 1984 Winter Olympics.

48 FAMOUS PERSONS

Dr. Alija Izetbegović has been the president of Bosnia and Herzegovina since December 1991. Haris Silajdžić was the prime minister in 1994. Dzemd Bijedic (1917–1977) was a leader of Yugoslavia from 1971 until 1977, when he was killed in a plane crash. The 1914 assassination of the Austrian Archduke Franz Ferdinand in Sarajevo led to World War I.

49 DEPENDENCIES

Bosnia and Herzegovina has no territories or colonies.

50 BIBLIOGRAPHY

Banac, Ovo. *The Nationality Question in Yugoslavia*. Ithaca, NY: Cornell University Press, 1984.

Borowiec, Andrew. *Yugoslavia Afer Tito*. New York: Praeger, 1977

Cataldi, Anna. *Letters from Sarajevo: Voices of a Besieged City*. Shaftesbury, Eng.: Element, 1994.

Donia, Robert J. *Islam under the Double Eagle: The Muslims of Bosnia and Herzegovina, 1878–1914*. New York: Columbia University Press, 1981.

Dunn, William N. & Josip Obradovic. *Workers' Self–Management and Organizational Power in Yugoslavia*. Pittsburgh: Univ. of Pittsburgh Press, 1978.

Filipović, Zlata. *Zlata's Diary: A Child's Life in Sarajevo*. New York: Viking, 1994.

Fine, John Van Antwerp. *The Bosnian Church: A New Interpretation*. New York: Columbia University Press, 1975.

Gapinski, James H., Borislav Skegko and Thomas W. Zuehlka. *Modeling the Economic Performance of Yugoslavia*. New York: Praeger, 1989.

Glenny, Michael. *The Fall of Yugoslavia: The Third Balkan War*. New York: Penguin, 1992.

Gutman, Roy. *A Witness to Genocide: The 1993 Pulitzer Prize-winning Dispatches on the "Ethnic Cleansing" of Bosnia*. New York: Macmillan, 1993.

Lockwood, William G. *European Moslems: Economy and Ethnicity in Western Bosnia*. New York: Academic Press, 1975.

Macesich, George, ed. *Essays on the Yugoslav Economic Model*. New York: Praeger, 1989.

Pinson, Mark (ed.) *The Muslims of Bosnia-Herzegovina: Their Historic Development from the Middle Ages to the Dissolution of Yugoslavia*. Cambridge, Mass.: Harvard University Press, 1994.

Shrenk, Martin et al. *Yugoslavia: Self Management Socialism and the Challenges of Development*. Baltimore: Johns Hopkins Univ. Press, 1979.

Sher, Gerson S. *Praxis: Marxism Criticism and Dissent in Socialist Yugoslavia.* Bloomington, Ind.: Indiana Univ. Press, 1977.

Sirc, Ljubo. *The Yugoslav Economy Under Self–Management.* New York: St. Martin's Press, 1979.

Sivrić, Ivo. *The Peasant Culture of Bosnia and Herzegovina.* Chicago: Franciscan Herald Press, 1982.

Stankovic, Slobodan. *The End of the Tito Era.* Stanford, Cal: Hoover Institution Press, 1981.

BULGARIA

Republic of Bulgaria
Republika Bulgaria

CAPITAL: Sofia (Sofiya).

FLAG: The flag is of white, green, and red horizontal stripes with the national seal in the upper left corner.

ANTHEM: *Bulgariya mila, zemya na geroi (Dear Bulgaria, Land of Heroes).*

MONETARY UNIT: The lev (Lv) of 100 stotinki has coins of 1, 2, 5, 10, 20, and 50 stotinki and 1 and 2 leva, and notes of 1, 2, 5, 10, 20, 50, and 100 leva. Lv1 = $1.209 (or $1 = Lv0.827).

WEIGHTS AND MEASURES: The metric system is the legal standard.

HOLIDAYS: New Year's Day, 1 January; Labor Days, 1–2 May; Education and Culture Day, 24 May; Christmas, 24–25 December.

TIME: 2 PM=noon GMT.

¹LOCATION, SIZE, AND EXTENT

Part of the Balkan Peninsula, Bulgaria has an area of 110,910 sq km (42,823 sq mi), and extends 330 km (205 mi) N–S and 520 km (323 mi) E–W. Comparatively, the area occupied by Bulgaria is slightly larger than the state of Tennessee. Bulgaria is bounded on the N by Romania, on the E by the Black Sea, on the SE by Turkey, on the S by Greece, and on the W by Macedonia and Serbia, with a total boundary length of 2,162 km (1,343 mi).

Bulgaria's capital city, Sofia, is located in the west central part of the country.

²TOPOGRAPHY

Bulgaria consists of a number of roughly parallel east-west zones. They are the Danubian tableland in the north, the Balkan Mountains (Stara Planina) in the center, and the Thracian Plain, drained by the Maritsa River, in the south. The Rhodope, Rila, and Pirin mountains lie in the southwestern part of the country. The average elevation is 480 m (1,575 ft), and the highest point, in the Rila Mountains, is the Musala, at 2,925 m (9,596 ft). The Danube (Dunav), Bulgaria's only navigable river, forms most of the northern boundary with Romania.

³CLIMATE

Bulgaria lies along the southern margins of the continental climate of Central and Eastern Europe. Regional climatic differences occur in the Danubian tableland, exposed to cold winter winds from the north, and the Thracian Plain, which has a modified Mediterranean climate and is protected by the Balkan Mountains against the northern frosts. January temperatures are between 0° and 2°C (32–36°F) in the lowlands but colder in the mountains; July temperatures average about 22° to 24°C (72–75°F). Precipitation is fairly regularly distributed throughout the year and amounts to an average of 64 cm (25 in).

⁴FLORA AND FAUNA

In the northeast lies the typical steppe grassland zone of the Dobrudja, merging into the wooded steppe of the Danubian tableland. Most trees in this area have been cut down to make room for cultivated land. The Balkan Mountains are covered by broadleaf forests at lower altitudes and by needle-leaf conifers at higher elevations. The vegetation of the Thracian Plain is a mixture of the middle-latitude forest of the north and Mediterranean flora. Clearing of forests has reduced the amount of wildlife, which includes bears, foxes, squirrels, elks, wildcats, and rodents of various types. Fish resources in the Black Sea are not extensive.

⁵ENVIRONMENT

Communist Party Decree No. 49 of 30 December 1982, dealing with problems of pollution and waste, provides for stiff penalties for automobile pollution; design and construction of a plant for recycling hard household waste (including paper and plastics) and coal dust into fuel briquettes; and limitation of industrial growth around Sofia. Bulgaria's air pollution problem results from the combined influence of industry, chemical production, and transportation. As of 1994, Bulgaria contributed 0.3% of the world's total gas emissions. Twenty-five percent of Bulgaria's forests have been significantly damaged by air-borne pollutants. A new forest-preservation law was passed in early 1983. Bulgaria's rivers and the Black Sea are also seriously affected by industrial and chemical pollutants. Four percent of the country's rural population does not have pure water. Industrial pollutants are also responsible for damage to 115 square miles of land in Bulgaria. Environmental protection responsibilities are vested in the State Council's Committee for Protection of Nature and Environment, in the Ministry of Forestry and Environment, and in the Scientific Center for Protection of Natural Environment and Water Resources. As of 1987, endangered species in Bulgaria included the Rosalia longhorn. In total, there are three mammals, 15 bird species, and one reptile that are endangered. Eighty-eight plant species in a total of 3,650 are also threatened as of 1994.

⁶POPULATION

According to the 1985 census, Bulgaria had 8,949,618 inhabitants, an increase of 2.5% over the 1975 census population of 8,727,771. About 64.8% of the population lived in towns. The population estimate in 1994 is 8,907,799. The projected population for the year 2000 is 8,897,000, assuming a crude birthrate of 13.5 per 1,000 population and a crude death rate of 12.2 during 1995–2000. The estimated average density in 1994 was about 80 persons per sq km (208 per sq mi). Sofia, the capital and principal city, had an estimated population of 1,141,142 in 1990. Other large cities (with their estimated 1990 populations) were Plovdiv,

379,083; Varna, 314,913; Burgas, 204,914; Ruse, 192,365; and Stara Zagora, 164,553.

7 MIGRATION

Emigration between 1948 and 1951 consisted mainly of Jews going to Israel and Turks going to Turkey. A high of 99,477 (of whom 98,341 were Turks) was reached in 1951. Most of the emigrants since the 1950s have been Turks bound for Turkey or other Balkan countries. A total of 313,894 emigrated to Turkey in 1989 because of government persecution. Some were forcibly expelled. More than 100,000 had returned to Bulgaria by February 1990. Meanwhile, about 150,000 ethnic Bulgarians also emigrated. In 1991 about 3 million Bulgarians were living abroad, including 1,200,000 in the former Yugoslavia, 800,000 in other Balkan countries, and 500,000 in the former USSR.

8 ETHNIC GROUPS

In the mid-1990s, Bulgarians accounted for an estimated 80–85% of the total population. The Turks, who number about 900,000–1,250,000 (10–14%) of the total, are settled mainly in the southern Dobrudja and in the eastern Rhodope Mountains. Between December 1984 and March 1985, the government compelled ethnic Turks and Pomaks (Bulgarian Muslims) to abandon their Turkish and Muslim names and to adopt Bulgarian and Christian ones. This action was reversed in 1990. The number of Gypsies is estimated at 450,000–700,000 and the number of Pomaks, 150,000–300,000. Macedonians live mainly in the Pirin region of southwestern Bulgaria. Romanian-speaking Vlachs live in the towns and countryside of northwestern Bulgaria. Greek-speaking Karakatchans are nomadic mountain shepherds of Romanian origin. The Gagauzi of northeastern Bulgaria are a Turkish-speaking group of Christian Orthodox religion. Bulgaria's cities have small minorities of Russians, Jews, Armenians, Tatars, and Greeks.

9 LANGUAGES

Bulgarian is classified as a Slavic language of the southern group, which also includes Macedonian, Serbo-Croatian, and Slovenian. Old Bulgarian, also known as Old Church Slavonic, was the first Slavic language fixed in writing (9th century). For this purpose, two Bulgarian monks, Cyril and Methodius, created a new alphabet, based partly on the Greek, that became known as the Cyrillic alphabet. Both the grammar and the vocabulary of modern Bulgarian show Turkish, Greek, Romanian, and Albanian influences.

In November 1991, the government made Turkish an optional subject four times weekly in schools in predominantly Turkish regions.

10 RELIGIONS

According to recent estimates, more than 88% of the population belongs at least nominally to the Eastern Orthodox Church, now considered the traditional religion of the state. There are also an estimated 9–13% Muslims and 3,000 Jews. After seizing power in 1946, the Communist regime eliminated its opponents from among the clergy. The government, whose aim was eventually to establish an atheistic society, sought during the ensuing period to replace all religious rites and rituals with civil ceremonies. The new constitution of 1991, however, guarantees freedom of religion to all. Diplomatic relations with the Vatican had already been established in 1990. The current government's Directorate of Religious Affairs oversees official relations with religious organizations.

11 TRANSPORTATION

Railroads are still the basic means of freight transportation in Bulgaria. Of the 4,294 km (2,668 mi) of railroad lines in use in 1991, about 94% were standard gauge. A cooperation agreement between Bulgaria and Greece was signed in February 1991, possibly allowing the restoration of the Thessaloniki-Sofia railway link.

In 1991, about 1,450,000 registered vehicles traveled on about 33,535 km (20,839 mi) of hard-surfaced roads, including 242 km (150 mi) of highways. Road transportation has grown steadily in recent years; a new 1,100 km (680-mi) highway network linking Sofia, the Black Sea coast, and Turkey is under construction.

Water transportation is also significant. At the end of 1991, Bulgaria's maritime fleet totaled 1.2 million GRT, as compared with 97,800 GRT in 1961. The major seaports are Burgas and Varna; principal river ports are Ruse, Lom, and Vidin.

Sofia's Vrazhdebna Airport is the major air center, but there are also international airports at Varna and Burgas, as well as five domestic airports. Initially a joint Soviet-Bulgarian concern, Bulgarian Airlines (BALKAN) passed into Bulgarian hands in 1954. Civilian airlines in Bulgaria performed 1,171 million passenger-kilometers (728 million passenger-miles) of service in 1992.

12 HISTORY

The Bulgarians have inhabited their present homeland for 13 centuries. They represent a merger of Bulgar invaders and local Slavic tribes which occurred in the 7th century. From the Slavs, who had migrated to the Balkans from the area north of the Carpathian Mountains in the 6th century, the Bulgarians received their language and cultural roots. From the Bulgars, a Central Asian Turkic tribe that had crossed the Danube in 679 to settle permanently in Bulgarian territory, the Bulgarians received their name and initial political framework.

The early Bulgarian state, which had adopted Christianity in 865, asserted itself against the Byzantine Empire and reached its greatest territorial extent under Simeon I (r.893–927), but by 1018 it had again fallen under Byzantine dominance. Bulgaria rose again as a major Balkan power in the 12th and 13th centuries, especially under Ivan Asen II (r.1218–41), who had his capital at Turnovo. By the end of the 14th century, Bulgaria was overrun by the Ottoman Turks, who ruled the country until 1878.

Through Russian pressure, the Treaty of San Stefano (3 March 1878) provided for the virtual independence of Bulgaria. This was somewhat curtailed by the Congress of Berlin (June–July 1878), which gave northern Bulgaria the status of an independent principality under Turkish suzerainty, with its capital at Sofia. Southern Bulgaria (then known as Eastern Rumelia) remained under Turkish rule as an autonomous province. A military coup in 1885 annexed Eastern Rumelia to Bulgaria. Stefan Stambolov, premier from 1887 to 1894, consolidated the country's administration and economy. In 1908, Bulgaria declared itself a kingdom completely independent of Turkey, and the ruling Bulgarian prince, Ferdinand of Saxe-Coburg-Gotha, assumed the title of tsar. Bulgaria joined the anti-Turkish coalition (consisting of Greece, Montenegro, and Serbia) in the First Balkan War (October 1912–May 1913), gaining its long-desired outlet to the Aegean Sea. But as a result of a dispute over Macedonia, Bulgaria became pitted against Greece, Romania, Serbia, and Turkey in the Second Balkan War (June–July 1913) and was defeated. The Treaty of Bucharest (10 August 1913) deprived Bulgaria of southern Dobrudja and a large part of Macedonia. Having sided with the Central Powers in World War I, Bulgaria also lost its outlet to the Aegean Sea through the Treaty of Neuilly (27 November 1919). By this time, Ferdinand had abdicated in favor of his son, Boris III, who ruled Bulgaria until his death in 1943. After an early period of stability and initial progressive reform under the leadership of Premier Alexander Stamboliski (assassinated 1923), growing political rivalries led to the introduction of authoritarian institutions; King Boris established a military government in 1934 and then personally assumed dictatorial powers in 1935.

When World War II broke out, Bulgaria moved toward an alliance with Germany in the hope of recovering lost territories. In

BULGARIA

0   25   50 Miles

0   25   50 Kilometers

ROMANIA

Bucharest

Zaječar
Vidin
Craiova
Silistra
Constanța

Dunărea

Dunav
Lom
Kozloduy
Alexandria
Ruse
Razgrad
Dobrich

Beleïe

Ogosta
Mikhaylovgrad
Pleven
Yantra
Shumen
Varna

Iskur
Vratsa
Veliko
Tûrnovo
Tùrgovishte

SERBIA

BALKAN
Sofia
Osum
Gabrovo
MOUNTAINS
Kamchiya
*Black
Sea*

Pernik
Stryama
Kazanlŭk
Sliven

Priboj
Panagyurishte
Tundzha
Burgas

Musala
9,596 ft.
2925 m.
Stara
Zagora
Yambol

Pazardzhik
Plovdiv
Maritsa
Elkhovo

Blagoevgrad
Asenovgrad

RHODOPE
Svilengrad

MACEDONIA
Struma
Mesta
Smolyan
Arda
Kŭrdzhali
TURKEY

Strumica
Rudozem
Madan
MTS.

GREECE

Alexandroupolis

*Aegean
Sea*

Thessaloníki

Bulgaria

LOCATION: 41°14′ to 44°13′N; 22°22′ to 28°37′E. **BOUNDARY LENGTHS:** Romania, 609 km (378 mi); Black Sea, 378 km (235 mi); Turkey, 259 km (161 mi); Greece, 493 km (306 mi); Yugoslavia, 506 km (315 mi). **TERRITORIAL SEA LIMIT:** 12 mi.

1940, Romania was forced to return southern Dobrudja, and, during the war, Bulgaria occupied Macedonia and western Thrace on the Aegean Sea. In September 1944, Soviet troops crossed the Danube and entered the country. At that time, the Bulgarian government severed relations with Germany and intended to sign an armistice with the Western Allies, but Moscow declared war on Bulgaria. A coalition government—the Fatherland Front (Otechestven Front)—was established, which, with the assistance of the Soviet army, came under the domination of the Communist Party. Subsequently, anti-Communist political elements were purged.

Elections for a national government, held in November 1945, were protested by the Western powers. The following September, a plebiscite replaced the monarchy with the People's Republic of Bulgaria. The 1947 peace treaty formally ending Bulgaria's role in World War II allowed the nation to keep southern Dobrudja and limited the size of its armed forces, but the latter provision was

later violated. A new constitution in 1947 instituted the nationalization of industry, banking, and public utilities and the collectivization of agriculture, each program following the Soviet pattern. Centralized planning was introduced for the development of the national economy through a series of five-year plans that from the outset stressed the expansion of heavy industry. Subsequently, Bulgaria joined the Warsaw Pact and CMEA, thus placing itself firmly within the Soviet bloc.

After the Soviet-Yugoslav rift of 1948, a large-scale purge was carried out inside the Communist ranks to expel "nationalist" elements led by Traicho Kostov, who was executed in December 1949. Thereafter, the Bulgarian government remained unquestionably loyal to Moscow and was unaffected politically or ideologically by the upheavals in Poland and Hungary in 1956 or the events that precipitated the Soviet invasion of Czechoslovakia in 1968. In the 1970s, Bulgaria sought to improve relations with neighboring Greece. Relations with

Yugoslavia, however, remained strained because of Bulgaria's historic claims on Macedonia.

Todor Zhivkov, first secretary of the Communist Party since 1954 and president since 1971, was by the mid-1980s one of the longest-ruling Communist leaders in the world. A cultural "thaw" took place in the late 1970s, under the leadership of Zhivkov's daughter, Lyudmila Zhivkova, who was closely involved in organizing the commemoration of what was claimed to be the 1,300th anniversary of the foundation of the Bulgarian state; she died in December 1981, two months before the celebration. In late 1982 and 1983, Bulgaria became a center of international attention because of allegations by Italian investigators that Bulgarian agents were involved in the attempted assassination of Pope John Paul II at the Vatican on 13 May 1981. In March 1986, however, an Italian court ruled that the evidence was insufficient to prove that Bulgaria had ordered or was involved in the assassination attempt. The 1984–85 campaign of forcible assimilation of ethnic Turks allegedly resulted in more than 1,000 deaths.

A program of far-reaching political and economic changes was announced in July 1987, including an administrative overhaul that was expected to reduce the number of Communist Party functionaries by as much as two-thirds, the introduction of self-management for individual enterprises, and liberalization of rules for joint ventures with foreign investors.

The radical changes which Mikhail Gorbachev was introducing in the Soviet Union, long Bulgaria's traditional "elder brother," encouraged reformist elements within the Bulgarian Communist Party, who were growing increasingly restive under Zhivkov. The long-time ruler, however, resisted attempts to change, and moved into a pattern of direct confrontation with Petar Mladenov, his Foreign Minister. Mladenov, who had close ties to Gorbachev, wanted to change Bulgaria's image, but Zhivkov's intensifying efforts to "assimilate" the country's ethnic Turks or, if that failed, to force them to emigrate, only reinforced international antipathy. Finally, in November 1989, Mladenov and other opposition figures were able to take advantage of an international environmental conference convened in Sofia to press for Zhivkov's resignation. When Defense Minister Dobri Dzhurov agreed to support Mladenov, Zhivkov was forced to resign.

Mladenov had intended to reform the Communist Party, not remove it from power, but the tide of popular sentiment ran against him. Coordinated by an umbrella opposition group called the Union for Democratic Reform, huge pro-democracy rallies gathered in the capital, demanding an end to the Communist monopoly on power, and calling for elections.

The Communists attempted to meet these demands by increments, first relinquishing their constitutional exclusivity, then ending Zhivkov's program of forced assimilation, and finally changing its name to Bulgarian Socialist Party. However, the opposition, now known as the Union of Democratic Forces (UDF), continued to insist on new elections, which were held in June 1991.

In something of a surprise, the Socialists received nearly 53% of the vote, while the UDF got only about a third; the rest of the votes went to the Movement for Rights and Freedoms, which represents the interests of the country's one million Turks. However, because the Socialists' votes came almost entirely from the countryside, while those of the UDF came from the city, the UDF decided to remain in opposition, and not enter any coalition. The Socialists' ability to form a government was further weakened by popular hostility to Mladenov, who was forced to resign about a month after the election.

That opened the way for the National Assembly to appoint Zhelyu Zhelev president. Leader of the UDF, Zhelev had spent 17 years under house arrest. The Socialists continued to have problems forming a government, however. Their first attempt, led by Prime Minister Andrei Lukanov, a Mladenov ally, collapsed after a few months; in December 1990 the replacement government of Dimitar Popov, an unaffiliated technocrat, outlined an ambitious program of economic reform.

However, because the Communists remained generally in charge of the government, very little reform was realized, and Bulgaria's economy continued to decline. In addition, a great deal of effort was devoted to the attempt to prosecute Zhivkov and his prominent cronies for malfeasance, incompetence, and other failings. Zhivkov fought back vigorously, exposing the sins of former colleagues who had remained in power. Although convictions were eventually obtained (in 1992, with additional charges brought in 1993), the exercise served to undermine public sympathy for the Socialists.

The National Assembly passed a new constitution in July 1991, making Bulgaria the first of the Eastern Bloc countries to adopt a new basic law. Among other things, this document called for new parliamentary elections, to be held in October 1991; another provision reduced the number of seats in the Assembly from 400 to 240, guaranteeing a wide-open election.

A form of proportional list voting was used, but a threshold of 4% to receive seats was set, in order to eliminate fringe parties. As a result, the same three parties were represented, although now in different proportions. The UDF received 34%, the Socialists 33%, and the MRF got 8%. The UDF adamantly refused to cooperate with the former Communists, instead taking as their coalition partners the Turks, who exacted a high price for their agreement.

Bulgaria's first non-Communist government since World War II was led by Filip Dimitrov, of the UDF; however, most of his ministers were chosen for technical expertise, rather than party affiliation. Dimitrov's cabinet, 60% were drawn from outside the National Assembly. Dimitrov undertook an ambitious program of economic and political transformation, although he was somewhat hampered by the necessity to obtain cooperation of the Socialists for any measures requiring constitutional changes, since that need a two-thirds majority vote of the Assembly.

Although it basically continued to perform poorly, the economy showed enough change to give Zhelev 45%, the greatest part of the popular vote, when direct presidential elections were held, in January 1992. However, his Socialist opponent, Velko Vulkanov, received 30%, indicating how closely the electorate is divided.

Bulgaria's economy, left in poor condition by Zhivkov, has continued to deteriorate. The consequent increased pressure on the government has exposed strains within the ruling UDF. In late 1992 the Dimitrov government was replaced by a minority coalition of the Socialists and the MRF, with some defecting UDF deputies, led by Lyuben Berov. Widely seen only as a caretaker prime minister meant only to take the country up to new elections, Berov has defied predictions, remaining in power for more than 15 months; this makes his the longest-lived government of the new era, a fact which Berov's serious health problems make even more remarkable.

However, surviving in power has been about the limit of the Berov government's achievments. The UDF majority in the Assembly is unrelenting in its hostility to Berov, whom it accuses of trying to "re-communize" Bulgaria. The UDF has submitted as many as six votes of no confidence in a single year; Berov won the most recent, in May 1994, by only four votes. In April 1994, President Zhelev announced that he no longer had confidence in Berov, but because the constitution denies him the power to dissolve the government, Berov has been able to keep his cabinet in position, dependent upon the support of the minority Socialists and MRF. This increasing political deadlock and the continued deterioration of Bulgaria's economy, however, make it seem increasingly likely that new elections will be called, probably in late 1994 or early 1995.

The outcome of such an election is difficult to predict. Hostility to the UDF is now high, with the Socialists managing to appear to be the more professional and capable party. The key to electoral success will be economic. Bulgaria's foreign debt is about $13 billion, and continues to grow, while the country has suffered heavily—disproportionately so, some argue—from the international sanctions against the former Yugoslavia.

13GOVERNMENT

The Constitution of July 1991 provides for a presidential-parliamentary form of republican government, in which no party enjoys constitutional primacy. No restrictions are made on party orientations, but the constitution does forbid ethnically exclusive parties, a clause which led to Bulgaria's first constitutional crisis. Importantly, the document provides clear-cut distinctions among the legislative, executive, and judicial branches of government.

The president, who is chief of state, is popularly elected. Among his duties is the naming of the prime minister, who must be confirmed by the National Assembly. It is generally agreed that the Constitution is ambiguous on the balance of power between the president and the Parliament, which has tended to exaggerate the gridlock of current politics; the constitutional weakness of the presidency, which, for example, allows only the Assembly to call for new elections, has also played a role. Nevertheless, the emerging tradition is that the president sets the overall direction of policy, while the prime minister and his cabinet, presently 14 people, are responsible for day-to-day implementation.

The legislative branch of government is the National Assembly, with 240 seats. Deputies are elected on a proportional voting basis, in which parties must receive at least 4% of the total national vote in order to receive seats. The legislature must approve the government, which it was generally assumed would be drawn from among its ranks. In practice, however, there has been a tendency toward "professional" governments, composed largely of unaffiliated technocrats. In the 1992 elections, the Union of Democratic Forces took 110 seats, the Bulgarian Socialist Party took 106 seats, and the Movement for Rights and Freedoms took 24 seats, giving this smallest party a disproportionate voice as the necessary coalition partner.

That fact, combined with the fact that the MRF is primarily made up of Bulgarian Turks, led a group of deputies to bring the charge in April 1992 that the MRF was "ethnic," and therefore unconstitutional. The issue was referred to the newly formed 11-member Constitutional Court. After some deliberation the Court demonstrated the judicial independence which has become one of the true successes of the new constitution, rejecting the claim by a vote of 6 to 5. In general the judiciary has been fairly successfully purged of Zhivkov-era judges, and public confidence in the courts is relatively high, especially by the standards of the region.

14POLITICAL PARTIES

Bulgaria did not develop the welter of political parties which most of the other post-Communist societies have enjoyed—or suffered. The fact that Bulgaria's "velvet revolution" was a two-stage affair, the first part of which was an internal coup within the Communist party, left the communists, particularly the reformist wing, with strong public support. Renamed the Bulgarian Socialist Party (BSP) in 1990, the party is generally committed to a program of economic reform and democratization, although there is an internal split between those pushing for fast reform and those wishing to brake it, or prevent it altogether. The Socialists did surprisingly well in the 1991 elections, gaining 53% of the vote. By 1992 their support had dropped to 33%, making them a minority party by four parliamentary seats. Although originally mostly rural in appeal, the Socialists have increasingly gained back urban voters disenchanted by the government's failure to deliver on promises, and by the generally chaotic parliamentary behavior of the Socialists' opponents. The Socialists prefer to delay the next elections until 1995, giving them the maximum time to consolidate their gains in popularity; whenever elections are held though, it is expected that the Socialists will do well.

The largest vote-getter in 1992 was the Union of Democratic Forces (UDF), an umbrella of opposition forces. Although President Zhelev was among this party's founders, the party has turned against him since it found itself maneuvered into opposition by the minority coalition of Socialists and Movement for Rights and Freedom (MRF). Since formation of the Berov government, the UDF has concentrated its efforts on trying to bring the government down, which has further crippled the ability of the Assembly to enact legislation. At the same time, though, tensions have appeared within the UDF itself; in July 1994, the membership rolls of the Democratic Party, the largest constituent of the UDF, were frozen, to prevent wholesale defection or a sundering of the umbrella organization.

As the stand-off between the Socialists and the UDF continues, there have been repeated efforts to unite smaller groups and defectors into a strong centrist party between the two. The most promising bid was that of the New Union for Democracy; however, in May 1994, the movement split into rival factions. Only the Bulgarian Agrarian National Union has been successful in linking together smaller parties, but the aggregate of this new party remains small, at least for the time being.

The third party, the MRF, primarily represents the interests of Bulgaria's large Turkish minority (about 11% of the population), which was subjected to savage, even bloody repression, during the Zhivkov years, and which still excites much nationalist antipathy among many Bulgarians.

A small but persistent part of that antipathy is organized in formal parties. Perhaps the largest is the Fatherland Party of Labor, a minor ally of the BSP, which had a strongly nationalist orientation. However, UDF concern that the Fatherland Party might receive a portfolio in the minority coalition government was sufficient to force the BSP to disavow any such possibility.

The Bulgarian National Radical Party, which got just over one percent of the vote in 1991, addresses Bulgarian irredentist populations in Romania and Macedonia, as well as seeks to rid Bulgaria proper of Turks. The party leader has signed a pact of cooperation with Russian ultra-nationalist Vladimir Zhirinovsky. Another smaller party is the Defense of National Interests, which is particularly strong in areas with mixed Bulgarian and Turkish populations; also openly racist is the Revival Movement, led by Father Georgi Gelemenov, who makes no secret of his admiration for Nazi ideology. In practice, however, support for the ultra-nationalist and xenophobic parties seems to be limited.

15LOCAL GOVERNMENT

Bulgaria is divided into eight counties, plus the city of Sofia. Local administrations are appointed by the central government, to whom they are responsible. However, much of the country is rural, with a strong peasant culture. In Zhivkov's day as much as 13% of the country's agriculture remained in private hands, which the Zhelev government is attempting to increase to 20% or more. Bulgaria has a long tradition of anti-capitalist peasant radicalism, which leaves the rural districts deeply hostile and resistant to many of the economic changes which the government is attempting to introduce. As elsewhere in the former Eastern Bloc, the increased turmoil of political life in the country's capital has meant that attention to local government has diminished, permitting a kind of organic and anarchic transformation to proceed.

[16]JUDICIAL SYSTEM

Under the 1971 constitution, members of the Supreme Court are elected by, and subordinate to, the National Assembly. A new law passed by the Assembly in November 1982 stipulated that all other judges would be similarly chosen; formerly, they were directly elected by the voting population. The Supreme Court is a court of original as well as appellate jurisdiction and is organized into criminal, civil, and military divisions; its professional and lay judges serve five-year terms. Below the Supreme Court there were, in 1985, 28 provincial courts and 105 regional courts. A law of 2 June 1961 provided for the already existing "comrades" courts to be established at all enterprises of 50 or more employees to deal with violations of labor discipline, peace, and property; sentences vary and cannot be appealed.

The chief prosecutor, elected by the National Assembly for a term of five years, exercises control over observance of the law by all officials and ordinary citizens. He appoints and discharges prosecutors on the lower levels.

The Bulgarian penal code sets a maximum 20-year term of imprisonment for all crimes except murder and certain crimes against the state, which may carry the death sentence. A new code passed in October 1974 expanded the power of the courts in matters of domestic security and brought the administration of Bulgarian law in closer alignment with Soviet procedures.

A Constitutional Court is responsible for judicial review of legislation and for resolving issues of competency of the other branches of government as well as impeachments and election law. A Supreme Court of Cassation called for by the constitution has not yet been established. Military courts handle cases involving military personnel and national security issues. The judiciary is independent of the legislative and executive branches.

[17]ARMED FORCES

The 1947 peace treaty limited the total strength of the Bulgarian armed forces to 65,000 men, with military training to be confined to personnel in these services. By 1993, however, the strength of the armed forces, consisting of ground, naval, and air elements, was estimated at 107,000 men, including 70,000 conscripts. The army numbered 75,000, the navy 10,000, and the air force 22,000, with some 259 combat aircraft. Organization and training follow former Warsaw Pact practices and doctrine.

Male citizens are subject to compulsory military service at the age of 19, but some may serve with a construction labor force instead. Length of service is two years in the army and air force, and three years in the navy.

A force of Frontier Guards (12,000 in 1993) is under the Ministry of Interior. Total reserve forces are estimated at 472,500. Defense expenditures are estimated at 4.4% of GDP. Bulgaria exports armaments valued at over $70 million a year, a sharp drop in what had been a $500-million enterprise.

[18]INTERNATIONAL COOPERATION

Bulgaria joined the UN on 14 December 1955 and participates in the ECE and all the nonregional specialized agencies except the IBRD, IDA, IFAD, IFC, and IMF. It belongs to the CMEA and WTO, and is a signatory of the Law of the Sea. Since the early 1970s, the Bulgarian government has tried to improve relations with other Balkan states. In 1971, a consular agreement was reached with Turkey. Bulgaria signed consular and cultural agreements with Greece in 1973, and a declaration of friendship and cooperation in 1986. A Bulgaro-Yugoslav Economic Chamber was set up in 1982 to promote mutual trade.

[19]ECONOMY

Before World War II, Bulgaria was an agricultural country, consisting mainly of small peasant farms; farming provided a livelihood for about 80% of the population. After the war, the Communist regime initiated an industrialization program. By 1947, a sizable portion of the economy was nationalized, and collectivization of agriculture followed during the 1950s. Until 1990, the country had a centrally planned economy, along Soviet lines, and its sequence of five-year economic plans, beginning in 1949, has emphasized industrial production. In 1956, according to official Bulgarian statistics, industry contributed 36.5% of national income, and agriculture and forestry, 32.9%; in 1992, the respective contributions were 42.5% and 12%.

Although Bulgaria has brown coal and lignite, iron ore, copper lead, zinc, and manganese, it lacks other important natural resources and must export in order to pay for needed commodities. Because it relied on the USSR and other CMEA countries for essential imports and as the major market for its exports, and lacks foreign exchange, the Bulgarian economy was greatly influenced by the breakup of the Soviet bloc and the switch to hard-currency foreign trade. In the 1970s, the economic growth rate was quite high (6.8% annually), but the pace of growth slowed in the 1980s, mainly because of energy shortages. The average annual growth rate was only 2% in that decade. With the disintegration of Soviet-bloc trade and payments arrangements, GDP declined by about 10% in 1990, 13% in 1991, 8% in 1992, and an estimated 4% in 1993. Meanwhile, Bulgaria began an economic reform program supported by the IBRD and IMF. But the economy remained largely state controlled. The private sector accounted for only about 20% of GDP in 1993, lowest in Eastern Europe. The unemployment rate was 16% in 1993; the inflation rate was 73%.

[20]INCOME

In 1992, the GNP was $11,906 million at current prices, or $1,330 per capita. For the period 1985–92 the average inflation rate was 30.7%, resulting in a real growth rate in per capita GNP of –3.6%.

In 1992 the GDP was $10,848 million in current US dollars. It is estimated that in 1991 agriculture, hunting, forestry, and fishing contributed 15% to GDP; manufacturing, 43%; construction, 5%; wholesale and retail trade, 8%; transport, storage, and communication, 8%; and other sources, 21%.

[21]LABOR

In 1992, total employment amounted to 3,112,900. Of this total, 40.2% was employed in industry and construction (45.5% in 1985); 18% in agriculture and forestry (20.9% in 1985); 10.6% in trade (8.4% in 1985); 7.8% in transport and communications (6.6% in 1985); and 23.5% in social, cultural, health, and other services (18.5% in 1985). Women represent about half of all agricultural workers outside the collective farms, where their participation is even greater, and nearly half the industrial labor force.

The 1991 constitution guarantees the right of all to form or join trade unions of their own choosing. Bulgaria has two large trade union confederations, the Confederation of Independent Trade Unions of Bulgaria (KNSB), and Podkrepa. The KNSB is the successor to the former Communist party, but now claims independence from the BSP. Podkrepa, formed in 1989, was one of the earliest opposition forces but, as of 1992, was no longer a member of the ruling UDF coalition. A new labor code passed in December 1992 recognizes the right to strike when other means of conflict resolution have been exhausted.

The average monthly earnings were Lv2,123 in 1992. The law establishes a standard workweek of 42.5 hours. The trilateral commission sets the minimum wage, although most of the population fell below the minimum income in 1991 due to a drop in real wages.

[22]AGRICULTURE

In 1991, the total agricultural land area covered 6,161,000 hectares (15,224,000 acres), of which 4,162,000 hectares

(10,284,000 acres) were fields and 1,999,000 hectares (4,940,000 acres) were meadows and pastures. The agricultural growth rate was –3.5% for 1980–85, –0.6% for 1985–90, and was –7.7% for 1992. That year agriculture (including fishing and forestry) made up 18% of employment.

Collectivized agriculture became the norm under the Communist government after 1958. In March 1991, the government adopted a land law which restored ownership rights to former owners of expropriated land. These owners were to receive 20–30 hectares (49–74 acres) each of land approximating the type and location of the former holdings, regardless of whether or not the owner cultivates that land. After February 1991, full price liberalization for producers and consumers was to occur. However, as of August 1993, the agricultural sector was still shrinking due to the lack of progress in the implementation of privatization and property restitution.

The principal grain-growing areas are the Danube tableland and southern Dobrudja. The following table shows the production of major crops (in thousands of tons):

	ANNUAL 1990	AVERAGE 1992
Wheat	5,292	3,270
Corn	1,221	2,300
Barley	1,387	1,100
Sunflower seeds	389	470
Tobacco	77	90
Soybeans	15	16

Bulgaria is a major supplier of grapes, apples, and tomatoes to Europe and the former Soviet Union. Potatoes and paprika are also important crops.

Machinery available to agriculture has increased significantly. Tractors rose from 25,800 units in 1960 to 53,800 units in 1985, before falling to 51,171 in 1991; combines increased from 7,000 to 16,000 in 1985, but by 1991 numbered only 8,000 in use. About 30% of the cultivated area is irrigated.

[23] ANIMAL HUSBANDRY
Meadows and pastures make up about 18% of the total land area. Bulgaria had 6.7 million sheep, 21 million fowl, 3 million hogs, 329,000 donkeys, and 113,000 horses in 1992. Meat production (in carcass weight) in 1992 amounted to 614,000 tons. In the same year, the country produced 1,550,000 tons of milk and 88,300 tons of eggs.

[24] FISHING
Fishing resources in the Black Sea are less than abundant. Before 1960, the annual catch was slightly above 5,000 tons. Fishing output reached a high of 167,100 tons in 1976, then fell to 115,607 tons in 1982. In 1991, the total catch was 49,915 tons. Whiting account for about 40% of the catch. Fishing vessels are based at the ports of Varna and Burgas, where the government built canning and processing plants.

[25] FORESTRY
Forests cover over 35% of Bulgaria's territory, with about 24% coniferous and 76% deciduous. The principal lumbering areas are the Rila and western Rhodope Mountains in the southwest and the northern slopes of the Balkan Mountains in the center. In 1991, Bulgaria produced 3.6 million cu m of timber.

Intensive exploitation and neglect before and during World War II and even more intensive exploitation since the war have contributed to the deterioration of the forests. The government has given considerable attention to reforestation. Between 1945 and 1965, 860,000 hectares (2,125,000 acres) were reforested; the 20-year plan (1961–80) called for the planting of 1.4 million hectares (3.5 million acres). During the 1980s, annual reforestation averaged 50,000 hectares (123,500 acres).

[26] MINING
Coal is the most important mineral fuel, but of the 28.1 billion tons produced in 1991, lignite accounted for 89% and brown coal for 10.7%.

The principal metallic ores are copper, iron, lead, and zinc. Most of the copper deposits are within a 30 mile wide swatch from Burgas in the east to the former Yugoslavia in the west. In 1991, more than 90% of total copper ore production (6 million tons) came from the three mining complexes of Elatzite, Medet, and Assarel, located between Sofia and Panagyurishte. That year, more than 80% of total iron ore production (1 million tons) came from the open pit mine at Kremikovtsi. Lead and zinc are mined chiefly in the eastern Rhodope Mountains at Madan and Rudozem and are smelted at nearby Kurdzhali and Asenovgrad. Other minerals mined are manganese (45,000 tons in 1991), uranium, and gold.

[27] ENERGY AND POWER
In the 1980s, Bulgaria produced only about 35% of its energy needs. Of the 38,917 million kwh produced in 1991, 36,476 million kwh were produced by thermal stations (including 13,184 million kwh by nuclear power plants) and 2,441 million kwh by hydroelectric plants. Lignite and brown coal are major sources (98%) for thermal power plants, which are located primarily in the coal-mining areas, including the Maritsa East Basin. The Maritsa East thermoelectric station has a capacity of about 650,000 kw.

In 1991, Bulgaria had a net installed capacity of 11,025,000 kw. In September 1974, Bulgaria's first nuclear power station—with a 440-Mw reactor—opened at Kozloduy in the northwest. A second reactor was added in 1975, and a third and fourth in 1981 and 1982. By 1991, nuclear plants supplied about 40% of Bulgaria's power. Continuous problems with the two oldest reactors contributed to the decline of the country's overall electrical production; the reactors were shut down as of 1991. Work on the second nuclear power plant in Beleňe has reportedly ceased.

Petroleum was discovered in the early 1950s in southern Dobruja (along the Black Sea), and in 1968 about 475,000 tons were produced; output subsequently declined to a low of 117,000 tons in 1976 and then rose to an estimated 1,000,000 tons in 1987, before falling to 500,000 tons in 1991. Petroleum processing began in 1963. In September 1974, a Soviet-Bulgarian natural gas pipeline was opened with an annual carrying capacity of 5 million cu m. In 1991, Libya doubled its crude oil deliveries to Bulgaria to 160,000 tons per month, in order to offset declining exports from the former USSR.

[28] INDUSTRY
Before World War II, Bulgarian industry, construction, mining, and handicrafts contributed only 17% to the net national income and accounted for only 8% of employment. Handicrafts in 1939 contributed almost half the net industrial output, followed by textiles and food processing. In the postwar period, the Communist regime nationalized industry and, through economic planning, emphasized a heavy industrialization program that resulted in a substantial increase in the metalworking and chemical industries. Between 1950 and 1960, the annual rate of growth of output in industry (including mining and power production) was 14.8%, according to the official index of gross output. Official statistics indicate that industrial output grew by 1100% between 1956 and 1980, with the production of capital goods increasing by 1500% and the production of consumer goods by 658%. Industrial output increased by 9.1% annually during 1971–75, 6% during 1976–80, 6.8% during 1980–85, and 2.7% during 1985–90. It fell 12.5% in 1990, 18.6% in 1991, and 11% in 1992. Ferrous metallurgy was given special emphasis in the 1960s, machine-building and

chemicals in the 1970s and early 1980s, and high technology in the mid-1980s.

The following table shows the output of main industrial products (in tons, except where noted):

	1985	1992
Cement	5,200,000	2,132,000
Crude steel	2,926,000	1,551,000
Pig iron and ferroalloys	1,754,000	853,000
Sulfuric acid	810,000	404,208
Canned vegetables and fruit	626,000	102,148
Refined sugar	174,300	97,596
Washing machines (units)	155,900	68,604
Television sets (units)	110,600	61,380

29 SCIENCE AND TECHNOLOGY

In 1993, Bulgaria had 25 scientific and technological learned societies and 66 scientific research institutes. There were 62,247 technicians, engineers, and scientists in 1987. The Bulgarian Academy of Sciences, founded in 1869, is the main research organization. The Academy of Medicine, founded in 1972, has five higher medical institutes. Expenditures on research and development in 1989 amounted to Lv1 billion. A large-scale program of scientific and technological cooperation of CMEA countries was adopted at the end of 1985.

Bulgaria has 14 universities and colleges offering degrees in basic and applied sciences.

30 DOMESTIC TRADE

Marketing and distribution, including price fixing, were state controlled before 1990. Trade was administered on the lower levels by province party committees and people's councils. Province trade enterprises were the distribution agencies for both urban and rural areas. There are general and specialty shops; self-service shopping is growing steadily. In 1992, retail trade turnover in state and cooperative trade came to Lv43,346.5 million. In 1993, private outlets accounted for 57% of total output.

Newspapers and magazines are the important means of advertising to the population at large. Radio advertisements are permitted for half an hour each day.

Offices are open from 8:30 AM to 12:30 PM and from 1:30 to 5:30 PM, Monday through Friday. Normal banking hours are 8 AM to 12 noon, Monday-Friday, and 8 to 11 AM on Saturday.

31 FOREIGN TRADE

Foreign trade was a state monopoly under the Ministry of Foreign Trade until 1990. Before World War II, 90% of exports consisted of agricultural products, primarily foodstuffs; machinery, finished consumer goods, fuels, and raw materials were the major imports. Postwar industrialization is reflected in the commodity composition of Bulgaria's trade. In 1992, the principal exports were rolled sheet metal, cigarettes, industrial trucks, tobacco, urea, wines, zinc, and footwear, in that order. The principal imports were crude oil, natural gas, motor card, diesel fuel, fuel oil, coal, and pharmaceuticals.

Principal imports in 1990 (in millions of foreign exchange leva) were as follows:

Machinery and equipment	6,238.7
Foodstuffs, beverages, and	
tobacco products	1,277.2
Other industrial consumer goods	1,084.9
Fuels, mineral raw materials and metals	810.5
Chemicals, fertilizers, and rubber	408.0
Raw materials for food production	259.5
Building materials	204.7
Other exports	276.0
TOTALS	10,314.9

Geographic distribution of trade has changed radically twice: since World War II and the collapse of the Soviet bloc. Whereas before the war Bulgaria traded mainly with the countries of Western and Central Europe, after the war, trade shifted almost entirely to the countries of the Communist bloc. After 1990, trade with Western Europe, Greece, the former Yugoslavia, and Turkey became much more important. In 1991, 49.8% of all exports still went to the former USSR and 43.2% of all imports still came from the former USSR.

Principal trade partners in 1992 (in millions of dollars) and excluding a breakdown of trade with the former USSR, were as follows:

	EXPORTS	IMPORTS	BALANCE
Germany	354.4	615.8	261.4
Italy	213.1	240.2	−27.1
Turkey	172.1	88.6	83.5
Greece	144.4	182.8	−38.4
The Former Yugoslavia	214.5	188.4	26.1
France	116.1	251.0	−134.9
Other countries	1,377.7	1,406.0	−28.3
TOTALS	2,592.3	2,972.8	−380.5

32 BALANCE OF PAYMENTS

During the postwar industrialization program, Bulgaria had a trade imbalance, made up largely by credits, particularly from the former USSR. From 1952 to 1958, the country had visible export surpluses, but another industrialization drive resulted in a trade imbalance during 1959–61, and there were persistent imbalances during the latter part of the 1960s. In the early 1970s, export surpluses were reported for most years; there were also small surpluses in 1979, 1980, and 1984. With the collapse of COMECON trade, Bulgaria has begun exporting agricultural products and light manufactures in exchange for consumer goods. During the first nine months of 1992, Bulgaria recorded its first surplus in many years. Since 1991, reforms have included an agreement on debt service payments and partial interest payments to commercial creditors. The non-interest current account recorded a surplus of 2.3% of GDP in 1992, as a result of turnaround in external trade.

In 1992 merchandise exports totaled $5,093 million and imports $4,609 million. The merchandise trade balance was $485 million. The following table summarizes Bulgaria's balance of payments for 1991 and 1992 (in millions of US dollars):

	1991	1992
CURRENT ACCOUNT		
Goods, services, and income	−146	409
Unrequited transfers	69	43
TOTALS	−77	452
CAPITAL ACCOUNT		
Direct investment	56	42
Portfolio investment	—	—
Other long-term capital	440	247
Other short-term capital	−401	−233
Exceptional financing	—	—
Other liabilities	—	—
Reserves	−17	−553
TOTALS	77	−497
Errors and omissions	0	45
Total change in reserves	−4	−573

33 BANKING AND SECURITIES

All banks were nationalized in 1947 in accord with Soviet banking policies. Until 1969, the Bulgarian National Bank was the chief banking institution handling deposits of state and local governments and national enterprises. It was the bank of issue and was authorized to credit enterprises with funds for facilities and activities not covered by the capital investment plan. In 1969 it was renamed the Bulgarian Central bank and remained the bank of issue. Two new banks—the Industrial Bank and the Agricultural and Trade Bank—assumed the functions of providing credit for industry and for agriculture and individuals, respectively. In 1968, the Bulgarian Foreign Trade Bank as established as a joint-stock company. The State Savings Banks was the chief savings institution.

When Bulgaria achieved independence in 1991, a two-tier banking system was formed. The Bulgarian National Bank became the country's central bank. The country has a state savings bank with 491 branches. There are 80 commercial banks in Bulgaria. Fifteen of the commercial banks are cross-border banks that are involved in the foreign exchange market. Some of the banks licensed for cross-border foreign exchange include: Agricultural and Co-operative Bank (1987), Balkenbank (1987), Biochim Commercial Bank (1987), Bulgarian Post-Office Bank, Economic Bank (1991), Hemus Commercial Bank, and the Bank for Economic Enterprise (December 1991).

[34]INSURANCE

Private insurance companies were nationalized in 1947 and absorbed into the State Insurance Institute. Property insurance and life insurance are compulsory for collective farms and voluntary for cooperatives, social organizations, and the population in general. Insurance policies and premiums have increased steadily for both. All foreign insurance and reinsurance is handled by the Bulgarian Foreign Insurance and Reinsurance Co.

[35]PUBLIC FINANCE

An annual budget for all levels of government, becoming effective on 1 January, is voted by the National Assembly, after having been prepared by the Ministry of Finance. The disintegration of the communist system in November 1989 and the subsequent collapse of the Soviet trade bloc caused severe economic disruption, pushing the government's budget deficit to 8.5% of GDP in 1990 (not including interest payments on commercial foreign debt). By the end of 1993, the budget deficit totaled Lv32.2 billion ($894.4 million), due to a 25% drop in tax collections.

The following table shows actual revenues and expenditures for 1990 and 1992 in millions of leva.

	1990	1992
REVENUE AND GRANTS		
Tax revenue	19,110	58,944
Non-tax revenue	12,971	8,539
Capital revenue	—	8
Grants	—	313
TOTAL	32,081	67,804
EXPENDITURES & LENDING MINUS REPAYMENTS		
General public service	886	—
Defense	1,870	—
Public order and safety	420	—
Education	2,075	—
Health	1,459	—
Social security and welfare	5,703	—
Housing and community amenities	2,290	—
Recreation, cultural, and religious affairs	586	—
Economic affairs and services	15,567	—
Other expenditures	2,386	—
Adjustments	—	—
Lending minus repayments	2,978	−80
TOTALS	36,372	77,046
Deficit/Surplus	−4,291	−9,242

In 1992, Bulgaria's total public debt stood at Lv118,221 million, of which Lv79,838 million was financed abroad. By 30 September 1993, state and cooperative debts totaled Lv167 billion ($4.7 million).

[36]TAXATION

The turnover tax (basically a sales tax), imposed on the prices of goods and services, is by far the most important source of revenue. Deductions from the profits of enterprises are also a major item. Direct taxes on individuals—on income, real estate, inheritance, bachelors, unmarried women, widowers, childless married couples, and childless divorced couples—provide relatively minor revenues.

[37]CUSTOMS AND DUTIES

Import licenses are required for a limited list of goods, including radioactive elements, rare and precious metals and stones, ready pharmaceutical products, and pesticides. The Ministry of Foreign Trade supervises the collection of customs duties. The amount collected is not published.

Goods arriving from foreign points to be unloaded in Bulgaria must have customs manifests and other shipping documents as specified by law. Customs duties are paid ad valorem. As of 1992, a temporary 15% import tax was levied on most goods, as well as a 0.5% customs clearance fee. Duty must be paid on all goods except those specifically exempt, such as works of art, scientific and educational items for research, and those for the diplomatic corps. In August 1987, the National Assembly adopted a law to establish tariff-free zones to attract foreign investment beginning in January 1988.

[38]FOREIGN INVESTMENT

Soviet-bloc credits contributed greatly to Bulgaria's economic programs. In the early 1970s, several "turnkey" projects were undertaken by West European countries in Bulgaria; once completed, these projects were turned over to Bulgarian hands.

Under a 1991 law, foreign investors may hold up to 100% of an investment but may not own land, real estate, or natural resources. They may freely repatriate earnings and other income from their investments at the market rate of exchange.

Foreign investment in high-tech sectors, agriculture, and food processing is exempt from profit taxes for five years. Foreign investors have expressed interest in tourism in the Black Sea and mountainous regions. By mid-1991, about 800 foreign entities worth $400 million in equity were registered in Bulgaria. Direct foreign investment was about $200 million during 1992–93, and the total number of ventures with foreign investment was estimated at around 1,500.

[39]ECONOMIC DEVELOPMENT

The economy was almost entirely nationalized or cooperatively owned until 1990, and operated on the basis of state plans. These were designed to expand the economy as a whole, with emphasis on the growth of heavy industry (fuels, metals, machinery, chemicals) and on the development of export goods. In 1971, productive enterprises were grouped into more than 60 state concerns responsible for almost all nonagricultural production.

Bulgaria's first five-year plan (1949–53) emphasized capital investment in industry. The period was marked by a slow pace in agricultural production (owing largely to collectivization and small investment), an inadequate supply of consumer goods, and a poor livestock output. The 1953–57 plan provided for a decrease in industrial investment, with a resultant improvement in agriculture, housing, and living conditions. The food-processing industry, important for export, began to receive greater attention in 1958, as did textiles and clothing. The lagging rate of growth during the early 1960s was due mainly to poor agricultural output and to a slower industrial pace. The third five-year plan (1958–62), with its "big leap forward" (1959–60), was claimed to have reached its goals by the end of 1960, but definite shortcomings remained. The fourth plan (1961–65) devoted 70% of total investment to industry, while agriculture received only 6.5%. Investments directed by the fifth plan (1966–70) adhered essentially to precedent, with some shift toward agriculture, and this trend continued under the sixth plan (1971–75). Of total investment during 1971–73, over 40% went to industry and 15% to agriculture. The 1976–80 plan resulted in a 35% increase in industrial output and a 20% increase in agricultural output. The overall growth rate began to slow down in the late 1970s, and the 1981–85 plan reflected the concept of a more gradual economic growth. Under the 1986–90 plan, it was projected that national income would grow by 22–25%, industrial output by 25–30%, and agricultural production by 10–12%. Priority was to be given to the development of high technology.

Economic reforms establishing profit incentives and greater decentralization were tentatively introduced in the late 1960s, but subsequent modifications undermined these measures. The New Economic Mechanism, introduced in agriculture in 1979 and in industry, construction, trade, and transport in 1982, represented another attempt at least partly to decentralize economic decision making. It provided for gradual elimination of subsidies to unprofitable enterprises and for reduction of centralized planning, and encouraged the economic self-sufficiency of individual enterprises by linking wages to output.

The post-Communist government began a program of privatization and reform of the nation's economy. It rescheduled the foreign debt, abolished price controls, and became a member of the IMF and IBRD.

[40]SOCIAL DEVELOPMENT

Social insurance is administered by the trade unions and is comprehensive. A state employee qualifies for sickness benefits after three months of employment; for temporary incapacity, the benefits vary from 70% (with up to five years' employment) to 90% (with 15 and more years' employment) of wages. Disability pension depends on the class of disability and income group, ranging from 40% to 75% of previous earnings.

Old age pensions vary from 55–80% of previous earnings according to category of work. Survivors' disability pensions and survivors' old age pensions are provided, the latter ranging from 50% (for one survivor), to 75% (for two), to 100% (for three or more survivors) of the insured's pension.

Special benefits include a grant upon birth of a child and monthly family allowances for children, the amounts increasing with the number of offspring; in 1991, the allowance was Lv15 for the first child, Lv60 for the second, and Lv115 for the third. As of 1991, paid maternity leave was 100% of earnings for 10–14 months, depending on the number of other children. Abortions are legal for married women with two or more living children, for married women over 40 with one child, and for all unmarried women. The fertility rate was 1.9 in 1985–90.

Although women have equal rights under the constitution, they have not had the same employment opportunities as men. Their rate of unemployment in 1993 was 2.6% higher than that of men.

[41]HEALTH

The Ministry of Health is the controlling and policymaking agency for the health system in Bulgaria, spending $1,154 million in 1990. In February, 1991, the Bulgarian government passed a bill restoring the right of the private sector to practice medicine and permitting the establishment of private pharmacies, dentists, and opticians. Bulgarian citizens resident in the country will still have use of the free national health service. Medical care has never been well funded, but the shift from a centrally planned to a private enterprise system has left the medical sector in disarray. Doctors continue to receive low wages, and operate inadequate and outdated machinery, and patients on the whole receive minimal health services. In 1993, the World Bank assessed the country's problems and recommended numerous changes and improvements. The Ministry of Health was seeking funding for 19–21 additional health centers and the rehabilitation of 67 secondary centers served by 283 emergency medical teams.

In 1990, there were 28,497 doctors, 4,366 pharmacists, 6,109 dentists, 5,318 nurses, and 7,466 midwives. From 1988 to 1992, Bulgaria had 3.19 doctors per 1,000 people (in 1990, one physician to 320 people). In 1990, there were 90,000 hospital beds (10 per 1,000). Mortality in 1993 was 12 per 1,000 (compared with 8.1 in 1960). Stroke mortality is the highest in Europe and circulatory diseases account for almost 60% of deaths. Smoking is on the increase; alcohol consumption is high; physical activity is low; and obesity is common. Bulgarians have a high intake of fats, sugars, and salt. One out of 8 people has high blood pressure. Improved maternal and child care lowered infant mortality from 108.2 per 1,000 in 1951 to 16 per 1,000 in 1992. Between 1990 and 1992, Bulgaria immunized children up to one year old as follows: tuberculosis (100%); diphtheria, pertussis, and tetanus (99%); polio (99%); and measles (97%). There were 111,000 births in 1992 (12.5 per 1,000 people in 1993), and from 1980 to 1993, an estimated 76% of married women (ages 15 to 49) used contraception. In 1990, 99% of the population had access to safe drinking water, and the life expectancy in 1992 was 72 years on the average.

[42]HOUSING

Although housing construction during 1976–85 averaged about 60,000 units per year, the housing shortage continues, especially in the larger cities, because of the influx into urban areas of new workers and because of the emphasis placed on capital construction. In 1975, to curb urban growth, the government instituted tight restrictions on new permits for residences in major cities. In December 1982, the Communist Party decreed that, in order to halt the growth of Sofia, a number of enterprises in the capital would be closed or moved elsewhere.

Capital investment for housing construction during 1976–80 amounted to Lv3.5 billion. At the end of 1985 there were 3,092,000 dwelling units in the country, 24% more than in 1975; by 1991, this figure had risen to 3,406,000. The number of new houses built plummeted from 62,926 in 1988 to 40,154 in 1989, 26,200 in 1990, and 19,423 in 1991.

[43]EDUCATION

Illiteracy has been decreasing steadily; the government claims that literacy is complete, but Western sources estimate 5% illiteracy. Education is free and compulsory for eight years between the ages of 7 and 15. "Socially useful work," an integral part of the curriculum, begins in the lowest grades as a required class subject and involves increasingly longer periods of practical work in the higher grades, with students performing manual work in agriculture, industry, or on construction projects.

In 1991 there were 2,827 primary level schools with 62,012 teachers and 920,694 students. At the secondary level, there were 28,874 teachers and 383,825 students, 233,528 of them in vocational courses.

There are over 30 higher education institutions, including four universities. The most important is the University of Sofia, founded in 1888. The others are: University of Plovdiv (founded 1961), University of Veliko Tarnovo (founded 1971), and American University in Bulgaria (founded 1991). All higher level institutions had a total of 185,914 students and 23,954 teaching staff in 1991.

44LIBRARIES AND MUSEUMS

The St. Cyril and St. Methodius National Library, established in 1878 in Sofia, is the largest in Bulgaria (2,239,000 volumes); since 1964, the Elin Pelin Bulgarian Bibliographic Institute has been attached to it. In the mid-1980s, the library contained 2.5 million volumes, including almost 11,000 manuscripts and over 7,000 old and rare publications, and about 115,000 maps, prints, and portraits. Other important libraries are the Central Library of the Scientific Information Center (with 1,535,700 volumes), the Sofia University Library (1,608,000 volumes), and the Ivan Vazov National Library in Plovdiv (with 1,300,000 volumes).

Among Bulgaria's 223 museums in 1990, the more important were the National Archaeological Museum (attached to the Academy of Sciences) and the National Art Gallery (with a collection of national and foreign art), both in Sofia. Other museums are devoted to history, science, and the revolutionary movement.

45MEDIA

Postal and telecommunications systems are owned and operated by the state. Telex service to the rest of the world improved markedly in 1982, when a new computerized telegraph exchange was put in service. By the mid-1980s, most communities were connected by telephone; telephones numbered 2.7 million in 1991. In the same year there were 3,970,000 radio receivers and 2,260,000 TV sets. There are 20 AM and 15 FM stations and 29 TV stations. Television was instituted in 1959; in 1992 there were two television channels.

In 1991, Bulgaria published 728 newspapers, with a total annual circulation of 1,079 million; the 13 dailies had an annual circulation of 760,200. The principal Sofia papers, with their publishers and estimated daily circulations (1992), are:

	PUBLISHER	CIRCULATION
24 Chasa	NA	320,000
Democraciya	NA	105,000
Trud	Central Committee of Trade Unions	250,000
Otechestven Vestnik	Dimitrov Union of People's Youth	100,000
Vecherni Novini	Communist Party	90,000
Zemedelsko Zname	Agrarian National Union	30,000

46ORGANIZATIONS

Bulgaria's important economic organizations include the Bulgarian Chamber of Commerce and Industry (1985) and organizations dedicated to promoting Bulgaria's exports in world markets. Important trade unions include the Confederation of Independent Trade Unions of Bulgaria. The organization was founded in 1901 and taken over by the Communists after World War II. In 1990, it became an independent organization. It has 75 member federations and 4 association members. Three million people belonged to the union in 1990.

47TOURISM, TRAVEL, AND RECREATION

Despite the country's economic troubles, tourism in Bulgaria has risen rapidly since the end of Communist rule. The tourist industry is in the process of becoming totally privatized, a development that is expected to improve the quality of the tourism infrastructure. Bulgaria is rich in mineral waters and has numerous tourist spas. Visitors are attracted to the Black Sea resorts and the Balkan mountains. Foreign visitors to Bulgaria must have a passport and, depending on their nationality, may require a visa. In 1990, tourist receipts totaled approximately US$320 million. The number of foreign visitors was estimated at 6.8 million in 1991, of whom 3.2 million came from Europe and 2.7 million from the Middle East and Turkey.

48FAMOUS BULGARIANS

The founders of modern Bulgarian literature, writing before the end of Turkish rule, were Georgi Rakovski (1821–67), Petko Slaveikov (1827–95), Lyuben Karavelov (1835–79), and Kristo Botev (1848–76), who was one of Bulgaria's greatest poets. The most significant writer after the liberation of 1878 was Ivan Vazov (1850–1921), whose *Under the Yoke* gives an impressive picture of the struggle against the Turks. Pentcho Slaveikov (1866–1912), the son of Petko, infused Bulgarian literature with philosophical content and subject matter of universal appeal; his epic poem *A Song of Blood* recalls an insurrection suppressed by the Turks in 1876. In the period between the two world wars, Nikolai Liliyev (1885–1960) and Todor Trayanov (1882–1945) were leaders of a symbolist school of poetry. Elin Pelin (1878–1949) and Iordan Iovkov (1884–1939) wrote popular short stories on regional themes. More recent writers and poets include Nikola Vaptzarov, Christo Shirvenski, Dimiter Dimov, Orlin Vassilev, and Georgi Karaslavov. Elias Canetti (b.1905), Bulgarian born but living since 1938 in the UK, received the Nobel Prize for literature in 1981. Ivan Mrkvicka (1856–1938), a distinguished Czech painter who took up residence in Bulgaria, founded the Academy of Fine Arts in Sofia.

A prominent Bulgarian statesman was Alexander Stamboliski (1879–1923), Peasant Party leader who was premier and virtual dictator of Bulgaria from 1920 until his assassination. The best known modern Bulgarian, Georgi Dimitrov (1882–1949), was falsely charged in 1933 with burning the Reichstag building in Berlin; he became general secretary of the Comintern until its dissolution and prime minister of Bulgaria in 1946. Traicho Kostov (1897–1949), an early revolutionary leader, was a principal architect of Bulgaria's postwar economic expansion. Caught up in the Tito-Stalin rift, he was expelled from the Politburo and executed in December 1949. Todor Zhivkov (b.1911) was first secretary of the Bulgarian Communist Party between 1954 and 1989, the longest tenure of any Warsaw Pact leader. His was marked by ardent and steadfast support of Soviet policies and ideological positions. Zhivkov's daughter Lyudmila Zhivkova (1942–81), a Politburo member since 1979, was regarded by Western observers as second only to her father in power and influence. Zhivkov was replaced by Dimitar Popov as premier of a coalition government headed by the Socialist Party (formally the Communist Party).

49DEPENDENCIES

Bulgaria has no territories or colonies.

50BIBLIOGRAPHY

Bell, John D. *The Bulgarian Communist Party from Blagoev to Zhikov.* Stanford, Calif.: Hoover Institute Press, 1985.

Bokov, Georgi, ed. *Modern Bulgaria.* Sofia: Sofia Press, 1981.

Bulgaria: A Country Study, 2nd ed. Washington, D.C.: Government Printing Office, 1993.

Clarke, James Franklin and Dennis P. Hupchick (eds.). *The Pen and the Sword: Studies in Bulgarian History.* Boulder, Colo.: East European Monographs, 1988.

Constant, Stephen. *Foxy Ferdinand, Tsar of Bulgaria.* London: Sidgwick & Jackson, Ltd., 1979.

Crampton, R. *A Short History of Modern Bulgaria.* Cambridge, England: Cambridge University Press, 1987.

———. *Bulgaria.* Santa Barbara, Calif.: Clio, 1989.

Hosch, Edgar. *The Balkans: A Short History from Greek Times to the Present Day.* London: Faber & Faber, 1972.

Lampe, John R. *The Bulgarian Economy in the Twentieth Century.* New York: St. Martin's, 1981.

Lendvai, Paul. *Eagles in Cobwebs: Nationalism and Communism in the Balkans.* Garden City: Doubleday, 1969.

MacDermott, Mercia. *A History of Bulgaria, 1393–1885.* New York: Praeger, *1962.*

Oren, Nissan. *Revolution Administered: Agrarianism and Communism in Bulgaria.* Baltimore: John Hopkins Press, 1973.

Perry, Duncan M. *The Politics of Terror: The Macedonian Liberation Movements, 1893–1903*. Durham, N.C.: Duke University Press, 1988.

Petkov, Petko. *The United States and Bulgaria in World War I*. Boulder, Colo.: East European Monographs, 1991.

Rothschild, Joseph. *The Communist Party of Bulgaria, 1833-1936*. New York: Columbia University Press, 1960.

Welsh, William A. *Bulgaria*. Boulder, Colo.: Westview, 1986.

CROATIA

Republic of Croatia
Republika Hrvatska

CAPITAL: Zagreb.

FLAG: Red, white, and blue horizontal bands with the Croatian coat of arms (red and white checkered).

ANTHEM: *Lijepa Nasa Domovina.*

MONETARY UNIT: The Croatian kuna was introduced in 1994. us$1 = 5.7 kuna as of fall 1994, but exchange rates are expected to fluctuate.

WEIGHTS AND MEASURES: The metric system is the legal standard.

HOLIDAYS: New Year's Day, 1 January; Epiphany, 6 January; Labor Day, 1 May; Republic Day, 30 May; National Holiday, 22 June; Assumption, 15 August; Christmas, 25–26 December.

TIME: 7 PM = noon GMT.

¹LOCATION, SIZE, AND EXTENT

Croatia is located in southeastern Europe. Comparatively, the area occupied by Croatia is slightly smaller than the state of West Virginia with a total area of 56,538 sq km (21,829 sq mi). Croatia shares boundaries with Slovenia on the w, Hungary on the n, Serbia on the e, Bosnia and Herzegovina on the s and e, and the Adriatic Sea on the w, and has a total boundary length of 7,633 km (4,743 mi). Croatia's capital city, Zagreb, is located in the northern part of the country.

²TOPOGRAPHY

The topography of Croatia is geographically diverse, with flat plains along the Hungarian border, as well as low mountains and highlands near the Adriatic coast. Approximately 32% of Croatia's land is arable. Croatia's natural resources include: oil, some coal, bauxite, low-grade iron ore, calcium, natural asphalt, silica, mica, clays, and salt. Croatia's natural environment experiences effects from frequent earthquakes, air pollution from metallurgical plants, coastal pollution from industrial and domestic waste, and forest damage.

³CLIMATE

Croatia's climate features hot summers and cold winters. Along the coast, the climate is Mediterranean with mild winters and dry summers.

⁴FLORA AND FAUNA

The region's climate has given Croatia a wealth of diverse flora and fauna. Ferns, flowers, mosses, and common trees populate the landscape. Along the Adriatic Sea there are subtropical plants. Native animals include deer, brown bears, rabbits, fox, and wild boars.

⁵ENVIRONMENT

Air pollution (from metallurgical plant emissions) and deforestation are inland environmental problems; coastal water systems have been damaged by industrial and domestic waste. Environmental management is becoming more decentralized, thereby empowering city and municipal administrations to determine environmental policy.

⁶POPULATION

The population of Croatia was 4,784,265 in 1991. It was projected by the World Bank to be 4,800,000 in 2010, based on a crude birth rate of 12 per 1,000 people, a crude death rate of 11, and a net natural increase of 1. The population density in 1991 was 85 per sq km (219 per sq mi). Zagreb, the capital, had a population of 706,770. Other cities and their 1991 populations, included Split, 189,388; Rijeka, 167,964; and Osijek, 104,761.

⁷MIGRATION

At the end of 1992, Croatia was accommodating 648,000 refugees. Some of these were Croats from Bosnia and Herzegovina. Others were from areas of Croatia in Serbian hands. Some 160,000 people had fled to other Yugoslav republics by mid-1991, and about 120,000 had fled abroad.

⁸ETHNIC GROUPS

Croats made up 78% of the population in 1991. Serbs were 12% and Muslims 1%. About 2% said they were Yugoslavs. There were smaller numbers of Slovenes, Hungarians, Italians, and other nationalities. A 1991 law guarantees Serbs autonomy in areas where they constitute the majority, but only after permanent peace is achieved.

⁹LANGUAGES

Serbo-Croatian is the native language. Since 1991, Croats have insisted that their tongue (now called Croat) is distinctive. The spoken language is basically the same, but Serbs use the Cyrillic alphabet and Croats the Roman alphabet. The Croatian alphabet has the special consonants č, ć, š, ž, dj, dž, lj, and nj, representing sounds provided by the Cyrillic alphabet.

¹⁰RELIGIONS

The Republic of Croatia declared its independence of the former Yugoslav federated republic in June of 1991. Christianity was introduced into the area in the 7th century. Under the Yugoslav Socialist Republic, churches—Roman Catholic in particular—experienced repression by the state. This moderated in 1966, when an agreement with the Vatican recognized a religious role for the clergy. The census of 1991 recorded a Catholic population of 76.5%, with 11.1% Serbian Orthodox, and 1.2% Muslims.

¹¹TRANSPORTATION

Croatia's railroads consist of two main routes. An east-west route originating in Serbia nearly parallels the Sava before reaching Zagreb and continuing on to Slovenia and Hungary. The north-south route connects the coastal cities of Split and Rijeka to Zagreb. Another railway connects Dubrovnik to Bosnia and Herzegovina. As of 1991, there were 2,698 km (1,677 mi) of railroads, 34.5% of which were electrified.

Highways totaled 32,071 km (19,929 mi) in 1990, including 23,305 km (14,482 mi) of paved roads, 8,439 km (5,244 mi) of gravel roads, and 327 km (203 mi) of earthen paths.

Rijeka, Split, and Kardeljevo (Ploče) are the main seaports along the Adriatic. There are 785 km (488 mi) of perennially navigable inland waters; Vukovar, Osijek, Sisak, and Vinkovci are the principal inland ports.

¹²HISTORY

Origins through the Middle Ages

Slavic tribes had penetrated slowly but persistently into the Balkan area since the 5th century. The Croats moved from the White Croatia area north of the Carpathian Mountains along the Oder and Vistula rivers south to the old Roman Illirycum. Their migration was presumably upon the invitation of the Byzantine Emperor Heraclius in AD 626, who had also invited Serbian tribes at the same time, to assist him in repelling the destructive inroads of the Avars. A coalition of Byzantine and Croat forces succeeded in forcing the Avars out of Dalmatia first, and then from the remainder of Illirycum and the lands between the Drava and Sava rivers. The Croats settled on the lands they had freed from the Avars and established their own organized units which included Slavic tribes who had settled in the area from earlier times.

Prince Vojnomir, ruler of Croatians of Pannonia and Slavonia in the late 8th century, acknowledged Frankish authority following Charlemagne's defeat of the Avars in AD 790. Along the Adriatic coast of Dalmatia in the area south of Rijeka, Croats held the territory to a line between today's Split and Dubrovnik, while territory to the south of this region was settled by Serbian tribes. However, most of the islands and fortified coastal cities held out against the Slavic invaders and for a long time maintained their Roman/Italian character while acknowledging Byzantine suzerainty. Since communications with Byzantium were very difficult over Slavic-dominated areas, the coastal cities maintained a high degree of political, cultural, and economic autonomy while maintaining strong ties to the Italian mainland across the Adriatic Sea.

The Franks who took control over Northern Dalmatia sent Christian missionaries from Aquileia. The first Christian Croatian ruler was Višeslav (AD 800–810) who, with assistance from the Franks, unified under him the Croatian tribes headed by their "Zupans" from today's port city of Rijeka south along the Dalmatian coast to the Cetina river. After Charlemagne's death in AD 814, Croats became restless under the Franks and in AD 819, Prince Ljudevit of Croatian Pannonia rebelled against them. He was joined in battle by Pannonian Slovenes and Timok Slavs, and together they attempted to unify Pannonia with the Slavs of Istria and Dalmatia, whose prince had been defeated by Borna Ljudevit. But in AD 822, a large Frankish army defeated Ljudevit and his allies. Ljudevit fled to the Serbs first, and then accepted asylum from Borna's successor in Dalmatia. He was eventually murdered in AD 823. When the Frankish Empire was split in AD 843, Istria and Dalmatian Croatia came under Frankish Italy's control while Frankish Germany took over Pannonian Croatia and Slavonia. From the east, the Bulgars conquered the territory of East Slavonia and Northern Bosnia (to the river Bosnia).

With Byzantium reasserting its authority over the Dalmatian city states, Croatian princes established good relationships with the empire. This earned them tributes from the coastal cities formerly paid to Byzantium for defense against Arab and Slavic Narentan pirate raids. In this way, Slavic pillaging of coastal cities was reduced. The Frankish attempt to reassert authority over the Dalmatian Croats backfired and led to the successful revolt by Croatian Prince Domagoj in AD 876 that ended the Franks' over-lordship in Dalmatia. The Venetians, formally a vassal of Byzantium but otherwise very independent, prevented Domagoj's attempt to take over Istria. Freed of the Franks, Dalmatian Croatia was independent and in AD 879 received Papal recognition under Prince Branimir.

It was not until the reign of Tomislav, however, that the two Croatian states were unified. This was achieved when he was asked to assist the Pannonian Croats in their fight against the Hungarians, who were trying to expand their territory. Tomislav, who had increased his army and navy, was able to repel the Hungarians several times and established the Croatian frontier along the Drava River. With the unification of the two Croatian states, the authority of the Franks was ended and Tomislav's lands were extended along the Adriatic coast, approximately from Rijeka to the Cetina River and north through Western Bosnia to Croatia proper and Slavonia. The old Roman/Italian coastal cities still recognized Byzantium's suzerainty, although they remained independent in practice. Tomislav also successfully established good relationships with both Rome and Byzantium.

When the Bulgarians under Tsar Symeon expanded their lands at the Byzantine Empire's expense, Tomislav allied himself with Byzantium and was able to defeat Symeon's attacking forces. Crowned King by Pope John X, Tomislav died sometime between AD 928–940 without a clear successor. A struggle for power followed, undermining the central authority Tomislav had established. Bulgarian Tsar Symeon had also died (AD 927) and Serbia, having regained its independence from Byzantium under Caslav, took over most of Bosnia. Kresimir II (AD 949–969) brought back stability to Croatia and took back the western part of Bosnia after Caslav's death in about AD 960. His son, Stephen Držislav (AD 969–997), received royal insignia from Byzantine Emperor Basil II in AD 986 and was apparently given authority over the Byzantine islands and cities of Dalmatia as "Rex Croatiae et Dalmatiae." While Držislav's sons quarreled among themselves, Venice was granted "sovereignty" over the Dalmatian islands and towns by the Byzantine Empire. By the year 1000, Venice, having defeated the Croatian fleet, controlled the entire Adriatic coast and was able protect its own growing trade from attacks by Arab and Croatian Narentan pirates. Venetian influence grew over future centuries, enabling the Roman/Italian character of the coastal cities to survive the intensified Slavic pressure into the 19th and 20th centuries.

Kresimir and his brother Gojslav succeeded in joining the Narentan area along the Neretva River and Delta to Croatia, but further attempts by Kresimir (AD 1000–1030) and his son Stephen I (AD 1030–1058) to regain control of the coastal cities—still ruled by Venice—failed, despite support from the Hungarian King Saint Stephen. Success came later with King Kresimir IV (1058–1073) when, around 1069, the Byzantines made Kresimir their representative to the Dalmatia Theme. This made the Dalmatian coastal cities accountable to Kresimir, while Byzantine suzerainty was preserved. The coastal cities, while welcoming the Italian cultural influence of Venice, feared its potential domination over their trading interests with the enormous Balkan hinterland. Thus Dubrovnik—the old Ragusa—with its growing fleet, preferred to remain tied to the more distant Byzantine Empire as its separate province (Theme).

Slavonia at this time was administered by Zvonimir, who was the son-in-law of the Hungarian King Bela I. After Kresimir had

CROATIA

0 25 50 75 Miles

0 25 50 75 Kilometers

SLOVENIA

HUNGARY

Prelog

Varaždin

Koprivnica

Kumrovec

BILO GORA

Drava

Sljeme 3,395 ft. 1035 m.

Zagreb

Bjelovar

Beremend

Batina

Zumberacka 3,874 ft. 1181 m.

Virovitica

Stari Trg

Ozalj

Podravska Slatina

Ilirska Bistrica

Koper

Vinica

Kupa

Sisak

PAPUK

Osijek

Umag

Rijeka

Karlovac

Sava

Slavonska Požega

Vukovar

Ogulin

Dubica

Novska

Dakovo

Vinkovci

Istria

KAPELA

Cetingrad

Dvor

Bosanska Dubica

Slavonski Brod

Baderna

Malinska

Vrbnik

Krk

Bihat

Derventa

Drenovci

Pula

Cres

Belej

Jablanac

GREMEČ

DINARIC

Unije

Gospic

VELEBIT

BOSNIA & HERZEGOVINA

Pag

Povljana

Premuda

ALPS

Molat

Zadar

Dinara 6,007 ft. 1831 m.

Dugi Otok

Knin

DALMATIA

Kornat

Sibenik

Prolog

Croatia

Ancona

Sinj

Buško Blato

Adriatic

Split

Brač

Ugljane

Sea

Hvar

Biokovo 5,781 ft. 1762 m.

Neretva

Vis

Vis

Korčula

Opuzen

SERBIA

Pescara

Lastovski Kanal

Zavala

ITALY

Mljet

Dubrovnik

Gruda

LOCATION: 45°10′N 15°30′E. **BOUNDARY LENGTHS:** Total boundary lengths, 1,843 km (1,145 mi); Bosnia and Herzegovina (east), 751 km (467 mi); Bosnia and Herzegovina (southeast), 91 km (57 mi); Hungary , 292 km (181 mi); Serbia, 239 km (149 mi); Montenegro, 15 km (9.3 mi); Slovenia, 455 km (283 mi); **COASTLINE:** 5,790 km (3,619 mi); mainland coastline, 1,778 km (1,111 mi); islands coastline, 4,012 km (2,506 mi).

disappeared, Zvonimir was crowned King of Croatia in 1075 by a Papal legate at Split; he concurred with the Pope's policy banning the Slavic-language liturgy. He also attempted to limit the power of the regional nobles by replacing them with his own supporters. Zvonimir died in 1089 or 1090, and so did his son. His widow, a Hungarian, took over, but the nobles opposed her. Her brother, the King of Hungary, intervened to protect her interests (and his own) by occupying Pannonian Croatia. This area was recovered in 1095 by Peter Svačić from Knin (1093–97). Peter, the last independent King of Croatia, was killed in battle in 1096 by King Koloman of Hungary, who then conquered Croatia. The area he now controlled included the Croatian port city of Bio-

grad. King Koloman concluded a non-aggression pact with Venice, which had retained control of the coastal islands and cities. The Croats then rebelled against Koloman and repelled his forces back to the Drava River frontier.

Royal Union with Hungary

In 1102, Koloman regrouped and attacked Croatia. He stopped at the Drava River, however, where he invited the nobles representing the twelve Croatian tribes to a conference. They worked out the so-called *Pacta Conventa*, an agreement on a personal royal union between Hungary and Croatia whereby the two would share the same King, but would otherwise be separate nations. Koloman promised to respect the ancestral privileges of the Croatian nobility, to respect the Croatian Diet (Sabor), to provide for a separate coronation of new kings of Croatia (dispensed with in 1235), undertook the obligation to defend Croatia, and made Latin the official language of both states. The overall administration of the state would be by a "Ban" (viceroy) appointed by the King, while regional and local administration were to stay in the hands of the Croatian nobles. This legal arrangement, with some practical modifications, remained the basis of the Hungarian-Croatian personal royal union and relationship until 1918. In practice, this union applied only to Croatia proper (Pannonian), and it was never truly integrated into the Hungarian state. By the 1180s, Bosnia had become practically independent (even though under Hungarian suzerainty), while Dalmatia continued to be the battleground among Venetians, Byzantines, Hungarians, and others.

Once joined with Hungary, Croatia lost its independence in foreign affairs. Its territorial interests, however, coincided to a large extent with Hungary's. Internally the Hungarian influence varied in different regions—from minimal in Croatia proper, where the old Croat hereditary nobles were quite autonomous, to considerable in Slavonia, where Hungarian Kings were able to grant land fiefs to Hungarian nobles and Hungarian law and church hierarchy prevailed. Since the 1190s, Croatia and Slavonia were ruled by Dukes of Croatia, usually brothers of the King of Hungary and Croatia. The reign of King Andrew II (1205–1235) was characterized by continuous instability due to the King's inefficient rule, long absences on expeditions, participation in a crusade, squandering of resources, and the selling of the port city of Zadar to Venice.

The Croatian and Hungarian nobles revolted and forced King Andrew to issue a Charter in 1222 that defined the rights of the nobility and thus limited the power of the King. The *Golden Bull*, as the charter was called, also granted the nobles and Church hierarchy the right to rise against a ruler who violated the *Golden Bull*. Through the internal struggles for the succession to the Hungarian throne following King Ladislas' death without sons in 1290, several Croatian noble families emerged with greater power. Among them were the Šubići. One of them, Paul Šubić, became the Ban of Croatia and Dalmatia and, in 1299 "Lord of Bosnia" and "Lord of all Bosnia" in 1305. So great was Ban Šubić's authority that he exercised it without any reference to the King of Hungary. The Šubić dynasty continued in power after Paul's death in 1312. His successor, Mladen II, supported Hungary against Serbia in 1318 and 1319. During this campaign Stjepan Kotromanić became Ban of Bosnia and a Šubić vassal. However, the Šubić's power generated a strong opposition among Croatian nobles, and they were successful in defeating Mladen. Stjepan Kotromanić, as Ban of Bosnia, became a direct vassal of the Hungarian King and also his leading ally.

The internal warfare among Croatia's nobility weakened its overall ability to resist the inroads of Venice, which acquired, with few exceptions, control of the coastal area between the Cetina River, Split, and Nin by 1329. The struggle for the coastal cities continued between the Hungarian-Croatian Kingdom and Venice until Venice was defeated in 1385, and was forced by the treaty of Zadar to surrender all rights to the coastal cities all the way to Durazzo in today's Albania. Dubrovnik also gained its independence from Venice, recognized the sovereignty of the Hungarian-Croatian King. Yet it continued to enjoy its quasi-independence and, later on, became a center of Croatian culture. Meanwhile, Tvrtko (1353–1390), Steven Kotromanić's successor, gained control of the Zahumlje region along the Adriatic coast and some Serbian lands along the upper Drina and Lim Rivers. In 1377, he proclaimed himself King of the Serbs, Bosnia, and the Croatian coast.

The civil war for the Hungarian Crown raging between Ladislas and Sigmund in the late 14th and early 15th centuries, divided the loyalties of the Croatian nobles. This gave Venice an opportunity to again take possession of most of the coastal towns of Dalmatia. This action was solidified when Ladislas agreed to sell his holdings and rights to them for 100,000 ducats in July 1409. By 1420, Venice was in possession of most of Dalmatia—through purchase or war—and by 1481, had taken possession of territory as far as Bar in the south and the island of Krk in the north. Only Dubrovnik retained its independence.

Defense against the Turks

In the mid-15th century Croatia—and the Hungarian Crown as well—were preoccupied with the growth of the Frankopan family holdings that, directly or through marriage and inheritance, made up most of Croatia. Meanwhile the threat from both Turks and Venice was growing more ominous, leading King Sigismund to establish three military defense regions in 1432. As these defensive regions were further developed, they attracted new, mostly Serbian, settlers/fighters who never assimilated into their Croatian surroundings, becoming a strong Serbian minority population in Croatia. The concern with the Ottoman threat brought about the election in 1440 of Vladislav Jagiellon, the King of Poland, as King of Hungary and Croatia. Vladislav was succeeded in 1445 by Ladislas, son of Albert of Hapsburg, and therefore King of both Austria and Hungary/Croatia. Since Ladislas was a minor, John Hunyadi, a brilliant general and the Vojvoda of Transylvania, was appointed regent. Hunyadi then had to face up to the Counts of Celje who had reclaimed the Ban of Slavonia title when they conquered Slavonia, including Zagreb.

In 1453, the Counts of Celje also claimed the title of Ban of Croatia, thus adding Croatia and Slavonia to their extensive holdings of Slovenian lands in Styria, Carniola, and Carinthia. Ulrich, one of the Counts of Celje, had meanwhile grown too powerful and fell victim to Ladislas Hunyadi's assassins at the defense of Belgrade from the Turks in 1456. This murder was avenged by King Ladislas V, who had the younger Hunyadi executed in 1456. Ladislas Hunyadi's younger brother, Matthew Corvinus, was then elected king. The kingdom Matthew Corvinus inherited was a land under attack by the Ottoman Turks who had overtaken Serbia and Bosnia by 1463. In spite of the defense pressures, Matthew Corvinus wanted to consolidate his control over Croatia and, in order to achieve it, he decided to eliminate the power of the Frankopan family that had turned for help to both the Hapsburgs and Venice. The Frankopan's holdings were thus taken over by the King, although the island of Krk—center of the Frankopan family and one of the last bastions of the Slavic liturgy—was taken by Venice in 1480.

Matthew Corvinus died in 1490 and Vladislav II of Bohemia was elected king by a Council of nobles. By 1493, the Turkish invaders were already conducting plundering raids into Croatian and even Slovenian lands. Left without effective defenses, caused in large part by the bitter infighting among the nobles, many Croatian noblemen began paying tribute to the Turks.

After 1520, the Turks began effective rule over some Croatian territory, having overtaken Belgrade and Sabac in Serbia in 1521. By 1526, the Turks had conquered Eastern Slavonia and had advanced north into Hungary. On 29 August 1526, in a massive battle at Mohacs, they defeated the Hungarian and Croatian forces, killing King Louis. By 1528, the Ottomans held the southern part of Croatia and by 1541, had conquered Budapest. Dubrovnik, on the other hand, had accepted the Ottoman suzerainty in 1483, keeping its autonomy through its extensive trade with the Turkish empire. Most coastal towns were under the protection of Venice, with its good trade relations with the Turks.

In 1526, after King Louis' death at Mohacs, Ferdinand of Hapsburg was elected King of Hungary and Croatia, even though opposed by John Zapolja. This ushered in a new chapter in

Croatia's history. While defending Croatia in heroic battles against the invading Turks, the Croatian nobility slowed down the Turkish onslaught across Croatia towards Italy. Thus, the Turks moved forward to the north over the Hungarian plains and towards Vienna. In Croatia, the Hapsburg rulers began to encroach on the rights of Croats, by turning the throne from a traditionally elected position into a hereditary one, and by allocating Croatian lands as fiefs to their supporters, thus turning the Croatian peasants from free men into serfs. Many of the newer overlords were foreigners and the Croatian peasants, caught between their oppression and the suffering caused by Turkish invasions, began to rebel. One such rebellion, led by Matia Gubec in 1572, spread from Croatia to Slovenian lands and threatened the feudal system before being suppressed brutally in 1573.

The defense of Croatia, Hungary, and all of Western Europe from the Ottomans' expansion required a sustained effort, led during this period by Duke Charles of Styria, King Rudolph's uncle. The original military defense regions instituted under King Sigismund in 1432 were expanded, with a new one created between the Sava and Drava Rivers. All these military regions were subject directly to the King's military authorities, in spite of the protestations of Croatia's Council and Bans. As the defense against the Turks required ever more support, the military regions attracted large numbers of lifelong soldier-refugees from Turk occupied areas—mostly of Serbian Orthodox background. As territory continued to fall to Turkish occupation, additional military regions were taken from Croatia's control. Furthermore, Croatian participation on the side of the Catholic League in the 30-year war (1618–1648) sapped energies, resources, and human lives that would otherwise have been available for Croatia's own defense.

King Ferdinand III (r.1637–1657) consolidated Hungary and Croatia under Hapsburg rule. Under Ferdinand's son, Leopold I (who in 1658 had also become the German Emperor), the status of Hungary and Croatia continued to deteriorate. Special statutes and rights were eliminated, while all power was centralized in the hands of the King/Emperor and his Court. Leopold wanted to emulate the absolutist model practiced by Louis XIV of France. The Turkish offensives of 1663 were successfully repelled by the Croatian brothers Nicholas and Peter Zrinski (in southern Hungary and Croatia, respectively). The two highly admired brothers, in their opposition to Hapsburg absolutism and their determination to free their lands from the Turks, together became the hope of Hungarians and Croats. Following the defeat of the Turks at Saint Gotthard in western Hungary in 1664, Leopold I unilaterally concluded a 20-year peace treaty with the Turks based essentially on the pre-war situation.

The Peace of Vasvar proved to the Hungarians and Croats that the Hapsburg Court was not interested in freeing Hungary and Croatia from the Turks. This situation led to a conspiracy by the Zrinski brothers and key Hungarian nobles against the Hapsburg Court. But the Turks betrayed the conspiracy to the Hapsburgs, and Peter Zrinski and his co-conspirator Francis Frankopan were executed in Wiener Neustadt on 30 April 1671 (Nicholas Zrinski had died in 1664). The Hungarian leaders Francis Nadasdy and Erasm Tattenbach were also executed. This essentially eliminated the two most powerful noble families of Croatia, and Leopold I took advantage of the situation and confiscated their enormous properties, while suspending for ten years the office of the Croatian Ban as the symbol of Croatian statehood and autonomy. Thus Leopold I moved closer to his goal of making Hungary and Croatia his hereditary lands. Leopold was forced to abandon Vienna on 12 April 1683 when Sultan Mehmed's 250,000-man army appeared at its gates. Vienna was later saved by Polish King Jan Sobjeski who, with this victory over the Turks, caused the beginning of the slow decline of the Ottoman Empire.

A Holy League of Leopold with Poland, Venice, and other

forces pursued the Turks in retreat for over 16 years. Leopold, encouraged by his successes, restored the Croatian Ban, but declared Hungary and Croatia hereditary lands of the Hapsburg male line. From then on the Kings were no longer elected—only crowned. Leopold also voided article 31 of the Golden Bull, giving the Croatian nobles the right to rebel against a King who violated the rights and privileges of the united Hungarian and Croatian Kingdoms.

The Turks were driven out of Hungary and Croatia through Serbia and into Macedonia. The Holy League had a chance of driving the Turks out of Europe into Asia Minor, but Louis XIV of France attacked Germany and reached the Rhine River, thus occupying their armies. This attack from the west, combined with a decimating plague, caused the retreat of the Holy League forces in 1690 from Macedonia, followed closely by the Turks. In 1690, the Serbs' fear of revenge by the Turks caused their mass emigration, led by their Patriarch Arsenije Crnojević, north into Srijem and southern Hungarian lands. The Turks were forced to make peace in 1699, signing the Treaty of Karlowitz which returned much of their territories to the Hapsburgs, who refused to return the liberated lands to Croatia. Instead, they added the territories to the Military Regions, which further alienated the Croatian nobility.

The situation in Croatia did not improve in the 18th century, other than some territorial gains from battles against the Turks. The last king of the male Hapsburg line was Charles III (r.1711–1740). In 1722, during his reign the Hungarian parliament agreed to extend the Hapsburg hereditary right to its female line (Charles had no son), something already agreed to by the Croatian parliament in 1712. At the same time the Hungarians obtained a legal guarantee on the indivisibility of the realm of the Crown of Saint Stephen, which included Croatia. Charles was thus followed by his daughter Maria Teresa (r.1740–1780) who, by decree, rendered the Croatian Ban and Sabor (Parliament) useless. She accomplished this by dividing the country into regions headed by her appointees, who followed direct orders from Vienna. Her decree regulating the relationship of serfs and landlords also weakened the nobility. The enlightened absolutism of Maria Teresa was continued by Joseph II, her son, who emancipated the serfs, established rules on the distribution of land, tried to improve education, tried to impose the German language on all as a unifying force, closed monasteries in an attempt to control the Catholic Church, and decreed religious toleration. In the 1788 war against the Turks, Joseph II suffered a devastating defeat, and unrest spread during his reign.

Joseph II died in 1790, succeeded by his brother Leopold II who recognized Hungary and Croatia as kingdoms with separate constitutions. Hungarian replaced Latin as the official language of the Hungarian Parliament. Hungarians then began trying to establish the Hungarian language in Croatia, Slavonia, and Dalmatia, thus initiating a hundred-year struggle of the Croats against Magyarization.

Napolean and the Spring of Nations

Meanwhile the French Revolution and Napoleon's campaigns brought about a new era in Europe, with new ideas and related movements of national consciousness and rebirth along with territorial changes. With the peace treaty of Campoformio ending the war against Napoleon in 1797, Austria obtained the territories of the Venice Republic, including the Adriatic coast as far as Kotor. In 1806, Napoleon seized Dubrovnik, and in 1809 he obtained control of Slovenian and Croatian territories from Carinthia, Carniola, the Littoral region with Trieste, and Croatia to the Una River. Out of all these areas, Napoleon created his Illyrian Provinces. For a few years, these provinces enjoyed an orderly administration—respectful and supportive of the Slovenian and Croatian national individuality and aspirations—and encouraged education and cultural development in national languages. The French regime was, however, oppressive in terms of heavy taxation and conscription into Napoleon's armies. The armies suffered heavy casualties, particularly during his Russian campaign. With Napoleon's defeat, all of Dalmatia reverted back to direct Austrian administration until the end of World War I in 1918.

In 1825, Francis I called the Hungarian Parliament into session and the Hungarians resumed their pressure to introduce the Hungarian language throughout "Hungary," with Hungarian being introduced into Croatian schools in 1827. However, the Magyarization drive only produced a more determined opposition from the younger generation of Croats who had studied in Vienna, Graz, and Prague, and who were imbued with the newly developing Croatian national consciousness. Ljudevit Gaj became the leader of the movement calling for the reassertion of the independent Kingdom of Croatia and advocated the introduction of "Illyrian" (Croatian) as the official language to replace Latin. A member of the Illyrian movement, Count Janko Drašković, also promoted the idea of reorganizing the Hapsburg lands into a federation of political units based on each of the various nations, with co-equal rights. The Croatian parliament ("Sabor") then nullified the previous agreement on using Hungarian, and Croatian became the language of the Croatian Parliament

On the cultural front, numerous clubs and associations were formed promoting the study of Croatian history, language, literature, and culture with "Matica Hrvatska" (Croatian Queen Bee) becoming the foremost of these. At the 1836 session of the Hungarian parliament, Croatian delegates stood their ground on the language issue and declared that the Croats would fight for the introduction of Croatian as the official language in Croatia. In 1835, the first newspaper and literary journal were published in the local kajkavian Croatian dialect. The following year the Štokavian dialect was adopted as common to both Croats and Serbs under the term "Illyrian." In 1840, the Croatian Sabor voted for the introduction of Croatian as the language of instruction in all Croatian schools and at the Zagreb Academy. The struggle over the Croatian language and national identity brought about the establishment of the first political parties in Croatia. The Croatian-Hungarian Party supported a continued Croato-Hungarian Commonwealth. The Illyrian Party advocated an independent kingdom of Croatia comprising all the Croatian lands including Bosnia and Herzegovina with the ultimate goal of uniting all the "Illyrian" South Slavs (Croats, Slovenes, Serbs, Bulgarians). Because of partisan fighting, the Austrian government banned the term "Illyrian" and the name of the Illyrian party of Ljudevit Gaj and Draskovic was changed to the National Party. But the seeds of a South Slavic union were planted and they kept growing.

At the next session of the Hungarian Parliament in 1843, the Croatian delegation walked out when not permitted to use Latin instead of the Hungarian language. The parliament had been a joint Hungarian and Croatian body with Latin as its official language, but the Hungarians insisted on using only Hungarian. Emperor Ferdinand supported the Hungarians while sanctioning the Croatian Sabor decision to introduce Croatian as the official language of Croatia. The Croatian National Party submitted to the Emperor its demands to reestablish an independent Government of Croatia, elevate the Zagreb Academy to University status, and raise the Zagreb Bishopric to the Archbishopric rank. The lines were thus drawn between the Hungarian and Croatian nationalists. The Hungarians were bent on "Magyarizing" all nations from the Carpathian Mountains to the Adriatic Sea under the leadership of Louis Kossuth. The Croats were determined to fight for their own independence, even though their lands were subject to Austrian, Hungarian, and Turkish controls.

This situation came to a head in 1848 when great unrest and revolts developed in Austria and Hungary. Kossuth pressed for the formation of an independent government for Hungary and the complete elimination of Croatian autonomy. Popular demonstrations broke out in Vienna forcing Emperor Ferdinand to promise constitutions and freedoms to all the nationalities of his Empire. The Croats felt extremely threatened and reacted by having Baron Josip Jelačić, head of the military border region, appointed Ban and promoted to General. The National Party also submitted its demands for the unification of all Croatian lands (Croatia, Slavonia, the Military region, Dalmatia, Rijeka), the abolition of serfdom and class privileges, a permanent elected Sabor, and an independent government for Croatia. Ban Jelačić severed all relations with the Hungarian Government and a new Sabor was elected on 18 May 1848 that included representation from the Military region. The feudal system was ended with the abolition of serfdom, and the Sabor advocated a Swiss Confederacy type of reorganization. Ban Jelačić was also appointed to the Governorship of Dalmatia and Rijeka, and thus unified the Croatian lands, with the exception of Istria and the lands still held by the Turks.

Autonomy or Independence

Francis Joseph I (r.1848–1916) had ascended to the Hapsburg throne on 2 December 1848 and ruled for a long time, vacillating between absolutism and limited constitutional government, while favoring the Hungarians against the Croats. Croatian parties had split between the pro-Hungarian union and those advocating Croatian independence based on ancient state rights. The latter evolved into the "Yugoslav" (South Slavic) movement led by Bishop Josip Juraj Strossmayer and the "Pravaši" movement for total Croatian independence led by Ante Starčević. While the Croatian parties vacillated on the issue of cooperation with Austria or Hungary, the latter two resolved their problems by agreeing on the "Dual Monarchy" concept on 28 July. The Hungarian half of the dual monarchy consisted of Hungary, Transylvania, Croatia, Slavonia, and Dalmatia. A separate settlement ("Nagodba") was forced on the Croats and became the constitutional framework of the Croatian-Hungarian relationship. A Ban would be appointed by the Emperor-King of Hungary upon the recommendation of the Hungarian premier, who would usually nominate a Hungarian noble. Croatia-Slavonia-Dalmatia was recognized as a nation with its own territory, the Croatian language was allowed, and it was granted political autonomy in internal affairs. But in reality, the Hungarians dominated the political and economic life of Croatia. In spite of the settlement, Dalmatia and Istria remained under direct Austrian administration, while the port city of Rijeka had a special status under direct Hungarian administration.

In the 1870s, Ivan Mažuranić was appointed Ban of Croatia. He implemented general administrative reform and a modern system of education. The Sabor instituted a supreme court and a complete judicial system. The 1878 Congress of Berlin resulted in a decision to allow Austria's military occupation and administration of Bosnia and Herzegovina and the Sandžak area (lost by the Turks after their defeat by Russia in 1877). The Croatian Sabor then requested the annexation of those areas, along with Dalmatia and the military regions, but Austria and Hungary refused. Croatia and Serbia were deeply disappointed, and Serbia began supporting irredentism and terrorist activities against the Austrians in those areas Serbia considered its own. In 1881, the Military Region was joined to Croatia, thus increasing the size of its Serbian Orthodox population. This offered the Hungarian Ban Khuen Hedervary the opportunity to play Serbs against Croats in order to prevent their joint front. The relations between Croats and Serbs continued to deteriorate as Magyarization continued.

Yugoslavism

By 1893, there was a united Croatian opposition that called for equality with Hungary, the unification of all Croatian lands, and which invited the Slovenes to join Croatia in the formation of a new state within the framework of the Hapsburg Monarchy. This united opposition took the name of Croatian Party of Right ("Stranka Prava"). By 1905, several other political parties developed, among them the Croatian People's Party, the Croatian People's Peasant Party, the Social Democrats, the Christian Socialists, and several Serbian parties. The Peasant Party represented the plight of the Croatian peasantry that, emancipated from serfdom and without any resources, became prey to speculators and loan sharks that drove thousands of Croatian peasants into bankruptcy and massive emigration. National unification, however, had strong opposition from powerful forces: the Hungarians with their Great Hungary Drive; the Serbs, who wanted to annex Bosnia and Herzegovina to Serbia; the Italians, claiming Istria, Rijeka, and Dalmatia; and the Austrians, and their Pan-Germanic partners.

While a strong movement in Hungary agitated for complete independence of the Austrian Crown, Croats and Serbs formed a Croat-Serbian coalition. The Croat-Serbian coalition won a simple majority in the 1908 Croatian parliament elections, followed by the Party of Right and the Peasant Party, led by the brothers Anthony and Stephen Radić. Also in 1908, the direct annexation of Bosnia and Herzegovina by Austria took place, opposed by the Hungarians because it would increase the influence of the Croats and Serbs in support of a "trialist" reorganization of the Monarchy and therefore grant a co-equal status to the unified South-Slavic nations. The Party of Right and the Peasant Party supported the annexation, hoping that the next step would be Bosnia and Herzegovina's incorporation into a unified Croatia. On the other hand, Serbia, enraged by the annexation, allowed the increased activities of Serbian irredentist groups in Bosnia supported by the "Narodna Odbrana" (National Defense) Society. Assassination attempts increased and led to the assassination of Archduke Ferdinand and his wife in Sarajevo on 28 June 1914. These tragedies followed the Serbian victories and territorial expansion in the wake of the 1912 and 1913 Balkan wars.

The idea of a separate state uniting the South Slavic nations ("Yugoslavism") grew stronger during World War I, fostered by Austro-Hungarian persecutions and sympathy for the plight of the Serbian nation. An emigre "Yugoslav Committee" was formed and worked for the unification of the South Slavs with the Kingdom of Serbia. In 1917, an aggreement was reached on the Greek island of Corfu between the "Yugoslav Committee" and the Serbian Government in exile on the formation of a "Kingdom of Serbs, Croats, and Slovenes" upon the defeat of Austro-Hungary.

Royal Yugoslavia

The unification of Croatia and the new "Kingdom of Serbs, Croats, and Slovenes" on 1 December 1918 was flawed by the inability to work out an acceptable compromise between Serbian unitarists and Croat-Slovene Federalists. The 1917 Corfu Declaration had left the decision on the nature of the post-World War I South Slavic state to the "qualified majority" of a constituent assembly. The National Council for all Slavs of former Austro-Hungary was formed on 12 October 1918 in Zagreb (Croatia) and was chaired by Monsignor Anton Korošec, head of the Slovenian People's Party. The Croatian parliament (Sabor) delegated its authority to the National Council which, on 29 October 1918, proclaimed the separation of the South Slavs from Austro-Hungary and the formation of a new, separate state of Slovenes, Croats, and Serbs of the former Austro-Hungary. The Zagreb Council intended to negotiate a federal type of union between the new state and the Kingdom of Serbia that would preserve the respective national autonomies of the Slovenes, Croats, and Serbs. Msgr. Korošec had negotiated a similar agreement in principle with Serbian Prime Minister Nikola Pašić in Geneva, but the

Serbian government reneged on it. While Msgr. Korošec was detained in Geneva, a delegation of the National Council went to Belgrade and submitted to Serbia a declaration expressing the will to unite with the Kingdom of Serbia. In order to prevent any delays, there were no conditions requested at the time on the type of union the National Council expected, and Serbia readily agreed. On 1 December 1918, Prince Alexander of Serbia declared the unification of the "Kingdom of Serbs, Croats, and Slovenes," a unitary Kingdom with a strongly centralized government. Serbia viewed its expansion as liberation of its Slavic brethren from Austro-Hungary, as compensation for its tremendous war sacrifices, and as the uniting of all Serbian lands into an essentially Serbian-influenced Kingdom, the realization of its "Greater Serbia" dream.

The Slovenes and Croats, on the other hand, while freed from the Austro-Hungarian domination, were nevertheless the losers in terms of the political and cultural autonomy they had hoped for. In addition, they suffered painful territorial losses to Italy (some 700,000 Slovenes and Croats were subjected to all kinds of persecutions by Fascist Italy) and to Austria (a similar fate for some 100,000 Slovenes left within Austria in the Carinthia region).

The provisional assembly convened in 1918, with the addition to the Serbian Parliament of representatives from the other south Slavic historical regions, while the Croatian "Sabor" was deprived of its authority. The elections to the Constituent Assembly were held on 28 November 1920 but the 50-member delegation of the Croatian Republican Peasant Party refused to participate, and instead held its own Assembly in Zagreb calling for a Croatian Republic. By that time the Serbian bureaucracy and military had been able to establish a unitary administrative system throughout the new state ahead of any constitutional provisions. The new constitution, based on the unitary Serbian one, was adopted on 28 June 1921 by a vote of 223 to 35, with 111 abstentions. The provision of the Corfu Declaration called for a "qualified majority" vote by the Constituent Assembly on the nature of the new state. In the absence of the Croatian Delegation with 50 votes, the Serbian side was able to obtain a "simple majority" vote of 223 of the 419 total seats. The opposition, mainly Croats and Slovenes, had supported a two-thirds vote as the Corfu "qualified majority" requirement, and therefore doubts have persisted on the legality of the 1921 constitution.

Another irritant to Croats and Slovenes was the law adopted in April 1922 that dispensed with the historical administrative areas and substituted 33 departments in the French mode. The period between 1921 and 1929 was a confused one, with a sequence of 23 governments, a parliament without the Croatian delegation's 50 votes and the Communist Party's 58 votes (it continued its work underground). This situation assured control to the Serbian majority, which was able to play one coalition against another while building a centralized bureaucracy and state. But in the long run it was not possible to govern the new country effectively without the participation of the Croats, the second largest nation.

Finally, in 1925, Prime Minister Pašić invited Stjepan Radić, head of the Croatian Peasant Party, to form a government with him. This had become possible after Radić dropped his opposition to the Monarchy and endorsed the constitution while pressing for an autonomous Croatia. However, not much was accomplished. Pašić died just a few years later and the bickering resumed in Parliament after Radić resigned from the Government. Tensions continued to escalate in Parliament, and on 20 June 1928 Radić was shot in Parliament and subsequently died in July. While Stjepan Radić was viewed as a charismatic but erratic leader, he did show a considerable degree of pragmatism, changing from his initial advocating of an independent Croatian Republic to the acceptance of the union with the Serbian Monarchy. Radić's greatest success, however, was the building of a massive national movement based on the needs and participation of the Croatian peasants.

Dr. Vlatko Maček, the new Croatian Peasant Party leader declared that "there is no longer a constitution, but only king and people." A coalition government under Prime Minister Msgr. Anton Korošec, head of the Slovene People's Party, lasted only until December 1928. The crisis was so serious that King Alexander even considered the option of separating Slovenia and Croatia into a state of their own by leaving Vojvodina, Southern Dalmatia, and Bosnia and Herzegovina to Serbia. But the Serbs of Croatia opposed a plan that would leave them outside of a common state with Serbia, and proposed a federalist solution that was rejected by the Serbian parties. With no other solution possible, the king dissolved the parliament on 6 January 1929, abolished the 1921 constitution, and established his own personal dictatorship as a temporary arrangement.

At first, most people accepted King Alexander's dictatorship as a necessity, which gave the country an opportunity to focus on building its economy from the foundation of post-war reconstruction. However, a series of royal decrees established a system of constraints and imposed uniformity in all areas of public life. Sanctions of death or 20 years in prison were set for terrorism, sedition, or Communist activities. All elected local councils were dissolved along with the traditional political parties. Freedom of the press was severely constrained and government permission was required for any kind of association. All power was centralized and exercised by the king through a council of ministers accountable only to him.

On 3 October 1929, the law on administrative reorganization regrouped the 33 departments into 9 "banovinas" headed by appointed Bans directly accountable to the Belgrade government. The country was renamed the Kingdom of Yugoslavia, and the Banovinas were named after rivers to emphasize the king's opposition to national names for territorial units. Thus the first Yugoslav experiment was initiated aiming at the creation of a unified Yugoslav nation out of a number of smaller, and different, historical nations represented by the motto "one King, one country, one nation." One of the consequences of the dictatorship and its harsh measures against political opposition and cultural/nationalism was the emigration of some political opponents, among them some of the top leadership of the Croatian Peasant Party and the leader of the Ustaša movement, Ante Pavelić.

The leaders of the traditional Serbian political parties, accustomed to a well-established parliamentary process, became quickly disenchanted with the royal dictatorship, even though it turned out to be another version of Serbian majority rule. In principle, the new constitution, promulgated by King Alexander on 3 September 1931 was a return to civil liberties and freedoms of association, assembly, and expression. But in reality all such freedoms were limited by the king's decrees that remained in force. Parliament was to consist of two houses with a council of ministers still accountable directly to the king. The Croatian opposition grew stronger, and in the winter of 1932, the Zagreb Manifesto called for the removal of Serbian hegemony, and for popular sovereignty. In reaction, the regime interned or imprisoned political opponents such as Dr. Maček, Msgr. Korošec, and Dr. Spaho, leader of the Muslim organization. Croatia was seething with rebellion, and the sentence of three years in prison for Dr. Maček would have sparked an open revolt, were it not for the danger of Italy's intervention.

The worldwide economic depression hit Yugoslavia hard in 1932, and contributed to greater opposition to the king's dictatorship, which had not proffered any solutions to the so-called Croatian question. Following his state visit to France in October 1934, the king was going to take measures to ease this opposition. He planned to release Dr. Maček from prison, reintroduce a real parliamentary system, and try to reach some compromise

between Serbs and Croats. Unfortunately, King Alexander was assassinated in Marseille on 9 October 1934 by agents of the Ustaša group, which was trained in terrorism in Hungary with the support of Italy's Mussolini. Prince Paul, King Alexander's cousin, headed a regency and released Dr. Maček and other political leaders, but otherwise continued the Royal Dictatorship. On 5 May 1935, the elections for a new Parliament were so scandalously improper that a boycott of Parliament began. To resolve the crisis, regent Paul consulted with Dr. Maček. As a result, a new government of reconstruction was formed by Dr. Milan Stojadinović that included Msgr. Korošec and Dr. Spaho. While not rushing to return to true parliamentarianism, the new government did initiate serious discussions with Dr. Maček on a federal system and a limited autonomous Croatian entity that would be empowered on all matters except the armed forces, foreign affairs, state finance, customs, foreign trade, posts, and telegraphs.

Since 1937, the thorniest issue discussed had been the make up of the federal units. Serbs wanted to unite Macedonia, Vojvodina, and Montenegro with Serbia. Croatia wanted Dalmatia and a part of Vojvodina. Slovenia was recognized as a separate unit while Bosnia and Herzegovina posed a real problem, with both Croats and Serbs claiming it and the Bosnian Muslims being caught in the middle. Meanwhile, intense trade relations with Germany and friendlier relations with Italy implemented by Premier Stojadinović were bringing Yugoslavia closer to the Axis Powers. Hitler's annexation of Austria and Czechoslovakia in 1938 made it imperative that Yugoslavia resolve its internal problem before Hitler and Mussolini attempted to destabilize and conquer Yugoslavia.

Upon Stojadinović's resignation (engineered through the resignation of five of his ministers), Regent Paul appointed Dragiša Cvetković as prime minister, and charged him with the task of reaching a formal agreement with the Croatian opposition. The agreement was concluded on 26 August 1939 as a major first step towards a federal reorganization of Yugoslavia. Dr. Maček became the new vice-premier, a Banovina of Croatia was established that included Dalmatia and western Herzegovina and was headed by a Ban appointed by the Crown, and the traditional Sabor (Parliament) of Croatia was revived. But autonomy for Croatia was not received well by most of Serbia. Concerned with the status of Serbs in Croatia, Serbia was anxious to incorporate most of Bosnia and Herzegovina into a Banovina of Serbia. Even less satisfied was the extreme Croatian nationalist Ustaša movement, whose goal was an independent greater Croatia inclusive of Bosnia and Herzegovina. For Ustaša, this goal was to be achieved by any means and at any cost, including violence and support from foreign powers. Tensions between the extremes of the failed Yugoslavism are symbolized by the three mottos—*Protect my Yugoslavia; Three Tribes, one nation; My brother is dear, whatever his religion*—contrasted with urgings by the clandestine Ustaša—*Hang the Serbs from willow trees*—broadcast on radio.

World War II

Meanwhile the clouds of World War II had gathered with Italy's takeover of Albania and its war with Greece, and Hitler's agreement with Stalin followed by his attack on Poland in the fall of 1939, resulting in its partitioning. Hungary, Romania, and Bulgaria had joined the Axis powers and England and France had entered the war against Germany and Italy. With the fall of France in 1940, Hitler decided to assist Mussolini in his war with Greece through Bulgaria, and therefore needed Yugoslavia to join the Axis so Germany would be assured of ample food and raw materials.

The Yugoslav Government had limited choice—either accept the possibility of immediate attack by Germany, or join the Axis, with Hitler's assurance that no German troops would pass through Yugoslavia towards Greece. Prince Paul felt that Yugoslavia would be spared from war, at least for a while and perhaps permanently, if Hitler were to attack the Soviet Union first. The regent was aware of Yugoslavia's weak defense capabilities and the inability of England to assist Yugoslavia against the Axis. Yugoslavia signed the treaty with Hitler on 26 March 1941 and on 27 March a *coup d'etat* by Serbian military officers forced the regent to abdicate. The military declared Prince Peter of age and the new king, and formed a government with General Dušan Simović as premier and Dr. Maček his vice-premier. The new government tried to temporize and placate Hitler, who was enraged by the deep anti-German feeling of the Yugoslav people who, on the whole, supported the coup by shouting in demonstrations, *Bolje rat nego pact, (Better war than the pact)*. Feeling betrayed, Hitler unleashed the German fury on Yugoslavia on 6 April 1941 by bombing Belgrade and other centers without any warning or formal declaration of war.

The war was over in 11 days, with the surrender signed by the Yugoslav Army Command while the Yugoslav government (with young King Peter II) fled the country for allied territory and settled in London. Yugoslavia was partitioned among Germany, Italy, Hungary, Bulgaria, and Italian-occupied Albania, while Montenegro, under Italian occupation, was to be restored as a separate kingdom. Croatia was set up as an independent kingdom with an Italian prince to be crowned Tomislav II. Ante Pavelić was installed by the Italians and Germans as head of independent Croatia (after Dr. Maček had declined Hitler's offer). Croatia had to cede to Italy part of Dalmatia with most of its islands, and the Boka Kotorska area. In exchange, Croatia was given the entire Bosnia and Herzegovina and the Srijem region up to Belgrade.

On 10 April 1941, the "resurrection of our independent State of Croatia" was proclaimed in Zagreb by Slavko Kvaternik for Ante Pavelić, who was still in Italy with some 600 of his Ustaše. With Pavelić's arrival in Zagreb five days later, the Ustaša regime was established, with new laws that expressed the basic Ustaša tenets of a purely Croatian state viewed as the bulwark of Western civilization against the Byzantine Serbs. Slavko Kvaternik explained how a pure Croatia would be built—by forcing one third of the Serbs to leave Croatia, one third to convert to Catholicism, and one third to be exterminated. Soon Ustaša bands initiated a bloody orgy of mass murders of Serbs unfortunate enough not to have converted or left Croatia on time. The enormity of such criminal behavior shocked even the conscience of German commanders, but Pavelić had Hitler's personal support for such actions which resulted in the loss of lives of hundreds of thousands of Serbs in Croatia and Bosnia and Herzegovina. In addition, the Ustaša regime organized extermination camps, the most notorious one at Jasenovac where Serbs, Jews, Gypsies, and other opponents were massacred in large numbers. The Serbs reacted by forming their own resistance groups ("Cetniks") or by joining with the Communist-led partisan resistance, and thus struck back at the Ustaša in a terrible fratricidal war encouraged by the Germans and Italians.

The Ustaša regime organized its armed forces into the homeguard (*Domobrani*), its Ustaša shock troops, and the local gendarmerie. Its attempt at organizing the Croatian people in the fascist mode failed, however. Most Croats remained faithful to the Croatian Peasant Party Democratic principles, or joined the Partisan movement led by Josip Broz-Tito that offered a federative political program. With respect to Bosnia and Herzegovina, the Ustaša regime never attained real control. The continuous fighting generated by Cetniks and Partisans fighting one another while being pursued by the Ustašas, the Germans, and the Italians made it impossible for the Ustašas to dominate. Most Croats rejected (and deeply resented) the trappings of an imported Fascist mystique and the abuse of their Catholic faith as a cover or justification for the systematic slaughter of their Serbian neighbors.

By the spring of 1942, the Ustaša regime began to retreat from its policy and practice of liquidation of Serbs. But the terrible harm was done, and one consequence was the deep split between the Serbian members and their Croatian colleagues within the cabinet of the Yugoslav government-in-exile. The Serbs held the entire Croatian nation accountable for the Ustaša massacres, and reneged on the 1939 agreement establishing the Croatian Banovina as the basis for a federative reorganization in a post-war Yugoslavia. This discord made the Yugoslav government-in-exile incapable of offering any kind of leadership to the people in occupied Yugoslavia, and also weakened the appeal of General Mihajlović's movement because of its lack of a clear political program for a future Yugoslavia. The fortunes of war and diplomacy favored the Communist Partisans—after Italy's surrender in September 1943, it handed over to the Partisans armaments and supplies from some ten Italian divisions. More and more Croats left their homeguard, and even some Ustaša units, to join the Partisans. Some Ustaša leaders, on the other hand, conspired against Pavelić in order to negotiate with the allies for recognition of the "independent" state of Croatia. But they were caught and executed in the summer of 1944.

With the entry of Soviet armies into Yugoslav territory in October 1944, the Partisans swept over Yugoslavia in pursuit of the retreating German forces. Pavelić and his followers, along with the Croatian homeguard units, moved north to Austria at the beginning of May 1945 to escape from the Partisan forces and their retaliation. The Partisans took over Croatia, launching terrible retaliation in the form of summary executions, people's court sentences, and large scale massacres, carried out in secret, of entire homeguard and other units.

Communist Yugoslavia

Such was the background for the formation of the second Yugoslavia as a Federative People's Republic of five nations—Slovenia, Croatia, Serbia, Macedonia, Montenegro—with Bosnia and Herzegovina as a buffer area with its mix of Serbs, Muslims, and Croats. The problem of large Hungarian and Muslim Albanian populations in Serbia was solved by creating the autonomous regions of Vojvodina (Hungarian minority) and Kosovo (Muslim Albanian majority) that assured their political and cultural development. Tito attempted a balancing act to satisfy most of the nationality issues that were carried over unresolved from the first Yugoslavia, but failed to satisfy anyone.

Compared to pre-1941 Yugoslavia where Serbs enjoyed a controlling role, the numerically stronger Serbs had lost the Macedonian area they considered Southern Serbia, lost the opportunity to incorporate Montenegro into Serbia, and had lost direct control over both the Hungarian minority in Vojvodina and Muslim Albanians of Kosovo, which had been viewed as the cradle of the Serbian nation since the Middle Ages. They could no longer incorporate into Serbia the large Serbian-populated areas of Bosnia, and had not obtained an autonomous region for the large minority of Serbian population within the Croatian Republic. The Croats—while gaining back from Hungary the Medjumurje area and from Italy the cities of Rijeka (Fiume), Zadar (Zara), some Dalmatian islands, and the Istrian Peninsula—had lost the Srijem area to Serbia and Bosnia and Herzegovina, which had been part of the World War II independent Croatian state under the Ustaša leadership. In addition, the Croats were confronted with a deeply resentful Serbian minority that became ever more pervasive in public administrative and security positions.

The official position of the Marxist Yugoslav regime was that national rivalries and conflicting interests would gradually diminish through their sublimation into a new Socialist order. Without capitalism, nationalism was supposed to wither away. Therefore, in the name of unity and brotherhood, nationalistic expression of concern was prohibited, and repressed by the dictatorial and centralized regime of the League of Yugoslav Communists acting through the Socialist Alliance as its mass front organization. Thus Croatia shared in the post-World War II history of the second experiment in Yugoslavism.

After a short post-war coalition government, the elections of 11 November 1945, boycotted by the non-communist coalition parties, gave the Communist-led People's Front 90% of the votes. A constituent assembly met on 29 November, abolished the monarchy and established the Federative People's Republic of Yugoslavia. In January 1946, a new constitution was adopted, based on the 1936 Soviet constitution.

The Communist Party of Yugoslavia took over total control of the country and instituted a regime of terror through its secret police. To destroy the bourgeoisie, property was confiscated, individuals were declared "enemies of the people" and executed or imprisoned. Large enterprises were nationalized, and forced-labor camps were formed. The church and religion were persecuted, properties confiscated, religious instruction and organizations banned, and education used for Communist indoctrination. The media was forced into complete service to the totalitarian regime, and education was denied to "enemies of the people."

The Stalin-engineered expulsion of Yugoslavia from the Soviet-dominated Cominform Group in 1948 was actually a blessing for Yugoslavia after its leadership was able to survive Stalin's pressures. Survival had to be justified, both practically and in theory, by developing a "road to Socialism" based on Yugoslavia's own circumstances. This new "road map" evolved quickly in response to Stalin's accusations and Yugoslavia's need to perform a balancing act between the NATO alliance and the Soviet bloc. Tito also radically changed the economy, pushing the nationalization of the economy through a policy of forced industrialization supported by the collectivization of the agriculture.

The agricultural reform of 1945–46 limited private ownership to a maximum of 35 hectares (85 acres). The limited free market (after the initial forced delivery of quotas to the state at very low prices) had to be abandoned because of resistance by the peasants. The actual collectivization efforts were initiated in 1949 using welfare benefits and lower taxes as incentives, along with direct coercion. But collectivization had to be abandoned by 1958 simply because its inefficiency and low productivity could not support the concentrated effort of industrial development.

By the 1950s, Yugoslavia had initiated the development of what would become its internal trademark: self-management of enterprises through workers' councils and local decision-making as the road to Marx's "withering away of the state." Following the failure of the first five-year plant (1947–51), the second five-year plan (1957–61), was completed in four years by relying on the well-established self-management system. Economic targets were set from the local to the republic level and then coordinated by a federal planning institute to meet an overall national economic strategy. This system supported a period of very rapid industrial growth in the 1950s. But a high consumption rate encouraged a volume of imports financed by foreign loans that exceeded exports. In addition, inefficient and low productivity industries were kept in place through public subsidies, cheap credit, and other artificial protective measures, leading to a serious crisis by 1961. Reforms were necessary and, by 1965, market socialism was introduced with laws that abolished most price controls and halved import duties while withdrawing export subsidies.

The Government relaxed its restrictions to allow labor migration, particularly large from Croatia, to West Germany where workers were needed for its thriving economy. Foreign investment was encouraged (up to 49%) in joint enterprises, and barriers to the movement of people and exchange of ideas were largely removed. The role of trade unions continued to include transmission of instructions from government to workers, allocation of perks, the education/training of workers, monitoring of legislation, and overall protection of the self-management system. Strikes were legally neither allowed nor forbidden, but until the 1958 miners' strike in Trbovlje, Slovenia, were not publicly acknowledged and were suppressed. After 1958, strikes were tolerated as an indication of problems to be resolved. Unions, however, did not initiate strikes, but were expected to convince workers to go back to work.

Having survived its expulsion from the Cominform in 1948 and Stalin's attempts to take control, Yugoslavia began to develop a foreign policy independent of the Soviet Union. By mid-1949, Yugoslavia ceased its support of the Greek Communists in their civil war against the then-Royalist government of Greece. In October 1949, Yugoslavia was elected to one of the non-permanent seats on the UN Security Council and openly condemned North Korea's aggression towards South Korea. Following the rapprochement opening with the Soviet Union initiated by Nikita Khrushchev and his 1956 denunciation of Stalin, Tito intensified his work on developing the movement of non-aligned "third world" nations. This would become Yugoslavia's external trademark, in cooperation with Nehru of India, Nasser of Egypt, and others. With the September 1961 Belgrade summit conference of non-aligned nations, Tito became the recognized leader of the movement. The non-aligned position served Tito's Yugoslavia well by allowing Tito to draw on economic and political support from the Western powers while neutralizing any aggressiveness form the Soviet bloc.

While Tito had acquiesced, reluctantly, to the 1956 Soviet invasion of Hungary for fear of chaos and its liberalizing impact on Yugoslavia, he condemned the Soviet invasion of Dubček's Czechoslovakia in 1968, as did Romania's Ceausescu, both fearing their countries might be the next in line for "corrective" action by the Red Army and the Warsaw Pact. Just before his death on 4 May 1980, Tito also condemned the Soviet invasion of Afghanistan. Yugoslavia actively participated in the 1975 Helsinki Conference and Agreements, and the first 1977–78 review conference that took place in Belgrade, even though Yugoslavia's one-party communist regime perpetrated and condoned numerous human rights violations. Overall, in the 1970s and 1980s, Yugoslavia maintained fairly good relations with its neighboring states by playing down or solving pending disputes—such as the Trieste issue with Italy in 1975—and developing cooperative projects and increased trade.

Though ravaged by war, occupation, resistance, and civil war losses and preoccupied with carrying out the elimination of all actual and potential opposition, the Communist government faced the double task of building its Socialist economy while rebuilding the country. As an integral part of the Yugoslav federation, Croatia was, naturally, impacted by Yugoslavia's internal and external political developments. The main problems facing communist Yugoslavia and Croatia were essentially the same as the unresolved ones under Royalist Yugoslavia. As the Royal Yugoslavism had failed in its assimilative efforts, so did the Socialist Yugoslavism fail to overcome the forces of nationalism. In the case of Croatia, there were several key factors sustaining the attraction to its national identity: More than a thousand years of its historical development, the carefully nurtured tradition of Croatian statehood, a location bridging central Europe and the Balkan area, an identification with Western European civilization, and the Catholic religion with the traditional role of Catholic priests (even under the persecutions by the Communist regime). In addition, Croatia had a well-developed and productive economy with a standard of living superior to most other areas of the Yugoslav Federation other than Slovenia. This generated a growing resentment against the forced subsidizing by Croatia and Slovenia of less developed areas, and for the build-up of the Yugoslav army. Finally, the increased political and economic autonomy enjoyed by the Republic of Croatia after the 1974 constitution and particularly following Tito's death in 1980, added impetus to the growing Croatian nationalism.

Tito's motto of unity and brotherhood was replaced by freedom and democracy to be achieved through either a confederative rearrangement of Yugoslavia or by complete independence. The debates over the reforms of the 1960s led to a closer scrutiny, not only of the economic system, but also of the decision-making process at the republic and federal levels, particularly the investment of funds to less-developed areas, where Slovenia and Croatia felt funds were poorly managed, if not squandered. Other issues fueled acrimony between individual nations. An example is the 1967 Declaration in Zagreb claiming a Croatian linguistic and literary tradition separate from the Serbian one, thus undermining the validity of the "Serb-Croatian" language. Also, Kosovo Albanians and Montenegrins, along with Slovenes and Croats, began to assert their national rights as superior to the right of the federation. The eighth congress of the League of Communists of Yugoslavia (LCY) in December 1964 acknowledged that ethnic prejudice and antagonism existed in socialist Yugoslavia, and went on record against the position that Yugoslavia's nations had become obsolete and were disintegrating into a socialist Yugoslavism. Thus the republic, based on individual nations, became a bastion of a strong federalism that advocated the devolution and decentralization of authority from the federal to the republic level. Yugoslav Socialist Patriotism was at times defined as a deep feeling for both one's own national identity and for the overall socialist self-management framework of Yugoslavia. Economic reforms were the other focus of the eighth LCY congress led by Croatia and Slovenia, with emphasis on efficiencies and local economic development decisions based on profit criteria.

Croatian Spring

The liberal bloc (Slovenia, Croatia, Macedonia, Vojvodina) prevailed over the conservative group, and the reforms of 1965 did away with central investment planning and political factories. The positions of the two blocs hardened into a national-liberal coalition that viewed the conservative, centrist group led by Serbia as the Greater Serbian attempt at majority domination. The devolution of power in economic decision making, spearheaded by the Slovenes, assisted in the federalization of the League of Communists of Yugoslavia as a league of quasi-sovereign republican parties. Under strong prodding from the Croats, the party agreed in 1970 to the principle of unanimity for decision making. In practice, this meant each republic had veto power. However, the concentration of economic resources in Serbian hands continued, with Belgrade banks controlling half of total credits and some 80% of foreign credits. Fear of Serbian political and cultural domination continued, particularly with respect to Croatian language sensitivities aroused by the use of the Serbian version of Serbo-Croatian as the norm, with the Croatian version as a deviation.

The language controversy thus exacerbated the economic and political tensions between Serbs and Croats, spilling easily into ethnic confrontations. To the conservative centrists the devolution of power to the republic level meant the subordination of the broad Yugoslav and Socialist interests to the narrow nationalist interest of national majorities. With the Croat League of Communists taking the liberal position in 1970, nationalism was rehabilitated as long as it didn't slide into chauvinism. Thus the "Croatian Spring" bloomed and impacted all the other republics of Yugoslavia. Meanwhile, through a series of constitutional amendments in 1967–68 that limited federal power in favor of republics and autonomous provinces, the federal government came to be viewed by liberals as an inter-republican problem-solving mechanism bordering on a confederative arrangement. A network of inter-republican committees established by mid-1971 proved to be very efficient, resolving a large number of difficult issues in a short time. The coalition of liberals and nationalists in Croatia, however, also generated sharp condemnation in Serbia, where its own brand of nationalism grew stronger, but as part of a conservative-centrist alliance. Thus, the liberal/federalist versus conservative/centrist conflict became entangled in the rising nationalism within each opposing bloc.

Particularly difficult were the situations in Croatia and Serbia because of their minorities issues. Serbs in Croatia sided with the Croat conservatives and sought a constitutional amendment guaranteeing their own national identity and rights. In the process, the Serbs challenged the sovereignty of the Croatian nation. The conservatives prevailed, and the amendment declared that "the Socialist Republic of Croatia (was) the national state of the Croatian nation, the state of the Serbian nation in Croatia, and the state of the nationalities inhabiting it."

Meanwhile, Slovenia, not burdened by large minorities, developed in a liberal and nationalist direction. This fostered an incipient separatist sentiment opposed by both the liberal and conservative party wings. Led by Stane Kavčić, head of the Slovenian Government, the liberal wing gained as much political local latitude from the Federal level as possible during the "Slovenian Spring" of the early 1970s. By the summer of 1971, the Serbian Party leadership was pressuring President Tito to put an end to what was in their view the dangerous development of Croatian nationalism. While Tito wavered because of his support for the balancing system of autonomous republic units, the situation quickly reached critical proportions. Croat nationalists, complaining about discrimination against Croats in Bosnia and Herzegovina, demanded the incorporation of western Hercegovina into Croatia. Serbia countered by claiming southeastern Hercegovina for itself. Croats also advanced demands for a larger share of their foreign currency earnings, the issuance of their own currency, their own national bank that would directly negotiate foreign loans, the printing of Croatian postage stamps, to a Croatian army, to recognition of the Croatian Sabor as the highest Croatian political body and, finally, to Croatian secession and complete independence.

Confronted with such intensive agitation, the liberal Croatian Party leadership could not back down and did not try to restrain the maximalist public demands nor the widespread university students' strike of November 1971. This situation caused the loss of support from the liberal party wings of Slovenia and even Macedonia. Tito intervened, condemning the Croatian liberal leadership on 1 December 1971 and supporting the conservative wing. The liberal leadership group resigned on 12 December 1971. When Croatian students demonstrated and demanded an independent Croatia, the Yugoslav army was ready to move in if necessary. A wholesale purge of the party liberals followed with tens of thousands expelled. Key functionaries lost their positions, several thousands were imprisoned (including Franjo Tudjman who later became President of independent Croatia), and leading Croatian nationalist organizations and their publications were closed. On 8 May 1972 the Croatian Party also expelled its liberal wing leaders and the purge of nationalists continued through 1973.

However, the issues and sentiments raised during the "Slovene and Croat Springs" of 1969–71 did not disappear. Tito and the conservatives were forced to satisfy nominally some demands, and the 1974 Constitution was an attempt to resolve the strained inter-republican relations as each republic pursued its own interests over and above any conceivable overall Yugoslav interest. The repression of liberal-nationalist Croats was accompanied by the growing influence of the Serbian element in the Croatian Party (24% in 1980) and police force (majority). This influence contributed to the ongoing persecution and imprisonments of Croatian nationalists into the 1980s. Tito's widespread purges of the "Croatian Spring" movement's leadership and participants in 1971 had repressed the reawakened Croatian nationalism, but could not eliminate it. Croatian elites had realized the disadvantages of the Croatian situation and expressed it in 1970–71 through the only channel then available—the Communist Party of Croatia and its liberal wing. With the purges, this wing became officially silent in order to survive, but remained active under the surface, hoping for its turn. This came with the 1974 constitution and its devolution of power to the republic level, and was helped along by the growing role of the Catholic church in Croatia. The Catholic church, as the only openly organized opposition force in the country, became the outspoken defender of Croatian nationalism. As a result, Catholic leaders and priests were subjected to persecution and furious attacks by the Communist establishment.

Yugoslavia—a House Divided

After Tito's death in 1980, relations between the Croatian majority and the Serbian minority became strained. Demands for autonomy by the half million Serbs in Croatia were brushed aside by the Croats, who pointed out the absence of such autonomy for Croats in Vojvodina and Bosnia and Herzegovina. Thus the conservatives' control of the League of Communist of Croatia between 1972 and 1987 could not prevent the resurfacing of the Croat question, which led in a few years to Croatia's disassociation from Yugoslavia and to war.

As the Communist parties of the various republics kept losing in membership and control, the clamoring for multiparty elections became irresistible. The first such elections were held on 8 April 1990 in Slovenia where a coalition of non-Communist parties (*Demos*) won, and formed the first non-Communist Government since 1945. In Croatia, the Croatian Democratic Union (HDZ) under the leadership of Dr. Franjo Tudjman, had worked illegally since 1989 and had developed an effective network of offices throughout Croatia and in Vojvodina and Bosnia and Herzegovina. The HDZ had also established its branches abroad from where, particularly in the US, it received substantial financial support. Thus, in the elections of late April-early May 1990 the Croatian Democratic Union was able to obtain an overwhelming victory with 205 of 356 seats won and a majority in each of the three chambers of the Croatian Assembly. In the most important Socio-Political Chamber, Dr. Tudjman's party won 54 of the 80 seats, with the Communists and their allies obtaining only 26 seats. On 30 May 1990, Dr. Tudjman was elected President of Croatia with 281 of 331 votes and Stipe Mesić became Prime Minister. Krajina Serbs voted either for the former Communists or for their new Serbian Democratic Party (SNS) led by Jovan Rašković, a psychiatrist from the Adriatic City of Zadar. The Serbian Democratic Party gained five delegates to the parliament and became the main voice of the Serbs in Croatia.

The overwhelming victory of Dr. Tudjman's party made the Serbs very uncomfortable. Their traditional desire for closer political ties to Serbia proper, the prospect of losing their overrepresentation (and jobs) in the Croatian Republic's administration, and fear of the repetition of the World War II Ustaša-directed persecutions and massacres of Serbs made them an easy and eager audience for Slobodan Milošević's policy and tactics of unifying all Serbian lands to Serbia proper. Tensions between Croats and Serbs increased when Tudjman proposed constitutional amendments in June 1990 defining Croatia as the Sovereign State of the Croats and other nations and national minorities without specifically mentioning the Serbs of Croatia. The Serbs feared they would be left unprotected in an independent Croatia and therefore strongly supported Milošević's centralist policies. This fear, and the anti-Croatian propaganda from Belgrade prevailed and caused Jovan Rašković to reject the invitation from Tudjman to

join the new government as its deputy prime minister. Instead, Rašković ended the participation in legislative activities of the five Serbian Democratic Party deputies. At the end of August 1990, a new Serbian National Council adopted a "Declaration on the Sovereignty and Autonomy of the Serbian People" implying the need for cultural autonomy for the Serbs if Croatia were to remain a member of the Yugoslav Federation, but claiming political autonomy for the Serbs if Croatia were to secede from the Yugoslav Federation. A referendum held on 18 August 1990 by Serbs in Croatia gave unanimous support to their "Declaration on Sovereignty" as the foundation for the further development of their Knin Republic—as their intercommunal council of Serbian-majority communes was called, from the name of the Dalmatian city of Knin where it was based.

The Tudjman government refrained from taking any action against the Knin Republic in order to avoid any reason for interference by the Yugoslav Army. But Tudjman made very clear that territorial autonomy for the Serbs was "out of the question." When in December 1990 Croatia proclaimed its sovereignty and promulgated its new constitution, the Serbs of Croatia established a "Serbian Autonomous Region," immediately invalidated by the constitutional court of Croatia. Then in February 1991, Croatia and Slovenia declared invalid all federal laws regarding the two republics. On 28 February, the Krajina Serbs declared their autonomy in response to Croatia's call for disassociation from Yugoslav Federation. Violence spread in many places with clashes between the Serbian paramilitary and special Croatian police units with Yugoslav army units ordered to intervene. The Yugoslav Army was also used in Serbia in March 1991 to aid Serbian authorities against large Serbian opposition demonstrations in Belgrade. The sight of Yugoslav tanks in the streets of Belgrade, with two dead and some 90 wounded, signaled the decision of the Yugoslav Army to defend Yugoslavia's borders and oppose interethnic clashes that could lead to a civil war. Clearly the Serbian leadership and the Yugoslav army top command (mostly Serbian) had cemented their alliance, with the goal of preserving Yugoslavia as a centralized state through pressuring Slovenia and Croatia into disarming their territorial defense units and by threatening forceful intervention in case of their refusal. But Slovenia and Croatia continued to buy arms for their defense forces, and to proclaim their intentions to gain independence.

At the end of March 1991, there were again bloody armed clashes between the Krajina Serbs and Croatian police, and again the Yugoslav army intervened around the Plitvice National Park, an area the Serbs wanted to join to their Knin Republic. For President Tudjman this Serbian action was the last straw—Croatia had been patient for eight months, but could wait no longer. The overall determination of Serbia to maintain a unitary Yugoslavia hardened, as did the determination of Slovenia and Croatia to attain their full independence. This caused the Yugoslav army leadership to support Serbia and Slobodan Milošević, who had made his position clear by the spring of 1991 on the potential unilateral separation of Slovenia, Croatia, and Bosnia and Herzegovina. Since there was no substantial Serbian population in Slovenia, its disassociation did not present a real problem for Milošević. However, separation by Croatia and Bosnia and Herzegovina would necessitate border revisions in order to allow for lands with Serbian populations to be joined to Serbia. This position was practically the same as Serbia's Prime Minister Pasić's in 1918. Pasić was not opposed to federation in principle, but refused to allow the two million Serbs then outside Serbia proper to be divided among several federal units.

Independence

A last effort to avoid Yugoslavia's disintegration was made by Bosnia and Herzegovina and Macedonia with their 3 June 1991 compromise proposal to form a Community of Yugoslav Republics whereby national defense, foreign policy, and a common market would centrally be administered while all other areas would fall into the jurisdiction of the member states, other than armed forces and diplomatic representation. But it was already too late. Serbia opposed the confederal nature of the proposal and this left an opening for the establishment of separate armed forces. In addition, Milošević and the Yugoslav army had already committed to the support of the Serbs' revolt in Croatia. In any case, both Milošević and Tudjman were past the state of salvaging Yugoslavia. They met in Split on 12 June 1991 to discuss how to divide Bosnia and Herzegovina into ethnic cantons.

The international community stood firmly in support of the preservation of Yugoslavia, of the economic reforms initiated by the Marković government, and of the peaceful resolution of the centralist/confederal conflict. The US and the European community had indicated that they would refuse to recognize the independence of Slovenia and Croatia if they unilaterally seceded from the Yugoslav Federation, while Slovenia and Croatia defined their impending separation as a disassociation by free members as sovereign nations, based on a negotiated process. With the Soviet Union also supporting Socialist Federal Yugoslavia, Milošević was thus assured of strong backing. The Yugoslav army interpreted the international support as a possible green light for military intervention. Slovenia and Croatia went ahead and declared their independence on 25 June 1991.

As a shrewd politician, Milošević knew that a military attack on a member republic would deal a mortal blow to both the idea and the reality of a "Yugoslavia" in any form. Thus, following the Yugoslav Army's attack on Slovenia on 27 June 1991, Milošević and the Serbian leadership concentrated on their primary goal of uniting all Serbian lands to Serbia.

This position led to the direct use of the Yugoslav army and its superior capabilities in support of the Serbian goal of establishing the Serbian autonomous region of Krajina in Croatia. Increased fighting from July 1991 caused tremendous destructions of entire cities (for example, Vukovar) and large scale damage to medieval Dubrovnik. Croatia, poorly armed and caught by surprise, fought over a seven-month period and suffered some 10,000 deaths, 30,000 wounded, over 14,000 missing and lost to the Krajina Serbs (and to the Yugoslav army), and lost about one-third of its territory from Slavonia to the west and around the border with Bosnia and south to northern Dalmatia.

The federal government of Yugoslavia ceased to exist effectively when its last president (Stipe Mesić) and prime minister (Ante Marković)—both Croatian—resigned in December 1991 after both Croatia and Slovenia reaffirmed their decision to disassociate from federal Yugoslavia after the three-month moratorium on such action agreed to in the Brioni Declaration of 7 July 1991. The European Community held a conference on Yugoslavia, chaired by Lord Carrington, where a series of unsuccessful cease-fires was negotiated for Croatia. The conference had also attempted to negotiate new arrangements based on the premise that the Yugoslav Federation no longer existed, a position strongly rejected by Serbia, who viewed with great suspicion Germany's support for the independence of Slovenia and Croatia. Germany granted recognition to Slovenia and Croatia on 18 December 1991, while other European community members and the US followed suit. The European community continued its efforts to stop the killing and destruction in Croatia, along with the UN special envoy, Cyrus Vance, who was able to conclude a peace accord on 3 January 1992 calling for a major UN peace-keeping force in Croatia. Part of the accord was also an agreement by the Serbian side to hand over to the UN units their heavy weapons and to allow the return to their homes of thousands of refugees. (The latter provision has not been honored as of August 1994.) Milošević had every good reason to press the Krajina Serbs and the Yugoslav army to accept the cease-fire because the Serb forces had already achieved control of about one-third of Croatian territory. He was confident that the UN forces would actually protect the Serb-occupied territories from the Croats.

[13]GOVERNMENT

Croatia is a unitary republic with a mix of parliamentary and presidential forms of government. The parliament of Croatia, as formed on 30 May 1990, adopted a constitution for Croatia on 22 December 1990. The executive authority is held by a president, elected for five years, and a government cabinet headed by a prime minister. Legality is assured by the constitutional court. In 1994, the president was Dr. Franjo Tudjman and the Prime Minister, Nikica Valentić.

The Bicameral parliament is composed of the House of Representatives (138 seats) and the House of Counties (68 seats) with the Chairman of the House of Representatives serving as the Parliament Chairman.

The President appoints the Prime Minister and the cabinet and is the Supreme Commander of the armed forces, declares war and concludes peace on the basis of the parliament's decisions.

[14]POLITICAL PARTIES

The last presidential elections were held in August 1992 when Dr. Franjo Tudjman was reelected President.

There are some 50 political parties registered in Croatia, but only 9 had elected representatives in the Croatian parliament (Sabor) following the August 1992 elections:

	Seats
Croatian Democratic Union (HDZ) President: Dr. Franjo Tudjman (Christian Democratic/Center Right)	122
Croatian Social Liberal Party (HSLS) President: Dražen Budiša	30
Croatian Peasant Party (HSS) President: Drago Stipac	8
Croatian People's Party (HNS) (Former Liberal Communists) President: Savka Dabčević-Kučar	7
Istrian Democratic Assembly (IDS) (Regional Party) President: Ivan Jakovčić	7
Dalmatian Action (Regional Party) President: Mira Ljubić-Lorger	—
Social Democratic Party (SDP) (Reformed Communists) President: Ivica Račan	7
Croatian Party of the Right (HSP) (Radical Party) President: Boris Kandare	5
Serbian People's Party (SNS) President: Milan Djukić	3

[15]LOCAL GOVERNMENT

Local government in Croatia consists of municipalities that are grouped into 21 counties. Citizens are guaranteed the right to local self-government with competencies to decide on matters, needs, and interest of local relevance. Counties consist of areas determined by historical, transportation, and other economic factors. The 21 counties are: Zagreb, Kradina-Zagorje, Sisačko-Moslavačka, Karlovac, Varaždin, Koprivnica-Križevci, Bjelovar-Bilogora, Hrvatsko Primorje-Gorski Kotar, Lika-Senj, Virovitica-Podravina, Požega-Slavonija, Slavonski Brod-Posavina, Zadar-Knin, Osijek-Baranja, Šibenik, Vukovar-Srijem, Dalmatia-Split, Istria, Dubrovnik-Neretva, Medjimurje, City of Zagreb.

[16]JUDICIAL SYSTEM

The judicial system is comprised of municipal and district courts, a Supreme Court, and a Constitutional Court. A High Judicial

Council (made up of the president and 14 other members) appoints judges and public prosecutors. The judicial system, supervised by the justice and administration ministry, remains subject to ethnic bias and political influence.

[17]ARMED FORCES

Upon declaring its independence in 1991, Croatia formed an active armed forces of 105,000 and 100,000 reservists. The army of 100,000 is half regular, half mobilized reservists. The separate air defense service has 4,000 members; the air force, 250 and increasing; and the navy, 5,000 sailors. There are also 40,000 armed police. Armed with Russian weapons, the army has 9 brigades and 5 separate regiments of combined arms. With only 400 tanks and APCs, the Croatian army is basically a mountain and urban infantry defense force. Croatia is also garrisoned by 12 UN infantry battalions (UNPROFOR), an added barrier to Serbian invasion and communal violence. The navy controls one submarine and 12 coastal combat and patrol vessels and craft, none larger than a small corvette. Croatia provides no reliable estimates of defense spending or arms trade, but appears to receive subsidies from Germany.

[18]INTERNATIONAL COOPERATION

Croatia was admitted to the UN on 22 May 1992. It is also a member of the CSCE, and is applying for membership in other international organizations. The country's sovereignty is recognized by the US and EC countries. The UN sent peacekeeping troops to Croatia in the spring of 1992 to mediate an ongoing civil war in the region.

[19]ECONOMY

Before the dissolution of the Yugoslav SFR, Croatia was its second-most prosperous and industrialized area (after Slovenia). Per capita output in Croatia was comparable to that of Portugal and about 33% above the Yugoslav average. As of early 1994, Croatian Serb nationalists controlled about one-third of Croatia's territory; the resolution of this territorial dispute is paramount to Croatia's long-term political and economic stability. Croatia's economic problems are largely inherited from a legacy of Communist mismanagement and a bloated foreign debt. More recently, fighting has caused massive infrastructural and industrial damage to bridges, power lines, factories, buildings, and houses.

Croatia's economy also earned the burden of 800,000 refugees and displaced persons from Bosnia and occupied Croat territories in 1993, with some 80% of the refugees finding shelter with families in Croatia. Extensive Western aid, especially in the tourist and oil sectors, may help salvage the economy from its fragile position.

[20]INCOME

In 1991, the estimated GDP purchasing power equivalent was $26.3 billion, or $5,600 per capita. The national product's real growth rate fell by some 25% in 1991. As of December 1992, consumer prices experienced a monthly inflation rate of 50%.

[21]LABOR

In 1992, about 1,159,000 persons were employed in the following areas: manufacturing, 34%; community, social, and personal services, 23%; transportation and communication, 9%; construction, 7%; agriculture, 5%; public utilities, 2%; mining, 1%; and other services, 19%. In 1992, about 23% of the labor force was either unemployed or informally employed.

All workers, except the military and police, may form and join unions of their own choosing without prior authorization. There are three national labor federations, and unions generally are independent of the government and political parties. The right to strike and bargain collectively is protected by law, and several short work stoppages occurred during 1992 over wages and working conditions.

National minimum wage standards are in place, but are insufficient in providing a worker and family with a decent living standard. The 42 hour workweek is standard, and regulations provide for overtime pay, half-hour work breaks, and 18 days per year of paid vacation.

[22]AGRICULTURE

An estimated 1.5 million hectares (3.7 million acres), or 26% of total land, was cultivated in 1991. Permanent pasture land amounted to 1.6 million hectares (3.9 million acres), or 28% of total land area.

Civil war has generally reduced agricultural output since the breakup of the Yugoslav SFR, as evidenced by the following table of major crops (in thousands of tons):

	1990	1992
Wheat	1,602	658
Corn	1,950	1,538
Sugar beets	1,206	525
Grapes	398	380
Apples	70	62
Plums	31	62

As of mid-1993, the World Bank and European Investment Bank were considering the provision of technical support to restructure and privatize the agricultural sector in Croatia.

[23]ANIMAL HUSBANDRY

About 28% of the total land area consists of meadows and pastures. In 1992, there were 1,183,000 pigs, 590,000 cattle, 539,000 sheep, 27,000 horses, and 13,000,000 chickens. That year, 246,000 tons of meat were produced, including 135,000 tons of pork, 58,000 tons of poultry, 50,000 tons of beef, and 3,000 tons of mutton. Milk production in 1992 totaled 645,000 tons; eggs, 38,700 tons; and cheese, 11,600 tons.

[24]FISHING

With a mainland coastline of 1,778 km (1,105 mi) and island coastlines totaling 4,012 km (2,493 mi) on the Adriatic, Croatia is suited to the development of marine fishing.

[25]FORESTRY

About 36% of the total area is forest. Despite the political unrest from the demise of the Yugoslav SFR, Croatia is still able to supply small but good quality oak and beech. The Croatian wood industry has traditionally been oriented to the Italian market (accounting for over 35% of exports), but has been badly hurt by the civil war. Since 1991, production of lumber and panels has fallen by 50%. Normally, Croatian exports of hardwood lumber consist of 50% beech, 30% oak, and 6% ash. Panels and veneer are also exported and Croatia is starting to increase the output of value-added products while seeking foreign private joint ventures. The forestry sector along with the whole of Croatian industry is also attempting to produce in accordance with European standards and develop standardized contracts.

[26]MINING

Apart from the petroleum deposits north of the Sava, Croatia contains deposits of bauxite, which are mined at Obravac, Drniš, and Rovinj. Cement is produced at Solin, Omiš, and Kaštel Sucuraċ. Marine salt is processed at Pag Island.

[27]ENERGY AND POWER

In 1991, Croatia had an installed electrical capacity of 3,570,000 kw. That year, some 8,830 million kwh were produced and consumption per capita amounted to 1,855 kwh. Oil fields in

Slavonia, natural gas fields at Bogsic Lug and Molve, and coal mines at Labin and Potpican provide Croatia with energy resources. Much of the energy network has been made inoperable by the civil war, and the oil refining industry has been severely damaged.

[28]INDUSTRY

Light industry, especially for the production of consumer goods, is more advanced in Croatia than in the other republics of the former Yugoslav SFR. Croatia's main manufacturing industries include: chemicals and plastics, machine tools, fabricated metal products, electronics, pig iron and rolled steel products, aluminum processing, paper and wood products (including furniture), building materials (including cement), textiles, shipbuilding, petroleum and petroleum refining, and food processing and beverages. Due to the civil unrest and uncertainty created from the breakup of the Yugoslav SFR, estimated industrial production declined by nearly one-third in 1991.

[29]SCIENCE AND TECHNOLOGY

Croatia's oldest pharmacy was founded in 1271 in Trogir and was the first in Europe. Increased foreign trade in recent years has made computers and related products more accessible.

[30]DOMESTIC TRADE

Domestic trade occurs mainly between urban industry and rural agriculture.

[31]FOREIGN TRADE

In 1990, Croatia's exports amounted to $2.9 billion, of which machinery and transport equipment accounted for 30%; other manufactures, 37%; chemicals, 11%; food and live animals, 9%; raw materials, 6.5%; fuels and lubricants, 5%; and other products, 1.5%. Exports were shipped primarily to the other republics of the former Yugoslav SFR. Imports in 1990 totaled $4.4 billion, of which machinery and transport equipment accounted for 21%; fuels and lubricants, 19%; food and live animals, 16%; chemicals, 14%; manufactured goods, 13%; miscellaneous manufactured articles, 9%; raw materials, 7%; and beverages and tobacco products, 1%.

[32]BALANCE OF PAYMENTS

Before the civil war, Croatia led the Yugoslav SFR in worker remittances, as thousands of Croats held factory jobs in Germany and elsewhere. In order to provide a framework for economic recovery, the government has organized the Ministry for Reconstruction, which plans to rebuild war-damaged regions and infrastructure for tourism, which could bring in much needed foreign currency. Foregone tourism alone is costing Croatia an estimated $4 billion annually in lost earnings.

[33]BANKING AND SECURITIES

The National Bank of Croatia was founded in 1992. It has the responsibility of issuing currency and regulating the commercial banking sector. The Croatian dinar was issued 23 December 1991, and was replaced in 1994 by the kuna.

Commercial banks in Croatia include: Dalmatinska Banka, Zadar (1957), Dubrovačka Banka, Dubrovnik (1990), Slavonska Banka, Samobor (1873), Istarska Banka, Pula, and Osijek (1990).

[34]INSURANCE

No recent information is available.

[35]PUBLIC FINANCE

The fiscal year follows the calendar year. As of 1993, Croatia was seeking assistance from the EBRD to repair economic imbalances from war and to curb hyperinflation. The EBRD is considering financial support for infrastructural, telecommunications, and energy projects which otherwise would be unobtainable by the Croatian government. The external debt of $2.6 billion provides for Croatia to assume some part of the foreign debt of the former Yugoslav SFR.

[36]TAXATION

The personal income tax rate varies from 25–35%; corporate taxes are levied at a flat rate of 25%. Also levied are a 20% turnover tax slated to be replaced by a value-added tax; a withholding tax that ranges from zero to 20%; and a social security tax paid at rates of 21.7% by the employer and 26.32% by the employee.

[37]CUSTOMS AND DUTIES

No recent information is available.

[38]FOREIGN INVESTMENT

Foreign companies desiring to establish a fully or jointly owned company in Croatia are required to be certified by the Ministry of Tourism and Trade. In the first half of 1992, Italy established 127 fully owned or joint venture companies in Croatia; Germany, 106; Austria, 62; and the US, 10.

[39]ECONOMIC DEVELOPMENT

In October 1993, the government adopted an ambitious three-phase program intended to stabilize the economy through fiscal stabilization, currency reform, and accelerated privatization. The plan, however, relies upon cooperation with international financial organizations.

Croatia is a member of the IMF, IBRD, and EBRD (as one of the Yugoslav SFR's successor states). Upon the outbreak of conflict in Yugoslavia, the US suspended all benefits to Yugoslavia under the General System of Preferences, but benefits under this program were subsequently extended on 11 September 1992 to all the former Yugoslav SFR republics except Serbia and Montenegro. Despite the economic adversity, foreign investors have been keen to identify business opportunities in Croatia's relatively well-adapted economy.

[40]SOCIAL DEVELOPMENT

The effects of the 1991 war, the great refugee burden, the disruptions of the Bosnian war, the absence of significant international aid and other factors have combined to strain the country's social fabric and economy. In 1993, the average standard of living stood at less than 50% of its level before 1991. Over 400,000 Croats were displaced by the war and its aftermath.

Women have apparently borne a disproportionate share of the unemployment caused by economic disruption. Zagreb and several other major cities have started family crisis associations, such as the Women of Vukovar, for women who have missing relatives, and Tresnjevka, a group working to open a support center for wartime rape victims from Bosnia.

[41]HEALTH

Availability of Croatia's health care statistics has been adversely affected by the civil war that has been raging since 1991. Between 1991 and 1992, there were 25,000 war-related deaths; in addition, deaths for 1993 and 1994 were not yet reported as of late 1994. Separate health care data is not yet available for the independent regions that made up Yugoslavia: Bosnia and Herzegovina, Croatia, Slovenia, and Macedonia.

[42]HOUSING

As of mid-1994, nearly 800,000 displaced persons and refugees from Bosnia and occupied Croat territories were in Croatia, of which approximately 640,000 have found housing with families in Croatia. The remainder are housed in refugee centers and hotels. Refugees continued to arrive at an average rate of 300–500 per day.

⁴³EDUCATION

Education at the elementary level is free and compulsory for children between the ages of 6 to 15 years. Secondary education lasts from two to five years and is of three kinds: grammar; technical and specialized; and mixed-curriculum.

In higher education, there are four universities and three polytechnic institutes: University of Osijek (founded in 1975); University of Rijeka (founded in 1973); University of Split (founded in 1974); and University of Zagreb (founded in 1669).

⁴⁴LIBRARIES AND MUSEUMS

Croatia has 130 museums and art galleries, and four opera houses at Zagreb, Split, Osijek, and Rijeka.

⁴⁵MEDIA

In 1990, there were 1,143,376 telephones. Government controlled Croatian Radio-Television (Hrvatska Radiotelevizija) has charge of all broadcasting. Croatian Radio runs 14 AM and 8 FM stations. Croatian television broadcasts on three channels. In 1991, there were 1,160,000 radios and 1,055,000 television sets.

In 1992, there were 9 daily newspapers with a combined circulation of 342 million, and 603 non-dailies (including 64 weeklies); there were 401 periodicals. In 1990, there were 2,413 book titles published.

⁴⁶ORGANIZATIONS

The Chamber of Economy of Croatia, the Association of Independent Businesses and the Zagreb Trade Fair coordinate and promote trade and commerce in world markets.

⁴⁷TOURISM, TRAVEL, AND RECREATION

Civil unrest since Croatian independence has decimated the lucrative tourist business formerly enjoyed by Adriatic coastal resorts, including Dubrovnik and Split, where thousands of European tourists flocked annually to enjoy the climate, scenery, and excellent swimming from April to October.

⁴⁸FAMOUS CROATS

Dr. Franjo Tudjman has been president of Croatia since May 1990. Nikica Valentić has been prime minister since April 1993.

Two Nobel prize winners have come from Croatia: Lavoslav Ružička and Vladimir Prelog.

Josip Broz Tito (1892–1980) was the leader of Communist Yugoslavia for many years after World War II. In 1948, he led his country away from the Communist Bloc formed by the Soviet Union. Tito served in the Red Army during the Russian Civil War and led the Yugoslav resistance movement during World War II.

There are several internationally known figures in literature and the arts: Ivan Gundulic (1589–1638) wrote about the Italian influences in Croatia in *Dubravka*. Count Ivo Vojnović (1857–1929) is best known for *A Trilogy of Dubrovnik*. Miroslav Krleya (1857–1981) captured the concerns of pre-revolutionary Yugoslavia in his trilogy of the Glembay family (1928–32) and in novels like *Return of Philip Latinovicz* (1932) and *Banners* (1963).

Double-agent Duško Popov (1912–1981), who worked during World War II, was the model for Ian Fleming's James Bond. The wartime figure, Andrija Artuković (1899–1988), known as "Butcher of the Balkans" for his activities in support of Germany, is from Croatia. Religious leader Franjo Seper (1884–1981) was born in Croatia. Musician Artur Radzinski (1894–1958) became conductor of the New York Philharmonic in 1943, and of the Chicago Symphony in 1947. Zinka Kumc Milanov (1906–) was a dramatic opera soprano with the New York Metropolitan Opera in the 1950s and 1960s. Mathilde Mallinger (1847–1920) was a famous Croatian soprano, who performed with Berlin Opera from 1869–1882.

⁴⁹DEPENDENCIES

Croatia has no territories or colonies.

⁵⁰BIBLIOGRAPHY

Cuvalo, Ante. *The Croatian National Movement, 1966–1972.* New York: Columbia University Press, 1990.

Gazi, Stephen. *A History of Croatia.* New York: Philosophical Library, 1973.

Glenny, Michael. *The Fall of Yugoslavia: The Third Balkan War.* New York: Penguin, 1992.

Guldescu, Stanko. *The Croatian-Slavonian Kingdom, 1526–1792.* The Hague: Mouton, 1970.

——. *Economic Wealth of Croatia.* Philadelphia, Dorrance, 1973.

——. *History of Medieval Croatia.* The Hague: Mouton, 1964.

Omrcanin, Ivo. *Diplomatic and Political History of Croatia.* Philadelphia: Dorrance, 1972.

CZECH REPUBLIC

Czech Republic
Ceskaá Republika

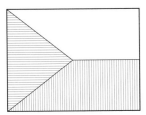

CAPITAL: Prague (Praha).

FLAG: The national flag consists of a white stripe over a red stripe, with a blue triangle extending from hoist to midpoint.

ANTHEM: *Kde domov můj (Where Is My Native Land).*

MONETARY UNIT: The koruna (Kc) is a paper currency of 100 haléru, replacing the Czechoslovak koruna (Kcs) on 8 February 1993. There are coins of 1, 5, 10, 20, and 50 heller and of 1, 2, 5, 10, 20, and 50 koruny, and notes of 10, 20, 50, 100, 200, 500, 1,000, 2,000, and 5,000 koruny. Kc = $0.0340 (or $1 = Kc29.404).

WEIGHTS AND MEASURES: The metric system is the legal standard.

HOLIDAYS: New Year's Day, 1 January; Labor Day, 1 May; Anniversary of Liberation, 9 May; Day of the Apostles, St. Cyril and St. Methodius, 6 July; Christmas, 25 December; St. Stephen's Day, 26 December. Easter Monday is a movable holiday.

TIME: 1 PM = noon GMT.

¹LOCATION, SIZE, AND EXTENT

The Czech Republic is a strategically located landlocked country in Eastern Europe. It sits astride some of the oldest and most significant land routes in Europe. Comparatively, the Czech Republic is slightly smaller than the state of South Carolina with a total area of 78,703 sq km (30,387 sq mi). It shares boundaries with Poland (on the NE), Slovakia (on the SE), Austria (on the S), and Germany (on the W and NW) and has a total boundary length of 1,880 km (1,168 mi). The capital city of the Czech Republic, Prague, is located in the northcentral part of the country.

²TOPOGRAPHY

The topography of the Czech Republic consists of two main regions. Bohemia in the west is comprised of rolling plains, hills, and plateaus surrounded by low mountains. Moravia in the east is very hilly.

³CLIMATE

The Czech Republic has a Central European moderate and transitional climate, with variations resulting from the topography of the country. The climate is temperate with cool summers, and cold, cloudy, and humid winters. The average temperature in Prague ranges from about –1°C (30°F) in January to 19°C (66°F) in July. A generally moderate oceanic climate prevails in the Czech lands. Rainfall distribution is greatly influenced by westerly winds, and its variation is closely correlated to relief. Over three-fifths of the rain falls during the spring and summer, which is advantageous for agriculture. The precipitation range is from 56 cm (22 in) to more than 127 cm (50 in); rainfall is below 58 cm (23 in) in western Bohemia and southern Moravia.

⁴FLORA AND FAUNA

Plants and animals are Central European in character. Almost 70% of the forest is mixed or deciduous. Some original steppe grassland areas are still found in Moravia, but most of these lowlands are cultivated.

Mammals commonly found in the Czech Republic include the fox, hare, hart, rabbit, and wild pig. A variety of birds inhabit the lowlands and valleys. Fish such as carp, pike, and trout appear in numerous rivers and ponds.

⁵ENVIRONMENT

The Czech and Slovak republics suffer from air, water, and land pollution caused by industry, mining, and agriculture. The air in both nations is contaminated by sulfur dioxide emissions traceable, in large part, to the use of lignite as an energy source. In July 1986 annual emissions of sulfur dioxide were reported at 23.4 tons per sq km (60.6 tons per sq mi), the highest level in Europe. In the same year, a program of desulfurization was initiated by the government of the former Czechoslovakia, which earmarked Kcs2.9 billion during 1986–90 to combat pollution. Together, the Czech and Slovak republics contribute 0.7% of the world's total gas emissions, and lung cancer is prevalent in areas with the highest pollution levels.

The Czech and Slovak republics have a total of 6.7 cu mi of water, of which 9% is used for farming and 68% is used for industry; their cities produce 2.9 million tons of solid waste per year. Airborne emissions in the form of acid rain, combined with air pollution from Poland and the former GDR, have destroyed much of the forest in the northern part of the former Czechoslovakia; in 1994, 75% had been damaged by air pollution. Land erosion caused by agricultural and mining practices is also a significant problem.

As of 1994, 2 mammal and 18 bird species in the Czech and Slovak republics were endangered, as well as 2 types of fish and 29 types of plants.

⁶POPULATION

According to the 1991 census, the population was 10,302,215, compared to 10,291,927 in the 1981 census. Average density in 1991 was 131 per sq km (338 per sq mi). Prague, the capital and principal city, had a population of 1,215,076 in 1991. Other major cities, with 1991 populations, include Brno, 392,614; Ostrava, 327,371; and Pilsen (Plzeň), 173,008.

[7]MIGRATION

After World War II, nearly 2.5 million ethnic Germans were expelled from the Sudeten region. The emigration wave from Czechoslovakia after the communist takeover in February 1948 included some 60,000 people; another 100,000 persons left the country after the invasion of the Warsaw Pact countries in August 1968. Emigration slowed during the 1970s to about 5,000 annually, but during the 1980s, some 10,000 people (according to Western estimates) were leaving each year. Average annual legal emigration in the years 1965–69 was 9,457; in 1970–74, 5,899; in 1975–79, 3,734; and in 1980–85, 3,240. In 1991 Czechoslovakia received 5,782 immigrants; emigrants totaled 3,896.

[8]ETHNIC GROUPS

Between 1945 and 1948, the deportation of the Sudeten Germans altered the ethnic structure of the Czech lands. Since the late 1940s, most of the remaining Germans have either assimilated or emigrated to the West. Slovaks came to 3% of the population in 1991. There are small numbers of Poles and an uncertain number of Gypsies.

[9]LANGUAGES

Czech, which belongs to the Slavic language group, is the major and official language. In addition to the letters of the English alphabet, the Czech language has both vowels and consonants with acute accents (indicating length) and háčeks (ˇ): á, é, í, ó, ú, ý, č, dč, ě, ň, ř, š, ť, ž; as well as ů (the circle also indicates length). In Czech, q, w, and x are found only in foreign words. There are numerous dialects. Many older Czechs speak German; many younger people speak Russian and English.

[10]RELIGIONS

In 1990, about 4.7 million Czechs were Roman Catholic. Seventeen other faiths are nationally recognized, the most important among them the Evangelical Church of the Czech Brethren. Protestants (mainly Lutherans), Greek Catholics, and Russian Orthodox are also present in significant numbers. In 1991, the Jewish population in the Czech Republic was only 4,500.

The constitution of 1960 provided for religious freedom and stated that religious practices could be observed insofar as they did not transgress the law. Religious orders were abolished, and members of the clergy were considered civil servants of the state. All houses of worship were controlled by the Office for Church Affairs. After the fall of the communist state in 1989, the Vatican began to appoint bishops in Czechoslovakia. In the next year, diplomatic relations were established. The Czechoslovakian Ecumenical Council of Churches continues to represent churches in both new republics.

[11]TRANSPORTATION

There are some 9,434 km (5,862 mi) of railroads in the Czech Republic, connecting Prague with Plzeň, Kutná Hora, and Brno. Highways cover 55,890 km (34,730 mi); the majority are hard surfaced. As a landlocked nation, the Czech Republic relies on coastal outlets in Poland, Croatia, Slovenia, and Germany for international commerce by sea. The principal river ports are Prague on the Vltava, and Děčin on the Elbe. Ruzyne airport at Prague is the nation's primary commercial airlink; in 1991 it served some 1,342,000 passengers and 17,300 tons of freight. In all, Czech airports in 1992 performed 2,158 million passenger-km and 230 million freight ton-km of service. At the end of 1992, there were 517 and 524 holders of private and commercial pilot's licenses, respectively.

With the separation of Czechoslovakia, the new Czech Republic has rapidly replaced its former Eastern European trading partners with Western ones (primarily Germany and the rest of the EC). This shift in the direction of transportation of goods into and out of the Czech Republic has overloaded the current infrastructure of roads, airports, and railroads. In 1993, the government targeted several goals to develop the transportation network, including: the development of priority connections between Prague and Vienna, Berlin, Warsaw, Nuremburg, Munich, and Linz; the construction of 264 km (164 mi) of new highways over the next 8–10 years for improved trucking links; expansion of the Prague Ruzyne airport; and connection to Western Europe's high-speed rail system, and the acquisition of better rolling stock.

Most goods are shipped by truck. Currently, underdeveloped railroads and waterways often can not accommodate intermodal transport.

[12]HISTORY

The first recorded inhabitants of the territory of the present-day Czech Republic were Celts, who settled there about 50 BC. They were displaced in the early modern era by Slavs, who pushed in from the east. The first unified state in the region was that of a Frankish merchant named Samo, who reigned until his death, in 658. In the 9th century an empire grew up, centered in Moravia. It was wooed by missionaries from both the Eastern and the Western Church. Although two Orthodox monks, Cyril and Methodius, succeeded in converting large numbers of people (introducing as they did so an alphabet they had devised in which to write the Slavic dialect—still called "Cyrillic"), the Roman Catholic missionaries were in the end more successful.

The Moravian Empire was destroyed at the end of the 9th century by invading Magyars (Hungarians), who incorporated the eastern lands into their own, while the Kingdom of Bohemia inherited the lands and peoples of the west. The Premyslid Dynasty took control of the kingdom, allying with the Germans to prevent further Magyar expansion. The German Emperors recognized the right of Bohemian nobles to elect their own kings, but insisted that the Holy Roman Emperor held ultimate authority. In the 13th century there was substantial migration of Germans into Bohemia and Moravia. In the 14th century Charles IV was King of Bohemia, as well as Holy Roman Emperor, ushering in the Czech "Golden Age." In 1348 he founded Charles University in Prague, beginning the city's tradition as a seat of learning. In the 15th century Bohemia became a center of passionate opposition to the Catholic church, and to German domination, led by Jan Hus. Burned at the stake for heresy in 1415 by German Emperor Sigismund, Hus become a national martyr and hero, and the country was in open rebellion from 1420–1436. In 1462 Hungary extended its control over Bohemia, which lasted until 1526, when Ferdinand of Hapsburg was elected to the Crown of St. Wenceslas, making Bohemia the property of the House of Hapsburg.

The Czechs were predominantly Protestant, while their rulers were Catholic, guaranteeing continued civil tensions. Although Protestants were able to secure certain civil freedoms, including of worship, peace was fragile. In 1618 two Protestant churches were closed, leading Protestants to throw two royal governors out of the windows of Prague Castle, an act known since as the "Defenestration of Prague." In the Thirty Years' War which followed, the Czechs deposed their Catholic king, installing instead Frederick of the Palatinate, a Protestant. The Protestant forces were defeated in 1620, at the Battle of White Mountain, and the Catholics again took the throne. This represented a disaster for the Czechs, who had their lands seized, their leaders executed, and nearly 30,000 of their number flee. The war ended in 1648, with the Peace of Westphalia, which sanctioned large-scale immigration of Germans, and the gradual Germanification of Czech territory. Under Empress Maria-Theresa (1740–1780) Bohemia became part of Austria, one result of which was that it became the most industrialized part of the Austrian Empire. Czech cul-

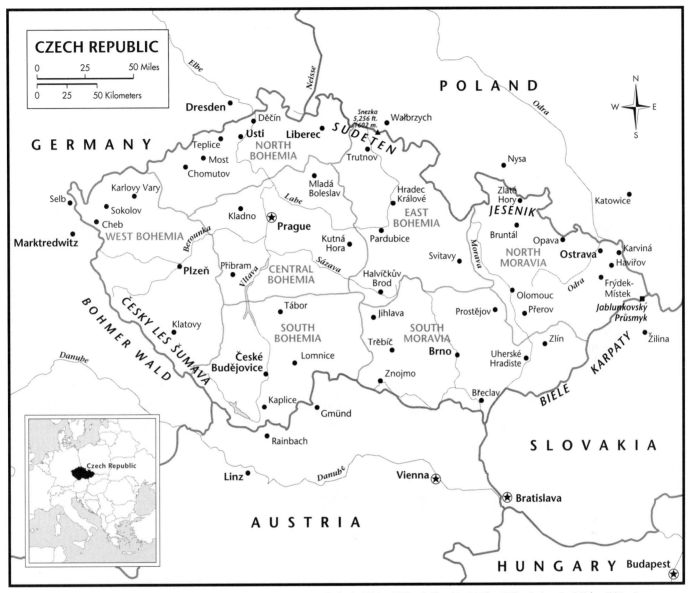

LOCATION: 49°26′ to 51°3′ N; 12°6′ to 18°54′ E. BOUNDARY LENGTHS:Poland, 658 km (409 mi); Slovakia, 214 km (133 mi); Austria, 362 km (225 mi); Germany, 646 km (401 mi).

ture and language were suppressed.

Political tranquillity was broken by the riots which broke out across Europe in 1848. On 11 March 1848, a demonstration in Prague demanded freedom of the press, equality of language, a parliament to represent Czech interests, and an end to serfdom. A Pan-Slav Congress was convened in Prague in June of the same year, under Francis Palacky, a Bohemian historian. The Austrian authorities responded by imposing a military dictatorship, which struggled to restrain a steadily rising tide of nationalist aspirations.

When World War I began, thousands of Czech soldiers surrendered to the Russians, rather than fight for the Austro-Hungarians. They were reformed as the Czech Legion, which fought on the Russian side, until the Russian Revolution of 1917. Although Austria retained nominal control of Bohemia until the war's end, a Czech National Council began functioning in Paris as early as 1916.

Formation of the Czechoslovak Republic

It was the members of that Council, especially Eduard Benes and Tomas Masaryk, who were instrumental in gaining international support for the formation of an independent Czech and Slovak

state at war's end. The Czechoslovak Republic, established 18 October 1918 under President Tomas Masaryk, was a contentious mix of at least five nationalities—Czechs, the so-called Sudeten Germans, Slovaks, Moravians, and Ruthenians. All were granted significant rights of self-determination, but many groups wished for full independence. In 1938 Adolph Hitler demanded that the Sudeten German area, which was the most heavily industrialized part of the country, be ceded to Germany. A four-power conference, of Germany, Italy, France, and Great Britain, was convened, without Czechoslovakian representation. Ignoring the mutual assistance pacts which Czechoslovakia had signed with both France and the USSR, this conference agreed on 30 September 1938 that Germany could occupy Sudetenland. The following spring, on 15 March 1939, Hitler took the remainder of the Czech lands, ending the first republic.

Many prominent Czechs managed to escape the Germans, including Eduard Benes, the president, who established a Provisional Government in London, in 1940, and Klement Gottwald, the communist leader, who went to Moscow. In 1945, negotiations between Benes, Gottwald, and Josef Stalin established the basis for a postwar government, which was formed in the Slovak city of Kosiče in April 1945 and moved to Prague the following month.

The government was drawn entirely from the National Front, an alliance of parties oriented toward Soviet Russia, with whom Czechoslovakia now had a common border, after the USSR incorporated what had been Ruthenia. Although deferring to the communists, the National Front government managed to run Czechoslovakia as a democracy until 1948. The communists had been the largest vote-getter in the 1946 elections, but it seemed likely that they might lose in 1948. Rather than risk the election, they organized a putsch, with Soviet backing, forcing President Benes to accept a government headed by Gottwald. Benes resigned in June 1948, leaving the presidency open for Gottwald, while A. Zapotocky became prime minister. In a repeat of Czech history, Jan Masaryk, Foreign Minister at the time, and son of T. Masaryk, was thrown from a window during the coup, a "defenestration" which was reported as a suicide.

Once Czechoslovakia became a People's Republic, and a faithful ally of the Soviet Union, a wave of purges and arrests rolled over the country, from 1949 to 1954. In 1952 a number of high officials, including Foreign Minister V. Clementis and R. Slansky, head of the Czech Communist Party, were hanged for "Tito-ism" and "national deviation."

Gottwald died a few days after Stalin, in March 1953, setting off a slow but eventually significant erosion of communist control. Zapotocky succeeded to the Presidency, while A. Novotny became head of the party; neither enjoyed the authority which Gottwald had, but both clung to the Stalinist methods which, after Nikita Khrushchev's secret denunciation of Stalin in 1956, had begun to change even in the USSR. Novotny took the presidency upon Zapotocky's death in 1957, holding Czechoslovakia in a tight grip until well into the 1960s.

The Khrushchev-led liberalization in the USSR encouraged liberals within the Czechoslovak party to try to emulate Moscow. Past abuses of the party, including the hanging of Slansky and Clementis, were repudiated, and Novotny was gradually forced to replace many of his most conservative allies, including the head of the Slovak Communist Party.

The new head of that party, Alexander Dubček, attacked Novotny at a meeting in late 1967, accusing him of undermining economic reform and damaging Slovak interests. Two months later, in January 1968, the presidency was separated from the party chairmanship, and Dubček was named head of the Czechoslovak Communist Party, the first Slovak ever to hold the post.

After an unsuccessful Army coup on his behalf, Novotny resigned, in March 1968, and Czechoslovakia embarked on a radical liberalization, which Dubček termed "socialism with a human face." The leaders of the other eastern bloc nations and the Soviet leaders viewed these developments with alarm. Delegations went back and forth from Moscow during the "Prague Spring" of 1968, warning of "counter-revolution." By July the neighbors' alarm had grown; at a July meeting in Warsaw they issued a warning to Czechoslovakia against leaving the socialist camp. Although Dubček himself traveled to Moscow twice, in July and early August, to reassure Soviet party leader Brezhnev, the Soviets remained unconvinced.

Finally, on the night of 20–21 August 1968, military units from all the Warsaw Pact nations save Romania invaded Czechoslovakia, to "save it from counter-revolution." Dubček and other officials were arrested, and the country was placed under Soviet control. Repeated efforts to find local officials willing to act as Soviet puppets failed, so on 31 December 1968 the country was made a federative state, comprised of the Czech Socialist Republic and the Slovak Socialist Republic. In April Gustav Husak, once a reformer, but now viewing harmony with the USSR as the highest priority, was named head of the Czech Communist Party.

A purge of liberals followed, and in May 1970 a new Soviet-Czechoslovak friendship treaty was signed; in June Dubček was expelled from the party.

Between 1970 and 1975 nearly one-third of the party was dismissed, as Husak consolidated power, re-establishing the priority of the federal government over its constituent parts and, in May 1975, reuniting the titles of party head and republic president. The formation of civil rights groups within the country, a group of whom in 1977 published a manifesto in the West called "Charter 77," did not seriously impinge upon Husak's power.

Once again it was liberalization in the USSR which set off political change in Czechoslovakia. Husak ignored Soviet leader Mikhail Gorbachev's calls for perestroika and glasnost until 1987, when Husak reluctantly endorsed the general concept of Party reform, but delayed implementation until 1991. Aging and in ill health, Husak announced his retirement in December 1987, declaring that Milos Jakes would take his post; Jakes had been a life-long compromiser and accommodator who was unable to control dissenting factions within his party, which were now using the radical changes in the Soviet Union as weapons against one another.

Even greater pressure came in early autumn 1989, when the West German Embassy in Prague began to accept East German refugees who were trying to go west. Increasingly the East German government was being forced to accede to popular demand for change, which in turn emboldened Czech citizens to make similar demands. On 17 November 1989 a group of about 3,000 youths gathered in Prague's Wenceslas Square, demanding free elections. On Jakes's orders, they were attacked and beaten by security forces; this ignited a swell of public indignation, expressed in ten days of non-stop meetings and demonstrations. This so-called "velvet revolution" ended on 24 November, when Jakes and all his government resigned. Novotny resigned his presidency soon after.

Although Alexander Dubček was put forward as a possible replacement, he was rejected because he was Slovak, and the choice fell instead on Vaclav Havel, a playwright and dissident, founder of the Charter 77 group, who was named president by acclamation on 29 December 1989.

Dismantling of the apparatus of a Soviet-style state began immediately, but economic change came more slowly, in part because elections were not scheduled until June 1990. In the interim, the old struggle between Czechs and Slovaks resulted in the country being renamed the Czech and Slovak Federal Republic.

In the June elections the vote went overwhelmingly to Civic Forum and its Slovak partner, and economic transformation was begun, although there were continued tensions between those who wished a rapid move to a market economy and those who wanted to find some "third way" between socialism and capitalism. Equally contentious was the sentiment for separation by Slovakia, the pressure for which continued to build through 1991 and 1992. In the June 1992 elections the split between the two parts of the country became obvious, as Czechs voted overwhelmingly for the reform and anti-communist candidates of V. Klaus' Civic Democratic Party, while Slovaks voted for V. Meciar and his Movement for Democratic Slovakia, a leftist and nationalist party. Legislative attempts to strengthen the federative structure, at the expense of the legislatures of the two constituent republics, failed, and the republics increasingly began to behave as though they were already separate so that, for example, by the end of 1992, 25.2% of Czech industry had been privatized, as opposed to only 5.3% of Slovak industry. The prime ministers of the two republics eventually agreed to separate, in the so-called "velvet divorce," which took effect 1 January 1993.

Havel was reconfirmed as president by a vote of the 200-member Czech parliament on 26 January 1993.

13 GOVERNMENT

The constitution of the Czech Republic was adopted by the Czech legislature in December 1992. It mandates a bi-cameral legislative body, consisting of an 81-member Senate and a 200-member lower body, or parliament. How exactly those seats should be filled, however, has proven a contentious point. The former Czech assembly was transformed into the parliament upon the dissolution of Czechoslovakia, but the Senate remains unfilled. The majority Civic Democratic Party (CDP) argued that the Senate should be filled with deputies from the now-defunct Federal Assembly, who in many cases were the various parties' stronger members. The parliamentary deputies and members of smaller parties objected, claiming this would give the CDP an advantage, as well as undercut their own authority; in the absence of a Senate, the Parliament fills that function, which makes it impossible for the President to call for new elections. Controversy also continues over whether to create 81 single-senator districts, as the CDP urges, or to create 27 three-senator districts, to which parties could nominate only one candidate, which works to the benefit of minority parties. In general the country remains undecided whether to move in the direction of a senate chosen by individual vote, which would reduce the importance of parties, or to move to a party-style system, in which voters would select parties, who would then fill seats based upon proportional voting.

The head of the executive branch is the president, who will eventually be elected popularly. The present incumbent, Vaclav Havel, was elected by the Parliament at the time of the republic's formation. Although sympathetic to elements of the parties which seek to diminish party influence and raise the role of individual citizens, Havel belongs to no party, and has attempted to remain above political fighting.

The government is headed by the prime minister, who comes from the majority party, or a coalition. Current incumbent is Vaclav Klaus, who had become prime minister of the Czech part of Czechoslovakia after his party's victory in the June 1992 elections.

14 POLITICAL PARTIES

At present the strongest political grouping in the republic is the Civic Democratic Party (CDP), headed by Prime Minister Vaclav Klaus. It is generally pro-democracy and pro-market economy, although Prime Minister Klaus has increasingly disputed President Havel's attempts to empower individual citizens, arguing that at least for the transitional period it is necessary to have a strong central authority.

The CDP has an unbreakable majority in parliament because of its coalition with three other parties, the Civic Democratic Alliance, Christian Democratic Union, and Christian Democratic Party. There are two more left-leaning parties, the Czech Social Democrats, and the Czech People's Party, but neither has a large following. There are a number of small nationalist parties, which have xenophobic or otherwise extreme platforms; however, only one, the Republic Party, is represented in parliament, because it won nearly 6% of the popular vote in the 1992 parliamentary elections. Although Republic Party members have been implicated in attacks on gypsies, Vietnamese, and other foreigners, their over-all influence is said to be waning.

15 LOCAL GOVERNMENT

The future form of local administration in the Czech Republic is currently at issue. Because the use of a federal structure had fueled the separation of Slovakia from the Czech Republic, which most Czechs were against, further division of the state into, for example, Bohemia and Moravia, has been rejected. It has been broadly decided to subdivide the nation into several regions, which would take up some responsibilities presently borne by the central government. How precisely those regions should be created, and what their powers should be, remains unresolved. A bill was introduced in June 1994 to create 13 regions, but it was rejected, leaving power in the hands of voting districts, which remain the only unit of state administration. The current centers of debate are the prime minister, who wishes to continue the tradition of strong central government, and the president, who wishes to create strong local governments, in order to foster the growth of what he calls "civil society."

16 JUDICIAL SYSTEM

Under the 1992 constitution, the judiciary has been completely reorganized to provide for a system of courts which includes a Supreme Court, a Supreme Administrative Court, high, regional, and district courts, and a Constitutional Court. The Supreme Court is the highest appellate court. The 15-member Constitutional Court created in 1993 rules on the constitutionality of legislation. Constitutional Court judges are appointed by the president, subject to Senate approval, for ten-year terms. Military courts were abolished in 1993 and their functions transferred to the civil court system. The new judiciary is independent from the executive and legislative branches and appears to be impartial in its application of the law.

17 ARMED FORCES

Before splitting into two republics, Czechoslovakia had universal military service for all males between 17 and 50, calling about 75,000 conscripts a year for 18 months of service, followed by service in the 475,000-man reserves.

The Czech and Slovak republics' armed forces in 1993 totaled 145,000. The army, with 72,000 regular troops and 450,000 reserves, was organized into 3 tank divisions, 6 motorized rifle or infantry divisions, 3 artillery brigades, 1 airborne brigade, and 7 engineering brigades, plus smaller combat units. The air force had 44,800 regulars, 45,000 reserves, with 304 combat aircraft and 56 attack helicopters. The air force also provided transport helicopters and air defense missile units. Paramilitary forces included 11,000 border troops and a part-time People's Militia of about 120,000. Defense expenditures in 1990 were equivalent to US$1.6 billion, or 3.2% of GNP.

The Košice Agreement of 1945 provided for military organization, equipment, and training to be modeled after those of the former USSR. Czechoslovakia was a signatory to the Warsaw Pact of 14 May 1955, which provided for military cooperation with the USSR and other Soviet-bloc countries and for a joint command with headquarters in Moscow. Soviet forces of 80,000 remained stationed in Czechoslovakia until 1991.

Czechoslovakia was a leading manufacturer and exporter of armaments until the fall of its Communist Party. From a $1–2 billion a year business in the 1980s, Czech arms exports fell to $270 million a year in 1991. Czech arms imports also showed a steep drop, falling from $280 million in 1990 to $50 million in 1991.

18 INTERNATIONAL COOPERATION

A charter member of the UN since 24 October 1945, Czechoslovakia participated in ECE and all the nonregional specialized agencies except IBRD, IDA, IFAD, IFC, and IMF. It was also a signatory of GATT and of the Law of the Sea, and a member of the WTO and of CMEA, which coordinated economic planning among the Socialist nations. The Czech Republic became a member of the UN on 8 January 1993, and is also a member of the CEI, CERN, CSCE, EBRD, IBRD, IDA, IFC, and IMF.

19 ECONOMY

Before World War II, Bohemia and Moravia were among the most agriculturally and industrially developed areas in Europe. In 1993, the Czech Republic emerged from 40 years of centralized

economic planning in the communist era (including the more balanced economic development of the 1960s) with a more prosperous and less debt-ridden economy than most other post-
communist countries. It enjoys an extensive industrial sector
strong in both heavy and precision engineering, self-sufficiency in
a variety of agricultural crops as well as an exportable surplus of
meat, extensive timber resources, and adequate coal and lignite to
supply two-thirds of its total energy needs.

The GDP dropped 7.1% in 1992 and, after further contraction
early in 1993, is estimated to have returned to the 1992 level. Statistics showed a trade surplus of us$268 million for the first 9
months of 1993 as exports to Western markets increased, and
tourism generated over us$1 billion in revenues over the same
period. The annual rate of inflation almost doubled from 11% in
1992 to 20% in 1993.

[20]INCOME

In 1992, the Czech Republic's GNP was $25,313 million at cur-
rent prices, or $2,440 per capita. For the period 1985–92 the
average inflation rate was 8.5%, resulting in a real growth rate in
per capita GNP of –5.3%.

It is estimated that in 1991 agriculture, hunting, forestry, and
fishing contributed 6% to GDP; mining, quarrying, and manufacturing, 44%; electricity, gas, water, and construction, 6%;
wholesale and retail trade, 10%; transport, storage, and communication, 4%; finance, insurance, real estate, and business
services, 10%; community, social, and personal services, 5%;
and other sources 15%.

[21]LABOR

As of April 1993 the labor force was estimated at over 5.2 million, with some 2.7% of that total unemployed. As of September
1992, there were over 1.1 million private entrepreneurs constituting 11.4% of the total population and 18% of all economically
active individuals (up from only 2% in 1990). Over three-quarters of all employees belong to one of the 20 labor unions. Wages
are expected to be comparable to EC wages within ten years.
While nominal wages rose at the start of 1993, productivity
declined by 2–3%.

Unemployment is expected to increase due to restructuring
and bankruptcy. While there has been little labor or social unrest
since independence, a severe housing shortage seriously impairs
labor mobility, which impedes workers in areas of high unemployment from moving to a place like Prague, with 0.3% unemployment.

[22]AGRICULTURE

Agriculture is a small but important sector of the economy which
has steadily declined since the "velvet revolution" of 1989. In
1992, agricultural production fell nearly 12% from the previous
year, with a further decline of 10–15% estimated in 1993.

The principal crops are grains (wheat, rye, barley, oats, and
corn), which support the Czech Republic's 70 breweries. At 166
liters (44 gallons) per person, the Czech Republic is the world's
highest per capita beer-consuming nation. There is a long tradition of brewing in the Czech Republic; some of the world's oldest
brands were invented there.

Agriculture lags behind other sectors in the restoration of private properties seized after 1948. As of June 1993, only 50,000
cases out of 400,000 had been settled. During 1993–95, the government plans to phase out inefficient production methods and
chronic over-production. As of 1993, agricultural subsidies were
restricted to the formation of new farms, and the production of
wheat, dairy products, and meat. Over the long term, the government estimates that over 250,000 agricultural workers will need
to find employment in other sectors, and that arable land in use
will decrease by 9%.

[23]ANIMAL HUSBANDRY

Hogs, cattle, and poultry are the main income-producers in the
livestock sector. In 1990 there were an estimated 3.5 million head
of cattle. The number of hogs that year reached an estimated 4.9
million; sheep, 451,000; and horses, 28,000.

Meat, poultry, and dairy production have been oriented
toward quantity rather than quality. As of 1993, some Czech
food processing companies had entered into joint ventures with
western countries.

[24]FISHING

Fishing is a relatively unimportant source of domestic food supply. Production is derived mostly from pond cultivation and, to a
lesser extent, from rivers.

[25]FORESTRY

The Forest Code (1852) of the Austro-Hungarian Empire was
incorporated into the laws of the former Czechoslovakia and governed forest conservation until World War II. Most forests were
privately owned, and during the world wars, they were exces-
sively exploited. Since the Czech government began property restitution, the need for wood products has far outstripped domestic
supply, especially for furniture and construction materials. Forests cover about one-third of the total area of the Czech Republic.

[26]MINING

The Czech Republic's nonfuel mineral resources include clay, tin-
tungsten, lead-zinc, and uranium. Copper is mined at small
underground operations at Zlaté Hory in Moravia. Nuclear electric facilities are powered with fuel produced from uranium ore
extracted from Pribram, North and South Bohemia, and South
Moravia. Cement production has increased, due to the construction boom. In 1992, 6.1 million tons of cement was produced, up
from 5.6 million tons in 1991. In 1992, lime production
amounted to 1.2 million tons (down from 2.1 million tons in
1991).

[27]ENERGY AND POWER

As of 1992, the Czech Republic had a yearly electrical energy
supply totaling 55,370 million kwh, of which 64.5% was produced by thermal power plants, 20.7% was generated at nuclear
facilities, 12% came from industrial power plants, and 2.8%
came from hydroelectric sources. The per capita consumption of
electric power is almost 100 kwh per day, or about half the US
per capita average.

As of the end of 1993, eight regional electricity companies
were to be privatized, while the high voltage network of 100 kilo-
watts and higher will remain a state entity. The state natural gas
monopoly will be broken up into six or seven regional companies.

Domestic coal mining supplied the former Czechoslovakia
with 55% of its annual energy needs. In the Czech Republic, lignite is mined at Brno, Kladno, Most, Plzeň, Sokolov, and Trut-
nov; bituminous coal comes from underground mines at the East
Bohemia, West Bohemia, Kladno, and Ostrava-Karviná coal
fields. Uranium for domestic nuclear plants comes from Přibram,
North and South Bohemia, and South Moravia.

[28]INDUSTRY

Before World War II, Czechoslovakia favored traditional export-
oriented light industries, including food processing. Concentration on the production of capital goods since the war has been at
the expense of consumer goods and foodstuffs, although there
have been increases in the metalworking industry and in the production of glass, wood products, paper, textiles, clothing, shoes,
and leather goods. Some of these and other consumer goods—
such as the world-famous pilsner beer, ham, and sugar—had fig-

ured prominently in the pre-World War II export trade, but machinery was predominant under the communist regime.

The extent of Czechoslovakian industry still ranks both the Czech and Slovak republics among the world's most industrialized countries. In 1988, industrial production accounted for 60% of Czechoslovakia's national revenue, 69% of GDP, and 37% of employment. Heavy industry, including machinery, chemicals, and rubber, was still predominant but is likely to decline in importance as the new republics seek export markets to replace those lost in the breakup of the Comecon alliance. Major industries in the Czech Republic include textiles, glass, china, wood and paper, iron, steel, coal, machine tools, and chemicals.

29 SCIENCE AND TECHNOLOGY

The Czech Republic has universities offering degrees in medicine, natural sciences, mathematics, engineering, and agriculture.

30 DOMESTIC TRADE

In the communist period, virtually the entire internal trade network was within the socialized sector.

Marketing and distribution, including price-fixing, were controlled by the federal government; administration on the lower levels was handled by the national committees. Cooperative farms sold the bulk of their produce to the state at fixed prices, but marginal quantities of surplus items were sold directly to consumers through so-called free farmers' markets. Starting in 1958, the government operated a program of installment buying for certain durable consumer goods, with state savings banks granting special credits. Most retail transactions, however, were for cash.

Retail trade is currently undergoing rapid privatization along with other sectors of the economy. More than 20,000 shops, restaurants, and workshops in both the Czech and Slovak republics were transferred to private owners by public auction in a wave of "small" privatization.

31 FOREIGN TRADE

Czechoslovak foreign trade has traditionally involved the import of raw materials, oil and gas, and semi-manufactured products and the export of semi-finished products and consumer and capital goods. In 1989, trade with former Eastern bloc nations accounted for 56% of Czechoslovakia's total foreign trade; by the end of 1992 their share had dropped to 27%. As of 1993, EC and EFTA countries accounted for 59% of trade by the Czech and Slovak republics. Their most important trading partners are Germany, the CIS, Austria, and Poland, followed by Italy, Switzerland, and France.

In 1992, total exports were valued at US$11,155 million, and total imports at US$12,406 million. In 1993, Czech exports (some 80% of which went to Western markets) expanded by over 16%, reversing continued GDP contraction in the face of declining industrial output. At the end of 1993, exports accounted for more than 50% of GDP.

32 BALANCE OF PAYMENTS

In 1992, the Czech Republic had an estimated trade deficit of $664 million, but service exports have been particularly strong since 1990, and have more than covered trade deficits. The transportation sector, vehicle transit fees, and tourism continue as the key foreign exchange earners in the services sector. Following the dissolution of Czechoslovakia, foreign exchange reserves increased rapidly, reaching $1.9 billion by June 1993.

33 BANKING AND SECURITIES

The Bank of the Czech Republic is the country's central bank, charged with issuing currency and regulating the state's commercial banking sector. The bank has reserves of Kc164,564 million and foreign assets of Kc185,197 million in 1993. The money sup-

ply, as measured by M2, was Kc697,406 million in 1993.

There are 36 commercial and savings banks in the Czech Republic. The state has 1 state financial bank, 21 Czech joint-stock companies, 6 partly owned foreign banks, and 7 foreign banks. The commercial banks had reserves of Kc71,445 million, foreign assets of Kc83,948 million, demand deposits of Kc210,961 million and time, savings and foreign currency deposits of Kc428,214 million in 1993.

The Prague Stock Exchange has been trading debt securities (mostly government and bank issues) since April 1993. Volume in mid–1993 was Kc18 million, of which two-thirds were listed issues.

34 INSURANCE

The pre-World War II insurance companies and institutions of the former Czechoslovakia were reorganized after 1945 and merged, nationalized, and centralized. Starting in 1952, the insurance industry has been administered by the State Insurance Office, under the jurisdiction of the Ministry of Finance, and two enterprises conducted insurance activities, the Czech and the Slovak Insurance Enterprises of the State.

In 1991, life insurance policies represented 41% (US$210 million) of premium income (and 72% of premium income collected from individuals). Personal property and liability insurance premiums amounted to US$81 million in 1991, as did industrial insurance premiums. Property insurance and car insurance are used by more than 80% of the population in the Czech Republic. Competition entered the insurance industry with the passage of a new law that went into effect in 1992. By 1993, the Czech Republic's state insurance enterprise, Ceska Pojistovna, had been joined by 16 other firms, including branches of foreign companies. Most offer standard life and health insurance, as well as property coverage and commercial insurance.

35 PUBLIC FINANCE

The Czech Republic's 1993 budget was balanced at $14.5 million. From January to May 1993, the state budget had a surplus totaling Kc4.8 billion. Tax collections from 1992 along with the collection of new taxes (especially VAT) have boosted revenues. Such new taxes represent approximately 80% of total revenues. Social spending was the largest expenditure in 1993. In June 1993, the external debt stood at $6.2 billion.

The following table shows actual revenues and expenditures for 1990 and 1991 in billions of koruny.

	1990	1991
REVENUE AND GRANTS		
Tax revenue	368.2	421.1
Non-tax revenue	40.9	55.6
TOTALS	400.2	489.4
EXPENDITURES & LENDING MINUS REPAYMENTS		
General public service	10.9	20.8
Defense	32.3	27.9
Public order and safety	11.5	17.4
Education	8.5	38.2
Health	1.9	28.8
Social security and welfare	112.9	159.7
Housing and community amenities	9.5	10.5
Recreation, cultural, and religious affairs	15.7	33.5
Economic affairs and services	130.5	85.4
Other expenditures	66.9	88.6
Adjustments	0.9	−0.2
Lending minus repayments	3.8	6.2
TOTALS	405.3	516.8
Deficit/Surplus	−5.1	−27.4

36TAXATION

A new system of personal and corporate income taxes and sales taxes was instituted on 1 January 1993. The turnover tax—basically a sales tax on goods, including foodstuffs—has been replaced by a conventional VAT system with a standard rate of 23% on most goods and services. Businesses with a taxable turnover of Kc1.5 million for the preceding quarter have to register for VAT. Personal income tax rates vary from 15% on incomes of Kc60,000 to 47% on Kc1,080,000 and over, and individual income taxes are levied on all services of income outside of employment.

Corporations pay a flat tax of 45%, to which individual republics can add up to 5%. The general payroll tax rate is 50%, and capital gains are treated as normal income.

37CUSTOMS AND DUTIES

After 1 August 1954, most goods imported into the former Czechoslovakia were dutiable except those exempted by the customs tariff or by international treaty. In 1993, the Czech Republic replaced the turnover tax, luxury tax, and import surcharges with a value-added tax.

38FOREIGN INVESTMENT

A competitive exchange rate and low wages have been conducive to foreign investment; total foreign investment reached US$1.2 billion in 1992. Moody's Investors Service gave the Czech Republic the first investment-grade rating to be awarded to a former Soviet bloc country. At the end of 1993, almost 7,000 joint ventures with some foreign participation and about 5,300 ventures with 100% foreign participation were registered in the Czech Republic. As of 1992, companies from the US, France, Germany, Austria, and Belgium ranked as the largest investors.

New investors may apply for a tax holiday of up to two years, although it will only apply if the company is profitable within that period. Free-trade zones have been established in Ostrava, Pardubice, Zlín, Třinec, and Cheb.

39ECONOMIC DEVELOPMENT

Economic recovery has been implemented by development of the private sector, particularly in the trade and services areas, increased exports to industrialized nations, control of inflation, and achievement of a positive trade balance. The most promising growth sectors are those involving advanced technology, environmental protection, biotechnology, and, generally, high value-added production. In 1992, the Czech-Moravian Guarantee and Development Bank was formed to provide guarantees for new ventures and implement government programs offering grants to newly created small and medium-size companies. At the end of 1993, approximately 60% of the Czech Republic's large companies had been privatized, mostly in the first wave of voucher privatization, through which nearly 6 million Czechs bought vouchers exchangeable for shares in companies that were to be privatized.

40SOCIAL DEVELOPMENT

Social welfare programs in the former Czechoslovakia dated back to the Austro-Hungarian Empire. During the First Republic (1918–39), social insurance was improved and extended. After World War II, new social legislation made sickness, accident, disability, and old age insurance compulsory. The trade unions administered health insurance and family allowances. The government's Bureau of Pension Insurance administered the pension insurance program, which was funded by the government and employers. In 1960, social welfare committees were established within the regional and district national committees to exercise closer control.

In recent years, women have played an increasingly greater role in Czech society. They exceed the number of men employed in farming, trade, health and social welfare, and education. Although the principle of equal pay for equal work is generally followed, women hold a disproportionate share of lower-paying positions. Women's median wages in 1993 were significantly lower than those of men. During the mid-1980s, an estimated 66% of married women in the former Czechoslovakia practiced contraception. Induced abortions are legal.

41HEALTH

In 1992, there were 135,000 births in the Czech Republic (giving it a birthrate of 13 per 1,000). An insurance scheme is already in place to encourage private medical practice. Insurance companies are required by law to pay the doctor within 5 days of treatment.

Health activities are directed by the Ministry of Health through the National Health Service. Factories and offices have health services, ranging from first-aid facilities in small enterprises to hospitals in the largest. All school children receive medical attention, including inoculations, X-rays, and annual examinations. Between 1990 and 1992, children up to 1 year of age were immunized for the following diseases: tuberculosis (98%); diphtheria, pertussis, and tetanus (99%); polio (99%); and measles (97%).

Special attention has been devoted to preventive medicine, with campaigns waged against tuberculosis, veneral diseases, cancer, poliomyelitis, diphtheria, and mental disturbances. Free guidance and care given to women and children have resulted in a low infant mortality rate of 11 per 1,000 live births in 1992. Average life expectancy in 1992 was 72 years for men and women, with an overall death rate of 11 per 1,000 people the same year.

42HOUSING

Currently, the lack of affordable housing, which inhibits labor mobility, is a major factor slowing economic growth in the Czech Republic. Problems include lack of financing, shortages of materials and labor, and a poorly developed infrastructure. As of July 1992, the government was drafting a new housing policy which, among other things, would lift existing restrictive legal provisions barring occupants from buying and reselling flats and differentiate rents according to quality and location of flats. According to the March 1991 census, there were 5,320,095 flats in the former Czechoslovakia. Housing starts totaled 10,000 in 1991, down nearly 80% from 1990.

43EDUCATION

Education in the former Czechoslovakia was under state control and free, up to and including the university level, for all who could obtain admittance. There was virtually no illiteracy. At the start of the 1991 school year, 1,898,470 students were enrolled in 6,480 nine-year (or primary) schools; 848,721 students attended secondary schools; 367,652 attended vocational schools; and 8,957 attended teacher training schools

Over 36 universities, colleges, and advanced schools in the former Czechoslovakia had a total of 177,110 students in 1991. Universities in the current Czech Republic include the world-famous Charles University at Prague (founded 1348); Palacký University at Olomouc (1576; reestablished 1946); and J. E. Purkyně University at Brno (1919; reestablished 1945).

44LIBRARIES AND MUSEUMS

The State Library of the Czech Socialist Republic (5.5 million volumes in 1985) was established in Prague in 1958, the result of an amalgamation of six Prague libraries, including the venerable University Library, founded in 1348. Other collections of significance are the university libraries at Brno and Olomouc.

Castles, mansions, churches, and other buildings of historical interest are public property. Many serve as museums and galleries. There are about 190 museums. The largest museum is the world-famous National Museum in Prague. The National Gallery, also in Prague, contains outstanding collections of medieval art and 17th-century and 18th-century Dutch paintings. Other outstanding museums and galleries are located in Brno and Plzeň. The Prague Botanical Gardens are among the finest in Europe.

45MEDIA

The telecommunications sector is one of the key industry sectors and a major infrastructural bottleneck in the Czech Republic. Partial privatization was underway in 1993. At the end of 1992, there were 1.8 million direct exchange lines serving 4.1 million telephones, of which 1.6 million were residential subscribers.

Investment of Kc130 billion for a system upgrade is expected to increase the number of telephones from 17 to 34 per 100 inhabitants by 1999. The waiting time for new telephone service currently is from five to ten years. In 1992, about 150 private companies provided cable television to some 5% of the 3.4 million Czech households. Several broadcast radio and television channels also operate.

Formerly, the Communist Party and the government controlled all publishing. Formal censorship, via the government's Office for Press and Information, was lifted for three months during the Prague Spring of 1968, but prevailed after that time until the late 1980s.

The following table lists major newspapers, their publishers, and estimated 1991 circulations:

PRAGUE	PUBLISHER	CIRCULATION
Lidove Noving	NA	450,000
Mladá Fronta	Socialist Union of Youth	391,000
Rudé Právo	Communist Party	370,000
Svobodné Slovo	Socialist Party	314,000
Práce	Revolutionary Trade Union Movement	235,000
Lidová Demokracie	Czechoslovak People's Party	122,500

46ORGANIZATIONS

The Czech Republic's 1991 Constitutional Law Guarantees its workers the right to form and join unions. Seventy percent of all Czech workers belong to a labor organizations, The most important umbrella labor organization is the Czech and Slovak Confederation of Trade Unions, an organization that promotes democracy. Other important political associations include the Czech Democratic Left Movements and the Civic Movement.

47TOURISM, TRAVEL, AND RECREATION

A passport is required for all foreign nationals, whether temporary visitors or transit passengers. Visitors from some countries (including the United States and the United Kingdom) do not need visas. Tourism has doubled since the overthrow of Communism. Hotel space in the Czech Republic is limited; many visitors are invited to rent a room in a private house or apartment. Several new luxury hotels were slated to open in 1993, including the Hotel Traha, the former Communist Party lodgings taken over by the Hyatt chain.

Prague, which survived World War II relatively intact, has numerous palaces and churches from the Renaissance and Baroque periods. There are many attractive mountain resorts, especially in northern Bohemia. Football (soccer), ice hockey, skiing, canoeing, swimming, and tennis are among the favorite sports.

48FAMOUS CZECHS

Perhaps the two most famous Czechs are the religious reformer John Huss (Jan Hus, 1371–1415) and the theologian, educator, and philosopher John Amos Comenius (Jan Amos Komenský,

1592–1670), an early advocate of universal education. *The History of the Czech People* by František Palacký (1798–1876) inspired Czech nationalism. Karel Havlíček (1821–56) was a leading political journalist, while Alois Jirásek (1851–1930) is known for his historical novels. The most famous woman literary figure is Božena Němcová (1820–62), whose *Babička (The Grandmother)*, depicting country life, is widely read to this day. A poet of renown, Jaroslav Vrchlický (1853–1912) wrote voluminous poetry and translations. *The Good Soldier Schweik* by Jaroslav Hašek (1883–1923) is a renowned satire on militarism. Karel Capek (1890–1938), brilliant novelist, journalist, and playwright, is well known for his play *R.U.R.* (in which he coined the word *robot*). Bedřich Smetana (1824–84), Antonín Dvořák (1841–1904), Leoš Janáček (1854–1928), and Bohuslav Martinů (1890–1959) are world-famous composers. The leading modern sculptor, Jan Stursa (1880–1925), is best known for his often-reproduced *The Wounded*.

The founder of modern Czechoslovakia was Tomáš Garrigue Masaryk (1850–1937), a philosopher-statesman born of a Slovak father and a Czech mother. Eduard Beneš (1884–1948), cofounder with Masaryk of the Czechoslovak Republic, was foreign minister, premier, and president of the republic (1935–38 and 1940–48). Jan Masaryk (1886–1948), son of Tomáš G. Masaryk, was foreign minister of the government-in-exile and, until his mysterious death, of the reconstituted republic. Klement Gottwald (1896–1953) became a leader of the Czechoslovak Communist Party in 1929 and was the president of the republic from 1948 to 1953; Antonín Zápotocký (1884–1957), a trade union leader, was president from 1953 to 1957. Alexander Dubček (b.1921) was secretary of the Czechoslovak Communist Party and principal leader of the 1968 reform movement that ended with Soviet intervention. Gen. Ludvík Svoboda (1895–1979) was president of the republic from 1968 to 1975. Gustáv Husák (b.1913) was general secretary of the Communist Party from 1969 to 1987; he became president of the republic in 1975. Parlimentary elections at the end of 1989 saw the rise of the playright Vaclav Havel (b. 1936) to power. The Czech and Slovak republics decided to split in 1992. Havel was elected president of the Czech Republic in parliametary elections. Vaclav Klaus was elected prime minister.

Prominent 20th-century Czech personalities in culture and the arts include the writers Vladislav Vančura (1891–1942) and Ladislav Fuks (b.1923), the painter Jan Zrzavý (1890–1977), and the Czech filmmakers Jiří Trnka (1912–69) and Karel Zeman (b.1910). Leaders of the "new wave" of Czechoslovak cinema in the 1960s were Ján Kadár (1918–79) and Miloš Forman (b.1932), both expatriates after 1968. The best-known political dissidents in the 1970s and 1980s were the playwrights Pavel Kohout (b.1928) and Václav Havel (b.1936), and the sociologist Rudolf Battěk (b.1924). The novelist Milan Kundera (b.1929), who has lived in France since 1975, is the best-known contemporary Czech writer. Two Czechs have become top world tennis players: Martina Navrátilová (b.1956), expatriate since 1975, and Ivan Lendl (b.1960).

There have been only two Czechoslovak Nobel Prize winners: in chemistry in 1959, Jaroslav Heyrovský (1890–1967), who devised an electrochemical method of analysis; and in literature in 1984, the poet Jaroslav Seifert (1901–84).

49DEPENDENCIES

Czechoslovakia has no territories or colonies.

50BIBLIOGRAPHY

Batt, Judy. *Economic Reform and Political Change in Eastern Europe: A Comparison of the Czechoslovak and Hungarian Experiences.* New York: St. Martin's Press, 1988.
Beneš, Eduard. *Memoirs: From Munich to New War and New*

Victory. Boston: Houghton Mifflin, 1954.

Brablcová, V., *et al*. *Czechoslovak Social Policy*. Prague: Orbis, 1974.

Bradley, J. F. N. *Czechoslovakia: A Short History*. Chicago: Aldine-Atherton, 1972.

——. *Czechoslovakia's Velvet Revolution: A Political Analysis*. New York: Columbia University Press, 1992.

——. *Politics in Czechoslovakia, 1945–1990*. New York: Columbia University Press, 1991.

Brisch, Hans, and Ivan Volgyes (eds.). *Czechoslovakia: The Heritage of Ages Past*. Boulder, Colo.: East European Quarterly, 1979.

Czechoslovakia: Industrial Transformation and Regeneration. Cambridge, MA: Blackwell, 1992.

Gawdiak, Ihor (ed.). *Czechoslovakia, A Country Study*. 3d ed. Washington, D.C.: Library of Congress, 1989.

Golan, Galia. *The Czechoslovak Reform Movement: Communism in Crisis, 1962–68*. Cambridge: Cambridge University Press, 1971.

Hinby, Peter. *Fools and Heroes: The Changing Role of Communist Intellectuals in Czechoslovakia*. New York: Pergamon, 1980.

Kalvoda, Josef. *The Genesis of Czechoslovakia*. New York: Columbia University Press, 1986.

Kaplan, Karel. *The Short March: the Communist Takeover in Czechoslovakia, 1945–1948*. New York: St. Martin's, 1987.

Kennan, George F. *From Prague after Munich: Diplomatic Papers, 1937–1940*. Princeton, N.J.: Princeton University Press, 1968.

Korbel, Josef. *Twentieth-Century Czechoslovakia: The Meanings of Its History*. New York: Columbia University Press, 1977.

Krejči, Jaroslav. *Social Change and Stratification in Postwar Czechoslovakia*. New York: Columbia University Press, 1972.

Kriseova, Eda. *Vaclav Havel: the Authorized Biography*. New York: St. Martin's Press, 1993.

Kusin, Vladimir V. *From Dubček to Charter 77: A Study of "Normalisation" in Czechoslovakia, 1968–1978*. New York: St. Martin's, 1978.

——. *The Intellectual Origins of the Prague Spring*. Cambridge: Cambridge University Press, 1971.

Lettrich, Jozef. *History of Modern Slovakia*. New York: Praeger, 1955.

Magocsi, Paul R. *The Rusyns of Slovakia: An Historical survey*. New York: Columbia University Press, 1993.

Mamatey, Victor S., and Radomia Luža (eds.). *A History of the Czechoslovak Republic, 1914–1948*. Princeton, N.J.: Princeton University Press, 1973.

Masaryk, Thomas [Tomáš]. *The Meaning of Czech History*. Chapel Hill: University of North Carolina Press, 1974.

Myant, M. R. *The Czechoslovak Economy, 1948–1988: The Battle for Economic Reform*. New York: Cambridge University Press, 1989.

Population Policy in Czechoslovakia. Prague: Orbis, 1974.

Schwartz, Harry. *Prague's 200 Days: The Struggle for Democracy in Czechoslovakia*. New York: Praeger, 1969.

Seton-Watson, Robert William. *A History of the Czechs and Slovaks*. London: Hutchinson, 1944.

Shawcross, William. *Dubcek*. New York: Simon & Schuster, 1990.

——. *Dubcek: Dubcek and Czechoslovakia, 1968–1990*. London: Hogarth, 1990.

Short, David. *Czechoslovakia*. Santa Barbara, Calif.: ABC-Clio, 1986.

Šik, Ota. *Czechoslovakia: The Bureaucratic Economy*. White Plains, N.Y.: International Arts and Sciences Press, 1972.

Skilling, H. Gordon. *Czechoslovakia's Interrupted Revolution*. Princeton, N.J.: Princeton University Press, 1976.

—— and Paul Wilson (eds.). *Civic Freedom in Central Europe: Voices from Czechoslovakia*. New York: St. Martin's Press, 1991.

Suda, Zdenek L. *Zealots and Rebels: A History of the Communist Party of Czechoslovakia*. Stanford, Calif.: Hoover Institution Press, 1980.

Szulc, Tad. *Czechoslovakia Since World War II*. New York: Viking, 1971.

Taborsky, Edward. *Communism in Czechoslovakia, 1948–1960*. Princeton, N.J.: Princeton University Press, 1961.

Teichova, Alice. *The Czechoslovak Economy, 1918–1980*. New York: Routledge, 1988.

Thomson, Samuel Harrison. *Czechoslovakia in European History*. Princeton, N.J.: Princeton University Press, 1953.

Ulč, Otto. *Politics in Czechoslovakia*. San Francisco: Freeman, 1974.

Unterberger, Betty Miller. *The United States, Revolutionary Russia, and the Rise of Czechoslovakia*. Chapel Hill: University of North Carolina Press, 1989.

Valenta, Jiri. *Soviet Intervention in Czechoslovakia, 1968*. Rev. ed. Baltimore: Johns Hopkins University Press, 1991.

Volgyes, Ivan, and Hans Brisch (eds.). *Czechoslovakia: The Heritage of Ages Past*. New York: Columbia University Press, 1986.

Windsor, Philip, and Adam Roberts. *Czechoslovakia 1968: Reform, Repression and Resistance*. New York: Columbia University Press, 1969.

Zinner, Paul E. *Communist Strategy and Tactics in Czechoslovakia, 1918–1948*. New York: Praeger, 1963.

DENMARK

Kingdom of Denmark
Kongeriget Danmark

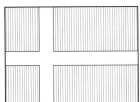

CAPITAL: Copenhagen (København).

FLAG: The Danish national flag, known as the Dannebrog, is one of the oldest national flags in the world, although the concept of a national flag did not develop until the late 18th century when the Dannebrog was already half a millennium old. The design shows a white cross on a field of red.

ANTHEM: There are two national anthems—*Kong Kristian stod ved hojen mast (King Christian Stood by the Lofty Mast)* and *Der er et yndigt land (There Is a Lovely Land).*

MONETARY UNIT: The krone (Kr) of 100 øre is a commercially convertible paper currency with one basic official exchange rate. There are coins of 25 and 50 øre, and 1, 5, 10, and 20 kroner, and notes of 50, 100, 500, and 1,000 kroner. Kr1 = $0.1515 (or $1 = Kr6.599).

WEIGHTS AND MEASURES: The metric system is the legal standard, but some local units are used for special purposes.

HOLIDAYS: New Year's Day, 1 January; Constitution Day, 5 June; Christmas Day, 25 December; Boxing Day, 26 December. Movable religious holidays include Holy Thursday, Good Friday, Easter Monday, Prayer Day (4th Friday after Easter), Ascension, and Whitmonday.

TIME: 1 PM = noon GMT.

¹LOCATION, SIZE, AND EXTENT

Situated in southern Scandinavia, the Kingdom of Denmark consists of Denmark proper, the Faroe Islands, and Greenland. Denmark proper, comprising the peninsula of Jutland (Jylland) and 406 islands (97 of them inhabited), has an area of 43,070 sq km (16,629 sq mi) and extends about 400 km (250 mi) N–S and 355 km (220 mi) E–W. Comparatively, the area occupied by Denmark is slightly more than twice the size of the state of Massachusetts. The Jutland Peninsula accounts for 29,767 sq km (11,493 sq mi) of the total land area, while the islands have a combined area of 13,317 sq km (5,142 sq mi). Except for the southern boundary with Germany, the country is surrounded by water—Skagerrak on the N, Kattegat, Øresund, and Baltic Sea on the E, and the North Sea on the W. Denmark's total boundary length is 7,382 km (4,587 mi).

Bornholm, one of Denmark's main islands, is situated in the Baltic Sea, less than 160 km (100 mi) due E of Denmark and about 40 km (25 mi) from southern Sweden. It has an area of 588 sq km (227 sq mi) and at its widest point is 40 km (25 mi) across.

Denmark's capital city, Copenhagen, is located on the eastern edge of the country on the island of Sjaelland.

²TOPOGRAPHY

The average altitude of Denmark is about 30 m (98 ft), and the highest point, in southeastern Jutland, is only 173 m (568 ft). In parts of Jutland, along the southern coast of the island of Lolland, and in a few other areas, the coast is protected by dikes. All of Denmark proper (except for the extreme southeast of the island of Bornholm, which is rocky) consists of a glacial deposit over a chalk base. The surface comprises small hills, moors, ridges, hilly islands, raised sea bottoms, and, on the west coast, downs and marshes. There are many small rivers and inland seas. Good natural harbors are provided by the many fjords and bays.

³CLIMATE

Denmark has a temperate climate, the mildness of which is largely conditioned by the generally westerly winds and by the fact that the country is virtually encircled by water. There is little fluctuation between day and night temperatures, but sudden changes in wind direction cause considerable day-to-day temperature changes. The mean temperature in February, the coldest month, is 0°C (32°F), and in July, the warmest, 17°C (63°F). Rain falls fairly evenly throughout the year, the annual average amounting to approximately 61 cm (24 in).

⁴FLORA AND FAUNA

Plants and animals are those common to middle Europe. There are many species of ferns, flower, fungi, and mosses; common trees include spruce and beech. Few wild or large animals remain. Birds, however, are abundant; many species breed in Denmark and migrate to warmer countries during the autumn and winter. Fish and insects are plentiful.

⁵ENVIRONMENT

Denmark's most basic environmental legislation is the Environmental Protection Act of 1974, which entrusts the Ministry of the Environment, in conjunction with local authorities, with antipollution responsibilities. The basic principle is that the polluter must pay the cost of adapting to environmental requirements; installations built before 1974, however, are eligible for government subsidies to cover the cost of meeting environmental standards. Land and water pollution are two of Denmark's most significant environmental problems. The quality of the land is endangered by over 3,100 dumping areas for harmful chemicals. In 1994, Denmark produced 447.3 thousand tons of solid waste. Much of Denmark's industrial and household waste is recycled. In 1985, some 312,000 tons of wastepaper, representing 31% of paper consumed, was collected, and recycled wastepaper accounted for 60% of paper production that year. A special treatment plant at Nyborg, on the island of Fyn, handles dangerous chemical and oil wastes. Pollution results from contamination by annual waste and the seepage of industrial pollutants into the waters within the North Seas around Denmark. Denmark's cities produce 2.6 million tons of solid waste per year. The nation has 2.6 cubic miles of water. Forty-three percent is used for farming, and 27% for industrial purposes. Remaining environmental problems include air pollution, especially from automobile emissions; excessive noise, notably in the major cities; and the pollution of rivers, lakes, and open sea by raw sewage. Denmark contributes 0.2% of the world's total gas emissions. It produces 160.9 tons of hydrocarbon emissions. In 1994, Denmark had 23 protected wildlife sites, with an area of 1,631 square miles of about 9.8% of the total land area. By 1994, one of Denmark's 49 species of mammals and 16 of its 190 bird species are endangered. Seven of the nation's 1,000 bird species are also endangered.

6POPULATION

At the beginning of 1992, the population of Denmark proper was 5,162,126; the projected population for the year 2000 was 5,245,000, assuming an estimated birthrate of 12.7 and a death rate of 11.3, for a net natural increase of 1.4 for the 1995–2000 period. The Faroe Islands had 47,449 people at the end of 1990 and Greenland 55,117 at the end of 1992. In 1992, 84.9% of the total population lived in urban areas. Excluding the Faroe Islands and Greenland, the population density in 1992 was 120 per sq km (310 per sq mi). The population of Copenhagen, the capital and principal city, was 464,566 at the beginning of 1992 (1,339,395 including suburbs). Other large towns and their 1992 populations are Aarhus (Arhus), 267,873; Odense, 179,487; Aalborg (Alborg), 156,614; Esbjerg, 80,843; and Randers, 61,440.

7MIGRATION

Emigration is limited, owing mainly to the relatively high standard of living in Denmark. Most of the 22,167 Danes who emigrated in 1991 went to the US (2,317), the UK (2,715), Germany (2,754), or other Scandinavian and European countries. In the same year, 20,430 immigrants entered Denmark (excluding Danes). At the end of 1992, Denmark was harboring 58,300 refugees. The total number of foreigners was 180,103, of whom 33,653 were Turks. Total internal migration was 855,125 in 1991, of which 307,984 was from one municipality to another.

8ETHNIC GROUPS

The population of Denmark proper is of indigenous northern European stock, and the Danes are among the most homogeneous peoples of Europe. There is a small German minority in southern Jutland.

9LANGUAGES

Danish is the universal language. In addition to the letters of the English alphabet, it has the letters ae, ø, and å. A spelling reform of 1948 replaced aa by å, but English transliteration usually retains the aa. There are many dialects, but they are gradually being supplanted by standard Danish. Modern Danish has departed further from the ancient Nordic language of the Viking period than have Icelandic, Norwegian, and Swedish (to which Danish is closely related), and there is a substantial admixture of German and English words. Danish may be distinguished from the other Scandinavian languages by its change of k, p, and t to g, b, and d, in certain situations and by its use of the glottal stop. Many Danes have a speaking knowledge of English and German, and many more are capable of understanding these languages.

10RELIGIONS

Religious freedom is provided by the constitution of 1849. About 91% of the people adhere to the official religion, the Evangelical Lutheran Church, which is supported by the state and headed by

the sovereign. There are small groups of Roman Catholics, Jews, and members of other faiths.

11TRANSPORTATION

Transportation is highly developed. At the end of 1991 there were 66,482 km (41,312 mi) of public roads, of which 97% were paved. The road system is well engineered and adequately maintained. Among the most important bridges are the Storstrom Bridge linking the islands of Sjaelland and Falster, and the Little Belt Bridge linking Fyn and Jutland. A new train and auto link from Sjaell and to Fyn (18 km/11 mi) is expected to be completed by 1996; a new bridge connecting Denmark to Sweden is expected to open by 2000. At the end of 1991, Denmark had 1,593,960 private cars, and 306,456 commercial vehicles. The bicycle is a very popular form of transportation.

The total length of the portion of the railway system owned and operated by the Danish State Railways was 2,120 km (1,317 mi) at the end of 1991, when only 555 km (345 mi) of railway were privately operated. In 1990, Danish State Railways performed some 4,851 million passenger-km of service, and transported 7,973,000 tons of freight. Danish State Railways also owns and operates motorbus lines.

The Danish merchant fleet at the end of 1991 was composed of 296 ships of 5,145,000 GRT. Over 90% of these vessels belonged to the Danish International Registry, an offshore registry program allowing foreign-owned vessels to sail under the Danish flag. Denmark, which pioneered the use of motor-driven ships, has many excellent and well-equipped harbors, of which Copenhagen is the most important.

Kastrup Airport near Copenhagen is a center of international air traffic, and accommodated 11,109,000 arriving and departing passengers in 1991. Domestic traffic is handled by Danish Airlines in conjunction with SAS, a joint Danish, Norwegian, and Swedish enterprise. In 1991, Danish airports accommodated 5,028,000 international passengers from 197,501 flights.

12HISTORY

Although there is evidence of agricultural settlement as early as 4000 BC and of bronze weaponry and jewelry by 1800 BC, Denmark's early history is little known. Tribesmen calling themselves Danes arrived from Sweden around AD 500, and Danish sailors later took part in the Viking raids, especially in those against England. Harald Bluetooth (d.985), first Christian king of Denmark, conquered Norway, and his son Sweyn conquered England. During the reign of Canute II (1017-35), Denmark, Norway, and England were united, but in 1042, with the death of Canute's son, Hardecanute, the union with England came to an end, and Norway seceded. During the next three centuries, however, Danish hegemony was reestablished over Sweden and Norway, and in the reign of Margrethe (1387-1412) there was a union of the Danish, Norwegian, and Swedish crowns. In 1523, the Scandinavian union was dissolved, but Norway remained united with Denmark until 1814.

The Reformation was established in Denmark during the reign of Christian III (1534-59). A series of wars with Sweden during the 17th and early 18th centuries resulted in the loss of Danish territory. Meanwhile, under Frederik III (r.1648-70) and Christian V (r.1670-99), absolute monarchy was established and strengthened; it remained in force until 1849. Freedom of the press and improved judicial administration, introduced by Count Johann von Struensee, adviser (1770-72) to Christian VII, were abrogated after his fall from favor. Having allied itself with Napoleon, Denmark was deprived of Norway by the terms of the Peace of Kiel (1814), which united Norway with Sweden; and as a result of the Prusso-Danish wars of 1848-49 and 1864, Denmark lost its southern provinces of Slesvig, Holstein, and Lauenburg. Thereafter, the Danes concen-

LOCATION: 54°33′31″ to 57°44′55″N; 8°4′36″ to 15°11′59″E. **BOUNDARY LENGTHS:** Germany, 68 km (42 mi); total coastline, 7,314 km (4,545 mi).
TERRITORIAL SEA LIMIT: 3 mi.

trated on internal affairs, instituting important economic changes (in particular, specialization in dairy production) that transformed the country from a nation of poor peasants into one of prosperous smallholders. Denmark remained neutral in World War I, and after a plebiscite in 1920, North Slesvig was reincorporated into Denmark.

Disregarding the German-Danish nonaggression pact of 1939, Hitler invaded Denmark in April 1940, and the German occupation lasted until 1945. At first, the Danish government continued to function, protecting as long as it could the nation's Jewish minority and other refugees (some 7,200 Jews eventually escaped to neutral Sweden). However, when a resistance movement developed, sabotaging factories, railroads, and other installations, the Danish government resigned in August 1943 rather than carry out the German demand for the death sentence against the saboteurs. Thereafter, Denmark was governed by Germany directly, and conflict with the resistance intensified.

After the war, Denmark became a charter member of the UN and of NATO. In 1952, it joined with the other Scandinavian nations to form the Nordic Council, a parliamentary body.

Having joined EFTA in 1960, Denmark left that association for the EEC in 1973. Meanwhile, during the 1950s and 1960s, agricultural and manufacturing production rose considerably, a high level of employment was maintained, and foreign trade terms were liberalized. However, the expense of maintaining Denmark's highly developed social security system, growing trade deficits (due partly to huge increases in the price of imported oil), persistent inflation, and rising unemployment posed political as well as economic problems for Denmark in the 1970s and 1980s, as one fragile coalition government succeeded another.

Economic performance continued to be a major issue in the 1990s. Voters narrowly rejected the Maastricht Treaty on European Union in 1992, but later approved it in 1994 after modifications were made in Denmark's favor.

13 GOVERNMENT

Denmark is a constitutional monarchy. Legislative power is vested jointly in the crown and a unicameral parliament (Folketing), executive power in the sovereign—who exercises it through his ministers—and judicial power in the courts. The revised constitution of 1953 provides that powers constitutionally vested in Danish authorities by legislation may be transferred to international authorities established, by agreement with other states, for the promotion of international law and cooperation.

The sovereign must belong to the Lutheran Church. The crown is hereditary in the royal house of Lyksborg, which ascended the throne in 1863. On the death of a king, the throne descends to his son or daughter, a son taking precedence.

Executive powers belong to the crown, which enjoys personal integrity and is not responsible for acts of government. These are exercised by the cabinet, consisting of a prime minister and a variable number of ministers, who generally are members of the political party or coalition commanding a legislative majority. No minister may remain in office after the Folketing has passed a vote of no confidence in him.

The single-chamber Folketing, which has been in existence since 1953, is elected every four years (more frequently, if necessary) by direct and secret ballot by Danish subjects 18 years of age and older. Under the 1953 constitution there are 179 members, 2 of whom are elected in the Faroe Islands and 2 in Greenland. Of the remaining 175 members, 135 are elected by proportional representation in 17 constituencies, and 40 supplementary seats are divided among the parties in proportion to the total votes cast.

A parliamentary commission, acting as the representative both of the Folketing and of the nation, superintends civil and military government administration.

14 POLITICAL PARTIES

Until 1849, the Danish form of government was autocratic. The constitution of 1849 abolished privileges, established civil liberties, and laid down the framework of popular government through a bicameral parliament elected by all men over 30. In 1866, however, the National Liberal Party, composed largely of the urban middle class, succeeded in obtaining a majority for a constitution in which the upper chamber (Landsting) was to be elected by privileged franchise, the great landowners gaining a dominant position. This proved the starting point of a political struggle that divided Denmark until 1901. Formally, it concerned the struggle of the directly elected chamber, the Folketing, against the privileged Landsting, but in reality it was the struggle of the Left Party (made up largely of farmers, but after 1870 also of workers) to break the monopoly of political influence by the Right Party (consisting of the landowning aristocracy and the upper middle class). Meanwhile, the workers established trade unions, their political demands finding expression in the Social Democratic Party. In 1901, Christian IX called on the Left to

form a government, and thereafter it was the accepted practice that the government should reflect the majority in the Folketing.

In 1905, the Left Party split. Its radical wing, which seceded, became a center party, the Social Liberals, and sought to collaborate with the Social Democrats. In 1913, these two parties together obtained a majority in the Folketing, and a Social Liberal government led Denmark through World War I. A new constitution adopted in 1915 provided for proportional representation and gave the vote to all citizens, male and female, 25 years of age and older (changed in 1978 to 18 years). In an attempt to obtain a broader popular base, the old Right Party adopted the name Conservative People's Party, and thenceforth this party and the Moderate Liberals (the old Left Party), the Social Liberals, and the Social Democrats formed the solid core of Danish politics. The Social Democrats briefly formed governments in 1924 and in 1929, in association with the Social Liberals.

During the German occupation (1940–45), a coalition government was formed by the main political parties, but increasing Danish popular resistance to the Germans led the Nazis to take over executive powers. From 1945 to 1957, Denmark was governed by minority governments, influence fluctuating between the Social Democrats on the one hand and the Moderate Liberals and Conservatives on the other, depending on which of the two groups the Social Liberals supported. In 1953, a new constitution abolished the Landsting and introduced a single-chamber system in which parliamentarianism is expressly laid down.

Aims of the Social Democratic Party are to nationalize monopolies, redistribute personal incomes by taxation and other measures, partition farm properties to form independent smallholdings, and raise working-class living standards through full employment. It supports the principle of mutual aid, as practiced in a combination of social welfare and widespread public insurance schemes. The Conservative Party advocates an economic policy based on the rights of private property and private enterprise and is firmly opposed to nationalization and restrictions, though it is in favor of industrial protection. It calls for a national contributory pensions scheme that would encourage personal initiative and savings. The major parties support the UN and NATO and favor inter-Scandinavian cooperation.

Issues in the 1970s focused less on international matters than on policies affecting Denmark's economy. The general elections of December 1973 resulted in heavy losses for all the established parties represented in the Folketing and successes for several new parties, notably the center-left Democratic Center Party and the "Poujadist" Progress Party led by Mogens Glistrup, an income tax expert who reputedly became a millionaire by avoiding taxes and providing others with advice on tax avoidance. The Progress Party, established early in 1973, advocated the gradual abolition of income tax and the dissolution of over 90% of the civil service. The Social Democrats, who had been in power, lost significantly in this election, and their chairman, Anker Jørgensen, resigned as prime minister. In mid-December, Poul Hartling was sworn in as prime minister, with a Liberal Democratic cabinet. The 22 Liberal members in the Folketing made up the smallest base for any government since parliamentary democracy was established in Denmark.

When it became clear in December 1974 that the Folketing would not approve the drastic anti-inflation program the Hartling government had announced, general elections were again called for. In the January 1975 balloting, the Liberals almost doubled their representation in the Folketing. However, because most of the other non-Socialist parties had lost support and because three of the four left-wing parties simultaneously gained parliamentary seats, the preelection lack of majority persisted, and Hartling resigned at the end of the month. After several attempts at a coalition by Hartling and Anker Jørgensen, the latter's alignment of Social Democrats and other Socialist-oriented minority parties finally succeeded in forming a new government. Jørgensen remained prime minister through general elections in 1977, 1979, and 1981. In September 1982, however, dissension over Jørgensen's plan to increase taxes in order to create new jobs, boost aid to farmers, and reduce the budget deficit led the government to resign. A four-party coalition led by Poul Schlüter, the first Conservative prime minister since 1901, then took power as a minority government, controlling only 66 seats out of 179. After the defeat of his 1984 budget, Schlüter called for new elections, which were held in January 1984 and increased the number of seats controlled by the coalition to 79. Following elections in September 1987, however, the number of seats held by the coalition fell to 70.

Following the 1990 general election, a new center-right coalition government was formed with Paul Schlüter remaining as prime minister. The coalition was reformed in 1994 composed of the Social Democrats, the Social Liberals, the Centre Democrats, and the Christian People's Party. Paul Rasmussen (Social Democrat) was appointed prime minister.

15LOCAL GOVERNMENT

A major reform of local government structure took effect on 1 April 1970. The city of Copenhagen, together with a number of adjacent municipalities, continues to have a separate status; it is governed by an elected City Council (Borger representation) of 55 members and an executive (magistrat) appointed by the council and consisting of a chief burgomaster (overborgmester), five burgomasters (borgmestie), and five aldermen (radmaend). The previous distinction between boroughs and urban and rural districts was abolished, and the number of counties was reduced from 25 to 14. The primary local units, reduced from 1,400 to 275, are governed by an elected council (kommunalbestyrelse) composed of 5 to 25 members who, in turn, elect a mayor (borgmester) who is vested with executive authority. Each county is governed by an elected county council (amtsiåd), which elects its own chairman, or county mayor (amstborgmester). County councils look after local matters, such as road building and maintenance, health and hospital services, and general education.

The Faroe Islands and Greenland enjoy home rule, with Denmark retaining responsibility for foreign affairs, defense, and monetary matters.

16JUDICIAL SYSTEM

As a rule, cases in the first instance come before the Copenhagen city court, the Aarhus city court, or one of 84 local courts. Certain major cases, however, come under the High Courts (Landsrettes), in Copenhagen and Viborg, in the first instance; otherwise these courts function as courts of appeal. The Supreme Court (Hojesteret) is made up of 15 judges, usually functioning as two divisions, each having at least 5 judges; it serves solely as a court of appeal for cases coming from the High Courts. Special courts include the Maritime and Commercial Court and the Tax Tribunal. An Ombudsman elected by and responsible to Parliament investigates citizen complaints against the government or its ministers.

The judiciary is fully independent of the executive and legislative branches. Judges are appointed by the monarch on recommendation of the Minister of Justice and serve to age 70. They may be dismissed only for negligence or for criminal acts.

17ARMED FORCES

Since 1849 Danish military defense has been based on compulsory national service. All young men must register at the age of 18 and are subject to 9–12 months service. Voluntary military service is popular because of educational benefits.Women may volunteer (1,600 serving in 1993) for service, including service on combat vessels. The army consists of 17,300 personnel, the navy 4,900, and the air force 7,000. There are also 72,500 members of the reserves and 70,000 in the volunteer home guard. Military expenditures for 1990 amounted to $2.1 million or 2% of GDP. No foreign troops or nuclear weapons are allowed on Danish territory, but a NATO headquarters in Denmark manages the defense of the approaches to the Baltic. Denmark has 1,300 military personnel abroad on peacekeeping assignments.

18INTERNATIONAL COOPERATION

Denmark became a charter member of the UN on 24 October 1945 and belongs to ECE and all the nonregional specialized agencies. In association with WHO, Denmark has supported UN relief work by supplying medical personnel to assist developing countries and by sending out the hospital ship *Jutlandia* during the Korean War. The European regional office of WHO is in Copenhagen. Denmark participates actively in multilateral technical aid programs, and the Danish Council for Technical Cooperation provides additional aid to developing countries in Asia and Africa. The nation also assists the Asian Development Bank and IDB. Denmark is a member of NATO and of various inter-European organizations including the Council of Europe and the OECD. Until 1 January 1973, when it joined the EC, Denmark had been a member of EFTA.

Denmark, a member of the Nordic Council, cooperates with other northern countries—Finland, Iceland, Norway, and Sweden—in social welfare and health insurance legislation and in freeing its frontiers of passport control for residents of other Scandinavian countries. The nation has signed GATT and the Law of the Sea.

19ECONOMY

Denmark is traditionally an agricultural country. Since the end of World War II, however, manufacturing has gained rapidly in importance and now contributes more than does agriculture to national income. Denmark has always been a prominent maritime nation, and since much Danish shipping operates entirely in foreign waters, it contributes considerably to the nation's economy. Denmark also has important investments abroad.

Danish living standards and purchasing power are relatively high, but the domestic market is limited by the small population, and most important industries must seek foreign markets in order to expand. Natural resources are limited, and therefore Denmark must export in order to pay for the raw materials, feeds, fertilizers, and fuels that must be imported. As a result, and because international competition makes it difficult for Denmark to accumulate adequate foreign exchange reserves, the national economy has been greatly influenced by trends and developments abroad, over which it can exercise little or no control. Since the Danes joined the EC on 1 January 1973, this problem has been alleviated somewhat. Integration into the Community's common agricultural policy has considerably improved Danish terms of trade by providing higher prices.

Productivity increased greatly in the postwar period. In agriculture the volume index for production rose steadily, while the agricultural labor force decreased. Similarly, improved techniques and mechanization in industry enabled production to increase, despite a percentage decline in the number of persons employed.

From 1961 to 1971, the average annual rate of price increases in Denmark was 6.1%; in 1972, it was 6.6%; in 1973, 9.3%; and in 1974, partly because of rising oil costs, 15.2%. Throughout the remainder of the 1970s and through 1982, inflation remained in the 9–12% bracket. It then dropped from 6.9% in 1983 to 1.3% in 1993. Economic activity slackened during the 1970s, with GDP growth at 2.3% a year, down from a rate of about 4.5% during 1960–70. Growth remained moderate during the 1980s averaging 2% a year. The GDP grew by 2.2% in 1990, but only at 1% in 1991, 12% in 1992, and 1.1% in 1993. Recessions in 1974–75 and 1980–81 spurred a substantial rise in unemployment. From a rate of 0.9% in 1973, unemployment reached 12.3% in 1993. Throughout the 1970s and through most of the next six years, Denmark's trade balance was in chronic deficit, but a surplus was registered in 1987 and grew in each of the succeeding five years. The central government deficit fell from a peak of 10% of GDP in 1982 to 2.9% in 1990.

[20]INCOME

In 1992, Denmark's GNP was $133,941 million at current prices, or $25,930 per capita. For the period 1985–92 the average inflation rate was 3.4%, resulting in a real growth rate in per capita GNP of 1.2%.

In 1992 the GDP was $94.2 billion in current US dollars. It is estimated that in 1991 agriculture, hunting, forestry, and fishing contributed 3% to GDP; mining and quarrying, 1%; manufacturing, 16%; electricity, gas, and water, 2%; construction, 5%; wholesale and retail trade, 12%; transport, storage, and communication, 8%; finance, insurance, real estate, and business services, 17%; community, social, and personal services, 5%; and other sources, 31%.

[21]LABOR

The Danish labor force has grown steadily since World War II. In 1991, it totaled 2,844,000; male participation rates remained stable in the 1980s, while female participation rates went from 51% in 1970 to 75.9% in 1989. Of those employed in 1990, 31.2% were in public service; 30.1% in trade and services; 20.3% in manufacturing; 6.4% in building and construction; 5.6% in agriculture and fishing; 5.3% in transportation; and 1.1% in other services. Unemployment increased from 1% of the work force in 1970 to 7% in 1980, to an estimated 11% in 1992. The 1982–90 period brought a 1.3% decline in agricultural employment, a slight decrease in employment in manufacturing, and a large increase in employment in services, especially government services (education, social welfare, etc.). With the aim of holding down unemployment, the government offers the option of early retirement, apprenticeship and trainee programs, and special job offerings for the long-term unemployed.

An estimated 80% of all wage-earners, mostly blue-collar workers and government employees, are organized in trade unions. In 1991, the 31 trade union federations had some 1.4 million members. Most of the unions are limited to particular trades. Among the leading labor organizations, the Federation of Civil Servants and Salaried Employees had some 325,000 members as of 1990.

Virtually all wage agreements covering industrial, craft, and agricultural workers expire and are renewed every other year. Wages have increased annually since 1962 pursuant to escalation provisions. In September 1990, average hourly earnings of skilled blue-collar workers were Kr126.11. The rise in hourly wages and salaries during 1991 amounted to some 3.1% in the private sector and 2.7% in the public sector. Employers are responsible for payment of benefits during the first five weeks of a period of illness. The workweek in the private sector was shortened from 40 to 39 hours in December 1986 (with no reduction in compensation) and further reduced to 37 hours in 1991.

Consultation between labor and management is carried on in individual companies by means of joint industrial committees; in March 1981, these committees were given the additional task of negotiating the use of new technology, disagreements over which are dealt with by an appointed technology tribunal. One-third (or at least two) of the members of the executive boards of large limited companies must be workers' representatives. Disputes concerning the interpretation or alleged violation of collective agreements are settled by a court of arbitration.

Unemployment insurance is voluntary but widespread. Funds have been established by trade unions, but state and local governments make considerable contributions, as do employers. Since 1898, employers have had to insure their staffs against accidents incurred at work. Those disabled by work accidents are entitled to medical attention and compensation. Legislation lays down certain minimum requirements regarding the nature of industrial premises and the prevention of accidents in connection with dangerous machinery. There are also laws protecting women and children, agricultural workers, salaried employees, and seamen.

[22]AGRICULTURE

About 60% of the land in 1991 was devoted to agriculture, much of it to natural or sown pastures, most of the arable part to feed and root crops. Although agriculture is of great significance to the Danish economy, its relative importance declined from 19% of the GDP in 1961 to 4% in 1991, when employment in the agricultural sector amounted to 5.5%.

The majority of farms are small and medium-sized. In 1991, 18% of all farms were less than 10 hectares (25 acres); 23.4% were between 10 and 20 hectares (25–49 acres); 37.6% were between 20 and 50 hectares (49–124 acres); and 21% were greater than 50 hectares. Thousands of smallholdings have been established since 1899 under special legislation empowering the state to provide the land by partitioning public lands, by expropriation, and by breaking up large private estates. In the more newly established holdings, the farmer owns only the buildings (for which the state advances loans), the land being owned by the state and the smallholder paying an annual rent fixed under the land-tax assessment. Comparatively few new holdings have been established since 1951.

Grain growing and root-crop production are the traditional agricultural pursuits, but considerable progress has been made in recent decades in apple growing and the production of field, forage, flower, and industrial seeds. Although the soil is not particularly fertile and holdings are kept deliberately small, intensive mechanization and widespread use of fertilizers and concentrated feeds result in high yields and excellent quality. In 1991 there were 160,387 tractors and 32,542 harvester-threshers.

The following table shows plantings and crop yields of major crops for 1992:

PLANTINGS	HECTARES	ACRES	(EST.) YIELD (TONS)
Barley	904,000	2,234,000	3,022,000
Wheat	591,000	1,460,000	3,648,000
Rye	92,000	227,000	333,000
Sugar beets	65,000	161,000	3,300,000
Potatoes	44,000	109,000	1,500,000
Roots and Tubers	44,000	109,000	1,500,000

Cereal, vegetable, and fruit exports supplied 3.2% of the value of Danish exports in 1991. Farm products provide materials for industrial processing, and a significant share of industry supplies the needs of domestic agriculture.

The Danish government devotes particular effort to maintaining the volume, price, quality, and diversity of agricultural products, but internal regulation is largely left to private initiative or exercised through private organizations, notably the cooperatives.

[23]ANIMAL HUSBANDRY

Denmark is generally regarded as the world's outstanding example of intensive animal husbandry. It maintains a uniformly high standard of operations, combining highly skilled labor, scientific experimentation and research, modern installations and machinery, and versatility in farm management and marketing. The excellent cooperative system guarantees the quality of every product of its members. Meat, dairy products, and eggs contribute a most important share of Danish exports. There is a close relationship between cost of feed and export prices.

The livestock population in 1992 included 2,185,000 head of cattle, 10,345,000 hogs, 160,000 sheep, 32,000 horses, and

15,000,000 fowl. Mink, fox, polecat, finnraccoon, and chinchilla are raised for their pelts.

The value of exported meat products in 1992 amounted to $3,916.2 million; exported dairy products and eggs totaled $1,297.2 million. Production included 4,600,000 tons of milk, 63,000 tons of butter, and 288,000 tons of cheese. In addition, egg production was 88,000 tons.

[24] FISHING

The country's long coastline, conveniently situated on rich fishing waters, provides Denmark with excellent fishing grounds. Fishing is an important source of domestic food supply, and both fresh and processed fish are important exports. For many years the government has encouraged fishing by various aids, especially by extending loans for boats and equipment. The catch is composed mainly of herring and sprat, cod, mackerel, plaice, salmon, and whiting; but sole and other flatfish, tuna, and other varieties are also caught. Both trout and eel are important. In 1991, the saltwater fishing catch amounted to 1,765,634 tons.

[25] FORESTRY

A law of 1805 placing all forestland under reservation stated that "where there is now high forest there must always be high forest." Various measures were adopted to maintain forest growth. Later revisions of the law compelled all woodland owners to replant when trees are felled and to give adequate attention to drainage, weeding out of inferior species, and road maintenance. As a result, forests, which occupied only 5% of Denmark's land area and were actually in danger of extinction at the beginning of the 19th century, now make up over 11% of the land and are in excellent condition. Spruce and beech are the most important varieties. In 1991, approximately 2.3 million cu m of broadleaved trees and conifers were cut. Denmark is a large importer of softwood lumber, especially from the other Scandinavian countries, and is a large particleboard consumer.

[26] MINING

According to the constitution, subsurface resources belong to the nation, and concessions to exploit them require parliamentary approval.

In 1991 there were some 90 pits in Denmark from which clay was mined; this material is used primarily by the cement, brickmaking, and ceramic tile industries. The production of sand, gravel, and crushed stone has become more important in recent years, not only in meeting domestic demand, but also as an export to Germany and other Scandinavian countries. Kaolin, found on the island of Bornholm, is used mostly for coarse earthenware, furnace linings, and as a filler for paper. There are important limestone, chalk, and marl deposits in Jutland. Limonite (bog ore) is extracted for gas purification and pig iron production. Large deposits of salt were located in Jutland in 1966; during 1991, some 537,000 tons were mined.

[27] ENERGY AND POWER

Denmark has virtually no waterpower, and no nuclear power plants; 97.8% of all electric power generation is thermal. Geothermal production accounted for most of the remainder. Some domestic lignite and peat are used, and diesel power is employed in some small energy-generating plants, but the main sources of energy are imported coal and fuel oil. Municipal plants predominate in the cities and towns, and cooperative-owned plants are prominent in rural districts. In 1991, 36.3 billion kwh of electricity was generated; the net installed capacity was 9,578 Mw.

Between 1988 and 1991, Denmark's energy consumption rose by nearly 5%. In 1991, 52% of Denmark's final energy consumption was of petroleum products, 18% of electricity, 6% of solid fuels, 9% of gases, and 15% from geothermal heating. As a result

of the slow rate of progress in developing Denmark's North Sea gas and oil resources—exploratory drilling had been conducted in fewer than 25% of the fields by the end of 1980—the Danish government in 1981 decided to nationalize most of the fields. The Gorm oil and gas field, with estimated oil reserves of 100 million tons, went into production in mid-1982, and indications of additional hydrocarbon deposits were found nearby during 1983. By 1990, the Gorm Field's cumulative output was 12.7 million tons. Production of oil in 1992 totaled 7.8 million tons, at a rate of 160,000 barrels per day, up 11% from 1991.

[28] INDUSTRY

Manufacturing has greatly expanded since the end of World War II and now accounts for a far greater share of national income than does agriculture. In 1992, manufacturing (including mining and utilities) accounted for 18.9% of the GDP, employing 20.4% of the total working population. The value of industrial production totaled Kr332,131 in 1992. In the important food and drink industry, which tends to be relatively stable, the pattern differs for various branches, but meat packing has developed remarkably. The chemical, metalworking, and pharmaceutical industries have made notable progress. Handicrafts remain important, and Danish stone, clay, glass, wood, and silver products are world famous. The industrial share of total commodity exports increased from 31% in 1951 to 50% in 1969, and to 70% in 1992. In the world market, Danish manufacturers, having a limited supply of domestic raw materials, a relatively small home market, and a naturally advantageous geographic position, have concentrated on the production of high-quality specialized items rather than those dependent on mass production. For example, Denmark became the world's largest supplier of insulin, the raw materials for which come from livestock intestines, and, because of a social law creating a large domestic market, Denmark came to produce 20% of the world's hearing-aid spectacles.

Machinery, by far the most important industrial export, includes cement-making machinery, dairy machinery, diesel engines, electric motors, machine tools, and refrigeration equipment. Other important exports are canned foods, chemicals and pharmaceuticals, furniture, metal and paper products, ships, and textiles.

The following table shows turnover by manufacturing in 1991 for the various branches of Danish industry (in millions of kroner):

	TURNOVER
Fabricated metal products, machinery, etc.	107,407
Food, beverages, and tobacco	107,966
Chemical, petroleum, coal, rubber, and plastic products	52,174
Paper and paper products, printing, and publishing	27,949
Textiles, wearing apparel, and leather	15,257
Nonmetallic mineral products	12,376
Wood and wood products, including furniture	17,570
Basic metals	4,393
Other manufacturing industries	6,773
TOTAL	351,865

[29] SCIENCE AND TECHNOLOGY

The Research Secretariat, under the Ministry of Education, assists and coordinates the activities of the eight government research councils and the Research Planning Council, which consists partly of members appointed from and by the eight research units. The Technology Council allocates government funds for technological research, but most industrial research is funded by the industries concerned. Among the principal public research institutions are the major universities, the Technological University of Denmark near Copenhagen, the National Hospital in Copenhagen, the Nuclear Research Institute at Risø (near Roskilde), the Danish Institute for Fisheries and Marine Research at near Copenhagen, and the Meteorological Institute at Copenhagen. Many of the world's preeminent theoretical nuclear physicists have worked at the Niels Bohr Institute of Copenhagen University.

Research and development expenditures in 1989 totaled an estimated Kr12 billion; 14,786 technicians and 10,662 scientists and engineers were engaged in research and development. Government grants supply almost half of all funding for research activities.

30 DOMESTIC TRADE

Some 165,504 persons held jobs in wholesaling and 197,742 in retailing in November 1991; together, these occupations accounted for 14% of the employed work force. Large units are becoming more common in wholesale as well as retail trade, ordering directly from local manufacturers and foreign suppliers. Retail operations now include purchasing organizations, various types of chains, cooperatives, self-service stores, supermarkets, and department stores.

In 1989, total retail sales amounted to Kr152,529 million. Danish retail trade is marked by keen competition between independent retailers, manufacturers' chains, and consumer cooperatives. About 30% of all Danish retail establishments are in the greater Copenhagen area, and these account for almost 40% of all retail sales.

Business opening hours vary between 8 and 9 AM; closing is between 5:30 and 7 PM for stores and 4 to 4:30 PM for offices. Early closing (1 PM) on Saturdays is now standard. Banking hours are from 9:30 AM to 4 PM, Monday through Friday; also, 4 to 6 PM on Thursday.

General, trade, and technical periodicals are important media, and direct-mail and film advertising are used extensively. Radio and television commercials are prohibited. The most important trade exhibition, the International Fair, takes place every spring in Copenhagen.

31 FOREIGN TRADE

The Danish economy depends heavily on foreign trade. Raw materials for use in production account for more than half the value of imports. Farm products traditionally comprised the bulk of total Danish exports, but since 1961, industrial exports have exceeded agricultural exports in value. In 1992, industrial products accounted for 70% of Denmark's total commodity exports by value; agricultural and fishing exports accounted for 18%.

To curb domestic demand, the government introduced several fiscal restraint measures in 1986, resulting in a decline in imports. Such measures and a tight-money policy have curbed inflation and made Danish exports more competitive, leading to a trade surplus in every year since 1987.

Exports in 1992 (in millions of kroner) were as follows:

Machinery and instruments	56,095.2
Meat and meat preparations	24,720.7
Fish, shellfish, and preparations	12,724.7
Fuels and lubricants	9,303.5
Dairy products and eggs	7,479.1
Furniture	10,321.8
Transport equipment	15,101.5
Chemical goods	14,621.7
Textiles	11,504.5
Medical and pharmaceutical products	9,541.7
Other exports	74,870.6
TOTAL	246,285.0

Imports in 1992 (in millions of kroner) were as follows:

Petroleum and petroleum products	12,482.1
Transport equipment	13,615.2
Iron and steel	7,772.5
Electrical machinery, apparatus, and appliances	5,150.6
Food, beverages, and tobacco	17,895.1
Clothing	8,267.6
Textile yarns, fabrics, and related products	8,483.5
Office machinery and data processing equipment	6,215.1
Paper and paper products	6,583.3
Plastic materials	7,399.5
Other imports	117,094.5
TOTALS	210,959.0

In 1992, Denmark's principal trade partners (in millions of kroner), based on incomplete data, were the following:

	EXPORTS	IMPORTS	BALANCE
Germany	56,765.4	45,539.0	11,226.4
Sweden	25,239.0	22,009.4	3,229.6
UK	24,171.0	16,692.6	7,478.4
US	10,155.2	11,505.7	−1,350.5
Norway	13,767.0	10,964.1	2,802.9
Netherlands	10,705.1	11,193.1	−488.0
France	13,712.0	11,403.8	2,308.2
Italy	10,764.8	8,452.7	2,312.1
Japan	8,768.6	8,406.6	362.0
Other countries	65,864.2	57,368.7	8,495.5
TOTALS	239,912.3	203,535.7	−36,376.6

Denmark terminated its membership in EFTA on 1 January 1973 and, along with Ireland and the UK, became a member of the EC. Denmark's trade with EC members in 1992 comprised 54.3% of exports and 53.4% of imports. Germany accounted for 23.1% of Denmark's total trade.

32 BALANCE OF PAYMENTS

The decline in Denmark's trade balance since the end of World War II has resulted in a serious deterioration in the balance-of-payments position, particularly since 1960. In the late 1960s, the course of Denmark's international economic activity paralleled trends in continental Europe, with high trade and capital flow levels being accompanied by a deteriorating current-account position; this condition continued into the early 1970s. The Danish government had hoped that Denmark's entry into the EC would reduce the country's persistent deficit and bring the balance on current account into a more favorable position, but this was not the case in the late 1970s. Although current-account deficits were reduced somewhat in 1980–81, thanks to the devaluation of the kroner and the restrictive income and fiscal policies implemented in 1979–80, the deficit again increased in 1982 and by 1985 was at the highest level since 1979. In 1990, after a century of deficits, the balance of payments showed a surplus of $1.3 billion, which increased to nearly $2.2 billion in 1991. These improvements were partially offset by increased transfer payments, including development assistance and foreign debt interest payments. The surplus has allowed Denmark to begin repaying its large foreign debt, which peaked in 1988 at Kr294 billion ($44 billion), or 40% of GDP.

In 1992 merchandise exports totaled $40,632 million and imports $33,442 million. The merchandise trade balance was $7,189 million. The following table summarizes Denmark's balance of payments for 1991 and 1992 (in millions of US dollars):

	1991	1992
CURRENT ACCOUNT		
Goods, services, and income	2,663	5,192
Unrequited transfers	−495	−492
TOTALS	2,167	4,700
CAPITAL ACCOUNT		
Direct investment	−299	−1,219
Portfolio investment	1,854	10,127
Other long-term capital	−3,477	−4,857
Other short-term capital	−1,364	−9,042
Exceptional financing	—	—
Other liabilities	399	4,301
Reserves	2,903	−4,075
TOTALS	16	−4,764
Errors and omissions	−2,183	64
Total change in reserves	3,179	−3,668

33BANKING AND SECURITIES

By an act of 7 April 1936, the Danish National Bank, the bank of issue since 1818, was converted from an independent to an official government corporation. Its head office is in Copenhagen, and it has branches in provincial towns. Money in circulation at the end of 1993 totaled Kr471.06 billion. The Bank performs all the usual functions of a central bank, and it holds almost all the nation's foreign exchange reserves. Foreign assets at the end of 1993 amounted to Kr70.88 billion, with $478 million in gold.

At the end of 1993 there were 19 major commercial banks and 3 large savings banks in Denmark. Foreign reserves of commercial banks amounted to Kr35.33 billion in 1993, and demand deposits by the public amounted to Kr255.44 billion.

Commercial banks provide short-term money to business and individuals, almost always in the form of overdraft credits, which are generally renewable. The official discount rate rose from 11% to 13% in February 1980 and returned to 11% in October 1980, where it stood through late 1982. It fell to 8.5% in March 1983 and to 7.5% a month later; in October it fell to 7%, where it stood through the end of 1986. In 1993, the lending rate was 11.7%.

Credit and mortgage societies are active in Denmark. In 1982, index-linked real estate loans were introduced, initially carrying nominal interest rates of 2.5% per year, with balance and installments adjusted yearly according to variations in the consumer price index and wage indexes. In 1992 the lending rate was 11.7%.

The stock exchange (or Bourse) in Copenhagen was built during 1619–30 by Christian IV. He subsequently sold it to a Copenhagen merchant, but it reverted to the crown and in 1857 was finally sold by Frederik VII to the Merchants' Guild. Although it is the oldest building in the world built as an exchange and still used as one, the nature of the business transacted in it has greatly changed. Originally a commodity exchange equipped with booths and storage rooms, the Bourse is now almost exclusively a stock exchange. In 1970, the Stock Exchange was placed under the jurisdiction of the Ministry of Commerce with a governing committee of 11 members. Only a few bond issues are made by manufacturing firms each year.

34INSURANCE

The Danish insurance industry is regulated by the Insurance Supervision Service. Danish companies do most stock insurance business. Some government-owned insurance companies sell automobile, fire, and life insurance and handle the government's war-risk insurance program. The state-owned State Life Assurance Institute has about 25% of the life insurance market. In 1989, Denmark had 236 insurance companies. Premiums totaled

us$1,219 per capita in 1990, or 4.5% of the GDP. In 1992, life insurance in the amount of Kr759,153 million was in force.

35PUBLIC FINANCE

The finance bill is presented to the Folketing yearly; the fiscal year follows the calendar year. As a general rule, the budget is prepared on the "net" principle, the difference between receipts and expenditures—surplus or deficit—of public undertakings being posted to the revenue accounts. By far the largest amounts of public expenditure are for social security, health, education and research, unemployment insurance, pensions, allowances, and rent subsidies.

The 1993 Finance Act services as an example of how revenue is only to a limited degree spent on the public sector's own operational and initial expenditure, but mainly repaid to citizens. Out of the Kr340 billion the government had at its disposal in 1993, 46% was to be sent back to individual citizens as income transfers. In addition, the government transferred 12% of the budget to municipalities in the form of block grants, which also will largely end up as transfer payments to individuals.

The following table shows actual revenues and expenditures for 1990 and 1991 in millions of kroner.

	1990	1991
REVENUE AND GRANTS		
Tax revenue	266,257	275,875
Non-tax revenue	45,362	44,569
Capital revenue	2,516	5,933
Grants	4,276	5,100
TOTALS	318,412	331,477
EXPENDITURES & LENDING MINUS REPAYMENTS		
General public service	18,059	—
Defense	16,091	—
Public order and safety	6,921	—
Education	31,268	—
Health	3,437	—
Social security and welfare	12,214	—
Housing and community amenities	4,831	—
Recreation, cultural, and religious affairs	5,396	—
Economic affairs and services	25,910	—
Other expenditures	85,850	—
Adjustments	—	—
Lending minus repayments	1,983	2,000
TOTALS	323,961	338,677
Deficit/Surplus	−5,549	−7,200

In 1991, income taxes and duties accounted for 59% and 32.7% of revenues, respectively. Also, in 1991 Denmark's total public debt stood at Kr33,718 million, of which Kr13,698 million was financed abroad.

36TAXATION

Danish residents are liable for tax on global income and net wealth. Non-residents are liable only for tax on certain types of income from Danish sources. Taxes payable for 1993 included national income tax, gift and inheritance taxes, stamp tax, and a national wealth tax. A tax reform program that took effect in 1987 separated capital from personal income for individuals and lowered the maximum rate of total tax that an individual can be charged from 73 to 68%. Capital gains and investment income are taxed at a rate of 50%.

The imposition of a 9% value-added tax at the wholesale level, effective from August 1962, and its increase to 15% in 1970 and eventually to 25% in 1993, together with the replacement of progressive income tax by proportional income tax for 90% of the individual taxpayers and for all joint-stock companies, represented a shift of the burden of public revenues from income to consumption. A significant reason for the changeover from the national income tax to indirect taxation of consumption was the need to provide additional long-term incentives for private capital formation.

Corporations and private limited companies are subject to a single proportional income tax. Corporate income is taxed at a rate of 34% of the year's net earnings. Corporations also pay a value-added tax, which is 25% added to the price of goods and services sold in the home market, but in return they may deduct from their tax liability the amount of tax they have paid on goods and services supplied to them, such as new plants and equipment. Excise taxes are levied on tobacco, alcoholic beverages, gasoline, and television sets, among other products; and there is a tax by weight on motor vehicles.

[37]CUSTOMS AND DUTIES

Denmark—a consistent advocate of free and fair conditions of international trade—had until recently the lowest tariff rate in Europe. However, owing to shortages of foreign currency, Denmark did impose quantitative restrictions on imports, and as late as 1959 about 64% of Danish industrial production was so protected. On joining EFTA on 8 May 1960, Denmark began eliminating tariff rates and quantitative restrictions on industrial products from other EFTA countries, and by 1 January 1970, those that remained were abolished. On 1 January 1973, Denmark ended its membership in EFTA and became a member of the EC, which not only represents a free trade area but also seeks to integrate the economies of its member states.

Denmark adheres to provisions of GATT on import licensing requirements although certain industrial products must meet Danish and EC technical standards. Denmark converted to the Harmonized System of import duties on 1 January 1988. Most products from European countries are duty free. Duty rates for manufactured goods range from 5–14% of c.i.f. value, and a 25% VAT is applied to imported, as well as domestic, products.

[38]FOREIGN INVESTMENT

Foreign investors are treated on an equal footing with Danish investors; investment capital and profits may be freely repatriated. Since the late 1950s, Denmark has attracted a moderate amount of foreign investment. In 1993, cumulative direct foreign investment in Denmark totaled $8 billion.

[39]ECONOMIC DEVELOPMENT

For many years, Danish governments followed a full-employment policy and relied chiefly on promotion of private enterprise to achieve this end. Beginning in the late 1970s, however, the government increased its intervention in the economy, in response to rising unemployment, inflation, and budget deficits. Inflation has been curbed and budget deficits reduced. This bolstered the currency from devaluation, but at the cost of restraining growth, and unemployment continued to rise.

Government influence on private enterprise through the exercise of import and export licensing has diminished in recent years. The discount policy of the National Bank is of major importance to the business community. Control of cartels and monopolies is flexible. The government has a monopoly or majority interest in railways, domestic air traffic, airports, and communications. Most of the country's power stations are owned and operated by local governments and municipalities.

Capital incentives are available to assist new industries, mainly in the less-developed areas of Denmark. Municipalities also provide infrastructure, industrial parks, or inexpensive land. Under a 1967 provision, the Regional Development Committee (composed of representatives of a number of special-interest organizations

and central and local authorities) can grant state guarantees or state loans for the establishment of enterprises in less developed districts.

In 1978, Denmark reached the UN target for official developmental assistance in the mid-1970s: 0.7% of GNP. It reached 0.96% of GNP in 1991, second only to Norway. Denmark's official assistance to developing countries amounted to $1,205 million in 1991, of which $691 million was bilateral. The UNDP was the largest single recipient of Danish multilateral aid, with 19%, and Tanzania the largest recipient of bilateral aid, with 6.9%. Wherever possible, Danish assistance focuses on the poorest levels of society in the least developed countries ($446 million in 1991).

[40]SOCIAL DEVELOPMENT

Denmark was one of the first countries in the world to establish efficient social services with the introduction of relief for the sick, unemployed, and aged. As of 1988, Denmark was ninth in the world in expenditures on social security, and housing, allotting 40.4% of its budget to these areas. According to the constitution, any incapacitated person living in Denmark has a right to public relief. Benefits such as maintenance allowances for the children of single supporters, maternity allowances, day care, and others, involve neither repayment nor any other conditions; some others are regarded as loans to be repaid when possible. Family allowances are paid to families with incomes below a certain threshold; rent subsidies require a means test. The 1976 Social Assistance Act was designed to provide a broad range of help on the basis of family need, with an emphasis on preventive treatment. The act provides for an advisory service for persons undergoing social hardship, cash grants in situations not covered by pension law, a home-help service, and assistance in caring for young people experiencing difficulties.

All Danish citizens over 67 years of age may draw old age pensions. Disability pensions, equal in amount to old age pensions plus special supplements, are paid to persons with a stipulated degree of disablement. Old persons are cared for at homes that have been established in many parts of Denmark.

The state is primarily responsible for the care, education, and support of physically and mentally handicapped persons, including the crippled and deformed, the blind, the deaf, epileptics, the mentally retarded, and the mentally ill. There are allowances for unmarried mothers, for the children of widows, and in some cases for the children of widowers.

Social welfare expenditure—including health insurance, health and hospital services, insurance for occupational injuries, unemployment insurance and employment exchange services, old age and disability pensions, rehabilitation and nursing homes, family welfare subsidies, general public welfare, payments for military accidents, and the general administration of the above—amounted to Kr177,984 million in 1984.

In 1985, 29,322 marriages were registered, for a rate of 5.73 per 1,000 population, up from 4.75 in 1982—the lowest rate ever recorded in Denmark. There were 14,385 divorces in 1985, or 2.81 per 1,000 population, down from a high of 2.89 in 1983. The average age at first marriage has been steadily rising, reaching 29 for males and 26.3 for females in 1985. The fertility rate has fallen steadily since the 1940s. It was 1.5 in 1985–90, up 8.5% from the previous 5-year period. Since 1975, abortion has been available on demand to any woman during the first 12 weeks of pregnancy.

In 1993, women made up 46% of the work force (including 23% of all supervisors). Roughly 75% of all women between the ages of 16 and 66 worked. Laws guarantee equal pay for equal work, and women have and use legal recourse if they feel discriminated against. There are 34 crisis centers that counsel and shelter victims of domestic violence.

41HEALTH

Approximately $3,000 is invested in the social and medical well-being of every Dane annually, although health care expenditures have declined over the last decade. The administration of hospitals and personnel is dealt with by the Ministry of the Interior, while primary care facilities, health insurance, and community care are the responsbility of the Ministry of Social Affairs. Anyone can go to a physician for no fee, and the public health system entitles each Dane to his/her own doctor. Expert medical/surgical aid is available, and a qualified nursing staff. Costs are borne by public authorities, but high taxes contribute to these costs. In 1990 there were 14,277 physicians (278 per 100,000 people), and from 1988 to 1992, the nurse to doctor ratio was 5.6. In 1991 there were 23,000 hospital beds (544 per 100,000 inhabitants), and 50,195 beds in nursing homes and old-age homes. In 1984, the central government paid for 11% of the cost of the public health care system, local authorities 80%, and employers 9%. Total health care expenditures in 1990 were $8,160 million. In 1992 there were 64,000 births (a rate of 12 per 1,000 people). Studies show that between 1980 and 1993, 63% of married women (ages 15 to 49) used contraception. In 1990, there were only 7 reported cases of tuberculosis per 100,000 people. In 1991, there were 204 AIDS cases and 19,729 abortions. Danish citizens may choose between two systems of primary health care: medical care provided free of charge by a doctor whom the individual chooses for a year, and by those specialists to whom the doctor refers the patient; or complete freedom of choice of any physician or specialist at any time, with state reimbursement of about two-thirds of the cost for medical bills paid directly by the patient. Most Danes opt for the former. All patients receive subsidies on pharmaceuticals and vital drugs; everyone must pay a share of dental bills.

Responsibility for the public hospital service rests with county authorities. Counties form public hospital regions, each of which is allotted 1 or 2 larger hospitals with specialists and 2 to 4 smaller hospitals where medical treatment is practically free. State-appointed medical health officers, responsible to the National Board of Health, are employed to advise local governments on health matters. Public health authorities have waged large-scale campaigns against tuberculosis, venereal diseases, diphtheria, and poliomyelitis. The free guidance and assistance given to mothers of newborn children by public health nurses have resulted in a low infant mortality rate of 7 per 1,000 live births (1992). Medical treatment is free up to school age, when free school medical inspections begin. Between 1990 and 1992, children up to 1 year of age were vaccinated against diptheria, pertussis, and tetanus (99%); polio (99%); and measles (86%). In 1993, life expectancy at birth was 72 years for males and 77 years for females. The overall death rate was 12 per 1,000 people in 1992.

42HOUSING

In recent decades, especially since the passage of the Housing Subsidy Act of 1956, considerable government support has been given to housing. For large families building their own homes, government loans have been provided on exceptionally favorable terms, and special rent rebates have been granted to large families occupying apartments in buildings erected by social building societies or in buildings built with government loans since 1950. Subject to certain conditions, housing rebates have been granted to pensioners and invalids. An annual grant is made to reduce householders' maintenance expenses. This extensive support helped to reduce the wartime and immediate postwar housing shortage. The total number of dwellings in 1992 was 2,386,384, of which 635,552 had five or more rooms and a kitchen. In 1991, 20,035 new dwellings were completed, down from 27,237 in 1990. As of 1989, 39% of all housing units were apartments, 41% were detached houses, 11% were un- or semi-detached, 7% were farms, and 1% were youth hostels. Roughly 55% were owner occupied and 44% were rented.

43EDUCATION

Virtually the entire Danish adult population is literate. Primary, secondary, and, on the whole, university and other higher education are free, and public expenditure on education is therefore high. Preschools are operated by private persons or organizations with some government financial aid.

Since 1814, education has been compulsory for children aged 7 to 14. The Danish primary school system, known as the "Folkes Kole," has a nine-year duration and many opt for an additional tenth year. English is included in the curriculum from the fifth grade. After basic schooling, two-thirds of the pupils apply for practical training in a trade or commerce at special schools. The remaining one-third go to secondary schools, which finish after three years with student examination and paves the way for higher education at universities. Municipal authorities, with some financial aid from the central government, have been responsible for providing schools for these children. Among the 954,073 receiving education in 1990, 655,169 were in public and secondary schools; 169,401 were undergoing vocational education in schools for business, maritime, and other studies; and 129,503 were in tertiary educational institutions such as the colleges and universities. Girls and women comprise almost 50% of those receiving education at all levels.

Adult education exists side by side with the regular school system. Founded as early as 1844, the folk high schools are voluntary, self-governing high schools imparting general adult education. In addition, there are hundreds of schools for higher instruction of pupils without previous special training.

There are four universities—the University of Copenhagen (founded in 1479), the University of Aarhus (founded as a college in 1928 and established as a university in 1933), the University of Odense (opened in 1966), and the University Center at Roskilde (founded in 1970). Attached to the various faculties are institutes, laboratories, and clinics devoted primarily to research, but also offering advanced instruction. Many specialized schools and academies of university rank provide instruction in various technical and artistic fields. All these institutions are independent in their internal administration.

44LIBRARIES AND MUSEUMS

Denmark's national library, the Royal Library in Copenhagen, founded by Frederik III in the 1660s, is the largest in Scandinavia, with 4.2 million volumes. Three other large libraries are the University Library in Copenhagen, Copenhagen Public Libraries and the State Library at Aarhus. As of 1990 there were 250 free public libraries throughout the country. That year, the public libraries had a total of more than 34 million volumes.

Denmark had 285 public and private museums and 5 zoological and botanical gardens in 1990. Among the largest museums are the National Museum (with rare ethnologic and archaeological collections), the Glyptotek (with a large collection of ancient and modern sculpture), the State Art Museum (containing the main collection of Danish paintings as well as other Scandinavian artists), the Thorvaldsen Museum, the Hirshsprung Collection, and the Rosenborg Palace, all in Copenhagen; and the National Historical Museum in Frederiksborg Castle, at Hillerød.

45MEDIA

Although the government telephone service owns and operates long-distance lines and gives some local service, the bulk of local telephone service is operated by private companies under government concession and with government participation. Continuous efforts are being made to expand and modernize the system. As of

1991 there were 4,398,000 telephones in Denmark proper, or approximately 856 telephones per 1,000 inhabitants. Telegraph services are owned and operated by the government. The radio broadcasting services are operated by the Danish State Radio System, on long, medium, and short waves. Television broadcasting hours are mainly devoted to current and cultural affairs and to programs for children and young people. There is no commercial advertising on radio or television; owners of sets pay an annual license fee. At the end of 1991 there were 5,310,000 radios and 2,760,000 television sets. In that year, Denmark had 334 movie theaters and produced 11 feature length films.

Complete freedom of the press is guaranteed under the constitution. The 46 daily newspapers in 1991 had an average daily net circulation of 1,842,000. The following table lists average daily circulation figures for 1991 for the largest newspapers:

	ORIENTATION	CIRCULATION
COPENHAGEN		
Ekstrabladet	Independent Social-liberal	231,700
B.T.	Independent Conservative	209,380
Politiken	Independent Social-liberal	156,720
Berlingske Tidende	Independent Conservative	132,480
PROVINCES		
Jyllands-Posten (Aarhus)	Independent	127,870
Aalborg Stiftstidende (Aalborg)	Independent	73,390
Aarhus Stiftstidende (Aarhus)	Independent	71,180
Fyens Stiftstidende (Odense)	Independent	71,989

During 1991, book and pamphlet production included 10,198 titles.

46ORGANIZATIONS

Nearly every Danish farmer is a member of at least one agricultural organization and of one or more producer cooperatives. The oldest agricultural organization, the Royal Agricultural Society of Denmark, was established in 1769, but most of the other organizations have been founded since 1850. They promote agricultural education and technical and economic development. Local societies have formed provincial federations, which in turn have combined in two national organizations, the Federation of Danish Agricultural Societies and the Federation of Danish Smallholders Societies. The Cooperative Movement of Denmark comprises three groups: agricultural cooperatives, retail cooperatives, and urban cooperatives. Owners of estates and large farms belong to separate organizations specializing in the affairs of larger agricultural units.

The first producer cooperatives were formed in the 1880s at a time when Danish farming changed its emphasis from cultivation to animal husbandry. Since then, the voluntary cooperation among the farmers of Denmark has been without parallel. There is almost nothing that Danish farmers buy, sell, or export that is not handled through cooperatives. Most consumers' cooperative societies belong to the Danish Cooperative Wholesale Society, which makes bulk purchases for member societies and also manufactures various products.

The Federation of Danish Industries and the Industrialists' Association in Copenhagen, which represent industrial undertakings and trade associations, safeguard and promote the interests of industry and deal with trade questions of an economic nature. The Council of Handicrafts represents various crafts, trades, and industries and gives subsidies to technical and trade schools. The leading organizations of the wholesale trade are the Copenhagen Chamber of Commerce and the Provincial Chamber of Commerce.

47TOURISM, TRAVEL, AND RECREATION

Dozens of castles, palaces, mansions, and manor houses, including the castle at Elsinore (Helsingør)—site of Shakespeare's *Hamlet*—

are open to the public. Tivoli Gardens, the world-famous amusement park, built in 1843 in the center of Copenhagen, is open from May through mid-September. Copenhagen is an important jazz center and holds a jazz festival in July. The Royal Danish Ballet, of international reputation, performs in Copenhagen's Royal Theater, which also presents opera and drama. Greenland, the world's largest island, is part of the Kingdom of Denmark and attracts tourists to its mountains, dog sledges, and midnight sun. In 1991 there were 37,056 hotel rooms with 92,524 beds in Denmark with a 36% occupancy rate.

No passport is required for Scandinavian nationals. Citizens of Canada, the US, and South and Central American countries, as well as those of most Commonwealth nations, most West European countries, and certain other nations may enter Denmark without a visa. All others must have a valid passport with entry and exit or transit visa. Most travelers cannot remain in Denmark longer than three months without extension or possession of a residence permit. In 1991, an estimated 1,429,000 tourists visited Denmark and spent $3.47 billion.

48FAMOUS DANES

Denmark's greatest classic writer and the founder of Danish literature is Ludvig Holberg (1684–1754), historian, philologist, philosopher, critic, and playwright, whose brilliant satiric comedies are internationally famous. Another important dramatist and poet is Adam Gottlob Oehlenschlaeger (1779–1850). The two most celebrated 19th-century Danish writers are Hans Christian Andersen (1805–75), whose fairy tales are read and loved all over the world, and the influential philosopher and religious thinker Søren Kierkegaard (1813–55). Nikolaj Frederik Severin Grundtvig (1783–1872), noted theologian and poet, was renowned for his founding of folk high schools, which brought practical education to the countryside. The leading European literary critic of his time was Georg Morris Brandes (Cohen, 1842–1927), whose *Main Currents in 19th-Century European Literature* exerted an influence on two generations of readers. Leading novelists include Jens Peter Jacobsen (1847–85); Martin Anderson Nexø (1869–1954), author of *Pelle the Conquerer* (1906–10) and *Ditte* (1917–21); and Johannes Vilhelm Jensen (1873–1950), who was awarded the Nobel Prize for literature in 1944 for his series of novels. Karl Adolph Gjellerup (1857–1919) and Henrik Pontoppidan (1857–1943) shared the Nobel Prize for literature in 1917. Isak Dinesen (Karen Blixen, 1887–1962) achieved renown for her volumes of gothic tales and narratives of life in Africa. Jeppe Aaksjaer (1866–1930), poet and novelist, is called the Danish Robert Burns. A great film artist is Carl Dreyer (1889–1968), known for directing *The Passion of Joan of Arc, Day of Wrath,* and *Ordet*. Famous Danish musicians include the composers Niels Gade (1817–90) and Carl Nielsen (1865–1931), the tenors Lauritz Melchior (1890–1973) and Aksel Schiøtz (1906–75), and the soprano Povla Frijsh (d.1960). Notable dancers and choreographers include August Bournonville (1805–79), originator of the Danish ballet style; Erik Bruhn (1928–86), who was known for his classical technique and was director of ballet at the Royal Swedish Opera House and of the National Ballet of Canada; and Fleming Ole Flindt (b.1936), who has directed the Royal Danish Ballet since 1965. The sculptor Bertel Thorvaldsen (1770–1844) is the artist of widest influence.

Notable scientists include the astronomers Tycho Brahe (1546–1601) and Ole Rømer (1644–1710); the philologists Ramus Christian Rask (1787–1832) and Otto Jespersen (1860–1943); the physicist Hans Christian Ørsted (1777–1851), discoverer of electromagnetism; Nobel Prize winners for physics Niels Bohr (1885–1962) in 1922 and his son Aage Niels Bohr (b.1922) and Benjamin Mottelson (b.1926) in 1975; Niels Rybert Finsen (b.Faroe Islands, 1860–1904), August Krogh (1874–1949), Johannes A. G. Fibiger (1867–1928), and Henrik C. P. Dam

(1895–1976), Nobel Prize-winning physicians and physiologists in 1903, 1920, 1926, and 1944, respectively. Frederik Bajer (1837–1922) was awarded the Nobel Prize for peace in 1908. Knud Johan Victor Rasmussen (1879–1933), explorer and anthropologist born in Greenland, was an authority on Eskimo ethnology.

Queen Margrethe II (b.1940) became sovereign in 1972.

49 DEPENDENCIES

Faroe Islands

The Faroe Islands (Faerøerne in Danish and Føroyar in the Faroese language), whose name stems from the Scandinavian word for sheep (får), are situated in the Atlantic Ocean, due N of Scotland, between 61°20′ and 62°24′N and 6°15′ and 7°41′w. The 18 islands, 17 of which are inhabited, cover an area of 1,399 sq km (540 sq mi). Among the larger islands are Streymoy (Strømø) with an area of 373 sq km (144 sq mi), Eysturoy (Østerø) with 286 sq km (110 sq mi), Vágar (Vaagø) with 178 sq km (69 sq mi), Suduroy (Syderø) with 166 sq km (64 sq mi), and Sandoy (Sandø) with 112 sq km (43 sq mi). The maximum length of the Faroe Islands is 112 km (70 mi) N–S and the maximum width is 79 km (49 mi) NE–SW. The total coastline measures 1,117 km (694 mi).

The population as of July 1992 was 48,588. Most Faroese are descended from the Vikings, who settled on the islands in the 9th century. The Faroes have been connected politically with Denmark since the 14th century. During World War II, they were occupied by the British, and in this period important political differences emerged. The Faroese People's party advocated independence for the islands; the Unionists preferred to maintain the status quo; and the Faroese Social Democrats wanted home rule. After the war, it was agreed to establish home rule under Danish sovereignty, and since 23 March 1948, the central Danish government has been concerned only with matters of common interest, such as foreign policy and foreign-currency exchange. The Faroes have their own flag, levy their own taxes, and issue their own postage stamps and banknotes. The Faroese language, revived in the 19th century and akin to Icelandic, is used in schools, with Danish taught as a first foreign language.

The Faroese parliament, or Lagting, dates back to Viking times and may be Europe's oldest legislative assembly. Distribution of seats in the 26-member Lagting has been fairly evenly divided among the four major parties. An administrative body, the Landsstyre, is elected by the Lagting. A judge, chief constable, and six district sheriffs carry out legal and police duties. The islands send two members to the Folketing.

In keeping with the islands' name, sheep raising was long the chief activity, but in recent years the fishing industry has grown rapidly. Annual fish catch is 360,000 metric tons (396,720 short tons). Principal varieties of fish caught are cod, herring, and haddock; almost the entire catch is exported. Exports go mainly to Spain, South American countries, and Denmark; imports come mainly from Denmark and the UK. Agriculture is limited to the cultivation of root vegetables, potatoes, and barley.

The economy is regulated by an agreement with Denmark whereby the central government facilitates the marketing of Faroese fisheries products and guarantees to some extent an adequate supply of foreign currency.

Greenland

Greenland (Grønland in Danish, Kalaallit Nunaat in Greenlandic) is the largest island in the world. Extending from 59°46′ to 83°39′N and from 11°39′ to 73°8′w, Greenland has a total area of 2,175,600 sq km (840,000 sq mi). The greatest N–S distance is about 2,670 km (1,660 mi), and E–W about 1,290 km (800 mi). Greenland is bounded on the N by the Arctic Ocean, on the E by the Greenland Sea, on the SE by the Denmark Strait (separating it from Iceland), on the S by the Atlantic Ocean, and on the W by Baffin Bay and Davis Strait. The coastline measures 39,090 km (24,290 mi). The ice-free strip along the coast, rarely exceeding 80 km (50 mi) in width, is only 296,900 sq km (114,630 sq mi) in area, while the coastal islands total 44,800 sq km (17,300 sq mi). The rest of the area, covered with ice measuring at least 2,100 m (7,000 ft) thick in some places, amounts to 1,833,900 sq km (708,070 sq mi). Greenland has a typically arctic climate, but there is considerable variation between localities, and temperature changes in any one locality are apt to be sudden. Rainfall increases from north to south, ranging from about 25 to 114 cm (10–45 in). Land transport is very difficult, owing to the ice and rugged terrain, and most local travel must be done by water. SAS operates flights on the Scandinavia-US route via Greenland, and tourists are being attracted by Greenland's imposing scenery.

The population, grouped in a number of scattered settlements of varying sizes, totaled 537,407 in July 1992. Greenlanders are predominantly Eskimos, with some admixture of Europeans. The Greenlandic language, an Eskimo-Aleut dialect, is in official use. Most native Greenlanders were engaged in hunting and fishing, but a steadily increasing number are now engaged in administration and in private enterprises. The Europeans chiefly follow such pursuits as administration, skilled services, and mining.

The Vikings reached Greenland as early as the 10th century. By the time Europeans rediscovered the island, however, Norse culture had died out and Greenland belonged to the Eskimos. Danish colonization began in the 18th century, when the whale trade flourished off Greenland's western shore. In 1933, the Permanent Court of Arbitration at The Hague definitively established Danish jurisdiction over all Greenland. Up to 1953, the island was a colony; at that time it became an integral part of Denmark. Greenland held that status until 1979, when it became self-governing after a referendum in which 70% of the population favored home rule. The number of members in the Landsting (parliament) varies from 23 to 26. In 1984 elections, the left-wing Siumut Party won 11 seats, the right-wing Atassat Party won 11 seats, and the Eskimo Movement (Invit Ataqatigiit), allied with the Siumut Party, won 3 seats. The five-member Executive Council (Landsstryet) was composed entirely of Siumut adherents. Greenland elects two representatives to the Folketing. In 1985, Greenland withdrew from the EC.

Fishing, hunting (mainly seal, and to a lesser extent fox), and mining are the principal occupations. Greenland's total fish catch in 1988 was 135,500 metric tons (148,770 short tons). Agriculture is not possible in most of Greenland, but some few vegetables are grown in the south, usually under glass.

At Ivigtut, on the southwest coast, a deposit of cryolite has long been worked by a Danish government-owned corporation, but reserves are believed to be nearing depletion. The government has a controlling interest in the lead-zinc mine at Mestersvig, on the east coast. Production began in 1956 and has continued sporadically. Low-grade coal mined at Disko Islands, midway on the west coast, is used for local fuel needs. Fish and fish products make up the bulk of exports. Trade is mostly with Denmark. Raw materials are administered jointly by a Denmark-Greenland commission. Underground resources remain in principle the property of Denmark, but the Landsting has veto power over matters having to do with mineral development.

A US Air Force base is situated at Thule, in the far north along the west coast, only 14° from the North Pole; Greenland also forms part of an early-warning radar network. An international meteorological service, administered by Denmark, serves transatlantic flights. In 1960, a 1,500-kw atomic reactor was set up in northern Greenland to supply electric power to a new US scientific base built on the icecap, 225 km (140 mi) inland from Thule.

⁵⁰BIBLIOGRAPHY

Anderson, Robert T., and Edward Hohfeld. *Denmark: Success of a Developing Nation.* Cambridge, Mass.: Schenkman, 1975.

Holbraad, Carsten. *Danish Neutrality: a Study in the Foreign Policy of a Small State.* New York: Oxford University Press, 1991.

Jensen, Jorgen. *The Prehistory of Denmark.* New York: Methuen, 1983.

Johansen, Hans Chr. *The Danish Economy in the Twentieth Century.* New York: St. Martin's Press, 1987.

Jones, W. Glyn. *Denmark: A Modern History.* Wolfeboro, N.H.: Longwood, 1986.

Lauring, Palle. *Denmark.* Philadelphia: Nordic Books, 1986.

MacHaffie, Ingeborg S., and Margaret A. Nielsen. *Of Danish Ways.* New York: Harper & Row, 1984.

Miller, Kenneth E. *Denmark.* Santa Barbara, Calif.: Clio Press, 1987.

——. *Denmark, a Troubled Welfare State.* Boulder, Colo.: Westview Press, 1991.

Nielsen, Niels (ed.). *Atlas over Denmark* (Atlas of Denmark). Copenhagen: Hagerup, 1949.

Oakley, Stewart. *A Short History of Denmark.* New York: Praeger, 1972.

Pedersen, Clemens (ed.). *The Danish Co-operative Movement.* Copenhagen: Det Danske Selskab, 1977.

Petersen, Jørn Henrik. *The Development of the Danish Welfare State and Its Present Status.* Odense: University of Odense, 1978.

Starcke, Viggo. *Denmark in World History.* Philadelphia: University of Pennsylvania Press, 1963.

ESTONIA

Republic of Estonia
Eesti Vabariik

CAPITAL: Tallinn.

FLAG: Three equal horizontal bands of blue (top), black, and white.

ANTHEM: *Mu isamaa, mu õnn ja rõõm (My Native Land, My Pride and Joy).*

MONETARY UNIT: The Estonian kroon (EEK) was introduced in August 1992, replacing the Russian rouble.

WEIGHTS AND MEASURES: The metric system is in force.

HOLIDAYS: New Year's Day, 1 January; Independence Day, 24 February; Good Friday, 14 April; Labor Day, 1 May; Victory Day, anniversary of the Battle of Vonnu in 1919, 23 June; Midsummer Day, 24 June; Christmas, 25–26 December.

TIME: 2 PM = noon GMT.

¹LOCATION, SIZE, AND EXTENT

Estonia is located in northeastern Europe, bordering the Baltic Sea, between Sweden and Russia. Comparatively, the area occupied by Estonia is slightly larger than the states of New Hampshire and Vermont combined, with a total area of 45,100 sq km (17,413 sq mi). Estonia shares boundaries with the Baltic Sea on the N and W, Russia on the E, and Latvia on the S. Estonia's boundary length totals 1,950 km (1,212 mi). Estonia's capital city, Tallinn, is located in the northern part of the country along the Baltic Sea coast.

²TOPOGRAPHY

The topography of Estonia consists mainly of marshy lowlands.

³CLIMATE

The proximity of the Baltic Sea influences the coastal climate. At the most western point, Vilsandi Saar, the mean temperature is 6°C (42.8°F). At the country's most eastern points, the mean temperature is between 4.2 and 4.5°C (36 to 40°F). Rainfall averages 50 cm (20 in) on the coast. Inland, rainfall averages 70 cm (28 in). Rainfall is heaviest during the summer and lightest in the spring.

⁴FLORA AND FAUNA

Calcareous soil and a relatively mild climate permit rich flora and fauna in western Estonia. Native plants number 1,500 species. The abundance of woodland and plant species provide a suitable habitat for elk, deer, wild boar, wolf, lynx, bear, and otter.

⁵ENVIRONMENT

Air, water, and land pollution rank among Estonia's most significant environmental challenges. The combination of 300,000 tons of dust from the burning of oil shale within Estonia plus air-borne pollutants from industrial centers in Poland and Germany creates a hazardous living environment for its inhabitants.

Estonia's water resources have been affected by industrial and agricultural pollutants. Some rivers and lakes within the country have been found to contain toxic sediments in excess of 10 times the accepted level for safety.

The nation's land pollution problems are aggravated by the 15 million tons of pollutants that are added yearly to the existing 250 million tons of pollutants that have accumulated. In 1994, 24,000 acres of the country's total land area are affected. Radiation levels from the nuclear accident at Chernobyl exceed currently accepted safety levels.

According to UN sources, as of 1992, 14 types of plants and 38 forms of lichens are extinct. Sixty-six types of plants are threatened with extinction. The Estonian government has placed 59 plant and 189 animal species under state protection.

⁶POPULATION

The population of Estonia was 1,572,916 in 1989. It was estimated at 1,526,177 at the beginning of 1993. A population of 1,576,000 is projected for 2000, based on a crude birthrate per 1,000 population of 14, a crude death rate of 11.1, and a natural increase of 2.9 for 1995–2000. The estimated population density at the beginning of 1993 was 34 per sq km (87 per sq mi). The population was 71% urban at that time. Tallinn, the capital, had an estimated population of 452,840. Other large cities and their populations were Tartu, 109,133; Narva, 80,491; Kohtla-Järve, 56,141; and Pärnu, 52,085.

⁷MIGRATION

Newly independent in 1918, Estonia was occupied and annexed in 1940 by the Soviet Union. It was occupied by German troops the following year. When the Soviet army returned in 1944, more than 60,000 Estonians fled to Sweden and Germany. Other Estonians were sent to Soviet labor camps. Many Russians migrated to Estonia under Soviet rule. Some left after Estonia became independent again. A 1990 immigration law sets annual quotas. In 1992 there were 3,615 registered immigrants and 37,293 registered emigrants.

⁸ETHNIC GROUPS

In 1989, Estonians made up 61.5% of the population, Russians, 30%, Ukrainians, 3%, Belorussians, 2%, and Finns, 1%. Non-Estonians were found chiefly in the northeastern industrial towns, while rural areas were 87% Estonian. Citizenship is by birth only if at least one parent is an Estonian citizen. Naturalization requires three years' residence and competence in Estonian. Only 12% of the Russians in Tallinn knew Estonian in 1989.

⁹LANGUAGES

Estonian is a member of the Finno–Ugric linguistic family. It is closely related to Finnish and distantly related to Hungarian.

Standard Estonian is based on the North Estonian dialect. Most of the sounds can be pronounced as either short, long, or extra long. Changing the duration of a sound in a word can alter the grammatical function of the word or change its meaning completely. The language is highly agglunative, and there are no less than 14 cases of noun declension. Most borrowed words are from German. The alphabet is Roman. The first text written in Estonian dates from 1525.

[10]RELIGIONS

Christianity was introduced into Estonia in the 11th century. During the Reformation it converted largely to Lutheranism, although political events in the 18th and 19th century occasioned a strong Russian Orthodox presence. Independence from the Soviet Union, achieved in 1991, relieved the pressure under which religious groups had labored since 1940. Although Estonians are overwhelmingly Lutheran, Seventh-day Adventist, Baptist, and Methodist churches have begun to establish themselves as well. In 1990, 3,500 Jews were living in Estonia.

[11]TRANSPORTATION

Some 1,030 km (640 mi) of railroads provide Tallinn, Haapsalu, Pärnu, Tartu, and Narva with rail access to Russia, Latvia, and the Baltic Sea. In order to overcome problems in rolling stock shortages and load fluctuations, a second line of tracks is being laid along the Tallinn-Narva route.

Highways in 1990 totaled 30,300 km (18,800 mi), including 29,200 km (18,100 mi) of hard-surfaced and 1,100 km (680 mi) of dirt roads. Motor vehicles dominate domestic freight transportation, carrying nearly 75% of all dispatched goods. Buses carry some 430 million passengers annually.

The Baltic Sea (with the Gulf of Finland and Gulf of Riga) provides Estonia with its primary access to international markets. The principal maritime posts are Tallinn and Pärnu. The merchant fleet includes 65 vessels (of which 51 are cargo ships) for a total capacity of 386,634 GRT in 1991. Sea transportation has increased especially since the completion of Tallinn's new harbor and the acquisition of high capacity vessels. Ships carry grain from North America and also serve West African cargo routes. In 1990, a ferry service opened between Tallinn and Stockholm.

Tallinn has direct air links to Helsinki and Stockholm. In 1992, Estonian Air, the principal international airline, carried some 146,300 passengers.

[12]HISTORY

What is now Estonia was ruled in turn by the Danes, the Germans, and the Swedes from the Middle Ages until the 18th century. Russia annexed the region in 1721. During the 19th century, an Estonian nationalist movement arose which by the early 20th century sought independence.

After the 1917 Bolshevik Revolution and the advance of German troops into Russia, Estonia declared independence on 24 February 1918. But after the German surrender to the Western powers in November 1918, Russian troops attempted to move back into Estonia. The Estonians, however, pushed out Soviet forces by April 1919, and the following year Soviet Russia recognized the Republic of Estonia.

The Nazi–Soviet Pact of 1939 assigned Estonia to the Soviet sphere of influence. The Red Army invaded in June 1940 and "admitted" the Estonian Soviet Socialist Republic into the USSR in August 1940. However, Hitler's forces invaded the USSR in June 1941 and took control of Estonia shortly thereafter. The German Army retreated in 1944 and Soviet forces once again occupied Estonia.

Taking advantage of the relatively greater freedom which Mikhail Gorbachev allowed, an Estonian nationalist movement, the Popular Front, was launched in 1987. Estonia declared its

independence from Moscow on 20 August 1991. A new constitution was adopted on 28 June 1992.

Most Russian troops have been withdrawn from Estonia, but about 2,500 of them are still there. The Estonian government called for Russia to withdraw them all by 31 August 1994, but on 10 July 1994, Russian President Boris Yeltsin stated that Moscow would not do so. Yeltsin said his decision was due to Estonia's unwillingness to grant citizenship or provide housing for retired Russian military personnel living in Estonia.

[13]GOVERNMENT

Estonia adopted a new post-Soviet constitution on 28 June 1992. It declares Estonia a parliamentary democracy with a unicameral parliament. The parliament is known as the Riigikogu. The president, prime minister and the cabinet make up the executive branch of government. The president is the head of state while the prime minister, is the head of government. Both the parliament and the president are elected by direct universal suffrage of citizens 18 years or older.

[14]POLITICAL PARTIES

Political parties in Estonia are still evolving. Party adherence seems based more on personal loyalties than on commitments to specific policy goals. Several political parties have emerged since the declaration of independence.

The Independent Communist Party of Estonia split from the Communist Party of the Soviet Union in January 1991. The Pro Patria Party, the Estonian Social Democratic Party, the Christian-Democratic Union of Estonia, the Estonian National Independence Party, and Estonian Green Movement are among the many parties that have emerged in the past few years. The Popular Front of Estonia, founded in 1988 to unite pro-independence forces, has lost much of its influence and role since the attainment of independence. The non-Estonian, mainly Russian, interests are represented by the Inter-Movement of the Working People of Estonia and the Union of Work Collectives, both founded in 1988. In addition, a Russian Democratic Movement has emerged that specifically represents the Russian-speaking population of Estonia.

[15]LOCAL GOVERNMENT

While only citizens are allowed to vote in Estonia's national elections, residents of Estonia, including non-citizens, are allowed to vote in local elections. Non-citizens, however, cannot be candidates in local (or national) elections.

[16]JUDICIAL SYSTEM

The 1992 constitution established a court system consisting of three levels of courts: (1) rural and city courts, (2) district courts, and (3) state courts. The upper two levels of courts may engage in constitutional review of legislation.

The 1992 interim criminal code abolishes a number of political and economic crimes under the former Soviet Criminal Code. Estonia is now in the process of drafting new criminal and civil procedural codes. The judicial reform law of 1993 will not be implemented until vacant judicial seats are filled.

[17]ARMED FORCES

Still in the process of forming a national army, Estonia plans to have 15 months obligated service in order to form a border guard, a rapid reaction force, and many territorial defense battalions. There were about 2,000 men on duty in 1994. The Russians have 23,000 soldiers, airmen, and air defense troops still in Estonian garrisons.

[18]INTERNATIONAL COOPERATION

Estonia was admitted to the UN on 17 February 1991. The country is a member of the CSCE, EBRD, FAO, IAEA, IMF,

UNCTAD, and the World Bank, and is applying for membership in other international organizations. The country's sovereignty is recognized by the US, EC countries, and many others. Estonia has especially close ties with the countries of the European Community. It is not a member of the CIS.

19 ECONOMY

Estonia has one of the strongest economies among the former Soviet republics. Its mineral resources include 60% of former Soviet oil shale deposits, as well as phosphates. Light manufacturing dominates industry, with major sectors that include textiles, furniture, and electronics. Agriculture is based mainly on rearing livestock, but dairy farming is also significant.

Estonia has successfully begun to integrate its economy into the European mainstream following the break-up of the Soviet Union, which disrupted its supply of inexpensive fuel and raw materials and collapsed traditional export markets.

20 INCOME

In 1992, the GNP was $4,297 million at current prices, or $2,750 per capita. For the period 1985–92 the average inflation rate was 23.7%, resulting in a real growth rate in per capita GNP of 3.0%.

In 1992 the GDP was $429 million in current US dollars. It is estimated that in 1991 agriculture, hunting, forestry, and fishing contributed 17% to GDP; mining and quarrying, 2%; manufacturing, 33%; electricity, gas, and water, 2%; construction, 6%; wholesale and retail trade, 8%; transport, storage, and communication, 6%; finance, insurance, real estate, and business services, 2%; community, social, and personal services, 4%; and other sources, 21%.

21 LABOR

In 1990, the total economically active population was estimated at 795,500, or 50.5% of the total population. Of the 790,000 employed in 1991, 32.5% were engaged in manufacturing, 25.1% in community, social, and personal services, 12.8% in agriculture, hunting, forestry, and fishing, 9.9% in construction, 8.7% in commerce, 8.5% in transportation and communication, and 2.5% in other sectors.

The new Estonian constitution guarantees the right to form and freely join a union or employee association. The Central Organization of Estonian Trade Unions (EAKL) was founded in 1990 as a voluntary and culturally Estonian organization to replace the Estonian branch of the Soviet labor confederation. In 1992, the EAKL claimed 500,000 members, organized in 30 unions. Collective bargaining, though legal, is still developing among the neophyte unions.

The statutory minimum employment age is 16. The government supervises the setting of the minimum wage rate. The standard workweek is legally set at 41 hours.

22 AGRICULTURE

During the Soviet period, forced collectivization reduced the share of labor in agriculture from 50% to less than 20%. Agriculture accounted for 15.1% of GDP in 1991 and 17.1% in 1992, despite a decline of 6.5% in that sector in 1991.

Principal crops in 1992 included potatoes, 648,000 tons; barley, 302,000 tons; rye, 150,000 tons; vegetables and melons, 115,000 tons; wheat, 90,000 tons; and fruit (excluding melons), 24,000 tons.

23 ANIMAL HUSBANDRY

Over 10% of the total land area is meadow or pastureland. In 1992, there were 799,000 pigs, 708,000 head of cattle, 143,000 sheep, and 5,000,000 chickens. Meat production is well developed and provides a surplus for export. In 1992, 60,000 tons of

LOCATION: 59°0'; 26 °0' **BOUNDARY LENGTHS:** Total boundary length 1,950 km (1,212 mi); Latvia 267 km (166 mi); Russia, 290 km (180 mi).

beef, 90,000 tons of pork, and 23,000 tons of poultry were produced. Cattle breeding was the main activity during the Soviet era, and production quotas were set extremely high, which required massive imports of feed. Pork production has risen in recent years to offset the decline in the total cattle herd. Dairy production is being encouraged.

24 FISHING

Estonia's Baltic and Atlantic catch is marketed in the former Soviet Union, in spite of its own need for quality fish products. The fishing industry is seen as an important way to acquire access to the world market, but scarcity of raw materials currently limits its development.

25 FORESTRY

Some 31% of the land area is covered by forests and woodlands. The production of wood and wood products is the second-largest industry after textiles; two cellulose plants (at Tallinn and Kehra) use local raw material, but have caused significant environmental problems. There is also a fiberboard processing plant (for furniture making) at Püssi. In 1990, exports of wood and paper products accounted for 4.2% of total exports.

26 MINING

Oil shale, found in the Northeast Estonian Basin, is the primary mineral of importance. Phosphate is quarried at the Maardu deposit, and there is also one uranium mining and concentrating complex at Sillamäe.

27 ENERGY AND POWER

Domestic electrical production comes from locally mined oil shale from 11 mines. About 90% of the annual 23–24 million tons mined is burned to produce electricity at the Estonian Thermal Power Station and the Baltic Thermal Power Station. Nearly 50% of the electricity generated is supplied to Latvia and the Russian Federation. If, however, atmospheric pollution from the oil shale fuel is not cut to 50% of the 1980 level by 1995, then the production of electricity from oil shale is scheduled to be reduced. Electrical generating capacity from the two large thermal plants at Narva totaled 3,045 million kw. In 1991, Estonia produced 16 billion kwh of electricity and exported 7.9 billion kwh.

28INDUSTRY

Industry is the principal sector of Estonia's economy. In 1991, 26.6% of industrial output was accounted for by the food industry, 25.9% by light industry, 12.7% by machine-building and metalworks, 10.3% by the timber industry, and 8.5% by chemicals. The textile mills of Kreenholmi Manufacturer in Narva and Balti Manufacturer in Tallinn are the country's largest industrial enterprises.

29SCIENCE AND TECHNOLOGY

The Academy of Sciences, founded in 1938, has sections of astronomy and physics, informatics and technical sciences, and biology, geology, and chemistry. The Research Institute of Avian Diseases is in Tartu, and the Research Institute of Epidemiology, Microbiology, and Hygiene is in Tallinn. Tallinn Technical University offers engineering degrees. Tartu University has faculties of biology and geography, mathematics, medicine, and physics and chemistry. Estonian Agricultural University has 2,461 students.

30DOMESTIC TRADE

Before the collapse of the Soviet Union, Estonia's domestic trade was underdeveloped by international standards. Most trading companies were owned either by the state or by cooperatives. In recent years, many shops have been privatized or municipalized, new private shops established, and the assortment of goods widened.

By the end of 1991, there were 4,026 shops in Estonia, occupying a total of 352,000 square meters. In 1992, the state sector accounted for only 34% of retail goods turnover.

31FOREIGN TRADE

During the Soviet era, Estonia's foreign trade was characterized by large net imports, 80–85% of which came from other Soviet republics, the destination of 95% of Estonian exports. Beginning in 1992, the value of exports began to surpass that of imports, and the share of the ruble zone states in Estonia's trade diminished. In 1992, the value of exports totaled EEK5.4 billion and that of imports EEK5.1 billion. The majority of exports went to Finland (21%) and Russia (20%), which also supplied most of the imports (23% and 29%, respectively). The main export articles were timber, wood products, and metal.

32BALANCE OF PAYMENTS

Since independence, Estonia has dismantled a Soviet-era system of trade barriers and tariffs to become one of the world's most free-trading nations. Exports to the west quadrupled in 1991/92, which consequently generated a strong surplus of approximately $100 million in the current account. Net private investment that year approached $60 million.

33BANKING AND SECURITIES

The country's central bank, Eesti Bank, was founded in 1989, is charged with issuing currency and regulating Estonia's 20 commercial banks. The commercial banks include the Bank of Tallinn (1990), Estonian Commercial Bank of Industry (1991), Cand Bank of Estonia (1990), and South Estonian Development Bank. Savings banks include the Estonian Savings Bank, a bank with 432 branches.

There are two stock exchanges in Estonia: the Estonian Stock Exchange and the Tallinn Stock Exchange.

34INSURANCE

Since Estonia regained its independence, it has sought to develop a system of health insurance involving the decentralization of medical care.

35PUBLIC FINANCE

The new government exercises fiscal responsibility, as was evidenced by a balanced 1992 budget which produced a surplus. No transfers or preferential credits are given to public enterprises, and governmental borrowing from the central bank is forbidden.

The following table shows actual revenues and expenditures for 1991 in millions of rubles.

	1991
REVENUE AND GRANTS	
Tax revenue	4,077.4
Non-tax revenue	399.8
Capital revenue	3.7
Grants	149.4
TOTAL	4,630.3
EXPENDITURES & LENDING MINUS REPAYMENTS	
General public service	251.4
Defense	—
Public order and safety	145.7
Education	285.2
Health	156.9
Social security and welfare	1,696.2
Housing and community amenities	78.8
Recreation, cultural, and religious affairs	144.0
Economic affairs and services	801.8
Other expenditures	446.6
Adjustments	—
Lending minus repayments	164.0
TOTAL	4,210.8
Deficit/Surplus	419.5

It is difficult to determine the quantity of Estonian debt within the Soviet external debt. Discussions with the countries of the CIS on this matter are ongoing.

36TAXATION

Individuals are taxed on income from employment, self-employment, and other sources. Rates range from 16% to EEK346 plus 33% of any amount over EEK1,800. Most capital gains are not taxed, and employers must pay a 20% social security contribution. The corporate income tax rate is a flat 35%. A value-added tax of 18% is levied on the sale of goods and services, including imports.

37CUSTOMS AND DUTIES

Estonia's 1991 economic program looked ahead to eventual Estonian participation in the EC. Estonia has a temporary customs agreement with Russia.

38FOREIGN INVESTMENT

Estonia has successfully attracted a large number of joint ventures with Western companies, benefiting from a well-developed service sector and links with Scandinavian countries. The foreign investment act passed by the Supreme Council in September 1991 offers tax relief to foreign investors. As of May 1992, there were 1,200 joint ventures, with capital contributions by non-resident investors estimated at around $150 million; firms from Sweden, Finland, and the CIS were the largest investors.

[39] ECONOMIC DEVELOPMENT

After passing an ownership act in June 1990, the government began "minor" privatization at the beginning of 1991. Close to half of the nearly 500 state-owned companies have since passed into new hands. Five companies have been sold as part of the "major" privatization program.

[40] SOCIAL DEVELOPMENT

The average family size in 1989 was 3.1 members, and the divorce rate was 8.9 per 1,000 women. The fertility rate in 1990 was 2.05 children per woman. Discrimination based on race, sex, nationality, or religion is illegal under the constitution. Men and women generally receive equal pay for equal work. Women constitute slightly more than half the work force. During 1993, public attention focused increasingly on the welfare of children in the wake of family crises caused by economic dislocation. Several safe havens for children were established.

In 1989, there were 9.7 alcohol-related deaths per 100,000 persons and 0.9 drug-related crimes.

[41] HEALTH

In 1992, there were 22,000 births (a rate of 14 per 1,000 people). From 1990 to 1992, Estonia immunized children up to one year old against tuberculosis (96%); diphtheria, pertussis, and tetanus (70%); polio (71%); and measles (75%). In 1990, there were 210 people per physician in the country. In 1992, the infant mortality rate was 20 per 1,000, and the overall death rate was 12 per 1,000 people. Life expectancy in 1992 averaged 71 years.

[42] HOUSING

As of 1989, 60% of all privately owned urban housing had running water, 60% had sewer lines, 17% had central heating, and 15% had hot water. On 1 January 1991, 51,000 households (or 12%) were on waiting lists for urban housing. Housing space per capita totaled 20.3 square meters at the end of 1991, and 34.3 million square meters altogether, of which 10.1 million were privately owned.

The housing costs of low-income families are subsidized and most housing will be privatized in a few years.

[43] EDUCATION

The country's adult literacy rate in 1990 was 99.7%, with men estimated at 99.9% and women at 99.6%.

Prior to the 1990s, the Soviet system of education was in existence. This was modified after its separation from USSR. Both Russian and Estonian are popularly taught. Estonian language schools have 12 years of schooling with nine years of primary and three years of secondary education. Russian-language schools have a total of 11 years of schooling. There are two well-known universities: the University of Tartu, founded in 1632, teaches both Estonian and Russian; and the Talliva Technical University, founded in 1936, mainly offers engineering. In 1991–92, all higher level institutions had 25,643 pupils.

[44] LIBRARIES AND MUSEUMS

The National Library of Estonia in Tallinn, founded in 1918, contains 4.3 million volumes. Other important libraries located in Tallinn include the Estonian Technical Library (11.8 million volumes) and the Library of the Academy of Sciences (3.3 million). The Tartu State University Library is the largest academic library with over 5 million volumes.

The Estonian History Museum in Tartu was established in 1864. It contains 230,000 exhibits which follow the history of the region's people from ancient times to the present. The Estonian National Museum in Tallinn, established in 1909, features exhibits about the living conditions of Estonians. Also in Tallinn is the Art Museum of Estonia.

[45] MEDIA

Recent improvements in Estonia's international telecommunications capacity include an optical cable under the Gulf of Finland, a new central telephone exchange for Tallinn, and satellite computer links. Domestic lines and exchanges, however, still require modernization. Estonian Radio began regular broadcasting in 1926. In 1937, the highest radio tower in Europe (196.7m) was built in Türi. In the 1970s, Estonian Radio was the first in the former Soviet Union to carry advertising. It broadcast in Estonian, Russian, Finnish, and several other languages. In 1991, the first local radio stations were opened, some with private funding. Estonian television began broadcasting in 1955, and started color broadcasts in 1972. It broadcasts on four channels in Estonian and Russian.

Journalism was subject to varying degrees of censorship from the Russian occupation in 1940 until the late 1980s. In 1989, 111 newspapers were officially registered. The most popular daily newspapers (with 1993 circulation figures) are the *Postimees* (73,500) and the *Rahva Hääl* (the Voice of the People) (62,600). The most widely read weeklies are the *Maaleht* (Country News, 65,200) and the *Eesti Ekspress* (Estonian Express, 40,000).

Estonia has an active publishing industry, although it faced economic difficulties in the early 1990s. The ISBN code has been used in Estonia since 1988. There were 15,939,600 books published in 1992.

[46] ORGANIZATIONS

The Chamber of Commerce and Industry of the Republic of Estonia promotes trade and commerce with its neighbors. Also, there is a chamber of commerce in Tartu. The Trade Union's activities are coordinated by the Estonia Trade Union Head Office. Many journalists in Estonia belong to the Journalists Union. In 1989 Estonian sports were reorganized and the Soviets reduced control of Estonia's sports system. In the same year the National Olympic Committee was restored.

[47] TOURISM, TRAVEL, AND RECREATION

After languishing under Soviet rule, tourism is becoming one of the major sectors of Estonia's economy. Visitors are drawn to the country's scenic landscapes, Hanseatic architecture, music and dance festivals, regattas, and beach resorts. Since May 1990, tourism has been coordinated by the National Tourist Board, and there are approximately 300 joint ventures and other companies operating in the tourist industry. The ancient town of Tallinn, noted for its architectural preservation, is a major tourist attraction and is linked by regular ferries to Helsinki and Stockholm. In 1992, 1.5 million passengers used its port.

[48] FAMOUS ESTONIANS

Lennart Meri and Mart Laar have been president and prime minister of Estonia since October 1992, respectively. Writer Friedrich Reinhold Kreutzwald wrote the epic *Kalevipoeg* [Son of Kalev.]. It was published by the Estonian Learned Society between 1857–61. The epic marked the beginning of Estonian national literature.

The Revolution of 1905 forced many Estonian writers to flee the country. In 1906 a stable government was established in Estonia and a literary movement took hold, Birth of Young Estonia. The movement was led by poet Gustav Suits. He fled to Finland in 1910 but returned after the Russian Revolution of 1917. Later, Suits became a professor of literature at Tartu University. His fellow writers and poets between the revolution of 1917 and 1940 included Friebert Tuglas and Marie Under. Writers who fled abroad during World War II include Karl Rumor and Arthur Adson. Estonian writers banned or exiled during the Soviet period include the playwright Hugo Raudsepp.

[49]DEPENDENCIES

Estonia has no territories or colonies.

[50]BIBLIOGRAPHY

Estonia: the Transition to a Market Economy. Washington, D.C.: World Bank, 1993.

Parming, Marju Rink. *A Bibliography of English-language Sources on Estonia.* New York: Estonian Learned Society in America, 1974.

Parming, Tonu and Elmar Jarvesoo (eds.). *A Case Study of a Soviet Republic: the Estonian SSR.* Boulder, Colo.: Westview Press, 1978.

Rank, Gustav. *Old Estonia, the People and Culture.* Bloomington: Indiana University, Research Center for Language and Semiotic Studies, 1976.

Raun, Toivo U. *Estonia and the Estonians.* 2d ed. Stanford, Calif.: Hoover Institution Press, 1991.

Taagepera, Rein. *Estonia: Return to Independence.* Boulder, Colo.: Westview Press, 1993.

———. *Softening Without Liberalization in the Soviet Union: the Case of Juri Kukk.* Lanham, Md.: University Press of America, 1984.

Urban, William L. *The Baltic Crusade.* DeKalb: Northern Illinois University Press, 1975.

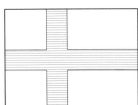

FINLAND

Republic of Finland
Suomen Tasavalta

CAPITAL: Helsinki.

FLAG: The civil flag contains an ultramarine cross with an extended right horizontal on a white background; the state flag flown on government buildings is the same but also includes, at the center of the cross, the coat of arms, consisting of a gold lion and nine white roses on a red background.

ANTHEM: *Maammelaulu* (in Swedish, *Vårt land; Our Land*).

MONETARY UNIT: The markka (M) of 100 penniä is a convertible currency with one official exchange rate. There are coins of 10 and 50 penniä and 1 and 5 markkaa, and notes of 10, 50, 100, 500 and 1,000 markkaa. M1 = $0.1829 (or $1 = M5.4678).

WEIGHTS AND MEASURES: The metric system is the legal standard.

HOLIDAYS: New Year's Day, 1 January; May Day, 1 May; Independence Day, 6 December; Christmas, 25–26 December. Movable holidays include Good Friday, Easter Monday, Whitsun, and Midsummer Day (late June). Epiphany, Ascension, and All Saints' Day are adjusted to fall always on Saturdays.

TIME: 2 PM = noon GMT.

¹LOCATION, SIZE, AND EXTENT

Part of Fenno-Scandia (the Scandinavian Peninsula, Finland, Karelia, and the Kola Peninsula), Finland has an area of 337,030 sq km (130,128 sq mi), of which 9.9% is inland water. Comparatively, the area occupied by Finland is slightly smaller than the state of Montana. Its length, one-third of which lies above the Arctic Circle, is 1,160 km (721 mi) N–S; its width is 540 km (336 mi) E–W.

Finland borders on the former USSR to the E, the Gulf of Finland to the SE, the Baltic Sea to the SW, the Gulf of Bothnia and Sweden to the W, and Norway to the NW and N, with a total boundary length of 3,754 km (2,333 mi).

Finland's capital, Helsinki, is located on the country's southern coast.

²TOPOGRAPHY

Southern and western Finland consists of a coastal plain with a severely indented coastline and thousands of small islands stretching out to the Åland Islands. Central Finland is an extensive lake plateau with a majority of the country's 60,000 lakes; 24.5% of the area of Mikkelin Province is water. Northern Finland is densely forested upland. The highest elevations are in the Norwegian border areas; northwest of Enontekiö rises Halti, a mountain 1,328 m (4,357 ft) above sea level. Extensive, interconnected lake and river systems provide important natural waterways.

³CLIMATE

Because of the warming influence of the Gulf Stream and the prevailing wind patterns, Finland's climate is comparatively mild for the high latitude. During the winter, the average temperature ranges from −14°C to −3°C (7–27°F), while summer mean temperatures range from 13°C to 17°C (55–63°F). Snow cover lasts from about 90 days in the Åland Islands to 250 days in Enontekiö. Average annual precipitation (including both rain and snow) ranges from 40 cm (16 in) in northern Finland to 70 cm (28 in) in southern Finland.

⁴FLORA AND FAUNA

Forests, chiefly pine, spruce, and birch, are economically the most significant flora. There are more than 1,200 native species of higher plants; flora is richest in southern Finland and the Åland Islands. Of 22,700 species of fauna, more than 75% are insects. At least 67 species of mammals are native to Finland. Fur-bearing animals (otter, marten, ermine) are declining in number, while elk, fox, and beaver have increased. Of some 370 species of birds, half of which nest in Finland, perhaps the best known is the cuckoo, the harbinger of spring. Of some 70 species of fish, 33 have some economic importance; in fresh waters, the perch, walleyed pike, great northern pike, and others are plentiful. Salmon remains the favorite of fly rod enthusiasts.

⁵ENVIRONMENT

Finland's main environmental issues are air and water pollution, and the preservation of its wildlife.

Finland's principal environmental agency is the Ministry of the Environment, established in 1983. Beginning in 1987, environmental protection boards were established for every community with more than 3,000 inhabitants. To preserve the shoreline profile, 30–50% of the shores suitable for recreational use may not be built on. As of mid-1986, only 2% of Finland's surface water was of poor quality; 18% was considered satisfactory, and 80% good or outstanding. Nevertheless, half the population lives on water systems that are polluted by municipal waste. Industrial pollutants from within the country and surrounding countries affect the purity of both the nation's air and water supplies. Acid rain from high concentrations of sulphur in the air has damaged the nation's lakes. Finland's cities produce 2.8 million tons of solid waste per year. The nation has 2.8 cubic miles of water with 85% used for industry and 12% used in domestic and urban areas. In 1993, the Finnish Council of State introduced new approaches to the control of water pollution to begin in 1995. By 1986, emissions of sulfur compounds had decreased about one-third from their peak, in the 1970s, of 600,000 tons annually. Lead-free gasoline was introduced in 1985. Finland contributes

0.2% of the global total for gas emissions and produces 199.5 tons of hydrocarbon emissions per year.

Care is taken to protect the flora and fauna of the forests, which are of recreational as well as economic importance. Closed hunting seasons, nature protection areas, and other game-management measures are applied to preserve threatened animal species. In 1994, 3 of the nation's 67 mammal species and 12 of its 370 bird species were threatened, as well as 1 type of freshwater fish and 11 plant species out of 1,450. In total, 1,011 of the nation's 40,000 species of plants and animals are threatened with extinction.

[6]POPULATION

As of the November 1990 census, Finland's population was 4,998,478, with 38.4% living in rural areas and 61.6% in cities and towns. The projected population for the year 2000 is 5,113,000, assuming a crude birthrate of 128 per 1,000 population and a death rate of 10.1 for 1995–2000. Distribution is uneven, with the density generally increasing from northern and inland regions to the southwestern region. The largest cities at the end of 1991 were Helsinki, 497,542; Tampere, 173,797; Turku, 159,403; Espoo, 175,670; and Vantaa, 157,274.

[7]MIGRATION

From 1866 to 1930, a total of 361,020 Finns emigrated, mostly to the US and, after the US restriction of immigration, to Canada. After World War II, about 250,000 to 300,000 Finns permanently emigrated to Sweden. This migration had ended by the 1980s because of a stronger Finnish economy. In 1988, Finland had 9,540 immigrants and 8,318 emigrants, for a net gain of 1,222. The number of foreigners was 34,618 in 1991—only 0.7% of the population. Europeans constituted two-thirds of the total.

More than 400,000 people fled the Soviet occupation of Karelia during World War II. There was also a heavy migration from rural areas, particularly the east and northeast, to the urban, industrialized south, especially between 1960 and 1975. By 1980, 90% of all Finns lived in the southernmost 41% of Finland.

[8]ETHNIC GROUPS

The Finns are thought to be descended from Germanic stock and from tribes that originally inhabited west-central Russia. Excluding the Swedish-speaking minority of about 250,000, there are only two very small non-Finnish ethnic groups: Lapps and Gypsies. In 1990 there were about 4,400 Lapps. Several societies have been established to foster the preservation of the Lappish language and culture. The Gypsy population numbers about 5,000 to 6,000.

[9]LANGUAGES

From the early Middle Ages to 1809, Finland was part of the Kingdom of Sweden, and its official language was Swedish. Finnish did not become an official language until 1863. At the end of 1991, 93.3% of the population was primarily Finnish-speaking, and 5.9% was primarily Swedish-speaking (comparable percentages in 1890 were 86.07% and 13.56%). Swedish-speaking Finns make up more than 95% of the population of the Åland Islands, and Swedish-speaking majorities are also found in parts of Uudenmaan, Turun-Porin, and Vaasan provinces. Swedish, the second legal language, is given constitutional safeguards. In 1990, only 24,783 individuals had another language as the mother tongue, principally Russian, English, or German. Finnish belongs to the Finno-Ugric language group and is closely related to Estonian, remotely to Hungarian.

[10]RELIGIONS

Freedom of religion has been guaranteed since 1923. As of 1990, 87.8% of the inhabitants belonged to the Evangelical Lutheran Church, which enjoys state support. An elected Church Assembly makes legislative proposals to the Parliament, which can be approved or rejected, but not altered. Approximately 1.1% of the inhabitants, largely evacuees from the Karelian Isthmus, were members of the Orthodox Church in Finland, which also receives state support; the church has three dioceses, in Helsinki, Karelia, and Oulu, and owes allegiance to the Ecumenical Patriarch of Constantinople. Other religious bodies include the Free Church, Jehovah's Witnesses, Adventists, Roman Catholics, Methodists, Mormons, Baptists, Swedish Lutherans, and Jews. The Civil Register comprises those individuals who prefer not to affiliate with any church (about 9.7% at the end of 1989).

[11]TRANSPORTATION

In 1991 there were 103,000 km (64,000 mi) of roads, of which 34% were paved. That same year, registered motor vehicles included 1,922,541 passenger cars, 264,390 trucks, and 8,968 buses.

There were 5,924 km (3,681 mi) of railway lines in operation in 1991, of which 99% were operated by the Finnish State Railways. They performed 3,230 million passenger-km (up from 2,156 million in 1970) and 7,634 million freight ton-km (up from 6,270 million in 1970) of service in 1991. In the same year, the merchant fleet had a combined GRT of 609,000. At the end of 1991 there were 160 passenger vessels, 19 tankers, and 268 dry cargo vessels. Import traffic is concentrated at Naantali, Helsinki, Kotka, and Turku, while the ports of Kotka, Hamina, Kemi, Oulu, and Rauma handle most exports. In 1990, imports and exports by sea totaled 58,872,000 tons; 10,834,000 passengers arrived or departed Finland by sea. Icebreakers are used to maintain shipping lanes during winter months. In 1991 there were 6,675 km (4,148 mi) of navigable inland waterways, of which 3,700 km (2,300 mi) are suitable for steamers. An agreement was signed in Moscow on 27 September 1962 for the reopening of the important Saimaa Canal under Finnish control, one-half of the canal having been incorporated into the former USSR in 1947. After extensive reconditioning, the canal began operating in 1968.

State-run Finnair is engaged in civil air transport over domestic and international routes. In 1992, Finnair served 3,247,600 revenue passengers and performed 112,900,000 freight ton-kilometers of service. In 1962, Finnair took over Kar-Air, the second-largest air carrier in Finland.

[12]HISTORY

Finland, a province and a grand duchy of the Swedish kingdom from the 1150s to 1809 and an autonomous grand duchy of Russia from 1809 until the Russian Revolution in 1917, has been an independent republic since 1917. Ancestors of present-day Finns—hunters, trappers, agriculturists—came to Finland by way of the Baltic regions during the first centuries AD, spreading slowly from south and west to east and north. Swedish control was established gradually, following several religious crusades, the first around 1154. By 1293, Swedish rule had extended as far east as Karelia (Karjala), with colonization by Swedes in the southwest and along the Gulf of Bothnia. As a result of over six centuries of attachment to the Swedish realm, Finnish political institutions and processes (marked by growing constitutionalism and self-government), economic life, and social order developed largely along Swedish lines.

After Sweden's military defeat in 1808–09, Finland was transferred to Russia. Alexander I granted Finland a privileged autonomous status, continuing the grand duchy's constitutional heritage. He, like his successors, took a solemn oath to "confirm and ratify the Lutheran religion and fundamental laws of the land as well as the privileges and rights which each class and all the inhabitants have hitherto enjoyed according to the constitution." Toward the end of the 19th century, a Russian drive to destroy Finland's autonomy ushered in several decades of strained relations, broken only for a few years by the Revolution of 1905, as a result of which Finland gained a modern political structure with universal suffrage. After the Bolshevik seizure of power in Russia in the fall of 1917, Finland declared its independence on 6 December. A short civil war ensued (28 January—10 May 1918) between Reds and Whites, won by the latter, with intervention by both the Russian Bolsheviks and Germany.

In July 1919, Finland became a democratic parliamentary republic. In the nearly two decades of peace following the settlement of disputes with Sweden (over the Åland Islands) and the former USSR (East Karelia) there were noteworthy economic and social advances. Despite its neutral pro-Scandinavianism in the 1930s, the country was unavoidably entangled in the worsening relations between the great powers. Negotiations with the former USSR, which demanded certain security provisions or territorial concessions, broke down in 1939, and two wars with that nation followed: the Winter War, lasting from 30 November 1939 to 13 March 1940, and the Continuation War, from 26 June 1941 to 19 September 1944. The armistice terms of 1944, later confirmed by the Paris Peace Treaty of 10 February 1947, provided for cession of territory and payment of reparations to the Soviets and required Finland to expel the German troops on its soil; this resulted in German-Finnish hostilities from October 1944 to April 1945. Relations with the German Democratic Republic (GDR) and the Federal Republic of Germany (FRG) were not normalized until 1973–74.

Postwar Finland's economic recovery has been striking. Since World War II, Finland has pursued a policy of neutrality and good relations with its neighbors. Traditional ties with other Nordic countries have been maintained and strengthened. Relations with the former USSR were based on the 1948 Treaty of Friendship and Mutual Alliance. The dominant figure of postwar politics was Urho Kekkonen, the Agrarian (later Center) Party leader who held the presidency from 1956 to 1981, when he resigned because of ill health. The cornerstone of his policy was maintenance of a center-left coalition (including the Communists) and good relations with the former USSR. Social Democratic leader Mauno Koivisto, the prime minister, became acting president in October 1981 and was elected president in his own right in January 1982 and reelected in 1988. In the presidential elections of February 1994, Martti Ahtisaari, of the Finnish Social Democratic Party, was elected president, defeating Elisabeth Rehn (Defense Minister) of the Swedish People's Party in a runoff.

In March 1987, the conservative National Coalition Party made such strong gains in parliamentary elections that it was able to form Finland's first conservative-led government since World War II. The new prime minister, Harri Holkeri, led a four-party cabinet that included his own National Coalition Party, the Social Democrats, and two smaller conservative parties. The conservative trend continued in March 1991 with the Center Party leading a new four-party center-right coalition under Esko Aho.

The collapse of the Soviet Union has led Finland to reassess its relationship with Europe and, in February 1993, Finland applied for membership in the EC. Finland's relationship with the EC has become a major issue of political debate even within the governing coalition. Economic difficulties brought about by the decline of markets in the east have resulted in the worst recession in Finland's history. Austerity measures, including spending cuts, have made the current government extremely unpopular.

13 GOVERNMENT

Finland is a parliamentary republic. The constitution of 17 July 1919 vests supreme executive power in a president, who presides over and is assisted by a Council of State (cabinet), which must

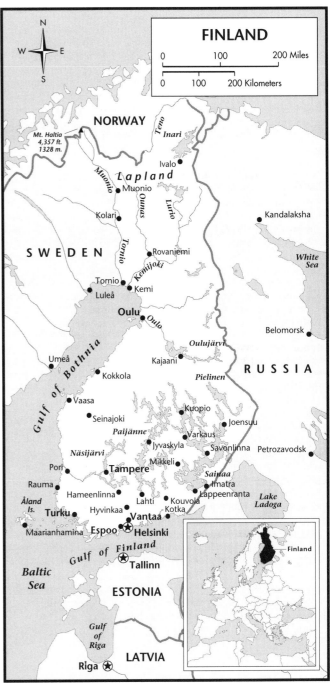

LOCATION: 59°30′10″ to 70°5′30″N; 19°7′3″ to 31°35′20″E.
BOUNDARY LENGTHS: Former USSR, 1,269 km (789 mi); Sweden, 586 km (364 mi); Norway, 716 km (445 mi); total coastline, 1,100 km (684 mi). **TERRITORIAL SEA LIMIT:** 4 mi.

enjoy the confidence of the parliament. The president is elected directly (since 1991) for a six-year term. The election is conducted on the basis of two rounds. The president appoints the prime minister, other ministers, and public officials and, in consultations with the prime minister, has the power to dissolve the legislature and order new elections. In addition, the President initiates legislation, issues decrees, directs foreign relations, and serves as commander-in-chief of the armed forces as well as appointing the highest civil servants.

The parliament (Eduskunta) is a single-chamber legislative body originally set up in 1906. Its 200 members are elected for four-year terms by proportional representation under universal suffrage at age 18. Finland was the first country in Europe to grant suffrage to women in national elections (1906). The Council of State is collectively responsible for its acts to the Eduskunta, but the overthrow of a cabinet (which has not been infrequent in postwar years) does not affect the exercise of supreme executive authority of the president, a factor ensuring a certain continuity of policy. The president can veto legislation by not signing a bill, but if the Eduskunta after a general election passes it again without amendment, it becomes law. The Eduskunta also has the right to alter the constitution, and its acts are not subject to judicial review.

[14]POLITICAL PARTIES

Four major partisan groupings have dominated political life in Finland, although none commands a majority position among the electorate. The Finnish Social Democratic Party (Suomen Sosiali-demokraattinen Puolue—SSDP) was organized in 1899 but did not become a significant political force until 1907, following the modernization of the country's parliamentary structure. Swedish-speaking Socialists have their own league within the SSDP. The party's program is moderate, and its emphasis on the partial nationalization of the economy has in recent decades given way to support for improvement of the condition of wage earners through legislation. The SSDP has generally worked closely with the trade union movement and has been a vigorous opponent of communism.

The Center Party (Keskusrapuolue—KESK; until October 1965, the Agrarian League—Maalaisliitto) was organized in 1906. While initially a smallholders' party, it has won some support from middle and large landowners but virtually none from nonagricultural elements. In an effort to gain a larger following in urban areas, the party changed its name and revised its program in 1965. In February 1959, an Agrarian League splinter party, the Finnish Small Farmers' Party, was formed; in August 1966, it took the name Finnish Rural Party (Suomen Maaseudun Puolue—SMP). The Liberal People's Party (Liberaalinen Kansan-puolue—LKP) was formed in December 1965 as a result of the merger of the Finnish People's Party and the Liberal League; in 1982, the LKP merged with the KESK. Esko Aho, leader of the KESK, became prime minister in 1991.

The National Coalition Party (Kansallinen Kokoomus—KOK), also known as the Conservative Party, was established in 1918 as the successor to the conservative Old Finnish Party. Its program, described as "conservative middle-class," has traditionally emphasized the importance of private property, the established church, and the defense of the state.

The Finnish Christian League (Suomen Kristillinen Liitto—SKL), founded in 1958, was formed to counter the increasing trend toward secularization and is usually found on the political right with the KOK.

The Swedish People's Party (Svenska Folkpartiet—SFP), organized in 1906 as the successor to the Swedish Party, has stressed its bourgeois orientation and the need for protecting the common interests of Finland's Swedish-speaking population.

The Finnish People's Democratic League (Suomen Kansan Demokraattinen Liitto—SKDL) represents the extreme left. Emerging in 1944, and illegal before then, the SKDL was a union of the Finnish Communist Party (organized in 1918) and the Socialist Unity Party. The SKDL had urged close relations with the former USSR and the Communist bloc, but in recent years it has moderated its demands for the establishment of a "people's democracy" in Finland. In 1986, a minority group within the SKDL was expelled; for the 1987 elections, it established a front called the Democratic Alternative (DEVA). Following the collapse of the Soviet Union, the SKDL in May 1990 merged with other left parties to form the Left Alliance (Vasemmistoliitto—VL).

The Greens, an environmentalist alliance, won four seats in the Eduskunta in 1987, although they were not formally organized as a political party.

From the end of World War II until 1987, Finland was ruled by a changing center-left coalition of parties that included the SSDP, KESK, SKDL, LKP, SFP, and SMP. The government formed on 30 April 1987 included seven members of the KOK, including the prime minister, Harri Holkeri; eight from the SSDP; two from the SFP; and one from the SMP. Conservative gains in the 1987 election put non-Socialists in their strongest position in parliament in 50 years. Following the general election of March 1991, the Center Party led by Esko Aho emerged as the largest single party in parliament. A new four-party, center-right coalition was formed composed of the Center Party, the National Coalition Party, the Swedish People's Party, and the Finnish Christian League.

The party composition of the Eduskunta after the March 1991 elections was as follows: Center Party (55), Social Democratic Party (48), National Coalition Party (40), Left Alliance (19), Swedish People's Party (12), Green League (10), Finnish Christian League (8), Finnish Rural Party (7), and the Liberal People's Party (1).

[15]LOCAL GOVERNMENT

There is an ancient and flourishing tradition of local self-government extending back to the 14th century. The present law on local government was enacted in 1976. There are 12 provinces (lääni), each headed by a governor appointed by the president. One of them, Ahvenanmaa (Åland Islands), has long enjoyed special status, including its own elected provincial council, and a statute effective 1 January 1952 enlarged the scope of its autonomy. The other provinces are directly responsible to the central government.

Below the provincial level, the local government units in 1994 included over 460 municipalities. Each local government unit is self-governing and has a popularly chosen council. Local elections are held every four years; being partisan in nature, they are regarded as political barometers. The councillors are unsalaried. Local administration is carried out under the supervision of council committees, but day-to-day affairs are usually run by professional, full-time managers. The functions of local government include education, social welfare, utilities, and collection of local taxes.

[16]JUDICIAL SYSTEM

There are three levels of courts: local, appellate, and supreme. In 1986 there were 72 rural district courts of the first instance, each with a judge and a jury of 5 to 12 lay persons. Some are divided into assize divisions, of which there were 147 in 1986. There were 28 municipal courts of the first instance, staffed in each case by a magistrate and two councillors. Each of the 6 appellate courts is headed by a president and staffed by appellate judges. In certain criminal cases these courts have original jurisdiction. The final court of appeal, the Supreme Court (Korkeinoikeus), sits in Helsinki under a president and 23 justices. There are also the Supreme Administrative Court, a number of provincial administrative courts, and some special tribunals. The administration of justice is under the supervision of a chancellor of justice and a parliamentary ombudsman.

The judiciary is independent form the executive and legislative branches. Supreme Court Judges are appointed to permanent positions by the president and are independent of political control. They may retire at age 63; retirement is mandatory at age 70. Supreme Court Justices appoint the lower court judges.

[17]ARMED FORCES

The Paris Peace Treaty of 1947 restricted the scope of Finland's armed forces to "tasks of an internal character and the local defense of the frontiers," imposing the following limits: army, 34,400 personnel; navy, 4,500 personnel and ships totaling 10,000 tons; air force, 3,000 personnel and 60 planes. Actual strength is lower. In 1993, the army had 27,300 personnel; the navy, 2,500 personnel and 53 vessels of various types; and the air force, 3,000 personnel and 116 combat aircraft. Of the 32,800 active duty personnel, 24,100 are conscripts serving from 8–11 months. Finland maintains 500,000 reservists, of whom 50,000 receive annual training.

Finland is also prohibited from possessing or constructing atomic weapons, submarines, bombers and certain other naval weapons. With the consent of the signatory powers of the Paris Treaty, Finland has acquired air defense missiles. There is compulsory military service for all males at age 17. A paramilitary frontier guard numbers 4,000 with 20,000 reserves. Defense expenditures are around $2 billion a year or about 2% of gross domestic product. Normally, Finland has produced a third of its arms, bought a third from the former USSR, and imported a third from other countries.

Finland provided 1,400 soldiers to 7 different peacekeeping operations in 1993.

[18]INTERNATIONAL COOPERATION

Finland has been a UN member since 14 December 1955; it is also affiliated with ECE and all the nonregional specialized agencies and is a signatory to GATT and the Law of the Sea.

Finland has actively participated in UN peacekeeping operations in Cyprus and in the Middle East on the Golan Heights between Israel and Syria, as a part of the UN forces there. Finnish officers serve in UN observer groups that police cease-fire lines in Kashmir and the Israeli-Egyptian border.

Finland participates in UN development activities and channels a substantial part of its development aid funds through the UN and other multilateral agencies. In addition, Finland plays a role in the African Development Bank, Asian Development Bank, and IDB, and is involved in a number of bilateral projects, primarily in African countries.

Finland has a close relationship with the other Scandinavian (Nordic) countries. The main forum of cooperation is the Nordic Council, established in 1952; Finland joined in 1955. A common labor market was established in 1954, granting citizens of member states the right to stay and work in any other Scandinavian country without restrictions.

Finland became associated with EFTA in 1961. In 1967, tariffs and other barriers to trade between Finland and EFTA members were eliminated; in 1986, Finland became a full member of EFTA. By agreement, the former USSR enjoys the same tariff benefits from Finland as those accorded the EFTA countries. Tariffs on most industrial goods from the EC have been phased out. In 1969, Finland joined the OECD; four years later, Finland became the first non-Communist country to sign a special agreement on economic and technical cooperation with CMEA.

Officially neutral, Finland seeks to maintain friendly relations with both the US and the former USSR, its powerful eastern neighbor. Finland has hosted many major meetings and conferences, including rounds I, III, V, and VII of the Strategic Arms Limitation Talks (SALT) between the US and USSR (1969–72). In November 1972, the multilateral consultations on the Conference on Security and Cooperation in Europe (CSCE) began in Helsinki. These initial consultations were followed by the first phase of CSCE at the foreign ministerial level and then by the third phase at the highest political level, culminating with the signing of the Final Act in Helsinki on 1 August 1975. The foreign ministers of the US, Canada, and 33 European countries met in Helsinki on 30 July 1985 to commemorate the 10th anniversary of the signing of the Final Act.

[19]ECONOMY

At the end of World War II, Finland's economy was in desperate straits. About 10% of the country's productive capacity had been lost to the former USSR, and over 400,000 evacuees had to be absorbed. Between 1944 and 1952, Finland was burdened with reparation payments to the USSR, rising inflation, and a large population growth. However, the GNP reached the prewar level by 1947, and since then the economy has shown consistent growth.

Handicapped by relatively poor soil, severe northern climate, and lack of coal, oil, and most other mineral resources necessary for the development of heavy industry, the Finns have nonetheless been able to build a productive and diversified economy. This was made possible by unrivaled supplies of forests (Finland's "green gold") and waterpower resources ("white gold"), as well as by the Finnish disposition toward hard work, frugality, and ingenuity. Agriculture, long the traditional calling of the large majority of Finns, has been undergoing continuous improvement, with growing specialization in dairying and cattle breeding. The industries engaged in producing timber, wood products, paper, and pulp are highly developed, and these commodities make up an overwhelming proportion of the country's exports. After World War II, and partly in response to the demands of reparations payments, a metals industry was developed, its most important sectors being foundries and machine shops, shipyards, and engineering works. Dependent on foreign sources for a considerable portion of its raw materials, fuels, and machinery, and on exports as a source of revenue, the Finnish economy is very sensitive to changes at the international level.

The annual growth of the GNP averaged 4.3% between 1986 and 1989, after which it was hard hit by the collapse of the former USSR, formerly Finland's chief trading partner. For 40 years, Finland and the USSR had conducted trade on a barter basis, a practice that ended in 1991. GDP was flat in 1990, fell by 7.1% in 1991, a further 4% in 1992, and 3.6% in 1993. The unemployment rate reached 17.9% in 1993.

[20]INCOME

In 1992, Finland's GNP was $116,309 million at current prices, or $22,980 per capita. For the period 1985–92 the average inflation rate was 5.1%, resulting in a real growth rate in per capita GNP of 0.7%.

In 1992 the GDP was $79.4 billion in current US dollars. It is estimated that in 1991 agriculture, hunting, forestry, and fishing contributed 5% to GDP; mining, quarrying, and manufacturing, 17%; electricity, gas, and water, 2%; construction, 8%; wholesale and retail trade, 9%; transport, storage, and communication, 7%; finance, insurance, real estate, and business services, 18%; community, social, and personal services, 5%; and other sources, 29%.

[21]LABOR

In proportion to the total population, the labor force of Finland is large. In 1991, about 66% of the population aged 15–74 years—a total of 2,484,000—participated in the labor force. The percentages of the labor force in the major sectors of the economy in 1991 were public administration, education, medical, social and other personal services, 30.3%; commerce, 15%; industry, 21%; finance and business services, 10.1% agriculture, forestry and fishing, 8.6%; transport and communications, 7.7%; construction, 7.2%; and unknown, 0.1%. The Employment Acts of 1956 and 1963 gave the government major responsibility for creating new jobs, maintaining full employment through economic measures, and providing work for the unemployed. From the mid-1960s to the mid-1970s, the rate of unemployment fluctuated between 1.5% and 4% of the total work force. Since then, however, the unemployment rate has crept upward, reaching 7.6% in 1991. In 1990, unemployment was only at 3.4%, but loss of export sales (specifically to the then-collapsing Soviet Union), structural rigidities, and excessive labor costs and borrowing created a deep recession in 1991.

The major trade union federations are the Central Organization of Finnish Trade Unions (SAK), which had 24 affiliated unions at the end of 1991, with a combined membership of 1,086,590; and the Confederation of Salaried Employees of Finland (TVK), with 15 affiliated unions and 423,994 members. At the end of 1991, the Confederation of Unions for Academic Professionals in Finland (AKAVA) had 33 affiliated organizations, with 294,623 members. The Confederation of Technical Employee Organizations in Finland (STTK) had 16 member organizations totaling 168,370 workers in February 1992. That year, over 80% of both workers and employers were members of trade unions and employers' collective bargaining associations.

Labor relations are generally regulated by collective agreements, usually one or two years in duration. Disputes over their terms are heard by a labor court, the verdict of which is final. Although mediation of labor disputes is provided for by law, work stoppages have occurred. Impasses over money frequently were avoided by the government's simultaneous addition of subsidies for industry and social benefits for laborers. This policy, however, put Finnish labor costs among the world's highest, thus creating the recent economic vulnerability. In 1992 there were a total of 1,165 industrial disputes involving 102,560 workers; a total of 76,090 days of work were lost.

22AGRICULTURE

Finnish farming is characterized by the relatively small proportion of arable land under cultivation, the large proportion of forestland, the small-sized landholdings, the close association of farming with forestry and stock raising, and the generally adverse climatic and soil conditions. Farming is concentrated in southwestern Finland; elsewhere, cultivation is set within the frame of the forest. The median farm has about 13.5 hectares (33 acres) of arable land. Small-sized farms were encouraged by a series of land reforms beginning with the Lex Kallio of 1922. The Land Use Act of 1958 sought to improve the conditions of existing farms by increasing the land area, amalgamating nonviable farms, and introducing new land-use patterns. The agricultural labor force declined from some 780,000 in 1950 to 203,000 in 1992, or 8% of the economically active population.

The principal crops in 1992 (in tons) were barley, 1,531,000; oats, 998,000; sugar beets, 1,049,000; potatoes, 673,000; and wheat, 212,000. A total of 2,579,000 hectares (6,373,000 acres) were classified as arable in 1991.

23ANIMAL HUSBANDRY

Livestock production contributes about 70% of total agricultural income. Livestock in 1992 included cattle, 1,263,000 head; hogs, 1,357,000; sheep, 61,000; and horses, 49,000. There were 5,000,000 poultry that same year. Some 350,000 reindeer are used by the Lapps as draft animals and for meat.

In recent years, Finland has attained exportable surpluses in some dairy and meat products. Production in 1992 included pork, 176,000 tons; beef, 117,000 tons; eggs, 67,500 tons; butter, 56,660 tons; and cheese, 88,321 tons. Milk production in 1992 was 2,399,000 tons.

24FISHING

In 1991, some 2,000 people took part in commercial fishing, but only half were full-time professional fishermen. The total catch in that year was about 82,813 tons and exports of fishery commodities totaled $10.6 million, or 1.5% of total agricultural exports. The most important catch is Atlantic herring, with 51,546 tons caught in 1991. Other important species are pike, salmon, rainbow trout, and cod.

25FORESTRY

Forestry in Finland has been controlled since the 17th century. Since 1928, the government has emphasized a policy of sustainable yields, with production reflecting timber growth. The forest area covered 23.2 million hectares (57.3 million acres), or about 76% of the total land area, in 1991. The most important varieties are pine (45% of the total growing stock), spruce (37%), birch, aspen, and alder. In 1990, the origin of raw wood material for Finland's forestry sector came from private (74%), company (6%), state (8%), and foreign (12%) forests. About 63% of the productive woodland is privately owned; 24% is owned by the state; the remainder is owned by companies, communes, and religious bodies. Some 5,000 sawmills were operating in 1992. In 1991, the total timber felled for sale (chiefly spruce pulpwood, birch pulpwood, pine pulpwood, fuel wood, sawn logs, and veneer logs) was 34 million cu m. Forestry engaged some 72,000 persons in 1992, including 46,000 in the chemical wood processing industry. In the 1980s, production of paper and paperboard rose significantly, while the mechanical wood processing industry went into decline. Over 70% of annual Finnish forestry output is exported, including 90% of all printing paper and 35% of all particleboard produced. Over 80% of forestry product exports are sent to Western Europe. In 1992, exports of forestry products accounted for 36% of the total export value.

26MINING

Overall, mining and metal processing employed about 65,000 persons in Finland as of 1991. Of that total, about 825 were employed in mining and quarrying, down from 860 in 1989. About 42% of the workers were in open pit operations, the remainder in underground mines. A chromium mine on the Gulf of Bothnia near the Swedish border is the only chromium mine in Scandinavia and one of the largest in the world, with estimated reserves of 150 million metric tons. Zinc metal production in 1991 was 170,400 tons; feldspar came to 53,000 tons; and chromite to 458,000 tons. Other processed minerals were nickel, selenium, cobalt, silver, and gold. Mineral reserves are declining, and many are expected to be soon exhausted due to extensive mining activity over the last 400 years.

27ENERGY AND POWER

During the period 1945–62, consumption of electric energy increased about 8.7% per year, largely from expansion of the energy-intensive wood-processing industry and the comprehensive electrification of rural areas. Production of electric energy rose from 6,600 million kwh in 1956 (of which 5,139 million kwh came from waterpower) to 58,137 million kwh in 1991 (13,096 million kwh from water power, 19,502 million kwh from nuclear power, and 25,539 from thermal power). Finland's net installed capacity in 1991 totaled 13.3 million kw. Finland has four nuclear power plants.

Most of Finland's waterpower resources are located along the Oulu and Kemi rivers. Oil—all imported—accounted for 35% of the energy used in 1991.

28INDUSTRY

Since the end of World War II, industrial progress has been noteworthy. Contributing factors include the forced stimulus of reparation payments, large quantities of available electric power, increased mining operations, growing mechanization of agriculture and forestry, development of transportation and communications, and steady foreign demand for Finnish exports. In terms of value of production and size of labor force, the metals industry is the most important, accounting for 16.6% of the industrial labor force (including power industries, mining, and quarrying) and 20.1% of the value added by industrial output in 1991. Also highly significant are the food, pulp and paper, machinery, chemical, and electrical products and instruments industries. In recent years impressive growth has been registered by the basic metals industry. The most important industrial regions center around Helsinki, Tampere, Turku, Lappeenranta, Lahti, Jyväskylä, and the valleys of the Kymi and Kokemäki rivers, and coastal towns like Kotka, Rauma, and Pori. The state owns a majority of the outstanding stock in many industrial companies.

Industrial production in 1991 (in millions of markkaa) included machinery and equipment (22,356) paper, printing, and publishing (57,948); fabricated metal products (70,234); food, beverages, and tobacco (50,637); chemical, petroleum, coal, rubber, and plastic products (33,489); basic metal products (17,760); wood and wood products (13,285); textiles, garments, and leather (6,784); and electricity (31,467).

29SCIENCE AND TECHNOLOGY

Scientific research is carried out at state research institutes, private research centers, and institutions of higher learning. The Technology Development Center, established in 1983 under the Ministry of Trade and Industry, oversees technological research and coordinates international research activities. The Academy of Finland, a central governmental organ for research administration, reports directly to the Ministry of Education. It promotes scientific research and develops national science policy by maintaining research fellowships, sponsoring projects, and publishing reports. In 1989, expenditure on research and development was about 8.9 million markkaa. Business enterprises, including those in which the central or local government owns major shares, finance more than half of the nation's research. In 1989 there were 21,195 scientists and technicians engaged in research and experimental development. In addition to faculties of sciences and technology at the universities, there are numerous learned societies and research institutes engaged in these fields. The principal learned societies, all in Helsinki, are the Federation of Finnish Scientific Societies. the Finnish Academy of Science and Letters, and the Finnish Society of Sciences and Letters; preeminent in technological development is the Finnish Technical Research Center at Espoo.

30DOMESTIC TRADE

Domestic trade is carried on through the customary wholesale and retail channels. Total wholesale receipts rose from M6,896 million in 1958 to M197,188 million in 1992; during the same period, retail sales increased from M4,982 million to M157,013 million. Employment in wholesale and retail trade was 253,836 in 1991. Wholesale trade is concentrated in the following groups: the Finnish Wholesalers and Importers Association and its customers; Kesko, a central marketing association controlled by rural retailers; the cooperative wholesalers SOK and OTK; producer cooperative wholesalers such as Valio and Hankkija; and specialized wholesalers such as the Central Federation of Technical Wholesalers, an association of importers. Price controls became effective on a permanent basis on 1 February 1977 but have been relaxed considerably in recent years.

Office hours are from 8 AM to 4:30 PM, Mondays through Fridays; government offices are open from 8 AM to 4 PM (3 PM in summer). Stores and shops are open from 9 AM to 6 PM, Monday through Friday, and 9 AM to 4 PM on Saturday. Summer hours are a little shorter.

There is growing acceptance of modern advertising techniques. Television advertising is sold by a state-licensed company; there is no commercial radio. Advertising of tobacco products and alcoholic beverages is prohibited, and promotion of food products, vitamins, and pharmaceuticals is strictly supervised.

31FOREIGN TRADE

In 1992, exports of goods and services represented 27% of Finland's GNP. Finland is highly dependent on imported energy.

Merchandise exports in 1992 (in millions of markkaa) were as follows:

Engineering and other metal products (incl. ships)	14,814
Paper industry	28,762
Nuclear reactors, boilers, and parts	14,285
Wood industry	7,343
Mineral fuels	3,504
Electrical machinery and equipment	8,593
Transport vehicles	5,352
Plastics and plastic articles	3,164
Other exports	21,646
TOTAL	107,463

Merchandise imports in 1992 (in millions of markkaa) were as follows:

Mineral fuels	12,228
Nuclear reactors, boilers, and parts	13,720
Electrical machinery and equipment	9,575
Transport vehicles	6,832
Plastics and plastic articles	3,920
Other imports	48,672
TOTAL	94,947

In 1992, EFTA countries took 19.5% of Finland's exports and supplied 19% of its imports. EC countries bought 53.2% of Finnish exports and supplied 47.2% of Finland's imports. The former Soviet bloc accounted for 6.8% of exports. By country, Finland's main customers in 1992 (in millions of markkaa) were as follows:

	IMPORTS	EXPORTS	BALANCE
Germany	16,085	16,804	719
Sweden	11,133	13,769	2,636
UK	8,215	11,518	3,303
US	5,792	6,365	573
France	4,382	7,204	2,822
Russia	6,700	3,020	−3,680
Norway	3,818	3,775	−43
Netherlands	3,458	5,628	2,170
Italy	3,425	4,302	877
Denmark	3,192	3,857	665
Other countries	28,747	31,221	2,474
TOTALS	94,947	107,463	12,516

32BALANCE OF PAYMENTS

With rare exceptions, Finland's foreign trade account has shown a deficit ever since the liberalization of foreign trade in the late 1950s. There have been fairly large year-to-year variations, mainly because of the cyclical sensitivity of forest industry exports. The services account of the balance of payments has traditionally been in surplus, transport income being the largest item. Economic policies were tightened markedly in 1975 in order to bring down the current account deficit and thus curb the growth of the country's foreign indebtedness, which reached a peak of over 21% of GDP in 1977.

In 1992, rising debt service payments, losses of subsidiaries abroad, and a deficit in the services trade all contributed to a continued large deficit in the current acount (4.6% of GDP). A quickly increasing trade suruplus, however, was expected to eliminate the deficit by 1994. Dwindling foreign exchange reserves caused the government to float the markka in September 1992, with reserves mostly replenished by the end of that year.

In 1992 merchandise exports totaled $23,554 million and imports $19,703 million. The merchandise trade balance was $3,851 million.

The following table summarizes Finland's balance of payments for 1991 and 1992 (in millions of US dollars):

	1991	1992
CURRENT ACCOUNT		
Goods, services, and income	−5,689	−4,231
Unrequited transfers	−1,005	−873
TOTALS	−6,694	−5,104
CAPITAL ACCOUNT		
Direct investment	−1,304	−791
Portfolio investment	9,333	7,993
Other long-term capital	3,628	350
Other short-term capital	−6,287	−4,110
Other liabilities	3	13
Reserves	1,886	2,150
TOTALS	7,229	5,604
Errors and omissions	−534	−500
Total change in reserves	2,035	2,395

33 BANKING AND SECURITIES

The central bank is the Bank of Finland, established in 1811, with headquarters in Helsinki and 7 branch offices. Possessing extensive autonomy though subject to parliamentary supervision, and endowed with extensive monetary and fiscal powers, the Bank is administered by a six-member board of management appointed by the president of the republic. It has an exclusive monopoly over the issuance of notes. The central bank on 31 December 1985 held foreign assets of M376.9 million in gold.

Other banking and credit institutions at the end of 1993 included 14 commercial, five mortgage banks, and 86 saving banks. Finland also has 329 co-operative banks.

Time deposits in the banking system as of 31 December 1993 totaled M155,705 million; demand deposits totaled M131,365 million. The Bank of Finland's discount rate was 5.50% in 1993. An exchange at Helsinki (established in 1912) is authorized to deal in stocks.

34 INSURANCE

Insurance is highly developed and diversified. In 1989 there were 56 Finnish insurance companies, 16 of them engaged in life insurance. In 1990, premium income amounted to $US1,901 per capita, or 6.5% of the GDP.

In 1992, life insurance in force totaled M70 billion. Workers' compensation and automobile third-party insurance are compulsory. Other forms of insurance include fire, burglary, water damage, maritime, funeral, livestock, fidelity guarantee, and credit.

35 PUBLIC FINANCE

Budget estimates are prepared by the Ministry of Finance and submitted to the legislature. They are referred to the finance committee and subsequently reported back to the full body. Supplementary budgets are usual.

The following table shows actual revenues and expenditures for 1990 and 1991 in millions of markkaa.

	1990	1991
REVENUE AND GRANTS		
Tax revenue	143,961	137,098
Non-tax revenue	16,232	16,981
Capital revenue	50	62
Grants	3,867	4,173
TOTALS	164,110	158,314

	1990	1991
EXPENDITURES & LENDING MINUS REPAYMENTS		
General public service	7,942	9,279
Defense	7,525	7,854
Public order and safety	4,782	5,035
Education	23,558	25,604
Health	17,755	5,970
Social security and welfare	54,856	82,518
Housing and community amenities	3,082	4,025
Recreation, cultural, and religious affairs	2,498	2,766
Economic affairs and services	30,118	33,398
Other expenditures	6,547	7,776
Lending minus repayments	4,490	8,185
TOTAL	163,163	192,410
Deficit/Surplus	947	−34,096

Finland's budget balance continued its sharp deterioration in 1992, as the deep recession resulted in decreased tax revenues and increased social expenditures. Extensive government support for the fragile banking system and increased interest expenditures were also responsible. Central government revenue decreased in 1992 by 5%, while expenditures increased by 11%. Net government borrowing to finance the deficit more than doubled, increasing from M26 billion ($6 billion) in 1991 to M68 billion ($15 billion) in 1992. About 35% of the budget was financed by borrowing, with two-thirds of the new borrowing to cover the deficit from foreign markets.

In 1990, Finland's total public debt stood at M57,038 million. Total debt of the central government as a proportion of GDP soared from just over 10% in 1990 to over 35% in 1992.

36 TAXATION

In 1992, the state corporate income tax rate was 23%, municipal taxes were 14–19% and there was a 1% church tax. The sales tax (22% in 1993) was slated for replacement by a value-added tax in 1994. The individual income tax was graduated between 7% and 39% in 1992. Other taxes included a wealth tax on property of individuals owning certain assets valued in excess of M1.1 million, an estate and gift tax, and a stamp tax.

37 CUSTOMS AND DUTIES

Since 1956, trade conditions, including duties, have been progressively liberalized. Raw materials are normally free of duty, and goods from developing countries and many other countries are duty-free. Exports are free of duty, and licensing is required only for metal scrap. Import licenses are required for some products. Roughly 85% of all imports are duty-free, and the average tariff rate on manufactured goods is 5.5%. Finland has implemented the GATT provisions on import licensing.

38 FOREIGN INVESTMENT

The government and the Bank of Finland are favorably disposed toward foreign investment, and there generally is no ban on wholly foreign-owned enterprises. Regulations have been liberalized over the years and are generously interpreted. Repatriation of capital and remittance of dividends require notification to the Bank of Finland. A commission for foreign investments has been established, subordinate to the Ministry of Trade and Industry.

By international standards, the amount of direct investment in Finland is relatively modest. However, the inflow of foreign exchange arising from the investments has been growing steadily. Total investments in Finland amounted to an estimated $4.07 billion in 1992. Most investment comes from Sweden, the UK, US, Germany, and France. Finnish investment abroad is in the form of long-term export credits and direct investment by private companies.

³⁹ECONOMIC DEVELOPMENT

Problems arising from World War II—reparations, loss of resources in the ceded territories, compensation to the evacuated and displaced population, and reconstruction—have dictated the main lines of Finnish economic policy.

Reparations were originally fixed at $300 million (1938 price level), payable in six years. They were subsequently scaled down to $226.5 million, payable in eight years. The value of goods delivered was very much higher in current prices; one carefully worked-out estimate put the total indemnity bill at $949 million at 1944 prices (reparations plus impositions laid down in the Paris Peace Treaty and at the Potsdam Conference). The reparations payments amounted to 6.4% of the total net product in 1945, declining to about 2.1% in 1951. During the first year, 78% of all exports were reparations goods; the reparations payments of the first six years were the equivalent of 340,000 freight carloads of goods. Finland's success in meeting these heavy obligations was due mainly to four factors: (1) the rapid development of industry and of productivity per worker; (2) a favorable export situation for forest products; (3) foreign capital investments and loans; and (4) remission of most of the penalty payments on reparations.

Extensive governmental control over supplies, prices, wages, rents, foreign trade, and foreign exchange was inevitable. A crucial role was played by the Bank of Finland, which was charged with maintaining the value of the markka against serious inflationary pressures, safeguarding foreign exchange, creating employment, and stimulating industrial expansion. In 1965, the Bank imposed restrictions on lending by financial institutions and introduced measures to help lower the level of imports and to improve the balance-of-payments position. In October 1967, the Bank was finally forced to devalue the markka by 24%. Exports rose while the demand for imports fell off sharply, and by 1969 the inflationary spiral had been largely brought under control.

Finland remains principally a free enterprise economy, although government-owned enterprises play a part. The only true state monopoly is of the production, import, and sale of alcoholic beverages. Government interests, however, dominate the railroads, airlines, broadcasting, and telecommunications, and the government owns a majority of the shares in many joint stock companies, particularly in utilities, mining, and industry.

Finland does not engage in formal economic planning, but it is making a serious attempt at industrial expansion and diversification. Incentives are provided for investment in four development zones in mining, manufacturing, tourism, breeding of fur-bearing animals, fishing, and nursery cultivation. Firms that establish operations in northern Finland are granted tax concessions. There are also special incentives for the shipbuilding industry.

Finland is a donor to the IDA and to the African, Asian, and Inter-American development banks. Economic aid to less developed countries totaled $951 million in 1991, of which $606 million was bilateral. Finland also aids developing countries by providing duty-free entry of goods from these countries.

⁴⁰SOCIAL DEVELOPMENT

Social welfare legislation in Finland is patterned largely on Scandinavian models. The system has evolved gradually and unevenly in response to social needs. Major benefits include employees' accident insurance, old age and disability insurance, unemployment insurance, sickness insurance, compensation for war invalids, and family and child allowances. The National Pensions Act (1957) governs old age and disability insurance. A 1962 amendment provides for both full-time and part-time wage earners, and legislation coming into force in 1970 added farmers and other self-employed persons. Unemployment funds are established on a vocational basis. A general and compulsory sickness insurance

plan was enacted in 1963 and became fully operative on 1 January 1967. Payments are also made to veterans and, upon their death, to dependent survivors. On 1 October, 1969, the National Survivors' Pension Act took effect, providing for payment of a pension to the widow and children of any male resident in Finland, with certain restrictions. Total social and housing expenditure in 1988 was estimated at 36.1% of government outlays.

Each local governmental unit is required to establish and maintain a social welfare board under the supervision of the National Board of Social Welfare. There are also private welfare organizations; some, like the Mannerheim Child Welfare League, have won widespread recognition. The Ministry for Social Affairs and Health is also responsible for such matters as health insurance, workers' protective legislation, unemployment insurance, labor exchange, and pensions.

Each municipality operates a maternal and child-care clinic. There is a maternity allowance, which covered 170 weekdays as of 1 January 1991. The father may share in a portion of this time and also gets a 12-day paternity leave at the time of birth. Abortion is allowed, but in 1978 the limit on social grounds was reduced from 16 weeks to 12 weeks of pregnancy. The fertility rate for 1985–90 was 1.7.

Women have a high level of education and hold a large number of elective political posts. However, they seldom hold high-paying management positions and earn on average only 80% of what men do. In 1986, Finland signed the UN Convention on the Elimination of All Forms of Discrimination Against Women, and a new act outlawing discrimination against women came into effect in 1987.

⁴¹HEALTH

In Finland, the local authorities are responsible for the majority of health services. The entire population is covered by health insurance, which includes compensation for lost earnings and treatment cost. This program is run by the Social Insurance Institution and is supplemented by private services. In 1991, a new Private Health Care Act took effect to enhance the quality of services provided.

With a total population in 1993 of 5 million, Finland had 64,000 births in 1992; 12,350 physicians (2.47 per 1,000 population); approximately 4,545 dentists; and a nurse-to-doctor ratio of 4 to 3. In 1989, there were 7,067 pharmacists; in 1990, 49,861 nurses, 34,212 practical nurses, and 6,232 physical therapists. In 1991, there were 539 midwives. From 1980 to 1993, 80% of married women (ages 15 to 49) were using contraceptives.

In 1990, there were an estimated 440 hospitals (including 57 mental facilities and 40 private institutions) with just over 67,000 total beds. In addition, from 1990 to 1992, one-year-old children were vaccinated against the following diseases: tuberculosis (99%); diphtheria, pertussis, and tetanus (95%); polio (97%); and measles (97%). There were 15 known cases of tuberculosis per 100,000 people in 1990. In 1991, there were 26 registered cases of AIDS and, in 1990, 12,433 abortions.

The death rate was 10 per 1,000 in 1992, and the infant mortality rate was 6 per 1,000 that same year, one of the world's lowest. The major causes of death in 1990 were: cardiovascular diseases (24,589); cancer (10,082); respiratory diseases (3,746); gastrointestinal diseases (1,847); other diseases (5,088); accidents/violence (4,735); and suicides (1,512). Life expectancy in 1992 was 76 years and, in 1991, total health expenditures for Finland were $26,926,000.

While female health is good by international standards, male mortality in the over-25 age bracket is much higher in Finland than in most industrial countries. The main reason for the excessive male death rate is cardiovascular diseases. In addition, there has been an increase in suicide among young men. Alcohol-related problems are also on the increase.

42HOUSING

At the end of World War II, Finland faced a critical housing shortage. About 14,000 dwellings had been severely damaged during the war; only a modest amount of new housing had been built from 1939 to 1944. Some 112,000 dwellings were lost to the ceded territories, and homes had to be found for the displaced persons. Government participation was inevitable in this situation. Two measures passed in the late 1940s, the Land Acquisition Act and the Arava Law, made large-scale credit available on reasonable terms. During 1949–59, a total of 334,000 dwellings were built, including 141,900 supported by the Land Acquisition Act and 89,400 supported by the Arava Law.

The migration into urban centers that continued throughout the 1950s and 1960s resulted in a constant urban housing shortage even after the war losses had been replaced. During 1960–65, the number of new dwellings averaged about 37,000 annually. To stimulate housing construction, the government passed the Housing Act in 1966 providing for increased government support. As a result of this Act, the number of new dwellings supported by government loans rose rapidly. During 1966–74, a total of 466,900 dwellings were completed, of which 214,700 were supported by government loans.

From 1974 through 1985, another 558,000 new units were added to the housing stock. In 1991, 51,803 new dwellings were completed, down from 65,397 in 1990. The total number of dwellings in 1990 was 2,209,556, of which the greatest number (672,496) had two rooms and a kitchen. The standard of new dwellings is relatively high, and the overall housing stock is young; about 75% of the present stock has been built since 1950. The housing density was about 0.78 persons per room in 1980.

43EDUCATION

Elementary teaching remained under the direction and inspection of the Evangelical National Lutheran Church until 1921, when the Compulsory Education Act was passed, providing for nationwide compulsory public education by 1937. A new Primary School Act came into force in 1958. The Act on the Principles of the School System, issued in 1968, and a decree issued in 1970 further transformed the educational system.

The new school system unites the primary school and lower secondary school into a compulsory nine-year comprehensive school, with a six-year lower level and a three-year upper level. Instruction is uniform at the lower level. At the upper one, there are both required and elective courses. The upper secondary school (gymnasium) and vocational schools have also been reformed, with enrollments expanding year by year. In 1991 pupils numbered 394,299. Virtually all adults are literate.

Higher education falls into three categories: universities and institutions of university status; people's high schools or colleges; and workers' academies. Entrance to the universities is through annual matriculation examinations. There were 13 universities and 12 colleges and institutes in 1991, with a total of 173,702 students. Among the best known are the University of Helsinki (founded 1640), Turku University (founded 1922), the Helsinki School of Economics, and the University of Tampere. University study is free of charge.

People's high schools and workers' academies are evidence of the widespread interest in popular or adult education. Although they are owned by private foundations or organizations, these ventures also receive state subsidies.

44LIBRARIES AND MUSEUMS

The largest library in Finland is the Helsinki University Library, with 2,800,000 volumes in 1990; it acts both as the general library of the university and as the national library. Next in size are the Helsinki City Library (2,059,690 volumes), the Turku University (1,730,000 volumes) and Åbo Academy (1,550,000).

There are about 400 research and university libraries in Finland, most of which are small. In 1989 there were 460 central public libraries and 1,429 branch libraries. Over 76.5 million books were borrowed by 2,356,009 people.

The museum movement has grown rapidly since the war, and there are more than 300, representing a wide range of interests. Many are open-air museums depicting local or rural history, which are accessible only from May to September. Among the betterknown museums are the National, Mannerheim, and Municipal museums and the Ateneumin art museum in Helsinki; the Turku art museum and provincial museum; the Runeberg Museum at Porvoo; and the outdoor museums at Helsinki and Turku.

45MEDIA

Freedom of the press is guaranteed by the constitution. In 1991, 66 daily newspapers with a total circulation of 2,707,000 were published in Finland. Major newspapers and their net daily circulation in 1991 were the following:

NEWSPAPER	ORIENTATION	CIRCULATION
Helsingen Sanomat (Helsinki)	Independent	482,400
Ilta-Sanomat (Helsinki)	Independent	215,300
Aamulehti (Tampere)	Conservative	145,100
Turun Sanomat (Turku)	Independent	134,700
Maaseudun Tulevaisuus (Helsinki)	Independent	124,800
Kaleva (Oulu)	Independent	96,900
Savon Sanomat (Kuopio)	Center Party	90,600
Keskisuomalainen (Jyväskylä)	Center Party	81,400
Etelä-Suomen Sanomat (Lahti)	Independent	71,200
Vaasa (Vaasa)	Conservative	63,500
Hufvudstadbladet (Helsinki; Swedish)	Independent	67,200
Satakunnan Kansa (Pori)	Conservative	62,600
Kansan Uutiset (Helsinki)	Finnish People's Democratic League	43,400

The leading weekly journals in 1991 were Seura (circulation 272,300) and Apu (279,200).

Postal and telegraph services are operated by the government Post and Telegraph Office. Telephone lines are both state and privately owned, but long-distance service is a state monopoly. In 1991 there were 3,140,000 telephones in use. Broadcasting is run by Yleisradio, a joint-stock company of which the government owns over 90%, and MTV, a commercial company. The number of radios was estimated at 4,980,000 in 1991. Regular television transmission began in 1958. The number of television sets was 2,760,000 in 1991.

46ORGANIZATIONS

The right to organize is guaranteed by the constitution, and organizations play a central role in all areas of Finnish life. The cooperative movement is highly developed. Cooperatives have developed extensive educational and informational programs, including a lively cooperative press and many training schools. They are divided into three major groups. Pellervo-Seura is the Central Organization of Farmers' Cooperatives. It provides educational and advisory services to its 800 member organizations. All the agricultural cooperative central organizations are members of Pellervo: the Cooperative Dairy Association, Meat Producers' Central Federation, Central Cooperative Egg Export Association, a wholesalers' cooperative for farm inputs and products, and the forest products cooperative. The Kulutusosuuskuntien Keskusliitto (KK) Cooperative Organizations, the so-called progressive cooperatives, include the KK (educational union of KK cooperatives), OTK (general wholesalers for KK cooperatives), and insurance associations. The FSA Cooperative Organizations are the Swedish-speaking cooperatives. Among their members are the FSA (general union of the Swedish-Finnish cooperatives), Labor (cooperative purchasing wholesalers), Åland

Central Cooperative (a central cooperative for cooperative dairies on the Åland Islands), cooperative marketing associations for eggs and dairy products, and the Central Fish Cooperative.

Occupational and trade associations are numerous. In the agricultural sector the most influential is the Central Union of Agricultural Producers, a nonpolitical farmers' trade union. The Federation of Agricultural Societies concentrates on advisory and educational functions. Important in industry and commerce are the Confederation of Finnish Industries, Central Federation of Handicrafts and Small Industry, Central Board of Finnish Wholesalers' and Retailers' Associations, and the Finnish Foreign Trade Association. The Central Chamber of Commerce of Finland has its headquarters in Helsinki.

Cultural and philanthropic organizations are also numerous; among the most influential are the Finnish Academy, the Finnish Cultural Fund, and the Wihuri Foundation. At the level of international cooperation are such organizations as the Norden societies and the League for the United Nations.

47TOURISM, TRAVEL, AND RECREATION

Finland offers natural beauty and tranquillity in forest cottages and on the tens of thousands of islands that dot the 60,000 lakes and the Baltic Sea. Winter offers cultural events and cross-country skiing. Finland is the original home of the sauna, a national tradition. In 1991, tourists spent 2,200,870 nights in hotels and other establishments. There were 47,997 rooms and 100,869 beds in hotels and other facilities, and tourism receipts totaled US$1.19 billion. In 1992, Finland celebrated the 75th anniversary of its independence. Anticipated EC membership in 1995 is expected to boost tourism by making Finland more competitive and accessible to visitors. Scandinavian nationals require no passports, and visa requirements have been dropped for visitors from the United States, OECD, Commonwealth, and many other countries.

From 1906 to 1984, Finns won 128 Olympic gold medals, 118 silver, and 142 bronze. Popular sports include skiing, running, rowing, and wrestling.

48FAMOUS FINNS

Great Finnish literary figures include Elias Lönnrot (1802–84), compiler of the national epic, the *Kalevala;* Johan Ludwig Runeberg (1804–77), the most important of the 19th-century Finnish-Swedish writers, known for his *Elk Hunters* and *Songs of Ensign Stål;* Aleksis Kivi (1834–72), the founder of modern Finnish-language literature and author of *The Seven Brothers;* Juhani Aho (1861–1921), master of Finnish prose; Eino Leino (1878–1926), perhaps the greatest lyric poet to write in Finnish; Frans Eemil Sillanpää (1888–1964), a Nobel Prize winner (1939), known to English-language audiences through his *Meek Heritage* and *The Maid Silja;* Toivo Pekkanen (1902–57), whose novels portray the impact of industrialization on Finnish life; Mika Waltari (1908–79), member of the Finnish Academy; Väinö Linna (b.1920), a Scandinavian Literature Prize winner (1963) and author of *The Unknown Soldier* (1954); and the antiwar novelist and playwright Veijo Meri (b.1928).

Finnish architects who are well known abroad include Eliel Saarinen (1873–1950) and his son Eero Saarinen (1910–61), whose career was chiefly in the US; Alvar Aalto (1898–1976); Viljo Revell (1910–64); and Aarne Ervi (1910–77). A leading sculptor was Wäinö Aaltonen (1894–1966); others well known are Eila Hiltunen (b.1922) and Laila Pullinen (b.1933). Five representative painters are Helena Schjerfbeck (1852–1946), Albert Edelfelt (1854–1905), Akseli Gallen-Kalléla (1865–1931), Pekka Halonen (1865–1933), and Tyko Sallinen (1879–1955). Arts and crafts hold an important place in Finnish culture: leading figures are Tapio Wirkkala (1915–85) and Timo Sarpaneva (b.1926). Finnish music has been dominated by Jean Sibelius (1865–1957).

Also notable are the composer of art songs Yrjö Kilpinen (1892–1957), the composer of operas and symphonies Aulis Sallinen (b.1935), and opera and concert bass Martti Talvela (b.1935).

Scientists of international repute are A. I. Wirtanen (1895–1973), Nobel Prize winner for chemistry in 1945; Rolf Nevanlinna (1895–1980), mathematician; Pentti Eskola (1883–1964), geologist; V. A. Heiskanen (1895–1971), professor of geodesy; Aimo Kaarlo Cajander (1879–1943), botanist and silviculturist; Edward Westermarck (1862–1939), ethnographer and sociologist; and Yrjö Väisälä (1891–1971), astronomer.

Outstanding athletes include Hannes Kolehmainen (1890–1966) and Paavo Nurmi (1897–1973), who between them won 14 Olympic medals in track. Another distance runner, Lasse Viren (b.1949), won gold medals in both the 1972 and 1976 games.

Major political figures of the 19th century were Johan Wilhelm Snellman (1806–81) and Yrjö Sakari Yrjö-Koskinen (1830–1903). Inseparably linked with the history of independent Finland is Marshal Carl Gustaf Emil Mannerheim (1867–1951), and with the recent postwar period President Juho Kusti Paasikivi (1870–1956). Sakari Tuomioja (1911–64) was prominent in UN affairs. President Urho Kekkonen (1900–86) was instrumental in preserving Finland's neutrality. Mauno Henrik Koivisto (b.1923) was elected president in 1982.

49DEPENDENCIES

Finland possesses no territories or colonies.

50BIBLIOGRAPHY

Alapuro, Risto. *State and Revolution in Finland.* Berkeley: University of California Press, 1988.

Allison, Roy. *Finland's Relations with the Soviet Union, 1944–1984.* New York: St. Martin's, 1985.

Arter, David. *Politics and Policy-making in Finland.* Sussex: Wheatsheaf Books; New York: St. Martin's Press, 1987.

Bako, Elemer. *Finland and the Finns: A Selective Bibliography.* Washington, D.C.: Library of Congress, 1993.

Engman, Max and David Kirby (eds.). *Finland: People, Nation, State.* Bloomington: Indiana University Press, 1989.

Irwin, John. *The Finns and the Lapps.* New York: Holt, Rinehart & Winston, 1973.

Jakobson, Max. *Finnish Neutrality: A Study of Finnish Foreign Policy Since the Second World War.* New York: Praeger, 1969.

Jutikkala, Eino. *A History of Finland,* translated by Paul Sjoblom. New York: Dorset Press, 1988.

Kekkonen, Urho. *A President's View.* London: Heinemann, 1982.

Kirby, D. G. *Finland in the Twentieth Century.* Minneapolis: University of Minnesota Press, 1980.

Maude, George. *The Finnish Dilemma: Neutrality in the Shadow of Power.* New York: Oxford University Press, 1976.

Nousiainen, Jaakko. *The Finnish Political System.* Cambridge, Mass.: Harvard University Press, 1971.

Polvinen, Tuomo. *Between East and West: Finland in International Politics, 1944–1947.* Minneapolis: University of Minnesota Press, 1986.

Puntila, L. A. *The Political History of Finland, 1809—1966.* New York: Crane-Russak, 1976.

Rajenen, Aini. *Of Finnish Ways.* Minneapolis: Dillon, 1981.

Rinehart, Robert (ed.). *Finland and the United States: Diplomatic Relations Through Seventy Years.* Washington, D.C.: Georgetown University, 1993.

Schwartz, A. J. *America and the Russo-Finnish War.* Westport, Conn.: Greenwood, 1975.

Singleton, Frederick Bernard. *A Short History of Finland.* Cambridge; New York: Cambridge University Press, 1989.

Smith, C. J. *Finland and the Russian Revolution, 1917–1922.* Athens: University of Georgia Press, 1958.

Solsten, Eric and Sandra W. Meditz (eds.) *Finland, a Country Study.* 2d ed. Washington, D.C.: Library of Congress, 1990.

Tanner, Wäinö A. *The Winter War.* Stanford, Calif.: Stanford University Press, 1957.

Upton, Anthony F. *The Finnish Revolution.* Minneapolis: University of Minnesota Press, 1981.

Wuorinen, John H. *A History of Finland.* New York: Columbia University Press, 1965.

FRANCE

French Republic
République Française

CAPITAL: Paris.

FLAG: The national flag is a tricolor of blue, white, and red vertical stripes.

ANTHEM: *La Marseillaise.*

MONETARY UNIT: The franc (Fr) is a paper currency of 100 centimes. There are coins of 5, 10, and 20 centimes and ½, 1, 2, 5, 10, and 20 francs, and notes of 20, 50, 100, 200, and 500 francs. Fr1 = $0.1751 (or $1 = Fr5.71).

WEIGHTS AND MEASURES: The metric system is the legal standard.

HOLIDAYS: New Year's Day, 1 January; Labor Day, 1 May; World War II Armistice Day, 8 May; Bastille Day, 14 July; Assumption, 15 August; All Saints' Day, 1 November; World War I Armistice Day, 11 November; Christmas, 25 December. Movable holidays include Easter Monday, Ascension, and Pentecost Monday.

TIME: 1 PM = noon GMT.

¹LOCATION, SIZE, AND EXTENT

Situated in Western Europe, France is the second-largest country on the continent, with an area (including the island of Corsica) of 547,030 sq km (211,209 sq mi). Comparatively, the area occupied by France is slightly more than twice the size of the state of Colorado. It extends 962 km (598 mi) N–S and 950 km (590 mi) E–W. France is bounded on the N by the North Sea and Belgium, on the NE by Luxembourg and the Federal Republic of Germany (FRG), on the E by Switzerland and Italy, on the S by the Mediterranean Sea, on the SW by Andorra and Spain, on the W by the Bay of Biscay and the Atlantic Ocean, and on the NW by the English Channel, with a total boundary length of 6,319 km (3,926 mi).

France's capital city, Paris, is located in the northcentral part of the country.

²TOPOGRAPHY

France topographically is one of the most varied countries of Europe, with elevations ranging from sea level to the highest peak of the continent, Mont Blanc (4,807 m/15,771 ft), on the border with Italy. Much of the country is ringed with mountains. In the northeast is the Ardennes Plateau, which extends into Belgium and Luxembourg; to the east are the Vosges, the high Alps, and the Jura Mountains; and along the Spanish border are the Pyrenees, much like the Alps in ruggedness and height.

The core of France is the Paris Basin, connected in the southwest with the lowland of Aquitaine. Low hills cover much of Brittany and Normandy. The old, worn-down upland of the Massif Central, topped by extinct volcanoes, occupies the south-central area. The valley of the Rhône (812 km/505 mi), with that of its tributary the Saône (480 km/298 mi), provides an excellent passageway from the Paris Basin and eastern France to the Mediterranean.

There are three other main river systems: the Seine (776 km/ 482 mi), draining into the English Channel; the Loire (1,020 km/ 634 mi), which flows through central France to the Atlantic; and the Garonne (575 km/357 mi), which flows across southern France to the Atlantic.

³CLIMATE

Three types of climate may be found within France: oceanic, continental, and Mediterranean. The oceanic climate, prevailing in the western parts of the country, is one of small temperature range, ample rainfall, cool summers, and cool but seldom very cold winters. The continental (transition) type of climate, found over much of eastern and central France, adjoining its long common boundary with west-central Europe, is characterized by warmer summers and colder winters than areas farther west; rainfall is ample, and winters tend to be snowy, especially in the higher areas. The Mediterranean climate, widespread throughout the south of France (except in the mountainous southwest), is one of cool winters, hot summers, and limited rainfall. The mean temperature is about 12°C (54°F) at Paris and 15°C (59°F) at Nice. In central and southern France, annual rainfall is light to moderate, ranging from about 68 cm (27 in) at Paris to 100 cm (39 in) at Bordeaux. Rainfall is heavy in Brittany, the northern coastal areas, and the mountainous areas, where it reaches more than 112 cm (44 in).

⁴FLORA AND FAUNA

France's flora and fauna are as variegated as its range of topography and climate. It has forests of oak and beech in the north and center, as well as pine, birch, poplar, and willow. The Massif Central has chestnut and beech; the subalpine zone, juniper and dwarf pine. In the south are pine forests and various oaks. Eucalyptus (imported from Australia) and dwarf pines abound in Provence. Toward the Mediterranean are olive trees, vines, and mulberry and fig trees, as well as laurel, wild herbs, and the low scrub known as maquis (from which the French resistance movement in World War II took its name).

The Pyrenees and the Alps are the home of the brown bear, chamois, marmot, and alpine hare. In the forests are polecat and marten, wild boar, and various deer. Hedgehog and shrew are common, as are fox, weasel, bat, squirrel, badger, rabbit, mouse, otter, and beaver. The birds of France are largely migratory; warblers, thrushes, magpies, owls, buzzards, and gulls are common.

There are storks in Alsace and elsewhere, eagles and falcons in the mountains, pheasants and partridge in the south. Flamingos, terns, buntings, herons, and egrets are found in the Mediterranean zone. The rivers hold eels, pike, perch, carp, roach, salmon, and trout; lobster and crayfish are found in the Mediterranean.

5ENVIRONMENT

The Ministry for the Environment is the principal environmental agency. France's basic law for the protection of water resources dates from 1964. Water pollution is a serious problem in France due to the accumulation of industrial contaminants, agricultural nitrates, and waste from the nation's cities. Only 52% of the population has adequate sewage facilities. France's cities produce 18.7 million tons of solid waste per year. France has 40.8 cubic miles of water with 69% used for industrial purposes and 15% used for farming. As of 1994, 20% of France's forests were damaged due to acid rain and other contaminants. The mid-1970s brought passage of laws governing air pollution, waste disposal, and chemicals. In general, environmental laws embody the "polluter pays" principle, although some of the charges imposed—for example, an aircraft landing fee—have little effect on the reduction of the pollutant (i.e., aircraft noise). Air pollution is a significant environmental problem in France. The nation contributes 1.7% of the world's total gas emissions. Official statistics reflect substantial progress in reducing airborne emissions in major cities: the amount of sulfur dioxide in Paris decreased from 122 micrograms per cu m of air in 1971 to 54 micrograms in 1985; in Lyon, from 110 to 61; Marseilles, 130 to 38; Lille, 110 to 37; and Rouen, 110 to 37. An attempt to ban the dumping of toxic wastes entirely and to develop the technology for neutralizing them proved less successful, however, and the licensing of approved dump sites was authorized in the early 1980s. As of 1985, recycling efforts were estimated annually to involve 7,750,000 tons of scrap iron, 2,200,000 tons of paper, 530,000 tons of glass, 290,000 tons of aluminum, 216,000 tons of copper, 190,000 tons of fabrics, 160,000 tons of lead, and 74,000 tons of plastic material.

In December 1984 there were six national parks, with a total area of 12,279 sq km (4,740 sq mi); as of 1 January 1986 there were 25 regional parks, with an area of 34,690 sq km (13,394 sq mi). In a total of 113 mammal species, 6 are currently threatened, as are 21 of 342 bird species, 2 of 36 types of reptiles, 1 of 29 types of amphibians, and 3 species of fresh-water fish in a total of 70. The greatest threat of extinction to France's flora and fauna concerns its plant species. Of 4,300–4,450 species, 143 are currently endangered. Endangered species in France in 1987 included the Mediterranean monk seal, the gray wolf, and the large blue butterfly. As of 1985, 25% of all species known to have appeared in France were extinct, endangered, or in substantial regression.

6POPULATION

The population, according to the census of 5 March 1990, was 56,634,299, compared with 54,295,692 in 1982. During 1982–90, the annual rate of population growth was about 0.5%. The estimated population as of mid-1994 was 57,289,648. Projected population for the year 2000 was 58,792,000, assuming a crude birthrate of 13 per 1,000 population and a crude death rate of 9.5, giving a net natural increase of 3.5 during 1995–2000. The 1990 population was 74.5% urban and 24.5% rural. Average density in 1990 was 104 persons per sq km (270 per sq mi). According to the 1990 census, 38 cities had more than 100,000 inhabitants. Paris proper, the capital, is the largest city, with a population in 1990 of 2,175,200, down from 2,188,960 in 1982. Greater Paris, with some 9,318,821 inhabitants in 1990, remained a heavily populated urban area, with a density of 3,920 people per sq km (10,153 per sq mi). The next largest cities, with

1990 populations, are Marseille, 807,726; Lyon, 422,444; Toulouse, 365,933; Nice, 345,674; Strasbourg, 255,937; Nantes, 252,029; Bordeaux, 213,274; Montpellier, 210,866; Rennes, 203,533; Saint-Étienne, 201,569; and Le Havre, 197,219.

7MIGRATION

In 1990 there were 3,607,590 recorded foreign residents of France. (Another 200,000 were believed to be in the country illegally.) The largest groups were the Portuguese (645,578), Algerians (619,923), Moroccans (584,708), Italians (253,679), Spaniards (216,015), Tunisians (207,496), and Turks (201,480). The growing presence of foreigners has become a political issue met by crackdowns on illegal immigrants and restrictions on citizenship. At the end of 1992 France was harboring 182,600 refugees.

8ETHNIC GROUPS

About 94% of the population holds French citizenship. Most of these citizens are of French ancestry, but there are also small groups of Flemings, Catalans, Germans, Armenians, Gypsies, Russians, Poles, and others. The largest resident alien groups are Algerians, Portuguese, Moroccans, Italians, Spaniards, Tunisians, and Turks.

9LANGUAGES

Not only is French the national language of France, but it also has official status (often with other languages) throughout much of the former French colonial empire, including about two dozen nations in Africa. In all, it is estimated that more than 300 million people have French as their official language or mother tongue. Moreover, French is the sole official language at the ICJ and UPU, and shares official status in most international organizations. Other languages spoken within France itself include Breton (akin to Welsh) in Brittany; a German dialect in Alsace and Lorraine; Flemish in northeastern France; Spanish, Catalan, and Basque in the southwest; Provençal in the southeast, and an Italian dialect on the island of Corsica.

10RELIGIONS

Church and state have been legally separate since 1905. In 1993, about 83.5% of the population was Roman Catholic and 2% was Protestant, mostly Calvinist or Lutheran. With the increased number of North Africans in metropolitan France, by 1992 the number of Muslims had risen to an estimated 1,900,000.

The French Jewish community, estimated at 530,000 in 1990, is the fourth-largest in the world, after the US, Israel, and the former USSR; more than half are immigrants from North Africa. Jews have enjoyed full rights of citizenship in France since 1791, and the emancipation of Central European Jewry was accomplished, to a large extent, by the armies of Napoleon Bonaparte. Anti-Semitism became a flaming issue during the Dreyfus affair in the late 1890s; in the 1980s, principal French synagogues were under police guard because of a wave of attacks by international terrorists.

11TRANSPORTATION

France has one of the most highly developed transportation systems in Europe. Its outstanding characteristic has long been the degree to which it is centralized at Paris—plateaus and plains offering easy access radiate from the city in all directions, and rivers with broad valleys converge on it from all sides. In 1991, the road network of 803,000 paved km (499,000 mi) included 33,400 km (20,755 mi) of national highways. By 1992 there were 23.8 million passenger cars and 5 million commercial vehicles. In 1991, 2,424,314 new private and commercial vehicles were registered.

All French railroads were nationalized in 1938 and are part of the national rail network Société Nationale des Chemins-de-Fer

LOCATION: 42°20′ to 51°5′N; 4°47′w to 8°15′E. **BOUNDARY LENGTHS:** Belgium, 630 km (391 mi); Luxembourg, 75 km (47 mi); FRG, 435 km (270 mi); Switzerland, 550 km (342 mi); Italy, 500 km (311 mi); Mediterranean Sea (including Monaco), 1,700 km (1,056 mi); Andorra, 60 km (37 mi); Spain, 690 km (429 mi); Bay of Biscay and Atlantic coastline (including islands), 1,800 km (1,118 mi); North Sea and English Channel coastline, 1,220 km (758 mi). **TERRITORIAL SEA LIMIT:** 12 mi.

Français, 51% of the shares of which are controlled by the government. As of the end of 1992, France ranked seventh in the world in the number of passengers carried and eighth in tons of freight transported. As of January 1992 there were 36,706 km (22,809 mi) of railway track, of which 32% were electrified. Only 2,138 km (1,329 mi) of track were privately owned as of 1991. Le Train à Grande Vitesse (TGV), the fastest train in the world, averaging 250 km (155 mi) per hour over most of its run, entered service between Paris and Lyon in 1981. TGV service between Paris and Lausanne became fully operational in 1985. The TGV set another world speed record on 18 May 1990 with a registered speed of 320.2 mph (515.2 kph). The Paris subway (métro), begun in the early 1900s but extensively modernized, and the city's regional express railways cover a distance of 472 km (293 mi). The métro has over one million passengers a day; Parisian bus lines carry about 800,000 passengers daily. Other cities with subways are Marseille, Lille, and Lyon, with construction underway in Toulouse.

Two high-speed rail tunnels under the English Channel will link Calais and Folkestone, England (near Dover). The 50-km (31-mi) project by Eurotunnel, a British-French consortium, was completed in 1993. From these terminals, people can drive their cars and trucks onto trains which can make the underground trek in about thirty minutes.

France, especially in its northern and northeastern regions, is well provided with navigable rivers and connecting canals, and inland water transportation is of major importance. In 1991 there were about 6,969 km (4,331 mi) of navigable waterways in heavy use. The French merchant marine, as of January 1992, had a total of 102 ships with 2.9 million GRT, of which 42 oceangoing tankers accounted for 1.7 million GRT and 48 tankers accounted for 984,000 GRT. Kerguelen, an archipelago in the French Antarctic Territory, offers an offshore registry program which is less regulatory than official French registry. As of the end of 1991, the Kerguelen merchant fleet numbered 33 ships with a capacity of 359,000 GRT. The leading ports are Marseille, Le Havre, Dunkerque, Rouen, Bordeaux, and Cherbourg. Other important ports include Boulogne, Brest, Fos-Sur-Mer, Sete, and Toulon. More than half of freight traffic to and from French ports is carried by French ships.

France's national airline, Air France, is government subsidized. It operates regularly scheduled flights to all parts of the world and carries about 79% (1992) of total passenger air traffic by French carriers. Its fleet as of 1991 included 42 Boeing 747s, 15 Boeing 727s, 28 Boeing 737s, 5 Boeing 767s, 16 A-300 Airbuses, and 5 Concordes. The Concorde, jointly developed by France and the UK at a cost of more than £1 billion, entered regular transatlantic service in 1976. In 1992, Air France flew 42,931 million passenger-km and transported 3,731,200 ton-km of freight. There are two major private airlines: the Union des Transports Aériens, which provides service to Africa and the South Pacific, and Air Inter, which operates within metropolitan France. The two international airports of Paris, Charles de Gaulle and Orly, lead all others in France in both passenger and freight traffic; together they handled 44.8 million passengers and 853,000 tons of freight in 1991.

12HISTORY

Cave paintings and engravings, the most famous of them at Lascaux, near Montignac in the southwest, attest to human habitation in France as early as 30,000 years ago. Relics from the period between 4000 and 1800 BC include some 4,500 dolmens (structures consisting of two vertical stones capped by a horizontal stone), nearly 1,000 of them in Brittany alone, and more than 6,000 menhirs (single vertical stones), 1.5–21.3 m (5–70 ft) high and weighing up to 350 tons. There may already have been 2–3 million people in France when Phoenician and Greek colonists founded cities on the southern coast around 600 BC.

Detailed knowledge of French history begins with the conquest of the region (58–51 BC) by Julius Caesar. The country was largely inhabited by Celtic tribes known to the Romans as Gauls. Under Roman rule the Gallic provinces were among the most prosperous and civilized of the empire. Roman roads, traces of which still may be seen, traversed the land. Numerous cities were founded. Latin superseded the Celtic dialects. Christianity spread rapidly in Roman Gaul after its introduction there in the 1st century, and by the time the empire began to disintegrate a few hundred years later, the Gauls were a thoroughly Romanized and Christianized people. Early in the 5th century, Teutonic tribes invaded the region from Germany, the Visigoths settling in the southwest, the Burgundians along the Rhône River Valley, and

the Franks (from whom the French take their name) in the north. The Germanic invaders probably never constituted more than a dominant minority of the population.

The first leader to make himself king of all the Franks was Clovis, who routed the forces of the last of the Roman governors of the province in 486 and was baptized a Christian in 496. Clovis conquered the southwest from the Visigoths and made himself master of western Germany as well, but after his death the kingdom disintegrated and its population declined. In 732, Charles Martel was able to rally the eastern Franks to inflict a decisive defeat on the Saracens—Muslim invaders who already controlled the Iberian Peninsula—between Poitiers and Tours. His grandson, Charlemagne (r.768–814), was the greatest of the early Frankish rulers. He gave the kingdom an efficient administration, created an excellent legal system, and encouraged the revival of learning, piety, and the arts. He added to the territories under his rule through wide conquests, eventually reigning over an area corresponding to present-day France, the FRG, the Low Countries, and northern Italy. On Christmas Day in the year 800, he was crowned emperor of the West by the pope in Rome.

After the death of Charlemagne, the vast Carolingian Empire broke up, the title of emperor passing to German rulers in the east. The territory of what is now France was invaded anew, this time by pagan tribes from Scandinavia and the north, and the region that later became known as Normandy was ceded to the Northmen in 911 by Charles III ("the Simple," r.898–923). At the end of the century, Hugh Capet (r.987–996) founded the line of French kings that, including its collateral branches, was to rule the country for the next 800 years. Feudalism was by now a well-established system. The French kings were the dukes and feudal overlords of the Île de France, centered on Paris and extending roughly three days' march around the city. At first, their feudal overlordship over the other provinces of France was almost entirely nominal. Some of the largest of these, like the Duchy of Brittany, were practically independent kingdoms. The Duchy of Normandy grew in power when William II, duke of Normandy, engaged in the Norman Conquest of England (1066–70) and became king as William I ("the Conqueror"), introducing the French language and culture. The powers of the French monarchy were gradually extended in the course of the 11th and early 12th centuries, particularly by Louis VI, who died in 1137. The power of his son Louis VII (r.1137–80) was challenged by Henry of Anjou, who, upon his accession to the English throne as Henry II in 1154, was feudal master of a greater part of the territory of France, including Normandy, Brittany, Anjou, and Aquitaine. Henry's sons, Richard and John, were unable to hold these far-flung territories against the vigorous assaults of Louis's son Philip Augustus (r.1180–1223). By 1215, Philip had not only reestablished the French crown's control over the former Angevin holdings in the north and west but also had firmly consolidated the crown's power in Languedoc and Toulouse. Philip's grandson Louis IX (St. Louis), in a long reign (1226–70), firmly established the strength of the monarchy through his vigorous administration of the royal powers. The reign of Louis's grandson Philip IV ("the Fair," 1285–1314) marks the apogee of French royal power in the medieval period. He quarreled with the papacy over fiscal control of the French clergy and other aspects of sovereignty. His emissaries arrested Pope Boniface VIII and after his death removed the seat of the papacy to Avignon, where the popes resided under French dominance (the so-called Babylonian Captivity) until 1377.

Philip the Fair was succeeded by three sons, who reigned briefly and who left no direct male heirs. In 1328, his nephew Philip VI (in accordance with the so-called Salic Law, under which succession could pass through a male line only) mounted the throne as the first of the Valois kings. The new king's title to the throne was challenged by Edward III of England, whose mother was the daughter of Philip the Fair. In 1337, Edward asserted a formal claim to the French crown, shortly thereafter quartering the lilies of France on his shield. The struggle that lasted from 1337 to 1453 over these rival claims is known as the Hundred Years' War. Actually it consisted of a series of shorter wars and skirmishes punctuated by periods of truce. Edward won a notable victory at Crécy in 1346, in a battle that showed the superiority of English ground troops and longbows against the French knights in armor. In 1356, the French royal forces were routed by the Prince of Wales at Poitiers, where the French king, John II, was taken prisoner. By terms of the Treaty of Brétigny (1360), the kingdom of France was dismembered, the southwest being formally ceded to the king of England. Under Charles V ("the Wise," r.1364–80), however, the great French soldier Bertrand du Guesclin, through a tenaciously conducted series of skirmishes, succeeded in driving the English from all French territory except Calais and the Bordeaux region.

It is estimated that between 1348 and 1400 the population dropped from 16 million to 11 million, mainly from a series of epidemics, beginning with the Black Death (bubonic plague) of 1348–50. In 1415, Henry V of England, taking advantage of civil war between the Gascons and Armagnacs, launched a new invasion of France and won a decisive victory at Agincourt. Charles VI (r.1380–1422) was compelled under the Treaty of Troyes (1420) to marry his daughter Catherine to Henry and to declare the latter and his descendants heirs to the French crown. Upon Henry's death in 1422, his infant son Henry VI was crowned king of both France and England, but in the same year, Charles's son, the dauphin of France, reasserted his claim, formally assumed the royal title, and slowly began the reconquest.

1422–1789

The first part of the Hundred Years' War was essentially a dynastic rather than a national struggle. The English armies themselves were commanded by French-speaking nobles and a French-speaking king. Although the legitimate succession to the French crown was the ostensible issue throughout the war, the emerging forces of modern nationalism came into play with the campaign launched by Henry V, whose everyday language was English and who, after Agincourt, became an English national hero. France owed no small measure of its eventual success to the sentiment of nationalism that was arising throughout the country and that found its personification in the figure of Joan of Arc. Early in 1429, this young woman of surprising military genius, confident that she had a divinely inspired mission to save France, gained the confidence of the dauphin. She succeeded in raising the siege of Orléans and had the dauphin crowned Charles VII at Reims. Joan fell into English hands and at Rouen in 1431 was burned at the stake as a heretic, but the French armies continued to advance. Paris was retaken in 1436, and Rouen in 1453; by 1461, when Charles died, the English had been driven from all French territory except Calais, which was recaptured in 1558.

Louis XI (r.1461–83), with the support of the commercial towns, which regarded the king as their natural ally, set France on a course that eventually destroyed the power of the great feudal lords. His most formidable antagonist, Charles the Bold, duke of Burgundy, who ruled virtually as an independent monarch, commanded for many years far more resources than the king of France himself. But after the duke was defeated and killed in a battle against the Swiss in 1477, Louis was able to reunite Burgundy with France. When Louis's son Charles VIII united Brittany, the last remaining quasi-independent province, with the royal domain by his marriage to Anne of Brittany, the consolidation of the kingdom under one rule was complete.

Under Charles VIII (r.1483–98) and Louis XII (r.1498–1515), France embarked on a series of Italian wars which were continued under Francis I (r.1515–47) and Henry II (r.1547–59). These wars developed into the first phase of a protracted imperialistic

struggle between France and the house of Habsburg. Although the Italian wars ended in a French defeat, they served to introduce the artistic and cultural influences of the Italian Renaissance into France on a large scale. Meanwhile, as the Reformation gained an increasing following in France, a bitter enmity developed between the great families that had espoused the Protestant or Huguenot cause and those that had remained Catholic. The policy of the French monarchy was in general to suppress Protestantism at home while supporting it abroad as a counterpoise to Habsburg power. Under the last of the Valois kings, Charles IX (r.1560–74) and Henry III (r.1574–89), a series of fierce religious civil wars devastated France. Paris remained a stronghold of Catholicism, and on 23–24 August 1572, thousands of Protestants were slaughtered in the Massacre of St. Bartholomew. Eventually, on the death of Henry III, the Protestant Henry of Navarre of the house of Bourbon, acceded to the throne. Unable to capture Paris by force, Henry embraced Catholicism in 1593 and entered the city peacefully the following year. In 1598, he signed the Edict of Nantes, which guaranteed religious freedom to the Huguenots. With the aid of his minister Sully, Henry succeeded in restoring prosperity to France.

Assassinated in 1610 by a Catholic fanatic, Henry IV was succeeded by his young son Louis XIII, with the queen mother, Marie de Médicis, acting as regent in the early years of his reign. Later, the affairs of state were directed almost exclusively by Cardinal Richelieu, the king's minister. Richelieu followed a systematic policy that entailed enhancing the crown's absolute rule at home and combating the power of the Habsburgs abroad. In pursuit of the first of these objectives, Richelieu destroyed the political power of the Protestants; in pursuit of the second he led France in 1635 into the Thirty Years' War, then raging in Germany, on the side of the Protestants and against the Austrians and the Spanish. Richelieu died in 1642, and Louis XIII died a few months later. His successor, Louis XIV, was five years old, and during the regency of his mother, Anne of Austria, France's policy was largely guided by her adviser Cardinal Mazarin. The generalship of the prince de Condé and the vicomte de Turenne brought France striking victories. The Peace of Westphalia (1648), which ended the Thirty Years' War, and the Peace of the Pyrenees (1659) marked the end of Habsburg hegemony and established France as the dominant power on the European continent. The last attempt of the French nobles to rise against the crown, the Fronde (1648–53), was successfully repressed by Mazarin even though the movement had the support of Condé and Turenne.

The active reign of Louis XIV began in 1661, the year of Mazarin's death, and lasted until his own death in 1715. Assisted by his able ministers Colbert and Louvois, he completed Mazarin's work of domestic centralization and transformed the French state into an absolute monarchy based on the so-called divine right of kings. Industry and commerce were encouraged by mercantilist policies, and great overseas empires were carved out in India, Canada, and Louisiana. By transforming the nobles into perennial courtiers, financially dependent on the crown, the king clipped their wings. Lavish display marked the early period of his reign, when the great palace at Versailles was built.

The reign of Louis XIV marked the high point in the prestige of the French monarchy. It was a golden age for French culture as well, and French fashions and manners set the standard for all Europe. Nevertheless, the Sun King, as he was styled, left the country in a weaker position than he had found it. Louis's old age was marked by increasing despotism. In 1685, he revoked the Edict of Nantes, and an estimated 200,000 Huguenots fled the country to escape persecution. Whole provinces were depopulated, and the economy was severely affected by the loss of many skilled and industrious workers. Louis undertook a long series of foreign wars, culminating in the War of the Spanish Succession (1701–14), in which England, the Netherlands, and most of the

German states were arrayed against France, Spain, Bavaria, Portugal, and Savoy. In the end, little territory was lost, but the military primacy of the country was broken and its economic strength seriously sapped.

The reign of Louis XV (1715–74) and that of his successor, Louis XVI (1774–93), which was terminated by the French Revolution, showed the same lavish display of royal power and elegance that had been inaugurated by the Sun King. At the same time, the economic crisis that Louis XIV left as his legacy continued to grow more serious. A series of foreign wars cost France its Indian and Canadian colonies and bankrupted the country. Meanwhile, the locus of the economic power in the kingdom had shifted to the hands of the upper bourgeoisie, who resented the almost wholly unproductive ruling class. Furthermore, the intellectual currents of the so-called Age of Reason were basically opposed to the old order. Voltaire attacked the Church and the principle of absolutism alike; Diderot advocated scientific materialism; Jean-Jacques Rousseau preached popular sovereignty.

1789–1900

In 1789, faced with an unmanageable public debt, Louis XVI convened, for the first time since the reign of Louis XIII, the States-General, the national legislative body, to consider certain fiscal reforms. The representatives of the third estate, the Commons, met separately on 17 June and proclaimed themselves the National Assembly. This action, strictly speaking, marked the beginning of the French Revolution, although the act that best symbolized the power of the revolution was the storming of the Bastille, a royal prison, by a Paris mob on 14 July—an event still commemorated as a national holiday. With the support of the mob, the Assembly was able to force Louis to accept a new constitution providing for a limited monarchy, the secularization of the state, and the seizure of Church lands. War with Austria, which wished to intervene to restore the status quo ante in France, broke out in 1792. The Assembly's successor, the National Convention, elected in September 1792, proclaimed the First French Republic. Louis XVI was convicted of treason and executed. The radical group of Jacobins under Maximilien Robespierre's leadership exercised strict control through committees of public welfare and a revolutionary tribunal. The Jacobins attempted to remake France in the image of an egalitarian republic. Their excesses led to a Reign of Terror (1793–94), carried out indiscriminately against royalists and such moderate republican groups as the Girondins. Manifold opposition to the Jacobins and specifically to Robespierre combined to end their reign in the summer of 1794. In 1795, a new constitution of moderate character was introduced, and executive power was vested in a Directory of five men. The Directory, weakened by inefficient administration and military reverses, fell in turn in 1799, when the military hero Napoleon Bonaparte engineered a coup and established the Consulate. Ruling autocratically as the first consul, Bonaparte established domestic stability and decisively defeated the Austrian-British coalition arrayed against France. In 1804, he had himself proclaimed emperor as Napoleon I and, until his downfall in 1814, he ruled France in that capacity.

Capitalizing on the newly awakened patriotic nationalism of France, Napoleon led his imperial armies to a striking series of victories over the dynastic powers of Europe. By 1808, he was the master of all Europe west of Russia with the exception of the British Isles. That year, however, the revolt in Spain—upon whose throne Napoleon had placed his brother Joseph—began to tax French military reserves. Napoleon's ill-fated attempt to conquer Russia in 1812 was followed by the consolidation of a powerful alliance against him, consisting of Russia, Prussia, Britain, and Sweden. The allies defeated Napoleon at Leipzig in 1813 and captured Paris in the spring of 1814. Napoleon was exiled to the island of Elba, just off the northwest coast of Italy, and Louis

XVIII, a brother of Louis XVI, was placed on the French throne. In March 1815, Napoleon escaped from Elba, rallied France behind him, and reentered Paris in triumph behind the fleeing Louis XVIII. He was, however, finally and utterly crushed by the British and Prussian forces at Waterloo (18 June 1815) and spent the remaining years of his life as a British prisoner of war on the island of St. Helena in the South Atlantic.

After the final fall of Napoleon, Louis XVIII ruled as a moderate and peaceful monarch until 1824, when he was succeeded by his brother Charles X, an ultraroyalist. Charles attempted to restore the absolute powers of the monarchy and the supremacy of the Catholic Church. In 1830, he was ousted after a three-day revolution in which the upper bourgeoisie allied itself with the forces of the left. Louis Philippe of the house of Orléans was placed on the throne as "citizen-king," with the understanding that he would be ruled by the desires of the rising industrial plutocracy. In 1848, his regime was overthrown in the name of the Second Republic. Four years later, however, its first president, Louis Napoleon, the nephew of Napoleon I, engineered a coup and had himself proclaimed emperor under the title Napoleon III. The Second Empire, as the period 1852–71 is known, was characterized by colonial expansion and great material prosperity. The emperor's aggressive foreign policy eventually led to the Franco-Prussian War (1870–71), which ended in a crushing defeat for France and the downfall of Napoleon III. France was stripped of the border provinces of Alsace and Lorraine (which had once belonged to the Holy Roman Empire) and was forced to agree to an enormous indemnity. A provisional government proclaimed a republic on 4 September 1870 and took over the responsibility for law and order until a National Assembly was elected in February 1871. Angered at the rapid capitulation to Prussia by the provisionals and the conservative National Assembly, the national guard and radical elements of Paris seized the city in March and set up the Commune. During the "Bloody Week" of 21–28 May, the Commune was savagely dispatched by government troops.

Democratic government finally triumphed in France under the Third Republic, whose constitution was adopted in 1875. Royalist sentiment had been strong, but the factions backing different branches of the royal house had been unable to agree on a candidate for the throne. The Third Republic confirmed freedom of speech, the press, and association. It enforced complete separation of church and state. Social legislation guaranteeing the rights of trade unions was passed, and elections were held on the basis of universal manhood suffrage. The Third Republic, however, was characterized by an extremely weak executive. A long succession of cabinets was placed in power and shortly thereafter removed from office by the all-powerful lower house of the national legislature. Nevertheless, the republic was strong enough to weather an attempt on the part of the highly popular Gen. Georges Boulanger to overthrow the regime in the late 1880s, as well as the bitter dispute between the left-wing and right-wing parties occasioned by the trumped-up arrest and long imprisonment of Capt. Alfred Dreyfus, a scandal in which Dreyfus's being Jewish was as much an issue as the treason he had allegedly committed. The eventual vindication of Dreyfus went hand in hand with the decisive defeat of the monarchists and the emergence of a progressive governing coalition, with Socialist representation.

The Twentieth Century

During World War I (1914–18), the forces of France, the UK, Russia, and, from 1917, the US were locked in a protracted struggle with those of Germany, Austria-Hungary, and Turkey. Although France, under the leadership of Georges Clemenceau, could claim a major share in the final Allied victory, it was in many respects a Pyrrhic victory for France. Almost all the bitter fighting in the west was conducted on French soil, and among the

Allies French casualties—including nearly 1,400,000 war dead—were second only to those sustained by Russia. The heavily industrialized provinces of Alsace and Lorraine were restored to France under the Treaty of Versailles (1919), and Germany was ordered to pay heavy war reparations. Nevertheless, the French economy, plagued by recurrent crises, was unable to achieve great prosperity in the 1920s, and the worldwide economic depression of the 1930s (exacerbated in France by the cessation of German reparations payments) was accompanied in France by inflation, widespread unemployment, and profound social unrest. Right- and extreme left-wing elements caused major disturbances on 6 February 1934. In 1936, the left-wing parties carried the parliamentary elections and installed a so-called Popular Front government under a Socialist, Léon Blum. Blum nationalized certain war industries, carried out agricultural reforms, and made the 40-hour week mandatory in industry. Increasing conservative opposition forced the Popular Front government from power, however, and in the face of the growing menace of Adolf Hitler's Germany, the leftists accepted the conservative government of Édouard Daladier in 1938. In a futile attempt to secure peace, Daladier acquiesced in British Prime Minister Neville Chamberlain's policy of appeasement toward Hitler. Hitler was not to be appeased, however, and when Germany invaded Poland in September 1939, France joined the UK in declaring war on Germany.

On 10 May 1940, the Germans launched a great invasion of the west through the Low Countries and the heavily wooded and sparsely defended Ardennes region. In less than a month, German forces outflanked the French Maginot Line fortifications and routed the French armies between the Belgian frontier and Paris. Marshal Pétain, the aged hero of World War I, hastily formed a government and sued for peace. With the exception of a triangular zone with its northern apex near Vichy, all France was placed under the direct occupation of the Germans. The Vichy regime ended the Third Republic and proclaimed a constitution based on the slogan "labor, family, fatherland," as opposed to the traditional republican "liberty, equality, fraternity." While the Vichy government did its best to accommodate itself to the German victory, French resistance gathered overseas around Gen. Charles de Gaulle, a brilliant career officer who had escaped to London on 18 June 1940 to declare that France had "lost a battle, not the war." De Gaulle organized the Provisional French National Committee, and this committee of the Free French later exercised all the powers of a wartime government in the French territories where resistance to the Germans continued. The Free French forces took part in the fighting that followed the Allied invasion of North Africa in 1942, and in 1943 a provisional French government was established at Algiers. Regular French units and resistance fighters alike fought in the 1944 campaign that drove the Germans from France, and shortly after the liberation of Paris, de Gaulle's provisional government moved from Algiers to the capital. It was officially recognized by the US, the UK, and the former USSR in October 1944.

France's postwar vicissitudes have been political rather than economic. De Gaulle resigned as head of the government early in 1946 over the issue of executive powers, and in spite of his efforts the Fourth Republic, under a constitution that came into effect in December 1946, was launched with most of the weaknesses of the Third Republic. Almost all powers were concentrated in the hands of the National Assembly, the lower house of Parliament, and there were numerous warring political parties.

Almost continuous fighting overseas, first in Indochina, which was lost in 1954, and later in Algeria, the scene of a nationalist rebellion among the Muslims, placed a heavy burden on France and led, especially after the Suez expedition of 1956, to disillusionment on the part of elements in the French army, which felt that its work was being undermined by a series of vacillating parliamentary governments. In May 1958, extremists among the

French settlers in Algeria, acting with a group of army officers, seized control of Algiers. Sympathetic movements in Corsica and in metropolitan France raised the specter of a right-wing coup. The government found itself powerless to deal with the situation, and on 1 June, Gen. de Gaulle, regarded as the only leader capable of rallying the nation, was installed as premier. He ended the threat peaceably, and in the fall of 1958, he submitted to a national referendum a new constitution providing for a strong presidency; the constitution won overwhelming approval. Elections held in November swept candidates pledged to support de Gaulle into office, and in December 1958, he was officially named the first president of the Fifth Republic.

Although the people of metropolitan France overwhelmingly approved de Gaulle's program for eventual Algerian independence, some French army officers and units attempted to overthrow the government by terrorism, which de Gaulle suppressed by temporarily assuming emergency powers. Peace negotiations were successfully concluded with Algerian rebel leaders, and Algeria gained independence on 1 July 1962. By then, nearly all of France's former African territories had attained independence. France has continued to provide economic assistance, and its ties with most of the former colonies have remained close.

During the mid-1960s, de Gaulle sought to distance France from the Anglo-American alliance. France developed its own atomic weapons and withdrew its forces from the NATO command; in addition, de Gaulle steadfastly opposed the admission of the UK to the EC, of which France had been a founding member in 1958.

The political stability of the mid-1960s ended in the spring of 1968, with student riots and a month-long general strike that severely weakened the Gaullist regime. In April 1969, Gen. de Gaulle resigned following a defeat, by national referendum, of a Gaullist plan to reorganize the Senate and regional government. In June, Georges Pompidou, a former premier in de Gaulle's government, was elected the second president of the Fifth Republic. Between 1969 and 1973, the Gaullist grip on the French populace continued to weaken. In 1974, after President Pompidou died in office, an Independent Republican, Valéry Giscard d'Estaing, narrowly won a national runoff election (with Gaullist help) and became the third president of the Fifth Republic. Giscard strengthened relations with the US but continued to ply a middle course between the superpowers in world affairs.

Although Giscard's center-right coalition held firm in the March 1978 legislative elections, a Socialist, François Mitterrand, was elected president in May 1981, and the Socialists captured a parliamentary majority in June. Mitterrand launched a program of economic reforms, including the nationalization of many industrial companies and most major banks. However, three devaluations of the franc, high unemployment, and rising inflation led to the announcement of an austerity program in March 1983. In foreign policy, Mitterrand took an activist stance, opposing the abortive US attempt in 1982 to halt construction of a natural gas pipeline between the former USSR and Western Europe, committing French troops to a peacekeeping force in Lebanon, and aiding the Chadian government against domestic insurgents and their Libyan backers.

In July 1984, Mitterrand accepted the resignation of Prime Minister Pierre Mauroy and named Laurent Fabius to replace him, signaling his intention to stress economic austerity and modernization of industry. In foreign affairs, the government attempted some retrenchment during 1984, withdrawing peacekeeping troops from Lebanon and announcing a "total and simultaneous" withdrawal of French and Libyan troops from Chad. However, Libyan troops did not actually withdraw as envisioned, and fighting there prompted a return of French troops in 1986. A major scandal was the disclosure in 1985 that French agents were responsible for the destruction in New Zealand, with the loss of a life, of a ship owned by an environmentalist group protesting French nuclear tests in the South Pacific.

In March 1986 elections, the Socialists lost their majority in the National Assembly, and Mitterrand had to appoint a conservative prime minister, Jacques Chirac, to head a new center-right cabinet. This unprecedented "cohabitation" between a Socialist president and a conservative government led to legislative conflict, as Chirac, with backing from the National Assembly, successfully instituted a program, opposed by Mitterrand, to denationalize 65 state-owned companies. Chirac encountered less success late in 1986 as he sought to deal with a wave of terrorist violence in Paris. In 1988, Chirac challenged Mitterand for the presidency, but in the May runoff election, Mitterand won a commanding 54% of the vote and a second seven-year term. Chirac then resigned, and Mitterand formed a minority Socialist government.

Economic and social problems as well as government scandals have strained relations between Mitterrand and the center-right government. Unemployment remains high and new legislation has increased police powers to combat illegal immigration. Several prominent politicians were the subject of corruption charges and in 1993 legal proceedings were instituted against former primer minister, Laurent Fabius, related to an HIV-infected blood scandal. A prominent Socialist prime minister, Pierre Beregovoy, committed suicide in May 1993 over media allegations of financial improprieties.

Presidential elections are scheduled for 1995. It is expected the legislative elections will follow shortly thereafter.

13 GOVERNMENT

Under the constitution of the Fifth Republic (1958), as subsequently amended, the president of the republic is elected for a seven-year term by direct universal suffrage. If no candidate receives an absolute majority of the votes cast, a runoff election is held between the two candidates having received the most votes. If the presidency falls vacant, the president of the Senate assumes the office until a new election can be held within 20–35 days. The president appoints the premier and, on the premier's recommendation, the other members of the cabinet. The president has the power to dissolve the National Assembly, in which event new elections must be held in 20–40 days. When the country is gravely menaced, the president is empowered to take special measures after consultation with the premier and other appropriate officials. The National Assembly, however, may not be dissolved during the exercise of exceptional powers. The president promulgates laws approved by the legislature, has the right of pardon, and is commander of the armed forces.

The Parliament consists of two houses, the National Assembly and the Senate. Under a system enacted in 1986, the National Assembly is composed of 577 deputies, each representing an electoral district. If no candidate receives a clear majority, there is a runoff among those receiving at least 12.5% of the vote; a plurality then suffices for election. All citizens aged 18 or over are eligible to vote.

The deputies' term of office, unless the Assembly is dissolved, is five years. The Senate consisted, as of September 1986, of 321 members indirectly elected to nine-year terms, one-third being chosen every three years. Of the total, 296 represented metropolitan France, 13, overseas departments and territories, and 12, French citizens residing abroad; all are chosen by electoral colleges.

To become law, a measure must be passed by Parliament. Parliament also has the right to develop in detail and amplify the list of matters on which it may legislate by passing an organic law to that effect. Regular parliamentary sessions are limited to two a year, one beginning on 2 October and lasting 80 days, the other beginning on 2 April and lasting not more than 90 days. A special session may be called by the premier or at the request of a majority of the National Assembly. Bills, which may be initiated by the executive, are introduced in either house, except finance bills, which must be introduced in the Assembly.

The premier and the cabinet formulate national policy and execute the laws. No one may serve concurrently as a member of Parliament and a member of the executive. Under certain circumstances, an absolute majority in the National Assembly may force the executive to resign by voting a motion of censure.

14 POLITICAL PARTIES

French political life has long been ruled both by considerations of political theory and by the demands of political expediency. Traditional issues such as the separation of church and state help to distinguish between right and left, but otherwise the lines separating all but the extremist political parties are difficult to draw. One result of this has been the proliferation of political parties, another the assumption by political parties of labels that seldom indicate any clear-cut platform or policy.

Broadly, since the late 1950s, French politics has been dominated by four political groups: the Gaullists, an independent center-right coalition, the Socialists, and the Communists. After the parliamentary elections of 23 and 30 November 1958, the first to be held under the constitution of the Fifth Republic, the largest single group in the Assembly was the Union for the New Republic (UNR), which stood for the policies of Gen. de Gaulle, elected president of the republic for a seven-year term in 1958. Independents of the right were the second-largest group, and the Christian Socialists (Mouvement Républicain Populaire) and several leftist groups followed. Only 16 members were elected by the center groups, and only 10 Communists.

In the November 1962 elections, the Gaullist UNR scored an unparalleled victory, polling 40.5% of the total votes cast. As a result of the elections, several old parliamentary groups disappeared, and new groups emerged: the Democratic Center (Centre Démocratique) with 55 seats; the Democratic Rally (Rassemblement Démocratique), 38 seats; and the Independent Republicans (Républicains Indépendants—RI), 33 seats. The UNR and the Democratic Workers Union (Union Démocratique du Travail—UDT), left-wing Gaullists, agreed to a full merger of their parties and together controlled 219 seats.

In the first presidential elections held by direct universal suffrage in December 1965, President de Gaulle was reelected on the second ballot with 55.2% of the total vote. In the March 1967 general elections, the UNR-UDT gained 246 seats against the Socialists' 116 and the Communists' 73. Following nationwide strikes and civil disturbances by workers and students in the spring of 1968, new parliamentary elections were held in June, in which de Gaulle's supporters won a sweeping victory.

The Union for the Defense of the Republic (Union pour la Défense de la République—UDR) emerged as the new official Gaullist organization. Political movements of the center joined to form the Progress and Modern Democracy group (Centre-PDM), while Socialists and the democratic left united under the Federation of the Left. Of the 487 Assembly seats, the UDR won 292 seats; RI, 61; Federation of the Left, 57; Communists, 34; Centre-PDM, 33; and independents, 10.

On 28 April 1969, following the defeat in a national referendum of a Gaullist plan to reorganize the Senate and regional government, President de Gaulle resigned. He was succeeded by former premier Georges Pompidou, a staunch Gaullist, who won 58% of the vote in elections held on 15 June 1969. During the Pompidou administration, Gaullist control was weakened by an alliance between the Communist and Socialist parties. In March 1973 elections, the Gaullist UDR lost 109 seats, falling to 183 of the 490 seats at stake. The Communists and Socialists increased their representation to 72 and 103, respectively. The remaining seats were won by the RI (55) and by centrists, reformists, and unaffiliated candidates (77).

On 2 April 1974, President Pompidou died. In elections held on 5 May, Gaullist candidate and former premier Jacques Chaban-Delmas was defeated, receiving only 15% of the votes cast. The leader of the leftist coalition, François Mitterrand, received over 11 million, and Valéry Giscard d'Estaing, the leader of the RI, over 8 million. However, as neither had won a majority, a runoff election was held on 19 May. Giscard, with the help of Gaullist votes, defeated Mitterrand by a margin of 50.7% to 49.3%. Jacques Chirac of the UDR was made premier, with a cabinet made up mainly of RI and UDR members.

A new Gaullist party, the Rally for the Republic (Rassemblement pour la République—RPR), founded by Chirac in 1976, received 26.1% of the vote in the second round of the 1978 legislative elections, winning 154 seats in the National Assembly. That year, the centrist parties had formed the Union for French Democracy (Union pour la Démocratie Française—UDF). The federation, which included the Republican Party (Parti Républicain), the successor to the RI, won 23.2% of the vote in the second round of balloting, giving the centrist coalition 124 seats in the National Assembly. The Socialists and Communists, who ran on a common platform as the Union of the Left, together won 199 seats (Socialists 113, Communists 86) and 46.9% of the vote. Independents, with the remaining 3.8%, controlled 14 seats, for a total of 491.

In the presidential elections of 26 April and 10 May 1981, Mitterrand received 25.8% of the vote on the first ballot (behind Giscard's 28.3%) and 51.8% on the second ballot, to become France's first Socialist president since the 1930s. Within weeks, Mitterrand called new legislative elections: that June, the Socialists and their allies won 49.2% of the vote and 285 seats, the RPR 22.4% and 88 seats, the UDF 18.6% and 63 seats, the Communists 7% and 44 seats; independents won the remaining 2.8% and 11 seats. In return for concessions on various political matters, four Communists received cabinet portfolios, none relating directly to foreign affairs or national security. The sweeping victory of the left was, however, eroded in March 1983 when Socialist and Communist officeholders lost their seats in about 30 cities in municipal balloting. Meanwhile, the Communists had become disaffected by government policies and did not seek appointments in the cabinet named when a new Socialist prime minister, Laurent Fabius, was appointed in July 1984.

In cantonal elections held in March 1985, the candidates of the left won less than 40% of the vote, while candidates on the right increased their share by 10–15%. The Socialists lost 155 of the 579 Socialist seats that were at stake. As a result, the Socialists introduced a new system of proportional voting aimed at reducing their losses in the forthcoming general election of 16 March 1986. The Socialists and their allies nevertheless won only 33% of the vote and 216 seats out of 577 in the expanded National Assembly. The RPR, the UDF, and their allies received 45% of the vote and 291 seats. The Communists, suffering a historic defeat, split the remaining 70 seats evenly with the far-right National Front, which won representation for the first time. The Socialists remained the largest single party, but the coalition led by the RPR and UDF had a majority; on that basis, Mitterrand appointed RPR leader Chirac as prime minister, heading a center-right government. Following his defeat by Mitterand in the May 1988 presidential election, Chirac resigned and a minority Socialist government was formed.

The National Assembly elections held in March 1993 represented a major defeat for the Socialist Party and their allies. The RPR and UDF won 247 and 213 seats, respectively, while the Socialists were reduced to 67 seats. The Communists also suffered losses, securing only 24 seats. Minor parties and independents won 26 seats.

15LOCAL GOVERNMENT

In 1972, Parliament approved a code of regional reforms that had been rejected when proposed previously by President de Gaulle in 1969. Under this law, the 96 departments of metropolitan France were grouped into 22 regions. Regional councils composed of local deputies, senators, and delegates were formed and prefects appointed; in addition, regional economic and social committees, made up of labor and management representatives, were created. This system was superseded by the decentralization law of 2 March 1982, providing for the transfer of administrative and financial authority from the prefect to the general council, which elects its own president; the national government's representative in the department is appointed by the cabinet. The 1982 law likewise replaced the system of regional prefects with regional councils, elected by universal direct suffrage, and, for each region, an economic and social committee that serves in an advisory role; the national government's representative in each region, named by the cabinet, exercises administrative powers. The first regional assembly to be elected was that of Corsica in August 1982; the first direct assembly elections in all 22 regions were held in March 1986.

Each of the 96 departments is further subdivided for administrative purposes into arrondissements, cantons, and communes. The basic unit of local government is the commune, governed by a municipal council and presided over by a mayor. A commune may be an Alpine village with no more than a dozen inhabitants, or it may be a large city, such as Lyon or Marseille. The majority, however, are small. In 1990, only 235 communes out of 36,551 had more than 30,000 inhabitants; 84% of all communes had fewer than 1,500 inhabitants, and 43% had fewer than 300. Municipal councillors are elected by universal suffrage for six-year terms. Each council elects a mayor who also serves as a representative of the central government. Several communes are grouped into a canton, and cantons are grouped into arrondissements, which have little administrative significance.

16JUDICIAL SYSTEM

There are two types of lower judicial courts in France, the civil courts (471 tribunaux d'instance and 181 tribunaux de grande instance in 1985, including overseas departments) and the criminal courts (tribunaux de police for petty offenses such as parking violations, tribunaux correctionnels for criminal misdemeanors). The function of the civil courts is to judge conflicts arising between persons; the function of the criminal courts is to judge minor infractions (contraventions) and graver offenses (délits) against the law. The most serious crimes, for which the penalties may range to life imprisonment, are tried in assize courts (cours d'assises); these do not sit regularly but are called into session when necessary. They are presided over by judges from the appeals courts. In addition, there are special commercial courts (tribunaux de commerce), composed of judges elected among themselves by tradesmen and manufacturers, to decide commercial cases; conciliation boards (conseils de prud'hommes), made up of employees and employers, to decide their disputes; and professional courts with disciplinary powers within the professions. Special administrative courts (tribunaux administratifs) deal with disputes between individuals and government agencies. The highest administrative court is the Council of State (Conseil d'État).

From the lower civil and criminal courts alike, appeals may be taken to appeals courts (cours d'appel). Judgments of the appeals courts and the courts of assize are final, except that appeals on the interpretation of the law or points of procedure may be taken to the highest of the judicial courts, the Court of Cassation in Paris. If it finds that either the letter or spirit of the law has been misapplied, it may annual a judgment and return a case for retrial by the lower courts. The High Court of Justice (Haute Cour de Justice), consisting of judges and members of Parliament, is convened to pass judgment on the president and cabinet members if a formal accusation of treason or criminal behavior has been voted by an absolute majority of both the National Assembly and the Senate. The death penalty was abolished in 1981.

The Conseil Constitutionnel, created by the 1958 Constitution, is now the only French forum available for constitutional review of legislation. Challenges to legislation may be raised by the President of the Republic, the Prime Minister, the President of the Senate, the President of the National Assembly, sixty Senators, or sixty Deputies of the National Assembly during the period between passage and promulgation (signature of President). Once promulgated, French legislation is not subject to judicial review.

The French judiciary is fully independent from the executive and legislative branches.

17ARMED FORCES

French military policy is formulated by the Supreme Defense Council (Conseil Supérieur de la Défense), presided over by the president of the republic. All French males between the ages of 18 and 45 are liable to 10 months of national service. There are four categories of national service: military service, defense service, technical aid service (designed to help in the development of French overseas departments and territories), and an international cooperative service. The annual conscript intake is around 200,000 a year. Women may volunteer, and 14,000 now serve.

In 1993 there were 431,700 regular personnel in the armed services and supporting medical and technical-staff services, including 260,900 in the army, 91,700 in the air force, 64,900 in the navy, 94,600 in the Gendarmerie Nationale, which is heavily armed, and 14,000 in various other service organizations. Reserves totaled 904,700, including 770,200 army reserves. About one-third of the reserve force is mobilizable. In 1992 the military budget was $35 billion or 3.6% of the GDP.

Although France withdrew from the integrated NATO military structure in 1966, it is part of the alliance and keeps liaison missions at all major NATO headquarters. In addition, it maintains a corps headquarters and an armored division in Germany (14,000 soldiers), and in 1988 it formed a mixed nationality brigade with the Bundeswehr. France has withdrawn its brigade of 2,700 from Berlin. The French maintain a field army of combined arms of six divisions (heavily reinforced with artillery and missiles) for European operations. Its Force Action Rapide (47,300) is an elite five-division force designed for rapid air deployment anywhere in the world. It can be further reinforced with about twenty additional battalions of the Foreign Legion and the Troupes de marine (the former colonial infantry). The French army uses weapons and equipment of French manufacture.

The French navy has 17 modern submarines (9 nuclear powered), 41 surface combatants (including 2 aircraft carriers), and around 60 other ships for mine warfare, amphibious operations, underwater replenishment, and intelligence operations. There is a 3,100-man commando and special operations marine force (fusiliers marins) and an 11,000-man naval air force with 145 combat aircraft, including the Super Étendard nuclear-capable fighter-bomber.

The French air force is divided into an air defense command, tactical air force, an air transport command, and a training command. France maintains a combat aircraft inventory of around 800 aircraft armed with advanced missiles. It has 19 air transport squadrons, and its helicopter fleet numbers about 120 for non-combat missions (the army and navy field more than 300 armed helicopters.)

France began building its own independent nuclear force during the deGaulle era and has conducted a number of atmospheric nuclear tests. There are several nuclear research centers in France, including an enriched uranium plant that began the first stage of production 1964. A thermonuclear test center is located in French Polynesia. The deployed strategic nuclear forces (17,000, all services) are 4 ballistic missile submarines (64 missiles), 18 air force IRBMs, 15 Mirage IVP Bombers, 23 army Pluton missiles, and 39 naval fighter–bombers.

France maintains substantial forces abroad in its colonies and protectorates, supported by two deployed naval squadrons in the Indian Ocean and Pacific. France has substantial garrisons in Antilles-Guyana, New Caledonia, Réunion Island, and Polynesia, and it provides military missions and combat formations to seven African nations. It has a composite air squadron in Turkey and almost 6,000 troops deployed on peacekeeping missions, to seven different countries including Croatia.

France is one of the world's leading makers and sellers of armaments, including the Mirage aircraft, Super Étendard fighter-bombers, and Exocet missiles, tanks, and armored vehicles. During 1981–91, French arms exports had a value of around $40 billion.

18INTERNATIONAL COOPERATION

France is a charter member of the UN, having joined on 24 October 1945, and actively cooperates in ECE, ECLAC, ESCAP, and all the nonregional specialized agencies; it is one of the five permanent members of the Security Council. France is also a founding member of the EC. Although France still belongs to NATO, in 1966 the nation withdrew its personnel from the two integrated NATO commands—Supreme Headquarters Allied Powers Europe (SHAPE) and Allied Forces Central Europe (AFCENT). France is a member of the Asian Development Bank, Council of Europe, IDB, OAS (as a permanent observer), OECD, PAHO (as a participating government), various community commissions and groups, and other intergovernmental organizations. In all, France belongs to more international governmental and nongovernmental organizations than any other country in the world. France is also a signatory of GATT and the Law of the Sea.

19ECONOMY

France is one of the most richly endowed countries of Europe. The favorable climate, extensive areas of rich soil, and long-established tradition of skilled agriculture have created ideal conditions for a thriving farm economy. Large deposits of iron ore, a well-integrated network of power plants, important domestic reserves of natural gas, good transport, and high standards of industrial workmanship have made the French industrial complex one of the most modern in Europe.

After World War II, France enjoyed an economic climate superior to that of the best interwar years. But on the debit side were the extremely high cost of France's colonial campaigns in Indochina and North Africa; the periodic lack of confidence of French investors in the nation's economy, resulting in the large-scale flight of funds; and the successive devaluations of the franc.

Through most of the 1960s and early 1970s, the French economy expanded steadily, with the GNP more than doubling between 1959 and 1967. However, the international oil crisis of 1974 led to a sharp rise in import costs; the resulting inflation eroded real growth to about 3% annually between 1977 and 1979. Further oil price increases in 1979–80 marked the beginning of a prolonged recession, with high inflation, high unemployment, balance-of-payments deficits, declining private investment, and shortages in foreign exchange reserves. However, GDP grew by an annual average of 2.5% between 1984 and 1991. In 1992, GDP was only 1.2% higher than in 1991. Consumer prices increased 1.9%, while the unemployment rate reached 10.2%.

20INCOME

In 1992, France's GNP was $1,278,652 million at current prices, or $22,300 per capita. For the period 1985–92 the average inflation rate was 3.1%, resulting in a real growth rate in per capita GNP of 2.2%.

In 1992 the GDP was $1.08 trillion in current US dollars. It is estimated that in 1991 agriculture, hunting, forestry, and fishing contributed 3% to GDP; mining, quarrying, and manufacturing, 21%; electricity, gas, and water, 2%; construction, 5%; wholesale and retail trade, 15%; transport, storage, and communication, 6%; finance, insurance, real estate, and business services, 22%; community, social, and personal services, 6%; and other sources, 20%.

21LABOR

In 1991, 24.6 million persons were active in the French economy. Of the resident employed population, as of 31 December 1992, 66.4% were employed in trade, transportation, and services, 28.5% in industry, and 5.1% in agriculture. As of 1991, the unemployment rate averaged 9.8%, up from 8.9% in 1990.

The oldest major labor organization, dating from 1895, is the communist-dominated Confédération Générale du Travail (CGT), an affiliate of the WFTU. Its membership in 1991 was estimated at 650,000. The Confédération Générale du Travail—Force Ouvrière (CGT–FO), with an estimated membership of 375,000, was founded in 1948 as a splinter group of the CGT; affiliated with the ICFTU, the CGT–FO draws its membership principally from white-collar workers and civil servants. Another labor group, the Confédération Française Démocratique du Travail, with some 425,000 members, split from the Confédération Française de Travailleurs Chrétiens (CFTC) at a union congress in November 1964. The CFTC regrouped around those minorities wishing to continue the traditions of Christian unionism; it has over 150,000 members. Among the smaller labor groups are the Fédération Nationale des Syndicats d'Exploitants Agricoles; the Fédération de l'Éducation Nationale, which claims some 350,000 members; the Confédération des Syndicats Libres; and the Confédération Française de l'Encadrement, a union of managerial and highly skilled technical personnel. In 1991, only 497,300 work days were lost from strikes, a drop of 30,000 from the previous year and the lowest since 1945.

The pay scale of wage earners is determined by collective bargaining. The government determines only the minimum hourly rate, Fr32.66 as of 1991. Workers' compensation and disability insurance are financed solely by employers.

In January 1982, a 39-hour workweek and a fifth week of paid vacation were introduced. The labor code and other laws provide for work, safety, and health standards. Union representatives may participate in board meetings of private companies, but only in an advisory capacity; the unions are actively represented on the boards of the nationalized and mixed enterprises. In 1992, there were 1,330 localized strikes involving 16,300 workers resulting in 359,100 lost workdays.

22AGRICULTURE

Agriculture remains a vital sector of the French economy, even though it employs only about 7% of the labor force and contributes less than 4% of the GDP. Since the early 1970s, the agricultural labor force has diminished by about 60%. France, whose farms export more agricultural food products than any other EC nation (accounting for more than one-fourth of the EC's total agricultural output), is the only country in Europe to be completely self-sufficient in basic food production; moreover, the high quality of the nation's agricultural products contributes to the excellence of its famous cuisine. France is one of the leaders in Europe in the value of agricultural exports—chiefly wheat, sugar, wine, and beef. Tropical commodities, cotton, tobacco, and vegetable oils are among the chief agricultural imports.

As of 1991, some 35% of the total land area was under cultivation. In 1983, 76.1% of all farmland was in holdings of less than 35 hectares (86.5 acres). Since the 1950s, the number of

farms has declined and the size of individual holdings has increased. By 1983 there were about 1.13 million farms, as compared to 2.3 million in 1955, and the mean area of farms was about 26 hectares (64 acres); the median area was about 16 hectares (40 acres). Because French law provides for equal rights of inheritance, traditionally much of the farmland came to be split up into small, scattered fragments. One of the major aims of postwar plans for rural improvement has been the consolidation of these through reallotment. Such consolidation also fosters the growth of mechanization. In 1991 there were 1,460,000 tractors (fourth in the world, after the US, Japan, and Germany) compared with 100,000 in 1948, and 1,327,900 in 1974.

Of the total productive agricultural area (30.4 million hectares/75.1 million acres in 1991), about 59% was under cultivation, 37% was pasture, and 4% vineyards. The most productive farms are in northern France, but specialized areas, such as the vegetable farms of Brittany, the great commercial vineyards of the Languedoc, Burgundy, and Bordeaux districts, and the flower gardens, olive groves, and orchards of Provence, also contribute heavily to the farm economy.

Among agricultural products, cereals (wheat, barley, oats, corn, and sorghum), industrial crops (sugar beets, flax), root crops (potatoes), and wine are by far the most important. In 1992, the wheat crop totaled 32,600,000 tons and barley, 10,474,000 tons. Other totals (in tons) included oats, 690,000; corn, 14,613,000; sugar beets, 31,334,000; and potatoes, 6,495,000. Wine production in that year came from 6,522,000 tons of crushed grapes (23% of world production). There is large-scale production of fruits, chiefly apples, pears, peaches, and cherries. Sericulture is also important. In 1991, France led the world in wine production, and ranked fifth in the production of wheat and eighth in corn production.

23ANIMAL HUSBANDRY

In 1992, farm animals included 20,928,000 head of cattle, 10,579,000 sheep, 12,384,000 hogs, 1,221,000 goats, and 340,000 horses. Poultry and rabbits are raised in large numbers, both for farm families and for city markets. Percheron draft horses are raised in northern France, range cattle in the central highlands and the flatlands west of the Rhône, and goats and sheep in the hills of the south. Meat production in 1992 included 1,780,000 tons of beef, 1,960,000 tons of pork, and 1,664,000 tons of poultry. In 1991, France ranked thirteenth in beef and veal production in the world.

Dairy farming flourishes in the rich grasslands of Normandy. Total cows' milk production in 1992 was 25,341,000 tons. France produces some 300 kinds of cheese; in 1992, production totaled about 1,522,700 tons. Butter production was 470,000 tons.

24FISHING

France's 4,716 km (2,930 mi) of coastline, dotted with numerous small harbors, has long supported a flourishing coastal and high-seas fishing industry. Total production in 1991 was 812,773 tons, including about 158,000 tons of oysters. Herring, skate, whiting, sole, mackerel, tuna, sardines, lobsters, and mussels make up the principal seafood catch, along with large quantities of cod, mostly from the fishing banks off northern North America, for centuries frequented by French fishermen.

25FORESTRY

Although much of the original forest cover was cut in the course of centuries, strict forest management practices and sizable reforestation projects during the last 100 years have restored French forests considerably. Since 1947, the government has subsidized the afforestation and replanting of 2.1 million hectares (5.2 million acres) of forest land along with thousands of miles of wood transport roads. The reforestation project in the Landes region of southwestern France has been particularly successful. About 66% of the forestland is covered with oak, beech, and poplar and 34% with resinous trees. There were some 14.8 million hectares (36.5 million acres) of forest in 1991. Production of roundwood in 1991 was 44.7 million cu m. In 1991, some 39,800 persons were engaged in forestry and logging.

[26]MINING

France is among the world's leading producers of coal. It also has sizable deposits of iron ore, antimony, bauxite, magnesium, pyrites, tungsten, and certain radioactive minerals. However, production of some of these resources has declined significantly. France is self-sufficient in salt, potash, and fluorspar. Reserves of lead and zinc are limited. In 1991, France was the fifth largest producer of uranium, at 2,907 metric tons. Due to low market prices, several uranium mines have recently been closed.

Coal mines are nationalized and are operated by Charbonnages de France, the French coal authority. The principal coal basins are in the north, in Lorraine, and in the Massif Central. Coal production (including lignite) decreased from a post–World War II high of over 60 million tons in 1958 to 25.6 million tons in 1975 and 12.3 million tons in 1991. Iron ore production fell from 49.7 million tons in 1975 to 29 million tons in 1980 and 7.4 million tons by 1991. Iron ore reserves are located principally in Lorraine. France is also a leading producer of bauxite (a mineral named after Les Baux, in the south of France), but production declined from 3.3 million tons in 1973 to 400,000 tons in 1991.

[27]ENERGY AND POWER

Small deposits of petroleum are located mainly in the Landes region. Production increased from 2.4 million tons in 1962 to 2.7 million tons in 1968; since then, however, production has fallen somewhat, and 1991 production revived to 2.8 million tons. Consumption, however, totaled 94.6 million tons in 1991. Production of natural gas in southwestern France totaled 4 million cu m in 1991, meeting only a small fraction of domestic requirements.

Primary energy sources in 1991 were oil, 35% (67% in 1973); coal, 9%; natural gas, 13%; nuclear fuels and hydroelectric power, 39%; and other sources (including solar power), 4%. During the 1950s, France became increasingly dependent on outside sources for petroleum. Although petroleum and natural gas continued to be produced in France itself, as they are today, the nation came to rely almost entirely on imports from oil fields in the dollar and sterling zones of the Middle East, putting a heavy strain on the country's foreign exchange reserves. Discoveries of large supplies of natural gas and petroleum in the Sahara changed the outlook radically; France in 1967 was able to meet almost half its fuel needs from countries within the franc zone. Petroleum production from the Saharan fields rose spectacularly from 8.7 million tons in 1960 to 53 million tons in 1970. Although France lost title to the Saharan deposits after the establishment of Algerian independence, arrangements were made with the Algerian government to keep up the flow of oil to France. France now receives most of its liquefied natural gas from Algeria.

Developments in the 1970s exposed the limitations of this strategy. Algeria took controlling interest in French oil company subsidiaries in 1971. The oil shocks of the mid- and late 1970s drove France's fuel and energy imports up; in 1975, fuel imports accounted for 22.9% of all imports. France began an energy conservation program in the mid-1970s; between 1973 and 1980, oil consumption increased by 7.2%. By 1980, fuel imports made up 26.6% of total imports. Consumption of petroleum declined by 9.4% in 1981 and 6.3% in 1982, in part because of the recession, but it continued to decline at a rate of around 4% a year through 1985. From 1986 to 1990, consumption increased by a total of only 4%; in 1991, consumption rose by 6%, but fell by 0.2% in

1992. In 1992, fuels accounted for 9.7% of total imports.

The burden of fossil fuel alternatives falls mainly, but not entirely, on nuclear power. A tidal power plant has been in operation at Rance, in Brittany, since 1967, and the world's first solar furnace was built at Odeillo in 1969. In addition, some dwellings were being equipped with solar converters, and some were being at least partially heated by geothermal sources. Since 1914, Paris has been burning its garbage to provide heat; by 1981, trash burning was supplying over 30% of the city's heating needs.

In 1991, net installed power capacity of thermal plants was 22.5 million kw; net installed capacity of hydroelectric plants was 24.9 million kw. Most major plants generating electricity are administered by Électricité de France, the state-owned power authority. Atomic energy is also controlled by the state. In 1991, net installed power capacity of nuclear plants amounted to 59.1 million kw. Although the Socialists had initially called for a freeze on nuclear power plant construction, most of the planned expansion of nuclear capacity (to 52,000 Mw by 1988) continued after the formation of a Socialist government in 1981. Of the total power production in 1991, 13.3% was produced by conventional thermal means, 13.9% by hydroelectric stations, and 72.8% by nuclear power plants. France was ranked second in 1991, behind the US, among producers of nuclear power, at 315 billion kwh. In 1991, France was the world's fifth largest producer of uranium, at an estimated 2,907 tons.

[28]INDUSTRY

Industry has expanded considerably since World War II, with particularly significant progress in the electronics, transport, processing, and construction industries. France is the fourth-leading industrial power, after the US, Japan, and Germany. In 1992, the industrial sector accounted for more than 31% of the labor force and over four-fifths of all exports. The state has long played an active role in French industry, but government involvement was greatly accelerated by a series of nationalization measures enacted by the Socialists in 1982. By 1983, about one-third of French industry—3,500 companies in all—was under state control. However, there was some privatization during 1986–88, later resumed in 1993, with 21 state-owned industries, banks, and insurance companies scheduled to be sold.

French ferrous metallurgy has long been one of the leaders in Europe. The steel industry, which employed some 77,300 workers in 1991 (down from 156,000 in 1979), suffered from the impact of worldwide recession in the early 1980s. In 1991, production included 18.5 million tons of crude steel and 12.8 million tons of pig iron. French plants produced 471,800 tons of aluminum.

The French automotive industry, which employed 356,200 workers in 1991, is one of the largest in the world. Some 3,190,000 automobiles were produced in 1991. The two leading companies are Peugeot and Renault, the latter state owned. In 1991, Renault, France's second largest company, had sales of $30 billion. The French aircraft industry, not primarily a mass producer, specializes in sophisticated design and experimental development. Some of its models, such as the Caravelle and the Mirage IV, have been used in over 50 countries. The aircraft industry employed 111,700 persons in 1991. Aérospatiale, among the world's leading makers of commercial aircraft, became a state company after World War II.

Chemicals, one of the fastest-growing industries in France, range from perfumes and cosmetics to such industrial materials as sulfuric acid. In 1991, chemical industries employed 97,600 persons. The electronics sector employed 214,400 people in 1991. In 1991, 2,549,000 television sets and 1,865,000 radios were produced. Refineries produced 82.1 million tons of petroleum products in 1991. The leading French firm by sales volume in 1991 was the government-owned oil giant Elf-Aquitaine ($37 billion), privatized in 1994.

The textile industry employed 168,700 workers in 1991. Production of textiles (in thousands of tons) in 1991 included cotton yarn, 153,800; wool yarn, 20,200; and synthetic fibers, 496,100. The food processing industry employed over 370,000 people in 1991. Products of this sector included, in 1991, 62 million hectoliters of wine produced, more than any other country.

The great concentrations of French industry are in and around Paris, in the coal basin of northern France, in Alsace and Lorraine, and around Lyon and Clermont-Ferrand. French industry, in general, is strong on inventiveness, inclined toward small-scale production of high-quality items, and reluctant in many branches to adopt modern methods of mass production. The French government offers subsidies and easy credit to firms undertaking relocation, reconversion, or plant modernization.

29SCIENCE AND TECHNOLOGY

French inventors played a pivotal role in the development of photography and the internal combustion engine; to French ingenuity the world also owes the first mechanical adding machine (1642), parachute (1783), electric generator (1832), refrigerator (1858), and neon lamp (1910). French industry has pioneered in the development of high-speed transportation systems—notably the supersonic Concorde and the TGV train—and French subway companies have built or provided equipment for mass-transit systems in Montreal, Mexico City, Rio de Janeiro, and other cities.

France is a leading exporter of nuclear technology and has developed the first commercial vitrification plant for the disposal of radioactive wastes by integrating them in special glass and then encasing the glass in stainless steel containers for burial. In 1965, France was the third nation, after the former USSR and the US, to launch its own space satellite. However, the French no longer launch their own satellites, preferring instead to contribute to the European Space Agency.

The Acádémie des Sciences, founded by Louis XIV in 1666, consists of eight sections: mathematics, physics, mechanics, astronomy, chemistry, cellular and molecular biology, animal and plant biology, and human biology and medical sciences. The Centre National de la Recherche Scientifique (CNRS), founded in 1939, controls more than 1,300 laboratories and research centers. In 1992, the CNRS employed nearly 10,000 research workers. In addition, there are well over 100 other scientific and technological academies, learned societies, and research institutes. In 1991, French government, industry, academic and nonprofit institutions spent 157 million francs on research and development. Research and development personnel in 1992 numbered 286,375 scientists and 296,572 engineers.

30DOMESTIC TRADE

The heart of French commerce, both domestic and foreign, is Paris. One-third of the country's commercial establishments are in the capital, and in many fields Parisian control is complete. The major provincial cities act as regional trade centers. The principal ports are Marseille, for trade with North Africa and with the Mediterranean and the Middle East; Bordeaux, for trade with West Africa and much of South America; and Le Havre, for trade with North America and northern Europe. Dunkerque and Rouen are important industrial ports.

In 1991, there were 2,678,088 workers in commerce. In 1992, metropolitan France had 53,613 wholesale enterprises, 379,240 retail firms, and 32,204 trade intermediaries. Supermarkets (7,420 in 1992, of which 950 were giant supermarket complexes), chain stores, and department stores have been increasing in number and in volume of sales. Among the 50 largest commercial companies in France are the department stores Au Printemps and Galeries Lafayette.

Business hours are customarily on weekdays from 9 AM to noon and from 2 to 6 PM. Normal banking hours are 9 AM to 4 PM, Monday–Friday. Most banks are closed on Saturdays; to serve a particular city or larger district, one bank will usually open Saturday mornings from 9 to noon. Most businesses close for three or four weeks in August.

Advertising in newspapers and magazines and by outdoor signs is widespread. A limited amount of advertising is permitted on radio and television. Trade fairs are held regularly in Paris and other large cities.

31FOREIGN TRADE

Leading French exports, by major categories, are capital goods (machinery, heavy electrical equipment, transport equipment, and aircraft), consumer goods (autos, textiles, and leather), and semifinished products (mainly chemicals, iron, and steel). Major imports are fuels, machinery and equipment, chemicals and paper goods, and consumer goods.

The French trade balance was favorable in 1961 for the first time since 1927; since then, however, imports have risen at a higher rate than exports. Trade deficits have thus generally increased since that time. From 1977 to 1985, the trade deficit nearly tripled. Among factors held responsible were heavy domestic demand for consumer products not widely produced in France, narrowness of the range of major exports, and a concentration on markets not ripe for expansion of exports from France, notably the EC and OPEC countries. In the following years, there was little change in the trade balance, but the deficit narrowed appreciably in 1992.

Germany continued to be France's most important trading partner, accounting for 18.7% of imports and 17.6% of exports in 1992. Other major trading partners are Italy, Belgium-Luxembourg, and the UK.

Principal trading partners in 1992 (in millions of francs) were as follows:

	EXPORTS	IMPORTS	BALANCE
Germany	215,519	236,072	−20,553
Italy	133,836	134,478	−642
Belgium-Luxembourg	112,923	108,909	4,014
UK	113,200	97,416	15,784
US	79,986	106,422	−26,436
Netherlands	59,857	64,176	−4,319
Spain	87,910	68,253	19,657
Switzerland	42,734	28,516	14,218
Sweden	12,417	18,751	−6,334
Portugal	20,396	14,261	6,135
Japan	22,730	51,700	−28,970
Other countries	325,997	334,980	−8,983
TOTALS	1,227,505	1,263,934	−36,429

32BALANCE OF PAYMENTS

Between 1945 and 1958, France had a constant deficit in its balance of payments. The deficit was financed by foreign loans and by US aid under the Marshall Plan, which totaled more than $4.5 billion. A 1958 currency reform devalued the franc by 17.5%, reduced quota restrictions on imports, and allowed for repatriation of capital; these measures, combined with increased tourist trade and greater spending by US armed forces in the franc zone, improved France's payments position.

With payments surpluses during most of the 1960s, gold and currency reserve holdings rose to $6.9 billion by the end of 1967. However, a massive deficit in 1968 led to another devaluation of the franc in 1969, and by 31 December 1969, gold and reserve holdings had dropped to $3.8 billion. After surpluses in 1970–72 raised international reserves to over $10 billion, price increases for oil and other raw materials resulted in substantial negative balances on current accounts in 1973 and 1974; because of this, France required massive infusions of short-term capital to meet its payments obligations.

Huge surpluses on the services account led to positive payments balances during 1977–80, when reserves rose by nearly $9.7 billion. After that, France's trade position deteriorated sharply. Foreign exchange reserves fell from $27,759 million as of March 1981 to $14,123 million by March 1983. To meet its payments obligation, France had to secure a $4 billion standby credit from international banks as well as loans from Sa'udi Arabia and the EC. During the mid-1980s, the trade deficit generally moderated; the current accounts balance recovered in 1985 from the heavy deficits of the past. In 1992, the merchandise trade account recorded a surplus of Fr31 billion, a large swing from the Fr30 billion deficit of 1990. Trade in industrial goods (including military equipment) and a surplus in the manufacturing sector (the first since 1986) were responsible for the boost in exports. In 1992 merchandise exports totaled $225,222 million and imports $223,561 million. The merchandise trade balance was $1,661 million. The following table summarizes France's balance of payments for 1991 and 1992 (in millions of US dollars):

	1991	1992
CURRENT ACCOUNT		
Goods, services, and income	959	12,608
Unrequited transfers	–7,979	–8,500
TOTALS	–7,020	4,109
CAPITAL ACCOUNT		
Direct investment	–8,783	–9,150
Portfolio investment	13,818	34,180
Other long-term capital	–2,839	–10,067
Other short-term capital	–7,680	–33,997
Other liabilities	665	11,519
TOTALS	332	–5,940
Errors and omissions	6,688	1,831
Total change in reserves	5,453	5,440

³³BANKING AND SECURITIES

The Banque de France, founded in 1800, came completely under government control in 1945. It is the bank of issue, sets discount rates and maximum discounts for each bank, regulates public and private finance, and is the Treasury depository. In 1945, a provisional government headed by Gen. de Gaulle also nationalized France's four largest commercial banks, and the state thus came to control 55% of all deposits. The four banks were Crédit Lyonnais, the Société Générale, the Banque Nationale pour le Commerce et l'Industrie, and the Comptoir National d'Escompte de Paris. In 1966, the Banque Nationale and the Comptoir merged and formed the Banque Nationale de Paris (BNP). The reserves of the BNP at the end of 1990 totaled Fr1,258.1 million; deposits stood at Fr13,559.7 million. At the same time, Crédit Lyonnais had reserves of Fr35,396 million and deposits of Fr1,380,725 million; and the Société Générale, reserves of Fr1,518.6 million and deposits of Fr78,214 million.

In 1982, Socialist President François Mitterrand nationalized 39 banks, bringing the state's control over deposits to 90%. Among leading banks nationalized in 1982 was the Crédit Commercial de France, but this bank and Société Générale were privatized in 1987. The government-owned Caisse Nationale de Crédit Agricole, the central agricultural credit association, with 94 member institutions. The Crédit Foncier grants medium- and long-term credits, fully guaranteed by mortgages or public securities.

The Ministry of Post, Telegraph, and Telephones (PTT), through its post offices, handles savings accounts. The money supply in France, as measured by M2, reached Fr2,446 billion as of 1992.

Public issues of stocks and bonds may be floated by corporations or by limited partnerships with shares. Publicly held companies that wish their stock to be traded on the exchange must receive prior authorization from the Stock Exchange Commission within the Ministry of Finance. In January 1962, the two principal Paris stock exchanges were merged. The six provincial exchanges specialize in shares of medium and small firms in their respective regions.

³⁴INSURANCE

Insurance is supervised by the government directorate of insurance, while reinsurance is regulated by the Ministry of Commerce. There were 607 insurance companies in 1989, of which 137 were life insurance companies. Premium income in 1987 amounted to US$50 billion, of which US$381.7 per capita was for life insurance and US$517.1 per capita for non-life. Total premiums accounted for 5.06% of the GDP.

In 1946, 32 major insurance companies were nationalized, and a central reinsurance institute was organized. All private insurance companies are required to place a portion of their reinsurance with the central reinsurance institute.

In 1991, life insurance in force totaled Fr9,453 billion.

³⁵PUBLIC FINANCE

The fiscal year runs from 1 January to 31 December. Deficits have been commonplace, but in recent years, efforts have been made to cut back on the growth of taxes and government spending and, since 1986, to remove major state enterprises from the expense of government ownership.

The French government had succeeded in progressively cutting the budget deficit until 1991, from 3.3% of GDP in 1985 to 1.9% in 1990. However, from 1991 to 1993 the sharp drop in economic growth led to a dramatic decline in revenues. Value-added tax receipts, which represent almost 60% of total central government revenues, declined largely due to weak consumption. In real terms, central government spending increased in 1991 less than 1%, and actually dropped in 1992. However, the deficit still soared to 1.8% of GDP in 1991, 3.3% in 1992, and was estimated at nearly 5% in 1993, the highest amount in over 20 years. Due to higher deficit and interest rates, interest payments as a percentage of central government spending increased from less than 8% in 1987 to more than 11% in 1992. Even though tax revenues have fallen more than expected, they have remained at approximately 44% of GDP, one of the highest rates among industrialized nations.

In 1989 France's external public debt stood at Fr29.4 billion. France's public debt management is market based and highly sophisticated. Servicing the overall national debt does not limit the national capacity to import.

³⁶TAXATION

Individual incomes are subject to a proportional tax, with tax rates indexed each year according to inflation. The top marginal rate on earned income was 56.8% in 1992.

The value-added tax (VAT), basically a sales tax on consumption, is assessed on the price of, or value added to, a product or service at each stage of its manufacture or distribution. In 1986, the normal rate of VAT was 18.6%, with reduced rate of 5.5% or 7% applied to most foodstuffs, books, medicines, and other basic items, and a luxury rate of 33.3% imposed on new cars, furs, tobacco products, phonograph records, and certain other items. The value-added tax applies to all imports. Levies imposed on business corporations include license taxes, organization taxes on initial capital and on capital stock increases, and taxes on industrial and commercial profits, distributed earnings, and sales volume. The basic corporate income tax rate was 34% in 1992. Various tax incentives are provided. The wealth tax was abolished in 1987. According to a 1987 OECD report, taxes accounted for about 45% of GDP.

37CUSTOMS AND DUTIES

Virtually all import duties are on an ad valorem c.i.f. basis. Minimum tariff rates apply to imports from countries that extend corresponding advantages to France. General rates, fixed at three times the minimum, are levied on imports from other countries. The recession of the early 1980s gave rise to calls for protectionist measures (e.g., against Japanese electronic equipment), but the Socialist government remained ostensibly committed to free trade principles. Observers noted, however, that cumbersome customs clearance procedures were being used to slow the entry of certain Japanese imports, notably videotape recorders, to protect French firms. France adheres to the EC's common external tariff and other uniform regulations for member nations. There is a standard 18.6% VAT on most imports.

38FOREIGN INVESTMENT

All direct investments in France require advance notification of—and in some cases approval by—the Treasury Department. Investments from other EC countries cannot be refused, but the department may specify whether the investment is to be financed from French or foreign sources. Direct foreign investment in France climbed from $6.5 billion in 1973 to $81.4 billion in 1992. The major investors were the US, Germany, and the UK.

39ECONOMIC DEVELOPMENT

Since World War II, France has implemented a series of economic plans, introduced to direct the postwar recovery period but later expanded to provide for generally increasing governmental direction of the economy. The first postwar modernization and equipment plan (1947–53) was designed to get the machinery of production going again; the basic economic sectors—coal, steel, cement, farm machinery, and transportation—were chosen for major expansion, and productivity greatly exceeded the target goals. The second plan (1954–57) was extended to cover all productive activities, especially agriculture, the processing industries, housing construction, and expansion of overseas production. The third plan (1958–61) sought, in conditions of monetary stability and balanced foreign payments, to achieve a major economic expansion, increasing national production by 20% in four years. After the successful devaluation of 1958 and an improvement in the overall financial and political situation, growth rates of 6.3% and 5% were achieved in 1960 and 1961, respectively. The fourth plan (1962–65) called for an annual rate of growth of between 5% and 6% and an increase of 23% in private consumption; the fifth plan (1966–70), for a 5% annual expansion of production, a 25% increase in private consumption, and the maintenance of full financial stability and full employment; and the sixth plan (1971–75), for an annual GDP growth rate of between 5.8% and 6% and growth of about 7.5% in industrial production. The sixth plan also called for increases of 31% in private consumption, 34% in output, and 45% in social security expenditure.

The seventh plan (1976–80) called for equalization of the balance of payments, especially through a reduction of dependency on external sources of energy and raw materials; a lessening of social tensions in France by a significant reduction in inequalities of income and job hierarchies; and acceleration of the process of decentralization and deconcentration on the national level in favor of the newly formed regions. Because of the negative impact of the world oil crisis in the mid-1970s, the targets of the seventh plan were abandoned in 1978, and the government concentrated on helping the most depressed sectors and controlling inflation.

In October 1980, the cabinet approved the eighth plan (1981–85). It called for development of advanced technology and for reduction of oil in overall energy consumption. After the Socialists came to power, this plan was set aside, and an interim plan for 1982–84 was announced. It aimed at 3% GDP growth and reductions in unemployment and inflation. When these goals were not met and France's international payments position reached a critical stage, the government in March 1983 announced austerity measures, including new taxes on gasoline, liquor, and tobacco, a "forced loan" equivalent to 10% of annual taxable income from most taxpayers, and restrictions on the amount of money French tourists could spend abroad. A ninth plan, established for the years 1984–88, called for reducing inflation, improving the trade balance, increasing spending on research and development, and reducing dependence on imported fuels to not more than 50% of total energy by 1990. The tenth plan, for 1989–92, gave as its central objective increasing employment. The main emphasis was on education and training, and improved competitiveness through increased spending on research and development.

French loans to its former African territories totaled CFA Fr50 billion by November 1972, when President Pompidou announced that France would cancel the entire amount (including all accrued interest) to lighten these countries' debt burdens. In 1991, official development assistance amounted to $7,526 million, or 0.62% of GNP. The major recipients of French aid in 1991 were, in addition to French dependencies, Côte d'Ivoire, Morocco, Senegal, Cameroon, Madagascar, Egypt, and Algeria.

40SOCIAL DEVELOPMENT

The Ministry of National Solidarity, created in May 1981, is in charge of social security, welfare, immigration, and social services. The social security fund is financed by contributions from both employers and employees, calculated on percentages of wages and salaries. A law of July 1966 made social insurance compulsory for the self-employed, thus adding 1.8 million persons to the social security system. In addition, ordinances of 1967, ratified in 1968, made voluntary insurance available to all persons living in France who are not affiliated with a compulsory or optional social security plan. By the early 1980s, virtually every person living in France was covered by some form of social assistance. As of 1988, France was tenth in the world in percentage of its budget spent on social security and housing (10%).

In addition to providing for the partial reimbursement of medical, pharmaceutical, and hospitalization expenses, health insurance guarantees the payment of cash benefits as partial compensation for loss of earnings during the period of disability. Maternity insurance provides for the payment of pharmaceutical, medical, surgical, and hospitalization expenses incurred during pregnancy, confinement, and postnatal treatment, as well as other benefits. Provided they fulfill certain legal requirements, unemployed workers receive daily payments not limited in time but reduced by 10% each consecutive year. Disability insurance pays a pension to the insured (but not to dependents) to compensate for the loss of earnings and costs of care. Old age insurance guarantees payment of a pension when the insured reaches age 65 (or at age 55 in special cases), provided the pensioner's contributions have been sufficient. Partial pension benefits are computed on the basis of years of coverage. Death insurance provides payment of a lump sum to the dependents of the insured.

Family allowances are paid to gainfully occupied heads of families to help them rear their children; the system is financed by a contribution paid solely by the employer. Monthly benefits are paid to employed heads of families having at least two dependent children. Maternity and prenatal allowances are also paid. Despite such pronatalist measures, the fertility rate for 1985–90 was only 1.8, less than the 2.1 considered necessary over the long term to maintain France's population at the present level. Induced abortions have been legal since 1975. In the mid-1980s, an estimated 79% of married women were using contraception. Women account for over one-third of the total labor force. The growth of the feminist movement in the 1970s led to the creation in 1974 of a special cabinet office for women's rights. Women's groups are active in lobbying for implementation of equal rights legislation. In 1992, the Penal Code was revised to include provisions stipulating up to one year in prison and up to the equivalent of us$20,000 in fines for workplace sexual harassment.

[41]HEALTH

Under the French system of health care, both public and private health care providers operate through centralized funding. Patients have the option of seeing a private doctor on a fee basis or going to a state-operated facility. Nearly all private doctors are affiliated with the social security system and the patients' expenses are reimbursed in part. Many have private health insurance to cover the difference. During the 1980s, there was a trend away from inpatient and toward outpatient care, with a growing number of patients receiving care at home.

In 1991, the financial condition of the French national health care system was poor. The social security system, which subsidizes approximately 75% of all health care costs, had Fr140 billion deficit by 1992.

Pharmaceutical consumption in France is among the highest in the OECD (exceeded only by Japan and the US). In 1992, the French government imposed a price-fixing mechanism on drugs.

The 1993 population of France was 57.5 million, with 742,000 births (a rate of 12.9 per 1,000 people). A study conducted from 1980 to 1993 indicated that 79% of France's married women (ages 15 to 49) used contraception.

As of 1989, France had approximately 169,051 physicians; 51,367 pharmacists; 37,931 dentists; and 10,705 midwives. From 1988 to 1992, there were 2.89 doctors per 1,000 people, with a nurse to doctor ratio of 1.6. In 1990, the population per physician was 350. In 1987, approximately 70% of physicians were operating in the private sector.

There were over 1,000 public hospitals with about 374,000 beds (1987), 2,700 private hospitals with 200,000 beds (1987), and 237 mental institutions (1982). There were also about 11,000 infants' and children's facilities of various kinds. In 1990, there were 9.9 beds per 1,000 people.

Life expectancy in 1992 averaged 77 years for men and women. The infant mortality rate was about 7 per 1,000 live births that same year. In 1993, the overall death rate was 9.1 per 1,000 people, with 523,000 deaths. Statistics indicate that from 1985 to 1990, major causes of death were: noncommunicable diseases (362 per 100,000); and injuries (76 per 100,000). In 1990, there were 16 reported cases of tuberculosis per 100,000 inhabitants.

Efforts to immunize children up to one year old between 1990 and 1992 were favorable: tuberculosis (80%); diphtheria, pertussis, and tetanus (95%); polio (85%); and measles (71%). Total health care expenditures in 1990 were $105,467,000.

[42]HOUSING

In 1984 there were 24,249,000 housing units in France, including 20,093,000 principal residences, 2,288,000 secondary residences, and 1,868,000 vacant units. By 1991, the total number of housing units had risen to 26,080,000. More than six million new dwellings were completed between 1970 and 1986. Living standards are high. As of May 1985, 97% of all French households had a refrigerator, over 90% a television set, 84% a washing machine, 73% an automobile, 35% a freezer, and 23% a dishwasher.

After World War II, in which 4.2 million dwellings were destroyed and 1 million damaged, the government took steps to provide inexpensive public housing. Annual construction rose steadily through the 1950s and 1960s; in 1970–75, housing construction of all types increased by an annual average of more than 6%. In 1975, the total number of new dwellings completed was

514,300. Construction slowed thereafter, and by 1992 the number had declined to 248,400.

In accordance with a law of 1953, industrial and commercial firms employing 10 or more wage earners must invest 1% of their total payroll in housing projects for their employees. These funds can finance either public or private low-cost housing. Concerns must undertake construction of low-cost projects either on their own responsibility or through a building concern to which they supply capital. Special housing allowances are provided for families who must spend an inordinately large share of their income on rent or mortgages.

[43]EDUCATION

The supreme authority over national education in France is the Ministry of Education. Education is compulsory for children from the age of 6 to 16 and is free in all state primary and secondary schools. Higher education is not free, but academic fees are low, and more than half of the students are excused from payment. Virtually the entire adult population is literate.

Since the end of 1959, private institutions have been authorized to receive state aid and to ask to be integrated into the public education system. In 1985, 17% of elementary-school children attended private schools, the majority of which are Roman Catholic. In Brittany especially, most children attend Catholic schools. Freedom of education is guaranteed by law, but the state exercises certain controls over private educational institutions, nearly all of which follow the uniform curriculum prescribed by the Ministry of Education. In 1991, the government budget for education was $43.9 billion (Fr247.8 billion).

In 1993, there were 6,610,046 pupils in primary schools (ages 6–11); 3,336,599 in secondary schools; and 2,230,512 in high schools. There are two levels of secondary instruction. The first, the collège, is compulsory; after four years of schooling are successfully completed, the student receives a national diploma (brevet des collèges). Those who wish to pursue further studies enter either the two-year lycée d'enseignement professionel or the three-year lycée d'enseignement général et technologique. The former prepares students for a certificate of vocational competence, the latter for the baccalauréat, which is a prerequisite for higher education. Choice of a lycée depends on aptitude test results.

University enrollment was 1,756,918 in 1991. There are 70 public universities within 26 académies, which now act as administrative units. Before the subdivision of these 26 units, the oldest and most important included Aix-Marseille (founded in 1409), Besançon (1691), Bordeaux (1441), Caen (1432), Dijon (1722), Grenoble (1339), Lille (1562), Montpellier (1180, reinstituted 1289), Nancy-Metz (1572), Paris (1150), Poitiers (1432), Rennes (1735, founded at Nantes 1461), Strasbourg (1538), and Toulouse (1229). The old University of Paris, also referred to as the Sorbonne, was the oldest in France and one of the leading institutions of higher learning in the world; it is now divided into 13 units, only a few of which are at the ancient Left Bank site. There are Catholic universities at Argers, Lille, Lyon, and Toulouse.

Besides the universities and specialized schools (such as École Normale Supérieure, which prepares teachers for secondary and postsecondary positions), higher educational institutions include the prestigious Grandes Écoles, which include the École Nationale d'Administration, École Normale Supérieure, Conservatoire National des Arts et Métiers, and École Polytechnique. Entrance is by competitive examination. Advanced-level research organizations include the Collège de France, École Pratique des Hautes Études, and École des Hautes Études en Sciences Sociales.

[44]LIBRARIES AND MUSEUMS

Paris, the leader in all intellectual pursuits in France, has the largest concentration of libraries and museums. The Bibliothèque

Nationale, founded in Paris in 1480, is one of the world's great research libraries, with a collection of 9 million books, as well as millions of manuscripts, prints, maps, periodicals, and other items of importance. The libraries of the 13-unit University of Paris system have collective holdings of more than 6 million volumes, and each major institution of higher learning has an important library of its own. The national archives are located in the Hôtel Rohan Soubise in Paris. In 1984 there were 94 central public libraries with a combined total of more than 413 million volumes; there were also 286 bookmobiles.

The Louvre, which underwent an extensive renovation in the 1980s, contains one of the largest and most important art collections in the world, covering all phases of the fine arts from all times and regions. The Cluny Museum specalizes in the arts and crafts of the Middle Ages. The Museum of Man is a major research center as well. The Centre National d'Art et de Culture Georges Pompidou opened in 1977 on the Beaubourg Plateau (Les Halles). Primarily a museum specializing in contemporary art, it also houses several libraries, children's workshops, music rooms, and conference halls. The Musée d'Orsay, a major new museum housing impressionist and postimpressionist paintings and many other works set in historical context, opened to the public in December 1986. Many of the 19th-century and 20th-century paintings in the Musée d'Orsay had previously been housed in the Musée du Jeu de Paume.

Most provincial cities have municipal libraries and museums of varying sizes. Many of the great churches, cathedrals, castles, and châteaus of France are national monuments.

45MEDIA

Postal, telephone, and telegraph systems are operated by the government under the direction of the Ministry of Post, Telegraph, and Telephones. Pneumatic tubes provide rapid delivery of letters in Paris. In 1991 there were 34,345,980 telephones.

The government-controlled Office de Radiodiffusion-Télévision Française was replaced in January 1975 by seven independent state-financed companies. A law of July 1982 allowed greater independence to production and programming organizations. Of the three state-owned television channels, TF-1, the oldest and largest, was privatized in 1987; a fourth, private channel for paying subscribers was started in 1984. Contracts were awarded in 1987 to private consortiums for fifth and sixth channels. In 1991, television sets numbered about 23.2 million. Under deregulation, many private radio stations have been established. In 1991 there were about 50.6 million radio receivers.

Traditionally, the French press falls into two categories. The presse d'information, including newspapers with the largest circulation, emphasizes news; the presse d'opinion, usually of higher prestige in literary and political circles but of much lower daily circulation, presents views on political, economic, and literary matters. The number of newspapers has consistently declined in the postwar period. Paris had only 14 dailies in 1986, compared with 28 in 1946. In 1991, there were 96 dailies in the country, and total circulation amounted to 9.3 million copies. Some of the important regional papers rival the Parisian dailies in influence and circulation.

The following table lists the estimated average daily circulation in 1991 of the leading newspapers:

	ORIENTATION	CIRCULATION
PARIS		
Le Figaro (m)	Moderate conservative; elite	433,500
Le Monde (e)	Independent; elite	382,000
Le Parisien Libéré (m)	Rightist; mass-appeal	365,660
France-Soir (e)	Mass-appeal	334,000
International Herald Tribune	English-language	209,000
La Croix (e)	Catholic	130,000
L'Humanité (m)	Communist	109,300

	ORIENTATION	CIRCULATION
PROVINCES		
Ouest-France (Rennes, m)	Mass-appeal	739,000
La Voix du Nord (Lille, m)	Conservative	381,000
Le Dauphiné Libéré (Grenoble, m)	Socialist	339,000
Sud-Ouest (Bordeaux, m)	Independent	339,000
La Dépêche du Midi (Toulouse, m)	Radical	260,000
Nice-Matin (Nice, m)	Radical independent	258,200

The Agence France-Presse is the most important French news service. It has autonomous status, but the government is represented on its board of directors. There are some 14,000 periodicals, of which the most widely read is the illustrated Paris-Match, with a weekly circulation of about 900,000. Several magazines for women also enjoy wide popularity, including Elle, (1991 circulation 360,000). Also for women are magazines publishing novels in serial form. The most popular political weeklies are L'Express (left-wing), with a circulation of about 555,300; the satirical Le Canard Enchaîné (left-wing), circulation 450,000; Le Nouvel Observateur (left-wing), circulation 372,300; and the newsmagazine Le Point (independent), circulation 310,900.

Filmmaking is a major industry, subsidized by the state. In 1991, 156 feature-length films were produced. There were 4,441 cinemas, with about 983,000 seats, in the same year.

46ORGANIZATIONS

The Confédération Générale d'Agriculture, originating in its present form in the resistance movement of World War II, has become the principal voice for farmers. The Société des Agriculteurs de France is considered the organization of landowners. Agricultural cooperatives, both producers' and consumers', are popular. There are also more than 44 large industrial trade organizations. Chambers of commerce function in the larger cities and towns. The International Chamber of Commerce has its headquarters in Paris, the national capital.

The Institute of France (founded in 1795) consists of five academies, including the famous French Academy (Académie Française). There are many scientific, artistic, technical, and scholarly societies and sports groups.

47TOURISM, TRAVEL, AND RECREATION

In 1991, France was the world's top tourist destination with an estimated 54.8 million overnight visitors, 49.8 million of them from other European countries. Receipts from tourism amounted to US$21.3 billion. Tourists need a valid passport and a visa to enter France; for a longer stay, police registration and a registration card (carte d'identité) are necessary.

France has countless tourist attractions, ranging from the museums and monuments of Paris (including the splendid Eiffel Tower, newly refurbished with glass elevators) to beaches on the Riviera and ski slopes in the Alps. More than 547,292 rooms with over 1 million beds in lodging establishments from small country inns to deluxe châteaus, accommodate both French and foreign tourists, with a 39.8% occupancy rate. Haute cuisine, hearty regional specialties, and an extraordinary array of fine wines attract gourmets the world over; the area between the Rhone River and the Pyrenees contain the largest single tract of vineyards in the world. In 1992 Euro Disneyland, 20 miles east of Paris, opened to great fanfare but was plagued by the European recession, a strong French franc, bad weather, and difficulty marketing itself to the French. Both the theme park and tourism in general are expected to receive a boost from the scheduled opening of the Channel Tunnel in 1994.

The most popular French sport is soccer (commonly called "le foot"). Other favorite sports are skiing, tennis, water sports, and bicycling. Between 1896 and 1984, France won 137 gold, 156 silver, and 158 bronze medals in the Olympic Games. Paris hosted the Summer Olympics in 1900 and 1924; the Winter

Olympics took place at Chamonix in 1924, Grenoble in 1968, and Albertville in 1992. Le Mans is the site of a world-class auto race.

⁴⁸FAMOUS FRENCH

Principal figures of early French history include Clovis I (466?–511), the first important monarch of the Merovingian line, who sought to unite the Franks; Charles Martel ("the Hammer," 689?–741), leader of the Franks against the Saracens in 732; his grandson Charlemagne (742–814), the greatest of the Carolingians, crowned emperor of the West on 25 December 800; and William II, Duke of Normandy (1027–87), later William I of England ("the Conqueror," r.1066–87). Important roles in theology and church history were played by St. Martin of Tours (b. Pannonia, 316?–97), bishop of Tours and founder of the monastery of Marmoutier, now considered the patron saint of France; the philosopher Pierre Abélard (1079–1142), traditionally regarded as a founder of the University of Paris but equally famous for his tragic romantic involvement with his pupil Héloïse (d.1164); and St. Bernard of Clairvaux (1090?–1153), leader of the Cistercian monastic order, preacher (1146) of the Second Crusade (1147–49), and guiding spirit of the Knights Templars. The first great writer of Arthurian romances was Chrétien de Troyes (fl.1150?).

The exploits of famous 14th-century Frenchmen were recorded by the chronicler Jean Froissart (1333?–1401). Early warrior-heroes of renown were Bertrand du Guesclin (1320–80) and Pierre du Terrail, seigneur de Bayard (1474?–1524). Joan of Arc (Jeanne d'Arc, 1412–31) was the first to have a vision of France as a single nation; she died a martyr and became a saint and a national heroine. Guillaume de Machaut (1300?–1377) was a key literary and musical figure. François Villon (1431–63?) was first in the line of great French poets. Jacques Coeur (1395–1456) was the greatest financier of his time. Masters of the Burgundian school of composers were Guillaume Dufay (1400?–1474), Gilles Binchois (1400?–1467), Jan Ockeghem (1430?–95), and Josquin des Prez (1450?–1521). Jean Fouquet (1415?–80) and Jean Clouet (1485–1541) were among the finest painters of the period. The flag of France was first planted in the New World by Jacques Cartier (1491–1557), who was followed by the founder of New France in Canada, Samuel de Champlain (1567–1635).

Modern French literature began during the 16th century, with François Rabelais (1490?–1553), Joachim du Bellay (1522–60), Pierre de Ronsard (1525–85), and Michel de Montaigne (1533–92). Ambroise Paré (1510–90) was the first of many surgeons, and Jacques Cujas (1522–90) the first of the great French jurists. Among the figures in the great controversy between Catholics and Protestants, Claude, duc de Guise (1496–1550), and Queen Catherine de Médicis (Caterina de'Medici, b.Florence, 1519–89) should be mentioned on the Catholic side, and Admiral Gaspard de Coligny (1519–72), a brilliant military leader, on the Protestant side. Two famous kings were Francis I (1494–1547) and Henry IV (Henry of Navarre, 1553–1610); the latter proclaimed the Edict of Nantes in 1598, granting religious freedom to his Protestant subjects. The poetic prophecies of the astrologer Nostradamus (Michel de Notredame, 1503–66) are still widely read today.

The era of Louis XIV ("le Roi Soleil," or "the Sun King," 1638–1715) was in many respects the golden age of France. Great soldiers—Henri de La Tour d'Auvergne, vicomte de Turenne (1611–75), François Michel Le Tellier, marquis de Louvois (1639–91), and Louis II de Bourbon, prince de Condé, called the Grand Condé (1621–86)—led French armies to conquests on many battlefields. Great statesmen, such as the cardinals Armand Jean du Plessis, duc de Richelieu (1585–1642), and Jules Mazarin (1602–61), managed French diplomacy and created the French Academy. Great administrators, such as Maximilien de Bethune, duc de Sully (1560–1641), and Jean-Baptiste Colbert (1619–83), established financial policies. Noted explorers in the New World were Jacques

Marquette (1637–75), Robert Cavalier, Sieur de La Salle (1643–87), and Louis Jolliet (1645–1700). Jean-Baptiste Lully (1632–87), Marc-Antoine Charpentier (1634–1704), and François Couperin (1668–1733) were the leading composers. Nicolas Poussin (1594–1665), Claude Lorrain (1600–1682), and Philippe de Champaigne (1602–74) were the outstanding painters. In literature, the great sermons and moralizing writings of Jacques Bénigne Bossuet, bishop of Meaux (1627–1704), and François Fénelon (1651–1715); the dramas of Pierre Corneille (1606–84), Molière (Jean-Baptiste Poquelin, 1622–73), and Jean Racine (1639–99); the poetry of Jean de La Fontaine (1621–95) and Nicolas Boileau-Despréaux (1636–1711); the maxims of François, duc de La Rochefoucauld (1613–80), and Jean de La Bruyère (1645–96); the fairy tales of Charles Perrault (1628–1703); the satirical fantasies of Savinien de Cyrano de Bergerac (1619–55); and the witty letters of Madame de Sévigné (1626–96) made this a great age for France. Two leading French philosophers and mathematicians of the period, René Descartes (1596–1650) and Blaise Pascal (1623–62), left their mark on the whole of European thought. Pierre Gassendi (1592–1655) was a philosopher and physicist; Pierre de Fermat (1601–55) was a noted mathematician.

1700–1900

During the 18th century, France again was in the vanguard in many fields. Étienne François, duc de Choiseul (1719–85), and Anne Robert Jacques Turgot (1727–81) were among the leading statesmen of the monarchy. Charles Louis de Secondat, baron de La Brède et de Montesquieu (1689–1755), and Jean-Jacques Rousseau (b.Switzerland, 1712–78) left their mark on philosophy. Denis Diderot (1713–84) and Jean Le Rond d'Alembert (1717–83) created the Great Encyclopedia (*Encyclopédie ou Dictionnaire Raisonné des Sciences, des Artes et des Métiers*). Baron Paul Henri Thiery d'Holbach (1723–89) was another philosopher. Jeanne Antoinette Poisson Le Normant d'Etoiles, marquise de Pompadour (1721–64), is best known among the women who influenced royal decisions during the reign of Louis XV (1710–74). French explorers carried the flag of France around the world, among them Louis Antoine de Bougainville (1729–1811) and Jean La Pérouse (1741–88). French art was dominated by the painters Antoine Watteau (1684–1721), Jean-Baptiste Chardin (1699–1779), François Boucher (1703–70), and Jean Honoré Fragonard (1732–1806) and by the sculptor Jean Houdon (1741–1828). Jean-Philippe Rameau (1683–1764) was the foremost composer. French science was advanced by Georges Louis Leclerc, Comte de Buffon (1707–88), zoologist and founder of the Paris Museum, and Antoine Laurent Lavoisier (1743–94), the great chemist. In literature, the towering figure of Voltaire (François Marie Arouet, 1694–1778) and the brilliant dramatist Pierre Beaumarchais (1732–99) stand beside the greatest writer on gastronomy, Anthelme Brillat-Savarin (1755–1826).

The rule of Louis XVI (1754–93) and his queen, Marie Antoinette (1755–93), and the social order they represented, ended with the French Revolution. Outstanding figures of the Revolution included Jean-Paul Marat (1743–93), Honoré Gabriel Riquetti, comte de Mirabeau (1749–91), Maximilien Marie Isidore Robespierre (1758–94), and Georges Jacques Danton (1759–94). Napoleon Bonaparte (1769–1821) rose to prominence as a military leader in the Revolution and subsequently became emperor of France. Marie Joseph Paul Yves Roch Gilbert du Motier, marquis de Lafayette (1757–1834), was a brilliant figure in French as well as in American affairs. This was also the period of the eminent painter Jacques Louis David (1748–1825) and of the famed woman of letters Madame Germaine de Staël (Anne Louise Germaine Necker, baronne de Staël-Holstein, 1766–1817).

During the 19th century, French science, literature, and arts all but dominated the European scene. Among the leading figures were Louis Jacques Mendé Daguerre (1789–1851), inventor of photography, and Claude Bernard (1813–78), the great physiologist. Other pioneers of science included Jean-Baptiste Lamarck (1744–1829) and Georges Cuvier (1769–1832) in zoology and paleontology, Pierre Laplace (1749–1827) in geology, André Marie Ampère (1775–1836), Dominique François Arago (1786–1853), and Jean Bernard Léon Foucault (1819–68) in physics, Joseph Louis Gay-Lussac (1778–1850) in chemistry, Camille Flammarion (1842–1925) in astronomy, and Louis Pasteur (1822–95) in chemistry and bacteriology. Louis Braille (1809–52) invented the method of writing books for the blind that bears his name. Auguste (Isidore Auguste Marie François Xavier) Comte (1798–1857) was an influential philosopher. Literary figures included the poets Alphonse Marie Louis de Lamartine (1790–1869), Alfred de Vigny (1797–1863), Alfred de Musset (1810–57), Charles Baudelaire (1821–67), Stéphane Mallarmé (1842–98), Paul Verlaine (1844–96), and Arthur Rimbaud (1854–91); the fiction writers François René Chateaubriand (1768–1848), Stendhal (Marie Henri Beyle, 1783–1842), Honoré de Balzac (1799–1850), Victor Marie Hugo (1802–85), Alexandre Dumas the elder (1802–70) and his son, Alexandre Dumas the younger (1824–95), Prosper Merimée (1803–70), George Sand (Amandine Aurore Lucie Dupin, baronne Dudevant, 1804–76), Théophile Gautier (1811–72), Gustave Flaubert (1821–80), the Goncourt brothers (Edmond, 1822–96, and Jules, 1830–70), Jules Verne (1828–1905), Alphonse Daudet (1840–97), Emile Zola (1840–1902), and Guy de Maupassant (1850–93); and the historians and critics François Guizot (1787–1874), Jules Michelet (1798–1874), Charles Augustin Sainte-Beuve (1804–69), Alexis de Tocqueville (1805–59), Ernest Renan (1823–92), and Hippolyte Adolphe Taine (1828–93). Charles Maurice de Talleyrand (1754–1838), Joseph Fouché (1763–1820), Adolphe Thiers (1797–1877), and Léon Gambetta (1838–82) were leading statesmen. Louis Hector Berlioz (1803–69) was the greatest figure in 19th-century French music. Other figures were Charles François Gounod (1818–93), composer of *Faust,* Belgian-born César Auguste Franck (1822–90), and Charles Camille Saint-Saëns (1835–1921). Georges Bizet (1838–75) is renowned for his opera *Carmen,* and Jacques Lévy Offenbach (1819–80) for his immensely popular operettas.

In painting, the 19th century produced Jean August Dominique Ingres (1780–1867), Ferdinand Victor Eugène Delacroix (1789–1863), Jean-Baptiste Camille Corot (1796–1875), Honoré Daumier (1808–79), and Gustave Courbet (1819–77), and the impressionists and postimpressionists Camille Pissarro (1830–1903), Édouard Manet (1832–83), Hilaire Germain Edgar Degas (1834–1917), Paul Cézanne (1839–1906), Claude Monet (1840–1926), Pierre Auguste Renoir (1841–1919), Paul Gauguin (1848–1903), Georges Seurat (1859–91), and Henri de Toulouse-Lautrec (1864–1901). Auguste Rodin (1840–1917) was the foremost sculptor; Frédéric Auguste Bartholdi (1834–1904) created the Statue of Liberty. The actresses Rachel (Elisa Félix, 1821–58) and Sarah Bernhardt (Rosine Bernard, 1844–1923) dominated French theater.

The Twentieth Century

In 20th-century political and military affairs, important parts were played by Georges Clemenceau (1841–1929), Ferdinand Foch (1851–1929), Henri Philippe Pétain (1856–1951), Raymond Poincaré (1860–1934), Léon Blum (1872–1950), Jean Monnet (1888–1979), Charles de Gaulle (1890–1970), Pierre Mendès-France (1907–82), François Maurice Marie Mitterrand (b.1916), and Valéry Giscard d'Estaing (b.1926). Winners of the Nobel Peace Prize include Frédéric Passy (1822–1912) in 1901, Benjamin Constant (1852–1924) in 1909, Léon Victor Auguste (1851–1925) in 1920, Aristide Briand (1862–1932) in 1926, Ferdinand Buisson (1841–1932) in 1927, and René Cassin (1887–1976) in

1968. Albert Schweitzer (1875–1965), musician, philosopher, physician, and humanist, a native of Alsace, received the Nobel Peace Prize in 1952. Famous scientists include the mathematician Jules Henri Poincaré (1854–1912); the physicist Antoine Henri Becquerel (1852–1908), a Nobel laureate in physics in 1903; chemist and physicist Pierre Curie (1859–1906); his wife, Polish-born Marie Sklodowska Curie (1867–1934), who shared the 1903 Nobel Prize for physics with her husband and Becquerel and won a Nobel Prize again, for chemistry, in 1911; their daughter Irène Joliot-Curie (1897–1956) and her husband, Frédéric Joliot-Curie (Jean-Frédéric Joliot, 1900–1958), who shared the Nobel Prize for chemistry in 1935; Jean-Baptiste Perrin (1870–1942), Nobel Prize winner for physics in 1926; the physiologist Alexis Carrel (1873–1944); and Louis de Broglie (1892–1987), who won the Nobel Prize for physics in 1929. Other Nobel Prize winners for physics include Charles Édouard Guillaume (1861–1938) in 1920, Alfred Kastler (1902–84) in 1966, and Louis Eugène Néel (b.1904) in 1970; for chemistry, Henri Moissan (1852–1907) in 1906, Victor Grignard (1871–1935) in 1912, and Paul Sabatier (1854–1941) in 1912. Also, in physiology or medicine: in 1907, Charles Louis Alphonse Laveran (1845–1922); in 1913, Charles Robert Richet (1850–1935); in 1928, Charles Jules Henri Nicolle (1866–1936); in 1965, François Jacob (b.1920), André Lwoff (b.1902), and Jacques Monod (1910–76); and in 1980, Jean-Baptiste Gabriel Dausset (b.1916). The philosopher Henri Bergson (1859–1941) received the 1927 Nobel Prize for literature. Émile Durkheim (1858–1917) was a founder of modern sociology. Pierre Teilhard de Chardin (1881–1955), a Jesuit, was both a prominent paleontologist and an influential theologian. Claude Lévi-Strauss (b.Belgium, 1908) is a noted anthropologist, and Fernand Braudel (1902–85) was an important historian.

Honored writers include Sully-Prudhomme (René François Armand, 1839–1907), winner of the first Nobel Prize for literature in 1901; Frédéric Mistral (1830–1914), Nobel Prize winner in 1904; Edmond Rostand (1868–1918); Anatole France (Jacques Anatole Thibaut, 1844–1924), Nobel Prize winner in 1921; Romain Rolland (1866–1944), Nobel Prize winner in 1915; André Paul Guillaume Gide (1869–1951), a 1947 nobel laureate; Marcel Proust (1871–1922); Paul Valéry (1871–1945); Colette (Sidonie Gabrielle Claudine Colette, 1873–1954); Roger Martin du Gard (1881–1958), Nobel Prize winner in 1937; Jean Giraudoux (1882–1944); François Mauriac (1885–1970), 1952 Nobel Prize winner; Jean Cocteau (1889–1963); Louis Aragon (1897–1982); André Malraux (1901–76); Jean-Paul Sartre (1905–80), who received the 1964 Nobel Prize; Simone Lucie Ernestine Marie Bertrand de Beauvoir (1908–86); Simone Weil (1909–43); Jean Genet (1910–86); Jean Anouilh (1910–87); Albert Camus (1913–60), Nobel Prize winner in 1957; Claude Simon (b.1913), a 1985 Nobel laureate; Marguerite Duras (b.1914); and Roland Barthes (1915–80). Romanian-born Eugene Ionesco (b.1912) and Irish-born Samuel Beckett (b.1906) have become writers in France. Significant composers include Gabriel Urbain Fauré (1845–1924), Claude Achille Debussy (1862–1918), Erik Satie (1866–1925), Albert Roussel (1869–1937), Maurice Ravel (1875–1937), Francis Poulenc (1899–1963), Olivier Messiaen (b.1908), and composer-conductor Pierre Boulez (b.1925). The sculptor Aristide Maillol (1861–1944) and the painters Henri Matisse (1869–1954), Georges Rouault (1871–1958), Georges Braque (1882–1963), Spanish-born Pablo Picasso (1881–1974), Russian-born Marc Chagall (1887–1985), and Jean Dubuffet (1901–85) are world famous.

Of international renown are actor-singers Maurice Chevalier (1888–1972), Yves Montand (Ivo Livi, b.1921), and Charles Aznavour (b.1924); actor-director Jacques Tati (Jacques Tatischeff, 1907–82); actors Charles Boyer (1899–1978), Jean-Louis Xavier Trintignant (b.1930), and Jean-Paul Belmondo (b.1933); actresses Simone Signoret (Simone Kaminker, 1921–85) and

Jeanne Moreau (b.1928); singer Edith Piaf (1915–63); master of mime Marcel Marceau (b.1923); and directors Georges Méliès (1861–1938), Abel Gance (1889–1981), Jean Renoir (1894–1979), Robert Bresson (b.1901), René Clément (b.1913), Eric Rohmer (Jean-Marie Maurice Scherer, b.1920), Alain Resnais (b.1922), Jean-Luc Godard (b.1930), Louis Malle (b.1932), and François Truffaut (1932–84).

⁴⁹DEPENDENCIES

French overseas departments include French Guiana, Guadeloupe, Martinique, and Saint-Pierre and Miquelon (described in the *Americas* volume under French American Dependencies) and Réunion (in the *Africa* volume under French African Dependencies). French overseas territories and collectivities include French Polynesia, French Southern and Antarctic Territories, New Caledonia, and Wallis and Futuna (see French Asian Dependencies in the *Asia* volume), and Mayotte (in the *Africa* volume). The inhabitants of French overseas departments and territories are French citizens, enjoy universal suffrage, and send elected representatives to the French Parliament.

⁵⁰BIBLIOGRAPHY

Agulhon, Maurice. *The French Republic, 1879–1992.* Oxford, UK; Cambridge, Mass.: B. Blackwell, 1993.

Aplin, Richard. *A Dictionary of Contemporary France.* London: Hodder & Stoughton, 1993.

Ardagh, John. *Cultural Atlas of France.* New York, NY: Facts on File, 1991.

Bell, Davis S. *Contemporary French Political Parties.* New York: St. Martin's, 1982.

Brogan, Denis. *The French Nation, from Napoleon to Pétain.* New York: Harper, 1957.

Cerny, Philip G. (ed.). *Social Movements and Protest in France.* New York: St. Martin's Press, 1982.

Chambers, Frances. *France.* Denver, Colo.: Clio Press, 1990.

Clough, Shepard B. *France: A History of National Economics, 1789–1939.* New York: Scribner's, 1939.

Cobban, Alfred. *A History of Modern France.* 3 vols. Harmondsworth and Baltimore: Penguin, 1965.

Cook, Don. *Charles De Gaulle: a Biography.* New York: G.P. Putnam's, 1983.

Cook, Malcolm (ed.). *French Culture Since 1945.* New York: Longman, 1993.

Corbett, James. *Through French Windows: an Introduction to France in the Nineties.* Ann Arbor, Mich.: University of Michigan Press, 1994.

Duby, Georges. *The Age of the Cathedrals: Art and Society, 980–1420.* Chicago: University of Chicago Press, 1981.

Evans, E. Estyn. *France: An Introductory Geography.* New York: Praeger, 1966.

Ewert, Alfred. *The French Language.* London: Faber & Faber, 1947.

Frears, J. R. *France in the Giscard Presidency.* Boston: Allen & Unwin, 1981.

Gildea, Robert. *The Past in French History.* New Haven: Yale University Press, 1994.

Goubert, Pierre. *The Ancien Régime: French Society, 1600–1750.* New York: Harper & Row, 1974.

Gough, Hugh and John Horne. *De Gaulle and Twentieth-century France.* New York: Edward Arnold, 1994.

Graham, Bruce Desmond. *Choice and Democratic Order: the French Socialist Party, 1937–1950.* New York: Cambridge University Press, 1994.

Greene, Nathanael. *From Versailles to Vichy: The Third French Republic, 1919–1940.* Arlington Heights, Ill.: Harlan Davidson, 1970.

Harrison, Michael M. *The Reluctant Ally: France and Atlantic Security.* Baltimore: Johns Hopkins University Press, 1981.

Harvey, Sir Paul, and Janet E. Heseltine (eds.). *The Oxford Companion to French Literature.* Oxford: Clarendon, 1959.

Heywood, Colin. *The Development of the French Economy, 1750–1914 the Economic History Society.* Houndmills, Eng.: Macmillan, 1992.

Hirsch, Arthur. *The French New Left: An Intellectual History from Sartre to Gorz.* Boston: South End, 1981.

Hollifield, James F. and George Ross (eds.). *Searching for the New France.* New York: Routledge, 1991.

Jackson, John Hampden (ed.). *A Short History of France from Early Times to 1958.* Cambridge: Cambridge University Press, 1959.

Keating, M. J. *Decentralisation and Change in Contemporary France.* Aldershot: Gower, 1986.

Lefebvre, Georges. *Napoleon: From Eighteen Brumaire to Tilsit, 1799–1807.* New York: Columbia University Press, 1969.

——. *Napoleon: From Tilsit to Waterloo, 1807–1815.* New York: Columbia University Press, 1969.

——. *The French Revolution.* 2 vols. New York: Columbia University Press, 1962–64.

Melitz, Jacques, and Charles Wyplosz (eds.). *The French Economy: Theory and Policy.* Boulder, Colo.: Westview, 1985.

Mitterrand, François. *The Wheat and the Chaff.* New York: Seaver, 1982.

Northcutt, Wayne. *The French Socialist and Communist Party Under the Fifth Republic, 1958–81.* New York: Irvington, 1985.

——. *Mitterrand: A Political Biography.* New York: Holmes & Meier, 1992.

Padover, Saul K., et al. *French Institutions: Values and Politics.* Stanford, Calif.: Stanford University Press, 1954.

Pinchemel, Philippe. *France: A Geographical, Social, and Economic Survey.* New York: Cambridge University Press, 1986.

Sutherland, Donald. *France: 1789–1815: Revolution and Counterrevolution.* Oxford: Oxford University Press, 1986.

Sydenham, M. J. *The First French Republic, 1792–1804.* Berkeley: University of California Press, 1974.

Thompson, James Matthew. *The French Revolution.* New York: Oxford University Press, 1945.

Tuppen, John N. *France under Recession, 1981–1986.* Albany: State University of New York Press, 1988.

Vinen, Richard Charles. *The Politics of French Business, 1936–1945.* New York: Cambridge University Press, 1991.

Weber, Eugen Joseph. *My France: Politics, Culture, Myth.* Cambridge, Mass.: Belknap Press of Harvard University Press, 1991.

Winchester, Hilary P. M. *Contemporary France.* New York: J. Wiley & Sons, 1993.

Wolf, John B. *Louis the Fourteenth of France.* New York: Norton, 1974.

Zeldin, Theodore. *France, 1848–1945.* 2 vols. Oxford: Clarendon Press, 1973–77.

GEORGIA

Republic of Georgia
Sakartveld Respublika

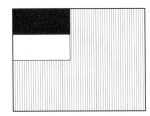

CAPITAL: T'bilisi (Tbilisi).

FLAG: Maroon field with small rectangle in upper hoist side corner; rectangle divided horizontally with black on top, white below.

ANTHEM: *National Anthem of the Republic of Georgia.*

MONETARY UNIT: The lari has not yet been issued since the introduction of government coupons began in April 1993. The coupons have replaced the Russian rouble (R) as the official currency.

WEIGHTS AND MEASURES: The metric system is in force.

HOLIDAYS: New Year's Day, 1–2 January; Christmas, 7 January; Independence Day, 26 May; St. George's Day, 22 November.

TIME: 3 PM = noon GMT.

¹LOCATION, SIZE, AND EXTENT

Georgia is located in southeastern Europe, bordering the Black Sea, between Turkey and Russia. Comparatively, the area occupied by Georgia is slightly larger than the state of South Carolina, with a total area of 69,700 sq km (26,911 sq mi). Georgia shares boundaries with Russia on the N and E, Azerbaijan on the E and S, Armenia and Turkey on the S, and the Black Sea on the W. Georgia's boundary length totals 1,771 km (1,100 mi). Its capital city, T'bilisi, is located in the southeastern part of the country.

²TOPOGRAPHY

The topography of Georgia is mainly mountainous, with the great Caucasus Mountains in the north and lesser Caucasus Mountains in the south. The Kolkhida Lowland opens to the Black Sea in the west and the Kura River basin lies in the east. Good soils occur in the river valley flood plains and in the foothills of the Kolkhida Lowland.

³CLIMATE

Georgia's climate along the Black Sea coast is Mediterranean. Farther in land the climate is continental, with warm summers and cold winters. July's mean temperature is 23°C (73.8°F). The mean temperature in January is -3°C (27.3°F). The annual rainfall in Georgia is 51 cm (20 in).

⁴FLORA AND FAUNA

The country's land is composed of gently rolling plains. The Caucasus Mountains in Georgia begin a series of high mountains in Central Asia. The subtropical zone of the Black Sea coast of the Caucasus Mountains has a distinctive vegetation: woods of black alder, oak, elm, and beech with a profusion of lianas and an admixture of evergreens. Mountain goats, Caucasian goats, Caucasian antelope, European wild boar, porcupine, and the leopard inhabit the Caucasus, and reptiles and amphibious creatures abound.

⁵ENVIRONMENT

The most significant environmental problems facing Georgia are land and water pollution. In 1994, 70% of the water was unsafe. Pesticides from agricultural areas have significantly contaminated the soil.

⁶POPULATION

The population of Georgia was 5,443,359 in 1989. The official estimate at the beginning of 1991 was 5,471,000. A population of 5,792,000 is forecasted for 2000, based on a crude birthrate of 14.9 per 1,000 people, a crude death rate of 8.8, and a natural increase of 6.1 for 1995–2000. The estimated population density at the beginning of 1991 was 78 per sq km (203 per sq km). The population of T'bilisi was estimated at 1,268,000 at the start of 1990. Kútáisi had an estimated population of 236,000 and Rustavi, 160,000.

⁷MIGRATION

Net emigration to other Soviet republics was only 5,600 during 1979–88. The number rose to 28,800 in 1989 and 39,900 in 1990. As many as 200,000 Georgians may have fled the fighting in Abkhazia in 1993. About 20,000 Georgians also fled the fighting in the autonomous region of South Ossetia in 1992.

⁸ETHNIC GROUPS

The population was 70% Georgian in 1989. The leading minorities were Armenian, 8%; Russian, 6%; Azerbaijani, 6%; Ossetian, 3%; Greek, 2%; Abkhazian, 2%; and Ukrainian, 1%.

⁹LANGUAGES

Georgian is a South Caucasian language called Kartveli by its speakers. There is no article and a single declension with six cases. The alphabet is a phonetic one with 33 symbols. Georgian literature dates from the 5th century AD. In addition to Georgian, Abkhaz, Ossetian, Armenian, Azari, Russian, and Greek are spoken.

¹⁰RELIGIONS

Georgia has existed as a state on a sporadic basis since classical times. In the 4th century AD Christianity enjoyed brief status as the official religion, but successive conquests by Mongols, Turks, and Persians left Georgia with a complex and unsettled ethnic and religious heritage.

Statistics available after the declaration of Georgian independence in 1991 reveal that the majority of the population is Christian (65%), primarily members of the Georgian Orthodox Church. There are also significant Muslim populations in various

161

ethnic groups (11%), as well as Russian and Armenian Orthodox, Roman Catholic (1%), and, in 1990, some 23,000 Jews.

[11]TRANSPORTATION

Railroads in Georgia consist of 1,570 km (975 mi) of track (not
including industrial lines). Railways serve primarily as connections to the Black Sea for inland cities like T'bilisi, Chiat'ura,
Jvari, and Tkvarcheli. Highways in 1990 totaled 33,900 km
(21,100 mi), 87% of which were hard-surfaced. The maritime
fleet of 54 ships (of 1,000 GRT or over) had a capacity of
715,802 GRT in 1991. Batumi and Poti are the principal Black
Sea ports.

[12]HISTORY

The first Georgian state can be traced to the 4th century BC.
Throughout its history Georgia has been conquered by the
Romans, Iranians, the Arabs, the Turks, the Mongols and the
Hordes of Tamerlane. Georgia did enjoy independence for short
periods of time from the 6th to the 12th centuries AD. The Mongols invaded and conquered Georgia by 1236. Later the Ottoman
and Persian empires competed for control of the region. Western
Georgia became a Russian protectorate in 1783. All of Georgia
was absorbed directly in the Russian empire during the 19th
century.

During the tumult of the Russian revolution, Georgia declared
its independence on 26 May 1918. Twenty-two countries recognized this new state, including Soviet Russia. The Red Army
invaded in February 1921 and Georgia's brief independence came
to an end.

Georgia's first multiparty elections were held in October 1990,
during the era of Gorbachev's perestroika in the Soviet Union. On
31 March 1991 the electorate endorsed independence in a referendum. Former dissident Zviad Gamsakhurdia was elected president in May 1991.

Gamsakhurdia's policies were increasingly criticized for being
dictatorial. He was accused of arresting and harassing political
prisoners, censoring the press and sponsoring laws that gave him
almost unlimited powers. These criticisms culminated with a
revolt that began on 21 December 1991 in T'bilisi. The revolt
continued for three weeks until Gamsakhurdia was expelled from
the parliament building.

Gamsakhurdia's opponents set up a provisional government
and in March 1992 invited former Soviet Foreign Minister Eduard Shevardnadze to be its leader (Shevardnadze had been the
Communist Party boss of Georgia from 1972 to 1985). Since the
beginning of 1992, Georgia has experienced secessionist movements, civil war, and economic collapse.

Georgia is a primarily Orthodox Christian country. There are
three regions within Georgia, though, which are predominantly
Muslim, or were so historically: South Ossetia, Abkhazia, and
Ajaria.

Although the Abkhaz are now a small minority within the
region, they have fought to secede from Georgia. This situation
culminated in 1993 when Abkhaz forces attacked Sokhumi, the
region's capital, reportedly with Russian military assistance. During the fall of 1993, Georgian forces were expelled from the
region. On 1 December, both sides signed a Memorandum of
Understanding intended to solve the conflict. It is not clear to
what extent Abkhaz or Russian forces are now running the
breakaway region.

Georgian forces have also battled secessionists in South Ossetia who want to join their region with North Ossetia, which is
inside the Russian Federation. Ajaria, however, has remained relatively calm.

After the loss of Abkhazia, civil war broke out again in Georgia itself during the latter part of 1993. Ousted President Gamsakhurdia and his supporters launched a rebellion in western

Georgia which was only defeated when Russia came to Shevardnadze's aid after he agreed to join the CIS.

[13]GOVERNMENT

Georgia is currently using its 1921 constitution. Shevardnadze,
though, is pushing for the adoption of a new constitution giving
the president additional powers.

A unicameral National Parliament with 234 seats was elected
in 1992; this body elected Shevardnadze as its chairman. A
November 1992 law proclaimed the chairman of the parliament
also to be president. The provisional government also has a prime
minister and cabinet of ministers that are appointed by the president and report directly to him.

[14]POLITICAL PARTIES

Communist Party deputies were banned from the legislature on 8
October 1991 when Gamsakhurdia was still in power.

A heterogeneous coalition of parties was created to overthrow
the Gamsakhurdia government. Since then, many of the members
of this coalition have maintained a role in the Provisional Government. Some of the most influential are the National Democratic Party, the National Independence Party, Charter 91, the
All-Georgian Merab Kostava Society, the Green Party, and others.
Many paramilitary organizations have a great influence on the
politics of Georgia even though they are not registered political
parties.

[15]LOCAL GOVERNMENT

Georgia had three autonomous republics: Abkhazia, South Ossetia, and Ajaria. The Georgian government has lost control over
Abkhazia, and has established direct rule over South Ossetia.

[16]JUDICIAL SYSTEM

Georgia's current legal system retains traces of the pre-Soviet era,
the Soviet period, the Gamsakhurdia presidency, and the State
Council period. Courts include district courts, a T'bilisi city
court, a supreme court in each of the two autonomous republics,
and the highest level Supreme Court of the Republic.

The judiciary remains subject to political pressures and other
influences. The supervisory role of the procuracy further compro-
mises the independence of the judiciary. The procuracy, for example, retains the Soviet-era prerogative to suggest that the Supreme
Court reconsider its own decisions.

[17]ARMED FORCES

Awash with civil strife and armed communal militias, Georgia
has a population of 500,000 men with military experience, but
no national army. It plans to have a conscripted army of 20,000,
supported by a national guard of 13,000. Only 3,000 armed
members of the national guard now serve the government. Russia
has a 20,000-man army corps and tactical air force in Georgia
awaiting repatriation. Only one Russian airborne battalion is
officially committed to peacekeeping. There are no reliable figures on defense spending available.

[18]INTERNATIONAL COOPERATION

Georgia was admitted to the UN on 21 July 1992. The country is
a member of the CSCE, IMF, and the World Bank, and Georgia is
applying for membership in other international organizations.
Georgia joined the CIS in 1993.

[19]ECONOMY

Georgia's mild climate makes it an important agricultural producer, raising a growing range of sub-tropical crops (including
tea, tobacco, citrus fruits, and flowers) in the coastal region and
exporting them to the northern republics in return for manufactured goods. Georgia supplied almost all of the former Soviet

LOCATION: 42°0′N; 44°0′E. BOUNDARY LENGTHS: Total boundary lengths, 1,461 km (908 mi); Armenia, 164 km (102 mi); Azerbaijan, 322 km (200 mi); Russia, 723 km (45 mi); Turkey, 252 km (157 mi).

Union's citrus fruits and tea, and much of its grape crop. The country has deposits of manganese, coal, iron ore, and lead, and a number of oil refineries operate in Batumi.

The economy, based largely on the country's mineral deposits and agricultural resources, has been slowed by political unrest.

20INCOME

In 1992, the GNP was $4,659 million at current prices, or $850 per capita. For the period 1985–92 the average inflation rate was 33.7%.

In 1992, the GDP was $4,660 million in current US dollars.

21LABOR

About 30% of the 2.8 million persons in the labor force are engaged in agriculture, with another 18% in industry. Since over half of Georgia's exports are agricultural products, the rapid privatization of farms which began in 1992 is expected to eventually strengthen the agricultural sector. Over 60% of farming lands had been distributed by mid-1993.

Employees have the right to form or join unions freely. A confederation of independent trade unions has emerged with the abandonment of old centralized Soviet trade unions, and some independent branch trade unions have emerged as well. Unions are neither required to form a single central trade union federa-

tion nor to register with government bodies. There were several politically motivated strikes in 1992. Wages are still primarily established by government bodies.

The minimum employment age is 14, and the standard workweek is 41 hours. The minimum wage has recently been adjusted upward by the government on a monthly basis to keep pace with hyperinflation.

22AGRICULTURE

About 11% of Georgia's total land area was considered arable before the dissolution of the Soviet Union. Since independence in April 1991, Georgian agriculture has become much more associated with the private sector; more than 60% of agricultural land is now privately owned. In 1992, agriculture accounted for 18.1% of GDP and 29% of NMP.

During the Soviet era, Georgia produced almost the entire citrus and tea crop and most of the grape crop for the entire Soviet Union. In 1992, production levels (in thousands of tons) included cereal grain, 459; tea, 100; vegetables, 820; fruit (excluding grapes), 24; and grapes, 550.

23ANIMAL HUSBANDRY

Meadows and pastures account for about 30% of the Georgian land area. In 1992, the livestock population included sheep,

1,400,000; cattle, 1,100,000; pigs, 850,000; and chickens, 19,000,000. Beef production in 1992 totaled some 45,000 tons; pork, 62,000 tons; and chicken, 20,000 tons. About 500,000 tons of milk were produced in 1992, as were 31,900 tons of eggs.

As of mid-1993, there was a temporary ban on the export of dairy products (including milk), cattle and poultry, meat and meat products, and leather. Georgia does not produce enough meat and dairy products to satisfy domestic demand.

24FISHING

The Black Sea and Kura River provide the domestic catch, but are heavily polluted. Commercial fishing is not a significant contributor to the economy.

25FORESTRY

About 3.7% of Georgia is forested. Production is primarily for domestic use; in 1990, paper and wood product exports comprised 1.3% of all exports by value in 1990.

26MINING

Georgia has a number of mineral resources, particularly arsenic, barite, copper, ferroalloys, lead-zinc, and manganese. The Madneuli region (west of Shaumyani) is a main site of barite, copper, and lead-zinc mining; manganese comes from the Chia'tura basin.

27ENERGY AND POWER

In 1992, electricity production amounted to 9.3 billion kwh. The two major power plants are a thermal plant at T'bilisi (with a capacity of 1,280,000 kw) and the Enguri hydroelectric plant (with a 1,325,000 kw capacity). Consumption of electricity in 1992 totaled 11.7 billion kwh.

Imports fulfill about 75% of Georgia's energy requirements. Oil comes primarily from Azerbaijan, natural gas and electricity from Russia.

Georgia plans on utilizing its Black Sea ports to become a significant transshipment point for oil produced by Azerbaijan (and the other republics of central Asia) which is destined for Eastern Europe. Additionally, improved ties with Iran will reduce dependence on energy imports from Russia, from which Georgia is trying to economically distance itself. Such an agreement might, in the future, lead to the extension of Iranian oil and natural gas pipelines that would run from Georgia through Azerbaijan.

Georgia is one of the 12 former Soviet republics to found the Intergovernmental Council on Oil and Gas (ICOG), which stresses international cooperation in the oil and natural gas industry and will entitle members to receive Russian energy resources in exchange for investment in Russia's oil and natural gas industries.

28INDUSTRY

Heavy industry, based on the country's mineral resources, predominates, and includes metallurgy, construction materials, and machine building. Light industry includes fund processing, beverage production, consumer durables, garments, and oil-processing.

29SCIENCE AND TECHNOLOGY

The Georgian Academy of Sciences has departments of mathematics and physics, earth sciences, applied mechanics and control processes, chemistry and chemical technology, agriculture science problems, biology, and physiology and experimental medicine. Georgia has 13 research institutes conducting mainly medical research. Seven colleges and universities offer degrees in basic and applied sciences.

30DOMESTIC TRADE

The war in Abkhazia severely disrupted domestic trade in 1993. Organized crime has allegedly acquired a virtual stranglehold on domestic gasoline supplies.

31FOREIGN TRADE

Georgia is heavily dependent on energy imports from other republics, especially Russia and Turkmenistan. External trade constituted 43% of the GDP in 1988–90. In 1988, total imports were valued at 5,300 million rubles, and exports at 3,400 million rubles.

32BALANCE OF PAYMENTS

As of 1992, Georgia's ability to earn foreign exchange depended upon the resolution of internal conflict, since several ports, highways, and railroads providing linkage for trade were blocked. Georgia's potential for exporting to hard currency markets is largely unknown.

33BANKING AND SECURITIES

The National Bank of Georgia, the state's central bank, was founded in 1991. At present, the banking system consists of the specialized banks of the former USSR and about 60 private commercial banks. The legal status of the Foreign Trade Finance Bank, (VEB-Georgia) is currently being redefined. It in not issuing letters of credits at present. The specialized government commercial banks were formed from the specialized banks of the former Soviet Union in 1991. This system is the core of the Georgian banking system. These banks presently provide more than 95% of total bank credit to the economy. VEB-Georgia is, in principle, an independent bank able to engage in all kinds of commercial banking operations. In practice, however, VEB-Georgia continues to operate as if it were a branch of VEB-Moscow. The bank was established in T'bilisi in 1989 to carry out all foreign exchange banking transactions in Georgia and to help domestic producers engaged in international trade operations. VEB-Georgia is now using correspondent accounts of banks (other than VEB) located in Moscow, but expects to open its own correspondent accounts overseas in the near future, enabling the rapid transfer of funds internationally.

Other commercial banks include the Agricultural Bank (1991), the Bank of Industry and Construction (1991), Housing Bank of Georgia (1991), and the State Savings Bank (1989). The Caucasian Exchange, a stock exchange, opened recently in Georgia.

Private commercial banks are rather new participants in the Georgian financial system. They started their operations in 1989 when the former USSR began to liberalize its financial system. At present they number approximately sixty. Although they provide only 5% of total bank credit to the economy, this deposit base is growing rapidly because of a very attractive interest rate for depositors. The activities of these banks is regulated by banking laws issued in August 1991.

34INSURANCE

Georgia's insurance system is largely inherited from government-controlled Soviet institutions. The civil war impairs any growth of the insurance sector.

35PUBLIC FINANCE

The government budget deteriorated from a surplus of 1.3% of GDP in 1990 to a deficit equivalent to 35% of GDP in 1992. Runaway inflation, revenue shortfalls, and civil conflict all exacerbated the deficit, which was largely financed by bank credit. The World Bank provides financing to Georgia for capital infrastructure projects, such as roads and railways, telecommunications, and port and power facilities. Georgia is also seeking assistance from the IMF and IBRD. The external debt in 1991 was estimated at $650 million.

36TAXATION

At the end of 1993, Georgia levied the following taxes: personal income (progressive from 12–40%); excise (10–90%); profit and value-added taxes (28% in most cases); payroll (38%), state enterprise profit tax (35%); and private enterprise profit tax (30%).

Compliance with the government tax program has been unsatisfactory; it was estimated that almost 80% of production enterprises underpaid their taxes in 1992.

37CUSTOMS AND DUTIES

Import duties range from 5–55% and customs taxes are generally charged at around 8%. Most former non-tariff trade barriers were eliminated in March 1992. Import licenses are still required for medical equipment, medications, plant chemicals, drugs, weapons, and ammunition.

38FOREIGN INVESTMENT

Georgia was one of the first former Soviet republics to adopt market reforms on foreign investment. However, political instability has hampered efforts to attract capital from abroad.

39ECONOMIC DEVELOPMENT

In late 1992, the government inaugurated its Medium-Term Program of Macroeconomic Stabilization and Systemic Change focusing on price and trade liberalization, budget constraints for public enterprises, and privatization. As part of a small enterprise privatization program, the first auction of small-scale assets was held in T'bilisi in March 1993. Practically all housing has been privatized, as well as 60% of agricultural land.

40SOCIAL DEVELOPMENT

Georgians experienced a significant decline in their standard of living in 1992, and unemployment increased sharply due to the republic's industrial slowdown.

The average family size was 4.1 members in 1989, and the divorce rate was 3.4 per 1,000 women. Women mostly work in low-paying, traditional occupations, often on a part-time basis. Female participation in politics has been discouraged by the widespread stereotype of the typical Gamsakhurdia supporter as a black-garbed female fanatic. Georgia's fertility rate was 2.2 in 1990. The previous year, there were 6.7 drug-related crimes and 1.6 alcohol-related deaths per 100,000 persons.

41HEALTH

Since the dissolution of the Soviet Union, there is little information about Georgia's health care system, other than statistics. In 1992, there were 84,000 births (a rate of 15 per 1,000 people), and the birth rate is projected at 18 per 1,000 through 1995.

From 1988 to 1992, there were 5.92 physicians per 1,000 inhabitants, with a nurse to doctor ratio of 2.2. In 1990, there was 1 physician per 170 people, and, between 1985 and 1990, there were 11.1 hospital beds per 1,000 people. Total health care expenditures in 1990 were $830 million, but immunization rates for the country was still relatively low from 1990 to 1992: children up to one year old were vaccinated against tuberculosis (63%); diphtheria, pertussis, and tetanus (45%); polio (45%); and measles (58%).

Life expectancy in 1992 was an average of 72 years, and the infant mortality rate was 25 per 1,000 live births. The overall mortality rate in 1993 was 9 per 1,000 people. There were approximately 2,000 civil war-related deaths in 1992. Studies also show that between 1985 and 1990, major causes of death were: communicable diseases and maternal/perinatal causes 69 per 100,000 people; noncommunicable diseases 591 per 100,000; and injuries 56 per 100,000. There were also 36 reported cases of tuberculosis per 100,000 people in 1990.

42HOUSING

In 1989, 64% of all privately owned urban housing had running water, 48% had sewer lines, 18% had central heating, and 14%

had hot water. In 1990, Georgia had 18.8 square meters of housing space per capita and, as of 1 January 1991, 128,000 households (or 16%) were on waiting lists for housing in urban areas.

43EDUCATION

Adult literacy was estimated at 99.0% in 1990, with men estimated at 99.5% and women at 98.5%. Georgia's educational system was based on the Soviet model until the late 1980s, when there was a de-emphasis of Soviet educational themes in favor of Georgian history and language. Georgian students are taught in a number of languages, including Georgian, Russian, Armenian, Azerbaijani, Abkhazian, and Ossetian. Several colleges and universities are located in Georgia. These include the Iran Dzhavakhiladze University of T'bilisi, Georgian Technical University, Abkhazian State University, and State University of Batumi.

44LIBRARIES AND MUSEUMS

Civil chaos has reduced the Georgian government's ability to maintain its extensive library system. Several museums and cultural institutions are located in T'bilisi.

45MEDIA

Georgia has international telecommunications links via landline to other former Soviet republics and Turkey. There is also a low capacity satellite earth station and connections via Moscow. As of January 1992, there were 339,000 telephone applications unfilled.

In 1989, Georgia had 149 newspapers. Of these, 128 were published in Georgian, with a combined circulation of 3.2 million.

46ORGANIZATIONS

Georgia's Chamber of Commerce and Industry promotes trade and commerce with its fellow members of the CIS. Union organizations in Georgia include the Confederation of Independent Trade Unions, an umbrella organization. Important political organizations include the all-Georgian Mecrab Kostava Society and the Paramilitary group Mkhredrioni.

47TOURISM, TRAVEL, AND RECREATION

Bounded by the Black Sea and the Caucasus Mountains, Georgia has been known for its lucrative tourist industry, but tourism has stagnated since independence due to political and economic turmoil. Mt. Shkhara, the ancient capital, is home to the Svetitskhoveli Cathedral, an 11th century edifice that is the spiritual center of the Georgian Orthodox Church and a major tourist attraction. The present-day capital, T'bilisi, is over 1,000 years old and offers historic citadels, cathedrals, and castles as well as warm springs and dramatic mountain views.

48FAMOUS GEORGIANS

Eduard A. Schvardnadze, a key figure in the Soviet government, has been president of Georgia since 1992. Joseph Stalin (1879–1953), a key figure in the Soviet period, was born in Gori, Georgia. The medieval poet Shota Rustaveli, who was from Georgia, wrote the masterpiece *Knight in the Tiger's Skin*. Nineteenth-century poets include Ilia Chavchavadze, Akaki Tsereteli, and Vazha Pshwda. Writers of that century include Titsian Tabidze, Gioigi Leonidze, and Irakli Abashidze. Painters include Niko Pirosmanashvili, and Irikli Toidze. Composers include Zarkavia Paliashvili and Meliton Balanchivadze.

49DEPENDENCIES

Georgia has no territories or colonies.

50BIBLIOGRAPHY

Allen, W. E. D. *A History of the Georgian People from the Beginning Down to the Russian Conquest in the Nineteenth*

Century. London: K. Paul, 1932.

Dolphin, Laurie. *Georgia to Georgia: Making Friends in the U.S.S.R.* New York: Tambourine Books, 1991.

Lang, David Marshall. *The Georgians.* New York: Praeger, 1966.

Pitskhelauri, G. Z. *The Longliving of Soviet Georgia.* New York: Human Sciences Press, 1982.

GERMANY

Federal Republic of Germany
Bundesrepublik Deutschland

CAPITAL: Berlin.

FLAG: The flag is a tricolor of black, red, and gold horizontal stripes—the flag of the German (Weimar) Republic from 1919 until 1933.

ANTHEM: *Einigkeit und Recht und Freiheit (Unity and Justice and Liberty).*

MONETARY UNIT: The deutsche mark (DM) is a paper currency of 100 pfennigs. There are coins of 1, 2, 5, 10, and 50 pfennigs and 1, 2, 5, and 10 deutsche marks, and notes of 5, 10, 20, 50, 100, 200, 500, and 1,000 deutsche marks. DM1 = $0.5981 (or $1 = DM1.6720).

WEIGHTS AND MEASURES: The metric system is the legal standard.

HOLIDAYS: New Year's Day, 1 January; Labor Day, 1 May; German Unity Day, 3 October; Repentance Day, Wednesday before the 3d Sunday in November (except Bavaria); Christmas, 25–26 December. Movable religious holidays include Good Friday, Easter Monday, Ascension, and Whitmonday. In addition, the movable Carnival/Rose Monday holiday and various provincial holidays are also celebrated.

TIME: 1 PM = noon GMT.

¹LOCATION, SIZE, AND EXTENT

Germany is located in western Europe, bordering the North Sea between France and Poland. Germany is slightly smaller than the state of Montana with a total area of 356,910 km sq (137,804 mi sq). Germany shares boundaries with Denmark and the Baltic Sea (north), Poland and the Czech Republic (east), Austria (southeast), Switzerland (south), France (southwest), Luxembourg, Belgium, and the Netherlands (west), and the North Sea (northwest). Germany's boundary length totals 6,010 km (3,734 mi). Germany's capital city, Berlin is located in the northeastern part of the country.

²TOPOGRAPHY

The topography of Germany is varied. The area along the Baltic coast is sandy, with dunes and small hills. Adjacent to the coast are forested ridges and numerous lakes of the Mecklenburg lake plateau. Around Berlin, the relief is less hilly. The southern limit of the lowland area is formed by a wide zone of fertile loess, reaching from Magdeburg to the highlands in the South. These highlands include the Harz Mountains; the densely wooded Thuringian Forest and the Erzgebirge (Ore Mountains), where the Fichtelberg rises to 1,214 m (3,983 ft). In the northeast, the wide German lowland—characterized by sandy North Sea shores, heath and moor (in the South), and highest altitudes of about 300 m (1,000 ft)—rises slowly to the central Germany uplands. These low, eroded mountains (1,070–1,520 m/3,500–5,000 ft) extend from the Rhine to the former border of East Germany. In the West are a wide rift valley and a narrow gorge carved by the Rhine River. A group of plateaus and low mountains, averaging 460 m (1,500 ft) in altitude and including the Black Forest and Odenwald Mountains (highest peak, the Feldberg, 1,493 m/4,898 ft), form the greater part of southern Germany. They merge gradually with the highest walls of the Bavarian Alps (2,440–2,740 m/ 8,000–9,000 ft), which form the boundary between Germany, Switzerland, and Austria; the Zugspitze (2,962 m/9,718 ft), on the Austrian border, is the highest point in Germany.

The only major lake is Lake Constance (Bodensee; within Germany, 305 sq km/118 sq mi), which is shared with Switzerland and Austria. Except in the extreme south, all of Germany is drained by rivers that empty into the North Sea. The Rhine (865 km/537 mi), with its two main tributaries, the Mosel and the Main, dominates the western areas; farther east are the Ems, the Weser, the Elbe, and the Oder. These rivers have estuaries that are important for the ports located there. In the South, the Danube flows (647 km/402 mi) from west to east. The East Frisian Islands are off the northwest coast; the North Frisian Islands lie along the coast of Schleswig. The small island of Helgoland is opposite the mouth of the Elbe River.

³CLIMATE

The climate is temperate; rapid changes in temperature are rare. Average temperatures in January, the coldest month of the year, range from 1.5°C (35°F) in the lowlands to –6°C (21°F) in the mountains. July is the warmest month of the year, with average temperatures between 18°C (64°F) in low-lying areas to 20°C (68°F) in the sheltered valleys of the south. The upper valley of the Rhine has an extremely mild climate. Upper Bavaria experiences a warm alpine wind (*Föhn*) from the south. The Harz Mountains form their own climatic zone, with cool summers, cold wind, and heavy snowfalls in winter.

Precipitation occurs throughout the year: in the northern lowlands, from 51 to 71 cm (20-28 in); in the central uplands, from 69 to 152 cm (27-60 in); in the Bavarian Alps, to more than 200 cm (80 in). The higher mountains are snow covered from at least January to March.

⁴FLORA AND FAUNA

Plants and animals are those generally common to middle Europe. Beeches, oaks, and other deciduous trees constitute one-third of the forests; conifers are increasing as a result of reforestation. Spruce and fir trees predominate in the upper mountains, while pine and larch are found in sandy soil. There are many species of ferns, flowers, fungi, and mosses. Fish abound in the rivers and the North Sea. Wild animals include deer, wild boar, mouflon, fox, badger, hare, and small numbers of beaver. Various migratory birds cross Germany in the spring and autumn.

5ENVIRONMENT

Industrialization has taken its toll on Germany's environment, including that of the former GDR, which, according to a 1985 UNESCO report, had the worst air, water, and ground pollution in Europe. In 1982, the FRG's total annual emission of sulfur dioxide was estimated at 1.86 million tons; nitrogen oxides, 893,000 tons; and carbon monoxide, 4.88 million tons. Germany produces 3.6% of the world's total gas emissions, and its particulate emissions total 295 tons per year. Since 1976, the Petrol Lead Concentration Act has limited the lead content of gasoline; for control of other automotive pollutants, the government looked toward stricter enforcement of existing laws and to technological improvements in engine design. The Federal Emission Protection Act of 1974, based on the "polluter pays" principle, established emissions standards for large industrial installations and manufacturing plants, agriculture and forestry operations, public utilities, and the private sector. Nevertheless, by 1994 50% of Germany's forests had been damaged by acid rain.

Germany has 23.0 cu m of water, of which 69.6% is used for industrial purposes and 19.6% for farming. Water pollution is evident in virtually every major river of the FRG. In the 1980s, the Rhine, from which some 10 million Germans and Dutch draw their drinking water, was 20 times as polluted as in 1949. Between November 1986 and January 1987 alone, 30 tons of mercury, 900 lb of pesticides, 540 tons of nitrogen fertilizers, and 10 tons of benzene compound were discharged into the river. The Effluency Levies Act, effective January 1978, requires anyone who discharges effluents into waterways to pay a fee reckoned in accordance with the quantity and severity of the pollutant; the proceeds of this act are allocated for the building of water treatment plants and for research on water treatment technology and reduced-effluent production techniques.

Germany produces 21.5 million tons of solid wastes and 15,659 tons of hazardous waste materials per year. The nation has set maximum levels for biocides in the soil, to protect food supplies. Under the nation's basic waste disposal law of 1972, some 50,000 unauthorized dump sites have been closed down and 5,000 regulated sites established; provisions governing toxic wastes were added in 1976. The FRG's principal environmental agency is the Ministry of Environment, Nature Conservation and Reactor Safety, created in June 1986.

As of 1986, the FRG had 67 nature parks and more than 2,000 nature reserves. In 1970, the first FRG national park, with an area of 13,100 hectares (32,370 acres), was opened in the Bavarian forest, and in 1978 a second national park (21,000 hectares/52,000 acres) was opened near Berchtesgaden. The third national park, in Schleswig-Holstein (285,000 hectares/704,250 acres), opened in 1985, and a fourth, in Niedersachsen (240,000 hectares/593,000 acres), opened in 1986. Of Germany's 94 animal species, 2 are endangered, as are 17 of 305 bird species and 3 freshwater fish species out of 70. In addition, 16 plant species are threatened with extinction. Endangered species in 1987 included Freya's damselfly and the European otter. Believed extinct were Spengler's freshwater mussel, the Bavarian pine vole, and the false ringlet butterfly.

6POPULATION

At the end of 1991, the population of Germany totaled 80,274,564. Average population density was 225 persons per sq km (582 per sq mi). A population of 82,583,000 was projected for the year 2000, assuming a crude birthrate of 11.1 per 1,000 population, a crude death rate of 10.6, and a net natural increase

of 0.5. Because of a low birthrate and an aging population, the FRG fell in population between 1973–78 and 1982–86. The GDR lost population through most of its existence, not only because of these factors but also because of emigration. A heavy influx of immigrants more than compensated for a slight population loss in the early 1990s because of more deaths than births.

An estimated 86% of the population was urban in 1995. Berlin, the capital, was the largest city in mid-1991, with a population of 3,437,900. Other big cities were Hamburg, 1,660,700; Munich (München), 1,236,500; Cologne (Köln), 955,500; Frankfurt am Main, 647,200; Essen, 626,100; Dortmund, 599,900; Stuttgart, 583,700; Düsseldorf, 576,700; Bremen, 552,300; Duisburg, 536,700; Hanover (Hannover), 514,400; Leipzig, 507,800; Nurenberg (Nürnberg), 494,400; and Dresden, 488,000. Bonn, still the working capital, had a population of 294,300.

7MIGRATION

From 1946 to 1968, 475,505 Germans emigrated to the US, 262,807 to Canada, and 99,530 to Australia and Oceania. During the same period, however, millions of people of German origin and/or speech migrated to the FRG from eastern Europe, notably from the former Czechoslovakia and GDR. Migration from the GDR to the FRG reached a climax just before the erection of the frontier wall in Berlin on 13 August 1961. It is estimated that about 4 million people—many of them skilled workers and professionals—crossed from the GDR to the FRG during the 40-year existence of the GDR. Immigration of ethnic Germans from Poland continued to be heavy after 1968, totaling about 800,000 between 1970 and 1989.

The number of foreigners in Germany at the end of 1991 was 5,882,300, or 7.3% of the population. In addition, there were thought to be 650,000 persons illegally present in the country. In 1991, 1,182,927 persons immigrated to Germany, of whom 940,491 were foreigners. A total of 582,240 emigrated from Germany, of which 497,476 were foreigners. According to German law, persons who are not ethnic Germans are foreigners (except for the few granted citizenship) even if they were born and have spent their entire lives in Germany. Conversely, ethnic Germans are not foreigners even if emigrating from birthplaces and homes in eastern Europe. The 1991 immigrants included 156,299 Germans arriving from the former Soviet Union. There were also 221,024 immigrants from the former Yugoslavia and 128,367 Poles (not counting 17,276 Polish Germans).

Germany is also the focal point in Europe for refugees seeking asylum. In 1992, 438,191 persons received asylum in Germany as refugees. Most of these were Yugoslavs (122,666) or were Romanians (103,787).

State-to-state migration came to 1,126,991 in 1991. By the end of the year the population of the former FRG was more than four times that of the former GDR. In 1991 the states of the former GDR had a net loss of 172,357 people to the west. There was a slight net movement from north to south. Schleswig-Holstein, Germany's northernmost state, had a net loss of 17,803 people.

8ETHNIC GROUPS

Until the late 1950s, the population was 99% German; the Danes in Schleswig-Holstein were the sole national minority. The influx of foreigners as "guest workers" beginning in the late 1950s led to an upsurge in the number of permanent foreign residents. Of the 5,882,300 foreigners in Germany at the end of 1991, Turks were by far the largest group, numbering 1,779,600. There were 775,100 Yugoslavs, 560,100 Italians, 336,900 Greeks, 271,000 Poles, 186,900 Austrians, 135,200 Spanish, and 93,000 Portuguese. It should be kept in mind that even persons born and reared in Germany are foreigners unless ethnically German or naturalized.

GERMANY

0   50   100 Miles

0   50   100 Kilometers

LOCATION: 47°16′ to 55°4′N; 5°52′ to 15°2′E. **BOUNDARY LENGTHS:** Denmark, 67 km (42 mi); Poland, 460 km (286 mi); Czech Republic, 810 km (503 mi); Austria (excluding Lake Constance), 784 km (487 mi); Switzerland (excluding Lake Constance), 334 km (208 mi); France, 446 km (277 mi); Luxembourg, 135 km (84 mi); Belgium, 155 km (96 mi); Netherlands, 576 km (358 mi). **TERRITORIAL SEA LIMIT:** 12 mi.

As joblessness increased in the 1980s and early 1990s, tensions arose between minority residents and young working-class youths, described as skinheads, who were influenced by neo-Nazi propaganda. This was true even in the former GDR, where there were only 191,190 foreigners (of which 60,607 were Vietnamese) at the end of 1989.

9LANGUAGES

German is the official language, and although dialectical variations are considerable, High German is standard. Low German, spoken along the North and Baltic Sea coasts and in the offshore islands, is in some respects as close to Dutch as it is to standard German. Sorbian (also known as Wendish or Lusatian) is a Slavic language spoken by the Sorbian minority of about 50,000–100,000. Under the GDR it was taught in schools in their settlement area. There was a daily newspaper in Sorbian and a publishing house for Sorbian literature. Many of Germany's sizable foreign-born population still speak their native languages, and there are numerous Turkish-speaking school children.

10 RELIGIONS

The reunification of Germany in 1990 ended some forty years of religious, as well as political separation. Freedom of religion is guaranteed, and although there is no official state religion, churches can receive financial support from the government. In 1993, the Evangelical (Protestant) Church, a federation of several church bodies, comprised some 41% of the population, primarily Lutherans, while Roman Catholics numbered 28,599,000 or 35.6%. A total of some 40,000 Jews lived in Germany in 1990. Protestants are in the majority in northern Germany and the new eastern provinces, while Catholics are dominant in the south, particularly in Bavaria, Saarland, and Rhineland-Palatinate. Free churches that do not rely upon state, tax-based support, including Methodists, Baptists, Mennonites, the Society of Friends, and the Salvation Army, are also represented. With the influx of immigrant workers, especially from Turkey, Muslims now comprise up to 3% of the entire population.

11 TRANSPORTATION

Although the German transportation network was heavily damaged during World War II, the FRG system is now one of the best developed in Europe (although much of the infrastructure in the former GDR needs significant improvement). Because of the FRG's central location, almost all continental surface traffic has to cross its terrain. In 1991, the railroad system consisted of 45,648 km (28,366 mi) of operational track, of which about 87% was operated by the government-owned Federal Railways System. About 32% of the trackage is electrified. In 1989, government and private railways carried 1.7 billion passengers and 310 million tons of goods through the pre-1991 FRG and the former GDR.

Highways and roads in 1991 totaled 590,909 km (367,191 mi), of which 8,290 km (5,151 mi) were autobahns. As of January 1991 there were 27,483,737 passenger cars, 1,390,052 trucks, and 69,710 buses that had been registered in the West before the reunification with the former German Democratic Republic, which had 6,300,000 passenger cars and 980,000 trucks registered at that time.

The total length of regularly used navigable inland waterways and canals was 7,541 km (4,686 mi) in 1991, and there were 31 major ports. Canals link the Elbe with the Ems, the Ems with the Dortmund, and the Baltic with the North Sea. The most important inland waterway consists of the Rhine and its tributaries, which carry more freight than any other European waterway. Duisburg-Ruhrort is the most important inland port.

Hamburg accounted for 53.8 million tons of overseas traffic in 1989; Wilhelmshaven, 14.5 million tons; Rostock, 20.8 million tons; Bremen, 14.8 million tons; and Bremerhaven, 15 million tons. These five ports handle about 70% of total merchandise traffic. Other major ports include Wismer and Stralsund, both on the Baltic Sea. In 1991, the FRG had a merchant fleet comprising 492 ships, including 396 tankers.

Lufthansa, organized in 1955, is the major air carrier; its route network includes both North and South America, the Near and Far East (including Australia), Africa, and Europe. In 1992, Lufthansa carried 26.9 million passengers and performed 4,284 million freight ton-kilometers of service. Major airports are at Hamburg, Hanover, Bremen, Düsseldorf, Cologne-Bonn, Frankfurt, Stuttgart, Nurenberg, Munich, and Berlin.

12 HISTORY

Hunting and gathering peoples roamed the land now known as Germany for thousands of years before the first farmers appeared in the sixth millennium BC. By the time these Indo-Europeans made contact with the Romans late in the 2d century BC, the Teutons of the north had driven most of the Celts westward across the Rhine. During the succeeding centuries, Germanic tribes such as the Alemanni, Burgundians, Franks, Lombards, Vandals, Ostrogoths, and Visigoths gradually developed in the territory between the Rhine estuary in the west, the Elbe River in the east, and northern Italy in the south. Some of these peoples, whom the Romans called barbarians (from the Latin *barbari*, meaning "foreigners"), overran Italy and helped destroy the Roman Empire; others settled in Britain, France, and Spain. The area on either side of the Rhine was contested until Charlemagne, king of the Franks (r.768–814), extended his domain to include most of Germany as far as the Elbe; he was crowned emperor at Rome in 800. Charlemagne's empire was eventually divided among his three grandsons, and the German sector itself was divided in the latter part of the 9th century.

Otto I, greatest of a new Saxon dynasty, united Germany and Italy and was crowned first Holy Roman emperor in 962. The strength of the rising Holy Roman Empire was undercut, however, by the two-pronged involvement in Italy and in eastern Europe. Successive generations of Germanic emperors and of various ducal families engaged in constant struggles within Germany as well as with the papacy, and dispersed their energies in many ventures beyond the confines of the empire. Frederick I (Barbarossa, r.1152–90), of the Hohenstaufen family, overcame the last of the powerful duchies in 1180. His grandson Frederick II (r.1212–50), the most brilliant of medieval emperors, reigned from Sicily and took little interest in German affairs. Four years after his death, the empire broke up temporarily, and there followed a 19-year interregnum. In 1273, Rudolf of Habsburg was elected emperor, but neither he nor any of his immediate successors could weld the empire into a manageable unit.

The Holy Roman Empire's loose and cumbersome framework suffered from lack of strong national authority at the very time when powerful kingdoms were developing in England, France, and Spain. In the ensuing period, the Holy Roman emperors tended to ally themselves against the nobility and with the prosperous German cities and with such potent confederations of towns as the Hanseatic and Swabian leagues. During the 15th century and part of the 16th, Germany was prosperous: commerce and banking flourished, and great works of art were produced. However, the already weak structure of the empire was further undermined by a great religious schism, the Reformation, which began with Martin Luther in 1517 and ended in the ruinous Thirty Years' War (1618–48), which directly and indirectly (through disease and famine) may have taken the lives of up to 2 million people. Thereafter, Germany remained fragmented in more than 300 principalities, bishoprics, and free cities. In the 18th century, Prussia rose to first rank among the German states, especially through the military brilliance of Frederick II ("the Great," r.1740–86).

During the French Revolution and the Napoleonic wars, German nationalism asserted itself for the first time since the Reformation. Although frustrated in the post-Napoleonic era, the nationalist and liberal movements were not eradicated, and they triumphed briefly in the Frankfurt parliament of 1848. Thereafter, a number of its leaders supported the conservative but dynamic Prussian chancellor, Otto von Bismarck. After a series of successful wars with Denmark (1864), Austria (the Seven Weeks' War, 1866), and France (the Franco-Prussian War, 1870–71), Bismarck brought about the union of German states (excluding Austria) into the Second Empire, proclaimed in 1871.

Germany quickly became the strongest military, industrial,

and economic power on the Continent and joined other great powers in overseas expansion. While Bismarck governed as chancellor, further wars were avoided and an elaborate system of alliances with other European powers was created. With the advent of Wilhelm II as German emperor (r.1888–1918), the delicate international equilibrium was repeatedly disturbed in a series of crises that culminated in 1914 in the outbreak of World War I. Despite initial successes, the German armies—leagued with Austria-Hungary and Turkey against the UK, France, Russia, and eventually the US—were defeated in 1918. As a consequence of the war, in which some 1,600,000 Germans died, the victorious Allies through the Treaty of Versailles (1919) stripped Germany of its colonies and of the territories won in the Franco-Prussian War, demanded the nation's almost complete disarmament, and imposed stringent reparations requirements. Germany became a republic, governed under the liberal Weimar constitution. The serious economic and social dislocations caused by the military defeat and by the subsequent economic depression, however, brought Adolf Hitler and the National Socialist (Nazi) Party to power in 1933. Hitler converted the republic into a dictatorship, consolidated Germany's position at home and abroad, and began a military expansion that by 1939 had brought a great part of Europe under German control, either by military occupation or by alliance, leading to World War II.

Germany signed a military alliance with Italy on 22 May 1939 and a nonaggression pact with the former USSR on 23 August. Hitler's army then invaded Poland on 1 September, and France and Britain declared war on Germany two days later. France surrendered on 22 June 1940; the British continued to fight. On 10 December 1941, Germany declared war on the US, three days after the attack on Pearl Harbor by its ally Japan. Hitler's troops were engaged on three major fronts—the eastern front (USSR), the North African front, and the western front (France). Hitler relied heavily on air power and bombed Britain continuously during 1941–42. But by 1943, German forces were on the defensive everywhere, thus marking the beginning of the end of the Nazi offensive thrusts. Finally, on 7 May 1945, after Hitler had committed suicide, the Allies received Germany's unconditional surrender. It is estimated that more than 35 million persons were killed during World War II. Of this number, at least 11 million were civilians. Among them were nearly 6 million Jews, mostly eastern Europeans, killed in a deliberate extermination by the Nazi regime known as the Holocaust; there were also about 5 million non-Jewish victims, including Gypsies, homosexuals, political dissidents, and the physically and mentally handicapped.

From Division to Reunification

After the surrender in 1945, Germany was divided into four occupation zones, controlled respectively by the former USSR, the US, the UK, and France. Berlin was likewise divided, and from April 1948 through May 1949 the USSR sought unsuccessfully to blockade the city's western sectors; not until the quadripartite agreement of 1971 was unimpeded access of the FRG to West Berlin firmly established. In 1949, pending a final peace settlement, Germany was divided into the Federal Republic of Germany, or West Germany, consisting of the former UK, French, and US zones of occupation, and the German Democratic Republic, or East Germany, consisting of the former Soviet zone of occupation. Territories in the east (including East Prussia), which were in German hands prior to 1939, were taken over by Poland and the former USSR.

The FRG's first chancellor (1949–63), Konrad Adenauer, the leader of the Christian Democratic Union (CDU), followed a policy of "peace through strength." During his administration, the FRG joined NATO in 1955 and became a founding member of the EC in 1957. That same year, the Saar territory, politically autonomous under the Versailles Treaty but economically tied to France after 1947, became a German state (Land) after a free election and an agreement between France and the FRG. A treaty of cooperation between those two nations, signed on 22 January 1963, provided for coordination of their policies in foreign affairs, defense, information, and cultural affairs. The cost of this program of cooperation with the West was further alienation from the GDR and abandonment, for the foreseeable future, of the goal of German reunification. Many citizens, including a significant number of skilled and highly-educated persons, had been covertly emigrating through Berlin in the West, and on 13 August 1961, East Berlin was sealed off from West Berlin by a wall of concrete and barbed wire. The Western Allies declared that they accepted neither the legality nor the potential practical consequences of the partition and reaffirmed their determination to ensure free access and the continuation of a free and viable Berlin.

On 16 October 1963, Adenauer resigned and was succeeded by former Finance Minister Ludwig Erhard, who is generally credited with stimulating the FRG's extraordinary postwar economic development—the so-called economic miracle. Kurt George Kiesinger of the CDU formed a new coalition government on 17 November 1966 with Willy Brandt, leader of the Social Democratic Party, as a vice-chancellor. Three years later, Brandt became chancellor, and the CDU became an opposition party for the first time. One of Brandt's boldest steps was the development of an "Eastern policy" (Ostpolitik), which sought improved relations with the Socialist bloc and resulted, initially, in the establishment of diplomatic ties with Romania and the former Yugoslavia. On 7 December 1970, the FRG signed a treaty with Poland reaffirming the existing western Polish boundary of the Oder and western Neisse rivers and establishing a pact of friendship and cooperation between the two nations. That August, the FRG had concluded a nonaggression treaty with the former USSR; a ten-year economic agreement was signed on 19 May 1973. Throughout the late 1960s and early 1970s, tensions over the Berlin division in particular and between the two Germanys generally eased markedly, as did, in consequence, the intensity of pressures from both Allied and Soviet sides over the issue of reunification. In an effort to normalize inter-German relations, FRG Chancellor Willy Brandt and GDR Chairman Willi Stoph exchanged visits in March and May 1970, the first such meetings since the states were established. A basic treaty between the two Germanys was reached on 21 December 1972 and ratified by the Bundestag on 17 May 1973; under the treaty, the FRG recognized the sovereignty and territorial integrity of the GDR, and the two nations agreed to cooperate culturally and economically. Two years later, the GDR and FRG agreed on the establishment of permanent representative missions in each others' capitals. Relations with Czechoslovakia were normalized by a treaty initialed 20 June 1973. The early 1970s brought an upsurge of terrorism on German soil, including the killing by Palestinians of Israeli athletes at the 1972 Summer Olympics in Munich. The terrorist wave, which also enlisted a number of German radicals, continued into the mid-1970s but declined thereafter.

Brandt remained chancellor until 6 May 1974, when he resigned after his personal aide, Günter Guillaume, was arrested as a spy for the GDR. Helmut Schmidt, Brandt's finance minister, was elected chancellor by the Bundestag on 16 May. Under Schmidt's pragmatic leadership, the FRG continued its efforts to normalize relations with Eastern Europe, while also emphasizing economic and political cooperation with its West European allies and with the US. Schmidt remained chancellor until the fall of 1982, when his governing coalition collapsed in a political party dispute. General elections in March 1983 resulted in a victory for the CDU, whose leader, Helmut Kohl, retained the chancellorship he had assumed on an interim basis the previous October. In January 1987 elections, Kohl was again returned to power, as the CDU and its coalition allies won 54% of the seats in the Bundestag.

The exodus of East Germans through Hungary in the summer of 1989 as well as mass demonstrations in several East German cities, especially Leipzig, led to the collapse of the German Democratic Republic in the fall of 1989. Chancellor Kohl outlined a 10-point plan for peaceful reunification, including continued membership in NATO and free elections in March 1990. Following these elections, the two Germanys peacefully evolved into a single state. Four-power control ended in 1991 and, by the end of 1994, all former Soviet forces will have left although British, French, and American forces will remain for an interim period.

Unification has been accompanied by disillusionment and dissatisfaction with politics and the economy. A falling GDP and rising unemployment have raised concerns that the costs of unification were underestimated. Various austerity measures have been negotiated including cuts in salaries and social welfare. Violent attacks by right-wing extremists have led to reform in Germany's asylum law, including agreements on the return of illegal immigrants.

Local elections have indicated a general loss of support for the major parties, and the general election in October 1994 confirmed that trend. In the election, Chancellor Helmut Kohl's governing coalition of Free Democrats and Christian Democrats was reduced from a 134-seat to a 10-seat majority in Parliament. Kohl's loss was attributed to resentment among many in the western part of the country about the costs of absorbing the east, and resentment in the east about the painful change to a market economy. The election strengthened the opposition Social Democrats and Greens.

Berlin has become the new capital of Germany, although the shift from Bonn to Berlin will take place over several years.

13GOVERNMENT

The federal government exercises complete sovereignty. On 3 October 1990, the Federal Republic of Germany and the German Democratic Republic were unified in accordance with Article 23 of the Basic Law (Grundgesetz) of 23 May 1949, under which the FRG is governed and which serves as a constitution. It may be amended by a two-thirds vote of the legislature.

The bicameral legislature (the federal parliament) consists of a federal council (Bundesrat) and a federal diet (Bundestag). Members of the Bundestag are elected for four-year terms by universal, free, and secret ballot, and may be reelected; voters and candidates must be at least 18 years of age. The Bundestag had 496 voting deputies through the 1976 elections, 497 as of 1980, 498 as of 1983, and 497 as of 1987; 22 nonvoting deputies represent West Berlin. Following unification, Bundestag membership was raised to 662 deputies. The Bundesrat, which has absolute veto power over legislation affecting the provinces (Länder), consists of 68 representatives appointed by the provincial governments according to the population of each province. Disagreements between the two chambers are handled by a conciliating committee.

The chancellor, the leader of the executive branch, is elected by a majority of the Bundestag and serves until a new Bundestag is elected or until a majority vote dismisses him. The chancellor determines and is responsible for policy, and selects the ministers who head the various administrative departments. The president, who is chief of state, performs the largely ceremonial functions of proposing the chancellor to the Bundestag, promulgating laws, formally appointing and dismissing judges and federal civil servants, and receiving foreign ambassadors. The president is elected for a five-year term by a federal convention composed of members of the Bundestag (including, for this purpose, the West Berlin deputies) and an equal number of delegates elected by the provincial legislatures.

14POLITICAL PARTIES

The "five percent clause," under which parties represented in the Bundestag must obtain at least 5% of the total votes cast by the electorate, has prevented the development of parliamentary splinter groups. Only three parties gained representation in the Bundestag following the elections of September 1965. The Christian Democratic Union (Christlich-Demokratische Union—CDU) and its Bavarian affiliate, the Christian Social Union (Christlich-Soziale Union—CSU), with 245 seats, remained the strongest group, as it had been since the first Bundestag was elected in 1949. The Social Democratic Party (Sozialdemokratische Partei Deutschlands—SPD) increased its seats to 202 and remained the major opposition party. The Free Democratic Party (Freie Demokratische Partei—FDP), winning 49 seats, joined with the CDU and the CSU to form the "small coalition" government of Chancellor Ludwig Erhard. The coalition government was dissolved in October 1966, following a budgetary disagreement between the CDU/CSU and the FDP. In November 1966, the CDU/CSU joined with the SPD to form a new coalition government, but following the general elections of September 1969, the SPD and FDP formed a coalition government with a combined strength of 254 seats. The elections of November 1972 resulted in a coalition composed of the SPD's 230 seats and the FDP's 42, over the CDU/CSU's 224 seats. Following the resignation of SPD leader Willy Brandt, Helmut Schmidt (SPD) was elected chancellor by the Bundestag in May 1974 by a 267–255 vote. The SPD/FDP coalition retained its majorities in the elections of 1976 (SPD 214, FDP 39) and 1980 (SPD 218, FDP 53).

After the breakup of the coalition in 1982, however, the CDU/CSU swept to victory in the voting of March 1983, winning 244 seats and 48.8% of the vote, compared with 226 seats (44.5%) in 1980 and 243 seats (48.6%) in 1976. The swing party, the FDP, took 34 seats (6.9%) of the vote and joined the CDU/CSU in a coalition behind Chancellor Helmut Kohl. The SPD polled 38.2% (down from 42.9% in 1980) and captured 193 seats, for a drop of 25.

In the general election of 25 January 1987, the results were as follows: CDU/CSU, 44.3% (223 seats); FDP, 9.1% (46 seats); SPD, 37% (186 seats); and the Greens, 8.3% (42 seats). The first all-Germany elections were held 2 December 1990. The results were as follows: CDU/CSU, 43.8% (319 seats); SPD, 33.5% (239 seats); FDP, 11.0% (79 seats); and Greens, 1.2% (8). The Party of Democratic Socialism (PDS), successor to the SED (Communist party), won 2.4% of the vote and 17 seats. East German parties were allowed to win seats if they received at least 5% of the vote in East Germany.

The CDU and CSU emphasize Christian precepts but are not denominational parties. They favor free enterprise and are supported by small business, professional groups, farmers, and Christian-oriented labor unions. In foreign policy, the CDU/CSU alliance supports European integration and the strengthening of NATO.

The SPD is the oldest and best organized of all German parties. In recent decades it has modified its traditional Marxist program and made an appeal not only to industrial workers but also to farmers, youth, professional people, and the petty bourgeoisie. Its revised Godesberg Program (1959) envisages a mixed economy, support for European integration and NATO, public ownership of key industries, a strong defense force, and recognition of religious values.

The FDP is a more heterogeneous organization, consisting of

both classical liberals and strongly nationalistic groups. The party is supported mainly by business interests and Protestant groups. It rejects socialism or state capitalism in principle. The Greens (Die Grünen), Germany's newest political party, constitute a coalition of environmentalists and antinuclear activists; in 1983, they became the first left-wing opposition party to gain a parliamentary foothold since the Communists won 15 seats in 1949. In 1990, in cooperation with Alliance 90, a loose left-wing coalition, the Greens were able to clear the 5% hurdle and win Bundestag seats.

The October 1994 elections saw a weakening of the Free Democratic and Christian Democratic coalition and a strengthening of the Social Democrats and the Greens. The Christian Democrats won 41.5% of the vote and the Free Democrats 6.9%. This gave the governing coalition 341 seats in parliament and a majority of only 10 seats as compared to its previous 134-seat edge. The combined opposition alliance took 48.1% of the vote (331 seats): the Social Democrats took 36.4%; the Greens, 7.3%; and the former Communists in eastern Germany (now called the Party of Democratic Socialism), 4.4%.

15 LOCAL GOVERNMENT

The Basic Law guarantees local self-government, and the states (Länder) are granted all powers not specifically reserved to the federal government. The Federal Republic consists of 16 Länder: Baden-Wurttemberg, Bayern, Berlin, Brandenburg, Bremen, Hamburg, Hessen, Mecklenburg-Vorpommern, Niedersachsen, Nordrhein-Westfalen, Rheinland-Pfalz, Saarland, Sachsen, Sachsen-Anhalt, Schleswig-Holstein, and Thuringen.

Länder have their own ministerial governments and legislatures. They have primary responsibility for the maintenance of law and order; jurisdiction over their own finances, taxes, and administration; and supreme authority in education and other cultural activities. Through the Bundesrat, the Länder have considerable influence in federal legislation.

Communes (Gemeinden) are the basic units of local government, apart from the municipalities, and have the right to regulate such local matters as those involving schools, building, cultural affairs, and welfare. Halfway between the Länder and the communes are the counties (Landkreise), which have autonomy in such matters as road building, transportation, and hospitals. They are administered by a Landrat, the chief official, and a Kreistag (country legislature).

16 JUDICIAL SYSTEM

Cases of the first instance are tried by local or Landkreis courts and the superior courts in each of the Länder. The Federal Courts of Justice in the cities of Karlsruhe and Berlin, the courts of last resort in regular civil and criminal cases, consist of members appointed by a committee that includes federal and Land ministers and several Bundestag members. A court of appeal and the several Land and Landkreis courts are subordinate to the Karlsruhe and Berlin tribunals. Special courts handle administrative, labor, financial, and social welfare matters. The Federal Constitutional Court, the highest court in the land, has competence to decide problems concerning the Basic Law and to test the constitutionality of laws. The court has 16 members: one 8-member panel elected by a committee of the Bundestag, the other by the Bundesrat.

In 1985 there were 664 civil and criminal courts and 193 labor, administrative, social, and financial courts.

The courts in the former German Democratic Republic (GDR) are in the process of being integrated into the West German court system and reformed to meet West German standards. There remains a shortage of qualified judges in the former GDR, many of the former judges having been removed because of their conduct under the former regime. As a result,

many of the new judges have been imported from the west. Most Justice Ministry officials, judges and prosecutors are from western Germany. There remain large backlogs and organizational problems in the administration of the new court system in the eastern states. The new courts have been criticized for being too lenient in sentencing right-wing extremists convicted of violent attacks.

The judiciary is independent of the legislative and judicial branches and remains free from interference or intimidation.

17 ARMED FORCES

The unification of Germany in 1991 brought the amalgamation of the People's Army of the German Democratic Republic and the Bundeswehr of the Federal Republic—on the Bundeswehr's terms, modified by political guidance. Essentially, West Germany abolished the East German ministry of defense and officer corps, but kept much of the GDR's Russian equipment and a few of its career officers and non-commissioned specialists. The Bundeswehr occupied East German military installations and found many of them beyond repair for training and suitable housing. The Bundeswehr moved eastward with all deliberate speed, especially since six Russian divisions and a tactical air force still remained in German installations. (With dependents these dispossessed Russians numbered almost 500,000.) Meanwhile, Germany's NATO allies still maintain an integrated ground and air field force of almost 250,000 troops in western Germany, although this force will shrink with the departure of the Canadian and Belgian forces and the reduction of the American and British contingents in the 1990s.

The Germany armed forces in 1993 numbered 447,000, about half of whom were conscripts performing twelve months of obligatory service. The army is divided into the field army (203,400) and the territorial army (64,000 cadre) with a supporting administrative and logistical establishment. The German army has large amounts of both western and Russian equipment: 7,000 main battle tanks, 4,500 artillery pieces, and 15,000 tactical vehicles (including 5000 Marder and BMP armored infantry fighting vehicles). The Germans have abundant air defense weapons, helicopters, engineering equipment, and sophisticated anti-tank weapons. Their army is by far the most formidable in Europe.

The navy (Bundesmarine) of 35,200 absorbed about 2,000 East German sailors and some of their vessels, but it is still very much the NATO German navy. It has 22 submarines, 14 major surface combat vessels, 43 patrol and coast combatants, and 40 mine warfare ships. It also mans about 50 additional ships for support services. The naval air arm (land-based except for ASW helicopters) has 118 combat aircraft and 19 armed helicopters. It is structured to support the fleet's main mission of anti-submarine warfare and sea approach reconnaissance.

The air force (Luftwaffe) has 95,000 officers and airmen, including about 9,000 former East Germans. None of the Soviet aircraft are being flown except for experimental purposes since the Luftwaffe already has more than 600 combat aircraft. All but a handful of MiG-29s will be scrapped to conform with the conventional arms limitation treaty for Europe (CFE). The Luftwaffe is principally a ground attack air force, armed with the Tornado and older German and Allied aircraft like the F-4. It also provides fixed and mobile air-defense units armed with missiles and an administrative helicopter force of about 180 helos. The air force also maintains a transport command and a training command; many German pilots train in the United States and Canada where the air space is more generous.

Germany also maintains an elite paramilitary border police force of 25,000 that provides counterterrorist units and narcotics control units as well as airport and train station security. Despite their martial appearance and fearsome arms, the Grenzpolizei are controlled by the Ministry of the Interior, not the Bundeswehr.

In 1991 Germany spent $39.5 billion for defense or about 2.5% of its gross domestic product. It has not yet taken a role in peacekeeping operations except to send 144 medical personnel to Cambodia (UNTAC).

[18] INTERNATIONAL COOPERATION

The FRG (along with the GDR) became a full member of the UN on 18 September 1973; it had previously belonged to all the non-regional specialized UN agencies. It is also an active participant in the Council of Europe, EC, ECE, NATO, and OECD, as well as a member of the Asian Development Bank and IDB and a permanent observer of the OAS. The country is a signatory to GATT but, like some of its Western allies, had declined, as of September 1987, to sign the Law of the Sea.

[19] ECONOMY

Germany has the world's third largest economy and the largest in Europe. Agriculture, forestry, and fishing accounted for only 1.2% of GDP in 1992, while industry, including construction, comprised 36.7%, and services the rest. Germany's unit of currency, the mark, is one of the strongest in the world.

In the western FRG, GNP increased at an annual average rate of 7% between 1950 and 1960 and 5.4% between 1960 and 1970. This rate slowed to 3.1% between 1970 and 1980 and 2.3% between 1980 and 1990. It was 3.7% in 1991 and 1.5% in 1992. Per capita income, estimated in 1992 at $20,833 (for western Germany only) was among the world's highest.

The former GDR was the wealthiest nation in the Soviet bloc. However, the unification of Germany in October 1990 proved a heavy economic burden on the west. In 1992 the former GDR Länder accounted for only 8% of GDP. Transfer payments and subsidies for the east resulted in a large public deficit. Alarmed at the potential for inflation, the Bundesbank pursued a tight-money policy. This boosted the value of the mark and had a recessionary effect on the European economy. Consumer prices averaged only 1.4% a year between 1985 and 1990 but rose 3.5% in 1991, 4% in 1992, and 4.2% in 1993. The unemployment rate in 1993 was 7.3% in the west, but 15.8% in the east because so many antiquated, inefficient enterprises were unable to compete in a market economy.

[20] INCOME

In 1992, Germany's GNP was $1,846,064 million at current prices, or $23,030 per capita. For the period 1985–92 the average inflation rate was 2.9%, resulting in a real growth rate in per capita GNP of 2.2%.

In 1992 the GDP was $1,928,400 million in current US dollars. It is estimated that in 1990 agriculture, hunting, forestry, and fishing contributed 1% to GDP; manufacturing, 29%; construction, 5%; wholesale and retail trade, 9%; transport, storage, and communication, 5%; finance, insurance, real estate, and business services, 12%; and other sources 29%. Easterners with jobs earn about 65% of what westerners are paid for comparable work.

[21] LABOR

With the reunification of the FRG and the GDR on 3 October 1990, the total labor force of the united FRG in 1991–92 numbered 39,011,000. As of September 1991, 1,973,000 were foreign workers (down 24% from the 1973 high), including 632,000 Turks, 325,000 Yugoslavs, and 172,000 Italians. Since reunification, large numbers of African and Vietnamese workers in eastern Germany have been repatriated, but illegal immigrant workers, especially from central Europe, have been perceived as putting an unacceptable strain on the job and housing markets

of the FRG. Overall unemployment in the united FRG averaged 6.7% in 1991–92, with the 5 states (Länder) of the former GDR at 10.3%, and the states of the pre-1990 FRG experiencing an unemployment rate of 5.5%. Roughly 28.9 million (45.5%) of the western population, and about 7.5 million (46.7%) of the easterners, including about 500,000 east-west commuters, were gainfully employed in 1991. The total labor force in the pre-1990 FRG was 30,575,000 (up 248,000 from 1990), and in the five new states it was 8,436,000 (down 510,000 from 1990).

The right to organize and to join trade unions is guaranteed by the federal and state constitutions; as of 1991–92, 41.7% of the total labor force was unionized. In 1991, the western trade unions successfully expanded eastward, where they created western structures in the new states, totally dominating overall development so that no GDR trade union survived reunification. The German Trade Union Federation (DGB)—the largest federation, with 13,749,000 members at the end of 1991—consists of 16 major industrial unions, including such giants as the Metal Workers' Union, with 3,624,000 members, and the Public Services, Transport, and Communications Union, with 2,138,000 workers. The average number of hours worked per week was 37.6 in the West and about 40 in the East. White-collar and salaried employees have formed the German Salaried Employees' Union, with 585,000 members in 1991, when the Confederation of German Civil Service Officials (DBB), had 1,053,000.

Disputes concerning the interpretation of labor agreements are settled before special labor courts. Wages and working conditions in virtually all commercial and industrial establishments are governed by collective bargaining agreements between employers' associations and trade unions. FRG workers in the coal, iron, and steel industries have had the right to co-determination in management since 1951. Under the Co-determination Act of 1976, this right was extended to all companies with over 2,000 employees.

Although the 40-hour workweek is common, the law establishes a maximum workweek of 5½ days or 48 hours (44 hours for women) in manufacturing and building; a 25% premium for overtime; paid holidays and vacations (15 workdays annually, minimum, and 18 days for employees over 35 years of age); and a 10% premium for night work. About 90% of the western German wage and salary earners are covered by a collective bargaining agreement, which partly explains the relatively high wages in the absence of a minimum wage law, and why working time and vacation provisions exceed legal requirements.

[22] AGRICULTURE

Although 34% of the total area of the FRG is devoted to crop production, production falls far short of satisfying industrial and consumer demand. Agriculture (including forestry and fishing) accounts for only 1% of GDP. The total amount of arable land in 1990 came to 11,971,000 hectares (29,580,300 acres), of which the former GDR accounted for 39%. The FRG is the world's second leading importer of tobacco (after the US), which accounted for over $920 million in imports in 1992.

Article 15 of the 1990 Treaty (for monetary, economic and social union) arranged for transitional price supports for GDR farmers until an integration within the EC agricultural market could occur. Before unification, agriculture had engaged about 6.1% and 3% of the economically active populations of the former GDR and old FRG, respectively. The former–GDR Länder contribute significantly to German agricultural production: grains, 31%; potatoes, 48%; fruits, 43%; and vegetables, 31%. The chief crops in order of yield in 1992 were sugar beets, 27,150,000 tons; wheat, 15,542,000 tons; barley, 12,196,000 tons; and potatoes, 10,975,000 tons. Apples and pears as well as cherries and peaches are significant fruit crops. Viticulture is important in the southwest, and the FRG is a renowned producer of wines for world consumption; 1,340,000 tons of wine were produced in 1992.

23 ANIMAL HUSBANDRY

The government regulates the marketing of livestock, meat, and some dairy products; it also controls the distribution of livestock for slaughter and meat. Livestock in 1992 included 17,134,000 head of cattle, 26,063,000 hogs, 2,488,000 sheep, 492,000 horses, 121,000,000 chickens, and 4,000,000 turkeys. Milk production amounted to 28.1 million tons in 1992, and meat production totaled 6.2 million tons. Some 954,000 tons of eggs were produced in 1992. Germany is the leading meat, milk, and honey producer of Europe.

24 FISHING

The importance of the fishing industry has declined in recent years. The total catch in 1991 amounted to 300,164 tons, including 34,406 tons of cod. The main fishing areas are the North Sea and the waters off Greenland. The total value of 1991 fishery exports was $715.9 million, only one-third the value of fish commodity imports.

25 FORESTRY

Total forest area amounted in 1991 to over 10,403,000 hectares (25,706,000 acres), more than 29% of the total land area. About two-thirds of the total woodland is coniferous, the remaining third comprising beeches, oaks, and other deciduous trees. The most thickly wooded of the federal Länder are Hessen and Rhineland-Pfalz. A total of 44.9 million cu m of timber was cut in 1991. In 1991, Germany was the world's leading producer of particleboard, at over 8.2 million cu m, or nearly 17% of world production. Output of paper totaled 13.5 million tons in 1991. High domestic labor costs compel Germany to import substantial quantities of value-added products such as veneers and panels.

26 MINING

In 1991, Germany was Western Europe's leading producer in alumina, refined copper, refined lead, lignite (of which it was the world's leading producer), pig iron, potash, salt, steel, and refined zinc. Germany ranked second in Western Europe in the production of primary aluminum metal, cadmium, cement, nitrogen in ammonia, elemental sulfur and hard (anthracite and bituminous) coal. Although mining of metals continues to decline, the processing of imported raw materials and the production of industrial mineral products (e.g., cement, limestone, potash, salt, and sulfur) contribute to the country's strong economic position. Lignite had been mined primarily in the eastern former-GDR states (the GDR was once the world's largest producer of lignite), but production is expected to be reduced there. Most of the hard coal mines are in the Saar and Ruhr regions.

In 1991, lead was mined at Lennestadt and Bad Grund. Potash primarily comes from Thüringen. In 1991, the uranium mine near Zwickau in the former GDR was deemed unprofitable and closed.

27 ENERGY AND POWER

With extensive coal reserves (about 80 billion tons in 1992), the FRG is the greatest producer of electric power in Western Europe and the fifth largest in the world, at 500 billion kwh in 1991. In 1991, net installed capacity was 123.1 million kw; total production of electric power amounted to 573 billion kwh, of which 68% was produced in conventional thermal plants (mainly fueled by hard coal), 4% in hydroelectric plants, and 28% in nuclear installations. Primary energy consumption in 1991 was from oil, 42%; anthracite, 18.6%; brown coal, 8%; natural gas, 18.1%; nuclear power, 11.6%; and other sources,

2.5%. As of 1991, there were 21 nuclear installations operating in the western states.

Natural gas reserves were estimated at 300 billion cu m in 1992. About one-third of the gas is produced domestically (18 billion cu m in 1992), with the remainder coming from such major foreign suppliers as the former USSR, the Netherlands, and Norway. A gas pipeline linking the former USSR and several West European countries, including the FRG, provided an estimated 22 billion cu m of gas per year to the FRG beginning in October 1984. Production of crude oil amounted to 3.4 million tons in 1991. Local production is not sufficient to cover consumption, which totaled 134.3 million tons in 1992. The lignite industry in the former GDR was drastically changed as a result of unification. In 1991, the eastern states produced only 167,727,000 tons of lignite, down from 249,000,000 tons in 1990. Total FRG production in 1991 was 279,403,000 tons. The strict environmental and safety laws of the pre-1991 FRG have caused some of the coal and nuclear operations in the eastern states to shut down.

28 INDUSTRY

The major industrial concentrations of western Germany are the Ruhr-Westphalia complex; the Upper Rhine Valley, Bremen and Hamburg, notable for shipbuilding; the southern region, with such cities as Munich and Augsburg; and the central region, with such industrial cities as Salzgitter, Kassel, Hanover, and Brunswick. In the east, most of the leading industries are located in the Berlin region or in such cities as Dresden, Leipzig, Dessau, Halle, Cottbus, and Chemnitz. The turnover by sector in 1991 (for western FRG only) included motor vehicles, DM 290.2 billion; chemical engineering, DM 231.9 billion; machinery, DM 227.8 billion; food, DM 211.5 billion; and chemicals, DM 207.6 billion.

The main industrial sectors in the former GDR were electrical engineering and electronics, chemicals, glass and ceramics. The optical and precision industries were important producers of export items. Following unification, wages in the east were allowed to reach levels far exceeding productivity. As a result, many factories closed and industrial production plunged by two-thirds before stabilizing.

Germany produced 4,227,000 passenger cars, 318,000 trucks and commercial vehicles, and 4,097,000 bicycles in 1992. The two leading automakers, Volkswagen and Daimler-Benz, ranked among the world's largest industrial corporations, with 1993 sales of $46.3 and $59.1 billion, respectively. Germany ranked fifth in the world as a steel producer in 1992, with a crude steel output of 32.6 million tons. Cement production totaled 41.7 million tons; motor fuel, 29.2 million tons; and diesel oil, 18.1 million tons.

29 SCIENCE AND TECHNOLOGY

The reunification of East and West Germany is creating great opportunities for all of its people but also placing great strains on the entire nation. Perhaps nowhere is this more evident than in science, engineering and technical education and vocational training. Germany maintains an excellent science and technology educational system and vocational training in many fields. By the mid-1990s, the nation will employ nearly 200 million scientists and engineers at universities, industries and in independent laboratories, a 25% increase from the mid-1980s. Nearly 140,000 science and engineering students will graduate per year through the end of this decade. Still, the challenge of incorporating the former German Democratic Republic (GDR) into a complete and modern German nation is daunting. Public and university research facilities in the former East Germany are old and poorly maintained, and science and engineering students have been found to be poorly trained and equipped to work in more modern West

German institutions and companies. It is believed that the German Government will need to completely rebuild the science and technology infrastructure in the former GDR before it can compare with more modern German facilities.

The German national science and technology budget of approximately DM80 billion ($47.5 billion) is applied to many areas of science and technology, and leading fields include traditional areas of German strength, like chemical, automotive and telecommunications R&D. The current policy emphasis is on applying science and technology to enhance Germany's economic and competitive standing while protecting the nation's health and the environment.

Germany supports national science and technology at many levels. There are independent laboratories, comprised of both the national laboratories and private research institutes like the Max Planck and Fraunhofer Societies. In addition, German industry supports many important types of R&D, and the German states, or Länder, provide still more resources for scientific research. The Ministry for Science and Technology (BMFT), an organization without parallel in the United States, both coordinates and sets priorities for the entire national science and technology program. Finally, Germany's participation in the European Union also has a significant science and technology component—Germany provides funding, scientists, and laboratories for broad European research and development.

30 DOMESTIC TRADE

Wholesalers, retailers, mail-order houses, door-to-door salespersons, department stores, consumer cooperatives, and factory stores all engage in distribution. Wholesale turnover in the FRG rose from about DM50 billion in 1949 to DM1,016 billion in 1991, while retail turnover rose from DM28 billion to DM606 billion in 1990. The number of retail businesses fell from about 445,000 in 1962 to 152,629 in 1990. Chain stores are common.

Usual business hours for retail stores are from 9 AM to 6:30 PM on weekdays and from 9 AM to 2 PM on Saturday. Wholesale houses and industrial plants usually have a half day (noon closing) on Saturday. Banks are open Monday–Friday from 8:30 AM to 1 PM and from 2:30 PM to 4 PM (5:30 PM on Thursday).

31 FOREIGN TRADE

Germany is one of the world's great trading nations. In some years—most recently, 1990—it has surpassed the US as the world's leading exporter. The volume of exports increased from DM8.4 billion in 1950 to DM671 billion in 1992, while the volume of imports increased from DM11.4 billion to DM637.5 billion. Manufactured products are the leading exports, accounting for 90% of the 1992 total. Germany generally enjoys a highly favorable trade balance, but it narrowed in 1991 and 1992.

Principal exports in 1992 (in millions of deutsche marks) were as follows:

Road vehicles	111,675
General industrial	46,718
Machinery and equipment	
chemical products	84,715
Electrical	47,070
Iron, steel, and sheet	
and metal goods	54,360
Textiles	21,646
Specialized machinery	40,782
Other exports	264,237
TOTAL	671,203

Principal imports in 1992 (in millions of deutsche marks) were as follows:

Foods, beverages, and tobacco	61,462
Mineral fuels	47,466
Chemical products	54,555
Electrical goods	34,286
Apparel and clothing	38,591
Road vehicles	63,726
Office machines and data	
processing equipment	28,584
Textiles	19,376
Other imports	289,500
TOTAL	637,546

In 1992, more than half of Germany's total trade was with EC countries. In the same year, Germany enjoyed a favorable trade balance with every EC country except Denmark, Ireland, and the Netherlands. Principal trade partners in 1992 (in millions of deutsche marks) were as follows:

	EXPORTS	IMPORTS	BALANCE
France	86,999.2	76,423.0	10,576.2
Netherlands	55,748.0	61,166.1	−5,418.1
US	42,704.3	42,357.7	346.6
UK	51,951.7	43,571.9	8,379.8
Italy	62,394.7	58,468.0	3,926.7
Belgium-Luxembourg	49,578.6	44,823.4	4,755.2
Switzerland	35,604.6	25,352.3	10,252.3
Austria	39,922.0	28,009.1	11,912.9
Spain	27,424.6	17,087.6	10,337.0
Japan	14,700.7	38,038.2	−23,337.5
Other countries	204,174.2	202,248.9	1,925.3
TOTALS	671,202.6	637,546.2	33,656.4

32 BALANCE OF PAYMENTS

After experiencing deficits during 1979–81, the FRG's current accounts balance rebounded to a surplus of about DM9.9 billion in 1982 and then kept rising to DM76.5 billion in 1986, primarily because of falling prices for crude oil and other imports, combined with appreciation of the deutsche mark relative to other European currencies. By 1989, Germany's current account surplus was nearly 5% of GNP. With reunification, however, this changed immediately. Imports rushed in as former-GDR residents sought newly available consumer goods, and exports fell as goods and services were diverted to the east. As a result, the current account balance fell from a surplus of DM108 billion in 1989 to a deficit of almost DM40 billion in 1992. In 1992, merchandise exports totaled $406.89 million and imports $374.03 million. The merchandise trade balance was $32.87 million. The following table summarizes Germany's balance of payments for 1991 and 1992 (in billions of US dollars):

	1991	1992
CURRENT ACCOUNT		
Goods, services, and income	16.77	6.42
Unrequited transfers	−36.35	−31.98
TOTALS	−19.57	−25.56
CAPITAL ACCOUNT		
Direct investment	−14.94	−8.98
Portfolio investment	24.25	49.52
Other long-term capital	−20.16	−1.93
Other short-term capital	22.98	29.47
Exceptional financing	—	—
Other liabilities	−8.11	−6.49
Reserves	5.97	−36.52
TOTALS	9.99	25.06
Errors and omissions	9.58	0.50
Total change in reserves	5.93	−36.32

33 BANKING AND SECURITIES

The central banking system of Germany consists of the German Federal Bank (Deutsche Bundesbank), located in Frankfurt, one bank for each of the Länder, and one in Berlin, which are the main offices for the Federal Bank. Although the Federal Bank is an independent institution, the federal government holds the bank's capital and appoints the presidents as well as the board of directors; the Central Bank Council acts as overseer.

The Federal Bank is the sole bank of issue. It determines credit and open market transactions, sets interest and discount rates, and is authorized to fix minimum reserve rations for the commercial banks and to grant credit to the federal government as well as to the provincial governments. Foreign assets of the Federal Bank were DM312.6 billion as of December 1993, and currency in circulation was DM2,048.1 million.

In 1991, Germany had 340 commercial banks with 6,600 offices, 220 regional banks, 2141 industrial cooperatives with 18,050 offices, and 80 foreign banks. The largest commercial banks are the Deutsche Bank, Dresdner Bank, and Commerzbank. Commercial reserves totaled DM109.1 in 1993. Foreign assets were DM797.1 in the same year while demand deposits were DM484.8 and time and savings deposits were DM1,350.5.

Under the constitution, the governments of the Länder regulate the operations of stock exchanges and produce exchanges. Stock exchanges operate in Berlin, Bremen, Düsseldorf, Frankfurt, Hamburg, Hannover, Munich, and Stuttgart. Germany has several other independent exchanges for agricultural items. While stock sales have remained fairly steady in recent years, the bond-debture total has risen dramatically.

34 INSURANCE

Spurred by demand in the new federal states, premium income grew 13% in 1991 to reach DM154 billion, or DM2,296 per capita. Over 80% of this revenue was earned by domestic companies. Private health insurance can be obtained to supplement or replace statutory health insurance. Life insurance in force totaled DM2,175 billion in 1992.

35 PUBLIC FINANCE

The 1967 Law for the Promotion of Economic Stability and Growth requires the federal and state governments to orient their budgets to the main economic policy objectives of price stability, high employment, balanced foreign trade, and steady commensurate growth. The Financial Planning Council, formed in 1968, coordinates the federal government, states, municipalities, and the Bundesbank in setting public budgets. Income, corporate, turnover, mineral oil, and trade taxes account for more than 80% of all tax revenue, with the federal government controlling just under half of it. Since the 1960s, social insurance provisions have accounted for the largest share of federal expenditures.

Germany's unification in 1990 raised special problems with regard to economic and financial assimilation. The Unification Treaty provided that the new states should be incorporated in the financial system established by the Basic Law as much as possible from the onset. Therefore, since 1991, the new states have basically been subject to the same regulations with regard to budgetary management and tax distribution as the western states. A "German Unity Fund" was initiated to provide financial support for the new states (and their municipalities); it is jointly financed by the western states, with most of the money being raised in the capital market.

The following table shows actual revenues and expenditures for 1990 and 1991 in billions of deutsche marks.

	1990	1991
REVENUE AND GRANTS		
Tax revenue	654.88	756.40
Non-tax revenue	42.88	47.90
Capital revenue	0.30	0.36
Grants	2.51	2.77
TOTAL	700.57	807.43
EXPENDITURES AND LENDING MINUS REPAYMENTS		
Current expenditures	682.54	802.20
Defense	30.95	53.71
Lending minus repayments	10.87	13.01
TOTALS	724.36	868.92
Deficit/Surplus	−39.55	−66.73

Of the 1992 federal budget total of DM422.1 billion, labor and social security accounted for DM91.3 billion in expenditures; the federal debt, DM55.1 billion; defense, DM52.1 billion; general fiscal administration, DM49.9 billion; transportation, DM40 billion; family and senior citizens, DM31.9 billion; economic affairs, DM15.4 billion; foodstuffs and agriculture, DM13.9 billion; pensions DM12 billion; research and technology development, DM9.3 billion; and other expenditures, DM51.2 billion.

In 1992, Germany's total public debt stood at DM389.44, of which DM32.29 was financed abroad.

36 TAXATION

A value-added tax (15% in 1993) is levied on most goods and services. Businesses with an annual turnover under DM25,000 can be exempted from VAT. Income tax is levied on a progressive scale. Rates and exemptions depend on the number of children, age, and marital status of taxpayer. Depreciation allowances are deductible. The top rate of income tax was 53%. Resident companies pay a corporate income tax of 50% on undistributed profits and 36% on distributed profits. Business activities are also subject to a 17% municipal trade tax. Other taxes include an inheritance and gift tax, a net worth tax, and a 2% real estate transfer tax.

37 CUSTOMS AND DUTIES

About 95% of all imports enter Germany duty free. As of January 1993, all imports from EC countries are duty free. Goods are classified according to the Harmonized System, with rates of 5–17% on most manufactured imports.

38 FOREIGN INVESTMENT

All foreign investment must be reported to the Bundesbank, but there are no restrictions on the repatriation of capital or profits. Only telecommunications is closed to foreign investment. There is no special treatment for foreign investors. Incentives for investment in the former GDR deemed to be desirable include accelerated depreciation and cash investment grants and subsidies.

Germany received $3.75 billion in foreign investment in 1992. Cumulative German investment abroad in that year totaled $29.2 billion.

39 ECONOMIC DEVELOPMENT

Outside of transportation, communications, and certain utilities, the government has remained on the sidelines of entrepreneurship. It has at the same time upheld its role as social arbiter and economic adviser. Overall economic priorities are set by the federal and Land governments pursuant to the 1967 Stability and Growth Act, which demands stability of prices, a high level of employment, steady growth, and equilibrium in foreign trade. In addition to the state, the independent German Federal Bank

(Bundesbank), trade unions, and employers' associations bear responsibility for the nation's economic health. In the international arena, Germany has acted as a leader of European economic integration.

Government price and currency policies have been stable and effective. Less successful have been wage-price policies, which have been unable to control a continued upward movement. Inflationary pressures have increased and combined with a general leveling off in productivity and growth. Attempts to neutralize competition by agreements between competitors and mergers are controlled by the Law Against Restraints of Competition (Cartel Act), passed in 1957 and strengthened since then. The law is administered by the Federal Cartel Office, located in west Berlin.

In 1991, Germany contributed $6.89 billion in development aid to other countries and multilateral development agencies. The leading recipients of German bilateral aid were, in descending order, Kenya, Turkey, Egypt, Zambia, Ghana, India, and China. Official development aid amounted to 0.41% of GNP in 1991.

40SOCIAL DEVELOPMENT

The social security system of the FRG remained in place following unification with the German Democratic Republic. However, the GDR system continued to apply on an interim basis within the former GDR territory. The two systems were merged effective 2 January 1992. The FRG's social insurance system provides for illness, workers' compensation, unemployment, and old age insurance; the program is financed by compulsory employee and employer contributions. As of 1988, the FRG spent 42.6% of its budget on social security and housing. Since 1968, old age and disability insurance has covered all salaried employees irrespective of income level; contributions amount to 8.85% of earnings by employee and an equivalent percentage by employer and are pegged to annual growth of the GNP; benefits are tied to the national index of wages. Self-employed persons are also covered. Accident insurance costs are shared equally between employer and employee; benefits are financed by the government. Special pension funds provide restitution to Nazi era victims for physical, emotional, and material damage suffered during World War II.

About 90% of the population is covered by statutory health insurance; contributions ranged from 4.0% to 23.2% of payroll in 1991, while employees contributed an equal percentage of earnings. Children's allowances, established in 1955, are granted to all families and in 1991 ranged from DM50 monthly for the first child to DM70 monthly for the second child and DM140 for every other child.

Women enjoy full legal equality with men under the Basic Law; legal parity within marriage was ensured by legislation in 1977. However, women tend to be concentrated in low-pay and low-status jobs and can have trouble obtaining training in traditionally male fields. Women's unemployment rate in the eastern states (21.7% in 1993) is high compared with that of men (11%); women accounted for almost 65% of unemployed workers in 1993. Since 1979, women have been entitled to six months' leave under the Maternity Act to care for their newborn babies. The estimated fertility rate in 1985–90 was a very low 1.4. In 1992, Parliament passed a bill that attempted to reconcile the abortion policy of the FRG with that of the former GDR. However, the following year a federal court struck down this compromise legislation and declared abortion unconstitutional, although first-trimester abortions are not subject to prosecution.

41HEALTH

In 1993, health insurance in Germany was available to everyone. Benefits are broad and nationally uniform, with only minor variations among plans. They include free choice of doctors; unlimited physician visits; preventive checkups; total freedom from out-of-pocket payments for physician services; unlimited acute hospital care (with a nominal co-payment); prescription drug coverage (with a minimal co-payment); comprehensive dental benefits (with a 25–30% co-payment); vision and hearing exams, glasses, aids, prostheses, etc.; inpatient and psychiatric care (and outpatient psychiatric visits); monthly home care allowances; maternity benefits; disability payments; and rehabilitation and/or occupational therapy. In 1993, Germany spent 80.9 billion marks on health care.

Between 1990 and 1992, Germany immunized its children up to one year old against tuberculosis (84%); diphtheria, pertussis, and tetanus (95%); polio (95%); and measles (80%).

In 1992, there were 242,000 physicians (a rate of 281 per 100,000 population, or 2.73 per 1,000), with a nurse to doctor ratio of 1.7). In the same year, there were 3,100 hospitals and clinics; 70,000 doctors' offices; 35,000 pharmacies; 11,000 medical aid shops; and 1,100 pharmaceutical companies. A 1991 study provided the following statistics: 228,368 physicians; 52,816 dentists; 411,437 nursing staff; 8,434 midwives; 39,510 pharmacists; 20,457 pharmacies; and 3,585 hospitals with 833,055 beds. Between 1985 and 1990, there were 8.7 hospital beds per 1,000 people.

There were 912,000 births in 1992, with an average life expectancy of 76 years. Infant mortality was 7 per 1000 live births in the same year. From 1990 to 1994, the birth rate was 11.4 per 1,000 live births, and the overall death rate was 11.4 per 1,000 people. Between 1985 and 1990, major causes of death per 100,000 people were: communicable diseases and maternal/perinatal causes (35); noncommunicable diseases, with cancer and circulatory/cerebrovascular problems among the highest (468); and injuries (45). There were 18 reported cases of tuberculosis per 100,000 people in 1990.

42HOUSING

Nearly 2.8 million of the country's 12 million dwellings were destroyed or made uninhabitable as a result of World War II. In the early 1950s, there were 10 million dwellings available for 17 million households. From 1949 to 1972, 12.8 million housing units were built, a construction rate of over 500,000 a year; since then, new construction has slowed, averaging 357,000 new units annually during 1980–85. By the end of 1985, the FRG had 27,081,000 dwellings, and the reunited country had roughly 33,860,000 dwellings in 1992, of which about 40% were owner occupied. Housing units in the western states and those in the states of the former East Germany differ considerably. In western Germany, each individual has about 36 square meters of living space, significantly more than is found in the eastern states. About 95% of all flats have a bath and 75% have central heating. The housing stock in the new federated states is older than that in the west; two-thirds of its houses were built before World War II, and many have deteriorated and lack modern sanitary facilities. Many new housing units must be built in eastern Germany and millions of old ones renovated.

43EDUCATION

Most German schools are state run, and private schools are few and far between. Each of the Länder, including the six new ones, is responsible for its own system. Therefore, though the overall structure is basically the same, it is difficult for a pupil to transfer from one school to another. Attendance at all public schools and universities is free.

German teachers are civil servants. They are required to have a teaching degree and paid according to a uniform salary scale. Children start school after their sixth birthday and are required to attend until they turn 18 years of age. Full-time attendance is mandatory for nine years (ten years in some Länder).

After four years of primary or elementary school (*Grundschule*), students choose from three types of secondary school. The best pupils go to a *gymnasium* which prepares them for the university maticulation examination, or *abitur*. Next is the *realschule*, a middle-level school leading to technical job training and middle management employment. The lowest type is the *hauptschule*, or general school.

The original East German school system has been abolished. There has, however, developed a network of correspondence courses geared for those who wish to continue studies while working on the side. In Germany, vocational training is the rule. On-the-job training in an authorized company is combined with instruction in a vocational school. Vocational training is concluded by taking a theoretical and practical examination before a Board of the Chamber, and those who pass are given a certificate. This system of vocational training has clearly reduced youth unemployment.

In 1990 there were 8,962,000 pupils in schools of general education; 2,570,000 pupils enrolled in vocational education; 97,000 in public health school. There were 1,318,000 students enrolled at universities, 29,000 in colleges of arts, and 373,000 in technical colleges. Teachers at schools of general education numbered 658,000; in schools of vocational education, 118,000; and in public health schools, 4,000.

44LIBRARIES AND MUSEUMS
Germany had no national library until 1913, when the German Library (6.8 million volumes in 1992) in Leipzig brought together all literature of the German language under one roof. The library also contains 3.9 million volumes of works written in exile by German authors during the Nazi era. Other prominent libraries are the Bavarian State Library in Munich (5.5 million books) and the Prussian Cultural Property State Library (3.7 million books) in Berlin. The Herzog-August Library in Wolfenbüttel (660,000 volumes) has an archive of 12,000 handwritten medieval books. One of the most important collections of German literature is at the Central Library of German Classics in Weimar. As of 1992, Germany had some 24,500 public libraries.

There are more than 4,030 state, municipal, association, private, residential, castle, palace, and church and cathedral treasures museums, which annually attract over 100 million visitors. Berlin has the Egyptian and Pergaman Museums, the Painting Gallery of Old Masters, and the National Gallery of Modern Art. The Germanic National Museum in Nurenberg has the largest collection on the history of German art and culture from antiquity to the 20th century. The German Museum in Munich is one of the most well-known natural sciences and technology museums in Europe. In addition, there are numerous smaller museums, ethnological and archeological institutions, scientific collections, and art galleries.

45MEDIA
Since reunification, postal services have been under the jurisdiction of the Deutsche Bundespost Postdienst and telecommunications under Deutsche Bundespost Telekom, which is in the process of upgrading the obsolete telephone network of the former GDR. By late 1991, 500,000 new telephone connections had been installed. In 1991, Germany had more than 45.7 million telephones. There were 11 regional broadcasting corporations, including Zweites Deutsches Fernsehen, which operates Channel Two nationally. In 1991, there were 70 million radios and 44.4 million television sets in Germany.

Germany has the world's fourth greatest number of newspapers. Daily newspapers numbered 410 per 1,000 inhabitants in 1992, and had a total average circulation of 29,953,000. The German Press Agency, owned by German newspaper publishers and publishers' organizations, furnishes domestic and international news. There are hundreds of small press agencies and services.

Of the newspapers sold on the street, the *Bildzeitung* has the largest circulation (4.5 million a day as of 1992). The largest subscription paper is the *Westdeutsche Allgemeine Zeitung* (1992 circulation 700,000). Other influential daily national newspapers (with 1991 circulation) are: the *Frankfurter Allgemeine Zeitung* (413,500); *Die Welt* (274,600); the *Süddeutsche Zeitung* (503,490), and the *Frankfurter Rundschau* (210,300). Major weeklies include *Die Zeit* (490,550), *Rheinischer Merkur* (no data), and *Deutsches Allgemeines Sonntagsblatt* (471,700). Over 20,000 periodicals are published in Germany. The best-known internationally is the news magazine *Der Spiegel* (1,101,130), which is modeled after the American *Time* magazine.

46ORGANIZATIONS
The Federation of German Industries, the Confederation of German Employers' Associations, the Federation of German Wholesale and Foreign Traders, and the Association of German Chambers of Commerce represent business in the FRG. There are about 14 regional associations of chambers of business and industry located in the largest cities; many maintain branch offices in smaller cities. The chambers are organized into provincial associations and are headed by the Permanent Conference of German Industry and Trade.

There are about 80 youth associations, most of which belong to the Federal Youth Ring. The scouting movement is highly active, and the political parties sponsor groups associated in the Ring of Political Youth. There are thousands of groups and associations for various professions, hobbies, and sports, as well as for patriotic and religious purposes. Civil action groups (Bürgerinitiativen) have proliferated in recent years. The private Association of Consumers operates more than 150 local advisory centers.

The cooperative movement is well developed. Consumer cooperatives are represented in the International Cooperative Alliance by the Central Association of German Cooperatives, founded in 1949; it also represents credit cooperatives. The central association of agricultural cooperatives, the German Raiffeisen Society, is located in Wiesbaden. The Association of German Peasants is the largest society of farmers. There is also a Central Association of German Artisan Industries.

47TOURISM, TRAVEL, AND RECREATION
In 1991, 15,648,000 foreign tourists visited the newly reunited Germany. Receipts from tourism were US$10.9 billion, and there were over a million hotel beds with a 44 percent occupancy rate. Germany is famous for its beautiful scenery, particularly the Alps in the south and the river valleys of the Rhine, Main, and Danube; the landscape is dotted with castles and medieval villages. Theater, opera, and orchestral music abound in the major cities. The area that was formerly the GDR offers a number of Baltic beach resorts and scenic Rügen Island. Residents of the US, Canada, the UK, Mexico, South Africa, Australia, New Zealand, and many other countries need only a valid passport to enter Germany for a period of under three months. All border formalities for residents of other EC countries were abandoned with the lifting of trade barriers in 1993.

Facilities for camping, cycling, skiing, and mountaineering are abundant. Football (soccer) is the favorite sport; Germany hosted and won the World Cup competition in 1974. Tennis has become more popular since Boris Becker won the Wimbledon Championship in 1985. The Olympic Games were held in Berlin in 1936, during the Hitler years, and at Munich in 1972.

48FAMOUS GERMANS
The roster of famous Germans is long in most fields of endeavor. The name of Johann Gutenberg (1400?–1468?), who is generally regarded in the Western world as the inventor of movable preci-

sion-cast metal type, and therefore as the father of modern book printing, might well head the list of notable Germans. Martin Luther (1483–1546), founder of the Reformation, still exerts profound influence on German religion, society, music, and language.

The earliest major names in German literature were the poets Wolfram von Eschenbach (1170?–1220?), Gottfried von Strassburg (d.1210?), and Sebastian Brant (1457?–1521). Hans Sachs (1494–1576) wrote thousands of plays, poems, stories, and songs. Hans Jakob Christoffel von Grimmelshausen (1620?–76) created a famous picaresque novel, *Simplicissimus*. The flowering of German literature began with such renowned 18th-century poets and dramatists as Friedrich Gottlieb Klopstock (1724–1803), Gotthold Ephraim Lessing (1729–81), Christoph Martin Wieland (1733–1813), and Johann Gottfried von Herder (1744–1803), and culminated with the greatest German poet, Johann Wolfgang von Goethe (1749–1832), and the greatest German dramatist, Johann Christoph Friedrich von Schiller (1759–1805). Leaders of the Romantic movement included Jean Paul (Jean Paul Friedrich Richter, 1763–1825), August Wilhelm von Schlegel (1767–1845), Novalis (Friedrich von Hardenberg, 1772–1801), Ludwig Tieck (1773–1853), E. T. A. (Ernst Theodor Wilhelm—the A stood for Amadeus, the middle name of Mozart) Hoffmann (1776–1822), and Heinrich Wilhelm von Kleist (1777–1811). The brothers Jakob Grimm (1785–1863) and Wilhelm Grimm (1786–1859) are world-famous for their collections of folk tales and myths. Heinrich Heine (1797–1856), many of whose poems have become folksongs, is generally regarded as the greatest German poet after Goethe. Other significant poets are Friedrich Hölderlin (1770–1843), Friedrich Rückert (1788–1866), Eduard Mörike (1804–75), Stefan Georg (1868–1933), and Rainer Maria Rilke (1875–1926). Playwrights of distinction include Friedrich Hebbel (1813–63), Georg Büchner (1813–37), Georg Kaiser (1878–1945), Ernst Toller (1893–1939), and Bertolt Brecht (1898–1957). Two leading novelists of the 19th century were Gustav Freytag (1816–95) and Theodor Storm (1817–88). Germany's 20th-century novelists include Ernst Wiechert (1887–1950), Anna Seghers (Netty Reiling, 1900–1983), and Nobel Prize winners Gerhart Johann Robert Hauptmann (1862–1946), Thomas Mann (1875–1955), Nelly Sachs (1891–1970), and Heinrich Böll (1917–86). Other major writers of the 20th century include German-born Erich Maria Remarque (1898–1970), Günter Grass (b.1927), and Peter Handke (b.1942).

Leading filmmakers include G. W. (Georg Wilhelm) Pabst (b. Czechoslovakia, 1885–1967), F. W. (Friedrich Wilhelm Plumpe) Murnau (1888–1931), Fritz Lang (b.Austria, 1890–1976), German-born Ernst Lubitsch (1892–1947), Max Ophüls (Oppenheimer, 1902–57), Leni (Helene Bertha Amalie) Riefenstahl (b.1902), Volker Schlöndorff (b.1939), Werner Herzog (b.1942), and Rainer Werner Fassbinder (1946–82). Outstanding performers include Emil Jannings (Theodor Friedrich Emil Janenz, b.Switzerland, 1886–1950), Marlene Dietrich (1901–1992), Klaus Kinski (Claus Günther Nakszynski, b.1926).

The two giants of German church music were Heinrich Schütz (1585–1672) and, preeminently, Johann Sebastian Bach (1685–1750). Significant composers of the 18th century were German-born Georg Friedrich Handel (1685–1759), Carl Philipp Emanuel Bach (1714–88), and Christoph Willibald von Gluck (1714–87). The classical period and music in general were dominated by the titanic figure of Ludwig von Beethoven (1770–1827). Romanticism in music was ushered in by Carl Maria von Weber (1786–1826), among others. Outstanding composers of the 19th century were Felix Mendelssohn-Bartholdy (1809–47), Robert Schumann (1810–56), Richard Wagner (1813–83), and Johannes Brahms (1833–97). Major figures of the 20th century are Richard Strauss (1864–1949), Paul Hindemith (1895–1963), Carl Orff (1895–1982), German-born

Kurt Weill (1900–50), Hans Werner Henze (b.1926), and Karlheinz Stockhausen (b.1928). Important symphonic conductors included Otto Klemperer (1885–1973), Wilhelm Furtwängler (1886–1954), Karl Böhm (1894–1981), and Eugen Jochum (1902–87). Among Germany's outstanding musical performers are singers Elisabeth Schwarzkopf (b.1915) and Dietrich Fischer-Dieskau (b.1925), and pianists Walter Gieseking (1895–1956) and Wilhelm Kempff (b.1895).

Veit Stoss (1440?–1533) was one of the greatest German sculptors and woodcarvers of the 15th century; another was Tilman Riemenschneider (1460?–1531). Outstanding painters, engravers, and makers of woodcuts were Martin Schongauer (1445?–91), Matthias Grünewald (1460?–1528?), Hans Holbein the Elder (1465?–1524), Lucas Cranach (1472–1553), Hans Holbein the Younger (1497?–1543), and above all, Albrecht Dürer (1471–1528). More recent artists of renown are the painters Emil Nolde (1867–1956), Franz Marc (1880–1916), Max Beckmann (1884–1950), the US-born Lyonel Feininger (1871–1956), Otto Dix (1891–1969), and Horst Antes (b.1936); the painter and cartoonist George Grosz (1893–1959); the sculptors Ernst Barlach (1870–1938) and Wilhelm Lehmbruck (1881–1919); the painteretcher-sculptor Käthe Kollwitz (1867–1945); and the architects Walter Gropius (1883–1969), leader of the Bauhaus School of Design, Ludwig Mies van der Rohe (1886–1969), Erich Mendelsohn (1887–1953), Gottfried Böhm (b.1920), and Helmut Jahn (b.1940).

Scholars and Leaders

German influence on Western thought can be traced back at least as far as the 13th century, to the great scholastic philosopher, naturalist, and theologian Albertus Magnus (Albert von Bollstädt, d.1280) and the mystic philosopher Meister Eckhart (1260?–1327?). Philipp Melanchthon (Schwartzerd, 1497–1560) was a scholar and religious reformer. Gottfried Wilhelm von Leibniz (1646–1716) was an outstanding philosopher, theologian, mathematician, and natural scientist. The next two centuries were dominated by the ideas of Immanuel Kant (1724–1804), Moses Mendelssohn (1729–86), Johann Gottlieb Fichte (1762–1814), Friedrich Ernst Daniel Schleiermacher (1768–1834), Georg Wilhelm Friedrich Hegel (1770–1831), Friedrich Wilhelm Joseph von Schelling (1775–1854), Arthur Schopenhauer (1788–1860), Ludwig Andreas Feuerbach (1804–72), Karl Marx (1818–83), Friedrich Engels (1820–95), and Friedrich Wilhelm Nietzsche (1844–1900). In the 20th century, Oswald Spengler (1880–1936), Karl Jaspers (1883–1969), and Martin Heidegger (1889–1976) are highly regarded. One of the founders of modern Biblical scholarship was Julius Wellhausen (1844–1918).

Among the most famous German scientists are Johann Rudolf Glauber (1694–1768), Justus von Liebig (1803–73), Robert Wilhelm Bunsen (1811–99), and Nobel Prize winners Fritz Haber (1868–1934), Carl Bosch (1874–1940), Otto Hahn (1879–1968), Friedrich Bergius (1884–1949), Georg Wittig (1897–1987), Kurt Alder (1902–58), and Ernst Otto Fischer (b.1918) in chemistry; Karl Friedrich Gauss (1777–1855), Georg Simon Ohm (1787–1854), Hermann Ludwig Ferdinand von Helmholtz (1821–94), Heinrich Rudolf Hertz (1857–1894), and Nobel Prize winners Wilhelm Konrad Röntgen (1845–1923), Max Karl Ernst Ludwig Planck (1858–1947), Albert Einstein (1879–1955), Gustav Ludwig Hertz (1887–1975), Werner Heisenberg (1901–76), Walter Bothe (1891–1957), Carl-Friedrich von Weizsäcker (b.1912), and Rudolf Mössbauer (b.1929) in physics; Rudolf Virchow (1821–1902), August von Wassermann (1866–1925), and Nobel Prize winners Robert Koch (1843–1910), Paul Ehrlich (1854–1915), Emil von Behring (1854–1917), Otto H. Warburg (1883–1970), and Konrad Lorenz (b.Austria, 1903) in physiology and medicine; earth scientists Alexander von Humboldt (1769–1859) and

Karl Ernst Richter (1795–1863); and mathematician Georg Friedrich Bernhard Riemann (1826–66). Notable among German inventors and engineers are Gabriel Daniel Fahrenheit (1686–1736), developer of the thermometer; Gottlieb Daimler (1834–1900), Rudolf Diesel (b.Paris, 1858–1913), and Felix Wankel (b.1902), developers of the internal combustion engine; airship builder Count Ferdinand von Zeppelin (1838–1917); and rocketry pioneer Wernher von Braun (1912–77). Leading social scientists, in addition to Marx and Engels, were the historians Leopold von Ranke (1795–1886) and Theodor Mommsen (1817–1903), Nobel Prize winner in literature; the political economist Georg Friedrich List (1789–1846); the sociologists Georg Simmel (1858–1918) and Max Weber (1864–1920); and the German-born anthropologist Franz Boas (1858–1942). Johann Joachim Winckelmann (1717–68) founded the scientific study of classical art and archaeology. Heinrich Schliemann (1822–90) uncovered the remains of ancient Troy, Mycenae, and Tiryns; Wilhelm Dörpfeld (1853–1940) continued his work.

Outstanding figures in German political history are the Holy Roman emperors Otto I (the Great, 912–973), Frederick I (Barbarossa, 1123–90), Frederick II (1194–1250), and Spanish-born Charles V (1500–58); Frederick William (1620–88), the "great elector" of Brandenburg; his great-grandson Frederick II (the Great, 1712–86), regarded as the most brilliant soldier and statesman of his age; Otto Eduard Leopold von Bismarck (1815–98), the Prussian statesman who made German unity possible; Austrian-born Adolf Hitler (1889–1945), founder of Nazism and dictator of Germany (1933–45); and Konrad Adenauer (1876–1967), FRG chancellor (1948–63). Walter Ernst Karl Ulbricht (1893–1973), chairman of the Council of State (1960–73), and leader of the SED from 1950 to 1971, was the dominant political figure in the GDR until his death in 1973. Erich Honecker (1912–94) became first secretary of the SED in 1971 and was chairman of the Council of State and SED general secretary from 1976 until the FRG and GDR merged in 1990. Willi Stoph (b. 1914), a member of the Politburo since 1953, served as chairman of the Council of Ministers in 1964–73 and again from 1976 on. Willy Brandt (b.1913), FRG chancellor (1969–74) won the Nobel Peace Prize for his policy of Ostpolitik. Other Nobel Peace Prize winners were Ludwig Quidde (1858–1941), Gustav Stresemann (1878–1929), and Carl von Ossietzky (1889–1938).

Baron Friedrich Wilhelm Ludolf Gerhard Augustin von Steuben (1730–94) was a general in the American Revolution. Karl von Clausewitz (1780–1831) is one of the great names connected with the science of war. Important military leaders were Hellmuth von Moltke (1800–1891); Gen. Paul von Hindenburg (1847–1934), who also served as president of the German Reich (1925–34); and Gen. Erwin Rommel (1891–1944).

49DEPENDENCIES

The FRG has no territories or colonies.

50BIBLIOGRAPHY

Berg-Schlosser, Dirk and Ralf Rytlewski (eds.). *Political Culture in Germany.* New York: St. Martin's Press, 1993.

Berghahn, Volker Rolf. *Modern Germany: Society, Economy, and Politics in the Twentieth Century.* 2d ed. New York: Cambridge University Press, 1987.

Beyme, Klaus von. *The Political System of the Federal Republic of Germany.* New York: St. Martin's, 1983.

Bithell, Jethro. *Modern German Literature, 1880–1950.* London: Methuen, 1959.

Bullock, Alan Louis Charles. *Hitler: A Study in Tyranny.* Rev. ed. New York: Harper & Row, 1964.

Burdick, Charles, *et al.* (eds.). *Contemporary Germany: Politics and Culture.* Boulder, Colo.: Westview, 1984.

Carr, William. *A History of Germany, 1815–1985.* 3rd ed. London: E. Arnold, 1991.

Childs, David. *Honecker's Germany.* London: Allen & Unwin, 1985.

———. *Germany in the Twentieth Century.* 3rd ed. New York: Icon Editions, 1991.

Davidowicz, Lucy S. *The War Against the Jews, 1933–1945.* New York: Holt, Rinehart & Winston, 1975.

Fest, Joachim. *Hitler.* New York: Random House, 1975.

Gay, Peter. *Weimar Culture: The Outsider as Insider.* New York: Harper & Row, 1968.

Gortemaker, Manfred. *Unifying Germany, 1989–1990.* New York: St. Martin's Press, 1994.

Gutjahr, Lothar. *German Foreign and Defence Policy after Unification.* New York: St. Martin's Press, 1994.

Henderson, W. O. *The Rise of German Industrial Power, 1834–1914.* Berkeley: University of California Press, 1976.

Hertz, Friedrich Otto. *The Development of the German Public Mind: A Social History of German Political Sentiments, Aspirations and Ideas.* London: Allen & Unwin, 1957–62.

Hoffmann, Peter. *The History of the German Resistance, 1933–1945.* Cambridge, Mass.: MIT Press, 1977.

Holborn, Hajo. *A History of Modern Germany.* 3 vols. New York: Knopf, 1959–69.

Huelshoff, Michael G., Andrei S. Markovits, and Simon Reich (eds.). *From Bundesrepublik to Deutschland: German Politics after Unification.* Ann Arbor: University of Michigan Press, 1993.

James, Harold. *A German Identity: 1770–1990.* New York: Routledge, 1989.

Kahler, Erich. *The Germans.* Princeton, N.J.: Princeton University Press, 1974.

Koch, Hannsjoachim. *A Constitutional History of Germany in the Nineteenth and Twentieth Centuries.* New York: Longmans, 1984.

Maier, Charles S. *The Unmasterable Past: History, Holocaust, and German National Identity.* Cambridge, Mass.: Harvard University Press, 1988.

McAdams, A. James. *Germany Divided: From the Wall to Reunification.* Princeton, N.J.: Princeton University Press, 1993.

McCauley, Martin. *The German Democratic Republic Since 1945.* New York: St. Martin's, 1986.

Orlow, Dietrich. *The History of the Nazi Party.* 2 vols. Pittsburgh: University of Pittsburgh Press, 1969–73.

Pflanze, Otto. *Bismarck and the Development of Germany: The Period of Unification, 1815–1871.* Princeton, N.J.: Princeton University Press, 1963.

Raff, Diether. *A History of Germany: From the Medieval Empire to the Present.* New York: St. Martin's Press, 1988.

Ryder, A. J. *Twentieth-Century Germany: From Bismarck to Brandt.* New York: Columbia University Press, 1973.

Sanford, Gregory. *From Hitler to Ulbricht.* Princeton, N.J.: Princeton University Press, 1983.

Sarkar, Saral K. *Green-alternative Politics in West Germany.* New York: United Nations University Press, 1993.

Shirer, William L. *The Rise and Fall of the Third Reich.* New York: Simon & Schuster, 1960.

Smith, Gordon (ed.). *Developments in German Politics.* Durham: Duke University Press, 1992.

Speer, Albert. *Inside the Third Reich: Memoirs of Albert Speer.* Translated by Richard and Clara Winston. New York: Macmillan, 1970.

Stern, Fritz. *Gold and Iron: Bismarck, Bleichröder, and the Building of the German Empire.* New York: Knopf, 1977.

———. *Dreams and Delusions: the Drama of German History.* New York: Knopf, 1987.

Treverton, Gregory F. *America, Germany, and the Future of*

Europe. Princeton, N.J.: Princeton University Press, 1992.

Turner, Henry Ashby, Jr. *The Two Germanies Since 1945.* New Haven, Conn.: Yale University Press, 1987.

Valentin, Veit. *The German People: Their History and Civilization from the Holy Roman Empire to the Third Reich.* New York: Knopf, 1946.

Watson, Alan. *The Germans: Who are They Now?* London: Thames Methuen, 1992.

Wedgwood, Cicely Veronica. *The Thirty Years' War.* New Haven, Conn.: Yale University Press, 1939.

GREECE

Hellenic Republic

Elliniki Dhimokratia

CAPITAL: Athens (Athínai).

FLAG: The national flag consists of nine equal horizontal stripes of royal blue alternating with white and a white cross on a royal-blue square canton.

ANTHEM: *Ethnikos Hymnos (National Hymn),* beginning "Se gnorizo apo tin kopsi" ("I recognize you by the keenness of your sword").

MONETARY UNIT: The drachma (D) is a paper currency of 100 lepta. There are coins of 50 lepta and 1, 2, 5, 10, 20, and 50 drachmae and notes of 50, 100, 500, 1,000, and 5,000 drachmae. D1 = $0.0041 (or $1 = D246.02).

WEIGHTS AND MEASURES: The metric system is the legal standard.

HOLIDAYS: New Year's Day, 1 January; Epiphany, 6 January; Independence Day, 25 March; Labor Day, 1 May; Assumption, 15 August; National Day (anniversary of successful resistance to Italian attack in 1940), 28 October; Christmas, 25 December; Boxing Day, 26 December. Movable religious holidays include Shrove Monday, Good Friday, and Easter Monday.

TIME: 2 PM = noon GMT.

¹LOCATION, SIZE, AND EXTENT

Greece is the southernmost country in the Balkan Peninsula, with a total area of 131,940 sq km (50,942 sq mi); about a fifth of the area is composed of more than 1,400 islands in the Ionian and Aegean seas. Comparatively, the area occupied by Greece is slightly smaller than the state of Alabama. Continental Greece has a length of 940 km (584 mi) N–S and a width of 772 km (480 mi) E–W. It is bounded on the N by Macedonia and Bulgaria, on the NE by Turkey, on the E by the Aegean Sea, on the S by the Mediterranean Sea, on the SW and W by the Ionian Sea, and on the NW by Albania, with a total boundary length of 14,886 km (9,250 mi). The capital city of Greece, Athens, is located along the country's southern coast.

²TOPOGRAPHY

About four-fifths of Greece is mountainous, including most of the islands. The most important range is the Pindus, which runs down the center of the peninsula from north to south at about 2,650 m (8,700 ft). Mt. Olympus (Ólimbos; 2,917 m/9,570 ft) is the highest peak and was the legendary home of the ancient gods.

Greece has four recognizable geographic regions. The Pindus range divides northern Greece into damp, mountainous, and isolated Epirus (Ipiros) in the west and the sunny, dry plains and lesser mountain ranges of the east. This eastern region comprises the plains of Thessaly (Thessalía) and the "new provinces" of Macedonia (Makedonia) and Thrace (Thraki)—"new" because they became part of Greece after the Balkan wars in 1912–13. Central Greece is the southeastern finger of the mainland that cradled the city-states of ancient Greece and comprises such classical provinces as Attica (Atikí), Boeotia (Voiotia), Doris, Phocis, and Locris. Southern Greece consists of the mountainous, four-fingered Peloponnesus (Pelopónnisos), separated from the mainland by the Gulf of Corinth (Korinthiakós Kólpos). Islands of the Aegean comprise the numerous Cyclades (Kikládes); the Dodecanese (Dhodhekánisos), including Rhodes (Ródhos); and the two large islands of Crete (Kríti) and Euboea (Évvoia).

Greek rivers are not navigable. Many dry up in the summer and become rushing mountain torrents in the spring.

³CLIMATE

The climate in southern Greece and on the islands is Mediterranean, with hot, dry summers and cool, wet winters. Winters are severe in the northern mountain regions. The summer heat is moderated by mountain and sea breezes. Precipitation is heaviest in the north and in the mountains. Average annual rainfall varies from 50 to 121 cm (20–48 in) in the north and from 38 to 81 cm (15–32 in) in the south. The mean temperature of Athens is 17°C (63°F), ranging from a low of 2°C (36°F) in the winter to a high of 37°C (99°F) in the summer.

⁴FLORA AND FAUNA

Of the 6,000 species of plants recorded in Greece, about 600 are endemic to the country. Many pharmaceutical plants and other rare plants and flowers considered botanical treasures flourish in Greece. Vegetation varies according to altitude. From sea level to 460 m (1,500 ft), oranges, olives, dates, almonds, pomegranates, figs, grapes, tobacco, cotton, and rice abound. From 460 to 1,070 m (1,500–3,500 ft) are forests of oak, chestnut, and pine. Above 1,070 m (3,500 ft), beech and fir are most common.

Fauna are not plentiful, but bear, wildcat, jackal, fox, and chamois still exist in many sparsely populated areas. The wild goat (agrimi), which has disappeared from the rest of Europe, still lives in parts of Greece and on the island of Crete. Migratory and native birds abound, and there are more than 250 species of marine life. Natural sponges are a main export item.

⁵ENVIRONMENT

Among Greece's principal environmental problems is industrial smog and automobile exhaust fumes in metropolitan Athens. Fifty-nine percent of all industry is located in the greater Athens area. From June to August 1982, the air pollution became so oppressive that the government closed down 87 industries, ordered 19 others to cut production, and banned traffic from the city center. In July 1984, the smog again reached the danger point, and 73 factories were ordered to cut production and cars were banned from the city. In January 1988, the number of taxis in the center of Athens was halved, and private cars were banned from the city's three main thoroughfares. The smog regularly sends hundreds of Greeks to the hospital with respiratory and heart complaints. Greece produces 0.3% of the world's gas emissions. The nation's hydrocarbon emissions amount to 286.5 tons annually. This situation is the result of almost complete disregard for environmental protection measures during the rapid industrial growth of the 1970s, compounded by unbalanced development and rapid, unregulated urban growth. Water pollution is also a significant problem due to industrial pollutants, agricultural chemicals such as fertilizers and pesticides, and sewage. The Gulf of Saronikos is one of the most polluted areas because 50% of Greece's industrial facilities are located there. Since 1970, the use of agricultural chemicals has increased by 100%. Greece has 10.8 cubic miles of water with 63% used for farming and 29% used for industrial purposes. The nation's cities produce 3.5 million tons of solid waste per year. The incumbent government of George Papandreou has adopted a national policy that emphasizes rational use of natural resources, balanced regional development, protection of the environment, and increased public participation in environmental matters. Four environmental and planning services have been consolidated under the new Ministry for Physical Planning, Housing, and the Environment.

In 1994, 4 of Greece's mammal species and 19 of its bird species are endangered. Three types of reptiles and 6 types of freshwater fish are also endangered. Of the nation's 6,000 plant species, 526 are threatened with extinction. As of 1987, the Mediterranean monk seal, hawksbill turtle, and large copper butterfly were endangered species.

⁶POPULATION

The 1991 census reported a total population of 10,269,074, or 5.4% more people than at the 1981 census. The population for the year 2000 was projected at 10,324,000, assuming a crude birthrate of 10.4 per 1,000 population, a crude death rate of 10, and a net natural increase of 0.4 between 1995 and 2000. The 1991 population density was 78 per sq km (202 per sq mi). In 1995, 65% of the population was estimated as urban, and 35% rural. The greater Athens metropolitan area had 3,096,775 residents in 1991.

⁷MIGRATION

Under League of Nations supervision in 1923, more than 1 million Greek residents of Asia Minor were repatriated, and some 800,000 Turks left Greece. During the German occupation (1941–44) and the civil war (1944–49), there was a general movement of people from the islands, the Peloponnesus, and the northern border regions into the urban areas, especially the Athens metropolitan area, including Piraiévs. Between 1955 and 1971 about 1,500,000 peasants left their farms—about 600,000 going to the cities, the rest abroad. According to the 1981 census, 813,490 Greeks had migrated since 1975 to urban areas, and 165,770 had moved to rural areas. The growth rate of the Athens, Salonika, Pátrai, Iráklion, and Vólos metropolitan areas during 1971–81 far exceeded the population growth rate for the nation as a whole.

Many Greeks leave the country for economic reasons. In the years after World War II, the number of annual emigrants has varied from a high of 117,167 (in 1965) to a low of 20,330 (in 1975). The net outflow of Greek workers during the 1960s was 450,000; during the 1970s, however, there was a net inflow of 300,000. This mainly reflected declining need for foreign labor in western Europe.

In 1974, when the Greek military government collapsed, about 60,000 political refugees were living overseas; by the beginning of 1983, about half had been repatriated, the remainder being, for the most part, Communists who had fled to Soviet-bloc countries after the civil war of 1944–49. In 1989 there were 225,624 foreigners officially residing in Greece, of whom 52,138 formerly held Greek citizenship. American, British, and German were the leading nationalities. The numbers of illegal aliens in 1993 was estimated at 400,000–600,000, of whom 100,000–200,000 were believed to be Albanians.

⁸ETHNIC GROUPS

About 98% of the population was Greek in 1989. Minority groups include Turks, Macedonian Slavs, Albanians, Armenians, Bulgarians, Jews, and Vlachs. Although the 1923 Treaty of Lausanne provided for an exchange of most Greek nationals in Turkey and Turkish nationals in Greece, the Turks of western Thrace (now numbering perhaps 100,000) were allowed to stay.

⁹LANGUAGES

Modern Greek, the official language, is the first language of about 98% of the population. English, learned mostly outside the school system, and French are widely spoken. Turkish and other minority languages, such as Albanian, Pomakic, Kutzovalachian, and Armenian, also are spoken. The vernacular and the language of popular literature are called dimotiki (demotic). The official language—katharevousa—generally used by the state, the press, and universities, employs classical terms and forms. In 1976, the government began to upgrade the status of dimotiki in education and government. The liturgical language is akin to classical Greek.

¹⁰RELIGIONS

Under the constitution, the Eastern Orthodox Church of Christ is the established religion of Greece, but religious freedom is guaranteed. The church is self-governing under the ecumenical patriarch resident in Istanbul, Turkey, and is protected by the government, which pays the salaries of the Orthodox clergy. Members of the Orthodox Church account for about 97% of the population; the remaining 3% are Muslims, Roman Catholics, Protestants, and Jews.

¹¹TRANSPORTATION

Greek transportation was completely reconstructed and greatly expanded after World War II. The length of roads in 1991 was 38,938 km (24,196 mi), of which 16,090 km (9,998 mi) were paved, 13,676 km (8,498 mi) were crushed stone and gravel, 5,632 km (3,500 mi) were improved earth, and 3,540 km (2,200 mi) were of unimproved earth. Toll highways connect Athens with Lamía and Pátrai. In 1991 there were 2,592,334 motor vehicles, including 1,777,484 cars (more than double the 1980 total), 792,770 trucks, and 22,080 buses.

The Hellenic State Railways, a government organ, operates the railroads, which in 1991 had a total length of 2,479 km (1,540 mi). The agency also operates a network of subsidiary bus lines connecting major cities. The privately owned Hellenic Electric Railways operates a high-speed shuttle service between Piraiévs and Athens. Construction of a subway system for Athens was stopped in 1983 for financial reasons.

Principal ports are Elevsís, Salonika, Vólos, Piraiévs, Iráklion, and Thíra. The Greek merchant fleet, the sixth largest in the world, had 914 ships (down from 2,893 in 1982) and a total GRT of 23,004,000 at the end of 1991. In addition, Greek shipowners had many other ships sailing under Cypriot, Lebanese, Liberian, Panamanian or some other foreign registry. The Greek fleet was hard hit by the international shipping slump of the 1980s. The

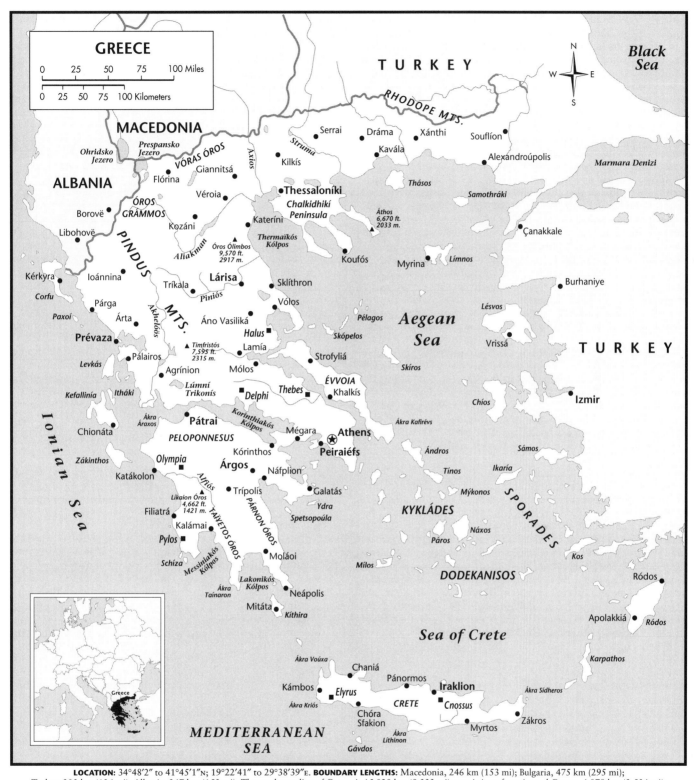

GREECE

0 25 50 75 100 Miles

0 25 50 75 100 Kilometers

TURKEY

Black Sea

MACEDONIA

Ohridsko Jezero

Prespansko Jezero

VÓRAS ÓROS

Axiós

Serrai   Dráma   Xánthi   Souflíon

RHODOPE MTS.

Struma

Kilkís   Kavála   Alexandroúpolis

ALBANIA

Florína

Giannitsá

Véroia

Marmara Denizi

Borovë

ÓROS GRÁMMOS

Kozáni

Katerhíni

Thessaloníki

Chalkidhikí Peninsula

Tháos

Samothráki

Libohovë

Áthos 6,670 ft. 2033 m.

Çanakkale

PINDUS MTS.

Ioánnina

Óros Ólimbos 9,570 ft. 2917 m.

Thermaïkós Kólpos

Koufós   Myrina   *Límnos*   Burhaniye

Kérkyra

Corfu

Trikala

Aliakman

Lárisa

Sklíthron

Piniós

Vólos

Pélagos

Skópelos

Lésvos

Vrissá

Paxoí

Párga

Árta

Akhelóös

Áno Vasiliká

Halus

Aegean Sea

Prévaza

Timfristós 7,595 ft. 2315 m.

Lamía

Strofyliá

Skíros

Izmir

Levkás

Pálairos

Agrínion

Mólos

Delphi

Thebes

Khalkís

ÉVVOIA

Chíos

Kefallinía   *Itháki*

Lúmní Trikonís

Ákra Áraxos

Korinthiakós Kólpos

Pátrai

Mégara

Athens

Ákra Kafirévs

Chionáta

PELOPONNESUS

Kórinthos

Peiraiéfs

Zákinthos

Olympia

Árgos

Náfplion

Ándros

Sámos

Katákolon

Alfiós

Trípolis

Galatás

Týnos

Ikaría

SPORADES

Likaion Óros 4,662 ft. 1421 m.

Ydra

KYKLÁDES

Mýkonos

Filiatrá

TAÏYETOS ÓROS

Kalámai

PÁRNON ÓROS

Spetsopoúla

Páros

Náxos

Kos

Pylos

Moláoi

Mílos

DODEKANISOS

Ródos

Schíza

Messiniakós Kólpos

Ákra Taínaron

Lakonikós Kólpos

Neápolis

Mitáta   *Kíthira*

Apolakkiá   *Ródos*

Sea of Crete

Karpathos

Ákra Voúxa

Chaniá

Pánormos

Iraklion

Ákra Sídheros

Kámbos

Elyrus

CRETE

Cnossus

Ákra Kriós

Chóra Sfakion

Myrtos   Zákros

MEDITERRANEAN SEA

Ákra Líthinon

Gávdos

Ionian Sea

Greece

LOCATION: 34°48′2″ to 41°45′1″N; 19°22′41″ to 29°38′39″E. **BOUNDARY LENGTHS:** Macedonia, 246 km (153 mi); Bulgaria, 475 km (295 mi); Turkey, 203 km (126 mi); Albania, 247 km (153 mi). The total coastline of Greece is 15,020 km (9,333 mi), consisting of continental Greece, 4,078 km (2,534 mi); the Ionian Islands, 1,004 km (624 mi); the Aegean Islands, 8,892 km (5,525 mi); and the Cretan Islands, 1,046 km (650 mi). **TERRITORIAL SEA LIMIT:** 6 mi.

inland waterway system consists of three coastal canals and three inland rivers, for a total of 80 navigable km (50 mi).

Athens Main Airport connects the capital by regular flights to major cities in Europe, the Middle East, and North America. Olympic Airways, nationalized in 1975, operates a large internal domestic network as well as international flights. In 1992, it carried 3,328,400 passengers on domestic flights and 2,137,100 on

international flights. During 1992, Greek airports performed 7,262 million passenger-kilometers (4,513 million passenger-miles) of service.

[12]HISTORY

Civilization in Greece first arose on Crete in the 3d millennium BC, probably as a result of immigration from Asia Minor (now

Turkey). The Minoan civilization (c.3000–c.1100 BC), named after the legendary King Minos (which may have been a title rather than a name), was centered in the capital of Knossos. Civilization on the mainland, known as Helladic (c.2700–c.1100 BC), probably originated from Crete. During the 2d millennium BC, Greece was conquered by Indo-European invaders: first the Achaeans, then the Aeolians and Ionians, and finally the Dorians. The Greeks, who called themselves Hellenes after a tribe in Thessaly (they were called Greeks by the Romans after another tribe in northwestern Greece), adapted the native culture to their own peasant village traditions and developed the characteristic form of ancient Greek political organization, the city-state (polis). The resulting Mycenaean civilization (c.1600–c.1100 BC), named after the dominant city-state of Mycenae, constituted the latter period of the Helladic civilization. The Mycenaeans destroyed Knossos about 1400 BC and, according to legend, the city of Troy in Asia Minor about 1200 BC. The Minoan and Mycenaean civilizations both came to a relatively abrupt end about 1100 BC, possibly as a result of the Dorian invasion, but the foundations had already been laid for what was to become the basis of Western civilization. It was the Greeks who first tried democratic government; produced the world's first outstanding dramatists, poets, historians, philosophers, and orators; and made the first scientific study of medicine, zoology, botany, physics, geometry, and the social sciences.

In the 1st millennium BC, overpopulation forced the Greeks to emigrate and to colonize areas from Spain to Asia Minor. The Greeks derived their alphabet from the Phoenicians during the 8th century BC. By the 6th century BC, the two dominant city-states were Athens and Sparta. The 5th century BC, recognized as the golden age of Athenian culture, brought the defeat of the Persians by the Athenians in the Persian Wars (490–479 BC) and the defeat of Athens and its allies by Sparta and its allies in the Peloponnesian War (431–404 BC). The inability of Greeks to unite politically led to the annexation of their territories by Philip II of Macedon in 338 BC and by his son Alexander the Great. Through Alexander's ambition for world empire and his admiration of Greek learning, Greek civilization was spread to all his conquered lands. The death of Alexander in 323 BC, the breakup of his empire, and the lack of national feeling among the Greeks prepared the way for their conquest by Rome at the close of the Macedonian Wars in 146 BC. Greece was made a Roman province, but Athens remained a center of learning, and the Greek language and culture were widely influential in Rome, in the Egyptian city of Alexandria, and elsewhere. For this reason, the period between the death of Alexander and the beginning of the Roman Empire is known as the Hellenistic period.

When the Roman Empire was officially divided in AD 395, Greece, by this time Christianized, became part of the Eastern Roman Empire, which became known as the Byzantine Empire (so named from Byzantium, the former name of Constantinople, its capital) after the fall of the Western Roman Empire in AD 476 and which lasted for more than a thousand years. During this period, Greek civilization continued to contribute to Byzantine art and culture.

The formal schism between Eastern Orthodox Christianity and Roman Catholicism came in 1054, when Pope Leo IX and Patriarch Michael Cerularius excommunicated each other. The continuity of Byzantine rule was broken by the fall of Constantinople in the Fourth Crusade in 1204. Under the Latin Empire of the East, which lasted until 1261, Greece was divided into feudal fiefs, with the Duchy of Athens passing successively under French, Spanish, and Florentine rulers.

The Ottoman Turks, who conquered Constantinople in 1453 and the Greek peninsula by the end of the decade, gave the Greeks a large degree of local autonomy. Communal affairs were controlled by the Orthodox Church, and Greek merchants ranged throughout the world on their business ventures, but Greece itself was poverty-stricken. Following an unsuccessful attempt to overthrow the Turks in 1770—an uprising aided by Russia, as part of Catherine the Great's plan to replace Muslim with Orthodox Christian rule throughout the Near East—the Greeks, led by the archbishop of Patras, proclaimed a war of independence against the Turks on 25 March 1821. The revolution, which aroused much sympathy in Europe, succeeded only after Britain, France, and Russia decided to aid the Greeks in 1827. These three nations recognized Greek independence through the London Protocol of 1830, and the Ottomans accepted the terms later in the year.

The same three powers also found for Greece a king in the person of Otto I of Bavaria. But he was never popular and was overthrown in 1862, in favor of Prince William George of Denmark, who ruled as King George I until he was assassinated in 1913. During the second half of the 19th century and until after World War II, Greece gradually added islands and neighboring territories with Greek-speaking populations, including the Ionian Islands, ceded by the British in 1864; Thessaly, seized from Turkey in 1881; Macedonia, Crete, and some Aegean islands in 1913; and the Dodecanese Islands and Rhodes, ceded by Italy in 1947.

For Greece, the first half of the 20th century was a period of wars and rivalries with Turkey; of republican rule under the Cretan patriot Eleutherios Venizelos; of occupation by Italy and Germany during World War II (in World War I, Greece had been neutral for three years and had then sided with the Allies); and of a five-year civil war (1944–49) between the government and the Communist-supported National Liberation Front, in which US aid under the Truman Doctrine played a significant role in defeating the insurgency. In September 1946, the Greeks voted back to the throne the twice-exiled George II (grandson of George I), who was succeeded upon his death in April 1947 by his brother Paul I. A new constitution took effect in 1952, the same year Greece joined NATO. For much of the decade, Greece backed demands by Greek Cypriots for *enosis,* or the union of Cyprus with Greece, but in 1959, the Greek, Turkish, and Cypriot governments agreed on a formula for an independent Cyprus, which became a reality in 1960.

King Paul died on 6 March 1964 and was succeeded by his son Constantine. Meanwhile, a parliamentary crisis was brewing, as rightist and leftist elements struggled for control of the army, and the government sought to purge the military of political influence. On 21 April 1967, a successful coup d'etat was staged by a right-wing military junta; leftists were rounded up, press censorship was imposed, and political liberties were suspended. After an unsuccessful countercoup on 13 December 1967, King Constantine and the royal family fled to exile in Italy. Lt. Gen. George Zoetakis was named regent to act for the king, and Col. George Papadopoulos was made premier. A constitutional reform was approved by 92% of the voters in a plebiscite held under martial law on 29 September 1968. Under the new constitution, individual rights were held to be subordinate to the interests of the state, many powers of the king and legislature were transferred to the ruling junta, and the army was granted extended powers as overseer of civil order. The constitution outlawed membership in the Communist Party. US military aid to Greece, suspended after the 1967 coup, was restored by President Richard M. Nixon in September 1970.

Following an abortive naval mutiny in 1973, Greece was declared a republic by the surviving junta. Papadopoulos became president, only to be overthrown by a group of officers following the bloody repression of a student uprising. The complicity of the junta in a conspiracy by Greek army officers on Cyprus against the government of Archbishop Makarios precipitated the final fall from power of Greece's military rulers in July 1974, when the Turkish army intervened in Cyprus and overwhelmed the island's

Greek contingent. Constantine Karamanlis, a former prime minister and moderate, returned from exile to form a civilian government that effectively ended eight years of dictatorial rule.

General elections held on 17 November 1974, the first since 1964, marked the recovery of democratic rule. In a referendum held on 8 December 1974, 69% of the electorate voted to end the monarchy and to declare Greece a parliamentary republic. On 7 June 1975, a democratic constitution was adopted by the new legislature, although 86 of the 300 members boycotted the session. Karamanlis became Greece's first prime minister under the new system, and on 19 June 1975, parliament elected Konstantinos Tsatsos as president.

Prime Minister Karamanlis, who had withdrawn Greece from NATO's military structure in 1974 to protest Turkey's invasion of Cyprus, resumed military cooperation with NATO in the fall of 1980 (a few months after he was elected president of Greece) and brought his nation into the EC effective 1 January 1981. With the victory of the Pan-Hellenic Socialist Movement (Panellinio Socialistikou Kinema—PASOK) in the elections of October 1981, Greece installed its first Socialist government. The new prime minister, Andreas Papandreou—the son of former Prime Minister George Papandreou and a man accused by rightists in 1967 of complicity in an abortive leftist military plot—had campaigned on a promise to take Greece out of the EC (although his government did not do so). In November 1982, he refused to allow Greek participation in NATO military exercises in the Aegean, which were then canceled. In January 1983, the government declared a general amnesty for the Communist exiles of the 1944–49 civil war.

In mid-1982, in an attempt to deal with the deepening economic crisis, the government created a ministry of national economy, which embraced industrial and commercial affairs. The proposed "radical socialization" of the economy, however, provoked widespread opposition, which limited it to the introduction of worker participation in supervisory councils; state control was imposed only on the pharmaceutical industry (in 1982), and of Greece's largest enterprises, only the Heracles Cement Co. was nationalized (in 1983). Relations with labor were strained as the government sought to balance worker demands that wages be indexed to inflation with the growing need for austerity; in late 1986, the government imposed a two-year wage freeze, which provoked widespread strikes and demonstrations.

In 1985, Prime Minister Papandreou unexpectedly withdrew his support for President Karamanlis' bid for a second five-year term and announced amendments to the constitution that would transfer powers from the president to the legislature and prime minister. Karamanlis resigned, and Papandreou proceeded with his proposed changes, calling an election in June and winning a mandate to follow through with them (parliament's approval was given in March 1986). Subsequently, however, the government began to lose power; the opposition made substantial gains in the 1986 local elections, and a 1987 scandal associated with Papandreou further weakened the government. In January 1988, Papandreou met with Turkish Premier Turgut Ozal in Switzerland; they agreed to work toward solving the problems between the two countries.

Two rounds of parliamentary elections were held in 1989; neither was conclusive. After the June vote, the center-conservative New Democracy (ND) party, with 146 of 300 seats, formed a government with left-wing parties and concentrated on investigating scandals of the Papandreou government, including those of the former prime minister himself. That government resigned in the fall and new elections were held in November. The ND and PASOK both improved their totals and an all-party coalition was formed to address economic reform. That government, however, also failed. In April 1990 elections, the ND emerged victorious to lead the government.

In the balloting of 10 October 1993, PASOK won 171 seats to 110 for the ND. Voters appeared dissatisfied with ND's economic reforms while PASOK won support for its hard-line foreign policy demanding that the former Yugoslav Republic of Macedonia change its name. Many Greeks believe the name of the newly independent state implies territorial designs on the northern Greek region which once formed part of historic Macedonia.

13GOVERNMENT

Before the 1967 coup, executive power was vested in the crown but was exercised by a Council of Ministers appointed by the king and headed by a premier. The 1975 constitution abolished the 146-year-old Greek monarchy and created the office of president as head of state. If a majority in parliament fails to agree on the selection of a president, the office is filled in a general election. The president, who is limited to two five-year terms, appoints the prime minister, who is head of government and requires the confidence of parliament to remain in power. (The constitution was amended in 1986 to reduce the power of the president, limiting his right to dissolve parliament on his own initiative and depriving him of the right to dismiss the prime minister, veto legislation, or proclaim a state of emergency; basically, these powers were transferred to parliament.) The prime minister selects a cabinet from among the members of parliament.

Legislative power is vested in a parliament (Vouli), a unicameral body of 300 deputies elected by direct, universal, secret ballot for maximum four-year terms. A proportional electoral system makes it possible for a party with a minority of the popular vote to have a parliamentary majority. In the 1974 elections, voting was made compulsory for all persons aged 21–70 residing within 200 km (124 mi) of their constituencies.

14POLITICAL PARTIES

Postwar political parties in Greece centered more around leaders than platforms. The Greek Rally, founded and led by Field Marshal Alexander Papagos, won control of the government in the 1951 elections. About 10% of the vote was received by the Union of the Democratic Left, a left-wing party founded in 1951 as a substitute for the Communist Party, outlawed since 1947. When Papagos died in October 1955, Constantine Karamanlis formed a new party called the National Radical Union, which won the elections of 1956, 1958, and 1961 and held power until 1963, when Karamanlis resigned and the newly formed Center Union, comprising a coalition of liberals and progressives and led by George Papandreou, subsequently won a narrow plurality, with Papandreou becoming prime minister. In elections held in February 1964, the Center Union won 174 out of 300 seats; however, King Constantine dismissed Papandreou in July 1965, and Stephanos Stephanopoulos formed a new government. This government, too, was short-lived. Political conflict came to a head when Panayotis Kanellopoulos, leader of the National Radical Union, who had been appointed premier of a caretaker government, set new elections for 28 May 1967. On 21 April, however, a military coup resulted in the cancellation of elections and suppression of political parties, which lasted until 1974.

On 28 September 1974, following his return from exile, Karamanlis formed the New Democracy Party (Nea Dimokratia—ND), advocating a middle course between left and right and promoting closer ties with Western Europe. The Center Union–New Forces (EKND), renamed the Union of the Democratic Center (EDHK) in 1976, rallied liberal factions of the former Center Union and announced a line that generally paralleled ND policies. The EDHK disintegrated following the 1981 elections. Other groups to emerge, most of them led by former opponents of the junta, included the Pan-Hellenic Socialist Movement (Panellinio Socialistikou Kinema—PASOK), led by Andreas Papandreou; the United Left (UL), which brought together elements of the Union of the Democratic Left and of the Communist Party to oppose the upcoming elections; and the National Democratic Union (NDU), which represented an amalgam of various elements, including some royalists and right-wing activists. Also in 1974, the Communist Party (Kommounistiko Komma Ellados—KKE) was made legal for the first time since 1947; the party later split into two factions, the pro-Soviet KKE-Exterior and the Eurocommunist wing, called the KKE-Interior. In May 1986, the KKE-Interior changed its name to the New Hellenic Left Party.

In the general elections held on 17 November 1974, the ND won an overwhelming majority in parliament, with the EKND forming the major opposition. The ND was again the winner in 1977, although its parliamentary majority dropped from 220 to 172. After parliament elected Karamanlis president in 1980, George Rallis succeeded him as prime minister. In the elections of 18 October 1981, Papandreou's PASOK won 48% of the popular vote and commanded a clear parliamentary majority. Although PASOK won again in the election of 2 June 1985, its share of the total votes cast fell to 45.8%.

In the elections of 10 October 1993, PASOK had about the same percentage (46.9%) and a majority of 171 seats. The ND followed with 110 seats and an offshoot party, Political Spring, had 10 seats. The Communists gained 9 places.

15 LOCAL GOVERNMENT

The 1975 constitution restored the large measure of local self-government initially provided for in the constitution of 1952 and reemphasized the principle of decentralization, although local units must depend on the central government for funding. Under the military regime of 1967–74, local units had been closely controlled by the central authorities.

Greece is divided into 13 regional governments (periferi-archis), which are subdivided into 51 prefectures or nomarchies (nomoi), in addition to Greater Athens and the autonomous administration of Mt. Áthos (Aghion Oros) in Macedonia. Each prefecture is governed by a *nomarch* who is nominally appointed by the minister of the interior. *Nomoi* are further divided into two or more provinces or *eparchies,* of which there were 147 in mid-1986. There were also 295 municipalities (cities of more than 10,000 inhabitants), administered by mayors; 5,728 communes (with 300 to 10,000 inhabitants), each run by a president and a community council; and 12,315 localities.

The rocky promontory of Mt. Áthos, southeast of Salonika, is occupied by 20 monasteries of the Greek Orthodox Church. Mt. Áthos is governed by a 4-member council and a 20-member assembly (1 representative from each monastery). The special status of Mt. Áthos was first formalized in the 1952 constitution.

16 JUDICIAL SYSTEM

The 1975 constitution designates the Supreme Court (Areios Pagos), made up of 11 judges, as the highest court of appeal. It consists of 2 penal and 4 civil sections. A Council of State does not hear cases but decides on administrative disputes, administrative violations of laws, and revision of disciplinary procedures affecting civil servants. The 1975 constitution also established a Special Supreme Tribunal as a final arbiter in disputes arising over general elections and referenda. Other elements of the judicial system include justices of the peace, magistrates' courts, courts of first instance, courts of appeal, and various administrative courts. Judges of the Supreme Court, the courts of appeal, and the courts of first instance are appointed for life on the recommendation of the Ministry of Justice. The president has the constitutional right, with certain exceptions, to commute and reduce sentences.

The constitution provides for an independent judiciary.

17 ARMED FORCES

The Hellenic armed forces are a member of NATO. All able-bodied men of 21 years of age are obliged to fulfill 19–23 months of military service, plus reserve service to age 50. The average annual call-up is about 50,000. The total reserves number 406,000. There were 159,300 in the army (125,800 male conscripts and 4,200 women volunteers), 19,500 in the navy, and 26,800 in the air force. The Greek field army has a large and varied combined arms structure, but only 2 of 9 divisions are kept combat ready. Two brigades are also maintained for rapid deployment. Two battalions (2,250) serve on Cyprus. The navy had 10 submarines, 9 destroyers, 4 frigates, 2 coastal minelayers, 37 patrol and coastal combatants, 14 minesweepers, 14 coastal minesweepers, and 26 other vessels as well as 15 armed helicopters. The air force had 381 combat aircraft. The gendarmerie numbered 26,500, and 4,000 customs and coast guards. Defense expenditures in 1991 were $3.8 billion or 5.6% of GDP. The US has one major naval base on Greek soil and several smaller installations.

Between 1981 and 1991, Greece received $5.6 billion in military aid, most of which came from the US. This aid dropped dramatically in 1990 to $120 million.

18 INTERNATIONAL COOPERATION

Greece is a charter member of the UN, having joined on 25 October 1945, and participates in ECE and all the nonregional specialized agencies. Greece was admitted to NATO in 1951 but suspended its military participation (1974–80) because of the Cyprus conflict. It belongs to the Council of Europe and OECD and is a signatory of GATT and the Law of the Sea. Greece is also a permanent observer at the OAS. The country, which had been an associate member of the EC, became a full member as of 1 January 1981. In August 1987, Greece and Albania signed a pact ending the state of war that had existed between them since World War II.

19 ECONOMY

The Greek economy suffers from a paucity of exploitable natural resources and a low level of industrial development relative to the rest of Western Europe. By 1992, it had fallen behind Portugal to become the poorest EC member. However, there is an unrecorded underground economy whose size is estimated at 30-50% of the official one. In the early 1990s, agriculture (with forestry and fishing) generated about 13% of the GDP but employed about 22% of the labor force. Agriculture produced 21% of 1992 exports, chiefly tobacco, cotton, wheat, raisins, currants, fresh fruits, olive oil, and olives. Industry and construction accounted for about 28% of the GDP and 25% of the labor force. Wholesale and retail trade and other services provided more than 50% of the GDP.

Next to food processing, textile manufacturing used to be the most important industry, but chemicals and metals and machinery have outstripped it in recent years. Paper products has been the fastest-growing industry since 1980. Greece has stimulated foreign investments in the development of its mineral resources by constitutionally providing guarantees for capital and profits. The government has encouraged tourism, which has developed into a major source of revenue. Greece continues to play a dominant role in the international shipping industry.

During the late 1950s and 1960s, the government took steps to reclaim land, develop new farms, increase credits and investments for agriculture, protect agricultural prices, and improve the agricultural product and utilize it to the best advantage; however, the country still depends on many imports to meet its food needs. Industrial output contributed substantially to the rapid increase in national income since 1960, and manufacturing and service industries were the fastest-growing sectors in the 1970s.In the 1980s, however, the economy retracted sharply because of the world recession and growth in real terms was sluggish. In the best year of the decade, 1988, GDP grew by 4.9%. It grew by 3.7% in

1989, dropped by 1.5% in 1990, then grew by 3.4% in 1991, and by 0.9% in 1992.

[20] INCOME

In 1992, Greece's GNP was $75,106 million at current prices, or $7,180 per capita. For the period 1985–92 the average inflation rate was 16.5%, resulting in a real growth rate in per capita GNP of 1.1%.

In 1992 the GDP was $79,016 million in current US dollars. It is estimated that in 1990 agriculture, hunting, forestry, and fishing contributed 13% to GDP; mining and quarrying, 1%; manufacturing, 14%; electricity, gas, and water, 2%; construction, 6%; wholesale and retail trade, 11%; transport, storage, and communication, 7%; finance, insurance, real estate, and business services, 8%; community, social, and personal services, 14%; and other sources, 24%.

[21] LABOR

In 1991, the total civilian labor force was estimated at 3.98 million people. Between 1970 and 1990, the estimated proportion of the labor force in agriculture declined from 56% to 22%, while the proportion of the work force in manufacturing remained steady at about 20% and services rose from 24% to 53%. Registered unemployment was 9.0% of the work force in 1991, compared with 2.4% in 1980, and the unemployment rate for young workers under age 25 in urban areas was strikingly high (41% in the second quarter of 1985). Females accounted for 37% of the work force in 1990, compared with 23% in 1971; women also accounted for 70% of those unemployed who had previously not been employed, indicating that women continue to enter the labor force. During the 1960s, with demand for labor high among the more developed countries of Western Europe, Greece exported its surplus laborers; from the 1970s through 1983, however, as available jobs overseas diminished, there was a net inflow of repatriates, which increased the labor force at an annual rate of 2% during that time.

Unions are organized on a territorial rather than a plant basis: all workers of a certain trade in a town usually belong to one union. On a nationwide scale, union members of the same trade or profession form a federation; the General Confederation of Greek Workers (GSEE), with 522,500 members, is the central core of the union movement. Government plays an important role in labor-management relations. Collective bargaining is provided by law, and if agreement is not reached, the Ministry of Labor may be called upon to mediate. If this fails, the dispute is referred to tripartite arbitration committees whose decisions are binding on both parties. In March 1992, public sector unions launched a series of successive strikes to protest the suspension of the right to collective bargaining for 1992. The EAS Blue Bus Union had a strike lasting two years in 1991–92, when, after failing to reach a consensus, the government dissolved the EAS Company, sold the assets to eight private companies, and laid off all 8,000 employees. As a result, a new wave of nationwide strikes and demonstrations hit the country in September 1992, resulting in blackouts and closures of state banks and post offices. In 1991 there were 161 strikes resulting in 5,839,650 lost workdays.

The maximum legal workweek is 40 hours in the private sector and 37½ hours in the public sector. As of 1 July 1992, the minimum monthly salary negotiated by the GSEE was D85,799, or D3,839 per week. As of mid-1990, the average weekly earnings for workers in manufacturing amounted to D26,692. The automatic indexation of wages and salaries to inflation was stopped as of 1 January 1991. Annual vacations with pay are provided by law, and in general, employment of children under the age of 14 is prohibited. Christmas bonuses customarily equal a month's wages, and Easter bonuses equal half a month's wages. Dismissal

wages vary with type of work. Industrial health and safety standards are set by law.

[22] AGRICULTURE

Agriculture in Greece suffers not only from natural limitations, such as poor soils and droughts, but also from soil erosion, lack of fertilizers, and insufficient capital investment.

About 30% of the land area is cultivable, and it supports over half of the population. Of the land under cultivation in 1991, about 73% was planted in seasonal crops, and 27% in orchards and vineyards. Almost 31% of the arable land was irrigated. Although agriculture accounts for 22% of the work force, its role in the economy is declining; in 1991 agriculture accounted for 13% of GDP, down from 25% in the 1950s.

In recent decades, Greek agriculture has been characterized by an increasing diversification of fruit crops for export. Agricultural production of principal crops in 1992 was estimated as follows (in thousands of tons): wheat, 2,786; corn, 1,955; olives, 1,700; tomatoes, 1,690; grapes, 1,300; potatoes, 965; oranges, 872; barley, 495; olive oil, 330; cotton, 275; tobacco, 182; rice, 95; and oats, 88.

Progress has been made toward modernization in machinery and cultivation techniques. Agricultural products, including processed foods, beverages, and tobacco, make up one-third of total exports. To expand agricultural production and encourage farm prosperity, the government exempts agricultural income from most taxes, extends liberal farm credits, and subsidizes agriculture. It also operates a service by which individual growers or cooperatives may hire heavy farm equipment at low prices, encourages the development of industries that use farm products, provides educational programs, and has sought to halt the trend toward ever-smaller farm holdings. More than 215,000 tractors, 6,650 harvester-threshers, and 9,300 milking machines were in use in 1991.

[23] ANIMAL HUSBANDRY

In 1992 there were 9,694,000 sheep, 5,832,000 goats, 1,150,000 hogs, 616,000 head of cattle, 165,000 donkeys, 140,000 horses and mules, and 27,000,000 poultry. Although production of milk, meat, and cheese has risen greatly since the end of World War II, Greece still must import substantial quantities of evaporated and condensed milk, cheese, cattle, sheep, hides, and meat. Livestock products in 1992 included (in thousands of tons) milk, 715; meat, 529; cheese, 222; eggs, 142.5; honey, 12; and butter, 5. Recent modernization in machinery has especially helped poultry and hog operations.

[24] FISHING

The fishing industry has expanded and been modernized in recent years. The total fish catch was 149,020 tons in 1991, valued at D24,217.6 million. A total of $86 million of fish and fish products were exported in 1992. In the north of Greece, freshwater fisheries have been restocked and developed.

Sponge fishing, formerly an important undertaking in the Dodecanese and other regions, decreased in volume from 135.5 tons of sponges in 1955 to 10 tons in 1991.

[25] FORESTRY

Forests cover about one-fifth of the total area. Much of the forest area was destroyed during the 1940s, but the government's reforestation program planted more than 100 million trees during the 1970s and 1980s. Pine, fir, and oak are the most common trees, and resin (11,879 tons in 1984) and turpentine (1,468 tons) are the principal products. In 1991, 360,000 cu m of sawn wood and 1,350,000 tons of firewood were produced. Production of timber is insufficient to meet the domestic demand, and many forestry products are imported.

[26]MINING

Greece has a wide variety of mineral deposits. Apart from bauxite, however, Greek mines operate far below their productive
capacity. The industrial processing of mineral ores was very limited until the 1960s and 1970s, when facilities for refining nick-
eliferous iron ore and bauxite were developed. Output of
bauxite rose from 884,000 tons in 1960 to 2,133,521 tons in
1991 (down from 3,095,000 tons in 1980). Production of iron
ore by gross weight has risen from 1,083,000 tons in 1987 to
2,023,678 tons in 1991. Other principal minerals and their
1991 production in crude form (in tons) were lignite,
50,537,241; magnesite, 590,180; asbestos, 400,000 (down from
4,500,000 in 1989); chromite, 75,000; and nickel, 24,284.
Other mineral deposits of commercial importance are antimony,
gold (placer dredger), asbestos, emery, Santorin earth, pumice,
sulfur, ceramic clay, marble, talc, gypsum, salt, and limestone.
As of 1991, estimated reserves of minerals (in millions of metric
tons), included lignite, 3,570; bauxite, 750; perlite, 200; iron,
70; and magnesite, 50.

[27]ENERGY AND POWER

Coal and oil are imported to supply power for the many small
generating plants spread over the country. Before World War II,
the Athens-Piraiévs Electricity Co. was the only modern plant in
Greece, and it, too, operated on imported coal. In 1950, the gov-
ernment-organized Public Power Corp. was established to construct and operate electricity generating plants and power
transmission and distribution lines; by 1955, it had erected four
major power plants. In 1965, the first two units of the Kremasta
hydroelectric station were opened; by 1992, installed capacity
totaled 8.9 million kw, of which hydropower accounted for 29%.
Production of electricity increased from 8,991 million kwh in
1970 to 35.8 million kwh in 1991, of which 91% was provided
by thermal power and 9% by hydroelectric stations.

Greece has actively explored offshore oil resources. A field off
Thásos in the northern Aegean began operations in July 1981.
Total production, as of 1991, reached 6 million barrels of oil and
180 million cu m of natural gas. A National Energy Council was
created in 1975 to coordinate and support energy development.

[28]INDUSTRY

Manufacturing, which now ranks ahead of agriculture as an
income earner, has increased rapidly owing to a vigorous policy
of industrialization. However, Greek industry must rely on
imports for its raw materials, machinery, parts, and fuel. Greece
has only a rudimentary iron and steel industry and does not manufacture basic transport equipment, such as cars and trucks.
Industry is concentrated in the Athens area, where 40% of the
industrial work force lived in 1988, and 36% of the manufacturing enterprises were located.

Chief industries in 1991 accounted for the following proportions of manufacturing's share of the GDP: food, beverages and
tobacco, 23%; metals and metals manufactures, machinery and
electrical goods, 16%; chemicals, 16%; textiles, 15%; nonmetallic minerals, 7.5%; clothing and footwear, 6%; and transport
equipment, 5.5%. Although the government controls certain
basic industries, such as electric power and petroleum refining,
most industry is privately owned. Selected industrial products in
1990 were sugar, 262,000 tons; wine, 231,000 tons; crude olive
oil, 197,000 tons; beer, 3,772,000 hectoliters; cigarettes, 27.7
million units; cotton yarn, 120,400 tons; anhydrous ammonia,
256,000 tons; nitrogenous fertilizers, 293,000 tons; sulfuric acid,
841,000 tons; paper and paperboard, 344,000 tons; cement,
13,151,000 tons; steel, 901,000 tons; and refrigerators, 85,000
units. Petroleum refinery products in 1991 included fuel oil,
5,374,000 tons; diesel fuel, 3,289,000 tons; and jet fuel,
1,488,000 tons.

[29]SCIENCE AND TECHNOLOGY

The Academy of Athens oversees the activities of research institutes
in astronomy and applied mathematics and in atmospheric physics
and climatology; scientific learned societies include the Association
of Greek Chemists, Greek Atomic Energy Commission, and Greek
Mathematical Society, all headquartered in Athens. In addition,
Greece has 7 scientific research institutes. Advanced technical
training is provided at 10 colleges and universities. In the early
1980s, the government established a Ministry of Research and
Technology to foster scientific and technological development.
Greece had 534 scientists and engineers and 488 technicians
engaged in research and development in 1986; expenditures on
research and development in 1986 amounted to D18 billion.

[30]DOMESTIC TRADE

Athens, Piraiévs, and Salonika are the principal commercial cities;
importers and exporters have offices in these cities and branches
in other centers. In 1988, there were 184,821 retail establishments, employing 338,132 people, and 30,720 wholesale outlets
with 115,402 employees.

In general, small shops specialize in particular lines of merchandise, but there are a few department stores in Athens. Most
people buy in the small shops, in the markets, and from itinerant
peddlers. Usual business hours are from 8 AM to 2:30 or 3 PM on
Mondays, Wednesdays, and Saturdays, and from 8 AM to 1 PM
and 5 to 8:30 PM on Tuesdays, Thursdays, and Fridays. Banking
hours are from 8 AM to 1PM Monday through Friday.

Advertising is used widely in the towns and cities, and several
advertising agencies are active in Athens and Salonika. The most
common media are newspapers, radio, films, billboards, neon
signs, and window displays. The principal annual trade fair is the
International Fair of Salonika, held in September.

[31]FOREIGN TRADE

Greece has an unfavorable balance of trade, with the annual
value of imports running more than double that of exports.

Principal exports in 1992 (in millions of drachmae) were as
follows:

Manufactured goods	413,766.9
Food and live animals	398,553.7
Miscellaneous manufacturing articles	452,453.8
Beverages and tobacco	124,367.1
Animal and vegetable oils and fats	105,245.6
Mineral fuels and lubricants	99,069.1
Machinery and transport equipment	90,264.9
Crude inedible materials (except fuels)	81,305.1
Chemicals and related products	71,448.2
Other exports	44,289.0
TOTAL	1,880,763.4

Principal imports in 1992 (in millions of drachmae) were as
follows:

Manufactured goods classified chiefly by raw material	804,422.6
Machinery and transport equipment	1,368,893.0
Miscellaneous manufactured goods	445,011.6
Mineral fuels and lubricants	437,812.4
Food and live animals	529,057.7
Inedible crude materials (except fuel)	143,546.3
Beverages and tobacco	88,792.7
Other exports	509,708.2
TOTAL	4,327,244.5

About two-thirds of Greece's trade is with other EC countries.
Principal suppliers of imports in 1992 included Germany, Italy,

and France. The principal trade partners in 1992 (in millions of drachmae) were as follows:

	EXPORTS	IMPORTS	BALANCE
Germany	445,305.1	914,530.2	-469,225.1
Italy	346,000.1	641,203.8	-295,203.7
France	135,999.2	353,745.8	-217,746.6
Netherlands	52,107.3	308,711.7	-256,604.4
Libya	11,869.7	94,329.6	-82,459.9
US	72,958.8	161,887.9	-88,929.1
Belgium-Luxembourg	47,729.0	158,135.9	-110,406.9
UK	132,228.5	247,051.2	-114,822.7
Japan	17,147.1	285,508.9	-268,361.8
Former USSR	23,775.2	83,000.0	-59,224.8
Switzerland	25,863.2	79,888.0	-54,024.8
Spain	46,532.4	99,663.0	-53,130.6
Iran	4,754.2	126,443.3	-121,689.1
Other countries	518,493.6	773,145.2	-254,651.6
TOTAL	1,880,763.4	4,327,244.5	-2,446,481.1

32BALANCE OF PAYMENTS

Because it imports more than twice the value of its exports, Greece has registered chronic annual deficits in its balance of payments. The major contributors to Greece's foreign exchange earnings are tourism, shipping services, and remittances from Greek workers abroad.

In 1992 merchandise exports totaled $6,009 million and imports $17,612 million. The merchandise trade balance was $-11,603 million.

The following table summarizes Greece's balance of payments for 1991 and 1992 (in millions of US dollars):

	1991	1992
CURRENT ACCOUNT		
Goods, services, and income	-7,757	-8,615
Unrequited transfers	6,183	6,475
TOTALS	-1,574	-2,140
CAPITAL ACCOUNT		
Direct investment	1,135	1,144
Portfolio investment	—	—
Other long-term capital	2,452	1,047
Other short-term capital	374	428
Exceptional financing	-544	186
Other liabilities	—	—
Reserves	-1,660	188
TOTALS	1,757	2,993
Errors and omissions	-183	-853
Total change in reserves	-1,792	327

33BANKING AND SECURITIES

The government-controlled Bank of Greece (founded in 1927) is the central bank and the bank of issue, and it also engages in other banking activities. Its foreign exchange reserve in 1993 totaled US$7,634 million.

About 70% of all banking business in the country is controlled by the National Bank of Greece, a commercial bank, which also controls the National Mortgage Bank of Greece. The Currency Committee, composed of five cabinet ministers, controls the eight specialized credit institutions: the Agricultural Bank, National Investment Bank S.A., National Investment Bank for Industrial Development, Hellenic Industrial Development Bank, National Mortgage Bank, Mortgage Bank S.A., Postal Savings Bank, and Consignments and Loans Fund. Domestic bank credit to the Greek economy outstanding in 1993 was D12,820.6 billion. The money supply in 1993, as measured by M2, was D8,900.8 billion.

The Athens Stock Exchange (Chrimatisterion) was founded by royal decree in 1876. In 1967, significant reforms were instituted, including more stringent listing requirements, bringing about a rapid increase in the number of listed securities.

34INSURANCE

In 1989 there were 151 insurance companies operating in Greece, in addition to offices of Lloyd's of London handling marine insurance only. In 1990, premiums totaled US$103.9 per capita or 1.6% of the GDP. In 1984, life insurance premiums written totaled D9,733 million; other insurance premiums, D32,848 million.

35PUBLIC FINANCE

The state budget includes ordinary revenues and expenditures and a special investment budget administered by the Ministry of Coordination. The net public sector borrowing requirement on a cash basis rose from 8% of GDP to 18% from 1980 to 1985, and fell to 16% in 1988.

In 1993, budget revenues amounted to $37.6 billion, and expenditures came to $45.1 billion, including capital expenditures of $5.4 billion. The following table shows actual revenues and expenditures for 1989 and 1990 in billions of drachmas.

	1989	1990
REVENUE AND GRANTS		
Tax revenue	2,587	3,417
Non-tax revenue	285	307
Capital revenue	9	10
Grants	132	200
TOTAL	2,997	3,913
EXPENDITURES & LENDING MINUS REPAYMENTS		
TOTAL	5,320	6,963
Deficit/Surplus	-2,323	-3,050

In 1990 Greece's total external debt stood about $23.5 billion, representing 42% of GDP. Greece faces a heavy repayment burden well until the mid-1990s.

36TAXATION

Individuals earning over D1 million a year are subject to income tax ranging from 5–40%, with certain distinctions being made in the tax rate in accordance with the source of income. Net income after deductions is taxable at proportional rates; employers are required to withhold tax on their payrolls. The stamp tax on sales is 1.2% to 3.6%.

Business enterprises (except small tradesmen and peddlers, who pay a license tax) pay taxes on annual income, with an allowance for profits reinvested in the business. Greek companies (with the exception of corporations) are taxed on the basis of each partner's income regardless of whether net profits are distributed. The effective corporate tax rate is generally 35% on profits. The personal income tax is progressive with special deductions for families whose income is derived primarily from their own work on agricultural enterprises. Indirect taxes include import and customs duties. A value-added tax of 8% on essentials and 18% on most other products and services was introduced on 1 January 1987; it replaced nearly half of Greece's 500 indirect taxes.

Other taxes include an excise duty on tobacco, alcohol, gasoline, and automobiles, a real estate transfer tax of 11–13%, and a 54–25% inheritance and gift tax.

37CUSTOMS AND DUTIES

The import tariff protects domestic products and provides a source of government revenue (2.1% of total indirect taxes in

1986). Many Greek industries are not yet large enough or sufficiently modern to compete in price with foreign products, either in markets abroad or in Greece itself. As a full member of the EC since 1981, Greece eliminated its remaining tariffs and quotas on imports from EC nations by 1986 and aligned its own tariffs on imports from other countries with those of EC members. Greek exports to EC countries are tariff-free. Imports from non-EC countries are subject to the EC's Common Customs Tariff, as well as a value-added tax of 8% to 18% and a University/Bank Charge based on c.i.f. value.

38FOREIGN INVESTMENT

The government encourages foreign capital investment and protects foreign investors against compulsory appropriation of their assets in Greece. Incentives include reduced tax rates and increased depreciation rates. Total direct foreign investment was estimated at $3.6 billion in 1992.

39ECONOMIC DEVELOPMENT

Until the mid-1970s, Greek governments devoted themselves principally to expanding agricultural and industrial production, controlling prices and inflation, improving state finances, developing natural resources, and creating basic industries. In 1975, the Karamanlis government undertook a series of austerity measures designed to curb inflation and redress the balance-of-payments deficit. A new energy program included plans for stepped-up exploitation of oil and lignite reserves, along with uranium exploration in northern Greece. Increased efforts at import substitution were to be undertaken in all sectors. On 7 March 1975, in an effort to strengthen confidence in the national currency, the government announced that the value of the drachma would no longer be quoted in terms of a fixed link with the US dollar, but would be based on daily averages taken from the currencies of Greece's main trade partners.

The Socialist government that took office in 1981 promised more equal distribution of income and wealth through "democratic planning" and measures to control inflation and increase productivity. It imposed controls on prices and credit and began to restructure public corporations. But the government was cautious in introducing what it called "social control in certain key sectors" of the economy, and it ordered detailed studies to be made first. Its development policies emphasized balanced regional growth and technological modernization, especially in agriculture. The conservative government that came to power in 1990 adopted a 1991–93 "adjustment program" that called for reduction of price and wage increases and a reduction in the public-sector deficit from 13% to 3% of GDP. Twenty-eight industrial companies were to be privatized.

Greece received $1,502.9 million in foreign aid in 1991, of which $904.5 million came from Japan and $515.4 million from Germany.

40SOCIAL DEVELOPMENT

The wars of the 1940s greatly multiplied the need for and the government's involvement in social welfare programs. The Social Insurance Foundation, the national social security system, is supported by contributions from employees (5.75–7.45% of salary in 1991) and employers (10.50–12.90% of payrolls, depending on the hazardousness of the occupation). Membership is compulsory for all wage earners and salaried persons. The system provides for treatment at dispensaries, home visits by doctors, laboratory examinations, X rays, prescriptions, and hospitalization; pays old-age pensions, disability pensions, and benefits to widows, orphans, and parents of deceased pensioners; and offers cash benefits for sickness, tuberculosis, accidents, maternity, and funeral expenses. As of 1988, Greece spent 32% of its budget on social security and housing.

In January 1983, Greece's family law was drastically changed by parliament to guarantee equality between marriage partners, make divorce easier, and abolish the traditional dowry as a legal requirement for marriage. The fertility rate for 1985–90 was 1.5; abortion is permitted on narrow medical grounds.

The General Secretariat for Equality of the Sexes works to remove barriers to equal employment opportunities for women. In 1993, figures showed that women earned 47% less than men in the manufacturing sector and 24% less in wholesale trade. The Secretariat opened a Center for Battered Women in Athens at the beginning of 1993.

41HEALTH

Since World War II, the government has broadened health services by building new hospitals and providing more clinics and medical personnel. In 1985, Greece had 552 hospitals with a total of 54,438 beds. From 1985 to 1990, there were 5.1 beds per 1,000 people. In 1988, there were 32,145 doctors and 6,941 pharmacists; in 1989, there were 9,628 dentists, 25,054 nurses, and 1,638 midwives. From 1988 to 1992, there were 1.73 doctors for every 1,000 people, with a nurse to doctor ratio of 1.6. In 1990, there were 580 people per 1 physician. The country spent a total of $3,609 million on health care in 1990. Pulmonary tuberculosis, dysentery, and malaria, which were once endemic, have been controlled. The incidence of typhoid, which was formerly of epidemic proportions, dropped to only 149 cases in 1985 following the application of US aid to improving sanitary conditions in more than 700 villages. In 1990, there were 12 reported cases of tuberculosis per 100,000 people. That same year, 95% of the population had access to safe water. In addition, between 1990 and 1992, Greece immunized children up to one year of age against tuberculosis (56%); diphtheria, pertussis, and tetanus (54%); polio (96%); and measles (76%). In 1992, the infant mortality rate was 8 per 1,000 live births, and there were 106,000 births (a rate of 10.4 per 1,000 people). That same year, life expectancy averaged 77 years. In 1993, the overall mortality rate was 9.8 per 1,000 people.

42HOUSING

Construction of new dwellings (including repairs and extensions) reached 88,477 units in 1985 and rose to 120,240 in 1990. In 1991, the total number of housing units was 3,428,000. Most new construction is in Athens or Salonika, indicating the emphasis on urban development. Considerable amounts of private investment have been spent on the construction of apartment houses in urban areas. In the mid-1980s, virtually the entire population had access to safe water. As of 1981, 97% of all housing units had lighting, 88% had piped indoor water, 84% had kitchen facilities, 70% had private toilets, 69% had private baths, 42% had a sewage disposal system, and 30% had central heating.

43EDUCATION

Adult literacy in 1990 was estimated at 93.2%: 97.6% for men and 89.1% for women. Education is free and compulsory for nine years beginning at age 6 and primary education is for 6 years. Secondary education includes two steps: first 3 years, followed by 3 more years in preparation for university. The central and local governments pay the cost of state schools, and private schools are state-regulated. In 1989 there were 5,474 nursery schools with 141,756 pupils; 7,755 primary schools with 834,688 pupils; secondary schools (gymnasiums) with 843,732 pupils; and technical, vocational, and ecclesiastical schools with 130,738 pupils. Greece's six major universities—Athens, Salonika, Thrace, Ioánnina, Crete, and Pátrai—together with the National Technical University of Athens, the new University of the Aegean, and the Technical University of Crete, plus seven special institutions of higher education, enrolled 194,419 students in 1989. Private universities are constitutionally banned.

In July 1982, the Socialist government began to democratize the higher-education system; a new law was approved that diminished the power of individual professors by establishing American-style departments with integrated faculties, and junior faculty members and representatives of the student body were granted a role in academic decision-making. The legislation also curbed university autonomy by establishing the National University Council, to advise the government on higher-education planning, and the Academy of Letters and Sciences, to set and implement university standards.

44LIBRARIES AND MUSEUMS

The National Library traces its origins to 1829, when it was established on the island of Aíyina; the library was moved to its present site in Athens in 1903 and today has more than 2 million volumes. Both the National Library and the Library of Parliament (1.5 million volumes) act as legal depositories for Greek publications and are open to the public. Public libraries are located mainly in provincial capitals, and there are regional libraries with bookmobile services for rural areas. Besides the libraries attached to the universities and other educational institutions, there are several specialized research libraries located in Athens. Outstanding special collections can be found at the Democritus Nuclear Research Center, the Center of Planning and Economic Research, the Athens Center of Ekistics, and the Gennadius Library, which houses a large collection on modern Greek history.

Most museums are devoted to antiquities and archaeology. One of the richest collections of Greek sculpture and antiquities is found at the National Archaeological Museum in Athens, which is also home to the Byzantine and Christian Museum, Benaki Museum, and Kanellopoulos Museum. The most impressive archaeological remains are the great temples and palaces at Athens (particularly the Parthenon and the Stoa of Attalos), Corinth, Salonika, Delphi, Olympia, Mycenae, the island of Delos, and Knossos, on Crete.

45MEDIA

The government owns and controls all communications. The Greek Telecommunications Authority operates domestic telegraph and telephone communications; in 1991 there were 4,522,834 telephones. The Hellenic National Radio and Television Institute operates radio stations. Radio Athens broadcasts are carried by provincial relay stations located in various parts of the country; other stations are operated by the Greek armed forces. There are three television channels. There were some 4,270,000 radios in 1991; television sets numbered 2 million.

The principal newspapers and magazines of Athens have nationwide circulation. Before the 1967 coup, most papers represented political views, and success in politics often depended to a considerable extent on newspaper support. This tradition made the newspapers particularly vulnerable to accusations of violating the junta's security regulations. Some newspapers voluntarily shut down, and others were ordered to suspend publication. The collapse of the military regime in 1974 led to constitutional restoration of freedom of the press. Many banned newspapers reappeared, and circulations steadily increased; the number of daily newspapers sold in Athens and Salonika totaled 307 million in 1983. In 1991 there were 117 daily newspapers. The largest Athens dailies (with estimated 1991 circulations) were *Ta Nea* (136,500), *Apogevmatini* (71,000), *Ethnos* (76,000), and *Avriani* (44,500).

46ORGANIZATIONS

Most of the larger cities and towns have associations of commerce, industry, handicrafts, and finance. Artists, writers, musicians, educators, and journalists are organized into professional associations. Scholarly societies include those devoted to archaeology, anthropology, geography, history, political science, and sociology. The Boy Scouts and other youth groups are active. There are some consumers' and producers' cooperatives; chambers of commerce and industry function in Athens, Piraiévs, and Salonika.

47TOURISM, TRAVEL, AND RECREATION

Tourism has surpassed shipping as the most important element in the Greek economy, with the active encouragement of the Greek National Tourist Organization. The government encourages tourists and facilitates their entry and accommodation. A passport is needed for admission, but for visitors from most countries, no visa is required. Citizens of the US, UK, Canada, and many other countries who remain in Greece for more than three months must obtain residence permits, which are valid for six months, and present sojourn and exit permits on leaving the country. Those wishing to reside in Greece permanently may be granted a residence permit valid for two years.

The number of foreign tourists visiting Greece in 1991, totaled 8,036,127, of whom 20.8% came from the UK, 19.4% from Germany, and 5.86% from France. Tourism receipts totaled us$2.56 million. There were 243,950 hotel rooms with 459,297 beds. Principal tourist sites, in addition to the world-famous Parthenon and Acropolis in Athens, include Mt. Olympus (the home of the gods in ancient mythology), the site of the ancient oracle at Delphi, the Agora at Corinth, and the Minoan ruins on Crete. Operas, concerts, ballet performances, and ancient Greek dramas are presented at the Athens Festival each year from July to September; during July and August, Greek classics also are performed in the open-air theater at Epidaurus, 40 km (25 mi) east of Árgos. Popular sports include swimming at the many beaches, sailing and water skiing, fishing, golf, and mountain climbing.

48FAMOUS GREEKS

The origins of Western literature and of the main branches of Western learning may be traced to the era of Greek greatness that began before 700 BC with the epics of Homer (possibly born in Asia Minor), the *Iliad* and the *Odyssey*. Hesiod (fl.700 BC), the first didactic poet, put into epic verse his descriptions of pastoral life, including practical advice on farming, and allegorical myths. The poets Alcaeus (620?–580? BC), Sappho (612?–580? BC), Anacreon (582?–485? BC), and Bacchylides (fl.5th cent. BC) wrote of love, war, and death in lyrics of great feeling and beauty. Pindar (522?–438? BC) celebrated the Panhellenic athletic festivals in vivid odes. The fables of the slave Aesop (b. Asia Minor, 620?–560? BC) have been famous for more than 2,500 years. Three of the world's greatest dramatists were Aeschylus (525–456 BC), author of the *Oresteia* trilogy; Sophocles (496?–406? BC), author of the Theban plays; and Euripides (485?–406? BC), author of *Medea, The Trojan Women,* and *The Bacchae*. Aristophanes (450?–385? BC), the greatest author of comedies, satirized the mores of his day in a series of brilliant plays. Three great historians were Herodotus (b. Asia Minor, 484?–420? BC), regarded as the father of history, known for *The Persian Wars;* Thucydides (460?–400? BC), who generally avoided myth and legend and applied greater standards of historical accuracy in his *History of the Peloponnesian War;* and Xenophon (428?–354? BC), best known for his account of the Greek retreat from Persia, the *Anabasis*. Outstanding literary figures of the Hellenistic period were Menander (342–290? BC), the chief representative of a newer type of comedy; the poets Callimachus (b. Libya, 305?–240? BC), Theocritus (b. Italy, 310?–250? BC), and Apollonius Rhodius (fl.3d cent. BC), author of the *Argonautica;* and Polybius (200?–118? BC), who wrote a detailed history of the Mediterranean world. Noteworthy in the Roman period were Strabo (b. Asia Minor, 64? BC–AD 24?), a writer on geography; Plutarch (AD 46?–120?), the father of biography, whose *Parallel Lives* of famous Greeks and Romans is a chief source of information about great figures of antiquity; Pausanias (b. Asia Minor, fl. AD 150), a travel writer; and Lucian (AD 120?–180?), a satirist.

The leading philosophers of the period preceding Greece's golden age were Thales (b. Asia Minor, 625?–547? BC), Pythagoras (570?–500? BC), Heraclitus (b. Asia Minor, 540?–480? BC), Protagoras (485?–410? BC), and Democritus (460?–370? BC). Socrates (469?–399 BC) investigated ethics and politics. His greatest pupil, Plato (429?–347 BC), used Socrates' question-and-answer method of investigating philosophical problems in his famous dialogues. Plato's pupil Aristotle (384–322 BC) established the rules of deductive reasoning but also used observation and inductive reasoning, applying himself to the systematic study of almost every form of human endeavor. Outstanding in the Hellenistic period were Epicurus (341?–270 BC), the philosopher of moderation; Zeno (b. Cyprus, 335?–263? BC), the founder of Stoicism; and Diogenes (b. Asia Minor, 412?–323 BC), the famous Cynic. The oath of Hippocrates (460?–377 BC), the father of medicine, is still recited by newly graduating physicians. Euclid (fl.300 BC) evolved the system of geometry that bears his name. Archimedes (287?–212 BC) discovered the principles of mechanics and hydrostatics. Eratosthenes (275?–194? BC) calculated the earth's circumference with remarkable accuracy, and Hipparchus (190?–125? BC) founded scientific astronomy. Galen (AD 129?–199?) was an outstanding physician of ancient times.

The sculptor Phidias (490?–430? BC) created the statue of Athena and the figure of Zeus in the temple at Olympia and supervised the construction and decoration of the Parthenon. Another renowned sculptor was Praxiteles (390?–330? BC).

The legal reforms of Solon (638?–559? BC) served as the basis of Athenian democracy. The Athenian general Miltiades (554?–489? BC) led the victory over the Persians at Marathon in 490 BC, and Themistocles (528?–460? BC) was chiefly responsible for the victory at Salamis 10 years later. Pericles (495?–429? BC), the virtual ruler of Athens for more than 25 years, added to the political power of that city, inaugurated the construction of the Parthenon and other noteworthy buildings, and encouraged the arts of sculpture and painting. With the decline of Athens, first Sparta and then Thebes, under the great military tactician Epaminondas (418?–362 BC), gained the ascendancy; but soon thereafter, two military geniuses, Philip II of Macedon (382–336 BC) and his son Alexander the Great (356–323 BC), gained control over all of Greece and formed a vast empire stretching as far east as India. It was against Philip that Demosthenes (384–322 BC), the greatest Greek orator, directed his diatribes, the *Philippics*.

The most renowned Greek painter during the Renaissance was El Greco (Domenikos Theotokopoulos, 1541–1614), born in Crete, whose major works, painted in Spain, have influenced many 20th-century artists. An outstanding modern literary figure is Nikos Kazantzakis (1883–1957), a novelist and poet who composed a vast sequel to Homer's *Odyssey*. Leading modern poets are Kostes Palamas (1859–1943), Georgios Drosines (1859–1951), and Constantine Cavafy (1868–1933), as well as George Seferis (Seferiades, 1900–1972), and Odysseus Elytis (Alepoudhelis, b. 1911),

winners of the Nobel Prize for literature in 1963 and 1979, respectively. Musicians of stature are the composers Nikos Skalkottas (1904–49), Iannis Xenakis (b. Romania, 1922), and Mikis Theodorakis (b. 1925); the conductor Dmitri Mitropoulos (1896–1960); and the soprano Maria Callas (Calogeropoulos, b. US, 1923–77). Contemporary filmmakers who have won international acclaim are Michael Cacoyannis (b. 1922) and Constantin Costa-Gavras (b. 1933). Actresses of note are Katina Paxinou (1900–1973); Melina Mercouri (b. 1925), who was appointed minister of culture and science in the Socialist cabinet in 1981; and Irene Papas (Lelekou, b. 1926).

Outstanding Greek public figures in the 20th century include Cretan-born Eleutherios Venizelos (1864–1936), prominent statesman of the interwar period; Ioannis Metaxas (1871–1941), dictator from 1936 until his death; Constantine Karamanlis (b. 1907), prime minister (1955–63, 1974–80) and president (1980–85) of Greece; George Papandreou (1888–1968), head of the Center Union Party and prime minister (1963–65); and his son Andreas Papandreou (b. 1919), the PASOK leader who became prime minister in 1981.

⁴⁹DEPENDENCIES

Greece has no territories or colonies.

⁵⁰BIBLIOGRAPHY

Alford, Jonathan (ed.). *Greece and Turkey: Adversity in Alliance.* New York: St. Martin's, 1984.

Clogg, Richard (ed.). *Greece, 1981–89: The Populist Decade.* New York: St. Martin's Press, 1993.

Clogg, Richard, and George Yannopoulos (eds.). *Greece under Military Rule.* New York: Basic Books, 1972.

Constas, Dimitris (ed.). *The Greek-Turkish Conflict in the 1990s.* New York: St. Martin's Press, 1991.

Dakin, Douglas. *The Greek Struggle for Independence, 1821-1833.* Berkeley: University of California Press, 1973.

——. *The Unification of Greece, 1770–1923.* New York: St Martin's, 1972.

Frazier, Robert. *Anglo-American Relations with Greece: The Coming of the Cold War, 1942–47.* New York: St. Martin's Press, 1991.

Hadas, Moses. *History of Greek Literature.* New York: Columbia University Press, 1950.

Jouganatos, George A. *The Development of the Greek Economy 1950–1991.* Westport, Conn.: Greenwood Press, 1992.

Kourvetaris, George A. and Betty A. Dobratz. *A Profile of Modern Greece, in Search of Identity.* New York: Clarendon Press, 1987.

Pettifer, James. *The Greeks: The Land and People Since the War.* London, England; New York: Viking, 1993.

Stobart, John Clarke. *The Glory That Was Greece: A Survey of Hellenic Cultures and Civilizations.* New York: Grove Press, 1962.

Wittner, Lawrence S. *American Intervention in Greece, 1943–49.* New York: Columbia University Press, 1982.

Woodhouse, C. M. *Modern Greece: A Short History.* 4th ed. London: Faber & Faber, 1986.

HUNGARY

Republic of Hungary
Magyar Népköztársaság

CAPITAL: Budapest.

FLAG: The national flag, adopted in 1957, is a tricolor of red, white, and green horizontal stripes.

ANTHEM: *Isten áldd meg a magyart (God Bless the Hungarians).*

MONETARY UNIT: The forint (Ft) of 100 fillérs is a paper currency with flexible rates of exchange. There are coins of 10, 20, and 50 fillérs and 1, 2, 5, 10, 20, 100, and 200 forints, and notes of 50, 100, 500, 1,000, and 5,000 forints. Ft1 = $0.0098 (or $1 = Ft102.041).

WEIGHTS AND MEASURES: The metric system is the legal standard.

HOLIDAYS: New Year's Day, 1 January; Anniversary of 1848 uprising against Austrian rule, 15 March; Labor Day, 1 May; Constitution Day, 20 August; Day of the Proclamation of the Republic, 23 October; Christmas, 25–26 December. Easter Monday is a movable holiday.

TIME: 1 PM = noon GMT.

¹LOCATION, SIZE, AND EXTENT

Hungary is a landlocked country in the Carpathian Basin of Central Europe, with an area of 93,030 sq km (35,919 sq mi), extending 268 km (167 mi) N–S and 528 km (328 mi) E–W. Comparatively, the area occupied by Hungary is slightly smaller than the state of Indiana. It is bounded on the N by Slovakia, on the NE by the Ukraine, on the E by Romania, on the S by Serbia and Croatia, on the SW by Slovenia, and on the W by Austria, with a total boundary length of 1,952 km (1,213 mi). Hungary's capital city, Budapest, is located in the north central part of the country.

²TOPOGRAPHY

About 84% of Hungary is below 200 m (656 ft) in altitude, its lowest point being 78 m (256 ft) above sea level and the highest being Mt. Kékes (1,014 m/3,327 ft) in the Mátra Mountains, northeast of Budapest. The country has four chief geographic regions: Transdanubia (Dunántúl), the Great Plain (Alföld), the Little Plain (Kisalföld), and the Northern Mountains. Hungary's river valleys and its highest mountains are in the northeast. Generally, the soil is fertile. The chief rivers are the Danube (Duna) and Tisza, which are navigable in Hungary for 417 km (259 mi) and 443 km (275 mi), respectively; the largest lake is Balaton, which is 78.1 km (48.5 mi) long and from 3.1 km (1.9 mi) to 14 km (8.7 mi) wide and has an area of 598 sq km (231 sq mi).

³CLIMATE

Hungary lies at the meeting point of three climatic zones: the continental, Mediterranean, and oceanic. Yearly temperatures vary from a minimum of –14°C (7°F) to a maximum of 36°C (97°F); over an average of 50 years, through the 1970s, the mean temperature in January was –2°C (28° F) and in July, 20°C (68°F). Rainfall varies, but the annual average is approximately 63 cm (25 in)—more in the west and less in the east—with maximum rainfall during the summer months. Severe droughts often occur in the summers.

⁴FLORA AND FAUNA

Plants and animals are those common to Central Europe. Oak is the predominant deciduous tree; various conifers are located in the mountains. Among the abundant wildlife are deer, boar, hare, and mouflon. The Great Plain is a breeding ground and a migration center for a variety of birds. Fish are plentiful in rivers and lakes.

⁵ENVIRONMENT

Protected areas in 1984 included national parks, 141,000 hectares (348,417 acres); conservation districts and reservations, 330,800 hectares (817,400 acres); and urban parks and greenbelts, 8,029 hectares (19,840 acres). According to official statistics, the highest concentrations of airborne dust in 1985 were in Várpalota, Dunaujváros, and Ajka. Chemical pollution of the air and water is extensive, but resources to combat pollution are scarce: only Ft30 billion was to be spent on water treatment during 1986–90. Pollution from sulphur and nitrogen oxides affects 41% of the population of Hungary, which has 1.4 cu mi of water, 55% used for industrial purposes and 36% used for farming activity. One-hundred percent of the city dwellers and 95% of people living in rural areas have pure water. The nation's cities produce 1.9 million tons of solid waste. Hungary's principal environmental agency is the National Council for Environment and Nature Conservation, under the auspices of the Council of Ministers. In 1992, the United Nations reported the extinction of 93 species of Hungary's plants and animals. As of 1994, two of Hungary's mammal species and 16 of its bird species are endangered. Twenty-one plant species are also endangered. Endangered species included the longicorn, the alcon large blue butterfly, the dusky large blue butterfly, and the Mediterranean mouflon.

⁶POPULATION

According to the census of 1 January 1990, the population totaled 10,374,823, a decline of 3.2% from 1980. As of 1 January 1992, it was estimated at 10,337,200, a decline of 0.36%. The same year, 62.7% of the population lived in cities, including 19.5% in Budapest. Average density in 1990 was 112 per sq km (289 per sq mi). Budapest, the capital and principal city, had a population of 2,015,955 at the beginning of 1992. Eight other cities had populations exceeding 100,000: Debrecen, 216,137; Miskolc, 192,355; Szeged, 177,679; Pécs, 170,542; Győr,

130,293; Nyíregyháza, 114,955; Székesfehérvár, 111,478; and Kecskemét, 104,563. Since the early 1950s, there has been a fundamental shift of the population from rural to urban areas; from 1976 to 1985, Hungary had a declining birthrate. A population of 10,507,000 is forecasted by the UN for the year 2000, assuming a crude birthrate of 13.7 per 1,000 population and a crude death rate of 13 during 1995–2000. But Hungary's own forecast for 2000 is no higher than 10,216,700.

[7] MIGRATION

Sizable migration during the two world wars resulted from military operations, territorial changes, and population transfers. Peacetime emigration in the decades before World War I was heavy (about 1,400,000 between 1899 and 1913). Emigration of non-Magyars was prompted by the repressive policy of Magyarization; groups also left because of economic pressures, the majority going to the US and Canada. In the interwar period, migration was negligible, but after 1947 many thousands left, despite restrictions on emigration. As a result of the October 1956 uprising, approximately 250,000 persons fled Hungary. The largest numbers ultimately emigrated to the US, Canada, the UK, the Federal Republic of Germany (FRG), France, Switzerland, and Australia. Emigation totaled 42,700 between 1981 and 1989. It is now virtually nonexistent; only 778 persons left in 1991, according to official statistics.

Since 1960 net migration from the villages to the cities has decreased, from about 52,000 that year to 20,814 in 1986. At the end of 1992 Hungary was harboring 32,000 refugees, of whom 29,000 were from the former Yugoslavia. There were 54,693 registered asylum seekers in 1991.

[8] ETHNIC GROUPS

Ethnically, Hungary is essentially a homogeneous state of Magyar extraction. According to the 1990 census, the ethnic composition in 1985 was as follows: Hungarians, 97.8%; Gypsies, 1.4%, Germans, 0.3%; Slovaks, 0.1%; Croats, 0.1%; Romanians, 0.1%; and others, 0.2%. These figures may be unrealistically low. An independent study found about 500,000 Gypsies in the 1980s, about 230,000 Germans, about 100,000 Slovaks, about 100,000 Yugoslavs, and about 30,000 Romanians. Between 1.7 million and 2.5 million Magyars live in Romania, where they have reportedly been victims of ethnic discrimination; another 600,000 Magyars live in Slovakia, 400,000 in Yugoslavia, and 180,000 in Ukraine.

[9] LANGUAGES

Magyar is the universal language. In addition to the letters of the English alphabet, it has the following letters and combinations: *á, é, í, ó, ö, ő, ú, ü, ű, cs, dz, dzs, gy, ly, ny, sz, ty, zs*. Written in Latin characters, Magyar belongs to the Finno-Ugric family, a branch of the Ural-Altaic language group. Magyar is also characterized by an admixture of Turkish, Slavic, German, Latin, and French words. In addition to their native language, many Hungarians speak English, German, French, or (since World War II) Russian.

[10] RELIGIONS

As of 1993, an estimated 63% of the people were Roman Catholics, with some two million Reformed Calvinists, members of the Hungarian Reformed Church. There were 100,000 Jews in 1991. Most of the remainder were nonreligious or atheistic. Laws passed in 1990 provide for separation of church and state and safeguard the liberty of conscience of all citizens and the freedom of religious worship. State relations with the Roman Catholic Church, hostile under the former Hungarian People's Republic, improved considerably in 1990 after Hungary reestablished diplomatic relations with the Holy See. The state contributes to the salaries of both Catholic and Protestant clergy. Church matters are handled by the state Department for Church Relations, established in 1990 and part of the Office of the Prime Minster. The first synagogue to be built after 1945 was opened in 1986, and about 50 Baptist churches were built between 1965 and 1986.

[11] TRANSPORTATION

Transportation facilities have improved steadily since the 1960s. Budapest is the transportation center. In 1991, roads totaled 130,000 km (80,800 mi), of which 28,701 km (17,835 mi) were part of the national highway system. In 1991, Hungary had 2,015,455 passenger cars and 201,039 trucks.

Railways carried nearly 45% of the total volume of mineral freight and 74% of the total amount of iron, steel, and nonferrous metal products in 1990. As of 1991, Hungary had 7,779 km (4,834 mi) of track, of which 97% was standard gauge. Most freight is carried by trucks; pipeline transport is of lesser importance, accounting for 40% of fuel transport in 1990. The railroad and bus networks are state owned.

Navigable waterways totaled 1,622 km (1,008 mi) in 1988, of which the Danube and Tisza rivers made up over half. In addition to the government shipping enterprises—which operate the best and largest ships and handle the bulk of water traffic—the Shipping Cooperative, an association of small operators, continues to function. In 1991, the merchant marine fleet consisted of 14 cargo ships and one bulk vessel (over 1,000 GRT) for a total capacity of 85,489 GRT.

Ferihegy Airport in Budapest, the most important center for domestic and international flights, handled 50,900 aircraft landings and takeoffs and 1,763,000 arriving and departing passengers in 1991. All domestic traffic is handled by the Hungarian Air Transportation Enterprise (Magyar Légiközlekedési Vallalat—MALÉV), which carried 910,700 passengers in 1991, but only 181,600 in 1992.

[12] HISTORY

Ancient human footprints, tools, and a skull found at Vértesszőllős date the earliest occupants of present Hungary at a period from 250,000 to 500,000 years ago. Close to that site, at Tata, objects used for aesthetic or ceremonial purposes have been discovered, among the earliest such finds made anywhere in the world.

Celtic tribes settled in Hungary before the Romans came to occupy the western part of the country, which they called Pannonia and which the Roman Emperor Augustus conquered in 9 BC. Invasions by the Huns, the Goths, and later the Langobards had little lasting effect, but the two subsequent migrations of the Avars (who ruled for 250 years and, like the Huns, established a khanate in the Hungarian plain) left a more lasting impression.

The Magyars (Hungarians) migrated from the plains south and west of the Ural Mountains and invaded the Carpathian Basin under the leadership of Árpád in AD 896. For half a century they ranged far and wide, until their defeat by Otto the Great, king of Germany and Holy Roman emperor, near Augsburg in 955. They were converted to Christianity under King Stephen I (r.1001–1038), who was canonized in 1083. The Holy Crown of St. Stephen became the national symbol, and a constitution was gradually developed. The Magna Carta of Hungary, known as the Golden Bull of 1222, gave the nation a basic framework of national liberties to which every subsequent Hungarian monarch had to swear fidelity. Hungary was invaded at various times during the medieval period; the Mongols succeeded in devastating the country in 1241–42.

Medieval Hungary achieved its greatest heights under the Angevin rulers Charles Robert and Louis the Great (r.1342–82), when Hungarian mines yielded five times as much gold as those of any other European state. Sigismund of Luxembourg, king of Hungary, became Holy Roman emperor in 1410, largely on the strength of this national treasure. During the 15th century,

LOCATION: 45°48′ to 48°35′N; 16°5′ to 22°58′E. **BOUNDARY LENGTHS:** Slovakia, 608 km (378 mi); Ukraine, 215 km (134 mi); Romania, 432 km (268 mi); Croatia and Serbia, 631 km (392 mi); Austria, 356 km (221 mi).

however, Turkish armies began to threaten Hungary. The Balkan principalities to the south and southeast of Hungary developed as buffer states, but they did not long delay the advance of the Turks; nor could the victories of János Hunyadi, brilliant as they were, ultimately stem the Turkish tide. With the Turks temporarily at bay, the Hungarian renaissance flourished during the reign of Hunyadi's son, Matthias Corvinus (1458–90), but his successors in the 16th century overexploited the gold mines, brutally suppressed a peasant revolt, and allowed the Magyar army to deteriorate. Hungary's golden age ended with the rout by the Turks at Mohács in 1526.

Thereafter, Hungary was split by warring factions, but power was gradually consolidated by the Habsburg kings of Austria. With the defeat of the Turks at Vienna in 1683, Turkish power waned and that of the Habsburgs became stronger. The Hungarians mounted many unsuccessful uprisings against the Habsburgs, the most important insurrectionist leaders being the Báthorys, Bocskai, Bethlen, and the Rákóczys. In 1713, however, the Hungarian Diet accepted the Pragmatic Sanction, which in guaranteeing the continuing integrity of Habsburg territories, bound Hungary to Austria.

During the first half of the 19th century, in the aftermath of the French Revolution and the Napoleonic wars, Hungary experi-

enced an upsurge of Magyar nationalism, accompanied by a burst of literary creativity. The inability of a liberal reform movement to establish a constitutional monarchy led to the revolt of 1848, directed by Lajos Kossuth and Ferenc Deák, which established a short-lived Hungarian republic. Although Hungarian autonomy was abolished as a result of intervention by Austrian and Russian armies, Austria, weakened by its war with Prussia, was obliged to give in to Magyar national aspirations. The Compromise (Ausgleich) of 1867 established a dual monarchy of Austria and Hungary and permitted a degree of self-government for the Magyars.

After World War I, in which Austria-Hungary was defeated, the dual monarchy collapsed, and a democratic republic was established under Count Mihály Károlyi. This was supplanted in March 1919 by a Communist regime led by Béla Kun, but Romanian troops invaded Hungary and helped suppress it. In 1920, Hungary became a kingdom without a king; for the next 25 years, Adm. Miklós von Nagybánya Horthy served as regent. The Treaty of Trianon in 1920 formally freed the non-Magyar nationalities from Hungarian rule but also left significant numbers of Magyars in Romania and elsewhere beyond Hungary's borders. The fundamental policy of interwar Hungary was to recover the "lost" territories, and in the hope of achieving that end, Hungary formed alliances with the Axis powers and sided with them during World War II. Hungary temporarily regained territories from Czechoslovakia, Romania, and Yugoslavia. In March 1944, the German army occupied Hungary, but Soviet troops invaded the country later that year and liberated it by April 1945.

In 1946, a republican constitution was promulgated, and a coalition government (with Communist participation) was established. Under the terms of the peace treaty of 1947, Hungary was forced to give up all territories acquired after 1937. The Hungarian Workers (Communist) Party seized power in 1948 and adopted a constitution (on the Soviet model) in 1949. Hungarian foreign trade was oriented toward the Soviet bloc, industry was nationalized and greatly expanded, and collectivization of land was pressed. Resentment of continued Soviet influence over Hungarian affairs was one element in the popular uprising of October 1956, which after a few days' success—during which Hungary briefly withdrew from the Warsaw Treaty Organization—was summarily put down by Soviet military force. Many people fled the country, and many others were executed. Since 1956, Hungary was a firm ally of the USSR. In 1968, the New Economic Mechanism was introduced in order to make the economy more competitive and open to market forces; reform measures beginning in 1979 further encouraged private enterprise. The movement toward relaxation of tensions in Europe in the 1970s was reflected in the improvement of Hungary's relations with Western countries, including the reestablishment of diplomatic relations with the FRG in 1973. A US-Hungarian war-claims agreement was signed that year, and on 6 January 1978 the US returned the Hungarian coronation regalia.

The New Economic Mechanism which had been instituted in 1968 was largely abandoned, at Soviet and Comecon insistence, a decade later. This compounded the blows suffered by Hungary's economy during the energy crisis of the late 1970s, leading to a ballooning of the country's foreign indebtedness. By the late 1980s the country owed $18 billion, the highest per capita indebtedness in Europe.

This indebtedness was the primary engine of political change. The necessity to introduce fiscal austerity was "sweetened" by the appointment of reform-minded Karoly Grosz as prime minister in 1987. Faced with continued high inflation, the government took the step the following year of forcing Janos Kadar out entirely, giving control of the Party to Grosz. In 1989 Grosz and his supporters went even further, changing the party's name to Hungarian Socialist Party, and dismantling their nation's section of the Iron Curtain. The action which had the most far-reaching consequences, however, came in October 1989 when the state constitution was amended so as to create a multi-party political system.

Although Hungarians had been able to choose among multiple candidates for some legislative seats since as early as 1983, the foundations of a true multi-party system had been laid in 1987–88, when large numbers of discussion groups and special interest associations began to flourish. Many of these, such as the Network of Free Initiatives, the Bajscy-Zsilinszky Society, the Hungarian Democratic Forum, and the Alliance of Free Democrats, soon became true political parties. In addition, parties which had existed before the 1949 imposition of Communist rule, such as the People's Party, the Hungarian Independence Party, and the Social Democrats, began to reactivate themselves.

An important indicator of Hungary's intentions came in June 1989, when the remains of Imre Nagy, hanged for his part in the events of 1956, were reinterred with public honors; politicians and other public figures used the occasion to press further distance from Communism and the removal of Soviet troops. Another sign of public sentiment was the first commemoration in 40 years of the anniversary of the Revolution of 1848.

All of these groups, or the parties which they had spawned, competed in the 1990 general election, the first major free election to be held in more than four decades. No party gained an absolute majority of seats, so a coalition government was formed, of the Democratic Forum, Smallholders', and Christian Democrats parties, with Forum leader Jozsef Antall as Prime Minister. Arpad Goncz, of the Free Democrats, was selected president.

Under Antall Hungary pursued a vigorous program of economic transformation, with the state goal of transferring 30–35% of state assets to private control by the end of 1993. Hungary's liberal investment laws and comparatively well-developed industrial infrastructure permitted the nation to become an early leader in attracting Western investors. However, there were large blocs in society, and within the Democratic Forum itself, which found the pace of transition too slow, particularly since the government did not kept to its own time schedule.

In addition to its economic demands, this radical-right contingent also has a strongly nationalist, or even xenophobic, agenda, which has tended to polarize Hungarian national politics. Approximately 10% of the Hungarian population is non-Hungarian, including large populations of Jews and Roma (Gypsies). There are also large Hungarian populations in neighboring states, particularly in Romania, all of whom had been declared dual citizens of Hungary in 1988. The appeal to "Hungarian-ness" has been touted fairly frequently, widening pre-existing tensions within the dominant Democratic Forum party, and weakening their coalition in parliament. The Smallholders Party withdrew from the coalition in 1992, and in 1993 other elements were threatening to do the same.

At its January 1993 congress, the leading coalition party, the Democratic Forum, accepted the necessity to expel its right wing, led by the populist, and openly anti-Semitic, Istvan Csurka. Csurka combined with other populists to form the Hungarian Justice and Life Party. However, this did little to help Antall's government, which continued to lose parliamentary and public support. Perhaps the greatest cause for dissatisfaction was the continued attempts by Antall's government to control the public media, which it claimed were serving the political opposition. The Forum's viability was also hurt by Antall's illness, which in December 1993 led to his death. He was replaced by Peter Boross, formerly Minister of Internal Affairs.

The Democratic Forum's loss of popularity was vividly exposed in the parliamentary elections of May 1994, when the party, led by acting head Sandor Leszak, lost almost one-third of the seats it had controlled. In that election voters turned overwhelmingly to the Hungarian Socialist Party, giving the former Communist party an absolute majority of 54%. Voter turn-out in the two-tier election was as high as 70%, leaving little doubt that Hungarian voters had repudiated the Democratic Forum and its programs of forced transition to a market economy.

The voters are likely to be disappointed if they hoped that by pushing the Democratic Forum from power they would also be ridding themselves of the stringencies of economic reform. Hungary's international indebtedness remains very high—the country ran a $936 million trade deficit for the first two months of 1994 alone—which obligates new Prime Minister Gyula Horn to continue most of the same economic reform programs which the Socialists' predecessors began. There is concern, however, that the Socialists' absolute majority, which makes them all but impervious to legislative challenge, could lead to reversal of some of the important democratic gains of the recent past. Those concerns sharpened in July 1994, when Prime Minister Horn unilaterally appointed new heads for the state-owned radio and television, who immediately dismissed or suspended a number of conservative journalists.

13 GOVERNMENT

Hungary's present constitution remains based upon the 1949 Soviet-style constitution, with major revisions made in 1972 and 1988. The 1988 revisions mandated the end of the Communist

Party's monopoly on power, removed the word *People's* from the name of the state, and created the post of president to replace the earlier Presidential Council.

The present system is a unitary multi-party republic, with a parliamentary government. There is one legislative house, with 386 seats. The head of state is the President, who is elected by the Parliament, for a five-year term. The current president is Arpad Goncz, whose term expires in 1995.

The head of the government is the prime minister, leader of the largest party seated in the Parliament. In the Antall government important ministerial and other posts were split among representatives of various parties, but the dominance of the Socialist Party in the 1994 elections, combined with the reluctance of other parties to share responsibility for the rigorous reforms which remain yet to be undertaken, probably mean that the Socialists will control virtually the entire government.

The lack of a new constitution has left Hungary with a number of remnants of the Communist era. This has been most noticeable in regards to the media, which have no constituitonal guarantee of freedom. The Antall government saw the press as hostile, and made serious moves to shut down or take over newspapers and television broadcasters which it viewed as hostile. There is also concern that lack of constitutional guarantees could affect other areas of civil liberties; a case in point is religion, the freedom of which was meant to have been guaranteed in 1990 by the Law on Religion, but which was curtailed for so-called "destructive sects" in 1993.

The rise of Hungarian nationalism, which in some quarters of the government and public life is crossing over into xenophobia, also creates concern for civil liberties, as attempts have been made to limit "non-Hungarian" activities.

14POLITICAL PARTIES

Each of the last two parliaments have seated representatives of the same six political parties. However, the relative numbers of seats shifted dramatically between 1990 and 1994.

At present the predominant party is the Hungarian Socialist Party, which took 209 of the legislature's 386 seats. The HSP is the Hungarian Communist Party renamed and, to a certain extent, reoriented. The party's platform indicates basic support for the market economy system, albeit with a wide net of social services. Like the Communists of the past, however, the HSP stresses party unity and discipline, making them a powerful legislative bloc.

The Alliance of Free Democrats (AFD) gained seventy seats. This party was a liberal opposition party during the Antall government, with positions strongly in favor of closer integration with Europe, cooperation with Hungary's neighbors, and support for alien Hungarians. In economic terms their platform is very similar to that of the HSP, which is the basis of their agreement to enter into a coalition with the HSP, giving the two parties two-thirds of the legislature.

The Hungarian Democratic Forum (HDF) was reduced to 38 seats, reflecting the public's disillusion with the processes unleashed by the Antall government. Especially with the party's right wing purged, the HDF is a party of strong support for the ethnic minorities within Hungary.

The Independent Smallholders' Party (ISP) is a center-right party which seeks to ensure Hungarian interests in the context of European integration. It draws particular support from rural districts and among farmers. The most junior member of the Antall coalition, the ISP broke with the HDF in 1992, but was unable to impose discipline on many of its members, who continued to vote with the Antall government. Perhaps as a consequence its representation fell to 26 seats in the new Parliament. Jozsef Torgyan, Party leader, is a populist who maintains contact with the skinheads and other radical right-wing groups.

The larger coalition partner was the Christian Democratic People's Party (CDPP), also a center-right group, but with a religious dimension. They too suffered from the anti-Antall vote, dropping to 22 seats.

The Alliance of Young Democrats (AYD) is similar in program to the AFD, but with narrower appeal. A technocrats' and intellectuals' party, the group is particularly interested in issues of integration with Europe.

The final parliamentary party is the Agrarian Alliance, which has a single seat. This party is primarily concerns with issues affecting the nation's farmers.

Before the election it was expected—and in some quarters feared—that the Hungarian Justice and Life Party (HJLP) would do well. Founded by Istvan Csurka, who was expelled from the HDF for his nationalist and anti-semitic sentiments, the party is populist in orientation, seeking to elevate "Hungarian values."

Two parties to the left of the HSP also did more poorly than expected. These were the Hungarian Social Democratic Party and the Workers' Party, both of which narrowly missed gaining seats in 1990. Perhaps in part because they are correct in their complaint that the HSP has siphoned away the entire leftist vote, both parties did about the same in 1994 as they had in 1990. There is also a small Labor Party, which continues to represent the position of Janos Kadar; it applauded the August 1991, efforts of Communists in Moscow to overthrow President Mikhail Gorbachev.

The National Democratic Alliance is another small party, oriented more toward the center. It tends toward policies of neutrality, and argues that defense of Hungarians outside of Hungary must be balanced with defense of non-Hungarians within the state.

On the extreme right Hungary has at least two groups which draw their inspiration from the fascist Arrow Cross movement, and its leader Ferenc Szalasi. One is the Hungarian National Front Line, led by Istvan Gyorkos, who claims contact with other neo-Nazi groups in Europe and the US; the other is the World National Popular Rule Party, led by Albert Szabo, a returnee from Australia.

Hungary also has a noticeable "skinhead" movement, which has provoked fights and other disturbances, especially with Gypsies. Their activities have been condoned and praised by Izabella Kiraly, who had won a parliamentary seat as an HDF member, but who then left to form her own radical right Hungarian Interest Party.

15LOCAL GOVERNMENT

Hungary is divided into 19 districts. In addition, the capital city of Budapest has status as an independent district. The capital has almost one-fifth of the nation's population, making it the dominant administrative force in the country. Regional administrators are appointed, and are still answerable primarily to the central administration.

16JUDICIAL SYSTEM

Cases in the first instance usually come before provincial city courts or Budapest district courts. Appeals can be submitted to county courts or the Budapest Metropolitan Court. The Supreme Court is basically a court of appeal, although it may also hear important cases in the first instance.

Supreme Court justices are elected by the National Assembly. Judges in the counties and districts are selected by the Presidential Council and appointed by the Ministry of Justice for an indefinite period. The courts of first instance have one professional judge and two lay assessors; in courts of appeal, all judges are professional.

The prosecutor-general, who exercises wide powers, is elected by and responsible to the National Assembly for a five-year term. The prosecutor-general appoints the prosecutors, who are responsible to him, and within this framework all act independently of the central and local governmental organs.

A Constitutional Law Council was established in April 1984 to verify the constitutionality of proposed laws. The Court's 15 members are elected by Parliament to 9-year terms which may be renewed.

[17] ARMED FORCES

In 1993, Hungary had an army of 63,500 men in four mixed divisions; an air force of 17,300 men and 91 combat aircraft; and a rivercraft brigade with 51 small craft. Security forces, consisting of frontier and border guards under the direction of the Ministry of the Interior, number about 20,000. There are about 4,000 paramilitary personnel and 192,000 military reservists. The defense budget was estimated at $1.16 billion in 1992 or around one percent of GDP. Arms purchases during 1985–89 were estimated at $800 million; they ended in 1990. Arms exports during the same period totaled $1 billion, but dropped $40 million in 1991.

Military service is compulsory; all males aged 18 to 55 are eligible for induction for 12 months' service. About 54,000 conscripts serve in the armed forces.

A Soviet military presence in Hungary since the end of World War II (65,000 in 1986) has gone away with the end of the Warsaw Pact. Hungary provides 24 UN observers abroad.

[18] INTERNATIONAL COOPERATION

Hungary has been a member of the UN since 14 December 1955 and participates in ECE and all the nonregional specialized agencies except the IDA, IFAD, and IFC; the nation became a member of the IBRD and IMF in 1982. As a member of CMEA and WTO, Hungary coordinates its economic and military plans with other Soviet-bloc countries. Hungary is also a signatory of GATT and the Law of the Sea.

[19] ECONOMY

Before World War II, industrial growth was slow because adequate capital was lacking. Since 1949, however, industry has expanded rapidly, and it now contributes a larger share than agriculture to the national income. The government has no capital investments abroad, but it participates in limited economic activities in developing countries. Potentially, the domestic market could be expanded, but the government has generally sought, through price-fixing, taxation, and other means, to regulate consumption and make more goods available for export in order to obtain essential raw materials and other imports. Substantial industrial growth continued through the 1960s and mid-1970s, but output in the socialized sector declined during 1979–80, and growth was sluggish in the 1980s. Hungary's gross debt to the West rose to about $24.5 billion as of December 1993, the largest per capita indebtedness of all European countries.

After the fall of Communism in 1989, Hungary began a painful transition to a market economy. Between 1990 and 1992, GDP dropped by about 20%. Freed to reach their own level, consumer prices rose 162% between 1989 and 1993. The rate of unemployment was 12.2% at the end of 1992. By late 1993, private-sector output was 35–40% of the GDP. About 18% of state holdings had been sold by the end of 1992. Hungary became an associate member of the EU in 1994.

[20] INCOME

In 1992, the GNP was $30,671 million, or $3,010 per capita. For the period 1985–92 the average inflation rate was 18.5%, resulting in a real growth rate in per capita GNP of –1.5%.

In 1992, the GDP was $35,218 million in current US dollars. It is estimated that in 1991 agriculture, hunting, forestry, and fishing contributed 10% to GDP; mining and quarrying, 3%; manufacturing, 22%; electricity, gas, and water, 3%; construc-

tion, 5%; wholesale and retail trade, 14%; transport, storage, and communication, 8%; finance, insurance, real estate, and business services, 8%; community, social, and personal services, 1%; and other sources, 25%.

[21] LABOR

Of the total employment of 4,710,000 in 1991, 29.6% were in industry; 19.3% in agriculture, 12.8% in trade; 8.7% in transportation; 6.5% in construction; and 23.1% in other branches of the economy, including administration, health, and education. Women constituted 52% of the civilian labor force.

Before World War II, trade unions had not developed substantially; their combined membership was only about 100,000, principally craftsmen. After the war, the government reduced the number of the traditional craft unions, organized them along industrial lines, and placed them under Communist Party control. The Central Council of Hungarian Trade Unions (SZOT) held a monopoly over labor interests for over 40 years. Since wages, benefits, and other aspects of employment were state-controlled, the SZOT acted as a social service agency, but was dissolved in 1990 with the shift away from centralization to democracy. The National Federation of Trade Unions is its successor, with 1.7 million members and assets of Ft5 billion ($63 million) in 1991. There are now several other large labor organizations in Hungary: the Democratic League of Independent Trade Unions, with some 240,000 members; the Autonomous Trade Unions, with 300,000 members; and the National Federation of Workers' Councils, with 120,000 members.

The average monthly wage of employees in the industrial sector was Ft17,400 as of 1991, up 29.9% from the previous year. Labor disputes are usually resolved by conciliation boards; appeal may be made to courts. In 1991, unemployment was at 8.4%, up from 1.6% in 1990.

Since 1991, most unions have been hesitant to strike, preferring instead to act as a buffer between workers and the negative side effects of economic reform.

In 1992, there were only four strikes involving 1,010 workers and 9,453 lost days. The eight-hour day, adopted in several industries before World War II, is now widespread. The five-day week is typical, but many Hungarians have second or third jobs. Minimum wage in January 1992 was Ft8,000 per month ($107). Paid leave is at least 15 workdays.

[22] AGRICULTURE

In 1991, 57% of the land (about 5.3 million hectares/13 million acres) was arable. More than half of Hungary's area lies in the Great Plain; although the soil is fertile, most of the region lacks adequate rainfall and is prone to droughts, requiring extensive irrigation. In 1991, some 145,000 hectares (358,300 acres) of land were irrigated. In 1992, agriculture contributed 7.1% to GDP.

Before World War II, Hungary was a country of large landed estates and landless and land-poor peasants. In the land reform of 1945, about 35% of the land area was distributed, 1.9 million hectares (4.7 million acres) among 640,000 families and 1.3 million hectares (3.2 million acres) in state farms. In 1949, the government adopted a policy of collectivization based on the Soviet kolkhoz, and by the end of 1952, 5,110 collectives, many forcibly organized, controlled 22.6% of total arable land. Peasant resentment led to a policy change in 1953, and many collectives were dissolved, but the regime returned to its previous policy in 1955. As a result of the 1956 uprising, collectives were again dissolved; but a new collectivization drive begun in 1959 was essentially completed by 1961. Meanwhile, the proportion of the economically active population employed in agriculture decreased steadily. In 1949, agricultural employees accounted for 55.1% of the total labor force; by 1992, the figure was about 8%.

Hungary has achieved self sufficiency in temperate zone crops, and exports about one-third of all produce, especially fruit and preserved vegetables. The traditional agricultural crops have been cereals, with wheat, corn (maize), and rye grown on more than half the total sown area. In recent years, considerable progress has been made in industrial crops, especially oilseeds and sugar beets. Fruit production (especially for preserves) and viticulture are also significant; the wine output in 1992 was 500,000 tons. That year, over 800,000 tons of grapes were produced on 135,000 hectares (333,600 acres).

The following table shows output of principal field crops in 1992:

| | AREA HARVESTED | | PRODUCTION |
	HECTARES	ACRES	(TONS)
Corn	1,159,000	2,863,900	4,910,000
Wheat	820,000	2,026,000	3,426,000
Sugar beets	97,000	239,700	3,560,000
Potatoes	43,000	106,200	1,200,000
Rye	72,000	178,000	134,000

23 ANIMAL HUSBANDRY

Although animal husbandry is second only to cereal cultivation in agricultural production, the number and quality of animals are much lower than in neighboring countries. An inadequate supply of fodder is one of the chief deficiencies. At the end of 1992 there were 5,993,000 hogs, 1,808,000 sheep, 1,420,000 head of cattle, and 75,000 horses; poultry numbered 36,000,000. The 1992 output of livestock products was 1,214,000 tons (live weight) of meat, 2,370,000 tons of milk, and 5,740 tons of wool; egg production was 228,000 tons.

As of 1992, the government undertook efforts to create an entrepreneurial type of agriculture, including a stockbreeding fund that promotes progress in improving and raising livestock.

24 FISHING

Fishing was unimportant before World War II, but production has increased in recent years. The best fishing areas are the Danube and Tisza rivers, Lake Balaton, and various artificial ponds. The catch is composed mainly of carp, catfish, and perch. The 1991 catch was 29,378 tons.

25 FORESTRY

Forests totaled 1,701,000 hectares (4,203,000 acres), or 18.4% of Hungary's total area, in 1991. Oak, ash, and beech are the most important varieties. Because of the relatively small forest area and the high rate of exploitation, Hungary traditionally has had to import timber. During the 1960s, a systematic reforestation program began. Production rose from 3.5 million cu m in 1960 to 6 million cu m in 1991. Reforestation affected about 440,000 hectares (1,087,000 acres) during 1960–68 but only about 65,000 hectares (161,000 acres) in 1970–74 and 64,322 hectares (158,942 acres) during 1975–81. From 1981–85, some 19,000 hectares (46,900 acres) were annually reforested.

26 MINING

Although the government has promoted privatization of state-owned companies since 1990, in 1991 the country's mineral industry was still state-owned. Mineral reserves are small and generally inadequate. In 1985, 115,300 people were employed in mining and quarrying. Bauxite, which is found in various parts of western Hungary, has been among the most important minerals; production in 1991 was 2,037,000 tons. Hungary produced 54,783 tons of manganese ore during the same year.

27 ENERGY AND POWER

All natural sources of power are state property, and all electric power plants are under state supervision. In 1990, installed capacity was 6.96 million kw, of which thermal electric generating plants accounted for 68%; nuclear power plants, 25%; and hydroelectric power facilities, 7%. By the end of 1963, all villages were connected with electric power. Most power is thermally generated, hydroelectric power development is not feasible. Major power plants are the oil-fueled Danube Thermal Power Plant at Százhalombatta (1,850 Mw); the Tisza Thermal Power Plant at Tiszaújváros (840 Mw); and the Gagarin Power Plant at Visonta (800 Mw) near Mt. Kékes, which uses lignite from an open-pit mine. The first Hungarian nuclear power plant, at Pécs, began production in 1982.

Oil and natural gas are rapidly replacing coal as the major energy source. Coal production in 1991 was 16,975,000 tons. Hard coal, mined near Pécs, comprised 10% of total production; brown coal, mined near Dorog, comprised 59%; and lignite, mined near Gyöngyös, accounted for the remaining 31%. Production of oil increased from 1,036,000 tons in 1959 to 1,893,000 tons in 1991; the government continues to sponsor oil exploration. Natural gas production totaled 5,041 million cu m in 1991. Uranium, discovered in 1953 near Pécs, is expected to supply its nuclear station until 2020.

Increased energy production has not kept up with consumption, and reliance on foreign power sources has been increasing. In 1991, imports accounted for about 50% of Hungary's total energy requirements and nearly 80% of its crude oil consumption. Beginning in 1962, direct links have been established between the power systems of Hungary and neighboring countries; the most important transmission line connects Vinnitsa in the Ukraine with Albertirsa in Hungary. Hungary has 5,604 km (3,482 mi) of oil, natural gas, and refined products pipelines. In 1990, these pipelines carried 40.3% of the total fuel transport.

28 INDUSTRY

Hungary is poor in the natural resources essential for heavy industry and relies strongly on imported raw materials. Industry, only partially developed before World War II, has expanded rapidly since 1948 and provides the bulk of exports. Industrial plants were nationalized by 1949, and the socialized sector accounted for about 98.5% of gross production in 1985.

Hungary has concentrated on developing steel, machine tools, buses, diesel engines and locomotives, television sets, radios, electric light bulbs and fluorescent lamps, telecommunications equipment, refrigerators, washing machines, medical apparatus and other precision engineering equipment, pharmaceuticals, and petrochemical products. Textile and leather production has decreased in relative importance since World War II, while chemicals grew to become the leading industry in 1992. Food processing, formerly the leading industry, provides a significant portion of exports; meat, poultry, grain, and wine are common export items.

The 1993 output of steel was 1,836,000 tons; crude aluminum, 27,879 tons; nitrogenous fertilizers, 220,574 tons (in terms of nitrogen); superphosphates, 424,563 tons (phosphoric acid); footwear, 11,963,000 pairs; and buses, 3,211. Other products, with 1993 output totals, include cement, 2,532,000 tons; television receivers, 188,021; TV sets, 185,000; washing machines, 134,258; refrigerators, 482,952; fluorescent tubes, 39,253,000; and cotton and woolen fabrics, 97.5 million sq m. In 1993, industrial production was only two-thirds of the 1985 level. The number of industrial employees increased from 1,323,600 in 1960 to 1,754,000 in 1974 but fell to 1,496,400 in 1985 and 842,800 in December, 1993.

29 SCIENCE AND TECHNOLOGY

In 1989, 14,113 technicians and 20,431 scientists and engineers were engaged in research and development. Expenditures on research and development that year amounted to Ft33 billion. Among major scientific organizations are the Hungarian Academy of Sciences (founded 1825), the Association for Dissemination of Sciences (founded 1841), and the Federation of Technical and Scientific Societies (founded 1948), with 32 scientific member societies.

30DOMESTIC TRADE

The total retail trade turnover was Ft1,682 billion in 1993, of which foodstuffs accounted for 31% and industrial articles, 24%. General department stores accounted for only 3%. Hungary's first supermarket was placed in operation in 1962 at Dorog and proved a success; the number of self-service stores is increasing.

Installment buying was inaugurated on 1 September 1958, with credit extended (6 to 18 months) by the National Bank to certain workers for durable consumer goods of "high value."

Business hours extend from 9 or 10 AM to 4 or 5 PM for offices and general stores and to 3 or 4 PM for banks. Early closing (between noon and 1 PM) on Saturdays is widespread; Sunday closing is general. Food stores open between 6 and 8 AM and close between 7 and 9 PM weekdays; a few remain open on Sundays.

Newspapers and general, trade, and technical magazines are used for advertising; there is also broadcast and outdoor advertising. A major industrial fair, held since 1906, takes place every spring and autumn in Budapest.

31FOREIGN TRADE

Hungary imports raw materials and semifinished products and exports finished products. Within that general framework, however, the structure, volume, and direction of Hungarian foreign trade have changed perceptibly in recent years. The total trade volume increased from Ft15,431.7 million (foreign exchange) in 1958 to Ft1,982.4 billion in 1993. While agricultural products made up 57% of total exports before World War II, they stood at 21.4% in 1993. There was a significant increase in exports of machinery and equipment, which made up 9.9% of the export total in 1938 and 28.8% in 1985, but only 13.9% in 1993. Other exports in 1993 were industrial consumer goods (25.2%), and raw materials and semifinished products (36.2%). Industrial consumer goods made up 21.2% of total imports in 1993; raw materials and semifinished products, 33.4%; machinery and equipment, 26.9%; and fuels and electric energy, 12.6%.

Exports and imports by major categories in 1993 (in billions of forints) were as follows:

	EXPORTS	IMPORTS
Raw materials, semi-finished products and spare parts	296.5	388.3
Machinery, transport equipment, and other capital goods	114.2	312.9
Raw materials for food industry, live animals, and processed food products	175.1	68.6
Industrial consumer goods	206.7	246.0
Fuels and electric power	27.5	146.7
TOTAL	819.9	1,162.5

The USSR used to be by far Hungary's most important supplier and customer. Germany has become the chief customer, with the former USSR second and (in 1993) still its chief supplier. Austria ranks third in both respects and Italy fourth. The EC countries took half of Hungary's exports in 1992. Following the conclusion of a most-favored nation agreement in 1978, Hungary's trade with the US grew considerably. An accord with the EC in 1992 lifted quotas on 60% of Hungary's exports.

Principal trade partners in 1993 (in millions of forints) were as follows:

	EXPORTS	IMPORTS	BALANCE
Former USSR	125,243	257,927	–132,684
Germany	218,246	250,891	–32,645
UK	18,703	29,609	–10,906
Austria	82,614	135,065	–52,451
Czech Republic and Slovakia	27,454	46,559	–19,105
US	34,629	45,406	–10,777
France	28,273	38,467	–10,194
Italy	65,544	69,555	–4,011
Other countries	219,210	289,013	–69,803
TOTAL	819,916	1,162,492	–342,576

32BALANCE OF PAYMENTS

Having scrapped central planning, the Hungarian government is attempting to stabilize the economy and tame inflation. Three years of current account surpluses, however, were expected to turn into a $1 billion to $1.7 billion deficit in 1993, due to falling exports. In 1992, exports had grown by 7.4%, but recession in export markets, western European protectionism, an appreciating forint, bankruptcies of firms producing one-third of exports, and drought caused Hungarian trade to slow down.

In 1992 merchandise exports totaled $10,097 million and imports $10,108 million. The merchandise trade balance was $–11 million. The following table summarizes Hungary's balance of payments for 1991 and 1992 (in millions of US dollars):

	1991	1992
CURRENT ACCOUNT		
Goods, services, and income	–464	–506
Unrequited transfers	867	858
TOTALS	403	352
CAPITAL ACCOUNT		
Direct investment	1,462	1,479
Portfolio investment	—	—
Other long-term capital	759	–1,696
Other short-term capital	–747	633
Exceptional financing	—	—
Other liabilities	—	—
Reserves	–1,795	–770
TOTALS	–321	–354
Errors and omissions	–82	2

33BANKING AND SECURITIES

Banking was nationalized in 1948, when the National Bank of Hungary was installed as the bank of issue, with a monopoly on credit and foreign exchange operations.

Following the 1987 reform of the banking system, the National Bank retained its central position as a bank of issue and its foreign exchange monopoly, but its credit functions were transferred to commercial banks. Three new commercial banks were established: the Hungarian Credit Bank, the Commercial and Credit Bank, and the Budapest Bank. Two other commercial banks, both founded in the 1950s, are the Hungarian Foreign Trade Bank and the General Banking and Trust Co. These six banks serve the financial needs of enterprises and government operations. The main bank for the general public is the National Savings Bank; in 1987 there were also 262 savings cooperatives. The Central Corporation of Banking Companies handles state property, performs international property transactions for individuals, and deals with the liquidation of bankrupt companies. The State Development Institution manages and controls development projects. In 1987 there were also three banks with foreign participation: the Central European International Bank (66% of shares held by six foreign companies), Citibank Budapest (80% owned by Citibank New York), and Unicbank (45% owned by three foreign companies). In 1991 there were 10 government owned commercial banks, 16 joint-stock owned commercial banks, 5 government owned specialized financial institutions, one offshore bank and 260 savings co-operatives. The Budapest stock exchange opened in June 1990.

34INSURANCE
Before World War II, 49 private insurance companies—25 domestic and 24 foreign—conducted business activities in Hungary. All insurance was nationalized in 1949 and placed under the State Insurance Institute, a government monopoly. A new institution, Hungária Insurance Co., was founded in 1986.

35PUBLIC FINANCE
In recent years, the government has presented its budget bill to the National Assembly sometime during the first several months of the year, but the budget itself becomes effective on 1 January, when the fiscal year begins. It is prepared by the Ministry of Finance.

The growing budget deficit is a crucial problem. State spending has been held in check, but unexpectedly large drops in GDP have depressed tax revenues. The 1991 target shortfall of Ft79 billion ended up at Ft114 billion, and the 1992 deficit target of Ft70 billion came in at Ft197 billion. In July 1993, Parliament passed a supplementary budget raising the 1993 projected deficit from Ft185 billion to Ft215 billion (6.8% of GDP). The budget problem is expected to persist without better tax collection and a restructuring of overly-generous social benefits.

Hungary has the heaviest per capita debt burden of Eastern Europe. Gross foreign debt at the end of 1993 was $24.5 billion, an estimated 65% of GDP and about 200% of 1991 hard currency exports. However, 80% of Hungary's external debt is in medium- and long-term loans. Hungary's refusal to reschedule its debt has encouraged international investment.

36TAXATION
Direct taxes include a 40% corporate profits tax, a progressive income tax (25–40% in 1992), and capital gains taxes. The major indirect taxes paid by the general population are transfer taxes on inheritance, gifts, and residential property, and a turnover tax based on the EC's VAT guidelines. The normal VAT rate is 25%, with a reduced rate of 15% for certain services and exemptions for many essentials.

37CUSTOMS AND DUTIES
Under Hungary's liberalized import policies, 93% of all imports do not require licenses. As a member of GATT, Hungary adheres to the Brussels Tariff Nomenclature. Most tariffs range from 12–13% with a maximum of 40–50%. Hungary plans to reduce tariffs to 8% to conform to GATT. All imports are also subject to value-added tax.

38FOREIGN INVESTMENT
Even before the repudiation of Communism, Hungary sought to enter joint ventures with Western countries. With the exception of the banking and service sectors, in which a greater share may be allowed, foreign investors' shares in Hungarian joint ventures are limited to 49%. To attract foreign investors, Hungary lowered profit taxes from 40% to 20% at the beginning of 1986. By the end of 1992, 13,218 registered joint ventures with Western companies had been agreed to. In 1993, a total of $5,576 million in foreign investment had been secured, more than half of all foreign investment in Eastern Europe. Incentives include tax concessions.

39ECONOMIC DEVELOPMENT
The economy of Hungary is under state control. Despite recent moves toward a more market-oriented economy, most industries and businesses are still organized into national enterprises operat-

ing with the current economic plan and according to directives issued by the pertinent ministries. During the first 20 years after World War II, Hungary had the following economic plans: the three-year plan (1947–49) for economic reconstruction; the first five-year plan (1950–54) which aimed at rapid and forced industrialization and which was slightly modified in 1951 and by the "new course" policy of 1953; the one-year plan of 1955; the second five-year plan (1956–60), designed to further industrialization but discarded as a result of the October, 1956 uprising; the three-year plan (1958–60), which also emphasized industrialization, although it allocated greater investment for housing and certain consumer goods; and the new second five-year plan (1961–65), which provided for a 50% increase in industrial production. These were followed by the third five-year plan (1966–70); the fourth five-year plan (1971–75), with greater emphasis on modernization of industrial plants producing for export and housing construction; the fifth five-year plan (1976–80), which called for amelioration of the gap in living standards between the peasantry and the working class; the sixth five-year plan (1981–85), emphasizing investment in export industries and energy conservation and seeking to curb domestic demand; and the seventh five-year plan (1986–90), which projected growth of 15–17% in NMP, 13–16% in industrial production, and 12–14% in agriculture.

Far-reaching economic reforms, called the New Economic Mechanism (NEM), were introduced on 1 January 1968. In order to create a competitive consumers' market, some prices were no longer fixed administratively, but were to be determined by market forces. Central planning was restricted to essential materials, and managers of state enterprises were expected to plan and carry out all the tasks necessary to ensure profitable production. In the early years of the NEM, the growth rate of industrial output surpassed target figures; national income rose substantially, surpassing any previous planning periods; and productivity increased significantly in all sectors of the national economy. However, following the huge oil price increases of 1973–74, the government returned to more interventionist policies in an attempt to protect Hungary's economy from external forces. Beginning in 1979, the government introduced a program of price reform, aimed at aligning domestic with world prices; changes in wage setting, intended to encourage productivity; and decentralization of industry, including the breakup of certain large enterprises and the creation of small-scale private ones, especially in services. New measures introduced in 1985 and 1986 included the lifting of government subsidies for retail prices (which led to sharp price increases) and the imposition of management reform, including the election of managers in 80% of all enterprises.

The 1991–95 economic program aimed to fully integrate Hungary into the world economy on a competitive basis. The program's main features were to accelerate privatization, control inflation, and institute measures to prepare the way for the convertibility of the forint.

40SOCIAL DEVELOPMENT
A national social insurance system was relatively well advanced before World War II for the nonagricultural population. A 1972 decree of the Council of Ministers extended this system to cover virtually the entire population, including craftsmen; by 1974, 99% of the population enjoyed the benefits of social insurance. Coverage includes relief for sickness, accidents, unemployment, and old age and incapacity, and provides maternity allowances for working women, allowances for children, and payment of funeral expenses.

Social welfare is centralized in the government-controlled, union-administered National Institute of Social Insurance. It is compulsory for all employees working or pensioned, for their family dependents, and for students. Payroll contributions of 43% are paid by the employer, and 10% of the employee's wage is deducted for pensions.

Women over 55 and men over 60 are eligible for old-age pensions if they have worked 20 years. For those working underground or in dangerous or unhealthful occupations, retirement ages are 50 for women and 55 for men. The pension amounts to 33% of the average monthly pay after 10 years of work, 55% after 20 years, and 75% after 42 years and over. Members of agricultural cooperatives receive a pension calculated in the same way as for employees. In case of accident or certain occupational diseases, the insured is entitled to medical treatment and compensation. A sick person receives 65–75% of the wage—70% (90% if the family breadwinner) if confined to a hospital. Persons disabled by an industrial accident receive fixed pensions regardless of the years of work.

Since 1967, an employed woman or, since May 1982, a father rearing his child alone, has been entitled to unpaid leave until the child is 3 years old. Monthly allowances for families with children up to 16 years of age (up to 19, if in day courses in secondary schools) are Ft800 for one child, Ft900 for two, and Ft1,000 for three, and an additional sum of Ft1,000 for each additional child. Women examined by an obstetrician during pregnancy receive a single maternity grant after the delivery, amounting to Ft6,000 per infant if four medical examinations have been carried out and Ft1,000 if not. Women receive their monthly average earnings during maternity leave, which lasts 24 weeks.

Between 1977 and 1985, the marriage rate in Hungary fell from 9.1 per 1,000 population to 6.9, and the number of divorces increased from 2.6 per 1,000 population to 2.8. The fertility rate for 1985–90 was 1.8. Fewer than 7% of Hungarian women aged 17–49 years used oral contraceptives in 1970; by 1985, the proportion had increased to 32.3%. During the same period, the abortion rate per 100 women aged 15–49 years fell from 7.2 to 3.2, and the actual number of abortions declined, according to official statistics, from 192,283 to about 82,400; the criteria by which married women (especially those under 40 years of age and with fewer than three children) may obtain abortions were significantly narrowed in 1974. Women have the same legal rights as men, including inheritance and property rights. They hold a large number of the positions in teaching, medicine, and the judiciary, which are all relatively low-paid professions.

Hungary has the world's highest suicide rate—44 deaths per 100,000 population in the mid-1980s.

41HEALTH

The Ministry of Health administers the state health service, with the counties and districts forming hospital regions. By the end of 1974, 99% of the population was covered by social insurance and enjoyed free medical services; those few not insured pay for medical and hospital care. Limited private medical practice is permitted. In 1992, The Ministry of Welfare proposed a compulsory health care scheme based on the German system, to be administered by the National Health Security Directorate. Total health care spending in 1990 came to $1,958 million.

In 1991, there were 33,859 doctors; in 1992, there were 2.98 physicians per 1,000 people, with a nurse to doctor ratio of 1.1. In 1990, there was 1 physician for every 340 people. In the same year, there were 4,504 pharmacists, 4,267 dentists, and 2,695 midwives. In 1989, there were 32,357 nurses. In 1991, there were 103,300 hospital beds (about 10 per 1,000 inhabitants). Hungary's birthrate in 1993 was 12.3 per 1,000 people. There were 127,000 births in 1992, with an average life expectancy of 70 years. Free professional assistance given to insured pregnant women and to the mothers of newborn children, maternity leave and grants, and improved hygienic conditions helped lower the infant mortality rate to 15 per 1,000 live births in 1992 (33.8 in 1973).

The country faces severe problems in maintaining an accept-

able level of health care for its population. The UN considers its death rate unacceptable (13.8 per 1,000 in 1993). Hungary has a declining population which is aging rapidly. Arteriosclerosis is a major cause of death (100 per 100,000 people). Contributing factors include the incidence of cardiovascular disease, which is directly related to stress through pressures of work, together with smoking and dietary factors. In 1990, major causes of death were generalized as follows: (1) communicable diseases and maternal/perinatal causes, 55 per 100,000; (2) noncommunicable diseases, 690 per 100,000; and (3) injuries, 90 per 100,000. In 1990, there were 38 reported cases of tuberculosis per 100,000 people, and in 1992, children up to 1 year old were vaccinated against tuberculosis (99%); diphtheria, pertussis, and tetanus (100%); polio (98%); and measles (100%).

42HOUSING

A total of 1,988,261 dwelling units were constructed between 1949 and 1981; during 1982–85, the number of new dwellings was 294,128. Of the 72,507 dwellings constructed in 1985, 12,956 were built by the state and 59,551 by private individuals (only 980 were built without any state funding). Although the housing stock increased from 3,122,000 units in 1970 to 3,846,000 in 1986, construction has not kept pace with the needs of Hungary's growing and increasingly urbanized population. The construction rate for new dwellings has been greater in smaller cities and towns than in Budapest, where as of 1980, 17.3% of all housing units were built before 1900 and 56.3% before 1945. In 1985 there were an average of 2.77 persons per dwelling unit and 1.26 occupants per room. In 1990, 57% of all housing units were made of brick, 22% were adobe, 14% were panel, and 7% were concrete. As of 1990, 78% of all dwellings were connected to a water system; 76% had flush toilets; 41% had piped gas; and 44% were connected to a public sewage system.

Low-income people and other private builders generally rely on the labor of family and friends, buying the essential materials little by little; they may apply for loans if necessary to complete the dwelling. In 1990, 76% of all dwellings were owner occupied and 24% were rented.

43EDUCATION

Virtually the entire adult population is literate. Primary (for eight years) and secondary (for four years) education is free. The state also pays the bulk of costs for higher education. The educational system is under the control of the Ministry of Education and is supervised by the local councils, which receive financial assistance from the central government.

Preschool programs are established and administered by local councils or enterprises. In 1991, the 4,706 kindergartens had 33,159 teachers and 394,091 children. Between 1945 and 1962, the eight-year school for children from 6 to 14 years of age was compulsory; in 1962, compulsory education was extended for two additional years, for children from 6 to 16. In 1991 there were 3,641 general elementary schools, with 89,276 teachers and 1,081,213 pupils, and general secondary schools, with 10,732 teachers and 130,378 students. The same year, 3,865 students were in teacher training and 390,908 were in vocational courses. Institutions of higher education had 107,079 students and 17,477 professors and lecturers in 1991.

Adult education has expanded since World War II, especially through workers' schools and correspondence courses. Politically acceptable students are given preference for admission to universities and high schools. Although there are university fees, many students are exempt from payment or pay reduced fees.

Before 1948, most schools were operated by religious bodies, especially the Roman Catholic Church; the school system was nationalized in 1948. Religious instruction for children, compulsory before the war, is now voluntary and is discouraged by the government.

44LIBRARIES AND MUSEUMS

Hungary's National Archives were established in 1756. Heavily damaged in World War II, the collection has been reorganized; among its treasures are some 100,000 items from the period prior to the Turkish occupation (1526). Hungary's National Széchényi Library is the largest and most significant in the country. Founded in Budapest in 1802, it has more than 2.5 million books and periodicals and more than 4.5 million manuscripts, maps, prints, and microfilms. Other important libraries are the Lóránd Eötvös University Library (1,400,000 volumes) and the Library of the Hungarian Academy of Sciences (1,942,000 volumes), both in Budapest; and the Central Library of the Lajos Kossuth University in Debrecen (3,768,000 volumes). As of 1987, there were 4,507 regional public libraries located throughout the country.

There were 571 museums (74 in Budapest) reported in 1990, and many zoological and botanical gardens. One of the largest institutions is the Hungarian National Museum, which displays relics of prehistoric times as well as artifacts reflecting the history of Hungary from the Magyar conquest through 1849, including the Hungarian coronation regalia. A branch of the National Museum is the Hungarian Natural History Museum. Other museums, all in Budapest, include the Ethnographical Museum, the Museum of History, the Hungarian National Gallery, and the Museum of Fine Arts.

45MEDIA

According to the constitution, all means of communication are government property and are administered by the central government. Budapest is the principal communications center. The postal, telegraph, and telephone systems are administered by a division of the Ministry of Transport and Communications. In 1991, there were 1,770,000 telephones. In 1990 Hungary had 32 AM and 15 FM radio stations and 41 television stations. There were 6,280,000 radios and 4,340,000 television sets in 1991 in Hungary. By early 1985, cable television was operating in 12 cities.

In 1991 there were 28 dailies, with an average combined daily circulation of 2.9 million. Budapest has always been Hungary's publishing center. The following table lists circulation figures for the larger Budapest dailies as of 1991:

	AFFILIATION	CIRCULATION
Népszabadság	Hungarian Socialist Workers' Party (HSWP)	327,000
Népszava	Hungarian Trade Unions	181,000
Kurir	NA	134,000
Magyar Nemzet	Patriotic People's Front	121,000
Esti Hírlap	Budapest Party Committee and Metropolitan Council	93,000

In 1991, 8,133 titles were published in Hungary, with a total of 99.9 million copies.

46ORGANIZATIONS

Hungary has 22 regional trade and professional associations, Also, there are 7,532 industrial, agricultural, and foreign trade organizations in the country. A chamber of commerce located in the capital promotes Hungary's goods and services in world markets.

The Act on Cooperatives, passed 6 January 1992, allows members of cooperatives to profit from their actions within cooperatives. As of 1992, the largest cooperatives in Hungary were: general consumer and seller cooperatives (AFESZ) with over 1 million members. Agricultural cooperatives in the country have over 800,000 members. Hungary's industrial cooperatives have

over 180,00 members. Savings cooperatives are the largest in Hungary with over 2 million members. In all there are 1,341 agricultural, 16 fishing, 3,450 industrial, 270 trade, 260 banking and saving, and 1,407 home-building and maintenance co-ops.

47TOURISM, TRAVEL, AND RECREATION

Hungary, at the crossroads of Central Europe, had the world's fifth-highest number of tourist arrivals (21.8 million) in 1991. Of Hungary's visitors, 26.2% came from Romania, 15.9% from Germany, 13.9% from Austria, and 8.6% from the former Yugoslavia. There were 25,549 hotel rooms with 59,339 beds and a 48.2% occupancy rate, and tourism receipts totaled US$1.03 billion.

A valid passport is required of all foreign visitors. Citizens of some countries (including the US, Canada, and the UK) do not need visas. Among Hungary's diverse tourist attractions are Turkish and Roman ruins, medieval towns and castles, more than 500 thermal springs (some with resort facilities), and Lake Balaton, the largest freshwater lake in Europe. Budapest, a city of over 2 million people, is a major tourist attraction and cultural capital, with two opera houses and several annual arts festivals.

Popular sports include handball, football (soccer), tennis, and volleyball. The Budapest Grand Prix, the only Formula-1 motor race in Eastern Europe, was inaugurated in August 1986.

48FAMOUS HUNGARIANS

The foundations for modern Hungarian literature begin with the movement known as the Period of Linguistic Reform, whose leaders were the versatile writer Ferenc Kazinczy (1759–1831) and Ferencz Kölcsey (1790–1838), lyric poet and literary critic. Among the outstanding literary figures was Dániel Berzsenyi (1772–1836) of the Latin School. Károly Kisfaludy (1788–1830) founded the Hungarian national drama. Mihaly Vörösmarty (1800–55), a fine poet, related the Magyar victories under Árpád in his Flight of Zalán. He was followed by Hungary's greatest lyric poet, Sándor Petöfi (1823–49), a national hero who stirred the Magyars in their struggle against the Habsburgs in 1848 with his Arise Hungarians. Another revolutionary hero was Lajos Kossuth (1802–94), orator and political author. János Arany (1817–82), epic poet and translator, influenced future generations, as did Mór Jókai (1825–1904), Hungary's greatest novelist. The outstanding dramatist Imre Madách (1823–64) is known for his Tragedy of Man. Endre Ady (1877–1919) was a harbinger of modern poetry and Western ideas. Lyric poets of the contemporary era include László Nagy (1925–78), János Pilinszky (1921–81), and Ferenc Juhász (b.1928). Gyula Illyés (1902–83), a poet, novelist, and dramatist, was one of the outstanding figures of 20th-century Hungarian literature. Ferenc Molnár (1878–1952) is known for his plays Liliom, The Swan, and The Guardsman. György Lukács (1885–1971) was an outstanding Marxist writer and literary critic. Hungarian-born Arthur Koestler (1905–83), a former radical, was a well-known anti-Communist novelist and writer.

János Fadrusz (1858–1903) and József Somogyi (b.1916) are among Hungary's best-known sculptors. The outstanding Hungarian painter Mihály Munkácsy (1844–1900) is best known for his Christ before Pilate. Victor Vasarely (b.1908), a world-famous painter of "op art," was born in Budapest and settled in France in 1930. Miklós Ybl (1814–91) was a leading architect; and Gyula Halasz (1899–1984), better known as Brassai, was a well-known photographer. The Hungarian-born Joseph Pulitzer (1847–1911) was a noted journalist and publisher in the US. Hungarian musicians include the composers Franz (Ferenc) Liszt (1811–86), Ernst (Ernö) von Dohnányi (1877–1960), Béla Bartók (1881–1945), and Zoltán Kodály (1882–1967), violinists Jenő Hubay (1858–1937) and Joseph Szigeti (1892–1973), and pianists Lili Kraus (1903–86) and Erwin Nyiregyhazi (1903–87). Renowned

Hungarian-born conductors who became famous abroad include Fritz Reiner (1888–1963), George Széll (1897–1970), Eugene Ormándy (1899–1985), Antal Doráti (b.1906), and Ferenc Fricsay (1914–63). Miklós Jancsó (b.1921) is a distinguished film director, and Vilmos Zsigmond (b.1930) a noted cinematographer; Béla Lugosi (Blasko, 1882–1956) and Peter Lorre (Laszlo Loewenstein, 1904–64) were famous actors.

Notable scientists include Lóránd Eötvös (1848–1919), inventor of torsion balance; Ányos Jedlik (1800–95), known for his research on dynamos; and the psychoanalyst Sándor Ferenczi (1873–1933). Ignaz Philipp Semmelweis (1818–65) pioneered in the use of antiseptic methods in obstetrics. Béla Schick (1877–1967) invented the skin test to determine susceptibility to diphtheria.

Hungarian-born Nobel Prize winners are Róbert Bárány (1876–1936) in 1914, Albert Szent-Györgyi (1893–1986) in 1937, and Georg von Békésy (1899–1972) in 1961 in physiology or medicine, Georg de Hevesy (1885–1966) in 1944 in chemistry, and Dénés Gábor (1900–79) in 1971 for physics. Budapest-born scientists who contributed to atomic research in the US were Leó Szilárd (1898–1964), Eugene Paul Wigner (b.1902), John von Neumann (1903–57), and Edward Teller (b.1908). Theodore van Karman (Todor Kármán, 1881–1963) is the father of aerodynamics.

Imre Nagy (1895?–1958) served as prime minister from 1953 to 1955, but was removed from office because of his criticism of Soviet policy; the uprising of October 1956 briefly brought Nagy back to the premiership. Arrested after the Soviet military intervention, Nagy was tried and executed in 1958. János Kádár (b.1912), first secretary of the HSWP since 1956, initially aligned himself with Nagy but subsequently headed the government established after Soviet troops rolled in. Kádár, who held the premiership from late 1956 to 1958 and again from 1961 to 1965, was the preeminent political leader in Hungary until his removal in May 1988.

49 DEPENDENCIES

Hungary has no territories or colonies.

50 BIBLIOGRAPHY

Berend, Ivan, and György Ránki. *The Hungarian Economy in the Twentieth Century.* New York: St. Martin's, 1985.

———. *The Hungarian Economic Reforms 1953–1988.* New York: Cambridge University Press, 1990.

Burant, Stephen R. (ed.). *Hungary: A Country Study.* 2d ed. Washington, D.C.: Government Printing Office, 1990.

Donáth, Ferenc. *Reform and Revolution: Transformation of Hungary's Agriculture, 1945–1970.* Budapest: Corvina, 1980.

Gati, Charles. *Hungary and the Soviet Bloc.* Durham, N.C.: Duke University Press, 1986.

Hankiss, Elemer. *East European Alternatives.* New York: Oxford University Press, 1990.

Hare, P. G., *et al.* (eds.). *Hungary: A Decade of Economic Reform.* Boston: Allen & Unwin, 1981.

Hoensch, Jorg K. *A History of Modern Hungary, 1867–1986.* New York: Longman, 1988.

Kádár, János. *Socialism and Democracy in Hungary.* Budapest: Corvina, Kiado, 1984.

Kovrig, Bennett. *Communism in Hungary from Kun to Kadar.* Stanford, Calif.: Hoover Institution Press, 1979.

Lasky, Melvin J. (ed.). *The Hungarian Revolution: The Story of the October Uprising.* New York: Praeger, 1957.

Macartney, Carlile Aylmer. *Hungary: A Short History.* Chicago: Aldine, 1962.

Ranki, Gyorgy (ed.). *Hungary and European Civilization.* Budapest: Akademiai Kiado, 1989.

Sugar, Peter F. (ed.). *A History of Hungary.* Bloomington: Indiana University Press, 1990.

Szekely, Istvan P. and David M. G. Newberry (eds.). *Hungary: an Economy in Transition.* Cambridge: Cambridge University Press, 1993.

Vardy, Steven Bela, and Agnes Huszar Vardy (eds.). *Society in Change.* Boulder, Colo.: East European Quarterly, 1983.

Volgyes, Ivan. *Hungary: A Nation of Contradictions.* Boulder, Colo.: Westview, 1981.

ICELAND

Republic of Iceland
Lýðveldið Ísland

CAPITAL: Reykjavík.

FLAG: The national flag, introduced in 1916, consists of a red cross (with an extended right horizontal), bordered in white, on a blue field.

ANTHEM: *O Guð vors lands (O God of Our Land).*

MONETARY UNIT: The new króna (K), introduced 1 January 1981 and equivalent to 100 old krónur, is a paper currency of 100 aurar. There are coins of 5, 10, and 50 aurar and 1, 10 and 50 krónur, and notes of 10, 50, 100, 500, 1,000 and 5,000 krónur. IsK1 = $0.0139 (or $1 = K71.690).

WEIGHTS AND MEASURES: The metric system is used.

HOLIDAYS: New Year's Day, 1 January; First Day of Summer, April; Labor Day, 1 May; National Holiday, 17 June; Bank Holiday, August; Christmas, 25–26 December. Movable religious holidays include Holy Thursday, Good Friday, Easter Monday, Ascension, and Whitmonday. Half-holidays are observed on Christmas Eve, 24 December, and New Year's Eve, 31 December.

TIME: GMT.

¹LOCATION, SIZE, AND EXTENT

Iceland, the westernmost country of Europe, is an island in the North Atlantic Ocean, just below the Arctic Circle and a little more than 322 km (200 mi) E of Greenland, 1,038 km (645 mi) W of Norway, and 837 km (520 mi) NW of Scotland. It has an area of 103,000 sq km (39,769 sq mi), extending 490 km (304 mi) E–W and 312 km (194 mi) N–S. Comparatively, the area occupied by Iceland is slightly smaller than the state of Kentucky. The total length of coastline is about 4,988 km (3,099 mi). The republic includes many smaller islands, of which the chief are the Westman Islands (Vestmannaeyjar) off the southern coast.

Iceland's capital city, Reykjavík, is located on the country's southwest coast.

²TOPOGRAPHY

Iceland consists mainly of a central volcanic plateau, with elevations from about 700 to 800 m (2,300–2,600 ft), ringed by mountains, the highest of which is Hvannadalshnúkur (2,119 m/6,952 ft), in the Öræfajökull glacier. Lava fields cover almost 11% of the country, and glaciers almost 12%. Among the many active volcanoes there is an average of about one eruption every five years. The largest glacier in Europe, Vatnajökull (about 8,400 sq km/3,200 sq mi), is in southeast Iceland. There are also many lakes, snowfields, hot springs, and geysers (the word "geyser" itself is of Icelandic origin). The longest river is the Thjórsá (about 198 km/123 mi) in southern Iceland. Most rivers are short and none are navigable, but because of swift currents and waterfalls, Iceland's rivers have important waterpower potential. There are strips of low arable land along the southwest coast and in the valleys. Good natural harbors are provided by fjords on the north, east, and west coasts.

³CLIMATE

Despite Iceland's northern latitude, its climate is fairly mild because of the Gulf Stream, part of which almost encircles the island. There are no extreme temperature variations between seasons, but frequent weather changes are usual, particularly in the south, which experiences many storms and heavy precipitation. Temperatures at Reykjavík range from an average of 11°C (52°F) in July to –1°C (30°F) in January, with an annual mean of about 4°C (39°F). Humidity is high, and there is much fog in the east. Annual rainfall in the north ranges from 30 to 70 cm (12–28 in); in the south, 80–130 cm (31–51 in); and in the mountains, up to 225 cm (89 in). Winters are long and fairly mild, summers short and cool. Summer days are long and nights short; in winter, days are short and nights long.

⁴FLORA AND FAUNA

Although there are a few small trees (ash, aspen, birch, and willow), the chief forms of vegetation are grass, mosses, and small shrubs (heather, willow, dwarf birch). Some 400 different species of flowers have been listed, but most of these are sparse.

The fox, the chief indigenous animal, is common. Wild reindeer, introduced in the 18th century and once abundant, were almost exterminated and therefore have been protected in recent years; they are found chiefly in the northeastern highlands. The waters around Iceland abound in whales, many types of seals, and many kinds of fish. Dolphin, grampus, porpoise, and rorqual are numerous. Cod, haddock, and herring are particularly abundant, but there are also sole, shark, halibut, redfish, saithe, and other fish. Salmon abound in many rivers, and trout in rivers and lakes. There are about 100 species of birds, both resident and migratory; most are aquatic. The chief resident birds are eiderduck (raised commercially for their down) and ptarmigan. Other characteristic indigenous birds are swan, eagle, falcon, and gannet, all rare now and protected. Iceland has no reptiles or frogs, and little insect life.

⁵ENVIRONMENT

Because of Iceland's sparing use of hydrocarbon fuels, its air is cleaner than that of most industrialized nations. However, its water supply is polluted by excessive use of fertilizers. (current estimates put Iceland's yearly usage of fertilizers at 2,500 pounds per acre). Population increases in the cities also contribute to water pollution. Iceland has 40 cubic miles of water with 63% used for industrial purposes and 6% used in farming activity. The nation's cities produce 0.1 million tons of solid waste. Hydrocarbon emissions amount to a yearly total of 14.3 tons. At the end of 1985 there were four national parks, with a total area of 619,300 hectares (1,530,315 acres); 27 nature reserves, covering 256,861 hectares (634,714 acres); and 34 other protected areas, comprising 65,224 hectares (161,171 acres). Principal environmental responsibility is vested in the Ministry of Social Affairs. As of 1994, one mammal species and two bird species were endangered, as well as two plant species. In 1987, the leatherback turtle and four species of whales were endangered.

6POPULATION

Total population as of 1 December 1991 was estimated at 259,577, as compared with 243,698 in 1986. A population of 283,000 was projected for the year 2000, assuming a crude birthrate of 17.3 per 1,000 population, a crude death rate of 7, and a net natural increase of 10.3 during 1995–2000. The average density as of December 1991 was 2.5 people per sq km (6.5 per sq mi). More than 91% of the population lives in towns and villages of more than 200 inhabitants and almost 58% is concentrated in the towns and districts surrounding and including Reykjavík, the capital (population 99,623), on the southwest coast. The next largest towns are Akureyri (14,436), on the north coast; Hafnarfjördur (15,623), about 10 km (6 mi) from Reykjavík; and Kópavogur (16,677), also south of Reykjavík.

7MIGRATION

Little immigration has occurred since the original settlement in the 9th and 10th centuries. In the last quarter of the 19th century, because of unfavorable conditions, about 12,000 residents of Iceland emigrated to Canada and the US. After 1900, net emigration decreased substantially. In 1991, the number of emigrants was 2,982; among the 15,745 emigrating during 1986–90, 4,147 went to Denmark, 4,506 to Sweden, 2,228 to Norway, and 1,473 to the US. Most of the 3,989 immigrants in 1991 (a record) were likewise from Nordic countries or the US.

8ETHNIC GROUPS

The population is almost entirely Icelandic, descended from the original settlers, who came chiefly from Norway (with a mixture of Scots and Irish) in the late 9th and early 10th centuries. In 1991 there were 5,395 foreigners, of whom 1,095 were Danish.

9LANGUAGES

Icelandic, the national language, derives from the Old Norse language that was spoken throughout Scandinavia at the time of settlement. It has changed little through the centuries, partly because of the country's isolation and partly because of the people's familiarity with the classical language, as preserved in early historical and literary writings. There is comparatively little difference between the old language and the modern, or between the written language and the spoken. To this day, Icelanders are able to read the great 13th-century sagas without special study.

10RELIGIONS

The Evangelical Lutheran Church, the national church, is endowed by the state, but there is complete freedom for all faiths, without discrimination. All Iceland constitutes a single diocese of the national church, headed by a bishop with his seat at Reykjavík; there are 281 parishes. About 93% of the people adhere to the established church. Of the remainder, 3.7% belong to other Lutheran denominations, and 1% are Roman Catholics.

11TRANSPORTATION

There are no railways or navigable inland waters. All important

towns and districts can be reached by bus and truck via interurban roads (12,343 km/7,670 mi in 1991), but 88% are dirt roads of poor quality. Registered passenger cars in 1991 numbered 120,862 and there were 16,012 commercial vehicles.

The merchant marine fleet consists of 12 ships (1,000 GRT/57,060 DWT) in 1991, including 5 cargo, 3 refrigerated cargo, 2 roll-on/roll-off cargo, 1 petroleum tanker, and 1 chemical tanker. In addition, there are about 1,000 civilian vessels, mostly small fishing craft. Registered civilian vessels at the end of 1991 totaled 963, with an aggregate of 140,349 GRT. Most of the import and export trade is handled in Reykjavík. Akureyri, on the north coast, is the largest port serving the outlying areas.

In the 1950s, Icelandic Airlines was the first transatlantic airline to offer fares drastically lower than those of the major carriers. Icelandair, formed by a merger of Icelandic Airlines and Iceland Air in the early 1970s, operates domestic routes as well as international flights to the UK, Scandinavia, and FRG, and transatlantic flights with stopovers at Reykjavík. In 1992, it carried 510,000 passengers on international routes and 257,100 on domestic routes. In 1991, the number of registered aircraft was 286, with a total of 3,077 seats.

12HISTORY

Iceland's first known settler, Ingólfur Arnarson, sailed from his native Norway to Iceland and settled at what is now Reykjavík in 874. During the late 9th and early 10th centuries, the island was settled by other Norwegians fleeing the oppressive rule of their king and by smaller groups of Scottish and Irish emigrants. In 930, a central legislative and judicial assembly, the Althing, was established, and a uniform code of laws for the entire country was compiled. Christianity was introduced in 1000, but the memory of the old pagan religion was preserved in 12th- and 13th-century Icelandic literature. Many of the early settlers were great seafarers and continued their westward voyages of discovery and exploration from Iceland. Most famous of these were Eric the Red (Eiríkur Thorvaldsson), who discovered and settled in Greenland in 982, and his son Leif Ericsson (Leifur Eiríksson), who around the year 1000 discovered the North American continent, which he called Vinland ("wineland") because of the grapes he found there. Icelanders acknowledged the sovereignty of Haakon IV of Norway in a treaty of 1262, which established a purely personal union, ending the independent republic or commonwealth. When all the Scandinavian countries came under the rule of Denmark at the end of the 14th century, Iceland became a Danish dominion. Lutheranism was introduced in the 1540s. Exclusive trading rights with Iceland were given in 1602 to a private Danish trading company. Danes had a complete monopoly of trade with Iceland until 1786, when trade was opened to all subjects of the kings of Denmark, including Icelanders.

The last decades of the 18th century were a period of economic ruin for Iceland, compounded by poor harvests, epidemics, and volcanic eruptions (notably that of 1783, the worst in Iceland's history); the population dwindled to 38,000 by 1800, less than half the number in the period of independence. In that year, the king abolished the Althing, long since reduced in power. Within a few decades, however, a nationalist movement had attained considerable strength, winning the reestablishment of the Althing (but only as an advisory body) in 1843, followed by the opening of trade with all countries in 1854. After a long constitutional struggle—led by a national hero, Jón Sigurðsson, who was both statesman and scholar—limited home rule was granted in 1874, and almost complete home rule in 1903. By agreement with Denmark in 1918, Iceland was declared a free and independent state, but personal union with the Danish crown was retained. The Danish king continued to function as king of Iceland, and Denmark conducted Iceland's foreign affairs; but Iceland had the right to terminate this union after 25 years. Cut off

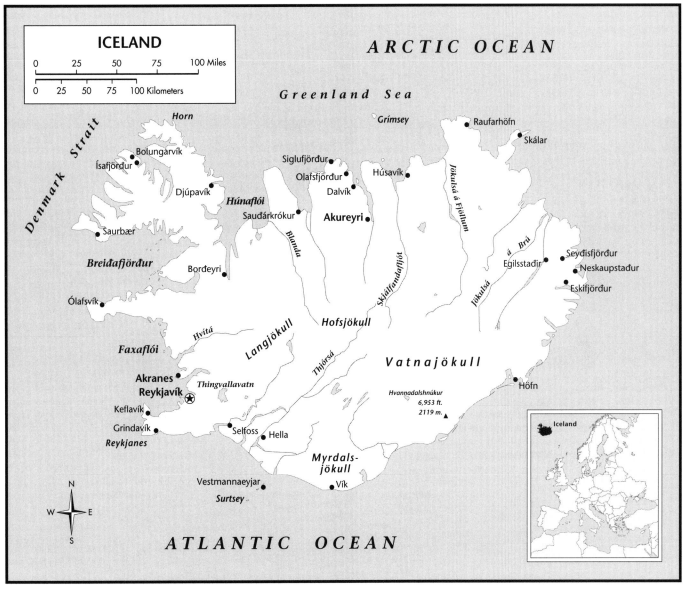

LOCATION: 63°19′ to 67°7′5″N; 13°16′7″ to 24°32′3″W. **BOUNDARY LENGTHS:** Total coastline, 4,970 km (3,090 mi). **TERRITORIAL SEA LIMIT:** 12 mi.

from Denmark during World War II by the German occupation of that country, Iceland established diplomatic relations with the UK and the US. British forces, who took over the protection of the island in 1940, were replaced the following year by US troops, who remained until early 1947. In a referendum held in May 1944, more than 97% of those participating voted to end the union with the king of Denmark and, on 17 June 1944, Iceland became an independent republic. In 1946, it was admitted to UN membership. Three years later, Iceland became a party to the Atlantic Pact (NATO), and a defense agreement was signed in 1951, providing for a US military presence. In March 1970, Iceland joined EFTA, and a tariff agreement was ratified with the EC in February 1973. To protect its fishing industry, Iceland unilaterally extended its fishing zone in 1958, and again in 1972 and 1975, provoking conflict with the UK and other countries. Casualties resulted from the most serious outbreak of the "cod war" with the UK in late 1975 and in February 1976. An agreement ended the conflict in June 1976, and relations with the UK improved.

In 1985, the parliament unanimously voted to declare Iceland a nuclear-free zone, banning any deployment of nuclear weapons.

Reykjavík was the scene of the 11/12 October 1986 summit meeting about nuclear disarmament between US President Ronald Reagan and Soviet leader Mikhail Gorbachev.

Depressed world fish prices continued to weaken the economy in the early 1990s, resulting in a no-growth GDP and higher unemployment. The government launched an austerity program including devaluation of the krona in an attempt to further reduce inflation.

13GOVERNMENT

Iceland is an independent republic. Executive power is vested in the president and the government, legislative power in the president and the legislative assembly (Althing). The president is elected by universal suffrage for a four-year term. Executive power is exercised by a prime minister selected by the president, and the prime minister in turn selects a cabinet composed of ministers responsible to the Althing for their acts.

All citizens who have reached the age of 18 may vote, provided they have resided in Iceland for the five years immediately preceding an election. By a system of proportional representation, they elect the 63 members of the unicameral (since 1981) Althing from eight constituencies at a general election held every four years, but sooner if the governing coalition loses its ability to command a legislative majority. The legislators elect one-third of their members to an upper house (Efrideilð), the rest constituting the lower house (Nedrideilð). Any citizen qualified to vote is eligible for the Althing. When any amendment to the constitution is voted, the Althing is dissolved and new elections are held; if the new Althing accepts the proposed amendment, it becomes law when ratified by the president.

14POLITICAL PARTIES

No one major party in recent years has been able to command a majority of the electorate, and coalition governments have been the rule. Principal parties include the Independence Party (Sjálf-stœðisflokkurinn) (IP), a conservative grouping, which, in the April 1991 election, won 26 seats in parliament; the Progressive Party (Framsóknarflokkurinn) (PP), an agrarian, left-center party, which won 13 seats; the Progressive Alliance (Althýðubandalag) (PA), a Communist-oriented party, which obtained 9 seats; and the Social Democratic People's Party (Althýðuflokkurinn) (SDP), a center-right group, which won 10 seats. An Independence Party splinter group, the Citizens' Party (CP), lost its parliamentary representation by securing no seats.

Of these parties, the Independence Party dates back to 1929, and the Progressive and Social Democratic People's (formerly Labor) parties to 1916; all three have been the source of various splinter groups. The People's Alliance became a distinct political party in 1970; it grew out of an alliance among Communist-oriented elements in the Social Democratic People's Party and other groups, and in effect replaced the earlier People's Union–Socialist Party (Sameiningarflokkur althyðu-Sósíalistaflokkurinn).

It was the issue of NATO and the US military presence that in March 1956 broke up an early alliance between Progressives and Independents, and the elections that year led to a new coalition of the Progressive, Labor, and People's Union–Socialist parties, all of which opposed the US military base on Iceland. (After the Hungarian uprising of October 1956, however, the Progressive and Labor parties reversed their stand.) That government fell because of Communist opposition to a proposed wage freeze, and after elections in October 1959, a government formed by the Independence and Labor parties came into office. This coalition endured for some time. But after the loss of four seats in the June 1971 general elections, a new government, composed of the Progressive Party, the People's Alliance, and the Liberal and Left Alliance (a party established in 1969 on a platform opposing Iceland's participation in NATO and its defense agreement with the US) came into power under Prime Minister Olafur Jóhannesson. Then, on 29 August 1974, after gains by the Independence Party in June elections, a coalition of Independents and Progressives was sworn in under Geir Hallgrímsson of the Independence Party.

Two short-lived coalition governments followed. The first, a leftist coalition including the Social Democrats, People's Alliance, and Progressive Party, led by Olafur Jóhannesson, was dissolved when the Social Democrats left the coalition in October 1979. Following an election that December, a second coalition was eventually formed from members of the Independence Party, the People's Alliance, and the Progressives, with Gunnar Thoroddsen, deputy chairman of the Independence Party, as prime minister. After three unsuccessful attempts by party leaders to form a governing coalition following the April 1983 elections, Vigdís Finnbogadóttir—who in August 1981 had been elected president, becoming the first woman to occupy that primarily ceremonial office—threatened to request the formation of a government of civil servants. Eventually, Progressive leader Steingrímur Hermannsson formed and headed a coalition of the Independence and Progressive parties. Following the 1987 elections, Thorsteinn Pálsson of the Independence Party replaced Hermannsson as prime minister.

The general election of April 1991 resulted in a new center-right coalition led by David Oddsson of the Independence Party and members of the Social Democratic People's Party. Vigdís Finnbogadóttir was reelected unopposed for a fourth four-year term in June 1992.

15LOCAL GOVERNMENT

Iceland is divided into 23 counties (sýslur) and 14 independent towns (kaupstaðir). Each county is administered by a magistrate or sheriff (sýslumaðour). Within the counties are more than 200 rural municipalities, each governed by a council: town councils are elected by proportional representation, rural councils by simple majority. The local government units supervise tax collections, police administration, local finances, employment, and other local affairs.

16JUDICIAL SYSTEM

The district magistrates (sýslumenn) and the town magistrates (bæjarfógetar) administer justice on a local level in 26 lower courts. Appeals are heard by the Supreme Court, consisting of eight justices (all appointed for life by the president), who elect one of their number as chief justice for a two-year term. There are special courts for maritime cases, labor disputes, and other types of cases.

The courts are free from political control. Although the Ministry of Justice administers the lower courts, the Supreme Court oversees independent and fair application of the law.

A recent reform project transferred all judicial authority for criminal and civil cases form local officials (chiefs of police) to newly established district courts. This complete separation of judicial and executive power in regional jurisdictions was completed in 1992.

17ARMED FORCES

Iceland is the only NATO member with no military force of its own, although the government does maintain armed fishery protection vessels and planes manned by 130 personnel. US forces (3,000) and Dutch (30) are stationed at Keflavík for air and anti-submarine defense.

18INTERNATIONAL COOPERATION

Iceland became a member of the UN on 19 November 1946 and belongs to ECE and all the nonregional specialized agencies except IFAD, UNIDO, and WIPO. It also belongs to the Council of Europe, EFTA, NATO, the Nordic Council, OECD, and other intergovernmental organizations. It is a signatory of GATT and the Law of the Sea.

19ECONOMY

Iceland's economy, once primarily agricultural, is now based overwhelmingly on fishing. Crop raising plays a small role, since most of the land is unsuitable for cultivation and the growing season is short. Sheep raising and dairying are the chief agricultural activities, with horse breeding also substantial. Iceland is generally self-sufficient in meat, eggs, and dairy products, but sugar and cereal products must be imported. Since Iceland has almost no known mineral resources and has had no concentrations of population until recent decades, industry is small-scale and local, depends heavily on imported raw and semimanufactured materials, and cannot compete favorably with foreign industry, especially with imports from low-income countries.

Although the economy is based on private ownership and operates mainly on a free-enterprise basis, public enterprises account for a sizable share of GDP (30% in 1993). The cooperative movement is important in rural trade, and the national and local governments own some productive facilities in certain fields requiring large amounts of capital not available from private sources. The economy developed rapidly after World War II, with a rate of capital investment so high at times as to strain available resources. GNP growth fell from 9% in 1977 to –3% in 1983 but recovered to 9% in 1987. After that, it averaged –0.4% through 1993. Inflation has been rapid, rising from 30 to 45% in the late 1970s to nearly 50% annually during 1981–85. It then moderated, dropping to only 3.7% in 1991 and 4.1% in 1992. Unemployment, traditionally low, rose to 3% in 1992 and 4.2% in 1993.

20INCOME
In 1992, Iceland's GNP was $6,177 million at current prices, or $23,670 per capita. For the period 1985–92 the average inflation rate was 16.8%, resulting in a real growth rate in per capita GNP of 0.5%.

In 1992 the GDP was $4.5 billion in current US dollars. It is estimated that in 1990 agriculture, hunting, forestry, and fishing contributed 10% to GDP; mining and quarrying, 0%; manufacturing, 14%; electricity, gas, and water, 3%; construction, 6%; wholesale and retail trade, 10%; transport, storage, and communication, 6%; finance, insurance, real estate, and business services, 13%; community, social, and personal services, 5%; and other sources, 32%.

21LABOR
In 1990, 18.4% of employment in Iceland was in fish processing or other manufacturing, 14.4% in commerce, 0.8% in electricity and steam production, 7.2% in community, social, and personal services, 8% in business services, 9.6% in construction, 6.4% in transportation and communications, 4.8% in agriculture, 5.6% in fishing, 18.4% in the public sector, and 6.4% in other sectors. About 76% of all workers belong to trade unions. Principal unions are the Icelandic Federation of Labor (associated with the ICFTU) and the Municipal and Government Employees' Association. Labor disputes are settled by direct negotiations or by special courts. In 1991, there were seven work stoppages, involving 751 employees and resulting in 3,000 lost working days. Wage increases were first pegged to the cost of living in 1939, and the practice has continued during most of the period since World War II. Inflation has been rampant in the nation for decades, but a new center-right coalition elected in April 1991 made fiscal restraint the focus of its policy, and began the overhaul of Iceland's extensive social welfare system. In 1985, nominal wage rates rose an estimated 32.6% over 1984, but real wage rates rose by only 0.2%. Unemployment is very low by international standards, averaging 1.5% in 1991. Expatriation for employment is common, and Icelanders can be found working all over the world, especially in the other Nordic countries, Europe, and the US. Most will inevitably repatriate once a suitable position opens, which sometimes only occurs through the retirement or death of someone already working in Iceland. The customary workweek is 46 hours.

22AGRICULTURE
About 78% of Iceland is agriculturally unproductive, and only about 1% of the land area is actually used for cultivation. Of this amount, 99% is used to cultivate hay and other fodder crops, with the remaining 1% used for potato and fodder root production. There were about 4,000 full-time farmers in 1991, with 75% living on their own land; some holdings have been in the same family for centuries. In the 19th century and earlier, agriculture was the chief occupation, but by 1930, fewer than 36% of the people devoted their energies to farming, and the proportion has continued to fall. Hay is the principal crop; other crops are potatoes, turnips, oats, and garden vegetables. In hot-spring areas, vegetables, flowers and even tropical fruits are increasingly being cultivated in greenhouses heated with hot water from the

springs. Agricultural output in 1991 included 3,360,000 cu m of hay and other fodder crops and 15,000 tons of potatoes. There are agricultural institutions in Borgarfjörður, Hjaltadalur, Hvanneyri, and Reykir; between 15–20% of all farmers have finished an agricultural degree program.

23ANIMAL HUSBANDRY
Sheep raising is extensive, and mutton and lamb are primary meat products. Sheep are permitted to find their own grazing pasture during the warmer months and are rounded up toward the middle of September and put in shed for the winter. Cattle are raised mainly for dairying, and their number has been rising steadily; beef production is negligible. Sheep at the end of 1992 numbered an estimated 487,300; cattle, 76,000 head; horses, 75,200; and poultry, 179,000. Estimated livestock products in 1992 included milk, 110,000 tons; mutton and lamb, 11,000 tons; and eggs, 3,900 tons. Iceland is self-sufficient in meat, dairy products, and eggs. Icelandic farm animals are directly descended from the sheep, cattle, goats, pigs, poultry, dogs, cats, and especially horses (which were an invaluable means of travel) brought by tenth-century Scandinavian settlers. In sparsely populated areas, such as the western fjords and on the east coast, farming is chiefly limited to raising sheep, although sheep farming exists in all areas of the country. Milk is produced mostly in the south and north. Except for poultry, egg, and pig production, farms are small in acreage and usually family-run. About 2,000 farmers are engaged in full-time sheep farming, and 1,000 more in mixed farming. There also are about 1,800 dairy farms in operation; Icelanders consume on average 175 liters (46.2 gal) of milk per capita per year, one of the highest amounts in the world. Cheese consumption is fourth highest, after France, Germany, and Italy. Horse-breeding is also a growing branch of animal husbandry in Iceland, as the popularity of the Iceland horse (which has five gaits) grows at home and abroad.

Animal farming is a highly mechanized industry carried out by well-educated farmers; nearly one-fifth of all farmers matriculate at one of three agricultural colleges in Iceland.

24FISHING
Accounting for about 17% of Iceland's employment, fishing and fish processing provide the primary source of foreign exchange, accounting for 82% (or $1,252.7 million) of total exports. Icelanders consume more fish per capita annually (over 90 kg/198 lb live weight equivalent) than any other people in Europe. Cod is caught during the first five months of the year off the southwest coast. Herring are taken off the north and northeast coasts from June to September and off the southwest from September to December. In 1992, the fish catch was 1,539,000 tons, up from 1,043,000 tons in 1991. The 1992 catch included 795,000 tons of capelin, 256,000 tons of cod, 102,000 tons of redfish, 75,000 tons of saithe, 44,000 tons of haddock, and 124,000 tons of herring.

The fishing fleet totaled 90,348 GRT as of 1992, and is being steadily modernized through the addition of new, larger trawlers and motorboats. Most fishing vessels are now equipped with telephones and computers. Through the early 1980s, about 250 whales a year were caught off the coast, providing lucrative export products. Although Iceland had agreed to phase out whaling in order to comply with the 1982 ban by the International Whaling Commission, in 1987 it announced its intention to take 100 whales a year for scientific purposes, but in 1991 no whales were reportedly taken.

Abundant quantities of pure water and geothermal heat give Iceland an advantage over other nations in fish farming. Aquaculture is being developed to offset lean years in the natural fish catch, and to produce more expensive and profitable species of fish.

25FORESTRY

There are no forests of commercial value, and the existing trees (ash, birch, aspen, and willow) are small. The originally extensive birch forests were cut down for firewood and to clear land for grazing sheep. In recent years, the remaining woods have been protected and reforestation has begun.

26MINING

Mineral resources are few. Deposits of spar and sulfur, once mined, are no longer worked extensively. Sulfur and lignite are now being processed experimentally, the former with the use of subterranean steam; diatomite extraction is underway near Lake Myvatn. Peat is common but is now little used. Iceland's mineral industry consists of one privately-owned aluminum plant and a 55% government-owned ferro-silicon plant, both of which use imported raw materials. Inexpensive hydroelectric and geothermal energy is used for production in these power-intensive industries. Although aluminum production increased in 1991 (88,768 tons) by 2.3% over the previous year, ferro-silicon production fell in 1991 (50,299 tons) by 20% from 1990.

27ENERGY AND POWER

Hydroelectric power potential from Iceland's many swift rivers and waterfalls is high, and is considered the key to further industrial development. An estimated 45 billion kwh per year is economically exploitable from the five principal glacial rivers, while the total potential is estimated at 64 billion kwh per year. Net installed capacity at the end of 1991 was 969,000 kw, of which 80% was hydroelectric. Electric energy output in that year was 4,494 million kwh, with hydroelectric output accounting for 94%. Per capita energy consumption in 1992 was 17,315 kwh. A government rural electrification program is designed to bring inexpensive public power to every family in Iceland. Peat, formerly an important source of heat on the farms, has been virtually abandoned.

Hot springs are used for heating greenhouses in which vegetables, fruit, and flowers are raised, and for heating public buildings. Since 1943, most of Reykjavík has been heated by water from hot springs at Reykir, some 160 km (100 mi) from the city. In 1992, some 85% of the population heated their houses with geothermal power. In recent years, however, a significant decline in flow from geothermal drill holes has raised concern that this energy resource may not be so boundless as was once thought.

28INDUSTRY

Fish processing is the most important industry. Facilities for freezing, salting, sun-curing, and reducing to oil or fish meal are flexible enough to allow shifting from one process to another in accordance with demand. By-products include fish meal and cod-liver oil.

Other industry is small-scale and designed to meet local needs. Chief manufactures include fishing equipment, electric stoves and cookers, paints, clothing, soaps, candles, cosmetics, dairy products, confectionery, and beer. Clothing factories are situated in Reykjavík and Akureyri. Icelandic ammonium nitrate needs are more than met by a fertilizer plant that produced 50,018 tons in 1992. A cement factory with a capacity of 120,000 tons a year supplies most domestic cement requirements; total production in 1992 amounted to 99,800 tons. Production of aluminum rose from 40,000 tons in 1970 to 89,478 tons in 1992. A ferro-silicon smelter, which began production in 1979, produced some 54,413 tons in 1992. A diatomite processing plant produced 19,946 tons.

29SCIENCE AND TECHNOLOGY

In 1983, a total of к461.8 million was spent on scientific and technological research and development, 65.7% of it in the form of government grants. Of that total, 50.9% was spent on research undertaken by the government, 17% on that by business, 26.6%

by higher education establishments, and 5.5% by private non-profit institutions. Of the 1,245 personnel engaged in scientific research in 1983, 641 had a university-level education. The National Research Council coordinates science policy and advises the government on scientific matters. It has four research institutes. Other research institutes and learned societies include the Surtsey Research Society, the Meteorological Office and .the Association of Chartered Engineers in Iceland.

The Icelandic Council of Science, an independent agency under the Ministry of Culture and Education, aims to stimulate and encourage scientific research. The University of Iceland has faculties of medicine, engineering, and science. Two agricultural colleges are located in Hólum í Hjaltadal and Hvanneyri. The Icelandic College of Engineering and Technology has 500 students.

30DOMESTIC TRADE

Foreign firms do not have branches in Iceland, and their business is conducted by Icelandic agents. Imports are handled by these agents, by wholesale or retail importers, or by the Federation of Iceland Cooperative Societies, and distribution is through private channels. Most advertising is translated and disseminated directly by agents. Foreign trade fairs are held from time to time.

Of the wholesale enterprises, 80–90% are concentrated in Reykjavík; more than half the retail establishments are likewise in the capital. Much trade is handled by cooperative societies, most of which are joined in the Federation of Iceland Cooperative Societies.

Business hours are from 9 AM to 6 PM on weekdays, and from 9 or 10 AM to noon on Saturdays. Banking hours are from 9:15 AM to 4 PM, Monday–Friday, with an additional hour from 5 to 6 PM on Thursday.

31FOREIGN TRADE

In recent years, Iceland's balance of trade has been unfavorable, but there was a surplus in 1993. Imports include almost all Icelandic requirements except fish, meats, dairy products, and some agricultural products. Leading imports are machinery and transport equipment, manufactures, mineral fuels and lubricants, and chemicals. Fish and fish products make up nearly 80% of total exports; the remainder consists of aluminum, ferro-silicon, meat, wool, sheepskins, and other material. The export of salt fish to Mediterranean countries was formerly the largest item, but frozen fish, exported mainly to the former USSR and the US, took first place after World War II. Iceland is a member of the EFTA.

The US, UK, and Germany are Iceland's major trade partners. After Iceland became a full member of EFTA in March 1970, trade with some EFTA countries has increased significantly, but this market became less important as the EC expanded to take in some EFTA members, such as the UK and Portugal. In 1993, trade with EFTA nations accounted for 9% of Iceland's exports and 23.7% of its imports; with the US, for 16% of exports and 9.3% of imports; and with the EC, 59.8% of exports and 48.4% of imports.

Principal trade partners in 1993 (in millions of krónur) were as follows:

	EXPORTS	IMPORTS	BALANCE
U.S.	15,164	8,511	6,653
UK	20,468	8,188	12,280
Germany	10,450	10,881	–431
Denmark	5,326	8,564	–3,238
Sweden	1,104	6,187	–5,083
Japan	8,777	5,058	3,719
France	7,796	3,108	4,688
Norway	3,187	11,299	–8,112
Netherlands	2,083	5,476	–3,393
Other countries	20,348	24,035	–3,687
TOTALS	94,703	91,307	3,396

[32]BALANCE OF PAYMENTS

The difference between imports and exports since World War II has been met by drawing from large wartime reserves, by Marshall Plan aid, and, since 1953, by income from US defense spending at Keflavík, the NATO airbase. Widely fluctuating current account deficits, attributable mainly to the trade imbalance, averaged more than 6.5% of GNP during 1971–75. During the next four years, although still largely negative, the current account balance improved; from 1980 through 1985, however, Iceland's current accounts position again deteriorated, this time because of large deficits in services. The balance of payments experienced a significant deterioration in 1991, especially on the current account and merchandise trade balances. The current account deficit more than doubled to $316 million in 1991, up from $133 million in 1990. The deficit grew because of a simultaneous 3% decrease in exports and 4% increase in imports in 1991. In 1992 merchandise exports totaled $1,529 million and imports $1,526.9 million. The merchandise trade balance was $–113.1 million.

The following table summarizes Iceland's balance of payments for 1991 and 1992 (in millions of US dollars):

	1991	1992
CURRENT ACCOUNT		
Goods, services, and income	–304.1	–203.1
Unrequited transfers	–5.2	–6.5
TOTALS	–309.3	–209.6
CAPITAL ACCOUNT		
Direct investment	24.1	–9.5
Portfolio investment	26.5	1.4
Other long-term capital	241.5	229.9
Other short-term capital	7.8	54.4
Reserves	–10.5	–80.8
TOTALS	289.4	195.4
Errors and omissions	19.9	14.2
Total change in reserves	–13.3	–48.9

[33]BANKING AND SECURITIES

In March 1961, the Central Bank of Iceland was founded to issue notes and assume other central bank functions previously exercised by the National Bank of Iceland, a wholly state-owned bank established in 1885. Other banks are the Agricultural Bank, a state bank founded in 1929; the Fisheries Bank, a private joint-stock bank founded in 1930, with most of its shares held by the government; the Industrial Bank, a joint-stock bank established in 1953, with part of the shares owned by the government; the Iceland Bank of Commerce, founded in 1961; the Cooperative Bank of Iceland, founded in 1963; and the People's Bank, founded in 1971. All banks have main offices in Reykjavík, and some have branches in other towns. Savings banks are distributed throughout the country.

In 1955, Iceland took the first step toward indexation of financial assets. The Economic Management Act of 1979 established a system of full indexation of savings and credit, most provisions of which were gradually implemented over the next two years. Most deposits are now indexed, and legislation that took effect in November 1986 gave banks increased power to determine their interest rate.

In 1990 the number of commercial banks in Iceland were reduced from seven to three. A number of banks were forced to merge into the Islandbanki because of financial trouble. At the end of 1992, the three commercial banks had total deposits of κ121,098 million.

Since 15 June 1973, the market rate of the Icelandic króna has been floating vis-à-vis other currencies. A currency reform that took effect 1 January 1981 introduced a new króna equivalent to 100 old krónur. The money supply, as measured by M2, totaled κ132,123 million in 1993.

There are no stock exchanges in Iceland. Residents of Iceland cannot own foreign securities.

[34]INSURANCE

There are many mutual insurance societies in addition to the national health and social insurance scheme. Almost all direct insurance is written by domestic companies that conduct business in the various kinds of property and life insurance. In 1989, there were 27 insurance companies operating. The total value of life insurance in force in 1992 was κ127 billion. Automobile liability insurance and homeowners' coverage against fire, floods, earthquakes, and volcanic eruptions are compulsory. The Ministry of Insurance Affairs is the principal supervisory body.

[35]PUBLIC FINANCE

Revenues generally exceeded expenditures in the 1960s, fell short during most of the 1970s, and alternated between surplus and deficit in the first half of the 1980s, before slipping back to deficit by the late 1980s. The budget proposal is presented to the Althing at the beginning of each regular session in October; the fiscal year coincides with the calendar year. The central government's accounts are subject to audits and control by the General Auditor's office, which operates as an independent entity under the Althing. The central government derives about 72% of its total tax revenue from indirect taxes, mainly the 24.5% value-added tax, tariffs, and excise charges.

The following table shows actual revenues and expenditures for 1990 and 1991 in millions of krónur.

	1990	1991
REVENUE AND GRANTS		
Tax revenue	92,153.2	101,493.4
Non-tax revenue	11,751.9	11,929.8
Capital revenue	811.7	1,135.9
Grants	3,120.7	2,879.2
TOTALS	107,837.5	117,438.3
EXPENDITURES & LENDING MINUS REPAYMENTS		
General public service	5,720.4	6,307.9
Public order and safety	4,624.6	5,063.2
Education	14,625.8	16,151.3
Health	27,406.7	30,564.4
Social security and welfare	24,317.0	27,780.9
Housing and community amenities	806.5	1,279.5
Recreation, cultural, and religious affairs	3,183.0	3,710.9
Economic affairs and services	24,270.9	26,435.0
Other expenditures	12,575.7	26,435.0
Lending minus repayments	–740.3	2,307.6
TOTALS	116,790.3	134,780.1
Deficit/Surplus	–8,952.8	–17,241.8

The fiscal deficit was 3.3% of GDP in 1991, up from only 1.3% in 1990, as public consumption grew nearly 5%. In 1991 Iceland's total public debt stood at κ127,655.8 million, of which κ67,953.1 million was financed abroad.

[36]TAXATION

Personal income is taxed at a flat rate of 39.85%; the corporate tax rate is 45%. The value-added tax stood at 24.5% in 1992. Iceland also levies a 1.6% capital tax with a 0.26% surcharge on individual and corporate net wealth.

[37]CUSTOMS AND DUTIES

Over 90% of imports are not subject to import restrictions or duties other than the same value-added tax applied to domestically produced goods. Special excise taxes are levied on sugar and some sugar products, potatoes, and motor vehicles. In March 1970, Iceland acquired full membership in EFTA. On 28 February 1973, Iceland ratified a trade agreement with the EC leading to the elimination of tariffs on industrial goods. A law authorizing the establishment of free trade zones went into effect in 1992.

[38]FOREIGN INVESTMENT

Icelanders have been reluctant to permit substantial foreign investment; nearly all such investment is limited to participation in joint ventures in which Icelandic interests hold a majority share. As of 1993, there was only one wholly foreign-owned industrial facility in the country, a Swiss alumina-processing facility. Two others, a ferro-silicon and a diatomite plant, had foreign equity participation. From the beginning of 1993, Icelanders have been free to invest abroad.

[39]ECONOMIC DEVELOPMENT

The national government and some local governments are involved in trawler fishing, herring processing, merchant shipping, electric power facilities, and certain other industries. To a considerable degree, the central government supervises the export-import trade and the fishing and fish-processing industries. It may set uniform prices of export commodities and may shift export and import trade to specific countries as balance-of-payments considerations require. It channels investment funds into fields it considers desirable.

The government supports farmers in the rebuilding or enlarging of their homes, livestock sheds, and barns, and assists them in the purchase of machinery. Equipped with crawler tractors and excavators, a government agency helps farmers enlarge cultivated areas and break, drain, and level new lands for the establishment of homesteads. Thousands of new acres have thus been brought under cultivation.

The government fixes prices of essential foods and other basic consumption items and subsidizes them, both to limit prices for the consumer and to maintain farm incomes. It also fixes mark-ups that manufacturers, wholesalers, retailers, and importers may place on a wide variety of products.

In the early 1990s, the government concentrated on maintaining the value of the króna by bringing down inflation, even at the cost of economic growth. Wage gains were restricted. In late 1992, plans were made public for a Fisheries Development Fund that would buy and scrap unneeded vessels and thereby promote efficiency. The Fund would also be used to help firms establish joint ventures abroad and buy fishing rights. Plans were also under way to sell several state-owned companies, with the money used for research and development and reducing the deficit.

[40]SOCIAL DEVELOPMENT

The national health insurance scheme, initiated in 1936 and revised and enlarged in 1947, includes insurance against sickness, accident, and unemployment; pensions for the aged and disabled; and a health service that provides protection and treatment and care of the sick. Benefits in all three categories were increased in 1963, and the administration of the whole scheme was unified under the supervision of the State Social Insurance Institution. The employer pays 2% of payroll for the pension system, and the government pays the rest. Old-age disability, and permanent widow's disability; pensions are paid at a flat rate of 11,497 crowns a month. Social security expenditures in 1984 included к3,546 million for old age and disability pensions and services, к1,891 million for family welfare, and к125 million in public assistance benefits.

Studies show that women earn about 40% less than men in comparable jobs. Since 1991, the Ministry of Social Affairs has handled complaints related to equal rights law. The emergency ward of the Reykjavik City Hospital now has an all-female staff to care for rape victims. In 1985 there were 1,252 marriages performed in Iceland, or 5.19 per 1,000 population (7.89 in 1971). The age at first marriage has been rising in recent decades, and in 1984 was 24.4 for females and 26.6 for males. The divorce rate rose from 0.25 per 1,000 population in 1921–30 to 1.48 in 1971 and 2.25 in 1985, but is still below the average of the other Nordic countries. Legal abortions in 1985 numbered 706, or 183.1 per 1,000 live births, the lowest such rate in the Nordic region.

[41]HEALTH

The Director of Public Health is responsible for all health matters. In 1989, there were 715 physicians (2.8 per 1,000 people), 164 pharmacists, 219 dentists, 1,713 nurses, and 197 midwives. In 1990, there were 53 hospitals, with 3,985 beds (621 beds per 100,000 people, or 64 people per bed). Two-thirds of the beds were in nursing and old-age homes, with the remaining one-third in hospitals.

The incidence of tuberculosis, once wide-spread, has been greatly reduced. Leprosy, also common in earlier times, has been virtually eliminated, with no new cases reported in recent decades. There were three reported cases of AIDS in 1990, and 658 abortions in 1991.

There were 4,500 births in 1992 in Iceland. Total population in 1993 was 263,000, with a birth rate of 17.4 per 1,000 inhabitants. In 1991 and 1992, 99% of Iceland's children were immunized against measles. Infant mortality in 1992 was 6 per 1,000 live births, while the overall death rate was 7.0 per 1,000 in 1993. Life expectancy for 1992 was 78 years (80 years for women and 76 for men), among the highest in the world and highest among the Nordic countries. Iceland spent $26,618,000 on health care in 1991.

[42]HOUSING

The total number of dwellings at the end of 1985 was 84,821. In 1991, 1,490 dwellings were completed, of which 795 were one- or two-family houses. Most rural buildings were at one time made of turf, then of wood, and most recently of stone and concrete. In the towns, turf houses long ago gave way to wooden ones, but for some decades most new housing has been concrete. Virtually all dwellings have electricity, piped water, and central heating.

[43]EDUCATION

There is virtually no adult illiteracy. Education is compulsory for children aged 7 to 15. There were 214 public schools in 1991. During the same year,there were 3,988 preprimary students; 25,809 students at the primary level (ages 7–12); 12,111 at the second level, first stage; 17,874 at the second level, second stage; and 6,161 at the postsecondary level. There were 49 schools operating at the secondary level in 1991 and 5 universities and colleges. Special schools include a commercial high school, a school of navigation, 2 schools of agriculture, and continuation schools. The University of Iceland in Reykjavík, founded in 1911, has faculties of law and economics, theology, medicine and dentistry, philosophy (art and humanities), and engineering. Tuition is free; only nominal registration and examination fees must be paid.

[44]LIBRARIES AND MUSEUMS

The leading libraries, all in Reykjavík, are the National Library (founded in 1918; 415,000 volumes), the Municipal Library (400,000 volumes), the University Library (300,000 volumes) and the National Archives, which contains a collection of documents covering 800 years. There were a total of 231 public libraries with combined holdings of 1,703,000 volumes in 1990.

Leading museums, all in Reykjavík, are the Icelandic National Museum (founded in 1863), the Natural History Museum (1889), and a museum devoted to the sculptures and paintings of Einar Jónsson.

45MEDIA

In 1991 there were 124,951 telephones (53 per 100 inhabitants). Radio and radiotelephone communications are maintained with Europe and America, and an underwater telegraph cable connects Iceland with Europe. The telephone, telegraph, and radio systems are publicly owned and administered. Icelandic radio broadcasts primarily on FM, via numerous public and private stations.Television was initiated in 1966, and two television stations broadcast seven days a week. In 1991 there were approximately 202,000 radios and 80,000 of television sets.

The three daily newspapers published in Reykjavík, with their political orientation and average daily circulation in 1991, were:

	ORIENTATION	CIRCULATION
Morgunblaðid	Independence Party	45,000
Tíminn	Progressive Party	14,000
Pjóðviljinn	Pro-labor	13,000

Nondaily newspapers are published in Reykjavík and other towns. Various popular and scholarly periodicals are published in Reykjavík.

46ORGANIZATIONS

Among the many organizations in Iceland are the Chamber of Commerce, the YMCA and YWCA, the Salvation Army, the Red Cross, the Iceland Sport Association, the Federation of Young People's Associations, the Federation of Icelandic Cooperative Societies, lodges of the Order of the Good Templar (temperance societies), the Employers' Federation, the Association of Steam Trawler Owners, and the Union of Icelandic Fish Producers.

Learned societies include the Icelandic Archaeological Society, the Icelandic Historical Society, the Icelandic Literary Society, the Music Society, the Icelandic Natural History Society, and the Agricultural Association. There are also the Icelandic Artists Association, the Iceland Association of Pictorial Artists, the Icelandic Actors Association, the Icelandic Musicians Association, the Icelandic Composers Society, the Icelandic Architects Association, and the Icelandic Writers Association. Among other cultural organizations are the Icelandic-American Society, the Danish Society, the Danish-Icelandic Society, the Anglo-Icelandic Society, the Alliance Française, the Nordic Society, and the Union of Women's Societies.

47TOURISM, TRAVEL, AND RECREATION

Iceland offers such diverse and unusual natural attractions as active volcanoes, glaciers, and hot springs. Among popular participatory sports are swimming (possible year-round in geothermal pools), salmon fishing, pony trekking, and golf. Tourists may arrange to stay in modern hotels or guest houses, on farms, or in youth hostels. In 1989, there were 3,368 hotel rooms with 6,405 beds and an occupancy rate of 39%. The approximate number of foreign visitors to Iceland in 1991 was 143,000, of whom 116,000 were from Europe. Receipts from these visits were about us$116 million. In June of 1994, tourists were drawn to celebrations of Iceland's 50th anniversary as an independent republic.

Citizens of the Scandinavian countries do not require a passport when visiting Iceland. Residents of some 60 countries (including the US, UK, and Canada) do not need visas for stays of up to three months but do need valid passports. Each visitor must have a return ticket, a reentry permit to the country of origin or permission to enter a third country, and sufficient funds for the intended period of the visit.

48FAMOUS ICELANDERS

Two famous early Icelanders were Eric the Red (Eiríkur Thorvaldsson), who discovered and colonized Greenland in 982, and his son Leif Ericsson (Leifur Eiríksson, b.970), who introduced Christianity to Greenland and discovered the North American continent (c.1000). Two famous patriots and statesmen were Bishop Jón Arason (1484–1550), who led the fight for liberty against the power of the Danish king, and Jón Sigurðsson (1811–79), Iceland's national hero, champion of the fight for independence.

Prominent writers were Ari Thorgilsson (1067–1148), father of Icelandic historical writing; Snorri Sturluson (1178–1241), author of the famous *Prose Edda*, a collection of Norse myths; and Hallgrímur Pétursson (1614–74), author of Iceland's beloved Passion Hymns. Leading poets include Bjarni Thorarensen (1786–1841) and Jónas Hallgrímsson (1807–45), pioneers of the Romantic movement in Iceland; Matthías Jochumsson (1835–1920), author of Iceland's national anthem; Thorsteinn Erlingsson (1858–1914), lyricist; Einar Hjörleifsson Kvaran (1859–1939), a pioneer of realism in Icelandic literature and an outstanding short-story writer; Einar Benediktsson (1864–1940), ranked as one of the greatest modern Icelandic poets; Jóhann Sigurjónsson (1880–1919), who lived much of his life in Denmark and wrote many plays based on Icelandic history and legend, as well as poetry; and the novelist Halldór Kiljan Laxness (b.1902), who received the Nobel Prize for literature in 1955.

Niels Ryberg Finsen (1860–1904), a physician who pioneered in the field of light (ray) therapy, received the Nobel Prize for medicine in 1903. Stefán Stefánsson (1863–1921) was the pioneer Icelandic botanist. Helgi Pjeturss (1872–1949), geologist and philosopher, was an authority on the Ice Age and the geology of Iceland. Einar Jónsson (1874–1954), Iceland's greatest sculptor, is represented in European and American museums.

49DEPENDENCIES

Iceland has no territories or colonies.

50BIBLIOGRAPHY

Auden, Wystan Hugh, and Louis MacNeice. *Letters from Iceland*. London: Faber & Faber, 1937.

Byock, Jesse L. *Medieval Iceland: Society, Sagas, and Power*. Berkeley: University of California Press, 1988.

Cary, Sturges E. *Volcanoes and Glaciers: The Challenge of Iceland*. New York: Coward-McCann, 1959.

Chamberlin, William Charles. *Economic Development of Iceland through World War II*. New York: Columbia University Press, 1947.

Durrenberger, E. Paul. *The Dynamics of Medieval Iceland: Political Economy & Literature*. Iowa City: University of Iowa Press, 1992.

Geisinger, Bruce E. *Icelandic Enterprise: Commerce and Economy in the Middle Ages*. Columbia: University of South Carolina Press, 1981.

Griffiths, John C. *Modern Iceland*. New York: Praeger, 1969.

Grondal, Benedikt. *Iceland: From Neutrality to NATO Membership*. Oslo: Universitetsforlaget, 1971.

Hastrup, Kirsten. *Culture and History in Medieval Iceland*. London: Oxford University Press, 1985.

———. *Nature and Policy in Iceland, 1400–1800*. New York: Oxford University Press, 1990.

Hermannsson, Halldór. *The Cartography of Iceland*. Islandica, vol. 21. Ithaca, N.Y.: Cornell University Press, 1931.

Jones, Gwyn. *The Norse Atlantic Saga: Being the Norse Voyages of Discovery and Settlement to Iceland, Greenland, America*. London: Oxford University Press, 1986.

Kristjansson, Jonas. *Icelandic Sagas and Manuscripts*. New York: Heinemann, 1980.

Roberts, David. *Iceland*. New York: H.N. Abrams, 1990.

Rutherford, Adam. *Origin and Development of the Icelandic Nation*. London: Ethnic Study Group, 1938.

Scherman, Katherine. *Daughter of Fire: A Portrait of Iceland*. Boston: Little, Brown, 1976.

Tomasson, Richard F. *Iceland: The First New Society*. Minneapolis: University of Minnesota Press, 1980.

Turville-Petre, Gabriel. *Origins of Icelandic Literature*. London: Oxford University Press, 1953.

IRELAND

Éire

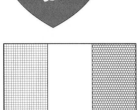

CAPITAL: Dublin (Baile Átha Cliath).

FLAG: The national flag is a tricolor of green, white, and orange vertical stripes.

ANTHEM: *Amhrán na bhFiann (The Soldier's Song).*

MONETARY UNIT: The Irish pound (£) of 100 pence, formerly exchangeable at par with the pound sterling, has floated within the European Monetary System since 1979. Decimal coinage was introduced in February 1971 to replace the former duodecimal system, in which the Irish pound had been divided into 20 shillings of 12 pence each. There are coins of 1, 2, 5, 10, 20, and 50 pence and notes of 1, 5, 10, 20, 50, and 100 pounds. £1 = $0.6970 (or $1 = £1.4347).

WEIGHTS AND MEASURES: As of 1988, Ireland has largely converted from the British system of weights and measures to the metric system.

HOLIDAYS: New Year's Day, 1 January; St. Patrick's Day, 17 March; Bank Holidays, 1st Monday in June, 1st Monday in August, and last Monday in October; Christmas Day, 25 December; St. Stephen's Day, 26 December. Movable religious holidays include Good Friday and Easter Monday.

TIME: GMT.

¹LOCATION, SIZE, AND EXTENT

An island in the eastern part of the North Atlantic, on the continental shelf of Europe, Ireland covers an area of 70,280 sq km (27,135 sq mi), of which 70,282 sq km (27,136 sq mi) are in the Irish Republic (Ireland) and the remainder in Northern Ireland, a part of the UK. Comparatively, the area occupied by Ireland is slightly larger than the state of West Virginia. The island's length is 486 km (302 mi) N–S, and its width is 275 km (171 mi) E–W. The Irish Republic is bounded on the N by the North Channel, which separates it from Scotland; on the NE by Northern Ireland; and on the E and SE by the Irish Sea and St. George's Channel, which separate it from England and Wales. To the W, from north to south, the coast is washed by the Atlantic Ocean.

Ireland's capital city, Dublin, is located on the Irish Sea coast.

²TOPOGRAPHY

Ireland is a limestone plateau rimmed by coastal highlands of varying geological structure. The central plain area, characterized by many lakes, bogs, and scattered low ridges, averages about 90 m (300 ft) above sea level. Principal mountain ranges include the Wicklow Mountains in the east and Macgillycuddy's Reeks in the southwest. The highest peaks are Carrantuohill (1,041 m/3,414 ft) and Mt. Brandon (953 m/3,127 ft), near Killarney, and Lugnaquillia (926 m/3,039 ft), 64 km (40 mi) south of Dublin.

The coastline, 3,169 km (1,969 mi) long, is heavily indented along the south and west coasts where the ranges of Donegal, Mayo, and Munster end in bold headlands and rocky islands, forming long, narrow fjordlike inlets or wide-mouthed bays. On the southern coast, drowned river channels have created deep natural harbors. The east coast has few good harbors.

Most important of the many rivers is the Shannon, which rises in the mountains along the Ulster border and drains the central plain as it flows 370 km (230 mi) to the Atlantic, into which it empties through a wide estuary nearly 110 km (70 mi) long. Other important rivers are the Boyne, Suir, Liffey, Slaney, Barrow, Blackwater, Lee, and Nore.

³CLIMATE

Ireland has an equable climate, because the prevailing west and southwest winds have crossed long stretches of the North Atlantic Ocean, which is warmer in winter and cooler in summer than the continental land masses. The mean annual temperature is 10°C (50°F), and mean monthly temperatures range from a mild 4°C (39°F) in January to 15°C (59°F) in July. Average yearly rainfall ranges from less than 76 cm (30 in) in places near Dublin to more than 254 cm (100 in) in some mountainous regions. The sunniest area is the extreme southeast, with an annual average of 1,700 hours of bright sunshine. Winds are strongest near the west coast, where the average speed is about 26 km/hr (16 mph).

⁴FLORA AND FAUNA

Since Ireland was completely covered by ice sheets during the most recent Ice Age, all native plant and animal life now extant originated from the natural migration of species, chiefly from other parts of Europe and especially from Britain. Early sea inundation of the land bridge connecting Ireland and Britain prevented further migration after 6000 BC. Although many species have subsequently been introduced, Ireland has a much narrower range of flora and fauna than Britain. Forest is the natural dominant vegetation, but the total forest area is now only 5% of the total area, and most of that remains because of the state afforestation program. The natural forest cover was chiefly mixed sessile oak woodland with ash, wych elm, birch, and yew. Pine was dominant on poorer soils, with rowan and birch. Beech and lime are notable natural absentees that thrive when introduced.

The fauna of Ireland is basically similar to that of Britain, but there are some notable gaps. Among those absent are weasel, polecat, wildcat, most shrews, moles, water voles, roe deer, snakes, and common toads. There are also fewer bird and insect species. Some introduced animals, such as the rabbit and brown rat, have been very successful. Ireland has some species not native to Britain, such as the spotted slug and certain species of wood lice. Ireland's isolation has made it notably free from plant and animal diseases. Among the common domestic animals, Ireland is particularly noted for its fine horses, dogs, and cattle. The Connemara pony, Irish wolfhound, Kerry blue terrier, and several types of cattle and sheep are recognized as distinct breeds.

5ENVIRONMENT

Industry is a significant source of pollution in Ireland. The nation produces 1.5 million tons of solid waste and 56,000 tons of hazardous wastes. The nation has 12.0 cubic miles of water with 74% used for industrial purposes and 10% used for farming activity. Ireland's cities produce 1.2 million tons of solid waste per year. Principal responsibility for environmental protection is vested in the Department of the Environment. The Department of Fisheries and Forestry, the Department of Agriculture, and the Office of Public Works also deal with environmental affairs. Local authorities, acting under the supervision of the Department of the Environment, are responsible for water supply, sewage disposal, and other environmental matters. Ireland enjoys the benefits of a climate in which calms are rare and the winds sufficiently strong to disperse atmospheric pollution. The nation produces 70.5 tons of hydrocarbon emissions and 128.9 tons of particulate emissions per year. It contributes 0.1% of the world's total gas emissions. As of 1994, none of Ireland's mammal species were endangered, but 10 of its bird species and 4 plant species were threatened with extinction.

6POPULATION

According to the official 1991 census, the population was 3,523,401, compared with 3,540,643 in the 1986 census, a decrease of 0.5%. In the period 1986–91, the average annual birthrate was 18.8 per 1,000, the death rate was 9.2, and the net natural increase 9.6. There were 1,752,389 males and 1,771,012 females in 1991. The UN has projected a population of 3,436,000 for the year 2000, based on a crude birthrate of 14.4 per 1,000 population, a crude death rate of 9.1, and a net natural increase of 5.3 for 1995–2000.

About two-fifths of the inhabitants live in rural areas. Population by provinces in 1991 was Leinster, 1,860,037; Munster, 1,008,443; Connacht, 422,909; and the three Irish Republic counties in Ulster, 232,012. The largest urban centers (excluding suburbs) were Dublin (477,675), Cork (127,024), Limerick (52,040), Galway (50,842), and Waterford (40,345). The population density was 50 persons per sq km (130 per sq mi) in 1991.

7MIGRATION

The great famine in the late 1840s inaugurated the wave of Irish emigrants to the US, Canada, Argentina, and other countries: 100,000 in 1846, 200,000 per year from 1847 to 1850, and 250,000 in 1851. Since then, emigration has been a traditional feature of Irish life, although it has been considerably reduced since World War II. The net emigration figure decreased from 212,000 for 1956–61 to 80,605 for 1961–66 and 53,906 for 1966–71. During 1971–81, Ireland recorded a net gain from immigration of 103,889. Between 1983 and 1990, however, the Irish Republic suffered a net emigraiton loss of 207,000—46,000 in 1989 alone. In 1992, there was a net gain from migration for the first time since 1981.

8ETHNIC GROUPS

Within historic times, Ireland has been inhabited by Celts, Norsemen, French Normans, and English. Through the centuries, the racial strains represented by these groups have been so intermingled that no purely ethnic divisions remain.

9LANGUAGES

Two languages are spoken, English and Irish (Gaelic). During the long centuries of British control, Irish fell into disuse except in parts of western Ireland. Since the establishment of the Irish Free State in 1922, the government has sought to reestablish Irish as a spoken language throughout the country. It is taught as a compulsory subject in schools, and all government publications, street signs, and post office notices are printed in both Irish and English. English, however, remains the language in common use. Only in a few areas (the Gaeltacht), mostly along the western seaboard, is Irish in everyday use.

10RELIGIONS

There is no established church, but in 1993, about 95% of the population was Roman Catholic. Members of the Church of Ireland were estimated at 4%, other Protestants 1%, and Jews 0.07%. For ecclesiastical purposes, the Republic of Ireland and Northern Ireland (UK) constitute a single entity. Both Roman Catholics and Episcopalian churches have administrative seats at Armagh in Northern Ireland. The Presbyterian Church has its headquarters in Belfast.

11TRANSPORTATION

The Irish Transport System (Córas Iompair Éireann—CIE), a state-sponsored entity, provides a nationwide coordinated road and rail system of public transport for goods and passengers. It is also responsible for maintaining the canals, although they are no longer used for commercial transport. Ireland's railroads, like those of many other European countries, have become increasingly unprofitable because of competition from road transport facilities. There were 1,947 km (1,210 mi) of track in 1991. CIE receives an annual government subsidy.

A network of good main roads extends throughout the country, and improved country roads lead to smaller towns and villages. Bus routes connect all the major population centers and numerous moderate-sized towns. In 1991 there were 92,294 km (57,351 mi) of roads, of which 87,422 km (54,324 mi) were surfaced and 4,872 km (3,027 mi) were gravel or crushed stone. Automobiles numbered 828,225; trucks, 148,882; motorcycles, 24,465; and public service vehicles, 9,731.

In 1991, Ireland's merchant fleet consisted of 42 vessels of 106,000 GRT. The state-supported shipping firm, the British and Irish Steam Packet Co. (the B & I Line), is largely engaged in cross-channel travel between Ireland and the UK, providing passenger and car ferry services as well as containerized freight services, both port to port and door to door. The Irish Continental Line operates services to France, linking Rosslare with Le Havre and Cherbourg; it also runs a summer service between Cork and Le Havre. Brittany Ferries operates a weekly service between Cork and Roscoff. Other shipping concerns operate regular passenger and freight services to the UK and freight services to the Continent. There are deepwater ports at Cork and Dublin and 10 secondary ports. Dublin is the main port, accounting by volume for 19% of imports and 17% of exports handled.

Aer Lingus (Irish International Airlines), the Irish national airline, operates services between Ireland, the UK, and the Continent as well as transatlantic flights. It carried 2,318,700 passengers in 1992. Many foreign airlines operate scheduled transatlantic passenger and air freight services through the duty-free port at Shannon, and most transatlantic airlines make nonscheduled stops there; foreign airlines also operate services between Ireland, the UK, and the Continent. The three state airports at Dublin, Shannon, and Cork are managed by Aer Rianta on behalf of the Ministry for Transport and Power. A domestic airline, Aer Árann Teo, connects Galway with the Aran Islands and Dublin.

12HISTORY

The pre-Christian era in Ireland is known chiefly through legend, although there is archaeological evidence of habitation during the Stone and Bronze ages. In about the 4th century BC, the tall, red-haired Celts from Gaul or Galicia arrived, bringing with them the Iron Age. They subdued the Picts in the north and the Érainn tribe in the south, then settled down to establish a Gaelic civilization, absorbing many of the traditions of the previous inhabitants. By the 3d century AD, the Gaels had established five permanent kingdoms—Ulster, Connacht, Leinster, Meath (North Leinster), and Munster—with a high king, whose title was often little more than honorary, at Tara. After St. Patrick's arrival in AD 432, Christian Ireland rapidly became a center of Latin and Gaelic learning. Irish monasteries drew not only the pious but also the intellectuals of the day, and sent out missionaries to many parts of Europe.

Toward the end of the 8th century, the Vikings began their invasions, destroying monasteries and wreaking havoc on the land, but also intermarrying, adopting Irish customs, and establishing coastal settlements from which have grown Ireland's chief cities. Viking power was finally broken at the Battle of Clontarf in 1014. About 150 years later, the Anglo-Norman invasions began. Gradually, the invaders gained control of the whole country. Many of them intermarried, adopted the Irish language, customs, and traditions, and became more Irish than the Gaels. But the political attachment to the English crown instituted by the Norman invasion caused almost 800 years of strife, as successive English monarchs sought to subdue Gaels and Norman-Irish alike. Wholesale confiscations of land and large plantations of English colonists began under Mary I (Mary Tudor) and continued under Elizabeth I, Cromwell, and William III. Treatment of the Irish reached a brutal climax in the 18th century with the Penal Laws, which deprived Catholics and Dissenters (the majority of the population) of all legal rights.

By the end of the 18th century, many of the English colonists had come to regard themselves as Irish and, like the English colonists in America, resented the domination of London and their own lack of power to rule themselves. In 1783, they forced the establishment of an independent Irish parliament, but it was abolished by the Act of Union (1800), which gave Ireland direct representation in Westminster. Catholic emancipation was finally achieved in 1829 through the efforts of Daniel O'Connell, but the great famine of the 1840s, when millions died or emigrated for lack of potatoes while landlords continued to export other crops to England, emphasized the tragic condition of the Irish peasant and the great need for land reform.

A series of uprisings and the growth of various movements aimed at home rule or outright independence led gradually to many reforms, but the desire for complete independence continued to grow. After the bloodshed and political maneuvers that followed the Easter Uprising of 1916 and the proclamation of an Irish Republic by Irish members of Parliament in 1919, the Anglo-Irish Treaty was signed in 1921, establishing an Irish Free State with dominion status in the British Commonwealth. Violent opposition to dominion status and to a separate government in Protestant-dominated Northern Ireland precipitated a civil war lasting almost a year. The Free State was officially proclaimed and a new constitution adopted in 1922, but sentiment in favor of a reunified Irish Republic remained strong, represented at its extreme by the terrorist activities of the Irish Republican Army (IRA). Powerful at first, the IRA lost much of its popularity when Éamon de Valera, a disillusioned supporter, took over the government in 1932. During the civil violence that disrupted Northern Ireland from the late 1960s on, the Irish government attempted to curb the "provisional wing" of the IRA, a terrorist organization that used Ireland as a base for attacks in the north. Beginning in 1976, the government assumed emergency powers to cope with IRA activities, but the terrorist acts continued, most notably the assassination on 27 August 1979 of the British Earl Mountbatten. The Irish government continues to favor union with Northern Ireland, but only by peaceful means. In November 1985, with the

LOCATION: 51°30′ to 55°30′N; 6° to 10°30′W. **BOUNDARY LENGTHS:** Northern Ireland, 434 km (270 mi); total coastline, 3,169 km (1,969 mi). **TERRITORIAL SEA LIMIT:** 3 mi.

aim of promoting peace in Northern Ireland, Ireland and the UK ratified a treaty enabling Ireland to play a role in various aspects of Northern Ireland's affairs.

The years since the proclamation of the Irish Free State have also witnessed important changes in governmental structure and international relations. In 1937, under a new constitution, the governor-general was replaced by an elected president, and the name of the country was officially changed to Ireland (Éire in Irish). In 1948, Ireland voted itself out of the Commonwealth of Nations, and on 18 April 1949, it declared itself a republic. Ireland was admitted to the UN in 1955 and became a member of the EC in 1973.

Early in the 1980s, Ireland's economy fell into recession. Unemployment rose to 18% in 1986—and to over 30% for recent graduates of high school or college. The result has been a resumption of emigration, particularly of young people; official estimates are that it will reach 250,000 people—7% of the population—by 1992. This estimate excludes large numbers of young persons taking up illegal residency in the US and other countries.

Unemployment and social issues (abortion, divorce, homosexuality) remained the major issues of the 1990s. A novel coalition of Fianna Fáil and the Labour Party formed in January 1993 sought to develop a five-year plan to lower the unemployment rate which is among the highest in the EC.

The problem of Northern Ireland has been the subject of ongoing discussions with the British government and several initiatives have been put forward. President Robinson paid a private visit to Northern Ireland in June 1993. Mary Robinson, who was elected president in November 1990, became the first woman to hold that office.

13GOVERNMENT

Under the constitution of 1937, as amended, legislative power is vested in the Oireachtas (national parliament), which consists of the president and two houses—Dáil Éireann (House of Representatives) and Seanad Éireann (Senate)—and sits in Dublin, the capital city. The president is elected by popular vote for seven years. Members of the Dáil, who are also elected by popular suffrage, using the single transferable vote, represent constituencies determined by law and serve five-year terms. These constituencies, none of which may return fewer than 3 members, must be revised at least once every 12 years, and the ratio between the number of members to be elected for each constituency and its population as ascertained at the last census must be the same, as far as practicable, throughout the country. Since 1981, there have been 166 seats in the Dáil.

The Seanad consists of 60 members: 43 elected from five panels of candidates representing (a) cultural and educational interests, (b) agricultural and allied interests and fisheries, (c) labor, (d) industry and commerce, and (e) public administration and social services; 6 elected by the universities; and 11 nominated by the taoiseach (prime minister). Elections for the Seanad must be held within 90 days of the dissolution of the Dáil; the electorate consists of members of the outgoing Seanad, members of the incoming Dáil, members of county councils, and county borough authorities. The taoiseach is assisted by a tánaiste (deputy prime minister) and as many as 14 other ministers. The constitution provides for popular referendums on certain bills of national importance passed by the Oireachtas. Suffrage is universal at age 18.

14POLITICAL PARTIES

The major political parties are the Fianna Fáil, the Fine Gael, the Progressive Democrats, the Workers' Party, and Labour. Because the members of the Dáil are elected by a proportional representation system, smaller parties—such as Seán MacBride's Clann na Poblachta and the Clann na talmhan (Farmers)—have also at times won representation in the Oireachtas. In 1986, Sinn Fein, the political arm of the Provisional IRA, ended its 65-year boycott of the Dáil and registered as a political party.

Fianna Fáil, the Republican party, was founded by Éamon de Valera. When the Anglo-Irish Treaty of 1921 was signed, de Valera violently opposed the dominion status accepted by a close vote of the Dáil. Until 1927, when the government threatened to annul their election if they did not fulfill their mandates, de Valera and his followers boycotted the Dáil and refused to take an oath of allegiance to the English crown. In 1932, however, de Valera became prime minister, a position he held continuously until 1947 and intermittently until 1959, when he became president for the first of two terms. From 1932 to 1973, when it lost its majority to a Fine Gael–Labour coalition, Fianna Fáil was in power for all but six years.

Fine Gael is the present name for the party that grew out of the policies of Arthur Griffith, first president of the Irish Free State, and Michael Collins, first minister for finance and commander-in-chief of the army. W. T. Cosgrave, their successor, accepted the conditions of the 1921 treaty as the best then obtainable and worked out the details of the partition boundary and dominion status. This party held power from the first general election of 1922 until 1932. Since 1948, as the principal opponent of Fianna Fáil, it has provided leadership for several coalition governments. The policies of Fine Gael traditionally have been far more moderate than those of Fianna Fáil, although it was an interparty coalition government dominated by Fine Gael and Labour that voted Ireland out of the Commonwealth in 1948.

In the general elections of 24 November 1982 (the third general election to be held within a year and a half), Fianna Fáil won 75 seats, Fine Gael 70, and the Labour Party 16. Two members of the Workers' Party and three independents were also elected. Garret FitzGerald was elected taoiseach, heading a Fine Gael-Labour coalition. It was the second time in a year that he had replaced Charles J. Haughey of the Fianna Fáil in that office. In December 1979, Haughey had replaced Jack Lynch as head of his party and become prime minister.

The 1987 elections saw Fianna Fáil raise its representation to 81 seats, 3 short of an overall majority in the 27th Dáil. Fianna Fáil's proportion of the vote dropped to 44.1%, from 45.2% in 1982. Fine Gael won 51 seats in the 1987 contest; its 27.1% of the vote was 12.1 percentage points lower than in 1982. The Progressive Democrats, who had held 5 seats at dissolution, elected 14 representatives and took 11.9% of the vote. Labour won 12 seats (down 2) and 6.5% of the vote. The Workers' Party doubled its representation, from 2 to 4, and other parties elected 4 members. In a bitter contest, Charles Haughey was elected taoiseach and formed a minority Fianna Fáil government.

An early general election in 1992 saw the two largest parties—Fianna Fáil and Fine Gael—lose seats to the Labour Party. The results were as follows: Fianna Fáil (68), Fine Gael (45), Labour Party (33), Progressive Democrats (10), Democratic Left (4), and others (6). Albert Reynolds (Fianna Fáil) was elected taoiseach of the Fianna Fáil-Labour Coalition.

15LOCAL GOVERNMENT

The provinces of Ulster, Munster, Leinster, and Connacht no longer serve as political divisions, but each is divided into a number of counties that do. Three counties in Ulster—Cavan, Donegal, and Monaghan—are among the 27 administrative counties of the Irish Republic, which are governed by county councils. The other divisions include the 5 county boroughs and 6 boroughs governed by municipal corporations, the 49 districts governed by urban district councils, and the 25 towns governed by town commissioners. The cities of Dublin, Cork, Limerick, Waterford, and Galway are county boroughs, while Dun Laoghaire, Wexford, Kilkenny, Drogheda, Sligo, and Clonmel are boroughs. Members of these authorities are elected under a system of proportional representation, normally every five years.

Local authorities' principal functions include planning and development, housing, roads, and sanitary and environmental services. Health services, which were administered by local authorities up to 1971, are now administered by regional health boards, although the local authorities still continue to pay part of the cost. Expenditures are financed by a local tax on the occupation of property (rates), by grants and subsidies from the central government, and by charges made for certain services. Capital expenditure is financed mainly by borrowing from the Local Loans Fund, operated by the central government, and from banking and insurance institutions.

16JUDICIAL SYSTEM

Responsibility for law enforcement is in the hands of a commissioner, responsible to the Department of Justice, who controls an unarmed police force known as the civil guard (Garda Síochána). In 1986, the force numbered 11,400. Justice is administered by a Supreme Court, a high court with full original jurisdiction, and circuit and district courts with local and limited jurisdiction.

Individual liberties are protected by the 1937 Constitution and by Supreme Court decisions. The Constitution provides for the creation of "special courts" to handle cases which cannot be adequately managed by the ordinary court system. The Offenses Against the State Act formally established a special court to hear cases involving political violence by terrorist groups. In such cases, in order to prevent intimidation, the panel of judges sits in place of a jury.

17ARMED FORCES

The army and its reserves, the air corps, and the naval service are a small but well-trained nucleus that can be enlarged in a time of emergency. In 1993, the permanent defense force numbered 13,000 and the reserve defense force 16,100. Recruitment is voluntary. The army (11,200 regulars, 15,000 reserves) consists of 11 battalions of infantry and smaller combined arms units with British and European weapons and equipment. A navy of 1,000 mans 7 patrol craft. The air force (800) has 16 combat aircraft and 15 armed helicopters. Ireland has committed 1 battalion (Lebanon) and about 80 observers to 9 peacekeeping operations. The defense budget in 1991 was $552 million or 1–2%of gross domestic product.

18INTERNATIONAL COOPERATION

Ireland, which became a member of the UN on 14 December 1955, belongs to ECE and all the nonregional specialized agencies. Irish troops have served in the Congo with UNOC, in Cyprus with UNFICYP, with UNEF in the Middle East, with UNIFIL in Lebanon, and with various other UN forces. On 1 January 1973, Ireland became a member of the EC. Ireland is also a founding member of OECD and the Council of Europe and a signatory of GATT and the Law of the Sea.

19ECONOMY

Until the 1950s, Ireland had a predominantly agricultural economy, with agriculture making the largest contribution to the GNP. However, liberal trade policies and the drive for industrialization have stimulated economic expansion. In 1958, agriculture accounted for 21% of the GNP, industry 23.5%, and other sectors 55.5%. By 1993, however, agriculture accounted for only 10.5% of the total, industry 44.5%, and other activities 45%.

Ireland's economy has been slower in developing than the economies of other West European countries. The government has carried on a comprehensive public investment program, particularly in housing, public welfare, communications, transportation, new industries, and electric power. Since the 1960s, the government has tried to stimulate output, particularly of goods for the export market, and manufactured exports grew from £78.4 million in 1967 to £11,510 million in 1992. Government spending accounts for about 40% of total investment, the difference between domestic savings and total investment being supplied by private capital inflow, the use of external assets, and some foreign borrowing. State-owned enterprises account for about 10% of GNP.

During the early 1980s, Ireland suffered from the worldwide recession, experiencing double-digit inflation and high unemployment. The economy continued to lag through 1986, but the GNP grew 30% between 1987 and 1992. Unemployment soared to 18% in 1986 (from 10% in 1981), and remained high; the rate was 16.8% in 1993. Inflation, however, was reduced from 20.4% in 1981 to 3% in 1987, its lowest level in 20 years. It has remained moderate since and was only 1.4% in 1993. Manufacturing output grew substantially in some years, but the impact on employment was minor.

20INCOME

In 1992, Ireland's GNP was $42,798 million at current prices, or $12,100 per capita. For the period 1985–92 the average inflation rate was 2.4%, resulting in a real growth rate in per capita GNP of 5.0%.

In 1992 the GDP was $42.4 billion in current US dollars. It is estimated that in 1990 agriculture, hunting, forestry, and fishing contributed 8% to GDP; mining, quarrying, manufacturing, electricity, gas, and water, 32%; construction, 5%; wholesale and retail trade, 13%; transport, storage, and communication, 5%; finance, insurance, real estate, and business services, 6%; community, social, and personal services, 14%; and other sources, 16%.

21LABOR

In 1992, the total civilian work force was estimated at 1,350,000, of whom 16.1% were unemployed. Of those employed in 1992, 13% were in agriculture, forestry, and fishing (down from 16% in 1986); 28% in industry (unchanged from 1986), and 59% in services (56% in 1986). In 1992, average weekly earnings in the industrial sector were £245.

About 58% of the labor force is organized into 70 trade unions (1992), affiliated with the Irish Congress of Trade Unions, formed in 1959 by the merger of the Irish Trade Union Congress and the Congress of Irish Unions. The standard workweek is 40 hours, based on 5 days at 8 hours a day. In 1992, there were 38 strikes involving 13,107 workers resulting in 190,609 lost workdays.

22AGRICULTURE

About 5.6 million hectares (13.9 million acres), or 82% of the total land area, are devoted to agricultural activities. In 1991, 16% of the agricultural acreage was used for growing grains, and root and green crops, and the balance for pasture and hay. Thus most of the farmland is used to support livestock, the leading source of Ireland's exports. Most farms are small, although there has been a trend toward consolidation. In 1992, agriculture accounted for 13% of Irish employment. Principal crops (with their estimated 1992 production) include barley, 1,300,000 tons; sugar beets, 1,380,000 tons; potatoes, 620,000 tons; wheat, 680,000 tons; and oats, 100,000 tons.

Over half of agricultural production, by value, is exported. The benefits of the EC's Common Agricultural Policy, which provides secure markets and improved prices for most major agricultural products, account in part for the increase of Ireland's agricultural income from £314 million in 1972 (before Ireland's accession) to £1,987 million in 1992. In 1992, gross agricultural output increased by 2.75% primarily as a result of lower input usage of feed and fertilizer. The EC's Common Agricultural Policy has kept the rate of increase of output prices below that of input prices, putting further downward pressure on farm incomes. Recent market devaluations, however, are expected to positively affect agricultural prices, causing farm incomes to rise.

The government operates a comprehensive network of services within the framework of the Common Agricultural Policy, including educational and advisory services to farmers. Under a farm modernization scheme, capital assistance is provided to farmers for land development, improvement of farm buildings, and other projects, with part of the cost borne by the EC. In 1974, pursuant to an EC directive, incentives were made available to farmers wishing to retire and make their lands available, by lease or sale, for the land reform program.

[23]ANIMAL HUSBANDRY

With some 90% of Ireland's agricultural land devoted to pasture and hay, the main activity of the farming community is the production of grazing animals and other livestock, which account for about 53% of agricultural exports. Cattle and cattle products accounting for about 17% of Ireland's agricultural exports and 4% of total exports. In 1992, live cattle exports alone were valued at $114.9 million.

The estimated livestock population in December 1992 was 6,073,000 head of cattle, 6,187,000 sheep, 1,134,000 hogs, and 9,000,000 poultry. In 1992, butter production totaled about 137,000 tons, cheese 85,250 tons, and wool (greasy) 19,000 tons. Milk production in 1992 was 5,494,000 tons.

Since livestock is a major element in the country's economy, the government is particularly concerned with improving methods of operation and increasing output. A campaign for eradication of bovine tuberculosis was completed in 1965, and programs are under way for eradication of bovine brucellosis, warble fly, and sheep scab.

[24]FISHING

Salmon, eels, trout, pike, perch, and other freshwater fish are found in the rivers and lakes; sea angling is good along the entire coast; and deep-sea fishing is done from the south and west coasts. The fishing industry has made considerable progress as a result of government measures to improve credit facilities for the purchase of fishing boats and the development of harbors; establishment of training programs for fishermen; increased emphasis on market development and research; establishment of hatcheries; and promotion of sport fishing as an attraction for tourists.

Leading varieties of saltwater fish are mackerel, herring, cod, whiting, plaice, ray, skate, and haddock. Lobsters, crawfish, and Dublin Bay prawns are also important. The value of exports of fish and fish products was $308.1 million in 1991. Salmon is Ireland's most important inland species; the salmon catch in 1991 totaled 9,300 tons. The total volume of the catch in 1991 was 240,703 tons, including 75,256 tons of Atlantic mackerel.

[25]FORESTRY

Once well forested, Ireland was stripped of timber in the 17th and 18th centuries by absentee landlords, who made no attempt to reforest the denuded land, and later by the steady conversion of natural forest into farms and grazing lands. In an effort to restore part of the woodland areas, a state forestry program was inaugurated in 1903; since then, over 350,000 hectares (865,000 acres) have been planted. More than half the planting is carried out in the western counties. In 1991, about 6% of Ireland was forested, up from 5% in 1980. About 95% of the trees planted are coniferous. The aim of the forestry program is to eliminate a large part of timber imports—a major drain on the balance of payments—and to produce a surplus of natural and processed timber for export. Roundwood removals totaled 1.7 million cu m in 1991.

[26]MINING

There was a marked increase in mining exploration beginning in the early 1960s, as a result of which Ireland has become a significant source of base metals. The largest lead-zinc field in Europe, near Navan, in County Meath, came into production in the late 1970's; in 1991, the mine produced 187,500 tons of zinc concentrates and 35,000 tons of lead concentrates. An upgrading project in 1992 was to have given the mine a capacity of 200,000 tons per year of zinc and 38,000 tons per year of lead concentrates. The country's output of zinc could double by the late 1990s if two new mines are developed as scheduled. Although coal reserves are relatively limited, they are believed sufficient to supply the country's anthracite needs if properly developed. In

addition, Ireland's 1.2 million hectares (3 million acres) of bogs provide an almost unlimited supply of fuel in the form of turf or milled peat. In 1991, over 6.2 million tons of peat were processed for fuel. In 1990, Ireland mined an estimated 45,000 tons of coal. Mineral production in 1991 included 429,000 tons of gypsum, 8,500,000 tons of limestone, and 80,000 tons of barites. Other commercially exploited minerals include copper, gypsum, salt, clays and shales, dolomite, diatomite, building stone, and aggregate building materials. In 1989, gold was discovered in County Mayo, with an estimated 498,000 tons of ore with at least 1.5 grams of gold per ton of ore.

[27]ENERGY AND POWER

Electric power is controlled by the government through the Electricity Supply Board (ESB), established in 1927. Government policy has been to provide adequate energy to meet industrial, commercial, and private domestic needs from native resources. Hydroelectric plants have been built on the Shannon, Lee, Liffey, and Erne rivers. Turf or peat from the extensive Irish bogs supplies the staple fuel for many homes and is utilized as intermediate fuel for electricity production.

Of all EC members, Ireland is still the most dependent on imported oil. Exploratory drilling in the Irish sector of the Atlantic Ocean began in 1973. By midyear, the Kinsale Head natural gas field, estimated to contain reserves of 1.5 billion cu ft, was discovered about 50 km (30 mi) south of Cork. Production of natural gas began in 1978 and is expected to be exhausted by 2000. The UK has guaranteed a continued supply. Production from the Kinsale field met an estimated 21% of Ireland's fuel needs in 1991. The Ballycotton natural gas field, in the vicinity of the Kinsale Field, was under development in 1991.

Net installed capacity as of 1991 was 3,811,000 kw; total power production was 15,147 million kwh, of which about 94% was produced by thermal coal and oil stations. Coal production consists of high-ash semibituminous from the Connaught Field, and is used for electricity production. By the beginning of the 1980s, Ireland's rural electrification program was virtually complete.

[28]INDUSTRY

Since the establishment of the Irish Free State, successive governments have encouraged industrialization by granting tariff protection and promoting diversification. Following the launching of the First Program for Economic Expansion by the government in 1958, considerable progress has been made in developing this sector of the economy, in which foreign industrialists have played a significant role. The Industrial Development Authority (IDA) administers a scheme of incentives to attract foreign investment. In addition, several government agencies offer facilities for consulting on research and development, marketing, exporting, and other management matters.

Official policy favors private enterprises. Where private capital and interest have been lacking, state-owned firms have been created to operate essential services and to stimulate further industrial development, notably in the fields of sugar, peat, electricity, steel, fertilizers, industrial alcohol, and transportation. Although efforts have been made to encourage decentralization, about half of all industrial establishments and personnel are concentrated in Dublin and Cork.

Industry grew by an average annual rate of more than 5% from 1968 to 1981, one of the highest rates in Europe. The growth rate during 1982–86 was 4.9%, with 1984 registering 12%; in 1985 and 1986, however, industry grew by only 2.7% and 2.8%, respectively. Between 1987 and 1992, it averaged 3.9%. The greatest growth was in high technology industries, like electronics and pharmaceuticals, where labor productivity also was growing substantially, thus limiting increases in the number of jobs. The most important products of manufacturing, by gross output, are food, metal and engineering goods, chemicals and chemical products, beverages and tobacco, nonmetallic minerals, and paper and printing.

In 1992, industry employed 18% of the labor force and accounted for 38% of GDP. Ireland's manufactured exports have grown from £78.4 million in 1967 to £11,510 million in 1992. Leading industrial products in 1991 included cement, 1,601,000 tons; nitrogenous fertilizers, 279,000 tons; motor fuels; 333,000 tons; and distillate and residual fuel oils, 1,329,000 tons.

29SCIENCE AND TECHNOLOGY

The major organizations doing scientific research in Ireland are the Agricultural Institute (established in 1958) and the Institute for Industrial Research and Standards (1946). The Dublin Institute of Advanced Studies, established by the state in 1940, includes a School of Theoretical Physics and a School of Cosmic Physics. The Royal Irish Academy, founded in 1785, promotes study in science and the humanities and is the principal vehicle for Ireland's partici- pation in international scientific unions. The Royal Dublin Society (1731) has a scientific library and publishes a journal.

Most scientific research is funded by the government; the gov- ernment advisory and coordinating body on scientific matters is the National Board for Science and Technology. Medical research is supported by the Medical Research Council and Medico-Social Research Board. Veterinary and cereals research is promoted by the Department of Agriculture, and the Department of Fisheries and Forestry and the Department of Industry and Energy have developed their own research programs. The UNESCO prize in science was awarded in 1981 for the development of clofaz- imines, a leprosy drug produced by the Medical Research Council of Ireland with aid from the Development Cooperation Division of the Department of Foreign Affairs.

Research and development personnel in 1988 numbered 7,642; expenditures totaled £186 million.

30DOMESTIC TRADE

Dublin is the financial and commercial center, the distribution point for most imported goods, and the port through which most of the country's agricultural products are shipped to Britain and the Continent. Cork, the second-largest manufacturing city and close to the transatlantic port of Cobh, is also important, as is Limerick, with its proximity to Shannon International Airport. Other important local marketing centers are Galway, Drogheda, Dundalk, Sligo, and Waterford.

Office business hours are usually 9 or 9:30 AM to 5:30 PM. Shops generally close at 5:30 PM, although most supermarkets are open until 9 PM on Thursday and Friday. Normal banking hours are 10 AM to 12:30 PM and 1:30 to 3 PM, Monday through Fri- day, and 3 to 5 PM on Thursday. Most offices are closed on Satur- day, and shops close on either Wednesday or Saturday afternoon.

31FOREIGN TRADE

Exports, of which machinery and transport equipment and food- stuffs and livestock made up 49% by value in 1992, provide a large proportion of national income, (71% of GNP in 1992). Imports, of which machinery, transport equipment, and manufac- tured articles made up 50.3%, account for a major part of pay- ments outflow. Trade deficits were formerly chronic, but a surplus has been recorded in every year since 1985. The 1992 trade surplus was a record. Most trade is carried on with Great Britain and Northern Ireland, although the US and Germany are increasingly important trade partners. In 1992, 31.5% of total Irish exports went to Great Britain and Northern Ireland, which concurrently provided 42.5% of Ireland's imports. Of the total trade volume in 1992, 70.8% was within the EC. After the UK, Ireland's most important trading partners in the EC were

Germany and France. The US received 8.2% of Ireland's exports and supplied 14.2% of its imports.

Principal exports in 1992 (in millions of Irish pounds) were as follows:

Machinery and transport equipment	4,482.7
Food and live animals	3,667.6
Chemicals and related products	3,211.2
Manufactured materials	1,255.5
Crude materials, excluding fuel	491.0
Miscellaneous manufactures	2,561.1
Other exports	471.9

The principal imports in 1992 (in millions of Irish pounds) were as follows:

Machinery and transport equipment	4,702.8
Manufactured materials	1,935.8
Chemicals and related products	1,713.0
Food and live animals	1,280.3
Fuel, lubricants	684.2
Miscellaneous manufactures	1,965.5
Other imports	373.7

The principal trade partners in 1992 (in millions of Irish pounds) were as follows:

	EXPORTS	IMPORTS	BALANCE
UK	5,232.4	5,601.8	−369.4
US	1,367.7	1,869.1	−501.4
Germany	2,122.3	1,103.7	1,018.6
France	1,603.1	587.1	1,016.0
Netherlands	1,160.5	581.3	579.2
Belgium-Luxembourg	809.8	273.3	536.5
Japan	480.0	660.5	−180.5
Other countries	3,853.0	2,518.2	1,334.8
TOTALS	16,628.8	13,195.0	3,433.8

32BALANCE OF PAYMENTS

Traditionally, Ireland has run a deficit in visible trade, covered by a large surplus in international transfers. In Ireland, merchandise trade is equivalent to over 105% of GDP; two out of every three manufacturing jobs are directly related to exporting, even though Ireland must import most raw materials and intermediate goods for manufacturing.

In 1992 merchandise exports totaled $27,901 million and imports $21,097 million. The merchandise trade balance was $6,804 million.

The following table summarizes Ireland's balance of payments for 1991 and 1992 (in millions of US dollars):

	1991	1992
CURRENT ACCOUNT		
Goods, services, and income	−1,742	−341
Unrequited transfers	3,186	2,969
TOTALS	1,444	2,629
CAPITAL ACCOUNT		
Direct investment	97	102
Portfolio investment	−1,070	−3,189
Other long-term capital	−1,568	−646
Other short-term capital	−660	−2,489
Exceptional financing	—	—
Other liabilities	—	1,337
Reserves	−464	2,166
TOTALS	−3,665	−2,719
Errors and omissions	2,221	91
Total change in reserves	−513	2,317

33BANKING AND SECURITIES

In 1979, Ireland joined the European Monetary System, thus severing the 150-year-old tie with the British pound. The Central Bank of Ireland, established in 1942, is both the monetary authority and the bank of issue. Its role has expanded considerably, particularly in monetary policy. Commercial deposits with the Central Bank have strongly increased since 1964, when legislation first permitted it to pay interest on deposits held for purposes other than settlement of clearing balances. Since July 1969, the Central Bank has accepted short-term deposits from various institutions, including commercial and merchant banks.

The powers of the Central Bank were greatly expanded by the Central Bank Act of 1971. This measure contained extensive provisions for the licensing and supervision of banks by the Central Bank in pursuance of "the orderly and proper regulation of banking," and it also strengthened the Central Bank's powers of monetary control by enabling it to require banks to maintain prescribed ratios between assets and liabilities. As a result, the bank now has status and powers comparable to those of other central banks in developed economies.

The major commercial banks in Ireland are known as associated banks. The principal banks numbered 22 in 1993. At the end of 1992 all banks held domestic demand deposits of £2,166 million as savings accounts (£12,880 million).

A number of other commercial, merchant, and industrial banks also operate. Additionally, Ireland's post office operates the Post Office Savings Banks and Trustee Savings Banks. The Irish stock exchange has its trading floor in Dublin. All stockbrokers in Ireland are member of this exchange.

34INSURANCE

In 1989 there were 72 insurance companies in Ireland. Insurance firms must be licensed by the Insurance Division of the Ministry of Industry, Trade, Commerce, and Tourism. Life insurance in force in 1992 totaled £51 billion.

35PUBLIC FINANCE

Ireland's fiscal year follows the calendar year.

Expenditures of local authorities are principally for health, roads, housing, and social welfare.

The following table shows actual revenues and expenditures for 1989 and 1990 in millions of pounds.

	1989	1990
REVENUE AND GRANTS		
Tax revenue	8,595	9,197
Non-tax revenue	556	639
Grants	284	466
TOTALS	9,435	10,302
EXPENDITURES & LENDING MINUS REPAYMENTS		
General public service	826	881
Defense	309	361
Education	1,266	1,333
Health	1,302	1,419
Social security and welfare	2,745	2,911
Housing and community amenities	293	260
Recreation, cultural, and religious affairs	36	43
Economic affairs and services	1,089	1,397
Other expenditures	2,085	2,282
Lending minus repayments	−166	−35
TOTALS	9,785	10,852
Deficit/Surplus	−350	−550

The government's budget estimates for 1992 called for a further increase in the exchequer borrowing rate to 2.4% (up from 2.1% in 1991). Fiscal difficulties were exacerbated in 1993, when the government was simultaneously faced with retroactive pay increases for public servants and the one-time loss of £200 million in revenue due to value-added tax collection changes by the EC, and further reductions in value-added and personal income tax rates.

In 1992 Ireland's total public debt stood at £27 billion, of which £10.9 billion was denominated in foreign currencies. The debt has generally been financed by the sale of government securities. The vast majority of the debt was accumulated in the 1970s and early 1980s as a result of oil price shocks and expansive social welfare programs and government employment.

36TAXATION

Standard income tax rates in 1993 ranged from 29% to 52%. Corporate profits tax is charged at 40%, with a reduced rate of 10% for certain companies. A value-added tax was instituted in 1972 to replace wholesale and turnover taxes. As of 1992, the standard rate was 21%, with reduced rates for certain goods and services.

To stimulate economic expansion and encourage investment in Irish industry, particularly in the area of industrial exports, tax adjustments have been made to give relief to export profits, expenditures for mineral development, shipping, plant and machinery, new industrial buildings, and investments in Irish securities.

Since 1969, the government has encouraged artists and writers to live in Ireland by exempting from income tax their earnings from their works of art. Royalties and other income from patent rights are also tax-exempt.

37CUSTOMS AND DUTIES

From the time of the establishment of the Irish Free State, government policy was to encourage development of domestic industry by maintaining protective tariffs and quotas on commodities that would compete with Irish-made products. Following Ireland's admission to the EC, the country's tariff schedule was greatly revised. The schedule vis-à-vis third-world countries and the US was gradually aligned with EC tariffs, and customs duties between Ireland and the EC were phased down to zero by July 1977. Certain goods still require import licenses, and tariffs are based on the Harmonized System. The Shannon Free-Trade Zone is located at the Shannon International Airport.

38FOREIGN INVESTMENT

To stimulate economic expansion, the Industrial Development Authority encourages and facilitates investment by foreign interests, particularly in the development of industries with export potential. Special concessions include nonrepayable grants to help establish industries in underdeveloped areas and tax relief on export profits. Freedom to take out profits is unimpaired. Total direct foreign investment in 1992 came to $14.4 billion, of which 50% was by the US. Engineering goods, computers, electronic products, electrical equipment, pharmaceuticals and chemicals, textiles, foodstuffs, leisure products, and metal and plastic products are among the items produced. Much of the new investment has occurred since Ireland became a member of the EC.

39ECONOMIC DEVELOPMENT

Government policies are premised on private enterprise as a predominant factor in the economy. Specific economic programs adopted in recent decades have attempted to increase efficiency in agriculture and industry, stimulate new export industries, create employment opportunities for labor leaving the agricultural sector, and reduce unemployment and net emigration. In pursuit of these objectives, the government provides aids to industry through the IDA, the Industrial Credit Co., and other agencies. Tax concessions, information, and advisory services are also provided.

The IDA seeks to attract foreign investment by offering a 10% maximum corporation tax rate for manufacturing and certain service industries, generous tax-free grants for staff training, ready-built factories on modern industrial estates, accelerated depreciation, export-risk guarantee programs, and other financial inducements. IDA also administers industrial estates at Waterford and Galway. The Shannon Free Airport Development Co., another government-sponsored entity, administers an industrial estate on the fringes of Shannon Airport, a location that benefits from proximity to the airport's duty-free facilities. A third entity, Udaras Na Gaeltachia, promotes investment and development in western areas where Irish is the predominant language. As of 1986 there were some 900 foreign-owned plants in Ireland.

Price control legislation was introduced under the Prices Act of 1958, amended in 1965 and 1972. In general, manufacturers, service industries, and professions are required to obtain permission from the Ministry of Commerce and Trade for any increase. Price changes are monitored by a National Prices Commission, established in 1971. The economic plan for 1983–87, called The Way Forward, aimed at improving the cost-competitiveness of the economy by cutting government expenditures and restraining the growth of public service pay, among other measures. The 1987–90 Program for National Recovery is generally credited with creating the conditions to bring government spending and the national debt under control. The 1991–93 Program for Economic and Social Progress was to further reduce the national debt and budget deficit and to establish a schedule of wage increases.

A 1994–99 national development plan calls for investment of £20 billion and aims to achieve an average annual GDP growth rate of 3.5%. The government hopes to create 200,000 jobs through this plan, with funding by the state, the EC, and the private sector. Half of the money is earmarked for industry, transport, training, and energy.

Ireland gave $73 million in foreign aid to developing countries in 1991.

40SOCIAL DEVELOPMENT

Since 1 April 1974, all wage and salary earners between the ages of 16 and 68 have been covered by a compulsory social insurance program, including unemployment insurance, disability benefits, retirement and old age pensions, widows' pensions, maternity benefits, and a death grant. The system is financed through weekly payments and administered by the Department of Social Welfare. In 1991, employees paid 5.5% of their earnings up to £17,300, and employers contributed 12.20% of their payroll up to £19,300 per employee. Old-age pensions were paid at a flat rate of £64.00 per week, disability pensions £56.40, and survivor pensions £58.20. The department is also responsible for administering programs of free travel, electricity, and radio and television licenses for certain pensioners. Additionally, it exercises general control over schemes of social assistance administered by local authorities, which include programs for school meals, welfare of blind persons, subsidized fuel, subsidized and free footwear, and home assistance. The 1986 expenditures for social insurance and assistance were estimated at £2,489 million. Total expenditures for social welfare amounted to approximately 22% of the GDP.

The predominance of the Roman Catholic Church has had a significant impact on social legislation. Both divorce and abortion are illegal in Ireland. In 1986, a referendum to pave the way for legalization of divorce under certain circumstances was defeated by a large margin. Contraceptives, the sale of which had been entirely prohibited, became available to married couples by prescription in the early 1980s. In 1985, the need for a prescription was abolished, and the minimum age for marriage was raised from 14 to 18 for girls and from 16 to 18 for boys. The fertility rate for 1985–90 was down 20.6% from the previous 5-year period.

In 1990, the government established the Second Commission on the Status of Women, to help bring about the participation of women in all aspects of Irish society. Areas of concentration include child care, education, employment opportunities, and legal rights. Despite the enactment of equal-pay legislation effective at the end of 1975, there was still a great disparity between men's and women's wage scales in the mid-1980s. Although the number of married women who hold paying jobs has increased in recent years, only a third of Irish women work outside the home.

41HEALTH

Health services are provided by regional boards under the administration and control of the Department of Health. A comprehensive health service, with free hospitalization, treatment, and medication, is provided for low-income groups. The middle-income population is entitled to free maternity, hospital, and specialist services, and a free diagnostic and preventive service is available to all persons suffering from specified infectious diseases. Insurance against hospital and certain other medical expenses is available under a voluntary plan introduced in 1957.

Since World War II, many new regional and county hospitals and tuberculosis sanatoriums have been built. Hospitals in 1987 numbered 185. In 1988, there were 5,590 doctors, 1,205 dentists, and 23,127 nurses. In 1992, there were 1.58 physicians per 1,000 people, with a nurse to doctor ratio of 4.7, and in 1990, there was 1 physician per 630 people and 3.9 hospital beds per 1,000 people.

While deaths from cancer, particularly lung cancer, and heart disease are rising, those from many other causes have been decreasing rapidly. Infant mortality has been reduced from 50.3 per 1,000 live births in 1948 to 18 in 1972 and 5 in 1992. Tuberculosis, long a major cause of adult deaths, declined from 3,700 cases in 1947 to only 18 per 100,000 in 1990. Average life expectancy at birth in 1992 was 75 years. The general mortality rate in 1993 was 9.2 per 1,000 people, and major causes of death in 1992 were cited as: communicable diseases and maternal/perinatal causes (57 per 100,000); noncommunicable diseases (526 per 100,000); and injuries (39 per 100,000).

Ireland's 1993 population was 3.5 million, with a birth rate of 14.4 per 1,000 people. There were 50,000 births in 1992 with children up to one year old immunized as follows: diphtheria, pertussis, and tetanus (65%); polio (81%); and measles (78%). Total health care expenditures in 1990 were $3,068 million.

42HOUSING

The aim of public housing policy is to ensure, so far as possible, that every family can obtain decent housing at a price or rent it can afford. Government subsidies are given to encourage home ownership, and local authorities provide housing for those unable to house themselves adequately. Housing legislation has encouraged private construction through grants and loans. In 1986, 23,000 new dwellings were constructed. Projected and existing housing needs are assessed regularly by local authorities, and their reports are the basis for local building programs, which are integrated with national programs and reconciled with available public resources. In 1985, capital expenditures for housing totaled £393.1 million. In 1992, 20,600 new private dwellings were completed. The value of residential construction grew by 13% to US$2.6 billion (a volume increase of 11% over 1991 levels). Further growth was projected for 1993 due to economic recovery and low interest rates. New public housing grew 10% in 1992 and was forecast to increase by 56% in 1993. Almost all public housing is concrete.

43EDUCATION

The Department of Education administers primary and postprimary education. Six years of primary education are free and education is compulsory for nine years. Postprimary education is free in over 90% of voluntary secondary day schools and in all vocational, comprehensive, and community schools. All secondary schools are private, and many are operated by religious orders. Most postprimary education is single-sex. The Department of Education makes grants and allowances to secondary and vocational schools, as well as to colleges, for training teachers of all religious denominations. It also pays the salaries of primary-, secondary-, comprehensive-, and community-school teachers.

In the secondary schools, the Department of Education allocates grants, on the basis of pupil enrollment, that serve to pay more than 90% of all teachers' salaries. Approximately 90% of the cost of maintaining vocational schools is paid from state funds; the rest is paid by local authorities.

Ireland has two universities: the University of Dublin (Trinity College) and the National University of Ireland, which consists of three constituent colleges in Dublin, Galway, and Cork. St. Patrick's College, Maynooth, is a recognized college of the National University. Universities are self-governing, but each receives an annual state grant, as well as supplementary grants for capital outlays. There are also various colleges of education, home economics, technology, and the arts.

In 1990, there were 416,747 pupils in 3,320 primary schools; 345,941 in postprimary schools; and 90,296 students in higher institutions. There were 15,614 teachers at the primary level; 20,830 at the general secondary level; and 5,598 at higher level institutions..

44 LIBRARIES AND MUSEUMS

Dublin, the center of cultural life in Ireland, has several museums and a number of libraries. The National Museum contains collections on Irish antiquities, folk life, fine arts, natural history, zoology, and geology. The National Gallery houses valuable paintings representing the various European schools from the 13th century to the present. The National Portrait Gallery provides a visual survey of Irish historical personalities over the past three centuries. The Municipal Gallery of Modern Art has a fine collection of works by recent and contemporary artists. There is a Heraldic Museum in Dublin Castle; the National Botanic Gardens are at Glasnevin; and the Zoological Gardens are in Phoenix Park.

Trinity College Library, which dates from 1591 and counts among its many treasures the Book of Kells and the Book of Durrow, two of the most beautiful illuminated manuscripts from the pre-Viking period, is the oldest and largest library in Ireland, with a bookstock of 3,000,000 volumes. Among other libraries in Dublin are the Chester Beatty Library, noted for one of the world's finest collections of Oriental manuscripts and miniatures, and the National Library of Ireland, founded in 1877, which houses 500,000 volumes. The Dublin public libraries have holdings of over 2,400,000 volumes and have special collections on Jonathan Swift and Yeats; political pamphlets and cartoons; and Dublin periodicals and 18th-century plays.

Public libraries and small museums, devoted mostly to local historical exhibits, are found in Cork, Limerick, Waterford, Galway, and other cities.

45 MEDIA

All postal, telegraph, telex, and telephone services are controlled and operated by the government through the Department of Posts and Telegraphs. In 1991 there were approximately 942,000 telephones in use. A statutory corporation, Radio Telefis Éireann, is the Irish national broadcasting organization; on 1 January 1976, this service celebrated 50 years of operation. Ireland's second radio service, Radio na Gaeltachta, broadcasting in Irish, was inaugurated in 1972; it broadcasts VHF from County Galway. There are two state-run color television stations (begun in 1961

and 1978), both run by Radio Telefis Éireann. There were some 2,200,000 radios and 829,000 television sets in 1991.

The four daily newspapers and three Sunday papers issued in Dublin circulate throughout the country, while the two dailies and one weekly published in Cork are read widely in the southern half. Ireland's major newspapers, with political orientation and estimated 1991 circulation, are as follows:

DUBLIN	ORIENTATION	CIRCULATION
Sunday World	Independent	255,000
Sunday Independent	Fine Gael	235,000
Sunday Press	Fianna Fáil	217,450
Irish Independent (m)	Fine Gael	154,000
Irish Times (m)	Independent	94,000
Irish Press (m)/ *Evening Press*	Fianna Fáil	62,780
CORK		
Cork Examiner (m)	Fine Gael	58,824
Cork Evening Echo	Fine Gael	33,806

Waterford, Limerick, Galway, and many other smaller cities and towns have their own newspapers, most of them weeklies.

46 ORGANIZATIONS

There are many types of organizations in Ireland: trade unions and trade organizations, farmers' groups, sport and athletic associations, religious clubs, political clubs, clubs for the preservation and promotion of the Irish language and culture, and societies devoted to art, literature, music, drama, science, and other branches of learning. Oldest and best known of the learned societies are the Royal Dublin Society, founded in 1731, and the Royal Irish Academy, founded in 1785.

47 TOURISM, TRAVEL, AND RECREATION

Among Ireland's numerous ancient and prehistoric sights are a restored Bronze Age lake dwelling (crannog) near Quin in County Clare, burial mounds at Newgrange and Knowth along the Boyne, and the palace at the Hill of Tara, the seat of government up to the Middle Ages. Numerous castles may be visited, including Blarney Castle in County Cork, where visitors kiss the famous Blarney Stone. Some, such as Bunratty Castle and Knappogue Castle, County Clare, and Dungaire Castle, County Galway, offer medieval-style banquets, and some rent rooms to tourists.

Among Dublin's tourist attractions are the Trinity College Library, with its 8th-century illuminated *Book of Kells;* Phoenix Park, the largest enclosed park in Western Europe and home of the Dublin Zoo; and literary landmarks associated with such writers as William Butler Yeats, James Joyce, Jonathan Swift, and Oscar Wilde. Dublin has long been noted for its theaters, foremost among them the Abbey Theatre, Ireland's national theater, which was founded in 1904 by Yeats and Lady Gregory. Dublin was the EC's Cultural Capital of Europe for 1991, during which time the National Gallery, Civic Museum, and Municipal Gallery were all refurbished and several new museums opened, including the Irish Museum of Modern Art.

Ireland has numerous golf courses, some of worldwide reputation. Fishing, sailing, horseback riding, hunting, horse racing, and greyhound racing are other popular sports. The traditional sports of Gaelic football, hurling, and camogie (the women's version of hurling) were revived in the 19th century and have become increasingly popular. The All-Ireland Hurling Final and the All-Ireland Football Final are held in September.

Traditional musical events are held frequently, one of the best known being the All-Ireland Fleadh at Ennis in County Clare. Numerous parades, concerts, and other festivities occur on and around St. Patrick's Day holiday of 17 March.

Income from tourism and travel has contributed significantly to the net invisible earnings in Ireland's balance of payments. A total of 3,535,000 tourists entered Ireland in 1991, of whom 86% were from Europe and 10% from North America. Visitors from OECD, Commonwealth, and most Latin American countries do not require a visa.

48FAMOUS IRISH

A list of famous Irish must begin with St. Patrick (c.385–461), who, though not born in Ireland, represents Ireland to the rest of the world. Among the "saints and scholars" of the 6th to the 8th centuries were St. Columba (521–97), missionary to Scotland; St. Columban (540?–616), who founded monasteries in France and Italy; and Johannes Scotus Erigena (810?–80), a major Neoplatonic philosopher.

For the thousand years after the Viking invasions, the famous names belong to warriors and politicians: Brian Boru (962?–1014), who temporarily united the kings of Ireland and defeated the Vikings; Hugh O'Neill (1547?–1616), Owen Roe O'Neill (1590?–1649), and Patrick Sarsfield (d. 1693), national heroes of the 17th century; and Henry Grattan (1746–1820), Wolf Tone (1763–98), Edward Fitzgerald (1763–98), Robert Emmet (1778–1803), Daniel O'Connell (1775–1847), Michael Davitt (1846–1906), Charles Stewart Parnell (1846–91), Arthur Griffith (1872–1922), Patrick Henry Pearse (1879–1916), and Éamon de Valera (b.US, 1882–1975), who, with many others, fought Ireland's political battles. The politician and statesman Seán MacBride (1904-88) won the Nobel Peace Prize in 1974.

Irishmen who have made outstanding contributions to science and scholarship include Robert Boyle (1627–91), the physicist who defined Boyle's law relating to pressure and volume of gas; Sir William Rowan Hamilton (1805–65), astronomer and mathematician, who developed the theory of quaternions; George Berkeley (1685–1753), philosopher and clergyman; Edward Hincks (1792–1866), discoverer of the Sumerian language; and John Bagnell Bury (1861–1927), classical scholar. The nuclear physicist Ernest T. S. Walton (b. 1903) won the Nobel Prize for physics in 1951.

Painters of note include Sir William Orpen (1878–1931), John Butler Yeats (1839–1922), his son Jack Butler Yeats (1871–1957), and Mainie Jellet (1897–1944). Irish musicians include the pianist and composer John Field (1782–1837), the opera composer Michael William Balfe (1808–70), the tenor John McCormack (1884–1945), and the flutist James Galway (b. Belfast, 1939).

After the Restoration, many brilliant satirists in English literature were born in Ireland, among them Jonathan Swift (1667–1745), dean of St. Patrick's Cathedral in Dublin and creator of *Gulliver's Travels;* Oliver Goldsmith (1730?–74); Richard Brinsley Sheridan (1751–1816); Oscar Fingal O'Flahertie Wills Wilde (1854–1900); and George Bernard Shaw (1856–1950).

Thomas Moore (1779–1852) and James Clarence Mangan (1803–49) wrote patriotic airs, hymns, and love lyrics, while Maria Edgeworth (1767–1849) wrote novels on Irish themes. Half a century later the great literary revival led by Nobel Prize-winning poet-dramatist William Butler Yeats (1865–1939), another son of John Butler Yeats, produced a succession of famous playwrights, poets, novelists, and short-story writers: the dramatists Lady Augusta (Persse) Gregory (1859?–1932), John Millington Synge (1871–1909), Sean O'Casey (1884–1964), and Lennox Robinson (1886–1958); the poets AE (George William Russell, 1867–1935), Oliver St. John Gogarty (1878–1957), Pádraic Colum (1881–1972), James Stephens (1882–1950); Austin Clarke (1890–1974), Thomas Kinsella (b. 1928), and Seamus Heaney (b. 1939); the novelists and short-story writers George Moore (1852–1932), Edward John Moreton Drax Plunkett, 18th baron of Dunsany (1878–1957), Liam O'Flaherty (1896–1984), Seán O'Faoláin (b. 1900), Frank O'Connor (Michael O'Donovan, 1903–66), and Flann O'Brien (Brian O'Nolan, 1911–66). Two outstanding authors of novels and plays whose experimental styles have had worldwide influence are James Augustine Joyce (1882–1941), the author of *Ulysses,* and Samuel Beckett (1906–89), recipient of the 1969 Nobel Prize for literature.

The Abbey Theatre, which was the backbone of the literary revival, also produced many outstanding dramatic performers, such as Dudley Digges (1879–1947), Sara Allgood (1883–1950), Arthur Sinclair (1883–1951), Maire O'Neill (Mrs. Arthur Sinclair, 1887–1952), Barry Fitzgerald (William Shields, 1888–1961), and Siobhan McKenna (1923–1986). For many years Douglas Hyde (1860–1949), first president of Ireland (1938–45), spurred on the Irish-speaking theater as playwright, producer, and actor.

49DEPENDENCIES

Ireland has no territories or colonies.

50BIBLIOGRAPHY

A New History of Ireland. Oxford: Clarendon Press, 1993.

Ayearst, Morley. *The Republic of Ireland.* New York: New York University Press, 1970.

Bell, J. Bowyer. *The Secret Army: The I.R.A., 1916–1979.* Dublin: Academy, 1979.

Boyce, D. George. *Nationalism in Ireland.* Baltimore: Johns Hopkins University Press, 1982.

Breen, Richard. *Understanding Contemporary Ireland: State, Class, and Development in the Republic of Ireland.* New York: St. Martin's Press, 1990.

Cairney, C. Thomas. *Clans and Families of Ireland and Scotland: an Ethnography of the Gael, A.D. 500–1750.* Jefferson, N.C.: McFarland, 1989.

——. *Ireland from the Flight of the Earls to Grattan's Parliament, 1607–1782.* Dublin: Fallon, 1949.

——. *Ireland from Grattan's Parliament to the Great Famine, 1783–1850.* Dublin: Fallon, 1949.

Carty, James (ed.). *Ireland from the Great Famine to the Treaty of 1921.* Dublin: Fallon, 1951.

Cullen, L. M. *An Economic History of Ireland Since 1660.* New York: Harper & Row, 1972.

Daly, Mary E. *Industrial Development and Irish National Identity, 1922–1939.* Syracuse, N.Y.: Syracuse University Press, 1992.

De Breffny, Brian (ed.). *Ireland: A Cultural Encyclopedia.* New York: Facts on File, 1984.

Edwards, Ruth Dudley. *An Atlas of Irish History.* New York: Harper & Row, 1974.

——. *A New History of Ireland.* Toronto: University of Toronto Press, 1972.

Foster, R. F. (ed.). *The Oxford Illustrated History of Ireland.* New York: Oxford University Press, 1989.

Freeman, Thomas Walter. *Ireland: Its Physical, Historical, Social and Economic Geography.* New York: Dutton, 1950.

Fulton, John, Dr. *The Tragedy of Belief: Division, Politics, and Religion in Ireland.* New York: Oxford University Press, 1991.

Hout, Michael. *Following in Father's Footsteps: Social Mobility in Ireland.* Cambridge, Mass.: Harvard University Press, 1989.

Inglis, Tom. *Moral Monopoly: The Catholic Church in Modern Irish Society.* New York: St. Martin's Press, 1987.

James, Francis Godwin. *Ireland in the Empire, 1688–1770.* Cambridge, Mass.: Harvard University Press, 1973.

Johnson, Paul. *Ireland, Land of Troubles—A History from the Twelfth Century to the Present Day.* London: Eyre Methuen, 1980.

Kennedy, Kieran Anthony. *The Economic Development of Ireland in the Twentieth Century.* London; New York: Routledge, 1988.

Lee, Joseph. *Ireland, 1912–1985: Politics and Society.* New York: Cambridge University Press, 1989.

Lyons, F. S. L. *Ireland Since the Famine*. New York: Scribner, 1971.

MacDonagh, Oliver, et al. (eds.), *Irish Culture and Nationalism, 1750–1950*. New York: St. Martin's, 1984.

Newman, Peter R. *Companion to Irish History 1603–1921: From the Submission of Tyrone to Partition*. New York: Facts On File, 1991.

O'Day, Alan and John Stevenson (eds.). *Irish Historical Documents since 1800*. Savage, Md.: Barnes & Noble Books, 1992.

O'Hegarty, Patrick Sarsfield. *History of Ireland Under the Union, 1801–1922*. London: Methuen, 1952.

Philpin, C. H. E. (ed.). *Nationalism and Popular Protest in Ireland*. New York: Cambridge University Press, 1987.

Sawyer, Roger. *'We are but Women': Women in Ireland's History*. New York: Routledge, 1993.

Shannon, Michael Owen. *Northern Ireland*. Santa Barbara, CA: Clio Press, 1991.

Somerset Fry, Plantagenet. *A History of Ireland*. New York: Routledge, 1988.

Wiles, James L. and Richard B. Finnegan. *Aspirations and Realities: A Documentary History of Economic Development Policy in Ireland since 1922*. Westport, Conn.: Greenwood Press, 1993.

ITALY

Italian Republic
Repubblica Italiana

CAPITAL: Rome (Roma).

FLAG: The national flag is a tricolor of green, white, and red vertical stripes.

ANTHEM: *Fratelli d'Italia (Brothers of Italy).*

MONETARY UNIT: The lira (L) is a paper currency of 100 centesimi. There are coins of 5, 10, 20, 50, 100, 200, 500 and 1,000 lire, and notes of 1,000, 2,000, 5,000, 10,000, 50,000, and 100,000 lire. The lira has floated freely since February 1973. L1 = $0.0006 (or $1 = L1,611.3).

WEIGHTS AND MEASURES: The metric system is the legal standard.

HOLIDAYS: New Year's Day, 1 January; Epiphany, 6 January; Liberation Day, 25 April; Labor Day, 1 May; Assumption, 15 August; All Saints' Day, 1 November; National Unity Day, 5 November; Immaculate Conception, 8 December; Christmas, 25 December; St. Stephen's Day, 26 December. Easter Monday is a movable holiday. In addition, each town has a holiday on its saint's day.

TIME: 1 PM = noon GMT.

¹LOCATION, SIZE, AND EXTENT

Situated in southern Europe, the Italian Republic, including the major islands of Sicily (Sicilia) and Sardinia (Sardegna), covers a land area of 301,230 sq km (116,306 sq mi). Comparatively, the area occupied by Italy is slightly larger than the state of Arizona. The boot-shaped Italian mainland extends into the Mediterranean Sea with a length of 1,185 km (736 mi) SE-NW and a width of 381 km (237 mi) NE-SW. It is bordered on the N by Switzerland and Austria, on the NE by Slovenia, on the E by the Adriatic and Ionian seas, on the W by the Tyrrhenian and Ligurian seas, and on the NW by France, with a total external boundary length of 6,895 km (4,284 mi). Situated off the toe of the Italian boot, Sicily has an area of 25,708 sq km (9,926 sq mi). Sardinia, which is about 320 km (200 mi) NW of Sicily, covers an area of some 24,090 sq km (9,300 sq mi). Within the frontiers of Italy are the sovereign Republic of San Marino, with an area of 61.2 sq km (23.6 sq mi), and the sovereign state of Vatican City, which covers 44 hectares (108.7 acres).

The long-disputed problem of Trieste, a 518-sq-km (200-sq-mi) area situated at the head of the Adriatic Sea, between Italy and Yugoslavia, was resolved in 1954, when Italy assumed the administration of Zone A, the city and harbor of Trieste, and Yugoslavia of Zone B, the rural hinterlands of the Istrian Peninsula. A treaty of October 1975 made the partition permanent.

Italy's capital city, Rome, is located in the westcentral part of the country.

²TOPOGRAPHY

Except for the fertile Po River Valley in the north and the narrow coastal belts farther south, Italy's mainland is generally mountainous, with considerable seismic activity. During Roman times, the city of Pompeii, near present-day Naples (Napoli), was devastated first by an earthquake in AD 63 and then by the eruption of Mt. Vesuvius (1,277 m/4,190 ft) in AD 79. In recent times, an earthquake in northeastern Italy on 6 May 1976 left more than 900 people dead, and a quake in the south on 23 November 1980 (and subsequent aftershocks) claimed at least 4,500 lives.

The Alpine mountain area in the north along the French and Swiss borders includes three famous lakes—Como, Maggiore, and Garda—and gives rise to six small rivers that flow southward into the Po. Italy's highest peaks are found in the northwest in the Savoy Alps, the Pennines, and the Graian chain. They include Mont Blanc (4,807 m/15,771 ft), on the French border; Monte Rosa (Dufourspitze, 4,634 m/15,203 ft) and the Matterhorn (Monte Cervino, 4,478 m/14,692 ft), on the Swiss border; and Gran Paradiso (4,061 m/13,323 ft). Marmolada (3,342 m/10,965 ft), in northeast Italy, is the highest peak in the Dolomites.

At the foot of the Alps, the Po River, the only large river in Italy, flows from west to east, draining plains covering about 17% of Italy's total area and forming the agricultural and industrial heartland. The Apennines, the rugged backbone of peninsular Italy, rise to form the southern border of the Po Plain. Numerous streams and a few small rivers, including the Arno and the Tiber (Tevere), flow from the Apennines to the west coast. The highest peak on the peninsula is Corvo Grande (2,912 m/9,554 ft). Vesuvius is the only active volcano on the European mainland.

While altitudes are lower in southern Italy, the Calabrian coast is still rugged. Among the narrow, fertile coastal plains, the Plain of Foggia in northern Apulia, which starts along the Adriatic, and the more extensive lowland areas near Naples, Rome, and Livorno (Leghorn) are the most important. The mountainous western coastline forms natural harbors at Naples, Livorno, La Spezia, Genoa (Genova), and Savona, and the low Adriatic coast permits natural ports at Venice (Venezia), Bari, Brindisi, and Taranto.

Sicily, separated from the mainland by the narrow Strait of Messina, has the Madonie Mountains, a continuation of the Apennines, and the Plain of Catania, the largest plain on the island. Mount Etna (3,369 m/11,053 ft) is an isolated and active volcano in the northeast.

Sardinia, in the Tyrrhenian Sea, is generally mountainous and culminates in the peak of Gennargentu (1,834 m/6,017 ft). The largest and most fertile plains are the Campidano in the south and the Ozieri in the north. The principal bay is Porto Torres in the Gulf of Asinara.

3CLIMATE

Climate varies with elevation and region. Generally, however, Italy is included between the annual isotherms of 11°C and 19°C (52°F and 66°F). The coldest period occurs in December and January, the hottest in July and August. In the Po Plain, the average annual temperature is about 13°C (55°F); in Sicily, about 18°C (64°F); and in the coastal lowlands, about 14°C (57°F). The climate of the Po Valley and the Alps is characterized by cold winters, warm summers, and considerable rain, falling mostly in spring and autumn, with snow accumulating heavily in the mountains. The climate of the peninsula and of the islands is Mediterranean, with cool, rainy winters and hot, dry summers. Mean annual rainfall varies from about 50 cm (20 in) per year, on the southeast coast and in Sicily and Sardinia, to over 200 cm (80 in), in the Alps and on some westerly slopes of the Apennines. Frosts are rare in the sheltered western coastal areas, but severe winters are common in the Apennine and Alpine uplands.

4FLORA AND FAUNA

Plants and animals vary with area and altitude. Mountain flora is found above 1,980 m (6,500 ft) in the Alps and above 2,290 m (7,500 ft) in the Apennines. The highest forest belt consists of conifers; beech, oak, and chestnut trees grow on lower mountain slopes. Poplar and willow thrive in the Po Plain. On the peninsula and on the larger islands, Mediterranean vegetation predominates: evergreens, holm oak, cork, juniper, bramble, laurel, myrtle, and dwarf palm.

Although larger mammals are scarce, chamois, ibex, and roe deer are found in the Alps, and bears, chamois, and otters inhabit the Apennines. Ravens and swallows are characteristic birds of Italy. Abundant marine life inhabits the surrounding seas.

5ENVIRONMENT

Italy has been slow to confront its environmental problems. Central government agencies concerned with the environment are the Ministry for Ecology (established in 1983), the Ministry of Culture and Environmental Quality, the National Council for Research, and the Ministry for Coordination of Scientific and Technological Research. Localities also have responsibility for environmental protection, but most of the burden of planning and enforcement falls on regional authorities. The most active environmentalist public group in the mid-1980s was Italia Nostra. The principal antipollution statute is Law No. 319 of 1976 (the Merli Law), which controls the disposal of organic and chemical wastes; enforcement, however, has proved difficult. Air pollution is a significant problem in Italy. United Nations sources estimate that carbon monoxide emissions increased by 12% in the period between 1985 and 1989. In 1994, Italy produced 911.4 tons of hydrocarbon emissions and 498.1 tons of particulate emissions. The nation contributes 1.8% of the world's total gas emissions. Water pollution is another important environmental issue in Italy. The nation's rivers and coasts are polluted by industrial and agricultural contaminants. In 1994, the nation had 43.0 cubic miles of water with 59% used in farming activity and 27% used for industrial purposes. Italy's cities produce 19.1 million tons of solid waste per year. In July 1976, the city of Seveso, north of Milan (Milano), gained international attention after an explosion at a small Swiss-owned chemical plant released a cloud of debris contaminated by a toxic by-product, dioxin. More than 1,000 residents were evacuated, and pregnant women were advised to have abortions.

The long-term threat posed by flooding, pollution, erosion, and sinkage to the island city of Venice was highlighted by a disastrous flood in November 1966, which also damaged priceless art treasures and manuscripts in Florence (Firenze). The digging of artesian wells in the nearby mainland cities of Mestre and Marghera so lowered the water table that the Venetian islands sank at many times the normal annual rate of 4 mm (0.16 in) a year between 1900 and 1975; with the wells capped as a protective measure, Venice's normal sinkage rate was restored. As of the mid-1980s, however, little effort has been made to control the number and speed of powerboats on the Grand Canal (the churning of whose waters causes buildings to erode), nor had the national government begun to implement a master plan for Venice approved in principle three years earlier. Meanwhile, in Rome, city authorities, in January 1983, announced the start of a project designed, in part, to protect the Roman Forum and other ancient monuments from the vibration and pollution of motor vehicles.

Of Italy's mammal species, 3 are endangered, as well as 19 bird species and 210 plant species. As of 1987, endangered species in Italy included the Italian gray partridge, Italian spadefoot toad, and the scarce large blue and false ringlet butterflies. The Sardinian pika and Spengler's freshwater mussel were extinct.

6POPULATION

The census of 20 October 1991 recorded a population of 56,411,290, an increase of 0.3% over the 1981 census total of 56,243,395. A population of 58,148,000 has been projected for the year 2000, assuming a crude birthrate of 10.5 per 1,000 population, a crude death rate of 10.1, and a net natural increase of 0.4 during the 1995–2000 period. The average population density in 1991 was 187 per sq km (485 per sq mi). In 1995, it was estimated that 70% of the population was urban.

Rome, the capital and largest city, had an estimated 2,791,354 inhabitants at the end of 1990. Other major cities were Milan, 1,432,184; Naples, 1,206,013; Turin (Torino), 991,870; Genoa, 701,032; Palermo, 734,238; Bologna, 411,803; and Florence, 408,403.

7MIGRATION

Emigration, which traditionally provided relief from overpopulation and unemployment, now represents only a fraction of the millions of Italians who emigrated during the two decades prior to 1914. From 1900 to 1914, 16 of every 1,000 Italians left their homeland each year; by the late 1970s, that proportion had declined to about 1.5 per 1,000. Of the 65,647 Italians who emigrated in 1989, 26,098 went to the FRG; 16,347 to Switzerland; 5,277 to France; 4,076 to the US; and 23,849 to other countries. Immigration in 1989 totaled approximately 81,201 people, of whom West Germans accounted for 13,198. In 1990, 781,100 immigrants lived in Italy. This figure did not include some 600,000 who were believed to be illegal immigrants.

The overall impetus to emigrate has been greatly reduced by economic expansion within Italy itself and by the shrinking job market in other countries, especially Germany. Nevertheless, Germany had 560,100 Italian residents at the end of 1991, and France had 253,679 in 1990. Particularly significant in the first two decades after World War II was the considerable migration from the rural south to the industrial north, but by the mid-1980s, this flow had become insignificant.

8ETHNIC GROUPS

Italy has been the home of various peoples: Lombards and Goths in the north; Greeks, Saracens, and Spaniards in Sicily and the south; Latins in and around Rome; and Etruscans and others in central Italy. For centuries, however, Italy has enjoyed a high degree of ethnic homogeneity. The chief minority groups are the German-speaking people in the Alto Adige (South Tyrol) region and the Slavs of the Trieste area.

9LANGUAGES

Italian, the official language, is spoken by the vast majority of people. While each region has its own dialect, Tuscan, the dialect of Tuscany, is the standard dialect for Italian. French is spoken in

0   100   200 Miles

0   100   200 Kilometers

GERMANY

LIECH.

SWITZERLAND

Brenner Pass

AUSTRIA

A L P S

Bolzano

Adige

Piave

Udine

SLOVENIA

Trieste

HUNGARY

FRANCE

A L P S

Bergamo

Milan

Brescia

Verona

Padova

Po

Turin

Po

Parma

Venice

Gulf of Venice

CROATIA

Genoa

La Spezia

A P E N N I N E S

Bologna

Rimini

Ligurian Sea

Pisa

Florence

Arno

Livorno

SAN MARINO

Ancona

Perugia

Tiber

Terni

Pescara

Sassari

BOSNIA AND HERZEGOVINA

SERBIA

Adriatic Sea

Elba

CORSICA (Fr.)

VATICAN CITY

Rome

Foggia

Bari

ALBANIA

Sassari

SARDINIA

Tyrrhenian Sea

Naples

Ischia

POMPEII

Capri

Salerno

Taranto

Cagliari

Cape Carbonara

Gulf of Taranto

Cape Santa Maria di Leuca

Cosenza

Ionian Sea

Stromboli

Eolie Is.

Palermo

Messina

Reggio di Calabria

Cape Spartivento

SICILY

Catania

Siracusa

Pantelleria

Cape Passero

MEDITERRANEAN   SEA

LOCATION: 47°05′ to 36°38′N; 6°37′ to 18°31′E. **BOUNDARY LENGTHS:** Switzerland, 744 km (462 mi); Austria, 430 km (267 mi); Slovenia, 209 km (130 mi); total coastline including islands of Sicily and Sardinia, 7,458 km (4,634 mi); France, 514 km (320 mi). **TERRITORIAL SEA LIMIT:** 12 mi.

parts of Piemonte and in Val d'Aosta, where it is the second official language; Fruilian (related to Romansch of Switzerland) and Slovene are spoken in the northern parts of the Fruilia-Venezia Giulia region. German is widely used in Bolzano Province, or South Tyrol (part of the Trentino–Alto Adige region), which was ceded by Austria in 1919; under agreements reached between Italy and Austria in 1946 and 1969, the latter oversees the treatment of these German-speakers, who continue to call for greater linguistic and cultural autonomy.

¹⁰RELIGIONS

In 1990, the overwhelming majority (97.6%) of Italians professed the Roman Catholic faith. Roman Catholicism, affirmed as the state religion under the Lateran Treaty of 1929, lost that distinction under a concordat with the Vatican ratified in 1985. The Federation of the Protestant Churches had about 50,000 members in 1993, the two major denominations being the Lutheran Church and the Waldensians. There were also approximately 45,000 Muslims and 32,000 Jews.

¹¹TRANSPORTATION

Italy's highway system, one of the world's best, in 1991 totaled 294,410 km (182,946 mi) of roads, of which 45,170 km (28,068 mi) were national roads and 5,900 km (3,666 mi) were super-highways (autostrade). These expressways carry heavy traffic along such routes as Milan–Como–Varese, Venice–Padua, Naples–Salerno, and Milan–Bologna–Florence–Rome–Naples. A major highway runs through the Mont Blanc Tunnel, connecting France and Italy. In 1991 there were an estimated 28,200,000 passenger cars, 2,443,000 trucks, and 78,000 buses.

In 1991, Italy maintained a total railway trackage of 20,085 km (12,481 mi). The government owns and operates 80% of the rail system, including the principal lines. Connections with French railways are made at Ventimiglia, Tenda, and Mont Cenis; with the Swiss, through the Simplon and St. Gotthard passes; with the Austrian, at the Brenner Pass and Tarvisio; and with the Slovenian, through Gorizia.

The navigable inland waterway system, totaling about 2,400 km (1,490 mi), is mainly in the north and consists of the Po River, the Italian lakes, and the network of Venetian and Po River Valley canals. There is regular train-ferry and automobile-ferry service between Messina and other Sicilian ports. Freight and passengers are carried by ship from Palermo to Naples. Sardinia and the smaller islands are served by regular shipping. Regular passenger service is provided by hydrofoil between Calabria and Sicily, and between Naples, Ischia, and Capri.

As of the beginning of 1992, Italy had the twelfth largest merchant fleet in the world, with 493 vessels totaling 6,826,000 GRT. Genoa and Savona on the northwest coast and Venice on the Adriatic handle the major share of traffic to and from the northern industrial centers. Naples, second only to Genoa, is the principal port for central and southern Italy, while Livorno is the natural outlet for Florence, Bologna, and Perugia. Messina, Palermo, and Catania are the chief Sicilian ports, and Cagliari handles most Sardinian exports.

Italy's one national airline, Alitalia, which is 97% government-owned, maintains an extensive domestic and international network of air routes; in 1992, it transported 13,037,800 passengers. Rome's Fiumicino and Milan's Malpensa and Linate are among the most important airports, being served by nearly every major international air carrier. In 1992, Italian civil aviation performed a total of 29,672 million passenger-kilometers (18,438 million passenger-miles) and accounted for 1,257 million ton-km of freight.

¹²HISTORY

The Italian patrimony, based on Roman antecedents—with a tradition that extends over 2,500 years—is the oldest in Europe, next to Greece's. The Ligurians, Sabines, and Umbrians were among the earliest-known inhabitants of Italy, but in the 9th century BC they were largely displaced in central Italy by the Etruscans, a seafaring people, probably from Asia Minor. Shortly thereafter there followed conquests in Sicily and southern Italy by the Phoenicians and the Greeks. By 650 BC, Italy was divided into ethnic areas: the Umbrians in the north, the Ligurians in the northwest, the Latins and Etruscans in the central regions, and the Greeks and Phoenicians in the south and Sicily. The Etruscan civilization, a great maritime, commercial, and artistic culture, reached its peak about the 7th century, but by 509 BC, when the Romans overthrew their Etruscan monarchs, its control in Italy was on the wane. By 350 BC, after a series of wars with both Greeks and Etruscans, the Latins, with Rome as their capital, gained the ascendancy, and by 272 BC, they managed to unite the entire Italian peninsula.

This period of unification was followed by one of conquest in the Mediterranean, beginning with the First Punic War against Carthage (264–241 BC). In the course of the century-long struggle

against Carthage, the Romans conquered Sicily, Sardinia, and Corsica. Finally, in 146 BC, at the conclusion of the Third Punic War, with Carthage completely destroyed and its inhabitants enslaved, Rome became the dominant power in the Mediterranean. From its inception, Rome was a republican city-state, but four famous civil conflicts destroyed the republic: Sulla against Marius and his son (88–82 BC), Julius Caesar against Pompey (49–45 BC), Brutus and Cassius against Mark Antony and Octavian (43 BC), and Mark Antony against Octavian. Octavian, the final victor (31 BC), was accorded the title of Augustus ("exalted") by the Senate and thereby became the first Roman emperor. Under imperial rule, Rome undertook a series of conquests that brought Roman law, Roman administration, and Pax Romana ("Roman peace") to an area extending from the Atlantic to the Rhine, to the British Isles, to the Iberian Peninsula and large parts of North Africa, and to the Middle East as far as the Euphrates.

After two centuries of successful rule, in the 3d century AD, Rome was threatened by internal discord and menaced by Germanic and Asian invaders, commonly called barbarians (from the Latin word *barbari,* "foreigners"). Emperor Diocletian's administrative division of the empire into two parts in 285 provided only temporary relief; it became permanent in 395. In 313, Emperor Constantine accepted Christianity, and churches thereafter rose throughout the empire. However, he also moved his capital from Rome to Constantinople, greatly reducing the importance of the former. From the 4th to the 5th century, the Western Roman Empire disintegrated under the blows of barbarian invasions, finally falling in 476, and the unity of Italy came to an end. For a time, Italy was protected by the Byzantine (Eastern Roman) Empire, but a continuing conflict between the bishop of Rome, or pope, and the Byzantine emperor culminated in a schism during the first half of the 8th century.

From the 6th to the 13th century, Italy suffered a variety of invaders and rulers: the Lombards in the 6th century, the Franks in the 8th century, the Saracens in the 9th, and the Germans in the 10th. The German emperors (of the Holy Roman Empire), the popes, and the rising Italian city-states vied for power from the 10th to the 14th century, and Italy was divided into several, often hostile, territories: in the south, the Kingdom of Naples, under Norman and Angevin rule; in the central area, the Papal States; and in the north, a welter of large and small city-states, such as Venice, Milan, Florence, and Bologna.

By the 13th century, the city-states had emerged as centers of commerce and of the arts and sciences; in particular, Venice had become a major maritime power, and the city-states as a group acted as a conduit for goods and learning from the Byzantine and Islamic empires. In this capacity, they provided great impetus to the developing Renaissance, which between the 13th and 16th centuries led to an unparalleled flourishing of the arts, literature, music, and science. However, the emergence of Portugal and Spain as great seagoing nations at the end of the 15th century undercut Italian prosperity. After the Italian Wars (1494–1559), in which France tried unsuccessfully to extend its influence in Italy, Spain emerged as the dominant force in the region. Venice, Milan, and other city-states retained at least some of their former greatness during this period, as did Savoy-Piedmont, protected by the Alps and well defended by its vigorous rulers.

The French Revolution was brought to the Italian peninsula by Napoleon, and the concepts of nationalism and liberalism infiltrated everywhere. Short-lived republics and even a Kingdom of Italy (under Napoleon's stepson Eugene) were formed. But reaction set in with the Congress of Vienna (1815), and many of the old rulers and systems were restored under Austrian domination. The concept of nationalism continued strong, however, and sporadic outbreaks led by such inveterate reformers as Giuseppe Mazzini occurred in several parts of the peninsula down to 1848–49. This

Risorgimento (national rebirth) movement was brought to a successful conclusion under the able guidance of Count Camillo Cavour, prime minister of Piedmont. Cavour managed to unite most of Italy under the headship of Victor Emmanuel II of the house of Savoy, and on 17 March 1861, the Kingdom of Italy was proclaimed with Victor Emmanuel II as king. Giuseppe Garibaldi, the popular republican hero of Italy, contributed much to this achievement and to the subsequent incorporation of the Papal States under the Italian monarch. Italian troops occupied Rome in 1870, and in July 1871, it formally became the capital of the kingdom. Pope Pius IX, a longtime rival of Italian kings, considered himself a "prisoner" of the Vatican and refused to cooperate with the royal administration.

The Twentieth Century

The new monarchy aspired to great-power status but was severely handicapped by domestic social and economic conditions, particularly in the south. Political reforms introduced by Premier Giovanni Giolitti in the first decade of the 20th century improved Italy's status among Western powers but failed to overcome such basic problems as poverty and illiteracy. During World War I, Italy, originally an ally of the Central Powers, declared itself neutral in 1914 and a year later joined the British and French in exchange for advantages offered by the secret Treaty of London. At the Versailles Peace Conference, Italy, which had suffered heavy losses on the Alpine front and felt slighted by its Western allies, failed to obtain all of the territories that it claimed.

This disappointment, coupled with the severe economic depression of the postwar period, created great social unrest and led eventually to the rise of Benito Mussolini, who, after leading his Fascist followers in a mass march on Rome, became premier in 1922. He established a Fascist dictatorship, a corporate state, which scored early successes in social welfare, employment, and transportation; in 1929, he negotiated the Lateran Treaties, under which the Holy See became sovereign within the newly constituted Vatican City State and Roman Catholicism was reaffirmed as Italy's official religion (the latter provision was abolished in 1984). The military conquest of Ethiopia (1935–36) added to Italy's colonial strength and exposed the inability of the League of Nations to punish aggression or keep the peace.

Italy joined Germany in World War II, but defeats in Greece and North Africa and the Allied invasion of Sicily toppled Mussolini's regime on 25 July 1943. Soon Italy was divided into two warring zones, one controlled by the Allies in the south and the other (including Rome) held by the Germans, who had quickly moved in, rescued Mussolini, and established him as head of the puppet "Italian Social Republic." When German power collapsed, Mussolini was captured and executed by Italian partisans.

The conclusion of the war left Italy poverty-stricken and politically disunited. In 1946, Italy became a republic by plebiscite; in the following year, a new constitution was drafted, which went into effect in 1948. Under the peace treaty of 10 February 1947, Italy was required to pay $360 million in reparations to the USSR, Yugoslavia, Greece, Ethiopia, and Albania. By this time, the Italian economy, initially disorganized by Mussolini's dream of national self-sufficiency and later physically devastated by the war, was in a state of near collapse. By the early 1950s, however, with foreign assistance (including $1,516.7 million from the US under the Marshall Plan), Italy managed to restore its economy to the prewar level. From this point, the Italian economy experienced unprecedented development through the 1960s and 1970s.

Politically, postwar Italy has been marked by a pattern of accelerating instability, with 48 different coalition governments through 15 March 1988. In May 1981, the coalition of Prime Minister Arnaldo Forlani was brought down after it was learned that many government officials, including three cabinet ministers, were members of a secret Masonic lodge, Propaganda Due (P-2),

that had reportedly been involved in illegal right-wing activities. Left-wing terrorism, notably by the Red Brigades (Brigate Rosse), also plagued Italy in the 1970s and early 1980s. In January 1983, 23 Red Brigade members were sentenced to life imprisonment in connection with the kidnapping and murder of Prime Minister Aldo Moro in 1978; another 36 members received sentences of varying lengths for other crimes, including 11 murders and 11 attempted murders, committed between 1976 and 1980.

By 1986, however, internal security had improved. A major effort against organized crime was under way in the mid-1980s; over 1,000 suspects were tried and the majority convicted in trials that took place in Naples beginning in February 1985 and in Sicily beginning in February 1986.

Revelations of corruption and scandals involving senior politicians, members of the government administration, and business leaders rocked Italy in the early 1990s. Hundreds of politicians, party leaders, and industrialists were either under arrest or under investigation. The scandals discredited the major parties which had governed Italy since 1948 and gave impetus to new reformist groups.

In August 1993, Italy made significant changes in its electoral system. Three-fourths of the seats in both the Chamber and the Senate would be filled by simple majority voting. The remainder would be allocated by proportional representation to those parties securing at least 4% of the vote. The first elections under the new system in March 1994 resulted in a simplification of electoral alliances and brought a center-right government to power. Silvio Berlusconi, founder of the "Go Italy" movement, emerged as prime minister. Berlusconi, a successful Italian businessman, was a newcomer to Italian politics. He was supported by the Alliance for Freedom coalition which had received over 42% of the vote and 366 seats. Berlusconi's government, however, remained troubled in 1994 and charges of government corruption continued to surface.

13 GOVERNMENT

In a plebiscite on 2 June 1946, the Italian people voted (12,700,000 to 10,700,000) to end the constitutional monarchy, which had existed since 1861, and establish a republic. At the same time, a constituent assembly was elected, which proceeded to draft and approve a new constitution; it came into force on 2 January 1948. Under this constitution, as amended, the head of the Italian Republic is the president, who is elected for a seven-year term by Parliament, together with a total of 58 regional representatives. To be elected, the presidential candidate must receive either a two-thirds majority within the first three ballots or a simple majority on any subsequent ballot. Elections for a new president must be held 30 days before the end of the presidential term. Presidential powers and duties include nomination of the prime minister, who, in turn, chooses a Council of Ministers (cabinet) with the approval of Parliament; the power to dissolve Parliament, except during the last six months of the presidential term of office; representation of the state on important occasions; ratification of treaties after parliamentary authorization; and the power to grant pardons and commute penalties. Although the constitution limits presidential powers, a strong president can play an important political as well as ceremonial role.

Legislative power is vested in the bicameral Parliament, consisting of the Chamber of Deputies and the Senate. Members of the 630-seat lower house, the Chamber of Deputies, must be at least 25 years old and are elected for five-year terms. The 315 elective members of the Senate must be at least 35 years old and are elected for five-year terms. Former presidents of the republic are automatically life senators, and the president may also appoint as life senators persons who have performed meritorious service. Parliament is elected by universal direct vote of all persons over 18 years of age for deputies and 25 years of age for senators.

The constitution gives the people the right to hold referenda to abrogate laws passed by the Parliament; a referendum requires at least 500,000 signatures. Four referenda had been held by 1987 (against the legalization of divorce in 1974, against increased police powers and state financing of the political parties in 1978, and against government cuts in wage indexation in 1985), and in all of them, the voters approved the parliamentary decisions.

Major changes were made in the electoral system in 1993.

14 POLITICAL PARTIES

Italy has a complex system of political alignments in which the parties, their congresses, and their leaders often appear to wield more power than Parliament or the other constitutional branches of government.

There are nine prominent political parties, each of which is divided into as many as four political factions; in addition, there are numerous splinter groups on both the right and the left. Basic party policy is decided at the party congresses—generally held every second year—which are attended by locally elected party leaders. At the same time, the national party leadership is selected.

The most important political party has been the Christian Democratic Party (Partito Democrazia Cristiana—DC), which stands about midway in the political spectrum. In the 1983 national elections, the DC commanded 32.9% of the vote and won 225 seats in the Chamber of Deputies, down from 38.3% and 262 seats in 1979; in 1987, however, its electoral strength increased again, to 34.3% and 234 seats. From 1948 until 1981, the prime minister of Italy was consistently drawn from the ranks of the DC, whose religious and anticlass base constitutes both its strength and its weakness. Its relationship with the Church gives it added strength but also opens it to criticism by lay parties. Since it attracts its membership from all classes, the DC is also the most prone to internal dissension. As a result of scandals and corruption charges, the DC has lost considerable support, especially to regional movements in the north. The DC is referred to as the Popular Party and contested the 1994 election under the Pact for Italy Coalition.

To the right and the left of the DC stand a wide range of parties. The most important of these is the Italian Communist Party (Partito Comunista Italiano—PCI), the largest Communist party in Western Europe. The PCI had been second in power and influence only to the DC, but in the 1980s, its electoral base declined, despite the fact that it has effectively severed its ties with both the former USSR and Marxism-Leninism. In 1987, the PCI won only 24.6% and 177 seats, down from 29.9% and 198 seats in 1983 and 34.4% and 228 seats in 1976. It is now two parties: Communist Refounding and the Democratic Party, or the left.

Two center-left parties, the Italian Socialist Party (Partito Socialista Italiano—PSI) and the Italian Social Democratic Party (Partito Socialista Democratico Italiano—PSDI) combined in 1966 to form the United Socialist Party, but following a split in 1969, both reemerged as separate parties. In 1987, the PSI won 94 seats in the Chamber of Deputies, a gain of 21 over 1983, and the PSDI took 17 seats, a decline of 6 from 1983.

The Italian Republican Party (Partito Repubblicano Italiano—PRI), which is liberal on civil and human rights but conservative on economic issues, scored impressive gains in 1983, raising its number of deputies from 16 to 29, but in 1987, it gained only 21 seats; during 1981–82, Giovanni Spadolini, PRI party secretary, served as prime minister, Italy's first non-DC head of government since 1948. The Italian Liberal Party (Partito Liberale Italiano—PLI) also advanced in 1983 by winning 16 seats, for a gain of 7, but gained only 11 seats in 1987. The Radical Party (Partito Radicale) has been active on social issues in Italy, having sponsored

the 1974 referendum on divorce; in 1983, it won 11 seats in the Chamber, and in 1987, 13 seats. Other parties include, on the extreme right, the Italian Social Movement (Movimento Sociale Italiano—MSI), which elected 42 deputies in 1983 and 35 in 1987, and, on the far left, the Proletarian Democracy (Democrazia Proletaria—DP), which elected 7 deputies in 1983 and 8 in 1987. The Greens, an environmentalist group which entered the elections for the first time in 1987, won 13 seats.

Between 1946 and 1962, the PSI acted in unity with the PCI, forming an opposition bloc of about 40% in the Chamber. In early 1962, a new type of government—a center-left coalition—was formed, uniting the DC with all the leftist parties except the PCI. The crux of this government was a working alliance between the DC and the PSI, which previously had been closely bound to the PCI. The objectives of the alliance were to isolate the PCI by drawing the PSI closer to the center parties and to undercut the Communists' popularity by legislating needed social and economic reforms. Center-left coalitions continued to form the governments after 1962, but these alliances were notoriously unstable. Furthermore, the alliance of the moderate left parties with the weakened DC actually strengthened the Communists as an opposition party in the 1970s.

In the late 1970s, a "historic compromise" was reached between the DC and the Communists, who were allowed to participate in the policy-making (1977–79) but had no direct role in the government. The strong gains made by the smaller political parties in 1983 led to the formation of a five-party coalition government (DC, PSI, PRI, PSDI, and PLI) under PSI leader Bettino Craxi on 4 August 1983. This marked the first time that a Socialist held the premiership. His government, which lasted until June 1986, was the longest postwar government. In July 1987, Giovanni Goria was confirmed by the Chamber of Deputies as the new DC prime minister; in November, however, his government collapsed when the PLI withdrew from the governing coalition. Goria formed a new government, but it collapsed in February 1988.

The elections of April 1992 failed to resolve Italy's political and economic problems. The election of March 1994 under new voting rules resulted in the following distribution of seats in the Chamber (lower House): Alliance for Freedom, 42.9% (Forza Italia, Northern League, National Alliance—366 seats); Progressive Alliance, 32.2% (Democratic Party, or the left, Communist Refounding, Democratic Alliance, Greens, Reformers—213 seats); and Pact for Italy, 15.7% (Popular Party, others—46 seats).

15 LOCAL GOVERNMENT

Under the terms of the 1948 constitution, Italy is divided into 20 regions. Five of these regions (Sicily, Sardinia, Trentino–Alto Adige, Friuli–Venezia Giulia, and the Valle d'Aosta) have been granted semiautonomous status, although the powers of self-government delegated from Rome have not been sufficient to satisfy the militant separatists, especially in Alto Adige. Legislation passed in 1968 granted the remaining 15 regions an even more limited degree of autonomy. All the regions elect regional councils, which have so far been dominated by the Christian Democrats and the Communists, although various regional movements have been gaining ground. The councils, which are elected by universal franchise under a proportional system analogous to that of the Parliament at Rome, are empowered to choose regional presidents and regional governing boards. A commissioner in each region represents the federal government.

The regions are subdivided into 94 provinces, which are, in turn, subdivided into communes—townships, cities, and towns—that constitute the basic units of local administration. Communes are governed by councils elected by universal suffrage for a four-year term. The council elects a mayor and a board of aldermen to administer the commune.

[16]JUDICIAL SYSTEM

Minor legal matters may be brought before conciliators, while civil cases and lesser criminal cases are tried before judges called pretori. There are 159 tribunals, each with jurisdiction over its own district; 90 assize courts, where cases are heard by juries; and 26 assize courts of appeal. The Court of Cassation in Rome acts as the last instance of appeal in all cases except those involving constitutional matters, which are brought before the special Constitutional Court. For many years, the number of civil and criminal cases has been increasing more rapidly than the judicial resources to deal with them.

The law assuring criminal defendants a fair and public trial is largely observed in practice. The 1989 amendments to the criminal procedure law both streamline the process and provide for a more adversarial system along the American model.

By law the judiciary is autonomous and independent of the executive branch. In practice, there has been a perception that magistrates were subject to political pressures and that political bias of individual magistrates could affect outcomes. Since the start of "clean hands" investigations of the judiciary in 1992 for kickbacks and corruption, magistrates have taken steps to distance themselves from political parties and other pressure groups.

[17]ARMED FORCES

Since 1949 Italy, as a member of NATO, has maintained large and balanced modern forces. The total strength in 1993 was 354,000 (211,000 conscripts), not including 111,400 carabinieri, or paramilitary national police. The total reserve strength was 584,000. Conscripted military service is for 12 months for all services.

Army personnel numbered 230,000, including 167,000 conscripts. Navy personnel totaled 48,000, including 19,000 conscripts and 800 marines, and 600 naval commandos. The air force had a total strength of 76,000 personnel, including 25,000 conscripts, and 449 combat aircraft. There were 20 air defense missile groups with 96 Nike Hercules missiles.

Italy's military budget for 1991 was $22.7 billion or 2.2% of gross domestic product. The nation was one of the world's major producers of armaments until 1985, after which its arms exports fell from $1.5 billion to $100 million by 1991.

Italy has troops committed to six peacekeeping operations.

[18]INTERNATIONAL COOPERATION

Italy has been a member of the UN since 14 December 1955 and participates in the ECE and all UN nonregional specialized agencies. It is a member of the Council of Europe, the EC, NATO, and the OECD and is a signatory to GATT and the Law of the Sea. Italy also participates in the Asian Development Bank and IDB and enjoys permanent observer status at the OAS. In 1982–83, Italy contributed military units to the international peacekeeping force in Beirut, Lebanon, and in 1987, it sent ships to protect tankers in the Persian Gulf.

[19]ECONOMY

As the Italian economy has expanded since the 1950s, its structure has changed markedly. Agriculture, which in 1953 contributed 25% of the GNP and employed 35% of the labor force, contributed in 1968 only 11% of the GNP and employed only 22% of the active labor force—despite continued increases in the value of agricultural production. Agriculture's contribution to the GDP further declined to 8.4% in 1974 and 3.3% in 1992. Conversely, the importance of industry has increased dramatically. Industrial output almost tripled between 1953 and 1968 and generally showed steady growth during the 1970s; in 1992, industry (including fuel, power, and construction) contributed 32.1% to the GDP. Precision machinery and motor vehicles have led the surge in manufacturing, and Italy has generally been a leader in

European industrial design and fashion in recent decades. By 1989, Italy had the fifth largest OECD economy.

Despite this economic achievement, a number of basic problems remain. Natural resources are limited, landholdings often are poor and invariably too small, industrial enterprises are of minimal size and productivity, and industrial growth has not been translated into general prosperity. The rise in petroleum prices during the mid-1970s found Italy especially vulnerable, since the country is almost totally dependent on energy imports. Partly because of increased energy costs, inflation increased from an annual rate of about 5% in the early 1970s to an annual average of 16.6% during 1975–81, well above the OECD average; but subsequently, inflation was brought down to 14.6% in 1983; 10.8% in 1984; 5.9% in 1986; and 4.7% in 1987. The 1988–92 average rate was 5.9% and the 1993 rate was 4.2%. From 1981 through 1983, Italy endured a period of recession, with rising budget deficits, interest rates above 20%, virtually no real GDP growth, and an unemployment rate approaching 10%. Between 1984 and 1991, GDP growth averaged 2.7% a year. The 1992 growth rate was 0.9%. In 1993, GDP fell 0.7%, the first yearly drop since 1975. Unemployment increased to 12% during 1987–89. It dropped to 10.9% in 1991 but rose again to 11.5% in 1992 and 13.8% in 1993.

[20]INCOME

In 1992, Italy's GNP was $1,186,568 million at current prices, or $20,510 per capita. For the period 1985–92 the average inflation rate was 6.6%, resulting in a real growth rate in per capita GNP of 2.3%.

In 1992 the GDP was $1.012 trillion in current US dollars. It is estimated that in 1991 agriculture, hunting, forestry, and fishing contributed 3% to GDP; mining, quarrying, and manufacturing, 21%; electricity, gas, and water, 5%; construction, 6%; wholesale and retail trade, 18%; transport, storage, and communication, 6%; finance, insurance, real estate, and business services, 25%; community, social, personal services, and other sources, 15%.

[21]LABOR

A substantial reduction in unemployment, a redistribution of the labor force, and record increases in wages constituted the most significant changes in the Italian labor sector during the expansionary 1954–73 period. Unemployment in 1954 had run as high as 3 million; the number decreased to 694,000 (or 3.5% of the labor force) at the end of 1968, but increased to 2,713,000 (11.3%) in January 1992. Overall employment, which was 19,633,000 in 1963, rose only to 21,366,000 in 1992. Employment in agriculture declined from 26.9% of the active labor force in 1963 to 16% in 1974 and to 7.9% in 1992. Employment in industry increased from 40.7% in 1963 to 42.4% in 1974 before dropping to 31.6% (including construction) in 1992. In recent years, employment in services has increased rapidly, accounting for 60.5% of total employment in 1992.

There are three major trade union confederations. The largest group, the General Confederation of Italian Workers (CGIL), has a membership of about 5.2 million workers and was controlled by the PCI. The Italian Confederation of Workers' Labor Unions (CISL), formed in 1950 and now the second-largest labor group, is closely affiliated with the DC; it has an estimated membership of 3.6 million. The Italian Union of Labor (UIL), with a membership of 1.6 million, is associated with the Socialists, Social Democrats, and Republicans. There are several other national federations, the largest being the Italian Confederation of National Workers' Unions (CISNAL). In all, about 200 unions exist in Italy, with 4 million members.

Collective labor contracts, which establish wages and salaries in every major field, generally provide for a 38-hour workweek, 10 paid statutory holidays, and a paid annual leave varying from

2 to 4 weeks. All employees in Italy receive an extra month's pay at the end of the year; contracts may also call for additional compulsory bonuses, and basic wages and salaries are adjusted quarterly to compensate for increases in the cost of living. In 1991, there were officially 791 strikes involving 2,952,240 workers resulting in 20,895,000 work hours not worked.

22AGRICULTURE

Of Italy's total land area of 29.4 million hectares (72.6 million acres), 11.9 million hectares (29.6 million acres), or 40.7% of the land, were under annual or permanent crops in 1991. Small, individually owned farms predominate, with the majority 3 hectares (7.4 acres) or less. In 1991, about 8% (1.7 million persons) of civilian employment was in the agricultural sector.

Despite government efforts, the agricultural sector has shown little growth in recent decades. The imports of agricultural products increased from $19.6 billion in 1987 to $24.5 billion in 1992. Italy has to import about half of its meat. The land is well suited for raising fruits and vegetables, both early and late crops, and these are the principal agricultural exports. Although yields per hectare in sugar beets, tomatoes, and other vegetable crops have increased significantly, both plantings and production of wheat declined between 1974 and 1981. Thus, although Italy remains a major cereal-producing country, wheat must be imported. The government controls the supply of domestic wheat and the import of foreign wheat.

Production of major agricultural products in 1992 (in millions of tons) included sugar beets, 14.3; wheat, 8.9; corn, 7.17; tomatoes, 5.49; potatoes, 2.49; oranges, 1.8; and lemons and limes, 0.73. In 1992, Italy produced 6.38 million tons of wine (second only to France) and 436,000 tons of olive oil. A scandal over adulterated wine in March–April 1986, when it transpired that the adulteration caused at least 20 deaths, was a serious blow to the industry. In 1992, tobacco production was 143,000 tons. In 1991, Italy had 1,459,000 tractors (fifth in the world) and 47,000 harvester-threshers.

23ANIMAL HUSBANDRY

In 1991, 4,880,000 hectares (12,058,000 acres) were being utilized as meadows and pastures. Both a growing need for fodder and insufficient domestic production compel Italy to import large amounts of corn. In 1992, the country had 8,549,000 hogs, 10,435,000 sheep, 1,314,000 goats, 384,000 horses, mules, and asses, and an estimated 139,000,000 chickens. That year, total meat production from indigenous hogs, cattle, sheep, and goats was 3,923,000 tons. Of the meat produced, 34% was pork, 27% was poultry, and 30% beef. Meat production falls short of domestic requirements, and about half of all meat consumed must be imported. Although Italy produced 9.8 million tons of cow milk in 1992 (production in 1979–81 was 10.5 million tons), dairy farming remains comparatively undeveloped. Both dairy and beef cattle are raised mainly in the north.

24FISHING

Although coastal and deep-sea fishing in the Mediterranean engage a sizable number of ships and men, the fishing industry is unable to meet domestic needs. The total catch in 1991 was 548,242 tons. Sponges and coral are commercially important.

25FORESTRY

The major portion of the 6.7 million hectares (16.6 million acres) of forest is in the Alpine areas of northern Italy; few extensive forests grow in central or southern Italy or on the islands. In 1991, a total of 8,393,000 cu m of roundwood were produced, with 51% used for fuel. Italy is a major importer of hardwood and softwood lumber, since its rugged terrain and disjointed forestland restrict domestic production.

26MINING

Italy is relatively poor in mineral resources, and production of most minerals declined in the late 1970s and early 1980s. Nevertheless, domestic production continues to supply a significant portion of Italy's need for some minerals, while mercury is exported. In 1991, 1,726,400 tons of low-grade coal (lignite and subbituminous) were mined, mostly in Sardinia. Alumina production has risen sharply, from 699,635 tons in 1987 to 804,596 tons in 1991. Production of other minerals in 1991 (in tons) included feldspar, 1,304,203 (world's leading producer); barite, 88,426; fluorspar, 98,518; cement, 40,000,000 (7th in the world); and pumice and pozzolan, 5,200,000 (1st in the world).

Marble and travertine quarrying from the famous mines at Massa and Carrara is still significant. Marble is quarried at hundreds of locations from the Alps to Sicily; the most important white marble-producing area was in the Apuan Alps near Tuscany. Important colored marble-producing areas include the Lazio region, Lombardy, the Po Valley, Puglia, Sicily, and Venice. The Carrara district produces 35% (700,000 tons) of the country's total white marble production. Reserves of several types are considered to be unlimited.

27ENERGY AND POWER

From 1970 to 1991, Italy's per capita consumption of energy rose by 70%. The National Hydrocarbon Agency (Ente Nazionale Idrocarburi—ENI), a state agency, controls the production and distribution of natural gas and petroleum. Natural gas production, which increased from 15 million cu m in 1937 to 15,273 million cu m in 1974, stood at 17,398 million cu m in 1991 and remains economically significant. Produced primarily in the Po River Valley, the gas is piped to the large cities of the north. Petroleum production rose dramatically from 14,000 tons in 1937 to 1,506,760 tons in 1968, and to 3,990,000 tons in 1991. Production falls far short of domestic needs; crude oil consumption in 1991 totaled 92.4 million tons.

Under a new energy plan adopted in October 1981 and revised in 1985, the government sought to reduce oil's share of the nation's primary energy requirement from 67% in 1980 to 50% by 1990; by 1992, however, oil accounted for 61.7% of primary energy consumption; natural gas, 26.9%; coal, 8.9%; and hydroelectricity, 2.5%. Italy imports about 75% of its energy; geothermal energy and hydroelectricity only represent 22% of national energy production. As of 1993, Italy's National Energy Plan called for an investment into the renewable energy sector (especially biomass, solar, and wind energy) of 4.5 trillion lira until the end of the decade.

The electric power industry was nationalized in 1962. Of the net installed capacity of 57.8 million kw in 1991, about 33% was in hydroelectric plants; this represents a decline from the early 1960s, when hydroelectric power accounted for 60% of installed capacity. National electrical output in 1991 was 222 billion kwh, an 11% increase from 1988. Of the 1991 output, conventional thermal plants produced 173.3 billion kwh (78%); hydroelectric, 45.6 billion kwh (21%); and geothermal, 3.1 billion kwh (1%).

28INDUSTRY

Characterized both by a few large industrial concerns controlling the greater part of industrial output and by thousands of small shops engaged in artisan-type production, Italian industry expanded rapidly in the postwar period. Industrial production almost tripled between 1955 and 1968 and has generally showed continued growth, although declines were registered in 1975 and 1981–83. In 1984, industrial production grew by 3.1%; in 1985, by 1.3%; in 1986, by 2.7%; and in 1987, by 3.9%. It averaged only 1.3% during 1988–92 and dipped in the last two years. In 1993, it dropped another 2.8%. The general index of industrial production—excluding the building industry—was 114.7 (1985 = 100) in

1992, with the lowest index for the extraction of solid combustibles (60) and the highest for office machinery and data processing (144.1). The lack of domestic raw materials and fuels represents a serious drag on industrial expansion.

Three state-holding companies have played a large role in industry: ENI (National Hydrocarbon Agency), IRI (Industrial Reconstruction Institute), and EFIM (Agency for Participation and Financing of Manufacturing Industry). IRI was the 16th-largest industrial company in the world in 1993, with sales of $50.5 billion; it had shareholdings in over 100 companies (including banks, electronics, engineering, and shipbuilding) and 333,600 employees in 1992. EFIM controls armaments and metallurgy industries. Debt-ridden EFIM was in the process of being dissolved in 1993, and privatization was being considered for the other two. Major private companies are the Fiat automobile company; the Olivetti company (office computers and telecommunications); the Montedison chemical firm; and the Pirelli rubber company. The bulk of heavy industry is concentrated in the northwest, in the Milan-Turin-Genoa industrial triangle. The government has made concerted efforts to attract industry to the underdeveloped southeast.

In 1992, steel production was 24,792,886 tons, down from 26,501,000 in 1980, and pig iron production totaled 10,432,447 tons. In 1992, refinery production included (in thousands of tons) gasoline, 18,951,375 tons; kerosene, 2,214,608; jet fuel, 1,868,743; diesel oil, 30,655,211; and residual fuel oil, 21,600,215.

The auto industry, which registered major gains during the 1960s and early 1970s, peaked in 1989, when 1,970,686 passenger cars were produced; in 1992, the production was 1,475,109 cars. Chemical industry output in 1992 included sulfuric acid, 2,773,478 tons; nitric acid, 1,773,741 tons; and caustic soda, 964,834 tons. The textile industry in 1992 produced 245,055 tons of cotton yarn. High-fashion items form a small but prestigious sector of the export market.

Production of other industrial commodities in 1992 was as follows: cement, 30,8778,000 tons; refrigerators, 4,010,639; washing machines, 5,132,477; television sets, 2,149,854; typewriters, 239,188; and 394,000 computers.

29SCIENCE AND TECHNOLOGY

The still-standing aqueducts, bathhouses, and other public works of both ancient republic and empire testify to the engineering and architectural skills of the Romans. The rebirth of science during the Renaissance brought the daring speculations of Leonardo da Vinci (including discoveries in anatomy, meteorology, geology, and hydrology, as well as a series of fascinating though ultimately impractical designs for a "flying machine"), advances in physics and astronomy by Galileo Galilei, and the development of the barometer by Evangelista Torricelli. To later Italian scientists and inventors the world owes the electric battery (1800), the electroplating process (1805), and the radiotelegraph (1895).

In 1988, Italy had 74,833 scientists and engineers and 38,287 technicians engaged in research and development. Expenditures on research and development totaled L13 billion. The National Research Council (Consiglio Nazionale delle Ricerche—CNR), founded in 1923, is the country's principal research organization. CNR institutes and associated private and university research centers conduct scientific work in mathematics, physics, chemistry, geology, technology, engineering, medicine, biology, and agriculture. Especially noteworthy are the National Institute of Nuclear Physics, in Rome, and the Enrico Fermi Center for Nuclear Studies, in Milan.

30DOMESTIC TRADE

Milan is the principal commercial center, followed by Turin, Genoa, Naples, and Rome. Genoa, the chief port of entry for

Milan and Turin, handles about one-third of Italy's trade; Naples is the principal entrepôt for central and southern Italy. Adriatic as well as Middle Eastern trade is carried through Ancona, Bari, and Brindisi.

Although small retail units predominate, department stores and supermarkets are playing an increasingly important role. In 1990 there were 373,942 food stores, 196,700 clothing stores, and 479,030 other outlets. There were also 229,966 mobile retail outlets.

Advertising in all forms is well developed, and the usual mass media (billboards, neon signs, newspapers and magazines, radio, cinema, and television) are used extensively. Market research is handled by over 100 firms.

Usual business hours in northern Italy are from 8 AM until noon and from 2 to 6 PM. In central and southern Italy, customary hours are 9 AM to 1 PM and 4 to 8 PM. Normal banking hours are 8:30 AM to 1:30 PM, Monday through Friday. Government offices are generally open weekdays from 8 AM to 2 PM.

31FOREIGN TRADE

Industrial products, textiles and apparel, and foodstuffs are Italy's most important exports. Fuels, meat, grain products, and various raw materials are among the major imports. Trade deficits were substantial between the end of World War II and 1955, but between 1956 and 1968 the deficit gradually declined, and Italy's trade balance continued in relative equilibrium through 1972. Then, as prices of crude oil and other raw-material imports rose, Italy again began registering growing trade deficits. In 1993, however, a large surplus was recorded because of an export boom that followed the devaluation of the lira in September 1992.

The bulk of manufactured imports come from EC countries and the US, which are also the leading customers for Italian exports. In 1992, over 58% of Italy's total trade was with other EC countries. Germany is Italy's single most active trading partner, accounting for 21% of total trade in 1992 (20.4% of exports and 21.6% of imports). France was next, with 14.5% in 1992. The US share of Italy's exports in 1992 was 7%, and the share of imports 5.2%. The Middle Eastern oil exporters' share of Italian trade increased sharply during the 1970s: Libya and Saúdi Arabia together accounted for 12.5% of Italy's 1981 import costs, but the share fell to 3.2% in 1992.

Italy's principal trade partners in 1992 (in billions of lire) were as follows:

	EXPORTS	IMPORTS	BALANCE
Germany	44,663	50,047	5,384
France	32,060	33,530	−1,490
U.S.	15,281	12,141	3,140
UK	14,392	13,284	1,108
Netherlands	6,879	13,713	−6,834
Switzerland	8,717	10,444	−1,727
Belgium/Luxembourg	7,297	11,239	−3,942
Spain	11,252	7,776	3,476
Other countries	78,895	79,917	−1,022
TOTALS	219,436	232,111	−12,675

32BALANCE OF PAYMENTS

Before the mid-1970s, Italy's payments position was relatively sound; one indication of Italy's financial strength during the 1950s and 1960s was its repayment to the US of postwar loans ahead of schedule. A 47% rise in import costs in 1974, due largely to a rise in the price of oil, helped throw Italy's balance of payments into a deficit exceeding $4.6 billion, financed in large part through IMF credits. Following large surpluses in the late 1970s (accomplished through huge net increases in services, especially tourism), Italy again registered deficits in the first half of the 1980s, except for 1983 when a small surplus ($555 million) was achieved. As tourism lagged, interest costs rose, and the cost of oil and coal imports more than doubled from L12,924 billion in 1979 to L30,397 billion in 1985. In 1992, Italy's trade surplus was an estimated L3.1 trillion, as compared with a trade deficit of L0.9 trillion in 1991. Following the devaluation and subsequent depreciation of the lira in 1992, Italian exporters have regained the competitiveness they had lost over the past several years due to high inflation and fixed exchange rates within the EC's exchange rate mechanism.

In 1992 merchandise exports totaled $177,650 million and imports $175,240 million. The merchandise trade balance was $2,410 million.

The following table summarizes Italy's balance of payments for 1991 and 1992 (in millions of US dollars):

	1991	1992
CURRENT ACCOUNT		
Goods, services, and income	−15,402	−19,650
Unrequited transfers	−6,029	−5,772
TOTALS	−21,432	−25,422
CAPITAL ACCOUNT		
Direct investment	−4,918	−2,944
Portfolio investment	−6,170	−13,129
Other long-term capital	15,856	−1,187
Other short-term capital	19,316	22,293
Reserves	6,407	31,717
TOTALS	30,491	36,750
Errors and omissions	−9,059	−11,328
Total change in reserves	14,248	21,036

33BANKING AND SECURITIES

The Bank of Italy (Banca d'Italia), the central bank, is the sole bank of issue and exercises credit control functions. It has branch offices in each provincial capital and headquarters in Rome. Currency in circulation increased from L968 billion at the end of 1948 to L11,704 billion at the end of 1974 and L46,841 billion in December 1986. In 1992 the money supply, as measured by M2, was L931.35 trillion.

As of 1991 there were 1,100 registered banks. Three banks are of nationwide standing: the Bank of Rome, Credito Italiano, and the Italian Commercial Bank. At the end of 1992 there were numerous foreign banks operating in Italy. The Istituto Mobiliare Italiano is the leading industrial credit institution; it also administers important government industrial investments. In 1987, the government privatized Mediobanca, another major industrial credit institution. As of December 1992, demand deposits at commercial banks totaled L445.73 trillion.

The Italian banking system was severely shaken by the bankruptcy in August 1982 of Banco Ambrosiano, following the mysterious death of its president, Roberto Calvi, in London. The bank's collapse, in which the Vatican Bank was implicated, came after it was unable to collect $1.4 billion in loans to Panamanian enterprises. Calvi was a member of P-2, the secret Masonic lodge, as was Michele Sindona, an Italian speculator whose financial collapse in 1974–75 had likewise embarrassed Italian and Vatican bankers.

There are 10 stock exchanges in operation. The most important is that in Milan (established in 1808). The others, in order of importance, are Rome (1812), Turin (1850), Genoa (1855), Bologna (1861), Florence (1859), Naples (1813), Venice (1600), Trieste (1755), and Palermo (1876). Since 1974, the markets have been regulated by the National Commission for Companies and the Stock Exchange.

34INSURANCE

The insurance industry is government supervised, and insurers must be authorized to do business. Automobile insurance was made compulsory in 1971, and coverage is also required for aircraft, powerboats, and yachts. In 1989 there were 248 insurance companies. Among the most important insurance companies in Italy are Assicurazioni Generali SpA, a joint-stock company, and the government-owned National Insurance Institute. Life insurance in force in 1992 totaled L250,000 billion. Insurance premiums for 1992 totaled an estimated $35.7 billion.

35PUBLIC FINANCE

Reflecting both increasing economic activity and the pressures of inflation, the Italian budget has expanded continually since 1950.

The following table shows actual revenues for 1988 and 1992 in billions of lire.

	1988	1992
REVENUE AND GRANTS		
Tax revenue	387,374	585,705
Non-tax revenue	10,982	17,108
Capital revenue	1,416	1,381
Grants	1,348	322
TOTAL	401,519	625,047
EXPENDITURES & LENDING MINUS REPAYMENTS		
General public service	37,899	—
Defense	18,415	—
Public order and safety	—	—
Education	41,890	—
Health	57,218	—
Social security and welfare	191,883	—
Housing and community amenities	2,881	—
Recreation, cultural, and religious affairs	4,857	—
Economic affairs and services	57,979	—
Lending minus repayments	12,332	—
TOTAL	516,857	—
Deficit/Surplus	−115,338	—

As the result of a budget reduction package, the 1993 public sector deficit was estimated at L150-170 trillion, or roughly 9.8%–10.9% of GDP.

In 1992 Italy's total public debt stood at 1,260,345 billion lire, of which 75,216 billion lire was financed abroad. The amount of Italy's public debt exceeded annual GDP in 1990, and interest payments are becoming an increasingly larger portion of the annual deficit.

36TAXATION

As of 1986, the major taxes on income included a personal income tax with progressive rates ranging from 10% on taxable incomes below L7.2 million to 51% on income exceeding L360 million; a corporate income tax with a normal rate of 36%; and a local income tax paid by individuals, corporations, and associations at a flat rate of 16.2%. Land and buildings are also taxed.

A turnover tax on goods and services (imposta generale sull'entrate) was replaced by a value-added tax (imposta sul valore aggiunto) in January 1973; the standard value-added tax rate was 19% in 1992. Other taxes on transactions include the stamp tax, contract registration tax, inheritance and gift taxes, a capital gains tax, and a transfer tax on land and buildings.

37CUSTOMS AND DUTIES

Italy's membership in the EC has greatly influenced its tariff structure. Duties on imports from EC members and their dependencies were gradually reduced following the Rome Pact in 1957 and disappeared by 1969, more than a year ahead of schedule. Duties on goods from Greece, which entered the EC in 1981, were reduced gradually and eliminated by 1986. Italy's adjustment of its tariff structure to that of the EC also has resulted in a substantial reduction of duties on products imported from areas other than the EC, including the US. Import duties average about 5%, and an excise tax is also levied.

38 FOREIGN INVESTMENT

Because of a lack of domestic venture capital, the government encourages foreign industrial investment through tax concessions on a case-by-case basis. Foreign ownership, however, is limited by law and includes the following regulations: foreign stockholders of "banks of national interest" have no voting rights; aircraft and airlines must be owned by Italians or by companies in which foreign investment is limited (33% maximum in aircraft and 40% in airlines); ships must be owned by firms established in Italy and in which Italians have a majority position; and insurance companies must obtain government authorization and appoint a resident Italian citizen as general agent. In an effort to increase confidence of foreign investors in Italy's economic development, the government has enacted legislation providing special incentives, particularly for investments in the south—Sicily, Sardinia, and the peninsula south of Rome. As of 1991, total direct foreign investment in Italy was $59.7 billion, up from $7.8 billion in 1973.

39 ECONOMIC DEVELOPMENT

Under Mussolini, business and labor were grouped into corporations that, in theory at least, jointly determined economic policy. Also, under the Fascist regime, direct government control over the economy was increased through the creation of powerful economic bodies, such as the Institute for Industrial Reconstruction. Although the corporative system disappeared after the fall of Mussolini, the concept of economic planning remained firmly implanted among the large Marxist parties, as well as among Christian Democratic leaders, who—by different means and for different reasons—sought to create a society free from the class warfare associated with a strictly liberal economic system.

Principal government objectives following World War II were (1) reconstruction of the economy; (2) stabilization of the currency; and (3) long-term, large-scale investment aimed at correcting the imbalance of the Italian economy and, in particular, the imbalance between northern and southern Italy. The first and second phases of this policy were accomplished by 1949. Then the government, supported by domestic financial and industrial groups and by foreign aid, principally from the US, embarked on the third and most important phase, best known as the Vanoni Plan (after former finance minister Ezio Vanoni). Notable in this development effort has been the Cassa per il Mezzogiorno, a government agency set up to develop southern Italy and attract private investment to the region. Between 1951 and 1978, total government spending on infrastructure in the south was $11.5 billion; additional low-cost loans totaled $13 billion, and outright grants amounted to $3.2 billion.

Simultaneously, direct government control of the economy has increased through such government agencies as ENI, whose activities expanded rapidly in the postwar era. The nationalization of the electric industry, in order to lay the industrial base for a more highly planned economy, and the creation of the National Economic Planning Board composed of leaders from government, industry, and labor are further indications of the importance attached to the concept of a planned Italian economy.

The combined effects of inflation, increased energy prices, and political instability posed serious economic problems during the 1970s. With Italy mired in recession in the early 1980s, economic policy was directed at reducing the public sector deficit,

tightening controls on credit, and maintaining a stable exchange rate, chiefly through a variety of short-term constraints. A period of recovery began in 1983, leading to expanded output and lower inflation but also to expanded unemployment. The economic policy aims in 1987 included the reduction of the public-sector deficit and unemployment. Furthermore, improvement in the external sector (due mainly to the fall of oil prices and depreciation of the dollar) led to liberalization of the foreign exchange market in May 1987.

Priorities of the early 1990s were cutting government spending, fighting tax evasion to reduce public debt, and selling off state-owned enterprises.

Italy provided $3,352 million in aid to developing countries in 1991, or 0.3% of GNP.

40 SOCIAL DEVELOPMENT

Social welfare legislation in Italy, begun in 1898, was redesigned by law in 1952 and has subsequently been expanded. Current social insurance is funded by employees, who pay under 8% of their salary, and by employers, whose contribution is roughly 19% or more of the total payroll. All workers and their families are covered and receive old-age, disability, and survivor pensions, unemployment and injury benefits, health and maternity coverage, and family allowances. Total current expenditures for social services in 1986 were L145,450 billion.

For 1985–90, the fertility rate was 1.3, down 14.2% from the previous 5-year period. Since 1978, abortion has been legal on unspecified grounds during the first 90 days of pregnancy; divorce, legalized by Parliament in 1970, was sanctioned by popular referendum in 1974.

Women fill only about 10% of managerial positions and are not well represented in the professions. They tend to work in areas such as teaching and public sector administrative jobs. Women are legally equal to men in marriage. Sexual harassment, while forbidden by labor agreements in some sectors, is not punishable by law. The government operates a public telephone service offering counseling to women on a variety of issues.

41 HEALTH

A national health plan, begun in 1980, seeks to provide free health care for all citizens, but certain minimum charges remain. It is financed by contributions from salaries, by employers, and by the central government. Most private hospitals have contracts with the national plan, but health care services are more highly concentrated in the northern regions of Italy. The shortage of medical personnel and hospital facilities in Italy's rural areas remains serious. Closure of a number of underutilized hospitals was planned, and the government has been making efforts to curb the state deficit in health expenditures; budgets and estimates are repeatedly more than demand. Total health care expenditures in 1990 were $82,214,000.

In 1989, there were 273,648 physicians, 53,948 pharmacists, 10,814 dentists, and 170,409 nurses. In 1992, there were 4.69 physicians per 1,000 people, with a nurse to doctor ratio of 0.6 and, in 1990, the population per physician was 210. In 1986, there were 1,798 hospitals (1,136 public and 662 private). In 1990, there were 7.5 hospital beds per 1,000 people with 481,000 beds.

The infant mortality rate, 72.1 per 1,000 live births in 1948, decreased to 8 per 1,000 by 1992. The overall mortality rate was 10.1 per 1,000 in 1993. Average life expectancy was estimated to be 77 years for women and men in 1992. The 1993 total population was 57.8 million, with a birth rate of 10 per 1,000 people. In 1992, there were 578,000 births with 78% of married women (ages 15 to 49) using contraception.

In 1992, immunization rates for children up to one year of age were: tuberculosis (6%); diphtheria, pertussis, and tetanus

(95%); polio (85%); and measles (50%). In 1990, major causes of death per 100,000 people were: communicable diseases and maternal/perinatal causes (38); noncommunicable diseases (425); and injuries (39). There were 25 reported cases of tuberculosis per 100,000 in 1990.

42HOUSING

Italy's housing and public building program was a major item in the general program of postwar reconstruction. Between 1940 and 1945, almost 20% of the habitable rooms in the country were destroyed. From June 1945 to June 1953, however, of the 6,407,000 rooms destroyed or severely damaged, 354,100 were rebuilt and 4,441,000 were repaired. Under a special housing program, originally instituted with funds from UNRRA and subsequently financed by employer and employee contributions, a total of 15 million rooms were constructed between 1953 and 1961, alleviating the nation's immediate housing problems. In 1981, 59% of all dwellings were owner occupied and 36% were rented. Almost 88% had indoor flush toilets, 99.5% had electricity, 59% had central heating, and 34% were heated by a stove or similar source. In 1985, a total of 39,385 new residential buildings were started. In 1992, the total number of housing units was 24,847,000.

43EDUCATION

In 1990, 97.1% adults were literate (males, 97.8% and females, 96.4%). Education is free and compulsory for eight years (for children between the ages of 6 and 14). In the academic year 1991, there were 22,911 public and private elementary schools providing education for 3,004,264 pupils. Also, 5,010,467 students were enrolled in secondary schools including 1,926,642 in vocational institutes and 183,711 in teacher training courses.

Higher education had a total enrollment of 1,533,202 in 1991 with 57,283 teaching staff. There are 41 state universities and 15 other universities, colleges, and higher learning institutes, including the University of Bologna (founded in the 11th century), the oldest in Italy and the University of Rome, which is the country's largest.

44LIBRARIES AND MUSEUMS

Italy, with its rich cultural heritage, is one of the world's great storehouses of books and art. Among its many of libraries, the most important are the national libraries in Florence (5,000,000 volumes), Rome (4,500,000), and Naples (1,672,000); the Este Library in Modena; the university libraries in Bologna and Naples; the Medici-Laurentian and Marucelliana libraries in Florence; and the Ambrosiana Library in Milan.

Numerous Italian cities, both large and small, boast world-renowned art collections. Among the more important are the Villa Giulia Museum and the National Gallery in Rome; the National Museum in Naples; the National Museum in Palermo; the Uffizi, Medici, Pitti, Bargello, and St. Mark's Museums in Florence; the National Museum in Cagliari, Sardinia; the Brera Museum in Milan; the Museum of Siena; the Archaeological Museum of Syracuse (Siracusa); the National Museum of Urbino; and the Academy of Venice.

45MEDIA

The Italian communications system is supervised or owned by the government. In 1991 there were 30,715,940 telephones in use. Post offices and telegraph offices also are operated by the government. Radiotelevisione Italiana (RAI), a government corporation, broadcasts on three radio and three television networks. Until 1976, RAI had a broadcasting monopoly, but since then, numerous private radio and television stations have begun operating. Advertising appears on RAI television, two of the three RAI radio networks, and on many private stations. In 1991

there were 24,300,000 television sets and 45,650,000 radios licensed in Italy.

Italy enjoys a free press, with vigorous expression of all shades of opinion. In 1991 there were 73 dailies with a combined daily circulation of some 6 million. The majority of papers are published in northern and central Italy, and circulation is highest in these areas. Rome and Milan are the most important publication centers. A considerable number of dailies are owned by the political parties, the Roman Catholic Church, and various economic groups. In general, the journalistic level of the Italian papers is high, and two dailies—Milan's *Corriere della Sera* and Turin's *La Stampa*—enjoy international respect.

The major daily newspapers (with their political orientations and estimated 1986 circulations) are as follows:

	ORIENTATION	CIRCULATION
La Repubblica (Rome)	Left-wing	882,600
Corriere della Sera (Milan)	Independent	715,000
La Stampa (Turin)	Liberal	586,400
Il Messaggero (Rome)	Left of center	379,000
La Nazione (Florence)	Right-wing	298,300
L'Unità (Rome-Milan)	Communist	281,000
Il Giornale (Milan)	Independent	266,000

The periodical press is becoming increasingly important. Among the most important periodicals are the pictorial weeklies—*Oggi, L'Europeo, Epoca, L'Espresso,* and *Gente.*

46ORGANIZATIONS

Italian society abounds with organizations of every description. Many of these are associated with or controlled by political parties, which have their ideological counterparts in labor organizations, agricultural associations, cultural groups, sports clubs, and cooperatives. Among the most important organizations are the National Confederation of Smallholders and the General Confederation of Italian Industry, which strongly influences economic policy. The General Confederation of Agriculture, the General Confederation of Trade, and the General Confederation of Master Craftsmen also are influential. There are chambers of commerce in most major cities. Catholic Action and the Catholic Association of Italian Workers are the most prominent of the religious organizations.

47TOURISM, TRAVEL, AND RECREATION

Tourism is a major industry in Italy, which ranked as the world's fourth most popular tourist destination in 1991, when 51,317,000 persons entered Italy as overnight tourists or same-day visitors. The greatest number of visitors (including repeaters) were from Switzerland, 10,228,678; Germany, 9,205,658; France 9,114,554; Austria, 5,540,654; and the former Yugoslavia, 4,367,181. In 1991, revenues from the tourist industry reached $19.67 billion. Citizens of the US and of many other countries need only a valid passport for short trips in Italy; for longer sojourns, a permit is necessary. No passport is required of nationals of EC member countries.

Among Italy's manifold tourist attractions are the artistic and architectural treasures of Rome and Florence; the thousands of historic churches and galleries in smaller cities; the canals and palaces of Venice; the ruins of ancient Pompeii; the Shroud of Turin, reputed to be the burial cloth of Jesus; and the delicacies of northern Italian cooking, as well as the heartier fare of the south. Tourists are also lured by Italy's many beaches and by excellent Alpine skiing. Italians enjoy a wide variety of sports, including football (soccer), bowling, tennis, track, and swimming. Italy won the World Cup in soccer three times, in 1934 (as host), 1938, and 1982. Cortina d'Ampezzo, in the Dolomites, was the site of the 1956 Winter Olympics, and Rome hosted the Summer Olympics in 1960.

⁴⁸FAMOUS ITALIANS

The Italian peninsula has been at the heart of Western cultural development at least since Roman times. Important poets of the republic and empire were Lucretius (Titus Lucretius Carus, 96?–55 BC), Gaius Valerius Catullus (84?–54 BC), Vergil (Publius Vergilius Maro, 70–19 BC), Horace (Quintus Horatius Flaccus, 65–8 BC), and Ovid (Publius Ovidius Naso, 43 BC–AD 18). Also prominent in Latin literature were the orator-rhetorician Marcus Tullius Cicero (106–43 BC); the satirists Gaius Petronius Arbiter (d.AD 66) and Juvenal (Decimus Junius Juvenalis, AD 60?–140?); the prose writers Pliny the Elder (Gaius Plinius Secundus, AD 23–79), his nephew Pliny the Younger (Gaius Plinius Caecilius Secundus, AD 61?–113?), and Lucius Apuleius (AD 124?–170?); and the historians Sallust (Gaius Sallustius Crispus, 86–34 BC), Livy (Titus Livius, 59 BC–AD 17), Cornelius Tacitus (AD 55?–117), and Suetonius (Gaius Suetonius Tranquillus, AD 69?–140). Gaius Julius Caesar (100?–44 BC), renowned as a historian and prose stylist, is even more famous as a military and political leader. The first of the Roman emperors was Octavian (Gaius Octavianus, 63 BC–AD 14), better known by the honorific Augustus. Noteworthy among later emperors are the tyrants Caligula (Gaius Caesar Germanicus, AD 12–41) and Nero (Lucius Domitius Ahenobarbus, AD 37–68), the philosopher-statesman Marcus Aurelius (Marcus Annius Verius, AD 121–180), and Constantine I (the Great; Flavius Valerius Aurelius Constantinus, b. Moesia, 280?–337), who was the first to accept Christianity. No history of the Christian Church during the medieval period would be complete without mention of such men of Italian birth as St. Benedict of Nursia (480?–543?), Pope Gregory I (St. Gregory the Great, 540?–604), St. Francis of Assisi (1182?–1226), and the philosopher-theologians St. Anselm (1033?–1109) and St. Thomas Aquinas (1225–74).

No land has made a greater contribution to the visual arts. In the 13th and 14th centuries there were the sculptors Niccolò Pisano (1220–84) and his son Giovanni (1245–1314); the painters Cimabue (Cenni di Pepo, 1240–1302?), Duccio di Buoninsegna (1255?–1319), and Giotto di Bondone (1276?–1337); and, later in the period, the sculptor Andrea Pisano (1270?–1348). Among the many great artists of the 15th century—the golden age of Florence and Venice—were the architects Filippo Brunelleschi (1377–1446), Lorenzo Ghiberti (1378–1455), and Leone Battista Alberti (1404–72); the sculptors Donatello (Donato di Niccolò di Betto Bardi, 1386?–1466), Luca della Robbia (1400–1482), Desiderio da Settignano (1428–64), and Andrea del Verrocchio (1435–88); and the painters Fra Angelico (Giovanni de Fiesole, 1387–1455), Sassetta (Stefano di Giovanni, 1392–1450?), Uccello (Paolo di Dono, 1397–1475), Masaccio (Tomasso di Giovanni di Simone Guidi, 1401–28?), Fra Filippo Lippi (1406?–69), Piero della Francesca (Pietro de' Franceschi, 1416?–92), Giovanni Bellini (1430?–1516), Andrea Mantegna (1431–1506), Antonio dei Pollaiuolo (1433–98), Luca Signorelli (1441?–1523), Perugino (Pietro Vannucci, 1446–1524), Sandro Botticelli (Alessandro Filipepi, 1447?–1510), Ghirlandaio (Domenico Currado Bigordi, 1449–94), and Vittore Carpaccio (1450–1522).

During the 16th century, the High Renaissance, Rome shared with Florence the leading position in the world of the arts. Major masters included the architects Bramante (Donato d'Agnolo, 1444?–1514) and Andrea Palladio (1508–80); the sculptor Benvenuto Cellini (1500–1571); the painter-designer-inventor Leonardo da Vinci (1452–1519); the painter-sculptor-architect-poet Michelangelo Buonarroti (1475–1564); and the painters Titian (Tiziano Vecelli, 1477–1576), Giorgione da Castelfranco (Giorgio Barbarelli, 1478?–1510), Raphael (Raffaelo Sanzio, 1483–1520), Andrea del Sarto (1486–1531), and Correggio (Antonio Allegri, 1494–1534). Among the great painters of the late Renaissance were Tintoretto (Jacopo Robusti, 1518–94) and Veronese (Paolo Cagliari, 1528–88). Giorgio Vasari (1511–74) was a painter, architect, art historian, and critic.

Among the leading artists of the Baroque period were the sculptor and architect Giovanni Lorenzo Bernini (1598–1680) and the painters Michelangelo Merisi da Caravaggio (1560?–1609), Giovanni Battista Tiepolo (1690–1770), Canaletto (Antonio Canal, 1697–1768), Pietro Longhi (1702–85), and Francesco Guardi (1712–93). Leading figures in modern painting were Umberto Boccioni (1882–1916), Amedeo Modigliani (1884–1920), Giorgio di Chirico (b. Greece, 1888–1978), and Giorgio Morandi (1890–1964). A noted contemporary architect was Pier Luigi Nervi (1891–1979).

Music, an integral part of Italian life, owes many of its forms as well as its language to Italy. The musical staff was either invented or established by Guido d'Arezzo (995?–1050). A leading 14th-century composer was the blind Florentine organist Francesco Landini (1325–97). Leading composers of the High Renaissance and early Baroque periods were Giovanni Pierluigi da Palestrina (1525–94); the madrigalists Luca Marenzio (1533–99) and Carlo Gesualdo, prince of Venosa (1560?–1613); the Venetian organists Andrea Gabrieli (1510?–86) and Giovanni Gabrieli (1557–1612); Claudio Monteverdi (1567–1643), the founder of modern opera; organist-composer Girolamo Frescobaldi (1583–1643); and Giacomo Carissimi (1605–74). Important figures of the later Baroque era were Arcangelo Corelli (1653–1713), Antonio Vivaldi (1678–1743), Alessandro Scarlatti (1660–1725), and his son Domenico Scarlatti (1683–1757). Italian-born Luigi Cherubini (1760–1842) was the central figure of French music in the Napoleonic era, while Antonio Salieri (1750–1825) and Gasparo Spontini (1774–1851) played important roles in the musical life of Vienna and Berlin, respectively. Composers of the 19th century who made their period the great age of Italian opera were Gioacchino Antonio Rossini (1792–1868), Gaetano Donizetti (1797–1848), Vincenzo Bellini (1801–35), and, above all, Giuseppe Verdi (1831–1901). Niccolò Paganini (1782–1840) was the greatest violinist of his time. More recent operatic composers include Ruggiero Leoncavallo (1853–1919), Giacomo Puccini (1858–1924), and Pietro Mascagni (1863–1945). Renowned operatic singers include Enrico Caruso (1873–1921), Luisa Tetrazzini (1874–1940), Titta Ruffo (1878–1953), Amelita Galli-Curci (1882–1963), Beniamino Gigli (1890–1957), Ezio Pinza (1892–1957), and Luciano Pavarotti (b.1935). Ferruccio Busoni (1866–1924), Ottorino Respighi (1879–1936), Luigi Dallapiccola (1904–75), Luigi Nono (b.1924), and Luciano Berio (b.1925) are major 20th-century composers. Arturo Toscanini (1867–1957) is generally regarded as one of the greatest operatic and orchestral conductors of his time; two noted contemporary conductors are Claudio Abbado (b.1933) and Riccardo Muti (b.1941). The foremost makers of stringed instruments were Gasparo da Salò (Bertolotti, 1540–1609) of Brescia, Niccolò Amati (1596–1684), Antonius Stradivarius (Antonio Stradivari, 1644–1737), and Giuseppe Bartolommeo Guarneri (del Gesù, 1687?–1745) of Cremona. Bartolommeo Cristofori (1655–1731) invented the pianoforte.

Italian literature and literary language began with Dante Alighieri (1265–1321), author of *The Divine Comedy,* and subsequently included Petrarch (Francesco Petrarca, 1304–74), Giovanni Boccaccio (1313–75), Lodovico Ariosto (1474–1533), Pietro Aretino (1492–1556), and Torquato Tasso (1544–95). An outstanding writer of the Baroque period was Metastasio (Pietro Trapassi, 1698–1782), and Carlo Goldoni (1707–93) was the most prominent playwright of the 18th century. The time of Italy's rebirth was heralded by the poets Vittorio Alfieri (1749–1803), Ugo Foscolo (1778–1827), and Giacomo Leopardi (1798–1837). Alessandro Manzoni (1785–1873) was the principal Italian novelist of the 19th century, and Francesco de Sanctis (1817–83) the greatest literary critic. Among the Italian literary figures of the late 19th and early 20th centuries, Giosuè Carducci (1835–1907; Nobel Prize winner, 1906), Giovanni Verga (1840–1922), Gabriele d'Annunzio (1863–1938), Luigi Pirandello (1867–1936;

Nobel Prize winner, 1934), and Grazia Deledda (1875–1936; Nobel Prize winner, 1926) achieved international renown. Leading writers of the postwar era are Ignazio Silone (Secondo Tranquilli, 1900–1978), Alberto Moravia (Pincherle, b.1907), Italo Calvino (1923–87), Umberto Eco (b.1932), and the poets Salvatore Quasimodo (1908–68; Nobel Prize winner, 1959) and Eugenio Montale (1896–1981; Nobel Prize winner, 1975). Outstanding film directors are Italian-born Frank Capra (b.1897-1991), Vittorio de Sica (1902–74), Luchino Visconti (1906–76), Roberto Rossellini (1906–77), Michelangelo Antonioni (b.1912), Federico Fellini (b.1920-93), Sergio Leone (b.1929), Pier Paolo Pasolini (1922–75), Franco Zeffirelli (b.1923), Lina Wertmüller (Arcangela Felice Assunta Wertmüller von Elgg, b.1928), and Bernardo Bertolucci (b.1940). Famous film stars include Italian-born Rudolph Valentino (Rodolfo Alfonso Raffaele Pierre Philibert Guglielmi, 1895–1926), Marcello Mastroianni (b.1924), and Sophia Loren (Scicoloni, b.1934).

In philosophy, exploration, and statesmanship, Italy has produced many world-renowned figures: the traveler Marco Polo (1254?–1324); the statesman and patron of the arts Cosimo de' Medici (1389–1464); the statesman, clergyman, and artistic patron Roderigo Borgia (Lanzol y Borja, b. Spain, 1431?–1503), who became Pope Alexander VI (r.1492–1503); the soldier, statesman, and artistic patron Lorenzo de' Medici, the son of Cosimo (1449–92); the explorer John Cabot (Giovanni Caboto, 1450?–98?); the explorer Christopher Columbus (Cristoforo Colombo or Cristóbal Colón, 1451–1506); the explorer Amerigo Vespucci (1454–1512), after whom the Americas are named; the admiral and statesman Andrea Doria (1468?–1540); Niccolò Machiavelli (1469–1527), author of *The Prince* and the outstanding political theorist of the Renaissance; the statesman and clergyman Cesare Borgia (1475?–1507), the son of Rodrigo; the explorer Sebastian Cabot (1476?–1557), the son of John; Baldassare Castiglione (1478–1529), author of *The Courtier;* the historian Francesco Guicciardini (1483–1540); the explorer Giovanni da Verrazano (1485?–1528?); the philosopher Giordano Bruno (1548?–1600); the political philosopher Giovanni Battista Vico (1668–1744); the noted jurist Cesare Bonesana Beccaria (1735–94); Giuseppe Mazzini (1805–72), the leading spirit of the Risorgimento; Camillo Benso di Cavour (1810–61), its prime statesman; and Giuseppe Garibaldi (1807–82), its foremost soldier and man of action. Notable intellectual and political leaders of more recent times include the Nobel Peace Prize winner in 1907, Ernesto Teodoro Moneta (1833–1918); the sociologist and economist Vilfredo Pareto (1848–1923); the political theorist Gaetano Mosca (1858–1941); the philosopher, critic, and historian Benedetto Croce (1866–1952); the educator Maria Montessori (1870–1952); Benito Mussolini (1883–1945), the founder of Fascism and dictator of Italy from 1922 to 1943; Carlo Sforza (1873–1952) and Alcide De Gasperi (1881–1954), famous latter-day statesmen; and the Communist leaders Antonio Gramsci (1891–1937), Palmiro Togliatti (1893–1964), and Enrico Berlinguer (1922–84).

Italian scientists and mathematicians of note include Leonardo Fibonacci (1180?–1250?), Galileo Galilei (1564–1642), Evangelista Torricelli (1608–47), Francesco Redi (1626?–97), Marcello Malpighi (1628–94), Luigi Galvani (1737–98), Lazzaro Spallanzani (1729–99), Alessandro Volta (1745–1827), Amedeo Avogadro (1776–1856), Stanislao Cannizzaro (1826–1910), Camillo Golgi (1843–1926; Nobel Prize winner, 1906), Guglielmo Marconi (1874–1937; Nobel Prize winner, 1909), Enrico Fermi (1901–54; Nobel Prize winner, 1938), Giulio Natta (1903–79; Nobel Prize winner, 1963), Daniel Bovet (b.1907; Nobel Prize winner, 1957), Renato Dulbecco (b.1914; Nobel Prize winner, 1975), Carlo Rubbia (b.1934; Nobel Prize winner, 1984), and Rita Levi-Montalcini (b.1909; Nobel Prize winner, 1986).

[49]DEPENDENCIES

Italy has no territories or colonies.

[50]BIBLIOGRAPHY

Albrecht-Carrié, Rene. *Italy from Napoleon to Mussolini.* New York: Columbia University Press, 1950.

Baldassarri, Mario (ed.). *Industrial Policy in Italy, 1945–90.* New York: St. Martin's, 1993.

———. *The Italian Economy: Heaven or Hell?* New York, N.Y.: St. Martin's Press, 1993.

Baranski, Zygmunt G. and Robert Lumley (eds.). *Culture and Conflict in Postwar Italy: Essays on Mass and Popular Culture.* New York: St. Martin Press, 1990.

Beales, Derek. *The Risorgimento and the Unification of Italy.* Winchester, Mass.: Allen & Unwin, 1971.

Berkeley, George Fitz-Hardinge, and Joan Weld Berkeley. *Italy in the Making: 1815 to November 16, 1848.* Cambridge: Cambridge University Press, 1932–40.

Burckhardt, Jakob. *The Civilization of the Renaissance in Italy.* 2 vols. New York: Harper & Row, 1958 (orig. 1860).

Cary, M., and H. H. Scullard. *A History of Rome.* New York: St. Martin's, 1976.

Coppa, Frank J. (ed.). *Dictionary of Modern Italian History.* Westport, Conn.: Greenwood, 1985.

Duggan, Christopher. *A Concise History of Italy.* New York: Cambridge University Press, 1994.

Francioni, Francesco (ed.) *Italy and EC Membership Evaluated.* New York: St. Martin's Press, 1992.

Furlong, Paul. *Modern Italy: Representation and Reform.* London; New York: Routledge, 1994.

Ginsborg, Paul. *A History of Contemporary Italy: Society and Politics, 1943–1988.* London: Penguin, 1990.

Grant, Michael. *The Etruscans.* New York: Scribner's, 1981.

———. *History of Rome.* New York: Scribner's, 1978.

Hearder, Harry. *Italy: A Short History.* New York: Cambridge University Press, 1990.

Hine, David. *Governing Italy: The Politics of Bargained Pluralism.* New York: Oxford University Press, 1993.

Hughes, Henry Stuart. *The United States and Italy.* Cambridge, Mass.: Harvard University Press, 1965.

Jemolo, A. O. *Church and State in Italy 1850–1950.* Oxford: Blackwell, 1960.

Kogan, Norman. *Italy and the Allies.* Cambridge, Mass.: Harvard University Press, 1982.

———. *A Political History of Postwar Italy: From the Old to the New Center Left.* New York: Praeger, 1981.

Lyttleton, Adrian. *The Seizure of Power: Fascism in Italy, 1919–1929.* New York: Scribner's, 1973.

Mack Smith, Denis. *Mussolini.* New York: Knopf, 1982.

Moss, David. *The Politics of Left-wing Violence in Italy, 1969–85.* New York: St. Martin's Press, 1989.

Pisano, Vittorfranco S. *The Dynamics of Subversion and Violence in Contemporary Italy.* Stanford, Calif.: Hoover Institution Press, 1987.

Pridham, Geoffrey. *Political Parties and Coalitional Behaviour in Italy.* New York: Routledge, 1988.

Pullan, Brian. *A History of Early Renaissance Italy.* New York: St. Martin's, 1973.

Sassoon, Donald. *Contemporary Italy: Politics, Economy, and Society Since 1945.* New York: Longman, 1986.

Spotts, Frederic, and Theodor Wieser. *Italy: A Difficult Democracy.* New York: Cambridge University Press, 1986.

Trevelyan, George Macaulay. *Garibaldi and the Making of Italy.* New York: Longmans, Green, 1948.

Wiskemann, Elizabeth. *The Rome-Berlin Axis: A History of the Relations Between Hitler and Mussolini.* London: Oxford University Press, 1949.

LATVIA

Republic of Latvia
Latvijas Republika

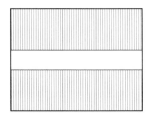

CAPITAL: Riga

FLAG: Three horizontal bands of red (top), blue (double width), and red with a large white disk centered in the blue band.

ANTHEM: *Dievs, svēti Latviju! (God bless Latvia!)*

MONETARY UNIT: The lat was introduced as the official currency in May 1993.

WEIGHTS AND MEASURES: The metric system is in force.

HOLIDAYS: New Year's Day, 1 January; Good Friday, 1 April; Midsummer Festival, 23–24 June; National Day, Proclamation of the Republic, 18 November; Christmas, 25–26 December; New Year's Eve, 31 December.

TIME: 2 PM = noon GMT.

¹LOCATION, SIZE, AND EXTENT

Latvia is located in northeastern Europe, bordering the Baltic Sea, between Sweden and Russia. Comparatively, Latvia is slightly larger than the state of West Virginia, with a total area of 64,100 sq km (24,749 sq mi). Latvia shares boundaries with Estonia on the N, Russia on the E, and Belarus on the S, Lithuania on the SW, and the Baltic Sea on the W. Latvia's boundary length totals 1,609 km (1,000 mi). Latvia's capital city, Riga, is located in the northern part of the country along the Baltic Sea coast.

²TOPOGRAPHY

The topography of Latvia consists mainly of a lowland plain.

³CLIMATE

The country's climate is influenced by is geographical location and by its closeness to the North Atlantic Ocean. The mean temperature in July is between 16.8°C and 17.6°C (62–64°C). In January the mean temperature is between –6.6°C and -2.6°C (20–27°F). The rainfall in the country is between 60–65 cm (24–26 in).

⁴FLORA AND FAUNA

Half of Latvia's soil is podsolic humus, which covers one-third of the country's arable land. Woodlands make up 41% of the country's territory, with one-half of the forests consisting of pines, birch, and firs. The woodlands and plant life support 14,000 different animal species. Species native to Latvia are the wild boar, Eurasian beaver, and brown bear. The routes of migratory birds pass along the Black Sea and over the country.

⁵ENVIRONMENT

Air and water pollution are among Latvia's most significant environmental concerns. In 1989, the nation released 584,780 tons of airborne pollutants into the environment. Cars and other vehicles account for 70% of the air pollution. Acid rain has contributed to the destruction of the nation's forests.

Latvia's water supply is perilously polluted with agricultural chemicals and industrial waste. Seventy percent of the nation's sewage does not receive adequate treatment. Almost half of the nation's water contains bacteria levels which are beyond accepted safety limits.

As of 1993, 119 of the nation's 12,700 species are endangered. One hundred twelve plant species, 20 types of lichen, and 32 types of mushrooms are also endangered.

⁶POPULATION

The population of Latvia was 2,680,029 in 1989. It was estimated at 2,606,176 at the beginning of 1993, of which 69% was urban. A population of 2,900,000 is estimated for 2010 by the World Bank, based on a crude birth rate per 1,000 people of 14, a crude death rate of 13, and a net increase of 1. The estimated population density in 1993 was about 41 per sq km (106 per sq mi). The population of Riga, the capital, was estimated at 874,172 at the end of 1992. Daugavpils had an estimated 124,887 people and Liepaja, 108,256. There were 75 urban localities.

⁷MIGRATION

Many Latvians fled Soviet occupation during World War II, and others were sent to Soviet labor camps. After the war many Russians moved to Latvia. Immigration from other former Soviet republics came to 4,590 in 1992. A total of 51,778 persons emigrated that year, 48,058 to former Soviet republics. Almost all of them went to Russia, Ukraine, or Belarus. Net internal migration was 52,171 in 1992, with slightly more than half moving to urban localities.

⁸ETHNIC GROUPS

In 1935, the population was 77% Latvian, but by 1993 the percentage of Latvians had dipped to only 53.5%. That year, 33% of the population was Russian, 4.2% Belorussian, 3.3 % Ukrainian, 2.2% Polish, and 1.3% Lithuanian. Nearly half the Russians and Ukrainians lived in Riga, where Russians formed a majority of the population. All residents of pre–1940 Latvia and their descendants are citizens. Naturalization requires 16 years' residence and fluency in Latvian.

⁹LANGUAGES

Latvian (also called Lettish) is a Baltic language written in the Roman alphabet. It is highly inflected, with seven noun cases and six verb declensions. The stress is always on the first syllable. There are three dialects. The macron is used for long vowels, and there is a hacek for "h." A cedilla adds the y sound. Education is now guaranteed in Latvian only. Instruction in higher education is given in Latvian only from the second year.

[10]RELIGIONS
After declaring independence from the Soviet Union in 1991, freedom of religion and worship was restored for the first time since 1941. Christianity had arrived in Latvia in the 12th century, and the Reformation made Lutheranism the primary religious persuasion after 1530. Ethnic Russians remaining after the Soviet period also comprise some 34% of the population (1992).

In 1993, some 18.6% of Latvians were Roman Catholics, with 190 congregations. Lutheran congregations numbered 282 and Orthodox 54. Baptists and Pentecostals are also present, and in 1990, 18,000 Jews lived in Latvia, the largest Jewish population in the Baltics.

[11]TRANSPORTATION
Railroads extend for 2,400 km (1,500 mi), linking port cities with Russia. More than 80% of railway use is for daily commuting. In 1990 there were 59,500 km (37,000 mi) of highways, of which 55% were hard-surfaced. Maritime ports include Riga, Ventspils, and Liepāja. The merchant fleet consists of 92 ships with a total of 917,979 GRT. From 1960 to 1989, marine transportation of goods increased by 14 times. In 1989, 38 million tons of freight (84% oil products) were transported through Latvian ports, mainly Ventspils. Ventspils is the terminus of the 421-km (262-mi) oil pipeline from Polotsk, Belarus, which carried 25% of all oil exported by the former Soviet Union in 1988.

In 1992, there were 327 licensed airline transport pilots. Riga has international air links to Helsinki, Stockholm, Copenhagen, and New York, as well as direct flights to Austria, Germany, Israel, Russia, and Belarus.

[12]HISTORY
Germans, Poles, Swedes, and Russians competed for influence in what is now Latvia from the Middle Ages until the 18th century, when it was incorporated into the Russian Empire. During the 19th century, a Latvian nationalist movement arose which by the early 20th century sought independence.

On 18 November 1918, the independent Republic of Latvia was proclaimed. Moscow recognized Latvian independence in the August 1920 Soviet-Latvian treaty. A secret protocol to the 1939 Nazi-Soviet pact assigned Latvia to the Soviet sphere of influence.

Soviet forces invaded Latvia on 17 June 1940, and Latvia was incorporated into the USSR. The Soviets, however, lost control of Latvia to the Germans in July 1941, shortly after Hitler launched his attack on the USSR. Soviet forces recaptured Latvia in 1944.

Soviet President Mikhail Gorbachev's policy of glasnost and perestroika allowed Latvians to voice their long-suppressed desire for national self-determination. The Latvian Popular Front (LPF) united independence forces and gained a majority in the elections for the Latvian Supreme Council in the spring of 1990. On 4 May 1990 provisional independence and a period of transitional rule were proclaimed.

On 21 August 1991—shortly after the failure of a coup against Gorbachev—Latvia proclaimed its full independence. The first post-independence elections for the new Saeima (parliament) were held on 5–6 June 1993.

On 30 April 1994, the Latvian and Russian governments signed a series of accords calling for the withdrawal of all Russian armed forces from Latvia by 31 August 1994, except for 599 soldiers at the Skrunda Radar Station which Russia may temporarily operate until 31 August 1998 and must completely dismantle by 29 February 2000.

[13]GOVERNMENT
The 1990 declaration of provisional independence reinstated the 1922 constitution. From 1990 to 1993, Latvia was in a state of transition and authority was held by the Supreme Council. The new Saeima (parliament) elected in June 1993 consists of a single chamber with 100 deputies. A party must receive at least 4% of the national vote to hold a seat in parliament.

The executive branch of government is made up of the president, prime minister, and the cabinet. The president is elected by the parliament. Executive power lies with the prime minister, who heads the Council of Ministers (cabinet).

[14]POLITICAL PARTIES
The Latvian Popular Front, established in 1988 to unite pro-independence forces, split apart after independence was achieved. As a result of the June 1993 elections, eight parties gained representation in the Saeima: Latvia's Way, the Farmers' Union, the National Independence Movement, Concord for Latvia, Equal Rights, the For the Fatherland and Freedom coalition, Christian Democrats, and the Democratic Center Party. A coalition government was formed by Latvia's Way and the Farmers' Union, which together won 48 of the 100 seats.

Only citizens of Latvia at the time of the 1940 Soviet invasion and their descendants were allowed to vote in the 1993 elections. This meant that an estimated 34% of the country's residents (primarily Russians) were ineligible to vote.

[15]LOCAL GOVERNMENT
Latvia's territory is divided into four historical districts—Kurzeme (western Latvia), Zemgale (southern Latvia), Vidzeme (northern Latvia), and Latgale (eastern Latvia).

[16]JUDICIAL SYSTEM
A 1991 constitution which supplements the reinstated 1922 constitution provides for a number of basic rights and freedoms. The courts are being reorganized along democratic lines. Regional courts are being added. More serious criminal cases are heard before a panel consisting of a judge and two lay assessors. There is a provision for a 12-member jury in capital cases, but the implementing laws are not yet in place.

[17]ARMED FORCES
The Latvian ground forces are organized in 10 battalions for border and coast defense with only one battalion ready for mobile warfare. The 12,000-man militia serves as a reserve. Latvia plans to assume control of the Russian air defense system within its borders, but it has not replaced the 40,000 Russians in the reinforced division, armed helicopters, 200 aircraft, and 250 SAM missiles that still garrison the country. No reliable financial estimates are available.

[18]INTERNATIONAL COOPERATION
Latvia was admitted to the UN on 17 September 1991. The country is a member of CSCE, EBRD, FAO, IAEA, IBRD, the IMF, and the World Bank. Its sovereignty is recognized by the US, EC countries, and many others. Latvia has especially close ties with the countries of the European Community. It is not a member of the CIS.

[19]ECONOMY
Latvia has a relatively well-developed infrastructure and a diversified industrial base, which accounts for about 60% of GNP. Agriculture constitutes approximately 20% of GNP and centers around the cultivation of potatoes, cereals, fodder, and other crops, as well as dairy farming.

Latvia's GDP fell about 30% in 1992 due to a steep decline in industrial exports to Russia, but the economy was expected to

LATVIA

0 — 25 — 50 Miles

0 — 25 — 50 Kilometers

ESTONIA

Pskovskoye Ozero

Pskov

Valka Valga

Irves Šaurums Kolkas Rags Salacgriva Burtnieku Ezers

Gulf of Riga

Limbaži Valmiera Alūksne Smiltene

Ventspils

Stende Cēsis

Usmas Ezers Talsi Gauja Sigulda Gulbene

Baltic Sea

Venta Balvi RUSSIA

Kuldīga Tukums Jūrmala Riga Ostrov

Pāvilosta Lielupe Ogre Gaizina 1,020 ft. 311 m. Lubānas Ezers

Kegums Plaviņas Aiviekste Malta

Liepāja Grobiņa Saldus Dobele Jelgava Daugava Costiņi Rēzekne

Auce Bauska Jēkabpils Rēznas Ezers

Memele Zalve

Rucava

Daugava

Šiauliai Daugavpils

Latvia

Navapolatsk

LITHUANIA

N W E S

BELARUS

LOCATION: 57°0′N; 25°0′E. **BOUNDARY LENGTHS:** Total boundary lengths, 1,078 km (670 mi); Belarus, 141 km (88 mi); Estonia, 267 km (166 mi); Lithuania, 452 km (282 mi); Russia, 217 km (135 mi).

rebound in the latter half of 1993, led by the service sector, trade, and light industry.

20 INCOME
In 1992, the GNP was $5,080 million at current prices, or $1,930 per capita. For the period 1985–92 the average inflation rate was 43.8%, resulting in a real growth rate in per capita GNP of –3.6%.

In 1992 the GDP was $5,081 million in current US dollars. It is estimated that in 1991 agriculture, hunting, forestry, and fishing contributed 20% to GDP; mining and quarrying, 0%; manufacturing, 34%; electricity, gas, and water, 2%; construction, 6%; wholesale and retail trade, 11%; transport, storage, and communication, 7%; finance, insurance, real estate, and business services, 5%; community, social, and personal services, 4%; and other sources, 11%.

21 LABOR
In 1992, 55% of the 1,350,000 persons employed in Latvia were women. Unemployment in 1992 was officially reported at 31,300 persons, or 2%, but actual unemployment in 1992 was at least 4% and growing. From 1985 to 1991, the labor force size annually grew by 0.4%. Approximately 16% of the labor force is engaged in agriculture, and 33% in industry.

Since 1991, Latvian workers have had the legal right to form and join labor unions of their own volition. As of 1992, about 70% of the labor force was unionized. Unions are generally nonpolitical, have the right to strike (with some limits), are free to affiliate internationally, can bargain collectively, and are mostly free of government interference in their negotiations with employers.

The minimum employment age is 16, and the mandatory maximum workweek is set at 40 hours. Latvian labor regulations also provide workers with four weeks of annual vacation and special assistance to working mothers with small children.

22 AGRICULTURE
As of 1991, out of a total land area of 6,205,000 hectares (15,333,000 acres), about 27.2% was crop land and 13.6% was permanent pastureland, with the remaining 59.2% consisting of forests, woodlands, roads, and urban areas. Agriculture accounted for 24.8% of GDP and one-sixth of employment in 1992.

Privatization of agriculture has progressed rapidly since 1991. By the beginning of 1993, over 50,000 private farms had been established, and many agricultural facilities were being privatized. Production of primary crops in 1992 (in thousands of tons) included wheat, 338; barley, 368; rye, 317; potatoes, 1,000; sugar beets, 380; vegetables, 236; and fruit, 100.

23ANIMAL HUSBANDRY

As of 1991, about 843,000 hectares (2,083,000 acres) of land were meadows and pastures, representing 13.6% of the total land area. In 1992, there were 1,383,000 head of cattle, 1,246,000 pigs, 184,000 sheep, 10,000,000 chickens, and 30,000 horses. In 1992, some 282,000 tons of meat were produced, over 90% of which was beef and pork. Milk and egg production in 1992 totaled 1,530,000 and 40,000 tons, respectively. Private sector production of milk and eggs in 1992 increased by 56% and 15%, respectively. In 1992, Latvian bees produced 2,500 tons of honey. Before World War II, Latvia was a prominent dairy producer; in the post-war period, the number of cattle, poultry, and pigs rose steeply. As of 1991, about 25% of meat and milk produced in Latvia came from individual farmers and subsidiary farms.

24FISHING

The total catch in 1989 was 547,000 tons. Fish packing is an important industry in Latvia; in 1989, some 233 million tins of preserved fish were canned.

25FORESTRY

Latvia's forests and woodlands covered 2.8 million hectares (6.9 million acres), or about 45% of the total land area in 1991. Before World War II (1939), the timber and paper industries accounted for 29% of employment; by 1990, the number had fallen to 9%. In 1939, the timber industry contributed 53.5% to total exports; in 1990, wood and paper exports accounted for 2.2% of total exports. Production amounts in 1989 included: sawn timber, 825,000 cu m; plywood, 95,000 cu m; paper, 138,000 tons; and cellulose, 51,900 tons.

26MINING

Coal, limestone for cement, and sand and gravel mines are spread throughout Latvia. Ceramic clays, dolomite, and gypsum also are produced. Peat is taken from 85 deposits, mostly east of Riga to Russia.

27ENERGY AND POWER

The hydroelectric power stations on the Daugava River, along with domestic wood and plant resources, produce only 12% of Latvia's consumed electricity; most electricity comes from Estonian or Lithuanian sources. During the first eight months of 1992, Latvia produced about 3 billion kwh of electricity, mostly from three hydroelectric plants at Plevinas, Riga, and Kegums, as well as by a conventional thermal plant in Riga.

Latvia imports nearly 100% of its required gas and petroleum products from Russia; in 1991, petroleum was consumed at a rate of 70,000 barrels per day and natural gas consumption totaled 100 billion cu ft.

28INDUSTRY

Latvia's industrial base centers mainly on heavy industries such as chemicals and petrochemicals, metal working, and machine building. Major manufactured items include railway carriages, buses, mopeds, washing machines, and telephone systems.

29SCIENCE AND TECHNOLOGY

The Latvian Academy of Sciences has divisions of physics, chemistry, and biology. Six institutes conduct scientific research. Five colleges and universities offer degrees in basic and applied sciences.

30DOMESTIC TRADE

Latvia's center of domestic commerce is in Riga, especially along Brīvības boulevard. In 1989, 3,109 shops and service businesses were operating, of which 1,291 provided service to urban areas and 1,818 to rural areas. In the early 1990s, the demand for services increased 50% in urban areas and 60% in the country side. In 1989, the most widely demanded domestic services included dressmaking and repair; house construction and repair; and automotive servicing. Shops are generally open from 9 or 10 AM to 7 or 8 PM.

31FOREIGN TRADE

Like most of the former Soviet republics, Latvia's trade was formerly dominated by the other Soviet states, but it has been relatively successful in achieving a wider range of trade partners, though constrained by cash shortages. Total imports in 1988 were valued at R5,000 million, and exports at R3,700 million. In that year, inter-republic trade accounted for 82% of imports and 92% of exports.

32BALANCE OF PAYMENTS

In 1989, imports exceeded exports by over R1 billion. Private investment from Scandinavian countries was beginning to grow in 1992. Exports and imports with Russia collapsed in 1991–92, when demand for hard currency payments began.

33BANKING AND SECURITIES

In 1991 banking matters were transferred to the Bank of Latvia from Soviet bank officials. The bank has the authority to issue Latvian rubles and regulate the commercial banking sector. Presently, there are 40 banks in Latvia, including the Baltic Transit Bank, Banka Atmoda, Latgale Stocj Commercial Bank, Latvian Credit Bank, Investment Bank of Latvia, and the Latvian Land Bank. Currency in circulation totaled R29,886 million in 1991. There are no security exchanges in Latvia.

34INSURANCE

No recent information is available.

35PUBLIC FINANCE

A stabilization program was commenced in 1992 (with IMF support), and a new currency (the lat) was issued in May 1993. Tight fiscal and monetary policy helped minimize public finance deterioration and curb inflation in 1992/93. In the second half of 1992, the Latvian budget deficit stood at $16 million. Internal and external loans were taken to alleviate the budget deficit. In November 1992, public debt stood at $159.6 million, including $45 million owed to the World Bank and $76.8 million to the IMF. Internal debt came to $12 million.

36TAXATION

Businesses which are at least 30% foreign-owned do not pay tax for the first two years, and are taxed at 50% the second two years. Locally owned businesses pay 35–65% with a standard rate of 25%. The personal income tax rate ranges from 25–35%. Also levied are a 10–18% turnover tax; a 10% excise tax; and a social security contribution of 37% by employers and 1% by employees.

37CUSTOMS AND DUTIES

Latvia has signed free trade agreements with more than 10 western countries. Imports from the West have included cars, clothes, and electrical equipment.

38FOREIGN INVESTMENT

In November 1991, a foreign investment act was passed permitting joint ventures in the form of either public or private limited companies. Businesses that are at least 30% foreign-owned receive a 2-year tax holiday, and a 50% tax abatement for the following 2 years. The government has also promised to allow non-citizens to own property and introduce a modern commercial code. There were some 230 joint ventures as of June 1992. By the end of 1992, American firms had invested $83 million in Latvia. Radisson planned to open a 380-room hotel in Riga in the spring of 1994.

39ECONOMIC DEVELOPMENT

The government began introducing economic reforms in 1990 to effect the transition to a market-driven economy. Individual and family-owned businesses, cooperatives, and privately- and publicly-held companies are now permitted. By January 1993, almost all agricultural land had been privatized and 50,000 private farms established. By the following month, over 55% of small enterprises had been privatized.

40SOCIAL DEVELOPMENT

In 1989, there were 478,000 old-age pensioners in Latvia. Average pensions equaled 38% of monthly earnings for nonfarm workers and 29% for farmers. Average family size was 3.1 members, and the divorce rate was 9.8 per 1,000 women. There were 0.9 drug-related crimes and 9.7 alcohol-related deaths per 100,000 persons. Prostitution is legal and is increasing, as is organized crime.

Employment discrimination based on gender is legally banned, although women are barred from certain occupations considered too dangerous. In practice, women face unequal treatment in terms of both pay and hiring, including discrimination stemming from the cost of legally mandated childbirth benefits if a woman is hired. In 1990, the fertility rate was 2.02.

41HEALTH

There were 37,000 births in 1993, a rate of 14 per 1,000 people. Life expectancy in 1992 was 71 years (77 years for females and 66 years for males). The infant mortality rate in 1992 was 22 per 1,000 live births, and the overall death rate was 12 per 1,000 inhabitants. The 1992 death rate exceeded the birth rate by 3,851.

In 1990, there was one physician for every 200 people, and one-year-old children were immunized against the following from 1990 to 1992: tuberculosis (94%); diphtheria, pertussis, and tetanus (87%); polio (92%); and measles (95%).

42HOUSING

Housing construction lags behind demand. In 1989, only 13.7% of capital investment in construction and renovation was allocated to housing while 42.9% went to industrial projects. At the beginning of 1990, 165,000 families (one out of five) were registered for new housing. Approximately 200,000 people lived in the 8% of existing housing stock that was in substandard condition.

43EDUCATION

The modern Latvian educational system is based on the reforms introduced in 1991. Compulsory preprimary and primary education lasts for nine years beginning at the age of six. Secondary education generally lasts for three years and is offered in general schools, specialized high schools, and trade schools. In the 1990–91 academic school year, there were 352,000 students enrolled in 962 secondary institutions.

Entrance examinations are a prerequisite for admission into universities. Higher education is offered by both private and public institutions. The state offers free higher education in some areas of specialized study. Latvia has two major universities: the University of Latvia and the Riga Technical University. Higher education is also offered in various other academies. In 1990–91, 46,000 students were enrolled in institutions of higher learning.

44LIBRARIES AND MUSEUMS

Traditionally, Latvia has supported a strong system of public and private libraries. After the occupation of Latvia in 1940, the libraries were nationalized and placed under state control. For the next 50 years the library system was poorly maintained. Today those libraries that remain open are over-crowded and in poor physical condition. However, the Latvian government has authorized the construction of a new National Library to be designed by the American architect G. Birkerts.

45MEDIA

International communications links are via leased connection to the Moscow international gateway switch and the Finnish cellular network. The Committee for Television and Radio controls broadcasting. Domestic and international programming in Latvian, Russian, Swedish, English, and German is broadcast by Latvian Radio. In 1991, there were about 1 million television sets. Latvia publishes many newspapers, periodicals, and books, in both Latvian and Russian.

46ORGANIZATIONS

Important economic organizations in Latvia include the Latvian Chamber of Commerce, an organization that promotes trade and commerce with its Baltic neighbors, Europe, and The Russian Federation. There are five business and trade organizations including: the Latvia International Commerce Center, Latvian Small Business Association, and the World Latvian's Businessmen's Association. The largest trade union in Latvia is the Association of Free Trade Unions, founded in 1990, an umbrella trade organization.

47TOURISM, TRAVEL, AND RECREATION

With a population of around 1 million, Riga is the major tourism center of the Baltic states. Its historic architecture has undergone extensive restoration in the past 20 years. Latvia's hotel industry is still underdeveloped but growing; joint ventures have modernized existing hotels in Riga to create Western-style accommodations. Tennis, horseback riding, fishing, hunting, sailing, water sports, and winter sports are available to visitors, as well as a ski marathon in February, the Sport Festival of Riga in May, and the International Riga Marathon in July. All visitors need passports and visas, except for nationals of the UK, Hungary, Poland and Denmark, who are exempt from visa requirements.

48FAMOUS LATVIANS

Guntis Ulmanis and Valdis Birkavs have been president and prime minister of Latvia since July 1993, respectively. Turis Alumans was Latvia's first poet. He started a school of poetry that produced the poets Krisjanis Barons and Atis Kronvalds in the 19th century. Romantic literature in the 20th century was symbolized by Janis Rainis's *Fire and Night*.

49DEPENDENCIES

Latvia has no territories or colonies.

50BIBLIOGRAPHY

Bilmanis, Alfreds, 1887–1948. *A History of Latvia*. Westport, Conn., Greenwood Press [1970], 1951.

Carson, George B. (ed.). *Latvia: An Area Study*. New Haven: Yale University Press, 1956.

Graham, Malbone W. *New Governments of Eastern Europe*. New York: H. Holt, 1927.

Karklins, Rasma. *Ethnopolitics and Transition to Democracy: the Collapse of the USSR and Latvia*. Baltimore: Johns Hopkins University Press, 1994.

Latvia. Washington, D.C.: International Monetary Fund, 1992.

Latvia: The Transition to a Market Economy. Washington, D.C.: World Bank, 1993.

Newman, E. W. Polson. *Britain and the Baltic*. London: Methuen, 1930.

Urch, Reginald Oliver Gilling. *Latvia; Country and People.* London: G. Allen & Unwin, 1938.

Watson, Herbert Adolphus Grant. *The Latvian Republic: The Struggle for Freedom*. London: G. Allen & Unwin, 1965.

LIECHTENSTEIN

Principality of Liechtenstein
Fürstentum Liechtenstein

CAPITAL: Vaduz.

FLAG: The national flag is divided into two horizontal rectangles, blue above red. On the blue rectangle, near the hoist, is the princely crown in gold.

ANTHEM: *Oben am jungen Rhein (On the Banks of the Young Rhine).*

MONETARY UNIT: The Swiss franc (SwFr) of 100 centimes, or rappen, has been in use since February 1921. There are coins of 1, 5, 10, 20, and 50 centimes and 1, 2, and 5 francs, and notes of 10, 20, 50, 100, 500, and 1,000 francs. SwFr1 = $0.7092 (or $1 = SwFr1.41).

WEIGHTS AND MEASURES: The metric system is the legal standard.

HOLIDAYS: New Year's Day, 1 January; Epiphany, 6 January; Candlemas, 2 February; St. Joseph's Day, 19 March; Labor Day, 1 May; Assumption, 15 August; Nativity of Our Lady, 8 September; All Saints' Day, 1 November; Immaculate Conception, 8 December; Christmas 25 December; St. Stephen's Day, 26 December. Movable religious holidays include Good Friday, Easter Monday, Ascension, Whitmonday, and Corpus Christi.

TIME: 1 PM = noon GMT.

¹LOCATION, SIZE, AND EXTENT

Liechtenstein, roughly triangular in shape, is a landlocked country situated in the Rhine River Valley. The fourth-smallest country in Europe, it is bordered by the Austrian province of Vorarlberg to the N and E, the Swiss canton of Graubünden to the S, and the Rhine River and the Swiss canton of St. Gallen to the W, with a total boundary length of 78 km (48.5 mi).

The principality has an area of 160 sq km (61.8 sq mi) and extends 24.5 km (15.2 mi) N-S and 9.4 km (5.8 mi) E-W. Comparatively, the area occupied by Liechtenstein is about 0.9 times the size of Washington, D.C.

Liechtenstein's capital city, Vaduz, is located in the western part of the country.

²TOPOGRAPHY

Liechtenstein is divided into a comparatively narrow area of level land bordering the right bank of the Rhine River and an upland and mountainous region occupying the remainder of the country; the level land occupies about two-fifths of the total surface area. The greatest elevation, Grauspitz (2,599 m/8,527 ft), is in the south, in a spur of the Rhaetian Alps.

³CLIMATE

Climatic conditions in Liechtenstein are less severe than might be expected from its elevated terrain and inland situation; the mitigating factor is a warm south wind called the Föhn. The annual lowland temperature varies between –4.5°C (24°F) in January and 19.9°C (68°F) in July. Late frost and prolonged dry periods are rare. Average annual precipitation was 105 cm (41 in) during 1974–83.

⁴FLORA AND FAUNA

The natural plant and animal life of Liechtenstein displays a considerable variety because of the marked differences in altitude. A number of orchid species are able to grow because of the warmth carried by the Föhn. In the higher mountain reaches are such alpine plants as gentian, alpine rose, and edelweiss. Common trees include the red beech, sycamore, maple, alder, larch, and various conifers. Indigenous mammals include the deer, fox, badger, and chamois. Birds, including ravens and eagles, number about 120 species.

⁵ENVIRONMENT

The Nature Conservation Act, adopted in 1933, was the nation's first major piece of environmental legislation; the Water Conservation Act dates from 1957, and air pollution laws were passed in 1973 and 1974. All wastewater is purified before being discharged into the Rhine. The great horned owl is now rare, and the European otter has become extinct.

⁶POPULATION

The census of 1990 reported a population of 28,877. The 1980 population was 25,215. The average annual growth rate during 1980–90 was 1.2%, down from 2.2% in the early 1970s. The overall population density as of 1990 was 180 per sq km (466 per sq mi).

The population is most heavily concentrated in the Rhine Valley, in which the two largest communes, Vaduz and Schaan, are located. In 1991, Vaduz had a population of 4,887, Schaan 5,035, and Balzers, 3,752.

The population density for the country as a whole is more than 166 persons per sq km (416 per sq mi). About 16% of the population lives in Vaduz, the capital. Most of the remainder of the population lives in ten other communities in the Rhine River Valley.

⁷MIGRATION

There were 11,021 foreign residents in Liechtenstein in 1991; the majority were Swiss (39%). Moreover, about 4,000 Austrians and Swiss commute to Liechtenstein every day. Several hundred Italian, Greek, and Spanish workers have migrated to the principality on a semipermanent basis.

[8] ETHNIC GROUPS

The indigenous population, accounting for 62.5% of the 1991 total, is described as being chiefly of Alemannic stock, descendants of the German-speaking tribes that settled between the Main and Danube rivers. German-speakers from Switzerland and Austria predominate among immigrant groups.

[9] LANGUAGES

German is the official language. The population speaks an Alemannic dialect.

[10] RELIGIONS

The state religion is Roman Catholicism, to which about 87% of the population adheres; however, absolute freedom of worship prevails. In 1992, 7.9% of the population was Protestant, while 5.8% was of other denominations.

[11] TRANSPORTATION

The line of the Arlberg express (Paris to Vienna) passes through Liechtenstein at Schaan-Vaduz, but few international trains stop. The main center for reaching Liechtenstein is Buchs, Switzerland, about 8 km (5 mi) from Vaduz.

Postal buses are the chief means of public transportation both within the country and to Austria and Switzerland. A tunnel, 740 m (2,428 ft) in length, connects the Samina River Valley with the Rhine River Valley.

In 1991, there were some 131 km (81 mi) of main roads and 192 km (119 mi) of byroads. A major highway runs through the principality, linking Austria and Switzerland.

The nearest airport is in Zürich, Switzerland.

[12] HISTORY

The territory now occupied by the Principality of Liechtenstein first acquired a political identity with the formation of the subcountry of Lower Rhaetia after the death of Charlemagne in 814. The County of Vaduz was formally established in 1342 and became a direct dependency of the Holy Roman Empire in 1396. The area (to which, in 1434, was added the Lordship of Schellenberg, in the north) was ruled in turn by various families, such as the counts of Montfort, von Brandis, van Sulz, and von Hohenems.

During the Thirty Years' War (1618–48), the area was invaded first by Austrian troops and then, in 1647, by the Swedes. After the von Hohenems line encountered financial difficulty, Prince Johann Adam of Liechtenstein purchased from them first Schellenberg (1699) and then Vaduz (1712). The Liechtenstein family thus added to its vast holdings in Austria and adjoining territories.

The Principality of Liechtenstein as such was created on 23 January 1719 by act of Holy Roman Emperor Charles VI, who made it a direct fief of the crown and confirmed the rule of Prince Anton-Florian, Johann Adam's successor, under the title of Prince von und zu Liechtenstein.

During the Napoleonic wars, Liechtenstein was invaded by both the French and the Russians. Following the Treaty of Pressburg (1805), Liechtenstein joined the Confederation of the Rhine, which made the principality a sovereign state. In 1815, following the downfall of Napoleon, Liechtenstein joined the newly formed Germanic Confederation.

With Prussia's victory over Austria in the Seven Weeks' War (1866), the Confederation was dissolved and the constitutional ties of Liechtenstein to other German states came to an end. In the war, Liechtenstein had furnished Austria-Hungary with 80 soldiers; two years later, the principality disbanded its military force for all time.

From 1852, when the first treaty establishing a customs union was signed, until the end of World War I, Liechtenstein was closely tied economically to Austria. After the war, the collapse of the Austrian currency and economy inclined the principality to seek economic partnership with its other neighbor, Switzerland. A treaty concluded with Switzerland in 1923 provided for a customs union and the use of Swiss currency.

Liechtenstein (like Switzerland) remained neutral in World War II, as it had in World War I. After Germany was defeated in 1945, Nazi sympathizers in Liechtenstein who had supported incorporation of the principality into Hitler's Third Reich were prosecuted and sentenced. The postwar decades have been marked by political stability and outstanding economic growth.

The reigning prince, Franz Josef II, who succeeded his granduncle, Franz I, in 1938, is the first reigning monarch actually to reside in Liechtenstein. On 26 August 1984, Franz Josef II handed over executive authority to his eldest son and heir, Crown Prince Hans Adam.

Liechtenstein has sought further integration into the world community. The country was admitted to the UN in September 1991. In Europe, Liechtenstein formed EFTA in 1991 and became a member of the European Economic Area (EEA) following a referendum in 1992. A referendum scheduled for 1994 will determine membership in the EC.

[13] GOVERNMENT

Liechtenstein is a constitutional monarchy ruled by the hereditary princes of the house of Liechtenstein. The monarchy is hereditary in the male line. The present constitution of 5 October 1921, as amended in 1987, provides for a unicameral parliament (Landtag) of 25 members elected for four years. Election is by universal adult male suffrage at age 20 and is on the basis of proportional representation. Since 1979, women have been allowed to vote in national referenda and on local candidates and issues. A new voting system that went into effect as of the 1974 national elections provides 9 representatives for the Upper Land district and 6 representatives for the Lower Land district.

The prince can call and dismiss the Landtag. On parliamentary recommendation, he appoints the prime minister, who must be of Liechtenstein birth, and the deputy prime minister for four-year terms. It is the regular practice for the prime minister to be of the majority party and the deputy prime minister to be selected from the opposition. The Landtag appoints four councillors for four-year terms to assist in administration. Any group of 1,000 persons or any three communes may propose legislation. Bills passed by the Landtag may be submitted to popular referendum. A law is valid when it receives majority approval by the Landtag and the prince's signed concurrence.

Two general elections were held in 1993 (February and October) resulting in a coalition government headed by Mario Frick of the Fatherland Union (VU). Although the VU remains the largest single party, Liechtenstein has had a coalition government since 1938.

[14] POLITICAL PARTIES

The two principal parties are the Fatherland Union (Vaterländische Union—VU) and the Progressive Citizens' Party (Fortschrittliche Bürgerpartei—FBP). In the general elections of October 1993, the VU, which has held a majority since 1978, won eleven seats in the Landtag and the FBP twelve. Other parties include the Free List (Frere Liste—FL), two seats; and the Liechtenstein Non-party List (Uberparteilische Liste Liechtensteins—ULL), which is not represented.

[15] LOCAL GOVERNMENT

The 11 communes (Gemeinden) are fully independent administrative bodies within the laws of the principality. They levy their own taxes. Liechtenstein is divided into two districts—the Upper Land and the Lower Land—for purposes of national elections.

¹⁶JUDICIAL SYSTEM

The principality has its own civil and penal codes, although in certain instances courts composed of Liechtenstein, Swiss, and Austrian judges have jurisdiction over Liechtenstein cases. Courts that function under sole Liechtenstein jurisdiction are the County Court (Landgericht), presided over by one judge, which decides minor civil cases and summary criminal offenses; the juvenile court; and the Schöffengericht, a court for misdemeanors. The remaining courts, with 5 judges each, have a mixed composition for purposes of impartiality: 3 Liechtenstein lay judges, 1 Swiss judge, and 1 Austrian judge. The criminal court (Kriminalgericht) is for major crimes. Other courts of mixed jurisdiction are the assize court (Schöffengericht-Vergehen), the superior court (Obergericht), and a supreme court (Oberster Gerichtshof). An administrative court of appeal hears appeals from government actions, and the State Court determines the constitutionality of laws. In June 1986, Liechtenstein adopted a new penal code abolishing the death penalty.

The constitution which dates from 1921 provides for public trials and judicial appeal. The judiciary is separate from the executive and legislative branches.

¹⁷ARMED FORCES

Since 1868, no military forces have been maintained in Liechtenstein, but there is obligatory military service for able-bodied men up to 60 years of age in case of emergency.

¹⁸INTERNATIONAL COOPERATION

Liechtenstein is not a member of the UN but does belong to IAEA, ICJ, ITU, UPU, and WIPO. It is a signatory of the Law of the Sea treaty. The principality participates in the Council of Europe, holds special status with EFTA, and has negotiated a special trade agreement with the EC. Liechtenstein has an embassy in Bern, Switzerland, but elsewhere is represented by the Swiss. In 1987, 34 consular representatives were accredited to Liechtenstein.

¹⁹ECONOMY

Despite its small size and limited national resources, Liechtenstein has developed since the 1940s from a mainly agricultural to an industrialized country and a prosperous center of trade and tourism. Factories produce a wide range of high-technology manufactures, especially precision instruments.

Special economic advantages enjoyed by very small nations of Europe (e.g., the issuance of new postage stamps, free exchange of currencies, and liberal laws that provide incentives for the establishment of bank deposits and of nominal foreign business headquarters) also play a part in this prosperity.

Liechtenstein has more than 50 factories, producing specialized small machinery in addition to precision instruments. Industrial products are manufactured almost exclusively for export.

²⁰INCOME

In 1990, Liechtenstein's GDP was $630 million in current US dollars, or $22,300 per capita.

²¹LABOR

In 1990, there were 19,905 persons in the labor force (11,933 foreigners), of whom 6,885 commuted to work from Switzerland and Austria. Foreigners make up almost 37% of the population.

The domestic labor force was estimated to be about 7,500 in 1994. Liechtenstein's workforce is highly skilled, but there are not enough workers to meet industry's need. The composition of the domestic labor force in 1990 was as follows: industry, commerce, and construction, 53.2%; services, 45%; and agriculture and forestry, 1.8%.

There is a Workers' Union Center in Vaduz; the Union of Artisans and Tradesmen is centered in Schaan. There is no minimum

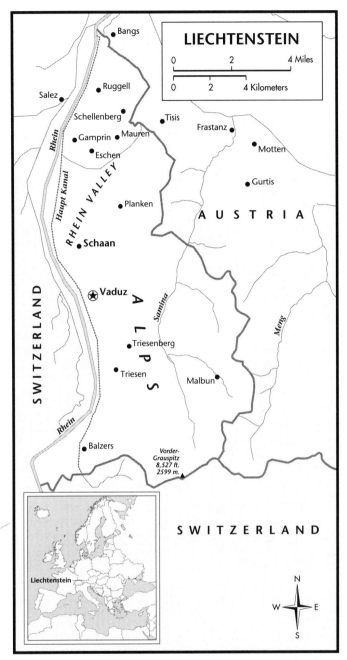

LOCATION: 47°3′ to 47°14′N; 9°29′ to 9°38′E. **BOUNDARY LENGTHS:** Austria, 34.9 km (21.7 mi); Switzerland, 41.1 km (25.5 mi).

wage, although wages are among the highest in the world. The legal workweek is 46 hours in the industrial sector and 50 hours in nonindustrial firms.

²²AGRICULTURE

Liechtenstein has only 912 hectares (2,254 acres) of arable land. Until the end of World War II, the economy was primarily focused on agriculture. In the Rhine Valley, the most productive area, the chief vegetables are corn, potatoes, and garden produce. On gradual mountain slopes, a variety of grapes and orchard fruits are grown.

²³ANIMAL HUSBANDRY

Alpine pasture, particularly well suited for cattle grazing, covers over 35% of the total land area.

In 1992, cattle numbered about 6,000; hogs, 3,000; and sheep, 3,000.

24FISHING

There is no commercial fishing in Liechtenstein. Rivers and brooks are stocked for sport fishing.

25FORESTRY

The forests of Liechtenstein not only supply wood but also have an important function in preventing erosion, landslides, and floods. Forests cover about 3,000 hectares (7,400 acres).

More than 90% of all forestland is publicly owned; of the 474 hectares (1,171 acres) of private forest, 158 hectares (390 acres) are the property of the prince. The most common trees are spruce, fir, beech, and pine.

26MINING

There is no mining of commercial importance.

27ENERGY AND POWER

The first Liechtenstein power station went into operation in 1927; its capacity is now 900 kw. Another station was constructed in 1947–49; it has an installed capacity of 9,600 kw. Total installed capacity in 1989 was 23,000 kw; production amounted to 150 million kwh. Since domestic production no longer meets local requirements, supplementary energy is imported from Switzerland, especially in winter.

28INDUSTRY

The industry of Liechtenstein, limited by shortages of raw materials, is primarily devoted to small-scale production of precision manufactures. The output includes optical lenses, high-vacuum pumps, heating equipment, electron microscopes, electronic measuring and control devices, steel bolts, knitting machines, and textiles.

Other products are artificial teeth, canned foods, furniture, pharmaceuticals, and leather goods. Handicrafts include decorated earthenware and wood carvings. In 1992, a total of 33 industrial enterprises were in operation. Liechtenstein's industry is completely geared to exports; industrial exports rose from SwFr196.7 million in 1967 to SwFr2,480.9 million in 1992.

29SCIENCE AND TECHNOLOGY

Like Swiss industry, manufacturing in Liechtenstein entails a high degree of precision and technological sophistication. Liechtenstein itself has no educational institutions offering advanced scientific training, but the Liechtenstein Institute, founded in 1986, conducts scientific research.

30DOMESTIC TRADE

Vaduz and Schaan, the chief commercial centers, have some specialty shops, but the smaller communities have only general stores. Business hours are generally from 8 AM to 6:30 PM. Normal banking hours are from 8:15 AM to noon and from 1:30 PM to 4 or 5 PM, Monday–Friday.

31FOREIGN TRADE

Goods to and from Liechtenstein pass freely across the Swiss frontier with Switzerland, with which Liechtenstein maintains a customs union. Exports in 1992 totaled SwFr2,021,711, as compared with SwFr893,385,000 in 1980.

Important exports include precision instruments, ceramics, textiles, and pharmaceuticals. Liechtenstein imports mainly raw materials, light machinery, and processed foods. In 1992, imports totaled SwFr1,074,566,000.

In 1991, 45.4% of total exports went to EC countries and 20.3% to EFTA countries. Liechtenstein became an EFTA member in 1991. The most important customer was Switzerland, with 14.9% of total exports.

32BALANCE OF PAYMENTS

A precise accounting of Liechtenstein's balance of payments cannot be ascertained because of the free flow of imports across the Swiss border.

33BANKING AND SECURITIES

Liechtenstein's banks form an important part of the economy, and they have experienced significant growth in the 1990s. As of 1994, the banking sector employs an estimated 4% of the work force.

The National Bank of Liechtenstein (Liechtensteinische Landesbank), founded in 1861, is the state bank of issue; in addition, it deals in real estate mortgages and ordinary banking operations. The Bank of Liechtenstein, a private bank founded in 1920, and the Private Trust Bank Corp., founded in 1956, play an important role in the finance and credit spheres of Liechtenstein's economy. The capital of the three banks was SwFr591 million in 1991. Banking is linked with the Swiss banking system, as is securities trading.

Because of Liechtenstein's strict bank secrecy, several thousand foreign businesses are nominally headquartered there.

34INSURANCE

Insurance activities in Liechtenstein are variously conducted by the government (old age and survivors' insurance), by private companies under government regulation (e.g., life, accident, health, and fire), and by farmers' associations.

35PUBLIC FINANCE

In 1990, budgeted revenues were equivalent to $259 million, while expenditures came to $292 million.

36TAXATION

The main taxes are levied on personal income and on business income and principal. Income tax rates range generally from 3.6% to 17.82% for individuals and from 7.5% to 15% for businesses.

Other levies include a capital gains tax on the sale of real estate; death, estate, and gift duties; a motor vehicle registration tax; and a turnover tax, remitted annually to Switzerland and amounting to 6.2% on retail goods and 9.3% for wholesale items.

Firms domiciled in Liechtenstein but conducting no gainful pursuits there benefit from extremely favorable tax arrangements, a prime factor in the establishment of nominal business headquarters. The communes may impose property and income taxes.

37CUSTOMS AND DUTIES

There are no customs between Switzerland and Liechtenstein. On the Austrian border, Switzerland collects the customs at its own rates. Liechtenstein's part of the duties is calculated on the basis of population, and the principality pays an annual indemnification to Switzerland for customs and administration.

38FOREIGN INVESTMENT

The Prince of Liechtenstein Foundation has established a number of ventures abroad, mainly in the field of investment management and counseling.

Several thousand foreign companies have established offices in Liechtenstein because taxes are very low, banking operates in strict secrecy, and the principality is politically stable. Some industrial establishments are owned and managed by Swiss interests.

39ECONOMIC DEVELOPMENT

The government generally encourages the increasing diversification of industry and the development of tourism. The principality's liberal tax policies and highly secret banking system is attractive to foreign corporations. Thousands of corporations have established nominal headquarters in Liechtenstein.

40SOCIAL DEVELOPMENT

Accident insurance has been obligatory since 1931, and old age and survivors' insurance since 1954. Family allowances have been granted since 1958, and disability insurance was added in 1960.

Unemployment insurance has been obligatory since 1969, and compulsory health insurance since 1971. The government established the Department of Social Welfare and the Department for the Care of Young People in 1965, the Department of Social and Preventive Medicine in 1977, and the Family Counseling Service in 1981.

A 1992 constitutional amendment guarantees women equality under the law, and several groups monitor and promote women's rights. Domestic violence laws have been enacted and are actively implemented.

41HEALTH

The government regulates the practice of medicine and subsidiary occupations, such as nursing and pharmacy. Liechtenstein's 1993 population was 28,000, with an estimated 104,000 births in 1990, and a life expectancy of about 76 years.

In 1992, Liechtenstein had an estimated 2.5 physicians per 1,000 population, with a nurse to doctor ratio of 2.1. In 1990, there were approximately 8.3 hospital beds per 1,000 people. A program of preventive medicine, introduced in 1976, provides regular examinations for children up to the age of 10.

42HOUSING

Houses in the countryside are similar to those found in the mountainous areas of Austria and Switzerland. Liechtenstein does not have a significant housing problem. In 1980, 82% of all dwellings had central heating, 89% had a kitchen, 91% had a private bath, 95% had hot water, and 88% had a common sewage system.

43EDUCATION

Education is conducted on Roman Catholic principles and is under government supervision. The present school system, introduced in 1929, underwent major reforms in the early 1970s. In 1974, the compulsory primary school attendance period was lowered from eight years to five, beginning at age seven.

Education is offered from kindergarten to the upper school, roughly equivalent to the French lycée or the German gymnasium. Many students continue their studies at universities in Switzerland, Austria, and Germany.

In 1990–91 there were 120 teachers in the primary schools. That same year, 1,985 students were enrolled in primary schools; 1,190 students were enrolled in secondary schools. There were 112 secondary school teachers.

Liechtenstein also has an evening technical school, a music school (with 76 teachers on the faculty and 2,175 students enrolled in 1985), and a children's pedagogic-welfare day school.

In 1985, Liechtenstein spent SwFr39.3 million on education. While there are no universities in Liechtenstein, students continue their education at universities abroad, especially in Germany, Austria, and Switzerland.

44LIBRARIES AND MUSEUMS

The National Library (founded in 1961) serves as the public, academic, and national library. It is located in Vaduz and has over 150,000 volumes. The National Museum, also located in Vaduz, includes collections from the Prince and the State.

The Prince Liechtenstein Art Gallery, founded in 1620 and located in Vaduz, is an important cultural institution in Liechtenstein.The museum is housed upstairs in the tourist information office.

45MEDIA

The post office (including telegraph and telephone services) is administered by Switzerland. Liechtenstein, however, issues its own postage stamps. The number of telephones in 1992 was 25,400; the Swiss dial system extends to the principality. Direct-dialing is used throughout the country and includes international service. Telegraph service is efficient. There were 18,000 radios and 9,000 television sets in 1991.

As of 1994, there are currently are no radio or television broadcasting facilities.

Two newspapers are published. The *Liechtensteiner Volksblatt* reflects the FBP's political outlook; it had a circulation of about 8,550 in 1991 and is published five times a week. The *Liechtensteiner Vaterland* reflects the views of the VU; it is published six times a week and had a circulation of about 8,690 in 1991.

46ORGANIZATIONS

Organizations include the Chamber of Industry and Commerce, the Historical Society of the Principality of Liechtenstein, three concert societies, and various other cultural organizations.

Charitable institutions include the Liechtenstein Caritas Society (founded in 1924) and the Liechtenstein Red Cross Society (1945).

47TOURISM, TRAVEL, AND RECREATION

The government actively encourages the tourist industry. In Vaduz, the lower country, and the Alpine regions there are hotels and guest houses. In 1991, the country had 1,134 hotel beds. The same year, an estimated 71,000 persons visited Liechtenstein, 61,000 of them from Europe.

Attractions include mountaineering and nature walks, the castles of Vaduz and Gutenberg (overlooking Balzers), the ruins of several fortresses, and the numerous local brass bands and choirs, as well as the operetta societies of Vaduz and Balzers. The most popular sports are swimming, tennis, hiking, and skiing. The ski resort of Malbun has 10 hotels and 6 ski lifts.

Modern, comfortable buses offer regular service throughout Liechtenstein, connecting with Austria and Switzerland.

48FAMOUS LIECHTENSTEINERS

Joseph Rheinberger (1839–1901), an organist and composer who lived in Munich, was the teacher of many famous composers. Prince Franz Josef II (b.1906), whose rule began in 1938, is Europe's longest-reigning sovereign. The heir apparent, Hans Adam (b.1945), took over executive power in 1984.

In 1980, Hanni Wenzel (b.1956) and her brother Andreas (b.1958) won the World Cup international skiing championships.

49DEPENDENCIES

Liechtenstein has no territories or colonies.

50BIBLIOGRAPHY

Kranz, Walter (ed.). *The Economy of the Principality of Liechtenstein.* Vaduz: Government Press and Information Office, 1982.
———. *The Principality of Liechtenstein: A Documentary Handbook.* 5th ed., rev. Schaan: Press and Information Office of Liechtenstein, 1981.
Meier, Regula A. *Liechtenstein.* Santa Barbara, CA: Clio Press, 1993.

Moore, Russell Franklin. *The Principality of Liechtenstein: A Brief History.* New York: Simmons-Boardman, 1960.

Raton, Pierre. *Liechtenstein: History and Institutions of the Principality.* Vaduz: Liechtenstein Verlag, 1970.

Statistisches Jahrbuch Fürstentum Liechtenstein. Vaduz: Amt für Volkswirkschaft (annual).

The Economy of the Principality of Liechtenstein. Press and Information Office of the Liechtenstein Government, 1967.

LITHUANIA

Republic of Lithuania
Lietuvos Respublika

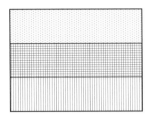

CAPITAL: Vilnius.

FLAG: Three equal horizontal bands of yellow (top), green, and red.

ANTHEM: *Lietuva Tevyne Musu.*

MONETARY UNIT: The Lithuanian lita of 100 cents has replaced the transitional system of coupons (talonas) which had been in force since October 1992, when the Soviet ruble was demonetized. There are coins of 1, 2, 5, 10, 20, and 50 cents and 1, 2, and 5 litas, and notes of 10, 20, 50, and 100 litas.

WEIGHTS AND MEASURES: The metric system is in force.

HOLIDAYS: New Year's Day, 1 January; Day of the Restoration of the Lithuanian State, 16 February; Good Friday, 1 April (movable); Anniversary of the Coronation of Grand Duke Mindaugas of Lithuania, 6 July; National Day of Hope and Mourning, 1 November; Christmas, 25–26 December.

TIME: 2 PM = noon GMT.

¹LOCATION, SIZE, AND EXTENT

Lithuania is located in eastern Europe, bordering the Baltic Sea, between Sweden and Russia. Comparatively, it is slightly larger than the state of West Virginia with a total area of 65,200 sq km (25,174 sq mi). Lithuania shares boundaries with Latvia on the N and NE, Belarus on the S and SE, Poland on the SW, Russia-Kaliningrad Oblaston the W, and the Baltic Sea on the NW. Lithuania's boundary length totals 1,381 km (858 mi).

Lithuania's capital city, Vilnius, is located in the southeastern part of the country.

²TOPOGRAPHY

The topography of Lithuania features lowland terrain with many scattered small lakes and fertile soil.

³CLIMATE

Lithuania's climate is transitional between maritime and continental. Yearly, the mean temperature is 6.1°C (43°F). The mean temperature in July is 17.1°C (63°F). Rainfall averages from 54 cm (21 in) to 93 cm (37 in) depending on location.

⁴FLORA AND FAUNA

The country is located in the mixed forest zone. The country's plantlife is a mixture of coniferous, broadleaf woodlands, arctic, and steppe species. There are 70 species of mammals, 293 bird species, 7 reptile species, 11 amphibian species, and 60 fish species. The country has rabbit, fox, red deer, roe, elk, wild boar, badger, raccoon dog, wolf, lynx, and gallinaceous birds. Roach, ruff, bream, and perch can be found in Lithuania's lakes and streams.

⁵ENVIRONMENT

Lithuania's environmental problems include air pollution, water pollution, and the threat of nuclear contamination. The cement industry produces 62,600 tons of airborne pollutants per year. In 1992, a UN report on Lithuania stated that air pollution had damaged about 68.4% of the nation's forests.

Water pollution results from uncontrolled dumping by industries and the lack of adequate sewage treatment facilities. In 1990, 42% of the nation's facilities were inoperative. In rural areas, 41.5% of the well water is unsafe.

After the nuclear accident at Chernobyl that contaminated much of Lithuania with excessive radiation, Lithuanians are concerned about nuclear energy development and the use of nuclear power generated by plants of the same kind as the one at Chernobyl.

Lithuania's pollution problems have also affected the nation's wildlife. Many of the country's original animal and plant species are now extinct.

⁶POPULATION

The population of Lithuania in 1989 was 3,689,779, of which 68% was urban. It was estimated at 3,751,400 in 1993. The World Bank projects a population of 4,100,000 in 2010, based on a crude birth rate of 15 per 1,000 people, a crude death rate of 11, and a natural increase of 4. The estimated population density in 1993 was about 57 per sq km (149 per sq mi). The biggest cities in 1989 were Vilnius, the capital, 576,747; Kaunas, 418,087; and Klaipėda (formerly Memel), 202,929.

⁷MIGRATION

Many Lithuanians unable to accept Soviet occupation in 1940 were deported to Siberia. However, Russian immigration to Lithuania was never as heavy as to the other Baltic republics. In 1992 there were 6,640 immigrants and 28,853 emigrants. Russians composed 40% of the former and 60% of the latter. Lithuanians made up 34% of the former and 5% of the latter.

⁸ETHNIC GROUPS

In 1989, Lithuanians formed 80% of the population. Russians accounted for 9.4%, Poles, 7%, Belorussians, 1.7%, and Ukrainians, 1.2%. Naturalization required 10 years' residence and competence in Lithuanian. More than 90% of all non-Lithuanians had been granted citizenship by early 1993.

⁹LANGUAGES

Lithuanian is noted for its purity in retaining ancient Indo-European language forms and has some remarkable similarities with

Sanskrit. It is highly inflected, with seven noun cases. Like Latvian, it has rising, falling, and short intonations. Its Roman alphabet has many special symbols, including the hacek, dot, and cedilla. In 1989, 99.6% of the Lithuanians in Lithuania, 95% of the Russians, 85% of the Poles, 51% of the Ukrainians, and 40% of the Belorussians spoke Lithuanian for their first tongue. Minorities have the right to official use of their languages where they form a substantial part of the population.

[10]RELIGIONS

Primarily Roman Catholic, the country witnessed extensive suppression of religious activities during the Soviet period. In 1993, some 80% of the population was Roman Catholic. Ethnic Russians include a representative group of Russian Orthodox adherents. Lutherans are also present and, in 1990, some 9,000 Jews.

[11]TRANSPORTATION

Railways extend 2,010 km (1,250 mi) across Lithuania, providing rail access to the Baltic Sea for Vilnius, Kaunas, and other major urban areas. About 80% of the 44,200 km (27,500 mi) of highways are hard-surfaced. In 1989, buses and trolleys carried 760 million and 288 million passengers, respectively. Sea routes link Klaipėda on the Baltic Sea with 200 foreign ports; Kaunas is the principal inland port. In 1991, the merchant fleet consisted of 66 ships (of 1,000 GRT or over) totaling 268,854 GRT; including 27 cargo vessels, 24 timber carriers, 3 railcar carriers, and 12 other vessels. A railway sea ferry from Klaipėda to Mukran (Germany) began in 1986. Two international airlines serve Lithuania: Lithuanian Airlines and Lietuva served 555,400 and 1,800 passengers, respectively, in 1992.

[12]HISTORY

From the 14th to the 18th centuries, the Grand Duchy of Lithuania was linked to the Kingdom of Poland. What is now Lithuania, though, was annexed to the Russian Empire in the final partition of the Polish-Lithuanian state in 1795. During the 19th century, a Lithuanian nationalist movement arose.

On 16 February 1918, Lithuania proclaimed its independence. The new Bolshevik government in Moscow attempted to establish Soviet power in Lithuania, but failed. In July 1920, Moscow recognized Lithuanian independence. A secret protocol to the 1939 Nazi-Soviet pact assigned Lithuania to the Soviet sphere of influence.

Wishing to avoid conflict, the Lithuanian government allowed Soviet forces to be stationed on its territory. The local government was forced to resign in June 1940. Rigged elections led to a parliament which proclaimed Lithuania to be a Soviet Socialist Republic in July 1940. Moscow lost control of Lithuania soon after Germany attacked the USSR in June 1941. Soviet forces recaptured Lithuania in 1944.

Soviet President Mikhail Gorbachev's policy of glasnost and perestroika allowed Lithuanians to voice their long-suppressed desire for national self-determination. Free elections to the Lithuanian Supreme Soviet on 24 February 1990 resulted in Sajudis—an anti-Communist Lithuanian reform movement—becoming the most influential force in the legislature at the expense of the Communists. On 11 March 1990, Lithuanian independence was proclaimed, but this was not generally recognized until after the abortive August 1991 coup attempt in Moscow.

Lithuania's first post-independence parliamentary elections were held in two rounds on 25 October and 15 November 1992. In these elections, a majority of seats was won by pro-independence former Communists. On 14 February 1993, former Communist Algirdas Brazauskas was elected president in a general election.

The withdrawal of Russian troops from Lithuania was completed on 31 August 1993.

[13]GOVERNMENT

On 25 October 1992, Lithuanian voters approved a new constitution which called for a 141-member unicameral legislature (Seimas) and a popularly elected president. The constitution requires whoever is elected as president to sever his or her formal party ties. All who were permanent residents of Lithuania in November 1989 have been granted the opportunity to become citizens, irrespective of their ethnic origins.

[14]POLITICAL PARTIES

The majority party in the Seimas since the 1992 parliamentary elections has been the Lithuanian Democratic Labor Party (LDLP), which won 73 out of 141 seats. The LDLP is comprised of Lithuanian ex-Communists who are also nationalists, and it seeks cooperative relations with Russia. The next largest is Sajudis and groups associated with it—extremely suspicious of Russia—which won 52 seats. There is also a Social Democratic Party and a Center Movement which together won 10 seats; they consider themselves to be "centrist" parties. The remaining seats were won by Polish and independent groups.

[15]LOCAL GOVERNMENT

Apylinkes (the smallest rural administrative units), urban-type settlements, and district towns make up the lowest level of local government. Districts and cities form the upper level. Local government is made up of the municipal council that is elected by its respective local population.

[16]JUDICIAL SYSTEM

The legal system is being transformed from that of the old Soviet regime to a democratic model. The system now consists of district courts and a Supreme Court which hears appeals from the district level courts. The Procurator General now exercises oversight responsibility through a network of local prosecutors. A newly created Constitutional Court began deliberations in 1993.

Implementation of the structural changes in the legal system, scheduled to take effect in 1992, were delayed pending enactment of new civil and criminal procedure codes which were expected to be enacted in 1994.

[17]ARMED FORCES

The army numbers 7,000, with 123,500 reserves for border and internal peacekeeping. Russia recently withdrew 43,000 soldiers and airmen in the equivalent of an army corps and ground attack air regiment.

[18]INTERNATIONAL COOPERATION

Lithuania was admitted to the UN on 17 September 1991. The country is a member of CSCE, EBRD, IAEA, ILO, IMF, UNCTAD, and the World Bank, and the country's sovereignty is recognized by the US, EC countries, and many others. Lithuania has especially close ties with the countries of the European Community. It is not a member of the CIS.

[19]ECONOMY

Until 1940, Lithuania's economy was primarily agricultural, and agriculture, mainly in the form of dairy farms and livestock raising, still provides roughly half the nation's GNP. The main industries are machine building and metalworking, although light industry and food processing are also well developed. Like the other Baltic states, Lithuania has few natural resources, primarily peat and amber.

[20]INCOME

In 1992, the GNP was $4,922 million at current prices, or $1,310 per capita. For the period 1985–92 the average inflation rate was 49.8%, resulting in a real growth rate in per capita GNP of –2.7%.

LOCATION: 56°0′N; 24°0′E. **BOUNDARY LENGTHS:** Total boundary lengths, 1,381 km (858 mi); Belarus, 502 km (312 mi); Latvia, 453 km (282 mi); Poland, 91 km (57 mi); Russia, 227 km (141 mi).

In 1992 the GDP was $4,922 million in current US dollars.

21LABOR

Lithuania's unwanted annexation by the former Soviet Union after World War II rapidly industrialized the country, forcing labor to move from agriculture to industry. As a result, Lithuania has a skilled work force, which had previously motivated central planners to establish sophisticated industries, leaving a legacy of considerable capacity in machine building, metal working, textile and leather industries, and agriculture and agro-processing. In 1992, the economically active population was estimated at 1.9 million, with industry and agriculture accounting for 25% and 20%, respectively.

Article 50 of the 1992 constitution recognizes the right for workers and employees to form and join trade unions. The Lithuanian Workers Union (LDS) emerged as an independent trade union in 1990, and claimed 50,000 dues-paying members in 1992, organized in 35 regional groupings. Article 51 of the 1992 Constitution provides the right to strike. During 1992, public service sector workers, hairdressers, photo studio operators, and truck and bus drivers engaged in strikes.

The legal minimum wage is periodically adjusted by the government for inflation, but these adjustments lag behind the inflation rate, which was about 800% in 1992.

22AGRICULTURE

Out of Lithuania's 4,551,000 hectares (11,245,000 acres) of land area, 37% and 17% consisted of cropland and permanent pastures, respectively. In 1991, agriculture contributed 21.2% to GDP, although the sector itself shrank by 9.3% that year.

Crops of importance in 1992 included potatoes, 1,079,000 tons; barley, 955,000 tons; wheat, 834,000 tons; sugar beets, 622,000 tons; rye, 342,000 tons; vegetables and melons, 334,000 tons, and oats, 51,000 tons.

[23]ANIMAL HUSBANDRY

About 238,000 hectares (588,100 acres) were classified as permanent pastureland in 1991, representing only 5.2% of the total land area. Livestock in 1992 included 2,197,000 head of cattle, 2,180,000 pigs, 16,000,000 chickens, 58,000 sheep, and 80,000 horses. Meat production in 1992 totaled 377,000 tons, of which 47% was beef, 43% was pork, 9% was chicken, and 1% other meat. Milk production exceeded 2.2 million tons in 1992, when 53,200 tons of eggs were produced.

By 1990, animal husbandry accounted for two-thirds of the output of collective and state farms. Livestock output grew by 7% from 1985–89. As of 1991, individual subsidiary plots accounted for one-third of total production.

[24]FISHING

Klaipéda's fishing port is the center of the fishing industry. In 1989, production totaled 417,900 tons of fish and marine products. As of 1989, there were two aquacultural facilities operating in Lithuania.

[25]FORESTRY

Forests and woodlands cover about 16% of Lithuania. The forestry, wood products, and paper industries are some of Lithuania's oldest—furniture, matches, and timber products were manufactured in Kaunas and Vilnius in the mid-1800s, and furniture-making prevailed from 1919–40. Currently, chemical timber processing, and the production of furniture, pulp, paper, wood fiber, wood chips, joinery articles, and cardboard, are the main activities of the forestry sector. Intensive timber processing, as well as the recycling of industrial waste are being expanded. Exports of wood and paper accounted for 3.1% of total exports in 1990. In 1989, 2.7 million cu m of timber was exported.

[26]MINING

Cement, clays, dolomite, limestone, and sand and gravel are the primary commodities extruded by more than 300 enterprises in Lithuania engaged in the production of industrial minerals. Peat is also extracted by 11 enterprises at 55 different sites.

[27]ENERGY AND POWER

Energy production in Lithuania has long depended on imported oil, natural gas, and coal. After World War II, Lithuania was completely without any domestic electricity generation capacity. By the late 1980s, there were seven electricity-generating facilities, including one hydroelectric and one nuclear power station. By 1990, consumption of electricity was primarily for industry (52%); agriculture was next (21.5%); followed by construction (1.6%); and transportation (1.5%). In 1991, installed capacity totaled 5,875,000 kw; production amounted to 25,500 kwh.

In October 1991, the Chernobyl-type Ignalina nuclear power plant was shut down due to a radioactive steam leak.

[28]INDUSTRY

Lithuania underwent rapid industrialization during the Soviet era and has significant capacity in machine building and metalworking, as well as the textile and leather industries, and agro-processing. The country's diverse manufacturing base also includes an oil refinery and high-tech minicomputer production.

[29]SCIENCE AND TECHNOLOGY

The Lithuanian Academy of Science, founded in 1941, has departments of mathematics, physics, chemistry, biology, medicine, and agriculture. Four institutes conduct research in medicine and forestry. Seven universities and colleges offer degrees in basic and applied sciences.

[30]DOMESTIC TRADE

Vilnius, Klaipéda, and Kaunas each have shopping areas and several markets; many smaller towns have a central market. Inflation (estimated at 125% in 1994) severely hinders domestic purchasing power. Organized crime has grown since independence and often extorts "protection" money from local businesses through intimidation (including bombings and arson).

[31]FOREIGN TRADE

Lithuania depends heavily on trade, particularly with other republics of the former Soviet Union. In 1988, total imports were valued at R7,800 million, and exports at R4,100. Inter-republican trade accounted for 83% of imports and 91% of exports. Since Lithuania's independence in 1990, growing disruptions in trade with Russia and the other republics have resulted in a steep decline in import volumes and numerous domestic shortages.

[32]BALANCE OF PAYMENTS

Inter-regional trade with other former Soviet republics, which had accounted for over one-half of Lithuania's exports in previous years, collapsed in 1991/92; hard currency is dearly needed to counteract a rising trade deficit, and Lithuania's reserves are the lowest among the Baltic nations.

[33]BANKING AND SECURITIES

Since 1991, Lithuania has reorganized its banking sector numerous times. On 3 July 1992 the government adopted a new currency unit, the litas, to replace the ruble. The banking sector consists of the Central Bank of Lithuania, four state banks, and 20 commercial banks. State banks in Lithuania include the Savings Bank, the Commercial Bank of Lithuania, and the Agricultural Bank. There are no security exchanges in the country.

[34]INSURANCE

Lithuania's health insurance system is reminiscent of the Soviet era through a state-run system of coverage for all residents.

[35]PUBLIC FINANCE

During the late 1980s, Lithuania's central and general government budgets typically ran deficits. In 1991, however, the general government budget recorded a surplus equivalent to 3% of GDP, due to new tax reform and collection measures, higher social security revenues, elimination of subsidies, and the end of transfers to the former USSR. In 1992, however, falling tax revenues and increasing expenditures for unemployment and other social benefits caused fiscal tensions. As a former Soviet republic, it is still uncertain how much debt Lithuania will be responsible for paying; Lithuania's official position is that it bears no responsibility for debt incurred during the Soviet period.

[36]TAXATION

The personal income tax rate varies from 10–33%; corporate income is taxed at a flat rate of 29%. Also levied are an 18% value-added tax, a 5% withholding tax, and a social security contribution of 30% by employers and 1% by employees.

[37]CUSTOMS AND DUTIES

Most foreign imports, including all raw materials, are duty-free. Exceptions include food products (5–10%), fabrics (10%), electronics (10%), cement (25%), and window glass (50%). Alcoholic beverages are subject to duties ranging from 10% for beer to 100% for some liquors. In 1991, the Baltic states announced their intention of forming a customers union modeled after the EC.

[38]FOREIGN INVESTMENT

In May 1991, a foreign investment law was passed permitting majority holdings by non-residents and guaranteeing the full transfer of profits. Lithuania expected investor interest from Scandinavia and other parts of Western Europe. As of May 1992, there were some 400 joint ventures, mostly with Poland, although the US had provided the majority of the capital.

[39]ECONOMIC DEVELOPMENT

In 1990, the Lithuanian government began a comprehensive economic reform program aimed at effecting the transformation to a market-driven economy. Reform measures include price reform, trade reform, and privatization. By mid-1993, 92% of housing and roughly 60% of businesses slated for privatization had been privatized.

[40]SOCIAL DEVELOPMENT

A national system of social insurance covers all of Lithuania's residents. Old age, sickness, disability, and unemployment benefits are paid on an earnings-related basis, from contributions by both employers and employees. The state also pays universal pensions and other benefits to those not covered through employment. Welfare benefits are paid by municipalities. At the end of 1989, 839,000 pensioners, including 206,000 farmers, received benefits averaging R85.4 per month. To qualify for earnings-related retirement benefits, men must be 60 years old with a 25-year work record. Women may retire at 50 after working 20 years. Disability payments amounted to R35 per month in 1989.

Legally, men and women have equal status, including equal pay for equal work, although in practice women are underrepresented in managerial and professional positions. Women receive maternity and day-care benefits. In 1990, the fertility rate was 2.04.

[41]HEALTH

The birthrate in 1993 was 14.8 per 1,000 people. In 1992, there were 56,000 births (a rate of 15 per 1,000 inhabitants). Life expectancy was 73 years in 1992 (79 for females and 68 for males). Total health expenditures for Lithuania in 1990 were $594 million.

In 1990, there was 1 physician for every 220 people. One-year-old children were immunized between 1990 and 1992 as follows: tuberculosis (94%); diphtheria, pertussis, and tetanus (78%); polio (88%); and measles (89%). In 1990, there were 82 cases of tuberculosis per 100,000 people.

The infant mortality rate in 1992 was 17 per 1,000 live births, and the overall death rate was 15 per 1,000 people. Mortality by cause of death for the years 1985 to 1990 were as follows: communicable diseases, maternal/perinatal causes, 25 per 100,000 people; noncommunicable diseases, 598 per 100,000; and injuries, 107 per 100,000.

[42]HOUSING

At the end of 1989, housing floor space totaled 70.8 million sq m, including 43.2 million sq m of state and cooperative apartments and 27.6 sq m of private housing. A total of 142,000 families (18% of all families) were on waiting lists for housing.

[43]EDUCATION

The adult literacy rate in 1990 was estimated as 98.4%, with men estimated at 99.2% and women at 97.8%. Education is free and compulsory for all children between the ages of six and 16 years (for 10 years). While Lithuanian is the most common medium of instruction, children also study Polish, Russian, and Yiddish.

At the postsecondary level institutions, over 55,000 pupils were enrolled in 1992–93. The four known universities are: Kaunas University of Technology (founded in 1950); Vilnius Technical University (founded in 1961); Vilnius University (founded in 1579); and Vytautas Magnus University (founded in 1922).

[44]LIBRARIES AND MUSEUMS

Founded in 1570 the Vilnius University Library has over 4 million volumes. Vilnius also has the Central Library of the Academy of Sciences, the Library of Trade Unions, and the Republican Scientific technical Library. Vilnius also has the Gediminas Castle Museum, the Memorial Museum of Writers, the National Art Museum, the Jewish Museum, and other museums for applied arts, history and ethnography, and architecture. Kaunas has several museums and galleries showing ceramics, photography, stained glass, and sculpture. There is a clock museum and an aquarium in Klaipėda.

[45]MEDIA

Lithuania has one of the best developed telephone systems in the former Soviet Union. There are approximately 22 telephones per 100 people. Broadcasting is controlled by Lithuanian Television and Radio Broadcasting. Radio Vilnius broadcasts in Lithuanian, Russian, Polish, and English. There are 13 AM and 26 FM radio stations and three television stations.

In 1991, there were 1,420,000 radios and 1,400,000 television sets. There were 456 newspapers and 104 periodicals published in 1990.

[46]ORGANIZATIONS

Important economic organizations include the Association of Chamber of Commerce and Industry, an organization that coordinates the activities of all the chambers of commerce in Lithuania. There are three umbrella trade union organizations in the country: the Lithuania Confederation of Free Trade Unions, the Lithuania Union of Trade Unions, and the Lithuanian Workers' Union.

[47]TOURISM, TRAVEL, AND RECREATION

The capital city of Vilnius has one of the largest historic districts in Eastern Europe, distinguished primarily by its Baroque churches, many of which have been reclaimed since independence by money and missionaries from abroad. Kaunas, Lithuania's second-largest city, offers the tourist old merchants' buildings and museums, and the seaside resort towns are active in the summer. There is a shortage of quality hotels, although some have been restored with foreign investment. The traveler can participate in tennis, fishing, sailing, rowing, and winter sports. Lithuanians have long distinguished themselves at basketball, and have contributed top players to the Soviet teams. Seven Lithuanians have Olympic gold medals, and the national basketball team won a bronze medal in Barcelona in 1992. Besides valid passports, all visitors need visas, except nationals of the UK, Hungary, Poland, and Denmark.

[48]FAMOUS LITHUANIANS

Algirdas Brazauskas and Adolfas Slezevicius have been president and prime minister of Lithuania since March 1993, respectively.

[49]DEPENDENCIES

Lithuania has no territories or colonies.

[50]BIBLIOGRAPHY

Graham, Malbone W. *New Governments of Eastern Europe.* New York: H. Holt, 1927.
Lithuania: Transition to a Market Economy. Washington, D.C.: World Bank, 1993.
Newman, E. W. Polson. *Britain and the Baltic.* London: Methuen, 1930.

Senn, Alfred Erich. *Lithuania Awakening.* Berkeley: University of California Press, 1990.

———. *The Emergence of Modern Lithuania.* New York: Columbia University Press, 1959.

Simutis, Anicetas. *The Economic Reconstruction of Lithuania after 1918.* New York: Columbia University Press, 1942.

Suziedelis, Simas (ed.). *Encyclopedia Lituanica.* Boston: J. Kapocius, 1970.

The Baltic and Caucasian States. London: Hodder and Stoughton, 1923.

Vardys, Vytas Stanley (ed.). *Lithuania under the Soviets; Portrait of a Nation, 1940–65.* New York: Praeger, 1965.

LUXEMBOURG

Grand Duchy of Luxembourg
French: *Grand-Duché de Luxembourg*
German: *Grossherzogtum Luxemburg*

CAPITAL: Luxembourg.

FLAG: The flag is a tricolor of red, white, and blue horizontal stripes.

ANTHEM: *Ons Hémecht (Our Homeland).*

MONETARY UNIT: The Luxembourg franc (LFr) of 100 centimes is a paper currency equal in value to the Belgian franc. There are coins of 25 and 50 centimes and ¼, 1, 5, 10, and 20 francs, and notes of 50 and 100 francs. Belgian currency is legal tender in Luxembourg, and bills of 500, 1,000, and 5,000 Belgian francs are regularly circulated. LFr1 = $0.0293 (or $1 = LFr34.115).

WEIGHTS AND MEASURES: The metric system is the legal standard.

HOLIDAYS: New Year's Day, 1 January; Labor Day, 1 May; public celebration of the Grand Duke's Birthday, 23 June; Assumption, 15 August; All Saints' Day, 1 November; Christmas, 25–26 December. Movable religious holidays include Shrove Monday, Easter Monday, Ascension, and Pentecost Monday.

TIME: 1 PM = noon GMT.

¹LOCATION, SIZE, AND EXTENT

A landlocked country in Western Europe, Luxembourg has an area of 2,586 sq km (998 sq mi), with a length of 82 km (51 mi) N-S and a width of 57 km (35 mi) E-W Comparatively, the area occupied by Luxembourg is slightly smaller than the state of Rhode Island. The eastern boundary with Germany is formed by the Our, Sûre (Sauer), and Moselle rivers. Luxembourg is bordered on the s by France and on the w and N by Belgium, with a total boundary length of 359 km (223 mi).

Luxembourg's capital city, Luxembourg, is located in the southcentral part of the country.

²TOPOGRAPHY

The country is divided into two distinct geographic regions: the rugged uplands (Oesling) of the Ardennes in the north, where the average elevation is 450 m (1,476 ft) and the highest point is 559 m (1,834 ft); and the fertile southern lowlands, called Bon Pays (Good Land), with an average altitude of 250 m (820 ft).

The entire area is crisscrossed by deep valleys, with most rivers draining eastward into the Sûre (160 km/99 mi within Luxembourg), which in turn flows into the Moselle (40 km/25 mi) on the eastern border. The northern region, comprising one-third of the country, is forested and has poor soil.

³CLIMATE

Luxembourg's climate is temperate and mild. Summers are generally cool, with a mean temperature of about 17°C (63°F); winters are seldom severe, average temperature being about 0°C (32°F). The high peaks of the Ardennes in the north shelter the country from rigorous north winds, and the prevailing northwesterly winds have a cooling effect. Rainfall is plentiful in the extreme southwest; precipitation throughout the country averages about 75 cm (30 in) annually.

⁴FLORA AND FAUNA

The principal trees are pine, chestnut, spruce, oak, linden, elm, and beech, along with fruit trees. There are many shrubs, such as blueberry and genista, and ferns; a multitude of lovely flowers; and many vineyards. Only a few wild animal species (deer, roe deer, and wild boar) remain, but birds are plentiful, and many varieties of fish are found in the rivers, including perch, carp, bream, trout, pike, and eel.

⁵ENVIRONMENT

The Ministry of the Environment is the main environmental agency. Government statistics indicate considerable improvement in pollution control. Luxembourg has 0.2 cu mi of water, with 45% used for industrial activity and 13% used in farming. The nation's cities produce 0.2 tons of solid waste and 817.7 tons of toxic substances. Luxembourg produces 3.3 tons of particulate emissions and 22 tons of hydrocarbon emissions per year. Emissions of particles of sulfur dioxide declined substantially from 1972 to 1983 and are well within EC standards.

Forest reserves have been severely depleted since 1800, when three-fourths of the country was forest; during World War II, heavy demands for fuel and German requisitions contributed to the depletion. There is one endangered mammal species in Luxembourg, as well as eight bird species and one species of plant. Animals extinct in Luxembourg include the wolf and European otter.

⁶POPULATION

The population according to the census of 1 March 1991 was 384,062 (364,602 in 1981), of whom 47% lived in cities. A population of 400,000 is projected for the year 2000. In 1991, Luxembourg had a crude birthrate of 12.9 per 1,000 population and a crude death rate of 9.6, for a net natural increase of 3.3. Average density in 1991 was 148.5 persons per sq km (385 per sq mi). The city of Luxembourg, the capital, had a population of 75,377 in 1991. The chief industrial city is Esch-sur-Alzette, with a population of 24,012. Other leading communes are Dudelange, 14,677; Differdange, 8,489; and Schifflange, 6,859.

⁷MIGRATION

During the 19th century, thousands of Luxembourgers emigrated, chiefly to the US. In 1870, however, rich deposits of iron ore were uncovered in southern Luxembourg, and during the period of industrialization and prosperity that followed, many persons from neighboring countries migrated to Luxembourg. In recent years, both emigration and immigration have been comparatively small. As of 1992, about 114,700 residents of Luxembourg were foreigners, chiefly "guest workers" from Portugal, Italy, France, Belgium, Germany, and other European countries.

8ETHNIC GROUPS

The indigenous inhabitants of Luxembourg consider themselves a distinct nationality, with a specific ethnic character. A strong indication of that character is the national motto, "Mir woelle bleiwe wat mir sin" ("We want to remain what we are"), for despite a history of long foreign domination, Luxembourgers have retained their individuality as a nation. There are also native-born residents of French, Belgian, or German ancestry, as well as a substantial immigrant population (29% of the total in 1991).

9LANGUAGES

Luxembourgers are a trilingual people who speak Letzeburgesch, the original dialect of the country, as well as French and German. All three are official languages. Letzeburgesch is a Germanic dialect related to the Moselle Frankish language that was once spoken in western Germany. It rarely appears in written form.

Letzeburgesch, French, and German are the languages of instruction in primary schools, while French is the most common language of instruction in secondary schools. Government publications are generally in French.

10RELIGIONS

There is complete religious freedom. Catholic priests, Protestant pastors, and Jewish rabbis are, however, paid by the state. In 1993, the population was estimated as 95% Roman Catholic, and 5% Protestant or other religions.

11TRANSPORTATION

Transportation facilities are excellent. The railways are consolidated into one organization, the Société Nationale des Chemins de Fers Luxembourgeois (CFL), with the government of Luxembourg controlling 51% of the stock and the remaining 49% divided between the French and Belgian governments. Railway lines, totaling 270 km (168 mi) in 1991, provide direct links with Belgium via Arlon, with France via Metz and Longwy, and with the FRG via Trier. There is through-train service to Paris and other points in France. CFL performed 282 million passenger-km and 672 freight ton-km of service in 1991.

In January 1992 there were 5,108 km (3,174 mi) of state and local roads. Direct roads connect all important towns, and the main arteries are suitable for heavy motor traffic. At the beginning of 1991, 200,739 cars, 12,881 trucks, and 777 buses were registered. As of 1990, a program to link Luxembourg's highways to those of Belgium, France, and Germany was being carried out.

The only river available for industrial transport is the Moselle, which for 37 km (23 mi) allows navigation of barges of up to 1,500 tons. In 1991, the merchant fleet comprised 47 ships with 1,593,000 GRT. The country's only airport is Findel, located near the city of Luxembourg, which served 1,092,000 passengers in 1992. Regular flights to other European cities are operated by Luxair, the national carrier, and by foreign airlines.

12HISTORY

The land now known as Luxembourg fell under the successive domination of the Celts, the Romans, and the Riparian Franks before its founding as the County of Luxembourg in 963 by Sigefroid, count of the Ardennes, who reconstructed a small ruined fortress called Lucilinburhuc (Little Burg) on the site of the present capital. The territory trebled in size during the reign of Countess Ermesinde (1196–1247). John, count of Luxembourg (r.1309–46) and king of Bohemia, became the national hero; although blind for many years, the inveterate knight-errant laid the foundations for a powerful dynasty before he fell in the Battle of Crécy, in northern France, during the Hundred Years' War. His son Charles (1316–78) was the second of four Luxembourg princes to become Holy Roman emperor. He made Luxembourg a duchy, but under his successors the country was ruined financially.

Luxembourg came under Burgundian rule in 1443 and remained in foreign hands for more than 400 years. Successively it passed to Spain (1506–1714, excepting 1684–97, when it was ruled by France), Austria (1714–95), and France (1795–1815). The Congress of Vienna in 1815 made Luxembourg a grand duchy and allotted it as an independent state to the king of the Netherlands, after ceding to Prussia its territory east of the Moselle, Sûre, and Our. Luxembourg lost more than half its territory to Belgium in 1839, but gained a larger measure of autonomy, although Dutch kings continued to rule as grand dukes. By the Treaty of London in 1867, Luxembourg was declared an independent and neutral state under the protection of the Great Powers, but was required to dismantle its mighty fortress. In 1890, the house of Nassau-Weilbourg, in the person of Grand Duke Adolphe (r.1890–1905), became the ruling house of Luxembourg. The country was occupied by German troops in World War I. In 1919, Grand Duchess Charlotte succeeded to the throne, and on 28 September 1919, in a referendum held to decide the country's future, a plurality supported her. In 1921, Luxembourg formed an economic union with Brussels.

The Germans again invaded the country in May 1940, but the grand ducal family and most members of the government escaped to safety. Under the Nazi occupation, the people suffered severely, particularly when their revolt in 1942 protesting compulsory service in the German army was savagely repressed. Luxembourg was liberated by Allied forces in September 1944.

That year, while still in exile, the government agreed to form an economic union with Belgium and the Netherlands; the first phase, the Benelux Customs Union, was effected in 1948. In February 1958, a treaty of economic union, which became effective in 1960, was signed by representatives of the three countries. During the postwar decades, Luxembourg also became an active member of NATO and the EC.

In April 1963, Luxembourg celebrated its 1,000th anniversary as an independent state. On 12 November 1964, Grand Duchess Charlotte abdicated in favor of her son, Jean, who became grand duke and who remained so as of 1994. His reign was marked by continued prosperity, as Luxembourg's economy shifted from dependence on steel to an emphasis on services, notably international banking.

In July 1992, Luxembourg approved the Maastrecht Treaty.

13GOVERNMENT

Luxembourg is a constitutional monarchy, governed by the constitution of 1868 as revised in 1919 (when universal suffrage and proportional representation were introduced) and subsequently. The grand ducal crown is hereditary in the house of Nassau-Weilbourg. Legislative power is vested in the Chamber of Deputies, the 60 (prior to 1984, 64 members) members of which (as of 1987) are elected for five-year terms. In addition, the Council of State, composed of 21 members appointed for life by the sovereign, acts as a consulting body in legislative, administrative, and judicial matters and has the right of suspensive veto.

Executive power rests jointly in the sovereign, who may initiate legislation, and a prime minister (president of the government), appointed by the monarch, who in turn selects a cabinet. The prime minister, together with the cabinet, must command a majority in the Chamber of Deputies. Voting is compulsory, and eligibility begins at age 18.

14 POLITICAL PARTIES

Since 1947, shifting coalitions among the three largest parties have governed the country. The Christian Social Party (Parti Chrétien Social—PCS) is a Catholic, promonarchist movement favoring progressive labor legislation and government protection for farmers and small business. Except for the period 1974–79, the PCS has been the dominant partner in all ruling coalitions since World War I. The Socialist Party (Parti Ouvrier Socialiste Luxembourgeois—POSL) supports improvement and extension of the present system of social welfare programs. The third major group, the Democratic Party (Parti Démocratique—PD), favors social reforms and minimal government activity in the economy. Other parties include the Luxembourg Communist Party (Parti Communiste—PC), which has its main strength with steelworkers in the industrialized south, and the Social Democratic Party (Parti Social-Démocrate Luxembourgeois—PSDL), which split from the POSL in 1971.

Two new minor parties have secured representation in parliament—the Green Alternative and the Five-Sixths Party. The latter is a single-issue party advocating pensions worth five-sixths of one's final salary for everyone.

Following the elections of 1994, party alignment in the Chamber of Deputies was PCS, 22; POSL, 18; PD, 11; and other groups, 9. Leading a PCS-POSL coalition as prime minister was Jacques Santer of the PCS.

15 LOCAL GOVERNMENT

Luxembourg is divided into 3 districts (Luxembourg, Diekirch, and Grevenmacher) comprising 12 cantons, which in turn make up 118 communes. The districts are headed by commissioners—civil servants who are responsible to the central government. Each commune elects an autonomous communal council headed by a burgomaster; the councils elect government officials at the local level. Local elections are held every six years and are next scheduled for 1995.

16 JUDICIAL SYSTEM

The legal system is similar to the French Napoleonic Code, except for the commercial and penal divisions, which are similar to their Belgian counterparts. Minor cases generally come before a justice of the peace. On a higher level are the two district courts, one in the city of Luxembourg and the other in Diekirch. The Superior Court of Justice acts as a court of appeal. The Court of Assizes, within the jurisdiction of the Superior Court, deals with criminal cases. The final judicial authority on matters relating to administration resides with a committee of 11 chosen from the Council of State. Judges are appointed for life terms. The death penalty was abolished in 1979. The prosecutor as well as the defendant may appeal verdicts in criminal cases. An appeal results in a completely new judicial procedure with the possibility that a sentence may be increased or decreased.

Luxembourg is the site of the European Court of Justice.

17 ARMED FORCES

In 1967, Luxembourg abolished conscription and created a volunteer military force that is part of NATO. Responsbility for defense matters is vested in the Ministry of Public Force, which also controls the police and gendarmerie.

In 1993 its army consisted of one infantry battalion of 800, and a gendarmerie of 560. Budgeted defense expenditures in 1991 were $100 million or 1.4 % percent of gross domestic product. NATO maintains 20 early warning aircraft with Luxembourg registration.

More than 5,000 American soldiers, including Gen. George S. Patton, are buried at the American Military Cemetery near the capital.

Luxembourg has no air force or navy.

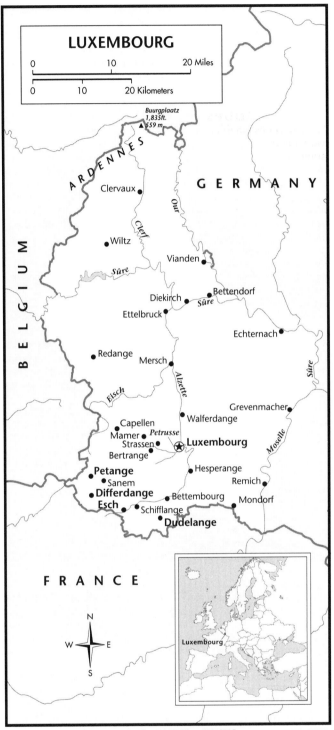

LOCATION: 49°26'52" to 50°10'58"N; 5°44'10" to 6°31'53"E. BOUNDARY LENGTHS: FRG, 135 km (84 mi); France, 73 km (45 mi); Belgium, 148 km (92 mi).

18 INTERNATIONAL COOPERATION

Luxembourg is a founding member of the UN, having joined on 24 October 1945, and participates in ECE and all the nonregional specialized agencies except IMO. Since 1921, it has been joined with Belgium in the Belgium-Luxembourg Economic Union (BLEU); it is a partner with Belgium and the Netherlands in the Benelux Economic Union.

Luxembourg is a member of the Council of Europe, the European Coal and Steel Community (headquartered in Luxembourg), the other EC agencies, NATO, OECD, and many other international organizations. Luxembourg has signed GATT and the Law of the Sea treaty.

[19]ECONOMY

In relation to its size and population, Luxembourg is one of the most highly industrialized countries in the world. Its standard of living rivals that of any country in Europe. Steelmaking, traditionally the most important industry, has been in recession since 1974, and its contribution to GDP declined from 21% in 1974 to 5.5% in 1992. To take up the slack, plastics, rubber and chemicals and other light industries were developed successfully, and service industries, most notably banking, expanded rapidly. Iron ore, formerly mined in limited quantities, is no longer produced because supplies have been exhausted.

The country's lack of industrial fuels makes it completely dependent on imports of coke for steel production. Agriculture is generally small-scale, with livestock and vineyards comprising the most important segment.

The worldwide recession of the early 1980s adversely affected Luxembourg's economy; between 1985 and 1992, however, GDP grew by 32%, or 4% per year. Inflation, as high as 9.4% in 1982, was only 0.3% in 1986 and averaged 3.3% during 1988–92. The unemployment rate averaged just 1.4% between 1984 and 1991 and was 2.2% in 1993.

[20]INCOME

In 1992, Luxembourg's GNP was $13,716 million at current prices, or $35,260 per capita. For the period 1985–92 the average inflation rate was 3.1%, resulting in a real growth rate in per capita GNP of 3.1%.

In 1988 the GDP was $7.38 billion in current US dollars. It is estimated that in 1991 agriculture, hunting, forestry, and fishing contributed 1% to GDP; mining and quarrying, 0%; manufacturing, 24%; electricity, gas, and water, 2%; construction, 7%; wholesale and retail trade, 16%; transport, storage, and communication, 7%; finance, insurance, real estate, and business services, 14%; community, social, and personal services, 15%; and other sources, 12%.

[21]LABOR

Of 167,532 economically active persons in 1991, 26,467 (15.8%) were employed in industry; 29,296 (17.5%) in trade, restaurants, and hotels; 52,690 (31.5%) in services and public administration; 14,042 (8.4%) in construction; 15,437 (9.2%) in credit and insurance; 10,623 (6.3%) in transportation and communications; 5,345 (3.2%) in agriculture and forestry; and 13,632 (8.1%) in other sectors. Unemployment was virtually nonexistent until the recession of the mid-1980s. In March 1991 there were 3,321 unemployed workers, slightly less than 2% of the work force.

Labor relations have been generally peaceful since the 1930s. Foreign investors are attracted by the positive relationship which exists in Luxembourg between employers and the labor force.

There is a strong trade union movement; about two-thirds of the labor force is organized, with half the members in the two largest unions. The Socialist-dominated General Confederation of Labor and the Confederation of Christian Trade Unions are the largest labor groups. Rapid industrial recovery after World War II was accompanied by progressive labor legislation. There are paid holidays and sick leave, and a legislated 40-hour workweek.

As of August 1992, workers who are at least 18 years of age with no dependents are entitled to a minimum wage. Wage agreements are generally arrived at by industry-wide bargaining between labor and management. Workers may strike only after their dispute is submitted to the National Conciliation Office and all mediation efforts have failed. No strikes occurred in 1992.

[22]AGRICULTURE

Almost 4% of the work force and 50% of the land (126,090 hectares/311,573 acres) were devoted to agriculture and grazing in 1990; the majority of agricultural land consisted of meadows and pastures. Farms are generally small and highly mechanized, although average farm size has been increasing. While the number of farms of 2 hectares (5 acres) or more fell from 10,570 in 1950 to 3,768 in 1985, the average holding increased from 13.16 to 33.33 hectares (from 32.52 to 82.36 acres) over the same period.

Vineyards including Ehnen, Stadtbredmis, and Bech-Kleinmacher are located in the Moselle River Valley. Wine and clover seeds are the important agricultural exports. In addition, millions of rosebushes, a major speciality crop, are exported annually. Chief fruits produced include apples, plums, and cherries.

[23]ANIMAL HUSBANDRY

Livestock breeding is relatively important, particularly because of Luxembourg's dairy product exports. In 1992, livestock included 209,335 head of cattle, 67,837 pigs, 6,924 sheep, and 1,835 equines. A total of 23,100 tons of meat and 260,400 tons of milk were produced in 1992.

[24]FISHING

There is some commercial fishing for domestic consumption and much private fishing for sport. The rivers teem with perch, carp, trout, pike, eel, and bream.

[25]FORESTRY

About 21% of the land area is woodland. Forestry production in 1990 included 246,470 cu m of round wood from deciduous trees and 445,032 cu m from conifers. Chief commercial woods are spruce and oak.

[26]MINING

Luxembourg's traditional source of mineral wealth was iron ore, concentrated on the southwestern border between Redange and Dudelange. Because of mine depletion, however, production declined from 2,079,000 tons in 1976 to 429,000 tons by 1981, at which time the last iron mines closed down. Production now depends on scrap and imported ores. However, the iron and steel industry is the single most important industrial sector of the economy. Slate quarrying is carried on primarily for export, and a few nonmetallic minerals (dolomite, gypsum, limestone, and sand and gravel) are mined for use in construction.

[27]ENERGY AND POWER

Net installed capacity in 1991 was 1,238,000 kw, of which 91% was hydroelectric. Gross production of electrical energy in 1991 amounted to 1,415 million kwh, of which 617 million kwh were produced by thermal power and 798 million kwh by three hydroelectric facilities. Electrical production has increased since the dams at Esch-sur-Sûre and Rosport were completed. The hydroelectric plant at Vianden has the largest pumping station in Europe. Virtually all of the country's hydroelectric potential has now been put to use. Electrical energy imported amounted to 4,500 million kwh, while exports reached 780 million kwh. Petroleum accounted for 52.5% of Luxembourg's total energy consumption in 1992; coal, 19.6%; natural gas, 13.1%; and other sources, 14.8%. In 1991, only 1% of total solid fuel requirements was domestically produced, mostly from the burning of waste material. The steel industry consumes 80% of total industrial energy demand.

[28]INDUSTRY

Luxembourg's industrial output declined about 14% between 1979 and 1982, but then made a recovery, growing 12% in 1984 and 5% in 1985. By 1989, output had grown another 18.6%, but it slumped 1% over the next three years. Massive restructuring of the steel industry and continuing diversification of the industrial base characterized the 1980s. Under the ongoing industrial diversification program, more than 80 new firms were launched between 1960 and 1985, providing jobs for 10,332 people. Chemicals, rubber, metal processing, glass, and aluminum became increasingly important, while some other industries, including construction, remained depressed; traditional light industries such as tanneries, glove-making plants, and textile mills were forced either to close down or to greatly reduce their scale of operations.

In 1992, steel was responsible for 36.1% of the industrial gross value added (at factor cost), down from 59.7% in 1970. Production of pig iron in 1992 was 2,255,200 tons (4,814,000 tons in 1970); steel, 3,945,000 tons (5,462,000 tons in 1970); and rolled steel products, 3,590,214 tons (4,252,000 tons in 1970). Luxembourg's blast furnaces and steel mills are located in the Bassin Minier of the southwest. Mergers have given ARBED, a private multinational firm with significant government shareholding, virtually complete control of the steel industry.

29 SCIENCE AND TECHNOLOGY

The Grand Ducal Institute, the central learned society, includes medical and scientific as well as historical, literary, artistic, linguistic, and folkloric sections. Two public research centers conduct scientific research. The University Center of Luxembourg has a science department. The Higher Institute of Technology has 550 students.

30 DOMESTIC TRADE

The commercial code is similar to that of Belgium, and trade practices are nearly identical. The city of Luxembourg is the headquarters for the distribution of imported goods within the country, and Antwerp in Belgium is the principal port of entry. Consequently, manufacturers' agents and importers maintain offices in one or both of those cities. French, German, and English are the languages of business correspondence.

Shopping hours are from 2 to 6 PM on Mondays and from 8 AM to 12 noon and 2 to 6 PM, Tuesday–Friday. Banking hours are on weekdays, 8:30 AM to 12 noon and 1:30–4:30 PM. Advertising is extensive, particularly in newspapers and on Radio-Télé-Luxembourg.

31 FOREIGN TRADE

Luxembourg remains dependent on foreign trade, even though domestic demand has become an increasingly important factor in fueling the economy. The nation's trade position has weakened with the decline of the steel industry: between 1974 and 1981, imports grew by 55% while exports rose only 7%, as the trade balance swung into deficit. Between 1985 and 1992, imports grew by 42% and exports rose only 24%.

Principal exports in 1992 (in millions of Luxembourg francs) were as follows:

Metals and minerals	67,559
Plastics, rubber, and tires	27,571
Chemical products	9,994
Machines and instruments	30,852
Textiles and clothing	14,712
Transport equipment	12,236
Animal and vegetable products	7,886
Food, beverages, tobacco	5,399
Stone, cement, and glass products	12,426
Other exports	19,493
TOTAL	208,128

Principal imports in 1992 (in millions of Luxembourg francs) were as follows:

Mineral and energy products	30,507
Metals and minerals	38,540
Chemicals	21,278
Plastics, rubber, and tires	13,508
Machines and instruments	48,291
Transport equipment	32,380
Food, beverages, tobacco	14,822
Textiles and clothing	14,120
Animal and vegetable products	12,654
Other imports	39,080
TOTAL	265,180

Trade with European nations accounted for 94.9% of imports and 89.5% of exports in 1992. With 30% of the total trade volume in 1992, Germany was Luxembourg's most important trading partner. Belgium ranked second, with 29%.

Principal trade partners (in millions of Luxembourg francs) were as follows:

	EXPORTS	IMPORTS	BALANCE
Germany	60,817	83,311	−22,494
Belgium	33,638	102,647	−69,009
France	34,976	30,459	4,517
Netherlands	10,678	12,042	−1,364
US	7,722	5,607	2,115
UK	11,875	4,512	7,363
Italy	11,738	5,354	6,384
Other countries	36,684	21,248	15,436
TOTALS	208,128	265,180	−57,052

32 BALANCE OF PAYMENTS

Luxembourg enjoyed a favorable trade balance from 1951 until 1975, when rising energy costs and structural weakness in the steel industry led to deterioration in terms of trade. The overall balance of payments has, however, tended to show a surplus, mainly because of income from banking services.

33 BANKING AND SECURITIES

Banking has been gaining in importance since the 1970s; by 1980, the sector accounted for 18% of the GDP. The principal bank and the sole bank of issue is the International Bank of Luxembourg (Banque Internationale à Luxembourg), founded in 1856. The Belgium-Luxembourg monetary agreement, as renewed for 10 years in 1991, provided for the establishment of the Luxembourg Monetary Institute to represent the nation at international monetary conferences and institutions. In December 1991 there were 187 banking firms in Luxembourg, most of them foreign, as compared with only 19 in 1960. In 1985, deposits in credit and savings accounts amounted to LFr1,384.6 billion in 1991, more than 20 times the figure for 1970. The banking sector has benefited from favorable laws governing holding companies. The European Investment Bank (an EC institution) and the European Monetary Fund are headquartered in Luxembourg. As of 31 December 1992, assets of the commercial banks totaled $376,499 million.

The Luxembourg Bourse, founded in 1929 in the city of Luxembourg, primarily handles stocks and bonds issued by domestic companies, although it also lists Belgian securities.

34 INSURANCE

Insurance was written by 155 firms in 1989. Third-party liability insurance is compulsory for all automobile owners. Domestic insurance companies issue both life and non-life policies. Of the total of 1,306,000 policies in force in 1985, 425,000 covered accidents, 202,000 fire, and 108,000 life. The volume of premiums in 1990 totaled $1,167 per capita, or 4.8% of the GDP.

35PUBLIC FINANCE

The budget of the Luxembourg government is presented to the Chamber of Deputies late in each calendar year and becomes effective the following year. Government budgets showed steady surpluses from 1984 to 1990. The 1990 surplus, amounting to 3.4% of GDP, enabled the government to channel additional monies into investment funds and into a budget reserve exceeding LFr6 billion ($160 million). That a budget reserve exists at all reflects the conservatively healthy management of Luxembourg's public finances. Deficits in 1991 and 1992 were largely caused by the continued funding of the government's investment program. To fund the program, the government draws from accumulated surpluses and raises capital in financial markes.

The following table shows actual revenues and expenditures for 1990 and 1991 in millions of francs.

	1990	1991
REVENUE AND GRANTS		
Tax revenue	134,594	143,037
Non-tax revenue	—	—
Capital revenue	1,550	721
Grants	954	613
TOTALS	137,098	144,371
EXPENDITURES & LENDING MINUS REPAYMENTS		
General public service	10,926	13,858
Defense	3,085	3,143
Public order and safety	2,593	2,730
Education	13,857	14,750
Health	3,420	3,404
Social security and welfare	67,945	76,824
Housing and community amenities	5,960	5,871
Recreation, cultural, and religious affairs	1,861	2,334
Economic affairs and services	22,814	23,632
Other expenditures	9,347	9,600
Adjustments	—	—
Lending minus repayments	3,022	8,514
TOTALS	144,830	164,660
Deficit/Surplus	16,949	–37,189

In 1991 Luxembourg's total public debt stood at LFr9,243 million. Since 1970, outstanding government debt as a percentage of GDP has steadily declined. Public debt is issued primarily to meet the institutional investment requirements of domestic pension plans and insurance companies.

36TAXATION

A graduated income tax, imposed on all net personal income, ranges from 10% to 50%. As of 1992, corporations were taxed at a flat rate of 33% plus a 1% unemployment surcharge. Holding companies are especially favored and are exempt from most taxes. Besides income taxes, levies include a municipal business tax, net worth tax, import tax, excise taxes, inheritance and gift taxes, and a value-added tax at a standard rate of 15%.

37CUSTOMS AND DUTIES

Tariff policies have been traditionally liberal. Duties have been reduced on nearly 90% of imports from countries belonging to the EC; as a member of the Benelux Customs Union, Luxembourg permits imports free of duty from Belgium and the Netherlands. The tariff on non-EC goods entering Luxembourg is the EC's common outer tariff (except for imports from some countries affiliated with the EC). Luxembourg levies its own value-added tax at the border on imports from all other countries, including members of the EC. Nontariff barriers exist also in the form of health, safety, and packaging regulations.

38FOREIGN INVESTMENT

Foreign capital investment in Luxembourg has traditionally been small. In recent years, however, US investments have risen substantially, with the value of direct investments in excess of $1 billion in 1993 in manufacturing alone. Moderate-sized investments by Luxembourg firms have been made in Germany, France, Belgium, and South American countries. To encourage private investment from abroad, the government grants tax relief for up to 10 years in certain cases. Profits from investment may be transferred out of the country, and invested capital may be repatriated with a minimum of regulation.

39ECONOMIC DEVELOPMENT

The keystone of the economic system is free enterprise, and the government has attempted to promote the well-being of private industry by every means short of direct interference. The full-employment policy pursued by every postwar government has produced a high ratio of economically active population to total population. The government encourages the diversification of industry by tax concessions and other means.

40SOCIAL DEVELOPMENT

An extensive system of social insurance covers virtually all employees and their families. In the late 1980s, Luxembourg ranked second in the world after Sweden in expenditures on social security and housing as a percentage of the national budget. Unemployment compensation is financed jointly by national and communal administrations. Sickness, maternity, old age, disability, and survivors' benefits are paid, with both employee and employer contributing and the government absorbing part of the cost.

Despite a system of family allowances and birth premiums paid by the government under the national social welfare system, Luxembourg has one of the world's lowest fertility rates; for 1985–90 the fertility rate was 1.45. Abortion is generally available during the first three months of pregnancy.

Women are legally entitled to equal pay for equal work, and no job discrimination suits have been filed. Women are well represented in politics and the professions, although their salaries on average are only 55% of men's earnings.

41HEALTH

Luxembourg has an advanced national health service, supervised by the Ministry of Public Health. Public health facilities are available to physicians, and treatment of patients is on a private basis. Hospitals are operated either by the state or by the Roman Catholic Church.

In 1992, there were 780 physicians (295 general practitioners and 485 specialists, which equates to 2 physicians per 1,000 inhabitants); in 1990, there were 307 pharmacists, 198 dentists, and 124 midwives. In 1992, there were 32 hospitals, with 4,438 beds (11.4 per 1,000 people). Luxembourg's 1993 population was about 385,000. Public health officials have waged efficient national campaigns against contagious diseases, and infant mortality has been reduced from 56.8 per 1,000 live births in 1948 to 9 by 1992. There were 4,700 births in 1992 (12.3 per 1,000 people in 1993), and 80% of the country's children were immunized against measles between 1991 and 1992. Average life expectancy in 1992 was 75 years (72.6 for males and 78.8 for females) with an overall death rate of 10.7 per 1,000 inhabitants in 1993. There were 4,021 deaths in 1992, with leading causes as follows: circulatory/heart diseases (1,686); cancer (996); road accidents (76);

and suicides (59). There were 12 cases of AIDS and 25 cases of tuberculosis in 1992 as well.

42 HOUSING
The immediate post-World War II housing shortage created by the considerable war damage has been alleviated by substantial construction of private homes and apartment buildings. The government has helped by making home loans at low interest rates available to buyers. In 1981 there were 128,281 private households in Luxembourg. Detached houses accounted for 60% of all housing units, apartments for 32% and farms for 4%. Owners occupied 60% of all dwellings, 40% were rented, 4% were occupied rent free, and 3% were occupied by a subtenant. In 1992, 4,316 new dwellings were built, down from 4,452 in 1991.

43 EDUCATION
There is virtually no adult illiteracy. School attendance is compulsory between the ages of 6 and 15. Pupils attend primary schools for six years and then enter secondary schools for a period of up to seven years. In 1990–91, school enrollment included 8,354 children in nursery schools, 26,612 elementary pupils, 11,207 pupils in technical secondary and 7,594 in general secondary schools. There were 305 pupils enrolled in the Superior Institute of Technology, 223 in pedagogic education and 590 in the Central University of Luxembourg (founded in 1969). Nearly 4,407 students were at foreign universities, including 664 in Belgium and 763 in France.

Luxembourg had 467 nursery teachers in 1991–92. There were 1,888 primary teachers and 1,998 secondary and university professors during the same school period.

The Central University of Luxembourg (founded in 1969) had about 500 students in the mid-1980s; most advanced students attend institutions of higher learning in Belgium and France.

44 LIBRARIES AND MUSEUMS
The National Library in Luxembourg is the largest in the country, with over 750,000 volumes. The Grand Ducal Institute maintains a few specialized collections in the city of Luxembourg, as does the government. In Esch-sur-Alzette the public library has 60,000 volumes and features a special collection of Luxembourgensia.

The National Museum of Historical Art (founded in 1845) exhibits fine arts as well as the history of Luxembourg. The home where the 19th-century French writer Victor Hugo lived as an exile is in Vianden.

45 MEDIA
Telephone, telegraph, and postal services are owned and operated by the government; in 1991 there were 230,000 telephones. Direct-dial telephone service is in use throughout the country, and includes efficient international service. Telegraph service is also widely available.

Radio-Télé-Luxembourg broadcasts on five radio channels (in Letzeburgesch, French, German, English, and Dutch) and two television channels (Letzeburgesch and French). The powerful commercial network reaches not only the domestic audience but millions of French, Germans, and other Europeans. A 16-channel television satellite was scheduled for launch in 1988. Within Luxembourg, licensed radio sets totaled about 237,000 and television sets some 100,000 in 1991.

The daily press is small in circulation but has high standards. Luxembourg does not have an independent news agency of its own but relies on foreign news agencies for information. There were five daily newspapers in 1991, including the *Luxemburger Wort* (German and French) (1991 circulation 81,500); *Tageblatt* (German and French) (24,500); and *La Républicaine Lorraine* (French) (24,000). Combined circulation for daily newspapers in 1991 was about 145,000.

46 ORGANIZATIONS
The principal agricultural organization is Centrale Paysanne Luxembourgeoise, under which are grouped all producer cooperatives and other farmers' societies. Organizations promoting the interests of industry include federations of artisans, manufacturers, merchants, and winegrowers. The Luxembourg Chamber of Commerce is active in representing local business interests.

47 TOURISM, TRAVEL, AND RECREATION
Picturesque Luxembourg, with approximately 130 castles, has long been a tourist attraction. Among the points of greatest attraction are Vianden; Clervaux, with its castle of the De Lannoi family, forebears of Franklin Delano Roosevelt; the famous abbey of Clervaux; Echternach, an ancient religious center; the Moselle region; and the fortifications of the capital.

In 1991, there were 861,000 tourist arrivals, and the country's 8,062 hotel rooms had a 40% occupancy rate. Popular sports for both residents and visitors include swimming, hiking, rock climbing, cycling, and golf. Most visitors from Western Europe and the US require a passport, but no visas are necessary for stays of less than three months. There are no restrictions on foreign currency exchanges by visitors.

More than 5,000 American soldiers are buried at the American Military Cemetery near the capital, including Gen. George S. Patton.

48 FAMOUS LUXEMBOURGERS
Count Sigefroid founded the nation in 963, and Countess Ermesinde (r.1196–1247) tripled the extent of the country. Other outstanding historical personages are Henry VII of Luxembourg (c.1275–1313), who became Holy Roman emperor in 1308; his son John the Blind (1296–1346), count of Luxembourg (1309–46) and king of Bohemia (1310–46), a national hero; and the latter's son Charles (1316–78), who became Holy Roman emperor as Charles IV (1346–78). Grand duke from 1890 to 1905 was Adolphe (1817–1905), one-time duke of Nassau (1839–66) and the founder of the present dynasty, the house of Nassau-Weilbourg, whose origins go back to 1059.

Joseph Bech (1887–1975), prime minister from 1926 to 1937 and from 1953 to 1958, served as foreign minister for 33 years. Luxembourg-born Robert Schuman (1886–1963), French premier (1947–48) and foreign minister (1948–53), was a key figure in the postwar movement for West European integration. Grand Duchess Charlotte (1896–1985) abdicated in 1964 in favor of her son Grand Duke Jean (b.1921), who has reigned since then; the heir apparent is Crown Prince Henri (b.1955). Gaston Thorn (b.1928), prime minister during 1974–79, became president of the Commission of the EC in 1981.

An artist of note was the expressionist painter Joseph Kutter (1894–1941). Gabriel Lippmann (1845–1921) was awarded the Nobel Prize in physics (1908) for his pioneering work in color photography.

49 DEPENDENCIES
Luxembourg has no territories or colonies.

50 BIBLIOGRAPHY
Clark, Peter. *Luxembourg*. New York: Routledge, 1994.

Dolibois, John. *Pattern of Circles: An Ambassador's Story*. Kent, Ohio: Kent State University Press, 1989.

Eyck, F. Gunther. *The Benelux Countries: An Historical Survey*. Princeton, N.J.: Van Nostrand, 1969.

Gade, John Allyne. *Luxembourg in the Middle Ages*. Leiden: Brill, 1951.

Hemmer, Carlo, and Marcel Schroeder. *Luxembourg*. Luxembourg: Bourg-Bourger, 1958.

Kurian, George Thomas. *Facts on File National Profiles. The*

Benelux Countries. New York: Facts on File Publications, 1989.

Margue, Paul. *A Short History of Luxembourg.* Luxembourg: Ministry of State, 1974.

Newcomer, James. *The Grand Duchy of Luxembourg.* Lanham, Md.: University Press of America, 1984.

MACEDONIA

Former Yugoslav Republic of Macedonia

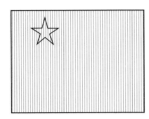

CAPITAL: Skopje.

FLAG: The flag consists of a gold sun on a red field.

ANTHEM: *Denec Nad Makedonija (Today over Macedonia)*

MONETARY UNIT: The currency in use is the denar. Denominations from smallest to largest are fifty deni, one denar, two denari, and five denari. In 1994, US$1 = 39 denars (1 denar = US$0.0256), but exchange rates are likely to fluctuate.

WEIGHTS AND MEASURES: The metric system is in effect in Macedonia.

HOLIDAYS: Orthodox Christmas, 7 January; national holiday, 2 August; Day of Referendum, 8 September.

TIME: 1 PM = noon GMT.

¹LOCATION, SIZE, AND EXTENT

Macedonia is a landlocked nation located in southeastern Europe. Macedonia is slightly larger than the state of Vermont with a total area of 25,333 sq km (9,781 sq mi). Macedonia shares boundaries with Serbia (north), Bulgaria (east), Greece (south), and Albania (west), and has a total boundary length of 748 km (465 mi). Macedonia's capital city, Skopje, is located in the northwestern part of the country.

²TOPOGRAPHY

The topography of Macedonia features a mountainous landscape covered with deep basins and valleys. There are two large lakes, each divided by a frontier line. Approximately five percent of Macedonia's land is arable. Natural resources include chromium, lead, zinc, manganese, tungsten, nickel, low-grade iron ore, asbestos, sulphur, and timber. Macedonia's natural environment suffers from a high seismic hazard and air pollution from metallurgical plants.

³CLIMATE

Macedonia's climate features hot summers and cold winters. Fall tends to be dry in the country. In July the mean temperature is between 20 and 23°C (70 and 73°F). The mean temperature in January is between –20 and 0°C (–4 and 32°F). Rainfall averages 48 cm (19 in) a year. Snowfalls can be heavy in winter.

⁴FLORA AND FAUNA

The terrain of Macedonia is rather hilly. Between the hills are deep basins and valleys, populated by European bison, fox, rabbits, brown bears, and deer. Ducks, turtles, frogs, raccoons, and muskrats inhabit the country's waterways.

⁵ENVIRONMENT

Air pollution from metallurgical plants is a problem in Macedonia, as in the other former Yugoslav republics. Earthquakes are a natural hazard.

⁶POPULATION

The population of Macedonia was 2,033,964 in 1991. It was projected by the World Bank to be 2.2 million in 2010, based on a crude birth rate of 17 per 1,000 people, a crude death rate of 7, and a net natural increase of 10. The population density in 1991 was 79 per sq km (205 per sq mi). Skopje, the capital, had a population of 563,301. The population was 58% urban and 42% rural.

⁷MIGRATION

Macedonia was home to 32,000 refugees at the end of 1992, mostly from Bosnia and Herzegovina, where there were 48,000 Macedonians in 1991. There were 95,743 Macedonians living abroad that year.

⁸ETHNIC GROUPS

Macedonians comprised 65% of the population in 1991. Another 21% were Albanians, mostly living in the west, particularly the northwest. Other groups included Turks, 5%; Gypsies and Muslims, 3% each; and Serbs, 2%.

⁹LANGUAGES

Macedonian is a southern Slavic tongue that was not officially recognized until 1944. Bulgarians claim it is merely a dialect of their own language. As in Bulgarian, there are virtually no declensions and the definite article is suffixed. Also as in Bulgarian—and unlike any other Slavic language—an indefinite article exists as a separate word. It is written in the Cyrillic alphabet, but with two special characters—*r* and *k*. Minority languages are officially recognized at the local level.

¹⁰RELIGIONS

As of 1993, 59% of the population was Eastern Orthodox, 26% Muslim, 4% Roman Catholic, and 1% Protestant. The remaining 10% belonged to other faiths or had no religious preference. The Macedonian Orthodox Church broke from the Serbian Orthodox Church in 1967, and is still officially unrecognized by the Serbian Orthodox Church.

¹¹TRANSPORTATION

A railway connects Skopje with Serbia to the north and Greece to the south. In 1991, there were 10,591 km (6,581 mi) of highways, of which 48% were paved, 13% were gravel, and 39% were dirt roads.

12HISTORY

Origin and Middle Ages

Macedonia is an ancient name, historically related to Philip II of Macedon, whose son became Alexander the Great, founder of one of the great empires of the ancient world. As a regional name, Macedonia, the land of the Macedons, has been used since ancient Greek times for the territory extending north of Thessaly and into the Vardar River Valley and between Epirus on the west and Thrace on the east. In Alexander the Great's time, Macedonia extended west to the Adriatic Sea over the area then called Illyris, part of today's Albania. Under the Roman Empire, Macedonia was extended south over Thessaly and Achaia.

Begining in the 5th century AD Slavic tribes began settling in the Balkan area, and by 700 they controlled most of the Central and Peloponnesian Greek lands. The Slavic conquerors were mostly assimilated into Greek culture except in the northern Greek area of Macedonia proper and the areas of northern Thrace populated by "Bulgarian" Slavs. That is how St. Cyril and Methodius, two Greek brothers and scholars who grew up in the Macedonian city of Salonika, were able to become the "Apostles of the Slavs," having first translated Holy Scriptures in 863 into the common Slavic language they had learned in the Macedonian area.

Through most of the later Middle Ages, Macedonia was an area contested by the Byzantine Empire, with its Greek culture and Orthodox Christianity, the Bulgarian Kingdom, and particularly the 14th century Serbian empire of Dušan the Great. The Bulgarian and Serbian empires contributed to the spread of Christianity through the establishment of the Old Church Slavic liturgy. After Dušan's death in 1355 his empire collapsed, partly due to the struggle for power among his heirs and partly to the advances of the Ottoman Turks. Following the defeat of the Serbs at the Kosovo Field in 1389, the Turks conquered the Macedonian area over the next half century and kept it under their control until the 1912 Balkan war.

Under Ottoman Rule

The decline of the Ottoman Empire brought about renewed competition over Slavic Macedonia between Bulgaria and Serbia. After the Russo-Turkish war of 1877 ended in a Turkish defeat, Bulgaria, an ally of Russia, was denied the prize of the Treaty of San Stefano (1878) in which Turkey had agreed to an enlarged and autonomous Bulgaria that would have included most of Macedonia. Such an enlarged Bulgaria—with control of the Vardar River Valley and access to the Aegean Sea—was, however, a violation of a prior Russo-Austrian agreement. The Western powers opposed Russia's penetration into the Mediterranean through the port of Salonika and, at the 1878 Congress of Berlin, forced the "return" of Macedonia and East Rumelia from Bulgaria to Turkey. This action enraged Serbia, which had fought in the war against Turkey, had gained its own independence, and had hoped to win control of Bosnia and Herzegovina, which had been given over to Austrian control, for itself.

In this situation both Serbia and Bulgaria concentrated their efforts on Macedonia, where Greek influence had been very strong through the Greek Orthodox Church. The Bulgarians obtained their own Orthodox Church in 1870, that extended its influence to the Macedonian area and worked in favor of unification with Bulgaria through intensive educational activities designed to "Bulgarize" the Slavic population. Systematic intimidation was also used, when the Bulgarians sent their terrorist units ("Komite") into the area. The Serbian side considered Macedonia to be Southern Serbia, with its own dialect but using Serbian as its literary language. Serbian schools predated Bulgarian ones in Macedonia and continued with their work.

While individual instances of Macedonian consciousness and language had appeared by the end of the 18th century, it was in the 1850s that "Macedonists" had declared Macedonia a separate Slavic nation. Macedonian Slavs had developed a preference for their central Macedonian dialect and had begun publishing some writings in it rather than using the Bulgaro-Macedonian version promoted by the Bulgarian Church and government emissaries. Thus, Macedonia, in the second half of the 19th century, while still under the weakening rule of the Turks, had become the object of territorial/cultural claims by its Greek, Serb, and Bulgarian neighbors. The most systematic pressure had come from Bulgaria and had caused large numbers of "Bulgaro-Macedonians" to emigrate to Bulgaria—some 100,000 in the 1890s—mainly to Sophia, where they constituted almost half the city's population and an extremely strong pressure group.

Struggle for Autonomy

More and more Macedonians became convinced that Macedonia should achieve at least an autonomous status under Turkey, if not complete independence. In 1893, a secret organization was formed in Salonika aiming at a revolt against the Turks and the establishment of an autonomous Macedonia. The organization was to be independent of Serbia, Bulgaria, and Greece and was named the Internal Macedonian Revolutionary Organization (IMRO), a group that became Socialist, revolutionary, and terrorist in nature. Much like Ireland's IRA, IMRO spread through Macedonia and became an underground paragovernmental network active up to World War II. A pro-Bulgarian and an independent Macedonian faction soon developed, the first based in Sophia, the second in Salonika. Its strong base in Sophia gave the pro-Bulgarian faction a great advantage and it took control and pushed for an early uprising in order to impress the western powers into intervening in support of Macedonia.

The large scale uprising took place on 2 August 1903 (Ilinden– "St. Elijah's Day") when the rebels took over the town of Kruševo and proclaimed a Socialist Republic. After initial defeats of the local Turkish forces, the rebels were subdued by massive Ottoman attacks using scorched earth tactics and wholesale massacres of the population over a three-month period. Europe and the US paid attention and forced Turkey into granting reforms to be supervised by international observers. However, the disillusioned IMRO leadership engaged in factional bloody feuds that weakened the IMRO organization and image. This encouraged both Serbs and Greeks in the use of their own armed bands—Serbian "Cetniks" and Greek "Andarte"—creating an atmosphere of gang warfare in which Bulgaria, Serbia, and Greece fought each other (instead of the Turks) over a future division of Macedonia. In the meantime, the Young Turks movement had spread among Turkish officers and military uprisings began in Macedonia in 1906. These uprisings spread and Turkish officers demanded a constitutional system. They believed that Turkey could be saved only by westernizing. In 1908 the Young Turks prevailed, and offered to the IMRO leadership agrarian reforms, regional autonomy, and introduction of the Macedonian language in the schools. However, the Young Turks turned out to be extreme Turkish nationalists bent on the assimilation of other national groups. Their denationalizing efforts caused further rebellions and massacres in the Balkans. Serbia, Greece, Bulgaria, and Montenegro turned for help to the great powers, but to no avail. In 1912 they formed the Balkan League, provisionally agreed on the division of Turkish Balkan territory among themselves, and declared war on Turkey in October 1912 after Turkey refused their request to establish the four autonomous regions of Macedonia—Old Serbia, Epirus, and Albania—already provided for in the 1878 Treaty of Berlin.

Balkan Wars

The quick defeat of the Turks by the Balkan League stunned the European powers, particularly when Bulgarian forces had reached the suburbs of Istanbul. Turkey signed a treaty in London on 30 May 1913 giving up all European possessions with the exception of Istanbul. However, when Italy and Austria vetoed a provision granting Serbia access to the Adriatic at Durazzo and Alessio and agreed to form an independent Albania, Serbia demanded a larger part of Macedonia from Bulgaria. Bulgaria refused and attacked both Serbian and Greek forces. This caused the second Balkan War that ended in a month with Bulgaria's defeat by Serbia and Greece with help from Rumania, Montenegro, and Turkey. The outcome was the partitioning of Macedonia between Serbia and Greece. Turkey regained the Adrianople area it had lost to Bulgaria. Romania gained a part of Bulgarian Dobrudja while Bulgaria kept a part of Thrace and the Macedonian town of Strumica. Thus Southern Macedonia came under the Hellenizing influence of Greece while most of Macedonia was annexed to Serbia. Both Serbia and Greece denied any Macedonian "nationhood." In Greece, Macedonians were treated as "slavophone" Greeks while Serbs viewed Macedonia as Southern Serbia and Serbian was made the official language of government and instruction in schools and churches.

First and Second Yugoslavia

After World War I, the IMRO organization became a mere terrorist group operating out of Bulgaria with a nuisance role against Yugoslavia. In later years, some IMRO members joined the Communist Party and tried to work toward a Balkan Federation where Macedonia would be an autonomous member. Its interest in the dissolution of the first Yugoslavia led IMRO members to join with the Croatian Ustaša in the assassination of King Alexander of Yugoslavia and French Foreign Minister Louis Barthou in Marseilles on 9 October 1934. During World War II, Bulgaria, Hitler's ally, occupied the central and eastern parts of Macedonia while Albanians, supported by Italy, annexed western Macedonia along with the Kosovo region. Because of Bulgarian control, resistance was slow to develop in Macedonia; a conflict between the Bulgarian and Yugoslav Communist parties also played a part. By the summer of 1943, however, Tito, the leader of the Yugoslav Partisans, took over control of the Communist Party of Macedonia after winning its agreement to form a separate Macedonian republic as part of a Yugoslav federation.

Some 120,000 Macedonian Serbs were forced to emigrate to Serbia because they had opted for Serbian citizenship. Partisan activities against the occupiers increased and, by August 1944, the Macedonian People's Republic was proclaimed with Macedonian as the official language and the goal of unifying all Macedonians was confirmed. But this goal was not achieved. However, the "Pirin" Macedonians in Bulgaria were granted their own cultural development rights in 1947, and then lost them after the Stalin-Tito split in 1948. The Bulgarian claims to Macedonia were revived from time to time after 1948.

On the Greek side, there was no support from the Greek Communist Party for the unification of Macedonian Slavs within Greece with the Yugoslav Macedonians, even though Macedonian Slavs had organized resistance units under Greek command and participated heavily in the post-war Greek Communists' insurrection. With Tito's closing the Yugoslav-Greek frontier in July 1949 and ending his assistance to the pro-Cominform Greek Communists, any chance of territorial gains from Greece had dissipated. On the Yugoslav side, Macedonia

LOCATION: 41°50′N; 22°0′E. **BOUNDARY LENGTHS:** Total boundary lengths, 748 km (465 mi); Albania, 151 km (94 mi); Bulgaria, 148 km (92 mi); Greece, 228 km (142 mi); Serbia and Montenegro, 221 km (137.3 mi).

became one of the co-equal constituent republics of the Federal Socialist Yugoslavia under the Communist regime of Marshal Tito. The Macedonian language became one of the official languages of Yugoslavia, along with Slovenian and Serbo-Croatian, and the official language of the Republic of Macedonia where the Albanian and Serbo-Croatian languages were also used. Macedonian was fully developed into the literary language of Macedonians, used as the language of instruction in schools as well as the newly established Macedonian Orthodox Church. A Macedonian University was established in Skopje, the capital city, and all the usual cultural, political, social, and economic institutions were developed within the framework of the Yugoslav Socialist system of self-management. The main goals of autonomy and socialism of the old IMRO organization were fulfilled, with the exception of the unification of the "Pirin" (Bulgarian) and "Greek" Macedonian lands.

All of the republics of the former Federal Socialist Republic of Yugoslavia share a common history between 1945 and 1991, the year of Yugoslavia's dissolution. The World War II Partisan resistance movement, controlled by the Communist Party of Yugoslavia and led by Marshal Tito, won a civil war waged against nationalist groups under foreign occupation, having secured the assistance, and recognition, from both the Western powers and the Soviet Union. Aside from the reconstruction of the country and its economy, the first task facing the new regime was the establishment of its legitimacy and, at the same time, the liquidation of its internal enemies, both actual and potential. The first task was accomplished by the 11 November 1945 elections of a constitutional assembly on the basis of a single candidate list assembled by the People's Front. The list won 90% of the votes cast. The three members of the "coalition" government representing the Royal Yugoslav Government in exile had resigned earlier in frustration and did not run in the elections. The Constitutional Assembly voted against the continuation of the Monarchy and, on 31 January 1946, the new constitution of the Federal People's Republic of Yugoslavia was promulgated. Along with state-building activities, the Yugoslav Communist regime carried out ruthless executions, massacres, and imprisonments to liquidate any potential opposition.

The Tito-Stalin conflict that erupted in 1948 was not a real surprise considering the differences the two had had about Tito's refusal to cooperate with other resistance movements against the occupiers in World War II. The expulsion of Tito from the Cominform group separated Yugoslavia from the Soviet Bloc, caused internal purges of pro-Cominform Yugoslav Communist Party members, and also nudged Yugoslavia into a failed attempt to collectivize its agriculture. Yugoslavia then developed its own brand of Marxist economy based on workers' councils and self-management of enterprises and institutions, and became the leader of the non-aligned group of nations in the international arena. Being more open to Western influences, the Yugoslav Communist regime relaxed somewhat its central controls. This allowed for the development of more liberal wings of Communist parties, particularly in Croatia and Slovenia, agitated for the devolution of power from the federal to the individual republic level in order to better cope with the increasing differentiation between the more productive republics (Slovenia and Croatia) and the less developed areas. Also, nationalism resurfaced with tensions particularly strong between Serbs and Croats in the Croatian Republic, leading to the repression by Tito of the Croatian and Slovenian "Springs" in 1970–71.

The 1974 constitution shifted much of the decision-making power from the federal to the republics' level, turning the Yugoslav Communist Party into a kind of federation (league) of the republican parties, thus further decentralizing the political process. The autonomous provinces of Vojvodina and Kosovo were also given a quasi-sovereign status as republics, and a collective Presidency was designed to take over power upon Tito's death. When Tito died in 1980, the delegates of the six republics and the two autonomous provinces represented the interests of each republic or province in the process of shifting coalitions centered on specific issues. The investment of development funds to assist the less developed areas became the burning issue around which nationalist emotions and tensions grew ever stronger, along with the forceful repression of the Albanian majority in Kosovo.

The economic crisis of the 1980s, with runaway inflation, inability to pay the debt service on over 20 billion dollars in international loans that had accumulated during Tito's rule, and low productivity in the less-developed areas became too much of a burden for Slovenia and Croatia, leading them to stand up to the centralizing power of the Serbian (and other) Republics. The demand for a reorganization of the Yugoslav Federation into a confederation of sovereign states was strongly opposed by the coalition of Serbia, Montenegro, and the Yugoslav army. The pressure towards political pluralism and a market economy also grew stronger, leading to the formation of non-Communist political parties that, by 1990, were able to win majorities in

multiparty elections in Slovenia and then in Croatia, thus putting an end to the era of the Communist Party monopoly of power. The inability of the opposing groups of centralist and confederalist republics to find any common ground led to the dissolution of Yugoslavia through the disassociation of Slovenia, Croatia, Bosnia and Herzegovina, and Macedonia, leaving only Serbia and Montenegro together in a new Federal Republic of Yugoslavia.

The years between 1945 and 1990 offered the Macedonians an opportunity for development in some areas, in addition to their cultural and nation-building efforts, within the framework of a one-party Communist system. For the first time in their history the Macedonians had their own republic and government with a very broad range of responsibilities. Forty-five years was a long enough period to have trained generations for public service responsibilities and the governing of an independent state. In addition, Macedonia derived considerable benefits from the Yugoslav framework in terms of federal support for underdeveloped areas (Bosnia and Herzegovina, Kosovo, Macedonia, Montenegro). Macedonia's share of the special development funds ranged from 26% in 1966 to about 20% in 1985, much of it supplied by Croatia and Slovenia.

In the wake of developments in Slovenia and Croatia, Macedonia held its first multiparty elections in November/December 1990, with the participation of over 20 political parties. Four parties formed a coalition government that left the strongest nationalist party (IMRO) in the opposition. In January 1991 the Macedonian Assembly passed a declaration of sovereignty.

Independence

While early in 1989 Macedonia supported Serbia's Slobodan Milošević in his recentralizing efforts, by 1991, Milošević was viewed as a threat to Macedonia and its leadership took positions closer to the confederal ones of Slovenia and Croatia. A last effort to avoid Yugoslavia's disintegration was made 3 June 1991 through a joint proposal by Macedonia and Bosnia and Herzegovina, offering to form a "community of Yugoslav Republics" with a centrally administered common market, foreign policy, and national defense. However, Serbia opposed the proposal.

On 26 June 1991—one day after Slovenia and Croatia had declared their independence—the Macedonian Assembly debated the issue of secession from Yugoslavia with the IMRO group urging an immediate proclamation of independence. Other parties were more restrained, a position echoed by Macedonian President Kiro Gligorov in his cautious statement that Macedonia would remain faithful to Yugoslavia. Yet by 6 July 1991, the Macedonian Assembly decided in favor of Macedonia's independence if a confederal solution could not be attained.

Thus, when the process of dissolution of Yugoslavia took place in 1990–91, Macedonia refused to join Serbia and Montenegro and opted for independence on 20 November 1991. The unification issue was then raised again, albeit negatively, by the refusal of Greece to recognize the newly independent Macedonia for fear that its very name would incite irredentist designs toward the Slav Macedonians in Northern Greece. The issue of recognition became a problem between Greece and its NATO allies in spite of the fact that Macedonia had adopted in 1992 a constitutional amendment forbidding any engagement in territorial expansion or interference in the internal affairs of another country. In April 1993, Macedonia gained membership in the UN, but only under the name of "Former Yugoslav Republic of Macedonia." Greece also voted against Macedonian membership in the Conference on Security and Cooperation in Europe on 1 December 1993. However, on 16 December 1993, the UK,

Germany, Denmark, and the Netherlands had announced the initiation of the recognition process for Macedonia and other countries joined the process which resulted in recognition of Macedonia by the US on 8 February 1994. Greece is still withholding its recognition of Macedonia as of June 1994. In fact, real needs were stronger than formalities and prevailed over the recognition concerns when the UN stationed some 700 Scandinavian and 300 US peacekeeping troops in 1993 at the Macedonian/Serbian border in order to monitor any possible military moves against Macedonia.

Of serious concern is the potential for severe internal problems and conflicts based on the ethnic composition of Macedonia's population that is 65% Macedonian and 21% Albanian, the rest consisting of Serbs, Turks, Gypsies, and others. In view of the fact that Macedonians had themselves experienced long-time domination by other groups that denied them their national rights, the hope remains that Macedonians will succeed in implementing guaranteed equal national, cultural, and political rights for all their citizens no matter what their national/ethnic backgrounds.

13GOVERNMENT

Macedonia became independent of former Yugoslavia on 20 November 1991, having adopted its constitution on 17 November 1991. Macedonia has a unicameral assembly of 120 seats, an executive branch consisting of a President (Kiro Gligorov) and a Council of Ministers (in 1994, the Prime Minister was Branko Crvenkovski).

14POLITICAL PARTIES

The last elections to Assembly seats were held on 11 November, 25 November, and 9 December 1990. The last presidential election was held on 27 January 1991 when Kiro Gligorov was elected President by the Assembly.

Four parties have formed a coalition government:

Social Democratic Union of Macedonia (former Communist Party)	
Branko Crvenkovski, President	31 seats
Party for Democratic Prosperity (Ethnic Albanian)	
Nevzat Halili, President	25 seats
Reformed Forces of Macedonia-Liberal	
Stojan Andov, President	17 seats
Socialist Party of Macedonia	
Kiro Popovski, President	5 seats

The main opposition party is the:

Internal Macedonian Revolutionary Organization-Democratic	
Party of Macedonian National Unity (IMRO-DPMNU)	37 seats

There are several other minor parties and political groups. New elections are scheduled for November 1994. The IMRO-DPMNU Party has lost some seats and a new Democratic Party was formed in the spring of 1994 led by Peter Gošev.

15LOCAL GOVERNMENT

Macedonia's 34 local governments are still based on the preexisting Yugoslav system. Under the 1974 Yugoslav constitution, the commune (opština) is the basic self-managed sociopolitical community. Each assembly consists of a chamber of work communities, composed of delegates from the working population; a chamber of local communities, composed of delegates of both workers and nonworkers residing in organized local communities; a sociopolitical chamber, composed of delegates of sociopolitical organizations such as labor unions and youth and veteran groups. The commune assembly elects an executive body which assumes administrative functions for the community and the

assemblies also elect the delegations that make up the assembly of the republic.

Reform legislation on local government has been submitted to the Assembly and is working its way very slowly through the legislative process.

16JUDICIAL SYSTEM

The judicial system is comprised of three tiers: municipal courts, district courts, and the Supreme Court. A Constitutional Court handles issues of constitutional interpretation, including protection of individual rights. The Constitution directs the establishment of a People's Ombudsman to defend citizens' fundamental constitutional rights, but implementing legislation is not yet in place. The Constitutional Court has not yet rendered any decisions in the area of protection of individual rights or liberties. The Constitution guarantees the autonomy and independence of the judiciary.

17ARMED FORCES

As of 1993, there were an estimated 484,700 males fit for military service. In January 1992, the Macedonian Assembly approved the formation of a standing army of 25,000–30,000 troops. However, the actual size of the military is estimated to be 11,000–12,000 regular soldiers, less than half the approved number. Reservists total 120,000. Defense-related expenditures amounted to about 7 billion denars in 1993. In July 1993, 300 US and 800 Scandinavian troops were stationed along the northern border to assist the Macedonian government in preventing the hostilities in Serbia from spilling over into Macedonia. That year, the police force numbered 8,000; there were also 65 pilots and 700 tank drivers and missileers, but no airplanes, armored vehicles, or missiles. Macedonia has two World War II-era Soviet-made T-34 tanks.

18INTERNATIONAL COOPERATION

Macedonia is a member of the UN. The country was admitted to the UN 8 April 1993. Macedonia is a member of FAO, IMF, INTERPOL, UNESCO, and UNICEF. The country is applying for membership in other international organizations. As of February 1994 the country's sovereignty had been recognized by the US and EC countries. Russia, Bulgaria, Turkey, and several other countries have also established diplomatic relations with Macedonia.

19ECONOMY

Although the poorest of the six former Yugoslav republics, Macedonia nevertheless can sustain itself in food and energy needs using its own agricultural and coal resources. Due to the scarcity of arable land in the Vardar River Valley and other valleys in the west, expatriate employment in Serbia and Germany has become more common.

In August 1992, because it resented the use of "Macedonia" as the republic's name, Greece imposed a partial blockade on Macedonia. This blockade, combined with the UN sanctions on Serbia and Montenegro, cost the economy some $1 billion in 1992.

20INCOME

In 1991, Macedonia's GDP was $7,100 million at current prices, or $3,110 per capita. In 1991, the inflation rate was 115%, resulting in a real growth rate in GDP of –18%.

21LABOR

Labor is primarily based on agriculture, mining, and light industry. The conflict in the region, with the imposition of international sanctions against Serbia and Montenegro and an increasing number of refugees, has severely disrupted the local economy and, understandably, has intensified unemployment.

The 1991 constitution guarantees citizens the right to form labor unions (with restrictions on the military, police, and government workers) and the right to strike. Much of the labor force is rural and unorganized. The Council of Trade Unions of Macedonia (SSSM) is the labor confederation which is the successor to the old Communist Party labor confederation, and is still the government's primary negotiating partner on social issues. The Union of Independent and Autonomous Trade Unions was formed in 1992 with six member unions.

Economic collapse, evidenced by fuel and currency shortages, resulted in high unemployment in 1992, with strikes a frequent occurrence. Teachers, railroad workers, farmers, and construction workers all had strikes during 1992.

Macedonia has adopted many provisions from the old Yugoslav SFR labor code, including a 42 hour workweek and a minimum employment age of 15 years.

22AGRICULTURE

As of 1991, there were some 555,000 hectares (1,371,000 acres) of arable land, representing 22% of the total land area. Estimated grain production in 1992 included: wheat, 200,000 tons; barley, 98,000 tons; corn, 95,000 tons; rice, 30,000 tons; and rye, 16,000 tons. Other important crops produced in 1992 included (in 1,000 tons): tomatoes, 106; green peppers, 70; potatoes, 66; sunflower seeds, 27; sugar beets, 75; tobacco, 23; and walnuts, 2.5. In 1992, 191,000 tons of grapes and 115,000 tons of wine were produced.

23ANIMAL HUSBANDRY

Meadows and pastures accounted for 27% (565,000 hectares/1,396,000 acres) of the total area in 1991. Livestock in 1992 consisted of 2,250,000 sheep, 282,000 head of cattle, 171,000 pigs, 48,000 horses, and 5,000,000 chickens. Beef production in 1992 amounted to 8,000 tons; pork, 12,000 tons; chicken, 2,000 tons; and mutton, 13,000 tons. Milk production in 1992 amounted to 99,000 tons.

24FISHING

Inland fishing occurs on Lake Ohrid, Lake Prespa, and the Vardar River. Macedonia has no direct access to the sea for marine fishing.

25FORESTRY

About 35% of the total area consisted of forests and woodlands in 1991, mostly in the eastern and southern regions. Bitola is the center for the wood products industry.

26MINING

Mineral resources of chrome, iron ore, marble, and zinc are found in Macedonia. Lead-zinc ore is mined at Kamenica and Probistip; iron ore at Tajmište, Demir Hisar, and Damjan. A nickel mine at Kavadarci was scheduled to reopen in 1992, after having been closed for eight years.

27ENERGY AND POWER

In 1991, 6,300 million kwh of electricity were generated. Installed capacity totaled 1,600,000 kw in 1991. Macedonia's only domestic mineral fuel is coal.

28INDUSTRY

Macedonia's industries are centered around Skopje. Steel and chemical production, along with textiles, furniture, and ceramics are important industries. In 1991, industrial production declined by an estimated 18%. Low levels of technology predominate in industrial production, as do overstaffing and other inefficient socialist strategies.

29SCIENCE AND TECHNOLOGY

Macedonia uses only low levels of technology for its agriculture and mining industries. Oil refining is performed by distillation only.

30DOMESTIC TRADE

Domestic commerce typically centers around an urban marketplace, where marketing of farm products is carried out.

31FOREIGN TRADE

In 1990, exports amounted to $578 million, of which manufactured goods accounted for 40%; machinery and transport equipment, 14%; other manufactured products, 23%; raw materials, 7.6%; food (rice) and live animals, 5.7%; beverages and tobacco, 4.5%; and chemicals, 4.7%. Imports in 1990 totaled $1,112 million, of which fuels and lubricants accounted for 19%; manufactured goods, 18%; machinery and transport equipment, 15%; food and live animals, 14%; chemicals, 11.4%; raw materials, 10%; other manufactured products, 8%; and beverages and tobacco, 3.5%. Macedonia's chief trading partners are the other former Yugoslav republics (especially Serbia and Montenegro), Greece, Germany, and Albania.

32BALANCE OF PAYMENTS

Macedonia, as the poorest former Yugoslav SFR republic, is heavily reliant on trade with Serbia. Regional conflict and the transition to a market economy, followed by the subsequent international sanctions against Serbia and Montenegro have devastated trade and the balance of payments; the government estimated the cost of sanctions to the Macedonian economy at $1.8 billion as of 1992.

33BANKING AND SECURITIES

In 1992, the National Bank of Macedonia was created to issue currency, conduct monetary polices, and regulate the banking sector of the country.

Commercial banks in Macedonia include the Komercijalna Banka, a.d., and Scopanska Banka, a.d., both in Skopje. The currency unit is the Macedonia denar. There are no security exchanges in the country.

34INSURANCE

No recent information is available.

35PUBLIC FINANCE

Regional conflict, sanctions against Serbia and Montenegro, and a transition to a market economy have severely disrupted the government's ability to account for public revenues and expenditures. The Macedonian government estimated in 1994 that it needed $200 million in immediate loans and another $500 million in soft loans to meet expenditures and commence the economic transition to recovery.

36TAXATION

Personal income taxes range from 1.28–2.17%; corporate rates vary from 1.5–5.5%. Also levied is a payroll tax of 8.8–43%.

37CUSTOMS AND DUTIES

No recent information is available.

38FOREIGN INVESTMENT

Macedonia's isolation, technological disadvantages, and penchant for political instability have all worked to create a poor climate for potential Western investors.

39 ECONOMIC DEVELOPMENT

As of 1993, the US donated $10 million in economic aid for humanitarian and technical assistance. The EC has promised an economic aid package. As of May 1994, the EBRD established a $10 million facility to guarantee Komercijalna Banka's designated correspondent banks against non-payment under confirmed letters of credit. By securing credit facilities, the bank's clients are able to stimulate production and increase exports.

40 SOCIAL DEVELOPMENT

Macedonia, historically the poorest of the former Yugoslav republics, has suffered further from the imposition of international sanctions against Serbia, the rising tide of refugees, and increasing unemployment.

Although women have the same legal rights as men, the traditional cultures of both Christian and Muslim communities have limited their advancement in society. A few women's advocacy and support groups began to organize in 1993.

Many of the state's social welfare programs for children have been inoperative due to the region's political and economic crises. Allowances to parents whose employers have gone bankrupt were delayed by five months in 1993. In the same year, however, the government initiated a vaccination program that reportedly covered at least 95% of the country's children.

41 HEALTH

As part of the former Yugoslavia, the availability of health care statistics for Macedonia has been hampered by the internal war that has been going since 1991. As of late 1994, separate health care data was not available for the independent regions that made up the former Yugoslavia, namely Bosnia and Herzegovina, Croatia, Slovenia, and Macedonia.

42 HOUSING

No recent information is available.

43 EDUCATION

Education at the elementary level is free and compulsory for eight years. There are also many secondary level schools. At the postsecondary level, there are two universities: the Bitola University, which was founded in 1979, and the University of Skopje, founded in 1949. The language of instruction is Macedonian and there are faculties of law, engineering, medicine, arts, science, physical education, architecture, and agriculture.

44 LIBRARIES AND MUSEUMS

Skopje is the cosmopolitan center for Macedonia's cultural institutions.

45 MEDIA

The Macedonian media remain mostly free of government influence. An independent television station, A–1, broadcasts from Skopje. State-sponsored newspapers include the Albanian-language *Flaka e Vlazerimit* and the Turkish-language *Birlik,* both of which are somewhat sympathetic to the government. In 1994, *Delo,* a new weekly with reportedly nationalist leanings began publication.

46 ORGANIZATIONS

The Chamber of Economy of Macedonia coordinates trade and commerce with the world. The Macedonian Academy of Science, founded in 1967, coordinates and finances scientific research conducted in Macedonia. The country has 26 learned societies and 13 natural and social scientific institutions.

47 TOURISM

As an isolated republic of the former Yugoslav SFR, tourism-related activities have traditionally not been emphasized in Macedonia.

48 FAMOUS MACEDONIANS

Kiro Gligorov has been the president of Macedonia since January 1991. Branko Crvenkovski was made prime minister in September 1992. Mother Teresa (b. 1910) is from Skopje, Macedonia, but left at age 17 to join a convent in Calcutta, India. In 1948, Mother Teresa left the convent to found the Missionaries of Charity. She won the Nobel Peace Prize in 1979.

Phillip II (382 BC–?) is the father of Alexander the Great. During Philip II's reign, he established a federal system of Greek States. Macedonian Alexander the Great (356 BC–297 BC) founded the largest Western Empire of the Western World from Greece to Northern India. Cassandar (353 BC–297 BC) succeeded Alexander the Great, and was king of Macedonia between 316 BC and 297 BC. To consolidate his power, Cassandar murdered Alexander's mother, widow, and son.

49 DEPENDENCIES

Macedonia has no territories or colonies.

50 BIBLIOGRAPHY

Banac, Ovo. *The Nationality Question in Yugoslavia.* Ithaca, NY: Cornell University Press, 1984.

Billows, Richard A. *Antigonos the One-eyed and the Creation of the Hellenistic State.* Berkeley: University of California Press, 1990.

Borowiec, Andrew. *Yugoslavia Afer Tito.* New York: Praeger, 1977

Dunn, William N. and Josip Obradovic. *Workers' Self–Management and Organizational Power in Yugoslavia.* Pittsburgh: Univ. of Pittsburgh Press, 1978.

Gapinski, James H., Borislav Skegko and Thomas W. Zuehlka. *Modeling the Economic Performance of Yugoslavia.* New York: Praeger, 1989.

Kofos, Evangelos. *National Heritage and National Identity in Nineteenth-and Twentieth-century Macedonia.* Athens: Hellenic Foundation for Defense and Foreign Policy, 1991.

Kophos, Euangelos. *Nationalism and Communism in Macedonia: Civil Conflict, Politics of Mutation, National Identity.* New Rochelle, N. Y.: A. D. Caratzas, 1993.

Macdermott, Mercia. *For Freedom and Perfection: The Life of Yane Sandansky.* London: Journeyman, 1988.

Macesich, George, ed. *Essays on the Yugoslav Economic Model.* New York: Praeger, 1989.

Perry, Duncan M. *The Politics of Terror: The Macedonian Liberation Movements, 1893–1903.* Durham: Duke University Press, 1988.

Shrenk, Martin et al. *Yugoslavia: Self Management Socialism and the Challenges of Development.* Baltimore: Johns Hopkins Univ. Press, 1979.

Sher, Gerson S. *Praxis: Marxism Criticism and Dissent in Socialist Yugoslavia.* Bloomington, Ind.: Indiana Univ. Press, 1977.

Sirc, Ljubo. *The Yugoslav Economy Under Self–Management.* New York: St. Martin's Press, 1979.

Sowards, Steven W. *Austria's Policy of Macedonian Reform.* Boulder, Colo.: East European Monographs, 1989.

Stankovic, Slobodan. *The End of the Tito Era.* Stanford, Cal: Hoover Institution Press, 1981.

Tachiaos, Anthony-Emil N. *The Bulgarian National Awakening and its Spread into Macedonia*. Thessaloniki: Society for Macedonian Studies, 1990.

Vacalopoulos, Apostolos E. *Contemporary Ethnological Problems in the Balkans*. Thessaloniki: Society for Macedonian Studies, 1991.

MALTA

The Republic of Malta
Repubblika Ta' Malta

CAPITAL: Valletta.

FLAG: The national flag consists of two equal vertical stripes, white at the hoist and red at the fly, with a representation of the Maltese Cross, edged with red, in the canton of the white stripe.

ANTHEM: *L'Innu Malti (The Maltese Hymn).*

MONETARY UNIT: The Maltese lira (LM) consists of 100 cents, with each cent divided into 10 mils. There are coins of 2, 3, and 5 mils and of 1, 2, 5, 10, 25, and 50 cents, and notes of 2, 5, 10, and 20 lira. Gold and silver coins of 1, 2, 4, 5, 10, 20, 25, 50, and 100 lira are also in circulation. ML1 = $0.3879 (or $1 = M2.5778).

WEIGHTS AND MEASURES: The metric system is the legal standard, but some local measures are still in use.

HOLIDAYS: New Year's Day, 1 January; National Day, 31 March; May Day, 1 May; Assumption, 15 August; Republic Day, 13 December; Christmas, 25 December. Movable holidays include Good Friday.

TIME: 1PM = noon GMT.

¹LOCATION, SIZE, AND EXTENT

Malta lies in the central Mediterranean Sea, 93 km (58 mi) south of Sicily and 290 km (180 mi) from the nearest point of the North African mainland. There are three main islands—Malta, Gozo to the NW, and Comino between them—as well as two small uninhabited islands, Cominotto and Filfla. Extending 45 km (28 mi) SE-NW and 13 km (8 mi)NE-SW, Malta's total area is 320 sq km (124 sq mi)—Malta, 245.7 sq km (94.9 sq mi); Gozo, 67.1 sq km (25.9 sq mi); Comino, 2.8 sq km (1.1 sq mi). Comparatively, the area occupied by Malta is slightly less than twice the size of Washington, D.C. The total coastline of the inhabited islands is 140 sq km (87 mi).

Malta's capital city, Valletta, is located on the east coast of the island of Malta.

²TOPOGRAPHY

The islands of Malta are a rocky formation (chiefly limestone) rising from east to northeast to a height of 240 m (786 ft), with clefts that form deep harbors, bays, creeks, and rocky coves.

³CLIMATE

The climate is typically Mediterranean, with fairly hot, dry summers and rainy, mild winters. The average winter temperature is 9°C (48°F); the average summer temperature, 31°C (88°F). Rainfall occurs mostly between November and January and averages about 56 cm (22 in) per year.

⁴FLORA AND FAUNA

The islands are almost treeless. Vegetation is sparse and stunted. Carob and fig are endemic, and the grape, bay, and olive have been cultivated for centuries. There are some rock plants.

The weasel, hedgehog, and bat are native to Malta. White rabbits and mice have been introduced. Many types of turtles, tortoises, and butterflies and several varieties of lizard also are found. Common varieties of Mediterranean fish, as well as the seal and porpoise, inhabit the surrounding waters.

⁵ENVIRONMENT

Malta's most significant environmental problems include inadequate water supply, deforestation, and the preservation of its wildlife. The nation's agriculture suffers from lack of adequate water for crops due to limited rainfall. Currently, 45% of Malta's land area is currently used for agricultural purposes. According to the United Nation reports in 1992, a significant proportion of Malta's animal and plant life is in danger of extinction. Malta was one of the first countries to ratify the 1976 Barcelona Convention for the protection of the Mediterranean from pollution. Malta's government has made recent efforts to control environmental damage including passage of the Environmental Protection Act of 1991 and the creation of a Ministry for the Environment. The Ministry of Health and Environment belongs to the International Union for the Conservation of Nature and Natural Resources. In cooperation with the World Wildlife Fund, the Ghadira wetland area was made a permanent nature reserve in 1980.

⁶POPULATION

The total resident population at the time of the 1985 census was 340,907, of whom 315,913 lived on Malta and 24,994 on Gozo and Comino. It was estimated at 355,910 at the end of 1990. The UN projects a population of 380,000 by the year 2000, assuming a crude birth rate of 15.1 per 1,000 population, a crude death rate of 7.9, and a net natural increase of 7.2 during 1995–2000. The 1990 estimate of 1,128 residents per sq km (2,921 per sq mi) makes Malta one of the most densely populated countries in the world. Valletta, the capital and chief port, had an estimated 1991 population of 9,183; other major cities, are Birkirkara (21,437), Qormi (19,525), and Sliema (13,541).

⁷MIGRATION

Because of overpopulation and a lack of sufficient employment opportunities in Malta, the government encourages emigration. In 1990, however, the 160 emigrants numbered fewer than the

858 Maltese who returned to the island. Most emigrants go to Australia (81 in 1990), the US (27), Canada (27), or the UK (10).

8ETHNIC GROUPS

Most Maltese are believed to be descended from the ancient Carthaginians, but there are considerable elements of Italian and other Mediterranean stock.

9LANGUAGES

Maltese, a Semitic language with Romance-language assimilations, is the national language and the language of the courts. Maltese and English are both official languages.

10RELIGION

Roman Catholicism is the official religion, but there is freedom of worship for all faiths. In 1993, an estimated 98% of the population was Catholic; religious minorities include some 3,900 Anglicans. Relations between the government and the Catholic episcopate deteriorated while Dom Mintoff was president. Legislation enacted by the Maltese parliament in 1983 that could have resulted in the expropriation of 75% of all properties owned by the church, the largest single property holder in Malta, was repealed by the new government in 1985.

11TRANSPORTATION

Malta has no railways. In 1991 there were 1,291 km (802 mi) of paved roads. Passenger cars in 1991 totaled 114,682; taxis, trucks, and buses, 21,237. Ferry and hydrofoil services connect Malta and Gozo.

The harbors of Valletta, among the finest in the Mediterranean, are a port of call for many lines connecting northwestern Europe and the Middle and Far East. Roughly 3,000 ships dock at Valletta each year. As of 31 December 1991, 640 vessels totaling 8,705,000 GRT were registered in Malta. The principal airport is at Luqa. A new terminal which is designed to handle 2.2 million passengers per year (or 2,000 at any given moment), was under construction in 1991. The national air carrier is Malta Airlines, which carried some 692,500 passengers in 1992.

12HISTORY

The strategic importance of the island of Malta was recognized in the time of the Phoenicians, whose occupation of Malta was followed by that of the Greeks, the Carthaginians, and the Romans. The apostle Paul was shipwrecked at Malta in AD 58, and the islanders were converted to Christianity within two years. With the official split of the Roman Empire in 395, Malta was assigned to Byzantium, and in 870 it fell under the domination of the Saracens. In 1090, it was taken by Count Roger of Normandy, and thereafter it was controlled by the rulers of Sicily—Norman and, later, Aragonese. The Emperor Charles V granted it in 1530 to the Knights of St. John, who had been driven from Rhodes by the Turks. The Knights surrendered Malta to Napoleon in 1798. Two years later, the British ousted the French garrison, with the aid of a revolt by the Maltese people. British possession of Malta was confirmed in 1814 by the Treaty of Paris.

During almost the entire 19th century, a British military governor ruled the colony. After World War I, during which the Maltese remained loyal to Britain, discontent and difficulties increased. The 1921 constitution granted a considerable measure of self-government, but political tensions reemerged, and the constitution, after having twice been suspended, was revoked in 1936. A new constitution in 1939 reinstated Malta as a British crown colony. In World War II the Maltese again remained loyal to the UK, and for gallantry under heavy fire during the German-Italian siege (1940–43), the entire population was awarded the George Cross.

Substantial self-government was restored in 1947. The Maltese, however, carried on negotiations with the UK for complete self-government, except in matters of defense and foreign affairs. In August 1962, Prime Minister Borg Olivier requested the UK to grant Malta independence, and Malta became a sovereign and independent nation within the Commonwealth of Nations on 21 September 1964. At the same time, mutual defense and financial agreements were signed with the UK. Under subsequent accords negotiated between 1970 and 1979, British troops withdrew from Malta, and the NATO naval base on the main island was closed.

On 13 December 1974, Malta formally adopted a republican form of government, and the former governor-general, Sir Anthony Mamo, became the first president. Dom Mintoff, leader of the Malta Labour Party and prime minister from 1971 through 1984, instituted socialist measures and initiated a nonaligned policy in foreign affairs. Although the Labour Party narrowly lost the popular vote in the 1981 elections, it retained its parliamentary majority; to protest the gerrymandering that allegedly made this possible, the opposition Nationalist Party boycotted parliament, and strikes and civil violence ensued. In January 1987, a new law guaranteed that, following future elections, the new government would be formed by the party that won a majority of the popular vote. In May 1987, the Nationalist Party won a popular majority but only 31 of 65 seats in parliament. In accordance with the new law, the Nationalists were given four additional seats, for a total of 35 in an expanded 69-seat parliament, and the Nationalist Eddie Fenech Adami became prime minister, replacing the Labourite Carmelo Mifsud Bonnici. The Nationalists were returned to power in February 1992 with a slightly higher majority. Eddie Fenech Adami remained prime minister. Vincent Tabone, president, had been elected in 1989.

Maltese politics have revolved around foreign policy issues, in particular, Malta's relationship with Europe. The Nationalist Party government has been a strong proponent of EC membership. In July 1990, Malta applied for full membership in the EC. The application was pending in 1994 awaiting various adjustments to the Maltese economy as well as changes to its legal structure.

13GOVERNMENT

The Malta Independence Constitution came into effect on 21 September 1964. Ten years later, Malta became a republic, while remaining within the Commonwealth of Nations. The unicameral parliament, the House of Representatives, consists of 65 members (1994) elected for a five-year term by universal adult suffrage (18 years of age and over), under a system of proportional representation. Additional seats may be allocated until a majority of one seat is obtained.

The House elects the head of state, the president of the republic, who holds office for five years. The president appoints the prime minister and, on the latter's advice, the other members of the cabinet. The prime minister, who is the leader of the majority party, is responsible for general direction and control of the government.

14POLITICAL PARTIES

There are two major political parties, the Nationalist Party (PN) and the Malta Labour Party (MLP), which have alternated in political power. The Nationalist Party was returned to government in 1987 after 16 years of Labour Party rule, and won reelection in February 1992 with a three-seat majority (34 to 31) in Parliament.

Parties not represented in Parliament include Democratic Alternative (AD), Malta Democratic Party (PDM) and the Malta Communist Party (PKM).

15LOCAL GOVERNMENT

There are no local government bodies as such, although Gozo has a limited form of home rule.

¹⁶JUDICIAL SYSTEM

The superior courts consist of the Constitutional Court (with the power to review laws and executive acts), the court of appeal, the court of criminal appeal, two civil courts, the criminal court, and the commercial court. The judiciary, appointed by the president on the advice of the prime minister, consists of nine superior court judges, including the chief justice, who is also president of the Constitutional Court and of the court of appeal, and ten inferior court magistrates. Retirement is at age 65. The judiciary operates in an independent manner. Defendants in criminal cases have the right to counsel of choice. Indigent defendants are afforded court-appointed counsel at public expense.

¹⁷ARMED FORCES

The volunteer army of 1,650 has one infantry battalion and a mixed air and naval battalion. The leasing of air and naval bases to UK units ended in 1979. Malta spends $21.9 million on defense (1989) or 1.3 % of gross domestic product.

¹⁸INTERNATIONAL COOPERATION

Malta joined the UN on 1 December 1964 and participates in ECE and all the nonregional specialized agencies except IAEA, IBRD, IDA, and IFC. A member of the Commonwealth of Nations, the Council of Europe, and G-77, Malta also is signatory to GATT and the Law of the Sea. In recent years, Malta has improved its relations with Libya and the former USSR, as well as with Italy. Malta considers itself to be part of the nonaligned movement.

¹⁹ECONOMY

Malta has few natural resources. Agriculture is limited by the rocky nature of the islands, and most food must be imported. Industrial raw materials are lacking and also must be imported. Until 1964, the dominant factor in the economy was the presence of British military forces; with the withdrawal of UK military personnel by 1979, the dockyards were converted to commercial use. Malta's economy now relies on light industry, tourism, and other service industries, in addition to shipbuilding, maintenance, and repairs. The government holds shares in a variety of enterprises, including joint ventures. A stock exchange opened in 1992.

²⁰INCOME

In 1992, Malta's GNP was $2,606 million at current prices, or $7,300 per capita. For the period 1985–92 the average inflation rate was 2.7%, resulting in a real growth rate in per capita GNP of 5.4%.

In 1988 the GDP was $2.5 billion in current US dollars. It is estimated that in 1990 agriculture, hunting, forestry, and fishing contributed 3% to GDP; mining and quarrying, 3%; manufacturing, 24%; electricity, gas, and water, 7%; construction, 0%; wholesale and retail trade, 13%; transport, storage, and communication, 5%; finance, insurance, real estate, and business services, 13%; community, social, and personal services, 8%; and other sources, 24%.

²¹LABOR

The employed work force in 1990 was 127,200, including 74,300 in agriculture and private industry and 52,900 in government service. Employed men numbered 94,330, and women, 52,900. As of mid-1993, Malta's labor force was about 135,000, of which 100,000 were men and 35,000 were women. The number of unemployed workers decreased from 8,499 in 1986 to 5,087 at the end of 1991, when unemployment stood at 3.8% of the total labor force. Labor is highly organized in Malta, and about 50% of industrial workers belongs to the General Workers' Union. Other large unions include the Union of United Workers (mostly

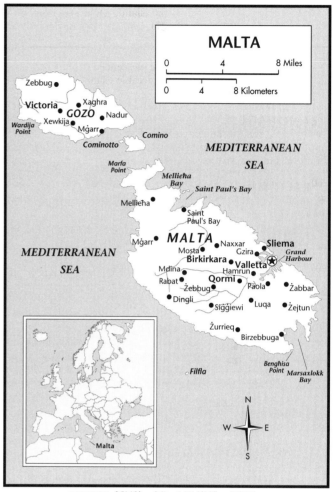

LOCATION: 35°48′ to 36°N; 14°10′30″ to 14°35′E.
TERRITORIAL SEA LIMIT: 12 mi.

nonindustrial workers) and the Confederation of Malta Trade Unions. The General Workers' Union was integrated with the Socialist Labor Party until 1992, when this affiliation was formally ended. In practice, however, the two are still closely related. In 1991, union membership represented about 30% of the total working population.

²²AGRICULTURE

Agriculture is carried out in small fields, consisting usually of strips of soil between rocks, and is characterized to a large extent by terracing. The total area under cultivation was about 13,000 hectares (32,100 acres) in 1991. Most farms are small. Wheat, barley, and grapes are the principal crops for domestic consumption, while potatoes, onions, wine, cut flowers, seeds, and fruit are the chief export crops. The total value of agricultural crops exported in 1992 was estimated at $23.5 million.

²³ANIMAL HUSBANDRY

Malta's livestock population in 1992 included 23,000 head of cattle, 107,000 pigs, 6,000 sheep, 5,000 goats, and 1,000,000 poultry. Animals slaughtered totaled 15,000 tons in 1992.

²⁴FISHING

Fishing is for local consumption. In 1991, the catch was 713.

²⁵FORESTRY

There are no forests on the islands.

26 MINING

In 1991, Malta's mineral industry produced 100 metric tons of salt, obtained during the desalination of sea water. Limestone, used in domestic construction, was also produced (600,000 cubic meters).

27 ENERGY AND POWER

Malta is totally dependent on imported fuel for its energy requirements. Electricity is the main source of power. In 1991, three thermal power stations with a net installed capacity of 250 Mw were in operation on the main island; Gozo and Comino are supplied with electric power by means of submarine cables. Production of electrical energy was 1,100 million kwh in 1991. On 5 February, 1991, a trade agreement was signed whereby Malta will reportedly import 75% of its required petroleum products from Libya.

28 INDUSTRY

Malta's principal industries are shipbuilding, maintenance, and repairs, food processing, electronics, and textiles and clothing. Other products include beverages, tobacco products, lace, metals, rubber products, and plastic goods. Total manufacturing production in 1991 was valued at LM188.2 million.

29 SCIENCE AND TECHNOLOGY

Malta's technological development has been confined largely to the shipbuilding and repair industry and the manufacture of electronic computer parts. The University of Malta has faculties of dental surgery, engineering, medicine, and science. In 1988, research and development expenditures amounted to LM10,000; 5 technicians and 34 scientists and engineers were engaged in research and development.

30 DOMESTIC TRADE

Valletta is the commercial center of Malta. Shopping hours are from 9 AM to 1 PM and from 3 to 7 PM; banks are open from 8:30 AM to 12:30 PM, Monday–Friday, and from 8:30 AM to noon on Saturday. Billboards, newspapers, radio, and television are the main advertising media.

31 FOREIGN TRADE

Because it depends on external sources for much of its food, fuel, raw materials, and manufactured articles, Malta imports considerably more than it exports.

Principal exports (including re-exports) in 1992 (in thousands of Maltese lira) were:

Manufactured articles	124,597
Machinery and transport equipment	274,651
Semimanufactured goods	31,540
Food, live animals, beverages, and tobacco	9,661
Chemicals	8,644
Other exports and reexports	41,216
TOTAL	490,309

Principal imports in 1992 (in thousands of Maltese lira) were:

Semimanufactured goods	126,723
Machinery and transport equipment	361,673
Manufactured articles	74,571
Food, live animals, beverages, and tobacco	74,636
Mineral fuels	35,053
Other imports	24,004
TOTAL	747,351

The UK was Malta's principal trade partner in the 1970s but was outstripped by Italy and Germany during the 1980s.

Principal trade partners in 1992 (in thousands of Maltese lira) were:

	EXPORTS	IMPORTS	BALANCE
Germany	69,845	80,316	–10,471
Italy	200,151	282,198	–82,047
UK	32,129	96,219	–64,090
US	28,430	23,648	4,782
Other countries	159,754	264,970	–105,216
TOTALS	490,309	747,351	–257,042

32 BALANCE OF PAYMENTS

Traditionally, Malta has had a large trade deficit because it must import most of its food and raw materials. The expansion of industry and the improvement of living standards in recent years have further increased the deficit, which is made up by other foreign receipts in the form of tourist revenues, transfers, and financial assistance, formerly from the UK and more recently from Italy and Libya. At the end of September 1993, the current account registered a deficit of $63 million, compared to a surplus of $6.6 million in September 1992. This deterioration was mainly due to the exceptional purchase of three aircraft by Malta's national airline. Malta's total net foreign assets at the end of September 1993 stood at $1.8 billion, up 5.9% from December 1992. In 1992 merchandise exports totaled $1,154.2 million and imports $1,753.0 million. The merchandise trade balance was $-598.8 million. The following table summarizes Malta's balance of payments for 1989 and 1990 (in millions of US dollars):

	1989	1990
CURRENT ACCOUNT		
Goods, services, and income	–107.9	–142.9
Unrequited transfers	104.4	87.5
TOTALS	–3.4	–55.4
CAPITAL ACCOUNT		
Direct investment	51.7	45.6
Portfolio investment	–57.7	–1.9
Other long-term capital	–13.8	–11.6
Other short-term capital	–27.0	–75.5
Reserves	–14.2	74.9
TOTALS	–61	31.5
Errors and omissions	64.4	23.9
Total change in reserves	104.3	–51.4

33 BANKING AND SECURITIES

In June 1968, activities of the Currency Board were transferred to the new Central Bank of Malta. Central Bank foreign assets as of December 1991 totaled LM 559.1 million. There are four commercial banks including the Bank of Valletta, Mid-Med Bank, and Lombard Bank Malta—as well as the National Savings Bank. Money supply, as measured by M2, was LM 1,365.9 million in 1993. A stock exchange was founded in 1992.

34 INSURANCE

All customary types of insurance are available. Many foreign insurance companies have representatives in Malta. Life insurance premiums totaled LM2.6 million in 1985, and other insurance premiums, LM10.3 million. In 1986, there were 1 life, 24 non-life, and 3 composite insurance companies in operation. In the same year, 20.3% of all premiums were written for life and 79.7% for non-life insurance.

35 PUBLIC FINANCE

The principal sources of recurrent revenues are income taxes, and customs and excise taxes.

The following table shows actual revenues and expenditures for 1990 and 1991 in millions of lira.

	1990	1991
REVENUE AND GRANTS		
Tax revenue	188.06	204.87
Non-tax revenue	92.11	96.56
Capital revenue	0.37	1.38
Grants	7.68	16.37
TOTAL	228.22	319.18
EXPENDITURES & LENDING MINUS REPAYMENTS		
General public service	25.51	31.97
Defense	6.19	6.49
Public order and safety	7.76	8.55
Education	28.89	32.54
Health	23.35	26.59
Social security and welfare	105.93	113.08
Housing and community amenities	27.31	30.80
Recreation, cultural, and religious affairs	5.69	5.87
Economic affairs and services	91.06	95.35
Other expenditures	5.51	9.14
Adjustments	—	—
Lending minus repayments	−0.92	−0.44
TOTAL	326.28	359.94
Deficit/Surplus	−38.06	−40.76

In 1991 Malta's total public debt stood at LM211.63 million, of which LM44.71 was financed abroad.

36TAXATION

In 1992, individuals paid income tax ranging from 18% on annual incomes of LM1,500 to 35% on incomes of LM4,4100 and over. Married people paid rates ranging from 10% to 35%. The basic corporate tax rate was 35% on total income. Other taxes include gift and inheritance taxes, excise taxes, and stamp taxes. Transactions with offshore companies are tax exempt.

37CUSTOMS AND DUTIES

Customs are collected mainly in the form of ad valorem duties; there are specific duties on petroleum, spirits, and tobacco. Preferential treatment is accorded to imports from the EC.

38FOREIGN INVESTMENT

Malta encourages foreign investment through tax holidays, export incentives, investment and accelerated depreciation allowances, reduced taxes on reinvested profits, grants to cover training costs and management services, a liberal attitude toward repatriation of profits and capital, and few restrictions on foreign ownership of Maltese firms.

39ECONOMIC DEVELOPMENT

The government's primary aim is to increase Malta's productive capacity. Under the LM123-million development plan for 1973–80, manufacturing, shipbuilding, and tourism expanded rapidly. The new Marsa shipyard and a 300,000-ton dock were completed by 1980; the Marsaxlokk harbor complex was to be developed into a free port.

Legislation adopted in 1988 provides for the establishment of offshore businesses and trusts. The Malta Development Corp. is a public agency that encourages new investment in industry. In the early 1990s, the government was planning to build a new telecommunications network, a larger power station, a new air terminal, and enlarged water purification and distribution systems.

Malta received $215.8 million in foreign aid during 1991.

40SOCIAL DEVELOPMENT

The National Insurance Act of 1956, as amended in 1965, provides benefits for sickness, unemployment, old age, widowhood, orphanhood, disability, and industrial injuries. These benefits are supplemented by social assistance under the National Assistance Act of 1956. Legislation establishing family allowances was enacted in 1974, and maternity benefits were mandated in 1981.

Women make up a growing portion of the labor force due to changing social patterns and economic necessity. A constitutional amendment effective July 1993 mandates government protection of all groups against economic, social, and political discrimination. In August 1993, Malta's Parliament passed legislation granting women equality in matters involving family law.

41HEALTH

In 1986 there were 3,142 beds in 8 government hospitals. In 1989, Malta had 692 doctors, 374 pharmacists, 92 dentists, 1,430 nurses, and 242 midwives. Infant mortality decreased from 23.3 per 1,000 live births in 1973 to 9 in 1992. Average life expectancy at birth in 1992 was 76 years. In 1993, Malta had a birth rate of 15.2 per 1,000 people, and a general mortality rate of 8 per 1,000 people. In 1992, there were 5,500 births, and 80% of Malta's children were vaccinated against measles.

42HOUSING

At the end of 1983, there were approximately 111,700 dwellings on Malta. New housing units completed during 1983 totaled roughly 2,400. In 1985, 45% of all dwellings were terraced, 20% were flats, 16% were terrans(self-contained rooms at ground level with a separate entrance accessible from the street), 11% were maisonettes, 3% were semi-detached, and 1% were farms. Roughly 94% had cooking facilities, 98% had a refrigerator, 80% had a washing machine, and 65% had a telephone.

43EDUCATION

Primary education is compulsory between the ages of 6 and 16 and is free in public schools. Maltese law requires that the teachings of the Roman Catholic Church be included in the public school curriculum. Some 30% of Maltese students in the mid-1980s received primary and secondary education in church schools, whose fees were frozen by the Mintoff government in 1982. Legislation passed the next year required all schools to provide free education. A compromise was reached in 1985 providing for the gradual phasing in of free education in church schools, but the Nationalist government that took office in 1987 seemed likely to change the original legislation.

In 1990, there were 115 primary schools with 1,780 teachers and 36,899 pupils enrolled. Total number of secondary school students were 32,544 with 2,688 teachers. There were 6,653 students enrolled in vocational schools. In 1990, all higher level institutions and universities had 252 teaching staff and 3,123 pupils.

44LIBRARIES AND MUSEUMS

The National Library of Malta (founded in 1555) is located in Valetta. The University of Malta Library (1769) is in Msidaan and contains over 318,000 volumes. The largest public library is the public library in Gozo with over 35,000 volumes. There are over 50 school libraries throughout Malta. Valletta is the site of the National Museum, with an archaeological collection, the Palace Armory, and the St. John's Museum. The Folk Museum and the Museum of Political History are at Vittoriosa.

45MEDIA

Malta's radio service transmits on two channels (one Maltese, one English). Television programs are received from a local service and from Italy. In 1991, there were 264,000 television sets and 187,000 radios; there were 172,973 telephones.

The press includes 2 Maltese daily newspapers, 1 English daily, 2 Maltese Sunday papers, and 1 English Sunday paper. Leading dailies (with estimated 1991 circulations) are *In Taghna* (Maltese, 20,000), *L'Orizzont* (Maltese, 25,000), and the *Times* (English, 23,000).

46 ORGANIZATIONS

Various cultural, recreational, religious, professional, political, industrial, and philanthropic organizations are active. There is a chamber of commerce in Valletta. In 1985, some 20 cooperative societies had 3,274 members.

47 TOURISM, TRAVEL, AND RECREATION

Tourism is a major industry, with 895,036 visitors in 1991 and gross earnings of $574 million. US citizens and most Western Europeans need no visa for visits of less than three months. About 51% of Malta's visitors in 1991 came from the UK, 15% from Germany, and 7% from Italy. There were 20,448 hotel rooms with 40,894 beds and a 55.9% occupancy rate. In 1992, a new $60 million air terminal was opened. Malta has many scenic and historical attractions, especially in Valletta, plus excellent beaches. Soccer is the national sport, and billiards and snooker are popular pastimes.

48 FAMOUS MALTESE

The city of Valletta is named after Jehan Parisot de la Vallette (1494–1568), Grand Master of the Knights of St. John, who successfully withstood a great Turkish siege in 1565. Dominic (Dom) Mintoff (b.1916), a founder of Malta's Labour Party, was prime minister during 1955–58 and 1971–84. Agatha Barbara (b.1923), a former cabinet minister, was elected the first woman president of Malta on 16 February 1982.

49 DEPENDENCIES

Malta has no territories or colonies.

50 BIBLIOGRAPHY

Blouet, Brian. *A Short History of Malta*. New York: Praeger, 1967.

Clews, Hilary A. (ed.). *The Year Book, 1987*. Sliema: De La Salle Brothers, 1987.

Dobie, Edith. *Malta's Road to Independence*. Norman: University of Oklahoma Press, 1967.

Elliott, Peter R. *The Cross and the Ensign: A Naval History of Malta, 1798–1978*. Annapolis, Md.: Naval Institute Press, 1980.

Evans, J. D. *The Prehistoric Antiquities of the Maltese Islands*. New York: Oxford University Press, 1971.

MOLDOVA

Republic of Moldova
Republica Moldoveneasca

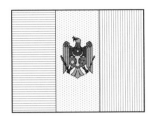

CAPITAL: Chisinau.

FLAG: Equal vertical bands of blue, yellow, and red; emblem in center of yellow stripe is Roman eagle with shield on its breast.

MONETARY UNIT: The leu is a paper currency, replacing the Russian Rouble.

WEIGHTS AND MEASURES: The metric system is in force.

HOLIDAYS: No information on holidays is available.

TIME: 2 PM = noon GMT.

[1] LOCATION, SIZE, AND EXTENT

Moldova is a landlocked nation located in eastern Europe, between Ukraine and Romania. Comparatively, it is slightly more than twice the size of the state of Hawaii with a total area of 33,700 sq km (13,012 sq mi). Moldova shares boundaries with Ukraine on the N, E, and S; and Romania on the W. Moldova's boundary length totals 1,389 km (864 mi).

Its capital city, Chisinau, is located in the south central part of the country.

[2] TOPOGRAPHY

The topography of Moldova consists of rolling steppe gradually sloping south toward the Black Sea.

[3] CLIMATE

The climate is of the humid continental type. The country is exposed to northerly cold winds in the winter and moderate westerly winds in the summer. The mean temperature in July is 20°C (68°F). The mean temperature in January is -4°C (24°F). Rainfall averages 58 cm (22.8 in) a year.

[4] FLORA AND FAUNA

Three-fourths of the country's terrain features chernozyom (black soil), which supports the natural vegetation of steppe-like grasslands. Carp, bream, trout, and pike populate the lakes and streams.

[5] ENVIRONMENT

The natural environment in Moldova suffers from the heavy use of agricultural chemicals (including banned pesticides such as DDT), which has contaminated soil and groundwater.

[6] POPULATION

The population of Moldova was 4,337,592 in 1989. It was estimated at 4,356,000 in 1993. A population of 5,200,000 is projected for 2010 by the World Bank, assuming a crude birth rate of 18 per 1,000 people, a crude death rate of 10, and a natural increase of 8. The population density in 1993 was about 129 per sq km (335 per sq mi). The estimated population at the beginning of 1990 for Chisinau (Kishinev), the capital, was 676,000. Tiraspol had an estimated 184,000 people; Balti (Beltsy), 162,000; and Tighina, 132,000.

[7] MIGRATION

There was a net emigration of 6,000 in 1979–88 to other Soviet republics. This grew to 16,300 in 1989 and 29,800 in 1990.

[8] ETHNIC GROUPS

The population was 64.5% Moldovan in 1989. Other groups included Ukrainian, 14%; Russian, 13%; Gagauzis, 3.5%; Bulgarians, 2%; and Jews, 1.5%.

[9] LANGUAGES

Moldovan is considered a dialect of Romanian rather than a separate language. It is derived from Latin but, unlike the other Romance languages, preserved the neuter gender and a system of three cases. There are a large numer of Slavonic-derived words. Under Soviet rule the language was written in the Cyrillic alphabet, but Roman script was restored in 1989. In the areas policed by the Russian army, a 1992 law made Russian and Ukrainian official languages of equal status with Moldovan, which continued to be written in the Cyrillic script.

[10] RELIGIONS

Ninety-five percent of Moldovans are Eastern Orthodox, 1–5% are Jewish, and about 1,000 people are Baptist. Almost all churchgoers are ethnic Moldovan; the Slavic population generally are not churchgoers.

[11] TRANSPORTATION

Railroads consisted of 1,150 km (715 mi) of track, not including industrial lines, in 1990. Highways that year totaled 20,000 km (12,400 mi), including 13,900 km (8,600 mi) of paved roads. Access to the sea is through Ukraine or Romania.

[12] HISTORY

The region that is now Moldova (also called Bessarabia) has historically been inhabited by a largely Romanian-speaking population. The region was part of the larger Romanian principality of Moldova in the 18th century, which in turn was under Ottoman suzerainty. In 1812, the region was ceded to the Russian Empire which ruled until March 1918 when it became part of Romania. Moscow laid the basis for reclaiming Moldova by establishing a small Moldovian Autonomous Soviet Socialist Republic on Ukrainian territory in 1924.

The 1939 Nazi-Soviet pact assigned Moldova to the Soviet sphere of influence. Soviet forces seized Moldova in June 1940. After the Nazi invasion of the USSR, Germany helped Romania to regain Moldova. Romania held it from 1941 until Soviet forces reconquered it in 1944.

Moldova declared its independence from the USSR on 27 August 1991. Russian forces, however, have remained on Moldovan territory east of the Dnister River and have supported the Russian minority (who form only 30% of the population in this small region) in proclaiming an independent "Transdnister Republic."

[13]GOVERNMENT

Elections to Moldova's first post-independence parliament were held on 27 February 1994. The new parliament consists of a single chamber of 104 seats. The president is elected separately in a popular election.

[14]POLITICAL PARTIES

Although 26 parties or coalitions of parties participated in the February 1994 elections, only four received more than the 4% of the national vote required to gain seats.

The Agrarian Party, which won 56 of the 104 seats, supports Moldovan independence. The Socialist/Unity Bloc won 28 seats; this pro-Russian party is supported primarily by ethnic Russians, and fears that independent Moldova will move closer to, and eventually rejoin, Romania. The other two parties (the Bloc of Peasants and Intellectuals, 11 seats; and the Popular Front Alliance, 9 seats) are pro-Romanian parties which advocate union with Romania.

[15]LOCAL GOVERNMENT

Local administration is divided into 38 districts, or rayons, and 10 cities.

The Russian minority on the east bank of the Dnister River have proclaimed their independence as the "Transdnister Republic." The Moldovan government is willing to allow this region a degree of autonomy, but the largely Communist Transdnister administration insists on independence.

[16]JUDICIAL SYSTEM

The judiciary is more independent now than when it was subject to the Soviet regime, but there is still no legal guarantee of an independent judiciary. There are courts of first instance at the city and district (rayon) levels with a Supreme Court acting as an appellate court. The Supreme Court is divided into civil and criminal sections.

Criminal defendants enjoy a presumption of innocence and afforded a number of due process rights, including a public trial and a right of appeal. In practice, a number of convictions have been overturned on appeal.

[17]ARMED FORCES

The military is organized into the Ground Forces, Air and Air Defense Force, and the Security Forces (internal and border troups). Approximately 850,000 males were considered fit for service in 1993.

[18]INTERNATIONAL COOPERATION

Moldova was admitted to the UN on 2 March 1992, and is a member of the CSCE, IMF, UNESCO, and the World Bank. A member of the CIS, the country is also applying for membership in other international organizations. Moldova has formal diplomatic relations with 90 countries. The US opened its embassy in the capital city 18 March 1992.

[19]ECONOMY

Agriculture is the most important sector of Moldova's economy, accounting for 42% of NMP in 1991. The country's wide range of crops provides significant export revenue and employment. The manufacturing base is small and concentrated mainly on food processing and other light industry. Droughts and trade disruptions following the dissolution of the former Soviet Union combined to cause steep declines in GDP between 1990 and 1992 after 20 years of growth.

[20]INCOME

In 1992, Moldova's GNP was $5,485 million at current prices, or $1,260 per capita. For the period 1985–92 the average inflation rate was 14.0%, resulting in a real growth rate in per capita GNP of –2.9%.

In 1992, the GDP was $5,637 million in current US dollars.

[21]LABOR

The total civilian employment in 1992 was 2,050,000 of which 20.6% were engaged in community, social, and personal services; 19.2% were in manufacturing; 40% in agriculture; 5.8% in construction; 5.4% in commerce; and 9% in other sectors.

Moldovan parliamentary decisions in 1989 and 1991 gave citizens the right to form all kinds of social organizations, including independent trade unions. The Federation of Independent Trade Unions of Moldova (FITU) is the successor to the previously existing Soviet trade union system. Various industrial unions still maintain voluntary membership in the FITU.

Government workers do not have the right to strike, nor do those in essential services such as health care and energy. In 1992, there were brief strikes by transport workers and teachers. That year, work stoppages amounted to 153,700 lost workdays involving 25,500 workers.

The minimum wage is supposedly linked to the inflation rate, but did not keep pace in 1992 enough to provide a decent standard of living for a worker and family. The labor code stipulates a standard workweek of 41 hours, with at least one day off weekly.

[22]AGRICULTURE

Cropland covers about 53% of the Moldovan land area. Agricultural activities engaged 40% of all employed persons in 1992. Agriculture is the most important sector of the Moldovan economy, accounting for 31.3% of GDP and 42% of NMP in 1991. The worst drought in the area since 1946 caused agricultural output to drop by 28% in 1991 and 25% in 1992. About 15% of all cropland is under irrigation.

Moldovan crops and their 1992 production amounts include (in tons): sugar beets, 2,200,000; wheat, 1,000,000; corn, 700,000; barley, 400,000; potatoes, 300,000; tobacco, 51,000; and soybeans, 30,000. Wine and tobacco products are important agricultural exports.

[23]ANIMAL HUSBANDRY

Less than 10% of the total area consists of pastureland. In 1992, the livestock population included 1,021,000 head of cattle, 1,404,000 pigs, 1,189,000 sheep, and 23,000,000 chickens. Pork production amounted to 99,000 tons in 1992; when 68,000 tons of beef were produced. In 1992, 1.2 million tons of milk and 44,800 tons of eggs were also produced. Milk and egg production were down by 7.7% and 37.3%, respectively, as a result of severe drought that season.

[24]FISHING

With no direct connection to the Black Sea, fishing is limited to the Dnister River. Commercial fishing is not economically significant.

25FORESTRY

Forested areas account for about 8% of the total. Production is largely domestically consumed; wood and paper product exports in 1990 made up just 2% of total exports.

26MINING

In Moldova, more than 100 deposits of gypsum, limestone, sand, and stone are exploited for industrial mineral production.

27ENERGY AND POWER

Moldova imports nearly all of its energy needs; there is only one small (40,000 kw) hydroelectric power plant at Dubásari that provides domestic production. Refined oil products and natural gas come from Russia, Ukraine, and Belarus, accounting for 99% of the fuel supply for Moldova's thermal power plants. Although Moldova traditionally has exported electricity to Ukraine and Bulgaria, recent shortages of imported fossil fuels have necessitated a strict system of electricity rationing.

In August 1993, Moldova agreed to assist in the construction of the proposed Iran-Azerbaijan-Ukraine natural gas pipeline. In April 1993, Russia threatened to cut off natural gas supplies to Moldova because of alleged outstanding debts.

In 1991, Moldovans consumed about 100,000 barrels of oil per day; natural gas consumption that year totaled 140 billion cu ft (3.96 billion cu m); coal, 3.9 million tons; and electricity, 9 billion kwh.

28INDUSTRY

Moldova's industry has been concentrated mostly in light manufacturing, including processed food and beverages and cigarettes, but other activities include consumer durables, garments, high-technology electrical motors, precision tools, and farm machinery.

29SCIENCE AND TECHNOLOGY

The Moldovan Academy of Sciences, founded in 1961, has departments of physics, engineering, mathematics, biology, and chemistry. Five scientific institutes conduct medical and agricultural research. Moldovan State University has faculties of physics, mathematics, chemistry, and biology. A polytechnic institute and a medical institute are located in Chisinau. M.V. Frunze Agricultural Institute has 7,900 students.

30DOMESTIC TRADE

Since two-thirds of Moldova is rural, local farm markets play an important role in the domestic economy.

31FOREIGN TRADE

Traditionally, Moldova maintained a trade surplus with the other Soviet republics and a trade deficit with the rest of the world. In 1988, total imports were valued at R5,100 million, and exports of R2,500. Inter-republic trade accounted for 82% of imports and 95% of exports.

32BALANCE OF PAYMENTS

Moldova maintains a trade surplus with the rest of the former USSR (because of price distortions), and a trade deficit with the rest of the world. The trade deficit has deteriorated since 1992, due to increased prices for energy imports, and a simultaneous increase in imports and decline in exports of agricultural products due to drought. In 1990, imports exceeded exports by R1.5 billion.

33BANKING AND SECURITIES

Moldova's banking sector will play a key role in the country's transition from a managed economy to a market economy. The banking system was reformed in 1991. The National Bank of Moldova is charged with implementing monetary policy and

LOCATION: 47°0′N; 29°0′E. BOUNDARY LENGTHS: Total boundary lengths, 1,389 km (864 mi); Romania, 450 km (280 mi); Ukraine, 939 km (584 mi).

issuing currency. State banks include the State Savings Bank, with 1,000 branches, and the Bank for Foreign Economic Exchange. Sixteen commercial banks include the Agroindbanc, Banca Sociala, and Moldindconbanc SA. Holdovers from the old Soviet system include three regional banks, which have been changed to joint-stock companies whose shares are owned by state enterprises. There is one private bank in the country. The currency unit is the leu. The country does not have a security exchange.

34INSURANCE

Moldova's insurance system is largely inherited from Soviet era governmental institutions.

[35]PUBLIC FINANCE

Moldova has traditionally enjoyed a budget surplus, and the fiscal position was essentially in equilibrium in 1991 as rising expenditures were covered partially by revenue measures. In 1992, however, a significant and sudden drop in revenue, together with unexpected expenditures related to the Transdnister conflict, increased public service wage expenses, and copious lending to public enterprises caused the fiscal deficit to swell to 21% of GDP. As of 1992, Moldova had not yet signed an agreement with Russia concerning its liability for former Soviet debt. During the first year of its independence, Moldova contracted debts of about $90 million with nations outside the former USSR.

[36]TAXATION

The personal income tax rate ranges from 10–50%; the corporate rate ranges from 15–40% with a standard rate of 32%. Also levied are a 20% value-added tax and a payroll tax of 4.7–30%.

[37]CUSTOMS AND DUTIES

Moldova's foreign trade environment is characterized by extensive export and import tariffs, license requirements, and export quotas. Trade within the former Soviet Union is carried out under specific bilateral agreements for various products.

[38]FOREIGN INVESTMENT

No recent information is available.

[39]ECONOMIC DEVELOPMENT

In March 1993, the Moldovan government inaugurated the Program of Activity of the Government 1992–95 to make the transition to a market-oriented economy. The first stage focuses on stabilization, including price liberalization, and the second stage concentrates on economic recovery and growth, including privatization, agrarian reform, infrastructure development, social protection, and trade reform.

[40]SOCIAL DEVELOPMENT

The average family size was 3.4 in 1989, and the divorce rate averaged 7.4 per 1,000 women. There were 1.8 drug-related crimes and 7.3 alcohol-related deaths per 100,000 inhabitants.

Although women are accorded equal rights under the law, they are underrepresented in government and other leadership positions and disproportionately affected by the country's growing unemployment. Several women's organizations participate in political or charitable activities. Moldova has comprehensive legislation for the protection of children, including programs for paid maternity leave and family allowances. There are extensive vaccination and other health care programs for children. The fertility rate in 1990 was 2.4.

[41]HEALTH

Moldova has been working on developing its own standards for health care, among other major programs. Its 1992 birth rate was 16 per 1,000 people, with 69,000 births that year. Average life expectancy was 68 years in 1992. The infant mortality rate for 1992 was 31 per 1,000 live births, and the overall death rate was 10 per 1,000 people. Major causes of death in 1990 were: communicable diseases and maternal/perinatal causes, 54 per 100,000 people; noncommunicable diseases, 704 per 100,000; and injuries, 104 per 100,000. In 1992, there were approximately 1,000 deaths from ethnic conflict within the country.

In 1990, there were 54 reported cases of tuberculosis per 100,000 people and, in 1992, Moldova's immunization rates for children up to one year old were: tuberculosis (96%); diphtheria, pertussis, and tetanus (89%); polio (93%); and measles (92%). Total health care expenditures in 1990 were $623 million.

In 1992, there were 4 physicians per 1,000 people, with a nurse to doctor ratio of 3.0. And, in 1990, there was 1 physician for every 250 people and 7.8 hospital beds per 1,000 people.

[42]HOUSING

In 1989, 18.2% of all privately owned urban housing had running water, 15.8% had sewer lines, 16% had central heating, and 91.3% had gas. In 1990, Moldova had 17.9 sq m of housing space per capita and, as of 1 January 1991, 218,000 households (or 33.3%) were on waiting lists for urban housing.

[43]EDUCATION

While Moldova was a part of the Soviet Union, its education system was based on the Soviet pattern and Russian was the language of instruction. However, after its separation, extensive changes were introduced in the education system. Over 21% of the country's total budget was allocated to education in the early 1990s. The Moldovan State University was founded in 1945, and uses both Moldovan and Russian as languages of instruction.

[44]LIBRARIES AND MUSEUMS

The State University at Chisinau has a large academic library; there are other research libraries associated with the Moldovan Academy of Sciences. Museums and cultural institutions are also focused in Chisinau.

[45]MEDIA

Telecommunications links are via land line to the Ukraine and through Moscow's switching center to countries beyond the former USSR. As of 1990, 215,000 telephone applications were unfilled. Radio Kishinev and Kishinev Television broadcast in Romanian and Russian.

In 1989, Moldova had 200 newspapers, with a combined circulation of 2.4 million.

[46]ORGANIZATIONS

The Chamber of Commerce and Industry of the Republic of Moldova handles the internal and external economic affairs of the country. Political associations and organizations in the country include the Union of Council of Labor Collectives (ULC), Ecology Movement of Moldova (EMM), the Christian Democratic League of Women of Moldova, and the Alliance of Working People of Moldova.

[47]TOURISM, TRAVEL, AND RECREATION

Civil unrest since Moldova's independence has prohibited the development of tourism.

[48]FAMOUS MOLDOVANS

Mircea Ion Snegur and Andrei Sangheli have been president and prime minister of Moldova, respectively, since July 1992.

[49]DEPENDENCIES

Moldova has no territories or colonies.

[50]BIBLIOGRAPHY

Bruchis, Michael. *Nations—Nationalities—People: A Study of the Nationalities Policy of the Communist Party in Soviet Moldavia.* Boulder, Colo.: East European Monographs, 1984.

Dima, Nicholas. *From Moldavia to Moldova: The Soviet-Romanian Territorial Dispute.* 2d ed. Boulder, Colo.: East European Monographs, 1991.

Hill, Ronald J. *Soviet Political Elites: The Case of Tiraspol.* New York: St. Martin's, 1977.

Moldova. Minneapolis: Lerner Publications Co., 1993.

Papacostea, Serban. *Stephen the Great, Prince of Moldavia, 1457–1504.* Bucharest: Editura Stiintifica si Enciclopedica, 1981.

MONACO

Principality of Monaco
Principauté de Monaco

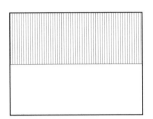

CAPITAL: The seat of government is at Monaco-Ville.

FLAG: The national flag consists of a red horizontal stripe above a white horizontal stripe.

ANTHEM: *Hymne Monégasque,* beginning "Principauté Monaco, ma patrie" ("Principality of Monaco, my fatherland").

MONETARY UNIT: Monaco uses the French franc (Fr), and all monetary restrictions in effect in France apply also in Monaco. Monégasque coins, on a par with French coinage, also circulate; denominations are 10, 20, and 50 centimes, and ½, 1, 2, 5, 10, and 50 francs. Fr1 = $0.1751 (or $1 = Fr5.71).

WEIGHTS AND MEASURES: The metric system is the legal standard.

HOLIDAYS: New Year's Day, 1 January; St. Dévôte, 27 January; Labor Day, 1 May; Assumption, 15 August; All Saints' Day, 1 November; National Day, 19 November; Immaculate Conception, 8 December; Christmas, 25 December. Movable religious holidays include Easter Monday, Ascension, Pentecost Monday, and Fête-Dieu.

TIME: 1 PM = noon GMT.

¹LOCATION, SIZE, AND EXTENT

The second-smallest country in Europe and the world after The Vatican, Monaco is situated in the southeastern part of the French department of Alpes-Maritimes. The area, including recent reclamation, is 195 hectares (482 acres), or 1.9 sq km (0.73 sq mi). Comparatively, the area occupied by Monoco is about three times the size of the mall in Washington, D.C. The principality's length is 3.18 km (1.98 mi) E–W, and its width is 1.1 km (0.68 mi) N–S. Bounded on the N, NE, SW, and W by France and on the E and SE by the Mediterranean Sea, Monaco has a total boundary length of 8.5 km (5.3 mi).

²TOPOGRAPHY

There are four main areas: La Condamine, the business district around the port; Monte Carlo, the site of the famous casino, which is at a higher elevation; Monaco-Ville, on a rocky promontory about 60 m (200 ft) above sea level; and Fontvieille, a 22-hectare (54-acre) industrial area of La Condamine that was reclaimed by landfill in the 1960s and 1970s.

³CLIMATE

Winters are mild, with temperature rarely below freezing and with a January average of about 8°C (46°F). Summer heat is tempered by sea breezes; the average maximum in July and August is 26°C (79°F). Rainfall averages about 77 cm (30 in) a year, and some 300 days a year have no precipitation whatsoever.

⁴FLORA AND FAUNA

Palms, aloes, carobs, tamarisks, mimosas, and other Mediterranean trees, shrubs, and flowers are abundant. Monaco does not have a distinctive fauna.

⁵ENVIRONMENT

Monaco is noted for its beautiful natural scenery and mild, sunny climate. The principality has sponsored numerous marine conservation efforts. Its own environment is entirely urban. According to UN reports in 1992, Monaco's environmental circumstances are very good. The nation has consistently monitored pollution levels in its air and water to ensure the safety of its citizens. One-fifth of the nation's land area (1.95 sq km) and two marine areas are protected by environmental statutes.

The government has also instituted a system of air pollution control facilities controlled by the Environmental Service. Citizens are encouraged to use public transportation to limit the amount of gas emissions.

Similar techniques have been applied to the protection of Monaco's water supply. Noise levels from industry and transportation are also monitored to ensure safe levels.

Monaco also has a sea-farming area which annually produces 800 tons of fish grown in clean water. Monaco is known for its activity in the field of marine sciences. The Oceanographic Museum, formerly directed by Jacques Cousteau, is renowned for its work and exhibits on marine life.

⁶POPULATION

The 1990 census placed the resident population at 29,876, of whom 6,200 were citizens of Monaco. Annual population growth rate is typically less than 1%. The residential population density in 1990 was 15,321 per sq km (39,669 per sq mi). Monaco-Ville has about 1,500 inhabitants.

⁷MIGRATION

There is a long waiting list for Monégasque citizenship. A 1992 law allows Monégasque women to confer citizenship on their children.

⁸ETHNIC GROUPS

On the evidence of certain place names, the native Monégasques are said to be of Rhaetian stock; they make up 15% of the population. The foreign residents are a highly cosmopolitan group, including more than half French and 17% Italians. French citizens are treated as if in France.

[9]LANGUAGES

French is the official language. English and Italian are also widely spoken. Many inhabitants speak the Monégasque language, which has its origins in the Genoese dialect of Italian and the Provençal language of southern France.

[10]RELIGIONS

Over 90% of the population adheres to Roman Catholicism, which is the official state religion. Freedom of worship is guaranteed by the constitution. Monaco is also part of the diocese of Gibraltar of the Church of England.

[11]TRANSPORTATION

French national roads join Monaco to Nice toward the west, and to Menton and the Italian Riviera toward the east. In 1991 there were 47 km (29 mi) of city streets. There is frequent bus service. The principality itself is served by motorbuses and taxicabs. In 1991 there were 17,000 passenger cars and 4,000 commercial vehicles. The southeastern network of the French national railroad system serves Monaco with about 1.6 km (1 mi) of track. Express trains on the Paris-Marseille-Nice-Ventimiglia line pass through the principality. Monaco is only 10 km (6 mi) from the international airport at Nice and is connected with it by bus and by a helicopter shuttle service. The harbor provides access by sea. As of 1 January 1992, Monaco had one oceangoing petroleum tanker of 3,268 GRT.

[12]HISTORY

The ruling family of Monaco, the house of Grimaldi, traces its ancestry to Otto Canella (c.1070–1143), who was consul of Genoa in 1133. The family name, Grimaldi, was adapted from the Christian name of Canella's youngest son, Grimaldo. The Genoese built a fort on the site of present-day Monaco in 1215, and the Grimaldi family secured control late in the 13th century. The principality was founded in 1338 by Charles I, during whose reign Menton and Roquebrune were acquired. Claudine became sovereign upon the death of her father, Catalan, in 1457. She ceded her rights to her husband and cousin, Lambert, during whose reign, in 1489, the duke of Savoy recognized the independence of Monaco. The first Monégasque coins were minted in the 16th century. Full recognition of the princely title was obtained by Honoré II in 1641.

The last male in the Grimaldi line, Antoine I, died in 1731. His daughter Louise-Hippolyte in 1715 had married Jacques-François-Léonor de Goyon-Matignon, Count of Thorigny, who adopted the name Grimaldi and assumed the Monégasque throne. France annexed the principality in 1793, but independence was reestablished in 1814. The following year, the Treaty of Stupinigi placed Monaco under the protection of the neighboring kingdom of Sardinia. In 1848, the towns of Roquebrune and Menton, which constituted the eastern extremity of Monaco, successfully rebelled and established themselves as a republic. In 1861, a year after the Sardinian cession of Savoy and Nice to France, Roquebrune and Menton also became part of that nation.

The economic development of Monaco proceeded rapidly with the opening of the railroad in 1868 and of the gambling casino. Since that time, the principality has become world famous as a tourist and recreation center. Monaco joined the United Nations on 28 May 1993.

[13]GOVERNMENT

Monaco is a constitutional monarchy ruled by the hereditary princes of the Grimaldi line. If the reigning prince should die without leaving a male heir, Monaco, according to treaty, would be incorporated into France.

Monaco's first constitution was granted by Prince Albert I on 7 January 1911. On 29 January 1959, Prince Rainier III temporarily suspended part of the constitution because of a disagreement over the budget with the National Council (Conseil National), and decreed that the functions of that body were to be assumed temporarily by the Council of State (Conseil d'État). In February 1961, the National Council was restored and an economic advisory council established to assist it.

A new constitution was promulgated on 17 December 1962. It provides for a unicameral National Council of 18 members elected by direct popular vote every five years; it shares legislative functions with the prince. Executive operations are conducted in the name of the prince by a minister of state (a French citizen) with the assistance of the Council of Government, consisting of three civil servants who are in charge of finances, public works, and internal affairs, respectively. All are appointed by the prince.

Women were enfranchised for municipal elections in 1945, and participated in elections for the National Council for the first time in February 1963. Suffrage is exercised only by true-born Monégasques of 25 and over. The electorate represents less than 15% of the resident population.

In January 1992, the National Council amended the citizenship laws for women. Women marrying a Monégasque no longer receive automatic citizenship but must apply after a five-year waiting period. Women can pass on Monégasque citizenship to their children.

[14]POLITICAL PARTIES

Monaco does not have political parties as such, but candidates compete on the basis of various lists. The major political groups have been the National and Democratic Union (Union Nationale et Democratique—UNI), founded in 1962; Communist Action (Action Communale—AC); Èvolution Communale (EC); and the Movement of Democratic Union (MUD).

In the general election of January 1993, the Campora List (Èvolution Communale) won 15 seats and the Medécin List (Action Communale) won two. One seat was won by René Giordano who ran as an independent.

[15]LOCAL GOVERNMENT

Municipal government is conducted by an elected council (Conseil Communal) of 15 members, headed by a mayor, all elected by universal suffrage for four-year terms. The three communes that made up Monaco before 1917—Monaco-Ville, La Condamine, and Monte Carlo—each had its own mayor from 1911 to 1917. Since that date, they have formed a single commune, together with Fontvieille.

Anne Marie Campora became mayor of Monte Carlo in 1991 succeeding Jean-Louis Médecin who had served as mayor since 1971.

[16]JUDICIAL SYSTEM

A justice of the peace tries petty cases. Other courts are the court of first instance, the court of appeal, the court of revision, and the criminal court. The highest judicial authority is vested in the Supreme Tribunal, established as part of the 1962 constitution. It has five full members and two assistant members, all of whom must be at least 40 years of age.

The Code Louis, promulgated by Prince Louis I (d.1701) and based on French legal codes, was formally adopted in 1919. Under the 1962 Constitution the Prince delegates his authority to the judiciary to render justice in his name.

The legal guarantee of a fair and public trial for criminal defendants is respected in practice. Defendants have the right to counsel at public expense if necessary.

[17]ARMED FORCES

France assumed responsibility for the defense of Monaco as part of the Versailles Treaty in 1919. There is no army in the principality.

A private guard protects the royal family, and a police force of 390 ensures public safety.

18INTERNATIONAL COOPERATION

A treaty providing in detail for mutual administrative assistance between France and Monaco became operative on 14 December 1954. Fiscal relations between the two countries are governed by a convention signed on 18 May 1963. France may station troops in Monaco and make use of Monaco's territorial waters. As a result of a customs union with France and French control of Monaco's foreign policy, the principality operates within the EC.

Monaco joined the UN on 28 May 1993 and is a member of the FAO, IAEA, ICAO, ITU, UNESCO, UPU, WHO, and WIPO. It is a signatory of the Law of the Sea, and has diplomatic or consular missions in 55 countries.

19ECONOMY

Monaco depends for its livelihood chiefly on income from tourism, real estate, financial services, and light industry. A substantial part of the principality's revenue from tourist sources comes from the operations of Sea-Bathing Co. (Société des Bains de Mer—SBM), in which the government holds a 69% interest. The SBM operates the gambling casino at Monte Carlo as well as several luxury hotels and motion-picture theaters. Monaco also serves as a tax haven for foreign non-French residents.

Statistics on the principality's economy are not published. However, under Prince Raineri, the economy has experienced economic and real estate development. Tourist facilities are being expanded and developed.

A 22-hectare landfill project at Fontvielle has increased Monaco's total land area.

20INCOME

In 1991 the GDP was $424 million, $16,000 per capita, in current US dollars.

21LABOR

There is virtually no unemployment in Monaco. The major employer of the working population is the SBM; others work in industry or in service establishments. In January 1987, the labor force was 25,560, of which 2,467 were in the public sector.

About two-thirds of all employees commute from France and Italy. The Inspectorate of Labor and the Bureau of Handicrafts enforce the labor code and statutes. The Industrial Court adjudicates labor disputes. Most people work a 40-hour week. Overtime is paid at the rate of time and a quarter; above 48 hours, at time and a half.

Owners and workers are each grouped in syndicates. There were some 35 unions grouped in a union federation, with about 4,000 members in 1992.

22AGRICULTURE

There is no agriculture.

23ANIMAL HUSBANDRY

There is a dairy industry serving local needs.

24FISHING

Some fishing is carried on to meet domestic requirements. The annual catch usually amounts to 2,000 tons. Monaco actively engages in marine science research, and in marine life preservation. The Oceanographic Institute has been studying the effects of radiation in the ocean since 1961.

25FORESTRY

There are no forests.

LOCATION: 43°43′49″N; 7°25′36″E. **BOUNDARY LENGTHS:** France, 5.4 km (3.4 mi); Mediterranean coastline, 7.3 km (4.5 mi). **TERRITORIAL SEA LIMIT:** 12 mi.

26MINING

There is no mining.

27ENERGY AND POWER

Services are provided by the Monégasque Electric Co. and Monégasque Gas Co. In 1991, standby electrical capacity totaled 10,000 kw; power is supplied by France.

28INDUSTRY

The tourist industry dominates Monaco's economic life, but small-scale industries produce a variety of items for domestic use and for export, contributing 27% of business turnover in 1990. Most industrial plants are located on Fontvieille. About 700 small businesses make pottery and glass objects, paper and cards, jewelry, perfumes, dolls, precision instruments, plastics, chemicals and pharmaceuticals, machine tools, watches, leather items, and radio parts. There are flour mills, dairies, and chocolate and candy plants, as well as textile mills and a small shipyard.

29SCIENCE AND TECHNOLOGY

Marine sciences have been the focus of scientific inquiry in the principality for several decades. Prince Albert (1848–1922), who reigned in Monaco during the early 1900s, was well-known internationally for his work as an oceanographer. His interest led to the establishment of a focus on oceanography for scientific pursuits in Monaco. Jacques-Yves Cousteau, popular oceonographer and activist, has been involved with Monaco's activities in marine life research.

In March 1961, in its first research agreement concluded with a member government, the IAEA, with the government of Monaco and the Oceanographic Institute in Monaco, undertook to research the effects of radioactivity in the sea. The Oceanographic Institute put at the disposal of the project a number of valuable facilities, including marine-biology laboratories, oceanographic vessels, specialized fishing equipment, and a wide variety of electronic and monitoring equipment.

The Scientific Center of Monaco conducts pure and applied research in oceanology and the environment.

30DOMESTIC TRADE

Domestic trade practices are similar to those in other towns along the French Riviera. Specialty shops deal in tourist souvenirs. The SBM controls most of the amusement facilities and owns most major hotels, sporting clubs, workshops, a printing press, and various retail shops.

Advertising media include magazines, billboards, and motion pictures. General business hours are from 8:30 AM to 12:30 PM and from 2 to 6 PM, Monday–Friday. Banking hours are 9 AM to 12 noon and 2 to 4 PM, Monday–Friday.

31FOREIGN TRADE

Statistical information is not available. Foreign trade is included in the statistics for France, with which Monaco has a customs union.

32BALANCE OF PAYMENTS

The economy is driven by such foreign currenty-earning activities as banking and tourism. Since separate records are not kept of Monaco's foreign trade transactions, payment statistics are not available.

33BANKING AND SECURITIES

Foreign currency circulates within Monaco under the supervision of the French government. The most important local bank is Crédit Foncier de Monaco, founded in 1922. In addition, there were 39 banks, including major French, Italian, US, and British banks, represented in Monaco in 1993. There is no securities exchange.

34INSURANCE

Branches of French insurance companies provide life, fire, accident, and other forms of insurance. Statistics are not available.

35PUBLIC FINANCE

Revenues are derived mostly from commercial and transactional taxes, income resulting from the customs agreement with France, the sale of postage stamps, and the sale of tobacco and matches. In 1991, budget revenues came to $424 million, while expenditures amounted to $376 million.

36TAXATION

There are no personal income taxes. Indirect taxes include the following: (1) a value-added tax, generally 18.6% but on some items as little as 5%; calculated on the sales price, including earlier taxes, it is charged by the manufacturer or distributor to the customer and is paid only once on a given article; (2) a service tax on compensation received by Monégasque firms for services rendered in Monaco and France; (3) excise taxes on alcoholic beverages; (4) registration fees; and (5) warranty duties on gold, platinum, and silver jewelry.

There is a tax of up to 35% on the profits of businesses that obtain more than one-fourth of their gross profits from operations outside Monaco. Corporations whose income is derived from royalties, licenses, trademarks, or other industrial or artistic property rights are subject to this tax, whether or not the income arises outside Monaco. There are no inheritance or gift taxes between spouses or between parents and children. Between brothers and sisters, the rate is 8%; between uncles or aunts and nephews or nieces, 10%; between other relatives, 13%; and between unrelated persons, 16%. Monaco grants no tax concessions to new businesses.

37CUSTOMS AND DUTIES

By treaty, France and Monaco form a customs union that treats the Monaco coast as part of France. The French customs service collects the duties on cargoes discharged in Monaco and pays a share to the principality.

Monaco imposes a duty on all exports to places other than France; the levy applies whether the transfer of goods is actual or fictitious.

38FOREIGN INVESTMENT

Monaco permits foreign businesses to establish their headquarters in its territory; the ownership and management must be made a matter of public record. Although both corporations and limited partnerships with shares are allowed, in fact only corporations are in existence. Two persons may form a corporation; the minimum capital must be fully subscribed and at least one-fourth paid up. Foreign companies may establish subsidiaries in Monaco. Low taxes on company profits are a considerable incentive for locating in Monaco.

39ECONOMIC DEVELOPMENT

The government strenuously promotes Monaco as a tourist and convention attraction. A government-financed International Convention Center offers large conference rooms, projection equipment, television and radio recording studios, telex communications, and simultaneous translation into five languages.

Two major development and reclamation projects have been undertaken under Prince Rainier. These are the major landfill and relcamation project at Fontvieille, and the Monte Carlo Bord de Mer. At Fontvieille, the government financed the reclamation of 220,000 sq m (2,368,000 sq ft) of inundated shore, creating a "platform" for residential construction and new port facilities.

The Monte Carlo seashore scheme, also government-financed, involved the relocation of railroad tracks underground in order to create a man-made beach, with a boardwalk and other tourist attractions. The beach lies between two other land reclamation projects: the Larvotto, a sports complex financed by SBM, and the Portier, an entertainment complex developed by the government.

Near the Larvotto the government has reserved a zone for the construction of residential and tourist accommodations. In the 1980s, Monaco concentrated on the development of business tourism, with the construction of the Monte Carlo Convention Center and the International Conference Center.

40SOCIAL DEVELOPMENT

Public social welfare organizations include the Pensions Office and the Social Services Benefits Office. Social security benefits are financed by payroll taxes, with monthly contributions by both employers and employees. There is a home for the aged attached to the Princess Grace Polyclinic.

Women have become increasingly visible in public life. As of 1993, 6 of Monaco's 19 lawyers were women, as were 6 of 41 physicians. In the same year, the Mayor of Monoco and one member of the National Council were also women. There is equal legal treatment of men and women who are born in Monoco, but women who are naturalized citizens cannot transmit citizenship to their children, whereas naturalized male citizens can.

41 HEALTH

In 1989, there were approximately 40 physicians, 30 dentists, 60 pharmacists, 290 nurses, and 10 midwives. In addition, in 1986, there were 432 hospital beds, and 16 pharmacies.

42 HOUSING

In 1991, there were 12,000 principal residences in Monaco. In recent years, the government has stressed the construction of luxury housing. All new construction or alteration of existing buildings requires government approval.

43 EDUCATION

Education is offered in Monaco from the preschool to the secondary and technical levels and is compulsory from age 6 to 16. Attendance is 90%, and virtually all adults are literate.

In 1991, Monaco's seven public primary schools had a total of 1,761 students enrolled. The primary schools had 60 teachers on the faculties. The public secondary schools had 2,858 students enrolled. Public technical schools had 475 students enrolled.

44 LIBRARIES AND MUSEUMS

The palace archives include the private collections of the princes of Monaco as well as a collection of money minted since 1640. The Louis Notari Library in Monaco has a collection of over 250,000 volumes.

The Oceanographic Museum, founded in 1910 by Prince Albert I and previously directed by the noted Jacques-Yves Cousteau, contains a library of 50,000 volumes, an aquarium, and displays of rare marine specimens. The Oceanographic Museum is located at Monaco-Ville. In addition to the museum, the Oceanographic Institute conducts research in various marine areas, including the effects of radiation on the sea and its life forms.

The Exotic Gardens include thousands of varieties of cacti and tropical plants. The National Museum was established 1972.

45 MEDIA

The postal and telegraphic services are operated by France, but Monaco issues its own postage stamps. Local telephone service is controlled by Monaco, while France is responsible for international service. In 1992 there were about 38,200 telephones.

Radio Monte Carlo and Télé Monte Carlo provide radio and television services and have had broadcast programs since 1954. As of 1991 there were 30,000 radios and 22,000 television sets in homes. Radio Monte Carlo's home service is broadcast in French. The system also provides overseas service in 12 foreign languages and is majority owner of the Cyprus-based Radio Monte Carlo relay station, a privately funded religious broadcasting service in 35 languages under the name Trans World Radio.

There is no daily press. The *Journal de Monaco*, an official publication, appears once a week, and the *Tribune de Monaco* is published biweekly.

Two dailies in Nice, *Nice-Matin* and *L'Espoir*, publish special editions for Monaco. International publications are readily available.

46 ORGANIZATIONS

Monaco is the seat of the International Academy of Tourism, which was founded in 1951 by Prince Rainier III. The academy publishes a quarterly, *Revue Technique du Tourisme*, and, in several languages, an international dictionary of tourism.

The International Hydrographic Bureau, which sponsors international conferences in its field, has its headquarters in Monaco.

The following international organizations also have their headquarters in Monaco:

International Commission for Scientific Exploration of the Mediterranean Sea,
International Center for Studies of Human Problems
International Commission for Legal-Medical Problems.

The IAEA has research laboratories in Monaco. Other organizations include the Monégasque Red Cross, the St. Vincent de Paul Society, the Society of Monégasque Traditions, the Commission for the Monégasque language (established 1985), and the Union of French Interests. The Prix Littéraire Prince Pierre de Monaco is an annual award presented to an eminent writer in the French language.

47 TOURISM, TRAVEL, AND RECREATION

Monaco has been famous for attracting wealth and titled tourists since its gambling casino was established at Monte Carlo in 1856. However, gambling now accounts for only about 3.3% of state revenue.

No restriction is placed on the entrance of persons from France into Monaco. Those remaining for longer than three months or who plan to work or conduct a business in Monaco must apply to the police for an identity card.

In 1990, 244,640 overnight tourists spent a total of 726,561 nights in hotels and other establishments.

Among the many attractions are the Louis II Stadium, the many museums and gardens, and the beach.

The Monte Carlo opera house was the site of many world premiere performances, including Massenet's *Le Jongleur de Notre Dame* (1902) and *Don Quichotte* (1910), Fauré's *Pénélope* (1913), and Ravel's *L'Enfant et les sortilèges* (1925). It was also the home of Serge Diaghilev's Russian Ballet (founded in 1911), later known as the Ballet Russe de Monte Carlo.

The principality has excellent sports facilities. The Monte Carlo Rally, a world-famous driving championship, ends with a finish line in Monaco.

48 FAMOUS MONÉGASQUES

Prince Albert (1848–1922), who reigned from 1889 to 1922, was famous as an oceanographer. In 1956, his great-grandson Rainier III (b.1923), reigning monarch since 1949, married Grace Patricia Kelly (1929–82), a US motion picture actress, whose death on 14 September 1982 following an automobile accident was mourned throughout Monaco. Their son, Prince Albert (b.1958) is the heir apparent.

49 DEPENDENCIES

Monaco has no territories or colonies.

50 BIBLIOGRAPHY

Bernardy, Françoise de. *Princes of Monaco: The Remarkable History of the Grimaldi Family*. London: Barker, 1961.

Canis, Louis. *Notre Passé*. Monte Carlo: Imprimerie Nationale de Monaco, 1964.

Englund, Steven. *Grace of Monaco: an interpretive biography*. Garden City, N.Y.: Doubleday, 1984.

Handley-Taylor, Geoffrey. *Bibliography of Monaco*. 2nd ed. Chicago: St. James, 1968.

Jackson, Stanley. *Inside Monte Carlo*. Briarcliff Manor, N.Y.: Stein & Day, 1975.

Labande, Léon Honoré. *Histoire de la principauté de Monaco*. Monaco: Archives du Palais, 1939.

Moncharville, Maurice. *Monaco: Son histoire diplomatique, la question des jeux*. Paris: Pedone, 1898.

Playfair, Giles, and Constantine FitzGibbon. *Little Tour: Andorra, Monaco, Liechtenstein, San Marino*. London: Cassell, 1954.

Sherman, Charles L. *Five Little Countries of Europe: Luxembourg,*

Monaco, Andorra, San Marino, Liechtenstein. Garden City, N.J.: Doubleday, 1969.

Smith, Adolphe. *Monaco and Monte Carlo.* London: Richards, 1912.

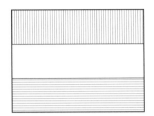

NETHERLANDS

Kingdom of the Netherlands
Koninkrijk der Nederlanden

CAPITAL: Constitutional capital: Amsterdam. Seat of government: The Hague ('s Gravenhage; Den Haag).

FLAG: The national flag, standardized in 1937, is a tricolor of red, white, and cobalt blue horizontal stripes.

ANTHEM: *Wilhelmus van Nassouwen (William of Nassau).*

MONETARY UNIT: The guilder (gulden; abbreviated f, designating the ancient florin) of 100 cents is a paper currency with one official exchange rate. There are coins of 5, 10, and 25 cents and 1, 2 ½, 5, 10, and 50 guilders, and notes of 5, 10, 25, 50, 100, 250, and 1,000 guilders. f1=$0.5322 (or $1=f1.8790).

WEIGHTS AND MEASURES: The metric system is the legal standard.

HOLIDAYS: New Year's Day, 1 January; Queen's Day, 30 April; National Liberation Day, 5 May; Christmas, 25–26 December. Movable religious holidays include Good Friday, Holy Saturday, Easter Monday, Ascension, and Whitmonday.

TIME: 1 PM = noon GMT.

¹LOCATION, SIZE, AND EXTENT

Situated in northwestern Europe, the Netherlands has a total area of 37,330 sq km (14,413 sq mi), of which inland water accounts for more than 2,060 sq km (795 sq mi). The land area is 33,920 sq km (13,097 sq mi). Comparatively, the area occupied by the Netherlands is slightly less than twice the size of the state of New Jersey. The Netherlands extends 312 km (194 mi) N–S and 264 km (164 mi) E–W. The land area increases slightly each year as a result of continuous land reclamation and drainage. The Netherlands is bounded on the E by Germany on the S by Belgium, and on the W and N by the North Sea, with a total boundary length of 1,478 km (918 mi).

The capital city of the Netherlands, Amsterdam, is in the western part of the country.

²TOPOGRAPHY

The country falls into three natural topographical divisions: the dunes, the lowlands or "polders" (low-lying land reclaimed from the sea and from lakes and protected by dikes), and the higher eastern section of the country. About 27% of the land lies below sea level. A long range of sand dunes on the western coast protects the low alluvial land to the east from the high tides of the North Sea, and farther east and southeast are found diluvial sand and gravel soil. The highest point of land, the Vaalserberg, is situated in the extreme south and is 321 m (1,053 ft) above sea level; the lowest point, 6.7 m (22 ft) below sea level, is an area of reclaimed land situated northeast of Rotterdam. The most extensive polder is that of East Flevoland in the province of Flevoland; it has an area of nearly 55,000 hectares (136,000 acres). Many dikes have been constructed along the lower Rhine and Meuse (Maas) rivers, as well as on a portion of the North Sea coast and along nearly the whole of the coast of the former Zuider Zee (formally called the IJsselmeer since its enclosure by a dike in 1932). There are many canals in the country, most of which have numerous locks.

³CLIMATE

The Netherlands has a maritime climate, with cool summers and mild winters. The average temperature is 2°C (36°F) in January

and 19°C (66°F) in July, with an annual average of about 10°C (50°F). Clouds generally appear every day, and in the winter months fog often abounds, while rainfall occurs frequently. Average annual rainfall is about 765 mm (30 in). The mild, damp climate is ideal for dairying and livestock raising, but the limited sunshine restricts the growing of food crops.

⁴FLORA AND FAUNA

Plants and animals that thrive in temperate climates are found in the Netherlands. The most common trees are oak, elm, pine, linden, and beech. The country is famous for its flowers, both cultivated varieties (best known among them the Dutch tulip) and wild flowers such as daisies and buttercups, and the purple heather that blooms on the heaths in September. Birds are those characteristic of Western and Central Europe, and large numbers of seagulls swarm over the coastal areas from time to time. Many kinds of fish abound along the North Sea coast and in the lakes and rivers. Wild or large animals are practically nonexistent.

⁵ENVIRONMENT

In recent years, as the result of rapid population and economic growth, the government has placed increased emphasis on preservation of the natural environment. One key concern is the pressure put on the countryside, traditionally the domain of the smallholder, by the demands of modern mechanized agriculture and the needs of a large urban population for recreational areas and waste disposal. To help solve this environmental problem, the government has instituted comprehensive land-use planning by means of a system of zoning that indicates the priorities for land use in each zone. Air and water pollution are significant environmental problems in the Netherlands. The nation contributes 0.06% of the world's total gas emissions. Recent efforts at controlling air pollution reduced sulphur dioxide emissions between 1980 and 1990 from 490,000 tons to 240,000 tons. Annual hydrocarbon emissions amount to 439.7 tons. Particulate emissions total 83.8 tons per year. Severe pollution of the country's rivers results from industrial and agricultural pollution. The Netherlands has 2.4 cubic miles of water of which 34% is used for farming and 61% is used for industrial purposes. Solid waste in the nation's cities amounts to 7.6 million tons yearly. Aggravating the situation are the prevailing southwesterly winds, which carry inland the pollutants from coastal industries, and the great rivers that carry pollution into the Netherlands from originating countries farther inland.

In 1971, the Ministry of Health and Environment was established; a countrywide system of air pollution monitoring by the National Institute of Public Health has been in place since 1975. Since the mid-1970s, discharges of heavy metals into industrial wastewater and emissions of most major air pollutants from industrial use of fossil fuels have been substantially reduced. Progress has also been recorded in reducing automotive emissions. An excise tax surcharge on gasoline and diesel fuel was imposed for pollution abatement in 1981. In 1994, 2 mammal species and 14 bird species were endangered and 7 plant species were threatened with extinction.

6POPULATION

The Netherlands had an estimated population of 15,010,445 as of 1 January 1991, with a density of 442 persons per sq km (1,145 per sq mi) of land, greater than that of any other West European country except Malta. A population of 16,073,000 was projected for the year 2000. With a crude birthrate in 1992 of 13 per 1,000 and a crude death rate of 8.6, the Dutch rate of natural increase was 4.4. In 1991, 74.8% of the population was over the age of 19.

About 89% of the population lived in urbanized areas in 1991, but only 26% lived in the 18 municipalities with more than 100,000 inhabitants. Major cities (with 1991 populations) are Amsterdam, 702,444; Rotterdam, 582,266; The Hague, 444,242; Utrecht, 231,231; Eindhoven, 192,895; Groningen, 168,702; Tilburg, 158,846; and Haarlem, 149,474. Over 45% of the population lives in the three most densely populated provinces: Utrecht, North Holland, and South Holland, which combined had a population density of 887 persons per sq km (2,297 per sq mi) in 1991.

7MIGRATION

Although the government has encouraged emigration to curb overpopulation, more people have migrated to the Netherlands than have left the country in recent years. Rapid economic growth in the 1960s drew many unskilled laborers from Mediterranean countries, and during the 1970s many people left Suriname for Holland when the former Dutch colony became independent. At first both groups settled mainly in the western region, but after 1970 the pattern of internal migration changed, as increasing numbers left the western provinces to settle in the east and south. The traditional pattern of migration from the countryside to the cities has likewise been altered, and since the 1970s the trend has been largely from the larger cities to small towns and villages.

In 1990, 57,344 persons left the Netherlands, of which 36,749 were Dutch nationals. Of these, 56% went to other European countries, 8% to the US, and 11% to the Netherlands Antilles or Suriname. In the same year, 81,264 immigrants arrived in the Netherlands, representing an increase of 24% over 1989. Of the total, 17% came from Suriname and the Netherlands Antilles, while about 13% were Turks.

Of the 692,000 aliens residing in the Netherlands in 1991 (4.6% of the population), 204,000 were Turkish nationals, 157,000 were Moroccan, 44,000 were Germans, and 39,000 were British. At the end of 1992 there were 26,900 refugees.

8ETHNIC GROUPS

The Dutch are an ethnically homogeneous people descended from Frankish, Saxon, and Frisian tribes. Ethnic homogeneity

slightly changed as a result of the arrival of some 300,000 repatriates and immigrants from Indonesia, mostly Eurasian, and more than 140,000 from Suriname. The influx of Turks and other workers from the Mediterranean area has further added to the ethnic mix.

9LANGUAGES

Dutch, or Holland, is the official language in all of the 12 provinces. It is also the universal tongue, except in Friesland, where most of the inhabitants speak the ancient Frisian language. Frisian, the native language of about 300,000 persons, is closely related to the Anglo-Saxon tongue but has many points in common with Dutch, which belongs to the Germanic language group. Many Netherlanders speak and understand English, French, and German, which are taught in secondary schools. Six Dutch dialects—notably Gelders and Groningen—are spoken in addition to Frisian.

10RELIGIONS

Complete religious liberty is provided for by the constitution, and a tradition of tolerance is well established. As of 1993, an estimated 37% were Roman Catholics, and 30% belonged to six major Protestant groups. Minority religious groups in 1986 included an estimated 338,000 Muslims and 72,000 Hindus or Buddhists. There were 25,700 Jews in 1990.

Most Protestants belong to Calvinist churches. The largest of these is the Dutch Reformed Church (Hervormde Kerk), with about 17% of the population aged 18 or more. Others are the Gereformeerde Kerk and the Christelijke Gereformeerde Kerk. The number of Lutherans in the Netherlands has never been large, comprising less than 1% of the total population. During the past three centuries, Baptists (Doopsgezinden) have been decreasing in number, and they now comprise less than 1%.

The Dutch Reformed Church, whose membership has declined by more than 50% since 1900, is strongest in Drenthe Province, in neighboring Groningen Province, and in Overijssel. Other reformed churches are particularly strong in Friesland and Zeeland. Roman Catholicism is widespread in North Brabant and Limburg. The largest growth has been among those professing no denomination, whose strength increased from 2.2% of the population in 1900 to 23.6% at the 1971 census and nearly 35% in 1984.

11TRANSPORTATION

Merchant shipping has always been of great economic importance to the seagoing Dutch. The Netherlands Maritime Institute is internationally famous, and the Dutch ship-testing station at Wageningen is known for its research in marine engineering. The Dutch merchant marine had 362 ships totaling 3,051,000 GRT in 1991. Emphasis has been placed on the development of new vessels suitable for container transport and on improving the Dutch tanker fleet. In 1992, 383 million tons of freight were handled at Dutch ports; the inland water transport fleet handled 250 million tons of freight in 1992. Rotterdam is the Netherlands' chief port and the world's largest; in 1990, it handled nearly 30% of all the goods in the EC transported by sea.

In 1991 there were 6,340 km (3,940 mi) of navigable waterways and 3,037 km (1,887 mi) of railroads. Passenger transport on railways is subsidized as part of the national policy for promoting public transport. In 1992, rail transported 315 million passengers and 17 million tons of freight. Public transport is provided for urban areas by municipal and regional transport companies, and minibus service in rural areas has ensured public transport for all towns with 1,000 residents or more. In 1991 there were 108,360 km (67,335 mi) of highways; motor vehicles in use in 1992 included 5,658,267 cars and 644,929 commercial vehicles. The number of privately owned bicycles was estimated

NETHERLANDS

0   25   50 Miles

0   25   50 Kilometers

North Sea

BELGIUM

GERMANY

FRANCE

East Frisian Islands

Emden

West Frisian Islands

Terschelling   *Schiermonnikoog*

Ameland

Vlieland   *Waddenzee*

Leeuwarden   Groningen

Texel   *Princess Margriet Canal*

Den Helder   *Dam with locks*

Heerenveen   Assen

IJsselmeer   Emmen

Northeast Polder   Hoogereen   Meppen

Alkmaar   Lelystad   Zwolle   Emlichheim

Noordzee-kanaal   *Flevoland Polder*   Roalte   Rheine

Zaanstad   *IJssel*

Haarlem   Enschede

★Amsterdam   Apeldoorn

Amsterdam-Rijnkanaal   Amersfoort   Winterswijk

Leiden   Utrecht   Arnhem   Borken

The Hague   *Nederrijn*

Delft   *Lek*

Rotterdam   *Waal*   Nijmegen

Dordrecht   *Maas*   's-Hertogenbosch   *Rhein*

Oosterschelde   *Wilhelminakanaal*   *Zuid-Willemskanaal*

Breda   Düsseldorf

Middelburg   Tilburg   Mönchengladbach

Westerschelde   Eindhoven

Antwerp

Gent   *Maas*

BELGIUM

★Brussels   Heerlen

Maastricht   Aachen

Liege   Netherlands

Schelde

LOCATION: 50°45′ to 53°52′N; 3°21′ to 7°13′E. **BOUNDARY LENGTHS:** FRG, 556 km (345 mi); Belgium, 407 km (253 mi); North Sea coastline, 642 km (399 mi).
TERRITORIAL SEA LIMIT: 12 mi.

at one million and mopeds numbered 68,000 in 1992. The state subsidizes the construction of urban and rural cycle paths.

The world's first airline from the standpoint of continuous corporate experience and operation is Royal Dutch Airlines (Koninklijke Luchtvaart Maatschappij—KLM), which began regularly scheduled operations in 1920. The Netherlands government owns a large part of the outstanding capital stock. Serving some 115 cities in 70 countries, KLM flew a total of 31.6 billion passenger-km, 8,349,400 passengers, and 2.4 billion freight ton-km in 1992. The major international airport is Schiphol, near Amsterdam, which handled 19.9 million passengers and 660,000 tons of freight in 1992.

12HISTORY

When, in about 55 BC, Julius Caesar conquered a large part of the lowlands near the mouths of the Rhine and Meuse (Maas) rivers, this region was populated by Celtic and Germanic tribes. To the north of the Rhine delta, several Germanic tribes had settled, among which the Batavi and the Frisians were the most important. The Batavi served with the Roman legions until they rebelled in AD 70, but even after the revolt was quelled, Batavian soldiers fought for Rome. About 300 years later, successive waves of powerful Germanic tribes, such as the Salic or West Franks, invaded this region, called the Low Countries, and gradually pushed the Frisians back to the east coast of the North Sea, except in the extreme northern section of the mainland where Saxons had settled. By the time of Charlemagne (742–814), the Saxons and Frisians had been completely conquered by the West Franks, and the Frankish language had replaced the languages of the Germanic tribes.

Soon after the death of Charlemagne and the disintegration of his realm, several duchies and counties were founded in the Low Countries by local leaders. With the coming of the Middle Ages, Holland (now the North and South Holland provinces) became the most important region and extended its power and territory under Count Floris V (r.1256–96). The ancient bishopric of Utrecht was another important principality. As the Middle Ages drew to a close, individual cities such as Amsterdam, Haarlem, and Groningen rose to eminence, together with the Duchy of Gelderland. In the 15th century, the dukes of Burgundy acquired, by various means, most of the Low Countries. Upon the extinction of the male line of the Burgundian dynasty and the marriage of Mary of Burgundy and Archduke (later Emperor) Maximilian I in 1477, however, the Austrian house of Habsburg fell heir to the lands.

The Habsburgs

Mary's son, Philip of Habsburg, married Joanna of Castile, heiress to the Spanish throne, and their son, Charles, became King Charles I of Spain in 1516 and Holy Roman Emperor Charles V in 1519. In 1547, he decreed the formal union of the Netherlands and Austria, and in 1549, the union of the Netherlands and Spain. By the end of his reign in 1555, he was master of the Low Countries. His son, Philip II, concentrated his efforts on the aggrandizement of Spain. To bring the Low Countries under his direct control, he tried to stamp out the rising force of Protestantism and suppressed the political, economic, and religious liberties long cherished by the population. As a result, both Roman Catholics and Protestants rebelled against him under the leadership of William the Silent, prince of Orange, who by marriage had acquired large properties in the Netherlands.

For 10 years, the 17 provinces comprising the Low Countries united in a common revolt. Much of the area was freed in 1577, with William as the acknowledged ruler, but not even his moderation and statesmanship sufficed to keep the northern and southern provinces united. In 1578, the southern region (now Belgium) began to turn against William. In 1579, the northern provinces concluded the Union of Utrecht, in which the province of Holland was the most prominent. The Union, or United Provinces, carried on the fight against Spain, and William was the soul of the resistance until his death by assassination in 1584. William's son Maurice, governor (stadtholder) of the republic from 1584 to 1624, carried on a successful campaign against Spain, but final recognition of Dutch independence by the Spanish government was not obtained until the Treaty of Westphalia (1648). Meanwhile, the southern provinces remained loyal to Spain and to the Roman Catholic Church, and were thereafter known as the Spanish Netherlands.

In the 17th century, the United Provinces became the leading commercial and maritime power in the world; its prosperity was nourished by Dutch settlements and colonies in the East Indies, India, South Africa, the West Indies, South America, and elsewhere. The government was oligarchic but based on republican and federative principles. The Dutch were noted for their religious freedom. They welcomed religious refugees—Spanish and Portuguese Jews, French Huguenots, and English Pilgrims.

Arts, sciences, literature, and philosophy flourished alongside trade and banking. At the peak of Dutch power, the Netherlands led several coalitions of European powers to victory over the aggressive France of Louis XIV. William III (r.1672–1702), great-grandson of William the Silent and grandson of the English King Charles I, and his English wife, Mary, were invited by the English Parliament to occupy the British throne in 1688, but they continued to take keen interest in Dutch affairs. The Dutch republic of which William had been governor survived for nearly a century after his death. Its position was continually threatened, however, by intense rivalries among and within the provinces. Four naval wars with Britain from the middle of the 17th century to the end of the 18th also sapped Dutch strength. In 1795, a much weakened republic was overrun by revolutionary French armies.

After the brief Napoleonic interlude, the great powers of Europe at the Congress of Vienna (1814–15) set up a new kingdom of the Netherlands, composed of the former United Provinces and the former Spanish or Austrian Netherlands, and installed a prince of the house of Orange as King William I. In 1830, a revolt by the southern provinces resulted in the establishment of the kingdom of Belgium. Thereafter, the much reduced kingdom was mainly concerned with domestic problems, such as the school conflict over secular versus religious instruction, social problems stemming from the industrialization of the country, and electoral reforms.

In foreign affairs, relations with Belgium were gradually improved after a decade of war and tension following Belgian independence, and Dutch claims to the principality of Luxembourg ended with the death of William III in 1890.

The World Wars to 1994

Foreign policies based on neutrality successfully met their test in World War I, and neutrality was preserved until the German war machine overran the country during World War II. Queen Wilhelmina (r.1890–1948) refused to surrender to the Germans, and instead fled to Britain with other officials of her government. Although Dutch resistance lasted only five days, destruction was widespread; nearly the whole of downtown Rotterdam was wiped out, and the cities of Arnhem and Nijmegen suffered great damage. In addition, Dutch factory equipment was carried away to Germany, bridges and railroads were blown up or removed, cattle were stolen, and part of the land was flooded. The Dutch withstood severe repressions until their liberation by Allied forces in May 1945. Wilhelmina abdicated in 1948 and was succeeded by her daughter, Juliana (r.1948–80).

The East Indies, most of which had been under Dutch rule for over 300 years, were occupied by Japanese forces in 1942. In 1945, a group of Indonesians proclaimed an independent republic and resisted Dutch reoccupation. After four years of hostilities and following UN intervention, the Netherlands recognized the independence of Indonesia in December 1949. Suriname (formerly Dutch Guiana), controlled by the Netherlands since 1815, became an independent nation on 25 November 1975. This Dutch colonial legacy was the root cause of several violent outbreaks during the late 1970s, as a group of South Moluccans, a few of the 40,000 Moluccans living in the Netherlands, used terrorism on Dutch soil to dramatize their demand for the independence of the South Molucca Islands from Indonesia. The Netherlands Antilles and Aruba continue to be dependent areas.

Reform of the social security system has been the major political issue in the 1990s, along with efforts to reduce public spending.

A number of radical social measures received parliamentary approval in recent years including conditions for administering euthanasia, legalization of prostitution, and laws banning discrimination.

Abdication of Queen Juliana

Queen Juliana abdicated in 1980 in favor of her daughter, Beatrix. In 1966, Beatrix had married Claus von Amsberg, a German diplomat, whose title remained that of Prince of the Netherlands when Beatrix became Queen. Their first-born son, Prince Willem-Alexander, is presumptive heir to the throne.

13GOVERNMENT

The Netherlands is a constitutional monarchy, under the house of Orange-Nassau. Executive power is exercised by the crown and the cabinet, which must have the support of a majority in the parliament. Cabinet ministers may not be members of the parliament. The Council of State, instituted in 1532, is appointed by and presided over by the sovereign; it is composed of a vice-president, 14 councillors, and 10 honorary members. The council considers all legislation proposed by the sovereign or the cabinet before it is submitted to the parliament. While functioning in an advisory capacity, the council has executive powers when it implements orders of the sovereign and it has judiciary powers when it acts in disputes concerning the government.

Legislative power is exercised jointly by the crown and the States-General (Staten-Generaal), a bicameral parliament. The upper house (Eerste Kamer) consists of 75 members elected for four years by the provincial representative councils on the basis of proportional representation. The lower house (Tweede Kamer) has 150 members elected for four years directly by the people, also on the basis of proportional representation. Only the lower house has the right to introduce bills and to move amendments, but the upper house can accept or reject bills passed by the other chamber.

All Dutch citizens who have reached the age of 18 years and reside within the Netherlands have the franchise. All citizens who have reached the age of 25 years are eligible for election to the States-General. In 1981, 1982, and 1986, more than 80% of the electorate participated in national elections.

Every year on the third Tuesday in September, the session of the States-General is opened at The Hague by the monarch. In the speech from the throne, the government's program for the year is announced. The monarch acts as an adviser to the cabinet, may propose bills, and signs all bills approved by the legislature. Theoretically she could refuse to sign a bill, but this never occurs in practice because the cabinet is responsible for the actions of the ruler. Thus, if the queen should refuse to sign a bill, the cabinet must resign and she must then find a new cabinet acceptable to the parliament.

A formateur is appointed by the sovereign to advise on the program and composition of the new cabinet, which he often does not join when it takes office. If he fails to bring together a new ministry, a new formateur is appointed, and so on until a new cabinet has been formed.

14POLITICAL PARTIES

Religion plays an important role in the political life of the Netherlands. During World War II, strenuous efforts were made to reduce this role, but denominational parties continue to exercise considerable influence. However, since the mid-1960s the general trend has been toward the polarization of politics into conservative and progressive parties, and denominational parties have lost voter support.

The religious political party with the largest membership is the Catholic People's Party (Katholieke Volkspartij—KVP), which favors democratic government and a middle-of-the-road social policy. The Labor Party (Partij van de Arbeid—PvdA), while calling itself socialist, has appealed mainly to national interests rather than to socialist ones, although it does favor state economic planning. The conservative People's Party for Freedom and Democracy (Volkspartij voor Vrijheid en Democratie—VVD) has advocated free enterprise, separation of church and state, and individual liberties. Smaller parties include the left-wing Pacifist Socialist Party (Pacifistisch Socialistische Partij—PSP), the Communist Party of the Netherlands (Communistische Partij van Nederland—CPN), the Farmers' Party (Boerenpartij—BP), and two very orthodox Calvinist groups: the State Reform Party (Staatkurdig Gerefoormeerde Partij—SGP) and the Reformed Political Association (Gerefoormeerd Politiek Verbond—GPV).

All parties except the CPN favor a foreign policy based on cooperation with the Western democracies. Since 1965, discontent with the major political parties and erosion of party discipline have led to the establishment of change-oriented parties like Democrats '66 (Democraten '66—D'66) and the Radical Party (Politieke Partij Radikalen—PPR). In 1991, the Communists formally dissolved and joined a new left-wing alliance known as the Green Left (Groen Links).

After World War II, the KVP and the PvdA vied for political leadership, polling about the same number of votes in national elections until 1972, when the PvdA won a plurality of nearly 25% of the total vote and emerged as the dominant member of a centrist coalition government. The KVP joined the Anti-Revolutionary Party (Anti-Revolutionaire Partij—ARP) and the right-wing Christian Historical Union (Christelijk-Historische Unie—CHU) to form the Christian Democratic Appeal (CDA) coalition to contest the 1977 elections, but the PvdA again won a plurality of parliamentary seats. It was unable to form a government, however, and a coalition of Christian Democratic and other parties took control. Despite discontent with the major parties and the subsequent regrouping of political forces in recent years, traditional political patterns have largely prevailed.

As no single party commands a majority in the States-General, the governing cabinet is a coalition of various party representatives, according to their numerical strength. The center-left coalition formed after the 1989 election was composed of the CDA and PvdA.

15LOCAL GOVERNMENT

As of 1994, the country was divided into 12 provinces, each governed by a representative provincial council (Provinciale Staten). Its members are elected by direct universal suffrage. The size of the council depends on the number of inhabitants in the province. Members are elected for four-year terms. From among their members, the councils elect provincial executives (Gedeputeerde Staten) with 6 to 8 members. Each province has a commissioner appointed by and representing the crown.

The municipalities (714 in 1986) are administered by municipal councils, which are elected directly for one-year terms by the local inhabitants and make local by-laws. The executive powers of the municipality are entrusted to a corporate board consisting of a burgomaster and 2–6 aldermen; the latter are elected from and by the council, while the burgomaster is appointed by the crown. The important function of flood control and water management is exercised by autonomous public authorities, some of which date as far back as the 13th century.

16JUDICIAL SYSTEM

The judiciary is independent and the judges irremovable except for malfeasance or incapacity. Roman law still is basic, but the judicial system is largely patterned on that of France. There is no jury system, and the state rather than the individual acts as initiator of legal proceedings. Administrative justice is separate from civil and criminal justice and not uniform in dispensation.

The supreme judiciary body is the High Court of the Netherlands (Court of Cassation). It is staffed by 24 justices and consists of a number of divisions of 5-member chambers. Its principal task is to supervise administration of justice and to review the judgments of lower courts. There are 5 courts of appeal (gerechtshoven), which act as courts of first instance only in fiscal matters. They are divided into chambers of 3 judges each. The 19 district courts (arrondissementsrechtsbanken) deal as courts of first instance with criminal cases and civil cases not handled by cantonal courts (kantongerechten); 62 of the latter handle petty criminal cases and civil cases involving sums of up to f500. Most of these courts are manned by single magistrates. There also are juvenile courts and special arbitration courts (for such institutions as the Stock Exchange Association and professional organizations).

[17] ARMED FORCES

Universal military training has been in force since the beginning of the 20th century. All able-bodied men reaching the age of 20 (about 43,000 a year) are subject to military training for 12 to 15 months. A small percentage of draftees invoke the Conscientious Objectors Act and are required to undertake alternative service. In 1993, the army (68,000, half conscripts) consisted of 6 mechanized infantry brigades, 3 armored brigades, and corps troops assigned to NATO. The navy had 15,500 officers and men, including 2,400 marines. Its fleet included 5 submarines, and 16 surface combatants, 26 anti-mine vessels, and 12 small landing craft. The naval air arm (900) is prepared for antisubmarine warfare (ASW). The air force of 12,000 men contained 8 combat squadrons and 12 air defense squadrons, as well as transport and special auxiliary groups. There were 188 combat aircraft. The constabulary numbers 3,900. The reserves for all services total 144,300, about 30,000 on short recall. The US stations 2,300 troops in the Netherlands. The nation spent $7.2 billion on defense (1991) or 3% of gross domestic product.

[18] INTERNATIONAL COOPERATION

The Netherlands is a founding member of the UN, having joined on 10 December 1945. It participates in ECE, ECLAC, ESCAP, and all the nonregional specialized agencies, and is a signatory both to GATT and to the Law of the Sea treaty. In addition, the Netherlands is a member of the Asian Development Bank, Council of Europe, EC, IDB, NATO, and OECD, and is a permanent observer at OAS and a participant in PAHO.

On 1 January 1948, Belgium, the Netherlands, and Luxembourg established a joint customs union, Benelux; since that time, the three countries have freed nearly all of their mutual imports from quantitative restrictions. On 3 February 1958, the Benelux Economic Union was established to make it possible for each participating country to apply itself more intensively to the production for which it is best suited as well as to extend the total market for the member countries.

[19] ECONOMY

An industrial nation with limited natural resources, the Netherlands bases its economy on the importation of raw materials for processing into finished products for export. Food processing, metallurgy, chemicals, manufacturing, and oil refining are the principal industries. Agriculture is particularly important to the economy, as about 60% of total agricultural production is exported.

Because of its geographic position on the sea, outstanding harbor facilities, and numerous internal waterways, the Netherlands became a trading, transporting, and brokerage nation. A major role in the economy has always been played by the service industries, such as banks, trading companies, shipping enterprises, and brokerage and supply firms. The economy, being dependent on international trade, is sharply affected by economic developments abroad—including fluctuations in prices of primary goods—over which the Netherlands has little or no control.

GDP grew by about 2% a year during 1988–92, but by only 0.2% in 1993. Inflation was low, averaging about 2% a year between 1986 and 1992. The unemployment rate fell from 10.5% in 1985 to 6.5% in 1993.

[20] INCOME

In 1992, Netherland's GNP was $312,340 million at current prices, or $20,590 per capita. For the period 1985–92 the average inflation rate was 1.5%, resulting in a real growth rate in per capita GNP of 2.1%.

In 1992 the GDP was $259.8 billion in current US dollars. It is estimated that in 1991 agriculture, hunting, forestry, and fishing contributed 4% to GDP; mining and quarrying, 3%; manufacturing, 19%; electricity, gas, and water, 2%; construction, 5%; wholesale and retail trade, 15%; transport, storage, and communication, 6%; finance, insurance, real estate, and business services, 20%; community, social, and personal services, 10%; and other sources, 16%.

[21] LABOR

As of 1 January 1992, the civilian labor force numbered 6,610,000. Some 723,000 persons were self-employed or unpaid family workers, and about 490,000 persons were registered as unemployed on average in 1991. The unemployed represented about 8% of the work force in 1992, compared with 1.2% in 1970 and 13% in 1985.

Most labor unions are organized on the basis of a specific religious, political, or economic orientation and belong to a similarly oriented central federation. In January 1993, the Federated Dutch Trade Union Movement (FNV), the largest Dutch labor union, had 1,091,854 members; the National Federation of Christian Trade Unions had 326,926. Total membership of all labor unions in 1992 was 25% of those employed.

The Social and Economic Council, on which labor is represented, advises the government on the main guidelines of wage policy. The average workweek (including overtime) for full-time workers in manufacturing was 39.9 hours in 1991, compared with 41 hours in 1983. The five-day workweek has been generally adopted. Workers receive workers' compensation, unemployment insurance, sick pay, payment for legal holidays, and paid vacations. The employment of women and adolescents for night work is forbidden.

Since the end of World War II, a main goal of government policy has been the maintenance of full employment; however, unemployment rose in the 1970s and, from 1983 to 1987, averaged more than 12.8% yearly. Seasonal and, to some degree, structural unemployment is combated mainly by public-works projects that aim at a basic improvement of the area concerned or are designed to fit in with programs for improving the cultivable land. In addition, there is a major emphasis on reeducation of youth and of the growing numbers of long-term unemployed.

[22] AGRICULTURE

More than 26% of the total land area of the Netherlands is under seasonal or permanent crop production. Grasslands account for about 54% of all agricultural lands, which totaled 1,991,000 hectares (4,919,800 acres) in 1991. In 1993, agriculture's contribution to GDP was 90% smaller than manufacturing's contribution and 95% less than the amount services contributed to GDP. Most farms are effectively managed and worked intensively with mechanical equipment. The many cooperatives have added to the efficiency of production and distribution.

Although agricultural production has decreased in recent years, labor productivity in Dutch agricultural and horticultural industries has risen sharply. The number of holdings declined by over 17% from the mid–1970s to the mid–1980s. The farm labor force (regular active laborers) totaled 293,000 in 1991; of these, 72% were men. Agriculture (including processed foodstuffs and tobacco products) is an important export industry, contributing 24% of the total exports in 1992.

Much of the soil in the east and southeast is poor. Moreover, large regions are so moist because of their low altitude that only grass can be grown profitably, a condition that has led to the enormous development of the dairy industry. The best land is found in reclaimed polders. Gross agricultural output increased 4.2% in 1992, with crop output rising by 6%. Principal crops and output in 1992 (in millions of kg) were sugar beets, 8,251; potatoes, 7,595; wheat, 1,017; barley, 204; oats, 19; and rye, 34.

The Netherlands is famous for its bulbs grown for export, principally tulip, hyacinth, daffodil, narcissus, and crocus. Flower growing is centered at Aalsmeer (near Amsterdam), and nurseries are situated mainly at Boskoop. Bulb growing, done principally at Lisse and Hillegom, between Haarlem and Leiden, has been extended in recent years to areas of North Holland.

Since the beginning of this century, the government has been helping the agrarian sector through extension services, the promotion of scientific research, and the creation of specific types of agricultural education. In the 1930s, an extensive system of governmental controls of agricultural production was introduced, and after World War II, an even more active policy was initiated, which evolved into integrated planning covering practically every aspect of rural life. In recent years, the government has actively encouraged the consolidation of small landholdings into larger, more efficient units.

[23]ANIMAL HUSBANDRY

World-renowned Dutch dairy products outrank all other agricultural produce, and livestock provides two-thirds of total agricultural value. In 1992 there were 4.8 million head of cattle, 13.7 million pigs, 1.9 million sheep, and 105 million chickens. Milk production in 1992 totaled 10.8 billion kg. Meat production in 1992 was over 2.7 billion kg (pork and bacon, 1.5 billion; beef and veal, 630 million; poultry, 0.5 billion; mutton and horse meat, 17 million). Butter production was 150 million kg; cheese, 610 million kg.

Friesland is the most important region for the production of milk and butter. Excellent grazing lands and a long growing season have greatly helped the Frisian dairy industry, whose main support is the famed Frisian strain of cows. The making of cheese is connected with such famous brands as those named for Edam and Gouda, towns in the province of South Holland, and Alkmaar in North Holland.

[24]FISHING

Although no longer as important as it was in the 16th and 17th centuries, fishing still contributes substantially to the food supply. The total catch in 1991 was 443,097 tons, consisting primarily of plaice, mackerel, whiting, herring, cod, and mussels. Shrimp, oysters, sole, and other saltwater fish were also caught. Fishery exports have increased rapidly in recent years and amounted to $1.4 billion in 1992.

About half of the fish catch is landed at the ports of Scheveningen and IJmuiden.

[25]FORESTRY

One of the least forested countries in Europe, the Netherlands produces only about 8% of its wood requirements. Woodland, chiefly pine, covers about 300,000 hectares (750,000 acres), or only 8% of the total land area, of which state forest areas comprise some 100,000 hectares (240,000 acres). Productive woodlands total about 230,000 hectares (580,000 acres); output of timber was approximately 1.3 million cu m from 1988 to 1991.

Another 1.4 million cu m of roundwood are imported annually, and afforestation has not kept pace with increasing consumption. The Dutch government would like to become at least 25% self-sufficient in wood fiber by 2025. In order to meet this goal, some 3.9 million cu m of fiber would need to be produced annually (assuming current consumption trends). Currently, Dutch wood fiber production is only 1.2 million cu m.

[26]MINING

The only minerals of commercial importance are petroleum, natural gas, and salt. Coal was mined in small quantities in the province of Limburg until 1974, when the mines were closed under a governmental policy of halting internationally noncompetitive mining enterprises. The production of salt from the mines at Hengelo is one of the oldest industries in the country. Magnesia is produced in a plant at Veendam from extracted salt brines.

[27]ENERGY AND POWER

The Netherlands, which has no waterpower, depends on natural gas and petroleum as energy sources. The vast Slochteren reserve in Groningen Province, which began production in 1959 and is one of the world's largest producing natural gas fields, and lesser deposits in the North Sea have enabled the country to meet its energy demands largely from domestic supplies. Proved natural gas reserves totaled 1,900 billion cu m in 1993; production in 1992 was 70.2 billion cu m (fourth highest in the world), of which about half was exported.

The second principal energy source is oil, which provided almost one-third of the Netherlands' energy needs in the early 1990s. Increased domestic production of crude petroleum (2.9 million tons in 1991) from offshore deposits in the North Sea still left the nation 80% dependent on imported petroleum. An Arab oil embargo and the tripling of oil prices in 1973–74 led the government to introduce energy-saving programs; energy consumption increased by an average of only about 0.5% annually between 1975 and 1985 and by an average of 1.1% yearly from 1986 to 1992. The Netherlands reexports two-thirds of all imported petroleum in the form of refined oil products. Production of the petroleum-refining industry increased by 8.5% in 1988, but declined by 5.3% in 1990.

Production of electric power in 1991 totaled 74,252 million kwh, of which thermal power plants using oil and coal as fuel supplied 95%, and nuclear power plants 5%. Nuclear generating capacity is provided chiefly by a 450-Mw station in Borssele, Zeeland. From 1988 to 1991, per capita energy consumption increased by nearly 7%.

[28]INDUSTRY

Because of World War II and its consequences (the high rate of population increase and the severing of economic ties with Indonesia), drastic structural changes took place in the Dutch economy, and the further development of industry became important. Industry increased to such an extent that it produced 32% of the GDP in 1991. In 1991 there were 10,104 industrial enterprises with more than 10 employees. All told, 974,000 persons were employed in manufacturing as of 30 September 1993.

Since World War II, the metallurgical industry in particular has made tremendous progress. The Philips Electrical Co. at Eindhoven has become the greatest electrical products firm in Europe as well as one of the world's major exporters of electric bulbs and appliances; it had sales of $31.7 billion in 1993. Unilever, the British-Dutch consumer products company, has grown to become one of the world's largest corporations, with 1993 sales of $41.8 billion. Quite as phenomenal has been the success of Royal Dutch Petroleum, which began as a small concern in 1890 and was combined with the Shell Co. to form what was at one time the largest oil company in the world.

In 1993, it was the world's fourth-largest industrial corporation, with sales of $95.1 billion. Royal Dutch/Shell owns and operates one of the world's largest oil refineries at Curaçao, near Venezuela, and Rotterdam's suburb of Pernis has the largest oil refinery in Europe. Total refinery output in 1992 (in millions of kg) included motor fuel, 3,775; naphtha, 10,314; gas and diesel oil, 18,404; and residual fuel oils, 14,922. Among leading exports is pig iron, produced from imported ore at the Velzen-IJmuiden plant, situated where the canal from Amsterdam reaches the North Sea. The chemical industry has grown increasingly important, but the once prosperous textile industry in Enschede has declined because of foreign competition and lack of modern management.

Selected industrial products in 1992 (in millions of kg) were crude steel, 5,439; pig iron, 4,849; and pharmaceutical products sold, 2,810. In 1992, the Netherlands also produced 81,440 million cigarettes and 2,062 million liters of beer. Canned fish, cocoa and cocoa products, sugar, candies, biscuits, and potato flour are among other leading food products.

29 SCIENCE AND TECHNOLOGY

Advanced scientific research and development have provided the technological impetus for the Netherlands' economic recovery since World War II. Dutch universities have traditionally carried out fundamental scientific research, and the government has promoted research activities through the Central Organization for Applied Scientific Research. It also has supported scientific organizations such as the Energy Development Corp. and Energy Research Foundation, Aerospace Development Agency, National Aerospace Laboratory, and Netherlands Maritime Institute. The country's scientific infrastructure employed some 58,000 scientists, engineers, and technicians and accounted for about 2% of the GNP by the early 1990s.

The highly developed electrotechnical industry produces computers, telecommunications systems, electronic measurement and control equipment, electric switching gear and transformers, and medical and scientific instruments. Dutch firms designed and constructed the Netherlands' astronomical satellites and play a major role in the European Space Agency. The important aerospace industry is led by the world-famous firm of Fokker, which produced Europe's best-selling passenger jet aircraft, the F-27 Friendship, and has been active in the consortium that developed the European Airbus.

Expenditures on scientific research and development in 1989 were estimated at f10,283 million, of which 60% was spent by business enterprises, 22% by research institutes, and 18% by universities.

30 DOMESTIC TRADE

A considerable but declining part of Dutch retail business is still conducted by small enterprises, which are usually owner operated. Some of the larger department stores in the cities have branches in small towns, and there are several nationwide supermarket chains. Cooperatives are important in both purchasing and producing. In 1990 there were 181,700 retail units.

Amsterdam is the chief center for commerce and trade, with Rotterdam and The Hague next. Most foreign firms have a single representative for the whole country. Many companies use the Netherlands as a distribution center for European markets. Terms of sale usually call for payment within 90 days.

Business offices are generally open from 9 AM to 5 PM on weekdays and are closed Saturdays. Retail stores usually open between 8 and 9 AM and close between 6 and 7 PM on weekdays and Saturdays. The country's most important trade fair is held at Utrecht, twice each year, in the spring and fall.

31 FOREIGN TRADE

In recent years, the Netherlands has increased its trade in industrial products and decreased that in food products and foodstuffs. Principal Dutch exports today are manufactured goods, chemicals, petroleum products, natural gas, and foods. Chief imports are manufactures, crude petroleum, machinery, and chemicals. From 1981 through 1993, the Netherlands experienced trade surpluses each year.

Principal exports in 1992 (in millions of guilders) were as follows:

Manufactured goods	33,671
Chemical products	39,021
Petroleum products	13,459
Machinery	44,325
Natural and manufactured gas	6,909
Raw materials (inedible), except fuels	14,164
Vegetables and fruits	10,127
Eggs, milk and cream	3,388
Meat	8,487
Transport equipment	10,223
Other exports	62,087
TOTAL	245,861

Principal imports in 1992 (in millions of guilders) were as follows:

Manufactured goods	38,135
Petroleum and oil products	17,294
Machinery	52,898
Chemical products	25,378
Road vehicles	17,198
Raw materials (inedible), except fuels	11,193
Food and live animals	25,522
Other imports	48,541
TOTAL	236,159

Approximately 70% of Dutch trade is with other members of the EU. Principal trade partners in 1992 (in millions of guilders) were as follows:

	EXPORTS	IMPORTS	BALANCE
Germany	70,809	59,586	11,223
Belgium-Luxembourg	35,123	33,581	1,542
UK	22,615	20,420	2,195
US	9,983	18,322	−8,339
Italy	15,743	8,542	7,201
Japan	2,230	8,575	−6,345
Sweden	3,943	4,936	−993
Spain	6,381	3,675	2,706
Other countries	79,034	78,522	512
TOTALS	245,861	236,159	9,702

32 BALANCE OF PAYMENTS

Dutch merchandise and services exports have grown to represent more than 50% of GDP, making the Dutch economy one of the most internationally oriented in the world. Economic expansion of the Netherlands in the period immediately after World War II paralleled a generally favorable balance of payments. After occasional and minor deficits on current accounts during the mid-1960s, a major deficit occurred in 1970. Since then, the current-accounts balance has generally registered a surplus, despite increased costs of oil imports during the 1970s.

In 1992 merchandise exports totaled $128,487 million and imports $117,769 million. The merchandise trade balance was $10,718 million. The following table summarizes Netherlands balance of payments for 1991 and 1992 (in millions of US dollars):

	1991	1992
CURRENT ACCOUNT		
Goods, services, and income	12,096	11,557
Unrequited transfers	−4,409	−4,771
TOTALS	7,687	6,786
CAPITAL ACCOUNT		
Direct investment	−7,032	−5,928
Portfolio investment	−856	−8,918
Other long-term capital	1,936	−2,216
Other short-term capital	1,949	16,952
Exceptional financing		
Other liabilities	430	−309
Reserves	−507	−6,118
TOTALS	−4,077	−6,537
Errors and omissions	−3,610	−252
Total change in reserves	−314	−4,140

	1991	1992
REVENUE AND GRANTS		
Tax revenue	247.71	254.81
Non-tax revenue	22.89	24.05
Capital revenue	0.26	0.21
Grants	0.24	0.24
TOTAL	271.10	279.31
EXPENDITURES AND LENDING MINUS REPAYMENTS		
General public service	18.54	19.52
Defense	13.57	13.79
Public order and safety	6.38	6.97
Education	30.04	32.31
Health	36.45	41.36
Social security and welfare	107.50	110.16
Housing and community amenities	11.20	11.83
Recreation, cultural, and religious affairs	1.06	1.12
Economic affairs and services	18.15	17.97
Other expenditures	40.75	43.28
Lending minus repayments	0.73	0.68
TOTAL	284.37	298.99
Deficit/Surplus	−14.93	−19.11

In 1992 the Netherlands' total public debt stood at f358.82 billion of which f79.50 billion was financed abroad.

33BANKING AND SECURITIES

The Netherlands Bank, nationalized in 1948, is the central bank. It issues the currency and regulates its value, establishes the rates of foreign exchange, issues money permits to foreigners, and supervises the privately owned banks. Since the 1950s, the Netherlands Bank has used reserve regulations and the central bank discount rate as instruments of monetary policy.

Principal assets of the country's banks and other money-creating institutions amounted to f195,752 million in 1993. Principal liabilities included f1,355.2 billion in time, savings and foreign currency deposits, f111.9 billion in demand deposits, and f2.81 billion in reserves.

Leading commercial banks are the Algemene Bank Netherlands, Amsterdam-Rotterdam (AMRO) Bank, and RABO Bank (formerly farmers' credits banks), which are among the world's 30 largest banks. They form a substantial section of Dutch banking, both as savings banks and as loan banks. The amount of currency in circulation as of 1993 was f440.0 billion.

The Netherlands has the oldest stock exchange in the world, the Amsterdam Stock Exchange; founded in the early 17th century, it is now one of the largest stock exchanges in operation. The issuance of new securities on the exchange is supervised by the Netherlands Bank, acting in cooperation with the commercial banks and stockbrokers.

34INSURANCE

There are two sectors of the insurance industry in the Netherlands: the companies operating under control laws set down by the EC and supervised by the government, and the companies (mutuals, reinsurance, marine and aviation) not under official supervision. There were 811 life insurance companies operating in the Netherlands in 1989. Total premium receipts amounted to us$1613.2 per capita in 1990, accounting for 8.1% of the GDP. Life insurance in force totaled G1,000 billion in 1992. Compulsory third-party motor insurance has been in effect since 1935.

35PUBLIC FINANCE

Late in the year, the government submits to the lower house of the States-General its budget for the following calendar year. The government has gradually cut the deficit from 10% of GDP in 1983 to 3.4% in 1993. The deficit is largely financed by government bonds. As of 1 January, 1994, financing was also covered by issuing Dutch Treasury Certificates, which will replace a standing credit facility for short-term deficit financing with the Netherlands Central Bank. Under the Maastricht Treaty, the Netherlands Central Bank will be abolished.

The following table shows actual revenues and expenditures for 1991 and 1992 in billions of guilders.

36TAXATION

Principal taxes raised by the central government are income and profits taxes levied on individuals and companies, a value-added tax on goods and services transactions, and a tax on enterprises of public bodies (except agricultural enterprises); a wealth tax of 0.8% is also levied on nonexempt taxable capital of individuals. Provinces and municipalities are not authorized to impose taxes on income and may impose other taxes only to a limited extent; the most important tax levied by municipalities is a real estate tax. Residents are taxed on both their local and foreign incomes, but nonresidents pay taxes only on their sources of income within the country. Incomes are taxed on a graduated scale, with liberal deductions for dependents; taxes are withheld by the state on the incomes of wage earners. In 1992, the minimum personal income tax rate was 13%, with a 25.5% social security tax; the maximum rate was 60%.

The basic tax on the net profits of corporations and companies was 35% in 1992. Depreciation allowances and certain other business deductions are permitted. A value-added tax was introduced in 1969; export goods, medical, cultural, and educational services, and credit and insurance transactions are exempt. In 1992, the standard rate was 18.5%; certain essential goods and services were taxed at only 6%.

37CUSTOMS AND DUTIES

The Dutch government has a traditionally liberal policy on tariffs, and its membership in the Benelux Economic Union, the EC, and other international trade organizations has resulted in comparatively low import duties. Tariffs on imports from the dollar area have also been liberalized, and about 90% of imports from the US are unrestricted quantitatively. Raw materials are usually not subject to import duties.

Imports are subject to EC customs regulations and tariff rates, plus VAT and other charges levied at entry through customs.

38FOREIGN INVESTMENT

The government has encouraged foreign corporations to set up branch plants in the Netherlands and to establish joint ventures with Dutch companies in order to benefit from the introduction of new production techniques and improved methods of management that outside firms often bring. The government does not discriminate between foreign and domestic companies; foreign entrepreneurs have the same business privileges and obligations as Dutch businessmen. As a result, foreign companies operate in virtually all industries, including high-technology electronics, chemicals, metals, electrical equipment, textiles, and food processing.

At the end of 1993, total direct foreign investment in the Netherlands was $69.6 billion. The US has been the largest foreign investor in the Netherlands, with total direct investments by US companies aggregating $19.1 billion in 1993; Dutch investment in the US as of that same year was f25.8 billion, making it the third largest foreign investor in the US.

39 ECONOMIC DEVELOPMENT

The Netherlands government in the period since World War II has aimed at increased industrialization. To encourage industrialization, the maintenance of internal monetary equilibrium was vitally important, and the government has largely succeeded in this task. Successive governments pursued a policy of easy credits and a "soft" currency, but after the Netherlands had fully recovered from the war by the mid-1950s, a harder currency and credit policy came into effect. In the social sphere, stable relationships were maintained by a deliberate governmental social policy seeking to bridge major differences between management and labor. The organized collaboration of workers and employers in the Labor Foundation has contributed in no small measure to the success of this policy, and as a result, strikes (other than an occasional wildcat strike) are rare.

Successive wage increases helped bring the overall wage level in the Netherlands up to that of other EC countries by 1968. The Dutch government's policy, meanwhile, was directed toward controlling inflation while seeking to maintain high employment. In 1966, the government raised indirect taxes to help finance rising expenditures, particularly in the fields of education, public transportation, and public health. Further attempts to cope with inflation and other economic problems involved increased government control over the economy. Wage and price controls were imposed in 1970/71, and the States-General approved a measure granting the government power to control wages, rents, dividends, health and insurance costs, and job layoffs during 1974.

During the mid-1980s, the nation experienced modest recovery from recession; the government's goal was to expand recovery and reduce high unemployment, while cutting down the size of the annual budget deficit. The government has generally sought to foster a climate favorable to private industrial investment through such measures as preparing industrial sites, subsidizing or permitting allowances for industrial construction and equipment, assisting in the creation of new markets, granting subsidies for establishing industries in distressed areas, and establishing schools for adult training. In 1978, the government began, by means of a selective investment levy, to discourage investment in the western region (Randstad), while encouraging industrial development in the southern province of Limburg and the northern provinces of Drenthe, Friesland, and Groningen.

The Netherlands' largest economic development projects have involved the reclamation of land from the sea by construction of dikes and dams and by the drainage of lakes to create polders for additional agricultural land. The Zuider Zee project closed off the sea and created the freshwater IJsselmeer by means of a 30-km (19-mi) barrier dam in 1932, and subsequently drained four polders enclosing about 165,000 hectares (408,000 acres). After a storm washed away dikes on islands in Zeeland and South Holland in 1953, killing some 1,800 people, the Delta project was begun. This project, designed to close estuaries between the islands with massive dams, was officially inaugurated in 1986; the cost was $2.4 billion. The Delta works include a storm-surge barrier with 62 steel gates, each weighing 500 tons, that are usu-

ally left open to allow normal tidal flow in order to protect the natural environment. Another major engineering project was construction of a bridge and tunnel across the Western Schelde estuary in the south to connect Zeeland Flanders more directly with the rest of the country.

The Dutch government has long been active in the field of technical assistance to less developed areas. In addition to providing expert assistance to foreign governments and private groups, it has also created a variety of other programs, including fellowships to foreigners for technical education in the Netherlands. In 1991, total Dutch official development assistance came to $2,517 million and amounted to 0.88% of GNP, fourth after Norway, Denmark, and Sweden. The major recipients of these funds and credits were Indonesia, Suriname, the Netherlands Antilles, and India.

40 SOCIAL DEVELOPMENT

A widespread system of social insurance and assistance is in effect. Unemployment, accidents, illness, and disability are covered by insurance, which is compulsory for most employees and voluntary for self-employed persons. Unemployment benefits total 70% of earnings up to a daily maximum and can be extended for up to 5 years. Sickness benefits are paid at the same rate and can be extended up to 52 weeks. Maternity grants and full insurance for the worker's family are also provided, as are family allowances for children. There are also widows' and orphans' funds. A state pension is granted to all persons over 65. The actual administration of various social services is not centrally organized, the government's role being chiefly that of covering deficits. Total public expenditures in 1985 within the scope of social insurance amounted to f83,650 million, or 22.4% of the net national product.

Between 1970 and 1985, the number of marriages per 1,000 inhabitants declined from 9.5 to 5.7, while the divorce rate (calculated per 1,000 married males) rose from 3.3 to 9.9. A survey taken in 1985 showed that 70% of married women aged 21 to 34 were using contraception or had been voluntarily sterilized. The fertility rate in 1985–90 was 1.6. Abortion is available on request in nonprofit clinics.

Participation of women in the labor force rose by 4.5% each year between 1988 and 1991. In 1992, 46% of women aged 15 to 64 had full- or part-time jobs, and about 40% of the labor force was female. Women have equal legal status with men. Upon marriage, they may choose either community property or separate regimes for their property.

41 HEALTH

The Netherlands has a social insurance system similar to Germany's. About two-thirds of workers are covered by the social insurance program; the remainder are covered by private insurance. Under the Health Insurance Act, everyone with earned income of less than 50,900 guilders per year pays a monthly contribution in return for which they receive medical, pharmaceutical, and dental treatment and hospitalization. People who earn more than this have to take out private medical insurance. The state also pays for preventive medicine including vaccinations for children, and school dental services, medical research, and the training of health workers. Preventive care emphasizes education, a clean environment, and regular exams and screenings.

The general health situation has been excellent over a long period, as is shown by a death rate of 8.7 per 1,000 in 1993 and an infant mortality of only 6 per 1,000 live births in 1992, down markedly from the 12.7 rate in 1970. The low rates are attributable to a rise in the standard of living, improvements in nutrition, hygiene, housing, and working conditions, and the expansion of public health measures. In 1992, average life expectancy was 77 years.

Most doctors and hospitals operate privately. A system of hospital budgeting which was introduced in 1983 has helped contain costs. In 1990, a proposal to increase competition among insurers, eliminating the distinction between public and private insurers was developed. A reference price system—to control pharmaceuticals especially—was introduced in 1991. Total health care expenditures in 1990 were $22,423,000.

The Ministry of Public Health and Environment is entrusted with matters relating to health care, but health services are not centrally organized. There are numerous local and regional health centers and hospitals, many of which are maintained by religious groups.

In 1985 there were 207 hospitals with 68,500 beds, about one-fourth of which were in hospitals operated by public authorities. In 1992, there were 1.6 mental hospital beds per 1,000 people; 2.1 beds per 1,000 in institutions for the mentally disabled; 3.5 beds per 1,000 in nursing homes; and 4.1 beds per 1,000 in hospitals. As of 1990, there were 37,461 physicians (about 1 for every 410 people), 2,247 pharmacists, and 7,900 dentists. In 1989, there were 121,000 nurses and 1,137 midwives. In 1992, there were 2.43 doctors per 1,000 people, with a nurse to doctor ratio of 3.4.

In 1993, the total population was 15.3 million, with a birth rate of 13.7 per 1,000 people, and 76% of married women (ages 15 to 49) using contraception. There were 207,000 births in 1992.

Major causes of death in 1992 were categorized as follows, per 100,000 inhabitants: (1) communicable diseases and maternal/perinatal causes (40); (2) noncommunicable diseases (416); and (3) injuries (36). There were 339 deaths per 100,000 attributed to cardiovascular problems and 235 per 100,000 attributed to cancer. There were only 9 reported cases of tuberculosis per 100,000 in 1990.

Immunization rates for children up to one year old in 1992 were as follows: diphtheria, pertussis, and tetanus (97%); polio (97%); and measles (94%).

42HOUSING

During World War II, more than 25% of Holland's 2 million dwellings were damaged: 95,000 dwellings were completely destroyed, 55,000 were seriously damaged, and 520,000 were slightly damaged. The housing shortage remained acute until 1950, when an accelerated program of housing construction got under way, and in 1953 the government decided to increase the house-building program to a level of 65,000 dwellings a year. Since then, the production rate has far exceeded both the prewar rate and yearly forecasts. From 1945 to 1985, nearly 4 million dwellings were built. In 1985 alone, 98,131 dwellings were built, bringing the total housing stock to 5,384,100 units by the end of the year. Most of the new units were subsidized by the national government. Subsidies are granted to municipalities, building societies, and housing associations, which generally build low-income multiple dwellings. Government regulations, which are considerable, are laid down in the Housing Act of 1965 and the Rental Act of 1979. In 1985, the average price of a Housing Act dwelling was f70,130; of other government-aided houses, f79,930; and of privately financed homes, f112,510. In that year, 16% of the housing stock had been built before 1931; 22% between 1931 and 1959; 18% between 1960 and 1969; 23% in the 1970s; and 12% in the 1980s. The total number of housing units in 1992 was 6,044,000.

The government determines on an annual basis the scope of the construction program. On the basis of national estimates, each municipality is allocated a permissible volume of construction. Within this allocation, the municipalities must follow certain guidelines; central government approval is required for all construction projects exceeding a specific cost. All construction must conform to technical and aesthetic requirements, as established by the government.

43EDUCATION

The present Dutch education system has its origins in the Batavian Republic which was constituted after the French Revolution. The role of education gained importance in the Civil and Constitutional Regulations of 1789 and the first legislation on education was passed in 1801. After 1848, the municipalities, supported by state funds, were responsible for managing the schools. Private schools were not originally supported by the government. However, after 1917, private and state schools received equal state funding.

Illiteracy is virtually nonexistent in the Netherlands. School attendance between the ages of 6 and 16 is compulsory. Apart from play groups and crèches (which do not come under the Ministry of Education), there are no schools for children below the age of four. Children may, however, attend primary school from the age of four. Secondary school is comprised of three types: (1) general secondary school, with two options, the four-year junior general secondary school (MAVO) and the five-year senior general secondary school (HAVO); (2) preuniversity—the athenaeum and the gymnasium, both lasting for six years, prepares the children for university education; and (3) vocational secondary school and is of three kinds—junior (LBO), senior (MBO) and higher (HBO).

Special education is provided to children with physical, mental, or social disabilities at special primary and secondary schools. Whenever possible, these children are later transferred into mainstream schools for continued education.

Facilities have been opended in various municipalities for adult education. Open schools and open universities have also been introduced. The Netherlands allocates 17% of its national budget to education. Out of a population of 14.9 million people, nearly 4 million go to school.

Vocational and university education is provided at the eight universities and five institutes (Hogescholen), which are equivalent to universities. These are funded entirely by the government. There are also seven theological colleges..

44LIBRARIES AND MUSEUMS

The Netherlands has rich library collections and has broad use of those materials. In 1989 there were 477 main public libraries with a combined collection of 40.8 million books and records.

The largest public library is the Royal Library at The Hague, which has about 2.25 million volumes and 7,000 manuscripts. Outstanding libraries are found in the universities: Amsterdam, with over 4 million volumes; Leiden, 2.2 million volumes; Utrecht, 3.1 million volumes; Groningen, 2.1 million volumes; and Erasmus of Rotterdam, 820,000 volumes. The technical universities at Delft, Wageningen, and Tilburg also have outstanding collections. Libraries of importance are found in some provincial capitals, such as Hertogenbosch, Leeuwarden, Middelburg, and Maastricht. Also noteworthy are the International Institute of Social History at Amsterdam, which houses important collections of historical letters and documents, such as the Marx-Engels Archives; and the Institute of the Netherlands Economic-Historical Archive, which has its library in Amsterdam and its collection of old trade archives at The Hague.

In 1987, the Netherlands had 625 museums. Among Amsterdam's museums, particularly outstanding are the Rijksmuseum, the Stedelijk Museum (with special collections of modern art), the Van Gogh Museum, and the Museum of the Royal Tropical Institute. The Boymans–Van Beuningen Museum in Rotterdam has older paintings as well as modern works and a fine collection of minor arts. The Hague's Mauritshuis and the Frans Hals Museum at Haarlem have world-renowned collections of old masters.

Other collections of national interest are in the Central Museum in Utrecht, the National Museum of Natural History in Leiden, Teyler's Museum in Haarlem, and the Folklore Museum in Arnhem. In the past, the most important art museums were found mainly in the large population centers of western Holland, but there are now museums of interest in such provincial capitals as Groningen, Leeuwarden, Arnhem, and Maastricht. The government stimulates the spread of artistic culture by providing art objects on loan and by granting subsidies to a number of privately owned museums.

45MEDIA

The post office, telegraph, and telephone systems are operated by the government. The state's monopoly on postal services is confined to delivery of letters and postcards; about half of other deliveries are handled by private firms. In 1977, postal codes were introduced for addresses as part of a postal modernization program. As of 1991 there were 9,750,000 telephone connections, or 66 per 100 inhabitants.

There are four radio networks. The Netherlands Broadcasting Foundation, a joint foundation, maintains and makes available all studios, technical equipment, record and music libraries, orchestras, and other facilities. Broadcasting to other countries is carried on by the Netherlands World Broadcasting Service, which is managed by a board of governors appointed by the minister of cultural affairs. There are three television channels. Shortwave programs are transmitted in Dutch, Afrikaans, Arabic, English, French, Indonesian, Portuguese, and Spanish. Annual license fees are charged to radio and television set owners. Commercial advertising was introduced in 1967/68 and limited to fixed times before and after news broadcasts. In 1991, television sets totaled 7,300,000 and radios 13,650,000.

The Dutch were among the first to issue regular daily newspapers. The oldest newspaper, the *Oprechte Haarlemsche Courant,* was founded in 1656 and is published today as the *Haarlemsche Courant.* The Dutch press is largely a subscription press, depending for two-thirds of its income on advertising. Editorial boards, however, are usually completely independent of the commercial management. Complete freedom of the press is guaranteed by the constitution, and in general the press shows much restraint and fairness. Sunday editions are not issued.

In 1991, the largest national and regional newspapers, with daily circulations, were:

	CIRCULATION
De Telegraaf (Amsterdam, m)	720,000
Algemeen Dagblad (Rotterdam, m)	417,000
De Volkskrant (Amsterdam, m)	310,000
NRC Handelsblad (Rotterdam, e)	215,100
Haagsche Courant (Ryswyk, e)	176,600
Nieuwsblad van het Noorden (regional: Groningen, e)	136,300
Trouw (Amsterdam, m)	119,800

Book production in 1990 included 13,691 titles. In 1991, the Netherlands had 418 motion picture houses (admissions totaled 14.7 million).

46ORGANIZATIONS

The Netherlands possesses numerous and varied organizations. Learned societies include the Royal Netherlands Academy of Sciences, the Royal Antiquarian Society, the Netherlands Anthropological Society, the Historical Association, the Royal Netherlands Geographical Society, and similar bodies in the fields of botany, zoology, philology, mathematics, chemistry, and other sciences. The Royal Netherlands Association for the Advancement of Medicine, the General Netherlands Society for Social Medicine and Public Health, and the Netherlands Association for Psychiatry

and Neurology are some of the organizations active in the field of medicine. In the arts, there are such groupings as the Society for the Preservation of Cultural and Natural Beauty in the Netherlands, the Society of Netherlands Literature, the St. Luke Association, the Society for the Advancement of Music, the Royal Netherlands Association of Musicians, and national societies of painters, sculptors, and architects. The Netherlands Center of the International Association of Playwrights, Editors, Essayists and Novelists (PEN), the Netherlands Branch of the International Law Association, and the Netherlands Foundation for International Cooperation are among the organizations active internationally in their fields.

Associations established on the basis of economic interests include the Federation of Netherlands Industries, the Netherlands Society for the Promotion of Industry and Commerce, the Federation of Christian Employers in the Netherlands, the National Bankers Association, and chambers of commerce in Amsterdam, Rotterdam, The Hague, and other cities.

The Netherlands has Red Cross, Boy Scout, Girl Scout, and other voluntary societies, as well as numerous sports and social organizations.

47TOURISM, TRAVEL, AND RECREATION

The Netherlands is one of Europe's major tourist centers, and tourism is a labor-intensive industry of great economic importance. Income from tourism totaled $4.07 billion in 1991. Foreign visitors rarely need a visa for a stay of 30 days or less; valid passports usually suffice. In 1991, the number of foreign tourists arriving in the Netherlands totaled 5,842,000, of whom 4,922,000 came from Europe and 552,000 from the Americas. There were 112,583 hotel beds with an occupancy rate of 37.9%.

Travel in the Netherlands by public railway, bus, and inland-waterway boat service is frequent and efficient. Principal tourist attractions include the great cities of Amsterdam, Rotterdam, and The Hague, with their famous monuments and museums, particularly the Rijksmuseum in Amsterdam; the flower gardens and bulb fields of the countryside; and North Sea beach resorts. Modern hotels and large conference halls in the large cities are the sites of numerous international congresses, trade shows, and other exhibitions.

Recreational opportunities include theaters, music halls, opera houses, cinemas, zoos, and amusement parks. Of a total population of 14 million, 4.3 million people belong to sport clubs. Popular sports include soccer, swimming, cycling, sailing, and hockey.

48FAMOUS NETHERLANDERS

The Imitation of Christ, usually attributed to the German Thomas à Kempis, is sometimes credited to the Dutch Gerhard Groote (1340–84); written in Latin, it has gone through more than 6,000 editions in about 100 languages. Outstanding Dutch humanists were Wessel Gansfort (1420?–89), precursor of the Reformation; Rodolphus Agricola (Roelof Huysman, 1443–85); and the greatest of Renaissance humanists, Desiderius Erasmus (Gerhard Gerhards, 1466?–1536). Baruch (Benedict de) Spinoza (1632–77), the influential pantheistic philosopher, was born in Amsterdam.

The composers Jacob Obrecht (1453–1505) and Jan Pieterszoon Sweelinck (1562–1621) were renowned throughout Europe; later composers of more local importance were Julius Röntgen (1855–1932), Alfons Diepenbrock (1862–1921), and Cornelis Dopper (1870–1939). Bernard van Dieren (1887–1936), a composer of highly complex music of distinct individuality, settled in London. Henk Badings (b.Bandung, Java, 1907–87) is a prolific composer of international repute. Outstanding conductors of the Amsterdam Concertgebouw Orchestra include Willem Mengelberg (1871–1951), Eduard van Beinum (1901–59), and Bernard Haitink (b.1929), who also was principal conductor of the London Philharmonic from 1967 to 1979.

Hieronymus Bosch van Aken (1450?–1516) was a famous painter. Dutch painting reached its greatest heights in the 17th century, when Rembrandt van Rijn (1606–69) and Jan Vermeer (1632–75) painted their masterpieces. Other great painters of the period were Frans Hals (1580–1666), Jan Steen (1626–69), Jacob van Ruisdael (1628–82), and Meindert Hobbema (1638–1709). Two more recent painters—Vincent van Gogh (1853–90) and Piet Mondrian (1872–1944)—represent two widely divergent artistic styles and attitudes. Maurits C. Escher (1898–1972) was a skilled and imaginative graphic artist.

Hugo Grotius (Huig de Groot, 1583–1645), often regarded as the founder of international law, is famous for his great book *On the Law of War and Peace*. The outstanding figure in Dutch literature was Joost van den Vondel (1587–1679), poet and playwright. Another noted poet and playwright was Constantijn Huygens (1596–1687), father of the scientist Christian. Popular for several centuries were the poems of Jacob Cats (1577–1660). Distinguished historians include Johan Huizinga (1872–1945) and Pieter Geyl (1887–1966). Anne Frank (b.Germany, 1929–45) became the most famous victim of the Holocaust with the publication of the diary and other material that she had written while hiding from the Nazis in Amsterdam.

Jan Pieterszoon Coen (1587–1630), greatest of Dutch empire builders, founded the city of Batavia in the Malay Archipelago (now Jakarta, the capital of Indonesia). Two Dutch naval heroes, Maarten Harpertszoon Tromp (1597–1653) and Michel Adriaanszoon de Ruyter (1607–76), led the Dutch nation in triumphs in sea wars with France, England, and Sweden. Peter Minuit (Minnewit, 1580–1638) founded the colonies of New Amsterdam (now New York City) and New Sweden (now Delaware). Peter Stuyvesant (1592–1672) took over New Sweden from the Swedish and lost New Netherland (now New York State) to the British.

Leading scientists include the mathematician Simon Stevinus (1548–1620); Christian Huygens (1629–95), mathematician, physicist, and astronomer; Anton van Leeuwenhoek (1632–1723), developer of the microscope; Jan Swammerdam (1637–80), authority on insects; and Hermann Boerhaave (1668–1738), physician, botanist, and chemist. Among more recent scientists are a group of Nobel Prize winners: Johannes Diderik van der Waals (1837–1923), authority on gases and fluids, who received the award in 1910; Jacobus Hendricus van 't Hoff (1852–1911), chemistry, 1901; Hendrik Antoon Lorentz (1853–1928) and Pieter Zeeman (1865–1943), who shared the 1902 award for physics; Heike Kamerlingh Onnes (1853–1926), physics, 1913; Christiaan Eijkman (1858–1930), physiology, 1929; Petrus Josephus Wilhelmus Debye (1884–1966), chemistry, 1936; Frits Zernike (1888–1966), physics, 1953; Jan Tinbergen (b.1903), economic science, 1969; Dutch-born Tjalling Koopmans (1910–85), who shared the 1975 prize for economic science; and Simon van der Meer (b.1925), cowinner of the physics prize in 1984. The 1911 Nobel Prize for peace was awarded to Tobias Michael Carel Asser (1838–1913).

The head of state since 1980 has been Queen Beatrix (b.1938).

⁴⁹DEPENDENCIES

Aruba and the Netherlands Antilles are part of the Kingdom of the Netherlands; descriptions of them are given in the volume on the *Americas* under Netherlands American Dependencies.

⁵⁰BIBLIOGRAPHY

Andeweg, R. B. *Dutch Government and Politics*. New York: St. Martin's, 1993.

Barnouw, Adriaan Jacob. *The Dutch: A Portrait Study of the People of Holland*. New York: Columbia University Press, 1940.

———. *The Making of Modern Holland: A Short History*. New York: Norton, 1944.

Blok, Petrus Johannes. *History of the People of the Netherlands*. 5 vols. New York: Putnam, 1898–1912.

Boxer, C. R. *The Dutch Seaborne Empire, 1600–1800*. Atlantic Highlands, N.J.: Humanities Press, 1980.

Campen, S. I. P. *Quest for Security*. The Hague: Nijhoff, 1958.

Geyl, Pieter. *Orange and Stuart*. New York: Scribners, 1969.

———. *The Netherlands in the 17th Century*. 2 vols. New York: Barnes & Noble, 1961–64.

———. *The Revolt of the Netherlands (1555–1609)*. New York: Barnes & Noble, 1958.

Hirschfeld, Gerhard. *Nazi Rule and Dutch Collaboration: The Netherlands under German Occupation, 1940–1945*. New York: St. Martin's, 1988.

Hoogenhuyze, Bert van. *The Dutch and the Sea*. Weesp: Maritiem de Boer, 1984.

Huizinga, Johan. *The Waning of the Middle Ages: A Study of the Forms of Life, Thought and Art in France and the Netherlands in the XIVth and XVth Centuries*. New York: Doubleday, 1954.

Hyma, Albert. *A History of the Dutch in the Far East*. Ann Arbor, Mich.: Wahr, 1953.

Israel, Jonathan Irvine (ed.). *The Anglo-Dutch Moment: Essays on the Glorious Revolution and its World Impact*. New York: Cambridge University Press, 1991.

Israel, Jonathan Irvine. *Dutch Primacy in World Trade, 1585–1740*. New York: Oxford University Press, 1989.

Jacob, Margaret C. and Eijnand W. Mihnhardt (eds.). *The Dutch Republic in the Eighteenth Century: Decline, Enlightenment, and Revolution*. Ithaca: Cornell University Press, 1992.

Jong, L. de. *The Netherlands and Nazi Germany Simon Schama*. Cambridge, Mass.: Harvard University Press, 1990.

King, Peter. *The Netherlands*. Santa Barbara, Calif.: Clio, 1988.

Krewson, Margrit B. *The Netherlands and Northern Belgium, a Selective Bibliography of Reference Works*. Washington, D.C.: Library of Congress, 1989.

Lambert, A. M. *The Making of the Dutch Landscape: An Historical Geography of the Netherlands*. New York: Academic Press, 1971.

Lijphart, Arend. *Politics of Accommodation: Pluralism and Democracy in the Netherlands*. Berkeley: University of California Press, 1968.

Raven, G. J. A. and N. A. M. Rodgers (eds.). *Navies and Armies: the Anglo-Dutch Relationship in War and Peace, 1688–1988*. Edinburgh: J. Donald, 1990.

Renier, Gustaaf Johannes. *The Dutch Nation: An Historical Study*. London: Allen & Unwin, 1944.

Riemens, Hendrik. *The Netherlands: Story of a Free People*. New York: Eagle Books, 1944.

Schama, Simon. *The Embarrassment of Riches: An Interpretation of Dutch Culture in the Golden Age*. New York: Knopf, 1987.

Schilling, Heinz. *Religion, Political Culture, and the Emergence of Early Modern Society: Essays in German and Dutch History*. New York: E.J. Brill, 1992.

Schoffer, Ivo. *A Short History of the Netherlands*. Amsterdam: Albert de Lange, 1956.

Shetter, William Z. *The Netherlands in Perspective: The Organizations of Society and Environment*. Leiden: M. Nijhoff, 1987.

Vandenbosch, Amry J. *Dutch Foreign Policy since 1815: A Study in Small Power Politics*. The Hague: Nijhoff, 1959.

Vere, Francis. *Salt in Their Blood: The Lives of the Famous Dutch Admirals*. London: Cassell, 1955.

Vlekke, Bernard Hubertus Maria. *Evolution of the Dutch Nation*. New York: Roy, 1945.

Vries, Johannes de. *The Netherlands Economy in the 20th Century: An Examination of the Most Characteristic Features in the Period 1900–1970*. Assen: Van Gorcum, 1978.

Wee, Herman van der. *The Low Countries in Early Modern Times*. Brookfield, Vt.: Variorum, 1993.

Wels, C. B. *Aloofness and Neutrality: Studies on Dutch Foreign Relations and Policy Making Institutions*. Netherlands: Hes, 1983.

Wolters, Menno and Peter Coffey (eds.). *The Netherlands and EC Membership Evaluated*. New York: St. Martin's, 1990.

Zanden, J. L. van. *The Rise and Decline of Holland's Economy: Merchant Capitalism and the Labour Market*. New York: St. Martin's, 1993.

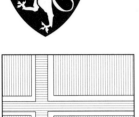

NORWAY

Kingdom of Norway
Kongeriket Norge

CAPITAL: Oslo.

FLAG: The national flag has a red field on which appears a blue cross outlined in white.

ANTHEM: *Ja, vi elsker dette landet (Yes, We Love This Country).*

MONETARY UNIT: The krone (Kr) of 100 øre is the national currency. There are coins of 50 øre and 1, 5, and 10 kroner, and notes of 20, 50, 100, 200, 500, and 1,000 kroner. Kr1 = $0.1370 (or $1 = Kr7.3005).

WEIGHTS AND MEASURES: The metric system is the legal standard.

HOLIDAYS: New Year's Day, 1 January; Labor Day, 1 May; National Independence Day, 17 May; Christmas, 25 December; Boxing Day, 26 December. Movable religious holidays include Holy Thursday, Good Friday, Easter Monday, Ascension, and Whitmonday.

TIME: 1 PM = noon GMT.

¹LOCATION, SIZE, AND EXTENT

Norway occupies the western part of the Scandinavian peninsula in northern Europe, with almost one-third of the country situated N of the Arctic Circle. It has an area of 324,220 sq km (125,182 sq mi). Comparatively, the area occupied by Norway is slightly larger than the state of New Mexico. In 1920, Norway's sovereignty over Svalbard was recognized by the League of Nations; Norway's total area including Svalbard and about 50,000 islands is 386,958 sq km (149,405 sq mi). Extending 1,752 km (1,089 mi) NNE-SSW, Norway has the greatest length of any European country; its width is 430 km (267 mi) ESE-WNW. Bounded on the N by the Arctic Ocean, on the NE by Finland and Russia, on the E by Sweden, on the S by the Skagerrak, on the SW by the North Sea, and on the W by the Norwegian Sea of the Atlantic Ocean, Norway has a boundary length of 24,440 km (15,186 mi).

Norway's capital city, Oslo, is in the southern part of the country.

²TOPOGRAPHY

Norway is formed of some of the oldest rocks in the world. It is dominated by mountain masses, with only one-fifth of its total area less than 150 m (500 ft) above sea level. The average altitude is 500 m (1,640 ft). The Glittertinden (2,472 m/8,110 ft, including a glacier at the summit) and Galdhøpiggen (2,469 m/8,100 ft), both in the Jotunheimen, are the highest points in Europe north of the Alpine-Carpathian mountain range. The principal river, the Glåma, 598 km (372 mi) long, flows through the timbered southeast. Much of Norway has been scraped by ice, and there are 1,700 glaciers totaling some 3,400 sq km (1,310 sq mi). In the Lista and Jaeren regions in the far south, extensive glacial deposits form agricultural lowlands. Excellent harbors are provided by the almost numberless fjords, deeply indented bays of scenic beauty that are never closed by ice and penetrate the mainland as far as 182 km (113 mi). Along many coastal stretches is a chain of islands known as the skjærgård.

³CLIMATE

Because of the North Atlantic Drift, Norway has a mild climate for a country so far north. With the great latitudinal range, the north is considerably cooler than the south, while the interior is cooler than the west coast, influenced by prevailing westerly winds and the Gulf Stream. Oslo's mean yearly temperature is 6°C (43°F) and ranges from a mean of –5°C (23°F) in January to 17°C (63°F) in July. The annual range of coastal temperatures is much less than that of the continental interior. The eastern valleys have less than 30 cm (12 in) of rain yearly, whereas at Haukeland in Masfjord the average rainfall is 330 cm (130 in).

Norway is the land of the midnight sun in the North Cape area, with white nights from the middle of May to the end of July, during which the sun does not set. Conversely, there are long winter nights from the end of November to the end of January, during which the sun does not rise above the horizon and the northern lights, or aurora borealis, can be seen.

⁴FLORA AND FAUNA

The richest vegetation is found in the southeast around Oslofjord, which is dominated by conifers (spruce, fir, and pine); at lower levels, deciduous trees such as oak, ash, elm, and maple are common. Conifers are seldom found at altitudes above 1,000 m (3,300 ft). Above the conifer zone extends a zone of birch trees; above that, a zone of dwarf willow and dwarf birch, and a zone of lichens and arctic plants. In areas exposed to salt sea winds, there is little tree growth. Of the larger wild animals, elk, roe deer, red deer, and badger survive, as do fox, lynx, and otter. Bird life is abundant and includes game birds such as capercaillie (cock of the woods) and black grouse. In the rivers are found trout, salmon, and char.

⁵ENVIRONMENT

Norway's plentiful forests, lakes, flora, and wildlife have suffered encroachment in recent years from the growing population and consequent development of urban areas, roads, and hydroelectric power. The forest floor and waterways have been polluted by Norway's own industry and by airborne industrial pollution from central Europe and the British Isles in the form of acid rain. The acid rain problem has affected the nation's water supply over an area of nearly 7,000 sq mi. Annual particulate emissions amount to 22 tons, hydrocarbon emissions amount to 270 tons, and The nation contributes 0.2% of the world's total gas emissions. Transportation vehicles account for 38% of the emissions. By the early

1980s, the government had enacted stringent regulations to prevent oil spills from wells and tankers operating on the Norwegian continental shelf. Coastal protection devices have since been installed, and new technologies to prevent oil damage have been developed. Industry, mining, and agriculture have polluted 16% of Norway's lake water. The nation has a total of 97.2 cu mi of water; 72% is used for industrial activity and 8% is used for farming. The nation's cities produce 2.2 million tons of solid waste per year. Pollution control laws operate on the premise that the polluter must accept legal and economic responsibility for any damage caused and for preventing any recurrence; the state makes loans and grants for the purchase of pollution control equipment. Municipal authorities supervise waste disposal.

Since its creation in 1972, the Ministry of the Environment has been Norway's principal environmental agency. Between 1962 and 1985, 15 national parks, with a total area of more than 5,000 sq km (2,000 sq mi), and more than 150 nature reserves were established. In 1994, 3 of Norway's mammal species and 8 of its bird species were endangered, and 13 plant species were also threatened. In 1987, animals likely to become endangered included the polar bear, wolf, and otter.

6POPULATION

The population in 1990 was 4,274,553, a 4.5% increase from the count of the 1980 census (4,091,132). The projection for the year 2000 is 4,485,000, assuming a crude birthrate of 15.2 per 1,000 population and a crude death rate of 10.5 during 1995–2000. In 1990, 71.3% of the population lived in towns and 28.7% in rural areas. Average density in 1990, not including Svalbard and Jan Mayen, was 13.1 per sq km (34 per sq mi). Oslo, the capital and principal city, had 467,090 inhabitants as of 31 December 1991. The only other towns with populations exceeding 100,000 were Bergen (215,967) and Trondheim (139,660). Most provincial cities are small, with only Stavanger (99,764), Kristiansand (66,398), and Drammen (52,062) having more than 50,000 at the end of 1991.

7MIGRATION

From 1866 on, North America received great waves of immigration from Norway, including an estimated 880,000 Norwegian immigrants to the US by 1910. The US and Canada still provide residence for many of the estimated 400,000 Norwegians living abroad. Emigration in recent years has not been significant. Norwegians moving abroad numbered 23,784 in 1990; immigrants totaled 25,494. Most emigrants went to Sweden (7,631), Denmark (2,756), the US (2,203), and the UK (1,980). Immigration was principally from the US (1,908), the UK (1,250), Denmark (2,356), and Sweden (5,053). There were about 143,304 foreigners residing in Norway at the end of 1990. At the end of 1992, Norway had 35,700 refugees.

8ETHNIC GROUPS

The Norwegians have for centuries been a highly homogeneous people of Nordic stock, generally tall and fair-skinned, with blue eyes. Small minority communities include some 20,000 Lapps and 7,000 descendants of Finnish immigrants.

9LANGUAGES

Norwegian, closely related to Danish and Swedish, is part of the Germanic language group. In addition to the letters of the English alphabet, it has the letters æ, å, and ø. Historically, Old Norse was displaced by a modified form of Danish for writing, but in the 19th century there arose a reaction against Danish usages. Many dialects are spoken. There are two language forms, Bokmål and Nynorsk; the former (spoken by a large majority of Norwegians) is based on the written, town language, the latter on country dialects. Both forms of Norwegian have absorbed many

modern international words, particularly from British and American English, despite attempts to provide indigenous substitutes. English is spoken widely in Norway, especially in the urban areas. The Lapps in northern Norway have retained their own language, which is of Finno-Ugric origin.

10RELIGIONS

The state church is the Evangelical Lutheran Church of Norway, with about 1,126 congregations grouped in 11 bishoprics. The king nominates the bishops, and the church receives an endowment from the state. About 89% of the population was registered as adhering to the state church in 1992. All religious faiths have freedom to function. Some 44,000 Norwegians belong to the Pentecostal movement, and a lesser number adhere to the Evangelical Lutheran Free Church. There are small numbers of Roman Catholics, Greek Orthodox, Methodists, Baptists, Anglicans, Muslims, and Jews, as well as followers of the Salvation Army and the Mission Covenant Church. About 3% of Norwegians have no religious affiliation.

11TRANSPORTATION

In spite of Norway's difficult terrain, the road system has been well engineered, with tunnels and zigzags, particularly in the fjordlands of the west; but there are problems of maintenance because of heavy rain in the west and freezing in the east. Road transport accounts for nearly 90% of inland passenger transport. At the end of 1991, the total length of highway was 79,540 km (49,246 mi), of which more than one-half was of gravel, crushed stone, or earth. At the end of 1991 there were 1,614,623 passenger cars, 311,063 trucks, and 23,288 buses. There are 2.2 inhabitants per car, second in Europe only to Germany. The state railway operates bus routes and has been steadily increasing its activities in this field, which is heavily subsidized by the government. At the end of 1991, 4,223 km (2,624 mi) of rail line was operational, of which 60% was electrified; most of the track is standard gauge. In 1991, the Norwegian National Railroad carried 35 million passengers and 22 million tons of freight.

With a merchant fleet of 830 vessels (21,699,000 GRT) at the end of 1991, Norway possessed the world's seventh-largest fleet—smaller only than those of Panama, Liberia, China, Cyprus, Japan, and Greece. The sale of Norwegian ships and their registration abroad, which increased considerably during the mid-1980s, severely reduced the size of the fleet. In 1988, the Norwegian International Ship Register program began, whereby ships could be registered offshore, thus allowing foreign vessels to operate under the Norwegian flag while reducing costs to shipowners. Oslo and Bergen have excellent harbor facilities, but several other ports are almost as fully equipped.

Fornebu Airport (Oslo), Flesland (Bergen), and Sola (Stavanger) are the main centers of air traffic, but there are 40 other airfields in Norway. External services are operated by the Scandinavian Airlines System (SAS), which is 21% Norwegian-owned. Braathens Air Transport operates most of the domestic scheduled flights. Important internal air services include that linking Kirkenes, Tromsø, and Bodø; 2,000 km (1,240 mi) long, this air route is reputed to be the most difficult to operate in western Europe. In 1991, Norway's four largest airports handled 10,559,000 passenger arrivals and departures, 4,592,000 of them on scheduled domestic flights. In 1991 there were 803 registered commercial pilots and 1,911 private pilots.

12HISTORY

Humans have lived in Norway for about 10,000 years, but only since the early centuries of the Christian era have the names of tribes and individuals been recorded. This was the period when small kingdoms were forming; the name Norge ("Northern Way") was in use for the coastal district from Vestfold to Hålogaland

NORWAY

| 0 | 75 | 150 Miles |
| 0 | 75 | 150 Kilometers |

Barents
Sea

Nordkapp

Hammerfest

Børselv

Kirkenes

Tana

Tromsø

Finnmarks-
vidda

RUSSIA

Vesterålen

Harstad   Innset

Muonio

Lofoten

Narvik

Bodo

Norwegian
Sea

Mo i Rana

Tornio

Strimasund

Hornavan

Luleå

Oulu

Kroken

Vågen

SWEDEN

Namsos

Steinkjer

Gulf of Bothnia

FINLAND

Kristiansund

Trondheim

Östersund

Umeå

Ålesund   Molde

TROLL-HEIMEN

Storsjön

Elgå

Galdhøpiggen
8,100 ft.
▲ 2469 m.

Hersvik

Urnes

Glåma

Lillehammer

Bergen

Gjøvik

Kinsarvik

Oslo

Gävle

Turku

Haugesund

Drammen

Arvika

Åland

Stavanger   Årdal

Skien

Fredrikstad

Stockholm

Egersund

Kristiansand

Vänern

Baltic
Sea

North
Sea

Skagerrak

Norrköping

DENMARK

Norway

LOCATION: 57°57′31″ to 71°11′8″N; 4°30′13″ to 31°10′4″E. **BOUNDARY LENGTHS:** Finland, 716 km (445 mi); USSR, 196 km (122 mi); Sweden, 1,619 km (1,006 mi); total coastline, 1,996 km (1,240 mi). **TERRITORIAL SEA LIMIT:** 4 mi.

before AD 900. The Viking period (800–1050) was one of vigorous expansion, aided by consolidation of a kingdom under Olav Haraldsson. From the death of Olav in 1030, the nation was officially Christian. During the next two centuries—a period marked by dynastic conflicts and civil wars—a landed aristocracy emerged, displacing peasant freeholders. A common legal code was adopted in 1274–76, and the right of succession to the crown was fixed. Shortly before, Iceland (1261) and Greenland (1261–64) came under Norwegian rule, but the Hebrides (Western Isles), also Norwegian possessions, were lost in 1266. Before 1300, Hanseatic merchants of the Baltic towns secured control of the essential grain imports, weakening the Norwegian economy.

Norway lost its independence at the death of Haakon V in 1319, when Magnus VII became ruler of both Norway and Sweden. The Black Death ravaged the country in the middle of the 14th century. In 1397, the three Scandinavian countries were united under Queen Margrethe of Denmark. Sweden left the union in 1523, but for nearly 300 more years Norway was ruled by Danish governors. Although the loss to Sweden of the provinces of Bohuslän (1645), Härjedalen (1658), and Jämtland (1645) was a handicap, gradual exploitation of the forest wealth improved Norwegian status. Denmark's alliance with France during the Napoleonic Wars resulted in the dissolution of the union. With the Peace of Kiel (1814), Norway was ceded to Sweden, but the Faroe Islands, Iceland, and Greenland were retained by Denmark. However, Norwegians resisted Swedish domination, adopted a new constitution on 17 May 1814, and elected the Danish Prince Christian Frederick king of Norway. Sweden then invaded Norway, but agreed to let Norway keep its constitution in return for accepting union with Sweden under the rule of the Swedish king. During the second half of the 19th century, the Storting (parliament) became more powerful; an upsurge of nationalist agitation, both within the Storting and among Norway's cultural leaders, paved the way for the referendum that in 1905 gave independence to Norway. Feelings ran high on both sides, but once the results were announced, Norway and Sweden settled down to friendly relations. The Danish Prince Carl was elected king of Norway, assuming the name Haakon VII.

Although Norway remained neutral during World War I, its merchant marine suffered losses. Norway proclaimed its neutrality during the early days of World War II, but Norwegian waters were strategically too important for Norway to remain outside the war. On 9 April 1940, Germany invaded; the national resistance was led by King Haakon, who in June escaped together with the government, representing the legally elected Storting, to England, where he established Norway's government-in-exile. Governmental affairs in Oslo fell to Vidkun Quisling, a Fascist leader and former Norwegian defense minister who had aided the German invasion and whose name subsequently became a synonym for collaborator; after the German surrender, he was arrested, convicted of treason, and shot. During the late 1940s, Norway abandoned its former neutrality, accepted Marshall Plan aid from the US, and joined NATO. King Haakon died in 1957 and was succeeded by Olav V.

The direction of economic policy has been the major issue in Norwegian postwar history, especially as related to taxation and the degree of government intervention in private industry. Economic planning has been introduced, and several state-owned enterprises established. Prior to the mid-1970s, Labor Party-dominated governments enjoyed a broad public consensus for their foreign and military policies. A crucial development occurred in November 1972, when the Norwegian electorate voted in a referendum to reject Norway's entry into the EC, this despite a strong pro-EC posture adopted by the minority Labor government. After the 1973 general elections, the Labor Party's hold on government policies began to erode, and in the 1981 elections, the party lost control of the government to the Conservatives. Although the non-Socialists retained a small majority in the 1985 elections, disagreements among them permitted Labor to return to office in 1986.

The EC issue has remained controversial in Norwegian political life while popular rejection of Norway's ascension to the EC is significant, Norway has taken steps to adopt its economic and social policies.

King Harold succeeded his father who died 17, January 1991.

13GOVERNMENT

Norway is a constitutional monarchy. The constitution of 17 May 1814, as subsequently amended, vests executive power in the king and legislative power in the Storting. Prior to 1990, sovereignty descended to the eldest son of the monarch. A constitutional amendment in May 1990 allows females to succeed to the throne. The amendment only affects those born after 1990. The sovereign must be a member of the Evangelican Lutheran Church of Norway, which he heads. Royal power is exercised through a cabinet (the Council of State), consisting of a prime minister and at least 7 other ministers of state (these numbered 17 in 1987). Since the introduction of parliamentary rule in 1884, the Storting has become the supreme authority, with sole control over finances and with power to override the king's veto under a specified procedure. While the king is theoretically free to choose his own cabinet, in practice the Storting selects the ministers, who must resign if the Storting votes no confidence.

The Storting is made up of 165 representatives from 18 counties. Election for a four-year term is by direct suffrage at age 18, on the basis of proportional representation. After election, the Storting divides into two sections by choosing one-fourth of its members to form the upper chamber Lagting, with the rest constituting the lower chamber Odelsting. The Odelsting deals with certain types of bills (chiefly proposed new laws) after the committee stage and forwards them to the Lagting, which, after approval, sends them to the king for the royal assent; financial, organizational, political, and other matters are dealt with in plenary session. Where the two sections disagree, a two-thirds majority of the full Storting is required for passage. Constitutional amendments also require a two-thirds vote. The constitution provides that the Storting may not be dissolved.

A special parliamentary ombudsman supervises the observance of laws and statutes as applied by the courts and by public officials. His main responsibility is to protect citizens against unjust or arbitrary treatment by civil servants.

14POLITICAL PARTIES

The present-day Conservative Party (Høyre) was established in 1885. The Liberal Party (Venstre), founded in 1885 as a counterbalance to the civil servant class, became the rallying organization of the Agrarian Friends' Association. The party's political program stresses social reform. Industrial workers founded the Labor Party (Arbeiderparti) in 1887 and, with the assistance of the Liberals, obtained universal male suffrage in 1898 and votes for women in 1913. The Social Democrats broke away from the Labor Party in 1921–22, and the Communist Party (Kommunistparti), made up of former Laborites, was established in 1923. The moderate Socialists reunited and revived the Labor Party organization in 1927. The Agrarian (Farmers) Party was formed in 1920; it changed its name to the Center Party (Senterparti) in 1958. The Christian People's Party (Kristelig Folkeparti), founded in 1933, and also known as the Christian Democratic Party, supports the principles of Christianity in public life.

For several decades, the Liberals were either in office or held the balance of power, but in 1935, as a result of the economic depression, an alliance between the Agrarian and Labor parties led to the formation of a Labor government. During World War II, the main parties formed a national cabinet-in-exile. Political differences between right and left sharpened in the postwar period. Attempts to form a national coalition among the four non-Socialist parties proved unsuccessful until the 1965 elections, when they gained a combined majority of 80 seats in the Storting. Per Borten, who was appointed in October 1965 to form a non-Socialist coalition government, retained office in the 1969 elections, although with a majority of only 2 seats.

In the 1973 general elections, the Labor Party received only 35.3% of the national vote; its representation in the Storting shrank to 62 seats, but with its Socialist allies, it was able to form a minority government. The Christian People's Party, meanwhile, registered gains, as did the Socialist Electoral League, a new coalition which was able to take a number of votes away from the Labor Party. In 1975, the Socialist Electoral League was transformed into a single grouping known as the Socialist Left Party, comprising the former Socialist People's Party, the Norwegian Communist Party, and the Democratic Socialist Party (formed in 1972); the transformation, which resulted in a platform that voiced criticism neither of the former USSR nor of Leninist ideology, marked the first occasion when a Western Communist Party voted to dissolve its organization and merge into a new grouping with other parties.

In the 1977 elections, Labor expanded its representation to 76 seats, but its Socialist Left ally won only 2 seats, and their coalition commanded a single-seat majority in the Storting. Odvar Nordli, who became prime minister in January 1976, succeeding the retiring Trygve Bratteli, formed a new cabinet and remained in office until February 1981, when he quit because of ill health. His successor was Gro Harlem Brundtland, Norway's first woman prime minister. Her term in office lasted only until September, when the non-Socialist parties obtained a combined total of more than 56% of the vote and a Conservative, Kåre Willoch, became prime minister of a minority government. In April 1983, the government was transformed into a majority coalition.

Following the loss of a vote of confidence, the coalition was replaced in May 1986 by a Labor minority government led by Brundtland, who formed a cabinet of 8 female ministers out of 18. With an average age of 47, her cabinet was the youngest ever in Norway.

Labor increased its support in the 1993 election, winning 67 seats. The Center Party became the second largest party while the Conservatives and other right-wing parties suffered a decline. The results were as follows: Labour Party (67), Center Party (32), Conservative Party (28), Christian People's Party (13), Socialist Left Party (13), Progress Party(10), and others (2). Unemployment and EC membership were dominant issues in the campaign.

15 LOCAL GOVERNMENT

Norway had 47 urban municipalities (bykommuner) and 407 rural municipalities (herredskommuner) in 1986, each administered by an elected municipal council. They are grouped into 18 counties (fylker), each governed by an elected county council. Each county is headed by a governor appointed by the king in council. Oslo is the only urban center that alone constitutes a county; the remaining 18 counties consist of both urban and rural areas. County and municipal councils are popularly elected every four years. The municipalities have wide powers over the local economy, with the state exercising strict supervision. They have the right to tax and to use their resources to support education, libraries, social security, and public works such as streetcar lines, gas and electricity works, roads, and town planning, but they are usually aided in these activities by state funds.

16 JUDICIAL SYSTEM

Each municipality has a conciliation council, elected by the municipal council, to mediate in lesser civil cases so as to settle them, if possible, before they go to court; under some conditions the conciliation councils also render judgments. The courts of first instance are town courts (byrett) and rural courts (herredsrett), which try both civil and criminal cases. Their decisions may be brought before a court of appeals (lagmannsrett), which also serves as a court of first instance in more serious criminal cases; there are five such courts, at Oslo, Skien, Bergen, Trondheim, and Tromsø. Appeals may be taken to the Supreme Court (Høyesterett) at Oslo, which consists of a chief justice and 17 judges, of whom 5 sit in a single case. Special courts include a Social Insurance Court and a Labor Disputes Court which mediates industrial relations disputes.

The judiciary is independent of both the legislative and the executive branches. In criminal cases, defendants are afforded free legal counsel. Indigent persons are granted free legal counsel in certain civil cases as well.

17 ARMED FORCES

The king is supreme commander of the armed forces. About 22,800 conscripts served in the armed forces of 32,700 officers and men in 1993. National service is compulsory and universal, but exemption is granted for religious reasons; those exempted are liable to two years' service in the civil labor corps. Adult males are subject to be called for military service from ages 20 to 44; conscripts serve 12 months in the army, 15 months in the navy and air force.

The army's total strength is 15,900 officers and men. The navy has a total complement of 7,300 men, including 2,000 men in the coastal artillery. The air force consists of 9,500 officers and men, with 85 combat aircraft. Joint services organizations have 300 men, reservists of all services number approximately 285,000, and the home guards has 85,000 men.

Norwegian materiel comes from domestic manufacture, the US, and European NATO members. A ready brigade and mountain warfare battalion are stationed on the Russian border. The navy mans 11 submarines, 5 frigates, and 35 coastal and patrol combatants, and maintaines artillery in 32 fortresses. The air force flies F-16s and ASW helos, and mans air defense guns and missiles. The paramilitary coast guard numbers 680.

Norway is the host nation for the NATO Allied Forces North a headquarters and provides troops for six peacekeeping operations. The nation spent $3.8 billion on defense in 1991 or 3.8% of gross domestic product.

18 INTERNATIONAL COOPERATION

Norway has been a member of the UN since 27 November 1945; the country participates in the ECE and all the nonregional specialized agencies. Norwegian experts serve in many countries under the UN Technical Assistance program, and Norwegian specialists served with UN forces in the Congo (now Zaire). The Norwegian Peace Corps, launched as an experiment in 1963, was made a permanent part of Norway's program of international aid in 1965.

Norway is a member of the Council of Europe, EFTA, NATO, the Nordic Council, and OECD, and is a signatory of GATT and the Law of the Sea.

In September 1972, a referendum on EC membership was rejected by nearly 54% of the electorate. In May 1973, however, the Norwegian government signed a Special Relations Agreement with the EC and the European Coal and Steel Community, providing for free trade in industrial products between Norway and EC members.

19 ECONOMY

Norway, with its long coastline and vast forests, is traditionally a fishing and lumbering country, but since the end of World War I it has greatly increased its transport and manufacturing activities. Without extensive inland mineral deposits, Norway has had to seek opportunities for income abroad, hence its vital interest in areas such as fishing, whaling, and shipping. The exploitation since the late 1970s of major new oil reserves in the North Sea has had considerable impact on the Norwegian economy.

Foreign trade is a critical economic factor. Exports bring in over 40% of the GDP. As a trading nation without a large domestic market, Norway was especially vulnerable to the effects of the worldwide recession of the early 1980s and is sensitive to fluctuations in world prices, particularly those of oil, gas, and shipping.

Since the early 1980s, Norway's exports have been dominated by petroleum and natural gas, which produce one-third of commodity exports by value and roughly 14% of GDP. In the early 1980s, the nation's economy became increasingly dependent on oil revenues, which stimulated domestic consumption and, at the same time, increased costs and prices, thus hampering the competitiveness of Norway's other export industries. The drastic decline of oil prices in 1986 caused the value of Norway's exports to fall by about 20%, making the need to remedy the structural imbalance in the Norwegian economy increasingly evident. Real GDP fell in 1988 for the first time in 30 years. Since 1989, GDP has grown each year—by an average of only 13% during 1989–91, but by 3.3% in 1992 and 2.3% in 1993. Unemployment, however, rose to a post-World War II high of 6% in 1993. Inflation fell from 8.7% in 1987 to 2.2% in 1993.

At considerable expense (6.2% of GDP in 1991), the government provides subsidies for industry, agriculture, and outlying regions. About half of the total goes to agriculture.

20 INCOME

In 1992, Norway's GNP was $110,465 million at current prices, or $25,800 per capita. For the period 1985–92 the average inflation rate was 4.5%, resulting in a real growth rate in per capita GNP of 0.2%.

In 1991 the GDP was $72.7 billion in current US dollars. It is estimated that in 1991 agriculture, hunting, forestry, and fishing contributed 3% to GDP; mining and quarrying, 13%; manufacturing, 13%; electricity, gas, and water, 4%; construction, 4%; wholesale and retail trade, 11%; transport, storage, and communication, 10%; finance, insurance, real estate, and business services, 14%; community, social, and personal services, 5%; and other sources, 22%.

21 LABOR

Employed workers in 1992 totaled 2,004,000, of whom 38.1% were engaged in community, social, and government services; 16% in industry; 17.6% in wholesale and retail trade; 7.8% in transportation, storage, and communications; 6.1% in construction; 5.5% in agriculture, forestry, fishing, and hunting; 7.6% in banking and financial services; and 1.3% in other sectors. From 1960–88, Norway's average unemployment rate was only 1.6%. Unemployment gradually increased during the 1970s, and jumped from 2.1% in 1987 to 5.5% in 1991.

The Norwegian Confederation of Trade Unions (LO), founded in 1899, had all national trade unions as its affiliates by 1905. In 1991, the 29 unions composing the LO represented some 776,773 workers, or 38.6% of the employed labor force. The Norwegian Employers' Confederation, founded in 1900, agreed in 1907 to national collective bargaining, but industrial disputes remained a chronic problem until the Trades Dispute Act of 1952 facilitated mediation in place of arbitration. A system of compulsory unemployment insurance was established in 1959, which provides in part for financial aid for vocational training. In 1919, the eight-hour day was established, together with paid holiday periods. In 1986, the workweek was reduced to 37.5 hours, effective January 1987. In 1992, employees averaged only 34.9 hours of actual work per week. Norwegian workers receive four weeks plus one day of annual vacation time with pay. Under the 1972 amendments to the Joint Stock Companies Act, workers must be represented on corporate boards of directors or other decision-making authorities in both private and public enterprises; generally, employee representatives make up one-third of a company board.

22 AGRICULTURE

Agricultural land in 1991 comprised 892,000 hectares (2,204,170 acres), or about 3% of the country's total land (excluding Svalbard and Jan Mayen). While the area under wheat and mixed grains has dropped sharply since 1949, that for rye, oats, and barley has more than doubled. The greater part of these crops is used to supplement potatoes and hay in the feeding of livestock. Of the 1991 land total, 49.4% produced hay and other fodder crops, 41.3% grains, and 2% potatoes; the balance consisted of other crops and pastures and meadows.

Although the proportion of larger farms has been increasing, most farms in 1990 were still small, with about 99% of the 84,635 farm holdings (including meadows) consisting of less than 50 hectares (124 acres) of arable land. Because of the small size of the holdings, many farm families pursue additional occupations, mainly in forestry, fishing, and handicrafts. Yields in 1991 for holdings of 0.5 hectares (1.24 acres) or more included 1,482,000 tons of grain, 415,000 tons of potatoes, 101,000 tons of fodder roots, and 3,420,000 tons of hay. Norway imports most of its grain and large quantities of its fruits and vegetables.

With steep slopes and heavy precipitation, Norway requires substantial quantities of fertilizers to counteract soil leaching. Smallholders and those in marginal farming areas in the north and in the mountains receive considerable government assistance for the purchase of fertilizers. Mechanization of agriculture is developing rapidly. In 1992, farmers with holdings of at least 0.5 hectares owned 156,000 tractors and 16,300 combines.

Since 1928, the state has subsidized Norwegian grain production; a state monopoly over the import of grains maintains the price of Norwegian-grown grains.

The Ministry of Agriculture has divisions dealing with agricultural education, economics, and other aspects. Each county has an agricultural society headed by a government official. These societies, financed half by the district and half by the state, implement government schemes for improving agricultural practices.

23 ANIMAL HUSBANDRY

Norway is self-sufficient in farm animals and livestock products. In 1992, on holdings of at least 0.5 hectares, there were 2,211,000 sheep, 1,011,000 head of cattle, 749,000 hogs, 20,000 horses, and 4,000,000 fowl. Norway is well known for its working horses. By careful breeding, Norway has developed dairy cows with very good milk qualities; artificial insemination is now widely used. In 1992, production included 83,000 tons of beef and veal, 90,000 tons of pork, 25,000 tons of mutton and lamb, and 55,000 tons of eggs. Norwegian production of milk, cheese, and meat satisfies local demand.

The breeding of furbearing animals has been widely undertaken, and good results have been obtained with mink. Nearly 200,000 reindeer graze in the north and on the lichen-clad mountains.

24 FISHING

Fishing is of modest importance, with 2,095,912 tons caught in 1991 by 26,000 fishermen. Cod, herring, haddock, mackerel, and sardines are the principal commercial species. The value of fish and fishery products exported in 1992 was $2.43 billion.

Cod spawn in March and April off the Lofoten Islands. The Lofoten fisheries are coastal, permitting the use of small craft, but there has been increased use of large trawlers that fish in the waters of Greenland, the Norwegian Sea, and the Barents Sea. Cod roe and liver (yielding cod-liver oil) are valuable by-products. The traditional wage system is on a share-of-the-catch basis. In view of the seasonal nature of the fisheries, many men work also in agriculture or forestry, and the supplementary income from part-time fishing is important to small farmers.

Aquaculture is also important in Norway, with over 800 facilities located along the entire coast from the Swedish border in the south to Finnmark far north of the Arctic Circle

In 1991, sealing expeditions hunting in the Arctic Ocean caught 14,719 seals. Norway was one of the four countries that did not agree to phase out whaling by 1986, having opposed a 1982 resolution of the International Whaling Commission to that effect. In 1991, only two minke whales were reportedly caught by Norwegian whalers.

25FORESTRY

Norway's forestland totals 8,330,000 hectares (20,583,000 acres), of which over 80% is owned by individuals, 9% by the state, and 7% by local governments; the remainder is held by institutions, companies, and cooperatives.

The state subsidizes silviculture and the building of forest roads. In 1991, removals amounted to 11 million cu m, of which 90% was coniferous timber, 19% pulpwood, and 8% fuel wood. The value of roundwood exported was $44.7 million in 1991. In 1992, Norway's trade surplus in forest products amounted to $808.2 million. The Norwegian Forest Research Institute has centers near Oslo and Bergen.

26MINING

Mining is Norway's oldest major export industry, and for a time silver, iron, and copper were important exports. Some of the mines now being worked were established more than 300 years ago. Copper, iron pyrites, and iron ore are still mined in considerable quantities. Known deposits of other minerals are small; they include limestone, quartz, dolomite, feldspar, and slate. In 1991, production of iron ore was 2,209,000 tons; titanium, 800,000 tons; copper, 17,393 tons; and zinc and lead, 22,403 tons. The largest titanium deposit in Europe is at Sokndal, in the southwest. Norway's only coal mines, at Spitsbergen in the Svalbard dependency, produced 389,000 tons in 1991. A large plant at Thamshavn uses half the Orkla mines' output of pyrites for sulfur production. Reserves for minerals generally have been depleted, except for olivine, which is abundant.

27ENERGY AND POWER

Norway, always well supplied with waterpower, has become self-sufficient in energy through the exploitation of vast petroleum and natural gas deposits in the North Sea. Reserves of the Ekofisk offshore oil field, discovered in 1969, were estimated at 2.2 billion barrels of petroleum, and of the Statfjord field (1972) at 3 billion barrels. As of 1992, the Ekofisk field was in danger of closing down due to safety concerns. In 1992, 39 new exploration wells were drilled, down from 44 in 1991. One of the world's largest offshore natural gas deposits, the Frigg field, was proved in 1972. Norway has an estimated 0.9% of world oil and 1.4% of world gas reserves. All together, the nation's remaining recoverable reserves of oil totaled 8.8 billion barrels as of 1 January 1993; of natural gas, 200 billion cu m. Companies licensed to exploit Norway's North Sea resources include the Phillips Petroleum Co. at Ekofisk, Statoil (the Norwegian state oil company), and Norsk Hydro at Statfjord; gas from the Frigg field is sold to the British Gas Corp. for transmission via pipeline to St. Fergus in Scotland. Statoil and Norsk Hydro were the first and second largest corporations in Norway (in terms of gross sales) in 1991. In 1992, Norwegian production of crude petroleum totaled an estimated 106,600,000 tons, or 3.4% of the world supply, and natural gas 28.1 billion cu m (1.4% of world supply). The value of oil and natural gas exports amounted to $13.7 billion and $2.7 billion, respectively, in 1991. Electric power production in 1991 totaled 110,950 million kwh, which was almost entirely hydroelectric. About 90% of the hydropower produced is from state-owned and municipal plants, and 10% from private enterprises. Approximately 25% of the total in 1993 was taken by energy-intensive industries, mainly electrochemical and electrometallurgical plants. Retail distribution is by municipal organizations; virtually the entire population is now served. The export value of Norwegian electricity was about $98.1 million in 1991. With the exhaustion of hydroelectric resources and an abundance of natural gas, the first gas-fired power plant is expected to open in the late 1990s.

Norway imports much coal and coke, and until 1960 imported almost all of its refined petroleum products. The importance of coal and other solid fuels, however, has steadily declined in recent years both in terms of total consumption and in relation to other forms of energy, while hydroelectric power and petroleum products have rapidly increased in importance.

28INDUSTRY

Manufacturing, mining, and crude petroleum and gas production accounted for nearly 30% of the GDP in 1993. The most important export industries are oil and gas extraction, metalworking, pulp and paper, chemical products, and processed fish. Products traditionally classified as home market industries (electrical and nonelectrical machinery, casting and foundry products, textiles, paints, varnishes, rubber goods, and furniture) also make an important contribution. Electrochemical and electrometallurgical products—aluminum, ferroalloys, steel, nickel, copper, magnesium, and fertilizers—are based mainly on Norway's low-cost electric power. Without any bauxite reserves of its own, Norway has thus been able to become a leading producer of aluminum (813,000 tons in 1992). Industrial output is being increasingly diversified.

About half of Norway's industries are situated in the Oslofjord area. Other industrial centers are located around major cities along the coast as far north as Trondheim. Oil refineries are located near Tönsberg (started 1960), at Sola near Stavanger (started 1967), and at Mongstad near Bergen (started 1975).

The gross value of all manufacturing was Kr435,454 million in 1991, when 11,532 establishments employed 298,982 persons.

The gross value of production (in millions of kroner) of the principal sectors is listed in the following table:

Food, beverages, and tobacco	79,822
Paper and paper products, printing and publishing	38,289
Basic metals and articles thereof	29,362
Machinery, except electrical	44,914
Petroleum refineries	14,983
Transportation equipment	22,923
Wood and wood products, including furniture	15,592
Industrial chemicals	15,693

29SCIENCE AND TECHNOLOGY

A highly advanced industrialized nation, Norway invested 1.5% of its GDP on basic scientific research and technological development in 1985. Public funds account for about 60% of research expenditures, either as direct grants from the central government or as proceeds from the State Football Pool, whose net receipts are divided between research and sports. In 1989, research and development expenditures amounted to 12 billion kroner; 8,600 technicians and 12,100 scientists and engineers were engaged in research and development.

The four principal research councils are the Agricultural Research Council of Norway, the Norwegian Research Council for Science and the Humanities, the Royal Norwegian Council for Scientific and Industrial Research, and the Norwegian Fisheries Research Council. The councils recruit researchers by means of fellowship programs and allocate research grants to universities. They are part of the Science Policy Council of Norway, an advisory board to the government on all research matters. Principal areas of current study are arctic research, specifically studies of the northern lights; oceanography, especially ocean currents; marine biology, with special attention to fish migration; and meteorology. The Royal Norwegian Society of Sciences and Letters, founded in 1760, has a Natural Sciences section.

30DOMESTIC TRADE

In 1991 there were 39,596 retail establishments employing 122,103 persons. Wholesale trade sales were Kr380,261 in 1991, and retail sales amounted to Kr183,770 million, excluding value-added tax.

Oslo, the principal merchandising center, handles the distribution of many import products; Bergen and Stavanger are other west coast distribution centers. Trondheim is the chief northern center; Tromsø and Narvik are also important. The largest number of importers, exporters, and manufacturers' agents are in Oslo and Bergen. In most cases, shopping hours are from 9 AM to 5 PM on weekdays and from 9 AM to 1 PM on Saturdays. Banks generally stay open from 9 AM to 3 PM Monday–Friday.

Cooperative societies are an important distribution factor, with local groups operating retail stores for many kinds of consumer goods, especially in the food sector. Food market chains have developed rapidly in recent years. The Norwegian Cooperative Union and Wholesale Society represents some 528 local societies, with 530,000 members, and accounts for over 10% of the total Norwegian retail turnover. Agricultural cooperatives are active in produce marketing, and cooperative purchasing societies (Felleskjöp) do much of the buying of farm equipment, fertilizer, and seed.

The Norwegian Consumer Council (established by the Storting in 1953) advances and safeguards the fundamental interests of consumers. It publishes comprehensive reports on accepted standards for key consumer goods, conducts conferences and buying courses in various parts of Norway, arranges consumer fairs, and cooperates closely with other organizations and institutions interested in consumer protection. Newspapers provide the main medium for advertisements; trade and other journals carry advertising, but the state-owned radio and television do not.

31FOREIGN TRADE

Foreign trade plays an exceptionally important role in the Norwegian economy, accounting, with exports of goods and services, for some 43% of the GDP in 1992. Exports are largely based on oil, natural gas, shipbuilding, metals, forestry (including pulp and paper), fishing, and electrochemical and electrometallurgical products. The manufacture of oil rigs, drilling platforms, and associated equipment has developed into a sizable export industry. Norway imports considerable quantities of motor vehicles and other transport equipment, raw materials, and industrial equipment. Exports tripled between 1974 and 1981, largely on the strength of the petroleum sector, which accounted for a negligible percentage of exports in 1974 but half the total export value in 1981. During the same period, imports advanced by 93%. Following years of trade deficits, Norway had surpluses from 1980 through 1985. However, the drastic fall in oil prices caused a decline in export value resulting in deficits between 1986–88. Since 1989, Norway has once again consistently recorded trade surpluses.

Principal exports in 1992 (in millions of kroner) were as follows:

Crude petroleum	82,658.4
Natural gas	14,499.3
Nonferrous metals	15,004.3
Transport equipment, excluding road vehicles	14,981.2
Fish and fish preparations	14,460.2
Iron and steel	5,691.3
Paper, paperboard, and manufactures	5,839.3
Plastics	3,741.1
General industrial machinery	3,734.1
Specialized machinery	2,785.0
Fertilizers, manufactured	2,010.2
Other exports	52,969.9
TOTAL	218,374.3

Principal imports in 1985 (in millions of Kroner) were as follows:

Road vehicles	9,961.8
Mineral fuels and lubricants	4,632.1
Chemicals and related products	4,977.6
Apparel and clothing accessories	8,535.8
General industrial machinery and equipment	8,582.6
Other transport equipment	11,784.7
Electrical machinery and apparatus	8,826.7
Specialized machinery	6,880.6
Food and live animals	8,941.4
Office machinery and data processing equipment	6,831.6
Iron and steel	7,274.9
Metalliferous ores and metal scrap	6,704.6
Paper, paperboard and manufactures	4,602.5
Telecommunications and sound recording and reproducing apparatus	4,525.4
Other imports	58,868.7
TOTAL	161,931.0

In 1992, EC countries accounted for 66% of Norway's exports and 49% of its imports; EFTA nations took 14% of exports and supplied 22% of imports. The UK was Norway's most important customer, followed by Germany, Sweden, the US, and Denmark.

Principal trade partners in 1992 (in millions of Kroner) were the following:

	EXPORTS	IMPORTS	BALANCE
UK	52,869.7	15,027.6	37,842.1
Germany	28,721.5	23,361.9	5,359.6
Sweden	20,461.2	24,988.0	−4,526.8
US	11,067.1	13,817.7	−2,750.6
Denmark	11,880.3	12,137.1	−256.8
Netherlands	15,592.0	6,384.0	9,208.0
France	16,799.9	6,578.4	10,221.5
Japan	3,597.0	10,187.3	−6,590.3
Finland	5,582.0	5,725.7	−143.7
Italy	5,683.7	5,439.7	244.0
Other countries	46,119.9	38,283.6	7,836.3
TOTALS	218,374.3	161,931.0	56,443.3

32BALANCE OF PAYMENTS

Norway's foreign exchange reserves have been built up to meet adverse developments in the balance of payments without the necessity of a retreat from the liberalization of imports. Until the oil boom of the late 1970s, imports regularly exceeded exports, but large deficits on current account were more than offset by the capital account surplus, giving a net increase in foreign exchange reserves. Norway has high earnings from services abroad and especially from its merchant marine. With the increase in oil revenues and the creation of a favorable trade balance, the government expected Norway to become a larger exporter of capital during the 1980s. However, falling oil prices reduced export income sufficiently to cause a large trade deficit in 1986.

Norway posted a record 1991 current account surplus of some $5 billion as compared to $3.7 billion in 1990. Offshore economic activity had been relatively buoyant in 1991. On external accounts, rising shipments of crude oil helped lift the value of exports, while imports remained somewhat stagnant. In 1992 merchandise exports totaled $35,170 million and imports $25,881 million. The merchandise trade balance was $9,285 million.

The following table summarizes Norway's balance of payments for 1991 and 1992 (in millions of US dollars):

	1991	1992
CURRENT ACCOUNT		
Goods, services, and income	6,573	4,719
Unrequited transfers	−1,523	−1,793
TOTALS	5,050	2,926

	1991	1992
CAPITAL ACCOUNT		
Direct investment	−2,180	493
Portfolio investment	−3,107	1,916
Other long-term capital	2,340	1,154
Other short-term capital	−4,634	−3,736
Exceptional financing	—	—
Other liabilities	—	—
Reserves	2,751	524
TOTALS	−4,830	351
Errors and omissions	−219	−3,274
Total change in reserves	−2,100	−1,292

33BANKING AND SECURITIES

The Bank of Norway was founded as a commercial bank in 1816; in 1949, all its share capital was acquired by the state. It is the central bank and the sole note-issuing authority. The bank discounts treasury bills and some commercial paper; trades in bonds, foreign exchange, and gold and silver; and administers foreign exchange regulations. The bank also receives money for deposit on current account but generally pays no interest on deposits. The head office is in Oslo, and there are 20 branches. The money supply totaled Kr314,900 million in August 1986.

In 1938 there were 105 commercial banks, but mergers brought the total down to only 31 in 1974 and 21 in 1984. As of 1993, the total was down to 20. The three largest—the Norske Creditbank, Bergen Bank, and Christiania Bank og Kreditkasse—account for more than half of the total resources of the commercial banks. Demand and time deposits of commercial and savings banks totaled Kr206,000 million at the end of 1991.

Ten state banks and other financial institutions serve particular industries or undertakings, including agriculture, fisheries, manufacturing, student loans, mortgages, and others. Although savings banks also have been merging in recent years, there were still 133 private savings banks and many credit associations in 1993. Savings banks had total assets of Kr250,000 million at the end of 1992.

A law of 1961 contains measures to implement the principle that banking policies are to be based on social as well as economic and financial considerations. The government appoints 25% of the representatives on the board of every commercial bank with funds of over Kr100 million. Guidelines for these banks are worked out cooperatively with public authorities.

The stock exchanges of Norway are at Oslo (the oldest, founded 1818), Trondheim, Bergen, Kristiansund, Drammen, Stavanger, Ålesund, Haugesund, and Fredrikstad.

34INSURANCE

Norwegian insurance can be undertaken only by joint-stock companies of mutual assistance associations. In 1989 there were 11 life insurance companies and 165 non-life companies. Foreign life insurance companies have practically ceased to operate in Norway. Life insurance policies and those for pension schemes are exempt from income tax and cannot be written by firms doing other insurance work. In 1992, Kr812,000 million in life insurance was in force.

The crown in 1767 initiated compulsory fire insurance in towns, and this fund still exists. In 1984, the 100 mutual fire insurance companies paid claims of Kr240.2 million and collected premiums worth Kr343 million.

For marine insurance, stock companies now are more important than mutual associations. While a number of foreign insurance underwriters transact business in Norway, there is considerable direct insurance of Norwegian vessels abroad, especially in London. Most other insurance, such as automobile and burglary, is underwritten by Norwegian concerns. In 1990, total premiums amounted to $1,289.7 per capita or 4.9% of the GDP.

35PUBLIC FINANCE

Norway's fiscal year coincides with the calendar year. Government expenditures amounted to Kr355 billion in 1992, with a fiscal budget deficit of about Kr40 billion that year. Approximately 70% of public expenditures are for transfers to the counties and municipalities as well as for private sector subsidies. About 30% of public commodities and services purchases go to the armed forces.

The following table shows actual revenues and expenditures for 1989 and 1990 in millions of kroner.

	1989	1990
REVEUNUE AND GRANTS		
Tax revenue	218,568	235,297
Non-tax revenue	57,903	70,288
Capital revenue	1,529	1,498
Grants	6,347	5,674
TOTAL	284,347	312,757
EXPENDITURES & LENDING MINUS REPAYMENTS		
General public service	13,265	14,731
Defense	21,485	23,861
Public order and safety	5,208	5,635
Education	24,903	28,123
Health	28,972	30,892
Social security and welfare	103,999	113,597
Housing and community amenities	3,567	3,804
Recreation, cultural, and religious affairs	3,457	3,599
Economic affairs and services	47,798	52,129
Other expenditures	26,863	28,538
Adjustments	−5,854	−6,262
Lending minus repayments	18,309	9,477
TOTALS	291,972	308,124
Deficit/Surplus	−7,625	−4,633

In 1990 Norway's total public debt stood at Kr146,837 million, of which Kr23,383 million was financed abroad. The government's stated policy is that the domestic private sector should cover the bulk of financing requirements related to Norway's external deficits. Since 1990, the government has allowed the private sector increased access to long-term foreign capital markets to facilitate improvements in the term-structure of its foreign debt.

36TAXATION

Both the central government and the municipal governments levy income and capital taxes. There is also a premium payable to the National Insurance Scheme. For individual taxpayers, income taxes and premiums adhere to the pay-as-you-earn system.

Central government personal income taxes are levied by progressive tax rates, which differ for single taxpayers and those with one or more dependents. Norwegians also pay a central government tax on net wealth, a fixed municipal income tax (21% in 1992), a municipal tax on net wealth, and an additional national income tax called a "top tax," at marginal rates of either 9.5% or 13%. The premium for the National Insurance Scheme is 7.8% of assessed income for wage earners, 3% for pensioners, and 10.7% for the self-employed. The marginal tax system allows for generous deductions from gross income, however. There is a general tax allowance for dependents.

Taxes on corporations are paid in the year following the income year. Corporate income taxes are levied at a flat rate of 28%. Also, employers contribute up to 16.7% of paid wages to the Social Security Scheme.

37CUSTOMS AND DUTIES

Heavily dependent on foreign trade, Norway has traditionally supported abolition of trade barriers. During the 1950s, direct control of imports was gradually abolished. Tariff rates on industrial raw materials and most manufactured goods are low; duties on finished textile products are levied at 15–25%.

A signatory of GATT and a member of EFTA, Norway has bilateral trade agreements with many countries, in every part of the world. In 1973, Norway signed a Special Relations Agreement with the EC, whereby both sides abolished all tariffs on industrial goods over the 1973–77 period. Other trade goods receiving gradual tariff reductions were fish, agricultural products, and wine.

38FOREIGN INVESTMENT

Foreign capital is largely centered in Norway's electrochemical and electrometallurgical industries, the primary iron and metal industry, and mining. The discovery of oil and natural gas in the North Sea area spurred foreign investments. The Ekofisk oil field was discovered in 1969 by an American Phillips Petroleum Co. consortium, including Petrofina of Belgium, ENI of Italy, and Norway's Petronord. A joint Norwegian-Phillips group company, Norpiepe, was formed in 1973 to construct the pipelines and to operate them for 30 years. Another U.S. company, McDermott International, was awarded a $150-million contract in 1982 to lay pipe from the Statfjord gas field in the North Sea to the Norwegian mainland. Foreign direct investment in Norway totaled about $15.7 billion in 1993. More than 2,000 enterprises have foreign investors holding at least 20% of the capital. At least half of the board of directors must be Norwegian nationals or have lived in Norway for the last two years.

39ECONOMIC DEVELOPMENT

The government holds shares in a number of large enterprises: a minority of shares in most industrial establishments and all or controlling shares in some armaments factories, as well as in chemical and electrometallurgical companies, power stations, and mines. The government also participates in joint industrial undertakings with private capital, in enterprises too large or risky for private capital, and in establishments with shares formerly held by German interests. Government policy also aims at attracting foreign investment.

Rapid industrial development and exploitation of resources are major governmental goals, with special emphasis on northern Norway, where development has lagged behind that of the southern areas. The Development Fund for North Norway, established in 1952, together with a policy of tax concessions, resulted in progress there at a rate more rapid than that of the rest of the country. The exploitation of offshore oil and natural gas reserves has had a profound effect on Norway's economy in recent years. Increased oil revenues have expanded both domestic consumption and investment. The government has used oil revenues to ease taxes and increase public investment in regional development, environmental protection, social welfare, education, and communications. In 1992, Norway's offshore oil and taxes amounted to Kr32,299 million.

A tax law permits industry and commerce to build up tax-free reserves for future investment, foreign sales promotion, and research. Designed to provide a flexible tool for influencing cyclical developments, the law's intent is to help ensure that total demand at any given time is sufficient to create full employment and strong economic growth. In the late 1970s, the government introduced combined price and wage agreements in an effort to restrain inflation and ensure real increases in buying power for consumers.

To stimulate industry, incentives are available for undertakings in the north as well as in other economically weak regions; companies may set aside up to 25% of taxable income for tax-free investment. Tariff incentives are available for essential imports. A Regional Development Fund grants low-interest, long-term loans

to firms to strengthen the economy of low-income, high-unemployment areas anywhere in the country.

In 1991, the government introduced a three-year program to improve infrastructure and reduce unemployment. This plan was to spend nearly Kr10 billion, primarily for road and rail communications, with the money coming from budget cuts in other areas.

Norway has been active in aiding developing nations under the Norwegian Agency for International Development. Norway's aid to developing countries of $1,178 million in 1991 came to 1.14% of GNP, higher than that of any of 19 other major developed countries. The leading recipients that year were Tanzania, Mozambique, Zambia, Bangladesh, Nicaragua, and Ethiopia. Multilateral aid rose from $162 million in 1978 to $443 million in 1991.

40SOCIAL DEVELOPMENT

Norway has been a pioneer in the field of social welfare and is often called a welfare state. Accident insurance for factory workers was introduced in 1894, unemployment insurance in 1906, compulsory health insurance in 1909, and accident insurance for fishermen in 1908 and for seamen in 1911. In the 1930s, further social welfare schemes were introduced: an old-age pension scheme; aid for the blind and crippled; and unemployment insurance for all workers except fishermen, whalers, sealers, civil servants, domestic servants, self-employed persons, salesmen, and agents. In the postwar period, health insurance became compulsory for all employees and available to self-employed persons; coverage includes dependents, with medical treatment including hospital and other benefits. Sickness benefits, family allowances during hospitalization, and grants for funeral expenses are paid. Costs of this scheme are met by deductions from wages and contributions by employers and by state and local authorities. Public assistance, available in Norway since 1845, supplements the foregoing programs. Social welfare has long included maternity benefits with free prenatal clinics.

The National Insurance Act, which came into effect in 1967, provides old-age pensions, rehabilitation allowances, disability pensions, widow and widower pensions, and survivor benefits to children. These separate programs were combined into the National Insurance Scheme in 1971. Membership is obligatory for all residents of Norway, including noncitizens, and for Norwegian foreign-service employees. Pensions begin at the age of 67. Benefits are graded according to the individual's previous income and years of employment. A wage earner is guaranteed a minimum annual income corresponding to about two-thirds of his average income during his 20 best years of earnings.

Workers' compensation covers both accidents and occupational diseases. Compensation is paid to a widow until she remarries, and to children up to the age of 18 (or for life if they are unemployable). Dependent parents and grandparents also are eligible for life annuities. Family allowance coverage, in force since 1946, is provided for children under the age of 16. In 1991, payments totaled Kr9,408 for the first child in a family, Kr9,900 for the second, and increasing amounts up to Kr12,324 for each child past the fourth one.

As the Norwegian birthrate has declined (to 12.4 live births per 1,000 population in 1985), so has the total fertility rate, which in 1985–90 was 1.7. A total of 14,577 legal abortions were performed in 1985, for a rate of 283.8 abortions per 1,000 live births or 475 per 1,000 women during their reproductive years.

Women made up about 43.3% of the labor force in 1985. In spite of a 1978 law mandating equal wages for equal work by men and women, economic discrimination persists, and the average pay for women in industry is lower than that for men. A shortage of day-care facilities has hampered the entry of married women as full-time wage earners.

41HEALTH

Since 1971, there has been a National Insurance Scheme. The public health service and the hospitals are the responsibility of the government. There are very few private hospitals in Norway. Hospital care is free of charge, but a minor sum is charged for medicine and primary health care. As of 1984, there has been a ceiling on the total amount one must pay for medical services. There is a three-part system made up of regional hospitals serving parts of the country, central hospitals serving the various counties, and local hospitals, also run by the counties. The country is in need of more nursing homes for the elderly.

The 1993 population was 4.3 million people. In 1988, there were 1,200 health institutions, including 92 hospitals, 681 nursing homes, and 171 psychiatric institutions, with 64,385 beds. This indicates a slight decrease since 1984 due to a decline in the number of somatic hospitals in Norway. In 1991, there were 15,533 hospital beds and 48,543 beds in nursing and old-age homes.

Most general hospitals are public; others are owned by the Norwegian Red Cross or other health or religious organizations. In 1991, there were 13,826 doctors, 5,084 dentists, and 58,561 nurses. In 1992, there were 2.43 doctors per 1,000 people, with a nurse to doctor ratio of 4.4.

On the local level, health councils (boards of health) are responsible for public health services, including tuberculosis control, school health services, and the like, and for environ- mental sanitation. Only in densely populated areas are public health officers appointed on a full-time basis; otherwise they engage in private practice as well. In some areas, they are the only physicians available.

Infant mortality has been appreciably reduced in recent years and, in 1992, stood at 6 per 1,000 live births, one of the lowest rates in the world. There was a 1993 birth rate of 14.8 per 1,000 people, and 63,000 births in 1992. In 1993, about 71% of married women (ages 15 to 49) were using contraception. Average life expectancy, among the highest in the world, was 77 years in 1992. The death rate for 1993 was 10.8 per 1,000 persons. Major causes of death per 100,000 people in 1990 were: (1) communicable diseases and maternal/perinatal causes (52); (2) non-communicable diseases (399); and (3) injuries (53). There were only 8 reported cases of tuberculosis per 100,000 people in 1990. In 1991, there were 60 cases of AIDS and 15,528 abortions.

In 1992, children up to one year of age were vaccinated against tuberculosis (95%); diphtheria, pertussis, and tetanus (91%); polio (86%); and measles (90%). Tuberculosis tests are given on a regular basis from infancy onward. Children go through a comprehensive vaccination program and also receive psychotherapy and dental care throughout their nine years of basic school.

42HOUSING

Before World War II, responsibility for housing rested mainly with the municipalities, but the state has since assumed the major burden. Loans and subsidies keep rents under a certain percentage of a family's income. Cooperative housing has made great progress in such densely populated areas as Oslo, where the Oslo Housing and Savings Society pioneered the practice for Norway. With housing problems compounded by wartime destruction and postwar increases in marriages and in the birthrate, Norway built more dwellings per 1,000 inhabitants than any other European country, completing between 31,000 and 42,000 units annually from 1967 through 1981. Construction of new dwellings has slowed in recent years, however; 41,257 units were completed in 1976, but only 26,114 in 1985 and 21,689 in 1991. As of 1990, Norway had 1,751,358 dwelling units. Since 1988, housing demand has fallen more than 50%. In 1992, investment in housing was 45% below the average annual rate for the period between 1985 and 1989. Tax reforms in 1992 contributed to the decline, making home ownership less attractive.

Home construction financing has come principally from two state loan organizations, the Norwegian Smallholdings and Housing Bank and the Norwegian State Housing Bank, but one-fourth of the nation's housing is still privately financed.

43EDUCATION

There is virtually no adult illiteracy in Norway. Elementary school education has been compulsory since the middle of the 18th century. The Basic Education Act of 1969 introduced a nine-year system of compulsory education for all children between the ages of 7 and 16. Local authorities generally provide school buildings and equipment and the central government contributes funds towards teachers' salaries and covers a considerable proportion of the cost of running the schools. Although there are private schools, government authorities bear a major share of the financial responsibility for these through a system of grants.

Secondary school for students from 16 to 19 involves theoretical, practical, or a combination of both types of education. In 1994, reforms in the secondary education system were to be introduced. The number of basic courses will be reduced from 100 to 13 and the fields of study made more generalized at this level with greater specialization at higher levels. Three-year general secondary schools (gymnasiums) prepare students for the university. In the 1991 academic year, 386,238 students were enrolled in the gymnasiums and other secondary schools. In recent years, it has become possible for students to enter a university without having passed through a gymnasium. Since 1976, the upper secondary school system has included vocational schools of various types, operated by the state, by local authorities, and by the industrial sector.

Norway's institutions of higher education include 215 colleges and 14 universities, with a total enrollment of 154,180 in 1991. In 1989–90, the University of Oslo (founded in 1811) had 25,500 students; the University of Bergen (1948) had 12,300; the University of Trondheim (1969) had 11,800 and the University of Troms (1969) had 3,500. There are also specialized institutions such as the Agricultural University of Norway (near Oslo); the Norwegian School of Economics and Business Administration (Bergen); and the Norwegian College of Veterinary Medicine (Oslo) representing fields not covered by the universities.

Universities and colleges in Norway serve a dual function—both learning and research. At the four universities, degrees are granted at three levels: Lower degree (a four-year study program); higher degree (five- to seven-year course of study); and doctorate degree. There are also courses lasting from five to seven years in law, medicine, agriculture, or engineering.

With a view to placing adults on an equal standing with the educated youth and giving them access to knowledge and job skills, a program of adult education was introduced in August 1977. An official administrative body for adult education exists in all municipalities and counties. However, the Ministry of Education and Research has the highest administrative responsibility for adult education. Folk high schools are associated with a long Scandinavian tradition of public enlightenment. There are more than 80 folk schools in Norway geared toward providing personnel growth and development rather than academic achievement.

44LIBRARIES AND MUSEUMS

Norway's 1,290 public libraries had 18,551,000 volumes in 1989, and the country's 99 academic libraries had a total of 8,718,000 volumes. Oslo University Library (founded in 1811), Norway's principal research library, is also the national library; it has 2,075,000 volumes in its central library and total holdings of 4,421,000 volumes, including those in institute libraries. Since 1882, copies of all Norwegian publications have had to be deposited in the national library; since 1939, copies have been deposited at Bergen and Trondheim as well. Bergen University Library has some 1,200,000 volumes, largely devoted to the natural sciences. The library of the Scientific Society in Trondheim, founded in 1760, is the country's oldest research library and has 1,100,000 volumes. The Tromsø Museum Library (180,000 volumes) has been organized to make it the research library for the north. There are technical and specialized libraries at many research institutes and higher educational centers. State archives are kept in Oslo, and there are record offices for provincial archives at Oslo, Kristiansund, Stavanger, Bergen, Hamar, Trondheim, and Tromsø.

The first municipal libraries were founded in the late 18th century. By law every municipality and every school must maintain a library; each such library receives financial support from state and municipality. In 1989 there were 3,383 school libraries with 6,858,000 books. Regional libraries also have been created. A special library service is provided for ships in the merchant navy, and a floating library service provides books to fishermen-farmers living in the sparsely populated regions.

There were 401 museums in 1989. There are natural history museums in Oslo, Stavanger, Bergen, Trondheim, and Tromsø. Oslo, Lillehammer and Bergen have notable art collections. A traveling "national gallery" was established in 1952. The most important museums in Norway are those dealing with antiquities and folklore, such as the Norwegian Folk Museum in Oslo. Oslo has a unique collection of ships from the Viking period. Open-air museums in Oslo and elsewhere show old farm and other buildings, as well as objects of Norwegian historical and cultural interest.

45MEDIA

Most of the telecommunications network is operated by the government-owned Televerket. The state owns all telephone facilities; telephones in 1991 numbered 2,579,000, or 62 for every 100 persons.

All radio and television broadcasting is controlled by the Norwegian Broadcasting Corp., an autonomous public corporation. Norway has over 300 radio broadcasting stations. Educational broadcasts supplement school facilities in remote districts. Radio license fees have not been required since 1977. Television programming on an experimental basis was initiated in 1958, and full-scale television transmission began in July 1960. Most households have at least one television set; in 1991 there were 3,390,000 radios and 1,805,000 television sets.

The Norwegian press is characterized by a large number of small newspapers. The 83 dailies appear six times a week; publishing newspapers on Sundays and holidays is prohibited by law. Net circulation of all daily newspapers in 1991 was 2,309,000. The following are the largest dailies with their circulations in 1991:

	ORIENTATION	CIRCULATION
OSLO		
VG-Verdens Gang	Independent	360,300
Aftenposten	Independent Conservative	267,000
Dagbladet	Liberal	214,600
Arbeiderbladet	Labor	57,000
OTHER CITIES		
Bergens Tidende (Bergen)	Independent	99,400
Adresseavisen (Trondheim)	Conservative	88,700
Stavanger Aftenblad (Stavanger)	Independent	67,500
Faedrelandsvennen (Kristiansund)	Independent	45,800
Drammens Tidende og Buskeruds		
Blad (Drammen)	Conservative	42,800
Sunnmorsposten (Ålesund)	Independent	38,700

46ORGANIZATIONS

Cooperative societies are numerous and important in Norway. About 2,500 agricultural cooperatives are active; these include purchasing, processing, and marketing organizations. Some 528 retail cooperatives are affiliated with the Norwegian Cooperative Union and Wholesale Society.

The Norwegian Academy of Science and Letters in Oslo is the central and leading learned society. Other learned and professional organizations include the Nobel Committee of the Storting, which awards the Nobel Peace Prize; the Norwegian Research Council for Science and the Humanities; and various legal, scientific, economic, literary, historical, musical, artistic, research, and other societies.

Doctors are organized in the Norwegian Medical Association and in local associations. Farming organizations and agricultural cooperatives are represented in the Federation of Agriculture. There are associations of small and large forest owners, fur breeders, and employers' organizations in most sectors of industry, as well as a central Norwegian Employers' Confederation.

Health organizations include the Norwegian Red Cross, the Norwegian Women's Health Organization, and societies to combat tuberculosis, poliomyelitis, and other diseases..

47TOURISM, TRAVEL, AND RECREATION

Norway's main tourist attractions are the cities of Oslo, Bergen, and Trondheim, which are connected by road, rail, and daily flights; the marvelous scenery of the fjord country in the west; and the arctic coast with the North Cape and "midnight sun." In 1991, foreign tourists numbered 2.1 million. There were 55,887 hotel rooms with 116,926 beds and a 36 percent occupancy rate. In the same year, income from tourism totaled $1.57 billion. A favorite method of tourist travel is by coastal steamer, sailing from Bergen northward to Kirkenes, near the Soviet frontier. Many cruise ships ply the Norwegian fjords and coastal towns as far north as Spitsbergen. Notable outdoor recreational facilities include the Oslomarka, a 100,000-hectare (247,000-acre) area located near Oslo, with ski trails and walking paths. To compensate for the shortness of winter days, several trails are illuminated for evening skiing. Other popular sports include ice skating, freshwater fishing, mountaineering, hunting (grouse, reindeer, and elk), and soccer. There are major theaters in Oslo and Bergen, as well as six regional theaters; Den Norske Opera in Oslo; and four symphony orchestras. International musical events include the Bergen Festival, held annually in late May or early June; and several jazz festivals in July. In 1994, Norway hosted the XVII Olympic Winter Games in Lillehammer. No passport is required of visitors from the Nordic area, but travelers arriving in Norway directly from non-Nordic countries are subject to passport control. A visa is not required for visits of less than three months

48FAMOUS NORWEGIANS

Ludvig Holberg (1684–1745), the father of Danish and Norwegian literature, was a leading dramatist whose comedies are still performed. Henrik Wergeland (1808–45), Norway's greatest poet, was also a patriot and social reformer; his sister Camilla Collett (1813–95), author of the first Norwegian realistic novel, was a pioneer in the movement for women's rights. Henrik Ibsen (1827–1906), founder of modern dramas, placed Norway in the forefront of world literature. Bjørnstjerne Bjørnson (1832–1910), poet, playwright, and novelist, received the Nobel Prize for literature in 1903. Other noted novelists are Jonas Lie (1833–1908); Alexander Kielland (1849–1906); Knut Hamsun (1859–1952), Nobel Prize winner in 1920; Sigrid Undset (1882–1949), awarded the Nobel Prize in 1928; and Johan Bojer (1872–1959).

Ole Bull (1810–80) was a world-famous violinist. Edvard Grieg (1843–1907) was the first Norwegian composer to win broad popularity. His leading contemporaries and successors were Johan Svendsen (1840–1911), Christian Sinding (1856–1941), Johan Halvorsen (1864–1935), and Fartein Valen (1887–1953). Kirsten Flagstad (1895–1962), world-renowned soprano, served for a time as director of the Norwegian State Opera. In painting, Harriet Backer (1845–1932), Christian Krohg (1852–1925), and Erik Werenskiold (1855–1938) were outstanding in the traditional manner; leading the way to newer styles was Edvard Munch (1863–1944), an outstanding expressionist, as well as Axel Revold (1887–1962) and Per Krohg (1889–1965). Norway's foremost sculptor is Gustav Vigeland (1869–1943); the Frogner Park in Oslo is the site of a vast collection of his work in bronze and granite.

Outstanding scientists are Christopher Hansteen (1784–1873), famous for his work in terrestrial magnetism; Niels Henrik Abel (1802–29), noted for his work on the theory of equations; Armauer (Gerhard Henrik) Hansen (1841–1912), discoverer of the leprosy bacillus; Vilhelm Bjerknes (1862–1951), who advanced the science of meteorology; Fridtjof Nansen (1861–1930), an oceanographer and Arctic explorer who won the Nobel Peace Prize in 1922 for organizing famine relief in Russia; Otto Sverdrup (1854–1930), Roald Amundsen (1872–1928), and Bernt Balchen (1899–1973), polar explorers; Johan Hjort (1869–1948), a specialist in deep-sea fishery research; Regnar Frisch (1895–1978), who shared the first Nobel Prize in Economic Science in 1969 for developing econometrics; Odd Hassel (1897–1981), co-winner of the 1969 Nobel Prize in chemistry for his studies of molecular structure; and Thor Heyerdahl (b.1914), explorer and anthropologist.

The first secretary-general of the UN was a Norwegian, Trygve (Halvdan) Lie (1896–1968), who served from 1946 to 1953. The historian Christian Louis Lange (1869–1938) was co-winner of the Nobel Peace Prize in 1921.

Sonja Henie (1913–69) was the leading woman figure skater of her time, and Liv Ullmann (b.1939) is an internationally known actress. Grete Waitz (b.1953) is a champion long-distance runner.

49 DEPENDENCIES

Svalbard
The Svalbard group includes all the islands between 10° and 35°E and 74° and 81°N: the archipelago of Spitsbergen, White Island (Kvitøya), King Charles' Land (Kong Karls Land), Hope Island, and Bear Island (Bjørnøya), which have a combined area of about 62,700 sq km (24,200 sq mi). The largest islands are Spitsbergen, about 39,400 sq km (15,200 sq mi); North-East Land (Nordaustlandet), 14,530 sq km (5,610 sq mi); Edge Island (Edgeøya), 5,030 sq km (1,940 sq mi); and Barents Island (Barentsøya), 1,330 sq km (510 sq mi). Svalbard's population totaled 3,181 at the end of 1991. The population is 64% Russian, 35% Norwegian, and 1% other.

Discovered by Norwegians in the 12th century and rediscovered in 1596 by the Dutch navigator Willem Barents, Svalbard served in the 17th and 18th centuries as a base for British, Dutch, Danish, Norwegian, German, and other whalers, but no permanent sovereignty was established. Russian and Norwegian trappers wintered there, and coal mining started early in the 20th century. Norway's sovereignty was recognized by the League of Nations in 1920, and the territory was taken over officially by Norway in 1925. Much of the high land is ice-covered; glaciers descend to the sea, where they calve to produce icebergs. The west and south coasts have many fjords, while the western coastal lowland is up to 10 km (6 mi) broad. The most important mineral, coal, occurs in vast deposits in Spitsbergen. The west coast is kept clear of ice for six months of the year by the relatively warm water of the North Atlantic Drift, but an air temperature as low as –62°C (–80°F) has been recorded. In this region there are 112 days without the sun's appearance above the horizon.

The chief official, a governor, lives at Longyearbyen; his administration is controlled by the Ministry of Industry. Coal mining is the main industry, with Norwegian-worked mines at Longyearbyen, Sveagruva, and Ny Ålesund and Russian worked mines at Barentsburg, Grumantbyen, and elsewhere. Russia has extraterritorial rights in the areas where they mine. Cod fishing takes place around Bear Island, but whaling has virtually ceased. Norwegian sealers hunt seals, polar bears, and walrus in the summer. For centuries, trappers wintered in Spitsbergen to catch fox and bear while the pelts were in the best condition, but few trappers have wintered there in recent years.

Communications are maintained during the summer months by ships from Tromsø carrying goods and passengers, while colliers put in frequently at the mine piers. There are no roads and no local ship services.

Jan Mayen
Located in the Norwegian Sea at 70°30′N and 8°30′W, 893 km (555 mi) from Tromsø, the island of Jan Mayen has an area of about 380 sq km (150 sq mi). The island is dominated by the volcano Beerenberg, 2,277 m (7,470 ft) high, which is responsible for its existence; a major eruption occurred in September 1970. Jan Mayen was discovered by Henry Hudson in 1607 and was visited in 1614 by the Dutch navigator Jay Mayen, who used it subsequently as a whaling base. In 1929, the island was placed under Norwegian sovereignty. It is the site of a meteorological station and an airfield.

Bouvet Island
Bouvet Island (Bouvetøya), situated at 54°26′S and 3°24′E in the South Atlantic Ocean, was discovered in 1739, and in 1928 was placed under Norwegian sovereignty. An uninhabited volcanic island of 59 sq km (23 sq mi), Bouvet is almost entirely covered by ice and is difficult to approach.

Peter I Island
Peter I Island (Peter I Øy), an uninhabited Antarctic island of volcanic origin, is located at 68°48′S and 90°35′W. It has an area of 249 sq km (96 sq mi), rises to over 1,233 m (4,045 ft), and is almost entirely ice-covered. The island was discovered in 1821 by a Russian admiral. In 1931, it was placed under Norwegian sovereignty, and by a parliamentary act of 1933 became a dependency.

Queen Maud Land
Queen Maud Land (Dronning Mauds land) consists of the sector of Antarctica between 20°W and 45°E, adjoining the Falkland Islands on the W and the Australian Antarctic Dependency on the E. It was placed under Norwegian sovereignty in 1939, and has been a Norwegian dependency since 1957. The land is basically uninhabited, except for several stations operated by Japan, South Africa, and Russia.

50 BIBLIOGRAPHY

Ausland, John. *Norway, Oil, and Foreign Policy.* Boulder, Colo.: Westview, 1979.

Brueckner, Hannes. *Geographic Survey of Norway.* New York: Columbia University Press, 1977.

Charbonneau, Claudette. *The Land and People of Norway.* New York: HarperCollins, 1992.

Derry, Thomas K. *A Short History of Norway.* Westport, Conn.: Greenwood, 1979.

Greve, Tim. *Haakon VII of Norway: The Man and the Monarch.* New York: Hippocrene, 1983.

Gustavson, Bjorn, and Gerry Hunius. *Improving the Quality of Life: The Case of Norway.* New York: Columbia University Press, 1981.

Hølaas, Odd. *The World of the Norsemen.* London: Bond, 1949.

Kersaudy, Francois. *Norway 1940.* New York: St. Martin's, 1991.

Kiel, Anne Cohen. *Continuity and Change: Aspects of Contemporary Norway.* New York: Oxford University Press, 1993.

Nelsen, Brent F. (ed.). *Norway and the European Community: the Political Economy of Integration.* Westport, Conn.: Praeger, 1993.

Popperwell, Ronald G. *Norway.* New York: Praeger, 1972.

Ramsey, Natalie Rogoff (ed.). *Norwegian Society.* New York: Humanities Press, 1974.

Sather, Leland B. *Norway, World Biographical Series No. 67.* Santa Barbara, Calif.: CLIO, 1986.

Skard, Sigmund. *The U.S. in Norwegian History.* Westport, Conn.: Greenwood, 1976.

Vanberg, B. *Of Norwegian Ways.* New York: Harper & Row, 1984.

POLAND

Polish People's Republic

Polska Rzeczpospolita Ludowa

CAPITAL: Warsaw (Warszawa).

FLAG: The national flag consists of two horizontal stripes, the upper white and the lower red.

ANTHEM: *Jeszcze Polska nie zginela (Poland Is Not Yet Lost)*.

MONETARY UNIT: The zloty (z) is a paper currency of 100 groszy. There are coins of 1, 2, 5, 10, 20, and 50 groszy and 1, 2, 5, 10, 20, 50, and 100 zlotys, and notes of 10, 20, 50, 100, 200, 500, 1,000, 2,000, 5,000, 10,000, 20,000, 50,000, 100,000, 200,000, 500,000, 1,000,000, and 2,000,000 zlotys. z1 = $0.00004 (or $1 = z22,119).

WEIGHTS AND MEASURES: The metric system is the legal standard.

HOLIDAYS: New Year's Day, 1 January; Labor Day, 1 May; National Day, 3 May; Victory Day, 9 May; All Saints' Day, 1 November; Christmas, 25–26 December. Movable holidays are Easter Monday and Corpus Christi.

TIME: 1 PM = noon GMT.

¹LOCATION, SIZE, AND EXTENT

Situated in eastern Europe, the Polish People's Republic has an area of 312,680 sq km (120,726 sq mi), extending 689 km (428 mi) E–W and 649 km (403 mi) N–S. It is bounded on the N by the Baltic Sea, on the N and E by Russia, Lithuania, Belarus, and Ukraine, on the S by Slovakia and the Czech Republic, and on the W by Germany, with a total boundary length of 3,605 km (2,240 mi). Comparatively, the area occupied by Poland is slightly smaller than the state of New Mexico.

Before World War II, Poland had encompassed a territory of nearly 390,000 sq km (150,600 sq mi). On 11 July 1920, an armistice mediated by Britain in a Polish-Soviet conflict established the "Curzon line" (named for George Nathaniel Curzon, the British statesman who proposed it), conferring the former Austrian territory of Galicia to the Soviet side. However, under the Treaty of Riga (1921), all of Galicia was assigned to Poland, and a boundary well to the east of the Curzon line prevailed until World War II. At the Yalta Conference in February 1945, the Allies accepted Soviet claims to eastern Poland, with a border running approximately along the Curzon line. On 21 April 1945, a Polish-Soviet treaty of friendship and cooperation was signed, followed by a new agreement on the Polish-Soviet border. To compensate for the loss of 46% of Poland's territory to the USSR, the Potsdam Conference of July–August 1945 placed former German territories east of the Oder (Odra) and western Neisse rivers under Polish administration, pending a final determination by a German peace treaty. On 6 August 1950, an agreement was signed between Poland and the GDR according to which both parties recognized the frontier on the Oder-Neisse line. The Federal Republic of Germany (FRG) recognized this boundary under the terms of a treaty signed with Poland on 7 December 1970 and ratified by the FRG on 23 May 1972. Poland's capital city, Warsaw, is located in the east central part of the country.

²TOPOGRAPHY

Poland's average altitude is 173 m (568 ft); 75.4% of the land is less than 200 m (656 ft) above sea level. The highest point, Mount Rysy (2,499 m/8,199 ft), is located in the Tatra Moun-

tains on the Slovakian border. The principal topographic regions are an undulating central lowland with a crystalline platform and warped bedrock; the Baltic highland in the north, a glaciated region with many lakes and sandy soils; and the coastland, a narrow lowland with promontories, bays, and lakes. The southern uplands are marked with rich loam and mineral deposits.

Several important navigable rivers drain into the Baltic Sea, among them the Vistula (Wisla), the Oder, the Bug, and the Warta. There are some 9,300 lakes in the northern lake region. Good harbors have been developed on the Baltic Sea.

³CLIMATE

Poland has a continental climate, conditioned especially by westerly winds. Only the southern areas are humid. Summers are cool, and winters range from moderately cold to cold. The average mean temperature is about 7°C (45°F); temperatures in Warsaw range, on average, from –6° to –1°C (21–30°F) in January and from 13° to 24°C (55–75°F) in July. Precipitation is greatest during the summer months, lasting 85 to 100 days. Annual rainfall ranges from about 50 cm (20 in) in the lowlands and 135 cm (53 in) in the mountains; the overall average is about 64 cm (25 in).

⁴FLORA AND FAUNA

Coniferous trees, especially pine, account for 70% of the forests; deciduous species include birch, beech, and elm. Lynx, wildcat, European bison, moose, wild horse (tarpan), and wild goat are among the few remaining large mammals. Birds, fish, and insects are plentiful.

⁵ENVIRONMENT

The main government agencies responsible for environmental protection are the Institute for Environmental Planning and the Ministry of Administration, Regional Economy, and Environmental Protection. Poland has yet to recover from the overexploitation of forests during World War II and the loss of about 1.6 million hectares (4 million acres) of forestland after the war. As of 1994, 75% of Poland's forests have been damaged by airborne contaminants.

Pollution of the air, water, and land are the most significant environmental problems facing Poland in the 1990s. Air pollution results from hazardous concentrations of airborne dust, carbon dioxide, and nitrogen compounds, fluorine, formaldehyde, ammonia, lead, and cadmium. The nation contributes 1.4% of the world's total gas emissions. Industry-related pollution affects particularly the Katowice region, where dust and sulfur dioxide emissions exceed acceptable levels. Water pollution in the Baltic Sea is 10 times higher than ocean water. Poland has 11.9 cu mi of reusable water. Twenty-four percent is used to support farming and 60% is for industrial purposes. Twenty-eight percent of the rural people do not have pure water. Six percent of all city dwellers also do not have pure water. According to a December 1985 government report, more than 90% of river waters are too polluted for safe human consumption. Poland's cities generate 5.7 million tons of solid waste per year. Its industrial sector contributes 200,000 tons of toxic pollutants each year. In 1989, 11% of the nation was considered endangered due to extreme levels of pollution and environmental damage. The nation's wildlife has also suffered degeneration of the habitat. In 1994, four mammal species were endangered. Sixteen bird species and 16 types of plants are also threatened with extinction. The cerambyx longicorn and rosalia longicorn were among the endangered species.

6POPULATION

According to the 1988 census, Poland's population was 37,879,000; as of mid-1994, the population was estimated at 38,513,000. The average annual rate of growth from 1978 to 1988 was 0.8%. A population of 39,508,000 is projected for the year 2000, assuming a crude birthrate of 14.5 per 1,000 population, a crude death rate of 9.8, and a net natural increase of 4.7 during 1995–2000. In 1988, density was 121 per sq km (314 per sq mi), with 61.2% of the population living in urban areas. Warsaw, the capital and principal city, had an estimated population of 1,653,300 at the end of 1991. Other cities with populations exceeding 250,000 at the end of 1991 were Lódz, 844,900; Cracow (Kraków), 751,300; Wroclaw, 643,600; Poznań, 589,700; Gdańsk, 466,500; Szczecin, 412,100; Bydgoszcz, 383,600; Katowice, 366,900; Lublin, 352,500; Bialystok, 273,300; Sosnowiec, 259,000; Czestochowa, 258,700; and Gdynia, 251,800.

7MIGRATION

Large-scale emigration from Poland took place before World War II, with the heaviest exodus in the decades before World War I. Between 1871 and 1915, a total of 3,510,000 Poles, Polish Jews, and Ukrainians emigrated, about half of them to the US. Emigration diminished greatly during the interwar period, when France became the chief country of destination. Between 1921 and 1938, some 1,400,000 Poles emigrated, while 700,000 returned. Poland suffered a net population loss of nearly 11,000,000 between 1939 and 1949 through war losses, deportations, voluntary emigrations, and population transfers arising out of territorial changes. An estimated 6,000,000 Germans left the present western territories of Poland when these territories came under Polish jurisdiction, and since the end of World War II more than 7,500,000 Poles have settled in the area. From the 1950s through the 1980s, Germans leaving for Germany constituted the bulk of emigrants; Jews also left in substantial numbers for Israel, both in the immediate postwar years and during the 1950s and 1960s. Another emigration wave occurred after the imposition of martial law in December 1981. According to official figures, net external migration was 233,600 during 1981–89. It was about 16,000 in 1991. Of the 20,977 emigrants, 14,502 went to Germany. These official figures seriously underestimate real emigration, however. Germany, for example, recorded 145,643 immigrants from Poland in 1991. There was a net rural-to-urban migration of 1,231,300 between 1981 and 1989, and of 106,400 in 1991.

8ETHNIC GROUPS

Before World War II, over 30% of the people living within the boundaries of Poland were non-Poles. According to the 1931 census, Polish was the mother tongue of 69% of Poland's 32 million people, Ukrainian and Ruthenian 14%, Belorussian 5.3%, and German 2.3%. Yiddish speakers also constituted a significant minority, and there were smaller numbers of Lithuanian, Czech, and Slovak speakers. As a result of World War II, and of the boundary changes and population transfers that followed, Poland today is a predominantly homogeneous state with about 2% of the population non-Polish. Ukrainians, Lithuanians, Belorussians, Germans, Gypsies, and Slovaks are the most numerous minorities.

9LANGUAGES

Polish, the universal language, is one of the western Slavic languages using the Latin alphabet and the only major Slavic language to preserve the old Slavic nasal vowels. It is easily distinguishable from other Slavic languages by the frequent accumulation of consonants. In addition to the letters of the English alphabet, it has the following letters and diphthongs: *a, ch, ci, cz, dż, dź, dzi, e, l, ń, ni, ó, rz, ś, si, sz, z, ż, ź*, and *zi*. It has no *q, v,* or *x*. Among the several dialects are Great Polish (spoken around Poznań), Kuyavian (around Inowroclaw), Little Polish (around Cracow), Silesian (around Katowice and Wroclaw), and Mazovian (around Warsaw and extending north and east). Some philologists consider that Kashubian, spoken along the Baltic, is not a Polish dialect but a separate language. Many Poles speak English, French, German, or Russian, and understand other Slavic languages in varying degrees.

10RELIGIONS

Poland is one of the world's most strongly Roman Catholic countries. During the period of Communist domination that began in 1945, that church suffered extensive repression by the state. A change in party leadership in October 1956, however, brought about a new relationship between church and state, which included voluntary religious instruction in schools and other guarantees to the Roman Catholic Church. In 1974, the Polish government established permanent working contacts with the Holy See. The position of the Church was further enhanced when the archbishop of Cracow, Karol Cardinal Wojtyla, became Pope John Paul II in 1978. Three visits by the Pope to Poland, 2–10 June 1979, 16–23 June 1983, and 8–14 June 1987, testified to the strength of Polish Catholicism; In 1989, the church was finally granted legal status and control of its schools, hospitals, and its university in Lublin. According to both state and other sources in 1993, 95% of Poles are Roman Catholics. In 1990, about 870,000 people were Russian Orthodox, and about 10,000 belonged to various Protestant groups.

On the eve of World War II, an estimated 3,351,000 Jews lived in Poland, more than in any other country; they constituted about 10% of the Polish population and nearly 20% of world Jewry. During the course of the Nazi occupation (1939–45), nearly 3,000,000 Polish Jews were killed, many of them in extermination camps such as Auschwitz (Oświecim), near Cracow. Most of the survivors had fled to the USSR; at the end of the war, only about 55,000 Jews remained in Poland. Repatriation raised the total Jewish population to 250,000 in 1946. However, the establishment of the State of Israel in 1948, combined with a series of anti-Semitic outbreaks in Poland (including a government-led campaign in 1968–69), induced most Jews to emigrate. By 1990, Poland had only 3,800 Jews.

11TRANSPORTATION

In 1991, the operational rail network of Poland was 27,041 km (16,803 mi) in length (90% standard gauge, 9% narrow gauge,

POLAND

Baltic Sea

LITHUANIA

LOCATION: 14°7′ to 24°8′E; 49° to 54°50′N. **BOUNDARY LENGTHS:** Baltic coastline, 491 km (304 mi); Russia, 432 km (268 mi); Lithuania 91 km (56 mi); Belarus, and Ukraine, 428 km (265 mi); Czech Republic, 658 km (408 mi); Slovakia, 444 km (275 mi); Germany, 460 km (286 mi). **TERRITORIAL SEA LIMIT:** 12 mi.

and 1% broad gauge), of which 11,016 km (6,845 mi) were electrified. Of the total trackage, 8,987 km (5,584 mi) was double-tracked. In 1992, the Polish railroads carried 201.7 million tons of freight.

There is a dense road and highway network. Improvement and repair have not kept up with the increased usage—an 800% increase in freight and an 1,800% increase in passenger transport between 1950 and 1970, and a 60% increase in freight traffic and a 70% increase in passenger transport during 1971–82. In 1991, out of a total of nearly 300,000 km (186,400 mi) of roads, improved hard-surface roads comprised 43.3%; unimproved hard-surface, 8%; earth roads, 33.3%; and various urban roads, 15.4%. In 1991 there were 6,112,171 passenger cars, and 1,238,409 commercial vehicles.

At the beginning of 1991, Poland had 230 merchant ships, totaling 2,950,000 GRT. Before World War II, Polish merchant marine operations were mainly with the Western countries, especially the US, but much of the current traffic is with Asian and African countries. The major ports are Szczecin, Gdynia, Gdańsk, and Swinoujście, which together handled 44.2 million metric tons of cargo in 1990. The ports were badly damaged during World War II but have since been rehabilitated and enlarged. There are

3,997 km (2,484 mi) of navigable rivers and canals; the principal inland waterways are the Oder, with Szczecin near its mouth, the Wista, and the Warta.

Polish Air Transport (Polskie Linie Lotnicze—LOT), organized in 1922 and reorganized after World War II, is a state enterprise, with Warsaw's Okecie International Airport as the center. In 1991, LOT's 27 aircraft carried 1,051,200 passengers and performed 38.1 million freight ton-km.

12HISTORY

The land now known as Poland was sparsely populated in prehistoric times. Slavic tribes are believed to have begun settling Poland more than 2,000 years ago, but by AD 800, the population was probably no more than 1 million. Rulers of the Piast dynasty united the Polish tribes of the Vistula and Oder basins about the middle of the 10th century. In 966, Mieszko I, a member of this dynasty, was baptized, and consequently Poland became a Christian nation. Thirty-three years later, his eldest son and successor, Boleslaw I ("the Brave"; r.992–1025), secured recognition of Polish sovereignty from Holy Roman Emperor Otto III.

During the next three centuries, Poland was continually embroiled in conflicts with the Germans to the west and with the

Eastern Slavs and the Mongol invaders to the east, while developing cultural relations with the Western civilizations. Foreign penetration and internal difficulties led to the division of Poland among members of the Piast dynasty. Under Casimir III ("the Great"; r.1333–70), the last of the Piast rulers, Poland was restored to unity and greatness. Casimir made peace with the Teutonic Knights, added Galicia to the realm, and welcomed Jewish refugees from the west; internally, law was codified, administration centralized, and a university was established at Cracow in 1364. In 1386, a Polish-Lithuanian federal union was created through a dynastic marriage, which also gave birth to the Jagellonian dynasty, named for Jagello, grand duke of Lithuania, who ruled Poland as Ladislas II (1386–1434). The union extended from the Baltic to the Black Sea and held control over other territories in Central Europe, notably West Prussia and Pomerania. The combined forces of the union annihilated the Teutonic Knights in 1410, in the Battle of Grunewald. In order to preserve the union during the reign of Sigismund II (1548–72), the last of the Jagellonians, provisions were made for an elective monarch to be chosen by a single parliament (Sejm) for Poland and Lithuania.

Although the 16th century marked the golden age of Polish literature and scholarship, its political reforms contributed to the nation's subsequent decline. The Polish gentry (szlachta) had progressively gained influence and power at the expense of the king. Meeting in the Sejm, the gentry adopted the legislative practice whereby a single dissenting voice was sufficient to prevent passage. The nobility imposed such far-reaching limitations upon the monarchy that national unity and integrity could not be maintained. Internal disorders, including the Cossack and peasant uprising (1648–49) led by Bogdan Chmielnicki against Polish domination of the Ukraine—a revolt that struck with particular ferocity against Polish Jews, many of whom had served as agents of the nobility in administering Ukrainian lands—further weakened the nation. In 1683, Polish and German troops led by John III Sobieski (r.1674–96) rescued Vienna from a Turkish siege, but in wars with Sweden, Russia, and other states, Poland fared poorly. A Russian, Prussian, and Austrian agreement led to the first partitioning of Poland in 1772; the second (1793) and third (1795) partitions led to the demise of Poland as a sovereign state. Galicia was ruled by Austria-Hungary, northwestern Poland by Prussia, and the Ukraine and eastern and central Poland by Russia, which extended its domains to include the Duchy of Warsaw, reconstituted as the Kingdom of Poland (under Russian imperial rule) at the Congress of Vienna in 1815. The Poles rebelled in 1830 and 1863 against the tsarist rulers, but each insurrection was suppressed. However, the peasants were emancipated by Prussia in 1823, by Austria in 1849, and by Russia in 1864. Galicia, which won partial autonomy from Austria following the Habsburg monarchy's constitutional reforms, became the cultural center of the Poles.

With the Russian Revolution of 1917 and the defeat of the Central Powers in World War I, Poland regained its independence. On 18 November 1918, Józef Pilsudski, leader of the prewar anti-Russian independence movement, formed a civilian government. The Soviet army, meanwhile, began a westward advance that was met by a Polish counteroffensive. The conflict, in which Poland, seeking a return to its 1772 eastern border, was aided by France, ended with the Treaty of Riga in 1921, under which Galicia was restored to Poland.

Poland struggled through the next two decades plagued by economic deterioration and political instability, and by increasingly menacing pressures from its Soviet and German neighbors. Following the Nazi-Soviet Pact in 1939, Germany invaded Poland on 1 September, overrunning the country in eight days. Meanwhile, the USSR occupied the Lithuanian region on 17 September, although Poland had nonaggression treaties with both the USSR and Germany. By 1941, Nazi forces were brutally oppressing

large segments of the Polish population while looting Poland's industrial sector and major resources—timber, coal, and wheat. Ghettos were set up in Warsaw and other cities for Jews, and numerous concentration camps were established on Polish territory, including the extermination camp at Auschwitz, where at least 1 million people perished between 1940 and 1944. Poland as a whole suffered tremendous losses in life and property during World War II. An estimated 6 million Poles were killed, half of them Jews; 2.5 million were deported for compulsory labor in Germany; more than 500,000 were permanently crippled; and the remaining population suffered virtual starvation throughout the Nazi occupation. Losses in property were evaluated at z258 billion (more than $50 billion).

The seeds of Poland's postwar political history were sown long before the war ended. A Polish government-in-exile was set up in France and later in the UK. Units of the Polish army fought with the Allies, while in Poland underground groups, organized along political lines, maintained resistance activities. The Armia Krajowa (home army) was the major non-Communist resistance group. In July 1944, the Polish National Council, a Soviet-backed resistance group, set up the Polish Committee of National Liberation as a provisional government in liberated Lublin, declaring the émigré Polish government illegal. On 17 January 1945, Warsaw was liberated by the Soviet and Polish armies, and the provisional government moved to the capital. At Yalta, the Allies agreed to accept the Curzon line, thereby awarding the USSR nearly half of former Polish territory (including Galicia) in return for a Soviet agreement to broaden the political base of the provisional government with the addition of non-Communist Polish leaders. After subsequent negotiations, the Provisional Government of National Unity was formally recognized by the US and UK in July 1945.

A bloc of four parties dominated by the Communists won the elections of January 1947. The Communists and the Socialists merged in December 1948 to form the Polish United Workers' Party (PZPR). The PZPR consistently followed a pro-Soviet policy. Domestically, the party pursued a reconstruction program stressing agriculture and industrial development. It shunned the Marshall Plan and, in its first two decades, renounced all dealings with the Western powers.

The first decade of Communist rule was dominated by tensions with the Roman Catholic Church and the question of Soviet influence, as symbolized by Konstantin Rokossovsky, a Soviet general of Polish birth who became Poland's defense minister in 1949 and served as deputy prime minister from 1952 until his resignation four years later. Rising nationalist sentiment, heightened by stagnating economic conditions, led to worker riots in Poznań on 28–29 July 1956. In response to the unrest, a new Polish Politburo, headed by Wladyslaw Gomulka (who had been purged from the PZPR in 1949 and subsequently imprisoned because of his nationalist leanings), introduced liberalizations, including the abolition of farm collectivization, and improved relations with the Church. By the late 1950s, however, the reform movement had been halted, and the government took a harder line against dissent. In 1968 there were student demonstrations against the government in the university centers; the Gomulka regime countered with a political offensive in which many government officials and party members accused of anti-Socialist or pro-Zionist sentiments were removed from office, and an estimated 12,000 Polish Jews left Poland.

Two years later, following a drought in 1969 and an exceptionally severe winter, demonstrations by shipyard workers in Gdańsk broke out on 16 December 1970 protesting economic conditions, including the planned implementation of a new incentive system (threatening the existing system of bonuses and overtime pay) and an announced rise in food prices. After widespread violence, in which at least 44 people were killed, Edward Gierek, a member of the Politburo, succeeded Gomulka as first secretary on 20 December. Another strike began in Szczecin on 23 January 1971. The government then postponed the controversial incentive system and froze prices at their new levels. After receiving a substantial long-term Soviet grant (estimated at $100 million), the Polish government rolled back prices to their pre-December 1970 levels, and labor peace was restored. In a move to bolster his support, Gierek reinstated Church control over thousands of religious properties in northwestern Poland to which the government had held title since 1945.

During the 1970s, Gierek's government vigorously pursued a policy of détente with the West. Three US presidents visited Poland, and Gierek himself traveled to the US and to several West European countries. Peace agreements governing the Oder-Neisse line and formally recognizing Polish sovereignty in former German territories were concluded with the FRG, and trade pacts were signed with the US, UK, France, Italy, Austria, and other nations.

As Polish trade with the West increased, so did Poland's indebtedness to Western creditors. In 1976, the government announced food price increases but had to rescind them after the workers responded by striking. During the next several years, the economic situation kept deteriorating, and Polish nationalism—buoyed in 1978 by the election of the archbishop of Cracow to the papacy as John Paul II—continued to rise. In July 1980, new meat price increases were announced, and within a few weeks, well-organized workers all over Poland demanded a series of economic and political concessions. The center of labor activity was the Lenin Shipyard in Gdańsk, where, in an historic public ceremony on 31 August, government officials agreed to allow workers the right to form independent trade unions and the right to strike. The independent labor movement Solidarity, headed by Lech Walesa, the leader of the Gdańsk workers, emerged in early September and soon claimed a membership of about 10 million. That month, Stanislaw Kania replaced Gierek as party first secretary.

For more than a year, the government and Solidarity leaders negotiated, with Catholic Church officials often acting as mediators. As Solidarity became more and more overtly political—demanding, for example, free parliamentary elections—Poland's Communist leaders came under increasing pressure from the USSR to stop the "anti-Socialist" and "anti-Soviet" forces. On 18 October 1981, Gen. Wojciech Jaruzelski, prime minister since February, replaced Kania as PZPR first secretary. On 13 December, after union leaders in Gdańsk called for a national referendum on forming a non-Communist government in Poland, Jaruzelski set up the Military Council for National Salvation and declared martial law. Almost the whole leadership of Solidarity, including Walesa, was arrested, and the union was suspended. Despite further strikes and rioting, which resulted in several deaths, the military had soon gained complete control. More than 10,000 people were arrested and detained for up to 12 months, and all rights and freedoms gained in the preceding year and a half were abolished. In January 1982, the US imposed sanctions against Poland, including withdrawal of most-favored-nation status, veto of Poland's entry into the IMF, and suspension of fishing rights in US waters and of LOT flights to the US. Protests and rioting continued sporadically into 1983, and some Solidarity leaders remained active underground, but these disturbances did not seriously threaten the military regime. On 22 July 1983, the government formally ended martial law and proclaimed an amnesty, but a series of legislative measures had meanwhile institutionalized many of the powers the government had exercised during the emergency, including the power to dissolve organizations, forbid public meetings, and run the universities.

The internal political situation stabilized to such a degree that in July 1984 the government proclaimed a general amnesty, and

the US began to lift its sanctions the following month (the last sanctions were lifted in early 1987). In October, however, an outspoken priest, Father Jerzy Popieluszko, was kidnapped and subsequently murdered by two secret police officers. In an unprecedented step, the government, in February 1985, permitted a trial to take place; four security officers charged with complicity in the killing were convicted and sentenced (two to 25 years each, one to 15, and one to 14). Another amnesty was proclaimed in September 1986, leading to the release of all remaining political prisoners.

The efforts of the Jaruzelski government to restore order were largely successful on the political level, for Poland remained a comparatively tolerant and progressive Eastern Bloc nation. Economically, however, the country proved impervious to incremental change. Continued declines in standards of living led to waves of strikes throughout Poland in spring and fall 1988, essentially paralyzing the nation. Significantly, the demands of strikers, most led by Solidarity, began to become political as well as economic.

By November 1987 public antipathy had so grown that, hoping to avoid repetition of strikes caused by the necessity to raise prices, the government called for the first public referendum to be held in Poland for more than 40 years, which also was the first open election to be held within the Warsaw Pact. Although the ballot itself asked only for public support of an accelerated economic reform package, the people of Poland understood the referendum to be a vote of confidence in the government itself. The final tally was approximately two-thirds in support of the government, but because of a Solidarity-inspired voter boycott, just 67% of the eligible voters cast their ballots. By the rules of the election, this meant that the referendum had failed to pass, making this a first-ever defeat for the government.

In autumn 1988, the entire government resigned, making clear that talks with labor activists were unavoidable. The negotiations leading up to the so-called "round-table talks," which finally opened in February 1989, were delicate and prolonged, as were the negotiations themselves. However, in April 1989 agreement was reached on a number of unprecedented concessions: Solidarity was recognized as a legal entity; the post of president was created, to be filled by legislative appointment; some antigovernment media were permitted legal operation; and the Catholic Church was given full legal status. Perhaps the most farreaching agreement, though, was to establish a Senate, complementing the existing *Sejm*, with the seats to be filled by open election, in June 1989. In addition, 35% of the seats in the *Sejm* were also made subject to direct election.

The government made it as difficult as it could for opposition candidates to run: only two months were allowed in which candidates could gather the petitions necessary to get on the ballot, and the ballots themselves listed candidates alphabetically, with no indication of party affiliation. However, these attempts only served to make Solidarity's victory more resounding; 99 of the 100 seats in the Senate went to Solidarity members. Even more striking, many government candidates in the *Sejm* managed to even lose seats, because voters crossed out the names of unopposed government candidates, thus denying them the necessary 50% of the total votes cast.

In June 1989, the newly elected parliament named General Wojtech Jaruzelski Poland's president by the slenderest of margins, 270 to 233, with 34 abstentions, making plain how dependent the Communists now were on Solidarity. Even so, the thought of a Solidarity-led government seemed impossible, even to many of the union's members. Thus the first prime minister under the new arrangement was General Czeslaw Kiszczak, named 2 August 1989.

However, impatience with the obviously discredited Communists was growing, feeding support for a formula advanced by senior Soldarity activist Adam Michnik, "Your President, Our

Prime Minister." After a mere 15 days in office, General Kiszczak succumbed to this pressure and resigned.

Although it was widely expected that Lech Walesa might lead the first Solidarity government, he demurred, instead putting forward Tadeusz Mazowiecki, who took office on 24 August 1989, the first non-Communist prime minister in the eastern bloc.

The wave of "velvet revolutions" across eastern Europe that autumn accelerated the de-Sovietization of Polish government. Freely contested local elections were held in May 1990, further weakening the Communists' grip on power.

Although Jaruzelski had been elected to a six-year term as president, Walesa made it known in early 1990 that he was now prepared to stand for president in open elections. Jaruzelski resigned in September 1990, opening the way for new elections.

Although there were six major candidates, across a political spectrum from ultra-nationalist to ex-communist, the race was widely assumed to be between Walesa and Mazowiecki, each of whom offered variations on a Solidarity presidency. Ironically, the movement's victory over Communism had also exposed dissension which had lain dormant during the years of struggle, now fracturing the movement into several rival factions.

The results of the November 25 preliminary election were a major political shock. Although the leader, Walesa had managed to get only 40% of the vote, second place was taken by Stanislaw Tyminski, a mysterious ex-patriate with a shadowy past, who took 23% of the popular vote. Mazowiecki received only 18%, provoking widespread fears of ill-defined but profesionally-managed conspiracies to stop the advance of Polish democracy.

However, in the run-off with Walesa, held 9 December 1990, Tyminski received just under 25% of the vote. Although the Canadian ex-patriate made some attempts to consolidate his popularity in a party, by the parliamentary elections of 1993 Tyminski's popularity had so diminished that his Party X received less than 3% of the vote.

After 1990, the success of Poland's "revolution," combined with economic dislocations caused by the country's rapid transition to a market economy, also demonstrated some of the drawbacks of ongoing democratization. The number of political parties ballooned, diluting the impact that any one party or group of parties was able to have, making it difficult to undertake such complex and contentious issues as large-scale privatization, economic rationalization of Soviet-era giant industry, and fundamental constitutional revision. The October 1991 election saw 69 parties competing, with 29 actually winning seats, none of them with more than 14% of the vote. Inevitably this resulted in coalition governments without clear mandates, giving Poland five prime ministers and four governments in 1991–93. Even so, the parliament enacted important legislation in that period, including the "Little Constitution" of 17 October 1992, which in the absence of a complete constitution provides much of the necessary framework for a democratic society.

This proliferation of parties reflected disparities among the electorate which emerged once the communists had been removed as a unifying focus for opposition. In addition to tensions between the clear winners and losers which economic transformation were producing, splits also became more apparent between the 40% of Poland which is rural, and thus desirous of continued protection for small-plot agriculture, and the 60% which is urban, and wishing to open Poland to European imports and influence. Also important were growing tensions between secular intellectuals and the powerful Catholic Church, which moved to assert close control on social issues like abortion, school curriculum, and women's role in society.

These issues, exacerbated by continued economic strains and growing uncertainty about the course of post-Communist Russia, contributed to the unexpected return to power of many ex-Communists in the September 1993 parliamentary elections. In that election the number of parties had dropped to 35, of which only five, plus a coalition, received seats. However the two most popular parties, the Polish Peasant Party (15.4%) and the Democratic Left Alliance (20.4%), were made up largely of ex-Communists or other figures from the governments of the past. Their influence was further amplified by voting rules which assigned the cumulative votes for parties which failed to reach the necessary thresholds for gaining seats to winning parties, thus giving the two "ex-Communist" parties a comfortable two-thirds majority.

This apparent rejection of the gains of Solidarity and the democrats was variously interpreted as a rejection of "shock-therapy" economic transformation, as the electorate's nostalgia for the more ordered life of the past, and as a vote against the Catholic Church, or at least its social agenda, the power of which had grown under Solidarity and its progeny. Another factor frequently mentioned was the greater professionalism of the ex-Communists, who ran much more effective campaigns than did most of their opponents. Finally, Walesa and his supporters were also seen to be suffering because they are now the responsible authorities, and hence provide the same target for opposition which they once found in the Communists.

However, local elections held 19 June 1994, suggest that fears of some return to Communism under the new government have proven unfounded. Voters demonstrated the ability to select representatives who would serve their own interests, returning about 20% of the incumbents to local office, and selecting other officials from across a broad political spectrum. The Democratic Left Alliance and Polish Peasant Party retained their dominance, but centrist and right-of-center parties also did well. This suggests that, although they differ from their predecessors on the pace of Poland's economic transformation, the government of Polish Peasant Party leader Waldemar Pawlak, and his Democratic Left Alliance partner, Aleksander Kwasniewski (now head of the Constitutional Commission), remains generally committed to Poland's course of democratization and economic transition. A further guarantee comes in President Walesa, who announced his intention, despite his very low popularity, to fight for a second term of office when presidential elections are next held, in December 1995.

13 GOVERNMENT

The form of government in Poland is in the midst of a protracted transformation, which leaves a number of its important features unclear. Aleksander Kwasniewski, leader of the Democratic Left Alliance (SLD) and present head of the Constitutional Commission, has announced his intention to produce a complete draft constitution during the current parliament, no later than the end of 1995. The absence of a dominant coalition, as well as the complexity of the issues which the Constitutional Commission must confront, make many observers doubt whether this timetable can be met.

Without a new formal constitution, Poland has been functioning on a much-amended form of its Communist-era constitution. The most important recent modifications were the Jaruzelski government's concessions of April 1989, which created both the Senate and the office of President, and a package of amendments passed in October 1992, which are collectively called the "Little Constitution." Another important modification was the agreement of 1990, which made the presidency a popularly elected post, rather than one of parliamentary appointment.

The present system is a difficult marriage of a presidential and a parliamentary system. The president is directly elected, for a term of six years. The post has traditional executive obligations and powers, such as the duty to sign into law or veto legislations, but also retains substantial legislative powers, including the right to introduce bills and draft legal amendments. The president has asserted the right to select the prime minister and other key ministers, such as finance and defense, from among candidates put forward by the ruling coalition or party; that right, however, was disputed by the Pawlak government, which sees the president's role as consultative. The current president, Lech Walesa, has also asserted, but not attempted to exercise, a presidential right to disperse parliament.

Walesa has fought to widen the powers of the presidency, arguing that, at least during this transition period, Poland requires a strong president who is able to resolve impasses and disputes on the basis of "practical experience," rather than on points of legal niceties. For the most part, though, this fight has been in vain.

The parliament consists of two houses, the *Sejm*, or lower house, with 460 seats, and the Senate, with 100 seats. Seats are filled on the basis of party lists; there is a minimum national vote threshhold of 5% for parties, or 8% for coalitions, with the votes for parties which fail to reach those minimums assigned to victorious parties. In the 1993 election, this magnified the gains of the SDL and PSL, giving them a total of 303 seats in the *Sejm* and 73 seats in the Senate.

The government, which appoints the Council of Ministers, is drawn from the party with majority parliamentary representation. In the absence of such a majority—which has been the case in every post-Communist parliament—coalitions are necessary.

During 1991–93, the period of the so-called "Solidarity" governments, there were reasonably cordial relations among the president, the parliament, and the governments, especially that of the last "Solidarity" government, headed by Prime Minister Hanna Suchocka, which permitted relatively smooth functioning of the assumptions of the "Little Constitution." The installation of the SLD-PSL government has exposed the dependency of the president on government and parliamentary support. With a party system determining the shape of the parliament, and a president who must sign legislation but who has no party representation in the parliament or government, the present system tends toward gridlock.

In the absence of a full constitution, the issue of the judiciary has remained largely unresolved. In general the Poles have been reluctant to undertake lustration of Communist-era judges, but fears about the fair-mindedness of people who served the earlier regime undermine the public's belief in the judiciary. An attempt was made to address this problem in a law enacted 9 September 1993, permitting removal of judges for "betraying principles of independence;" whether this law will have the desired effect remains to be seen.

Clearly the most crucial issue in Poland's immediate future is the passage of a constitution, which the present battles between president and government make more difficult. The government has announced intentions to conduct a national "pre-referendum" on the constitution, allowing the people to indicate their preferences on such basic issues as strong vs. weak presidency, and interventionist vs. laissez-faire economic policy.

14POLITICAL PARTIES

After the political poverty of its Communist past, Poland exploded in a rich exuberance of political parties, which ranged across the full political spectrum, from the rabidly xenophobic nationalism of the Polish National Front (whose leader, Janusz Bryczkowski, invited Russian extremist Vladimir Zhirinovsky to Poland in 1994) to the socialist party, Union of Labor (UP). In between, or sometimes even taking positions not to be found on ordinary political spectra, were special interest and even quirky parties, of which the best example may be the Polish Beerdrinkers' Party. A full 69 parties participated in the 1991 parliamentary elections, of which 29 gained seats, none of them with more than 14% of the total vote.

By 1993, however, the political scene was showing signs of stabilizing. Only 35 parties took part in that election; perhaps more significantly, only five received seats, as did members of a coalition of parties. That election, distorted in part by laws assigning the votes of unsuccessful parties to more successful ones, seemed to indicate a strong shift toward the left.

The local elections of 1994, however, indicated that Poland is coalescing into three basic political orientations, which are served by shifting coalitions of parties. On the right in that election were two large coalitions: the Alliance for Poland, which included the Christian National Union, the Center Alliance, the Movement for the Republic, the Peasant Alliance, and the Conservative Coalition; and the 11 November Agreement, which included the Conservative Party, the Party of Christian Democrats, the Christian-Peasant Alliance, and the Real Politics Union (a radical *laissez-faire* party). These parties generally favor a major role for the Catholic Church, and tend to draw their support from Poland's rural sectors; in 1994, they did best in the eastern districts. In general, though, public support for the right, especially the religious right, appears to be limited.

The center is dominated by Freedom Union (UW), which was formed in April 1994, when the Liberal Democratic Congress merged with the Democratic Union. The centrist position derives largely from the intellectual wing of the original Solidarity, favoring radical economic transformation, while being less concerned with immediate impact upon workers. UW draws much of its support from smaller cities, especially university ones, such as Cracow.

The left, which was almost entirely discredited in 1991, has shown remarkable resilience, demonstrated by their reluctance to join coalitions in 1994 balloting. The two major parties are the Democratic Left Alliance (SLD), which incorporates the Social Democracy of Republic of Poland party (SDRP), the formal inheritor of the Communist party, and the Communist-era trade union federation (OPZZ), and the Polish Peasant Party (PSL), which is the descendent of the Communist party's old ruling partner, the United Peasant Party (ZSL).

In the 1993 parliamentary election, SLD got 171 seats and PSL got 132 seats, making them by far the strongest parties in Poland. Although they share generally left-wing orientations, which favor extension of the social safety net, considerable government intervention in the functioning of the economy, and a more balanced position between Europe and Russia, the two parties serve different constituencies. SLD has its support in Warsaw and the other large industrial cities, especially Lodz (long known as "red Lodz"), while the PSL is an agricultural party, more interested in blocking food imports and preserving high subsidies for farmers. Both parties are secularist in orientation, and in concert have blocked passage of the Concordat with the Vatican which the previous parliament had arranged but not passed.

In the 1993 elections, President Walesa sponsored a Nonparty Bloc to Support Reforms (BBWR), in an effort to unite the post-Solidarity parties against the post-Communists, but none of the post-Solidarity parties wished to be identified with the President, who has become deeply unpopular in the country. As a consequence BBWR did poorly, barely reaching the parliament, and depriving Walesa of a party of support in parliament.

15LOCAL GOVERNMENT

Poland is divided into 49 administrative districts, or voivods, which were the basic administrative units under the Communists. One of the innovations of the 1989 Solidarity government was to replace that system with one in which the basic unit is the *gmina*, or local authority, which owns property and has responsibility for its own budget. The *gmina* elects a council, which appoints the executive officials actually responsible for day-to-day administration of the locality.

In 1994, there were 2,383 such local councils, to which the law provides a mixed system of election. In districts containing more than 40,000 people, of which there were 110 in 1994, council representation is proportionally determined, based upon party affiliation. In the smaller districts council representatives are elected by direct majority vote.

Originally these *gmina* councils were similar in make-up to the Solidarity Citizens Committees, from which they descended. Increasingly, however, the councils have differentiated themselves, some becoming controlled by national parties, while others remain dominated by personalities, who respond primarily to local issues.

When Prime Minister Pawlak's government assumed power, the attempt was made to shift the system towards greater proportional voting, with the goal of strengthening the hold of the PSL and SLD on local administrations, where the two leftist parties had done poorly in the 1990 elections. However, fearing a wholesale purge of existing administrations, the parliament refused to pass the necessary legislation, leaving the present system intact.

It is generally agreed that the *gmina* councils are a success, better able to determine local needs and priorities than were the national bodies which they replaced. It is said that council-run projects are run at 60–80% of the cost which national bodies once incurred.

[16] JUDICIAL SYSTEM

The judiciary is supervised by the Ministry of Justice, which also oversees the training and practice of lawyers. There is no private practice, and lawyers belong to legal collectives. The prosecutor-general, independent of the Ministry of Justice, is appointed by the Council of State and is responsible to it. He appoints the prosecutors on the lower administrative levels, who in turn are responsible to him and are independent of the local authorities.

The Supreme Court, the highest judicial organ, functions primarily as a court of appeal. Its judges are elected by the Council of State for five-year terms. The Supreme Court is divided into criminal, civil, military, and labor and social insurance chambers. In addition, there are voivodeship and other regional courts, as well as special courts such as military tribunals, children's courts, and courts for cases involving social insurance. Misdemeanor courts, supervised by the Ministry of Internal Affairs, were used extensively by martial-law authorities, while military courts tried major economic and social crimes.

In July 1993, legislation was passed reestablishing intermediate level appellate courts for the first time since before World War II. These courts will consider procedural issues only. There is now a Constitutional Tribunal which offers opinions on legislation and exercises no real authority of judicial review.

Most judges are holdovers from the Communist era who lack extensive legal training. A 1993 law makes it possible for the Ministry of Justice to recall a judge determined by a disciplinary commission to have failed to exercise "court independence." While purportedly designed to guarantee judicial independence, this law grants the executive the power to recall judges. This law is currently being challenged before the Constitutional Tribunal.

[17] ARMED FORCES

The conscription law of January 1959 provides for registration at 18 and service (18 months) at age 20. Polish armed forces numbered 296,500 (167,400 conscripts) in 1993, including 195,000 in 13 army divisions and 10 specialized brigades. Navy personnel totaled 19,300. The air force had 83,000 men and 424 combat aircraft of Soviet design. The reserve had about 435,000 active members in 1993.The Ministry of Interior had 20,000 troops and border guards. Defense expenditures for 1991, as officially reported, amounted to $2.4 billion. Arms exports during 1981–91 were valued at $7 billion and imports at $8 billion.

Poland provides 1,100 servicemen to 7 different nations as observers.

[18] INTERNATIONAL COOPERATION

Poland is a charter member of the UN, having signed on 24 October 1945. It participates in ECE and all the nonregional specialized agencies except IDA, IFAD, IFC, and ILO. Poland became a member of IBRD and IMF in 1986. Poland belongs to CMEA and WTO, and is a signatory to GATT and the Law of the Sea.

[19] ECONOMY

Until recently, Poland had a centrally planned economy that was primarily state controlled. Agriculture, however, was only partly socialized, with state farms and cooperatives accounting for 23% of the country's total farmland in 1984. Since World War II, agriculture's predominance in the economy has been waning; in 1990, it accounted for 16.2% of the NMP, compared to 22.7% in 1970. Poland, with its sizable coastline, has become a maritime nation of some note, having developed three major ports on the Baltic and a greatly expanded shipbuilding industry, which in 1991 produced 53 ships. Although Poland has rich coal deposits, it lacks important natural resources, such as petroleum and iron ore, and must export in order to pay for the raw materials it needs.

During 1971–75, Poland's NMP increased by about 12.8% annually; the growth was, to a substantial degree, the result of credits from the West. After 1975, however, Poland's economic performance deteriorated because of excessive investments, internal market problems, several bad harvests, the worldwide recession, and the political upheaval of 1980–81. An economic growth rate of 2.5% annually during 1976–78 was followed by declines of 2% in 1979, 4% in 1980, 12% in 1981, and 5.5% in 1982, while the debt to Western governments reached nearly $25 billion by 1983, rising to $33 billion in 1991, when the total hard-currency debt reached $52.5 billion. During 1980–91, the GNP grew at an annual average rate of only 1.2%. Inflation averaged 54.3% annually in the 1980s.

With Poland subjected to the "shock therapy" of a transition to a market economy, GDP fell 31.5% between 1990–92 before rising 4% in 1993. By 1992, the private sector accounted for almost half of economic activity. Consumer prices shot up almost sixfold in 1990, another 70% in 1991, 43% in 1992, and 35% in 1993. Unemployment rose to 15.7% at the end of 1993.

[20] INCOME

In 1992, the GNP was $75,268 million at current prices, or $1,960 per capita. For the period 1985–92 the average inflation rate was 124.2%, resulting in a real growth rate in per capita GNP of −1.9%.

In 1992, the GDP was $83,823 million in current US dollars.

[21] LABOR

The labor force in 1992 totaled 17,529,000 persons, with 21.4% of the workers engaged in agriculture. Some 3,884,000 were employed in community, social, and personal services. About 3,827,000 persons were engaged in mining, manufacturing, and utilities. Recorded private sector employment rose from 38% to 43% in 1991, and to 60% by mid-1993. There is considerable rural underemployment and some unemployment, due mainly to the large percentage of Poland's population aged 15 to 30 (27% in 1992). By the end of 1991, the total unemployment rate rose from 11.4% to 13.6%, and climbed to 14.6% by mid-1993, amounting to 2.7 million Poles without work. Official statistical omissions of rural unemployment are offset somewhat by those who work in the underground economy.

The trade union act of 1949 consolidated the existing unions into the Central Council of Labor Unions. Under labor legislation enacted during the first three decades of Communist rule, collective agreements were concluded yearly on such matters as production norms, socialist competition, and labor discipline, but wages, hours, pensions, sick leave, and vacations were established by law. After 1956, arbitration commissions, elected by workers' councils, were entrusted with the settling of labor disputes. Also established in 1956 were labor inspectors, attached to the provincial councils of the unions, to check for violations of labor laws by management. Workers were guaranteed sick pay, overtime pay, paid vacations, and paid maternity leave. Beginning in 1972, farm workers and their families were covered by a free medical care plan.

From the point of view of government planners, labor productivity rose too slowly in the 1960s, and overtime and absenteeism were considered excessive in some industries. In 1962, a system of bonuses linked to physical output quotas was introduced as an incentive for production. Gradually, however, such bonuses became more or less institutionalized as an expected and important part of the workers' pay. When, in 1970, the government sought to introduce a new system (originally scheduled for full implementation in 1971) in which bonuses would depend on a complex system of enterprise profit indicators, there was dissatisfaction over the possibility of pay losses and, further, of the loss of comfortable jobs in the more inefficient enterprises. It was in the context of these apprehensions that the consumer price increases decreed shortly before Christmas 1970 touched off widespread protests, sufficiently severe in the northern port cities to force a major changeover in the government. Unrest subsided only after the new government, on 25 January 1971, canceled the wage adjustment.

A pivotal chapter in Polish labor history began in August 1980, when, after a series of strikes in Gdańsk and elsewhere (including Silesia, where most of the coal mines were closed), the government authorized the formation of independent labor unions. On 5 September, a new national labor movement, called Solidarity, was born. Solidarity achieved legal status in October 1980—but only on condition that it recognize the "leading role" of the PZPR—and within a short time claimed a membership of almost 10 million. The goals of Solidarity included a five-day workweek, worker self-management, an easing of censorship, and other economic and political reforms. In May 1981, Rural Solidarity, a labor union of independent farmers, won legal recognition. At the first national congress of Solidarity, held in September and October 1981, Lech Walesa was elected national chairman. Walesa and other Solidarity leaders were detained in December 1981, when martial law was imposed. All existing labor organizations were outlawed on 8 October 1982. New unions, authorized at that time and formally constituted in January 1983, were to be confined to individual factories or workplaces and, although theoretically independent, were in fact closely supervised by the government. The rights to strike and to leave one's job were severely limited, and national coordination of individual unions was prohibited. In February 1986, the government issued a decree permitting an extension of the workweek to 46 hours (6 days), thus rescinding one of the few remaining concessions won by Solidarity. In 1988, strikes resumed, as a protest to the government's attempt to eliminate food subsidies. The Solidarity movement was permitted to resume at the demand of the workers. The government then resigned, and Solidarity earnestly participated in the negotiations with the interim Council of Ministers on economic and constitutional reforms. In 1989, Solidarity was legalized once again. In 1992, there were 6,351 work stoppages involving 752,500 workers resulting in 1,855,400 lost workdays.

Since the government forsook central planning, Poland has struggled with the transformation of over 8,000 state-owned enterprises into viable private corporations. By mid-1993, 2,400 enterprises had began the privatization process, with 777 completing privatization. The long-term goal of the government was 10% employee ownership of privatized enterprises.

22AGRICULTURE

In 1991, agriculture employed 26.7% of the Polish labor force (as compared with 53.5% in 1948 and 39.9% in 1967). About 62% of Poland's land is agricultural; of this area, 78% is cultivated. Overall agricultural output during 1971–75 rose by nearly 27%, or 5.4% annually. Between 1976 and 1982, agricultural production dropped by 10%; between 1985 and 1990, it declined by 0.5%. In 1992, the agricultural sector shrank by 16.9% due to the effects of a serious drought throughout Central Europe, which led to crop losses as high as 25%. In 1992, agriculture accounted for 6.5% of GDP, down from 14.5% in 1985.

The transition from an agricultural economy is due partly to territorial changes resulting from World War II; largely agricultural areas were transferred to the USSR, whereas the areas acquired in the west were predominantly industrial. During the war, approximately one-third of the Polish farms were completely or partly laid waste, and five-sixths of the hogs and two-thirds of the cattle and sheep were destroyed, leaving farmers almost without draft animals and fertilizer. At the same time, population transfers delayed cultivation in the areas of resettlement.

Land redistribution followed both world wars but was much more extensive after World War II. A 1944 decree expropriated all holdings larger than 100 hectares (247 acres); land belonging to Germans or collaborators was also expropriated. Attempts at collectivization were generally resisted; after 1956, most collective farms were disbanded and their land redistributed. As of 1992, about 3.7 million Poles were engaged in small plot farming (with an average farm size of 6 hectares/15 acres) on 2.1 million private farms, which produced about 75% of agricultural output.

In 1992, the principal crops and their yields (in thousands of tons) were potatoes, 23,388; meadow hay, 15,098; sugar beets, 11,052; wheat, 7,368; rye, 3,981; barley, 2,819; and oats, 1,236. Yields have been poor because of infertile soil, insufficient use of fertilizers, and inadequate mechanization, in addition to the drought. There were 1,178,000 tractors in 1991, up from 620,724 during 1979–81. Although grain production has been Poland's traditional agricultural pursuit, since World War II, Poland has become an importer—instead of an exporter—of grains, particularly wheat. Imports of wheat, barley, and corn amounted to 6,919,000 tons in 1980 but have fluctuated from 2,224,000 tons in 1985, to 1,561,000 tons in 1990 to 2,282,300 tons in 1992 because of foreign exchange.

23ANIMAL HUSBANDRY

The government has encouraged the development of livestock production through increased fodder supply and improvement in breeding stock and partial tax relief for hog raising. Emphasis has been placed on the raising of hogs and sheep. In 1992, there were 22.1 million pigs (of which 2.1 million were sows), 8.2 million head of cattle (of which 4.3 million were cows), 1.9 million sheep, 900,000 horses, and 58 million poultry.

A severe drought in 1992 adversely affected grain prices, causing livestock herds to shrink throughout the first half of 1993. Additionally, the EC (Poland's primary market for fresh agricultural products) banned meat imports from Poland because of concerns about hoof-and-mouth disease, just when farmers were marketing spring lamb and veal. Livestock products in 1992 included 2,989,000 tons of meat (down from 3,068,000 tons in 1991), 12.8 million tons of milk, and 389,000 tons of eggs.

24FISHING

Most of the fishing industry has been brought under state ownership. Sea fishing is conducted in the Baltic and North seas and in the Atlantic (Labrador, Newfoundland, and African waters), and there are inland fisheries in lakes, ponds, and rivers. The 1992 saltwater catch was 409,389 tons, predominantly herring and cod; freshwater fishing yielded about 48,000 tons.

25 FORESTRY

As of 1991, 29% of Poland's land was forested. Pine, larch, spruce, and fir are the most important varieties of trees. The Wielkopolski National Forest, a reservation in Rogalin, is famous for its thousand-year-old oak trees. Wood processing occurs in the Biala Podlaska region, while large areas of forest in the Zamosc region foster development in the furniture industry. Poland was once an exporter of timber, but given the booming construction of private homes, domestic production does not meet local demand. In 1991, wood amounting to 12.7 million cu m from coniferous trees and 4.3 million cu m from broad-leaved trees was produced. In 1992, production of wood and paper increased by 13.9% over 1991.

The government has been attempting to offset losses from territorial redistribution and wartime destruction by afforestation.

26 MINING

In 1991, dissolution of state price controls and subsidies and the gradual privatization of the economy resulted in lower production of most mineral commodities. The acquisition of former German territories in 1945 enriched Poland with hard coal and, to a lesser extent, zinc and lead. Iron ore is found around Czestochowa in south-central Poland, but in deposits of low metal content. Other deposits are uranium (found in Lower Silesia), salt, and sulfur.

The most significant raw material is hard coal. Poland's coal industry was the seventh largest in the world in 1991. The 1991 output consisted of 209 million tons of hard coal, 140 million tons of which were bituminous, and 69 million tons were lignite. Estimated hard-coal reserves total 65.5 billion tons, of bituminous and 12.8 billion tons of lignite.

In 1991, Poland ranked seventh in the world in mine output of copper, with 390,000 tons; ninth in refined copper production, with a reported 378,000 tons; eleventh in mine output of zinc, at 175,000 tons; seventh in silver mine output, at a reported 899,000 kg; and fifth in sulfur, with 3.8 million tons. Poland must import iron ore, nickel, manganese, cobalt, copper, and potash.

27 ENERGY AND POWER

The main domestic energy sources are coal, lignite, and peat; rivers remain a largely untapped source of power. In 1991, the net installed capacity was 30,984,000 kw and production was 134,696 million kwh (2.5% hydroelectric). In 1991, about 77% of Poland's total energy requirement was fulfilled by coal. In 1992, Poland produced about 198 million tons of coal. Proven coal reserves at the end of 1992 amounted to 41.2 billion tons (72% anthracite and bituminous, 28% subbituminous and lignite), or 4% of the world's total. Coal production decreased by 5.8% in 1992. Poland is the world's seventh largest coal producer and exporter. Poland has no oil deposits but produces over one-third of its natural gas needs; production was 3,900 million cu m in 1992. Poland is increasingly looking toward the Middle East for its oil supply, due to the current uncertain economic and political climate in the former USSR.

28 INDUSTRY

Leading industries in 1993 included food processing (21.5% of total output), fuel (16.2%), metals and metal products (8.9%), and chemicals (5.8%). Industrial production increased by 14.5% annually during 1971–75, but in the late 1970s, the growth rate began to fall. During the 1980s, it grew at an annual rate of 1.1%. With the destabilizing effects of the dissolution of the Soviet bloc and central planning, industrial production fell by 26% in 1990 and 12% in 1991. It grew by 5.6% in 1993, however. In 1991, private-sector industrial output grew to one-fourth of the total.

Poland produced 9.9 million tons of steel in 1993. Sulfur is another important industrial commodity; production in 1993 totaled 1,901 tons. The cement industry turned out 12.3 million tons during the same year. All these totals were lower than in the 1980s, however. Light industries were long relegated to a secondary position but, since the 1970s, Poland has increased its production of durable household articles and other consumer goods. In 1993, Poland produced 401,000 automatic washing machines, 584,000 refrigerators and freezers, 841,000 television sets, 307,000 radios, and 21,000 tape recorders and dictaphones.

29 SCIENCE AND TECHNOLOGY

Destruction of the Polish scientific community, buildings, and equipment during World War II was nearly total, requiring a tremendous rebuilding program. Attached to the various university faculties and government bodies are institutes, laboratories, and clinics devoted primarily to research, but some offering advanced instruction. In 1952, the Polish Academy of Sciences, established in Warsaw, replaced the old Polish Academy of Sciences and Letters of Cracow. As of 1993, 43 scientific and technological research institutes were affiliated with the Academy of Sciences, and there were 78 scientific and technological research institutes attached to government ministries. Research and development expenditures in 1989 amounted to z1.2 billion. Personnel engaged in research and development that year included 32,500 scientists and engineers.

30 DOMESTIC TRADE

As of 1980, 89.5% of the internal trade network, including all wholesale trade, was in the socialized sector. Marketing and distribution, including price fixing, were controlled and supervised by the Ministry of Internal Trade and the State Price Board; on the lower level, provincial and district councils administered the trade program, but cooperatives also participated in distribution. The state bought produce from private farmers under a system of long-term purchase contracts; farmers could sell their surplus on the free market. Food subsidies were cut by more than half in 1990 as part of a continuing program to reduce the budget deficit.

In 1985, Poland had 142,084 shops (20,690 private). The total number of retail trade establishments in 1985 was 219,759, of which 37,545 were private. Retail trade by volume fell by 2.7% in 1989 and 17.4% in 1990, but rose 7.4% in 1991. Private trade grew rapidly as the government moved to dismantle state monopolies.

Offices are open from 8 or 9 AM to 4 PM Monday through Friday. Food stores are open from 6 or 7 AM to 7 PM; other stores, from 11 AM to 7 or 8 PM; and banks, from 9 AM to 4 PM Monday through Friday, and 9 AM to 1 PM on Saturday. The most important trade exhibition, the Poznan International Fair, takes place in June.

31 FOREIGN TRADE

Until recently, foreign trade was a state monopoly under the control of the Ministry of Foreign Trade. After World War II, the orientation of Polish trade shifted from Western and Central European countries to Eastern Europe. This changed with the dissolution of the Soviet-bloc CMEA in 1991. In December of that year, Poland signed an association agreement with the EC.

Germany is Poland's most important supplier and customer, accounting for 23.9% of Poland's imports and 31.4% of its exports in 1992. The USSR used to be Poland's leading trade partner, but Russia fell to a distant second in the 1990s as hard currency replaced barter-type arrangements.

Principal exports for 1992 and 1993 included mineral fuels; chemicals and products; machinery and transport equipment; and food and live animals.

Principal trade partners in 1992 (in billions of zlotys) were as follows:

	EXPORTS	IMPORTS	BALANCE
Russia	9,925	18,702	–8,777
Germany	56,488	52,582	3,906
France	6,552	9,804	–3,252
Netherlands	10,752	10,386	366
UK	7,704	14,732	–7,028
Romania	9,980	15,236	–5,256
Austria	5,748	9,870	–4,122
Other countries	72,538	88,638	–16,100
TOTAL	179,687	219,950	–40,263

³²BALANCE OF PAYMENTS

Measured in terms of commodity trade figures, negative balances have been the rule in Poland in the post–World War II period. As of 1992, Poland was running a small trade deficit in its convertible currency account; the non-convertible currency account was in surplus. In 1991, the collapse of exports to the Soviet Union dealt a sharp blow to overall export performance. The requirement to exchange by means of hard currency for Soviet raw materials and energy prevented a repeat of the 1990 trade surplus.

In 1992, merchandise exports totaled $13,926 million and imports $14,000 million. The merchandise trade balance was $–134 million. The following table summarizes Poland's balance of payments for 1991 and 1992 (in millions of US dollars):

	1991	1992
CURRENT ACCOUNT		
Goods, services, and income	–2,914	–3,570
Unrequited transfers	768	466
TOTALS	–2,146	–3,104
CAPITAL ACCOUNT		
Direct investment	298	665
Portfolio investment	—	—
Other long-term capital	–2,616	–935
Other short-term capital	–1,286	–775
Exceptional financing	5,342	4,946
Other liabilities	—	—
Reserves	1,175	–649
TOTALS	2,913	3,252
Errors and omissions	–767	–148
Total change in reserves	1,204	–500

³³BANKING AND SECURITIES

The Banking Law of 1 July 1982 substantially reformed the Polish banking system by giving banks an effective role in setting monetary and credit policy, thereby allowing them to influence economic planning. The Council of Banks, consisting of top bank officers and representatives of the Planning Commission and the Ministry of Finance, is the principal coordinating body.

The National Bank of Poland (Narodowy Bank Polski), created in 1945 to replace the former Bank of Poland, is a state institution and the bank of issue. It also controls foreign transactions and prepares financial plans for the economy. On 1 January 1970, the National Bank merged with the Investment Bank and has since controlled funds for finance and investment transactions of state enterprises and organizations. The function of the Food Economy Bank and its associated cooperative banks is to supply short- and long-term credits to rural areas. The national commercial bank, Bank Handlowy w Warszawie, finances foreign trade operations. The General Savings Bank (Bank Polska Kasa Opieki—PKO), a central institution for per-

sonal savings, also handles financial transfers into Poland of persons living abroad.

Time, savings, and foreign currency deposits increased from z25.1 billion in 1975 to z1,351.1 billion in 1985 and z25,409 billion in 1992. In March 1985, two types of hard-currency accounts were introduced: "A" accounts, bearing interest, for currency earned in an approved way; and "B" accounts, for other currency, bearing no interest. "B" accounts can be converted into "A" accounts after one year. Banking laws in 1989 opened the country's banking system to foreign banks.

Major enterprises in Poland conduct their business by interaccount settlements through the National Bank rather than by check, and wages are paid in cash.

Poland has no stock exchange, nor are stocks traded.

³⁴INSURANCE

In 1948, all insurance other than social insurance was included in a centralized State Insurance Bureau, with the former reinsurance organization, Warta, continuing its activity. As of 1994, Warta had been privatized and was one of three major insurers who, together, controlled over 90% of Poland's insurance market. Since the 1990 liberalization of Poland's insurance law, 21 new firms have been licensed. In 1990, premiums totaled US $19.3 per capita, or 1.2% of the GDP. Claims totaled z15 trillion in 1992, and life insurance in force totaled z112,300 billion.

³⁵PUBLIC FINANCE

The annual budget is presented to the *Sejm* in December and becomes effective for the fiscal year beginning on 1 January. The state budget, prepared by the Ministry of Finance, constitutes a financial plan for the entire economy, and includes provincial and district budgets. The state budget for 1992 included z312.8 billion in revenues, and z381.9 billion in expenditures (including z19.5 billion in capital expenditures). The budget ran a deficit of z69.1 billion in 1992.

In 1990, Poland's total external debt with western creditors reached $46.6 billion (4.3 times annual export earnings), and had climbed to approximately $48 billion by the end of 1992 (3 times export earnings). The external debt in 1993 was equivalent to 28.8% of GDP, down from 32.8% in 1991.

³⁶TAXATION

Corporations are taxed at a flat rate of 40% of total taxable income. Companies must also pay a tax of 20% on wages paid to Polish workers. Polish residents pay tax on their worldwide income, while non-residents are taxed only on income earned in Poland. Tax rates for residents are progressive, ranging from 20–40%, with a 20% withholding tax. A 22% value-added tax took effect in 1993.

³⁷CUSTOMS AND DUTIES

Under the terms of a 1991 agreement, Poland uses the EC Nomenclature System of Tariff classification and has granted duty-free status to over 1,000 line items from EC countries. Tariffs range from 0–45%, averaging 14%.

³⁸FOREIGN INVESTMENT

Prior to World War II, considerable foreign capital was invested in the Polish economy, particularly in petroleum and mining, which were mostly foreign-owned. A nationalization decree in 1946 confiscated enemy properties and nationalized Poland's industries, eliminating foreign investments completely. The decree provided for no compensation procedures and foreign governments involved negotiated directly with Poland. The first joint venture with Western counterparts (one Austrian and one US company) was formed in early 1987 to build a new airport terminal in Warsaw. In mid-1991, there were 4,100 foreign registrations, worth

$506 million, and in 1993 another $2 billion in foreign investment entered Poland. Among the industrial companies sold to Western interests were Polam-Pila (light bulbs) to Phillips, Polkolor (TV sets) to Thomson, Pollena-Bydgoszcz (detergents) to Unilever, and Wedel (confectioneries) to Pepsico Foods.

39ECONOMIC DEVELOPMENT

After World War II, the economy of Poland was centrally planned and almost completely under state control, especially in nonagricultural sectors. The nationalized industries and businesses operated within the national economic plan and were governed by the directives issued by the pertinent ministries. After 1963, however, centralized planning and management were somewhat relaxed, and state-owned enterprises gained more freedom in the design and implementation of their programs. Private undertakings were confined to personal crafts and trades and agriculture.

Economic planning followed Soviet lines, setting production goals that determined tasks for each sector on a long-term basis. Under the three-year plan for 1947–49, principal emphasis was placed on the reconstruction of war-devastated areas and industries, in order to raise production and living conditions at least to their prewar levels. Under the six-year plan for 1950–55, the emphasis continued to be on heavy industry, and the housing, transport, agriculture, and consumer sectors lagged. The five-year plan for 1956–60, originally cast along the same lines, was modified after the 1956 disturbances. It called for a lessened rate of industrial expansion and for increases in agricultural output, housing, consumer goods, and social services. Under a long-range plan for 1961–75, which governed the three five-year plans falling within that period, emphasis was placed on a direct improvement in living standards. The first and second of these plans (1961–65 and 1966–70) were oriented toward investments intended (1) to develop the raw-material base of the country, especially the newly discovered resources of sulfur, copper, and lignite; (2) to secure employment opportunities for the rapidly growing population of working age; and (3) to improve Poland's international trade balance. The five-year plan for 1961–65 reached its industrial targets but fell short in the areas of agriculture and consumer goods. The period 1966–70 witnessed two poor agricultural years in addition to export lags, and there were shortages of basic food commodities in 1969–70.

In late 1970, violent protests erupted over the government's stepped-up efforts to increase production. After the change in political leadership from Gomulka to Gierek, government emphasis shifted from heavy industry to light, consumer-oriented production. In addition, through a concentration of investment in mechanization, fertilizers, and other farm improvements, the government sought and achieved a 50% increase in food production. Overall, the 1971–75 five-year plan achieved its main targets by a wide margin, with industrial production up about 73%. The 1976–80 plan, which aimed at a 50% increase in industrial production and a 16% increase in agricultural output, ran into difficulty almost from the beginning, and by 1979 the economy had entered a period of decline and dislocation that continued into 1982. An economic reform stressing decentralization of the economy was introduced in January, 1982, but it failed to produce any significant improvements. With price rises and consumer goods shortages continuing to fuel popular discontent, the government in March, 1983 announced a three-year austerity plan for 1983–85. Its aims included a general consolidation of the economy, self-sufficiency in food production, and increased emphasis on housing and the production of industrial consumer goods. By 1986, the economy had rebounded. The 1986–90 plan expected the national income to grow 3–3.5% annually, industrial output to increase by 3.2% each year, and exports to grow by 5% (in fixed prices) annually. These goals were not reached. A "second stage," proclaimed in 1986, called for more autonomy for individual enterprises and for more efficient management, with top jobs filled without regard to political affiliations.

The Economic Transformation Program adopted in January 1990 aimed to convert Poland from a planned to a market economy. Measures were aimed at drastically reducing the large budget deficit, abolishing all trade monopolies, and selling many state-owned enterprises to private interests.

40SOCIAL DEVELOPMENT

A social insurance institute administers social security programs through a network of branch offices. Social security, including social insurance and medical care, covers virtually the entire population.

Any incapacitated citizen is entitled to assistance. Old age, disability, and survivors' pensions are provided, as well as family allowances, sickness benefits, maternity benefits, workers' compensation, and unemployment. The retirement age for teachers, aviation and maritime workers, and workers in hazardous occupations is 60 for men and 55 for women; for most other workers it is 65 for men and 60 for women, if the former have been employed for 25 years and the latter for 20.

Special family allowances have been a part of the social security program since 1947 and are paid for each child after the first. Maternity benefits include full wages for a total of 16–18 weeks followed by a leave of 24–72 months paid at 25% of average monthly earnings (40% for single parents). In 1985–90, the fertility rate was 2.2, one of the highest in Europe. Because of a lack of effective contraceptives, abortion is often used as a method of birth control. Abortions are done free of charge at state hospitals, with a three-day medical leave provided. In 1985, women accounted for 45% of the labor force. The law prohibits women from working in 90 occupations, and unemployment affects women disproportionately compared with men.

41HEALTH

Poland's 1993 birth rate was 14.3 per 1,000 people, with 75% of married women (ages 15 to 49) using contraception. There were 550,000 births in 1992.

In 1990, Poland had 81,674 physicians (2.06 per 1,000 people in 1992), 18,219 dentists, 200,783 nurses, and 23,868 midwives. In 1989, there were 15,960 pharmacists. About 54% of the physicians and 81% of the dentists were women. Limited private practice by physicians and dentists continues, but health professionals in private practice must spend a minimum number of hours in state service, and complete socialization is the aim.

In 1991, there were 56.8 hospital beds per 10,000 population and 18.2 beds per 10,000 in social welfare houses and establishments. In 1990, there were 6.6 hospital beds per 1,000 inhabitants. Health care suffers from a lack of medicines, many of which must be imported from the West. The 1990 per capita pharmaceutical consumption was $16.1, and total health care expenditures were $3,157 million the same year. In 1992, Poland immunized children up to 1 year old against tuberculosis (94%); diphtheria, pertussis, and tetanus (98%); polio (98%); and measles (94%).

Life expectancy in 1992 averaged 72 years, and infant mortality was 14 per 1,000 live births. The general mortality rate was 10.1 per 1,000 people in 1993. Leading causes of death per 100,000 people in 1990 were: (1) communicable diseases and maternal/perinatal causes (73); (2) noncommunicable diseases (603); and (3) injuries (80). There were 70 reported cases of tuberculosis per 100,000 people in the same year.

42HOUSING

Almost 40% of all urban dwelling space was destroyed during World War II. Although investment in public housing has increased, and credits have been assigned for cooperative and private construction, the housing shortage remains critical. In the mid-1980s, the average wait for an apartment was about 15 years. In 1984 there were 10,253,000 dwelling units; 4.6% had only one room, 21% consisted of two rooms, 35.5% of three rooms, 25.7% of four rooms, and 13.2% of five or more rooms. An additional 193,000 dwelling units were constructed in 1985. As of 1992, there was a shortage of 1.3 million housing units, a figure that was expected to grow to 2.4 million by the year 2000. About 1.8 million apartments were expected to be lost due to deterioration by 2020. In 1991, 130,000 new housing units were constructed.

43EDUCATION

Virtually the entire Polish population is literate. Primary, secondary, and most university and other education is free. State and local expenditure on education is, therefore, substantial. Lower schools are financed by local budgets, higher and vocational schools from the state budget.

The school system, which is centralized, consists of an eight-year primary school followed by a four-year secondary general education school, five-year technical school, or basic three-year vocational training school. In 1991 there were 18,323 primary schools with 5,305,000 students and 328,900 teachers, and 1,131 general secondary schools, with 494,000 students. Some 1,722,000 students attended 9,413 vocational schools, studying technology, agriculture, forestry, economy, education, health services, and the arts. Another 394,313 students attended 98 institutions of higher learning in 1990–91.

Higher learning is under the jurisdiction of the Ministry of Higher Education and other ministries. A matriculation examination, which is common for all students, is required for admission to institutions of higher learning. Of the 98 third-level institutions, 11 are universities, 18 polytechnical schools, 17 art schools, 11 medical academies, and 3 theological academies. Jagiellonian University, among the oldest in Europe, was established at Cracow in 1364. Other prominent universities are the Warsaw University; the Central School of Planning and Statistics (Warsaw); the Higher Theater School (Warsaw); the Academy of Fine Arts (Cracow); and the Adam Mickiewicz University (Poznań). The only free private university in the Socialist bloc is the Roman Catholic University at Lublin. Evening and extramural courses are available for anyone who is interested and is not a part of the school system. Foreign students are also welcome to study in Poland, either as regular students or at their summer schools. During the 1990–91 academic year, 4,235 foreign students were enrolled.

44LIBRARIES AND MUSEUMS

The National Library, established in Warsaw in 1928, is the largest in Poland, with about 4,870,000 volumes, including periodicals, manuscripts, maps, illustrations, and music. Other important libraries are the Public, University, and the government departmental libraries in Warsaw; the Jagiellonian University Library in Cracow, which has 2.5 million volumes; and the Ossolineum Library in Wroclaw. In 1990 there were 10,269 public libraries, jointly holding almost 140 million volumes.

Of the 551 museums in Poland at the end of 1989, the foremost is the National Museum in Warsaw, which has an extensive and important art collection as well as a collection of Polish art from the 12th century to present day. Other important museums are the National Museum in Cracow, notable for its collection of Far Eastern Art, and the National Museum in Poznań, which has a celebrated collection of musical instruments.

45MEDIA

All communications services are government owned and operated. In 1991 there were 4,830,216 telephones.

In 1991 three radio networks were Polskie Radio, Radio Solidarnesc, and Radio Z, and television programming was broadcast by Telewizja Polskie. There were 27 AM and 27 FM radio stations and 40 TV stations. During the same year there were 11.3 million television sets and 16.6 million radios.

In 1991 there were 45 daily newspapers. The largest Polish dailies, with political orientations and 1991 circulations, were as follows:

	CIRCULATION
WARSAW	
Gazeta Wyborcza	510,000
Zycie Warszawy	250,000
Rzeczpespolita	216,000
Express Wieczorny	120,000
Trybuna	110,000
Sztandar Mlodych	102,000
Slowo Powszechne	60,000

46ORGANIZATIONS

The Polish Chamber of Commerce and the Chamber of Foreign Trade promote foreign trade by furnishing information, establishing or extending commercial relations, and arranging for Polish participation in trade fairs, and exhibitions abroad. There are also many cultural, sports and social, organizations in Poland.

The most important workers organizations in Poland is Solidarity, founded in 1980 by Lech Welesa.

47TOURISM, TRAVEL, AND RECREATION

Foreign visitors to Poland must have a valid passport. Citizens of over 30 countries, including the US and the UK, may stay up to 90 days without a visa. The number of foreign visitors was approximately 11.3 million in 1991, and tourist receipts amounted to $149 million. There were 43,688 hotel rooms with 88,392 beds.

The main tourist attractions include the historic city of Cracow, which suffered little war damage; the resort towns of Zakopane, in the Tatras, and Sopot, on the Baltic; and the restored Old Town in Warsaw, as well as the capital's museums and Palace of Science and Culture. Camping, hiking, and soccer are among the most popular recreational activities.

48FAMOUS POLES

Figures prominent in Polish history include Mieszko I (fl.10th century), who led Poland to Christianity; his son and successor, Boleslaw I ("the Brave," d.1025), the first king of sovereign Poland; Casimir III ("the Great," 1309–70), who sponsored domestic reforms; and John III Sobieski (1624–96), who led the Polish-German army that lifted the siege of Vienna in 1683 and repelled the Turkish invaders. Tadeusz Andrzej Bonawentura Kościuszko (1746–1817), trained as a military engineer, served with colonial forces during the American Revolution and then led a Polish rebellion against Russia in 1794; he was wounded, captured, and finally exiled. Kazimierz Pulaski (1747–79) fought and died in the American Revolution, and Haym Salomon (1740–85) helped to finance it. The reconstituted Polish state after World War I was led by Józef Pilsudski (1867–1935), who ruled as a dictator from 1926 until his death. Polish public life since World War II has been dominated by Wladyslaw Gomulka (1905–82), Edward Gierek (b.1913), and Gen. Wojciech Jaruzelski (b.1923), Communist leaders, respectively, during 1956–70, during 1970–80, and after 1981. Important roles have also been played by Stefan Cardinal Wyszynski (1901–81), Roman Catholic primate of Poland, archbishop of Gniezno and Warsaw, and frequent adversary of the postwar Communist regime; Karol Wojtyla (b.1920), archbishop of Cracow from 1963 until his elevation to the papacy as John Paul II in 1978; and Lech Walesa (b.1943), leader of the Solidarity movement during 1980–81, Nobel Peace Prize laureate in 1983, and President of Poland since 1990.

The father of Polish literature is Nicholas Rey (1505–69), one of the earliest Polish writers to turn from Latin to the vernacular. Poland's golden age is marked by the beginning of literature in Polish; its greatest poet was Jan Kochanowski (1530–84). Notable among 19th-century poets and dramatists was Adam Mickiewicz (1798–1855), whose *The Books of the Polish Nation and of the Polish Pilgrimage, Pan Tadeusz*, and other works exerted a paramount influence on all future generations. Other leading literary figures were the poets and dramatists Juliusz Slowacki (1809–49) and Zygmunt Krasiński (1812–59), whose *Dawn* breathed an inspired patriotism. Józef Kraszewski (1812–87), prolific and patriotic prose writer, is considered the father of the Polish novel. The leading late-19th-century novelists were the realists Aleksander Glowacki (1847–1912), who wrote under the pseudonym of Boleslaw Prus, and Henryk Sienkiewicz (1846–1916), Poland's first Nobel Prize winner (1905), whose *The Trilogy* described the 17th-century wars of Poland; he is internationally famous for *Quo Vadis?* Another Nobel Prize winner (1924) was the novelist Wladyslaw Reymont (1867–1925), acclaimed for *The Peasants*. A Pole who achieved stature as an English novelist was Joseph Conrad (Józef Teodor Konrad Korzeniowski, 1857–1924). Other important literary figures around the turn of the century were the playwright and painter Stanislaw Wyspiański (1869–1907), the novelist Stefan Zeromski (1864–1926), and the novelist Stanislaw Ignacy Witkiewicz (1885–1939). The best-known modern authors are novelist and short-story writer Isaac Bashevis Singer (1904–91), a Nobel Prize winner in 1978 and a US resident since 1935; the satirist Witold Gombrowicz (1904–69); science-fiction writer Stanislaw Lem (b.1921); the dissident novelist Jerzy Andrzejewski (1909–83); the poet Czeslaw Milosz (b.1911), a Nobel Prize winner in 1980 and resident of the US since 1960; and novelist Jerzy Kosinski (b.1933), who has lived in the US since 1957 and writes in English.

The greatest Polish composer was Frédéric Chopin (1810–49), born in Warsaw, who lived in Paris after 1831. A popular composer was Stanislaw Moniuszko (1819–72), founder of the Polish national opera and composer of many songs; he influenced such later composers as Wladyslaw Zeleński (1837–1921), Zygmunt Noskowski (1846–1909), and Stanislaw Niewiadomski (1859–1936). Other prominent musicians include the pianist Ignacy Jan Paderewski (1860–1941), also his country's first prime minister following World War I; the great harpsichordist Wanda Landowska (1877–1959); the renowned pianist Arthur Rubinstein (1887–1982); the violinist Wanda Wilkomirska (b.1929); the conductor Stanislaw Skrowaczewski (b.1923); and the composers Mieczyslaw Karlowicz (1876–1909) and Karol Szymanowski (1883–1937). Witold Lutoslawski (b.1913) and Krzysztof Penderecki (b.1933) are internationally known contemporary composers.

The first Polish painters of European importance were Piotr Michalowski (1800–55) and Henryk Rodakowski (1823–94). In the second half of the 19th century, Polish realism reached its height in the historical paintings of Jan Matejko (1838–93), Artur Grottger (1837–67), Juliusz Kossak (1824–99), and Józef Brandt (1841–1915), as well as in genre painting and the landscapes of Wojciech Gerson (1831–1901), Józef Szermentowski (1833–76), Aleksander Kotsis (1836–77), Maksymilian Gierymski (1846–74), Aleksander Gierymski (1849–1901), and Józef Chelmoński (1849–1914). Feliks Topolski (b.1907), who has lived in London since 1935, is well known for his oil paintings, watercolors, and drawings. Andrzej Wajda (b.1926), Roman Polański (b.1933), an expatriate since the mid-1960s, and Krzysztof Zanussi (b.1939) are famous film directors, and Jerzy Grotowski (b.1933) is a well-known stage director.

The outstanding scientist and scholar Nicolaus Copernicus (Mikolaj Kopernik, 1473–1543) is world renowned. Among Poland's brilliant scientists are Maria Sklodowska-Curie (1867–1934), a codiscoverer of radium and the recipient of two Nobel Prizes, and Casimir Funk (1884–1967), the discoverer of vitamins. Oskar Lange (1904–66) achieved renown as an economist.

49 DEPENDENCIES
Poland has no territories or colonies.

50 BIBLIOGRAPHY
Bernhard, Michael H. *The Origins of Democratization in Poland: Workers, Intellectuals, and Oppositional Politics, 1976–1980.* New York: Columbia University Press, 1993.

Blazyca, George and Ryszard Rapacki (eds.). *Poland into the 1990s: Economy and Society in Transition.* New York: St. Martin's, 1991.

Bromke, Adam. *The Meaning and Uses of Polish History.* New York: Cambridge University Press, 1986.

Davies, Norman. *Heart of Europe: A Short History of Poland.* New York: Oxford University Press, 1984.

Engel, David. *Facing a Holocaust: The Polish Government-in-exile and the Jews, 1943–1945.* Chapel Hill: University of North Carolina Press, 1993.

Fallenbuchl, Zbigniew M. *The Polish Economy in the Year 2000: Need and Outlook for Systematic Reforms, Recovery and Growth Strategy.* Pittsburgh: University of Pittsburgh Center for Russian and East European Studies, 1988.

Fiszman, Samuel (ed.). *The Polish Renaissance in its European Context.* Bloomington: Indiana University Press, 1988.

Goodwyn, Lawrence. *Breaking the Barrier: the Rise of Solidarity in Poland.* New York: Oxford University Press, 1991.

Hahn, Werner G. *Democracy in a Communist Party: Poland's Experience Since 1980.* New York: Columbia University Press, 1987.

Kaminski, Bartoomiej. *The Collapse of State Socialism: The Case of Poland.* Princeton, N.J.: Princeton University Press, 1991.

Kennedy, Michael D. *Professionals, Power, and Solidarity in Poland: A Critical Sociology of Soviet-type Society.* New York: Cambridge University Press, 1991.

Kurczewski, Jacek. *The Resurrection of Rights in Poland.* New York: Oxford University Press, 1993.

Marer, Pau and Wodzimierz Siwinski (eds.). *Creditworthiness and Reform in Poland: Western and Polish Perspectives.* Bloomington: Indiana University Press, 1988.

Ost, David. *Solidarity and the Politics of Anti-politics: Opposition and Reform in Poland since 1968.* Philadelphia: Temple University Press, 1990.

Polonsky, Antony. *Politics in Independent Poland, 1921–1939.* Oxford: Clarendon Press, 1972.

Rachwald, Arthur R. *In Search of Poland: The Superpowers' Response to Solidarity, 1980–1989.* Stanford, Calif.: Hoover Institution Press, 1990.

The Reconstruction of Poland, 1914–23. New York: St. Martin's Press, 1992.

Sanford, George. *Poland.* Santa Barbara, Calif.: Clio Press, 1993.

Shen, Raphael. *Economic Reform in Poland and Czechoslovakia: Lessons in Systemic Transformation.* Westport, Conn.: Praeger, 1993.

Simatupang, Batara. *The Polish Economic Crisis: Background, Causes and Aftermath.* New York: Routledge, 1994.

Staar, Richard F. (ed.). *Transition to Democracy in Poland.* New York: St. Martin's, 1993.

Walesa, Lech. *The Struggle and the Triumph: An Autobiography.* New York: Arcade, 1992.

Wedel, Janine R. (ed.). *The Unplanned Society: Poland During and After Communism.* New York: Columbia University Press, 1992.

PORTUGAL

Portuguese Republic
República Portuguesa

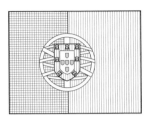

CAPITAL: Lisbon (Lisboa).

FLAG: The national flag, adopted in 1911, consists of a green field at the hoist and a larger red field at the fly. At the junction of the two, in yellow, red, blue, and white, is the national coat of arms.

ANTHEM: *A Portuguesa (The Portuguese).*

MONETARY UNIT: The escudo (E) is a paper currency of 100 centavos. There are coins of 1, 2.5, 5, 10, 20, 50, 100, and 200 escudos, and notes of 500, 1,000, 2,000, 5,000 and 10,000 escudos. E1 = $0.0057 (or $1 = E174.12).

WEIGHTS AND MEASURES: The metric system is the legal standard.

HOLIDAYS: New Year's Day, 1 January; Carnival Day, 15 February; Anniversary of the Revolution, 25 April; Labor Day, 1 May; National Day, 10 June; Assumption, 15 August; Republic Day, 5 October; All Saints' Day, 1 November; Independence Day, 1 December; Immaculate Conception, 8 December; Christmas, 25 December. Movable religious holidays include Carnival Day, Good Friday, and Corpus Christi.

TIME: GMT.

¹LOCATION, SIZE, AND EXTENT

The westernmost country of Europe, Portugal occupies the greater portion of the western littoral of the Iberian Peninsula. Portugal has an area of 92,080 sq km (35,552 sq mi), including the Azores (Açores) Archipelago, nine islands about 1,300 km (800 mi) W of Portugal, with an area of 2,247 sq km (868 sq mi), and Madeira and Porto Santo, more than 960 km (600 mi) to the SW, with an area of 794 sq mi (307 sq mi). Comparatively, the area occupied by Portugal is slightly smaller than the state of Indiana. The mainland of Portugal extends 561 km (349 mi) N-W and 218 km (135 mi) N-W. Bordered on the N and E by Spain and on the S and W by the Atlantic Ocean, Portugal has a total boundary length of 3,007 km (1,868 mi).

Portugal's capital city, Lisbon, is located on Portugal's west coast.

²TOPOGRAPHY

Portugal exhibits sharp topographic contrasts. Although the north is largely lowland or land of medium altitude, the distribution of highlands is unequal north and south of the Tagus (Tejo) River. From north to south, the principal mountain ranges are the Peneda (reaching a maximum height of 1,416 m/4,646 ft), Gerêz (1,507 m/4,944 ft), Marão (1,415 m/4,642 ft), Montemuro (1,382 m/4,534 ft), Açor (1,340 m/4,396 ft), and Lousã (1,204 m/3,950 ft), all north of the Tagus. The uplands of Beira, traversed by the Tagus on its way to the sea, contain Portugal's highest peak, Estrêla (1,991 m/6,532 ft). Westward lies the low coast of the Beira Littoral. The Tagus and Sado basins lie adjacent to the hilly area of Estremadura and rise to the hills of Alentejo on the east. The interior lowland of lower Alentejo, farther south, is limited by the hills of Algarve. The south coast, from the mouth of the Guadiana to Cape St. Vincent, is mainly steep, but northward from Cape St. Vincent to the Tagus, including the great Bay of Setúbal and the estuary of the Tagus, the coast is low. North of the Tagus, it rises steeply toward the hills of Sintra, beyond which is a low coast of dunes interrupted by the marshes of Aveiro.

Beyond the mouth of the Douro River, the coast is steep all the way to the Spanish frontier and the mouth of the Minho River. The larger rivers—the Minho, the Douro, the Tagus, and the Guadiana—all rise in Spain. The Douro has the longest course in Portugal (322 km/200 mi).

³CLIMATE

Marked seasonal and regional variations within temperate limits characterize the climate. In the north, an oceanic climate prevails: cool summers and rainy winters (average annual rainfall 125–150 cm/50–60 in), with occasional snowfall. Central Portugal has hot summers and cool, rainy winters, with 50–75 cm (20–30 in) average annual rainfall. The southern climate is very dry, with rainfall not exceeding 50 cm (20 in) along the coast. In Lisbon, the average temperature is about 21°C (70°F) in July and 4°C (39°F) in January. The annual mean temperature in Portugal is 16°C (61°F).

⁴FLORA AND FAUNA

Three types of vegetation can be distinguished in Portugal: the green forests of eucalyptus, pine, and chestnut in the north; the open dry grasslands, interrupted by stands of cork and other types of evergreen oak, in the central areas; and the dry, almost steppelike grasslands and evergreen brush in the south. Few wild animals remain in Portugal. The coastal waters abound with fish, sardines and tuna being among the most common species.

⁵ENVIRONMENT

Air and water pollution are significant environmental problems especially in Portugal's urban centers. Industrial pollutants include nitrous oxide, sulfur dioxides and carbon emissions. In total, the nation contributes 131.1 tons of particulate emissions and 171.9 tons of hydrocarbon emissions per year and 0.2 % of the world's total gas emissions. The nation's water supply is threatened by pollutants from the oil and cellulose industries. Portugal has 8.2 cubic miles of reusable water of which 48 % is used to support farming and 37% is for industrial activity. In total, the nation's cities produce 2.6 million tons of solid waste. Another environmental concern is handling the 180,000 tons of industrial contaminants that are produced yearly. The nation's wildlife and agricultural activities are threatened by erosion and desertification of the land.

The principal environmental agencies in Portugal include the Ministry of Quality of Life and the Office of the Secretary of State for the Environment. The nation's basic environmental legislation dates from 1976. In 1994, 6 of Portugal's mammal species and 18 of its bird species were endangered was well as 240 plant species. As of 1987, endangered species in Portugal included the Spanish Lynx, rosalia, Mediterranean monk seal, and Spanish imperial eagle. The São Miguel bullfinch and three species of turtle (green sea, hawksbill, and leatherback) were endangered in the Azores, and the Mediterranean monk seal and four species of turtle (green sea, hawksbill, Kemp's ridley, and leatherback) were endangered in Madeira.

6POPULATION

According to the 1991 census, the population of Portugal, including the Azores and Madeira, was 9,862,056, an increase of 0.7% since 1981; it was estimated by the US Bureau of the Census at 10,484,248 in mid-1994. The UN projection for the year 2000, however, is 9,932,000, assuming a crude birthrate of 11.8 per 1,000 population, a crude death rate of 10.3, and a net natural increase of 1.5 annually during 1995–2000. Average population density in 1991 was 107 per sq km (277 per sq mi). An estimated 64% of the population was rural and 36% urban in 1995. About two-thirds of the people lived in the coastal fourth of the country. Lisbon (Lisboa), the capital and principal city, had a metropolitan-area population of 1,851,063 in 1991.

7MIGRATION

Portuguese emigration, which decreased from an annual average of 48,000 persons during the decade 1904–13 to 37,562 in 1961, increased sharply after 1963 as a result of acute labor shortages in other European countries, especially in France and the Federal Republic of Germany (FRG). By 1970, it was estimated that more than 100,000 Portuguese were emigrating yearly. Legal emigration to the FRG continued to increase until November 1973, when the FRG suspended non-EC immigration. Overall, more than 130,000 Portuguese emigrated in 1973. Because of the loss of Portugal's African colonies in 1975, an estimated 800,000 Portuguese settlers returned to Portugal. Since then at least 25,000 return from abroad each year generally, from other European countries or America. Some 4,000,000 Portuguese are living abroad, mainly in France, Germany, Brazil, South Africa, Canada, Venezuela, and the US. Their remittances home came to 8.3% of the nation's GDP in 1989.

There were 121,513 legally registered foreigners in 1991, including 52,037 Africans.

8ETHNIC GROUPS

The Portuguese people represent a mixture of various ethnic strains. In the north are traces of Celtic influence; in the south, Arab and Berber influence is considerable. Other groups—Lusitanians, Phoenicians, Carthaginians, Romans, Visigoths, and Jews—also left their mark on the Portuguese people. The present-day Portuguese population is one of the most homogeneous in Europe, with no national minorities.

9LANGUAGES

Portuguese, the national language, evolved from ancient dialects of Latin; its rules of orthography were reformulated in 1911. Portuguese is also the official language of Brazil and the former African provinces. Spanish, French, and English are the most common second languages.

10RELIGIONS

Although most Portuguese are Roman Catholic, other religions enjoy freedom of worship. In 1993, about 94% of the population was Roman Catholic; there were also some 80,000 Protestants, about 15,000 Muslims, and about 2,000 Jews. An estimated 100,000, who live mainly in the north, are nominally Roman Catholics but keep some Jewish practices; these are descendants of the Marranos, a Spanish term for those who outwardly converted to Christianity but secretly practiced Judaism after the expulsion of all professing Jews from Spain and Portugal at the end of the 15th century.

11TRANSPORTATION

The Portuguese railways are almost entirely owned and operated by the nationalized Portuguese Railway Co. The railway system, which is adequate for Portugal's needs, totals 3,614 km (2,246 mi) of track, comprised mostly of wide gauge (1.67 m) single track. Some 15% of this total has been electrified.

The length of usable highways in 1991 was 74,000 km (45,880 mi), of which 84% were paved. The principal highways connect Lisbon and Porto with La Coruña in Spain, and Lisbon with Madrid via Badajoz. Bus service links all Portuguese cities, towns, and principal villages. In 1991 there were 2,448,200 motor vehicles registered in continental Portugal, including 1,800,000 passenger cars, and 648,200 trucks, buses, and other commercial vehicles.

As of 1 January 1992, the Portuguese merchant fleet had 47 oceangoing vessels of over 1,000 gross tons, totaling 673,000 GRT. The main shipping firm is the Portuguese Maritime Transport Co., created after the private shipping companies were nationalized in 1975. It maintains scheduled services to the Azores, Madeira, Macao, and the former overseas territories in Africa; there is regular service to Brazil and North America. The chief ports—Lisbon (the largest), Porto, Ponta Delgada, and Sines—are all fully equipped and have adequate warehousing facilities. Portugal has created a captive register of convenience on Madiera for Portuguese-owned ships, allowing for taxation and crewing benefits.

Because of their geographical position, Lisbon's Portela Airport and Santa Maria in the Azores are of great importance in international aviation. Portela is one of the principal airports for overseas flights to North and South America and to western and central Africa; Santa Maria is a stopping point for transoceanic flights from Europe to North America. The most important aviation company in Portugal is Transportes Aereos Portugueses (TAP), which was nationalized in 1975 and carried 4,145,000 passengers in 1992.

12HISTORY

Portugal, known in antiquity as restored, derives its name from ancient Portus Cale (now Oporto), at the mouth of the Douro River, where the Portuguese monarchy began. The country's early history is indistinguishable from that of the other Iberian peoples. Lusitanians were successively overrun by Celts, Romans, Visigoths, and Moors (711). In 1094, Henry of Burgundy was given the county of Portugal by the king of Castile and León for his success against the Moors; his son, Alfonso I (Alfonso Henriques), became king and achieved independence for Portugal in 1143, beginning the Burgundy dynasty. By the mid-13th century, the present boundaries of Portugal were established, and Lisbon became the capital.

During the reign of King John (João) I, the founder of the powerful Aviz dynasty and husband of the English princess Philippa of Lancaster, the Portuguese defeated the Spanish in a war over the throne (1385), established a political alliance with England (by the Treaty of Windsor in 1386) that has endured to the present day, and inaugurated their most brilliant era. Prince

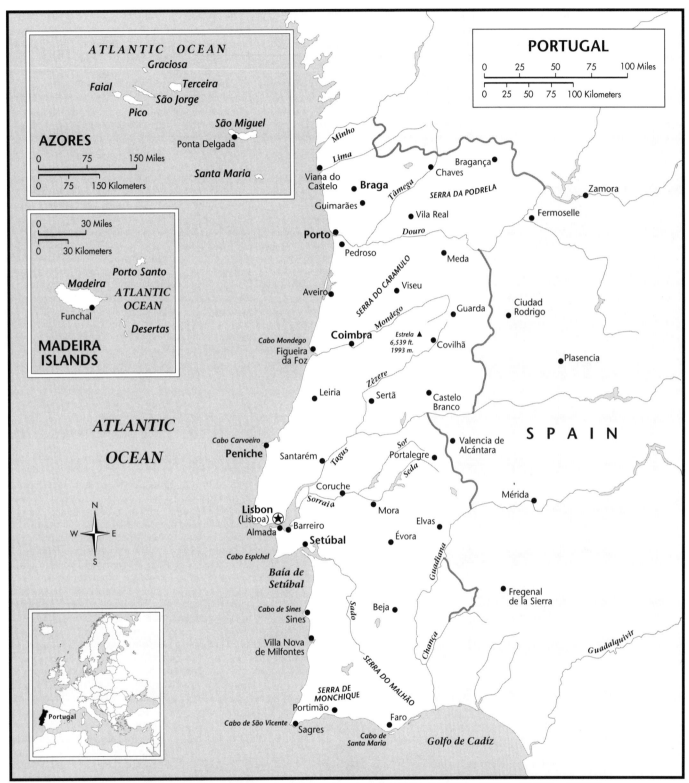

ATLANTIC OCEAN

Graciosa

Faial   *Terceira*
      São Jorge
   Pico

                    São Miguel
      Ponta Delgada

AZORES

0   75   150 Miles

0   75   150 Kilometers

      Santa Maria

PORTUGAL

0   25   50   75   100 Miles

0   25   50   75   100 Kilometers

0   30 Miles

0   30 Kilometers

Porto Santo
Madeira   ATLANTIC
      OCEAN
Funchal
      Desertas

MADEIRA ISLANDS

ATLANTIC

OCEAN

N
W   E
S

Portugal

Minho
Lima
Viana do
Castelo   **Braga**
Guimarães
      Tâmega
                  Bragança
            Chaves
                  SERRA DA PODRELA
      Vila Real
Porto
Pedroso   *Douro*
            Meda
      SERRA DO CARAMULO
Aveiro   Viseu
      Mondego   Guarda
Coimbra
Cabo Mondego   Estrela ▲
Figueira   6,539 ft.   Covilhã
da Foz   1993 m.
      Zêzere
Leiria   Sertã   Castelo
            Branco
Cabo Carvoeiro
Peniche   *Sor*
Santarém   *Tagus*   *Portalegre*
            Seda
Coruche
      Sorraia   Mora
Lisbon
(Lisboa) ✪   Elvas
Almada   Barreiro   Évora
      Setúbal
Cabo Espichel
Baía de
Setúbal   *Sado*
Cabo de Sines   Beja   *Guadiana*
Sines
Villa Nova   *Chança*
de Milfontes
      SERRA DO MALHÃO
SERRA DE
MONCHIQUE
      Portimão
Cabo de São Vicente   Faro
      Sagres   Cabo de   *Golfo de Cadíz*
            Santa Maria

Zamora
Fermoselle
Ciudad
Rodrigo
Plasencia
S P A I N
Valencia de
Alcántara
Mérida
Fregenal
de la Sierra
Guadalquivir

Azores—*See Africa continental map*; Madeira—*See Africa continental map*: **LOCATION:** 36°57′39″ to 42°9′8″N; 6°11′10″ to 9°29′45″W.
BOUNDARY LENGTHS: Spain, 1,215 km (755 mi); Atlantic coastline, 832 km (517 mi). **TERRITORIAL SEA LIMIT:** 12 mi.

Henry the Navigator (Henrique o Navegador), a son of John I, founded a nautical school at Sagres, where he gathered the world's best navigators, cosmographers, geographers, and astronomers and commenced a series of voyages and explorations that culminated in the formation of the Portuguese Empire. In the 15th and 16th centuries, the golden age of Portugal, Portuguese explorers sailed most of the world's seas; made the European discovery of the Cape of Good Hope, Brazil, and Labrador; founded Portugal's overseas provinces in western and eastern Africa, India, Southeast Asia, and Brazil; and poured the vast riches of the empire into the homeland. In 1580–81, Philip II of Spain, claiming the throne, conquered Portugal and acquired its empire, but national sovereignty was restored by the revolution of 1640 and the accession of John IV, founder of the Bragança dynasty, to the Portuguese throne. John IV ushered in Portugal's silver age, the 17th and 18th centuries, when the wealth of Brazil once more made Lisbon one of the most brilliant of European capitals. The city was largely destroyed by a great earthquake in 1755 but was subsequently rebuilt. During the Napoleonic wars, Portugal, faithful to its British alliance, was the base of British operations against the French in the Iberian Peninsula. The royal family, however, withdrew to Brazil, and from 1807 to 1821, Rio de Janeiro was the seat of the Portuguese monarchy. In 1822, Brazil, ruled by Pedro, the son of King John VI of Portugal, formally declared its independence; Pedro became Emperor Pedro I of Brazil but was deposed in 1831.

The Bragança dynasty, which had ruled Portugal since 1640, came to an end with the revolution of 1910, when the monarchy was replaced by a republican regime. Lack of stability under the new republic led to a military dictatorship in 1926. Marshal António Carmona served as president from 1926 to 1951. António de Oliveira Salazar, brought to the government in 1928 as minister of finance, emerged as Portugal's prime minister in 1932. In 1933, Salazar proclaimed a new constitution, which consolidated his regime and established Portugal as a corporative state. During World War II, Portugal supported the Allies but did not take part in combat; it subsequently became a member of NATO.

Despite its reduced status as a European power, Portugal attempted to maintain its overseas empire, especially its resource-rich African provinces. In 1961, Portugal surrendered Goa, Daman, and Diu to India. In the same year, uprisings in Angola began, organized by the Union of Angolan Peoples in protest against Portugal's oppressive policies in the territory. These uprisings led to serious disagreements between the UN and Portugal; following Portugal's refusal to heed its recommendations for liberalization of policies with a view toward eventual self-government, the UN General Assembly passed a resolution in 1965 calling for a worldwide economic and arms boycott of Portugal in order to force it to grant independence to its African dependencies. Subsequently, the Assembly passed a number of resolutions condemning Portugal for its policies in its African territories. Meanwhile, guerrilla movements in Angola, Mozambique, and Guinea-Bissau were met by a steadily increasing commitment of Portuguese troops and supplies.

Salazar, who served as prime minister of Portugal from 1932 to 1968, died in July 1970 at the age of 81. When he was incapacitated in September 1968, he was succeeded by Marcello Caetano. The unwillingness of the Caetano regime to institute democratic and economic reforms, coupled with growing discontent over the continuance of the ever more costly colonial war in Africa, led to a military coup by the left-wing Armed Forces Movement in April 1974. Broad democratic liberties were immediately granted and opposition political parties legalized, while the corporate state apparatus was gradually dismantled. A decolonization program was also begun, resulting by November 1975 in the independence of all of Portugal's African provinces.

The first provisional coalition government came to power in May 1974, with Gen. António Sebastião Ribeiro de Spínola, whose book *Portugal and the Future* had played a key role in focusing antiwar sentiment among the military, as president. In September 1974, after a power struggle with the leftist forces, Gen. Spínola resigned and was replaced by Gen. Francisco da Costa Gomes. Following an unsuccessful right-wing coup attempt in March 1975, Gen. Spínola was forced to flee the country, along with a number of officers. The continued dissension between right and left—and between Communist and Socialist factions on the left—was evidenced by the numerous provisional

governments that followed the coup. In April 1975, general elections were held for a Constituent Assembly, whose task was to draw up a new constitution. Legislative elections were held in April 1976 and presidential elections in June. Gen. António dos Santos Ramalho Eanes was elected president, and the leader of the Portuguese Socialist Party, Mário Alberto Nobre Lopes Soares, became prime minister. Mainly as a result of policy differences within the governing coalition, this administration fell in July 1978 and was replaced by a caretaker cabinet.

After a succession of different coalitions, the Socialist Party won a 35% plurality in the parliamentary elections of April 1983, and Soares was again named prime minister, forming a coalition government with the center-right Social Democratic Party (Partido Social Democratico—PSD). Political turbulence increased after the election, and in 1984, urban terrorism appeared. In the following year, Portugal entered the EC, boosting the economy. Political instability continued, however, and a general election was called in October 1985. The vote brought the PSD to power with a slim plurality; Prof. Aníbal Cavaço Silva was able to form a minority government. In 1986, four candidates ran for president; none was able to win a majority, and in the ensuing runoff election, former prime minister Soares won a narrow victory to become the nation's first civilian president in 60 years. In 1987, the government lost a vote of confidence, and Soares called a general election; the PSD under Silva won a majority in the Assembly, achieving the first such government since democracy was restored in 1974.

The PSD was returned to power in 1991 and Mario Soares was reelected president for a second five-year term on 13 January 1991. Economic recession, government deficits, and regional development initiatives have been major concerns in the 1990s. The government has also taken steps to restruct the right of political asylum.

¹³GOVERNMENT

A constitution made public on 9 April 1975 and effective 25 April 1976 stipulated that the Armed Forces Movement would maintain governmental responsibilities as the guarantor of democracy and defined Portugal as a republic "engaged in the formation of a classless society." The document provided for a strong, popularly elected president, empowered to appoint the prime minister and cabinet. This constitution was substantially revised in 1982 and later in 1989; the most important new provisions were the elimination of the military Council of the Revolution and the limitation of presidential power. The new government system is parliamentary.

According to the constitution as amended, the president is elected by popular vote for a five-year term. The president appoints the prime minister and, at the prime minister's proposal, other members of the government. The main lawmaking body is the unicameral Assembly of the Republic, the members of which (230 in 1994) are directly elected to four-year terms, subject to dissolution. Suffrage is universal from age 18.

¹⁴POLITICAL PARTIES

Under the Salazar regime, although the constitution did not prohibit political activity, the National Union (União Nacional) was the only political party represented in the legislature. Candidates of the old Center parties, which had been active prior to 1926–28, were allowed to participate in national elections starting in 1932, although none were ever elected.

After the 1974 revolution, several right-wing parties were banned, and various left-wing parties that had functioned underground or in exile were recognized. Among these was the Portuguese Communist Party (Partido Comunista Português—PCP), which was founded in 1921 and is Portugal's oldest political party. It is especially strong among industrial workers and southern farm workers. The government also recognized the Portuguese Socialist Party (Partido Socialista Português—PSP), founded in exile in 1973, and the Popular Democratic Party (Partido Popular Democrático—PPD), formed during the Caetano regime; both the PSP and the PPD favored the establishment of a Western European-style social democracy. Tied to the policies of the Caetano regime was the Social Democratic Center (Centro Democrático Social—CDS), founded in 1974, which held its first conference in January 1975 and became a target for left-wing disruptions. In June 1976, Gen. António Ramalho Eanes, the army chief of staff, who was supported by the major non-Communist parties, won election as Portugal's first president.

In 1979, the right-of-center Democratic Alliance (Aliança Democrática—AD) was formed by the Social Democratic Party (Partido Social Democrático—PSD), founded in 1974; the CDS; and the People's Monarchist Party (Partido Popular Monárquico—PPM). The left-wing United People's Alliance (Aliança Povo Unido), also formed in 1979, included the People's Democratic Movement (Movimento Democrático Popular—MDP), dating from 1969, and the PCP.

The Republican and Socialist Front (Frente Republicana e Socialista—FRS), formed in 1980, consisted of the PSP; the Union of the Socialist and Democratic Left (União da Esquerda Socialista Democrática—UESD), founded in 1978; and Social Democratic Independent Action (Acção Social Democrata Independente—ASDI), founded in 1980. The People's Democratic Union (União Democrática Popular—UDP), dating from 1974, comprised political groups of the revolutionary left.

In October 1985, former President Eanes's centrist Democratic Renewal Party (Partido Renovador Democrático—PRD) entered the ballot for the first time, taking 18% of the vote. In 1991, the seats were distributed as follows: PSO, 135; PSP, 72; CDU, 17; Center Democrats, 5; National Solidarity, 1. The latter was formed in 1990 to address the needs of pensioners.

15LOCAL GOVERNMENT

Portugal is grouped into 22 districts, including 18 on the mainland and 4 in the autonomous regions of the Azores and Madeira islands. Each district has a governor, appointed by the minister of the interior, and an assembly. There are more than 300 municipalities, subdivided into parishes.

16JUDICIAL SYSTEM

Justice is administered by ordinary and special courts, including the Supreme Court of Justice in Lisbon, consisting of a president and 29 judges; four courts of appeal, at Lisbon, Évora, Coimbra, and Oporto; courts of first instance in every district; and special courts. The jury system was reintroduced in 1976, but it is used only when requested by either the prosecutor or the defendant.

The judiciary is independent and impartial. Citizens enjoy a wide range of protections of fundamental civil and political rights which are outlined in the Constitution with specific reference to the Universal Declaration of Human Rights. An Ombudsman, elected by the Assembly of the Republic (legislature) to a four-year term, serves as the nation's chief civil and human rights officer.

17ARMED FORCES

The armed forces are maintained by conscription, with terms of 8–12 months for all services. As of 1993, the army had 32,700 personnel (24,800 conscripts), the navy 15,300 (including 2,500 marines), and the air force, 10,300 personnel, and 83 combat aircraft. The defense budget in 1991 was $1.7 billion, or 2.8% of the GDP. The US maintains an important airbase in the Azores, and NATO has one headquarters at Lisbon. Paramilitray police and special guards have increased to 50,000. Portugal has 190,000 reservists.

18INTERNATIONAL COOPERATION

Portugal joined the UN on 14 December 1955 and participates in ECE and all the nonregional specialized agencies except IDA. The nation is one of the 12 original signatories to NATO, a signatory to GATT and the Law of the Sea, and a member of OECD and EFTA. It also participates in IDP, and has permanent observer status at OAS. Seeking to broaden its sphere of external cooperation, Portugal since 1974 has established diplomatic relations and signed economic, technical, and cultural cooperation agreements with the former USSR and most other Eastern European countries. Portugal began negotiating for entry into the EEC in 1978; entry was granted officially in 1985.

19ECONOMY

Manufacturing and construction together accounted for 32.8% of Portugal's GDP in 1992. The largest industries are clothing, textiles, footwear, and food processing. Agriculture employed 11.3% of the work force in 1992 but contributed only 4.7% of the GDP (in constant prices). Productivity has been hampered by low investment and a lack of machinery and fertilizers. Two traditional Portuguese foreign exchange sources are income from tourism and remittances by emigrant workers in Western Europe. Despite the economic progress recorded since World War II, stimulated in part by Marshall Plan support, Portugal remains one of the poorest countries in Europe.

From the end of 1973 through 1983, the energy crisis and insufficient liquidity jeopardized economic growth, which dropped still further following the overthrow of the Caetano regime in April 1974. GNP growth in 1974 fell to 2–3% from 8.1% in the previous year. The decline was caused by a sharp drop in new offers of investment and credit from abroad (investors feared rising Communist influence and government takeovers of private firms), coupled with a decline in tourism and a massive increase in unemployment primarily resulting from the return of Portuguese settlers and soldiers from newly independent Angola. During the late 1970s, Portugal adopted an austerity program and succeeded in lowering inflation to 16.6% and increasing GDP growth to 5.5% in 1980. However, adverse interest and exchange rates and a severe drought during 1980–81 resulted in a resurgence of inflation (an estimated 22.5% in 1982) and sluggish economic growth (1.7% in 1981 and 2% in 1982).

In mid-1983, the Soares government implemented an IMF stabilization plan of drastic internal tightening, which brought steady economic improvement. The persistent current-account deficits ended in 1985, partially as a result of the decline in world oil prices and entry into the EC. The Silva government's economic liberalization emphasized competitiveness and accountability. The GDP grew by an average of 3.6% a year between 1985 and 1992 and fell by 1% in 1993. Inflation has been a problem, with consumer prices rising by an average of 12.1% a year between 1985 and 1992. Unemployment fell from 8.7% in 1985 to 4.1% in 1992, but rose to 5.5% in 1993.

The unofficial, or underground, economy is estimated at 20% of official GDP, about the same level as that of Spain and Italy.

20INCOME

In 1992, Portugal's GNP was $73,336 million at current prices, or $7,450 per capita. For the period 1985–92 the average inflation rate was 13.6%, resulting in a real growth rate in per capita GNP of 5.5%.

In 1992 the GDP was $79,547 million in current US dollars. It is estimated that in 1990 agriculture, hunting, forestry, and fishing contributed 6% to GDP; mining, quarrying, and manufacturing, 28%; electricity, gas, and water, 3%; construction, 7%; wholesale and retail trade, 20%; transport, storage, and communication, 5%; business services, 13%; community, social, and personal services, 3%; and other sources, 15%.

21LABOR

The labor force in Portugal, including the Azores and Madeira, at the end of 1992 totaled 4,737,200, of whom 194,100 (or 4.1%) were unemployed. Manufacturing employed 1,126,100 persons (23.8% of the total labor force); agriculture, 536,600 (11.2%); services, 1,290,900 (27.3%); commerce, 935,600 (19.8%); construction, 386,000 (8.1%); transportation and communications, 224,800 (4.7%); and other sectors, 237,200 (5.1%).

Between 1974 and 1976, there was only one coordinating association of trade unions, the pro-Communist Intersindical Nacional; its monopoly was revoked in October 1976. In 1985, the Intersindical still represented the majority of organized labor. The pro-Socialist General Union of Workers of Portugal (União Geral dos Trabalhadores—UGT), founded in 1978, is a pluralist democratic federation affiliated with the International Confederation of Free Trade Unions and the European Trade Union Confederation.

Extensive labor and social security laws were adopted in the mid-1970s. The government approves all collective bargaining contracts and regulates such matters as social insurance, pensions, hours of labor, and vacation provisions. A minimum wage was established in 1975; in 1991, the minimum monthly salary was 40,100 escudos per month.

22AGRICULTURE

In 1992, 34% of the land was under cultivation and 14.9% of the economically active population was engaged in agriculture, which accounts for 7% of GDP. Estimates of agriculture production in 1992 included potatoes, 1,293,000 tons; tomatoes, 700,000 tons; corn, 616,000 tons; wheat, 301,000 tons; olives, 221,000 tons; rice, 155,000 tons; and rye, 80,000 tons. Production of olive oil reached 40,000 tons in 1991. Wine, particularly port and Madeira from the Douro region and the Madeira islands, is an important agricultural export; production totaled 724,000 tons in 1992, down from 1,137,000 tons in 1990. Portugal is the world's seventh-largest producer of wine, although Portugal's wines are mostly unknown internationally apart from port and rosé. Portugal's wines are mostly unknown internationally. In 1992, the value of agricultural products imported by Portugal exceeded that of agricultural exports by three times.

According to government estimates, about 900,000 hectares (2,200,000 acres) of agricultural land were occupied between April 1974 and December 1975 in the name of land reform; about 32% of the occupations were ruled illegal. In January 1976, the government pledged to restore the illegally occupied land to its owners, and in 1977, it promulgated the Land Reform Review Law. Restoration of illegally occupied land began in 1978.

Agriculture is the main problem area of the economy; yields per hectare are less than one-third of the European average, with a severe drought in 1991/92 only exacerbating the problem. The situation has actually been deteriorating since the mid-1970s, with many yields falling and arable and permanent crop areas declining. With the reform of the EC's Common Agriculture Policy (CAP), a significant reduction in the number of producers through consolidation (especially in the north) will result in the end of traditional, subsistence-like based agriculture.

23ANIMAL HUSBANDRY

In 1992, the livestock population included 5,847,000 sheep, 2,580,000 hogs, 1,370,000 head of cattle, 862,000 goats, 250,000 donkeys and mules, 18,000,000 chickens and 6,000,000 turkeys. Mules and donkeys, as well as horses and oxen, often provide draft power for the farms. The main districts for cattle are northern and north-central Portugal; most of the sheep, goats, and pigs are raised in the central and southern sections. In 1992, Portugal produced about 1,547,000 tons of milk, 55,824 tons of cheese, and 531,000 tons of meat (down from 553,000 tons in 1991). The

Alentejo region is Portugal's grazing heartland. In 1992, a severe drought caused livestock and dairy production to fall.

24FISHING

Three main fields of activity make up the Portuguese fishing enterprise: coastal fishing, with sardines as the most important catch; trawl fishing on the high seas; and cod fishing on the Grand Banks, off Newfoundland. The total catch fell from 375,413 tons in 1973 to 247,596 tons in 1983 but increased to 325,349 tons in 1991.

25FORESTRY

With about 32% of the total land area forested, Portugal is an important producer of forestry products. The country is the world's leading producer of cork, ordinarily supplying about half the world output. Portugal is also an important producer of resin and turpentine. In 1992, timber and other forest product exports amounted to $1.9 billion, or 11% of the national total. Exports in 1992 consisted of cork, 29%; pulp, 26%; logs and lumber, 20%; paper, 17%; furniture, 5%; and resins, 3%. Wine stoppers account for 55% of cork export value. Cork demand has fallen in recent years, and production is limited by the botanical fact that a single tree can only be stripped once every nine years. Eucalyptus logs (the crux of the pulp industry) are exported as well; forestation of eucalyptus is a major national controversy, with opponents charging that it displaces traditional farmers and damages the soil and water table. Various pine species account for most lumber exports. In 1990, about 10,000 people were engaged in forestry and logging.

26MINING

Portugal is moderately rich in minerals, with tungsten, tin, and iron ore in the north; anthracite coal and lignite in the central region; and copper pyrites in the south. Tungsten, tin ore, and beryl are exported, while coal and pyrites are used at home; the government has also utilized the iron ore to develop a domestic steel industry. Mineral production has generally grown in recent years. Production in 1991 included iron pyrites, 138,760 tons; anthracite, 237,000 tons; tungsten, 1,400 tons; and tin, 10,360 tons (up from 63 tons in 1989). Output of copper ore was reported at 654,129 tons (up from 800 in 1987). The discovery and development of the rich copper and tin deposit at Neves-Corvo has helped rejuvenate the Portuguese mining industry. In 1991, copper reserves were estimated at 32.5 million metric tons.

27ENERGY AND POWER

Between 1951 and 1976, 16 hydroelectric plants were constructed in Portugal. Total production of electric power (including the Azores and Madeira) was 29,871 million kwh in 1991 (compared with 6,215 million kwh in 1968), 31% from hydroelectric sources. In 1991, Portuguese power stations had a net capacity of 7,414,000 kw. Portugal lacks adequate fuel resources, and large quantities of coal and oil are imported, especially as the electricity sector is switching away from oil; there are no gas reserves and no nuclear power plants in Portugal. In 1991, oil consumption accounted for 72% of total energy consumption, as compared with 78% in 1985 and 69.3% in 1979. As of 1992, oil accounted for 82% of primary energy needs, the highest rate in the EC. Coal accounts for about 4% of total energy consumption. The Germunde Mine at Castelo de Paiva, Portugal's only coal mine, was scheduled to close in 1994 because of high production costs and difficult mining conditions. Portugal has no petroleum resources. Mining operations yielded 125 tons of uranium in 1991.

28INDUSTRY

Industry (including construction, energy, and water) employed 33% of the labor force in 1993, and its contribution to the national economy has grown significantly in recent decades. Portuguese industry is mainly light; the development of heavy industry has been hampered by a shortage of electric power. Textiles—especially cottons and woolens—are the oldest and most important of Portugal's manufactures. Other principal industries are automotive assembly, electronics, glass and pottery, footwear, cement, cellulose and paper, rubber and chemicals, cork and cork products, and food industries (mainly canned fish). Small artisan industries, such as jewelry and homespun and hand-embroidered clothing, are of local importance.

Manufactured goods in 1991 included 7,342,000 tons of cement, 1,619,000 tons of wood pulp, 537,000 tons of crude steel for ingots, 1,037,000 tons of paper and paperboard, 1,522,000 radio receivers, and 318,000 television sets.

29 SCIENCE AND TECHNOLOGY
In 1993, Portugal had 16 scientific and technological learned societies, and 21 scientific and technological research institutes. The leading scientific academy is the Lisbon Academy of Sciences, founded in 1779. Total government expenditure on research and development was ɛ30 billion in 1988, and the number of technicians, scientists and engineers involved in research was 8,575.

30 DOMESTIC TRADE
Lisbon and Porto are the two leading commercial and distribution centers. The usual business hours are from 9 AM to 1 PM and from 3 to 7 PM, Monday through Friday, with a half-day on Saturday; some firms close on Saturday. Banking hours are 8:30 AM to 12 noon and 1 to 2:30 PM, Monday through Friday. An increasing number of shopping centers in urban areas have more flexible hours.

The most common advertising media are newspapers and outdoor billboards; movie theaters also carry advertisements.

31 FOREIGN TRADE
Portugal's foreign trade balance has regularly shown a heavy deficit. The principal exports are raw and processed cork, textiles and clothing, footwear, electrical machinery, and road vehicles and parts. Imports include fuels, foodstuffs, raw materials, machinery and equipment, and chemicals.

The principal trade partners in 1991 (in billions of escudos) were as follows:

	EXPORTS	IMPORTS	BALANCE
EC countries, of which	1,769.2	2,740.9	−971.7
France	337.9	454.8	−116.9
Germany	450.0	570.5	−120.5
Italy	93.9	390.6	−296.7
UK	251.9	285.4	−33.5
Netherlands	134.9	232.2	−97.3
Spain	351.3	602.6	−251.3
EFTA countries	228.5	233.1	−4.6
US	89.7	129.7	−40.0
OPEC	13.0	181.2	−168.2
Former colonies	98.4	18.1	80.3
Other countries	304.6	712.9	−408.3
TOTALS	2,354.1	3,811.1	−1,457.0

32 BALANCE OF PAYMENTS
Despite chronic trade deficits, Portugal until 1973 managed to achieve a balance-of-payments surplus through tourist revenues and remittances from emigrant workers. With the economic dislocations of 1974, net tourist receipts fell 30%; the trade deficit almost doubled; and emigrant remittances stagnated—thus, the 1973 payments surplus of $255.7 million became a $647.7 million deficit in 1974. Emigrant remittances grew steadily between 1976 and 1980, when they peaked at $2,946 million. Because of this, Portugal's balance of payments improved and in 1979 even showed a surplus of $761 million. Subsequently,

however, increasing trade deficits resulted in balance-of-payments deficits that reached $3.2 billion in 1982. By 1985, however, the deficit had become a surplus of $0.4 billion, which rose to $1.1 billion in 1986; the chief reason was the weakening dollar, which boosted the value of tourism earnings and remittances. The 1990 Portuguese external payments surplus stabilized at the previous year's record level of nearly $4 billion. Afer a few years of surplus boom, mainly due to the enormous influx of foreign capital and transfers to Portugal following EC membership in 1986, measures were taken in July 1990 to restrict foreign credit and investment thereby helping the authorities get better control over monetary aggregates. These measures, along with the hiatus in international investment caused by the Gulf crisis and some deterioration in the merchandise trade account contributed to halting the growth of the total nonmonetary balance. In 1992 merchandise exports totaled $18,195 million and imports $27,735 million. The merchandise trade balance was $9,540 million.

The following table summarizes Portugal's balance of payments for 1991 and 1992 (in millions of US dollars):

	1991	1992
CURRENT ACCOUNT		
Goods, services, and income	−6,691	−8,010
Unrequited transfers	5,974	7,826
TOTALS	−717	−184
CAPITAL ACCOUNT		
Direct investment	1,985	1,185
Portfolio investment	1,895	−3,064
Other long-term capital	−180	1,015
Other short-term capital	539	−87
Exceptional financing	—	—
Other liabilities	—	—
Reserves	−5,713	156
TOTALS	−1,474	−795
Errors and omissions	1,160	1,893
Total change in reserves	−513	1,197

33 BANKING AND SECURITIES
All banks in Portugal, except for three foreign-owned ones (Banco do Brasil, Credit Franco-Portugais, and the Bank of London and South America), were nationalized in 1975. A 1983 law, however, permitted private enterprise to return to the banking industry. Since then, 18 domestic private banks have been set up, and the establishment of 13 foreign banks has been authorized. The Bank of Portugal, the central bank (founded in 1846), functions as a bank of issue and rediscount, controls gold and foreign exchange movements, and sets the discount rate. Total assets of the bank on 31 December 1993 were $14,877 million. The money supply in December 1993, as measured by M2, totaled ɛ10,712 million. The escudo was regularly devalued by 0.6% a month after October 1986, but the Bank of Portugal has periodically intervened to adjust the exchange rate.

The state-owned General Savings Bank dominates the savings field, holding over 70% of time deposits. The National Development Bank, established in January 1960, administers long-term loans. Commercial and savings bank demand deposits were ɛ 2,908.7 billion at the end of 1993.

Portugal's two stock exchanges, located in Lisbon and Porto, were closed after the coup of April 1974. The Lisbon exchange reopened in 1976, and the Oporto exchange in 1981. The role of the stock exchange is relatively minor.

34 INSURANCE
Portugal's domestic insurance companies were nationalized in 1975. Foreign companies were required to accept government

representatives among their directors. A new law, approved in 1983, allowed the private sector to reenter the domestic insurance industry. Almost all Portuguese companies sell life and non-life insurance; some specialize in reinsurance only. In 1989 there were 13 life, 37 non-life, and 14 composite insurance companies. Premiums totaled US$206.3 per capita in 1990. The supervising authority is the National Insurance Institute.

35PUBLIC FINANCE

Portugal's budgets (accounting for the effects of loans and transfers) have been in deficit since 1974. The deficit is caused by accumulated debt service, which is shrinking due to a sustained policy of public debt prepayment that has reduced the public debt from a record 74.5% of GDP in 1988 to 63.8% in 1991. To finance the deficit, the government issues bonds in the domestic market, which also serves the monetary policy purpose of absorbing excess liquidity. The fiscal deficit narrowed in 1992 to 5.2% of GDP (down from 6.5% in 1991), primarily due to a large increase in indirect taxes, in the form of a value-added tax.

The following table shows actual revenues and expenditures for 1989 and 1990 in billions of escudos.

	1989	1990
REVENUE AND GRANTS		
Tax revenue	2,346.0	2,795.3
Non-tax revenue	139.7	250.6
Capital revenue	4.0	19.2
Grants	126.0	144.5
TOTAL	2,675.8	3,212.0
EXPENDITURES & LENDING MINUS REPAYMENTS		
General public service	234.9	296.8
Defense	168.8	188.0
Public order and safety	—	—
Education	345.0	426.6
Health	217.8	286.3
Social security and welfare	795.0	972.9
Housing and community amenities	22.6	27.3
Recreation, cultural, and religious affairs	24.5	27.4
Economic affairs and services	326.4	374.1
Other expenditures	770.5	989.9
Adjustments	−32.2	−21.6
Lending minus repayments	−28.0	−93.1
TOTAL	2,845.3	3,474.7
Deficit/Surplus	−169.5	−262.7

In 1992 Portugal's total public debt stood at the equivalent of $53,540 million.

36TAXATION

Corporate tax rates in 1993 were 36%, to which was added a 5–10% surcharge (formerly the municipal tax). Income tax varied from 16–40%. The payroll tax on normal pay comprised 24.5% for social security. Also levied are taxes on transactions (value-added, real estate, transfers, capital gains, and stamp duties) and taxes on property (real estate and investment income).

37CUSTOMS AND DUTIES

Portugal has a two-column tariff; maximum rates are applicable to countries having no specific commercial treaties with Portugal and minimum rates to those that have such treaties or are members of GATT. Specific duties are levied on gross, legal net, or actual net weight; ad valorem duties are assessed on the c.i.f. value. Import and export permits must be authorized by the government; in March 1978, Portugal introduced quota restrictions.

With Portugal's entry into the EC on 1 January 1986, tariffs were to be lowered during the following seven years to conform with the EC schedule. Quotas on car imports were to be abolished by 1988; tariff barriers and quota restrictions between Spain and Portugal were to be eliminated largely by 1989 and entirely by 1991. Portugal levies the EC Common Tariff on non-EC and non-EFTA goods. However, duty rates for agricultural and fishery goods were still higher in 1993 but slated for adjustment.

38FOREIGN INVESTMENT

As a member of the EU, Portugal abides by the investment rules that govern the rest of the union. New foreign investment legislation was enacted in 1986. The Institute of Foreign Investment (ICEP) is the supervising agency. Foreign investment is permitted in all sectors except power production, ports, air and rail services, and the arms industry. Even in these areas, however, deregulation is under way. The foreign investment code contains liberal profit remittance regulations and tax incentives.

Direct foreign investment in Portugal totaled $2.9 billion in 1992. Main investing countries are the UK, Spain, and France. The financial sector accounted for 63% of all new foreign investment in 1992.

39ECONOMIC DEVELOPMENT

In 1975, radical economic transformations were accomplished through a series of decrees that nationalized the domestically owned parts of major sectors of the national economy. These decrees affected the leading banks, insurance companies (representing 99% of insurance companies' capital), petroleum refineries, the transportation sector, the steel industry, and eventually Portugal's leading privately owned industrial monopoly, Companhia União Fabril. At the same time, large-scale agrarian reform measures led to expropriation of many of the country's privately owned large landholdings; other holdings were seized illegally by peasants. In an attempt to stimulate agricultural production, the government decreed a 30% reduction in the price of fertilizer to farm workers and small and medium farmers. When the nationalization and agrarian reform measures met with only limited success, partly because of liquidity problems, an emergency austerity plan was approved by the Council of Ministers in October 1975. The program included wage and import controls and the reduction of subsidies on consumer goods.

As a result of Portugal's entry into the EC, the highly protected, unresponsive, and inefficient economy is being transformed. State intervention is being reduced, and the physical infrastructure is being modernized. Privatization began in 1989, with the share of GDP for non-financial public enterprises reduced from 17.9% in 1985 to 10.7% in 1991. In 1992, $3.6 billion was raised as banks, insurance companies, and a 25% interest in Petrogal—the state oil company—were sold. The government estimated that privatized companies would represent half of stock market capitalization by the end of 1994.

40SOCIAL DEVELOPMENT

The government-run social security system provides old-age, disability, sickness, and unemployment benefits, family allowances, and health and medical care. The system is funded by payroll contributions from employers and employees. According to law, women must receive equal pay for equal work. In 1985, women accounted for 42% of the total labor force. The fertility rate in 1985–90 was 1.6.

Human rights conditions improved substantially after the 1974 coup. The secret police was dismantled, and civil and political rights were restored. A vaguely worded 1978 law prohibits activities related to fascism; through the mid-1980s, no charges had been brought under this statute. The maximum penalty for any crime is 28 years of imprisonment.

Women have full legal equality under the Civil Code. The Commission for Equality and Rights of Women has been a leading advocate for women's rights since 1976. In 1993, the government released a study on sexual harassment in the workplace calling for increased legal means of combating this problem.

41 HEALTH

The public health care sector is by far the largest. As of 1993, the country planned to construct 12 new hospital districts, 84 health centers, 5 technical schools for nurses, and to enlarge or remodel several hospital centers, hospital districts, and maternity wards. The Santa Maria Hospital in Lisbon is the largest hospital in Portugal. In 1990, there were 28,016 doctors (1 doctor for every 490 people), 5,438 pharmacists, and 4.2 hospital beds per 1,000 people. In 1992, there were 2.57 doctors per 1,000 inhabitants, with a nurse to doctor ratio of 0.8. The 1993 population of Portugal was 9.9 million, with a birthrate of 11.6 per 1,000 people, and 66% of married women (ages 15 to 49) using contraception. There were 114,000 births in 1992. The infant mortality rate decreased from 61 to 11 per 1,000 live births from 1968 to 1992. The general mortality rate was 10.2 per 1,000 people in 1993. Average life expectancy in 1992 was 75 years. The leading natural causes of death are circulatory disorders, cancer, and respiratory disorders. Statistics for 1990 indicated that major causes of death per 100,000 people were: (1) communicable diseases and maternal/perinatal causes (70); (2) noncommunicable diseases (429); and (3) injuries (78). There were 57 reported cases of tuberculosis in 1990. In 1992, children up to one year of age were vaccinated against tuberculosis (89%); diphtheria, pertussis, and tetanus (95%); polio (95%); and measles (96%). Total health care expenditures in 1990 were $3,970 million.

42 HOUSING

According to the 1981 census, Portugal had 2,548,064 residential buildings, with 3,426,702 dwelling units. In 1984, 44,132 new residential buildings were completed. In the early 1990s, Portugal built an average of 40,000 housing units annually, of which about 12,000 were for low-income housing, 4,000 were rental units for relocated residents, and 24,000 were constructed for the open market by the private sector. The total number of housing units in 1991 was 3,630,000. In May 1993, the government announced a $2 billion program designed to clear urban slums, which included the construction of 20,000 low-income units in Lisbon by the year 2000.

43 EDUCATION

Education has been compulsory since 1911. In 1990, adult literacy rates were an estimated 85–88.8% for men and 81.5% for women. Primary level education, which is for six years, is compulsory. Secondary level education is in two stages of three years. In 1990, preprimary schools numbered 4,879 with 9,700 teachers and 181,450 pupils. In 1991 primary schools had 998,529 pupils with 12,303 teachers. At the secondary level, during 1990, there were 64,513 teachers and 670,035 pupils. Of these, 32,274 pupils were in vocational schools.

Coimbra University, founded in 1290, is Portugal's oldest institution of higher learning, and the universities of Lisbon and Porto are two of the largest. In 1990, total enrollment in institutions of higher learning was 185,762, with 14,432 instructors. There are also art schools, music schools, and a school of tropical medicine.

44 LIBRARIES AND MUSEUMS

Portugal had 1,058 libraries reported in 1990, with a total book stock of over 15 million. The leading libraries are the National Library (about 2.2 million volumes) and the Library of the Academy of Sciences (360,000) in Lisbon, the University Library in Coimbra (1 million), and the Municipal Library in Porto (1.3 million).

There were 314 museums in 1990; most featured exhibits relating to Portuguese history. Lisbon has the National Museum of Ancient Art, the Museum of Decorative Arts, the Calouste Gulbenkian Museum, and the Center for Modern Art, as well as the National Museum of Natural History. The Abbey of the Friars of St. Jerome in Belém and the Battle Abbey in Batalha contain some of the finest specimens of Portuguese art.

45 MEDIA

The domestic telegraph and telephone systems are wholly government-operated. In 1991 there were 2,258,315 telephones in Portugal. Direct radiotelephone service connects Portugal with its former and current overseas provinces in Africa and Asia. The government broadcasting network, Radiodifusão Portuguesa, and Radio Renascenca, a religious network, operate AM and FM stations. In 1991, Portugal had about 2.2 million radios. The state-owned television network, Radiotelevisão Portuguesa, offers color broadcasts on two channels. There were 1.8 million television sets in 1991.

In 1991, 28 daily newspapers were published in Portugal, including the islands. The constitution of 1976 guaranteed freedom of the press. The principal daily newspapers (with their estimated 1991 circulations) include the following:

	AFFILIATION	CIRCULATION
LISBON		
Correo da Manhã	Independent	78,000
Diario de Noticias	Communist—influenced	70,000
Publico	NA	66,500
A Capital	Leftist—influenced	48,400
O Dia	NA	20,000
Diario Popular	Leftist—influenced	40,000
PORTO		
Jornal de Noticias	Leftist	75,500
O Comercio do Porto	Moderate	35,000
O Primeiro de Janeiro	Conservative	27,100

During the factional struggles of 1975, the press became a battleground between Communists and other left-wing factions. The most noteworthy episode was the takeover of the Socialist *República* by Maoist printers in May 1975. Communist influence in the press was abruptly curtailed after the nation's press was closed down by the new center-left coalition government in November 1975 and subsequently reorganized. Nearly all the newspapers had reappeared by the end of the year, in more moderate guises. In 1976, the government nationalized several newspaper publishing groups. The circulations of state-owned newspapers decreased during the late 1970s.

46 ORGANIZATIONS

Under the Salazar and Caetano regimes, the cooperative movement was generally superseded by state-controlled groups called juntas nacionais. The principal current organizations are syndicates, the majority of which are linked to the national trade union confederation; residents' commissions; workers' commissions; and popular assemblies. Many of these associations, particularly in rural areas, are involved in local community improvement projects as well as political and cultural activities. There are four chambers of commerce and three main industrial organizations, the oldest of which, the Industrial Association of Porto, dates from 1849.

47 TOURISM, TRAVEL, AND RECREATION

Tourism has become a major contributor of foreign exchange earnings ($3.7 billion in 1991) and a stimulus to employment and investment in the hotel industry and related services. In 1991, the number of tourists was 8,656,956; of these, 47% came from

Spain, 13% from the UK, 9% from Germany, and 7% from France. There were 82,575 hotel rooms with 188,501 beds and a 41.7% occupancy rate. Portugal's historic cities—Lisbon, Porto, Coimbra, and others—offer numerous museums, old churches, and castles. Most villages still celebrate market days with dances and other festivities. There are more than 800 km (500 mi) of beaches. The Portuguese bullfight (differing from the Spanish variety in that the bulls are not killed) is a popular spectator sport; the season lasts from Easter Sunday to October. Soccer is popular as both a participant and a spectator sport. Generally, a valid passport is required for entry, but air and sea travelers with an onward ticket may stay in Portugal for up to 10 days without a visa.

[48]FAMOUS PORTUGUESE

During Portugal's golden age, the 15th and 16th centuries, the small Portuguese nation built an overseas empire that stretched halfway around the globe. Prince Henry the Navigator (Henrique Navegador, 1394–1460) laid the foundations of the empire. Among the leaders in overseas exploration were Bartholomeu Dias (1450?–1500), the first European to round the Cape of Good Hope; Vasco da Gama (1469–1524), who reached India and founded Portuguese India in 1498; and Pedro Alvares Cabral (1460?–1526), who took possession of Brazil for Portugal in 1500. Ferdinand Magellan (Fernão de Magalhães, 1480?–1521) led a Spanish expedition, the survivors of which were the first to sail around the world, although Magellan himself was killed after reaching the Philippines. Afonso de Albuquerque (1453–1515) was foremost among the builders of Portugal's Far Eastern empire.

Famous literary figures of the golden age include the historians Diogo do Couto (1542–1616) and João de Barros (1496–1570); Portugal's greatest writer, Luis Vas de Camões (1524?–80), the author of Os Lusiadas, the Portuguese national epic, and of lyric and dramatic poetry; the dramatists Gil Vicente (1465?–1537?) and Francisco de Sá de Miranda (1482–1558); the poets Bernardim Ribeiro (1482?–1552) and Diogo Bernardes (1532?–96?); and the travel writer Fernão Mendes Pinto (1509–83). Portugal's leading painter was Nuno Gonçalves (fl.1450–80).

Among the noted Portuguese of more recent times are Sebastião José de Carvalho e Mello, marquis de Pombal (1699–1782), the celebrated prime minister of King Joseph Emanuel (José Manuel, 1715–77); the novelists Camilo Castelo Branco, viscount of Correia-Botelho (1825–90), and José Maria Eça de Queiróz (1843–1900); the poets João Baptista da Silva Leitão, viscount of Almeida-Garrett (1799–1854), Antero Tarquinio de Quental (1842–91), João de Deus Nogueira Ramos (1830–96), Teófilo Braga (1843–1924), and Abilio Manuel Guerra Junqueiro (1850–1923); the satirist José Duarte Ramalho Ortigão (1836–1915); and the painter Domingos António de Sequeira (1768–1837). António Caetano de Abreu Freire Egas Moniz (1874–1955) won the Nobel Prize in physiology in 1949.

António de Oliveira Salazar (1889–1970), prime minister for more than 30 years, was Portugal's best-known modern leader. Gen. (later Marshal) António Sebastião Ribeiro de Spínola (b.1910) played a key role in the revolution of April 1974. Gen. António dos Santos Ramalho Eanes (b.1935) became president in 1976 and was reelected in 1980. The main political leaders of the late 1970s and early 1980s were the Socialist Mário Alberto Nobre Lopes Soares (b.1924), prime minister in 1976–78 and 1983–85 and president since 1986; Francisco Sá Carneiro (1934–80), a

leader of the Social Democratic Party and prime minister in 1979–80; and economics professor Aníbal Cavaco Silva (b.1939), another Social Democratic leader and prime minister since 1985.

[49]DEPENDENCIES

Between 1974 and 1976, all of Portugal's overseas possessions in Africa—including Angola, the Cape Verde Islands, Portuguese Guinea (now Guinea-Bissau), Mozambique, and São Tomé and Príncipe—became independent countries in accordance with the Armed Forces Movement's decolonization policy. After the Portuguese withdrew from East Timor, in the Indonesian archipelago, the former colony was invaded by Indonesian forces in 1975 and became a province of Indonesia in 1976, however, neither Portugal nor the UN has officially recognized the annexation. Macau, on the south coast of China, has been a "Chinese territory under Portuguese administration" since 1975 and will become a Chinese territory in 1999; see Portuguese Asian Dependency in the *Asia* volume.

[50]BIBLIOGRAPHY

Bruneau, Thomas C., and Alex Macleod. *Politics in Contemporary Portugal: Parties and the Consolidation of Democracy.* Boulder, Colo.: Lynne Rienner, 1986.

Clarence-Smith, Gervase. *The Third Portuguese Empire, 1825–1975.* Wolfeboro, N.H.: Longwood, 1985.

Graham, Lawrence F., and Harry M. Makler (eds.). *Contemporary Portugal: The Revolution and Its Antecedents.* Austin: University of Texas Press, 1979.

——. *The Portuguese Military and the State: Rethinking Transitions in Europe and Latin America.* Boulder, Colo.: Westview Press, 1993.

Harvey, Robert. *Portugal: Birth of a Democracy.* New York: St. Martin's, 1978.

Herr, Richard (ed.). *The New Portugal: Democracy and Europe.* Berkeley: University of California at Berkeley, 1992.

Kaplan, Marion. *The Portuguese: The Land and its People.* London: Viking, 1991.

Livermore, Harold Victor. *A New History of Portugal.* 2d ed. New York: Cambridge University Press, 1977.

MacDonald, Scott B. *European Destiny, Atlantic Transformations: Portuguese Foreign Policy Under the Second Republic, 1974–1992.* New Brunswick, N.J: Transaction Publishers, 1993.

Machado, Diamantino P. *The Structure of Portuguese Society: the Failure of Fascism.* New York: Praeger, 1991.

Oliveira Marques, A. H. de. *History of Portugal.* New York: Columbia University Press, 1972.

Opello, Walter C. *Portugal: From Monarchy to Pluralist Democracy.* Boulder, Colo.: Westview Press, 1991.

Payne, Stanley G. *A History of Spain and Portugal.* Madison: University of Wisconsin Press, 1973.

Pitcher, M. Anne. *Politics in the Portuguese Empire: The State, Industry, and Cotton, 1926–1974.* New York: Oxford University Press, 1993.

Solstein, Eric (ed.). *Portugal: A Country.* 2d ed. Washington, D.C.: Library of Congress, 1993.

Wheeler, Douglas L. *Historical Dictionary of Portugal.* Metuchen, N.J.: Scarecrow Press, 1993.

Wiarda, Howard J. *Politics in Iberia: The Political Systems of Spain and Portugal.* New York, NY: HarperCollins, 1993.

ROMANIA

Romania

CAPITAL: Bucharest (Bucuresti).

FLAG: The national flag, adopted in 1965, is a tricolor of blue, yellow, and red vertical stripes.

ANTHEM: *Trei culori (Three Colors).*

MONETARY UNIT: The leu (L) is a paper currency of 100 bani. There are coins of 25 bani and 1, 3, 5, 10, 20, 50, and 100 lei, and notes of 10, 25, 50, 100, 200, 500, 1,000, and 5,000 lei. L1 = $0.0006 (or $1 = L1,650).

WEIGHTS AND MEASURES: The metric system is the legal standard.

HOLIDAYS: New Year's Day, 1 January; International Labor Day, 1–2 May; Liberation Day, 23 August; National Day, 1 December; Christmas Day, 25 December.

TIME: 2 PM = noon GMT.

¹LOCATION, SIZE, AND EXTENT

Situated in eastern Europe, north of the Balkan Peninsula, Romania has a total area of 237,500 sq km (91,699 sq mi). Comparatively, the area occupied by Romania is slightly smaller than the state of Oregon. The dimensions of the country are 789 km (490 mi) E–W and 475 km (295 mi) N–S. It is bounded on the N and NE by Ukraine and Moldova, on the E by the Black Sea, on the S by Bulgaria, on the SW by Serbia, and on the W by Hungary, with a total boundary length of 2,733 km (1,698 mi). Romania's capital city, Bucharest, is located in the south central part of the country.

²TOPOGRAPHY

The backbone of Romania is formed by the Carpathian Mountains, which swing southeastward and then westward through the country. The southern limb of this arc-shaped system is known as the Transylvanian Alps, whose compact, rugged peaks rise to 2,543 m (8,343 ft) in Mt. Moldoveanu, Romania's highest. The eastern Carpathians have an average elevation of 1,000 m (3,300 ft) and exceed 1,900 m (6,200 ft) only in the highest ranges. On the eastern and southern fringes of the Carpathian arc are the low plateaus and plains of Moldavia and Walachia, extending to the Prut River (Moldovan border) in the east and to the Danube (Bulgarian border) in the south. On the inside of the Carpathian arc is the Transylvanian Basin, a hilly region dissected by the wide, deep valleys of the Mures and Somes rivers. The Dobruja, located between the lower Danube and the Black Sea, is an eroded plateau with average elevations of 400 to 600 m (1,310–1,970 ft). Except for the low-lying, swampy Danube Delta in the north, the Black Sea coast of the Dobruja is steep, facing the sea with almost vertical cliffs.

An earthquake that struck Romania on 4 March 1977 destroyed or severely damaged some 33,000 buildings and left more than 34,000 families homeless. The shock, measuring 7.2 on the open-ended Richter scale, was the most severe in Europe since a series of shocks in October–November 1940, also in Romania.

³CLIMATE

Romania's climate is of the moderate humid continental type, exposed to predominant northerly cold winds in the winter and moderate westerly winds from the Atlantic in the summer. Average January temperatures range from –4°C to 0°C (25–32°F). During the summer, the highest temperatures are recorded in the Danube Valley (24°C/75°F). Temperatures decrease toward the high elevations in the northwest and toward the southeast, where the Black Sea exerts a moderating influence. Precipitation decreases from west to east and from the mountains to the plains, with an annual average of between 100 and 125 cm (about 40 and 50 in) in the mountains and about 38 cm (15 in) in the delta.

⁴FLORA AND FAUNA

Natural vegetation consists mainly of steppelike grasslands in the Moldavian and Walachian lowlands, with tall, deep-rooted grasses in the more humid sections and short, shallow-rooted grass in the drier parts. The Carpathian system is covered with forests, with deciduous trees at lower elevations and conifers at altitudes above 1,070–1,220 m (3,500–4,000 ft). Alpine meadows occupy the highest parts of the mountains. Wild animals, including the black chamois, Carpathian deer, wolves, hares, marten, brown bear, lynx, boar, and fox, have sought refuge in the sparsely inhabited and forested Carpathians. Water birds flourish in the Danube Delta, and sturgeon abound in the waters of the lower Danube. Carp, bream, and pike populate the lakes; dace, barbel, and trout are found in rivers and streams.

⁵ENVIRONMENT

The National Council for Environmental Protection is the main environmental agency. Rapid industrialization since World War II has caused widespread water and air pollution, particularly in Prahova County, an oil-refining region. The nation has 8.9 cubic miles of water with 59% used to support farming and 33% used for industrial purposes. Romania's cities produce 3.0 million tons of solid waste per year. Air pollution is heaviest in the nation's cities where industry produces hazardous levels of sulphur dioxide. Romania contributes 0.7% of the world's total gas emissions. Damage to the nation's soils from erosion and pollution has decreased agricultural production by 50% in some areas. Acid rain originating in Hungary is another environmental problem. Some water conservation programs were initiated in the mid-1980s, but the Environmental Protection Law of 1972 has not been strictly enforced. Romania's forests and natural steppelands have been encroached on by farmers. Radioactivity from the Chernobyl nuclear site, two floods, and two earthquakes have also contributed to the nation's environmental problems. Moreover, intensive exploitation of forests before, during, and immediately after World War II necessitated a reforestation program that, between 1950 and 1964, resulted in the replanting of 1,159,600 hectares (2,865,400 acres). In 1994, two of Romania's mammal species, 18 of its bird species, and 67 plant types are endangered. The Romanian bullhead perch was among those listed as endangered. Romania had 12 national parks in 1986.

6POPULATION

According to the 1992 census, Romania's total population was 22,810,035; the population was estimated at 23,777,056 in mid-1994. A population of 24,039,000 was projected for the year 2000, assuming a crude birthrate of 16.5 per 1,000 population, a crude death rate of 10.7, and a net natural increase of 5.8 during 1995–2000. The average density as of 1995 was 96 per sq km (248 per sq mi). The urban population represented 54% of the total in 1992. Bucharest (Bucuresti), the capital and principal city, had a population of 2,067,545 in 1992. Other major cities and their 1992 populations (excluding suburbs) were Brasov, 323,736; Constanta, 350,581; Timisoara, 334,115; Iasi, 344,425; Cluj-Napoca, 328,602; Galati, 325,788; Craiova, 303,959; Braila, 234,110; and Ploiesti, 252,715.

7MIGRATION

Population shifts numbering in the millions occurred as a result of the two world wars—because of territorial changes, deportation and liquidation of Jews by the Nazis, flight before the Soviet military forces, deportations to the USSR, expulsion of the Volksdeutsche (ethnic Germans), and departures following the Communist takeover and before stringent security measures halted the flow. About 117,950 Jews emigrated to Israel between 1948 and 1951; another 90,000 were permitted to emigrate during 1958–64. Some 120,000 ethnic Germans left Romania between 1978 and 1988, and some 40,000 ethnic Hungarians fled in 1987 alone. In 1990, 80,346 people left, 78% to Germany, 9% to Hungary. Some 44,160 Romanians emigrated in 1991 and 31,152 in 1992. In 1992, 103,787 Romanians were given asylum in Germany, but in September of that year Germany returned 43,000 refugees, over half of whom were Gypsies.

8ETHNIC GROUPS

Romanians constitute by far the majority group (89.5%, according to the 1992 census), but the population includes two important ethnic minorities: Hungarians (7.1% of the total population) and Germans (0.5%), both concentrated in Transylvania. The number of Hungarians may be understated by as much as 40%, however, and the number of Germans by even more. The number of Gypsies, officially put at 401,087, has been estimated elsewhere at 2.3 million. Lesser numbers of minorities (totaling 1.1%) include Ukrainians, Turks, Russians, Serbs, Croats, Jews, Poles, Bulgarians, Czechs, Greeks, Armenians, Tatars, and Slovaks.

Under the new government, as under the Communist regime, ethnic Hungarians have vainly sought the full restoration of secondary and university teaching in their language. They also criticize the failure of the new constitution to guarantee the use of minority languages in court. Since 1989 Gypsies have been targets of an organized campaign of violence throughout Romania.

9LANGUAGES

Romanian is the official language. It is a Romance language derived from the Latin spoken in the Eastern Roman Empire, and Latin word elements make up 85% to 90% of the modern Romanian vocabulary. In the 2,000 years of its development, the language was also influenced by contacts with Slavonic, Albanian, Hungarian, Greek, and Turkish. Of the loanwords, Slavonic elements are the most numerous. Earliest Romanian written texts still extant date from the 16th century. In addition to letters of the English alphabet, Romanian has the letters ă, î, â, ş, and ţ. Hungarian is spoken by a large percentage of the inhabitants of Transylvania.

10RELIGIONS

The great majority of Romanians (estimated at 87% in 1993) are affiliated with the Romanian Orthodox Church, one of the autocephalous Eastern Orthodox churches. Under Bulgarian influence, Slavonic rite was maintained in the Romanian Church until the 17th century, when Romanian became the liturgical language. The Romanian Church enjoyed a large measure of autonomy in the Middle Ages and, after Romania achieved full independence from the Turks in 1878, was formally declared independent of the Patriarchate of Constantinople; it is now headed by its own patriarch. The Greek Catholic (Uniate) Church was formed in 1698 by the Transylvanian Orthodox, who acknowledged the jurisdiction of the Holy See. In October 1948, the new Communist regime compelled the Uniate Church to sever its ties with Rome and to merge with the Romanian Orthodox Church.

There are 13 other legally recognized denominations. About 3.2 million persons belonged to the Roman Catholic Church in 1993. Greatly weakened under earlier Communist pressure, Roman Catholics had no official connection with Rome since 1948, when the Communist regime unilaterally annulled the concordat with the Vatican. In 1990, relations with the Vatican were restored. There were about 17,500 Jews in 1988. Other denominations include the Reformed (Calvinist) Church of Romania, with an estimated 600,000 members; the German-minority Evangelical Church of the Augsburg Confession, 150,000; and the Unitarian Church (mostly Hungarian), 60,000. There are small numbers of Baptists, Seventh-Day Adventists, Pentecostals, and Muslims.

11TRANSPORTATION

The length of Romania's railroad network in 1991 was 10,860 km (6,750 mi) of standard-gauge track and 45 km (28 mi) of broad-gauge track; 3,411 km (2,120 mi) was electrified and 3,060 km (1,901 mi) was double track. There were 72,799 km (45,235 mi) of roads at the end of 1991, of which 35,970 km (22,352 mi) were paved. In 1992, there were 1,593,029 passenger cars and 378,677 commercial vehicles in use.

Only the Danube and, to a lesser extent, the Prut rivers are suitable for inland navigation, which accounts for only about 1% of the total freight traffic. The main Danube ports include Galati, Braila, and Giurgiu. At Giurgiu, on the main transportation line between Romania and Bulgaria, a road-and-rail bridge was completed in 1954, replacing the former Danube ferry to Ruse, Bulgaria. A major project, the Danube–Black Sea Canal, designed to bypass the shallow, silted arms of the Danube Delta, was started in 1949 but abandoned in 1953; it was revived in the early 1980s and opened in 1984. The canal is 64 km (40 mi) long and connects Cernavoda with Constanta. The Romanian merchant fleet consisting of 282 vessels, totaled 3.5 million GRT in 1991, and was based in Constanta, the nation's chief Black Sea port.

Romanian Air Transport (Transporturile Aeriene Române—TAROM) and Romanian Air Lines (Liniile Aeriene Române—LAR) are the primary air carriers. Otopeni International Airport, near Bucharest, was opened in 1970 and remains the nation's principal international air terminal. Baneasa Airport, also near Bucharest, handles local traffic.

12HISTORY

Archaeological excavations show that the land now known as Romania has been inhabited for thousands of years. Agriculture

ROMANIA

| 0 | 50 | 100 Miles |
| 0 | 50 | 100 Kilometers |

LOCATION: 48°15′06″ to 43°37′07″N; 20°15′44″ to 29°41′24″E. **BOUNDARY LENGTHS:** Ukraine 531 km (329 mi); Moldova, 450 km (279 mi); Black Sea coastline, 234 km (145 mi); Bulgaria, 608 km (377 mi); Serbia and Montenegro, 476 km (295 mi); Hungary, 445 km (277 mi). **TERRITORIAL SEA LIMIT:** 12 mi.

was introduced in the 6th millennium BC, and by the 3d millennium BC the Cucuteni civilization had produced polychrome pottery. The Dacians, of Thracian stock, had become a distinct people by the end of the 1st millennium BC. The kingdom of Dacia reached the highest stage of its development toward the end of the 1st century AD, in the reign of Decebalus (87–106), but after four years of war, Dacia fell to the Roman Emperor Trajan in AD 106. The withdrawal of the Romans in AD 271 left the Romanians a partly Christianized Dacian-Roman people, speaking Latin and living in towns and villages built on the Roman pattern. In the following centuries, as Dacia was overrun by successive waves of invaders, the early Romanians are believed to have sought refuge in the mountains or to have migrated south of the Danube River. There the Dacian-Romanians, assimilating Slavic influences, became known by the 7th century as Vlachs (Walachians). The Vlachs apparently remained independent of their neighbors, but came under Mongol domination in the 13th century.

The establishment of the two principalities of Walachia and Moldavia in the late 13th and early 14th centuries opened one of the most important chapters in the history of Romania. Walachia came under Turkish suzerainty in 1476 and Moldavia in 1513; 13 years later, Transylvania, which had been under Hungarian control since 1003, also passed into Turkish hands. The tide of Ottoman domination began to ebb under Russian pressure in the second half of the 17th century; in 1699, under the Treaty of Karlowitz, Transylvania was taken by Austria (later Austria-Hungary), and in 1812, Russia obtained Bessarabia, a section of Moldavia, from the Turks. The Congress of Paris in 1856, which ended the Crimean War, guaranteed the autonomy of the principalities of Walachia and Moldavia and forced Russia to return the southernmost part of Bessarabia to Moldavia. The two principalities formed a union in 1859, with Alexandru Ioan Cuza as its first prince, but he was replaced in 1866 by Carol I of the house of Hohenzollern-Sigmaringen, under a new governing document that proclaimed Romania a constitutional monarchy. At the Congress of Berlin in 1878, Romania obtained full independence from Turkey but returned southern Bessarabia to Russia. Under the rule of Carol I, Romania developed into a modern political and economic unit.

As a result of the Balkan Wars in 1912–13, Romania gained southern Dobruja from Bulgaria. Carol I died in 1914 and was succeeded by Ferdinand I. In World War I, Romania joined the Allies, and as a result acquired Bessarabia from Russia, Bukovina from Austria, and Transylvania from Hungary. The establishment of a greatly expanded Romania was confirmed in 1919–20 by the treaties of St. Germain, Trianon, and Neuilly. In the early postwar period, Ion Bratianu (son of a 19th-century premier) instituted agrarian and electoral reforms. Both Ferdinand and Bratianu died in 1927. A brief regency period under Iuliu Maniu, Peasant Party leader, was followed in 1930 by the return to Romania of Carol II, who, having earlier renounced his right of succession, now deposed his nine-year-old son, Michael (Mihai), and established a royal dictatorship.

As economic conditions deteriorated, Fascism and anti-Semitism became increasingly powerful, and Carol II sought to appease both Germany and the USSR, which by August 1939 had concluded their nonaggression agreement. In 1940, Romania ceded Bessarabia and northern Bukovina to the USSR, northern Transylvania to Hungary, and southern Dobruja to Bulgaria. In the same year, Carol II abdicated in favor of his son Michael, and German troops entered the country. Romania joined the Axis in war against the Allies in 1941. As Soviet forces drove into Romania in 1944, a coup overthrew the wartime regime of Gen. Ion Antonescu on 23 August, and Romania joined the Allies against Germany. A Communist-led coalition government under Premier Petru Groza was set up in March 1945. King Michael was forced to abdicate on 30 December 1947, and the Romanian People's Republic was proclaimed. The Paris Peace Treaty of 1947 fixed Romania's frontiers as of 1 January 1941, with the exception of the border with Hungary, which was restored as of 1 January 1938, so that northern Transylvania was once again part of the Romanian state.

The Communist constitution of 1948 was superseded in 1952 by a constitution patterned more directly on that of the USSR. In international affairs, Romania followed a distinctly pro-Soviet line, becoming a member of CMEA and the Warsaw Pact. Internally, the regime nationalized the economy and pursued a policy of industrialization and the collectivization of agriculture. During the 1960s, however, and especially after the emergence of Nicolae Ceausescu as Communist Party and national leader, Romania followed a more independent course, increasing its trade with Western nations and avoiding a definite stand in the Sino-Soviet dispute. In 1967, Romania was the only Communist country that did not break diplomatic relations with Israel following the Six-Day War. In 1968, Romania denounced the Soviet intervention in Czechoslovakia, and the USSR-Romania treaty of friendship and cooperation expired; a new accord was not signed until 1970. Further examples of Romania's independent foreign policy in the 1970s were the gradual improvement of relations with China, numerous bilateral agreements with the nations of Western Europe, and President Ceausescu's state visit in December 1973 to Washington, where he signed a joint declaration on economic, industrial, and technical cooperation with the US. In the 1970s and early 1980s, Romania also became increasingly involved in the nonaligned movement. In 1982, Ceausescu called on the USSR to withdraw from Afghanistan.

In contrast to some other East European countries, there was relatively little political and cultural dissent in Romania during the first 30 years of Communist rule. In 1977, however, about 35,000 miners in the Jiu Valley, west of Bucharest, went on strike because of economic grievances. Afterwards, the Romanian

Communist Party hierarchy was frequently reshuffled, ostensibly to improve economic management, with Ceausescu and several members of his family (particularly his wife, Elena) increasing their power.

In the early and mid-1980s, there were a number of work stoppages and strikes caused by food and energy shortages. In early 1987, Ceausescu indicated that Romania would not follow the reform trend initiated by Mikhail Gorbachev in the USSR.

The progress of perestroika (restructuring) in the Soviet Union, intensified by the wave of "velvet revolutions" which rolled across Eastern Europe in autumn 1989, only served to highlight the repressiveness of the Ceausescu regime, which had all but starved and frozen the country to death in its attempt to repay international indebtedness, which President Ceausescu said in April 1989 had been $10 billion. The regime was also single-mindedly pushing ahead with the "systemization plan" begun in March 1988, which intended to force about half the country's peasants into urbanized "agro-industrial" complexes by bulldozing their villages.

The policy was especially offensive to the 2.5 million Hungarians in Romania's western regions, who understood the policy to be an attempt to further undercut their cultural autonomy. In mid-December 1989, abysmal economic conditions and ethnic tension led to spontaneous demonstrations in the western city of Timisoara. When the Securitate, Romania's dreaded secret police, attempted to deport Laszlo Toekes, a popular clergyman who had been a leading spokesperson for the local Hungarians, thousands of people took to the streets. Troops were summoned, and two days of rioting ensued, during which several thousand citizens were killed.

News of the riot, and of the government's handling of it, fanned further demonstrations around the country. Probably unwisely, President Ceausescu went ahead with a planned three-day visit to Iran. Upon his return, he convened a mass rally at which he attempted to portray his opponents as fascists. However, the rally turned into an anti-government demonstration, in which the army sided with the demonstrators.

Ceausescu and his wife attempted to flee the country, but were apprehended, tried, and summarily executed, on 25 December 1989. Several days of fighting raged, as the Securitate and the army battled for power. A hastily assembled Council of National Salvation took power, repealing a number of Ceausescu's most hated policies and laws. The Council's president was Ion Iliescu, a former secretary of the Communist Party, who had been one of several signatories to a letter which had accused Ceausescu of gross mismanagement of Romania's economy, made public in March 1989. The Prime Minister, Peter Roman, was also a prominent Communist.

Although the Council contained some non-Communists, the majority had been prominent officials in Ceausescu's regime, which prompted almost continuous public protests. Despite a continued government monopoly on media, political opposition groups managed to rally public support to demand the banning of the Communist Party, and the widening of the government. In February 1990, Iliescu agreed, replacing the 145-member Council of National Salvation with a 241-member Council of National Unity, which included members of opposition parties, national minorities, and former political prisoners; it also contained the full membership of the former Council, and Iliescu remained president.

Parliamentary elections were held in May 1990 against a background of continued civil unrest, especially in the Hungarian west. Although international observers considered the elections to have been generally fair, the National Salvation Front—now a political party—made ruthless use of its media monopoly to take about two-thirds of the parliamentary seats from a divided, disorganized, and inexperienced opposition. Iliescu was elected president, with about 85% of the votes, in a contest in which there had been more than 94% voter turn-out.

The conviction that ex-Communists had "stolen" the election brought continued demonstrations in Bucharest and elsewhere. In April 1990, in a move which was criticized internationally, the Iliescu government trucked in miners from the northern part of the country, urging them to beat up and disperse the demonstrators, ending what threatened to become a coup d'etat against Iliescu.

After the failure of those demonstrations, the opposition began to link up into parties, hoping to challenge Iliescu and his party in the next parliamentary elections, to be held in 1992. Popular discontent, however, continued to find more direct expression. Angry that the promises which had brought them to Bucharest in June had not been kept, the miners returned in September 1991, this time to link up with many of the opposition figures whom they earlier had attacked, now to mount a mass attack on the government. Iliescu had no choice but to dismiss Prime Minister Roman, replacing him with Theodor Stolojan, an economist who managed to contain popular discontent until the general elections of September 1992, largely by delaying implementation of economic reforms. The parliamentary elections demonstrated a wide diffusion of political support. Iliescu's National Salvation Front won 28% of the seats, making it the largest party, but the Democratic Convention, an anti-Communist opposition coalition with a strong monarchist wing, took 20%, while former Prime Minister Roman's National Salvation Front, now opposed to Iliescu, took 10%. The remaining 42% of the seats were divided among 5 other parties.

The popular vote for president showed that Iliescu still had support, although it had dropped just above 60% of the electorate. The success of his opponent, Emil Constantinescu, a former rector of Bucharest University, demonstrated the continuing hostility to Iliescu and the other ex-Communists who had managed to retain power.

Iliescu's dismissal of Stolojan, in November 1992, was widely seen as a recognition of that significant minority's opposition. Iliescu chose Nicolae Vacaroiu as Prime Minister, who had had no earlier ties to the Ceausescu or Iliescu governments. However, the move was addressed as much to the International Monetary Fund (IMF) and the rest of the international financial community, which has emerged as Romania's chief source of support. Continued political instability and the fitful pace of privatization, combined with a strong nationalist bloc in the parliament which warns against "selling out" Romania to foreigners, have all kept foreign investment quite low, a total of only about $785 million for all of 1990–94. As a consequence Romania has had to rely upon loans from Western sources, especially the IMF, piling up foreign debt at the rate of about $1 billion a year. In return for this infusion of cash the foreign donors have set stringent requirements of economic reform, which Romania is not finding easy to meet.

Romania's fitful progress toward democratization exacerbates the social pressures of its continued economic decline. Romanians began the post-Ceausescu period as among the poorest people in Europe, and their economy has only grown worse since. Inflation for 1992 was 210%, and more than 300% for 1993, while unemployment was almost 10%. Most significantly, production has fallen consistently, dropping 22% in 1993 against the preceding year.

As a consequence, more Romanians appear to be seeking miracles, either of the religious sort, as was the case with the huge crowds which descended on Bucharest in October 1993 to venerate the relics of an Orthodox saint, or of the economic sort, as was the case with the 4 million people who had put their money—estimated to be about 50% of the country's total savings—into a pyramid investment scheme set up in 1992 by a company called Caritas. In November 1993, Caritas collapsed, wiping out the savings of hundreds of thousands of people.

¹³GOVERNMENT

The Council for National Unity enacted a new constitution for Romania in November 1991, but the document carries many of the hallmarks of Soviet-era constitutions, granting rights in some articles which it revokes in others. In practice, government remains largely centralized and relatively secretive, with power more diffuse than it was in the Ceausescu period, but still far from democratic.

The present arrangement has a directly elected president, who is head of state. The current president, Ion Iliescu, resigned from the National Salvation Front, of which he was a founding member, upon taking office; it is not clear, however, whether this was constitutionally required. Among the president's powers is the right to name the government, which is headed by a prime minister. The present lack of a dominant party encouraged Iliescu to chose Nicolae Vacariou as Prime Minister, an economist without party affiliations.

The legislature is made up of two houses, the Senate, with 143 seats, and the Assembly of Deputies, with 341 seats, 13 of them appointive, rather than elective. Although the legislature has the formal duty to propose and pass laws, in practice the bodies have been weak, so that much of the country's function appears still to be conducted by decrees and orders, as in the past. In addition the present legislature is badly split, with a large opposition able to combine for negative votes, but not able to maintain a coherent program themselves, since they combine socialists, monarchists, and nationalist extremists, some of whom wish to return to the Ceausescu past, others of whom find their inspiration in the pre-war fascist Iron Guard.

The 1991 constitution affords the Romanian judiciary nominal independence, which is meant to be insured by a Constitutional Court. However, since the Court's findings carry only "consultative" status, in practice the judiciary remains responsive to central authority.

¹⁴POLITICAL PARTIES

After the coup against Ceausescu, some 80 political parties appeared, some new, others, like the Liberals and the Peasant Party, revivals of pre-war parties which the Communists had outlawed. The dominant party in the 1990 elections, however, proved to be the National Salvation Front (NSF), which took two-thirds of the seats in the National Assembly.

By 1992, the NSF had split over the issue of whether or not to support Iliescu. The main party renamed itself the Party of Social Democracy in Romania (PSDR), while a pro-Iliescu wing became the Democratic National Salvation Front, and an anti-Iliescu wing, headed by ex-Prime Minister Roman, became the Front for National Salvation. The PSDR took 28% of the vote, while the FSN got about 10%.

The second-largest party in the 1992 elections was a coalition, called the Democratic Convention of Romania (DCR), which incorporated such parties as the National Peasant Party Christian Democratic, the Movement of Civic Alliance, the Party of Civic Alliance, Liberal Party '93, and the Social Democratic Party. Comprising monarchists, pro-republicans, and strong nationalists, the DCR is able to agree on little beyond their opposition to Iliescu, whom they have moved to impeach, and Vacariou, in whom they have repeatedly attempted to vote "no confidence."

A total of 42% of the National Assembly is held by five other parties, none of them large enough to influence policy alone, but all of them able to exaggerate their influence through coalition building. These include the Magyar Democratic Union, the Agrarian Democratic Party, the National Unity Party, Democratic National Salvation Front, and others.

Their support of the minority PSDR government gave exaggerated importance to two ultra-nationalist parties, the Party of Romanian National Unity and the Greater Romania Party, and to the Communists, now reborn as the Socialist Labor Party. Despite superficial political differences, all three parties are anti-Hungarian, anti-Gypsy, and anti-Semitic, as well as anti-democratic.

Romania also has small but active neo-fascist parties, which find their inspiration in the Iron Guards and other fascist movements of the pre-war past. One group, lead by the Movement for Romania, exalts the Iron Guard of Corneliu Codreanu (d. 1938), while the Party for the Fatherland prefers the fascism of Codreanu's successor, Horia Sima (died in exile in 1993).

15 LOCAL GOVERNMENT

Romania is divided into 40 counties, as well as the municipality of Bucharest, which has separate status. In the Ceausescu era these localities were administered by appointees of the center, whose reponsibility was solely to Bucharest. The Iliescu government has attempted to reshape local government, but most sources agree that the result has been only to remove authority from the countryside, not to replace it. Much of Romania is deeply rural, with almost no contact between localities or with the center. The Iliescu government stopped the Ceausescu "systemization" plan and, in 1990, passed legislation intended to return land to individual peasant control. Indications are, however, that enactment of those provisions is spotty, suggesting that much of the countryside remains in a sort of administrative limbo, no longer tightly controlled by the center but not yet self-governing.

16 JUDICIAL SYSTEM

The 1992 law on reorganization of the judiciary establishes a four-tier legal system, including the reestablishment of appellate courts which existed prior to Communist rule in 1952. The four tiers consist of courts of first instance, intermediate appellate level courts, a Supreme Court, and a Constitutional Court. The Constitutional Court, six of whose nine members are chosen by the Parliament and three by the President, has judicial responsibility for judicial review of constitutional issues. The intermediate appellate courts had not yet been established as of 1993 due to lack of personnel and funding. The Justice Ministry has had difficulty recruiting lawyers and judges because of the fact that private practice has become financially more attractive to many attorneys.

Under the law, the courts are independent of the executive branch. The Constitution vests authority for selection and promotion of judges in the Ministry of Justice. Judges are appointed for life by the President upon recommendation from a panel of judges and prosecutors selected by Parliament.

Alongside this ordinary court system is a three-tiered military court system which handles cases involving military personnel.

17 ARMED FORCES

The revolution of 1989–90 destroyed the Communist armed forces and security establishment. Reorganization continues. In 1993, the armed forces numbered about 200,000 officers and men: 161,000 in the army, 19,000 in the navy, and 20,000 in the air force, which had 486 combat aircraft and 220 armed helicopters. In addition, frontier guards and security troops, both militarized, totaled some 37,000 men, and the militia (Patriotic Guard) totaled about 900,000. Conscripts (126,700) serve in all branches.

Military service is compulsory, and all able-bodied men at the age of 20 may be drafted into the armed forces for 12–18 months. Budgeted defense expenditures in 1991 may have been $500 million or about 1.5% of GDP. Arms imports during 1981–91 were estimated at $3.5 billion, and arms exports at $3.1 billion until ended in 1990. Military equipment and arms are Russian. The Ministry of Interior controls 15,000 border guards and 34,800 national police.

18 INTERNATIONAL COOPERATION

Romania, which became a member of the UN on 14 December 1955, participates in ECE and all the nonregional specialized agencies except the IDA and IFC. Although Romania is also a member of CMEA and WTO, its demonstrated independence from the Soviet-era line in foreign policy matters allows the nation to participate in G-77, the only Warsaw Pact member to do so. Romania is a contracting party to GATT and receives favorable consideration from the EC as a developing nation. The nation is also a signatory to the Law of the Sea.

19 ECONOMY

Before World War II, the economy was predominantly agricultural, with agriculture and forestry contributing 38.1% of the national income in 1938, and industry (including construction) 35.2%. As a result of the industrialization program of the Communist government, this ratio has changed greatly. In 1993, agriculture contributed 23.4% to national income; industry, 43.8%; construction, 4%; transport, 5.1%; trade, 10.8%; and other branches 12.9%. Within industry, structural changes reflected the government's emphasis on the development of heavy industry, particularly machine-building, as opposed to consumer goods. The relative neglect of the agricultural sector, in addition to peasants' resistance to collectivization, resulted in agricultural difficulties, including shortages.

The basic organization of economic management in Romania was highly centralized, like its original Soviet model, with few of the modifications introduced elsewhere in Eastern Europe. During the late 1970s and in the 1980s, the continued emphasis on industrial expansion and consequent neglect of agriculture led to food shortages and rationing. Romania's economic problems in the 1980s were exacerbated by the government's program to reduce foreign debt: the debt was indeed reduced, from $10.5 billion in 1981 to $6.6 billion at the end of 1987, but at the cost of reduced industrial development. In addition, two extremely harsh winters (1985 and 1987) resulted in widespread power shortages and loss of production.

The transition to a market economy also proved extremely painful. In 1992, grain production was only two-thirds of the 1989 level, and in 1993 industrial output had fallen to 47% of the 1989 level. GDP fell by 38% between 1989 and 1992 before rising 1% in 1993. After price controls were lifted from all but a few goods, the consumer price index soared to 32 times the 1969 level, more than tripling in 1992 and almost quadrupling in 1993. Unemployment, formerly virtually nonexistent, reached 10.5% of the labor force in 1993. In that year, the private sector had grown to 30% of GDP.

20 INCOME

In 1992, the GNP was $24,865 million at current prices, or $1,090 per capita. For the period 1985–92 the average inflation rate was 30.9%, resulting in a real growth rate in per capita GNP of –5.5%.

In 1992 the GDP was $24,438 million in current US dollars. It is estimated that in 1991 agriculture, hunting, forestry, and fishing contributed 19% to GDP; mining, quarrying, manufacturing, electricity, gas, and water, 44%; construction, 5%; wholesale and retail trade, 8%; transport, storage, and communication, 5%; finance, insurance, real estate, and business services, 2%; community, social, and personal services, 3%; and other sources, 14%.

21 LABOR

An estimated 10,785,800 people were employed in 1991, of whom 29.8% worked in agriculture (compared with 57.1% as of a 1966 census); 35.2% in industry (including mining and public utilities); 14.8% in trade, transportation, and communications; 4.6% in construction; and 15.6% in other sectors. Officially, unemployment was at 8.4% in 1992. Labor legislation adopted in 1991 guarantees the right of private sector employees to associate freely, organize and join unions, bargain collectively, and carry out strikes. Romania's trade unions belonged to the General Confederation of Romanian Trade Unions (UGSR), a state controlled body for many years. Many of the new unions joined the umbrella organizations the Organization of Free Trade Unions and Alfa Carta. The eight major unions in Romania include: Infratirca, Justice of Brotherhood Union, and the Convention of Non-Affiliated Trade Unions of Romania.

Most employees work a 5-day, 40-hour week. According to official figures, non-agricultural earnings increased by 29% during 1983–90. The average monthly pay, excluding farmworkers, was L7,265 in 1991. Since the overthrow of the Ceausescu regime some small-scale privatization has occurred, including over 3,000 small shops and restaurants, and much of retail trade and personal services.

22AGRICULTURE

Although under Communism the emphasis had been on industrialization, Romania is still largely an agricultural country. Of the total land area, 64% was devoted to agriculture in 1991, when agriculture accounted for 21% of total employment and 18.5% of GDP.

The government began forming collective farms in 1949 and had largely completed the collectivization process by 1962. By 1985, of a total of 15,020,178 hectares (37,115,460 acres) of agricultural land, 29.7% was in state farms, with another 60.8% in large cooperative farms. The socialized sector consisted of 3,745 collectives, 419 state farms, and 573 farming mechanization units by 1985. The Land Reform of 1991 returned 80% of agricultural land to private ownership, resulting in Romania now having some 5,500,000 farmers on holdings of up to 10 hectares (25 acres). In 1993, agriculture was carried out by 17 state-owned companies, 14 private companies, 10 state-owned service and repairing companies, and 4 research companies.

Grain growing has been the traditional agricultural pursuit, but the acreage has been reduced since World War II, and more area has been assigned to industrial and fodder crops. The following table shows 1980, 1985, and 1992 production totals (in thousand tons) for major crops:

	1980	1985	1992
Wheat and rye	6,467	5,712	3,261
Corn	11,513	15,238	6,829
Sugar beets	5,562	6,446	2,875
Potatoes	4,135	7,294	2,600

Romania is an important grape producer. Grape production in 1992 was 906,000 tons; wine output in 1992 reached 750,000 tons. The 1992 harvest also included 2,075,000 tons of fruit and 3,140,000 tons of vegetables.

23ANIMAL HUSBANDRY

Animal production in Romania has developed somewhat more rapidly than crop production. The 1970 value of total livestock production, including the increase in herds and flocks as well as livestock products, was slightly more than double the level of 1938, and the 1974 value was 34% above that of 1970. In view of the initially low level of Romanian livestock production, development has been slow, however. The major reasons for the inadequate increases had been lack of economic incentives, insufficient fodder, and inadequate shelter. Since the overthrow of the Ceausescu regime in 1989, privatization of much of the grazing land has begun. In order to improve livestock raising, the government continues to stress agricultural modernization.

The following table shows livestock numbers in thousands for 1971, 1986, and 1992:

	1971	1986	1992
Cattle	5,216	7,077	4,355
Hogs	6,539	14,319	10,954
Sheep	13,818	18,609	13,879
Poultry	54,333	124,770	106,000

Output of livestock products for 1992 comprised 1,397,000 tons (live weight) of meat, including 846,000 tons of pork, 131,000 tons of beef, and 330,000 tons of poultry; 2.8 million tons of milk; 340,000 tons of eggs; and 10,000 tons of honey. Some 53,000 tons of wool were also produced.

24FISHING

Romania lost an important fishing region and nearly all its caviar-producing lakes with the cession of Bessarabia to the USSR in 1940. But the Black Sea, the Danube and its floodlands, as well as other rivers, lakes, and ponds, are favorable to the development of the fishing industry, which expanded rapidly during the early 1970s. About 32% of the fish comes from the Danube floodlands and delta and from the Black Sea, and the rest is from fishing operations in the Atlantic. In 1991, the total catch was 124,933 tons, as compared with 267,618 in 1988 and 16,000 in 1960.

25FORESTRY

Forests, representing 29% of the total area of Romania, are found mainly in the Carpathian Mountains and in Transylvania. Forests became state property in 1948. From 1946 to 1954, Romania's forest industries were administered by a joint Soviet-Romanian company, which passed entirely into Romanian hands in 1954. Forestry and forestry products are still important to the economy. Roundwood production in 1991 was 14,760,000 cu m. Between 1976 and 1985, 580,000 hectares (1,433,200 acres) were reforested.

26MINING

Output of coal, mainly of the lignite variety, rose from about 3.9 million tons in 1950 to 61.3 million tons in 1989, but fell to 37.4 million tons in 1991. The main mines are located in the Jiu River Valley. In addition to fuels, Romania mines iron ore (2 million tons in 1991), as well as copper, gold, silver, nonferrous metals, and uranium. There are large salt mines; Romania is a leading salt producer (6,500,000 tons in 1991—9th in the world). Barite, bentonite, diatomite, feldspar, graphite, gypsum, kaolin, limestone, and other industrial minerals were also mined at about 60 deposits throughout the country.

27ENERGY AND POWER

Under the stimulus of industrialization, electric power generation rose from 2.1 billion kwh in 1950 to 7.6 billion in 1960, 35.1 billion in 1970, and 75.5 billion in 1986. Production in 1991 totaled 56.9 billion kwh. Installed capacity increased from 1,863,000 kw in 1961 to 22,268,000 kw in 1991. Before the 1989 revolution, there were frequent power shortages and strict energy rationing measures.

Most thermal electric power is generated with natural gas and low-quality coal, with the latter replacing fuel oil in recent years. Two nuclear reactors being built at Cernavoda, near Constanta, were scheduled to begin operation in 1985, but as of 1991, only one reactor was 50% completed. In September 1991, Canada reportedly approved a $277 million loan for Romania to complete the first 685 Mw reactor, which is scheduled to begin operating in 1995.

As of the early 1970s, Romania was Europe's second-largest petroleum producer, next to the USSR. Oil production reached its prewar peak of 8.7 million tons in 1936 and rose to 14.5 million by 1974; by 1991, however, oil output was down to 6.8 million tons, and Romania has had to import oil since 1979. The

Ploiesti fields, once among Europe's richest, are becoming depleted, and production from new fields on the Moldovan slopes of the Carpathians and elsewhere has not taken up the slack. In 1981, new deposits were discovered in the Romanian part of the Black Sea. A major fuel source is natural gas, which is associated with oil or occurs in separate deposits in Transylvania. Output rose from 11.1 billion cu m in 1960 to 37.4 billion cu m in 1987, before falling to 24.4 billion cu m in 1991. Reserves of natural gas were estimated at 485 billion cu m in 1991. In addition to supplying Romania's industries, natural gas is sent by pipeline to Hungary.

28 INDUSTRY

Industrial development received about half of all investment during the 1951–80 period. As officially measured, the average annual growth rate in gross industrial production between 1950 and 1980 was 12.3%, one of the highest in Eastern Europe. In 1993, however, industrial production was at only 47% of the 1989 level. The leading sectors in 1993 were food and drink (14.7%), metallurgy (10.6%), electric power (10.9%), chemicals and synthetic fibers (8.9%), and machines and equipment (7.5%).

The machine-building industry produces tractors, internal-combustion engines, electric motors and power transformers, drilling installations, ships, and diesel locomotives, among other items. Of total exports, machinery and equipment contributed 28.3% in 1985 but only 11% in 1992. Endowed with petroleum and gas resources, Romania has rebuilt and developed processing plants and produces drilling equipment for export. Output of petroleum products in 1992 included 2,923,000 tons of motor fuel and 3,693,000 tons of distillate fuels. Steel production increased from 555,000 tons in 1950 to 13,795,000 tons in 1985 but fell to 5,376,000 tons in 1992. A large iron and steel combine, completed in 1970 at the Danube port of Galati, had an annual capacity of 4 million tons of steel. Among the chemical products, those exported in greatest quantity include chemical fertilizers, sulfuric acid, soda ash, and caustic soda. A new industrial complex for the chemical industry, constructed in central Romania, began operating in the early 1970s. Chemical production in 1992 included 372,000 tons of caustic soda, 572,000 tons of sulfuric acid, and 1,398,000 tons of chemical fertilizers. Other industrial products in 1992 were 74,000 automobiles, 273,000 DWT of seagoing vessels, 481 million sq m of woven goods, 113,000 tons of artificial fibers, 36,000 tons of synthetic rubber, and 44,000,000 pairs of footwear. All these figures were lower than in the mid-1980s.

29 SCIENCE AND TECHNOLOGY

The Academy of Medical Sciences and the Academy of Agricultural and Forest Sciences were founded in 1969. In 1993, Romania had 71 research and development institutes. In 1989, total research and development expenditures amounted to L21 billion; 42,931 technicians and 59,670 scientists and engineers were engaged in research and development.

30 DOMESTIC TRADE

Wholesale and retail trade were entirely in the socialized sector before 1990. In 1993, however, 50% of retail trade had been privatized. In 1992, wholesale trade came to L906,856 million, of which 93% was state owned and the rest cooperative. Retail trade totaled L1,627,176 million in 1992. There were 25,148 state stores, 26,907 cooperative shops, and 84,488 private ones. Of the total retail trade in 1992, foodstuffs accounted for 44%. Stores are open daily except Sunday from 10 AM to 6 PM. Food shop and retail department store hours are 7 AM to 9 PM Monday to Saturday and 7 AM to 12 noon on Sundays. Offices generally open at 7 or 8 AM and close at 3 or 4 PM. Exchange counters in banks transact public business from 8 AM to 12 noon, but exchange offices at border crossings remain open 24 hours a day.

31 FOREIGN TRADE

Before 1990, foreign trade was a state monopoly carried out through export-import agencies under the administration of the Ministry of Foreign Trade. Since World War II, the orientation and structure of Romanian foreign trade have shifted. Before the war, cereals, oil, timber, livestock, and animal derivatives accounted for over 90% of total exports, while consumer goods (60%) and raw materials (20%) accounted for the bulk of the imports. Under the Communist industrialization program, structural changes were particularly striking in exports, with machinery and nonedible consumer goods emerging as important export items. Foreign trade was in surplus throughout the 1980s, but fell into deficit in the 1990s.

Exports in 1992 totaled L1,376,902 million and imports L1,745,554 million. Of this 31.6% was in the private sector. The major export categories, by value, are minerals, metals, and fuels (30.4% in 1992); machinery and electric equipment (11%); textiles (10.6%), transport vehicles and equipment (10.4%), and chemicals and products (9.8%). Principal import categories during the same year were minerals, metals, and fuels (36.6%); machinery and equipment (15.3%), textiles (9.5%), and chemicals (7%).

The former USSR remains Romania's most important supplier and customer, followed by Germany. Trade with Eastern Europe has declined sharply. Trade with the EU countries, especially Germany, has increased substantially, largely because of Romania's need for advanced Western technology and equipment. It accounted for 32.6% of exports and 37.5% of imports in 1992.

Principal trade partners in 1992 (in millions of lei) were as follows:

	EXPORTS	IMPORTS	BALANCE
Former USSR	179,476	274,635	–95,159
of which Russia	129,003	189,536	–60,534
Germany	153,550	264,238	–110,688
Italy	84,961	156,079	–71,118
France	54,880	114,534	–59,654
UK	50,482	60,122	–9,640
China	63,593	23,574	40,019
Iran	38,741	149,470	–110,729
Netherlands	35,198	48,600	–13,402
US	26,754	71,219	–44,465
Turkey	70,216	56,526	13,690
Hungary	25,937	57,031	–31,094
Other countries	593,114	469,526	123,588
TOTAL	1,376,902	1,745,554	–368,652

32 BALANCE OF PAYMENTS

Trade with Western countries has involved growing amounts of credits in recent years. As a result of a series of devaluations of the Romanian leu dating from February 1990, western imports have become increasingly costly. While the monetary value of imports has risen, the volume of imports has declined.

In 1992 merchandise exports totaled $4,364 million and imports $5,558 million. The merchandise trade balance was $–1,194 million.

The following table summarizes Romania's balance of payments for 1991 and 1992 (in millions of US dollars):

	1991	1992
CURRENT ACCOUNT		
Goods, services, and income	–1,230	–1,571
Unrequited transfers	218	65
TOTALS	–1,012	–1,506

	1991	1992
CAPITAL ACCOUNT		
Direct investment	37	73
Portfolio investment	—	—
Other long-term capital	245	1,134
Other short-term capital	38	173
Exceptional financing	—	—
Other liabilities	—	—
Reserves	677	138
TOTALS	997	1,518
Errors and omissions	15	–12
Total change in reserves	758	–179

³³BANKING AND SECURITIES

Romanian banks were nationalized in 1948. The bank of issue is the National Bank of the Socialist Republic of Romania, which also extends short-term loans to state enterprises and supervises their financial activities. The Romanian Bank for Development (1990) finances investments of state enterprises and institutions and grants long-term credit. As investments increased in volume, this bank was required to intensify its control over the use of funds allocated for investment. The Romanian Bank for Foreign Trade conducts operations with foreign countries. Savings are deposited with the Loans and Savings Bank. In 1974, New York's Manufacturers Hanover Trust opened an office in Bucharest, the first such instance for a Western commercial bank in a Communist nation. There is no securities trading.

³⁴INSURANCE

During the Communist era, all commercial insurance was nationalized. Since 1991, casualty, automobile, and life insurance have been made available through private insurers with foreign partners. Private insurers are only legally permitted as joint stock or limited liability companies. Policies available include life, automobile, maritime and transport, aircraft, fire, civil liability, credit and guarantee, and agricultural insurance. Foreign insurance companies and agencies are now allowed to set up representative offices within Romania.

³⁵PUBLIC FINANCE

The annual budget is presented to the Grand National Assembly around December and becomes effective for the fiscal year on 1 January. The state budget, prepared by the Ministry of Finance, is a central part of the financial plan for the whole economy. The reduction of the growth rate of expenditures during the early 1980s was in keeping with an economic stabilization program designed to hold down domestic investment and consumption. As a result of fiscal reforms begun since the fall of the Ceausescu regime in December 1989, adherence to IMF fiscal targets, and an unanticipated inflation-fed revenue windfall during the first half, the central government unofficially recorded a relatively modest deficit for 1991. Subsidies for energy imports constituted a major share of the deficit. Taxes on salaries and retail turnover provide three-fourths of revenues.

The following table shows actual revenues and expenditures for 1990 and 1991 in millions of lei.

	1990	1991
REVENUE AND GRANTS		
Tax revenue	265.37	274.19
Non-tax revenue	29.99	63.75
Capital revenue	2.55	34.87
TOTAL	292.81	372.81

	1990	1991
EXPENDITURES & LENDING MINUS REPAYMENTS		
General public service	3.88	15.44
Defense	29.81	80.42
Public order and safety	4.58	18.21
Education	7.86	78.16
Health	25.20	71.75
Social security and welfare	91.23	206.81
Housing and community amenities	—	0.61
Recreation, cultural, and religious affairs	1.84	3.69
Economic affairs and services	110.94	257.45
Other expenditures	14.53	47.43
TOTAL	289.87	779.98
Deficit/Surplus	8.04	42.83

In 1993 Romania's external public debt stood at $3.4 billion.

³⁶TAXATION

Companies are taxed 30% on profits up to L1 million and 45% on profits exceeding that amount. Dividends are taxed 10%. Wage taxes range from 6–25% of monthly income. Indirect taxes consist of a turnover tax (maximum 30%) and excise taxes (maximum 70%) as well as a tax on services, stamp taxes, and customs duties.

³⁷CUSTOMS AND DUTIES

Romania joined EFTA in December 1992 and signed an association agreement with the EC early in 1993 which provides for Romania to adapt to EC economic-commercial standards over a 10-year period. Under an interim collaborative agreement effective 1 May 1993, a revised Romanian import tariff schedule was introduced with preferential tariffs for imports from EC and EFTA member nations.

³⁸FOREIGN INVESTMENT

Foreign investment was negligible before the overthrow of the Communist regime. A new 1991 foreign investment law was enacted in 1991. Incentives to foreign investors include tax holidays and reduction, full foreign ownership of an enterprise, and full conversion and repatriation of after-tax profits. However, the latter is a drawn-out process because of the central bank's shortage of hard currency. In 1993, 28,805 foreign investors had $746.9 million in investments in Romania.

³⁹ECONOMIC DEVELOPMENT

The economy of Romania before 1990 was centrally planned and, for the most part, under complete state control. The nationalized industries and other economic enterprises operated within the state economic plan and were governed by the directives issued by the pertinent ministries. Economic planning, conducted by the State Planning Commission, emulated the Soviet example.

Nationalization of industry, mining, transportation, banking, and insurance on 11 June 1948 was followed by one-year economic plans in 1949 and 1950. These were succeeded by the first five-year plan (1951–55), which laid the groundwork for rapid industrialization, with emphasis on heavy industry, primarily machine-building. The state's second five-year plan (1956–60) provided for an increase of industrialization by 60–65%. Greater attention was given to consumer goods and to agriculture. A subsequent six-year plan (1960–65) envisaged an overall industrial increase of 110%, especially in producer goods. The five-year plan for 1966–70 realized an overall industrial increase of 73%. The five-year plans for 1971–75, 1976–80, and 1981–85 called for further industrial expansion and, according to official figures, during 1966–85 industrial production grew by 9.5% annually. The eighth five-year plan, for 1986–90, projected a 13.3–14.2% annual increase in Romania's net industrial production.

In the farming sector, the government has assiduously pursued a policy of collectivization. By virtue of the 22 March 1945 land reform, most farms over 50 hectares (123 acres)—a total of about 1.5 million hectares (3.7 million acres)—were confiscated without compensation. In 1949, the remaining large private farms were seized, and their 500,000 hectares (1,236,000 acres) organized into state farms. Various pressures, including coercion, were used to force peasants into joining. In April, 1962, collectivization was announced as virtually completed. Agricultural development in following years was comparatively neglected.

As of 1 January 1979, Romania began implementing the "new economic-financial mechanism," an attempt to introduce into the Romanian economy the principle of workers' self-management as previously developed elsewhere in Eastern Europe, notably in Yugoslavia and Hungary. Accordingly, autonomous production units were expected to plan for their own revenues and expenditures and manpower needs. These separate plans were, however, to be harmonized with the national economic plan, so that Romania's centralized system of goal and price setting was not significantly altered.

One of the major economic targets in the 1980s was the reduction of foreign debt, which was achieved but at the cost of drastic austerity measures and reduced industrial growth. After the fall of Communism, a major objective was the privatization of 6,200 state enterprises. The economy was to be completely restructured, with the emphasis on private ownership and adherence to the market for the allocation of resources. By late 1992, 70% of all agricultural land was privately held.

40 SOCIAL DEVELOPMENT

The Ministry of Health and Social Welfare controls the social welfare system through regional and district councils, with assistance provided by the trade unions. Social security covers all wage earners, those in military service, those who have rendered exceptional service to the country, and their dependents. Old-age pensions are granted at age 60 for men and at 55 for women. Those engaged in hazardous or arduous work are eligible for retirement at 55 and 50, respectively. The pension equals 85% of a reference wage calculated by average base earnings and increments.

Survivors' benefits are payable to the spouse, father and mother, and brothers and sisters who are dependents of the deceased, and to children up to age 16. Workers' compensation and unemployment insurance are also provided.

For workers who do not meet the conditions of duration of employment at retirement age, social assistance is provided. Pensioners and their families are entitled to medical assistance. Sickness and maternity benefits equal 50% of earnings. Families with children under age 16 receive family allowances and a birth grant of L1,500 (as of 1991) for each child. In addition to state social insurance, other schemes cover members of artisans' cooperatives, the clergy, and the professions. Collective farmers have their own programs. Coverage is not provided for private farmers.

In 1985, women represented 45% of the labor force; the constitution guarantees equal pay for equal work. Abortion was virtually unrestricted from 1957 until 1966, when, presumably alarmed by the nation's low birthrate, the government restricted fully elective access to abortion to women over 45 years of age (lowered to 40 in 1972) or supporting four or more children. In 1984, new pronatalist measures were introduced, including lowering of the minimum marriageable age for women to 15 years, strict penalties (up to the death penalty) for doctors who perform illegal abortions, and mandatory monthly pregnancy tests for women aged 20–30 years. The fertility rate in 1985–90 was 2.3.

Legally, women have the same rights and privileges as men, although they face employment discrimination in Romania's harsh economic climate. It is difficult to bring rape cases to trial because the victim's testimony is not considered sufficient evidence, and witnesses are required.

41 HEALTH

The Ministry of Public Health and Social Welfare is the central controlling agency for the health system in Romania. It organizes, plans, and directs the activities of all medical institutions. In 1989, Romania had 41,938 physicians, 6,432 pharmacists, and 7,116 dentists. There was 1 doctor for every 560 people in 1990 and, also in 1992, there were 1.79 doctors per 1,000 people. Private practice was virtually abolished in 1959. In 1990, there were 8.9 hospital beds per 1,000 people. Through social insurance, all workers and employees, pensioners, and their dependents are covered for medical care and medicine; members of collective farms and their families also are included in the medical program. Increased mother and child care lowered the infant mortality rate from 143 per 1,000 live births in 1948 to 23 in 1992. The general health of the population has likewise improved, with several previously serious diseases eliminated (e.g., recurrent fever, malaria) or greatly reduced (e.g., diphtheria, tuberculosis). In 1990, there were 70 reported cases of tuberculosis per 100,000 inhabitants. Overall mortality was 11.2 per 1,000 people in 1993; major causes of death per 100,000 people in 1990 were: communicable diseases and maternal/perinatal causes (93); noncommunicable diseases (685); and injuries (65). Maternal mortality in 1991 was 72 per 100,000 live births. Average life expectancy in 1992 was 70 years. Romania's birth rate in 1993 was 15.7 per 1,000 people, and 58% of married women (ages 15 to 49) used contraception. There were 363,000 births in 1992. Immunization rates for children up to one year old in 1992 were: tuberculosis (99%); diphtheria, pertussis, and tetanus (97%); polio (90%); and measles (92%). Per capita pharmaceutical consumption in 1990 was $11.5, and total health care expenditures were $1,455 million.

42 HOUSING

Inadequate housing has been a serious problem since World War II. Romanian housing suffered from the 1940 earthquake, war damage, neglect, and inadequate repair and maintenance after the war. An increase in the urban population caused by industrialization and emphasis on capital construction exacerbated the problem.

Between 1951 and 1965, the number of dwellings constructed totaled 1,500,093, more than two-thirds of them in rural areas. About 266,000 apartment units were constructed during 1960–65, some 30,000 units short of the government's plan for the period. Houses built without any state aid numbered 527,435, predominantly in the rural areas. Since 1965, the government has encouraged private construction by state support in the form of credits and expertise. During 1976–80, 840,644 new units were built, of which only 85,301 were built entirely from private resources. In 1984, 131,901 new dwelling units were built, of which 9,429 were funded by private owners; in 1985, the corresponding figures were 105,610 and 8,608, respectively. Since 1987, construction of new housing units has plummeted from 110,400 to 60,400 in 1989; 48,600 in 1990; and 28,000 in 1991. Total housing stock numbered 7,839,000 in 1991.

43 EDUCATION

Adult illiteracy in 1990 was 3.1% (males, 1.4% and females, 4.8%). In 1948, the government established compulsory education for at least four years in rural areas and for seven years in urban areas, with the hope that the seven-year school would be general. A decree of 30 September 1961 provided for the transition to an eight-year general, compulsory, and free education for children between 7 and 15 years of age; since 1968, the compulsory span has lengthened to 10 years. According to the Education Law of 1978, Romania's educational system consists of preschool (ages 3–6), primary school (grades 1–4), gymnasium (grades 5–8), lyceum or college in two steps (each consisting of 2 years), vocational schools and schools for foremen, higher education, and postgraduate education. In 1991, there were 36,326 teachers in 12,600 nurseries and kindergartens, with 742,232 pupils; and 13,730 general education schools (primary schools and gymnasiums), with 2,608,914 students and 153,187 teachers. The total number of secondary level students were 1,208,630 with 58,413 teachers. Of these students, 13,026 were in teacher training schools and 946,856 were in vocational schools, and over 44 institutions of higher learning had 164,507 students and 11,696 teachers in 1989.

Admission to an advanced institution depends on a variety of factors, including the student's social background. Over half the students receive government assistance. Yearly quotas are established by the Ministry of Education according to manpower needs. Students in some fields must first complete six months of practical work in industry or agriculture.

In 1959, the Romanian Victor Babes University (founded 1919) and the János Bolyai University (1945) for Hungarian minority students, both in Cluj-Napoca, were merged into the Babes-Bolyai University in order to strengthen "socialist patriotism." There are six other universities—in Bucharest (founded in 1864), Brasov (1971), Craiova (1966), Galati (1948), Iasi (1860), and Timisoara (1962).

Like the other formerly Communist countries, Romania has emphasized polytechnic education in recent years. This "link of education with life" in the early grades means studying practical subjects; but beginning in the upper grades there are work programs, often directly in enterprises, in workshops, or on collective farms, depending on the locality.

44 LIBRARIES AND MUSEUMS

Many of the important libraries are located in Bucharest, including the National Library which contains 8.5 million volumes and was founded in 1955. Public and school libraries are found throughout the country. University libraries at Bucharest, Iasi, and Cluj-Napoca hold 1.9, 2.9, and 0.75 million volumes, respectively. Romania's 471 museums in 1991 attracted 1.8 million visitors. Bucharest is home to many of the important museums in Romania including the National History Museum of Romania, the National Museum of Art, and the newer Historical Museum of Bucharest (founded in 1984).

45 MEDIA

There were 2.3 million telephone subscribers in 1990. There were 12 AM and 5 FM radio broadcasting stations in 1990 and 13 TV stations. In 1991, there were 4,620,000 radios and 1,840,000 television sets. In 1991 there were 34 daily newspapers with a total annual circulation of 3,648,000. The leading daily newspapers (with 1991 circulation figures) are *Adevarul* (380,000); *Romania Libera* (300,000); *Libertatea* (250,000); and *Tineretul Liber* (200,000). A total of 2,178 authorized book titles were printed in 1991.

46 ORGANIZATIONS

Economic organizations concerned with Romania's internal and external economic activities include the Romanian Chamber of Commerce and Industry of Romania. In 1992 the Council for National Minority Affairs was formed for the discussion of minority issues. The organization helps the government formulate policies favorable to the minorities of the country. The body is headed by the Secretary General of the government. Representatives from 16 officially recognized minorities groups and 12 government ministries make up the organization.

There are also many cooperatives in key sectors of the economy. Many Romanian farmers belong to the private Farmers'

Federation. In total there are 4,000 farming cooperatives and 41 district unions. A large cooperative located in the manufacturing and consumers sectors of the economy is the Central Union of Commerce and Credit Cooperative. In total, there are over 2,500 production and 850 credit cooperatives. Another important cooperative is the Central Union of Handi Craft Cooperatives.

47 TOURISM, TRAVEL, AND RECREATION

The Romanian tourist industry, like its other state monopolies, is undergoing privatization. The Carpathian Mountains, the Black Sea coast, and the Danube region are being developed to attract and accommodate larger numbers of tourists. In 1991, visitor arrivals (including same-day visitors) numbered 5,360,128; 40% came from the former USSR, 15% from Bulgaria, and 14% from Hungary. Tourism payments totaled $103 million. There were 87,100 hotel rooms with 166,268 beds. The government is expected to sell a number of state-owned hotels to international buyers.

Major tourist attractions include many old cities and towns (Brasov, Constanta, Sibiu, Sighisoara, Suceava, Timisoara, and others) and more than 120 health resorts and spas. The monasteries in Bukovina are famous for their exterior frescoes. Castle Dracula, the castle of Prince Vlad of Walachia, has been a tourist attraction since the 1970s.

Popular sports are soccer, skiing, hiking, swimming, canoeing, wrestling, handball, and gymnastics. Between 1965 and 1984, Romanian athletes won 176 Olympic medals (48 gold, 52 silver, and 76 bronze). Romania was the only Socialist country to send athletes to the 1984 games in Los Angeles; all the others, following the USSR's lead, boycotted these games. All visitors to Romania must have a visa, obtainable from Romanian embassies abroad or at border stations.

48 FAMOUS ROMANIANS

Perhaps the most famous historical figure in what is now Romania was Vlad (1431?–76), a prince of Walachia who resisted the Turkish invasion and was called Tepes ("the impaler") and Dracula ("son of the devil") because of his practice of impaling his enemies on stakes; he was made into a vampire by Bram Stoker in his novel *Dracula*. The first leader of Communist Romania was Gheorghe Gheorghiu-Dej (1901–65), who held the office of premier from 1952 to 1955 and of president of the State Council from 1961 until his death. Nicolae Ceausescu (1918–89) was general secretary of the Communist Party between 1965 and 1989 and head of state from 1967 to 1989; his wife, Elena (1919–89), was a member of the Permanent Bureau of the Executive Committee of the Communist Party.

Ion Heliade-Radulescu (1802–72) founded the Bucharest Conservatory and the National Theater and became first president of the Romanian Academy. Mihail Kogalniceanu (1817–91), a leading statesman in the early Romanian monarchy, inaugurated modern Romanian historiography. Vasile Alecsandri (1821–90) was a leader of the traditionalist school of writers, which sought its inspiration in the Romanian past rather than in imitations of foreign writers. Mihail Eminescu (1850–89) is regarded as an outstanding poet, famous for romantic lyricism. His friend Ion Creanga (1837–87) drew from folklore and wrote with a gaiety and gusto recalling Rabelais. The nation's greatest playwright was Ion Luca Caragiale (1852–1912), who excelled in social comedy; an internationally famous Romanian-born playwright, Eugène Ionesco (b.1912), settled in Paris in 1938. Mihail Sadoveanu (1880–1961) was an important novelist in the period between the two world wars. Romanian-born Elie Wiesel (b.1928), in the US from 1956, is a writer on Jewish subjects, especially the Holocaust, and a winner of the Nobel Peace Prize in 1986. Romanian-born Mircea Eliade (1907–86) was a scholar in comparative religion and comparative mythology, in the US from 1948. Romanian-born Tristan Tzara (1896–1963), a literary and artistic critic who settled in Paris, was one of the founders of Dadaism. Nicolae Grigorescu (1838–1907) and Ion Andreescu (1850–82) were leading painters, as was Theodor Aman (1831–91), a modern artist and founder of the School of Fine Arts in Bucharest. Sculpture was greatly advanced by Constantin Brâncusi (1876–1957). Perhaps the greatest names Romania has given to the musical world are those of the violinist and composer Georges Enescu (1881–1955), known for his *Romanian Rhapsodies,* and the pianist Dinu Lipatti (1917–50). A prominent tennis player is Ilie Nastase (1946–94); gymnast Nadia Comaneci (b.1961) won three gold medals at the 1976 Olympics.

49DEPENDENCIES

Romania has no territories or colonies.

50BIBLIOGRAPHY

Bachman, Ronald D. (ed.). *Romania: A Country Study.* 2d ed. Washington, D.C.: Library of Congress, 1991.

Castellan, Georges. *A History of the Romanians.* New York: Columbia University Press, 1989.

Ceausescu, Ilie. *Romanian Military Doctrine: Past and Present.* New York: Columbia University Press, 1988.

——. *War, Revolution, and Society in Romania: The Road to Independence.* Boulder, Colo.: East European Quarterly, 1983.

Deletant, Andrea, and Dennis Deletant. *Romania* [Bibliography]. Santa Barbara, Calif: ABC-Clio Press, 1985.

Dima, Nicholas. *From Moldavia to Moldova: The Soviet-Romanian Territorial Dispute.* 2d ed. New York: Columbia University Press, 1991.

Fischer, Mary Ellen. *Nicolae Ceausescu: A Study in Political Leadership.* Boulder, Colo.: L. Rienner Publishers, 1989.

Fischer-Galati, Stephen A. *Twentieth Century Rumania.* 2d ed. New York: Columbia University Press, 1991.

Jowitt, Kenneth. *Revolutionary Breakthroughs and National Development.* Berkeley: University of California Press, 1971.

King, Robert R. *History of the Romanian Communist Party.* Stanford, Calif.: Hoover Institution Press, 1980.

Linden, Ronald Haly. *Communist States and International Change: Romania and Yugoslavia in Comparative Perspective.* Boston: Allen & Unwin, 1987.

Lungu, Dov B. *Romania and the Great Powers, 1933–1940.* Durham: Duke University Press, 1989.

Otetea, Andrei, and Andrew MacKenzie (eds.). *A Concise History of Romania.* New York: St. Martin's, 1985.

Saiu, Liliana. *The Great Powers and Rumania, 1944–1946: A Study of the Early Cold War Era.* New York: Columbia University Press, 1992.

Shafir, Michael. *Romania: Politics, Economics and Society.* Boulder, Colo.: Lynne Rienner, 1985.

Verdery, Katherine. *National Ideology under Socialism: Identity and Cultural Politics in Ceausescu's Romania.* Berkeley: University of California Press, 1991.

Verona, Sergiu. *Military Occupation and Diplomacy: Soviet Troops in Romania, 1944–1958.* Durham: Duke University Press, 1992.

RUSSIA

Russian Federation
Rossiyskaya Federatsiya

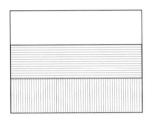

CAPITAL: Moscow

FLAG: Equal horizontal bands of white (top), blue, and red.

ANTHEM: *Patriotic Song.*

MONETARY UNIT: The rouble (R) is a paper currency of 100 kopecks. There are coins of 1, 2, 3, 5, 10, 15, 20, and 50 kopecks and 1 rouble, and notes of 100, 200, 500, 1,000, 5,000, 10,000 and 50,000 roubles.

WEIGHTS AND MEASURES: The metric system is the legal standard.

HOLIDAYS: New Year's Day, 1–2 January; Christmas, 7 January; Women's Day, 8 March; Spring and Labor Day, 1–2 May; Victory Day, 9 May; State Sovereignty Day, 12 June; Socialist Revolution Day, 7 November.

TIME: 3 PM Moscow = noon GMT.

¹LOCATION, SIZE, AND EXTENT

Russia is located in northeastern Europe and northern Asia. It is the largest country in the world—slightly more than 1.8 times the size of the US, with a total area of 17,075,200 sq km (6,592,771 sq mi). Russia shares boundaries with the Arctic Ocean on the N, northern Pacific Ocean on the W, China, Mongolia, Kazakhstan, the Caspian Sea, Azerbaijan, Georgia on the S, and the Black Sea, Ukraine, Belarus, Latvia, Estonia, Finland on the W with a total boundary length of 57,792 km (35,910 mi). Russia's capital city, Moscow, is located in the eastern part of the country.

²TOPOGRAPHY

The topography of Russia features a broad plain with low hills west of the Ural Mountains with vast coniferous forests and tundra in Siberia. There are uplands and mountains along the southern border region. Despite its size, only a small percentage of Russia's land is arable, with much of it too far north for cultivation.

³CLIMATE

Most of the country has a continental climate, with long, cold winters and brief summers. There is a wide range of summer and winter temperatures and relatively low precipitation. January temperatures range from 6°C (45°F), on the southeastern shore of the Black Sea, to as low as –71°C (–96°F) in northeastern Siberia. The lowest temperatures of any of the world's inhabited regions are found in Siberia, and in many areas the soil never thaws for more than a foot. The Siberian village of Oymyakon registered -71°C (-96°F) in 1974, the lowest temperature ever recorded in a permanently inhabited place on this planet.

Annual precipitation decreases from about 64–76 cm (25–30 in) in the European region to less than 5 cm (2 in) a year in parts of Central Asia. The tundra has long winters, with summers lasting one or two months, and receives from 8 to 12 months of snow or rain. The far northern forest, like most of the country, has long severe winters, short summers, and extremely short springs and autumns. Precipitation is low but falls throughout the year, varying from 53 cm (21 in) at Moscow to between 20 and 25 cm (8–10 in) in eastern Siberia. The steppes have very cold winters and hot, dry summers.

⁴FLORA AND FAUNA

Russia has several soil and vegetation zones, each with its characteristic flora and fauna. Northernmost is the so-called arctic desert zone, which includes most of the islands of the Arctic Ocean and the seacoast of the Taymyr Peninsula. These areas are characterized by the almost complete absence of plant cover; only mosses and lichens are to be found. Birds and mammals associated with the sea, (sea calf, seal, and walrus) are typical of this zone.

The tundra, which extends along the extreme northern part of Asia, is divided into arctic, moss-lichen, and shrubby tundra subzones. Only dwarf birches, willows, lichens, and mosses grow in the thin layer of acid soil. Indigenous fauna include the arctic fox, reindeer, white hare, lemming, and common and willow ptarmigan.

South of the tundra is the vast forest zone, or taiga, covering half of the country; the soil here is podzolic. The northern areas of this zone are characterized by the alternation of tundra landscape with sparse growth of birches, other deciduous trees, and spruce. Farther south are spruce, pine, fir, cedar, and some deciduous trees. There are subzones of mixed and broadleaf forests on the Great Russian Plain in the southern half of the forest zone. Wildlife in the taiga include moose, Russian bear, reindeer, lynx, sable, squirrel, and among the birds, capercaillie, hazel-grouse, owl, and woodpecker. In the broadleaf woods are European wild boar, deer, roe deer, red deer, mink, and marten.

Farther south is the forest-steppe zone, a narrow band with the boundaries of the Great Russian plain and the West Siberian low country. Steppes with various grasses alternate with small tracts of oak, birch, and aspen. Still farther south, the forest-steppe changes to a region of varied grasses and small plants. The black and chestnut soils of this zone produce the best agricultural land in Russia. Typical mammals are various rodents (hamsters and jerboas); birds include skylarks, cranes, eagles, and the great bustard.

In the semi-desert zone, plant cover includes xerophytic grasses and shrubs. Typical animals are the wildcat and saiga antelope; lizards, snakes, and tortoises are common. The semi-desert areas and the deserts of Central Asia and Kazakhstan make up a separate subregion.

5 ENVIRONMENT

Decades of Soviet mismanagement have resulted in the catastrophic pollution of land, air, rivers, and seacoasts, although the USSR did manage reforestation with some success. Air pollution is especially a problem in the Urals and Kuznetsk (where vast populations are exposed to hazardous emissions from metal-processing plants) as well as in the Volga and Moscow regions. About 75% of Russia's surface water is unsuitable for drinking. The Volga River has been damaged through rash exploitation of hydroelectric power. Lake Baikal is the largest fresh water reservoir in the world, but has been heavily polluted through agricultural and industrial development. Accidental and intentional dumping of radioactive materials in the 1950s and 1960s had left several areas still uninhabitable as of 1990.

6 POPULATION

The population of Russia was 147,021,869 in 1989. It was estimated at 148,673,000 in 1993. The population was projected at 155,240,000 in 2000, assuming a crude birth rate of 13.8 per 1,000 people, a crude death rate of 9.4, and a natural increase of 4.4 for 1995–2000. The estimated population density in 1993 was 8.7 per sq km (22.6 per sq mi). The biggest city is Moscow, the capital, with an estimated population at the beginning of 1990 of 8,801,000. Other big cities, with their estimated 1990 populations, include St. Petersburg (formerly Leningrad), 4,468,000; Nizhniy Novgorod (formerly Gorkiy), 1,443,000; Yekaterinburg (formerly Sverdlovsk), 1,367,000; and Samara (formerly Kuybyshev), 1,258,000.

7 MIGRATION

During 1979–88, Russia gained 1,747,040 people through net migration from other Soviet republics. In 1989, net migration was 83,000, and in 1991, 164,000. Since then Russian refugees from other parts of the Soviet Union have flooded the country—at least 1,500,000 in 1993 alone, according to one account. Official figures reported that 73,742 people emigrated from Russia in 1991. Since Germany took in 156,299 former Soviet Germans in 1991, emigration is probably underreported.

8 ETHNIC GROUPS

In 1989, 81.5% of the population was Russian. Minorities included Tatars, 3.8%, Ukrainians, 3%, and a wide variety of other peoples.

9 LANGUAGES

Russian is a member of the eastern group of Slavic languages. It is highly inflected, with nouns, pronouns, and adjectives declined in six cases. There are three grammatical genders. The language is written in the Cyrillic alphabet of 33 letters and has been written since about 1000 AD. A variety of other Slavic, Finno–Ugric, Turkic, Mongol, Tungus, and Paleo–Asiatic languages are also spoken.

10 RELIGIONS

Russians are predominantly Russian Orthodox, followed by Protestants and Roman Catholics, Jews, and Moslems. The Russian Orthodox Church (ROC) dates back to the "Kievan Rus" period (the first organized Russian state). In 988, Prince Vladimir, in order to gain an alliance with the powerful Byzantine Empire, declared Christianity as the religion of his realm, and mandated the baptism of Kiev's population and the construction of cathedrals. During the Mongol occupation (1240-1480), the head of the ROC (Metropolitan) was moved to Moscow. Throughout the reign of the tsars, Orthodoxy was synonymous with autocracy and national identity. After the Communist revolution of 1917, the Soviet government, based on Marxism, imposed a dogma of militant atheism and subordinated the ROC through fear and persecution. Other Christians, Moslems, and Jews were also oppressed (anti-Semitism was widespread before and after the 1917 revolution). Since 1985 and the subsequent dissolution of the Soviet Union, thousands of churches have been reopened; freedom of religion was incorporated into the draft constitution of 1993.

11 TRANSPORTATION

Russia's transportation system is extensive, but much has widely fallen into disrepair. Maintenance, modernization, and expansion are required for Russia's infrastructure, much of which operates beyond capacity.

Railroads have long been an important means of transportation in Russia. In the 1890s, a vast state-sponsored program of railway construction commenced, with the goal of nurturing private enterprise, exploiting natural resources, and expanding heavy industry (especially metallurgy and mineral fuels). The Trans-Siberian Railroad was the cornerstone of this development; from 1898–1901, more than 3,000 km (1,900 mi) of track were constructed per year. Railroad development also figured prominently during the Soviet era. Railways in 1993 extended some 140,000 km (87,000 mi), primarily with 1.52 m-gauge track.

There were 879,100 km (546,200 mi) of highways in 1990, including 652,500 km (405,400 mi) of paved roads and 226,600 km (140,800 mi) of earth roads. Compared with other developed countries, Russia has few passenger cars on the road, but many imports from Europe are increasingly arriving in Russia. Russia's ratio of population per car is four times that of Europe.

Marine access has been important to Russia ever since the construction of St. Petersburg was ordered by Peter the Great on the marshland adjoining the Gulf of Finland, in order to provide imperial Russia with a "window on the west." Other important maritime ports include Kaliningrad, on the Baltic Sea; Murmansk and Arkhangel'sk, both on the Barents Sea; Novorossiysk, on the Black Sea; Vladivostok and Nakhodka, both on the Sea of Japan; Tiksi on the Laptev Sea; and Magadan and Korsakov on the Sea of Okhotsk (the latter is on Sakhalin). Major inland ports include Nizhniy Novgorod, Kazan', Khabarovsk, Krasnoyarsk, Samara, Moscow, Rostov, and Volgograd. The merchant fleet consisted in 1991 of 842 ships (of 1,000 GRT or over), totaling 8,151,393 GRT. Almost three-fifths of the merchant fleet consists of cargo vessels. Late in 1994, a new port was scheduled to be built in the Batareynaya Harbor of the Baltic Sea about 70 km (43 mi) southwest of St. Petersburg. The new facility will handle oil shipments.

12 HISTORY

The history of Russia is usually dated from the 9th century AD when a loose federation of the eastern Slavic tribes was achieved under the legendary Rurik. At this time, Kiev was the political and cultural center. Vulnerable due to the flat land that surrounded them, the Kievan rulers sought security through expansion—a policy that subsequent Russian leaders frequently pursued.

By the 11th century, Kievan Rus had united all the eastern Slavs. However, over the next two centuries, Kievan dominance was eroded by other Slavic and non-Slavic centers of power. The Mongol conquest of Russia marked the eclipse of Kiev as a center of power. When Mongol power declined and collapsed in the 14th and 15th centuries, it was Moscow that emerged as the new Russian power center. The military victories of Grand Duke Ivan III (r. 1462–1505) in particular established Moscow's predominance over almost all other Russian principalities. In 1547, Grand Duke Ivan IV was crowned as the first "Tsar of All the Russias."

When the Rurik dynasty died out in 1598, Russia experienced internal political turmoil and territorial encroachment from the West. In 1618, the first of the Romanovs was crowned tsar, and

RUSSIA

LOCATION: 60°0′N; 30°0′E. **BOUNDARY LENGTHS:** Total land boundary lengths, 20,139 km (12,514 mi); Azerbaijan, 284 km (177 mi); Belarus, 959 km (596 mi); China (southeast), 3,605 km (2,240 mi); China (south), 40 km (25 mi); Estonia, 290 km (180.2 mi); Finland, 1,313 km (816 mi); Georgia, 723 km (450 mi); Kazakhstan, 6,846 km (4,254 mi); North Korea, 19 km (12 mi); Latvia, 217 km (135 mi); Lithuania, 227 km (141 mi); Mongolia, 3, 441 km (2,138 mi); Norway, 167 km (104 mi); Poland 432 km (268 mi); Ukraine, 1,576 km (980 mi); total coastline 37,653 km (23,398 mi).

Russia set about regaining the territory it had lost. In the 17th century, Russian power expanded across Siberia to the Pacific Ocean. Under Peter I (r. 1682–1725), Russian power was extended to the Baltic Sea in the early 18th century. It was under Peter that the Russian capital was moved from Moscow to St. Petersburg, on the Baltic Sea.

Russian power expanded further into Europe and Asia during the 18th century. The French Emperor, Napoleon, attacked Russia in 1812. Despite the considerable advances that he made, he was forced to withdraw from Russia and back across Europe in 1814. By the end of the Napoleonic wars in 1815, Russia had acquired Bessarabia (Moldova), Finland, and eastern Poland.

Russia's European borders remained relatively stable in the 19th century. It was during this period, though, that Russia completed its conquest of the Caucasus, Central Asia, and what became its Maritime Province (Vladivostok).

From the rise of Moscow after the Mongols until the early 20th century, Russia was ruled as an autocracy. Peter I founded a senate, but this was an advisory and honorific body, not a legislative one.

Some reform was made. Alexander II (r. 1855–81) emancipated the serfs of Russia in 1861. Alexander II appeared to be embarking on a course of political reform involving elections

when he was assassinated by revolutionaries in 1881. His son, Alexander III (r. 1881–94) ended political reform efforts and reverted to autocratic rule. Under him, however, economic development made considerable progress in Russia.

The autocratic nature of Tsarist rule generated growing opposition in Russia, beginning with the abortive "Decembrist" uprising of 1825. By the reign of the last tsar, Nicholas II (r. 1894–1917), many opposition groups had arisen. With the Tsarist regime's weakness evident as a result of its defeats in the 1905 Russo-Japanese War, a revolutionary movement grew up in Russia that same year. Under the leadership of the socialists, revolutionary "soviets" or councils seized power in parts of St. Petersburg and Moscow. The government was able to defuse the revolutionary impetus through promising an elected Duma (parliament). The First Duma (1906) met only briefly; its demands for land reform were unacceptable to the tsar, who dissolved it. The Second Duma (1907) was also dissolved shortly after it was convened. A Third Duma (1907–11) and Fourth Duma (1912–17) were elected on more restrictive franchises. While the Third Duma in particular made some progress in economic and social reform, the Tsar and his ministers retained firm control over the government.

It was Russia's disastrous involvement in World War I that led to the end of the monarchy. By early 1917, Russia had suffered a number of defeats in its struggle with superior German forces. The war and continued autocratic rule had grown increasingly unpopular. Riots broke out in the major cities in March 1917. The Tsar attempted to dissolve the Fourth Duma, but it refused to be dissolved. "Soviets" again rose up in Petrograd (St. Petersburg had been renamed in 1914) and Moscow. Nicholas II was forced to abdicate on 15 March 1917.

A Provisional Government, based on the old Fourth Duma, was declared. But its authority was challenged by the Soviets. In addition, the Provisional Government refused to end Russia's involvement in the war. This was seen as a major decision which only a duly elected government could make. Over the course of 1917, the Mensheviks (socialists) increasingly gained control over the Provisional Government but lost control over the Soviets to the Bolsheviks, led by Vladimir Lenin. On the night of 6 November 1917, the Bolsheviks seized control of St. Petersburg.

Elections for a Constituent Assembly organized by the Provisional Government did take place on 25 November 1917—Russia's freest elections until the 1990s. Only 168 of the 703 deputies elected were Bolsheviks. The Constituent Assembly convened on 18 January 1918, but was prevented from meeting again by Bolshevik forces.

Lenin moved quickly to end Russia's involvement in World War I. In March 1918, he agreed to a peace treaty with Germany which deprived Russia of considerable territory (it was at this time that the Bolsheviks moved the capital back to Moscow). From 1918 to 1921, the Bolsheviks fought a civil war against a large number of opponents, whom they defeated. After the German surrender to the Western powers in November 1918, Lenin's forces moved to take back the territory it had given up. Except for Finland, Poland, the Baltic states (temporarily), and Bessarabia (Moldova), Lenin's forces succeeded in regaining what they had given up.

The Bolshevik regime was based on Marxist-Leninist ideology. It sought to overthrow the rule of economic "oppressors" (the aristocracy and the bourgeoisie) and replace it with rule by the proletariat. There were two main concepts in Lenin's political theory: the dictatorship of the proletariat, and democratic centralism. In Lenin's view, the working class had to impose dictatorial rule over its class enemies to prevent them from regaining power. But within the instrument of this class dictatorship—the Communist Party—there was to be freedom of debate. Once a policy question had been resolved, however, debate was to cease.

Theoretically, power in the Communist Party was vested in an elected party congress which then elected a smaller Central Committee which in turn elected an even smaller Politburo to run day-to-day affairs. In fact, it was the top party leadership—Lenin and his Politburo colleagues—who established and maintained dictatorial control.

After the civil war, Lenin relented on his ambitious plans for the state to control the entire economy. He ushered in the New Economic Policy (NEP) which allowed peasants to own land and sell their produce at market, and permitted private business to operate (though the state retained control of large enterprises). Lenin died on 21 January 1924. A power struggle among the top Communist leaders broke out. By 1928, Joseph Stalin had eliminated all his rivals and achieved full power. He then ended NEP and ushered in a brutal period of forced industrialization and collectivization of agriculture. Stalin's rule was especially harsh in the non-Russian republics of the USSR. Scholars estimate that as many as 20 million Soviet citizens died during the 1928–38 period either because of state terror or famine.

In August 1939, the infamous Nazi-Soviet pact was signed dividing Eastern Europe into spheres of influence. Under this agreement, the USSR regained most of the territories that had belonged to the Russian Empire but had been lost during the Russian Revolution (eastern Poland, the Baltic states, and Bessarabia [Moldova]). But on 22 June 1941, Hitler's forces invaded the

USSR and Moscow quickly lost all the territory that it had recently gained. German forces reached the outskirts of Moscow. With the help of massive materiel shipments from the US and other Western countries, Soviet forces were able to rally and drive the Germans back. By the end of the war in May 1945, the USSR had reconquered everything it lost. With the Red Army in Eastern Europe, Stalin was able to establish satellite Communist regimes in Poland, Czechoslovakia, Hungary, Romania, Bulgaria, and East Germany. (Communist regimes also came to power in Yugoslavia and Albania, but did not remain allied to Moscow.)

Stalin's rule was especially harsh during the last years of his life. He died in 1953 and the ensuing power struggle was eventually won by Nikita Khrushchev. Khrushchev ended the terror of the Stalin years, but the basic features of the Stalinist system (Communist Party monopoly on power, centralized economy allowing for little private initiative, limited opportunities for free expression) remained until Mikhail Gorbachev came to power in March 1985.

Realizing that the old Stalinist system had led to a stagnant economy which would undermine the USSR's ability to remain a superpower, Gorbachev sought to reform the Communist system. But although greater freedom of expression led to an enhanced understanding of the serious economic and ethnic problems the USSR faced, Gorbachev was unwilling to implement the economic and other reforms that would have weakened party control. The intense division on how to solve the problems faced by the USSR led ultimately to the ultimate dissolution in 1991 of the nation into its separate republics.

For the first time, relatively free multi-party elections were held in Russia in March 1990. In May 1990, the new Russian Supreme Soviet elected Boris Yeltsin as its chairman. Yeltsin had been an ally of Gorbachev until they disagreed over the pace of reform and Yeltsin was pushed out of the Politburo and his other positions. On 12 June 1991, the first elections to the Russian presidency were held, and Yeltsin won. Yeltsin also played an instrumental role in foiling the August 1991 coup attempt by Soviet conservatives.

On 8 December 1991, Yeltsin, together with the leaders of Ukraine and Belarus, formed the nucleus of the Commonwealth of Independent States (CIS), which spelled the end of the USSR later that month. Like the other former Soviet republics, Russia had become an independent sovereign state.

In early 1992, Yeltsin and his acting Prime Minister, Egor Gaidar, sought to introduce rapid economic reform. Price controls were lifted on all but a few items. Prices rose rapidly, and as time passed, public opposition to economic reform grew. The Yeltsin government's relations with the legislature also grew increasingly acrimonious. Many of the deputies had close ties with the state-run economy and bureaucracy, which were threatened by economic reform.

Much of Russian politics in 1993 consisted of bitter squabbling between Yeltsin and the legislature. No progress was made on drafting a new constitution to replace the much amended Soviet-era constitution that still governed Russia.

On 21 September 1993, Yeltsin unilaterally dissolved the Supreme Soviet and introduced rule by presidential decree until new parliamentary elections and a referendum on his draft constitution could be held on 12 December. Many of the anti-Yeltsin parliamentarians refused to accept Yeltsin's suspension, and barricaded themselves inside the parliament building. On 3 October, forces loyal to the parliament briefly occupied the office of the mayor of Moscow and attempted to seize the Ostankino television center. Forces loyal to Yeltsin then attacked and seized the parliament building. A state of emergency and press censorship were briefly introduced.

The referendum and parliamentary elections were held as planned. The electorate approved the new constitution, which called for a strong presidency. In the parliamentary elections, though, the Communist and ultra-nationalist forces did well.

13GOVERNMENT

A new post-Soviet constitution for Russia was approved in a referendum held 12 December 1993. The constitution establishes a bicameral legislature known as the Federal Assembly. The lower house (State Duma) consists of 450 elected deputies while the 178-member upper house (Council of the Federation) is composed of representatives of the provinces and autonomous republics that make up Russia. The president is elected separately for a five-year term.

The president appoints the cabinet and other top government posts subject to confirmation by the legislature. Presidential appointments of prime minister, deputy prime ministers, and chairman of the central bank are subject to confirmation by the State Duma while appointments of high court judges and the prosecutor general are subject to confirmation by the Council of the Federation. The president can refuse to accept the State Duma's rejection of an appointment to the prime ministership. If the State Duma refuses three times to confirm a new prime minister, the president may dissolve the lower house and hold new elections to it. If the State Duma votes twice within three months a no-confidence motion against the prime minister and cabinet, the president may respond either by dismissing the cabinet or dissolving the State Duma. The president, however, cannot dissolve the State Duma due to its passing a no-confidence motion during the first year of the State Duma's term of office. The president may declare war or a state of emergency on his own authority.

Impeachment of the president is provided for in the constitution, but is very difficult. Two-thirds of the State Duma must vote to initiate the impeachment process. Both the Constitutional Court, established to arbitrate any disputes between the executive and legislative branches, and the Supreme Court must review the charges. The findings of all three organizations are then submitted to the Council of the Federation, which can impeach the president by a two-thirds majority vote. This process must be completed within three months from beginning to end.

The State Duma has jurisdiction over the budget and economic policy, most of which must then be approved of by the Council of the Federation. The Council has jurisdiction over issues affecting the provinces and autonomous republics, including border changes and the use of force within the Russian Federation.

14POLITICAL PARTIES

In the elections to the State Duma held 12 December 1993, 225 of the 450 seats were elected on the basis of proportional representation from party lists which had to receive a minimum of 5% of the national vote to gain representation. The other 225 seats were elected from single member districts.

The party to receive the largest number of seats (76) was the radical reformist Russia's Choice led by Yeltsin's ex-acting Prime Minister, Egor Gaidar. The centrist New Regional Policy group (which was actually formed by non-aligned deputies from single member districts after the election) won 65. Vladimir Zhirinovsky's ultra-nationalist, anti-democratic Liberal Democratic Party won 63. The pro-Communist Agrarian Party won 55 seats, while the Communist Party of the Russian Federation won 45. Six other parties or blocs (some of which were also formed after the election) won between 12 and 30 seats each.

Deputies to the 178-seat Council of the Federation were elected in two-member districts where they mostly ran as individuals. Of the 171 seats that were filled, only 27 identified themselves with a particular party. Nevertheless, while the ultranationalists, Communists, and their sympathizers predominate in the State Duma, Yeltsin supporters appear to have the upper hand in the Council.

15LOCAL GOVERNMENT

Russia has a complicated patchwork of regional and local governments. Russia is divided into six krais, 49 oblasts, one autonomous oblast, 10 autonomous okrugs, and two independent cities (Moscow and St. Petersburg). There are also 21 autonomous republics where non-Russian minorities predominate, or used to predominate.

For all but the 21 autonomous republics, President Yeltsin issued decrees reorganizing the system of local government in October 1993. Each unit has an elected legislature. Most of these are unicameral, though two (Magadan Oblast and Altai Krai) have opted for bicameral ones.

Each head of local administration (governor), however, is appointed by the Russian president. The head of administration cannot be removed by the local legislature, and may appoint a staff without consulting it. The heads of administration cannot dissolve the local legislature.

By contrast, the Russian president does not appoint the heads of the 21 autonomous republics. These (usually called president) are selected in whatever manner is prescribed by their individual constitutions. In some, the president is directly elected by the voters, while in others the president is elected by the legislature.

16JUDICIAL SYSTEM

A Constitutional Court was established to arbitrate any disputes between the executive and legislative branches. The Supreme Court reviews charges brought against the executive and legislative branches.

17ARMED FORCES

Still formidable in terms of weapons and equipment, the Russian armed forces reached a low state of morale and effectiveness in 1993. With the collapse of the original CIS in 1992, Russia established a separate Ministry of Defense and military establishment upon the wreckage of the Soviet armed forces. The attempted coup of 1991 and economic woes have thrown the armed forces into confusion, and reorganization continues along with a withdrawal from other countries in Europe and the former Soviet Union. No reliable defense expenditures can be cited, but may be around $130 billion, probably a reduction of 50% since 1989. Russia has assumed the responsibility of the Soviet Union to reduce by treaty its strategic arsenal and conventional forces in Europe. The former is proceeding with US technical and financial assistance; civilians and military personnel of the On-Site Inspection Agency (517 in 1991) furnish this assistance. Although equipment numbers and force structure remain impressive, the Russian armed forces have been "hollowed" by low-manning, the failure of draft calls, diversion to survival tasks rather than training, and lack of discipline. Nevertheless, the very size and modernity of the Russian armed forces still make them a force of global significance, especially to smaller and weaker neighbors.

The active Russian armed forces may number 2.7 million (1.5 million conscripts) with 3 million recent veterans in the first-line reserve and 20 million in the general reserves until age 50. Russian males have an 18-month service training obligation, but failures to serve are now common.

Russia remains the world's second most formidable nuclear nation. The Strategic Rocket Forces (144,000) control 1,400 silo-based and mobile ICBMs with 6,620 warheads and provide ground defense forces to defend ICBM launch sites and warhead storage facilities. Strategic aviation forces control 581 long-range bombers with a tanker and reconnaissance aircraft fleet of 150 aircraft in a support role; these Russian bombers may be capable of carrying more than 700 missiles and bombs. The Russian navy provides 55 fleet ballistic missile submarines of six different classes armed with 832 missiles (2,700 warheads). These strategic nuclear forces appear to be under good order and relatively prepared to stop rogue behavior or terrorist attack, but international observers are concerned about the rise of a Russian flea-market in nuclear weapons. Russian forces also man 100 anti-ballistic-missile missiles and associated radars in the name of the defunct CIS.

The Russian navy has surrendered little of its strength to the break-away republics. It retains the vast majority of the combat capability in the Soviet navy, and it shares only its Black Sea installations with others, although it has lost control of its major Baltic base at Riga. The navy (320,000) controls 183 attack submarines and other types of submarines, 192 surface combatants (including 2 carriers and 33 cruisers), 305 patrol and coastal combatants, 218 mine warfare ships and craft, and more than 700 amphibious and support vessels. The naval air arm (60,000) has 1,100 combat aircraft and 290 armed helicopters. Naval infantry numbers 12,000 and coastal defense forces (designed for naval base defense) deploy 15,000 troops with ground combat artillery, and missile weapons. The navy remains organized in four major fleets with regional and global missions stationed in Arctic Russia, four Baltic bases, three Black Sea bases, and Vladivostok.

The Russian army has declined to 1.4 million, of whom perhaps one million are unwilling conscripts. The 400,000 officers and non-commissioned officers retain high-skill levels, but probably cannot maintain a force structure of over 100 divisions and 60 specialized separate brigades. The weapons inventory remains formidable: 29,000 main battle tanks, 28,000 armored infantry fighting vehicles, 23,000 reconnaissance and specialized mobile warfare vehicles, 28,000 towed and self-propelled artillery pieces, and 3,200 attack and transport helicopters. Russian fixed and mobile air defense systems are still the most numerous and effective in the world. Almost 200,000 troops remain in Germany and Poland awaiting demobilization or restationing, while Russian soldiers remain in nine of the new republics that formed the CIS, some of them involved in continuing peacekeeping missions.

The Russian air force, a separate service from the missile forces and air defense air arm, claims 300,000 airmen (about half conscripts) of whom 25,000 are assigned to the strategic nuclear air forces. The principal weapons systems remain MiG and Su fighters and fighter-attack aircraft and armed helicopters, which number 2,700 aircraft and helos. Additional aircraft probably number 1,500–2,000. The air defense force (VPVO) has 356,000 personnel and 2,200 frontline interceptors as well as airborne command and battle management aircraft.

The remnants of the state internal security forces (KGB) still number 220,000 with another 250,000 paramilitary forces assigned to specialized security functions for border protection, river patrols, customs duties, installation and plant protection, transportation security, and riot duty.

Although Russia has scaled back the Soviet Union's imperial presence, the Russian armed forces still maintain a global presence. In addition to troops remaining in Warsaw Pact nations and CIS members, Russia maintains major military missions or units in Cuba, Algeria, Libya, India, Cambodia, Syria, Yemen, Mongolia, and Vietnam. Russian units participate in seven separate peacekeeping missions, five UN-sponsored. Although Russian arms exports and imports dropped dramatically in 1991, Russia's desperate search for foreign currency kept arms exports at the level of $6.6 billion, but it is doubtful that Russia will return to its 1980s level of $18–22 billion a year. Given the large numbers of unused Russian military equipment, Russian arms deals are likely to remain a global problem for years to come.

[18]INTERNATIONAL COOPERATION

Russia has taken the former Soviet Union's place in the UN and in its membership in international organizations. Russia, in one form or another, has held a seat in the UN since 24 October 1945. It is a member of the CSCE, ECO, IAEA, ICAO, ILO, IMF, IMO, ITV, UPU, WHO, WIPO, WMO, and the World Bank. It has observer status in GATT. It is a founding member of the CIS. The country has assumed the foreign relations established by the former Soviet Union. The US has recently negotiated a multibillion dollar aid package with the country. It is hoped the money will be used to establish a free market economy in Russia and encourage foreign investment.

[19]ECONOMY

Russia's is the largest economy within the former Soviet bloc. It is undergoing a transformation from a centrally planned economy to a market-oriented one with limited public ownership. The largest sector is industry (31% of GDP in 1993); the manufacturing centers in Moscow and St. Petersburg are the most important in the entire former USSR. Russia has rich energy and mineral resources, including large deposits of iron ore, coal, phosphates, and non-ferrous metals, as well as one-fifth of the world's gold deposits and substantial oil and gas beds. There are also vast forest resources. Agricultural production is almost up to self-sufficiency levels and accounted for 4% of GDP in 1993. There is an acute excess demand for goods, especially consumer goods.

Russia's economic situation has deteriorated steadily since the break-up of the Soviet Union. National income and industrial production fell by 18% and 13% respectively in the first half of 1992. By the end of 1993, unofficial figures placed unemployment at over 10%.

[20]INCOME

In 1992, the GNP was $397,786 million at current prices, or $2,680 per capita. For the period 1985–92 the average inflation rate was 13.6%.

In 1992 the GDP was $387,476 million in current US dollars.

[21]LABOR

In 1993, the labor force was estimated at 75 million, of which production and economic services employees accounted for 83.9%, and government workers 16.1%. Wages were set by the government during the Soviet era. Since the dissolution of the USSR, hyperinflation has outpaced wage hikes—real wages fell by about 40% in 1992. By the end of 1993, unemployment surpassed 10%. Women accounted for about 50% of the work force but 90% of the unemployed in 1992. Overstaffing had accounted for an estimated 20–25% of the work force at the end of 1991. The development of the labor force is expected to be a structural and generational process. As reforms progress, the role of unions is expected to grow as a reaction to widespread unemployment. The Russian Labor Code standardizes a 40 hour working week, paid sick leave allowances, four weeks of paid vacation, and forbids wage reductions based on a worker's sex, age, race, nationality, religion, or voluntary association. As of 1 January 1994, the monthly minimum wage was set at R14,620. A legacy from the Soviet era, the Federation of independent Russian Trade Unions still dominates organized labor. The mining and air transport industries (along with the state sector) are highly unionized.

[22]AGRICULTURE

Russian agriculture accounts for about 18% of GDP and utilizes some 13% (including permanent pastures) of the total land area. In 1992, gross agricultural output dropped by 8% (mostly from a decline in livestock production), whereas grain production grew by 20% due to favorable weather. The 1992 harvest included (in 1,000 tons): wheat, 46,000; potatoes, 37,800, barley, 25,500; sugar beets, 25,500; rye, 13,900; vegetables and melons, 12,500; oats, 11,500; dry peas, 3,800; sunflower seeds, 3,070; soybeans, 50; and grapes, 520. The government is promoting the expansion of small-plot farming; about 150,000 new farms have begun operating since 1991, primarily in the south.

23ANIMAL HUSBANDRY

Some 83 million hectares (205 million acres) are pastureland, representing just under 5% of the total area. Russia's pastures occupy about the same amount of land as those of all the nations of Europe combined. As of 1992, the livestock population included: cattle, 54,677,000; sheep, 52,535,000; pigs, 35,384,000; goats, 2,765,000; horses, 2,610,000; chickens, 628,000,000; and turkeys, 24,000,000. Russia ranked second in the world in number of turkeys (after the US), and third in chickens and pigs (after China and the US). Russia's sheep population also ranked third largest, after China and New Zealand.

In 1992, livestock production dropped sharply, causing gross agricultural output to fall by about 8%. The 1991 (and 1992 in parentheses) meat production amounts included (in 1,000 tons): beef, 3,989 (3,500); pork, 3,190 (2,700); mutton, 342 (280); and poultry, 1,751 (1,577). Milk production in 1992 totaled 46.9 million tons (down 9.5% from 1991), and egg production amounted to 2.4 million tons in 1992 (down 9.6% from 1991). Infrastructural and distributional problems have only exacerbated the declining production. By September 1993, the absence of available food resources left Moscow short of 55% of its inhabitants' meat requirements, which prompted the consideration of purchasing meat abroad and/or price subsidies.

24FISHING

Russia's fishing fleet is second only to Japan's in size. The total catch in 1992 was 5.4 million tons, down 22% from 1991. Exports of fish in 1991 accounted for 2.4% of total exports. Overfishing and pollution of territorial waters have forced fishermen farther away from traditional fishing waters. For example, pollutants like mercury have partly caused the decline of the sturgeon and pike perch catches, which fell by 50% and 90%, respectively, from 1974 to 1987 in the Caspian Sea. Additionally, the fishing fleet's vessels are old, and fuel shortages are common. Whereas fish exports in 1992 totaled 2.5 million tons, exports in 1993 were expected to reach only 1.5 million tons.

Despite problems with pollution, the Russian catch expanded during the 1980s (the marine catch by 24%, the freshwater catch by 26%) due to intensified fishing in dam reservoirs, consumption substitution toward non-traditional fish stocks, and acceptance of higher levels of contaminants.

25FORESTRY

Russia's forested areas are vast. In the early 1980s an estimated 760 million hectares (1,878 million acres) were classified as forested—an area about as large as the total land area of Australia. The forest stock in Russia is 80% coniferous, consisting mainly of spruce, fir, larch, and pine in sub-arctic areas. Deciduous trees (oak, ash, maple, elm) grow further south. From 1917 to 1980, the area covered by forests declined by only about 16%. The Russian wood products industry has been adversely affected by turmoil in the macroeconomy, industrial reorganization, and poor utilization of its resource base. As of early 1993, outputs of commercial timber, sawn timber, and paper fell by 25–30% from the previous year. By April 1993, preliminary estimates indicated production declines of 23% for commercial timber, 27% for sawn timber, 25% for plywood, 29% for particleboard, 23% for paper, and 33% for paperboard from 1992 levels.

Privatization in the forest products industry is expected to eventually rejuvenate the sector's output. In the spring of 1993, auctions in St. Petersburg included the privatization of the timber trading port, a woodworking combine, and the Zevsapmebel combine, a large furniture manufacturer which sells to western markets. The combine in Syas'stroy, the biggest producer of sanitary papers in Russia, was privatized in March 1993. The Ust-Ilim combine, one of the biggest forest products companies in Russia, was vertically integrated so that a single parts depart-

ment, raw material commodity exchange, chemical pulp and sawmill were split into separate companies through privatization. In April 1993, export regulations were lifted on firewood, pallets, parquetry, and structural goods, enabling Russian producers to enter into export contracts without governmental intervention.

26MINING

Russia has bountiful and diverse mineral resources. Mining activities are concentrated near the Arctic Circle (nickel, cobalt, phosphate, uranium, gold, tin, and mercury); in the Ural region (titanium, vanadium, nickel-cobalt, soda ash, asbestos, magnesite, vermiculite, talc, bauxite, copper, bismuth, beryllium, lead, zinc, and iron ore); and in Siberia (tungsten, molybdenum, fluorospar, mica, asbestos, diamond, talc, iron ore, gold, tin, lead, and zinc).

Ferroalloy production in 1991 amounted to 1.7 million tons, down 15% from 1990. Russian gold production was estimated at 147,000 kg that year. Iron ore production, at 90.9 million tons in 1991, was 18% below the previous year's level; the shortage of coking coal resulted in a 19% reduction in pig iron (to 84 million tons). More than 40% of the iron production was from the Kursk Magnetic Anomaly, about 20% from the Kola Peninsula (Kol'skiy Poluostrov) and Karelia combined, and about 20% each from the Urals and Siberia.

27ENERGY AND POWER

Russia possesses enormous reserves of oil, natural gas, and coal, which provide a significant source of foreign revenue as well as a large degree of self-sufficiency in energy resources. In 1992, petroleum exports accounted for $13.2 billion, or 35% of total exports.

The Tartarstan and Chechen-Ingushetia republics and the Tyumen oblast (west Siberia) are the main regions where oil is produced. Production has fallen from 569.5 million tons in 1987 (about 11 million barrels per day) to 396 million tons in 1992 (about 8 million barrels per day). Production fell by 14.1% from 1991 to 1992. At the beginning of 1993, 31,900 wells (more than 20% of all wells) were inactive. Nevertheless, in 1992, Russia ranked third in total oil production, after Saudi Arabia and the US. Refineries in Russia are generally antiquated and inefficient, relying on western Siberian crude oil delivered via pipeline. Pipelines are also used to export up to one million barrels per day of oil to Eastern Europe; tankers are used through the major oil ports of St. Petersburg and others. At the end of 1992, Russia had some 6.6 billion tons (48.4 billion barrels), or 4.8% of the world's proven oil reserves.

Natural gas production is also centered in western Siberia, namely at the Urengoi Field. Natural gas exports now are limited to the parts of Europe which are served by the west Siberian and Ural pipelines. In 1992, Russia produced 604 billion cu m (21.3 trillion cu ft), down from 606.5 billion cu m (21.4 trillion cu ft) in 1991. Proven reserves of natural gas in Russia at the end of 1992 totaled 1,681.2 trillion cu ft (47.6 trillion cu m), or 34.4% of the world's total reserves. Future production will depend on exploiting inaccessible fields, which will require a significant amount of investment capital.

Coal production in 1993 was estimated at 278 million tons, which met 97% of domestic consumption requirements. In 1992, natural gas contributed 48% to Russia's primary energy consumption; oil, 27%; coal, 20%; nuclear energy, 3.3%; and hydroelectric power, 1.7%.

The World Bank estimated that Russia would need $50 billion to stop the declining oil output; furthermore, a loan of $610 million was initiated in August 1993 to restore 1,300 wells and replace 800 miles of pipeline in Western Siberia. In July 1993, the US Export-Import Bank approved $2 billion in credit to refit existing natural gas and oil refining and processing facilities.

Several western petroleum companies, including Texaco, Conoco, and Occidental, are assisting in Russia's oil and natural gas development through joint venture projects.

The revitalization of Russia's weakening energy sector depends on the economic success of privatization, the abolition of price controls, and currency reform.

28INDUSTRY

Major manufacturing industries include crude steel, cars and trucks, aircraft, chemicals (including fertilizers), plastics, cement and other building materials, paper, television sets, and appliances. Industrial expansion is mainly in consumer goods and food processing, often embraced by enterprises converting from military production, which dominated industry output in the former Soviet Union.

29SCIENCE AND TECHNOLOGY

The Russian Academy of Sciences, founded in 1725, is the chief coordinating body for scientific research in Russia through its science councils and commissions. It controls a network of approximately 300 research establishments. The Russian Academy of Agricultural Sciences, founded in 1929, comprises 18 specialized research complexes, 9 regional divisions and 5 specialized sections. It supervises a number of research institutes, experimental and breeding stations, dendraria and arboreta. The Russian Academy of Medical Sciences, founded in 1944, comprises 79 research establishments and 47 research councils. Russia has 258 institutes conducting scientific research.

30DOMESTIC TRADE

A central marketplace is a common feature of urban areas in Russia. Many consumer goods, which were often traded via the black market during the Soviet era, are now openly available. However, inflation and slow economic recovery severely constrain domestic purchasing power. Since the underground economy was so well-developed during the Soviet period distribution and trade through informal channels is still common. The appearance and rapid development of organized crime in post-Soviet Russia may also be seen as a result of Russia's affinity for informal domestic economic activity; local businesses are often forced to pay protection money to organized crime. Commercial advertisement, virtually unknown during the Soviet era, is now commonly used.

31FOREIGN TRADE

Principal exports have traditionally been oil (accounting for about 20% of earnings), gas, minerals, military equipment and weapons, gold, shipping, and transport services. In 1988, total imports were valued at R101,900 million, and exports at R132,700. Inter-republic trade accounted for 51% of imports and 68% of exports. In 1992, the trade balance showed a surplus of us$7.4 billion. Almost half of Russia's trade in that year was with the Baltics and Eastern Europe, followed by Germany, France, Spain, and Switzerland.

32BALANCE OF PAYMENTS

Foreign trade was largely deregulated in early 1992, and the trade balance contracted throughout the year; exports declined by 35% to $15.4 billion, while imports fell by 24% to $14.9 billion during the first half of 1992 compared with the same period of 1991. The current account deficit was estimated at $4 billion in 1992, due to the significant decrease in imports. As of the beginning of 1993, there was a dire shortage of hard currency reserves, which severely limited importation possibilities of consumer and capital goods.

33BANKING AND SECURITIES

The Central Bank of the Russian Federation was created in January 1992 from the old Soviet banking system headed by Gosbank (The Soviet State Bank). The bank heads a two-tier banking system, and implements a monetary policy and regulates the commercial banking sector by setting the reserve requirements and the discount rate. The currency unit of Russia is the rouble, a currency that is in the process of becoming fully convertible with world currency. Russia, along with a few other countries of the former Soviet Union, decided to keep the rouble as its currency. The other important state bank is the Rosevneshtorgbank (Bank for Foreign Trade of the Russian Federation).

Commercial banks in the Russian Federation numbered about 10 in 1993. The total number of banks in Russia is about 2,000. Commercial banks include the Commercial Bank Industriaservis, the Commercial Credit Bank, the Commercial Conservation Bank, the Commercial Innovation Bank, the International Moscow Bank, St. Petersburg's Investment Bank, and the Construction Bank. The International Bank is a bank whose shares are owned by western banks, such as Citibank NA (US) and the Barclays Groups Ltd. (UK), interested in doing business in the country.

Russia had a small stock market in 1992. The market is considered an emerging market by western investors with the potential for significant growth in coming years.

34INSURANCE

As of 1993, 1,524 Russian companies had been licensed to sell insurance and another 750 companies had applied for licenses. However, fewer than 2% of the operating firms had assets over R100 million (us$80,000), and premium volume for the first nine months of 1993 amounted to only 1.3% of the GDP (as compared with volume of 2.9% for the former Soviet Union in 1990).

Property insurance is the largest segment of the market with 880 companies. There are 775 cargo insurance firms, and 600 that sell life insurance. The various companies are gradually consolidating into groups.

35PUBLIC FINANCE

Since the breakup of the COMECON and the Soviet Union, trade disruptions and friction between Russia and the governments of the former Soviet republics had led to an enormous expansion of the fiscal deficit. During the first half of 1992, the government maintained relatively cautious fiscal and monetary policies after most prices were allowed to adjust to market levels in January 1992. During the latter half of 1992, however, a huge expansion of credit from the central bank in the form of loans to state enterprises severely deteriorated the fiscal position and led to hyperinflation.

In mid-1992, Russia was granted admission into the IMF, and was given drawing rights equivalent to $4.15 billion. The external debt of the CIS in convertible currency was estimated at $75 billion in 1992; Russia's external debt was reported at $40 billion at the end of 1991.

36TAXATION

A January 1992 tax law significantly changed the existing corporate tax rate structure. The standard rate was cut from 32% to 18%, except for income for certain services, which varies from 25–45%. Under the new law, there is a withholding tax of 18% on dividends, interest, royalties, and other Russian source income.

Under a December 1991 law, the personal income tax rate varies from 12–40%, and all income is taxable. All goods produced or sold in Russia are subject to a 20% value-added tax.

37CUSTOMS AND DUTIES

Russia has eliminated many of the import restrictions imposed by the former Soviet Union. An August 1992 law established a 15% import duty on goods from countries receiving most-favored nation status from Russia, and implemented further adjustments to reflect Russia's most-favored nation treatment by the US.

38FOREIGN INVESTMENT

In September 1991, a foreign investment law promoting the transfer of capital, technology, and know-how went into effect. Non-residents may acquire partial shareholdings or form wholly-owned subsidiaries in Russia. Foreign firms may obtain licenses to exploit natural resources. Foreign investors can be exempted from import duties and export taxes, and there is limited relief from profits tax, varying by sector and region. However, foreign investment was low through 1992 due to political and economic instability.

39ECONOMIC DEVELOPMENT

In 1991, Russia's parliament enacted legislation aimed at fully privatizing the commercial and service sector by 1994 and placing about half the medium and large companies in private hands by 1995. By the end of 1992, about 6,000 firms had applied to become joint-stock companies, and 1,560 had completed the process; almost one-third of Russia's approximately 250,000 small businesses had been privatized. Housing privatization began late in 1992, and over 2.6 million apartments—about 8% of the total—had been privatized by the end of 1993.

40SOCIAL DEVELOPMENT

The Russian Republic had enacted its own pension legislation in November 1990, before the collapse of the Soviet Union. While it followed the USSR model in many respects, it raised the minimum old age pension from 70 to 100 roubles a month (with corresponding increases in other benefits), and linked pensions to a "minimum subsistence" figure instead of to the minimum wage. However, rapid price increases in 1992 pressured the Yeltsin government into once again indexing pensions to the minimum wage. For cash benefit programs, the minimum pension rose from 342 roubles a month in January 1992 to 900 rubles by May. As of June 1992, the payment on the birth of a child was 2,700 roubles, and the monthly allowance ranged from 200 to 500 roubles.

In 1989, the average family size was 3.5 members, and the divorce rate was 8.5 per 1,000 women. There were 4.4 drug-related crimes and 9.9 alcohol-related deaths per 100,000 persons.

41HEALTH

With Moscow the seat of practically all major political activity, Russia had many social systems in place and was the most influential sector of the former USSR. The 1993 birth rate was 16 per 1,000 people. There were 1.81 million births in 1992. Infant mortality was 28 per 1,000 live births in 1992, and average life expectancy was 69 years. The general mortality rate was 11 per 1,000 inhabitants in 1993.

In 1992, there were 4.69 physicians per 1,000 people; in 1990, the population per physician was 210. In 1991, there were 13.8 hospital beds per 1,000 population. Children up to one year of age were immunized in 1992 against tuberculosis (88%); diphtheria, pertussis, and tetanus (73%); polio (69%); and measles (83%). Total health care expenditures in 1990 were $23,527 million.

42HOUSING

In 1989, 46.7% of all privately owned urban housing had running water, 35.2% had sewer lines, 36.3% had central heating, and 17.2% had hot water. In 1990, Russia had 16.4 square meters of housing space per capita and, as of 1 January 1991, 9,456,000 households (25.6%) were on waiting lists for urban housing.

43EDUCATION

The illiteracy rate in 1990 was estimated at 1.3%, with males at 0.4%, and females at 2.1%. Education, mostly free and state funded, is also compulsory for 10 years. The state also provides a stipend for higher education. Although Russian is the most common medium of instruction, other languages are also taught, especially at the secondary level. In the early 1990s, many privately owned institutions were opened and the education system was modified with the introduction of a revised curriculum.

At the higher level, there were 42 universities with a total enrollment of 2,824,500 students in 1990–91 school year. The St. Petersburg State University, which was founded in 1724, is well known for its education.

44LIBRARIES AND MUSEUMS

Museums throughout Russia have some of the world's finest collections, including the Hermitage in St. Petersburg and a museum of Czarist treasures in the Kremlin. During the Soviet era, the contents of libraries and museums were controlled by the government. Ironically, many of the churches closed by the state (1930s–60s) and converted into museums have once again become functioning churches.

45MEDIA

Russia has about 36 million telephone lines, of which only about 3% are switched automatically, and there are approximately 11 telephones per 100 persons.

Broadcasting is overseen by All-Russian State Television and Radio (Ostankino). There are 1,050 AM, FM, and short wave radio stations, which reach 98.6% of the population, and 310 television stations with 580 reporters.

In 1991 there were 723 daily newspapers with a total circulation of 133,979,000. In 1992, Russia's major newspapers, all published in Moscow, were (with circulation figures): *Komsomalskaya Pravda* (3,400,000); *Trud* (3,100,000); *Krasnaya Zvezda* (2,500,000); *Moskovski Komsomolyets* (1,200,000); and *Selskaya Zhizn* (1,200,000).

46ORGANIZATIONS

The leading opposition movement to the non-partisan leadership of Russia is Democratic Russia, one of the grassroots political and social organizations that have emerged in Russia. They are allowed to publicize their activities and operate freely as long as they register with the government. The International Red Cross and the Red Crescent operate branches throughout the federation, A chamber of commerce that promotes the economic and business activities of the country to the rest of the world operates in Moscow.

47TOURISM, TRAVEL, AND RECREATION

In September 1992, Russia lifted its travel restrictions on foreigners, opening the entire country to visitors and tourists. Tourist attractions in Moscow include the Kremlin, monasteries and churches, museums, and other cultural attractions, including opera and ballet at the world-famous Bolshoi Theater. Nearby tourist destinations include St. Petersburg (formerly Leningrad) and Kiev.

48FAMOUS RUSSIANS

Notable among the rulers of pre-revolutionary Russia were Ivan III (the Great, 1440–1505), who established Moscow as a sovereign state; Peter I (the Great, 1672–1725), a key figure in the modernization of Russia; Alexander I (1777–1825), prominent both in the war against Napoleon and the political reaction that followed the war; and Alexander II (1818–81), a social reformer who freed the serfs. Boris Yeltsin, President of Russia, (b. 1931) was born in the Sverdlovsk region of the Urals. Mikhail Gorbachev (b. 1931) came to power in 1985 and initiated many reforms of the old Communist system.

Mikhail Lomonosov (1711–65), poet and grammarian, also was a founder of natural science in Russia. The poet Gavrila

Derzhavin (1743–1816) combined elements of topical satire with intimate, lyrical themes. Aleksandar Radishchev (1749–1802) criticized both religion and government absolutism. Nikolay Karamzin (1766–1826), an early translator of Shakespeare, was the founder of Russian Sentimentalism. The fables of Ivan Krylov (1768/69?–1844) exposed human foibles and the shortcomings of court society. Russia's greatest poet Aleksandr Pushkin (1799–1837) was also a brilliant writer of prose. Other outstanding poets were Fyodor Tyutchev (1803–73), Mikhail Lermontov (1814–41), and Afanasy Fet (Shen-shing 1820–92). Nikolay Gogol (1809–52), best known for his novel *Dead Souls* and his short stories, founded the realistic trend in Russian literature. Vissarion Belinsky (1811–48) was an influential critic. Noted radical philosophers were Aleksandr Hertzen (1812–70). Nikolay Chernyshevshy (1828–89), and Nikolay Dobrolyubov (1812–91), satirized the weakness of Russian society. Ivan Turgenev (1818–83) is noted for his sketches, short stories, and the novel *Fathers and Sons*. Fyodor Dostoyevsky (1821–81) wrote outstanding psychological novels (*Crime and Punishment*, *The Brothers Karamazov*). Leo (Lev) Tolstoy (1828–1910) perhaps the greatest Russian novelist (*War and Peace*, *Anna Karenina*), also wrote plays, essays and short stories. Aleksandr Ostrovsky (1823–86) was a prolific dramatist. The consummate playwright and short-story writer Anton Chekhov (1860–1904) was the greatest Russian writer of the late 19th century. Leonid Nikolayevich Aandreyev (1871–1919) wrote plays and short stories. The novels, stories, and playas of Maksim Gorky (Aleksey Peshkov, 1868–1936) bridged the tsarist and Soviet periods. Ivan Bunin (1870–1953) received the Nobel Prize in 1933 for his novels and short stories. Georgy Plekhanov (1856–1918), a Marxist philosopher and propagandist, also was a literary critic and art theorist, as was Anatoly Lunacharsky (1875–1933).

Russian composers of note include Mikhail Glinka (1804–57), Aleksandar Borodin (1833–87), also a distinguished chemist, Mily Balakirev (1837–1910), Modest Mussorgsky (1839–81), Pyotr Ilyich Tchaikovsky (1840–93), Nikolay Rimsky-Korsakov (1844–1908), Aleksandr Skryabin (1871–1915), Sergey Rakhmaninov (1873–1943), Igor Stravinsky (1882–1971), Sergey Prokofyev (1891–1953), Aram Ilyich Khachaturian (1903–78), Dmitry Kabalevsky (1904–87), and Dmitry Shostakovich (1906–75). Two of the greatest bassos of modern times are the Russian-born Fyodor Chaliapin (1873–1938) and Alexander Kipnis (1891–1978). Serge Koussevitzky (1874–1951), noted conductor of the Boston Symphony Orchestra, was important in Russian musical life before the Revolution.

Outstanding figures in the ballet are the impresario Sergey Diaghilev (1872–1929); the choreographers Marius Petipa (1819–1910), Lev Ivanov (1834–1901), and Mikhail Fokine (1880–1942); the ballet dancers Vaslav Nijinsky (1890–1950), Anna Pavlova (1881–1931), Tamaara Karsavina (1885–1978), Galina Ulanova (b. 1909), and Maya Plosetskaya (b. 1925); and the ballet teacher Agrippina Vaganova (1879–1951).

Outstanding figures in the theater include Kostantin Stanislavsky (Alekseyev, 1863–1938), director, acotor and theorectician; Vladimir Nemirovich-Danchenko (1858–1943), director, playwright, and founder, with Stanislavsky, of the Moscow Art Theater; and Vsevolod Meyerhold (1873–1942), noted for innovations in stagecraft. Important film directors were Vsevolod Pudovkin (1893–1953), Aleksandr Dovzhenko (1864–1956), Sergey Eisenstein (1898–1948, Vasily Shiksin (1929–74), and Andrei Tarkovsky (1932–87).

Varfolomey (Bartolomeo Francesco) Rastrelli (1700–1771) designed many of the most beautiful buildings in St. Petersburg. Other important Russian architects include Vasily Bazhenov (1737–99), Matvey Kazakov (1733–1812), Andreyan Zakharov (1761–1811), and Ivan Starov (1806–58), Vasily Perov (1833/34–82), Vasily Vereshchagin (1842–1904), Ilya Repin (1844–1930),

Mikhail Vrubel (1856–1910, Leon (Lev) Bakst (Rosenberg, 1866–1924), and Aleksansr Benois (1870–1960). Modern Russian artists whose work is internationally important include the Suprematist painters Kasimir Malevich (1878–1935) and El (Lazar) Lissitzky (1890–1941), the "Rayonist" painters Natalya Goncharova (1881–1962) and Mikhail Larionov (1881–1964), the Constructivist artist Vladimir Tatlin (1885–1953), and the Spatial sculptor Aleksandar Rodchenko (1891–1956). Famous Russian-born artists who left their native country to work abroad include the painters Alexei von Jawlensky (1864–1941), Vasily Kandinsky (1866–1944), Marc Chagall (1897–1985), and Chaim Soutine (1894–1943) and the sculptors Antoine Pevsner (1886–1962), his brother Naum Gabo (1890–1977), Alexander Archipenko (1887–1964), and Ossip Zadkine (1890–1967).

Prominent Russian scientists of the 19th and 20th centuries include the chemist Dmitry Ivanovich Mendeleyev (1834–1907), inventor of the periodic table, Aleksandr Mikhailovich Butlerov (1828–86), a creator of the theory of chemical structure, Nikolay Yegorovich Zhukovsky (1847–1921), a founder of modern hydrodynamics and aerodynamics; Pyotr Nikolayevich Lebedev (1866–1912), who discovered the existence of the pressure of light; Nikolay Ivanovich Lobachevsky (1792–1856), pioneer in non-Euclidean geometry; Ivan Petrovich Pavlov (1849–1936); creator of the theory on the higher nervous systems of animals and man, who received the Nobel Prize in 1904 for his work on digestive glands; Ilya Ilyich Mechnikov (Elie Metchnikoff, 1845–1916), who received the Nobel Prize in 1908 for his Phagocyte theory; Kliment Arkadyevich Timiryazev (1843–1920), biologist and founder of the Russian school of plant physiology; and Aleksandr Stepanovich Popov (1859–1906), pioneer in radio transmission. Among later scientists and inventors are Ivan Vladimirovich Michurin (1855–1935), biologist and plant breeder; Konstantin Eduardovich Tsiolkovsky (1857–1935), scientist and the inventor in the field of the theory and technology of rocket engines, interplanetary travel and aerodynamics; Vladimir Petrovich Filatov (1875–1956), ophthalmologist; Ivan Pavlovich Bardin (1883–1960), metallurgist, Yevgeny Nikanorovich Pavlovsky (1884–1965), parasitologist; and Nikolay Ivanovich Vavilov (1887–1943), geneticist.

49DEPENDENCIES

The Russian Federation has no territories or dependencies.

50BIBLIOGRAPHY

Aslund, Anders (ed.). *Economic Transformation in Russia*. New York: St. Martin's, 1994.

Aslund, Anders, and Richard Layard (eds.). *Changing the Economic System in Russia*. New York: St. Martin's, 1993.

Buckley, Mary. *Redefining Russian Society and Polity*. Boulder, Colo.: Westview Press, 1993.

Dallin, Alexander (ed.). *Political Parties in Russia*. Berkeley: International and Area Studies, University of California at Berkeley, 1993.

Durgo, A.S. (ed.). *Russia Changes: The Events of August 1991 and the Russian Constitution*. Commack, N.Y.: Nova Science, 1992.

Khasbulatov, R.I. *The Struggle for Russia: Power and Change in the Democratic Revolution*. New York: Routledge, 1993.

McFaul, Michael. *The Troubled Birth of Russian Democracy: Parties, Personalities, and Programs*. Stanford, Calif.: Hoover Institution Press, Stanford University, 1993.

The Modern Encyclopedia of Russian, Soviet and Eurasian History. Gulf Breeze, Fla.: Academic International Press, 1994.

Steele, Jonathan. *Eternal Russia: Yeltsin, Gorbachev and the Mirage of Democracy*. Boston: Faber, 1994.

Yeltsin, Boris Nikolayevich. *The Struggle for Russia*. New York: Times Books, 1994.

SAN MARINO

The Most Serene Republic of San Marino

La Serenissima Repubblica di San Marino

CAPITAL: San Marino.

FLAG: The flag is divided horizontally into two equal bands, sky blue below and white above, with the national coat of arms superimposed in the center.

ANTHEM: *Onore a te, onore, o antica repubblica (Honor to You, O Ancient Republic).*

MONETARY UNIT: San Marino principally uses the Italian lira (L) as currency; Vatican City State currency is also honored. The country issues its own coins in standard Italian denominations in limited numbers as well. Coins of San Marino may circulate in both the republic and in Italy. L1 = $0.0006 (or $1 = L1,611.3).

WEIGHTS AND MEASURES: The metric system is the legal standard.

HOLIDAYS: New Year's Day, 1 January; Epiphany, 6 January; Anniversary of St. Agatha, second patron saint of the republic, and of the liberation of San Marino (1740), 5 February; Anniversary of the Arengo, 25 March; Investiture of the Captains-Regent, 1 April and 1 October; Labor Day, 1 May; Fall of Fascism, 28 July; Assumption and August Bank Holiday, 14–16 August; Anniversary of the Foundation of San Marino, 3 September; All Saint's Day, 1 November; Commemoration of the Dead, 2 November; Immaculate Conception, 8 December; Christmas, 24–26 December; New Year's Eve, 31 December. Movable religious holidays include Easter Monday and Ascension.

TIME: 1 PM = noon GMT.

1 LOCATION, SIZE, AND EXTENT

San Marino is the third-smallest country in Europe, with an area of 60 sq km (232 sq mi), extending 13.1 km (8.1 mi) NE-SW and 9.1 km (5.7 mi) SE-NW. Comparatively, the area occupied by San Marino is about 0.3 times the size of Washington, D.C. It is a landlocked state completely surrounded by Italy, with a total boundary length of 39 km (24 mi).

2 TOPOGRAPHY

The town of San Marino is on the slopes and at the summit of Mt. Titano (749 m/2,457 ft), and much of the republic is coextensive with the mountain, which has three pinnacles. Each of the peaks is crowned by old fortifications, that on the north by a castle and the other two by towers. Level areas around the base of Mt. Titano provide land for agricultural use.

3 CLIMATE

The climate is that of northeastern Italy: rather mild in winter, but with temperatures frequently below freezing, and warm and pleasant in the summer, reaching a maximum of 26°C (79°F). Annual rainfall averages about 89 cm (35 in).

4 FLORA AND FAUNA

The republic has the same flora and fauna as northeastern Italy.

5 ENVIRONMENT

Information on the environment is not available.

6 POPULATION

The resident population was 23,719 at the 1992 census. Density was 388 persons per sq km (1,004 per sq mi). At the end of 1990, 4,185 people lived in the capital, also called San Marino. In 1992, the crude birthrate was 9.9 per 1,000 population; the crude death rate 7.2; and the net natural increase 2.7. The population increased 0.55% annually from 1985 to 1990.

7 MIGRATION

Immigrants come chiefly from Italy; emigration is mainly to Italy, the US, France, and Belgium. Foreigners who have been resident in San Marino for 30 years can become naturalized citizens.

8 ETHNIC GROUPS

The native population is predominantly of Italian origin.

9 LANGUAGES

Italian is the official language.

10 RELIGIONS

With few exceptions, the population is Roman Catholic, and Roman Catholicism is the official religion.

11 TRANSPORTATION

Streets and roads within the republic total about 220 km (140 mi), and there is regular bus service between San Marino and Rimini. Motor vehicle registrations in 1991 included 20,508 passenger cars and 3,357 commercial vehicles. An electric railroad, 32 km (20 mi) long, between Rimini and San Marino was inaugurated in 1932; damaged as a result of a British air raid on 26 June 1944, it has been out of service since that time. The government operates a cable-car service from the city of San Marino to Borgo Maggiore. There is helicopter service between San Marino and Rimini in summer.

12 HISTORY

San Marino, the oldest republic in the world, is the sole survivor of the independent states that existed in Italy at various times from the downfall of the Western Roman Empire to the proclamation of the Kingdom of Italy in 1861. (The Vatican City State, which is also an independent enclave in Italy, was not constituted in its present form until the 20th century.)

According to tradition, the republic was founded in the 4th century AD by Marinus, a Christian stonecutter who fled from Dalmatia to avoid religious persecution; later canonized, St. Marinus is known in Italian as San Marino. If founded at the time asserted by tradition, San Marino is the oldest existing national state in Europe. There was a monastery in San Marino in existence at least as early as 885.

Because of the poverty of the region and the difficult terrain, San Marino was rarely disturbed by outside powers, and it generally avoided the factional fights of the Middle Ages. For a time, it joined the Ghibellines and was therefore interdicted by Pope Innocent IV in 1247–49. It was protected by the Montefeltro family, later dukes of Urbino, and in 1441, with Urbino, it defeated Sigismondo Malatesta and extended the size of its territory. It was briefly held by Cesare Borgia in 1503, but in 1549 its sovereignty was confirmed by Pope Paul III. In 1739, however, a military force under a papal legate, Cardinal Giulio Alberoni, occupied San Marino and unsuccessfully attempted to get the Sanmarinese to acknowledge his sovereignty over them. In the following year, Pope Clement II terminated the occupation and signed a treaty of friendship with the tiny republic. Napoleon allowed San Marino to retain its liberty; the Sanmarinese are said to have declined his offer to increase their territory on the grounds that smallness and poverty alone had kept them from falling prey to larger states.

In 1849, Giuseppe Garibaldi, the liberator of Italy, took refuge from the Austrians in San Marino; he departed voluntarily shortly before the Austrians were to invade the republic to capture him. San Marino and Italy entered into a treaty of friendship and customs union in 1862. This treaty was renewed in March 1939 and amended in September 1971.

During the period of Mussolini's rule in Italy, San Marino adopted a Fascist type of government. Despite its claim to neutrality in World War II, it was bombed by Allied planes on 26 June 1944. The raid caused heavy damage, especially to the railway line, and killed a number of persons. San Marino's resources were sorely taxed to provide food and shelter for the over 100,000 refugees who obtained sanctuary during the war.

The elections of 1945 put a coalition of Communists and left-wing Socialists in control of the country. In 1957, some defections from the ruling coalition were followed by a bloodless revolution, aided by Italy, against the government. The leftists surrendered, and some were imprisoned. The rightists, chiefly Christian Democrats, won the election of 1959 and remained in power until 1973, chiefly in coalition with the Social Democrats. In March 1973, after splitting with the Social Democrats, the Christian Democrats formed an unstable coalition with the Socialists. After new elections in May 1978, the Communists, the Socialists, and the Socialist Unity Party, who together commanded a one-seat majority in the legislature, formed a governing coalition; San Marino thus became the only West European country with a Communist-led government. This coalition governed until 1986, when it was replaced by a Communist–Christian Democratic coalition; this was the first coalition government formed by these two parties in San Marino's history.

13GOVERNMENT

Legislative power is exercised by the Grand and General Council (Consiglio Grande e Generale) of 60 members, regularly elected every five years by universal suffrage at age 18. The Council elects from among its members a State Congress (Congresso di Stato) of 10 members (3 secretaries of state and 7 ministers of state), which makes most administrative decisions and carries

them out. In 1960, universal manhood suffrage was established in place of the previous system, whereby only heads of families voted. Women also received the franchise effective in 1960 and were first permitted to run for office in 1974. Nearly 100% of eligible voters participate in elections.

Two members of the Council are named every six months to head the executive branch of the government; one represents the town of San Marino and the other the countryside. The terms of these officials, called captains-regent (capitani reggenti), begin on 1 April and 1 October. The captains-regent, who must be native-born citizens, are eligible for reelection after three years.

14POLITICAL PARTIES

The political parties in San Marino have close ties with the corresponding parties in Italy: the Christian Democrats (Partito Democratico Cristiano Sammarinese—DCS), Communists (Partito Communista Sammarinese—PCS), Socialists (Partito Socialista Sammarinese—PSS), and Social Democrats (Partito Socialista Democratico Independente Sammarinese—PSDIS).

15LOCAL GOVERNMENT

San Marino consists of nine administrative divisions or castles (castelli): Acquaviva, Borgo Maggiore, Chiesanuova, Domagnano, Faetano, Fiorentino, Montegiardino, San Marino, and Serravalle. Each castle has an auxiliary council, elected for a four-year term. It is headed by an official called the captain of the castle, who is elected every two years.

16JUDICIAL SYSTEM

There is a civil court, a criminal court, and a superior court, but most criminal cases are tried before Italian magistrates because, with the exception of minor civil suits, the judges in Sanmarinese cases are not allowed to be citizens of San Marino. Appeals go, in the first instance, to an Italian Judge residing in Italy. The highest appellate court is the Council of Twelve, chosen for six-year terms from members of the Grand and General Council. The rights of the accused, including the rights to a public trial, legal counsel and other procedural safeguards, are guaranteed by law and observed in practice.

17ARMED FORCES

The San Marino militia nominally consists of all able-bodied citizens between the ages of 16 and 55, but the armed forces actually maintained are principally for purposes of ceremonial display; these include the noble guard used in various functions.

18INTERNATIONAL COOPERATION

Although not a UN member, San Marino does belong to some UN specialized agencies, including ILO, ITU, UNESCO, UPU, and WHO, and it maintains a permanent observer mission at the UN in Geneva. San Marino sends its own delegation to the 35-nation Conference on Security and Cooperation in Europe and is a member of the World Tourism Organization and the European Conference of Postal and Telecommunications Administrations.

19ECONOMY

Farming was formerly the principal occupation, but it has been replaced in importance by light manufacturing. However, the main sources of income are tourism and remittances from Sanmarinese living abroad. Some government revenue comes from the sale of postage stamps and coins and from Italy's subsidy to San Marino (about L9,000 million annually) in exchange for which San Marino does not impose customs duties.

20INCOME

In 1992, San Marino's GDP was $465 million at current prices, or $20,000 per capita. In 1992 the average inflation rate was 5%.

21LABOR

Most of the inhabitants are farmers or stock raisers. The labor force in 1991 totaled about 13,322 persons, most of whom worked in manufacturing plants or were engaged in service occupations, especially during the summer. There is little unemployment (493 in 1991). The Democratic Federation of Sanmarinese Workers, affiliated with the International Confederation of Free Trade Unions, had about 2,500 members in 1992; the General Federation of Labor had 2,400. About 50% of the work force of 12,000 (including 2,000 Italians) is unionized. In 1991, there were 6 strikes involving 119 workers.

22AGRICULTURE

About 17% of the land is arable. Annual crop production includes wheat and grapes, as well as other grains, vegetables, fruits, and fodder.

23ANIMAL HUSBANDRY

Livestock raising uses some 1,400 hectares (3,500 acres), or about 23% of the total area. Cattle, hogs, sheep, and horses are raised.

24FISHING

There is no fishing.

25FORESTRY

Small quantities of wood are cut for local use.

26MINING

San Marino has no commercial mineral resources.

27ENERGY AND POWER

Electric power is imported from Italy.

28INDUSTRY

Manufacturing is limited to light industries such as textiles, bricks and tiles, leather goods, clothing, and metalwork. Cotton textiles are woven at Serravalle; bricks and tiles are made in La Dogana, which also has a dyeing plant; and cement factories and a tannery are located in Acquaviva, as well as a paper-making plant. Synthetic rubber is also produced. The pottery of Borgo Maggiore is well known. Gold and silver souvenirs are made for the tourist trade. Other products are Moscato wine, olive oil, and baked goods.

29SCIENCE AND TECHNOLOGY

Sanmarinese students generally pursue their scientific and technical training abroad, since science and technology resources are domestically limited.

30DOMESTIC TRADE

There are small general stores in the capital and the smaller towns. Billboards and newspapers are the main advertising medium. A weekly market is held at Borgo Maggiore, and there is an annual fair for the sale of cattle and sheep.

31FOREIGN TRADE

Records of foreign trade are not published, but it is known that imports far exceed exports. Principal exports are wine, textiles, furniture, quarried stone, ceramics, and handicrafts. The chief imports are raw materials and a wide variety of consumer goods. San Marino has a customs union with Italy.

32BALANCE OF PAYMENTS

Since imports and exports are not subject to customs duties, no record is kept of foreign payments transactions. Receipts from

LOCATION: 12°27′E and 43°56′N.

tourism, remittances from Sanmarinese working abroad, and sales of postage stamps to foreign collectors are principal sources of foreign exchange.

33BANKING AND SECURITIES

The principal bank, the Cassa di Risparmio, was founded in 1882. Other banks include the Banca Agricola and the Cassa Rurale. There are no securities transactions in San Marino.

34INSURANCE

Several major Italian insurance companies have agencies in San Marino.

35PUBLIC FINANCE

The government derives its revenues mainly from the worldwide sale of postage stamps, direct and indirect taxes, and yearly subsidies by the Italian government. State budgets have increased sharply in recent years. In 1987, the budget totaled L409,424 million, compared with L199,021 million in 1983.

36TAXATION

Legislation introducing San Marino's first income tax was passed by the Grand and General Council in October 1984. A general income tax is applied progressively to individuals (12–50% in 1992) and a flat rate of 24% to corporations. Also levied are a stamp duty, registration tax, mortgage tax, and succession duty.

37 CUSTOMS AND DUTIES

San Marino's trade policy is governed by its customs union with Italy. There is a one-phase duty system on imported goods, which closely follows the rates of the Italian VAT system. In 1992, there was a 14% tax on imports.

38 FOREIGN INVESTMENT

Information on foreign investment is not available.

39 ECONOMIC DEVELOPMENT

In addition to promoting tourism in San Marino, the government has encouraged the establishment of small-scale industries and service-oriented enterprises (40–60 employees) by offering tax exemptions for 5–10 years.

40 SOCIAL DEVELOPMENT

Since 1956, the government has maintained a comprehensive social insurance program, including disability, family supplement payments, and old-age pensions. In 1982, Sanmarinese women who married foreign citizens were given the right to keep their citizenships. Divorce was first allowed in 1986.

41 HEALTH

Public health institutions include the State Hospital (opened in 1975), a dispensary for the poor, and a laboratory of hygiene and prophylaxis. All citizens receive free, comprehensive medical care.

San Marino's population for 1993 was 23,000. The infant mortality rate for 1992 was estimated at 10 per 1,000 live births and estimated average life expectancy was 77 years. The estimated crude death rate was 10 per 1,000 people in 1992, and the estimated maternal mortality was 5 per 100,000 live births in 1991.

42 HOUSING

In 1986, San Marino had 7,926 dwellings, virtually all with electricity and piped-in water. Most new construction is financed privately.

43 EDUCATION

Primary education is compulsory for all children between the ages of 6 and 14; the adult literacy rate is about 98%. The program of instruction is patterned after the Italian curriculum, and San Marinese school certificates are recognized by Italy. Children go through five years of primary education followed by three years of secondary education at the first stage and a further five years of higher secondary and preuniversity education. In 1991, there were 15 preprimary schools, with 750 students, and 14 elementary schools, with 1,200 students and 218 teachers; middle and upper-secondary schools enrolled 1,158 pupils during the same year. Of these, 137 were in vocational schools. Sanmarinese students are able to pursue higher education at Italian universities. There are also vocational training schools and a technical institute.

44 LIBRARIES AND MUSEUMS

In the capital city is the Palazzo del Valloni, containing a library of some 60,000 books, documents, and pamphlets. There is also a museum in Borgia Maggiore devoted to objects connected with Garibaldi's stay in the republic. The Palazzo del Valloni also houses the state archives, as well as a collection of rare coins and medals. The Palazzo del Governo (built in 1894) and most other large buildings in the capital are of comparatively recent date, but many monuments have been rebuilt in an earlier style. There are nine museums; one of them is devoted to the postage stamps of San Marino and other countries. The National Gallery of Modern Art is also in San Marino. The 14th-century church of San Francesco has paintings by several minor masters. The three old fortresses of Guaita, Fratta, and Montale are situated on the three pinnacles of Mt. Titano.

45 MEDIA

Telegraphic communication with Italy has been in service since 1879, and connections with the Italian telephone system were established in 1904. There are nine post offices, one for each castle. There are no local radio or television stations, but there were 14,000 radios and 8,000 television sets in 1991. An automatic telephone system integrated into Italy's system served 11,707 telephones in 1986.

Daily newspapers are not published in San Marino, but political papers are issued by the political parties: the Christian Democratic *San Marino,* the Social Democratic *Riscossa Socialista,* the Socialist *Il Nuovo Titano,* and the Communist *La Scintilla.* At regular intervals the government issues the *Bolletino Uffiziale* for the publication of statutes and official and legal notices.

46 ORGANIZATIONS

Information on organizations is not available.

47 TOURISM, TRAVEL, AND RECREATION

The government has promoted tourism so successfully that in summer during the 1980s the number of San Marino residents was often exceeded by the number of visitors (20,000–30,000 daily). There were 22 hotels and 35 restaurants in 1986. Growth in the tourist industry has increased the demand for San Marino's stamps and coins, gold and silver souvenirs, handicrafts, and pottery. In 1987, an estimated 3 million people visited San Marino.

Principal attractions are the three medieval fortresses at the summit of Mt. Titano and the magnificent view from there of Rimini and the Adriatic Sea. The State Tourism, Sports, and Entertainment Board maintains various recreational facilities. Visitors arriving from Italy do not need visas or inoculations

48 FAMOUS SANMARINESE

Giambattista Belluzzi, a 16th-century military engineer in the service of Florence, was born in San Marino. Well-known Italians who were associated with San Marino include Cardinal Giulio Alberoni (1664–1752), who attempted to subject the republic to papal domination in 1739–40; Count Alessandro Cagliostro (Giuseppe Balsamo, 1743–95), a Sicilian adventurer, imposter, and alchemist; Bartolommeo Borghesi (1781–1860), an antiquarian, epigrapher, and numismatist, who resided in San Marino from 1821 to 1860; and Giuseppe Garibaldi (1807–82), the great Italian patriot, who obtained refuge from the Austrians in San Marino in 1849.

49 DEPENDENCIES

San Marino has no territories or colonies.

50 BIBLIOGRAPHY

Arzilli, M. *La Repubblica di San Marino: Panorama Storicoturistico.* San Marino, 1950.

Bent, James Theodore. *A Freak of Freedom; or, The Republic of San Marino.* Port Washington, N.Y.: Kennikat Press, 1970 (orig. 1879).

Brugnoli, M. V., and E. Zocca. *Guida di San Marino.* Rome: Libreria dello stato, 1953.

Crocioni, Giovanni. *Bibliografia Delle Tradizioni Populari di San Marino.* San Marino: Artigrafiche della Balda, 1947.

Delfico, Melchiorre. *Memorie Storiche della Repubblica di San Marino.* Naples, 1865.

Fattori, Marino. *Ricordi Storici della Repubblica di San Marino.* Florence: Le Monnier, 1956.

Johnson, Virginia Wales. *Two Quaint Republics: Andorra and San Marino.* Boston: Estes, 1913.

Kochwasser, Friedrich. *San Marino: die Älteste und Kleinste Republik der Welt.* Herrenalb: Horst Erdmann, 1961.

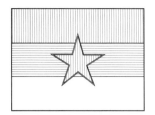

SERBIA AND MONTENEGRO

PROCESS

The dissolution of the former Yugoslavia into five separate and independent states after 74 years of common history poses several questions for historians. The Yugoslavia that was formed in 1918 as the Kingdom of Serbs, Croats, and Slovenes was a composite of distinct nations, each with a separate 1,400 year history. Histories of Yugoslavia have been written generally by using a period description of each component part in its relationship to the whole of Yugoslavia, considering the latter as a logical and final goal of their historical development. With Yugoslavia's dissolution in 1991, each of the five independent states is writing its own separate history with the logical goal of justifying its separate identity with its own history in order to solidify its independence. Thus, the 74-year period of common history is no longer viewed as an achieved goal but only as a detour towards independence.

YUGOSLAVIA OVERVIEW

All of the republics of the former Federal Socialist Republic of Yugoslavia shared a common history between 1945 and 1991, the year of Yugoslavia's dissolution. The World War II partisan resistance movement, controlled by the Communist party of Yugoslavia led by Marshal Tito, won a civil war waged against nationalist groups under foreign occupation, having secured the assistance, and recognition, from both the Western Powers and the Soviet Union. Aside from the reconstruction of the country and its economy, the first task facing the new regime was the establishment of its legitimacy and, at the same time, the liquidation of its internal enemies, both actual and potential. The first task was accomplished by the 11 November 1945 election of a constitutional assembly on the basis of a single candidate list assembled by the People's Front. The list won 90% of the votes cast. The three members of the coalition government representing the Royal Yugoslav Government in exile had resigned earlier in frustration and did not run in the elections. The Constitutional Assembly voted against the continuation of the Monarchy and, on 31 January 1946, the new constitution of the Federal People's Republic of Yugoslavia was promulgated. Along with the state-building activity the Yugoslav Communist regime carried out ruthless executions, massacres, and imprisonment to liquidate any potential opposition.

The Tito-Stalin conflict that erupted in 1948 was not a real surprise considering the differences the two had had about Tito's refusal to cooperate with other resistance movements against the occupiers in World War II. The expulsion of Tito from the Cominform group separated Yugoslavia from the Soviet Bloc, caused internal purges of pro-Cominform Yugoslav Communist Party members, and also nudged Yugoslavia into a failed attempt to collectivize its agriculture. Yugoslavia then developed its own brand of Marxist economy based on workers' councils and self-management of enterprises and institutions, while becoming the leader of the non-aligned group of nations in the international arena. Being more open to Western influences, the Yugoslav Communist regime relaxed somewhat its central controls. This allowed for the development of more liberal wings of communist parties, particularly in Croatia and Slovenia, that agitated for the devolution of power from the federal to the individual republics' level in order to better cope with the increasing differentiation

between the more productive republics (Slovenia and Croatia) and the less developed areas. Also, nationalism resurfaced with tensions particularly strong between Serbs and Croats in the Croatian Republic leading to the repression by Tito of the Croatian and Slovenian Springs in 1970–71.

The 1974 constitution shifted much of the decision-making power from the federal to the republic level, turning the Yugoslav Communist Party into a kind of federation (League) of the republican parties, thus decentralizing further the political process. The autonomous provinces of Vojvodina and Kosovo were also given a quasi-sovereign status as the republics, and a collective Presidency was designed to take over power upon Tito's death. When Tito died in 1980 the delegates of the six republics and the two autonomous provinces represented the interests of each republic or province in a process of shifting coalitions centered on specific issues. The investment of development funds to assist the less developed areas became the burning issue around which nationalist emotions and tensions grew ever stronger along with the forceful repression of the Albanian majority in Kosovo.

The economic crisis in the 1980s—marked by runaway inflation, inability to pay the debt service on over 20 billion dollars in international loans accumulated during Tito's rule, and low productivity in the less developed areas—became too much of a burden for Slovenia and Croatia, leading them to stand up to the centralizing power of the Serbian (and other) Republics. The demand for a reorganization of the Yugoslav Federation into a confederation of sovereign states was strongly opposed by the coalition of Serbia, Montenegro and the Yugoslav Army. The pressure towards political pluralism and a market economy also grew stronger, leading to the formation of non-Communist political parties that were able by 1990 to win majorities in multiparty elections in Slovenia first, then in Croatia. The inability of the opposing groups of centralist and confederalist republics to find any common ground led to the dissolution of Yugoslavia through the disassociation of Slovenia, Croatia, Bosnia and Herzegovina, and Macedonia, leaving only Serbia and Montenegro together in a new Federal Republic of Yugoslavia.

SERBIA

Origins and Middles Ages

The Serbs, one of the large family of Slavic nations, first began settling in the Balkans around the 7th century in the areas now known as Bosnia, Kosovo, and Montenegro, straddling the line that since AD 395 had divided the Eastern and Western halves of the Roman Empire. The line went from the Sava River south along the Drina River and across Montenegro to the Adriatic Sea by the Skadar (Scutari) lake. Other Slavic tribes had settled the Balkans since the late 4th century and had slowly taken over most areas by destroying old Roman settlements, except for strongholds along the Adriatic Coast.

The origins of the Serbs (and Croats) have kept historians very busy in controversial directions, but there seems to be a prevailing consensus on their Sarmatian (Iranian) origin. Having assimilated into the Slavic tribes, the Serbs migrated with them west into central Europe (White Serbia) in the Saxony area and from there moved to the Balkans around AD 626 upon an invitation by the

Byzantine Emperor Heraclius to assist him in repelling the Avar and Persian attack on Constantinople. Having settled in the Balkan area the Serbs organized several principalities of their own, made up of a number of clans headed by Zpans. Both the Byzantine Empire and the Bulgars tried to conquer them, but the very fact of the absence of a centralized political unit worked against the permanence of any agreements. One of the early Serbian rulers, Vlastimir, was able to unify a larger area and thus oppose the Bulgar invasion of Serbia between AD 839 and 850. Having defeated the Bulgars, Vlastimir increased his lands by marrying his daughter to the neighboring Zupan of Trebinje mentioned in Emperor Constantine Porphyrogenitus' reports. Between the 9th and 12th centuries, several Serbian principalities evolved, among them Raška in the mountainous north of Montenegro and southern Serbia, and Zeta (south Montenegro along the Adriatic coast) whose ruler Mihajlo (Michael) was anointed King by Pope Gregory VII in 1077.

In the late 10th century the Bulgarian Khan Samuilo extended his control over Bosnia, Raška, and Zeta, north to the Sava River, and south over Macedonia. There, a hundred years earlier, in AD 863, the two Greek scholars Constantine (Cyril) and Methodius had learned the area's Slavic language and had translated Holy Scriptures into Slavic using an original alphabet of their invention for a mission to Moravia to convert the Moravians to Christianity through the use of their own Slavic tongue. Their disciples came to Bulgaria where Tsar Boris supported their work of conversion of the Bulgars to Christianity already initiated by Greek missionaries. Thus the liturgy in the old church Slavic language was introduced in Bulgaria, Macedonia and, from there to Serbia and also old Russia, in competition with the usual liturgy in Greek.

Raška became the area from where the medieval Serbian empire developed. Stephen Nemanja, grand Zupan of Raška, fought against the Byzantines in AD 1169, added Zeta to his domain in 1186. He built several Serbian monasteries, including Hilandar on Mount Athos. His son, Rastko, became a monk (Sava) and the first Serbian Archbishop of the new Serbian Autocephalous Church in 1219. The second son, Stephen, received his crown from Pope Innocent IV in 1202 and was successful in further developing his lands and political alliances that, following his death in 1227, allowed Serbia to resist the pressure from Bulgaria and, internally, keep control over subordinate Zupans. Archbishop Sava (later Saint Sava) preferred the Byzantine Church and utilized the Orthodox religion in his nation-building effort. He began by establishing numerous Serbian-Orthodox monasteries around Serbia. He also succeeded in turning Zeta from Catholicism to Serbian Orthodoxy.

The medieval Serbian empire, under Stephen Dušan the Mighty (1331–55) extended from the Aegean Sea to the Danube (Belgrade), along the Adriatic and Ionian coasts from the Neretva River to the Gulf of Corinth and controlled, aside from the central Serbian lands, Macedonia, Thessaly, the Epirus, and Albania. The Serbian Church obtained its own Patriarchate, with its center in Peć. Serbia became an exporting land with abundant crops from the Kosovo region and minerals from numerous mines. Dušan, who was crowned Tsar of "The Serbs and Greeks" in 1346, gave Serbia its first code of laws based on a combination of Serbian customs and Byzantine law. His attempt to conquer the throne of Byzantium failed, however, when the Byzantines called on the advancing Ottoman Turks for help in 1345. Even though Dušan withstood the attacks from the Turks twice (in 1345 and 1349), the gates to Europe had been opened and the Ottoman Turks had initiated their campaign to subjugate the Balkans.

Under Ottoman Rule
Dušan's heirs could not hold his empire together against the Turks and the Nemanja dynasty ended with the death of his son

Stephen Uroš in 1371, the same year his brothers Vukašin and Ivan Ugleš were killed at the battle of Marica. The defeat of the Serbs at Kosovo Polje in 1389 in an epochal battle that took the lives of both Sultan Murad I and Serbian Prince Lazar left Serbia open to further Turkish conquest. Following a series of wars betweeen the Turks and the Serbs, Hungarians, Albanians, Venetians, and other Europeans, the Turks succeeded in overtaking Constantinople in 1453 and all of Serbia by 1459. For the next three-and-a-half centuries, Serbs and others had to learn how to survive under Ottoman rule. The Turks did not make any distinctions based on ethnicity, but only on religion. Turkish Muslims were the dominant class while Christians and Jews were subordinated to the Muslim Sultan, although they enjoyed a system of autonomy within their own communities. The local leaders were accountable for both tax collection and law and order. While maintaining their religious and cultural autonomy, the non-Turks developed most of the non-military administrative professions and carried on most of the economic activities, including internal trade and trade with other countries of the Christian world. There was no regular conscription of non-Turks into the Sultan's armies, but non-Turks had to pay a tax for defense support. They were also subjected to the practice of forceful wrenching of Christian boys between the age of eight and twenty from their families to be converted to Islam and trained as "Janissaries" or government administrators. While many of these former Christians became persecutors, others rose into the higher administrative echelons and some even became grand viziers (advisers) to sultans.

Urban dwellers under Ottoman rule, involved in crafts, trade, and the professions, fared much better then the Christian peasantry, who were forced into serfdom. Heavy regular taxes were levied on the peasants; additional taxation was imposed to support the Sultans' wars and ceremonial needs, with corruption making the load so unbearable as to provoke peasant rebellions not unlike the ones in the Christian world across the Ottoman borders. Two distinct cultures lived side by side—Turkish Muslim in cities and towns as administrative centers and Christian Orthodox in the countryside of Serbia. The numerous Serbian monasteries built around the country since the Nemanja dynasty became the supportive network for Serbian survival. This, despite the fact that the Serbian Church was subjected after 1459 to the Greek patriarchate that appointed non-Serbian—mostly Greek—Bishops. One hundred years later, however, with the assistance of Grand Vizier Mehmet Sokollu/Sokolović, a former "Janissary" from Bosnia, a Serbian patriarchate emerged again and was headed by a sequence of four members of the Sokolović family. Because of the extent of the Ottoman lands, the Serbian patriarchate covered a large area from north of Ohrid to the Hungarian lands north of the Danube and west through Bosnia.

The Serbian Diaspora
Over the two centuries since 1459 many Serbs left their lands and settled north of the Sava and Danube Rivers where Hungary had promised their leader ("Vojvoda") an autonomous arrangement in exchange for military service against the Turks. The region is called "Vojvodina" by Serbs, even though the Hungarians had reneged on their promise of autonomy. Priests and bishops also came with their people, and Serbian churches and monasteries were built, such as the ones around Fruška Gora, becoming centers of Serbian national culture. The Serbian Diaspora was continuously reinforced by a series of mass migrations from the areas of Kosovo and central Serbia north across the Sava and Danube Rivers and west into Bosnia and contiguous Croatian lands before and following the Turkish occupation of Bosnia (1463) and Herzegovina (1483). Fleeing the Turkish conquest many Serbs and Croats settled in Venetian occupied Dalmatia and continued fighting against the Turks from fortified areas. Others

were engaged by the Austrians as lifetime soldiers in the military frontier organized in Croatia beginning in 1578, in exchange for privileges such as free status, land, and their own Orthodox church. Thus, they were able to create their own Serbian institutions and never assimilated to their otherwise Croatian environment. The wars between Austria and the Turks in the late 17th through the mid-18th centuries had caused both the mass migrations from Serbia led by Serb Patriarchs and the hardening of Ottoman treatment of their Christian subjects.

Following the defeat of the Turks in 1683 at the gates of Vienna by a coalition led by Poland's King Jan Sobieski, the Christian armies pursued the Turks all the way to Macedonia and had a good chance to drive the Turks off the European continent. The Serbian people had joined in the fight against the Turks, hoping for final liberation. However, when Louis XIV of France attacked Germany the Austrian armies, already decimated by plagues, had to retreat from Macedonia and Serbia. Before doing so, they first set fire to Skopje, a city compared in size to Prague by the Austrian commander. The fear of retribution from the Turks caused the Serbian leaders, including Patriarch Arsenije III Crnojević, to join the Austrian retreat into Hungary with over 30,000 families in 1689, leaving a serious void of resistance among the Serbian population.

Turk reprisals were violent and took two directions with serious long-term consequences. The Serbian lands left depopulated—particularly the Kosovo region—were settled by Albanians, whom the Turks favored because they were mostly Muslims. Conversion to Islam increased considerably. A second large scale migration took place 50 years later, after the 1736–39 Austrian defeat by the Turks. This migration was again led by a Serbian Patriarch, Arsenije IV šakabent. In addition, numerous Serbian families migrated into northern Serbia from the Kosovo and Sandžak area that were again populated by Muslim Albanians. All these movements of population resulted in the loss of the Kosovo area—the cradle of Serbian nationhood—to Albanians. This situation resulted in the Serbs being unable to cannot give up control over an area to which their collective national consciousness feels a tremendously deep emotional attachment, even though they represent only about ten percent of its population.

Serbian Revolts and Independence

Meanwhile, two areas of active Serbian national activity developed, one under the Turks in the northern Šumadija region and the other in Hungary with the growth of the Serbian diaspora in direct contact with central European cultural life. Šumadija, a forested region, became the refuge for numerous Serbs from the southern areas and the center for many hajduks (Serbian "Robin Hoods" also active in Bosnia) that raided Turkish establishments. These hajduks were legendary heroes among the Serbian people. When Austria joined in the Crimean War against Turkey, it seized the Belgrade area from the Turks in 1788. An insurrection joined by hajduk bands followed in Šumadija, while at the same time Austria formed a corps of Serbian volunteers to fight the Turks. One of the volunteers was Djordje Petrović, called, who otherwise made a living in Šumadija as a pig dealer. He continued the fight against the Turks as a hajduk after Austria returned the Belgrade area to the Turks in 1791.

Later Karadjordje became the leader of the first Serbian general revolt against the Turks in 1804, which started as a peasant uprising in response to the Janissaries' oppression and murder of a group of prominent Serbs. In 1805, the Serbs defeated the Turks and gained control of the Belgrade region. The Sultan agreed to Serbian terms for political autonomy in September 1806. A partially elected government structure was established, and by 1811 the Serbian assembly confirmed Karadjordje as supreme leader with hereditary rights. The drive of Serbia for complete independence was thwarted, however, by the Great Powers agreement to leave Serbia under Ottoman rule. The Turks reoccupied Serbia by 1813 and revenged themselves with a terrible reign of terror. Turk retaliation included pillaging, looting, enslaving women and children, while killing all males over age 15 and torturing any captured leader that was not able to escape into the Vojvodina region.

A second uprising by the Serbs occurred in 1815 and spread all over Šumadija. It was led by Miloš Obrenović, who had participated in the first revolt, survived the Turkish reprisals and, after 1913, served in the administration along with other Serbs following an amnesty proclaimed by the Turks. Successful in repelling Turkish forces, Miloš gained the support of the Russian tsar, and after some six months he negotiated an agreement giving Serbia a *de facto* autonomy in its internal administration. In 1817, on Miloš's orders, Karadjordje was murdered upon his return to Ser-

bia to support the Greeks on a general uprising of Christians against the Turks. The 1825 Greek war of independence generated more concessions to the Serbs, and by 1830, Serbia had gained its autonomy and Miloš was recognized as an hereditary Prince of Serbia. Serbia was internationally accepted as a virtually independent state, though still paying an annual tribute to the Sultan.

The Serbian communities in Vojvodina and elsewhere in Hungary had, in the meanwhile, prospered. Their elite were educated in Austrian and Hungarian schools and worked closely with cultural leaders among the Slovenes and Croats of Austria. This brought about the "Illyrian" movement of South Slavic cooperation, including the 1850 Vienna agreement on a joint Serbo-Croatian language.

Miloš Obrenović, like Karadjordje, was an authoritarian ruler who had to be forced to promulgate a constitution for Serbia establishing a council of chiefs sharing power with him. This provision was opposed by both Austria and the Sultan, and Miloš set it aside. But the Sultan, under pressure from Russia, promulgated a constitution for Serbia in 1838 with Russia as a guarantor. A council was appointed to pass laws and taxes, a council of ministers was created, and provisions were formulated for an eventual assembly. Miloš was forced to abdicate in 1839 and went into exile, succeeded by 16-year-old son Mihajlo. A coup d'etat in 1842 overthrew the Obrenović dynasty, and an assembly in Belgrade appointed Alexander Karadjordjević the new ruler until he himself was deposed in 1858 by an assembly called by Ilija Garašanin, his own prime minister. Ilija Garašanin is credited with advocating a "Greater Serbia" in 1844, based on Tsar Dušan's empire. In 1848, a Serbian assembly demanded the incorporation of Vojvodina into Serbia, taking advantage of the Kossuth revolt against Austria. The "Greater Serbia" concept became an overall goal of Serbian foreign policy until realized with the creation of Yugoslavia in 1918.

The 1858 Assembly restored Miloš Obrenović to power but he died in 1860 and was succeeded, again, by his son Mihajlo, then 35 years old. He built up the Serbian army in anticipation of a war of liberation against the Turks as a first step towards the goal of a Greater Serbia. His private life, however, scandalized the people and he was murdered in 1868. In spite of his personal problems, Mihajlo had developed a highly centralized state organization, a functioning parliament, two political parties, a judicial system, and urban educational institutions. Mihajlo's successor, his cousin Milan, acquired more territory and total independence, proclaimed in 1882, from the Ottomans. However, it was during his watch that Bulgaria almost succeeded in seizing Macedonia, and Austria conquered Bosnia and Herzegovina, both badly wanted by Serbia. But Milan's army was no match for the Turks when he attacked them in 1876 to support the Bosnian revolt. They were saved by Russia's 1877 attack on Turkey. Milan's 1885 attack on Bulgaria in response to their repeated threat to Macedonia was a failure. Milan became dependent on Austria when that country saved Serbia from an invasion by Bulgaria.

All these failures alienated Milan Obrenović from his people and he abdicated in 1889 in favor of his son Alexander. Alexander continued to rely on Austria, abolished the constitution, led a corrupt and scandalous life, and was murdered along with his wife, the premier, and other court members by a group of young officers in June 1903, thus ending the Obrenović dynasty. The assembly then called on Peter, Alexander Karadjordjević's son, to take the crown, despite the fact that there were indications that he had been aware of the plot to murder his father. Under Peter Karadjordjević, Serbia regained its constitution, and a period of stable political and economic development ensued, interrupted by the 1908 Austrian annexation of Bosnia and Herzegovina, the 1912 and 1913 Balkan wars, and World War I.

The Balkan Wars

Austria's annexation of Bosnia and Herzegovina was carried out in 1908 at the time of the Young Turks crisis in Turkey and with the full backing of Germany. This fact deterred Russia from giving any encouragement to the infuriated Serbs, who saw Austria's move as a serious blow to their goal of a Greater Serbia with an outlet to the Adriatic Sea through Bosnia and Herzegovina. They therefore turned in the direction of the only other possible access routes by the sea—Macedonia, with its port city of Salonika and the northern coast of Albania. With the backing of Russia, the Balkan countries (Serbia, Bulgaria, Montenegro, and Greece) formed the Balkan League, agreed provisionally among themselves on territorial divisions, and attacked Turkey in 1912. The League quickly defeated the Turks and drove them to the gates of Constantinople, while Serbian units reached the Adriatic coast of Albania. Austria and Italy opposed a Serbian outlet to the Adriatic in Albania, supporting instead an independent Albanian state and assisted its establishment in 1913. Serbia and Greece divided Macedonia between themselves, while Bulgaria gained Thrace and access to the Aegean Sea. Serbia, deprived of access to the sea, requested it from Bulgaria. Bulgaria responded to the request by attacking Serbia and Greece, hoping to obtain all of Macedonia. The second Balkan war ended with the defeat of Bulgaria by Serbia, Montenegro, Greece, Romania, and Turkey itself, which gained back Adrianople and Thrace. Romania gained northern Dobrudja, Serbia kept central and northern Macedonia, and Greece was given control over the southern part with Salonika and Kavalla in addition to southern Epirus. Serbia and Montenegro divided the Sandžak area between themselves. But Serbia had to withdraw from the Albanian coast following a sharp ultimatum from Austria that made Serbia even more determined to fight over Bosnia and Herzegovina.

World War II and Royal Yugoslavia

Austria viewed Serbian expansion with great alarm, fearing it would serve as an impetus to the restless South Slavic nations of its empire, who had been demanding a "tri-alist" reorganization of the "dualist" Austro-Hungarian crown. In resisting the ever stronger Germanization of the Slovenes and Magyarization of the Croats and Serbs, the South Slavs had begun to look at the option of separating from Austria-Hungary and joining with Serbia in a new "Yugoslav" (South Slavic) configuration that would, in their hopes, assure each nation its cultural and political autonomy. Thus the "Greater Serbia" plans became a serious threat to the Austro-Hungarian empire. This "tri-alist" solution was viewed as the first phase in the dissolution of the empire, and therefore the Austro-Hungarians felt Serbia had to be restrained by whatever means, including war. Naturally, the large Serbian population in Bosnia and Herzegovina looked at Serbia with great hopes for their liberation. In Serbia and Bosnia, secret organizations were operating in support of pro-Serbian and terrorist acts. The Austro-Hungarian political and military leadership, bent on war against Serbia, needed only a spark to ignite a conflagration. The result would be total defeat and subordination of Serbia, and preservation intact of the Austro-Hungarian empire as the bridgehead for further expansion into the Balkans.

The spark was provided by the 28 June 1914 assassination in Sarajevo of Austria's Archduke Ferdinand and his wife. The archduke was a supporter of the "tri-alist" approach and therefore dangerous to both the Austro-Hungarian "centrists" and to Serbia's "Greater Serbia" proponents. His visit to Sarajevo during large scale maneuvers was viewed as a provocation by Bosnian Serbs, and they conspired to assassinate him with the assistance of the Serbian secret organization, Black Hand, which had also been behind the murder of Serbian King Miloš and his wife in 1903. Austria presented an ultimatum to Serbia on 23 July with ten requests that were accepted by Serbia in a desperate effort to

avoid a war. Servia also withdrew its troops from the border areas while mobilizing its armed forces. Austria, however, ignoring the opinion of German Emperor Wilhelm that "the wishes of the dual monarchy have been acceeded to," declared war on Serbia on 28 July 1914. They began bombing Belgrade the same day, and sent armies across the Danube and Sava Rivers to invade Serbia on 11 August 1914, taking the Serbs by total surprise. The Serbian army twice repelled the Austrian forces in 1914, with tremendous losses in men and materials and civilian refugees. In addition, a typhus epidemic exacted some 150,000 victims among Serbian soldiers and civilians throughout Serbia, where there were almost no doctors or medical supplies. Later in 1915, the Austrians were able to bring additional German and Bulgarian forces against Serbia, whose army refused to surrender and chose, along with countless civilians, to retreat to the Adriatic Sea and the island of Corfu. A trek across the dangerous mountain ranges of Albania and Montenegro caused tremendous losses of men, women, and children who perished from cold, starvation, and sickness. Still, an army of some 120,000 men made it through and was able to join the Allied forces holding the Salonika front in the fall of 1916. From there, after two years, they were sucessful in driving the Austrian forces out of Serbia in October 1918.

Meanwhile, political initiatives and negotiations had taken place that impacted the future of the South Slavic nations following the end of World War I. Aside from survival, the Serbian elite's political goal for the main outcome of the war was the same—a greater Serbia, with the liberation of their South Slavic brethren, particularly Serbs, from the Austro-Hungarian yoke. This liberation was viewed as an annexation of South Slavic lands to the Kingdom of Serbia as a victor in World War I. The Western powers, on the other hand, still considered the restoration of prewar Montenegro and Serbia and the autonomous development of the South Slavs of Austria-Hungary as their overriding goal, while allocating to Italy the areas of Austria promised to it in the 1915 Treaty of London. The dissolution of the Austro-Hungarian Empire was not yet an operational concept. But the South Slavic representatives that had constituted the Yugoslav Committee in November 1914 had as their goal a federation of Slovenes, Croats, and Serbs from Austria-Hungary with Serbia as equal partners in a new South Slavic state. However, Serbia was not conceding its dominant role and the Yugoslav Committee signed the Corfu Declaration of 20 July 1917 with Serbia. This declaration consisted of 14 points delineating the future joint state of Serbs, Croats, and Slovenes while treating both Macedonians and Montenegrins as Serbs.

But Austro-Hungary was losing the war and disintegrating from the inside. In May 1917, the "Yugoslav Club" in the Vienna Parliament, consisting of deputies from Slovenia, Istria, and Dalmatia led by Catholic Slovene People's party leader Monsignor Anton Korošec, issued a declaration demanding the independence of all Slovenes, Croats, and Serbs united in one national state. (The phrase "under the sceptre of the Hapsburgs" was added to their delcaration for safety reasons, to avoid prosecution for treason.) Poles, Czechs, and Slovaks were also agitating for their independence and they all had received support from their communities in the US. President Woodrow Wilson's 14 points supported the concept of self-determination and greatly impacted the work of the Slavic groups toward their independence. On 20 October 1918, President Wilson declared his support for the independence of all the nation subjects of the Austro-Hungarian monarchy.

Under the leadership of Monsignor Korošec, a council of Slovenes, Croats, and Serbs was formed in Zagreb, Croatia as their joint provisional government charged with negotiating a union with the Kingdom of Serbia. The Serbian army entered Belgrade on 1 November 1918 and proceeded to take over the Vojvodina region. The armistice ending World War I was signed on 3

November 1918, and on 6–9 November a conference was held in Geneva by Serbia's Prime Minister Nikola Pašić, Monsignor Korošec, and the Yugoslav Committee. The conference was empowered by the Zagreb Council to negotiate for it with the Allies. The sudden appearance on the scene by the Zagreb National Council had surprised Prime Minister Pašić but he could not ignore the provisional government set up by elected representatives of the Slovenes, Croats, and Serbs of Austro-Hungary. Thus, Pašić signed a declaration for the Serbian government setting up a joint provisional government with the right of the National Council in Zagreb to administer its territories until a constitutional assembly could be elected to agree on the form of government for the new state. However, the Serbian government reneged on Pašić's commitment. The National Council delegation with Monsignor Korošec was detained abroad and, given the pressures from the on-going Italian occupation of Slovene and Croat territories and the urgent need for international recognition, the National Council sent a delegation to Belgrade on 27 November 1918 to negotiate terms for unification with Serbia. But time was running out and the unification was proclaimed on 1 December 1918 without any details on the nature of the new state, since Bosnia and Herzegovina, Vojvodina, and Montenegro had already voted for their union with Serbia.

The Corfu declaration of 1917 had left open the issue of the unitarist or federalist structure of the new state by providing for a constitutional assembly to decide the issue on the basis of a "numerically qualified majority." Serbs interpreted this to mean a simple majority whereas others advocated a two-thirds majority. Following the 28 November 1920 elections, the simple majority prevailed and a constitution (mirroring the 1903 constitution of Serbia) for a unitary state was approved on 28 June 1921 by a vote of 223 to 35, with 111 abstentions out of a total of 419 members. The 50 members of the Croatian Peasant Party refused to participate in the work of the assembly, being opposed to the Serbian Monarchy and advocating an independent Croatian Republic.

After ten years of a contentious parliamentary system that ended in the murder of Croatian deputies and their leader Stjepan Radić, King Alexander abrogated the 1921 constitution, dissolved the parliament and political parties, took over power directly, renamed the country "Yugoslavia," and abolished the 33 administrative departments. These deparments had replaced the historic political/national regions in favor of administrative areas named mostly after rivers. A new policy was initiated with the goal of creating a single "Yugoslav" nation out of the three "tribes" of Serbs, Croats, and Slovenes. But in practice, this meant the Serbian King's hegemony over the rest of the nation. The reaction was intense and King Alexander himself fell victim to Croat-Ustaša and Macedonian terrorists and was assassinated in Marseilles in 1934. A regency ruled Yugoslavia headed by Alexander's cousin, Prince Paul, who managed to reach an agreement in 1939 with the Croats. An autonomous Croatian banovina headed by Ban Ivan Subašić was established, including most Croatian lands outside of the Bosnia and Herzegovina area. Strong opposition developed among Serbs because they viewed the Croatian Banovina as a privilege for Croats while Serbs were split among six old administrative units with a large Serbian population left inside the Croatian Banovina itself. Still, there was a chance for further agreements that might have satisfied the Serbs and Slovenes. But there was no time left—Hitler and his allies (Italy, Hungary, Bulgaria) attacked Yugoslavia on 6 April 1941. This came after a coup on 27 March 1941 had deposed Prince Paul's government, which had yielded to Hitler's pressures on 25 March. Thus the first Yugoslavia, born out of the distress of World War I, had no time to consolidate and work out its problems and was dismembered by aggressors. Still, the first Yugoslavia had allowed the Serbs a chance to bring all Serbs into a single state that they could control simply because of their relative size, unitary administration, and holding of key positions of political and economic leverage.

World War II

The aggression against Yugoslavia on 6 April 1941 by Germany, Italy, Hungary, Romania, and Bulgaria resulted in its occupation and division among Germany and its allies. Slovenia was split between Germany and Italy. Croatia, including Bosnia and Herzegovina but minus parts of Dalmatia taken by Italy, was established as an "independent" state under German/Italian control headed by the leader of the Ustaša movement. Montenegro was under Italian control along with Albania, who occupied the Sandžak, Kosovo, and Western Macedonian areas, all with sizable Muslim populations. The rest of Macedonia and Southeast Serbia was taken by Bulgaria, while Hungary occupied the Vojvodina area. Germans controlled the rest of Serbia and the Banat area. Serbia was put under the administration of General Milan Nedić who was allowed to organize his own military force for internal peacekeeping purposes. Resistance movements were initiated in various areas of Yugoslavia by both nationalist groups and by Communist-led partisans, the latter particularly following Hitler's attack on the Soviet Union on 22 June 1941. In Serbia the resistance was led by Colonel Draža Mihajlović as the Yugoslav army in the homeland, popularly called "Cetniks." The Cetniks recognized the authority of the Yugoslav government-in-exile, which, in fact, promoted Mihajlović to general and appointed him its Minister of War. In the fall of 1941 Mihajlović and Josip Broz Tito, who led the Communist partisan movement, met to seek agreement on a common front against the Nazis. However, Mihajlović saw that Tito's goal was to conquer Yugoslavia for Communism. Mihajlović could not go along with this, nor could he accept Tito's request that he subordinate his command to Tito.

A civil war between the two movements (under foreign occupation) followed. Meanwhile, in Croatia the Ustaša had mounted a genocidal campaign against Serbs, Jews, Gypsies, and others who opposed them. Wholesale massacres were committed, estimated at 300,000 to 500,000 in the Serb-populated areas of Croatia and Bosnia. Large numbers of Serbs fled to the mountain areas and initiated a guerilla war in retaliation and self-defense. Many of them joined the partisans, while others sought refuge in the Dalmatian areas under Italian control. Politically, the partisan movement was promising a federal Yugoslavia, with each nation forming its own republic. Mihajlović could not match the partisans' federal program because the Yugoslav government-in-exile could not work out an agreement between Serbs and Croats. In fact, the Serbian members, partly as a reaction to the massacres of Serbs in Croatia, could not confirm the 1939 agreement on the Croatian banovina as the basis for a post-World War II Yugoslavia. On the other hand Winston Churchill, convinced by reports that Mihajlović was collaborating with the Germans while the partisans under Marshal Tito were the ones who killed more Germans, decided to recognize Tito as the only legitimate Yugoslav resistance. Though aware of Tito's communist allegiance to Stalin, Churchill threw his support to Tito. This forced the Yugoslav government-in-exile into a coalition government with Tito, who had no intention of keeping the agreement. In fact, Tito would have fought along with the Germans against an Allied landing in Yugoslavia.

When Soviet armies, accompanied by Tito, entered Yugoslavia from Romania and Bulgaria in the fall of 1944, military units and civilians that had opposed the partisans had no choice but to retreat to Austria or Italy. Among them were the Cetnik units of Draža Mihajlović, and "homeguards" from Serbia, Croatia, and Slovenia that had been under German control but were pro-Allies in their convictions and hopes. Also in retreat were the units of the Croatian Ustaša, who had collaborated with Italy and Germany in order to achieve (and control) an independent greater Croatia. In the process, Ustaša had committed terrible and large scale massacres of Serbs, Jews, Gypsies and others.

After the end of the war, the Communist-led forces took control of Serbia and Yugoslavia and instituted a violent dictatorship that committed systematic crimes and human rights violations on an unexpectedly large scale. Thousands upon thousands of their former opponents who were returned from Austria by British military authorities were tortured and massacred by partisan executioners. General Mihajlović was captured in Bosnia in March 1946 and publicly tried and executed on 17 July 1946.

Communist Yugoslavia

Such was the background for the formation of the second Yugoslavia as a Federative People's Republic of five nations (Slovenes, Croats, Serbs, Macedonians, Montenegrins) with their individual republics and Bosnia and Herzegovina as a buffer area with its mix of Serb, Muslim, and Croat populations. The problem of large Hungarian and Muslim Albanian populations in Serbia was solved by creating for them the autonomous region of Vojvodina (Hungarian minority) and Kosovo (Muslim Albanian majority) that assured their political and cultural development. Tito attempted a balancing act to satisfy most of the nationality issues that were carried over, unresolved, from the first Yugoslavia. However, he failed to satisfy anyone. Compared to pre-1941 Yugoslavia, where Serbs enjoyed a controlling role, the numerically stronger Serbs had suffered many losses. They had lost the Macedonian area they considered Southern Serbia; lost the opportunity to incorporate Montenegro into Serbia; lost direct control over the Hungarian minority in Vojvodina and Muslim Albanians of Kosovo (viewed as the cradle of the Serbian nation since the Middle Ages); were not able to incorporate into Serbia the large Serbian-populated areas of Bosnia; and had not obtained an autonomous region for the large minority Serbian population within the Croatian Republic. The Croats, while gaining back from Hungary the Medjumurje area and from Italy the cities of Rijeka (Fiume), Zadar (Zara), some Dalmatian islands, and the Istrian Peninsula had, on the other hand, had lost the Srem area to Serbia and also Bosnia and Herzegovina. (Bosnia and Herzegovina had been part of the pre-World War II independent Croatian state under the Ustaša leadership). In addition, the Croats were confronted with a deeply resentful Serbian minority that became ever more pervasive in public administrative and security positions. The official position of the Marxist Yugoslav regime was that national rivalries and conflicting interests would gradually diminish through their sublimation into a new Socialist order. Without capitalism, nationalism was supposed to wither away. Therefore, in the name of their unity and brotherhood motto, any nationalistic expression of concern was prohibited and repressed by the dictatorial and centralized regime of the League of Yugoslav Communists, with the Socialist Alliance as its mass front organization.

After a short post-war coalition government, the elections of 11 November 1945—boycotted by the non-communist coalition parties—gave the Communist-led People's Front 90% of the vote. A Constituent Assembly met on 29 November, abolished the monarchy and established the Federative People's Republic of Yugoslavia. In January 1946, a new constitution was adopted based on the 1936 Soviet constitution. The Stalin-engineered expulsion of Yugoslavia from the Soviet-dominated Cominform Group in 1948 was actually a blessing for Yugoslavia, after its leadership was able to survive Stalin's pressures. Survival had to be justified, both practically and in theory, by developing a road to Socialism based on Yugoslavia's own circumstances. This new road map evolved rather quickly in response to Stalin's accusations and Yugoslavia's need to perform a balancing act between

the NATO alliance and the Soviet bloc. Tito quickly nationalized the economy through a policy of forced industrialization, supported by the collectivization of the agriculture.

The agricultural reform of 1945–46 included limited private ownership of a maximum of 35 hectares (85 acres) and a limited free market (after the initial forced delivery of quotas to the state at very low prices), but had to be abandoned because of resistance by the peasants. The actual collectivization efforts were initiated in 1949 using welfare benefits and lower taxes as incentives, along with direct coercion. But collectivization had to be abandoned by 1958 simply because its inefficiency and low productivity could not support the concentrated effort of industrial development.

By the 1950s, Yugoslavia had initiated the development of its internal trademark: self-management of enterprises through workers councils and local decision-making as the road to Marx's withering away of the state. Following the failure of the first five-year plan (1947–51), the second five-year plan (1957–61) was completed in four years by relying on the well-established self-management system. Economic targets were set from the local to the republic level and then coordinated by a federal planning institute to meet an overall national economic strategy. This system supported a period of very rapid industrial growth in the 1950s from a very low base. But a high consumption rate encouraged a volume of imports, largely financed by foreign loans, far in excess of exports. In addition, inefficient and low-productivity industries were kept in place through public subsidies, cheap credit, and other artificial measures, leading to a serious crisis by 1961. Reforms were necessary and, by 1965, market socialism was introduced with laws that abolished most price controls and halved import duties while withdrawing export subsidies. After necessary amounts were left with the earning enterprise, the rest of the earned foreign currencies were deposited with the national bank and used by the state, other enterprises, or were used to assist less developed areas. Councils were given more decision-making power on investing their earnings and they also tended to vote for higher salaries in order to meet steep increases in the cost of living. Unemployment grew rapidly even though political factories were still subsidized.

Thus, the government relaxed its restrictions to allow labor migration particularly to West Germany, where workers were needed for its thriving economy. Foreign investment was encouraged up to 49% in joint enterprises, and barriers to the movement of people and exchange of ideas were largely removed.

The role of trade unions continued to be one of transmission of instructions from government to workers, allocation of perks along with the education/training of workers, monitoring legislation and overall protection of the self-management system. Strikes were legally neither allowed nor forbidden, but until the 1958 miners strike in Trbovlje, Slovenia, were not publicly acknowledged and were suppressed. After 1958, strikes were tolerated as an indication of problems to be resolved. Unions, however, did not initiate strikes but were expected to convince workers to go back to work.

Having survived its expulsion from the Comminform in 1948 and Stalin's attempts to take control, Yugoslavia began to develop a foreign policy independent of the Soviet Union. By mid-1949, Yugoslavia ceased its support of the Greek Communists in their civil war against the then-Royalist government of Greece. In October 1949, Yugoslavia was elected to one of the non-permanent seats on the UN Security Council and openly condemned North Korea's aggression in South Korea. Following the "rapprochement" opening with the Soviet Union initiated by Nikita Khrushchev and his 1956 denunciation of Stalin, Tito intensified his work on developing the movement of non-aligned "third world" nations as Yugoslavia's external trademark in cooperation with Nehru of India, Nasser of Egypt, and others.

With the September 1961 Belgrade summit conference of non-aligned nations, Tito became the recognized leader of the movement. The nonaligned position served Tito's Yugoslavia well by allowing Tito to draw on economic and political support from the Western powers while neutralizing any aggression from the Soviet bloc. While Tito had acquiesced, reluctantly, to the 1956 Soviet invasion of Hungary for fear of chaos and any liberalizing impact on Yugoslavia, he condemned the Soviet invasion of Dubček's Czechoslovakia in 1968, as did Romania's Ceausescu, both fearing their countries might be the next in line for corrective action by the Red Army and the Warsaw Pact. Just before his death on 4 May 1980, Tito also condemned the Soviet invasion of Afghanistan.

Yugoslavia actively participated in the 1975 Helsinki Conference and Agreements and the first 1977–78 review conference that took place in Belgrade, even though Yugoslavia's one-party communist regime perpetrated and condoned numerous human rights violations. Overall, in the 1970s and 1980s, Yugoslavia maintained fairly good relations with its neighboring states by playing down or solving pending disputes and developing cooperative projects and increased trade.

Though ravaged by the war, occupation, resistance and civil war losses, and preoccupied with carrying out the elimination of all actual and potential opposition, the Communist government faced the double task of building its Socialist economy while rebuilding the country. As an integral part of the Yugoslav federation Serbia was, naturally, impacted by Yugoslavia's internal and external political developments. The main problems facing communist Yugoslavia/Serbia were essentially the same as the unresolved ones under Royalist Yugoslavia. As Royal Yugoslavism had failed in its assimilative efforts, so did the Socialist Yugoslavism fail to overcome the forces of nationalism.

As nationalism was on the rise in Yugoslavia, particularly in Croatia and Slovenia, Serbs were facing a real dilemma with the rising of Albanian nationalism in Kosovo, considered by Serbs as the sacred cradle of their own nationhood since the middle ages. Kosovo had been increasingly populated by Muslim Albanians since the waves of Serb emigration from it under Turkish pressures and persecutions. Albanians had also taken control in Kosovo in World War II with Italian support and had terrorized the Serbian population into further migrations. After World War II, Tito had set up Kosovo as an autonomous province and the Albanians were able to develop their own political and cultural autonomy, including a university with instructors and textbooks from Albania. Immigration from Albania also increased and after Tito's death in 1980, Albanians became more assertive and began agitating for a republic of their own, since by then they comprised about 80% of Kosovo's population. Serbia used force to put down the Albanians' rebellious demonstrations, but the situation continued to deteriorate, generating more violence and increasing demands by Serbs for their protection in Kosovo.

The reverberations of the Kosovo events were very serious throughout Yugoslavia since most non-Serbs viewed the repression of the Albanians as a possible precedent for the use of force elsewhere. Serbs were accused of using a double standard—one for themselves in the defense of Serbs in Kosovo by denying the Albanians' political autonomy and violating their human rights, and a different standard for themselves by demanding political autonomy and human rights for Serbs in Croatia.

Prior to the formation of the second Yugoslavia, Serbian statehood had developed on the basis of a unitarian and centralized administration heavily influenced by its military element. Little, if any, tolerance was allowed for non-Serbian populations that were basically ignored or simply considered "Serbian." Serbian intellectuals and novelists began focusing on what they considered a very dangerous and tragic situation endangering the very existence of the Serbian nation. In 1986, the Serbian Academy of Arts

and Sciences issued a draft manifesto that called for the the creation of a unified Serbia whereby all lands inhabited by Serbs would be united with Serbia while bringing Kosovo under control to be eventually repopulated by Serbs. To accomplish this goal, the 1974 Constitution would need to be amended into an instrument for a recentralizing effort of both the government and the economy.

Recentralization vs. Confederation

In 1986, work was begun on amendments to the 1974 Constitution that, when submitted in 1987, created a furor, particularly in Slovenia and Croatia. The main points of contention were the creation of a unified legal system, the establishment of central control over the means of transportation and communication, the centralization of the economy into a unified market, and the granting of more control to Serbia over its autonomous provinces of Kosovo and Vojvodina. These moves were all viewed as coming at the expense of the individual republics. A recentralization of the League of Communists was also recommended but opposed by liberal/nationalist groups. Serbia also proposed changes to the bicameral federal Skupština (Assembly) by replacing it with a tricameral one where deputies would no longer be elected by their republican assemblies but through a "one person, one vote" nationwide system. Slovenia, Croatia, and Bosnia and Herzegovina strongly opposed the change as they opposed the additional Chamber of Associated Labor that would have increased the federal role in the economy. The debates over the recentralizing amendments caused an even greater focus in Slovenia and Croatia on the confederative structure based on self-determination by sovereign states and a multiparty democratic system as the only one that could maintain some semblance of a "Yugoslav" state.

Meanwhile, Slobodan Milošević had become the head of the Communist Party in Serbia in early 1987. An ardent advocate of the Serbs in Kosovo (and elsewhere), as well as a vocal proponent of the recentralizing constitutional amendments, he was able, through skillful manipulations and use of pressure with mass demonstrations, to take control of the leadership in Montenegro as well as in Vojvodina and impose Serbian control over Kosovo.

The Slovenian Communist Party had taken the leadership in opposing the recentralizing initiatives and in advocating a confederal reorganization of Yugoslavia. Thus a political dueling took place between Slovenia and Serbia. When Slobodan Milošević directed the organization of mass demonstrations by Serbs in Ljubljana, the capital city of Slovenia, and the Slovenian leadership vetoed it, the Serbs began a boycott of Slovenian products, withdrawing savings from Slovenian banks, and terminating economic cooperation and trade with Slovenia. Serbian President Milošević's tactics were extremely distasteful to the Slovenians and the use of force against the Albanian population of the Kosovo province worried the Slovenes (and Croats) about the possible use of force by Serbia against Slovenia itself. The tensions with Serbia convinced the Slovenian leadership of the need to undertake protective measures and, in September 1989, draft amendments to the constitution of Slovenia were published that included the right to secession, the sole right of the Slovenian legislature to introduce martial law, and the right to control deployment of armed forces in Slovenia. The latter seemed particularly necessary since the Yugoslav Army, largely controlled by a Serbian and Montenegrin officer corps dedicated to the preservation of a communist system, appeared to have a self-interest in preserving the source of its own allocations of some 51% of the Yugoslav federal budget.

A last attempt at salvaging Yugoslavia was to be made at the extraordinary congress of the League of Communists of Yugoslavia, convened in January 1990 to review proposed reforms such as free multiparty elections and freedom of speech. The Slovenian delegation attempted to broaden the spectrum of reforms but was rebuffed and walked out on 23 January 1990. They also pulled out of the Yugoslav League. The Slovenian Communists then renamed their party the Party for Democratic Renewal. The political debate in Slovenia intensified and some nineteen parties were formed by early 1990. On 10 April 1990 the first free elections since before World War II were held in Slovenia where there still was a three-chamber assembly: political affairs, associated labor, and territorial communities. A coalition of six newly formed democratic parties, called Demos, won 55% of the votes, with the remainder going to the Party for Democratic Renewal (former Communists), 17.3%; the Socialist Party, 5.4%; and the Liberal Democratic Party (heir to the Slovenian Youth Organization), 14.5%. The Demos coalition organized the first freely elected Slovenian Government of the post-Communist era with Dr. Lojze Peterle as the Prime Minister. Milan Kučan, former head of the League of Communists of Slovenia, was elected President with 54% of the vote in recognition of his efforts to effect a bloodless transfer of power from a monopoly by the Communist party to a free multiparty system and his standing up to the recentralizing attempts by Serbia.

Yugoslavia's Dissolution

In October 1990, Slovenia and Croatia published a joint proposal for a confederation of Yugoslavia as a last attempt at a negotiated solution, but to no avail. The Slovenian legislature also adopted in October a draft constitution proclaiming that "Slovenia will become an independent state . . . ." On 23 December, a plebiscite was held on Slovenia's secession from Yugoslavia if a confederate solution could not be negotiated within a six-month period. An overwhelming majority of 88.5% of voters approved the secession provision, and on 26 December 1990 a Declaration of Sovereignty was also adopted. All federal laws were declared void in Slovenia as of 20 February 1991 and, since no negotiated agreement was possible, Slovenia declared its independence on 25 June 1991. On 27 June 1991, the Yugoslav army tried to seize control of Slovenia and its borders with Italy, Austria, and Hungary under the pretext that it was its constitutional duty to assure the integrity of Socialist Yugoslavia. The Yugoslav Army units were surprised and shocked by the resistance they encountered from the Slovenian "territorial guards" that would surround Yugoslav Army tank units, isolate them, and engage in close combat along border checkpoints. These encounters often ended with Yugoslav units surrendering to the Slovenian forces. Fortunately, casualties were limited on both sides, but over 3,200 Yugoslav army soldiers surrendered. They were treated well by the Slovenes, who scored a public relations coup by having the prisoners call their parents all over Yugoslavia to come to Slovenia and take their sons back home. The war in Slovenia was ended in ten days after the European Community negotiated a cease fire. Also negotiated was a three-month moratorium of Slovenia's implementation of independence, giving the Yugoslav Army time to retreat from Slovenia.

The collapse of Communist regimes in Eastern Europe in 1989 had a deep impact in Yugoslavia. Communist leaders there realized that, in order to stay in power, they needed to embrace the goals of nationalistic movements. In Slovenia, the Communist Party agreed to shed its monopoly of power and lost in the first multiparty elections on 8 April 1990. The same happened in Croatia on 22 April 1990. In Serbia and Montenegro, the Communists won on 9 December 1990 on the basis of their strong Serbian nationalism, and practically maintained their monopoly of power. The only change was the party name—from Communist to Socialist. In its last years, Yugoslavia thus became a house divided, prompting the parliament of Slovenia to pass a resolution on 20 February 1991 proposing the division of Yugoslavia into two separate states.

Suppression of Kosovo and Revolt in Croatia

The situation in Kosovo had become very tense when, on 2 July 1990, the Albanian members of the Yugoslav legislature had declared the region a separate territory within the Yugoslav federation. But on 5 July 1990, the Serbian Parliament countered the Albanian move by suspending the autonomous government of Kosovo. Serbia also had to deal with the developments in Croatia. In August of 1990, an open insurrection against the Croatian government was initiated by the Serbs of the "Krajina" region, apparently with the support of Slobodan Milošević. On 17 March 1991, Milošević declared that Krajina, a region in Croatia, was a Serbian autonomous region. Negotiations were stalemated at the collective presidency of Yugoslavia, primarily by the firm but opposite positions of the presidents of Serbia and Croatia. The situation in Croatia caused clashes between the Serbian militia and Croatian police and the use of Yugoslav Army units to keep the peace. The latter were also used in Belgrade on 9–13 March 1991 against massive anti-Milošević demonstrations, causing two deaths and some 90 wounded.

The Serbian determination to maintain a unitary Yugoslavia hardened, while the determination of the Slovenes and Croats to gain their independence grew stronger. This caused the closing of ranks by the Yugoslav army command in support of the Serbian leadership and Slobodan Milošević, who made his position clear by the spring of 1991 on the potential unilateral secession of Slovenia, Croatia, and Bosnia and Herzegovina. Since there was no substantial Serbian population in Slovenia, its secession did not present a real problem. However, secession by Croatia and Bosnia and Herzegovina would necessitate border revisions to allow for lands with Serbian populations to be joined to Serbia. This position was practically the same as Prime Minister Pašić's in 1918. Pašić was not opposed to federation in principle, but refused to have two million Serbs then outside Serbia proper divided among several federal units.

The new constitution promulgated by Serbia in September 1990 provided for a unicameral legislature of 250 seats and the elimination of autonomy for Vojvodina and Kosovo. The first elections were held on 9 December 1990. More than 50 parties and 32 presidential candidates participated. Slobodan Milošević's Socialist Party of Serbia received two thirds of the votes and 194 out of the 250 seats. The Movement for Renewal, headed by Vuk Drašković received 19 seats while the Democratic Party won 7 seats. With the mandate from two-thirds of the electorate, Slobodan Milošević had complete control of Serbia. But with it also came the accountability for the actions that followed. Having gained control of Serbia, Montenegro, Kosovo, and Vojvodina, Milošević controlled four of the eight votes in the collective presidency of Yugoslavia. With the collective presidency—also responsible for the armed forces—stalemated, the top army leadership became even more independent of the normal civilian controls, and was able to make its own political decisions on rendering support to the Serbs in Croatia and their armed rebellion.

A last effort to avoid Yugoslavia's disintegration was made by Bosnia and Herzegovina and Macedonia with their 3 June 1991 compromise proposal to form a Community of Yugoslav Republics. In this community, national defense, foreign policy, and a common market would be centrally administered, while all other areas would fall to the jurisdiction of the member states (except for the armed forces and diplomatic representation). But it was already too late. Serbia disliked the confederal nature of the proposal, and objected to leaving an opening for the establishment of separate armed forces. In addition, Milošević and the army had already committed to the support of the revolt of the Serbs in Croatia. At their meeting in Split on 12 June 1991, Milošević and Croatia's president Tudjman were past the stage of salvaging Yugoslavia when discussing how to divide Bosnia and Herzegovina into ethnic cantons.

The international community stood firmly in support of the preservation of Yugoslavia, of the economic reforms initiated by the Marković government, and of the peaceful solution to the centralist vs. confederal conflict. The US and the European Community had indicated that they would not recognize the independence of Slovenia and Croatia if they unilaterally seceded from the Yugoslav Federation. However, Slovenia and Croatia had defined their impending separation as a "disassociation" by free members as sovereign nations based on a negotiated process. With the then-Soviet Union also supporting Socialist Federal Yugoslavia, Milošević was assured of strong backing, while the Yugoslav army interpreted such support as a possible green light for military intervention. Slovenia and Croatia proceeded with their declarations of independence on 25 June 1991.

As a shrewd politician, Slobodan Milošević knew that a military attack on a member republic would deal a mortal blow to both the idea and the reality of a Yugoslavia in any form. Thus, following the Yugoslav army's attack on Slovenia on 27 June 1991, Milošević and the Serbian leadership concentrated on their primary goal of uniting all Serbian lands to Serbia.

This position led to the direct use of the Yugoslav army and its superior capabilities in support of the Serbian goal of establishing the Serbian autonomous region of Krajina in Croatia. Increased fighting from July 1991 caused tremendous destruction of entire cities (Vukovar), and large scale damage to the medieval city of Dubrovnik. Croatia, which was poorly armed and caught by surprise, fought over a seven-month period. It suffered some 10,000 dead, 30,000 wounded, over 14,000 missing, and lost to the Krajina Serbs (and to the Yugoslav Army) about one-third of its territory, from Slavonia to the west and around the border with Bosnia and south to northern Dalmatia.

The intervention of the European Community (as earlier in the case of Slovenia) and the UN brought about a cease-fire on 3 January 1992. UN Peacekeepers were stationed by March 1991 to separate the Serb-controlled areas from Croatian army and paramilitary forces. Milošević had very good reasons to press the Krajina Serbs and the Yugoslav army to accept the cease-fire because the Serb forces had already achieved control of about one-third of Croatian territory. He was confident that the UN forces would actually protect the Serb-occupied territories from the Croats.

Aggression in Bosnia and Herzegovina

In the meantime, a far worse situation was developing in Bosnia and Herzegovina. The Yugoslav army, forced to retreat from Slovenia in October 1991, took its revenge against Croatia. Following the ceasefire in Croatia and the deployment there of UN peacekeepers, the Yugoslav army moved into Bosnia and Herzegovina. The latter had held a referendum in February 1992 on its sovereignty and independence in accordance with the European Community's conditions for eventual international recognition. The ethnic mix of Bosnia and Herzegovina according to the 1991 census was about 44% Muslim, 31% Serbian, 17% Croatian, and 6% Yugoslav. Milošević's goal of unifying all Serbian lands would become impossible with an independent Bosnia and Herzegovina. Therefore, Bosnian Serbs abstained from voting, while 64% of eligible voters approved of an independent Bosnia and Herzegovina by an almost unanimous 99.7%.

At the same time, a provisional agreement had been reached at a conference in Lisbon in late February 1992 on dividing Bosnia and Herzegovina into three ethnic units, with related central power sharing. This agreement was rejected by the Muslim side, and the Bosnian Serbs, who had earlier organized their territory into their own Serbian Republic of Bosnia and Herzegovina, prepared for hostilities with the support of the Yugoslav army and volunteers from Serbia and Montenegro.

The international recognition of Bosnia and Herzegovina on 6 April 1992, the anniversary of the 1941 Nazi invasion of Yugoslavia, added more credibility to the Serbian propaganda line about a German/Catholic conspiracy against the Orthodox Serbs. The terror whipped up by Serbia, using the fear of another genocidal Ustaša orgy against Serbs similar to the one of World War II memory, steeled the Serbs' determination to fight for their own survival. An incident on 1 March 1992 when a Serbian wedding party was attacked in the Muslim section of Sarajevo was the spark that ignited the fighting in Bosnia and Herzegovina that has yet to stop as of October 1994. Serbs pounded Sarajevo for two years, reducing it to rubble, took control of two-thirds of the territory, and carried out ferocious "ethnic cleansing" of Muslims in areas they intended to add to their own. Under international pressure, the Yugoslav army moved to Serbia, leaving to the Bosnian Serbs an abundance of weaponry and supplies.

In May 1992, the UN, convinced that Serbia and Montenegro (who had formed their own Federal Republic of Yugoslavia on 27 April 1992) were supporting the aggression against Bosnia and Herzegovina, imposed economic sanctions. In spite of the sanctions and worldwide opprobrium Milošević's Socialist Party won the elections of 22 December 1992 and he was elected President of Serbia by 56% versus 34% for his opponent, Milan Panić, a successful California businessman. The exhaustion of Serbia, the terrible inflation and unemployment, and savage corruption convinced Milošević to attempt some compromise and support the various plans proffered for bringing about peace in Bosnia and Herzegovina. However, the Bosnian Serbs felt assured of victory and Milošević seemed unable to convince them to agree to any plan, not even the one in the summer of 1994 that offered the combined Muslim-Croat Federation 51% and the Serbs 49% of Bosnia and Herzegovina's territory. The desperate economic situation of Serbia caused by its assistance to the Bosnian Serbs and the UN-imposed sanctions finally forced Milošević to disassociate Serbia from the Bosnian Serbs and to close the borders with Bosnia in September 1994, hopefully to obtain a gradual lifting of the economic sanctions. Even with the eventual settlement of hostilities in Bosnia and Herzegovina, Serbia will face serious internal political problems in addition to its ruined economy: the tradition of independence in Montenegro, the Albanian majority in Kosovo, the Muslims of the Sandžak area, the Hungarians in Vojvodina, and independent Macedonia.

Montenegro

Montenegro is the other constituent member, along with Serbia, of the third Yugoslavia formed by the two republics in April 1992. Montenegro's early history is as part of the medieval development of Serbia, known as Duklja or Zeta, north of Lake Scutari (Skadar). It remained a part of the enlarged Serbia of the Nemanja dynasty and, following the death of Dušan the Great in 1355, fell under the domain of the Balsa family from 1360 to 1421. By this time the Turks had already advanced into the Balkans and had defeated the Serbs at the 1389 battle of Kosovo Polje. Many Serbs fled from the Turks and settled in the mountainous regions of Zeta. A new dynasty was founded by Steven Crnojević when the male line of the Balsa family became extinct. Crnojević's successor, Ivan the Black, had to retreat into more inaccessible areas north of Lake Scutari, establishing the capital at Cetinje.

Bosnia fell to the Turks in 1463, to Albania in 1478, and to Herzegovina in 1482. Thus Montenegro became completely surrounded by the Turks and subjected to continuous fighting for 400 years. Living in a very harsh mountain territory, the Montenegrins were natural and fierce fighters and not even the large Turkish armies could conquer them. Ivan the Black, in spite of all the fighting, was able to establish a printing shop near Cetinje where books were printed in begining in 1493. He also built a monastery in Cetinje as the See of the Orthodox bishopric. In 1516, Montenegro, a name which came from the Venetians meaning "Black Mountain," became a theocracy when power was transferred from the last Crnojević to the Bishop of Cetinje.

For the next three centuries, until 1851, Montenegro was ruled by its bishops. These bishops were either elected by local assemblies from among the Cetinje monks or, after 1696, by designation of their own successors. The Bishops' role strengthened the Montenegrins' loyalty to the Orthodox Church and prevented their conversion to Islam, except in the lowlands and coastal areas occupied by the Turks. In 1696, Danilo Petrović Njegoš (1696–1737) was elected "Vladika" (Bishop) and his dynastic family ruled Montenegro until its unification with Serbia into the first Yugoslavia. Since the Vladikas were celibates, they would usually nominate a nephew as their successor.

The Montenegro area was an almost impregnable mountain fortress with some limited access from the Adriatic coast where the Turks had taken hold. The population was comprised of Slav and Albanian Muslims. Even within the fortress, though, there were renegade Muslims who aided the Turks. This was a dangerous situation, and Danilo solved it by carrying out a massacre of all Muslim men—Albanian, Turk, or Serb—on Christmas Eve in 1702. The Turkish attacks increased, and in 1714 they were able to occupy the capital of Cetinje. The Turks could not hold sustain their hold, however, because of difficulties in getting supplies, and constant guerrilla attacks by the Montenegrins.

Meanwhile, Peter the Great of Russia had recognized Montenegro's independence in 1715 viewing it as an allied Orthodox country valuable in his struggle against the Ottoman Empire. Having gained a greatly supportive ally in Russia, Danilo was successful in opposing the Turks with occassional support from Venice until his death in 1737. His successors had to struggle with the internal weakness of Montenegro, that is, the traditional competition and blood feuds among key Montenegrin families. Peter I (1782–1830) was able to bring together the feuding factions, reorganize his administration, issue the first Montenegrin Code of Laws in 1798, and defeat the Turks in 1799. Peter also obtained from the Turks a formal recognition of Montenegro's independence and even a key declaration that it had never been subject to the Ottoman Empire. In addition, Peter I succeeded in incorporating the Brda region into Montenegro at the expense of Turkey. During the Napoleonic wars, Montenegro, Russia's ally, fought the French over Dubrovnik and, in 1806, occupied the Gulf of Kotor, thus gaining access to the Adriatic sea. But Montenegro had to relinquish Kotor to Austria following the Congress of Vienna decisions in 1814–15.

Peter I died in 1830, having repelled again Turkish attacks in 1819–21 and 1828–29. Peter II, considered by many to be the greatest Serbian poet, established a senate of 12 members and centralized his authority by abolishing the office of civil governor, which had existed since 1516. However, his successor, Danilo II (1851–60), effected a radical change by proclaiming himself an hereditary prince in 1852. Because he wanted to marry, he also separated the office of bishop from that of prince, and designated it as a post to be held by Montenegrin aristocrats. Concentrating on secular concerns, Danilo II introduced a new legal code in 1855 that guaranteed civil and religious freedoms based on the constitution of 1852. During the 1856 Crimean War, Danilo II failed to assist Russia in its war with Turkey, causing internal opposition within Montenegro which led to a successful war against Turkey in 1858. Danilo died in 1860 of a wound inflicted by an exiled Montenegrin rebel.

Danilo had only one daughter, and therefore his nephew Nicholas took over as the last independent ruler of Montenegro from 1860 until the 1918 unification with Serbia and the first Yugoslavia. During his 58-year reign Nicholas saw the demise of the empires he needed to repel in order to maintain Montenegro's independence, namely the Austrian, Ottoman, and Russian empires. He also gained the nickname of "Father-in-Law of Europe" by marrying six daughters into Italian, Russian, Serbian, and German royal families. Through a series of wars with Turkey (1862, 1876, 1912, and 1913), Nicholas succeeded in more than doubling Montenegro's territory. Following the 1913 Balkan War, Montenegro and Serbia divided the Sandžak area and became neighbor states, both primarily populated by Serbs. Montenegro also gained access to the Adriatic Sea south of Lake Scutari (Skadar), which was divided in 1913 between Montenegro and the newly formed Albanian state.

Between 1880 and 1912, Montenegro took advantage of an era of relative peace to develop roads, education, agriculture, postal services, and banks, mostly with foreign investment especially from Italy, whose queen was Nicholas' daughter Elena. For higher education, most Montenegrins studied at the University of Belgrade and came back home with progressive and democratic ideas, along with deep and personal ties and commitment to the Serbian goals of national unification.

The first Montenegrin parliament met in 1905, with 62 elected and 14 ex-officio members. Following the successful Balkan wars, Serbian-Montenegrin relations grew closer, and by 1914, the two Serbian kingdoms proposed a union in which they would share their armed forces, foreign policy, and customs while maintaining their separate royal dynasties. World War I interrupted this process. Montenegro's poor defense of Mount Lovćen against Austrian attacks led to Austrian occupation for the better part of the war, based of the capitulation worked out by Prince Mirko, King Nicholas' son. Thus Montenegro ceased to officially participate in the war as an ally of Serbia and the Western Powers against Austria.

While King Nicholas and his ministers lived abroad, the Montenegrins at home, with Serbian Cetniks, carried out guerrilla warfare. Some of their regiments retreated to Corfu with the Serbian army and were incorporated into it. The civilian population suffered under a harsh Austrian occupation both from persecutions and shortages of food and other supplies. A Montenegrin Committee for National Union was formed by exiles in Paris who supported the 20 July 1917 Corfu Declaration on the establishment of a Kingdom of Serbs, Croats, and Slovenes. It was the Montenegrin Committee's view that the role of Montenegro as an independent state was at an end. As a purely Serbian country, the Montenegrin Committee felt the time had come to unite with the Kingdom of Serbs, Croats, and Slovenes. King Nicholas opposed such a move and had the support of Italy who opposed the formation of a strong South Slavic state under Serbian leadership. Most Montenegrins resented King Nicholas' surrender to Austria and at the end of World War I, the Montenegrins rose against the Austrians on 13 November 1918. Their assembly deposed King Nicholas and, on 24 November 1918, passed a resolution in favor of Montenegro's union with the Kingdom of Serbia. This was made easier by the presence of the Serbian armed forces. Thus, Montenegro became part of the first Yugoslavia on 1 December 1918, not as Montenegro but as part of the Kingdom of Serbia. The voting at the 1918 Assembly took place with white cards for the first group (therefore called "Bjelaši") and green cards for the second one (called "Zelenaši"). With the reorganization of the Kingdom of Serbs, Croats, and Slovenes into the Kingdom of Yugoslavia, Montenegro was part of the Zetska Banovina, and Montenegrins participated very actively in Yugoslavia's political life, mostly supporting the centralist Serbian positions.

During World War II, Italy controlled Montenegro and attempted unsuccessfully to revive the old Kingdom. Much fighting went on between Communist partisans and anti-Communist Montenegrin Cetniks. In the post-World War II Socialist Federative Yugoslavia, Tito reestablished Montenegro as a separate republic due in large part to strong Montenegrin representation in the circle of his closest collaborators, but also to balance the influence of Serbs in general. Most Montenegrins took the side of the Serbian centralists against the liberal elements in the League of Communists and, in the late 1980s and early 1990s, supported Slobodan Milošević. With the demise of Yugoslavia, Montenegro joined Serbia in forming the Federal Republic of Yugoslavia. Being a less-developed area, Montenegro depends heavily on Serbian assistance—difficult to obtain under the impact of economic sanctions. The old division between Bjelaši and Zelenaši is becoming more pronounced in Montenegro with the latter, as proponents of Montenegro's independence, appear to be gaining ground.

Kosovo and Vojvodina

Kosovo is a term deeply embedded in the Serbian national consciousness—it draws from the 1389 Serbian defeat by the Turks. Kosovo was the center of the Serbian Kingdom in the Middle Ages, full of old Serbian Orthodox churches and monasteries and other reminders of a fully developed medieval Serbian culture that had survived five centuries of harsh Ottoman rule until liberated in 1912. Firmly attached to their Christian faith and opposed to conversion into Islam, large numbers of Serbs were forced to leave the Kosovo region because of Turkish persecutions. In their place Muslim Albanians were settled in increasing numbers so that liberation of Serbian Kosovo in 1912 actually liberated an almost entirely Albanian area. By the end of World War II, the Kosovo area was already about 70% Albanian and claiming its right to join Albania itself. The Communist partisan leadership under Tito reneged on its promises and decided to keep Kosovo within a Serbian Republic of a Federal Yugoslavia by granting Kosovo a special autonomous status. This decision kept Serbian hopes alive that eventually Serbs could repopulate the Holy Ground of Kosovo and bring the underdeveloped region into the Serbian mainstream, both culturally and economically. But such hopes failed to materialize because, from the Serbian point of view, the autonomy mechanism favored the further growth of the Albanian population (with a much higher birth rate than the Serbian one). Serbs were being systematically pushed out by a new persecution, supposedly supported by the Communist regime.

The Albanians clamored for their right to self-determination and a republic of their own (still within Yugoslavia), and began to actively demonstrate against Serbian domination from Belgrade. Albanians increased their pressure on the remaining Serbian population, which had dwindled to some ten percent of the total by 1991. Cries of genocide were raised by Serbian media, and a series of bloody clashes justified Slobodan Milošević's administration to develop a new Serbian constitution of September 1990, drastically limiting Kosovo's autonomy. Serbia instituted direct controls of local security forces in Kosovo, took over the administrative structure by dismissing Albanians from thousands of positions, took over the educational system, imprisoned hundreds of Albanian activists and indicted their leader, Azem Vllasi, on charges of counterrevolutionary activity (he was acquitted in April 1990), and, finally, adjourned the Kosovo Assembly. The Albanians actively opposed such measures, and further clashes took place causing over 60 deaths and a world-wide outcry by mid-1990. But the Milošević regime continued its policies and the Albanians then organized their own political parties, the strongest of which became the Kosovo Democratic Alliance led by Ibrahim Rugova.

In a street meeting on 2 July 1990, the adjourned Kosovo assembly adopted a declaration proclaiming Kosovo a separate republican entity within Yugoslavia for an Albanian nation. Serbs reacted by suspending the Kosovo Assembly on 5 July 1990 and followed with a widespread purge of Albanian public employees and censorship of the Albanian media. The Albanians were undeterred and, on 7 September 1990, a secret meeting of their Assembly delegates took place. They adopted a constitution for a Sovereign Republic of Kosovo. Most of the Albanian delegates had to flee the country to avoid imprisonment and prosecution by Serbian authorities for illegitimate actions.

Albanians have since been forced to develop on their own parallel educational, cultural, and political structures to survive the strictures imposed by the Milošević regime, particularly during the years of wartime controls and deprivations. It is to be expected, however, that Serbian efforts to re-Serbianize Kosovo will play a critical role in the future of Kosovo, of Serbia, and of Albania, which is feared may intervene in defense of the Albanians in Kosovo.

According to the 1991 census, Serbia had a population of 9,721,177 with 5,753,825 in Serbia proper. These included 125,000 Muslims in the Sandžak area, 1,954,747 in Kosovo (of which 1,630,000 are Albanian), and 2,012,605 in Vojvodina, including 450,000 Hungarians and 100,000 Croats. The situation of the Hungarians in Vojvodina has become more precarious since the constitutional changes of 1990 abolished their minority rights and autonomy in the same way as was done in Kosovo. In addition, large numbers of Hungarians were forced to seek refuge in Hungary because of the war and intimidation by the numerous Serbian refugees from Croatia and Bosnia that have been resettled in Vojvodina. Any systematic increase in intimidation or of Bosnia-like atrocities as part of an ethnic cleansing operation against the Hungarian population would generate public opinion pressures on the Hungarian government to intervene in defense of its co-nationals igniting a further war. Serbia, however, knows that it could not repel the Hungarians in its current situation of near total exhaustion. In addition, Hungary could apply to Vojvodina the same historical possession argument Serbia used to justify its possession claims to the Kosovo region. Therefore, it is in the interest of Serbia to avoid any direct clash with Hungary.

The Sandžak region, the old Serbian Metohija, borders on Montenegro, Albania, Bosnia and Herzegovina, and the Kosovo province. Of its population of 440,000, about one-half is Muslim. They are culturally very similar to the Bosnian Muslims and therefore of suspect loyalty to Serbia. Serbia feels it must control the area that connects Serbia to Montenegro and the Adriatic Sea. Thus Serbia cannot afford to satisfy the autonomy claims of Sandžak, and has supported the Bosnian Serbs' ethnic cleansing of the Bosnian towns with Muslim majorities along the Drina River (Goražde and other towns) in order to also prevent their direct linking with the Sandžak Muslims.

Serbia finds itself in a very peculiar and dangerous situation. Through several past centuries the Serbian people have expanded their reach by forced mass migrations and wars that have contributed to the depopulation of its own cradle area—Kosovo. Now the Serbian claims to these lands are contested by neighboring states or other older populations. Serbia and Montenegro are isolated and facing adversary states. This situation does not bode well for Serbia's and Montenegro's futures if a spark from Kosovo ignites a conflagration with their neighbor states.

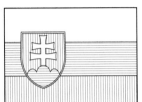

SLOVAKIA

Slovak Republic
Slovenska Republic

CAPITAL: Bratislava

FLAG: Horizontal bands of white (top), blue, and red superimposed with a crest of white double cross on three blue mountains.

ANTHEM: *Nad Tatru sa blyska (Over Tatra it lightens').*

MONETARY UNIT: The currency of the Slovak Republic is the Slovak koruna (Sk) consisting of 100 hellers, which replaced the Czechoslovak Koruna (Kcs) on 8 February 1993. There are coins of 10, 20, and 50 hellers and 1, 2, 5, and 10 korun, and notes of 20, 50, 100, 500, 1,000 and 5,000 korun.

WEIGHTS AND MEASURES: The metric system is the legal standard.

HOLIDAYS: New Year's Day, 1 January; Easter Monday, 4 April; May Day, 1 May; Anniversary of Liberation, 8 May; Day of the Slav Apostles, 5 July; Anniversary of the Slovak National Uprising, 29 August; Reconciliation Day, 1 November; Christmas, 24–26 December.

TIME: 1 PM = noon GMT.

¹LOCATION, SIZE, AND EXTENT

Slovakia is a landlocked country located in Eastern Europe. Comparatively, it is about twice the size of the state of New Hampshire with a total area of 48,845 sq km (18,859 sq mi). Slovakia shares boundaries with Poland (on the N), Ukraine (on the E), Hungary (on the S), and Austria and the Czech Republic (on the W), and has a total boundary length of 1,355 km (842 mi). Slovakia's capital city, Bratislava, is located on the southwestern border of the country.

²TOPOGRAPHY

The topography of Slovakia features rugged mountains in the central and northern part of the country, and lowlands in the south. The High Tatras (Tatry) mountains along the Polish border are interspersed between many lakes and deep valleys. Bratislava is situated in Slovakia's only substantial region of plains, where the Danube River forms part of the border with Hungary.

³CLIMATE

Slovakia's climate is continental, with hot summers and cold winters. In July the mean temperature is 21°C (70° F). January's mean temperature is –1°C (30°F). Rainfall averages roughly 49 cm (19.3 in) a year, and can exceed 200 cm (80 in) annually in the High Tatras.

⁴FLORA AND FAUNA

Over one-third of the land is forest. Some original steppe grassland areas can be found in Slovakia today. Mammals found in the country include fox, rabbits, and wild pig. A wide variety of birds inhabit the valleys of Slovakia. Carp, pike, and trout are found in the country's rivers, lakes, and streams.

⁵ENVIRONMENT

The Czech and Slovak Republics suffer from air, water, and land pollution caused by industry, mining, and agriculture. The air in both nations is contaminated by sulfur dioxide emissions trace-able, in large part, to the use of lignite as an energy source. In July 1986 annual emissions of sulfur dioxide were reported at 23.4 tons per sq km (60.6 tons per sq mi), the highest level in Europe. In the same year, a program of desulfurization was initiated by the government of the former Czechoslovakia, which earmarked Kcs2.9 billion during 1986–90 to combat pollution. Together, the Czech and Slovak republics contribute 0.7% of the world's total gas emissions, and lung cancer is prevalent in areas with the highest pollution levels.

The Czech and Slovak republics have a total of 6.7 cu mi of water, of which 9% is used for farming and 68% is used for industry; their cities produce 2.9 million tons of solid waste per year. Airborne emissions in the form of acid rain, combined with air pollution from Poland and the former GDR, have destroyed much of the forest in the northern part of the former Czechoslovakia; in 1994, 75% had been damaged by air pollution. Land erosion caused by agricultural and mining practices is also a significant problem.

The land has suffered from the loss of forest cover, erosion, and acid rain, with 75% of the trees and about 700,000 hectares (1,700,000 acres) of farmland affected. In 1994, 2 mammal species and 18 types of birds were endangered, and 29 types of plants were threatened with extinction.

⁶POPULATION

The population of Slovakia was 5,274,335 in 1991. The US Bureau of the Census projected a population of 5,432,383 for 1995 and 5,584,684 for 2000. The population density in 1991 was 107.5 per sq km (278.5 per sq mi). Bratislava, the capital, had a population of 442,197 in 1991. Košice had a population of 235,160.

⁷MIGRATION

Czechoslovakia received 5,782 immigrants in 1991, while emigrants totaled 3,896. There was no breakdown by region.

[8]ETHNIC GROUPS

The population was 85% Slovak in 1991. Hungarians, heavily concentrated in southern border areas, totaled 11.5%. Romany (Gypsies), came to 1.5%, Ruthenians, 1%, and Czechs, 1%. There were smaller numbers of Germans, Poles, and Ukrainians. The Gypsy population in eastern Slovakia is sizeable and underreported. Czechs have the option of dual citizenship.

[9]LANGUAGES

Slovak is the official language. It belongs to the western Slavic group and is written in the Roman alphabet. There are only slight diferences between Slovak and Czech, and the two are mutually intelligible. Slovak lacks the ě, ů, and ř in Czech but adds ä, ľ, ô, and ŕ. As in Czech, q, w, and x are found only in foreign words. A minority language like Hungarian may be used for official business if its speakers make up at least 20% of the population on the local level.

[10]RELIGIONS

The Slovak Republic was a strongly Catholic region, even during the period of communist repression of religion from 1944–89. In 1993 an estimated 74% of the population were Roman Catholics, although estimates vary widely, with some as low as 46%. Other churches with substantial memberships are the Slovak Evangelical Church of the Augsburg Confession (329,000 members in 1991) and the Orthodox Church (54,000 members in 1991). In the same year there were also 3,300 Jews, a remnant of what had been a much larger population prior to the Second World War.

[11]TRANSPORTATION

There were some 3,669 km (2,280 mi) of railroads in 1990, primarily consisting of the Bratislava-Košice route.

The road system totaled 17,737 km (11,022 mi) in 1992, including 601 km (373 mi) of express highways. In October 1992, the government announced plans to strengthen and widen about 300 km (185 mi) of main road during 1993–95.

As an inland country, Slovakia relies on the Danube for transportation of goods. Bratislava and Komárno are the major ports on the Danube, which connects with the European waterway system to Rotterdam and the Black Sea.

Air service in Slovakia is primarily through Ivanka Airport at Bratislava. In 1993, a joint Austrian-Slovakian airport project was proposed, involving cooperation between Vienna International Airport and Ivanka, which are only 50 km (31 mi) apart, in order to avoid harmful competition. In 1991, Ivanka Airport handled only 155,000 passengers, whereas Vienna International serviced about 6,000,000 passengers.

[12]HISTORY

The first known peoples of the territory of present-day Slovakia were Celts, who lived in the region about 50 BC. The Celts were pushed out by Slavs, who moved in from the east at the beginning of the modern era. A Frankish merchant named Samo formed the first unified state in the region in the mid-7th century. The Moravia Empire appeared in the 9th century, incorporating parts of present-day Slovakia. Although the first Christian missionaries active in the area were Orthodox (including the monks Cyril and Methodius, who introduced an alphabet of their own invention— still called Cyrillic—in which to write the Slavic languages), it was the Roman church that eventually established dominance. At the end of the 9th century the Magyars (Hungarians) began to move into Slovakia, incorporating the territory into their own. For many centuries the Hungarians treated the Slovaks as subject people, so it was not until the 13th century, when Hungary had been ravished by Tatar invasions, that the territory began to develop. Some contact with the Czechs, who speak a closely related language, began in the early 15th century, as refugees from the Hussite religious wars in Bohemia moved east.

After the Turkish victory at Mohacs in 1526 the Kingdom of Hungary was divided into three parts; so-called "Royal Hungary," which included Slovakia, was passed to the rule of the Hapsburg dynasty. Bratislava became the Hapsburg capital until the end of the 17th century, when the Turks were driven from Hungarian territory, and the Hungarian capital moved to Budapest. Although there was some religious spill-over of Protestantism from the west, Slovakia was solidly in control of the Catholic Counter-Reformation, establishing the long tradition of strong church influence in the region.

In the late 18th century the attempt of the Hapsburg rulers, especially Josef II (1765–1790), to Germanify the empire led to a rise in Hungarian nationalism, which in turn stimulated a rise in Slovak national self-consciousness. During the 1848 Revolution a program, "Demands of the Slovak Nation," was formulated, which called for the use of Slovak in schools, courts, and other settings, and demanded creation of a Slovak assembly. These demands were rejected, and the Hungarians continued their efforts to surpress Slovak nationalism. When the Austro-Hungarian Empire was formed in 1867, the Hungarians began a program of intense Magyarification. In the absence of a Slovak intellectual elite, nationalistic ideals were largely maintained by the local clergy.

When World War I began the Slovaks joined with the Czechs and other surpressed nationalities of the Austro-Hungarian Empire in pushing for their own state. Czech and Slovak immigrants in America were united in their efforts to prod the US to recognize a postwar combined Czech and Slovak state. The Czechs declared independence on 28 October 1918, and the Slovaks seceded from Hungary two days later, to create the Czecho-Slovak Republic.

The relationship between the two parts of the new state was never firmly fixed. The Czech lands were more developed economically, and Czech politicians dominated the political debate. Although they were supported by a portion of Slovak society, there remained a large constituency of Slovak nationalists, most of them in Jozef Tiso's People's Party, who wanted complete independence.

Attempts to deal with Slovak separatist sentiments occupied a good deal of legislative time during the first Czechoslovak Republic, particularly since economic development continued to favor the Czech lands over the Slovak.

In 1938 Adolph Hitler demanded that the Sudeten German area, in the Czech part of the country, be ceded to Germany. Rpreresentatives of Germany, Italy, France, and the UK met in Munich, without participation by Czechoslovakia, and decided that in order to achieve "peace in our time" Germany could occupy the Sudetenland, which it did in October 1938. Slovak nationalists argued that once the dismemberment of Czechoslovakia had begun, they too should secede, particularly because both Poland and Hungary also took advantage of the situation to seize parts of Slovakia. When Hitler's forces seized Prague in March 1939, a separate Slovak state was declared, which immediately fell under Nazi domination. Although nominally independent, the Slovakia of President Tiso was never more than a Nazi puppet.

During the war Slovak leaders like Stefan Osusky and Juraj Slavik cooperated with E. Benes' Czechoslovak government-in-exile, headquartered in London. There was also a small group of Slovak communists who took refuge in Moscow. In December 1943 a Slovak National Council was formed in opposition to the Tiso government, with both democratic and communist members. They began an uprising in Banska Bystrica in August 1944, which failed because of lack of support by both the West and the Soviet Union. When the war ended, the Slovak National Council took control of the country. Soviet attempts to use Slovak nation-

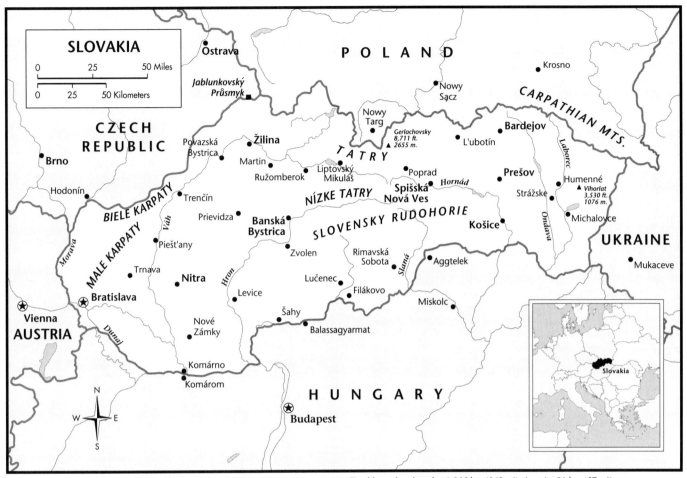

LOCATION: 47°44′ to 49°37′; 16°51′ to 22°34′E. **BOUNDARY LENGTHS:** Total boundary lengths, 1,355 km (842 mi); Austria, 91 km (57 mi); Czech Republic, 215 km (134 mi); Hungary, 515 km (320 mi); Poland, 444 km (276 mi); Ukraine, 90 km (56 mi).

alism as a tool of control failed in the 1946 elections, when non-communist parties received 63% of the vote. The communists switched their tactics to encouraging civil disorder and arresting people accused of participation in the wartime Slovak government. Tiso himself was executed in 1947.

Elsewhere in Czechoslovakia, the communists had been the largest vote-getters in the 1946 elections, but in 1948 it seemed that they might lose. Rather than risk the election, they organized a Soviet-backed coup, forcing President Benes to accept a government headed by Klement Gottwald, a communist. Benes resigned in June 1948, leaving the presidency open for Gottwald, while A. Zapotocky became prime minister.

Once Czechoslovakia became a People's Republic, and a faithful ally of the Soviet Union, a wave of purges and arrests rolled over the country, from 1949 to 1954. In 1952 a number of high officials, including Foreign Minister V. Clementis and R. Slansky, head of the Czech Communist Party, were hanged for "Tito-ism" and "national deviation."

Gottwald died in March 1953, a few days after Stalin, setting off the slow erosion of communist control. Zapotocky succeeded to the presidency, while A. Novotny became head of the party; neither had Gottwald's authority, and so clung even more tightly to the Stalinist methods which, after Nikita Khrushchev's secret denunciation of Stalin in 1956, had begun to be discredited even in the USSR. Novotny became president upon Zapotocky's death in 1957, holding Czechoslovakia in a tight grip until well into the 1960s.

Khrushchev's liberalization in the USSR encouraged liberals within the Czechoslovak party to try to emulate Moscow. Past abuses of the party, including the hanging of Slansky and Clementis, were repudiated, and Novotny was eventually forced to fire many of his most conservative allies, including Karol Bacilek, head of the Slovak Communist Party, and Viliam Siroky, premier for more than a decade. Slovaks detested both men because of their submission to Prague's continued policies of centralization, which in practice subordinated Slovak interests to those of the Czechs.

Alexander Dubček, the new head of the Slovak Communist Party, attacked Novotny at a meeting in late 1967, accusing him of undermining economic reform and ignoring Slovak demands for greater self-government. Two months later, in January 1968, the presidency was separated from the party chairmanship, and Dubček was named head of the Czechoslovak Communist Party, the first Slovak ever to hold the post.

Novotny resigned in March 1968, and Czechoslovakia embarked on a radical liberalization, which Dubček termed "socialism with a human face." The leaders of the other eastern bloc nations and the Soviet leaders viewed these developments with alarm. Delegations went back and forth from Moscow during the "Prague Spring" of 1968, warning of "counter-revolution." By July the neighbors' alarm had grown; at a meeting in Warsaw they issued a warning to Czechoslovakia against leaving the socialist camp. Although Dubček himself traveled to Moscow twice, in July and early August, to reassure Soviet party leader Brezhnev, the Soviets remained unconvinced.

Finally, on the night of 20–21 August 1968, military units from all the Warsaw Pact nations except Romania invaded Czechoslovakia, to "save it from counter-revolution." Dubček and other officials were arrested, and the country was placed under Soviet control. Difficulties in finding local officials willing to act as Soviet puppets caused the Soviets to play on Czech and Slovak antagonisms. On 31 December 1968 the country was made into a federative state, comprised of the Czech Socialist Republic and the Slovak Socialist Republic, each with its own legislature and government. In April Gustav Husak, once a reformer, but now viewing harmony with the USSR as the highest priority, was named head of the Czech Communist Party. A purge of liberals followed, and in May 1970 a new Soviet-Czechoslovak friendship treaty was signed; in June Dubček was expelled from the party.

Between 1970 and 1975 nearly one-third of the party was dismissed, as Husak consolidated power, re-establishing the priority of the federal government over its constituent parts and, in May 1975, reuniting the titles of party head and republic president.

Once again it was liberalization in the USSR which set off political change in Czechoslovakia. Husak ignored Soviet leader Mikhail Gorbachev's calls for perestroika and glasnost until 1987, when he reluctantly endorsed the general concept of Party reform, but delayed implementation until 1991. Aging and in ill health, Husak announced his retirement in December 1987, declaring that Milos Jakes would take his post; Jakes had been a life-long compromiser and accommodator who was unable to control dissenting factions within his party, which were now using the radical changes in the Soviet Union as weapons against one another.

Enthusiasm for political change was not as great in Slovakia as it was in the Czech west, where in November 1989 people had begun to gather on Prague's Wenceslas Square, demanding free elections. The so-called "velvet revolution" ended on 24 November, when Jakes and all his government resigned. Novotny resigned his presidency soon after.

Alexander Dubček was brought out of exile and put forward as a potential replacement, but the hostility of Czech intellectuals and activists, who felt that they had had to drag unwilling Slovaks into the new era, made it impossible to choose a Slovak as president. The choice fell instead on Vaclav Havel, a Czech playwright and dissident, who was named president by acclamation on 29 December 1989, while Dubček was named leader of the national assembly.

Dismantling the apparatus of a Soviet-style state began immediately, but economic change came more slowly, in part because elections were not scheduled until June 1990. The old struggle between Czechs and Slovaks intensified, as Slovaks grew increasingly to resist the programs of economic and political change being proposed in Prague. Slovak demands led to an almost immediate renaming of the country, as the Czech and Slovak Federal Republic.

In the June elections the Slovaks voted overwhelmingly for Public Against Violence, the Slovak partner of the Czech Civic Forum, which meant that economic transformation was begun. Again there was much greater enthusiasm for returning to private ownership in the west than there was in the east, intensifying Slovak separatism. In December 1990 the country's Federal Assembly attempted to defuse the problem by increasing the roles of the Czech and Slovak regional governments, but it also gave President Havel extraordinary powers, to head off attempts at Slovak secession. In Vladimir Meciar, the Slovak Premier, the nationalists found an articulate and persuasive voice for growing separatist sentiments.

During a visit to Bratislava in March 1991, President Havel was jeered by thousands of Slovaks, making obvious the degree of Slovak discontent. Meciar was replaced in April 1991, by Jan Carnogursky, but the easing of tensions was only temporary, since Carnogursky, too, favored an independent Slovakia.

Throughout 1991 and 1992 a struggle followed, with the Federal Assembly and president on one side, trying to devise ways of increasing the strength of the federal state, and the Czech and Slovak National Councils, or legislatures, on the other, seeking to shore up their own autonomy at the expense of the central authorities. Although polls indicated that most Slovaks continued to favor some form of union with the Czechs, the absence of any national figure able or willing to articulate what form that union might take, left the field to the separatists and the charismatic Meciar.

By June 1992 matters had reached a legislative impasse, so new federal elections were called. Slovakia chose to hold elections for its National Council at the same time. In July the new Slovak legislature issued a declaration of sovereignty and adopted a new constitution as an independent state, to take effect 1 January 1993.

In the federal election the vote split along national and regional lines, with the Czechs voting for right-of-center, reformist candidates, especially Vaclav Klaus's Civic Democratic Party, while the Slovaks voted for leftist and nationalist parties, especially Vladimir Meciar's Movement for a Democratic Slovakia. Although the federal government and President Havel continued to try to hold the state together, Czech Prime Minister Klaus made clear that the Czechs would offer no financial incentives or assistance to induce the Slovaks to remain in the union. Increasingly the republics began to behave as though they were already separate so that, for example, by the end of 1992, 25.2% of Czech industry had been privatized, while only 5.3% of Slovak industry had. By the end of 1992 it was obvious that separation was inevitable, so the two prime ministers, Klaus and Meciar, agreed to the so-called "velvet divorce," which took effect 1 January 1993. Czechs and Slovaks alike have objected that this move was never put to a popular referendum.

The new constitution created a 150-seat National Assembly, which elects the head of state, the president. Despite the strong showing of his party, Prime Minister Meciar was unable to get his first candidate through, and so put up Michal Kovac, a Dubček supporter and former Finance Minister in Slovakia, who had served as the last chairman of Czechoslovakia's federal parliament.

The Meciar government rejected the moves toward political and economic liberalization which the Czechs were pursuing, attempting instead to retain a socialist-style government, with strong central control. Swift economic decline, especially relative to the Czech's obviously growing prosperity, combined with Meciar's own erratic and autocratic manner, caused him to lose a vote of no-confidence in March 1994.

The new prime minister is Jozef Moravcik, representing a coalition of five parties, including Moravcik's Democratic Left Party (the former Communist Party), Common Choice, and the Christian Democratic Movement. New elections are scheduled for the end of September 1994, with polls putting Meciar's party slightly ahead of Moravcik's.

13 GOVERNMENT

The constitution which the Slovak National Assembly adopted in July 1992 calls for a unicameral legislature of 150 members. Voting is by party slate, with proportional seat allotment affecting the gains of the winner. Thus in the 1992 election Meciar's party gained 74 of the 150 seats, with only 36 percent of the popular vote. The government is formed by the leading party, or coalition of parties, and the prime minister is head of the government. Head of state is the president, who is elected by a three-fifths vote of the legislature. A continuing problem in Slovakia, as in the Czech republic, is that during the time the two states were joined, parties placed their best politicians in the federal assembly, rather than in the national assemblies, where power is presently centered.

14 POLITICAL PARTIES

There were 18 parties contesting the 150 seats of the National Assembly in the 1994 election, but only 7 or 8 were considered to be serious contenders, because of the necessity of receiving 5% of the total vote in order to take a seat. The single most popular party, with standings of 25% in opinion polls, is the Movement for a Democratic Slovakia, headed by V. Meciar, whom these polls also rank as the country's most popular politician. Common Choice, the strongest of the present coalition partners, is the second most popular party, with about 20%, while another coalition partner, the Christian Democratic Movement, also polls well. Combined with Prime Minister Moravcik's Democratic Left Party, the three could draw the 35% of the popular vote necessary to form a new coalition.

Meciar's most likely coalition partner, the Slovak National Party, which had almost 8% of the total vote in 1992, achieved its major goal with the formation of a separate state, and has since lost considerable following, so that it is not certain whether the party will clear the 5% representation "threshold." Another possible partner is the Association of Slovak Workers, currently polling about 6%; however, that party's leader, Jan Luptak, refuses to endorse either of the leading parties. There is also a Hungarian party, representing the country's approximately 60,000 Magyars, which is at about 11% in polls, but it is unlikely to join with Meciar, because of the ex-prime minister's earlier attempts to restrict Magyar cultural autonomy. At the same time, though, Muravcik has indicated that he will not entertain demands for greater Magyar self-rule either.

There is a small but persistent percentage of Slovak society which continues to honor the wartime Tiso government and its aims. Led by the Slovak National Unity Party, the Slovak People's Party, and the Association of Jozef Tiso, they have attempted such things as publicly marking the formation of the Tiso puppet state.

An important indicator of the current volatile state of Slovak politics, however, is a poll conducted in early 1994, which indicates that fully 50% of Slovaks support no parties and trust no politicians.

15 LOCAL GOVERNMENT

Slovakia is currently divided into 38 districts. The heads of these districts are appointed by the government, but were not expected to be politicized, since they have responsibilities for conducting elections and conducting censuses. However, the fall of the Meciar government moved some of these district heads to call for the resignation of President Kovac, whom they accused of having precipitated the crisis which brought about the vote of no-confidence. This in turn led the Muravcik government to replace 26 district chiefs, which opponents called a political purge. It seems likely that this weakness in the structure of local authority will be addressed by the new National Assembly.

16 JUDICIAL SYSTEM

The judicial system consists of a republic-level Supreme Court; regional courts in Bratislava, Banská Bystrica, and Kosice; and 38 local courts responsible for individual districts. The courts have begun to form specialized sections, including commercial, civil, and criminal branches.

The highest judicial body, the 10-judge Constitutional Court in Kosice, reviews the constitutionality of laws as well as the decisions of lower level courts and national and local government bodies.

The constitution declares the independence of the judiciary from the other branches of government. The Parliament appoints judges to the highest court while the Minister of Justice appoints others on the recommendation of their peers. Judges are appointed for life.

Defendants in criminal cases have the right to free legal counsel and are guaranteed a fair and open public trial.

17 ARMED FORCES

Because they are still in the process of reorganization, the armed forces of Slovakia cannot be described in detail at this time, but will probably include an active duty army and air force, recruited through conscription, of perhaps 80,000, armed with Warsaw Pact weapons and supplemented by East European paramilitary border guards and militarized police numbering perhaps 10,000.

18 INTERNATIONAL COOPERATION

Slovakia is a member of the UN, which it joined in 1993 when Czechoslovakia agreed to split into two parts. The country is a member of GATT, ICAO, IDA, IFC, ILO, IMF, ITU, UNESCO, UNIDO, UPU, WHO, WIPO, and the World Bank. The country's sovereignty is recognized by the US, the EC countries, and many other nations. It has diplomatic relations with the US and EC countries.

19 ECONOMY

The economy of the Slovak Republic is highly industrialized, although the industrial structure is less developed than that of the Czech Republic. In 1991, industry accounted for about 58% of GDP, and agriculture—which had been the largest sector of the economy before the rapid industrialization of the communist era—accounted for only about 7% of GDP and 11% of employment. Slovakia has extensive forest resources, and prospects for tourism in the 1990s are good.

20 INCOME

In 1992, Slovakia's GNP was $10,249 million at current prices, or $1,920 per capita. For the period 1985–92 the average inflation rate was 7.6%, resulting in a real growth rate in per capita GNP of –7.0%.

It is estimated that in 1991 agriculture, hunting, forestry, and fishing contributed 6% to GDP; mining and quarrying, 1%; manufacturing, 33%; electricity, gas, and water, 5%; construction, 4%; wholesale and retail trade, 10%; transport, storage, and communication, 6%; finance, insurance, real estate, and business services, 21%; community, social, and personal services, 2%; and other sources, 13%.

21 LABOR

Agriculture and industry accounted for 11% and 43% of employment, respectively, in 1991. In 1992, there were 317,261 private entrepreneurs registered in Slovakia, of whom 18.8% did business in the industrial sector, 20.2% in construction, and 54.5% in trade, services, and tourism. Registered unemployment was estimated at 370,000 persons, or 14.5% in 1993 (a 39.4% increase from 1992). About 78% of all workers are members of one of Slovakia's 22 unions.

22 AGRICULTURE

Agriculture contributed 5.6% to GDP in 1992, down from 7% in 1991, when it accounted for 11% of employment. Some 43% of the total land area is under cultivation. In 1990, there were 680 cooperatives spread out over 1,080,733 hectares (2,670,500 acres); 73 state farms utilized 226,313 hectares (559,220 acres).

Important crops in Slovakia in 1990 (in thousands of tons) included: wheat, 2,083; rye, 178; corn, 370; barley, 914; potatoes, 779; and sugar beets, 1,581. In 1990, 36,912 tractors and 6,536 combines were in use; the agricultural work force numbered nearly 351,000 persons.

Barley and hops are important agricultural exports of the new republic; fruit, wine, and seed oil are also produced for export.

23 ANIMAL HUSBANDRY

Some 808,000 hectares (1,996,500 acres) of land are classified as meadows and pastures, representing 16.5% of the total area. In

1990, there were some 1,563,000 head of cattle, 2,521,000 pigs, 16,478,000 chickens, 600,000 sheep, and 14,000 horses. The government is seeking to expand the development of livestock farming.

24FISHING

Fishing is only a minor source of the domestic food supply. Production comes mostly from mountain streams and stocked ponds. Some of the rivers and ponds near Bratislava are polluted with chemicals and petrochemical seepings, impairing the growth of fish stocks regionally.

25FORESTRY

Forests have been severely damaged by acid rain from coal-fired power stations. Slovakian forest product exports include paper, wood, and furniture. In 1990, paper production amounted to 333,649 tons. Forests cover an estimated 40% of Slovakia.

26MINING

Nonfuel mineral resources include antimony ore, mercury, iron ore, copper, lead, zinc, precious metals, magnesite, limestone, dolomite, gravel, brick soils, ceramic materials, and stonesalt.

Metallurgy represents one-seventh of the total industrial production. The government is seeking foreign investment for magnesite industry development, special ceramics production, and for the establishment of a new salt excavation and processing plant. In 1993, the EBRD Development Project approved a $110 million loan and $15 million equity investment to finance the modernization of the aluminum industry.

27ENERGY AND POWER

Over 50% of total electricity production is generated by nuclear power plants. As of 1992, of the total 5,666,000 kw of electrical generating capacity, nuclear plants accounted for 1,760,000 kw; thermal power plants, 1,990,000 kw; and hydroelectric plants, 1,916,000 kw. Slovensky Energeticky Podnik (SEP) is a state-owned enterprise which is the dominant producer and provider of electricity; its transmission system includes 1,519 km (943 mi) of high voltage lines with 14 substations, and 964 km (196 mi) of standard voltage lines with 11 substations.

In November 1993, the Gabcikovo Project began operating. Originally begun as a joint project with Hungary in 1977, it was delayed when all construction stopped in October 1989, because Hungary perceived it as environmentally hazardous to the Danube basin. By May 1992, Hungary agreed to a compromise which allowed the project's completion. The power station has eight Kaplan turbines and generators with an installed capacity of 720,000 kw, enough to satisfy peak demands.

Coal mining produces some 4.6 million tons per year, mostly from Prievidza. There are petroleum refineries at Bratislava, Strážske, and Zvolen.

28INDUSTRY

Major industries include heavy engineering, armaments, iron and steel production, non-ferrous metals, and chemicals.

29SCIENCE AND TECHNOLOGY

The Slovak Academy of Sciences, founded in 1953, has departments of technical sciences and natural sciences, and 33 affiliated learned societies. Eight universities offer scientific and technical degrees.

30DOMESTIC TRADE

In the communist period, virtually the entire internal trade network was within the socialized sector. Marketing and distribution, including price-fixing, were controlled by the federal government; administration on the lower levels was handled by the national committees. Cooperative farms sold the bulk of their produce to the state at fixed prices, but marginal quantities of surplus items were sold directly to consumers through so-called free farmers' markets. Starting in 1958, the government operated a program of installment buying for certain durable consumer goods, with state savings banks granting special credits. Most retail transactions, however, were for cash.

Retail trade is currently undergoing rapid privatization along with other sectors of the economy. More than 20,000 shops, restaurants, and workshops in both the Czech and Slovak republics were transferred to private owners by public auction in a wave of "small" privatization.

31FOREIGN TRADE

The Czech Republic accounts for roughly half of Slovakia's foreign trade. Trade with the former Soviet Union has declined in importance and has been increasingly replaced by OECD trade, which accounts for almost half of all Slovak exports.

32BALANCE OF PAYMENTS

The Slovak Republic's balance of payments showed a deficit of Sk1.3 billion in November 1992, far less than the deficit of Sk7.2 billion in November 1991. In 1992, imports exceeded exports by $400 million. The current account deficit stood at an estimated $200 million in 1992; foreign exchange reserves amounted to $130 million in mid-1993.

33BANKING AND SECURITIES

Four years after the Soviet system relinquished control over the eastern bloc, Slovakia formed a national bank. In January 1992 the banking system of Czechoslovakia was split. From that point on the National Bank of Slovakia was charged with the responsibility of circulating currency and regulating the banking sector. There are 12 commercial banks in the Slovak Republic, including the Investment and Development Bank (1992); People's Bank (1992); Postal Bank Inc. (1991); Industrial Bank, Inc. (1992); First Commercial Bank Inc. (1993); Slovak Credit Bank (1993); Slovak Agricultural Bank (1991); and the General Credit Bank (1990). The Bratislava Stock Exchange opened on 8 July 1990 and acts as a share holding company formed by all Slovakian financial institutions, banks and savings banks, and companies authorized to trade securities. Brokers and other mediators are not permitted in the trading system. The Bratislava Option and Futures Exchange was expected to open in 1994.

34INSURANCE

The pre-World War II insurance companies and institutions of the former Czechoslovakia were reorganized after 1945 and merged, nationalized, and centralized. Starting in 1952, the insurance industry has been administered by the State Insurance Office, under the jurisdiction of the Ministry of Finance, and two enterprises conducted insurance activities, the Czech and the Slovak Insurance Enterprises of the State.

As of 1993, health insurance was paid for by the state. Health insurance benefits expenditures amounted to Sk13.4 billion in 1993.

35PUBLIC FINANCE

Since the dissolution of Czechoslovakia, the Slovak government has implemented several measures to compensate for the large loss of fiscal transfers it received from the Federation, which were equivalent to between Sk20–25 billion in 1992. The Slovak government's initial budget was balanced at the beginning of 1992, with revenues and expenditures equivalent to Sk159 billion. Decreased subsidies, personnel layoffs, streamlining of social benefits, and the delay of investment projects helped reduce the budget by about 7% of GDP during 1992. During the first quarter of

1993, however, the budget was in deficit at about 4% of GDP. Further expenditure reductions and improved tax administration and collection were planned as a result. The external debt as of mid-1993 stood at $3.1 billion.

36TAXATION
The principal taxes are corporate income tax, personal income tax, and value-added tax. Individuals are liable for tax on all sources of worldwide income. Corporate income tax is levied on joint stock companies, limited liability companies, and limited partnerships. Owners of real estate are subject to an annual capital tax.

37CUSTOMS AND DUTIES
As a GATT signatory, Slovakia uses the Brussels Tariff Nomenclature. Goods imported into Slovakia are liable to three kinds of charges: customers duties, value-added tax, and excise tax. Duties for EC- and EFTA-source goods have been reduced under 1992 Association Agreements.

38FOREIGN INVESTMENT
Direct foreign investment totaled US$72 million in 1992, and total foreign investment amounted to $346.3 million as of September 1993, with the greatest percentage coming from Austria. The government is introducing tax incentives to attract more capital from abroad.

39ECONOMIC DEVELOPMENT
The government is expected to slow economic reforms due to the social burden imposed by the transformation to a market economy. Anticipated measures include stimulation of demand through price subsidies and public spending. Slovakia's most successful structural reform has been privatization. The first stage of large-scale privatization included 751 companies, and a second stage, which will involve 650 medium- and large-scale enterprises, was expected to be implemented by late 1993.

40SOCIAL DEVELOPMENT
Slovak law guarantees the equality of all citizens and prohibits discrimination. Health care, retirement benefits, and other social services are provided regardless of race, sex, religion, or disability.

Women and men are equal under the law, enjoying the same property, inheritance, and other rights, and receiving equal pay for equal work. The Democratic Union of Slovakia, the nation's largest women's organization, monitors observance of women's rights. Other women's groups include the Council of Women, the Slovak Women's Center, and the Federation of Women for World Peace. Despite legal safeguards, the small number of women in private and public leadership roles is evidence of continuing cultural barriers to full equality.

41HEALTH
Life expectancy in 1992 was 72 years, and infant mortality was 12 per 1,000 live births. In the same year, there were 79,000 births. Immunization rates for children up to 1 year old in 1992 were impressively high: tuberculosis (91%); diphtheria, pertussis, and tetanus (99%); polio (99%); and measles (96%). The country had 17,419 physicians in 1992 and 61,573 hospital beds.

42HOUSING
In 1992, the Slovak Association of Towns and Villages, comprised of some 2,000 towns, was engaged in recovering all housing units from former state administration authorities. With a shortage of 500,000 flats, the Slovak Republic planned to build 200,000 new flats by the year 2000. As of 1992, 80,000 people were waiting for flats.

43EDUCATION
Slovakia has an estimated adult literacy rate of 99%. Education is compulsory for 10 years, approximately up to the age of 18. Elementary education lasts for eight years followed by secondary education, which is provided in general or specialized and technical schools. In the school year 1989–90, approximately 721,687 children attended the elementary schools. Nearly 55,648 pupils attended the 132 general secondary schools while 237,130 pupils attended the 493 specialized and technical secondary schools.

Slovakia has 13 universities, with the oldest being Cornenius (Komensky) University in Bratislava. The Pavel Josef Šafařík University, founded in 1959, is in Košice. In 1989–90, nearly 54,350 students were enrolled at the universities.

44LIBRARIES AND MUSEUMS
The most important library in Slovakia is the Slovak National Library (4.9 million volumes), founded in 1863 and located at Martin. In 1992, some 715,000 registered readers averaged 32 book loans each from Slovakia's 2,682 public libraries. Some 60 museums had 2,172,400 visitors in 1992.

45MEDIA
Local and long-distance telephone, telegraph, and telex services are available. There is one radio station (Slovak Radio Bratislava) and one television station (Slovak Television). In 1992, radio and television broadcasting amounted to 24,600 and 8,720 hours, respectively. There are 12 major daily newspapers in Bratislava and one each in Kosice and Banská Bysterica.

The following table lists major newspapers, their publishers, and estimated 1991 circulations:

	PUBLISHER	CIRCULATION
BRATISLAVA		
Práca	Slovak Trades Union Council	230,000
Smena	Socialist Union of Youth	132,000

46ORGANIZATIONS
There are 17 trade unions in Slovakia including Trade Union Workers groups in the construction, energy, food processing, and glass industries. Important non-parliamentary political organizations in the country are the Green Party, the Democratic Party, and the Conservative Democrats Party. There are 13 academic organizations of higher learning in Slovakia including the Comenius University in Bratislava.

47TOURISM, TRAVEL, AND RECREATION
Slovakia's outdoor tourist attractions include mountains (the most famous being the High and Low Tatras), forest, cave formations, and over 1,000 mineral and hot springs. In addition, tourists can visit ancient castles, monuments, chateaux, museums, and galleries. In 1991, over 15 million foreign visitors arrived in Slovakia and spent an estimated US$135 million. There are over 1,000 hotels in Slovakia. All visitors are required to have valid passports.

48FAMOUS SLOVAKS
Ján Kollár (1793–1852), writer, poet, Slavist, and archaeologist, was a Slovak patriot who championed the Slav struggle against foreign oppression. Ludovít Štúr (1815–56) is the founder of the Slovak literary language and modern Slovak literature. Founder of scientific Slavic studies was Pavel Josef Šafačrík (1795–1861), whose *Slavonic Antiquities* had great scholarly influence. Andrej Hlinka (1864–1938) led the Slovak Catholic autonomist movement. The greatest Slovak poet, Pavel Hviezdoslav (1849–1921), translated foreign poetry, refined the language, and contributed to Slovak awakening. The Robin Hood of the Slovaks, Juraj Jánošík (1688–1713), fought the Hungarians. Milan Rastislav Štefánik

(1880–1919), military leader, astronomer, and ally of Tomáš Masaryk, represented the Slovaks in their struggle for liberty. Alexander Dubček (1921-92) was first secretary of the Czechoslovak Communist Party (1968-69). His attempt to increase civil liberties led to the invasion of Czechoslovakia by the Warsaw Pact in 1968. In 1989 he was elected the Federal Assembly's first speaker.

⁴⁹DEPENDENCIES
Slovakia has no territories or colonies.

⁵⁰BIBLIOGRAPHY

Fogel, Daniel S. (ed.). *Managing in Emerging Market Economies: Cases from the Czech and Slovak Republics.* Boulder, Co.: Westview Press, 1994.

Jelinek, Yeshayahu A. *The Parish Republic: Hlinka's Slovak People's Party: 1939–1945.* New York: Columbia University Press, 1976.

Johnson, Owen V. *Slovakia, 1918–1938: Education and the Making of a Nation.* New York: Columbia University Press, 1985.

Magocsi, Paul R. *The Rusyns of Slovakia: An Historical Survey.* New York: Columbia University Press, 1993.

Mikus, Joseph A. *Slovakia and the Slovaks.* Washington, D.C.: Three Continents Press, 1977.

Palickar, Stephen Joseph. *Slovakian Culture in the Light of History, Ancient, Medieval and Modern.* Cambridge, Mass., Hampshire Press, 1954.

Steiner, Eugen. *The Slovak Dilemma.* Cambridge, Eng.: Cambridge University Press, 1973.

SLOVENIA

Republic of Slovenia
Republika Slovenije

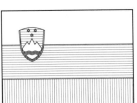

CAPITAL: Ljubljana

FLAG: Equal horizontal bands of white (top), blue, and red with seal superimposed on upper hoist side.

ANTHEM: *Zive naj vsi narodi.* (The anthem begins, "Let all nations live . . .")

MONETARY UNIT: The currency of Slovenia is the tolar (Slt), which consists of 100 stotinov. There are coins of 50 stotinov and 1, 2, and 5 tolars, and notes of 10, 20, 50, and 200 tolars.

WEIGHTS AND MEASURES: The metric system is in force.

HOLIDAYS: New Year, 1–2 January; Prešeren Day, Day of Culture, 8 February; Resistance Day, 27 April; Labor Days, 1–2 May; National Statehood Day, 25 June; Assumption, 15 August; Reformation Day, 31 October; All Saints' Day, 1 November; Christmas Day, 25 December; Independence Day, 26 December. Movable holidays are Easter Sunday and Monday.

TIME: 1 PM = noon GMT.

¹LOCATION, SIZE, AND EXTENT

Slovenia is located in central Europe. Slovenia is slightly larger than the state of New Jersey with a total area of 20,296 sq km (7,836 sq mi). Slovenia shares boundaries with Austria (north), Hungary (east), Croatia (south), and the Adriatic Sea and Italy (west), and has a total boundary length of 1,998 km (1,196 mi). Slovenia's capital city, Ljubljana, is located near the center of the country.

²TOPOGRAPHY

The topography of Slovenia features a small coastal strip on the Adriatic, an alpine region adjacent to Italy, and mixed mountains and valleys with numerous rivers in the east.

Slovenia's natural resources include lignite coal, lead, zinc, mercury, uranium, and silver. Approximately ten percent of Slovenia's land is arable.

³CLIMATE

Slovenia's climate is Mediterranean on the coast, and continental with mild to hot summers and cold winters in the plateaus and valleys to the east. July's mean temperature is 22°C (72°F). The mean temperature in January is 1°C (31°F). Rainfall averages 62 cm (24 in) a year.

⁴FLORA AND FAUNA

The region's climate has given Slovenia a wealth of diverse flora and fauna. Ferns, flowers, mosses, and common trees populate the landscape. There are subtropical plants along the Adriatic Sea. Wild animals include deer, brown bear, rabbit, fox, and wild boar. About half of Slovenia is mountainous; mainly, the mountains are located in the central and eastern part of the country. Farmers plant vineyards on the hillsides and raise livestock in the fertile lowlands of the country.

⁵ENVIRONMENT

The Sava River is polluted with domestic and industrial waste; heavy metals and toxic chemicals can be found along coastal water near Koper. Metallurgical and chemical emissions have exacerbated forest damage.

⁶POPULATION

Slovenia's natural environment suffers from damage to forests from industrial pollutants, water pollution, and is subject to flooding and earthquakes. The population of Slovenia was 1,974,839 in 1991, a 4.4% increase from the 1981 figure of 1,891,864. A population of 2.1 million was projected by the World Bank for 2010, based on a crude birth rate of 13 per 1,000 people, a crude death rate of 10, and a net natural increase of 3. The population density in 1991 was 97.5 per sq km (252.5 per sq mi). Ljubljana, the capital, had a population of 276,133 in 1991. Maribor had a population of 108,122.

⁷MIGRATION

In 1990, the number of immigrants was 6,842 and the number of emigrants, 4,720. Slovenia was harboring 47,000 refugees at the end of 1992. Most of them were from other republics of the former Yugoslavia.

⁸ETHNIC GROUPS

In 1991, the population was 88% Slovene. Croats comprised 3%, Serbs, 2%, and Muslim, 1%.

⁹LANGUAGES

Like Serbo-Croatian, Macedonian, and Bulgarian, Slovene is a language of the southern Slavic group. It is closest to Serbo-Croatian, but the two are not mutually intelligible. Slovene is written in the Roman alphabet and has the special letters č, š, and ž. The letters *q, w, x,* and *y* are missing.

¹⁰RELIGIONS

The former Socialist Republic of Slovenia, a member of the Yugoslav federation, became an independent nation in 1991. The largest denominational group is the Roman Catholic Church, estimated in 1993 at 84% of the population. There is also a Slovenian Old Catholic Church and some Eastern Orthodox. Although Calvinism played an important role here during the Reformation, the only well-established Protestant group is the Evangelical Lutheran Church of Slovenia, with some 18,900 members in 1993.

11TRANSPORTATION

Rail lines, emanating from Ljubljana, connect the capital to Kranj and Jesenice, Postojna and Novo Gorica, Celje and Maribor, and Nova Mesto before continuing to Austria, Italy, and Croatia. As of March 1993, there were some 1,200 km (750 mi) of railway tracks. With over 150 passenger stations and 140 freight stations, almost every town in Slovenia can be reached by train. Slovenian Railways uses high-speed trains and container transports.

In 1991, Slovenia had 14,553 km (9,043 mi) of roads, 72% of which were paved. Slovenia has two expressways: one extends 56 km (35 mi), connecting Ljubljana, Postojna, and Razdrto with the coastal region; the other is 25 km (16 mi) long and links Ljubljana with Kranj and the Gorenjska region in the northwest and with the Karawanken tunnel to Austria.

The principal marine port is Koper. There is no merchant fleet per se, but Slovenian owners control 21 vessels (1,000 GRT or over) totaling 334,995 GRT, all registered under St. Vincent and the Grenadines (a flag of convenience).

12HISTORY

Origins and Middle Ages

Slovenia has the unique distinction of being located in the central European area where Latin Germanic, Slavic, and Magyar people have come into contact with one another. The historical dynamics of these four different groups have heavily impacted the development and rather miraculous survival of a small nation in a geopolitically strategic area.

Traditional scholarship considers the Slovenes part of the large group of Slavic nations deriving their name from the ancient Slavic tribes that migrated from their ancestral lands north to the Novgorod area of Russia, west to northern Germany, and then south to the eastern Alps and the Adriatic Sea. More recent researchers, however, connect the origins of the Slovenes to the ancient *Venedi* people that populated the area of the Alps since 1200 BC.

Unlike most of the invading tribes that contributed to the demise of the Roman Empire and were consequently absorbed into the Romanized populations, the Slavs maintained their identity and territories they had conquered, except for some of the farthest areas of expansion such as Greece, central Germany, and Austria. Up to the 8th–9th centuries AD, Slavs used the same common Slavic language that was codified by St. Cyril and Methodius in their AD 863 translations of Holy Scriptures into the Slavic tongue. Later variations brought about the current large number of Slavic languages that identify the east, west, and south Slavic nations. The Germanic expansion towards eastern lands reduced considerably the territorial extent of the Slavs in Central Europe, particularly of the Serbs, Poles, and Slovenes. In this case Christianization also meant Germanization and the peoples most exposed to it were the westernmost Serbs (old White Serbs) of Saxony and the Slovenes. During this period of conversion and conquest, the Slovenes lost about two-thirds of their 9th century territory that extended from Vienna to Linz and the sources of the Drava and Mura rivers in Austria, the Friuli Plains in Italy and the Adriatic Sea, Lake Balaton in Hungary, and the current borders with Croatia.

Essentially an agricultural people, the Slovenes settled from around AD 550 in the Roman Noricum area of the eastern Alps known as Carantania and in the western Pannonian Plains. The ancestors of today's Slovenes developed their own form of politi-

cal organization in which power was delegated to their rulers through an "electors" group of peasant leaders/soldiers (the "Kosezi"). Part of the Slavic Kingdom of Samo in the mid-7th century, Carantania continued its existence as a Duchy of the Slovenes after Samo's death in AD 659 and included, in addition to Carinthia, the regions of Styria, Carniola, and parts of the Littoral region. Allies of the Bavarians against the Avars whom they defeated in AD 743, the Carantania Slovenes came under control of the numerically stronger Bavarians and both were overtaken by the Franks in AD 745. The ancestors of the Slovenes who had settled in the Pannonian area maintained their independence longer and established a principality of their own along the Mura and Drava rivers and north to Lake Balaton.

In 863, the Greek scholars Constantine (Cyril) and Methodius were sent to Moravia, having first developed an original alphabet (called "Glagolitic") and translated the necessary Holy Scriptures into the Slavic tongue of the time. The work of the two "Apostles of the Slavs" was opposed by the Frankish Bishops who accused them of teaching heresy and using a non-sacred language and script. Invited by Pope Nicholas I to Rome to explain their work, the brothers visited with the Slovene Prince Kocelj in 867 and took along some 50 young men to be instructed in the Slavic scriptures and liturgy that were competing with the traditionally "sacred" liturgical languages of Latin and Greek. Political events prevented the utilization of the Slavic language in Central European Churches with the exception of Croatia and Bosnia. However, the liturgy in Slavic spread among Balkan and Eastern Slavs. Slovenes view the installation of the Dukes of Carinthia with great pride as the expression of a non-feudal, bottom-up delegation of authority—by the people's "electors" through a ceremony inspired by olf Slavic egalitarian customs. All the people assembled would intone a Slovene hymn of praise—"Glory and praise to God Almighty, who created heaven and earth, for giving us and our land the Duke and master according to our will."

This ceremony lasted for 700 years with some feudal accretions and was conducted in the Slovenian language until the last one in 1414. The uniqueness of the Carinthian installation ceremony is confirmed by several sources, including medieval reports, the writing of Pope Pius II in 1509, and its recounting in Jean Bodin's *Treatise on Republican Government* (1576) as "unrivaled in the entire world." In fact, Thomas Jefferson's copy of Bodin's *Republic* contains Jefferson's own initials calling attention to the description of the Carinthian installation and therefore, to its conceptual impact on the writer of the American Declaration of Independence.

The eastward expansion of the Franks in the 9th century brought all Slovene lands under Frankish control. Carantania then lost its autonomy and, following the 955 victory of the Franks over the Hungarians, the Slovene lands were organized into separate frontier regions. This facilitated their colonization by German elements while inhibiting any effort at unifying the shrinking Slovene territories. Under the feudal system, various families of mostly Germanic nobility were granted fiefdoms over Slovene lands and competed among themselves bent on increasing their holdings.

The Bohemian King Premysl Otokar II was an exception, and attempted to unite the Czech, Slovak, and Slovene lands in the second half of the 13th century. Otokar II acquired the Duchy of Austria in 1251, Styria in 1260, and Carinthia, Carniola, and Istria in 1269, thus laying the foundation for the future Austrian empire. However, Otokar II was defeated in 1278 by a Hapsburg-led coalition that conquered Styria and Austria by 1282. The Hapsburgs, of Swiss origin, grew steadily in power and by the 15th century became the leading Austrian feudal family in control of most Slovene lands.

Christianization and the feudal system had supported the Germanization process and created a society divided into "haves"

SLOVENIA

LOCATION: 46°15′N; 15°10′E. **BOUNDARY LENGTHS:** Total boundary lengths, 999 km (621 mi); Austria 262 km (161 mi); Croatia, 455 km (238 mi); Italy, 199 km (124 mi); Hungary, 83 km (52 mi).

(German) and "have nots" (Slovene) elements, which were further separated into the nobility/urban dwellers versus the Slovene peasants/serfs. The Slovenes were deprived of their original, egalitarian "Freemen" rights and subjected to harsh oppression of economic, social, and political nature. The increasing demands imposed on the serfs due to the feudal lords' commitment in support of the fighting against the Turks and the suffering caused by Turkish invasions led to a series of insurrections by Slovene and Croat peasants in the 15th to 18th centuries, cruelly repressed by the feudal system.

Reformation

The Reformation gave an impetus to the national identity process through the efforts of Protestant Slovenes to provide printed materials in the Slovenian language in support of the Reformation movement itself. Martin Luther's translation of the New Testament into German in 1521 encouraged translations into other vernaculars, including the Slovenian. Thus Primož Trubar, a Slovenian Protestant preacher and scholar, published the first *Catechism* in Slovenian in 1551 and, among other works, a smaller elementary grammar (*Abecedarium*) of the Slovenian language in 1552. These works were followed by the complete Slovenian translation of the Bible by Jurij Dalmatin in 1578, printed in 1584. The same year Adam Bohorič published, in Latin, the first comprehensive grammar of the Slovenian language that was also the first published grammar of any Slavic language. A first Slovenian publishing house (1575) and a Jesuit

College (1595) were established in Ljubljana, the central Slovenian city and between 1550 and 1600 over fifty books in Slovenian were published. In addition, Primož Trubar and his coworkers encouraged the opening of Slovenian elementary and high schools. This sudden explosion of literary activity built the foundation for the further development of literature in Slovenian and its use by the educated classes of Slovenes. The Catholic Counter-Reformation reacted to the spread of Protestantism very strongly within Catholic Austria, and slowed down the entire process until the Napoleonic period. Despite these efforts, important cultural institutions were established, such as an Academy of Arts and Sciences (1673) and the Philharmonic Society in 1701 (perhaps the oldest in Europe).

The Jesuits, heavily involved in the Counter-Reformation, had to use religious literature and songs in the Slovene language, but generally Latin was used as the main language in Jesuit schools. However, some first Catholic books in Slovenian were issued by 1615 to assist priests in the reading of Gospel passages and delivery of sermons in Slovenian. The Protestant books in Slovenian were used for such purposes and they thus assisted in the further development of a standard literary Slovenian. Since Primož Trubar used his dialect from the Carniola region, it heavily influenced the literary standard. From the late 17th and through the 18th century the Slovenes continued their divided existence under Austrian control. But with the lessened Turkish threat more normal life was possible with much greater attention to economic progress and trade.

Standing over trade routes connecting the German/Austrian hinterland to the Adriatic Sea and the Italian plains eastward into the Balkan region, the Slovenes partook of the benefits from such trade in terms of both economic and cultural enrichment. Thus by the end of the 18th century, a significant change occurred in the urban centers where an educated Slovene middle class came into existence. Deeply rooted in the Slovene peasantry, this element ceased to assimilate into the Germanized mainstream and began to assert its own cultural/national identity. Many of their sons were educated in German, French, and Italian universities and thus exposed to the influence of the Enlightenment. Such a person was, for instance, Baron Ziga Zois (1749–1819), an industrialist, landowner and linguist, who became the patron of the Slovene literary movement. When the ideas of the French Revolution spread through Europe and the Napoleonic conquest reached the Slovenes, they were ready to embrace them.

During the reign of Maria Teresa (1740–80) and Joseph II (1780–90), the influence of Jansenism—the emancipation of serfs, the introduction of public schools (in German), equality of religions, closing of monasteries not involved in education or tending to the sick—weakened the hold of the nobility. On the other hand, the stronger Germanization emphasis generated resistance to it from an awakening Slovene national consciousness and the publication of Slovene non-religious works, such as Marko Pohlin's *Abecedika* (1765), a *Carniolan Grammar* (1783) with explanations in German, and other educational works in Slovenian, including a Slovenian-German-Latin dictionary (1781). Pohlin's theory of metrics and poetics became the foundation of secular poetry in Slovenian, that, only fifty years later, reached its zenith with France Prešeren (1800–1849), still considered the greatest Slovene poet. Just prior to the short Napoleonic occupation of Slovenia, the first Slovenian newspaper was published in 1797 by Valentin Vodnik (1758–1819), a very popular poet and grammarian. The first drama in Slovenian appeared in 1789 by Anton Tomaž Linhart (1756–1795), playwright and historian of Slovenes and South Slavs. Both authors were members of Baron Zois' circle.

Napoleon and the Spring of Nations

When Napoleon defeated Austria and established his Illyrian Provinces (1809–13) comprising the southern half of the Slovenian lands, parts of Croatia, and Dalmatia all the way to Dubrovnik with Ljubljana as the capital, the Slovene language was encouraged in the schools and also used, along with French, as an official language in order to communicate with the Slovene population. The four-year French occupation served to reinforce the national awakening of the Slovenes and other nations that had been submerged through the long feudal era of the Austrian Empire. Austria, however, regained the Illiryan Provinces in 1813 and reestablished its direct control over the Slovene lands.

The 1848 "spring of nations" brought about various demands for national freedom of Slovenes and other Slavic nations of Austria. An important role was played by Jernej Kopitar with his influence as librarian/censor in the Imperial Library in Vienna, as the developer of Slavic studies in Austria, as the mentor to Vuk Karadžić (one of the founders of the contemporary Serbo-Croatian language standard), as the advocate of Austro-Slavism (a state for all Slavs of Austria), and as author of the first modern Slovenian grammar in 1808. In mid-May 1848, the "United Slovenia" manifesto demanded that the Austrian Emperor establish a Kingdom of Slovenia with its own Parliament, consisting of the then separate historical regions of Carniola, Carinthia, Styria, and the Littoral, with Slovenian as its official language. This kingdom would remain a part of Austria, but not of the German Empire. While other nations based their demands on the "historical statehood" principle, the Slovenian demands were based on the principle of national self-determination some 70 years before American

President Woodrow Wilson would embrace the principle in his "Fourteen Points."

Matija Kavčič, one of 14 Slovenian deputies elected to the 1848/49 Austrian Parliament, proposed a plan of turning the Austrian Empire into a federation of fourteen national states that would completely do away with the system of historic regions based on the old feudal system. At the 1848 Slavic Congress in Prague, the Slovenian delegates also demanded the establishment of a Slovenian University in Ljubljana. A map of a United Slovenia was designed by Peter Kozler based on then available ethnic data. It was confiscated by Austrian authorities and Kozler was accused of treason in 1852, but was later released for insufficient evidence. The revolts of 1848 were repressed after a few years and absolutistic regimes kept control on any movements in support of national rights. However, recognition was given to equal rights of the Slovenian language in principle, while denied in practice by the German/Hungarian element that considered Slovenian the language of servants and peasants. Even the "minimalist" Maribor program of 1865 (a common assembly of deputies from the historical provinces to discuss mutual problems) was fiercely opposed by most Austrians that supported the Pan-German plan of a unified German nation from the Baltic to the Adriatic seas. The Slovenian nation was blocking the Pan-German plan simply by being located between the Adriatic Sea (Trieste) and the German/Austrian Alpine areas and therefore any concessions had to be refused in order to speed up its total assimilation. Hitler's World War II plan to "cleanse" the Slovenians was an accelerated approach to the same end by use of extreme violence.

Toward "Yugoslavism"

In 1867, the German and Hungarian majorities agreed to the reorganization of the state into a "Dualistic" Austro-Hungarian Monarchy in order to be better able to control the minority elements in each half of the empire. The same year, in view of such intransigence, the Slovenes reverted back to their "maximalist" demand of a "United Slovenia" (1867 Ljubljana Manifesto) and initiated a series of mass political meetings, called "Tabori," after the Czech model. Their motto became "Umreti nočemo!" ("We refuse to die!"), and a movement was initiated to bring about a cultural/political coalition of Slovenes, Croats, and Serbs of Austro-Hungary in order to more successfully defend themselves from the increasing efforts of Germanization/Magyarization. At the same time, Slovenes, Croats, and Serbs followed with great interest several movements of national liberation and unification, such as those in Italy, Germany, Greece, and Serbia, and drew from them much inspiration. While Austria lost its northern Italian provinces to the Italian "Risorgimento," it gained, on the other hand, Bosnia and Herzegovina through occupation (1878) and annexation (1908). These actions increased the interest of Slovenes, Croats, and Serbs of Austro-Hungary in a "Trialistic" arrangement that would allow the South Slavic groups ("Yugoslavs") to form their own joint (and "Third") unit within Austro-Hungary. A federalist solution, they believed, would make possible the survival of a country to which they had been loyal subjects for many centuries. Crown Prince Ferdinand supported this approach called "The United States of greater Austria" by his advisers also because it would remove the attraction of a Greater Serbia. But the German leadership's sense of its own superiority and consequent expansionist goals prevented any compromise and led to two world wars.

World War I and Royal Yugoslavia

Unable to achieve their maximalist goals, the Slovenes concentrated their effort at the micro-level and made tremendous strides prior to World War I in introducing education in Slovenian, organizing literary and reading rooms in every town, participating in economic development, upgrading their agriculture, organizing cultural societies and political parties, such as the Catholic People's Party in 1892 and the Liberal Party in 1894, and participating in the Socialist movement of the 1890s. World War I brought about the dissolution of centuries-old ties between the Slovenes and the Austrian Monarchy and the Croats/Serbs with the Hungarian Crown. Toward the end of the war, on 12 August 1918, the National Council for Slovenian Lands was formed in Ljubljana. On 12 October 1918, the National Council for all Slavs of former Austro-Hungary was founded in Zagreb, Croatia, and was chaired by Msgr. Anton Korošeć, head of the Slovenian People's Party. This Council proclaimed on 29 October 1918 the separation of the South Slavs from Austro-Hungary and the formation of a new state of Slovenes, Croats, and Serbs.

A National Government for Slovenia was established in Ljubljana. The Zagreb Council intended to negotiate a Federal Union with the Kingdom of Serbia that would preserve the respective national autonomies of the Slovenes, Croats, and Serbs. Msgr. Korošeć had negotiated a similar agreement in Geneva with Nikola Pašić, his Serbian counterpart, but a new Serbian government reneged on it. There was no time for further negotiations due to the Italian occupation of much Slovenian and Croatian territory and only Serbia, a victor state, could resist Italy. Thus, a delegation of the Zagreb Council submitted to Serbia a declaration expressing the will to unite with The Kingdom of Serbia. At that time, there were no conditions presented or demand made regarding the type of union and Serbia immediately accepted the proposed unification under its strongly centralized government and a unitary "Kingdom of Serbs, Croats, and Slovenes" was declared on 1 December 1918. Because of the absence of an initial compromise between the Unitarists and Federalists, what became Yugoslavia never gained a solid consensual foundation. Serbs were winners and viewed their expansion as liberation of their Slavic brethren from Austria-Hungary, as compensation for their tremendous war sacrifices, and as the realization of their "Greater Serbia" goal. Slovenes and Croats, while freed from the Austro-Hungarian domination, were nevertheless the losers in terms of their desired political/cultural autonomy. In addition, they suffered painful territorial losses to Italy (some 700,000 Slovenes and Croats denied any national rights by Fascist Italy and subject to all kinds of persecutions) and to Austria (a similar fate for some 100,000 Slovenes left within Austria in the Carinthia region).

After ten years of a contentious Parliamentary system that ended in the murder of Croatian deputies and their leader Stjepan Radić, King Alexander abrogated the 1921 Constitution, dissolved the Parliament and political parties, took over power directly, and renamed the country "Yugoslavia." He abolished the 33 administrative departments that had replaced the historic political/national regions in favor of administrative areas named mostly after rivers. A new policy was initiated with the goal of creating a single "Yugoslav" nation out of the three "Tribes" of Serbs, Croats, and Slovenes. But in practice this policy meant the King's Serbian hegemony over the rest of the nations. The reaction was intense and King Alexander himself fell victim of Croat-Ustaša and Macedonian terrorists and died in Marseilles in 1934. A regency ruled Yugoslavia, headed by Alexander's cousin, Prince Paul, who managed to reach an agreement in 1939 with the Croats. An autonomous Croatian "Banovina" headed by "Ban" Ivan Subašić was established, including most Croatian lands outside of the Bosnia and Herzegovina area. Strong opposition developed among Serbs because they viewed the Croatian Banovina as a privilege for Croats while Serbs were split among six old administrative units with a large Serbian population left inside the Croatian Banovina itself. Still, there might have been a chance for further similar agreements that would have satisfied the Serbs and Slovenes. But there was no time left—Hitler and his allies (Italy, Hungary, Bulgaria) attacked Yugoslavia on 6 April 1941, after a coup on 27 March 1941 had deposed Prince Paul's government, which had yielded to Hitler's pressures on 25 March. Thus the first Yugoslavia, born out of the distress of World War I, had not had time to consolidate and work out its problems in a mere 23 years and was then dismembered by its aggressors. Still, the first Yugoslavia allowed the Slovenes a chance for fuller development of their cultural, economic, and political life, in greater freedom and relative independence for the first time in modern times.

World War II

Slovenia was divided in 1941 among Germany, Italy, and Hungary. Germany annexed northern Slovenia, mobilized its men into the German army, interned, expelled, or killed most of the Slovenian leaders and removed to labor camps the populations of entire areas, repopulating them with Germans. Italy annexed southern Slovenia but did not mobilize its men. In both areas, particularly the Italian, resistance movements were initiated by both nationalist groups and by Communist-dominated Partisans, the latter particularly after Hitler's attack on the Soviet Union on 22 June 1941. The partisans claimed monopoly of the resistance leadership and dealt cruelly with anyone that dared to oppose their intended power grab. Spontaneous resistance to the Partisans by the non-Communist Slovenian peasantry led to a bloody civil war in Slovenia under foreign occupiers, who encouraged the bloodshed. The resistance movement led by General Draža Mihajlović, appointed Minister of War of the Yugoslav Government in exile, was handicapped by the exile government's lack of unity and clear purpose (mostly due to the fact that the Serbian side had reneged on the 1939 agreement on Croatia). On the other hand, Winston Churchill, convinced by rather one-sided reports that Mihajlović was "collaborating" with the Germans while the Partisans under Marshal Tito were the ones "who killed more Germans," decided to recognize Tito as the only legitimate Yugoslav resistance. Though aware of Tito's communist allegiance to Stalin, Churchill threw his support to Tito, and forced the Yugoslav government-in-exile into a coalition government with Tito, who had no intention of keeping the agreement and, in fact, would have fought against an Allied landing in Yugoslavia along with the Germans.

When Soviet armies, accompanied by Tito, entered Yugoslavia from Romania and Bulgaria in the fall of 1944, military units and civilians that had opposed the Partisans retreated to Austria or Italy. Among them were the Cetnik units of Draža Mihajlović, and "homeguards" from Serbia, Croatia, and Slovenia that had been under German control but were pro-Allies in their convictions and hopes. Also in retreat were the units of the Croatian Ustaša that had collaborated with Italy and Germany in order to achieve (and control) an "independent" greater Croatia and, in the process, had committed terrible and large-scale massacres of Serbs, Jews, Gypsies and others who opposed them. Serbs and Partisans counteracted and a fratricidal civil war raged over Yugoslavia. After the end of the war, the Communist-led forces took control of Slovenia and Yugoslavia and instituted a violent dictatorship that committed systematic crimes and human rights violations on an unexpectedly large scale. Thousands upon thousands of their former opponents that were returned, unaware, from Austria by British military authorities were tortured and massacred by Partisan executioners.

Communist Yugoslavia

Such was the background for the formation of the second Yugoslavia as a Federative People's Republic of five nations (Slovenes, Croats, Serbs, Macedonians, Montenegrins) with their individual republics and Bosnia and Herzegovina as a buffer area with its mix of Serb, Muslim, and Croat populations. The problem of large Hungarian and Muslim Albanian populations in Serbia was solved by creating for them the autonomous region of Vojvodina

(Hungarian minority) and Kosovo (Muslim Albanian majority) that assured their political and cultural development. Tito attempted a balancing act to satisfy most of the nationality issues that were carried over unresolved from the first Yugoslavia, but failed to satisfy anyone.

Compared to pre-1941 Yugoslavia where Serbs enjoyed a controlling role, the numerically stronger Serbs had lost the Macedonian area they considered "Southern Serbia," lost the opportunity to incorporate Montenegro into Serbia, and lost direct control over the Hungarian minority in Vojvodina and the Muslim Albanians of Kosovo, viewed as the cradle of the Serbian nation since the Middle Ages. They further were not able to incorporate into Serbia the large Serbian populated areas of Bosnia, and had not obtained an autonomous regions for the large minority of Serbian population within the Croatian Republic. The Croats, while gaining back the Medjumurje area from Hungary and from Italy, the cities of Rijeka (Fiume), Zadar (Zara), some Dalmatian islands and the Istrian Peninsula had, on the other hand, lost other areas. These included the Srem area to Serbia, and also Bosnia and Herzegovina, which had been part of the World War II "independent" Croatian state under the Ustaša leadership.

In addition, the Croats were confronted with a deeply resentful Serbian minority that became ever more pervasive in public administrative and security positions. The Slovenes had regained the Prekmurje enclave from Hungary and most of the Slovenian lands that had been taken over by Italy following World War I (Julian region and Northern Istria), except for the "Venetian Slovenia" area, the Gorizia area, and the port city of Trieste. The latter was initially part of the UN protected "Free Territory of Trieste," split in 1954 between Italy and Yugoslavia with Trieste itself given to Italy. Nor were the Slovenian claims to the southern Carinthia area of Austria satisfied. The loss of Trieste was a bitter pill for the Slovenes and many blamed it on the fact that Tito's Yugoslavia was, initially, Stalin's advance threat to Western Europe, thus making the Allies more supportive of Italy.

The official position of the Marxist Yugoslav regime was that national rivalries and conflicting interests would gradually diminish through their sublimation into a new Socialist order. Without capitalism, nationalism was supposed to wither away. Therefore, in the name of their "unity and brotherhood" motto, any nationalistic expression of concern was prohibited and repressed by the dictatorial and centralized regime of the "League of Yugoslav Communists" acting through the "Socialist Alliance" as its mass front organization.

After a short post-war "coalition" government period, the elections of 11 November 1945, boycotted by the non-communist "coalition" parties, gave the Communist-led People's Front 90% of the vote. A Constituent Assembly met on 29 November, abolishing the monarchy and establishing the Federative People's Republic of Yugoslavia. In January 1946 a new constitution was adopted, based on the 1936 Soviet constitution. The Stalin-engineered expulsion of Yugoslavia from the Soviet-dominated Cominform Group in 1948 was actually a blessing for Yugoslavia after its leadership was able to survive Stalin's pressures. Survival had to be justified, both practically and in theory, by developing a "Road to Socialism" based on Yugoslavia's own circumstances. This new "road map" evolved rather quickly in response to some of Stalin's accusations and Yugoslavia's need to perform a balancing act betweeen the NATO alliance and the Soviet bloc. Tito quickly nationalized the economy through a policy of forced industrialization, to be supported by the collectivization of the agriculture.

The agricultural reform of 1945–46 (limited private ownership of a maximum of 35 hectares (85 acres), and a limited free market after the initial forced delivery of quotas to the state at very low prices) had to be abandoned because of the strong resistance by the peasants. The actual collectivization efforts were initiated in 1949 using welfare benefits and lower taxes as incentives along with direct coercion. But collectivization had to be abandoned by 1958 simply because its inefficiency and low productivity could not support the concentrated effort of industrial development.

By the 1950s Yugoslavia had initiated the development of its internal trademark: self-management of enterprises through workers councils and local decision-making as the road to Marx's "withering away of the state." The second five-year plan (1957–61), as opposed to the failed first one (1947–51), was completed in four years by relying on the well-established self-management system. Economic targets were set from the local to the republic level and then coordinated by a Federal Planning Institute to meet an overall national economic strategy. This system supported a period of very rapid industrial growth in the 1950s from a very low base. But a high consumption rate encouraged a volume of imports far in excess of exports, largely financed by foreign loans. In addition, inefficient and low productivity industries were kept in place through public subsidies, cheap credit, and other artificial measures that led to a serious crisis by 1961.

Reforms were necessary and, by 1965, "market socialism" was introduced with laws that abolished most price controls and halved import duties while withdrawing export subsidies. After necessary amounts were left with the earning enterprise, the rest of the earned foreign currencies were deposited with the national bank and used by the state, other enterprises, or were used to assist less-developed areas. Councils were given more decision-making power in investing their earnings and they also tended to vote for higher salaries in order to meet steep increases in the cost of living. Unemployment grew rapidly even though "political factories" were still subsidized. The government thus relaxed its restrictions to allow labor migration, particularly to West Germany where workers were needed for its thriving economy. Foreign investment was encouraged up to 49% in joint enterprises, and barriers to the movement of people and exchange of ideas were largely removed.

The role of trade unions continued to be one of transmission of instructions from government to workers, allocation of perks along with the education/training of workers, monitoring legislation and overall protection of the self-management system. Strikes were legally neither allowed nor forbidden, but until the 1958 miners strike in Trbovlje, Slovenia, were not publicly acknowledged and were suppressed. After 1958 strikes were tolerated as an indication of problems to be resolved. Unions, however, did not initiate strikes but were expected to convince workers to go back to work.

Having survived its expulsion from the Cominform in 1948 and Stalin's attempts to take control, Yugoslavia began to develop a foreign policy independent of the Soviet Union. By mid-1949 Yugoslavia withdrew its support from the Greek Communists in their civil war against the then-Royalist government. In October 1949, Yugoslavia was elected to one of the non-permanent seats on the UN Security Council and openly condemned North Korea's aggression towards South Korea. Following the "rapprochement" opening with the Soviet Union, initiated by Nikita Khrushchev and his 1956 denunciation of Stalin, Tito intensified his work on developing the movement of non-aligned "third world" nations as Yugoslavia's external trademark in cooperation with Nehru of India, Nasser of Egypt, and others. With the September 1961 Belgrade summit conference of non-aligned nations, Tito became the recognized leader of the movement. The non-aligned position served Tito's Yugoslavia well by allowing Tito to draw on economic and political support from the Western powers while neutralizing any aggression from the Soviet bloc. While Tito had acquiesced, reluctantly, to the 1956 Soviet invasion of Hungary for fear of chaos and any liberalizing impact on Yugoslavia, he condemned the Soviet invasion of Dubček's Czechoslovakia in 1968, as did Romania's Ceausescu, both fearing their countries might be the next in line for "corrective" action by the Red Army and the Warsaw Pact. Just before his death on 4 May 1980, Tito also condemned the Soviet invasion of Afghanistan. Yugoslavia actively participated in the 1975 Helsinki Conference and agreements and the first 1977–78 review conference that took place in Belgrade, even though Yugoslavia's one-party Communist regime perpetrated and condoned numerous human rights violations. Overall, in the 1970s–80s Yugoslavia maintained fairly good relations with its neighboring states by playing down or solving pending disputes such as the Trieste issue with Italy in 1975, and developing cooperative projects and increased trade.

Compared to the other republics of the Federative People's Republic of Yugoslavia, the Republic of Slovenia had several advantages. It was 95% homogeneous. The Slovenes had the highest level of literacy. Their pre-war economy was the most advanced and so was their agriculture, which was based on an extensive network of peasant cooperatives and savings and loans institutions developed as a primary initiative of the Slovenian People's Party ("clerical"). Though ravaged by the war, occupation, resistance and civil war losses, and preoccupied with carrying out the elimination of all actual and potential opposition, the Communist government faced the double task of building its Socialist economy while rebuilding the country. As an integral part of the Yugoslav federation, Slovenia was, naturally, affected by Yugoslavia's internal and external political developments. The main problems facing communist Yugoslavia/Slovenia were essentially the same as the unresolved ones under Royalist Yugoslavia. As the "Royal Yugoslavism" had failed in its assimilative efforts, so did the "Socialist Yugoslavism" fail to overcome the forces of nationalism. In the case of Slovenia there were several key factors in the continued attraction to its national identity: more than a thousand years of historical development; a location within Central Europe (not part of the Balkan area) and related identification with Western European civilization; the Catholic religion with the traditional role of Catholic priests (even under the persecutions by the Communist regime); the most developed and productive economy with a standard of living far superior to most other areas of the Yugoslav Federation; and finally, the increased political and economic autonomy enjoyed by the Republic after the 1974 Constitution, particularly following Tito's death in 1980. Tito's motto of "unity and brotherhood" was replaced by "freedom and democracy" to be achieved through either a confederate rearrangement of Yugoslavia or by complete independence.

The debates over the reforms of the 1960s led to a closer scrutiny, not only of the economic system, but also of the decision-making process at the republic and federal levels, particularly the investment of funds to less developed areas that Slovenia and Croatia felt were very poorly managed, if not squandered. Other issues fueled acrimony between individual nations, such as the 1967 Declaration in Zagreb claiming a Croatian linguistic and literary tradition separate from the Serbian one, thus undermining the validity of the Serbo-Croatian language. Also, Kosovo Albanians and Montenegrins, along with Slovenes and Croats, began to assert their national rights as superior to the Federation ones.

In December 1964, the 8th Congress of the League of Communists of Yugoslavia (LCY) acknowledged that ethnic prejudice and antagonisms existed in socialist Yugoslavia and went on record against the position that Yugoslavia's nations had become obsolete and were disintegrating into a socialist "Yugoslavism." Thus the republics, based on individual nations, became bastions of a strong Federalism that advocated the devolution and decentralization of authority from the federal to the republic level. "Yugoslav Socialist Patriotism" was at times defined as a deep feeling for both one's own national identity and for the socialist self-management of Yugoslavia. Economic reforms were the other

focus of the Eighth LCY Congress, led by Croatia and Slovenia with emphasis on efficiencies and local economic development decisions with profit criteria as their basis. The "liberal" bloc (Slovenia, Croatia, Macedonia, Vojvodina) prevailed over the "conservative" group and the reforms of 1965 did away with central investment planning and "political factories." The positions of the two blocs hardened into a national-liberal coalition that viewed the conservative, centralist group led by Serbia as the "Greater Serbian" attempt at majority domination. The devolution of power in economic decision-making spearheaded by the Slovenes assisted in the "federalization" of the League of Communists of Yugoslavia as a league of "quasi-sovereign" republican parties. Under strong prodding from the Croats, the party agreed in 1970 to the principle of unanimity for decision-making that, in practice, meant a veto power for each republic. However, the concentration of economic resources in Serbian hands continued with Belgrade banks controlling half of total credits and some 80% of foreign credits. This was also combined with the fear of Serbian political and cultural domination, particularly with respect to Croatian language sensitivities, which had been aroused by the use of the Serbian version of Serbo-Croatian as the norm, with the Croatian version as a deviation.

The language controversy exacerbated the economic and political tensions between Serbs and Croats, which spilled into the easily inflamed area of ethnic confrontations. To the conservative centralists the devolution of power to the republic level meant the subordination of the broad "Yugoslav" and "Socialist" interests to the narrow "nationalist" interest of republic national majorities. With the Croat League of Communists taking the liberal position in 1970, nationalism was rehabilitated. Thus the "Croatian Spring" bloomed and impacted all the other republics of Yugoslavia. Meanwhile, through a series of 1967–68 constitutional amendments that had limited federal power in favor of the republics and autonomous provinces, the Federal Government came to be seen by liberals more as an inter-republican problem-solving mechanism bordering on a confederative arrangement. A network of inter-republican committees established by mid-1971 proved to be very efficient at resolving a large number of difficult issues in a short time. The coalition of liberals and nationalists in Croatia also generated sharp condemnation in Serbia whose own brand of nationalism grew stronger, but as part of a conservative-centralist alliance. Thus the liberal/federalist versus conservative/centralist opposition became entangled in the rising nationalism within each opposing bloc. The situation in Croatia and Serbia was particularly difficult because of their minorities issues—Serbian in Croatia and Hungarian/Albanian in Serbia.

Serbs in Croatia sided with the Croat conservatives and sought a constitutional amendment guaranteeing their own national identity and rights and, in the process, challenged the sovereignty of the Croatian nation and state as well as the right to self-determination, including the right to secession. The conservatives won and the amendment declared that "the Socialist Republic of Croatia (was) the national state of the Croatian nation, the state of the Serbian nation in Croatia, and the state of the nationalities inhabiting it."

Slovenian "Spring"

Meanwhile, Slovenia, not burdened by large minorities, developed a similar liberal and nationalist direction along with Croatia. This fostered an incipient separatist sentiment opposed by both the liberal and conservative party wings. Led by Stane Kavčič, head of the Slovenian government, the liberal wing gained as much local political latitude as possible from the Federal level during the early 1970s "Slovenian Spring." By the summer of 1971, the Serbian party leadership was pressuring President Tito to put an end to the "dangerous" development of Croatian nationalism. While Tito wavered because of his support for the balancing system of autonomous republic units, the situation quickly reached critical proportions.

Croat nationalists, complaining about discrimination against Croats in Bosnia and Herzegovina, demanded the incorporation of Western Herzegovina into Croatia. Serbia countered by claiming Southeastern Herzegovina for itself. Croats also advanced claims to a larger share of their foreign currency earnings, to the issuance of their own currency, the creation of their own national bank that would directly negotiate foreign loans, the printing of Croatian postage stamps, the creation of a Croatian army, and recognition of the Croatian *Sabor* (assembly) as the highest Croatian political body, and, finally, to Croatian secession and complete independence. Confronted with such intensive agitation, the liberal Croatian party leadership could not back down and did not try to restrain the maximalist public demands nor the widespread university students' strike of November 1971. This situation caused a loss of support from the liberal party wings of Slovenia and even Macedonia. At this point Tito intervened, condemned the Croatian liberal leadership on 1 December 1971, and supported the conservative wing. The liberal leadership group resigned on 12 December 1971. When Croatian students demonstrated and demanded an independent Croatia, the Yugoslav army was ready to move in if necessary. A wholesale purge of the party liberals followed with tens of thousands expelled, key functionaries lost their positions, several thousand were imprisoned (including Franjo Tudjman who later became President in independent Croatia), and leading Croatian nationalist organizations and their publications were closed.

On 8 May 1972, the Croatian party also expelled its liberal wing leaders and the purge of nationalists continued through 1973 in Croatia, as well as in Slovenia and Macedonia. However, the issues and sentiments raised during the "Slovene and Croat Springs" of 1969–71 did not disappear. Tito and the conservatives were forced to satisfy nominally some demands. The 1974 Constitution was an attempt to resolve the strained inter-republican relations as each republic pursued its own interests over and above an overall "Yugoslav" interest. The repression of liberal-nationalist Croats was accompanied by the growing influence of the Serbian element in the Croatian Party (24% in 1980) and police force (majority) that contributed to the continued persecution and imprisonments of Croatian nationalists into the 1980s.

Yugoslavia—House Divided

In Slovenia, developments took a direction of their own. The purge of the nationalists took place as in Croatia but on a lesser scale, and after a decade or so, nationalism was revived through the development of grassroots movements in the arts, music, peace, and environmental concerns. Activism was particularly strong among young people, who shrewdly used the regime-supported youth organizations, youth periodicals—such as *Mladina* (in Ljubljana) and *Katedra* (in Maribor)—and an independent student radio station. The journal *Nova Revija* published a series of articles focusing on problems confronting the Slovenian nation in February 1987; these included such varied topics as the status of the Slovenian language, the role of the Communist Party, the multiparty system, and independence. The *Nova Revija* was in reality a Slovenian national manifesto that, along with yearly public opinion polls showing ever higher support for Slovenian independence, indicated a definite mood toward secession. In this charged atmosphere, the Yugoslav army committed two actions that led the Slovenes to the path of actual separation from Yugoslavia. In March 1988, the army's Military Council submitted a confidential report to the Federal Presidency claiming that Slovenia was planning a counter revolution and calling for repressive measures against liberals and a *coup d'etat*. An army document delineating such actions was delivered by an army sergeant to the journal *Mladina*. But, before it could be published, *Mladina's* edi-

tor and two journalists were arrested by the army on 31 March 1988. Meanwhile, the strong intervention of the Slovenian political leadership succeeded in stopping any army action. But the four men involved in the affair were put on trial by the Yugoslav army.

The second army *faux pas* was to hold the trial in Ljubljana, capital of Slovenia, and to conduct it in the Serbo-Croatian language, an action declared constitutional by the Yugoslav Presidency, claiming that Slovenian law could not be applied to the Yugoslav army. This trial brought about complete unity among Slovenians in opposition to the Yugoslav army and what it represented, and the four individuals on trial became overnight heroes. One of them was Janez Janša who had written articles in *Mladina* critical of the Yugoslav army and was the head of the Slovenian pacifist movement and President of the Slovenian Youth Organization. (Ironically, three years later Janša led the successful defense of Slovenia against the Yugoslav army and became the first Minister of Defense of independent Slovenia.) The four men were found guilty and sentenced to jail terms from four years (Janša) to five months. The total mobilization of Slovenia against the military trials led to the formation of the first non-Communist political organizations and political parties. In a time of perceived national crisis, both the Communist and non-Communist leadership found it possible to work closely together. But from that time on the liberal/nationalist vs. conservative/centralist positions hardened in Yugoslavia and no amount of negotiation at the federal presidency level regarding a possible confederal solution could hold Yugoslavia together any longer.

Since 1986, work had been done on amendments to the 1974 Constitution that, when submitted in 1987, created a furor, particularly in Slovenia, due to the proposed creation of a unified legal system, the establishment of central control over the means of transportation and communication, centralization of the economy into a unified market, and the granting of more control to Serbia over its autonomous provinces of Kosovo and Vojvodina. This all came at the expense of the individual republics. A recentralization of the League of Communists was also recommended but opposed by liberal/nationalist groups. Serbia's President Slobodan Milošević also proposed changes to the bicameral Federal Skupština (Assembly) by replacing it with a tricameral one where deputies would no longer be elected by their republican assemblies but through a "one person, one vote" national system. Slovenia, Croatia, and Bosnia and Herzegovina strongly opposed the change as they opposed the additional Chamber of Associated Labor that would have increased the Federal role in the economy. The debates over the recentralizing amendments caused an even greater focus in Slovenia and Coatia on the concept of a confederative structure based on self-determination by "sovereign" states and a multiparty democratic system as the only one that could maintain some semblance of a "Yugoslav" state.

By 1989 and the period following the Serbian assertion of control in the Kosovo and Vojvodina provinces, as well as in the republic of Montenegro, relations between Slovenia and Serbia reached a crisis point: Serbian President Milošević attempted to orchestrate mass demonstrations by Serbs in Ljubljana, the capital city of Slovenia, and the Slovenian leadership vetoed it. Then Serbs started to boycott Slovenian products, to withdraw their savings from Slovenian banks, and to terminate economic cooperation and trade with Slovenia. Serbian President Milošević's tactics were extremely distasteful to the Slovenians and the use of force against the Albanian population of the Kosovo province worried the Slovenes (and Croats) about the possible use of force by Serbia against Slovenia itself. The tensions with Serbia convinced the Slovenian leadership of the need to take necessary protective measures. In September 1989, draft amendments to the Constitution of Slovenia were published that included the right to secession, and the sole right of the Slovenian legislature to introduce martial law. The Yugoslav army particularly needed the amendment granting control over deployment of armed forces in Slovenia, since the Yugoslav army, controlled by a mostly Serbian/Montenegrin officer corps dedicated to the preservation of a communist system, had a self-interest in preserving the source of their own budgetary allocations of some 51% of the Yugoslav federal budget.

A last attempt at salvaging Yugoslavia was to be made as the extraordinary Congress of the League of Communists of Yugoslavia convened in January 1990 to review proposed reforms such as free multiparty elections, and freedom of speech. The Slovenian delegation attempted to broaden the spectrum of reforms but was rebuffed and walked out on 23 January 1990, pulling out of the Yugoslav League. The Slovenian Communists then renamed their party the Party for Democratic Renewal. The political debate in Slovenia intensified and some nineteen parties were formed by early 1990. On 10 April 1990 the first free elections since before World War II were held in Slovenia, where there still was a three-chamber Assembly: political affairs, associated labor, and territorial communities. A coalition of six newly formed democratic parties, called *Demos,* won 55% of the votes, with the remainder going to the Party for Democratic Renewal, the former Communists (17%), the Socialist Party (5%), and the Liberal Democratic Party—heir to the Slovenia Youth Organization (15%). The *Demos* coalition organized the first freely elected Slovenian Government of the post-Communist era with Dr. Lojze Peterle as the Prime Minister.

Milan Kučan, former head of the League of Communists of Slovenia, was elected President with 54% of the vote in recognition of his efforts to effect a bloodless transfer of power from a monopoly by the Communist party to a free multiparty system and his standing up to the recentralizing attempts by Serbia.

Toward Independence

In October 1990, Slovenia and Croatia published a joint proposal for a Yugoslavian confederation as a last attempt at a negotiated solution, but to no avail. The Slovenian legislature also adopted in October a draft constitution proclaiming that "Slovenia will become an independent state." On 23 December 1990, a plebiscite was held on Slovenia's disassociation from Yugoslavia if a confederate solution could not be negotiated within a six-month period. An overwhelming majority of 89% of voters approved the secession provision and on 26 December 1990 a Declaration of Sovereignty was also adopted. All federal laws were declared void in Slovenia as of 20 February 1991 and, since no negotiated agreement was possible, Slovenia declared its independence on 25 June 1991. On 27 June 1991, the Yugoslav army tried to seize control of Slovenia and its common borders with Italy, Austria, and Hungary under the pretext that it was the army's constitutional duty to assure the integrity of Socialist Yugoslavia. The Yugoslav army units were surprised and shocked by the resistance they encountered from the Slovenian "territorial guards," who surrounded Yugoslav Army tank units, isolated them, and engaged in close combat, mostly along border checkpoints that ended in most cases with Yugoslav units surrendering to the Slovenian forces. Fortunately, casualties were limited on both sides. Over 3,200 Yugoslav army soldiers surrendered, and were well treated by the Slovenes, who scored a public relations coup by having the prisoners call their parents all over Yugoslavia to come to Slovenia and take their sons back home.

The war in Slovenia ended in ten days due to the intervention of the European Community, who negotiated a cease-fire and a three-month moratorium on Slovenia's implementation of independence, giving the Yugoslav army time to retreat from Slovenia by the end of October 1991. Thus Slovenia was able to "disassociate" itself from Yugoslavia with a minimum of casual-ties, although the military operations caused considerable physical damages estimated at almost $3 billion. On 23 December 1991, one year following the independence plebiscite, a new Constitution was adopted by Slovenia establishing a parliamentary democracy with a bicameral legislature. Even though US Secretary of State James Baker, in his visit to Belgrade on 21 June 1991, had declared that the US opposed unilateral secessions by Slovenia and Croatia and that the US would therefore not recognize them as independent countries, such recognition came first from Germany on 18 December 1991, from the European Community on 15 January 1992, and finally from the US on 7 April 1992. Slovenia was accepted as a member of the UN on 23 April 1992 and has since become a member of many other international organizations, including the Council of Europe in 1993 and the NATO related Partnership for Peace in 1994.

On 6 December 1992, general elections were held in accordance with the new Constitution, with twenty-two parties participating and eight receiving sufficient votes to assure representation. A coalition government was formed by the Liberal Democrats, Christian Democrats, and the United List Group of Leftist Parties. Dr. Milan Kučan was elected President and Dr. Janez Drnovšek became Prime Minister.

In the 1970s, Slovenia had reached a standard of living close to the one in neighboring Austria and Italy. However, the burdens imposed by the excessive cost of maintaining a large Yugoslav army, heavy contributions to the Fund for Less Developed Areas, and the repayments on a $20 billion international debt, caused a lowering of its living standard over the 1980s. The situation worsened with the trauma of secession from Yugoslavia, the war damages suffered, and the loss of the former Yugoslav markets. In spite of all these problems Slovenia has made good progress since independence by improving its productivity, controlling inflation, and reorienting its exports to Western Europe. Based on past experience, its industriousness, and good relationship with its trading partners, Slovenia has a very good chance of becoming a successful example of the transition from authoritarian socialism to a free democratic system and a market economy capable of sustaining a comfortable standard and quality of life.

[13]GOVERNMENT

Slovenia is a republic based on a constitution adopted on 23 December 1991, one year following the plebiscite that supported its independence. The president is Dr. Milan Kučan, elected in December 1992. The prime minister is Dr. Janez Drnovšek.

The constitution provides for a National Assembly as the highest legislative authority with 90 seats. Deputies are elected to four-year terms of office. The National Council, with 40 seats, has an advisory role and councilors represent social, economic, professional, and local interests. They are elected to five-year terms of office and may propose laws to the National Assembly, request the latter to review its decisions, and may demand the calling of a constitutional referendum.

The executive branch consists of a President of the Republic who is also Supreme Commander of the Armed Forces, and is elected to a five-year term of office, limited to two consecutive terms. The president calls for elections to the National Assembly, proclaims the adopted laws, and proposes candidates for prime minister to the National Assembly. Since 1993 the government has consisted of 15 ministries instead of the previous 27.

The current (July 1994) government is a coalition of three parties: Liberal Democratic, Christian Democrats, and The United List. Of the 16 members of the Council of Ministers, 6 are Liberal Democrats, 4 are Christian Democrats, 3 are from the Associated List of Social Democrats, 1 from the Greens, and 2 are not members of any party.

[14]POLITICAL PARTIES

The last parliamentary elections were held on 6 December 1992, with 22 parties participating and 8 of them receiving sufficient votes to gain representation in the National Assembly:

Liberal Democratic Party	22 seats
Slovene Christian Democrats	15 seats
Associated List of Social Democrats	14 seats
Includes:	
Party of Democratic Reforms	
Party of Slovene Pensioners	
Social Democratic Union	
Labor Party	
Slovene National Party	12 seats
Slovene People's Party	10 seats
Democratic Party	6 seats
Green Ecological Social Party	5 seats
Social Democratic Party	4 seats
Italian Minority	1 seat
Hungarian Minority	1 seat

Through some later realignments, the Democratic Party lost three deputies who joined the Liberal Democrats, the People's Party gained one deputy, while the Slovene National Party split into two groups and was left with five deputies.

[15]LOCAL GOVERNMENT

The National Assembly has been struggling for some time with legislation aimed at reforming the burdensome local government system inherited from the former Yugoslavia. Pending legislation could not gather sufficient support as of September 1994 and will need to be revised for passage. Under the 1974 Constitution of the former Yugoslavia, the commune (Občina) is the basic self-managed sociopolitical community. Each assembly consists of a chamber of work communities, composed of delegates from the working population; a chamber of local communities, composed of delegates of both workers and nonworkers residing in organized local communities; and a sociopolitical chamber, composed of delegates of sociopolitical organizations such as labor unions and youth and veteran groups. The commune assembly elects an executive body which assumes administrative functions for the community. The assemblies also elect the delegations that make up the Assembly of the Republic.

[16]JUDICIAL SYSTEM

The judicial system consists of local and district courts and a Supreme Court which hears appeals from these courts. A nine-member Constitutional Court resolves jurisdictional disputes and rules on the constitutionality of legislation and regulations. The Constitutional Court also acts as a final court of appeal in cases requiring constitutional interpretation.

Judges are elected by Parliament after nomination by a Judicial Council composed of 11 members—6 judges selected by their peers and 5 persons elected by the State Assembly on nomination of the President. The Constitution guarantees the independence of judges. Judges are appointed to permanent positions subject to an age limit.

The Constitution affords criminal defendants a presumption of innocence, open court proceedings, the right to an appeal, a prohibition against double jeopardy, and a number of other procedural due process protections.

[17]ARMED FORCES

The Slovenian armed forces number 15,000 active duty soldiers and 85,000 reservists who are required to give 7 months of service. The equipment is all dated, Warsaw-Pact material. The paramilitary police number 4,500 actives and 5,000 reserves. Defense spending is probably around $170 million (1991).

[18]INTERNATIONAL COOPERATION

Slovenia was admitted to the UN in 1992. It is also a member of the Council of Europe, CSCE, IAEA, ICAO, ILO, ITU, UNCTAD, UPU, and WIPO. Slovenia's sovereignty is recognized by the US and European countries.

[19]ECONOMY

Before its independence, Slovenia was the most highly developed and wealthiest republic of the old Yugoslav SFR, with a per capita income more than double that of the Yugoslav average, and nearly comparable to levels in neighboring Austria and Italy. The painful transition to a market-based economy has been exacerbated by the disruption of intra-Yugoslav trade. Whereas GDP fell by 9% in 1991 and 6% in 1992, the 1993 GDP was expected to fall by only 2%.

Slovenia freed prices and implemented a privatization law in November 1992, which has enabled private businesses to expand. To a lesser extent, privatization of socially owned enterprises has begun as well. As of mid-1992, 78% of all enterprises were private (up from 67% in 1990).

[20]INCOME

In 1992, Slovenia's GNP was $12,744 million at current prices, or $6,330 per capita. In 1992 the average inflation rate was 93%, resulting in a real growth rate in GDP of –7%.

[21]LABOR

As of the end of 1992, there were some 789,810 persons employed, excluding the armed forces. Forty-one percent of all employees were in manufacturing; 21% in community, social, and personal services; 11% in commerce; 6% in transportation and communication; 5% in construction; 9% in agriculture; and 7% in other sectors. About 47% of those employed in 1992 were women. The total economically active population (employees, self-employed, and unpaid family workers over age 15) in March 1991 totaled 945,766. Unemployment stood at 12% in 1992.

The 1991 Constitution provides that the establishment, activities, and recruitment of members of labor unions shall be unrestricted. There are three main labor federations, with constituent branches throughout the society. Virtually all workers except for police and military personnel are eligible to form and join unions. The right to strike is also guaranteed by the Constitution. Collective bargaining is still undergoing development, and the government still has the principal role in setting the minimum wage and other conditions, although increasingly, private businesses are setting pay scales directly with their employees' unions or representatives.

[22]AGRICULTURE

Some 247,000 hectares (610,300 acres), or 12% of the total land area, were in use as cropland in 1991. In 1992, agriculture contributed 5% to GDP. Slovenia was the least agriculturally active of all the republics of the former Yugoslav SFR. Major crops produced in 1992 included: wheat, 186,000 tons; corn, 207,000 tons; potatoes, 368,000 tons; sugar beets, 97,000 tons; and fruit, 340,000 tons (of which grapes accounted for 63%). Food industry products contributed 3% to total exports in 1992.

[23]ANIMAL HUSBANDRY

As of 1991, about 565,000 ha (1,396,000 acres), or 28% of the total land area, were permanent pastureland. Sheep and cattle breeding, as well as dairy farming, dominate the agricultural sector of the economy. In 1992, the livestock population included: cattle, 484,000; sheep, 28,000; pigs, 529,000; chickens, 12,000,000; and horses, 11,000. Meat production in 1992 included 50,000 tons of beef, 75,000 tons of pork, and 53,000 tons of poultry. Productivity rates for livestock and dairy farming are comparable to much of Western Europe. In 1992, 352,000 tons of milk and 15,800 tons of eggs were produced.

24FISHING

As of 1991, fishing and agriculture accounted for 5% of GDP. As of 1991, the fishing sector accounted for less than 1% of foreign investment in Slovenia.

25FORESTRY

In 1991, forests and woodlands covered just over 50% of the total area; they are Slovenia's most significant natural resource. In 1992, wood processing accounted for 4% of manufacturing; paper production for 9%. Paper, paperboard, and related products amounted to 5% of exports in 1992. The furniture-making industry is also a prominent consumer of forest products.

26MINING

Slovenia's nonfuel mineral resources include lead-zinc (from Mezica) and mercury (mined and smelted in Idrija). Imported ore is needed for the aluminum plant at Kidričevo, and for the iron and steel producing facilities at Jesenice, Ravne, and Štore.

27ENERGY AND POWER

In 1991, total installed electrical capacity was 2.9 million kw; production amounted to 12,250 million kwh that year. Slovenia is relatively well supplied with hydroelectricity. Several thermal plants and one nuclear power plant also supply electricity. Slovenia imports oil from the former republics of the USSR and the developing world which supplies a refinery at Lendava. Coal is mined at Velenje; the mine had an annual capacity of 5 million tons in 1991. Natural gas is used extensively for industry and is supplied by the former USSR and Algeria via 305 km (190 mi) of natural gas pipelines.

28INDUSTRY

Manufacturing is the prominent economic activity, and is widely diversified. Important manufacturing sectors include: electrical and non-electrical machinery, metal processing, chemicals, textiles and clothing, wood processing and furniture, transport equipment, and food processing. Industrial production fell by 12% in 1991 and an estimated 13% in 1992, due in part to the international sanctions against Serbia. In the composition of total value-added by economic activity, the share from industry declined from 50% in 1989 to 43% in 1991. The electronics industry employs some 46,000, predominantly in two firms: Iskra and Gorenje. Both companies export products such as telephones, digital telephone exchanges, electro-optical products, and electronics components.

29SCIENCE AND TECHNOLOGY

The Slovenian Academy of Sciences and Arts, founded in 1921, has institutes conducting research in biology and medicine, and four scientific learned societies. The Ljubljana Geological Institute was founded in 1946. The University of Ljubljana has faculties of natural science, engineering, medicine, and veterinary medicine. The University of Maribor has a college of agriculture and a center for applied mathematics and theoretical physics.

30DOMESTIC TRADE

Although Slovene is the official language, business is often conducted in English, German, Italian, or French. Slovenia's domestic economy has historically been small, thus necessitating an emphasis on exports.

31FOREIGN TRADE

Slovenia has reoriented much of its trade away from its former Yugoslav neighbors toward Western Europe. Sanctions imposed by the UN on trade with Serbia severed Slovenia from its largest foreign market. In 1992, 55% of Slovenia's exports were sent to the European Union, and only 30% to Croatia and the other former Yugoslav republics. In 1990, Slovenian exports totaled $4.12 billion, of which transport equipment and machinery accounted for 38%; other manufactured goods, 44%; chemicals, 9%; food and live animals, 5%; raw materials, 3%; and beverages and tobacco products, less than 1%. Imports in 1990 totaled nearly $4.68 billion, of which machinery and transport equipment accounted for 35%; other manufactured goods, 27%; chemicals, 15%; raw materials, 9%; fuels and lubricants, 7%; and food and live animals, 6%.

The European Union signed a cooperation agreement with Slovenia in April 1993, which provided for greater access to the EU market. Slovenia also entered into trade agreements with Hungary, the Czech Republic, and Slovakia in 1993 that will gradually eliminate most trade barriers.

32BALANCE OF PAYMENTS

In 1992, the balance of payments situation (excluding transactions with former members of the Yugoslav SFR) strengthened significantly. From January to November 1992, merchandise exports increased by 11% and imports fell by 0.2%, producing a trade surplus of $153 million. Buoyant receipts from non-factor services contributed a major share of the account surplus, which reached $825 million after ten months. Consequently, total foreign reserves grew to $1,142 million at the end of November, 1992, enough to cover about three months' imports.

In 1992 merchandise exports totaled $6.7 billion and imports $5.9 billion. The merchandise trade balance was $791.5 million. The following table summarizes Slovenia's balance of payments for 1992 (in millions of US dollars):

	1992
CURRENT ACCOUNT	
Goods, services, and income	846.2
Unrequited transfers	85.3
TOTALS	931.5
CAPITAL ACCOUNT	
Direct investment	113.0
Portfolio investment	8.8
Other long-term capital	−4.4
Other short-term capital	−114.5
Reserves	−632.5
TOTALS	−629.5
Errors and omissions	−301.9
Total change in reserves	−603.5

33BANKING AND SECURITIES

The Bank of Slovenia is the country's bank. There are 31 commercial, mixed, and state savings banks in the country. Commercial banks in the country include the Albania Joint-Stock Company. The currency unit is the tolar (Slt). The Ljubljana Stock Exchange, abolished in 1953, was reopened in December 1989. As of May 1993, it listed 30 securities and had 60 members. In 1992, 56% of the securities trading on the Ljubljana Stock Exchange consisted of bonds, 42% short-term securities, and 2% shares.

34INSURANCE

No recent information is available.

35PUBLIC FINANCE

Fiscal policy supports a cautious monetary position maintained by the Central Bank. In 1992, general government revenue was equivalent to 47% of GDP, while central government revenue came to 22% of GDP. The general government account recorded a surplus equivalent to 0.3% of GDP in 1992. General government expenditures in 1992 came to 47% of GDP, with budgets and pension funds accounting for over four-fifths of expenditures. At the end of February 1993, the total debt outstanding was $1,742 million.

36TAXATION

Corporate income is taxed at 30% of gross profits, and employers are taxed at 45.4% for employee pension funds, social security, and unemployment insurance. Personal income taxes are progressive, and average about 15%. There is a sales tax of 20% on consumer products and 10% on services, with special taxes on alcohol, tobacco, and fuel.

37CUSTOMS AND DUTIES

Imports to Slovenia are generally unrestricted, except for certain agricultural, textile, and wood products. Ninety-three percent of all goods are unrestricted, 6% are controlled by import quotas, and 1% require an import license. Imported goods are subject only to customs duties. Many import taxes have been abolished, and further liberalization is planned.

38FOREIGN INVESTMENT

Since independence, the foreign investment climate has steadily improved in Slovenia, despite constraints that had inhibited investment. The small domestic economy has been viewed by many prospective investors as the least risky of the former Yugoslav republics.

From 1985 to 1991, foreign investment flows came primarily from Germany (39%), Austria (26%), Italy (16%), France (11%), Australia (3%), and US (1%); other countries' investments made up the remainder. At the end of 1991, about 70% of foreign investments were contractual joint ventures, 27% equity joint ventures, and 2% directly from foreign companies. The majority of foreign capital has been directed toward automobile, electric/electronic, chemical, and machine-building industries.

39ECONOMIC DEVELOPMENT

Slovenia has become a member of the IMF as well as the World Bank, from which it has obtained an $80 million loan for financial rehabilitation. The EBRD has loaned Slovenia $50 million for the improvement of the railway sector.

40SOCIAL DEVELOPMENT

Women and men have equal status under the law. Discrimination against women or minorities in housing, jobs, or other areas, is illegal. Officially, both spouses are equal in marriage, and the Constitution asserts the state's responsibility to protect the family. Women are well represented in business, academia, and government, although they still hold a disproportionate share of lower-paying jobs. The Constitution provides for special protection against economic, social, physical, or mental exploitation or abuse of children.

41HEALTH

No recent information is available.

42HOUSING

No recent information is available.

43EDUCATION

Slovenia has a high literacy rate. There are 842 primary schools and 149 secondary schools; 5% of the population are pupils and the teacher-student ratio is 1:14.

In Slovenia there are two universities located at Ljubljana and Maribor. The University of Ljubljana, founded in 1919, has 25 faculties. In 1993, 26,190 pupils were enrolled, including 300 students from foreign countries. The University of Maribor had 12,000 students enrolled in 1992. It has a faculty for teaching, a faculty for economics and business, and a faculty for technology. There are also two colleges attached to it.

44LIBRARIES AND MUSEUMS

Slovenia has 15 galleries and museums. Ljubljana has the National Gallery, Museum of Modern Art, Museum of Architecture, National Museum of Slovenia, as well as five other galleries and museums. The Technology Museum of Slovenia is in Vrhnika. Eight cultural institutions and about a dozen theatres and opera houses are in Slovenia as well.

45MEDIA

In 1989, Slovenia had 630,000 telephones, 21 radio stations, and 2 television channels. In 1991, there were 710,000 radios and 560,000 televisions.

In 1989, there were 3 daily and 425 other newspapers and 250 periodicals. A total of 1,932 book titles were published in the same year.

46ORGANIZATIONS

The Slovenia Chamber of Commerce (Chamber of Economy of Slovenia) coordinated all economic activities within and outside the country. In 1990 two large associations of trade unions were formed. In March of 1991 the Confederation of New Trade Unions of Slovenia was created, and has 135,000 members. The Association of Independent Trade Unions was formed in April 1990. It has 420,000 members.

47TOURISM, TRAVEL, AND RECREATION

Visitors from Europe and most other countries can enter Slovenia without visas. There are 75,000 beds available in hotels and other types of accommodations. Slovenia has convention centers in Ljubljana and three other cities and international airports in Ljubljana, Maribor, and Portorož. Popular recreational activities include tennis, golf, mountain climbing, canoeing, and fishing.

48FAMOUS SLOVENIANS

Milan Kučan and Janez Drnovšek have been president and prime minister of Slovenia since 1992. In 1551, Primož Trubar translated the New Bible into Slovene. The poet, Valentin Vodnik (1754—1819), wrote poems in paise of Napoleon; literature in praise of the French flourished during the French occupation of Slovenia in 1813. Slovenian tennis star Mima Jausovec (b.1956) won the Italian Open in 1976 and the French Open in 1977.

49DEPENDENCIES

Slovenia has no territories or colonies.

50BIBLIOGRAPHY

Cerar, Miro, and Janez Kranjc (eds.). *Constitution of the Republic of Slovenia*. Ljubljana: Uradni list Republike Slovenije, 1992.

Glenny, Michael. *The Fall of Yugoslavia: The Third Balkan War.* New York: Penguin, 1992.

Gobetz, Edward, and Ruth Lakner (eds.). *Slovenian Heritage.* Willoughby Hills, Ohio: Slovenian Research Center of America, 1980.

Harriman, Helga H. *Slovenia Under Nazi Occupation, 1941–1945.* New York: Studia Slovenica, 1977.

SPAIN

Spanish State
Estado Español

CAPITAL: Madrid.

FLAG: The national flag, adopted in 1785, consists of three horizontal stripes: a yellow one—equal in size to the other two combined—between two red ones, with the coat of arms on the yellow stripe.

ANTHEM: *Marcha Real Granadera (March of the Royal Grenadier)*.

MONETARY UNIT: The peseta (P) is a paper currency of 100 centimos. There are coins of 50 centimos and 1, 5, 25, 50, and 100 pesetas, and notes of 1,000, 2,000, 5,000, and 10,000 pesetas. P1 = $0.0073 (or $1 = P137.38).

WEIGHTS AND MEASURES: The metric system is the legal standard.

HOLIDAYS: New Year's Day, 1 January; St. Joseph's Day, 19 March; Epiphany, 31 March; Day of St. Joseph the Artisan, 1 May; St. James's Day, 25 July; Assumption, 15 August; National Day and Hispanic Day, 12 October; All Saints' Day, 1 November; Immaculate Conception, 8 December; Christmas, 25 December. Movable religious holidays include Holy Thursday, Good Friday, Easter Monday, and Corpus Christi.

TIME: 1 PM = noon GMT.

¹LOCATION, SIZE, AND EXTENT

Occupying the greater part of the Iberian Peninsula, Spain is the third-largest country in Europe, with an area of 504,750 sq km (194,885 sq mi). Comparatively, the area occupied by Spain is slightly more than twice the size of the state of Oregon. This total includes the Balearic Islands (Islas Baleares; 5,014 sq km/1,936 sq mi) in the western Mediterranean Sea and the Canary Islands (Islas Canarias; 7,273 sq km/2,808 sq mi) in the Atlantic Ocean west of Morocco; both island groups are regarded as integral parts of metropolitan Spain. The Spanish mainland extends 1,085 km (674 mi) E–W and 950 km (590 mi) N–S. Bordered by the Bay of Biscay, France, and Andorra on the N, by the Mediterranean on the E and S, by Gibraltar and the Strait of Gibraltar on the S, by the Gulf of Cádiz on the SW, and by Portugal and the Atlantic on the W, Spain has a total boundary length of 6,867 km (4,267 mi). Spain also holds Ceuta, Melilla, and other "places of sovereignty" in the north of Morocco.

Spain has long claimed Gibraltar, a narrow peninsula on the south coast, which was taken by a British-Dutch fleet in 1704 and became a British colony under the Treaty of Utrecht (1713). Spain closed the border with Gibraltar in 1969. In 1980, agreement was reached with Britain to begin negotiations concerning Gibraltar's sovereignty; the border was opened to pedestrian traffic in December 1982 and fully reopened in February 1985. Talks between the UK and Spain were held in February and December 1985 and January 1987.

Spain's capital city, Madrid, is located in the center of the country.

²TOPOGRAPHY

Continental Spain is divided into five general topographic regions: (1) The northern coastal belt is a mountainous region with fertile valleys and large areas under pasture and covered with forests. (2) The central plateau, or Meseta, with an average altitude of about 670 m (2,200 ft), comprises most of Castilla y León, Castilla–La Mancha, and the city of Madrid. (3) Andalucía,

with Sevilla its largest city, covers the whole of southern and southwestern Spain and, except for the flat fertile plain of the Guadalquivir River, is a mountainous region with deep fertile valleys. (4) The Levante is on the Mediterranean coastal belt, with Valencia its chief city. (5) Catalonia (Cataluña) and the Ebro Valley comprise the northeastern region.

Spain has six principal mountain ranges—the Pyrenees, the Cordillera Cantábrica, the Montes de Toledo, the Sierra Morena, the Serranías Penibéticas, and the Sistema Ibérico. The principal peaks are Pico de Aneto (3,404 m/11,168 ft) in the Pyrenees and Mulhacén (3,478 m/11,411 ft) in the Penibéticas. The main rivers are the Tagus (Tajo), Duero, Guadiana, and Guadalquivir, which flow to the Atlantic, and the Ebro, which flows to the Mediterranean. The Duero and the Guadalquivir form broad valleys and alluvial plains and at their mouths deposit saline soils, creating deltas and salt marshes. The coastline has few natural harbors except the estuaries (rías) in the northwest, formed by glaciers, and those in the Levante and the south, created by sandbars during the Quaternary period.

The Canary Islands are a group of 13 volcanic islands, of which 6 are barren. They have a ruggedly mountainous terrain interspersed with some fertile valleys. Spain's highest mountain, Pico de Teide (3,718 m/12,198 ft), is on Tenerife. The Balearic Islands are a picturesque group with sharply indented coastlines; they combine steep mountains with rolling, fertile ranges.

³CLIMATE

The climate of Spain is extremely varied. The northern coastal regions are cool and humid, with an average annual temperature of 14°C (57°F); temperatures at Bilbao ranged in 1981 from an average of 10°C (50°F) in January–March to 19°C (66°F) during July–September. The central plateau is cold in the winter and hot in the summer; Madrid has a winter average of about 8°C (46°F) and a summer average of 23°C (73°F). In Andalucía and the Levante, the climate is temperate except in summer, when temperatures sometimes reach above 40°C (104°F) in the shade. The northern coastal regions have an average annual rainfall of 99 cm (39 in); the southern coastal belt has 41–79 cm (16–31 in); and the interior central plain averages no more than 50 cm (20 in) annually.

⁴FLORA AND FAUNA

Because of its wide variety of climate, Spain has more different types of natural vegetation than any other European country; some 8,000 species are cataloged. Nevertheless, vegetation is generally sparse. In the humid areas of the north there are deciduous trees (including oak, chestnut, elm, beech, and poplar), as well as varieties of pine. Pine, juniper, and other evergreens, particularly the ilex and cork oak, and drought-resistant shrubs predominate in the dry southern region. Much of the Meseta and of Andalucía has steppe vegetation. The Canaries, named for the wild dogs (*canariae insulae*) once found there, support both Mediterranean and African flora. A small, yellow-tinged finch on the islands has given the name "canary" to a variety of yellow songbirds widely bred as house pets. Animal life in Spain is limited by the pressure of population, and few wild species remain.

⁵ENVIRONMENT

Extensive forests are now limited to the Pyrenees and the Asturias-Galicia area in the north because centuries of unplanned cutting have depleted stands. Fire eliminates 700,000 to 1,000,000 heactares of forestland each year. Government reforestation schemes meet with difficulties where sheep and goats graze freely over large areas. During the 1980s, an average of 92,000 hectares (227,000 acres) were reforested annually. Erosion affects 18% of the total land mass Spain. Air pollution is also a problem in Spain. The nation produces 1.1% of the world's total gas emissions. Hydrocarbon emissions amount to 929.0 tons per year. Industrial and agricultural sources contribute to the nation's water pollution problem. Spain is also vulnerable to oil pollution from tankers which travel the shipping routes near the nation's shores. Spain's cities produce 13.8 million tons of solid waste per year. Principal environmental responsibility is vested in the Directorate General of the Environment, within the Ministry of Public Works and Urban Affairs. In 1994, 6 of the country's mammal species and 23 bird species were endangered, 25 were 936 plant specoes. As of 1987, endangered species included the Spanish lynx, Pyrenean ibex, Mediterranean monk seal, northern bald ibis, Spanish imperial eagle, Cantabrian capercaillie, dusky large blue and Nevada blue butterflies, and on the Canary Islands, the green sea turtle and Hierro giant lizard.

⁶POPULATION

The population of Spain in 1991 was 39,433,942, a 4.4% increase over the 1981 census figure of 37,746,260. Population density in 1991 was 78 inhabitants per sq km (202 per sq mi). A population of 39,640,000 is projected for the year 2000, assuming a crude birthrate of 11.3 per 1,000 inhabitants, a death rate of 9.4, and a net natural increase of 0.9 for 1995–2000. An estimated 81% of the population was urban in 1995, compared with 52.6% in 1950. Madrid is the largest city, with 3,010,492 inhabitants in 1985. Other large cities are Barcelona (1,643,542), Valencia (752,909), Seville (683,028), Zaragoza (594,394), and Málaga, 522,108.

⁷MIGRATION

Emigration of Spanish workers to the more industrialized countries of Western Europe, notably to the Federal Republic of Germany (FRG), France, Switzerland, and Belgium, increased markedly during the 1960s, but since 1973 the number of Spaniards returning to Spain has been greater than the number of those leaving. Nevertheless, more than 1.7 million Spanish citizens were residing outside the country in 1987. In 1991, Spain had 360,655 foreign residents. Some come there to retire, others to work. There were 75,422 British in 1991 and 49,513 Moroccans. Germans, French, Portuguese, and Argentinians were also well represented. In addition there were an estimated 300,000 illegal immigrants in Spain.

Internal migration was 685,966 in 1990. In the past it has been directed toward the more industrialized zones and the great urban centers, and away from the rural areas. Rural-to-urban and urban-to-rural migration is now roughly in balance.

⁸ETHNIC GROUPS

Ethnological studies reveal a homogeneous Latin stock in three-fourths of the country. The greatest contrasts are found between those of Celtic, Iberic, and Gothic antecedents in the north and those of southern lineage. The great mobility of the population toward the urban centers, the coast, and the islands has contributed to the diffusion of ethnic characteristics.

Cultural groups, but not properly distinct ethnic groups, include the Castilians of central Spain, the Asturians and the Basques of Vizcaya, Álava, Guipúzcoa, and (in part) Navarra provinces in the north, the Catalans of Catalonia, the Galicians of the far northwest, and the Andalusians of the south. The Basques, Galicians, and Catalans consider themselves separate nations within Spain; they enjoy considerable cultural, economic, and political autonomy. Estimates of the Gypsy population range from 50,000 to 450,000.

⁹LANGUAGES

According to the 1978 constitution, Spanish is the national language. Castilian, the dialect of the central and southern regions, is spoken by most Spaniards and is used in the schools and courts. Regional languages—Catalan, Galician, Basque, Bable, and Valencian—are also official in the respective autonomous communities, where the education is bilingual.

According to census data, regional languages were spoken by 16,307,921 persons in Spain. A majority (6,643,346) of those who live in the northeastern provinces and the Balearic Islands spoke Catalan, a neo-Latin tongue. Galician, close to Portuguese, was used in Galicia, in the northwest corner of Spain, by 2,753,836 people. Bable, a form of Old Castilian in Asturias (northwest), was spoken by 1,127,007 persons, and Valencian, a dialect of Catalan, was used by 3,648,765 inhabitants of the eastern province of Valencia. The 2,134,967 Basques in northern Spain spoke Basque, a pre-Roman language unrelated to any other known tongue and using an ancient script.

¹⁰RELIGIONS

Until 1978, Roman Catholicism was the official religion of Spain, but the constitution of 1978 established the principles of religious freedom and separation of church and state. In 1993, at least 95% of the population was Roman Catholic (organized into more than 21,000 congregations). Protestants, numbered at 250,000 in 1993, freely published magazines and had their own radio stations, publishing houses, libraries, seminaries, and schools. There are more than 15,000 Jews. In addition, about 200,000 who profess Roman Catholicism still keep some Jewish practices; these people are descendants of the Marranos, the Spanish term for those who officially converted to Christianity but secretly practiced Judaism for centuries after all professing Jews had been expelled from Spain in 1492. A 1985 aliens law threatened to force the expulsion of most of the 27,000 Muslims living in the Ceuta and Melilla enclaves. A joint commission of government and Muslim leaders was set up in mid-1986 to discover ways of integrating the Muslims fully into Spanish society. In 1993, Muslims numbered approximately 300,000 and there were small Bahai and Buddhist communities.

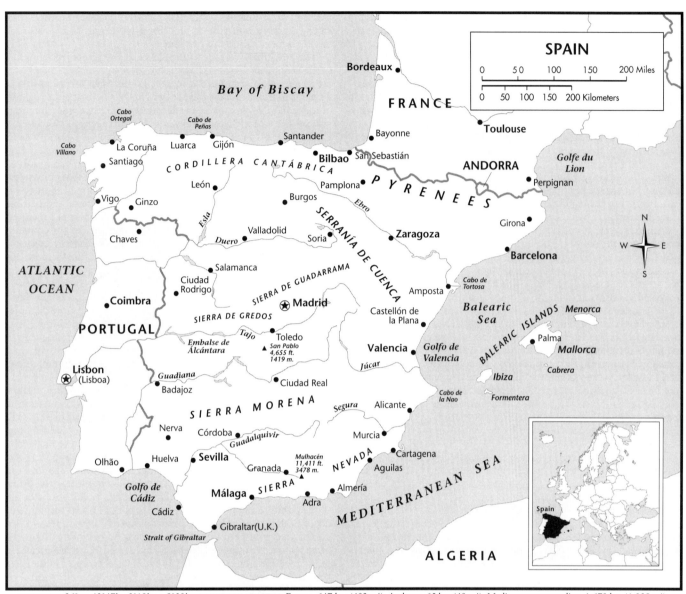

LOCATION: 36° to 43°47′N; 3°19′E to 9°30′W. **BOUNDARY LENGTHS:** France, 647 km (402 mi); Andorra, 65 km (40 mi); Mediterranean coastline, 1,670 km (1,038 mi); Gibraltar, 1 km (0.6 mi); Portugal, 1,232 km (766 mi); Atlantic and Bay of Biscay coastlines, 2,234 km (1,388 mi). The Balearic Islands extend from 1°12′ to 4°19′E and 38°38′ to 40°5′N; coastline, 910 km (565 mi). The Canary Islands extend from 13°20′ to 18°19′W and 27°38′ to 29°25′N; coastline, 1,126 km (700 mi). **TERRITORIAL SEA LIMIT:** 12 mi.

11 TRANSPORTATION

In 1991, Spain had 150,839 km (198,211 mi) of highways. State-operated national roads comprised 82,513 km (51,273 mi). About one-third of the road network is macadamized, with nearly 5,100 km (3,170 mi) of modern highways, of which the Mediterranean and Cantábrico routes are the most important. There were 15,152,132 vehicles in 1991, including 2,495,226 trucks and 46,604 buses.

The National Spanish Railway Network in 1991 encompassed 12,691 km (7,886 mi) of broad-gauge track, of which 6,184 km (3,843 mi) was electrified.

Of Spain's 200 ports, 26 are of commercial significance. The largest are Barcelona, Tarragona, and Cartagena on the Mediterranean, Algeciras on the Strait of Gibraltar, La Coruña on the Atlantic, and Las Palmas and Santa Cruz de Tenerife in the Canaries. The port of Bilbao, on the Bay of Biscay, can accommodate tankers of up to 500,000 tons. Substantial improvements were made during the 1970s at Gijón, Huelva, and Valencia. Scheduled ferry services connect Spain with neighboring countries

and North Africa. In 1991, the merchant fleet totaled 267 vessels, comprising 2,713,000 GRT, a decline of nearly 50% since 1985.

Spain has 61 airports, the most important being Madrid-Barajas, Barcelona-Prat, and Palma-Son San Juan. The state-owned Iberia Air Lines had regular connections with 50 countries and 89 cities in Europe, Africa, Asia (including the Middle East), and the Western Hemisphere and flew 194,800,000 km (121,050,000 mi), carrying some 15,411,600 passengers. Other Spanish airlines are Aviaco, Air Europa, Viva Air, Binter Canarias, and Spanair. Spanish airlines flew 27,400 million passenger-km and 586 million ton-km of freight in 1992.

12 HISTORY

Archaeological findings indicate that the region now known as Spain has been inhabited for thousands of years. A shrine near Santander, discovered in 1981, is believed to be over 14,000 years old, and the paintings discovered in the nearby caves of Altamira in 1879 are of comparable antiquity. The recorded history of Spain begins about 1000 BC, when the prehistoric Iberian culture was transformed by the invasion of Celtic tribes from the north and the coming of Phoenician and Greek colonists to the Spanish coast. From the 6th to the 2d century BC, Carthage controlled the Iberian Peninsula up to the Ebro River; from 133 BC, with the fall of Numantia, until the barbarian invasions of the 5th century AD, Rome held Hispania, from which the name Spain is derived. During the Roman period, cities and roads were built, and Christianity and Latin, the language from which Spanish originated, were introduced. In the 5th century, the Visigoths, or western Goths, settled in Spain, dominating the country until 711, when King Roderick was defeated by the invading Moors. All of Spain, except for a few northern districts, knew Muslim rule for periods ranging from 300 to 800 years. Under Islam, a rich civilization arose, characterized by prosperous cities, industries, and agriculture and by brilliant writers, philosophers, and physicians, including Jews as well as Muslims. Throughout this period (711–1492), however, Christian Spain waged intermittent and local war against the Moors. The most prominent figure in this battle was El Cid, who fought for both Christians and Moors in the 11th century. By the 13th century, Muslim rule was restricted to the south of Spain. In 1492, Granada, the last Moorish stronghold on Spanish soil, fell, and Spain was unified under Ferdinand II of Aragón and Isabella I of Castile, the "Catholic Sovereigns." Until then, Aragón (consisting of Aragón, Catalonia, Valencia, and the Balearic Islands) had been an independent kingdom, which had expanded toward the eastern Mediterranean, incorporating Sicily and Naples, and had competed with Genoa and Venice. In order to strengthen the unity of the new state, Moors and Jews were expelled from Spain; Catholic converts who chose to stay were subject to the terrors of the Inquisition if suspected of practicing their former religions. The year 1492 also witnessed the official European discovery of the Americas by Christopher Columbus, sailing under the Castilian flag. In 1519, Ferdinand Magellan, a Portuguese in the service of Spain, began the first circumnavigation of the world, completed in 1522 by Juan Sebastián Elcano.

The 16th century, particularly under Charles I, who was also Holy Roman Emperor Charles V, was the golden age of Spain: its empire in the Americas produced vast wealth; its arts flourished; its fleet ruled the high seas; and its armies were the strongest in Europe. By the latter part of the 16th century, however, under Philip II, the toll of religious wars in Europe and the flow of people and resources to the New World had drained the strength of the Spanish nation; in 1588, the "invincible" Spanish Armada was defeated by England. Spain's continental power was ended by wars with England, the Netherlands, and France in the 17th century and by the War of the Spanish Succession (1701–14), which also established the Bourbon (Borbón) dynasty in Spain. In 1808, the enfeebled Spanish monarchy was temporarily ended, and Napoleon Bonaparte's brother Joseph was proclaimed king of Spain. On 2 May 1808, however, the Spanish people revolted and, later assisted by the British, drove the French from Spain. In the post-Napoleonic period, the Bourbons were restored to the Spanish throne, but a spirit of liberalism, symbolized by the 1812 Constitution of Cádiz, remained strong.

Much of the 19th and early 20th centuries was consumed in passionate struggles between radical republicanism and absolute monarchy. Abroad, imperial Spain lost most of its dominions in the Western Hemisphere as a result of colonial rebellions in the first half of the 19th century; Cuba, Puerto Rico, and the Philippines were lost as a result of the Spanish-American War in 1898. Spain remained neutral in World War I but in the postwar period engaged in extensive military action to maintain its colonial possessions in Morocco.

Early defeats in the Moroccan campaign paved the way in 1923 for the benevolent dictatorship of Primo de Rivera, who successfully ended the war in 1927 and remained in power under the monarchy until 1930. In 1931, after municipal elections indicated a large urban vote in favor of a republic, Alfonso XIII left Spain and a republic was established.

The constitution of December 1931 defined Spain as a "democratic republic of workers," with "no official religion," respecting the "rules of international law, . . . renouncing war as an instrument of national policy and recognizing the principle of regional autonomy." Neither right nor left had a parliamentary majority, and on the whole the coalition governments were ineffective. On 17 July 1936, an army revolt against the republic took place in Spanish Morocco. On the following day, Gen. Francisco Franco landed in Spain, and for the next two and a half years, until 31 March 1939, Spain was ravaged by civil war. The two contending parties were the Republicans, made up partly of democrats and partly of antidemocratic left-wing groups, and the rebels (Nationalists), who favored the establishment of a right-wing dictatorship. Almost from the beginning, a number of foreign countries intervened. Germany and Italy furnished manpower and armaments to the Nationalists, while the USSR, Czechoslovakia, and Mexico supported the Republicans. Finally the Republicans were defeated, and Gen. Franco formed a corporative state. Under the Franco regime, Spain gave aid to the Axis powers in World War II but was itself a nonbelligerent.

The Post War Years
Diplomatically isolated following the end of World War II, Spain in succeeding decades improved its international standing, in part by signing economic and military agreements with the US in 1953 and 1963. Spain was admitted to the UN in 1955. While relations with its European neighbors approached normality, the repressive nature of the Franco regime kept Spain apart from the main social, political, and economic currents of postwar Western Europe.

On 22 July 1969, Juan Carlos de Borbón y Borbón was officially designated by Franco as his successor, to rule with the title of king; formally, Franco had been ruling as regent for the prince since 1947. On 20 November 1975, Gen. Franco died at the age of 82, thus ending a career that had dominated nearly four decades of Spanish history. Two days later, Juan Carlos I was sworn in as king. He reconfirmed Carlos Arias Navarro as prime minister on 5 December. Despite Juan Carlos I's announcement, in early 1976, of a program of moderate political and social reform, the new government was received with widespread demonstrations by labor groups and Catalan and Basque separatists. Continued political unrest, coupled with a sharp rise in living costs, led ultimately to the king's dismissal of Arias Navarro, who was replaced, on 7 July, by Adolfo Suárez González.

On 15 June 1977, the first democratic elections in Spain in 40 years took place, with the Union of the Democratic Center (Unión de Centro Democrático—UCD), headed by Suárez, winning a majority in the new Cortes. The Cortes prepared a new constitution (in many respects similar to that of 1931), which was approved by popular referendum and sanctioned by the king in December 1978. In the elections of March 1979, the UCD was again the victor, and in the April local elections it captured more than 75% of the municipalities.

When Suárez announced his resignation in January 1981, the king named Leopoldo Calvo Sotelo y Bustelo to the premiership. As the Cortes wavered over the appointment, a group of armed civil guards stormed parliament on 23 February and held more than 300 deputies hostage for 17 hours. The attempted coup was swiftly neutralized by the king, who secured the loyalty of other military commanders. The plotters were arrested, and Sotelo was swiftly confirmed. A year of political wrangling followed; by mid-1982 the UCD was in disarray, and Sotelo called new elections. In October 1982, the Spanish Socialist Worker's Party (Partido Socialista Obrero Español—PSOE), headed by Felipe González

Márquez, won absolute majorities in both houses of parliament. The new government was characterized by its relative youthfulness—the average age of cabinet ministers was 41—and by the fact that its members had no links with the Franco dictatorship. In the 1986 and 1989 elections, the PSOE again won majorities in both houses of parliament. The PSOE failed to win a majority in 1993 but governed with the support of the Basque and Catalan nationalist parties.

A continuing problem since the late 1960s has been political violence, especially in the Basque region. Political murders and kidnappings, mainly perpetrated by the separatist Basque Nation and Liberty (Euzkadi ta Askatasuna), commonly known as ETA, by the Anti-fascist Resistance Groups (GRAPO), and by several right-wing groups, abated only slightly in recent years. Another uncertainty in Spain's political future was the role of the military. Several army officers were arrested in October 1982 on charges of plotting a preelection coup, which reportedly had the backing of those involved in the February 1981 attempt. Spain joined NATO in 1982, but the membership question became so controversial that a referendum on it was held in March 1986; about two-thirds of the electorate voted, and 53% chose continued NATO membership. On 1 January of that year, Spain became a full member of the EC. In January 1988, the US, acceding to Spain's demands, agreed to withdraw 72 jet fighters based near Madrid.

Spain received considerable recognition with the holding of the 1992 Summer Olympics in Barcelona, and Expo 92, a world's fair, in Sevilla. Other notable events included the designation of Madrid as the culture capital of Europe in 1992.

13 GOVERNMENT

Between 1966 and 1978, Spain was governed under the Organic Law of the Spanish State. A new constitution, approved by the Cortes on 31 October 1978 and by the electorate in a national referendum on 6 December, and ratified by King Juan Carlos I on 27 December 1978, repealed all the laws of the Franco regime and confirmed Spain as a parliamentary monarchy. It also guaranteed the democratic functioning of all political parties, disestablished the Roman Catholic Church, and recognized the right to autonomy of distinct nationalities and regions.

According to the constitution, the king is the head of state, symbolizing its unity. Legislative power is vested in the Cortes Generales, consisting of two chambers: the Congress of Deputies (350 members in 1994) and the Senate (254 members). All deputies and 208 senators are popularly elected to four-year terms under universal adult suffrage. The remaining senators (46) are chosen by the assemblies in the 17 autonomous regions. The government, which is answerable to the Congress, consists of the president (prime minister), vice-president, and ministers, all appointed by the king. The supreme consultative organ of government is the Council of State. Also established by the constitution is the function of "defender of the people," inspired by medieval tradition and by the Scandinavian ombudsman. Suffrage is universal at age 18.

14 POLITICAL PARTIES

The Falange, known officially as the Nationalist Movement, was the only legally functioning party in Spain during the Franco regime. Founded in 1933 by José Antonio Primo de Rivera, it dated in its later form from 1937, when various right-wing groups were united under Gen. Franco. Nationalists, monarchists, and national syndicalists (Fascists) were the leading groups within the Falange. It lost some of its former power and much of its prestige during the last decades of Franco's regime. On 21 December 1974, the Franco government passed a law conferring a limited right of political association. On 9 June 1976, after Franco's death, the Cortes voted to legalize political parties; by

the 1977 parliamentary elections, no fewer than 156 political parties were organized, into 10 national coalitions and 12 regional alliances.

The Spanish political scene is characterized by changing parties and shifting alliances. The Union of the Democratic Center (Unión de Centro Democrático—UCD) was formed as an electoral coalition of smaller moderate parties. From 1977 to 1982, the UCD was the governing political body, headed first by Adolfo Suárez González and then by Leopoldo Calvo Sotelo y Bustelo. In late 1981, the UCD began to disintegrate; it won only 8% of the vote in the 1982 elections and was dissolved in February 1983. A new centrist party, the Democratic and Social Center (Centro Democrático y Social—CDS), was created in 1982. The Spanish Socialist Worker's Party (Partido Socialista Obrero Español—PSOE), which traces its lineage to the late 19th century, won absolute majorities in both chambers of the Cortes in October 1982 and June 1986.

The right is represented by the People's Alliance (CP), later the Popular Party or PP, embracing the Alianza Popular, the Christian Democratic Partido Demócrata Popular, and the Partido Liberal; the coalition took 26% of the 1986 vote. An extreme rightist party, New Force (Fuerza Nueva), lost its only seat in parliament in 1982 and thereupon dissolved. The Communist Party (Partido Comunista—PC), legalized in 1977, was one of the most outspoken "Eurocommunist" parties in the late 1970s, harshly criticizing the former USSR for human rights abuses. In the 1986 election, the PC formed part of the United Left coalition (Izquierda Unida—IU), which included a rival Communist faction and several socialist parties; the IU's share of the vote was 4.6%. Nationalist parties function in Catalonia, Andalucía, the Basque provinces, and other areas.

Despite charges of corruption and economic mismanagement, the PSOE secured electoral victories in 1989 and 1993; however, the party finished 17 seats short of a parliamentary majority in 1993. A noticeable shift toward the conservative PP was evident with a 34-seat gain between 1989 and 1993. PSOE secretary-general Felipe Gonzalez Marquez received endorsement for a fourth term as prime minister, receiving support from the small Basque and Catalan nationalist parties.

The results of the 1993 election were as follows: PSOE, 159; PP, 141; IV, 18; CIV, 17; and others, 15.

15 LOCAL GOVERNMENT

Spain is divided into 17 autonomous regions, each of which has an elected assembly and a governor appointed by the central government. Municipalities are gradually becoming consolidated; their number had declined to about 8,000 by 1987. Each municipality has a mayor (alcalde) and councilmen (concejales); the councilmen, directly elected by the people, elect the mayors.

The statutes governing the Basque and Catalan autonomous communities, providing for regional high courts and legislative assemblies, were approved by referendum in October 1979; the statutes for Galicia in December 1980; and those for Andalucía in October 1981. Autonomy statutes for the other 11 historic regions of continental Spain and the Balearic and Canary Islands were subsequently approved and a regular electoral process begun. Administration of the presidios (places of sovereignty) on the North African shore is by appointed officials, but this has been subject to review in recent years because of local Muslim pressure. Their administrative status remains unclear in 1994.

16 JUDICIAL SYSTEM

According to the 1978 constitution, the judiciary is independent and subject only to the rule of law. The highest judicial body is the seven-member Supreme Court (Tribunal Supremo), the president of which is nominated by the 20 judges of the General Council of the Judiciary and appointed by the king.

Territorial high courts (audiencias) are the courts of last appeal in the 15 regions of the country; provincial audiencias serve as appellate courts in civil matters and as courts of first instance in criminal cases. On the lowest level are the judges of the first instance and instruction, district judges, and justices of the peace.

The National High Court (Audiencia Nacional), created in 1977, has jurisdiction over criminal cases that transgress regional boundaries and over civil cases involving the central state administration. The constitution of 1978 also established the Constitutional Court (Tribunal Constitucional), with competence to judge the constitutionality of laws and decide disputes between the central government and the autonomous regions. The European Court of Human Rights is the final arbiter in cases concerning human rights.

Defendants in criminal cases have the right to counsel at state expense if indigent. The Constitution prohibits arbitrary arrest and detention. Suspects may be held for no more than three days without a judicial hearing.

[17]ARMED FORCES

Spain has a 9-month compulsory military service system but is moving toward a smaller, volunteer force. In 1993, the armed forces totaled 217,000, of whom 158,100 were conscripts, a one-third reduction since 1986. The 146,000-man army was organized into 5 divisions, and 8 special purpose brigades. The navy had 36,000 men and included 1 aircraft carrier, 15 missile frigates, 8 submarines, 39 coastal and patrol combatants, and various mine warfare and transport vessels. The air force had 35,000 men and about 207 combat aircraft. The Guardia Civil numbered about 65,000. Spain's arms imports for 1981–91 totaled $5 billion. The Socialist government has introduced a modernization program aimed at decreasing the size of the army and shifting its function from domestic order to external defense as part of NATO. In 1991 Spain spent $8.7 billion on defense, or 2% of gross domestic product. Spain contributes 164 observers to two UN missions and hosts 3,400 Americans at the Rota naval base.

[18]INTERNATIONAL COOPERATION

Spain, having joined the UN on 14 December 1955, participates in ECE, ECLA, and all the nonregional specialized agencies. Spain became a full member of the OECD in 1959. In June 1970, Spain signed a trade agreement with the EC calling for a mutual reduction of tariffs over a six-year period; the nation became a full member of the EC in 1986. Spain is also a member of the Council of Europe. The entry of Spain into NATO was approved in 1982 and confirmed by referendum in 1986.

In the 1970s, accords for double nationality, cultural assistance, and technical cooperation were signed with the majority of Latin American countries. Spain has observer status in the OAS and the Andean Pact and is also a member of IDB. In June 1975, Madrid was selected as permanent headquarters for the World Tourism Organization. Five years later, Madrid became the seat of the Conference on Security and Cooperation in Europe. Spain is a signatory of GATT and the Law of the Sea.

[19]ECONOMY

Agriculture, livestock, and mining—the traditional economic mainstays—no longer occupy the greater part of the labor force or provide most of the exports. In order to offset the damage suffered by the industrial sector during the Civil War and to cope with the problems created by Spain's post-World War II isolation, the Franco regime concentrated its efforts on industrial expansion. Especially after 1953, the industrial sector expanded rapidly. In terms of per capita income, however, Spain still ranks among the lowest in Western Europe, with an estimated GDP of $14,000 per person in 1993. From 1974 through the early 1980s,

the Spanish economy was adversely affected by international factors, especially oil price increases. The annual GDP growth rate during 1974–77 was 3%, higher than that in other OECD countries, but the inflation rate reached 24% in 1977. Real GDP growth slowed to about 1.6% during 1980–85 and averaged 3.5% between 1985 and 1992 but fell 1% in 1993. Consumer prices rose 25.1% between 1989 and 1993, and unemployment rose from 17.3% to 22.7%.

Tourism is a major source of foreign exchange, but its importance to the economy has declined. In 1992, tourism receipts made up 3.6% of GDP.

[20]INCOME

In 1992, Spain's GNP was $547,947 million at current prices, or $14,020 per capita. For the period 1985–92 the average inflation rate was 6.9%, resulting in a real growth rate in per capita GNP of 3.8%.

[21]LABOR

In 1991, civilian employment totaled 12,609,400, distributed as follows: services, 7,100,700; industry, 2,890,100; fishing and agriculture, 1,345,100; and construction, 1,273,500. Employment in agriculture has been in steady decline; many farm workers have been absorbed by construction and industry. The service sector has been the most dynamic in recent years. Unemployment averaged about 17% during 1991.

At the end of the Civil War, a system of national, or vertical, syndicates was formed through which the government controlled industry and labor. Almost all employees and employers were required to join one of the National Syndical Organization's 22 syndicates, each of which covered a basic field of industry or agriculture. The syndicates were financed by a levy on employees of 0.5% of all wages received and on employers of 1.5% of all wages paid. The status of the syndicates was that of public corporations, under close government supervision.

Collective bargaining was introduced in 1958. Strikes, though prohibited, became increasingly common during the late 1960s and early 1970s, and a law of May 1975 legalized work stoppages under limited conditions. The constitution of 1978 guarantees the freedom to form unions and the right to strike. In 1992, there were over 200 registered unions in Spain. The main trade unions are the General Union of Workers (Socialist), the Workers' Commissions (Communist), the Workers' Trade Union (independent), the Solidarity of Basque Workers (independent), and the National Confederation of Labor (anarchist).

Special labor courts hear disputes between workers and employers. In 1981, representatives of government, business, and unions signed an agreement aimed at slowing the wage increases that contributed to inflation and unemployment in the late 1970s. Short strikes are commonplace in Spain. In 1992, work stoppages were at their highest level since 1988 and included a nationwide strike on May 28.

[22]AGRICULTURE

During 1970–90, the proportion of the GDP from agriculture fell from 11.3% to less than 5%, and the proportion of workers employed in agriculture decreased from 26% to about 9.5% by 1992. Agricultural land in 1991 covered 20,089,000 hectares (49,640,000 acres), of which 76% was used for field crops, and 24% planted with olive trees, vineyards, and orchards. Pastureland comprised another 10,300,000 hectares (25,451,000 acres).

Agricultural production, in 1992, included (in millions of tons) barley, 6.0; potatoes, 5.2; wheat, 4.5; corn, 2.6; tomatoes, 2.6; oats, 0.3; and rice, 0.5. Fruit and nut production for 1992 (in thousands of tons) included oranges, 2,724; apples, 1,027; tangerines, 1,488; pears, 602; peaches, 964; lemons, 661; bananas, 355; almonds, 288; apricots, 193; plums, 141; and hazelnuts, 27.

Other important crops were grapes, 5,676,000 tons, and olives, 2,831,000 tons. Grapes are cultivated in every region; in 1992, 3,472,000 tons of wine were produced. Olive oil remains a major agricultural product, with 597,000 tons produced during 1992. The most important olive groves are in Andalucía. Within the domestic market, the use of sunflower oil and soybean oil has grown considerably.

Agricultural mechanization has been increasing steadily. In 1991 there were 755,743 tractors, and 48,821 harvester-threshers. The use of fertilizers has also increased. The Institute for Agrarian Development and Reform directly or indirectly regulates some 10 million hectares (25 million acres) of land, promoting intensive cultivation and irrigation to improve productivity.

23 ANIMAL HUSBANDRY

Because much of Spain is arid or semiarid, sheep are by far the most important domestic animals. In 1992, Spain's livestock population (in thousands) included sheep, 24,625; hogs, 17,240; cattle, 4,924; goats, 3,000; horses, 240; asses, 130; and mules, 100. In 1992, milk production was 5.8 million tons; egg production was an estimated 597,400 tons in 1992.

24 FISHING

Fishing is important, especially along the northern coastline. In 1991, the fish catch was 1,350,000 tons.

25 FORESTRY

Spain's forested area in 1991 was 15,858,000 hectares (39,185,000 acres). Roundwood production in 1991 totaled 17,272,000 cu m. Spain is one of the largest producers of cork, its most important commercial forest product. Scotch and maritime pine, as well as radiata pine, are the main softwood lumber species produced in Spain; eucalyptus and poplar are the principal hardwood species.

26 MINING

Almost all known minerals are found in Spain, and mining is still a notable, though much diminished, factor in the Spanish economy. Iron ore, mined in the north (Basque provinces, Asturias, León) and in Andalucía, is one of Spain's principal mineral assets; total reserves are estimated at 6 million tons of iron, with 3.9 million tons of ore produced in 1991. The principal coal mines are in Asturias and León; reserves are estimated at 500 million tons. In 1991, 5.8 million tons of anthracite, 14 million tons of bituminous coal, and 16 million tons of lignite were produced. Lead (50,000 tons in 1991) is mined mainly in Jaén, potash salts (760,000 tons) in Barcelona, and mercury (900,000 kg of processed metal in 1991, second only to the former USSR) in Ciudad Real. The Almadén mines constitute the richest mercury deposit in the world. Iron pyrites, copper, zinc, sulfur, manganese, and tungsten also are mined.

In 1990, the estimated value of Spanish mineral production was about $4.3 billion: 11% in the metals sector, 39% in industrial minerals, and 50% in the mineral fuels sector. Quarried natural stone accounted for 16% of the value of Spanish mining.

27 ENERGY AND POWER

Production of electricity in 1991 reached 155 billion kwh, as compared with 45.9 billion kwh in 1968. Per capita consumption increased from 420 kwh in 1955 to 3,972 kwh in 1991. In the same year, 46% of production was conventional thermal, 37% nuclear, and 17% hydroelectric in origin, up from 4.8% in 1981. As of 1991, the Spanish government continued the moratorium on construction of nuclear power plants due to cost, environmental considerations, and the need for energy diversification. The Hidro-Electrica Espanõla and Sevillana utilities are the plants most adversely affected by the termination of work on the Valdecaballeros power plant in western Spain. Increased use of coal

and natural gas for thermal plants is also envisioned, and increasing attention is being paid to solar energy. Coal production in 1992 totaled 33.9 million tons; known reserves were estimated at 500 million tons of hard coal in 1991.

In 1964, oil was struck near Burgos, and in 1971, offshore deposits were located near Amposta, in Tarragona. In 1992, Spanish wells were producing an estimated 20,000 barrels of crude oil per day. Consumption, however, totaled 1,065,000 barrels daily in 1992. In 1991, fuel imports accounted for 11% of total imports. Spain imports much of its natural gas from Algeria and Libya. In 1987, Spain signed an agreement to obtain natural gas from fields in northern Europe.

28 INDUSTRY

Industrial production fell by 4.7% in 1993 after averaging an annual growth of 1.7% during 1985–92. The chief sectors are food and beverages, energy, and transport materials. Chemical production, particularly of superphosphates, sulfuric acid, dyestuffs, and pharmaceutical products, is also significant. Of the heavy industries, iron and steel (1992 production 12,271,000 tons), centered mainly in Bilbao and Avilés, is the most important. Petroleum refinery production in 1991 totaled 54.8 million tons, and in 1992, 24.6 million tons of cement were produced. Other important products in 1992 included automobiles, 1,795,620 and commercial vehicles, 372,842. New ships totaling 442,000 GRT, 2,266,000 tons of plastics, and 7,686,000 domestic electric appliances were produced in 1990.

Government participation in industry is through the National Industrial Institute (INI), which owns mining enterprises, oil refineries, steel and chemical plants, shipbuilding yards, and artificial fiber factories, or through Patrimonio. Nearly 20 subsidiaries of INI and Patrimonio were sold between 1985 and mid-1993, mostly to foreign multinational companies.

29 SCIENCE AND TECHNOLOGY

The Council for Scientific Research, founded in 1940, coordinates research in science and technology. The Royal Academy of Exact, Physical, and Natural Sciences, founded in 1847, is the nation's chief scientific academy. In 1987, total expenditures on research and development amounted to 221 billion pesetas; 8,196 technicians and 20,890 scientists and engineers were engaged in research and development.

30 DOMESTIC TRADE

Madrid is the distribution center for the interior of Spain. Spain has no free ports, but free-zone privileges are granted at Barcelona, Bilbao, Cádiz, Vigo, and the Canary Islands. There are bonded warehouses at the larger ports. The government has established a market distribution program to regulate the flow of goods to and from the producing and consuming areas. Since 1972, wholesale market networks have been established in cities with more than 150,000 inhabitants. The National Consumption Institute promotes consumer cooperatives and credit unions.

Advertising is largely through newspapers, magazines, radio, and motion picture theaters. Usual business hours are from 9 AM to 8 PM, with an afternoon recess of two to three hours (from 1 to 4 PM). Banks are open from 9 AM to 2 PM, Monday through Friday, and to 1 PM on Saturday.

31 FOREIGN TRADE

Traditionally, exports consisted mainly of agricultural products (chiefly wine, citrus fruits, olives and olive oil, and cork) and minerals. While agricultural products and minerals remain important, they have, since the 1960s, been overtaken by industrial exports. Imports habitually exceed exports by a large margin.

Principal exports in 1992 (in millions of pesetas) were the following:

Machinery	521,673
Food, beverages, and tobacco	838,616
Automobiles	1,110,767
Other exports	4,134,611
TOTAL	6,605,667

Principal imports in 1992 (in millions of pesetas) were the following:

Machinery	1,213,723
Intermediate energy products	1,009,719
Food, drinks, and tobacco	774,626
Automobiles	684,336
Other imports	6,522,609
TOTAL	10,205,013

Principal trade partners in 1992 (in millions of pesetas) were the following:

	EXPORTS	IMPORTS	BALANCE
EC countries, of which	4,701,080	6,197,512	−1,496,432
France	1,335,045	1,619,268	−284,222
Germany	1,036,536	1,673,659	−637,123
UK	505,739	745,042	−239,302
Italy	719,441	1,003,081	−283,639
US and Canada	350,027	813,259	−463,232
EFTA countries	282,398	502,723	−220,325
Japan	61,631	475,643	−414,012
Latin America	271,017	425,706	−154,689
Other countries	939,514	1,790,172	−850,658
TOTALS	6,605,667	10,205,015	−3,599,348

32BALANCE OF PAYMENTS

Tourism, remittances from Spaniards living abroad, investment income, and loans to the private sector were the principal factors that helped to offset recurrent trade deficits in the 1970s and 1980s. In 1992, imports increased by 8.8%, but the rate of growth for imports fell sharply following currency devaluation late in 1992. Exports grew by 7.1% that year. In 1992 merchandise exports totaled $63,921 million and imports $−94,954 million. The merchandise trade balance was $−31,033 million. The following table summarizes Spain's balance of payments for 1991 and 1992 (in millions of US dollars):

	1991	1992
CURRENT ACCOUNT		
Goods, services, and income	−22,779	−24,292
Unrequited transfers	6,060	5,810
TOTALS	−16,718	−18,482
CAPITAL ACCOUNT		
Direct investment	6,919	6,758
Portfolio investment	18,725	−790
Other long-term capital	8,418	15,559
Other short-term capital	−2,086	−15,109
Exceptional financing	—	—
Other liabilities	—	—
Reserves	−14,141	17,472
TOTALS	17,835	23,890
Errors and omissions	−1,117	−5,407
Total change in reserves	−14,596	20,319

33BANKING AND SECURITIES

The banking and credit structure centers on the Bank of Spain,

the government's national bank of issue since 1874. The bank acts as the government depository as well as a banker's bank for discount and other operations. Other "official" but privately owned banks are the Mortgage Bank of Spain, the Local Credit Bank of Spain, the Industrial Credit Bank, the Agricultural Credit Bank, and the External Credit Bank.

In 1993, the private banking system consisted of over 100 banks, comprising national banks, industrial banks, regional banks, local banks, and foreign banks. The liberalization of the banking system and Spain's entry into the EC have raised the number and presence of foreign banks. The total assets of the private banks amounted to P117,311 million in 1993. In addition, Spain has 62 rural savings banks.

Spain has four major stock exchanges, in Madrid, Barcelona, Bilbao, and Valencia. These exchanges are open for a few hours a day, Tuesday through Friday. Since 1961, foreign investment in these exchanges has increased rapidly. The major commercial banks invest in the equity and debt securities of private firms and carry on brokerage businesses as well.

34INSURANCE

Insurance companies are supervised by the government through the Direccion General de Seguros. Life insurance in force in 1992 totaled P50 trillion. In the same year, there were roughly 500 insurance companies operating in Spain, although about 100 of these were in the process of going out of business, and it was estimated that 80% of the insurance market would be concentrated in about 54 firms by 1995. Insurance premiums totaled P1.7 trillion in 1991.

35PUBLIC FINANCE

The public sector deficit in 1993 was equivalent to 3.8% of GDP (down from 4.4% in 1992 and 5% in 1991), or about the same as in 1990. In order to cap the central government deficit in 1993, spending was to have been severely reduced. For example, defense procurements were to have been cut by 10%, and total payroll costs were slated to decline as well.

The following table shows actual revenues and expenditures for 1989 and 1990 in billions of pesetos.

	1989	1990
REVENUE AND GRANTS		
Tax revenue	13,471.7	14,430.1
Non-tax revenue	793.0	825.8
Capital revenue	37.9	76.1
Grants	219.2	228.9
TOTAL	14,521.8	15,560.9
EXPENDITURES & LENDING MINUS REPAYMENTS		
General public service	433.3	530.9
Defense	815.3	748.6
Public order and safety	535.9	577.0
Education	858.5	891.3
Health	2,088.2	1,182.2
Social security and welfare	5,627.7	6,536.2
Housing and community amenities	98.1	81.3
Recreation, cultural, and religious affairs	124.9	101.9
Economic affairs and services	1,666.6	1,687.3
Other expenditures	2,946.5	4,627.0
Adjustments	—	—
Lending minus repayments	341.4	216.5
TOTAL	15,536.4	17,180.2
Deficit/Surplus	−1,014.6	−1,619.3

In 1990 Spain's total foreign debt stood at P587.8 billion.

36TAXATION

The structure of the Spanish fiscal system was profoundly modified in 1977 and 1978. As of 1992, marginal personal income tax rates ranged from 20% to 56%, with few deductions allowed. The basic corporation tax rate is 35%. Indirect taxes include levies on inheritances, documents, sales, special products (alcohol, petroleum, and others), luxury items, and fiscal monopolies. As a condition of entry into the EC, Spain introduced a value-added tax on 1 January 1986. It replaced several taxes—such as the turnover, luxury, and equalization taxes—and coexists with the remainder.

37CUSTOMS AND DUTIES

Since 20 July 1959, when Spain became a member of the OECD, steps have been taken to liberalize customs restrictions. A new customs tariff paralleling that of other OECD countries became effective in 1960; new customs legislation was passed in 1977. Tariffs were relaxed further when Spain entered the EC. Spain adheres to GATT, so the basis for most duties is ad valorem. In some cases, an import permit is required, although the general policy on imports is described as "free trade."

38FOREIGN INVESTMENT

Since the decree laws of 1959, 1960, and 1963, foreign investments have developed into a vital element in Spain's economic growth. Foreign participation in Spanish enterprises is authorized up to 10% of equity except in certain sectors, such as military equipment, radio and television broadcasting, mining, shipping, air transport, public services, oil exploration, and gambling, where only minority participation is allowed. Free repatriation of principal, earnings, and capital gains of both portfolio and direct investment is permitted, and all restrictions on foreign capital have been lifted for selected industrial and capital endeavors. The liberalization associated with entry into the EC boosted foreign investment. In 1993, foreign investment in Spain totaled $15 billion, of which $1.5 billion came from the US.

39ECONOMIC DEVELOPMENT

After 1939, Spanish economic policy was characterized by the attempt to achieve economic self-sufficiency. This policy, largely imposed by Spain's position during World War II and the isolation to which Spain was subjected in the decade following 1945, was also favored by many Spanish political and business leaders. In 1959, following two decades of little or no overall growth, the Spanish government, acceding to reforms suggested by the IMF, OECD, and IBRD and encouraged by the promise of foreign financial assistance, announced its acceptance of the so-called Stabilization Plan, intended to curb domestic inflation and adverse foreign payment balances.

Long-range planning began with Spain's first four-year development plan (1964–67), providing a total investment of P355 billion. The second four-year plan (1968–71) called for an investment of P553 billion, with an average annual growth of 5.5% in GNP. The third plan (1972–75) called for investments of P871 billion; drastic readjustments had to be made in 1975 to compensate for an economic slump brought on by increased petroleum costs, a tourist slowdown, and a surge in imports. A fifth plan (1976–79) focused on development of energy resources, with investments to increase annually by 9% increments. A stabilization program introduced in 1977 included devaluation of the peseta and tightening of monetary policy. The economic plan of 1979–82 committed Spain to a market economy and rejected protectionism.

Accession to the EC generated increased foreign investment but also turned Spain's former trade surplus with the EC into a growing deficit: the lowering of tariffs boosted imports, but exports did not keep pace. The government responded by pursuing market liberalization and deregulation, in hopes of boosting productivity and efficiency to respond to EC competition. A number of projects, such as the construction of airports, highways, and a high-speed rail line between Madrid and Seville, received EC funding. To prepare Spain for a forthcoming European economic and monetary union, the government in 1992 planned to cut public spending. The currency was devalued three times in 1992–93.

40SOCIAL DEVELOPMENT

All employed persons aged 14 and older must subscribe to the national social security scheme. As of 1991, workers contributed 4.8% and employers 24% of base salary to a social insurance fund. The fund provides for health and maternity insurance, old age and incapacity insurance, a family subsidy, workers' compensation, and job-related disability payments. The fund also covers domestic workers and farmers. The voluntary insurance system includes retirement pensions and dowry insurance. A compulsory unemployment insurance system was substantially improved in 1984 to provide benefits of 80% of average earnings for the first 6 months, 70% for the next 6 months, 60% for an additional 12 months, and, after that, 75% of the minimum wage for 18 months.

Civil divorce was legalized in 1981, despite the strong opposition of the Roman Catholic Church. An estimated 51% of married women practiced contraception in 1985, a majority by traditional methods. Abortion in cases of rape or incest or on limited health grounds was legalized in 1985. The 1978 constitution abolished the death penalty.

One-third more women now work outside the home than a decade ago, but employment levels for women are still relatively low. A 1993 update of the 1988 Women's Institute plan for equal opportunities calls for cooperation between women's groups and government to assist battered women, improve access to job search networks, and promote equal sharing of family responsibilities.

41HEALTH

Spain's total health care expenditures were about $39.44 million in 1992. It is estimated that they will be between 8.1 and 8.3% of the GDP by the year 2000. Spanish officials say that public contributions to the cost of health care must be limited in the face of potentially unlimited demand.

The public sector in health care is the largest and continues to grow. In 1991, there were 354 public hospitals, 149 private hospitals, and 312 private business hospitals. There were a total of 175,375 beds of which 120,861 (68.9%) were public. In the nonprofit private sector (Red Cross, churches), there were 25,235 beds (14.4%); and, in the private business sector, there were 29,288 beds (16.7%). The public health sector contracts a significant number of beds from both types of private hospitals. In 1990, Spain had 148,717 doctors, 10,347 dentists, and 36,590 pharmacists; in 1988, there were 147,726 nurses and 6,291 midwives. In 1990, the population per physician was 280. In 1992, there were 3.60 doctors per 1,000 people, with a nurse to doctor ratio of 1.1. Recent programs have created special residences for elderly and retired people, eye clinics, a network of government health centers in the principal cities, and more than a dozen human tissue and organ banks for transplantation and research. Immunization rates for children up to one year old in 1992 were: diphtheria, pertussis, and tetanus (93%); polio (94%); and measles (97%).

In 1993, Spain had a birth rate of 10.8 per 1,000 people, with about 59% of married women (ages 15 to 49) using contraception. There were 422,000 births in 1992. Average life expectancy in 1992 was 77 years. The infant mortality rate in 1992 was 8 per 1,000 live births, down from 38 in 1965. The general mortality rate was 9.2 per 1,000 in 1993. Leading causes of death in

1990 were delineated as follows: communicable diseases and maternal/ perinatal causes (45 per 100,000 people); noncommunicable diseases (410 per 100,000); and injuries (42 per 100,000). There were about 49 cases of tuberculosis per 100,000 reported in 1990.

42 HOUSING

According to the 1980 housing census, the number of housing units was 6,516,589. Construction has generally fallen short of the 336,000 units required annually to keep pace with population growth and the deterioration of old buildings. The pressure for new housing has been especially great in rural areas, where as of 1980, 66% of the units had been built before 1960. The number of housing units completed in 1986 was 195,200, down from the high of 242,900 in 1982. In 1989, 233,063 units were completed and the total number of dwellings in 1991 was 15,974,000.

43 EDUCATION

According to the 1978 constitution, elementary education is compulsory and free, and university autonomy is recognized. During 1989, there were 19,331 schools with 140,285 teachers and 2,961,953 pupils. General secondary schools had 3,657,391 pupils with 187,934 teachers. The adult literacy rate in 1985 was estimated at 79% for women and 93% for men.

Students in higher education numbered 1,169,141 in 1989 and there were 59,136 instructors. The Pontifical University of Salamanca, founded in 1254, is the oldest university, while the University of Madrid has the largest student body.

44 LIBRARIES AND MUSEUMS

In 1990, Spain had 3,550 libraries under the following classifications: 1 national, 567 at institutions of higher learning, and 2,982 public. The National Library in Madrid, the Library of Catalonia in Barcelona, the university libraries of Salamanca, Valladolid, Barcelona, and Sevilla, and the public library in Toledo (with many imprints from the fifteenth to the eighteenth centuries) are among the most important collections. Spain also has 61 historical archives, among them the Archivo General de Indias in Sevilla, with 60,000 volumes and files, and the archives of Simancas, with 86,000 volumes and files.

The Prado, in Madrid, with its extensive collection of Spanish art, is the most famous museum of Spain and one of the best in the world. The National Archaeological Museum, also in Madrid, contains the prehistoric cave paintings of Altamira. The Museum of Modern Art, in Barcelona, houses excellent cubist and surrealist collections. There are also important art collections in the Escorial and Aranjuez palaces, near Madrid.

45 MEDIA

The government owns, operates, or supervises all internal telephone, telegraph, and radio and television service. Postal and telegraph facilities are provided by the Mail and Telecommunications Service. The National Telephone Co., an autonomous enterprise, operated 15,476,775 telephones in 1991. Since 1975 there had been only one official radio and television authority, but legislation ending its monopoly was awaiting approval in 1987. In 1991, radio transmissions were broadcast over more than 500 stations by four government and six private networks, and four state-owned television networks. In the same year, Spaniards had some 12.1 million radios and 15.6 million television sets.

There were 102 daily newspapers in 1991. Sunday editions have become increasingly common, with circulations often double the weekday runs. English-language papers are now printed in Madrid and Palma de Mallorca. There are also some 3,000 magazines, bulletins, and journals. Formerly, the Falange published the newspapers in all provincial capitals and controlled some 35% of the total national circulation; censorship was obligatory.

In 1966, a new press law abolished censorship but established stiff penalties for editors who published news "contrary to the principles of the national interest"; offending newspapers could be seized. The 1978 constitution guarantees freedom of the press.

The leading Spanish dailies, with 1991 circulations, included the following:

	CITY	CIRCULATION
El País	Madrid	375,800
ABC	Madrid and Sevilla	300,000
El Periódico	Barcelona	230,000
La Vanguardia Española	Barcelona	225,000
Diario 16	Madrid	200,000
Ya	Madrid	59,800

46 ORGANIZATIONS

Under the Falangist system of corporate organization, all branches of society were required to participate in business and in agricultural or professional syndicates. Despite this system, cooperatives emerged in various sectors of Spanish society, among them agricultural, consumer, credit, industrial, maritime, fishing, rural, housing, and educational organizations. Chambers of commerce function in all provincial capitals, and there are numerous industrial and trade associations.

47 TOURISM, TRAVEL, AND RECREATION

Tourism has become a vital industry. In 1991, Spain was the world's third most popular tourist destination, and Europe's second. In that year, 53.4 million people visited Spain, 22% from France, 19% from Portugal, and 14% from Germany. Tourism receipts totaled $19 billion. Many are attracted to Spain by its accessibility, warm climate, beaches, and relatively low costs. Among the principal tourist attractions are Madrid, with its museums, the Escorial Palace, and the nearby Valley of the Fallen (dead in the Civil War); Toledo, with its churches and its paintings by El Greco; the Emerald Coast around San Sebastián; the Costa Brava on the coast of Catalonia, north of Barcelona; Granada, with the Alhambra and the Generalife; Sevilla, with its cathedral and religious processions; and the Canary and Balearic islands. There were 627,055 hotel rooms in 1991, with 1,146,473 beds. Passports are required of all persons entering Spain, but US citizens may stay six months without a visa, and citizens of many other countries need no visas for stays of up to 90 days.

Soccer is the most popular sport in Spain, and many cities have large soccer stadiums; Spain was host to the World Cup competition in 1982. Barcelona was the site of the 1992 Summer Olympics and in the same year, an International Exposition was held in Sevilla. Among traditional attractions are the bullfights, held in Madrid from April through October, and pelota, an indoor ball game in which spectators bet on the outcome.

48 FAMOUS SPANIARDS

The Hispanic-Roman epoch produced the philosopher and dramatist Marcus (or Lucius) Annaeus Seneca (54 BC–AD 39), while the Gothic period was marked by the encyclopedist Isidore of Seville (560?–636), author of the *Etymologies*. Important Spanish thinkers of the Middle Ages included Averroës (Ibn Rushd, or Abu al-Walid Muhammad ibn Ahmad ibn Rushd, 1126–98), philosopher; Maimonides (Moses ben Maimon, also known as the Rambam, 1135–1204), the great Jewish physician and philosopher; Benjamin de Tudela (d.1173), geographer and historian; King Alfonso X (the Wise, 1226?–84), jurist, historian, musician, and astronomer; Juan Ruiz (1283?–1351?), archpriest of Hita, the greatest Spanish medieval poet; and Fernando de Rojas (1475?–1538?), a dramatic poet. El Cid (Rodrigo Díaz de Vivar, 1043?–99) has become the national hero of Spain for his fight against the Moors, although he also fought for them at times.

The golden age of Spanish exploration and conquest began with the Catholic Sovereigns, Ferdinand (1452–1516) and Isabella

(1451–1504), in the late 15th century. The first great explorer for Spain was Christopher Columbus (Cristoforo Colombo or Cristóbal Colón, 1451–1506), a seaman of Genoese birth but possibly of Judeo-Catalán origin, who made four voyages of discovery to the Americas, the first landing occurring on 12 October 1492 on the island of Guanahaní (probably on the island now called San Salvador) in the Bahamas. Among the later explorers, Alvar Núñez Cabeza de Vaca (1490?–1557?), Hernando de Soto (d.1542), and Francisco Vázquez de Coronado (1510–54) became famous for their explorations in the southern and southwestern parts of the present US; Juan Ponce de León (1460?–1521), for his travels in Florida; Vasco Núñez de Balboa (1475–1517), for his European discovery of the Pacific Ocean and claim of it for Spain; Francisco Pizarro (1470?–1541), for his conquest of Peru; and Hernán Cortés (1485–1547) for his conquest of Mexico. Juan de la Costa (1460?–1510) was a great cartographer of the period. Spanish power was at its greatest under Charles I (1500–1558), who was also Holy Roman Emperor Charles V. It began to decline under Philip II (1527–98).

In Spanish art, architecture, and literature, the great age was the 16th century and the early part of the 17th. Among the painters, El Greco (Domenikos Theotokopoulos, b.Crete, 1541–1614), Lo Spagnoletto (Jusepe de Ribera, 1589?–1652?), Francisco de Zurbarán (1598?–1660), Diego Rodriguez de Silva y Velázquez (1599–1660), and Bartolomé Esteban Murillo (1617–82) were the leading figures. In architecture, Juan de Herrera (1530–97), the designer of the royal palace, monastery, and tomb of the Escorial, and the baroque architect José Churriguera (1650–1723) are among the most important names. In literature, the dramatists Lope Félix de Vega Carpio (1562–1635) and Pedro Calderón de la Barca (1600–1681) and the novelist Miguel de Cervantes y Saavedra (1547–1616), author of *Don Quixote*, are immortal names. Other leading literary figures include the great poet Luis de Góngora y Argote (1561–1627), the satirist Francisco Gómez de Quevedo y Villegas (1580–1645), and the playwrights Tirso de Molina (Gabriel Téllez, 1571?–1648) and Mexican-born Juan Ruiz de Alarcón y Mendoza (1580?–1639). Outstanding personalities in the annals of the Roman Catholic Church are St. Ignatius de Loyola (Iñigo de Oñez y Loyola, 1491–1556), founder of the Jesuit order; St. Francis Xavier (Francisco Javier, 1506–52), Jesuit "apostle to the Indies"; and the great mystics St. Teresa of Ávila (Teresa de Cepeda y Ahumada, 1515–82) and St. John of the Cross (Juan de Yepes y Álvarez, 1542–91). The phenomenon of pulmonary blood circulation was discovered by Michael Servetus (Miguel Servet, 1511–53), a heretical theologian, while he was still a medical student.

The 16th century was also the golden age of Spanish music. Cristóbal de Morales (1500?–53) and Tomás Luis de Victoria (1549?–1611) were the greatest Spanish masters of sacred vocal polyphony. Important composers include Luis Milán (1500?–1565?), Antonio de Cabezón (1510–66), Alonso Mudarra (1510–80), and Miguel de Fuenllana. Juan Bermudo (1510?–55?), Francisco de Salinas (1513–90), and Diego Ortiz (b.1525?) were theorists of note. Two leading 18th-century composers in Spain were the Italians Domenico Scarlatti (1685–1757) and Luigi Boccherini (1743–1805). Padre Antonio Soler (1729–83) was strongly influenced by Scarlatti. Leading modern composers are Isaac Albéniz (1860–1909), Enrique Granados y Campina (1867–1916), Manuel de Falla (1876–1946), and Joaquín Turina (1882–1949). World-famous performers include the cellist and conductor Pablo Casals (1876–1973), the guitarist Andrés Segovia (1894–1987), operatic singers Victoria de los Angeles (Victoria Gómez Cima, b.1923) and Placido Domingo (b.1941), and the pianist Alicia de Larrocha (b.1923).

Francisco Goya y Lucientes (1746–1828) was the outstanding Spanish painter and etcher of his time. Pablo Ruiz y Picasso

(1881–1973) was perhaps the most powerful single influence on contemporary art; other major figures include Juan Gris (1887–1927), Joan Miró (1893–1983), and Salvador Dali (1904-89), who, like Picasso, spent most of his creative life outside Spain. The sculptor Julio González (1876–1942) was noted for his work in iron. A leading architect was Antonio Gaudí (1852–1926); an influential modern architect was José Luis Sert (1902–83), dean of the Graduate School of Design at Harvard University for 16 years.

Miguel de Unamuno y Jugo (1864–1936) and José Ortega y Gasset (1883–1955) are highly regarded Spanish philosophers. Benito Pérez Galdos (1843–1920) was one of the greatest 19th-century novelists. Other Spanish novelists include Pedro Antonio de Alarcón (1833–91), Emilia Pardo Bazán (1852–1921), Vicente Blasco Ibáñez (1867–1928), Pío Baroja y Nessi (1872–1956), Ramón Pérez de Ayala (1880–1962), and Ramón José Sender (1902-82). Prominent dramatists include José Zorrilla y Moral (1817–93), José de Echegaray y Eizaguirre (1832–1916), and Jacinto Benavente y Martínez (1886–1954). The poets Juan Ramón Jiménez (1881–1958) and Vicente Aleixandre (1900–84) were winners of the Nobel Prize for literature in 1956 and 1977, respectively. Other outstanding poets are Gustavo Adolfo Bécquer (1836–70), Antonio Machado Ruiz (1875–1939), Pedro Salinas (1891–1951), Jorge Guillén (1893–1984), Dámaso Alonso (b.1898), Federico García Lorca (1899–1936) and Luis Cernuda (1902–63). Ramón María del Valle-Inclán (1866–1936) was a novelist, dramatist, poet, and essayist. A noted novelist, essayist, and critic was Azorín (José Martínez Ruiz, 1876–1967). Salvador de Madariaga y Rojo (1886–1978) was an important cultural historian and former diplomat. Luis Buñuel (1900–83), who also lived in Mexico, was one of the world's leading film directors.

Santiago Ramón y Cajal (1852–1934), histologist, was awarded the first Nobel Prize for medicine in 1906. The physicians Gregorio Marañón (1887–1960) and Pedro Laín Entralgo (b.1908) were scholars and humanists of distinction. Juan de la Cierva y Codorniu (1896–1937) invented the autogyro. Severo Ochoa (b.1905), who lives in the US, won the Nobel Prize for medicine in 1959.

Francisco Franco (1892–1975), the leader of the right-wing insurgency that led to the Spanish Civil War (1936–39), was chief of state during 1939–47 and lifetime regent of the Spanish monarchy after 1947. After Franco's death, King Juan Carlos I (b.1938) guided Spain through the transitional period between dictatorship and democracy. Felipe González Márquez (b.1942), a Socialist, became prime minister in December 1982.

49 DEPENDENCIES

Spanish "places of sovereignty" on the North African shore, which are part of metropolitan Spain subject to special statutes owing to their location, include Alborán Island (at 35°56′N and 3°2′W), Islas de Alhucemas (at 35°13′N and 3°52′W), Islas Chafarinas (at 35°10′N and 2°26′W), and Perejil (at 35°54′N and 5°25′W). The two major places of sovereignty are Ceuta and Melilla. Ceuta (19 sq km/7.3 sq mi; population 71,403 in 1993) is a fortified port on the Moroccan coast opposite Gibraltar. Melilla (12.3 sq km/4.7 sq mi; resident population 55,613 in 1993), on a rocky promontory on the Rif coast, is connected with the African mainland by a narrow isthmus. Melilla has been Spanish since 1496; Ceuta since 1580. Since 1956, Morocco has repeatedly advanced claims to these areas. Under the 1978 constitution, Ceuta and Melilla are represented in the Cortes by 1 deputy and 2 senators each.

50 BIBLIOGRAPHY

Abel, Christopher, and Nissa Torrents (eds.). *Spain: Conditional Democracy.* New York: St. Martin's, 1984.

Altamira, Rafael. *A History of Spain.* New York: Van Nostrand, 1949.

Brenan, Gerald. *The Literature of the Spanish People: From Roman Times to the Present Day.* Cambridge: Cambridge University Press, 1953.

Carr, Raymond. *Spain, 1808–1939.* London: Oxford University Press, 1982.

Davies, Reginald Trevor. *The Golden Century of Spain, 1501–1621.* New York: St. Martin's, 1954.

Donaghy, P. J. *Spain: A Guide to Political and Economic Institutions.* New York: Cambridge University Press, 1987.

Gunther, Richard. *Spain after Franco: The Making of a Competitive Party System.* Berkeley: University of California Press, 1988.

———.(ed.). *Politics, Society, and Democracy: The Case of Spain.* Boulder, Colo.: Westview Press, 1993.

Herr, Richard. *The Eighteenth-Century Revolution in Spain.* Princeton, N.J.: Princeton University Press, 1958.

Hooper, John. *The Spaniards: A Portrait of the New Spain,* Harmondsworth, Eng.: Penguin Books, 1987.

Hume, Martin A. S. *Spain: Its Greatness and Decay (1479–1788).* Cambridge: Cambridge University Press, 1940.

Maxwell, Kenneth. *Spanish Foreign and Defense Policy.* Boulder, Colo.: Westview Press, 1991.

Olson, James S. (ed.). *Historical Dictionary of the Spanish Empire, 1402–1975.* New York: Greenwood Press, 1992.

Orwell, George. *Homage to Catalonia.* New York: Harcourt Brace Jovanovich, 1969.

Payne, G. Stanley. *The Franco Regime, 1936–1975.* Madison, Wis.: University of Wisconsin Press, 1987.

———. *A History of Spain and Portugal.* Madison: University of Wisconsin Press, 1973.

Perez Diaz, Victor. *The Return of Civil Society: The Emergence of Democratic Spain.* Cambridge, Mass.: Harvard University Press, 1993.

Preston, Paul (ed.). *Revolution and War in Spain, 1931–1939.* New York: Methuen, 1985.

Pritchett, V. S. *The Spanish Temper.* New York: Knopf, 1954.

Rubottom, Richard R., and J. C. Murphy. *Spain And The United States: Since World War II.* New York: Praeger, 1984.

Solsten, Eric and Sandra W. Meditz (eds.). *Spain: A Country Study.* 2d ed. Washington, D.C: Library of Congress, 1990.

Thomas, Hugh. *The Spanish Civil War.* Rev. ed. New York: Harper & Row, 1977.

SWEDEN

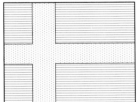

Kingdom of Sweden
Konungariket Sverige

CAPITAL: Stockholm.

FLAG: The national flag, dating from 1569 and employing a blue and gold motif used as early as the mid-14th century, consists of a yellow cross with extended right horizontal on a blue field.

ANTHEM: *Du gamla, du fria, du fjallhöga nord (O Glorious Old Mountain-Crowned Land of the North).*

MONETARY UNIT: The krona (Kr) is a paper currency of 100 öre. There are coins of 50 öre and 1, 2, 5, and 10 kronor, and notes of 5, 10, 20, 50, 100, 500, and 1,000 kronor. Kr1 = $0.1277 (or $1 = Kr7.828).

WEIGHTS AND MEASURES: The metric system is the legal standard, but some old local measures are still in use, notably the Swedish mile (10 km).

HOLIDAYS: New Year's Day, 1 January; Epiphany, 6 January; Labor Day, 1 May; Midsummer Day, Saturday nearest 24 June; All Saints' Day, 5 November; Christmas, 25–26 December. Movable religious holidays include Good Friday, Easter Monday, Ascension, Whitmonday.

TIME: 1 PM = noon GMT.

¹LOCATION, SIZE, AND EXTENT

Fourth in size among the countries of Europe, Sweden is the largest of the Scandinavian countries, with about 15% of its total area situated north of the Arctic Circle. Extreme length N–S is 1,574 km (978 mi) and greatest breadth E–W is 499 km (310 mi). Sweden has a total area of 449,964 sq km (173,732 sq mi): land area, 411,615 sq km (158,925 sq mi); water area, 38,349 sq km (14,807 sq mi), including some 96,000 lakes. Comparatively, the area occupied by Sweden is slightly smaller than the state of California. Sweden is bounded on the N and NE by Finland, on the E by the Gulf of Bothnia, on the SE by the Baltic Sea, on the SW by the Öresund, the Kattegat, and the Skagarrak, and on the W by Norway, with a total boundary length of 5,423 km (3,370 mi). The two largest Swedish islands in the Baltic Sea are Gotland and Öland. Sweden's capital city, Stockholm, is located on the Baltic Sea coast.

²TOPOGRAPHY

Northern Sweden (Norrland) slopes from the Kjölen Mountains along the Norwegian frontier (with the high point at Kebnekaise, 2,111 m/6,926 ft) to the coast of the Gulf of Bothnia. The many rivers—notably the Göta, the Dal, the circle Angerman, the Ume, and the Lule—flow generally toward the southeast and have incised the plateau surface; waterfalls abound. Central Sweden, consisting of a down-faulted lowland, has several large lakes, of which Vänern (5,585 sq km/2,156 sq mi) is the largest in Europe outside the former USSR. To the south of the lake belt rises the upland of Smaland and its small but fertile appendage, Skane. The lowlands were once submerged and so acquired a cover of fertile, silty soils. Much of Sweden is composed of ancient rock; most ice erosion has resulted in generally poor sandy or stony soils. The best, most lime-rich soils are found in Skane, and this southernmost district is the leading agricultural region; it resembles Denmark in its physical endowments and development.

³CLIMATE

Because of maritime influences, particularly the warm North Atlantic Drift and the prevailing westerly airstreams, Sweden has higher temperatures than its northerly latitude would suggest. Stockholm averages –3°C (26°F) in February and 18°C (64°F) in July. As would be expected from its latitudinal extent, there is a wide divergence of climate between northern and southern Sweden: the north has a winter of more than seven months and a summer of less than three, while Skane in the south has a winter of about two months and a summer of more than four. The increasing shortness of summer northward is partly compensated for by comparatively high summer temperatures, the greater length of day, and the infrequency of summer cloud; the considerable cloud cover in winter reduces heat loss by radiation. Annual rainfall averages 61 cm (24 in) and is heaviest in the southwest and along the frontier between Norrland and Norway; the average rainfall for Lapland is about 30 cm (12 in) a year. The maximum rainfall occurs in late summer, and the minimum in early spring. There is considerable snowfall, and in the north snow remains on the ground for about half the year. Ice conditions in the surrounding seas, especially the Gulf of Bothnia, often are severe in winter and seriously interfere with navigation.

⁴FLORA AND FAUNA

Vegetation ranges from Alpine-Arctic types in the north and in upland areas through coniferous forests in the central regions to deciduous trees in the south. Black cock, woodcock, duck, partridge, swan, and many other varieties of birds are abundant. Fish and insects are plentiful.

⁵ENVIRONMENT

Sweden's relatively slow population growth and an effective conservation movement have helped preserve the nation's extensive forest resources. By the end of 1985 there were 19 national parks covering 618,070 hectares (1,527,276 acres), 1,215 nature reserves of 870,748 hectares (2,151,653 acres), and 2,016 other protected landscape areas of 540,064 hectares (1,334,520 acres); together these reserves accounted for 4.9% of Sweden's total land area. However, about 15 million cu m of forestland are damaged each year. Sweden produces 187.3 tons of particulate emissions and 484.9 tons of hydrocarbon emissions yearly. The list of 2150

415

pollutants includes sulphur air, nitrogen compounds, oil, VOCs (volatile organic compounds), radon, and methane. The pollution of the nation's water supply is also a significant problem. Factory effluents represent a threat to water quality, however, and air-borne sulfur pollutants have so acidified more than 16,000 lakes that fish can no longer breed in them. By 1992, United Nation reports described acidification as Sweden's most serious environmental problem. Sweden has 42.2 cu mi of water with 9% used for farming and 55% used for industrial purposes. Principal responsibility for the environment is vested in the National Environmental Protection Agency.

One of the most controversial environmental questions in recent years was put to rest by a March 1980 referendum in which a small plurality of the electorate (39.3%) supported expansion of nuclear power to no more than 12 reactors by the mid-1980s, but with provisions for the nationalization of nuclear energy, for energy conservation, and for the phaseout of nuclear power within an estimated 20–25 years. In 1994, 1 of the nation's mammal species and 14 bird species were endangered, as well as 10 types of plants. In 1987, endangered species included the blue ground beetle and cerambyx longhorn. Protected fauna include the wild reindeer, golden eagle, and crane.

6POPULATION

The population of Sweden as of 31 December 1992 was estimated at 8,692,013, an increase of 1.1% over the 1990 census figure of 8,590,630, which was 3.2% higher than the 1980 figure. Since the start of the 20th century, Sweden's population has increased by less than 1% a year, primarily because of declining birthrates. In 1934, the country's birthrate was the lowest in the world; it later rose but then declined to an all-time low of 11.02 per 1,000 population in 1983. It then rose rapidly through 1990 before declining slightly in 1991 and 1992. In 1992 the birthrate was 14.17 per 1,000 population, while the death rate was 10.93, for a net natural increase of 3.24 per 1,000 population. As a result, the government has projected a population of 8,949,742 for the year 2000, an increase of 3% from the 1992 population.

The average population density was 21 persons per sq km (55 per sq mi) of land area in 1992. Some 84% of the population are urban dwellers, and 86% live in the southern 40% of the country. Stockholm, the capital and principal city, had a population of 684,576 at the end of 1992, with 1,517,285 in the greater Stockholm area. Other large cities and their 1992 populations are Göteborg, 433,811 and Malmö, 236,684. At the end of 1990 Uppsala had 109,497; Norrköping, 82,639; Örebro, 85,858; and Väster, 98,233.

7MIGRATION

In the period 1865–1930, nearly 1,400,000 Swedes, or about one-fifth of the country's population, emigrated; over 80% went to the US, and about 15% to other Nordic countries. The exodus ended by the 1930s, when resource development in Sweden started to keep pace with the population growth. In the 1960s there was a flood of immigration—especially by Finns—that increased the number of aliens in Sweden from 190,621 to 411,280. The number remained steady in the 1970s but increased, though at a slower rate, in the 1980s. In 1992, net immigration totaled some 19,622 persons, representing 41% of the population increase. There were 45,348 immigrants and 25,726 emigrants in 1992. There were 499,072 aliens in 1992 (5.7% of the population). This figure included 111,477 Finns, 39,578 Yugoslavs, 38,996 Iranians, 35,319 Norwegians, 27,176 Danes, 26,547 Turks, 17,872 Chileans, and 16,365 Poles.

8ETHNIC GROUPS

The Swedes are Scandinavians of Germanic origin. In addition to the resident foreign-born (929,909 in 1992), minorities include about 300,000 Finns in the north and approximately 20,000 Lapps.

9LANGUAGES

Swedish is the universal language. In addition to the letters of the English language, it has å, ä, and ö. Swedish is closely related to Norwegian and Danish. Many Swedes speak English and German, and many more understand these languages. The Lapps speak their own language. There is a spread of Finnish-speaking people from across the frontier.

10RELIGIONS

Religious freedom is provided for by the constitution, but 88% of the population was nominally affiliated with the Lutheran Church in 1993. Lutheranism, the state religion, must be the faith of the monarch and of cabinet members dealing with church matters. The archbishopric is at Uppsala. According to 1991 estimates, Roman Catholicism had 147,414 adherents; Pentecostal Church, 95,800; Mission Covenant Church of Sweden, 77,013; and Salvation Army, 26,600. In addition, there were an estimated 21,000 Baptists and 15–20,000 Jews.

11TRANSPORTATION

As of 1991, the total length of highways was 97,400 km (60,520 mi), of which 53% was paved. At the end of 1991 there were 3,619,000 passenger cars, 310,000 trucks, 15,000 buses, 204,000 vans, and 103,000 motorcycles in service. In 1967, Sweden changed from left- to right-hand traffic.

Sweden's railroad system of 12,000 km (7,450 mi) is operated by the state-owned Statens Järnvagar; about 70% of the track is electrified. Whereas the total tonnage of freight carried by rail has fallen from 71 million tons in 1970 to 54 million tons in 1991, the average haul per ton of freight increased from 243 km (151 mi) to 348 km (216 mi) during that time. Railway passenger traffic increased from 77 million to 93 million between 1977 and 1982, but declined to 88 million yearly by 1984. The average passenger journey has fallen from 75 km (47 mi) in 1970 to 64 km (40 mi) by 1991.

Since the 1960s, the number of ships in the merchant navy has decreased because of competition from low-cost shipping nations and, more recently, the slump in world trade. Sweden has an increasing number of special-purpose vessels, such as fruit tramps, ore carriers, and oil tankers. Most of the larger vessels, representing about 80% of Sweden's commercial tonnage, are engaged in traffic that never touches home ports, and only about two-fifths of Swedish foreign trade is carried in Swedish ships. Göteborg, Stockholm, and Malmö, the three largest ports, and a number of smaller ports are well equipped to handle large ocean-going vessels. At the start of 1992, the Swedish merchant fleet consisted of 172 ships with a combined capacity of 2.5 million GRT. Canals in central Sweden have opened the lakes to seagoing craft; inland waterways add up to 2,050 km (1,270 mi), navigable by small steamers and barges.

Arlanda international airport (Stockholm) received its first jet aircraft in 1960; other principal airports are Bromma (Stockholm), Sturup (Malmö), and Torslanda (Göteborg). The Scandinavian Airlines System (SAS) is operated jointly by Sweden, Denmark, and Norway, each of which owns a 50% share of the company operating in its own territory; the other half in Sweden is owned by private investors. Linjeflyg, a subsidiary of SAS, operates a domestic service to most of the larger cities and resorts.

12HISTORY

Sweden and the Swedes are first referred to in written records by the Roman historian Tacitus, who, in his *Germania* (AD 98), mentions the Suiones, a people "mighty in ships and arms." These people, also referred to as Svear, conquered their southern neighbors, the Gotar, merged with them, and extended their dominion over most of what is now central and southern Sweden. In the 9th and 10th centuries, Swedes pressed on raids southeastward across Russia to Constantinople, and tradition holds that the descendants of one of their chieftains, Rurik, founded the Kievan Russian state. Some other settled regions and placenames in various parts of Europe also show Swedish influence.

Christianization came gradually from the 9th through the 11th century. During the 12th century, the Swedish kingdom began to expand into the Baltic, incorporating Finland, partly as a result of religious crusades, between 1150 and 1300. Among the institutions established in Sweden during the 12th and 13th centuries were Latin education, new modes and styles of architecture and literature, town life, and a more centralized monarchy with new standards in royal administration—all with significant economic, legal, and social implications.

Norway and Sweden were united in 1319 under the infant king Magnus VII, but Waldemar IV, King of Denmark, regained Skane, the southern part of Sweden, and all the Scandinavian countries were united under his daughter Margaret (Margrethe) in 1397. For over a century, Sweden resisted Danish rule. In 1523, following a war with Denmark, the Swedes elected Gustavus Vasa (Gustaf I) to the Swedish throne. A great king and the founder of modern Sweden, Gustavus made Lutheranism the state religion, established a hereditary monarchy, and organized a national army and navy. His successors incorporated Estonia and other areas in Eastern Europe. The growth of nationalism, the decline of the Hanseatic League's control of Baltic trade, and Protestantism contributed to the rise of Sweden in the following century.

Another great king and one of the world's outstanding military geniuses, Gustavus Adolphus (Gustaf II Adolf, r.1611–32), is generally regarded as the creator of the first modern army. He defeated Poland and conquered the rest of Livonia, and by winning a war with Russia acquired Ingermanland and Karelia. In the period of the Thirty Years' War (1618–48), Sweden was the foremost Protestant power on the Continent, and for the following half century the Baltic Sea became a Swedish lake. Although the king was killed at Lützen in 1632, his policies were carried on during the reign of his daughter Christina by the prime minister, Axel Oxenstierna. By terms of the Peace of Westphalia (1648) Sweden gained Pomerania and the archbishopric of Bremen, part of the Holy Roman Empire. Swedish expansionism resulted, in 1658, in the recapture of the southern Swedish provinces that Denmark had retained since the early 16th century. Renewed wars extended the Swedish frontier to the west coast while reducing Danish control over trade by taking away the eastern shore of the Öresund.

Under young Charles XII (r.1697–1718), Sweden fought the Great Northern War (1700–1721) against a coalition of Denmark, Poland, Saxony, and Russia. Sweden at first was militarily successful, but after a crushing defeat by Russian forces under Peter the Great (Peter I) in 1709 at the Battle of Poltava, the nation lost territories to Russia, Prussia, and Hannover. Thereafter Sweden was a second-rate power. Throughout the 18th century there was internal dissension, marked principally by the conflicting policies of the pro-French faction, the Hats, and the pro-Russian faction, the Caps. From 1751 to 1814, the throne was occupied by the house of Oldenburg-Holstein-Gottorp, whose most interesting figure, Gustavus III (r.1771–92), a poet, playwright, and patron of the arts and sciences, was assassinated by a group of nobles.

Sweden entered the Napoleonic Wars in 1805, allying itself with Great Britain, Austria, and Russia against France. Russia switched sides in 1807, however, and the ensuing Russo-Swedish conflict (1808–9) resulted in the loss of Finland. King Gustavus

LOCATION: 55°20′ to 69°4′N; 10°58′ to 24°10′E. **BOUNDARY LENGTHS:** Finland, 586 km (364 mi); coastline, 2,390 km (1,485 mi); Norway, 1,619 km (1,006 mi). Gotland Island coastline, 400 km (249 mi); Öland Island coastline, 72 km (45 mi). **TERRITORIAL SEA LIMIT:** 12 mi.

IV was then overthrown by the army, and a more democratic constitution was adopted. In 1810, one of Napoleon's marshals, a Frenchman from Pau named Jean Baptiste Jules Bernadotte, was invited to become the heir to the Swedish throne. Three years later, he brought his adopted country once again over to the side of the allies against Napoleon in the last full-scale war fought by Sweden.

In 1814, Norway was united with Sweden and remained tied dynastically to the Swedish kings until 1905, when the union was dissolved. Bernadotte assumed the name Charles John (Carl Johan) and succeeded to the Swedish throne in 1818 as Charles XIV John. The Bernadotte dynasty, which has reigned successively since 1818, gradually relinquished virtually all of its powers, which were assumed by the Riksdag, and Sweden became one of the most progressive countries in the world. Industry was developed, the cooperative movement began to play an important part in the economy, and the Social Democratic Labor Party gained a dominant position in political life.

Sweden and Neutrality

Sweden remained neutral in both world wars; during World War II, however, Sweden served as a haven for refugees from the Nazis and allowed the Danish resistance movement to operate on its soil. After the war, Sweden did not join NATO, as did its Scandinavian neighbors Norway and Denmark, but it did become a member of the UN in 1946 and participated in some of the European Recovery Program benefits. In 1953, Sweden joined with Denmark, Norway, Iceland, and, later, Finland to form the Nordic Council, and was instrumental in creating EFTA in 1960. Subsequently Sweden declined an invitation to join the EEC with Denmark, Ireland, and the UK; a free-trade agreement with the EEC was signed 22 July 1972.

Carl XVI Gustaf has been king since the death of his grandfather, Gustav VI Adolf, in 1973. In September 1976, a coalition of three non-Socialist parties won a majority in parliamentary elections, ending 44 years of almost uninterrupted Social Democratic rule that had established a modern welfare state. The country's economic situation worsened, however, and the Social Democrats were returned to power in the elections of September 1982. Prime Minister Olof Palme, leader of the Social Democratic Party since 1969, was assassinated in February 1986. As of the end of 1987, investigators were unable to establish a motive for the killing.

Sweden's traditional policy of neutrality was strained in late October 1981 when a Soviet submarine ran aground inside a restricted military zone near the Swedish naval base at Karlskrona. The Swedish government protested this "flagrant violation of territorial rights" and produced reasons for believing that the submarine had been carrying nuclear weapons. Swedish naval vessels refloated the damaged submarine and permitted it to return to the Soviet fleet in early November. In 1984, a Swedish military report stated that at least ten "alien" submarines had been detected in Swedish waters.

The environment and nuclear energy were major political issues in the 1980s. In the 1990s, the major concerns have been conflicts over immigration policies, the economy, and Sweden's relationship to the European Communities. Sweden's economic crisis has led to large-scale public spending cuts by the center-right government. In 1991, Sweden applied for membership in the EC against a background of considerable opposition for accession. In May 1993, the Riksdag altered Sweden's long-standing foreign policy of neutrality. In the future, neutrality would only be followed in time of war. The Riksdag also opened up the possibility of Sweden's participation in defense alliances.

Major political issues in Sweden have been resolved by referenda in the past. A referendum on Sweden's accession to the EC is expected in 1994 following conclusion of the negotiations.

13 GOVERNMENT

Sweden developed as a constitutional monarchy under the constitution of 1809, which remained in effect until 1 January 1975, when a new instrument of government replaced it. Legislative authority is vested in the parliament (Riksdag). The sovereign

performs only ceremonial duties as the official head of state, his last political duty, regular participation in cabinet meetings, having been taken away under the new constitution. The king must belong to the Lutheran Church; the throne was hereditary only for male descendants until 1980, when female descendants were granted the right to the throne. The real chief executive is the prime minister, who is proposed by the speaker of the Riksdag and confirmed by the parliamentary parties. The prime minister appoints a cabinet consisting of 18–20 members. Ministers issue directives but administrative decisions are taken by central boards, which have their respective spheres of activity delimited by the Riksdag.

The Riksdag was bicameral until 1971, when a unicameral body of 350 members serving three-year terms was established; the 1975 constitution provided for 349 members. All members of the Riksdag are directly elected by universal suffrage at age 18. The unicameral system was designed to ensure almost exact equality in proportional representation among the constituencies. The constitution requires, however, that a party must gain at least 4% of the national popular vote or 12% in a constituency to be represented in the Riksdag. The Riksdag is empowered to undertake votes of censure against the cabinet as a whole or against individual cabinet members. If an absolute majority supports the censure motion, the cabinet or minister concerned must resign unless the government agrees to hold a new election within ten days. The Riksdag has direct control of the Bank of Sweden and the National Debt Office, although in practice the cabinet's influence on parliamentary policy in financial affairs is a matter of no small importance.

Sweden's first ombudsman was designated in 1766, and the institution has been in continuous existence since 1809. At present, the Riksdag elects one or more ombudsmen (four in 1981) who supervise the observance of laws and statutes as applied by the courts and by public officials, except in cabinet and military matters. The ombudsmen are concerned especially with protecting the civil rights of individual citizens and of religious and other groups, and may admonish or prosecute offenders, although prosecutions are relatively rare.

14 POLITICAL PARTIES

Except for a brief period in 1936, the Social Democratic Labor Party was in power almost uninterruptedly from 1932 to 1976, either alone or in coalition. In 1945, it dissolved the wartime cabinet, which had consisted of representatives of all parties except the Left Party Communists, and launched a program of social reform. In the general election of 1948, however, the opposition gained several seats. In order to get a working majority, the Social Democrats formed a coalition government with the Center Party (formerly the Agrarian Party) in 1951. Although inflation and other difficulties slowed the Social Democratic program, steadily mounting production encouraged the government to push through its huge social welfare program, sanctioned in principle by all major parties.

After holding or controlling all parliamentary majorities since 1957, the Social Democrats lost their parliamentary majority in the elections of September 1976, when a non-Socialist coalition won 180 of the 349 seats at stake (Center Party 86, Moderates 55, Liberals 39). The Social Democrats declined from 156 seats to 152, and the Communists fell from 19 seats to 17. The same coalition retained control in the 1979 election with a reduced majority of 175 seats (Moderates 73, Center Party 64, Liberals 38), compared to 154 seats for the Social Democrats and 20 for the Communists. In the election on 19 September 1982, however, the Social Democrats gained 12 seats and returned to power. Olof Palme, who had been the Social Democratic prime minister from 1969 to 1976, was able to put together a new coalition cabinet on 8 October 1982. His party remained in power, though with a reduction of seats, following the 1985 election. Palme was assassinated in February 1986; he was succeeded by Ingvar Carlsson.

The 1988 election marked a turning point in Sweden with the decline of the Social Democrats and the growth of the Moderates and Liberals. For the first time in 70 years, a new party gained representation in the Riksdag—the Environment Party (MpG) which obtained 20 seats. The Social Democrats were narrowly defeated in September 1991, and the government of Ingvar Carlsson gave way to that of Carl Bilt (Moderate Party), who headed a minority four-party, center-right coalition composed of Moderates, the Liberals, Center Party, and the Christian Democratic community. The coalition controlled 170 seats.

The 1991 election represented a gain for the Moderates (80 seats) and two previously unrepresented parties—Christian Democrats (26 seats) and New Democracy (25 seats)—who managed to exceed the 4% threshold. Losing parties included the Social Democrats (down to 138 seats from 156), the Liberals (26 seats), the Center Party (31 seats), and the Environment Party, which fell below the minimum 4% barrier losing 20 seats. The anti-immigration Progress Party, formed in 1989, demanded reform of Sweden's policies on refugees and political asylum. New Democracy emerged prior to the 1991 general election as a party of discontent urging tax cuts and reduced immigration. The Left Party-Communists was renamed the Left Party (VP) in 1990. In 1991, Inegerd Traedsson (Moderate Party) became the first woman to be elected Speaker of the Riksdag. This post is the second highest ranking office after the monarch.

15LOCAL GOVERNMENT

Decentralization is markedly characteristic of Sweden's governmental structure. The country is divided into 24 counties and some 278 municipalities, each with an elected council. Local government is administered by county councils and rural or urban district councils consisting of at least 20 members popularly elected, on a proportional basis, for four years. Under each council is an executive board with various committees. In addition there is a governor (prefect), the government-appointed head of the administrative board in each of Sweden's counties, who holds supreme police and other supervisory authority. Local authorities are responsible for most hospitals, elementary education, certain utilities, and the police force.

16JUDICIAL SYSTEM

Ordinary criminal and civil cases are tried in a local court (tingsrätt), consisting of a judge and a panel of lay assessors appointed by the municipal council. Above these local courts are six courts of appeal (hovrätter). The highest tribunal is the Supreme Court (Högsta Domstolen), with 24 justices. Special cases are heard by the Supreme Administrative Court and other courts. The Swedish judicial procedure uses a jury of the Anglo-US type only in press libel suits. Capital punishment, last employed in 1910, is expressly forbidden by the constitution.

The judiciary is independent of executive control or political influence. The right to counsel of criminal defendants is restricted to cases in which the maximum penalty possible is six month imprisonment or greater.

17ARMED FORCES

Sweden's policy of neutrality and nonalignment requires a strong, modern, and independent defense establishment. The budget allocated $6.2 billion for defense or 4% of gross domestic product.

Swedish military defense is based on general conscription of all male citizens between the ages of 18 and 47. The length of basic training for conscripts varies from 7½ to 15 months, depending on training specialization. In wartime a force of 700,000 reservists can be mobilized within 72 hours. The coastal defense is under the command of the Royal Swedish Navy. There are naval stations at Stockholm, Karlskrona, and Göteborg. Regular armed forces in 1993 totaled 60,500 (38,800 conscripts). The army had 43,500 half conscripts; mobilizable wartime strength included 4 armored brigades, 12 infantry brigades, and 5 arctic warfare brigades. The navy had 9,650 men on active service (5,900 conscripts); naval forces included 12 submarines, 3 ASW helicopter squadrons, 28 mine warfare vessels, and 33 fast attack craft. The air force, with 7,500 regulars (5,500 conscripts), had a total of 499 combat aircraft. Reserves in voluntary defense organizations totaled 40,000.

Many defenses have been dug in atom bomb-proof rock shelters along some 1,100 km (700 mi) of coastline. There is a civil defense service of about 230,000 persons—mainly women between the ages of 16 and 67 and men between 47 and 67. As part of the civil defense program, nuclear-resistant shelters were built over a 10-year period in the large urban areas. The shelters, completed in 1970, are used as garages in peacetime and can hold 6.3 million people in a national emergency. Sweden also manufactures most of its weapons and its arms export business totaled over $500 million per year until 1990.

18INTERNATIONAL COOPERATION

Having joined the UN on 19 November 1946, Sweden takes part in EEC and all the nonregional specialized agencies. The first UN Conference on the Human Environment was held in Stockholm in June 1972. Together with Denmark, Finland, Iceland, and Norway, Sweden has been a member of the advisory Nordic Council since 1953 and cooperates with these other Scandinavian countries in social welfare and health insurance and in freeing frontiers of passport control. Sweden is a signatory of GATT and the Law of the Sea. The nation is a member of the Asian Development Bank, Council of Europe, EFTA, and IDB. Since 1974, Sweden has exceeded the UN target of 0.7% for official development assistance. It contributed 1.02% of GNP for such assistance in 1982 and 0.86% in 1985, among the highest percentages in the world.

19ECONOMY

Sweden is a highly industrialized country. The shift from agriculture to industry began in the 1930s and developed rapidly during the postwar period. In 1992, manufacturing accounted for 25% of the GDP at value added factor cost, finance, insurance, real estate and business services, 31%; commerce, 14%; construction, 8%; transport and communication, 9%; agriculture, forestry, and fishing, 3%; public utilities, 4%; mining, 0.3%; and other services 25.7%. Average annual growth of the GDP declined from 4.3% in the 1960s to 2% in the 1970s and to 1.6% in the 1980s. It grew by 1.4% in 1990 but fell 1.4% in 1991, 1.9% in 1992, and 2.1% in 1993, the longest period of decline in the 20th century.

Swedish industry is outstanding in supplying quality goods and specialized products—ball bearings, high-grade steel, machine tools, glassware—that are in world demand. Intimate contact between trade, industry, and finance is a feature of the economy, as is the spread of factories to rural districts. Some natural resources are ample, the foremost being lumber, iron ore, and waterpower. Sweden's lack of oil and coal resources makes it dependent on imports for energy production, despite abundant waterpower.

Swedish living standards and purchasing power are among the highest in the world. However, inflation has been a chronic problem since the early 1970s, with the annual rise in consumer prices peaking at 13.7% in 1980. The rate of price increase declined thereafter, but was still 10.4% in 1990 and 9.4% in 1991 before falling to 2.2% in 1992. Unemployment shot up from 1.7% in 1990 to 8.2% in 1993.

20INCOME

In 1992, Sweden's GNP was $233,209 million at current prices, or $26,780 per capita. For the period 1985–92 the average inflation rate was 6.9%, resulting in a real growth rate in per capita GNP of 0.4%.

In 1992 the GDP was $145.6 billion. It is estimated that in 1991 agriculture, hunting, forestry, and fishing contributed 2% to GDP; mining and quarrying, less than 1%; manufacturing, 18%; electricity, gas, and water, 3%; construction, 7%; wholesale and retail trade, 9%; transport, storage, and communication, 6%; finance, insurance, real estate, and business services, 20%; community, social, and personal services, 4%; and other sources, 31%.

21LABOR

The labor force numbered 4,429,000 persons in 1992, of whom 52% were men and 48% women. During that year, the number of employed workers was 4,195,000, of whom 20% were employed in manufacturing, mining, electricity, or water service; 14.3% in wholesale and retail trade, restaurants, and hotels; 9.1% in financial and business services; 7.1% in transport and communication; 6.5% in construction; 3.3% in agriculture, forestry, hunting, and fishing; and 39.7% in other services. That year, 64.2% of the labor force was employed by private enterprise, 26.4% by local government, and 4.6% by national government. The unemployment rate averaged 4.8% in 1992, and was projected to rise in part due to defense downsizing as well as an aggressive effort to trim the large Swedish public sector.

More and more women work outside their homes. About 71% of all women between the ages of 16 and 74 years participated in the labor force in 1991. The trade unions have lent their support to closing the wage gap between the sexes; as of 1992, women's wages in manufacturing had risen to 90% of men's.

About 84% of Swedish wage earners are members of trade unions, and within certain industrial branches the percentage is even higher. The first unions in Sweden were organized in the 1870s, but for a long time the movement remained numerically weak relative to the rest of industrialized Europe. At the end of 1992, however, the Swedish Trade Union Confederation, which is closely allied to the Social Democratic Party, had 2.23 million members and was thus the largest organization of any kind in Sweden. The Swedish Confederation of Salaried Employees had a total membership of 1.3 million, and the Swedish Confederation of Professional Associations enrolled some 356,012, organized by occupation. The trade union movement is based on voluntary membership, and there is neither closed shop nor union shop. As of 1 June 1993, the Swedish Employers Confederation, the principal employer organization, had 43,000 members, who employed 1.2 million persons.

Agreements between employers and trade unions are as a rule worked out by negotiation. Public mediators or mediation commissions intervene if necessary. A labor court, made up of three impartial members and five representing employers, workers, and salaried employees, has jurisdiction over the application and interpretation of collective agreements already signed and may impose damages on employers, trade unions, or trade union members violating a contract. For many years, an overwhelming majority of the court's decisions have been unanimous, and since the end of the 1930s industrial peace has generally prevailed. In 1990, labor unrest resulted in 770,356 working days lost to work stoppages, but the number fell to 21,724 days in 1991; 28,141 days were lost in 1992. Swedish law requires employee representation on company boards of directors. A law passed in 1983 introduced employee funds, partly funded by contributions from profits of all Swedish companies, which give unions and employees equity in companies, while providing the companies with investment capital.

The present basic features of labor welfare were defined in a law of 1949. Working life commences at 16. The regular workweek cannot exceed 40 hours, and overtime is limited to 48 hours over a four-week period and a total of 200 hours a year. However, these regulations may be modified by collective bargaining agreement. A minimum of five weeks' holiday with pay is stipulated by law. More than half of all employees are covered by trade union employment insurance funds, which receive substantial government support. In 1974, a law established minimum conditions for notice of employment termination. The Swedish labor scene is currently in transition. New labor legislation may provide employers with more flexibility in hiring, firing, and terms of employment, as well as overall further decentralization of the wage formation process. The government created an independent commission in 1991 to help decrease the frequent rate of wage increases in order to cool the overheated economy.

22AGRICULTURE

Only about 3% of the people earned their living in agriculture in 1992, compared with more than 50% at the beginning of the 20th century and about 20% in 1950. Production exceeds domestic consumption; however, a considerable amount of food is imported. About 6.8% of the land area of Sweden, or 2,790,000 hectares (6,894,100 acres), is classed as land cultivated with permanent or temporary crops. In 1991 there were 93,554 holdings with more than 2 hectares (5 acres) of arable land. Farm holdings are intensively tilled; fertilizers are used heavily and mechanization is increasing.

Most farmers are elderly, and few small farms have a successor waiting to replace the present farmer. Government policy in recent years has been to merge small unprofitable farms into larger units of 10 to 20 hectares (25–50 acres) of arable land with some woodland, the size estimated able to support a family in the same living standard as an industrial worker. Most Swedish farmers are small landowners who also support themselves through forestry and fishing, and most farms are less than 20 hectares (50 acres) in extent. Farmer participation in the government's set-aside program resulted in about 300,000 hectares (741,300 acres) of cropland being retired from production in 1990, and again in 1991.

Grains (particularly oats, wheat, barley, and rye), potatoes and other root crops, vegetables, and fruits are the chief agricultural products. Sugar beet cultivation in Skåne is important and produces almost enough sugar to make Sweden self-sufficient. In 1992, Sweden produced 1,261,000 tons of barley; 807,000 tons of oats; 1,411,000 tons of wheat; 1,144,000 tons of potatoes; and 128,000 tons of rye. That year, the total crop production was down 21% from 1979–81. Agricultural exports (excluding fish) in 1992 totaled $789 million.

The Warfare Preparedness Program, developed after World War II, has protected Swedish agriculture, resulting in high costs and overproduction. In 1991, a five-year agricultural reform program came into effect, whereby most subsidies and price regulations will be eliminated, allowing consumer demand to determine production volumes.

23ANIMAL HUSBANDRY

Although the long winters necessitate indoor feeding from October to May, pastoral farming is important, and about 80% of farm income derives from animal products, especially dairy products. Cattle (2.2 million in 1992) are the most important livestock, with the percentage of dairy cows decreasing significantly as the number of beef calves has increased. Liquid milk production totaled 3,168,000 tons in 1992; butter, 58,900 tons; and cheese, 115,000 tons. Because the oversufficiency of butter before 1970 weakened Sweden's position in world markets, the government encouraged farmers to shift to meat production. A five-year agricultural reform program which began in 1991 will dismantle price regulations and subsidies for products like milk and meat in favor of market-oriented pricing. As a result, meat and dairy production fell in 1992. The sheep population was 448,000 in 1992, and pigs numbered 2,280,000. There were 12,000,000 chickens during the same year. Fur farms breed large numbers of mink and a declining number of fox. Reindeer are raised by 51 Sami (Lapp) communities in the north, and between 1970 and 1992 the reindeer population in Lapp villages increased from 166,200 to 300,000. Reindeer meat production declined in the aftermath of the Chernobyl nuclear disaster of 1986 in the former USSR.

24FISHING

Fish is an important item in the Swedish diet, and Sweden is both a major importer of fish products and a principal supplier to other countries. Göteborg, Bohus, and Halland are the principal fishing districts, but large quantities of fish are caught all along the coasts. Herring, cod, plaice, flounder, salmon, eel, mackerel, and shellfish are the most important saltwater varieties. Freshwater fish include trout, salmon, and crayfish, a national delicacy. The saltwater fish catch increased from 228,000 tons in 1971 to 259,000 tons in 1984, overcoming a significant drop in the 1974–79 period because of government conservation measures and the declining number of fishermen. However, the marine catch was down to 239,502 tons in 1991, and the total catch was 245,016 tons. That year, herring and cod accounted for 55% and 19% of the total catch, respectively.

25FORESTRY

Forests occupy some 57% of the land area and total 23,500,000 hectares (58,069,000 acres). The growing stock was estimated at 2,776 million cu m in 1991. The annual growth amounts to about 99 million cu m. Annual removals decreased from an average of 70.8 million cu m during 1970/71–1974/75 to an average of 55.5 million cu m during 1976/77–1980/81 but increased to roughly 65 million cu m during recent years. Important varieties include spruce (46% of commercial stands), pine (38%), birch (11%), and oak, beech, alder, and aspen (5% combined). Slightly less than half of the total forest area is owned by private persons and an additional one-fourth by private corporations and rural communes. The government owns most of the remaining forests, but they are located, for the most part, in the north, where climatic conditions slow the trees' growth.

Forestry and farming are interdependent everywhere except in the most fertile plains; in northern Sweden, almost one of every two men works in the woods for at least part of the winter. Both the number of workers and the productivity of those who stayed on declined in the late 1970s. Since the early 1970s, the number of employees in the forestry sector has fallen by 40%, to about 21,000 in 1992. Almost 4% of the labor force was occupied in forestry in 1991.

The exploitation of forest wealth ranks second in importance in the economy (after metal-based industry). Sweden competes with Canada for world leadership in the export of wood pulp and is the world's leading exporter of cellulose. In 1992, wood and wood products made up about 18% of exports. The total timber felled for sale in 1991 amounted to an estimated 51.7 million cu m. Mostly roads and trains are used to transport timber; only a few of the biggest rivers are used. About 70% of timber harvested comes from clear-cutting, and 30% from thinning. About 60% of Sweden's annual forestry production is exported every year. Sweden is the third largest exporter of paper and board, supplying 13% of the export market, with production amounting to 4% of the world's total.

A new forest policy introduced in 1980 coordinates forestry measures more closely with industrial needs and places increased emphasis on clear-cutting and more complete use of the forest biomass, including stumps and small trees. The government, through the Forest Commission, enforces pest control, the prevention of premature cutting, and the use of proper methods of preserving permanent forest cover.

26MINING

Since ancient days, mining and the iron industry have been of great importance in the economic life of Sweden. The Bergslagen region in central Sweden yields high-grade ores for quality steel. Sweden's iron ore reserves were estimated at 3 billion tons in 1991. Sweden accounts for about 2.2% of the world's iron-ore production and is a leading iron-ore exporter. Iron-ore production in 1991 was estimated at 19.3 million tons. Lead, copper, zinc, gold, silver, bismuth, cobalt, and huge quantities of arsenic are produced in the Skellefte (Boliden) region. Further south, phosphate, tungsten, kyanite, and pyrite are mined. Some low-grade coal is mined in Skane, but practically all coal and almost all oil have to be imported from abroad. Granite is quarried for domestic use and for export.

27ENERGY AND POWER

With many rivers, waterfalls, and lakes, Sweden has favorable conditions for waterpower. Northern and southern Sweden have their peak productions at different seasons; thus, they are complementary, and all large power stations are coordinated. In the north, underground installations provide power for iron-ore working, for iron smelting at Lulea, and for the Lapland railway. More than half the hydroelectric output is produced underground. Because of environmental considerations, high production costs, and low world market prices, Sweden's substantial uranium reserves—some 250,000–300,000 tons (or about 20% of the known world reserves)—have not been exploited.

Net installed electrical capacity in 1991 was 34,089,000 kw, of which 48% was hydroelectric, 29% nuclear, and 23% conventional thermal. That same year, Sweden's electricity production totaled 147,730 million kwh. In 1991, exports of Swedish electricity generated $149.3 million in revenues.

During the 1970s, as the price of Sweden's oil imports increased sevenfold, Swedes reduced their dependence on petroleum imports by conserving energy, so that their energy consumption rose by only 0.6% annually from 1973 to 1979.

The share of oil in the total energy supply declined from nearly 70% in 1979 to 40% in 1992. In 1991, electricity accounted for 55% of the total energy requirement; petroleum, 29%; coal, wood, and other solids, 11%; natural gas, 1%; and other sources, 4%. Sweden embarked on an ambitious nuclear energy program, under which seven nuclear reactors came into operation between 1972 and 1980. By 1986, 12 units offered a capacity of 9.4 million kwh; by 2010, all 12 will be shut down, with two reactors closing by 1995. Plants fired by natural gas will replace nuclear energy's role. Energy conservation, development of alternative energy sources, and increased use of imported coal are also planned.

28INDUSTRY

The basic resources for industrial development are forests, iron ore, and waterpower. Forest products, machinery, and motor vehicles made up 60% of total export value in 1992. The total value of manufacturing output in 1992 was Kr253 billion, or 25% of the GDP at value added factor cost.

Since the end of World War II, emphasis has shifted from production of consumer goods to the manufacture of export items. Swedish-made ships, airplanes, and automobiles are considered outstanding in quality. In 1991, 176,937 automobiles and about 75,000 trucks were manufactured. Swedish shipyards, however, built only eight seagoing merchant vessels that year, and the declining shipping industry is attempting to diversify. Sweden's motor vehicle producers are Volvo and SAAB-Scania.

The export value of iron and steel products was Kr18.5 billion in 1992. Before World War II, virtually the entire tonnage consisted of high-grade steels, but in recent years exports have included considerable quantities of commercial grades. Transport equipment and iron and steel are of declining importance, however, while exports of machinery, chemicals, and paper have been growing in value.

29SCIENCE AND TECHNOLOGY

Sweden's high-quality scientific and technological development is renowned throughout the world. Technological products invented or developed by Swedish firms include the self-aligning ball bearing, the cream separator, the three-phase electric motor, and a refrigerator without moving parts. Sweden's more recent applications of sophisticated technology range from powder metallurgy to the Hasselblad camera and the Viggen jet fighter. Of Sweden's 10 largest industrial corporations, six are engineering companies: Volvo, SAAB-Scania, ASEA, Electrolux, SKF, and L. M. Ericsson.

State-financed research, centering on the universities, is directed by the Council for Planning and Coordination of Research. Long-term industrial research and development is the responsibility of the government through the National Board for Technological Development. Nearly 3,000 Swedish students graduate per year with science and engineering degrees, accounting for 4.8% of all university students. The number of Swedish scientists and technicians working in industry, academia, and government is just under 500,000. Sweden's support of technological research amounted to about 2.6% of GNP, one of the highest such percentages in the world, and totaled 36,410 million kronor in 1991.

Institutions that have played an important role in the advancement of science, both in Sweden and throughout the world, are the Nobel Foundation, which sponsors annual awards in chemistry, physics, and physiology or medicine, as well as for peace, literature, and economic science; the Royal Swedish Academy of Sciences; and the Karolinska Institute, specializing in medical research.

30DOMESTIC TRADE

In 1991, Sweden had 53,122 retail establishments, with (in 1992) 240,462 employees and a total turnover of Kr229,099 million. Supermarkets, virtually nonexistent in Sweden before 1960, have proliferated in recent years.

Of the country's retail business, most is in private hands, but the turnover of cooperative societies represents more than 10% of total retail trade, making the consumer cooperative movement the country's largest retail organization. The local organizations belong to the Cooperative Union and Wholesale Society, a central buying and manufacturing organization with 2 million members, which operates factories, department stores, supermarkets, and specialized shops. Competition between the cooperatives and private enterprise has improved selling methods, so that Sweden's self-service shops are among the most modern in Europe. Department stores are located in the major cities.

Offices and stores are open on weekdays from 9 AM to 5 or 6 PM (in summer, sometimes to 3 or 4 PM) and close early on Saturdays. However, many stores stay open one night a week, and some department stores are open on Sundays.

31FOREIGN TRADE

The volume of Sweden's foreign trade has increased very rapidly since World War II, mainly as a result of the gradual liberalization of trade restrictions within the framework of OECD and EFTA. During 1992, Swedish exports amounted to about 32% of GDP.

Principal exports in 1992 (in millions of kronor) were as follows:

Nonelectrical machinery	50,738
Transport equipment	48,810
Paper, paperboard, and manufactures thereof	36,359
Chemicals	29,956
Electrical machinery and apparatus	14,342
Iron and steel	18,499
Petroleum products	8,490
Pulp and waste paper	8,512
Wood, lumber, and cork	11,669
Other exports	118,633
TOTAL	346,008

Principal imports in 1992 (in millions of kronor) were as follows:

Crude oil and petroleum products	22,128
Nonelectrical machinery	47,251
Transport equipment	28,855
Electrical machinery and apparatus	19,065
Food and live animals	17,774
Clothing	15,224
Iron and steel	9,151
Chemicals, plastics, and pharmaceuticals	30,592
Other imports	99,883
TOTAL	289,923

In 1992, most of Sweden's foreign trade continued to be with Western Europe. Imports from the EC represented 56% of the total, and exports to the EC also accounted for 56%; imports from and exports to fellow members of EFTA were 16% and 17% of the total, respectively. This represents a substantial change from the late 1960s, when trade volume with EFTA exceeded that with the EC; the entry of the UK into the EC accounts for some of the difference.

Principal trade partners in 1985 (in millions of kronor) were as follows:

	EXPORTS	IMPORTS	BALANCE
Germany	48,746	53,699	−4,953
UK	31,516	24,989	6,527
US	26,896	25,353	1,543
Norway	27,481	19,880	7,601
Denmark	23,320	22,586	734
Finland	16,861	17,947	−1,086
France	18,867	14,858	4,0009
Netherlands	18,241	12,439	5,802
Other countries	114,080	98,172	15,908
TOTALS	326,008	289,923	36,085

32BALANCE OF PAYMENTS

From 1974 through 1985, Sweden ran annual current-account deficits (except in 1984) because of increases in world oil prices and a decline in the competitiveness of Swedish export products on the world market. Until 1977, deficits were financed mainly through long-term foreign private borrowing by the private sector. Thereafter, however, central government borrowing expanded rapidly. The current account deficit improved from Kr35.1 billion in 1990 to an estimated Kr18.9 billion in 1991, representing 2l6% and 1.3% of GDP, respectively. A rebounding trade balance surplus and a turnaround in direct investment aided in the improvement. The lifting of controls on foreign direct investment, combined with improved competitiveness accruing from greater wage restraint and rising productivity, are expected to bring continued interest in investing in Sweden. In 1992 merchandise exports totaled $55,934 million and imports, $48,485 million. The merchandise trade balance was $6,949 million. The following table summarizes Sweden's balance of payments for 1991 and 1992 (in millions of US dollars):

	1991	1992
CURRENT ACCOUNT		
Goods, services, and income	–1,065	–2,430
Unrequited transfers	–2,050	–2,495
TOTALS	–3,115	–4,925
CAPITAL ACCOUNT		
Direct investment	–1,237	–1,048
Portfolio investment	7,143	477
Other long-term capital	12,289	17,712
Other short-term capital	–17,313	–9,788
Reserves	–431	–7,126
TOTALS	951	227
Errors and omissions	2,664	4,698
Total change in reserves	–344	–4,293

33 BANKING AND SECURITIES

The Central Bank of Sweden (Sveriges Riksbank), founded in 1656, is the oldest bank in the world. It is the bank of issue, regulates the value of Swedish currency, controls foreign exchange, and sets the discount rate. The largest commercial bank is the Skandinaviska Enskilda Banken. Recently, Swedish banks have suffered severe losses, the government was forced to intervene and support the commercial banks Nordbanken and Gota Bank and the savings bank Forsta Sparbanken. By 1992, the number of commercial banks in Sweden was only 9, as compared with 28 in 1937 and 80 in 1910. The smaller banks serve provincial interests. Deposit accounts at various lengths of call are used for short-term credit by industry and trade.

Mortgage banks of various types meet the needs of property owners, home builders, farmers, and shipbuilders. Credit also is extended by some 500 local rural credit societies and by about an equal number of agricultural cooperatives. There are four semi-governmental credit concerns, organized as business companies and created in cooperation with private commercial banks to facilitate long-term lending to agriculture, industry, small industry, and exports. The Riksbank discount rate was lowered from 9.5% to 8.5% in March 1986, to 8% a month later, and to 7.5% in September. On 8 October 1982, the bank devalued the krona by 16%, to 7.37 per the US dollar. Although the Riksbank's note issue is not tied to its gold reserves, there is an adjustable legal limit.

As of 1992, public demand, time, savings and foreign currency deposits totaled Kr630.9 billion. The money supply, as measured by M2, totaled Kr73,945 million the same year. The krona was allowed to float against foreign currency beginning on 19 November 1992, and soon devalued 20% against the currencies of Western Europe and the US dollar. Interest rates in 1992 averaged 11.4%.

The Riksbank lends money to the commercial banks and other credit associations against securities. Traditionally, the Swedish people have preferred to save by placing money in these banks rather than by direct investment. In 1992, 118 Swedish companies and 10 foreign companies were listed on the Stockholm Stock Exchange, which was computerized that year.

Profits from the sale of securities are taxable provided they have been owned for less than five years. The capital gain is wholly taxable for securities held less than two years, but only 40% of the gain is taxable if the shares have been held more than two years. For machinery and equipment a minimum write-off period of three years is prescribed. The 1985 deregulation of the credit market included the removal of ceilings on lending banks, finance houses, and housing credit institutions and had the effect

of diminishing part of Sweden's "gray market": direct contact between companies and private individuals with money for loans.

34 INSURANCE

The Swedish people are very life-insurance conscious; life insurance policies worth Kr1,980 billion were in force in 1992. In 1985 there were at least 560 Swedish insurance companies. Most companies were very small, however, and only 65 firms operated on a nationwide scale. The five largest companies held almost 80% of total insurance assets. Automobile liability insurance is compulsory.

The total nominal value of nationwide Swedish insurance company assets at the end of 1985 amounted to Kr229.8 billion, of which life insurance companies accounted for about 81%. In 1990, premiums totaled $1,326.1, or 4.8% of the GDP.

35 PUBLIC FINANCE

The financial year extends from 1 July to 30 June. Estimates are prepared in the autumn by the Ministry of the Budget and examined by the Riksdag early the following year. The budget contains two sections: an operating budget and a capital budget, the latter generally representing investments in state enterprises. The policy of running a surplus on the budget in boom years and a deficit in depression was used in the period between the two world wars and has been continued as a way of combating inflation. From 1982 to 1989, the budget balance improved from a deficit equivalent to about 13% of GDP to a surplus of nearly 2% of GDP. In 1990, however, a deficit reappeared, equivalent to 1.2% of GDP. In 1991 and 1992 the budget deficits widened to 4.3% and 9.6% of GDP, respectively.

The following table shows actual revenues and expenditures for 1991 and 1992 in billions of kronor.

	1991	1992
REVENUE AND GRANTS		
Tax revenue	—	526.84
Non-tax revenue	—	95.16
Capital revenue	0.05	0.61
Grants	—	—
TOTAL	624.96	622.61
EXPENDITURES & LENDING MINUS REPAYMENTS		
General public service	27.24	26.79
Defense	38.90	36.41
Public order and safety	17.95	18.40
Education	59.40	61.66
Health	5.22	4.97
Social security and welfare	320.79	335.94
Housing and community amenities	26.40	36.50
Recreation, cultural, and religious affairs	4.45	4.42
Economic affairs and services	49.07	—
Other expenditures	80.66	—
Adjustments	–14.56	–14.66
Lending minus repayments	–6.20	–7.91
TOTAL	609.32	654.65
Deficit/Surplus	15.64	–32.04

In 1992 Sweden's total public debt stood at Kr607.32 billion, of which Kr135.99 billion was financed abroad. The share of government domestic borrowing financed by household sector was around 21% in 1992.

36 TAXATION

With so many social services in effect, Sweden's taxation is the highest in the world. In 1992, personal income tax was levied at 20% for income above Kr186,400, with the highest marginal rate

50%. Municipal tax was charged at a flat rate of approximately 30%. It is virtually the only local tax in Sweden.

In contrast, corporations are taxed relatively lightly in comparison with those in many other countries. The national income tax rate on corporations was 30% in 1992 (separate municipal income tax on corporations was abolished as of 1985), with no distinction between distributed and undistributed profits.

Tax liability is determined according to a firm's books so long as these are properly kept. Companies are allowed considerable discretion in determining their net income for any particular year; they can take advantage of the flexible rules governing the valuation of stocks and the depreciation of equipment and machinery. Swedish companies may set aside an investment reserve in boom years and use this reserve in years of slack production.

For decades, the Swedish ratio of indirect taxes to total tax revenue was one of the lowest in the world. During World War II and the early postwar years, however, a national sales tax was in effect. On 1 January 1969, the national sales tax was replaced by a value-added tax with a rate of 10%; the rate was increased to 15% in January 1971 and stood at 22% of the taxable value (defined as total price charged) at the beginning of 1993. Almost all goods and most services are subject to this tax.

37 CUSTOMS AND DUTIES

Tariffs were established in the 19th century to allow for the development of Swedish industry, but the rates have been among the lowest in the world. Sweden subscribes to the OECD trade liberalization program, and imports, with few exceptions, are not subject to controls. As a member of EFTA, Sweden abolished customs duties against other EFTA countries by the end of 1966. Sweden declined an offer to join the EC but signed a free-trade agreement with the community in 1972. Some 90% of imports from developing countries are duty-free.

In general, the importation of raw materials is duty-free; import duties are based on weight rather than value. Import restrictions apply mainly to protected agricultural products, to automobiles, and to trade with Eastern Europe and the Far East.

38 FOREIGN INVESTMENT

Net direct Swedish investment abroad in 1993 was Kr15.5 billion, up from Kr8.9 billion in 1982. Of the total (less reinvested earnings), 36% was for investment in Italy, 27% in the UK, and 10% in France. Net foreign direct investment in Sweden in 1993 was Kr18.1 billion. Of these funds 17% was from Finland, 14% from the Netherlands, 14% from the US, and 13% from the UK. Sweden's corporate income tax rate of 28% is one of the lowest in Europe.

Some 370 US-owned subsidiaries employed 27,730 Swedes in 1992, down from 36,000 in 1982.

39 ECONOMIC DEVELOPMENT

Between 1946 and 1953, the Swedish economy was dominated by expansion. Thereafter, although production continued to increase (at a lessened rate), inflation was a matter of concern. Domestic investment has remained at about the same level as in 1939, but a larger share has come from public investment. Expansion of output slowed down during the international oil crisis and recession of 1974–75, largely as a result of a weakening of foreign demand for Swedish products, but employment remained high. Thus far, the economy has managed to contain inflationary trends within reasonable limits. Although some industries (the railways, ironore mines, etc.) have been nationalized for a long time, private concerns carry on most of Sweden's industry, in terms of both number of workers and value of output.

During periods of unemployment such as the world recession of 1980–81, the central government and the municipalities have expended funds to provide additional employment and to keep the unemployment rate relatively low. The jobless have been put to work building dwellings and highways, extending reforestation work, and constructing water and sewer installations, harbors, lighthouses, railroads, defense projects, and telecommunications facilities. Although the government resorted to stockpiling industrial goods to combat the economic slowdown in the mid-1970s, the cost was considered too high, and the policy was not repeated during the recession of the early 1980s. More recently, the emphasis has been on cutting costs and restraining inflation to make Swedish goods more competitive in the international marketplace.

Regional development has been fostered by the use of investment funds (a tax device permitting enterprises to set aside taxfree reserves during boom years to be used for investment during recessions), relief works, and government lending to small-scale industry. A national program for regional development was introduced in 1972 to develop services and job opportunities in provinces that have lagged behind in industrial development. Projects in northern Sweden benefited most from this program.

In 1991, the government announced a plan to privatize 35 wholly or partially state-owned firms with annual turnovers totaling Kr150 billion. This program was delayed by the economic recession, however. A 10-year, Kr110 billion program of infrastructure investment was announced in 1994. More than 90% of the money would be spent on the road and rail networks, and a bridge would link Malmö with Copenhagen.

Official development assistance totaled $2,116 million in 1991, of which 30.8% went through multilateral agencies. The principal recipients of Swedish aid were Tanzania (7%), India (3%), Viet Nam (3%), Mozambique (7%), and Zambia (3%).

40 SOCIAL DEVELOPMENT

Sweden has been called the model welfare state; every citizen is guaranteed a minimum subsistence income and medical care. Social welfare legislation was introduced relatively early and was greatly expanded after World War II. The system is financed partly by insurance premium payments and partly by state and local taxation. Basic benefits are often increased by cost-of-living supplements.

Old-age pensions are paid to everyone 65 years of age or older (about 2,000,000 persons, or 24% of the population at the end of 1986), but an earlier retirement is possible, with a reduction in pension benefits. As of 1991, benefits paid to a single pensioner entitled to little or no supplemental coverage amounted to Kr30,912 a year; to a married couple Kr50,544. A supplementary pension scheme, introduced in 1960, is designed to raise old-age pension benefits to two-thirds of the recipient's average income during the 15 most profitable years before retirement. The scheme also contains provisions for pensions to persons totally disabled before retirement age and for family pensions (widows and orphans). The first benefits under the new plan were paid out in 1963; the scheme became fully operational in 1981. Supplementary pensions for employees are wholly financed by employers' contributions, while self-employed persons are required to pay their own contributions.

Unemployment insurance is the only kind of voluntary social insurance in Sweden. Administered by the trade unions, it provides benefits according to salary (up to Kr3,801 weekly in 1991) to those who voluntarily enroll. More than half of all employees are covered. Unemployment relief, through monetary assistance or public works, is provided by the central government or by state-subsidized municipalities.

Compulsory health service was introduced in 1955. Hospital care is free for up to two years. Medical services and medicines are provided at substantially reduced rates or, in some cases, without charge. In the event of illness, employed persons and housewives receive cash payments and get further benefits according to income. Costs of confinement and maternity allowances for women are covered by health insurance. Half the cost of these health benefits is met by individual premium payments, one-fourth by employers, and one-fourth by the government. A national program of dental insurance financed through employer-employee contributions and general revenue took effect in 1974.

Since the beginning of 1955, workers' compensation has been coordinated with the national health service scheme. This type of insurance, financed entirely by employers, covers work time as well as travel to and from work for all employees. Benefits include free medical treatment, medicines, and appliances. Annuities are paid to persons permanently disabled, and funeral benefits and pensions to dependents are provided in case of death. Public assistance is provided for blind or infirm persons confined to their homes and to people who are in sanitariums, special hospitals, or charitable institutions.

The social services help meet the costs of rearing children. In 1991, family allowances began at Kr750 a month for families with one child under age 16. A housing allowance is also paid to families with children under 16 to assist them in acquiring modern and more spacious dwellings. For 360 days, a parental benefit is paid upon the birth or adoption of a child to the parent who stays home and takes care of the child. A law passed in 1985 provides that by 1991 at the latest every child between the age of 18 months and school age shall have a right to a place in a preschool, day nursery, parents' cooperative, or part-time care group. In 1987, an estimated 77% of children of preschool age were in some sort of child-care group. Schoolchildren receive free textbooks, and about 75% of public-school children are given free meals. A quarterly tax-free grant is made for every child under 16 years of age, and a monthly grant is given for children of 16 and 17 who attend school. Vacation camps for children, often with free travel, are supported by the government. In many cases, these benefits are increased by cost-of-living supplements.

Changes in the structure of family life have run parallel to those of other Scandinavian countries. The marriage rate declined from an average of 9.04 per 1,000 population during 1941–50 to 4.34 in 1983 (up to 4.59 in 1985), the lowest rate among the Nordic nations. The median age at first marriage among women increased from 23.6 during 1966–70 to 27.5 in 1985; among men, the rise was from 26 to 30.1. The divorce rate rose from 0.30 per 1,000 population during 1921–30 to 3.28 in 1974, before declining to 2.37 in 1985. During that year, there were 312 legal abortions for every 1,000 live births.

Women are underrepresented in higher paying jobs, and often receive less pay for equal work. The percentage of women in the work force fell in 1993, for the first time since World War II, to 75.9%, possibly as a result of the recession.

41HEALTH

The national health insurance system, financed by the state and employer contributions, was established in January 1955 and covers all Swedish citizens and alien residents. Total expenditure for national health insurance was 8.7% of the gross national product (a per capita sum of Kr13,000) in 1992. In 1991 Sweden spent $20,055 million on health care. Principal health care reform issues in the 1990s include universal and equal access to services; and equitable funding of health care.

In 1990 there were an estimated 28,000 physicians, more than one for every 350 inhabitants. In the same year, Sweden had 12,700 dentists, 108,000 nurses, 70,000 assistant nurses, 834 pharmacists, 10,700 physiotherapists, and 5,500 psychologists. For rural medical attention, doctors are supplemented by district nurses. Only about 5% of all physicians are in full-time private practice. The corresponding figure for private dentists, however, is more than 50%.

Swedish hospitals, well known for their high standards, had 35,990 short-term beds (hospital), 85,972 long-term beds (nursing/old-age homes), and 15,500 psychiatric beds in 1991.

Many health problems are related to environment and lifestyle (including tobacco smoking, alcohol consumption, and overeating). The predominant diseases are cardiovascular conditions and cancer. In 1990, leading causes of death were: heart and circulatory diseases (48,561 people); cancer (20,331 people); pneumonia (4,371); suicides (1,471); traffic accidents (747); and homicides/other (109). In 1991, there were 137 cases of AIDS and 35,788 abortions; and, in 1990, there were 7 reported cases of tuberculosis per 100,000 people. Periodic campaigns are conducted to reduce tuberculosis (with a nationwide X-ray survey), cancer, rheumatism, and venereal diseases. There is a well-developed prenatal service. Children receive free dental care until the age of 20.

In 1992, average life expectancy in Sweden was 74.8 years for males and 80.4 years for females. There were 122,699 births in 1992, and the birth rate in 1993 was 14 per 1,000 people. In 1993, there was a general mortality rate of 11.5 per 1,000 persons (94,678 deaths in 1992). Sweden's 1993 population was 8.7 million. Infant mortality has been sharply reduced, from 60 per 1,000 live births in 1920 to 5.8 per 1,000 in 1992, one of the lowest rates in the world.

42HOUSING

The total number of dwellings was 4,043,378 in 1990, with the greatest number (974,674) having two rooms and a kitchen. Construction of new dwellings declined from a peak of 109,843 in 1970 to 28,791 in 1986, but rose to 66,886 by 1991. There were 2.4 persons per dwelling unit as of 1980, and 60% of all homes were inhabited by only one or two persons. Most houses are built by private contractors, but more than half of new housing is designed, planned, and financed by nonprofit organizations and cooperatives. To ease the housing shortage, the government subsidizes new construction and reconditioning, helps various groups to obtain better housing, and extends credit at interest rates lower than those obtainable in the open market. In 1987, these interest subsidies totaled Kr12.4 billion; and housing allowances for low-income families were Kr7.5 billion.

A system of rent controls, introduced in 1942 and designed to freeze rents at the existing rate, was abolished in 1975. Many tenant organizations negotiate rental agreements with landlords, and rent increases can be reviewed by a tribunal. The average rental for a three-room apartment was Kr21,168 annually in 1985. In that year, 53% of all housing units were owner occupied, 32% were rented, and 12% were occupied by tenant-owners, or members of a housing cooperative.

43EDUCATION

Virtually the entire adult Swedish population is literate. Education is free and compulsory from age 7 to 17. A nine-year comprehensive course was introduced in 1962. All pupils receive the same course of instruction for six years; beginning in the seventh year the curriculum is differentiated, and students may choose between a classical and a vocational course. About 80% of all students then enter gymnasium (senior high school) or continuation schools. The gymnasium specializes in classical or modern languages or science; after the three-year course, students may take a final graduating examination. The continuation schools offer a two-year curriculum that is more practical and specialized than that of the gymnasium and leads more quickly to the practice of a trade. Both comprehensive schools and secondary schools are administered by local authorities, while the central government provides grants-in-aid to cover the greater part of the costs. In 1991 there were 944,792 comprehensive-course students and 293,482 students at the primary level and 291,866 at the secondary level, and 206,079 students enrolled in the universities.

More than 25% of secondary-school graduates attend college or university. Sweden's six universities, all largely financed by the state, are at Uppsala (founded in 1477), Lund (1666), Stockholm (1877), Göteborg (1891), and Umea and Linköping (both completed in 1963). Uppsala and Lund have four faculties each—law, theology, medicine, and philosophy (arts and sciences). Stockholm has faculties of humanities, law, mathematics, and science; Göteborg, medicine and humanities. There are also more than two dozen specialized schools and institutions of university rank for such subjects as medicine, dentistry, pharmacology, veterinary science, music, economics, commerce, technology, agriculture, and forestry. Tuition is free, except for some special courses; most university students receive government loans to help them meet their living expenses.

Sweden has an active adult education movement in which some 3 million persons participate each year. People's schools and other educational institutions give courses for all those who want to study. All the universities have extension divisions for general studies. There are more than 100 state-subsidized folk high schools for working adults that provide an annual period of study lasting 30 weeks.

44LIBRARIES AND MUSEUMS

The four major libraries, the Royal Library at Stockholm and the university libraries of Uppsala, Lund, and Göteborg, receive free copies of all Swedish publications; all except Göteborg have at least 3 million volumes. There are technical and other special libraries, and these, together with the university libraries, the state-aided municipal libraries, and the 24 county libraries, have an interlibrary loan scheme. The largest public libraries are those of Stockholm and Göteborg, which have over 1.5 million volumes each.

In 1991, Sweden had 375 public libraries. Altogether, the public library systems had a combined total of 47.2 million volumes. The Swedish Authors' Fund administers a library loan compensation system that pays an author royalties each time a book is borrowed.

A total of 14.5 million visits were made to Sweden's 195 museums in 1990. Most of the outstanding museums are in Stockholm. Especially renowned are the rich art collections of the Swedish National Art Museum and the sculptures of Carl Milles in the artist's former home at Millesgarden in Lidingö. Göteborg has a number of museums including the Goteborg Art Gallery and a maritime museum reflecting the interests of that city. The finest Swedish folk museum is in Skansen, near Stockholm.

45MEDIA

The Swedish press is said to be the oldest in which censorship is legally forbidden. The first regular newspaper, *Post-och Inrikes Tidningar,* appeared in 1645 and is still published. The first daily was *Norrköpings Tidningen* (1758). There were 107 daily newspapers in Sweden in 1991 with a combined average daily circulation of 4,387,000. There were also 69 nondaily newspapers with a total circulation of 392,000. There are no newspaper chains.

News is drawn largely from the Swedish News Agency (Tidningarnas Telegrambyra—TT), an agency owned by the Swedish press. The accompanying table lists political orientation and average daily circulation figures for leading newspapers during the first half of 1991:

STOCKHOLM	ORIENTATION	CIRCULATION
Expressen	Liberal	612,000
Dagens Nyheter	Independent	423,500
Aftonbladet	Labor	412,000
Svenska Dagbladet	Conservative	233,450

PROVINCES	ORIENTATION	CIRCULATION
Göteborgs-Posten (Göteborg)	Liberal	294,000
Sydsvenska Dagbladet (Malmö)	Independent Liberal	125,150
Nya Wermlands-Tidningen (Karlstad)	Conservative	75,300

In 1988 there were about 46 general interest magazines, with a total circulation of 4,947,000.

In 1993, the former Swedish Broadcasting Corporation was broken up and its subsidiaries became independent. One operates the two television networks, one is responsible for educational radio, and another for the four national and local radio channels and Radio Sweden, which broadcasts internationally in several languages. In 1991, Swedes owned 7,550,000 radios and 4,030,000 television sets.

46ORGANIZATIONS

Almost all farmers are members of agricultural cooperatives, which buy supplies and sell products for the farmers and represent farmers' interests to state agencies. Over 300,000 farmers belong to a member body of the Federation of Swedish Farmers, a powerful organization that provides farmers with legal and tax advice as well as educational services on agricultural matters. There are two farm credit institutions, a dairies association, a meat marketing association, and an egg marketing association. The National Union of Swedish Farmers (formed in 1905) supplies its members with fertilizer, seeds, feeds, and other supplies and buys their crops.

The Federation of Swedish Industries (founded 1910) is active in promoting trade. There are specialist industrial and trade associations such as those of the glass exporters and wood exporters. Chambers of commerce operate in all the principal cities and towns.

The three most distinguished scholarly organizations are the Swedish Academy (founded 1786), the Royal Academy of Letters, History, and Antiquities (founded 1753), and the Royal Academy of Arts and Sciences (founded 1776). There are professional organizations in agriculture, archaeology, art, engineering, ethnology, geography, geology, law, literature, mathematics, medicine, music, science, and other fields.

47TOURISM, TRAVEL, AND RECREATION

Tourism is a major industry in Sweden, although it has been stagnant since 1990 due to a value-added tax on hotels, restaurants and travel services. The number of foreign tourists to Sweden cannot be ascertained because of uncontrolled tourist movements across borders within Scandinavia; statistics of Scandinavian visitors to Sweden have not been kept since 1951. Approximately 80% of Sweden's tourism is domestic; international tourism is led by Norway and other Nordic countries. In 1991, Sweden had 83,932 hotel rooms and 166,104 beds with a 27% occupancy rate, and receipts from tourism totaled $2.72 billion. No passport is required for Scandinavian nationals. Citizens of Canada, the US, West European countries, and certain other nations may enter Sweden with a valid passport and do not require a visa.

Principal tourist sites include the Royal Palace in Stockholm, the "garden city" of Göteborg, the resort island of Öland off the Baltic coast, and the lake and mountain country in the north. Cultural centers in Stockholm are the Royal Opera, Royal Dramatic Theater, and Berwald Concert Hall. Popular recreational activities include soccer, skiing, ice skating, swimming, mountain climbing, and gymnastics.

48FAMOUS SWEDES

Esaias Tegnér (1782–1846), considered the national poet of Sweden, and Erik Gustaf Geijer (1783–1847), historian and poet, are the best-known Swedish writers of the early 19th century. A new impulse was given to literature by August Strindberg (1849–1912), a major literary figure whose powerful, socially oriented plays and stories reflected the advanced thought of the age. Selma Lagerlöf (1858–1940), who won the Nobel Prize for literature in 1909, showed in her novels a depth of narrative genius reminiscent of the Norse sagas. Other Swedish winners of the Nobel Prize for literature were the novelist and poet Karl Gustav Verner von Heidenstam (1859–1940), in 1916; the novelist and short-story writer Pär Lagerkvist (1891–1974), in 1951; and the novelists Eyvind Johnson (1900–1976) and Harry Edmund Martinson (1904–78), who shared the 1974 award. A noted contemporary novelist is Vilhelm Moberg (1889–1974).

The painter, etcher, and sculptor Anders Leonhard Zorn (1860–1920) and the sculptor Carl Milles (1875–1955) are the greatest figures in Swedish art. The outstanding Swedish musician of the 19th century was Franz Adolf Berwald (1796–1868), composer of symphonies, operas, and chamber music. August Johan Söderman (1832–76) is considered the leading Swedish operatic composer. Two famous sopranos were Jenny Lind (1820–87), the "Swedish nightingale," and Christine (Kristina) Nilsson (1843–1921). Outstanding 20th-century musicians are the composers Wilhelm Stenhammar (1871–1927), Hugo Alfvén (1872–1960), Ture Rangström (1884–1947), Kurt Atterberg (1887–1974), Hilding Constantin Rosenberg (1892–1985), and the singers Jussi Björling (1910–60) and Birgit Nilsson (b.1918).

Famous 18th-century scientists were the astronomer and physicist Anders Celsius (1705–44), who devised the temperature scale named after him; the chemist Karl Wilhelm Scheele (1742–86); and the botanist Carolus Linnaeus (Carl von Linné, 1707–78), who established the classification schemes of plants and animals named after him. Emanuel Swedenborg (1688–1772) was a scientist, philosopher, and religious writer whose followers founded a religious sect in his name.

Svante August Arrhenius (1859–1927), a great pioneer in physical chemistry, is renowned for his theory of electrolytic dissociation and his speculations in the field of cosmic physics; in 1903, he was awarded the Nobel Prize for chemistry. Other Swedish Nobel Prize winners in science or medicine are Gustaf Dalén (1869–1957), for his work in automatic beacons for coast lighting (1912); Allvar Gullstrand (1862–1930), for work on dioptics of the eye (1911); Karl Manne Georg Siegbahn (1886–1978), for work on X-ray spectroscopy (1924); The (Theodor) Svedberg (1884–1971), for work in colloidal chemistry (1926); Hans Karl August Simon von Euler-Chelpin (b. Augsburg, 1873–1964), for work in enzyme chemistry (1929); George Karl de Hevesy (b. Budapest, 1885–1966), for work on isotopes (1943); Arne Wilhelm Kaurin Tiselius (1902–71), for investigations in electrophoresis (1948); Axel Hugo Theodor Theorell (1903–82), for work on enzymes (1955); Ragnar Arthur Granit (b. Finland, 1900), for "discoveries in primary physiological and chemical visual processes in the eye" (1967); Hannes Olof Gösta Alfvén (b.1908), for work in magnetohydrodynamics (1970); and Ulf von Euler-Chelpin (b.1905), for work on the treatment of nervous and mental disorders (1970). In addition, Kai M. Siegbahn (b.1918) shared the 1981 Nobel Prize in physics for developing spectroscopy; and Sune Karl Bergström (b.1916) and Bengt Ingemar Samuelsson (b.1934) shared the 1982 prize in medicine for their research on prostaglandins. Bergström has also served as chairman of the Nobel Foundation.

Swedish inventors who have done much to promote manufacturing and technical advances include the Swedish-American John Ericsson (1803–89), who pioneered the screw propeller and designed the first Western armored-turret warship, the *Monitor;* Alfred Nobel (1833–96), inventor of dynamite and progenitor of the Nobel Prizes; Lars Magnus Ericsson (1846–1926), who contributed much to the development of telephones; and Gustaf de Laval (1845–1913), who developed steam turbines and invented a centrifugal cream separator.

Three distinguished political economists are Karl Gunnar Myrdal (1898–1987), who was awarded the 1974 Nobel Prize in economic science for work in the theory of money and economic fluctuations and whose 1944 book *An American Dilemma* contributed to the overthrowing of legally sanctioned racial segregation in the US; Bertil Gotthard Ohlin (1899–1979), who shared the 1977 prize for his contribution to international trade theory; and Dag Hammarskjöld (1905–61), who was secretary-general of the UN from 1953 until his death and was posthumously awarded the 1961 Nobel Prize for peace. Other Swedish winners of the Nobel Peace Prize were Klas Pontus Arnoldson (1844–1916), in 1908; Karl Hjalmar Branting (1860–1925), in 1921; Nathan Söderblom (Lars Olof Jonathan, 1866–1931), in 1930; and Alva Reimer Myrdal (1902–86), the wife of Gunnar Myrdal, in 1982.

One of the most noted film directors of our times is Ingmar Bergman (b.1918); other noted directors were Victor Seastrom (Sjöström, 1879–1960) and Mauritz (Moshe) Stiller (b.Finland, 1883–1928). Famous screen personalities have included Greta Garbo (Greta Louisa Gustafsson, 1905–90) and Ingrid Bergman (1917–82). More recent stars of Swedish theater and films include Erland Josephson (b.1923), Max Von Sydow (b.1929), Ingrid Thulin (b.1929), Harriet Andersson (b.1932), and Bibi Andersson (b.1935). Sweden's sports stars include five-time Wimbledon tennis champion Björn Borg (b.1956) and Alpine skiing champion Ingemar Stenmark (b.1956).

49 DEPENDENCIES

Sweden has no territories or colonies.

50 BIBLIOGRAPHY

Anderson, Ingvar. *History of Sweden.* New York: Praeger, 1969.

Bengtsson, Frans G. *The Long Ships.* Glasgow: William Collins Sons & Co., Ltd., 1984

Childs, Marquis. *The Middle Way on Trial.* New Haven and London: Yale University Press, 1980.

Einhorn, Eric, and John Logue. *Welfare States in Hard Times: Policy and Politics in Denmark and Sweden.* Kent, Ohio: Kent Popular Press, 1982.

Elstob, Eric. *Sweden: A Popular and Cultural History.* Totowa, N.J.: Rowman & Littlefield, 1979.

Hadenius, Stig. *Swedish Politics During the 20th Century.* Swedish Institute, 1985.

Heckscher, Gunnar. *The Welfare State and Beyond.* Minneapolis: University of Minnesota Press, 1984.

Heclo, Hugh and Henrik Madsen. *Policy and Politics in Sweden: Principled Pragmatism.* Philadelphia: Temple University Press, 1987.

Hellberg, Thomas, and Larsson, Lars Magnus. *Alfred Nobel.* Stockholm: Alno Production KB, 1984.

Linner, Birgitta. *Sex and Society in Sweden.* New York: Praeger, 1969.

Milner, Henry. *Sweden: Social Democracy in Practice.* New York: Oxford University Press, 1989.

Moberg, Vilhelm. *A History of the Swedish People.* New York: Pantheon Books, 1973.

Puffendorf, Samuel F. *The Compleat History of Sweden,* 2 vols. Folcroft, Pa.: Folcroft Library Editions, 1977.

Roberts, Michael. *The Age of Liberty: Sweden, 1719–1772.* New York: Cambridge University Press, 1986.

———. *Gustavus Adolphus.* 2d ed. New York: Longman, 1992.

Ruden, Bengt, and Villy Bergstrom (eds.). *Sweden: Choices for Economic and Social Policies in the 1980s.* Winchester, Mass.: Allen & Unwin, 1982.

Sandelin, Bo (ed.). *The History of Swedish Economic Thought.* London; New York: Routledge, 1991.

Sather, Leland B. *Sweden*. Santa Barbara, Calif.: Clio, 1987.

Scott, Franklin Daniel. *Sweden, the Nation's History*. Carbondale: Southern Illinois University Press, 1988.

Sundelius, Bengt (ed.). *The Committed Neutral: Sweden's Foreign Policy*. Boulder, Colo.: Westview Press, 1989.

Sweden in Brief. Stockholm: Swedish Institute, 1981.

SWITZERLAND

Swiss Confederation

[French:] *Suisse*, [German:] *Schweiz*, [Italian:] *Svizzera*, [Romanish:] *Svizra*,
Swiss Confederation, [French:] *Confédération Suisse*, [German:] *Schweizerische
Eidgenossenschaft*, [Italian:] *Confederazione Svizzera*, [Romansh:] *Confederaziun Helvetica*

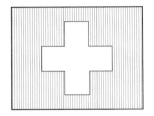

CAPITAL: Bern.

FLAG: The national flag consists of an equilateral white cross on a red background, each arm of the cross being one-sixth longer than its width.

ANTHEM: The Swiss Hymn begins "Trittst in Morgenrot daher, Seh' ich dich in Strahlenmeer" ("Radiant in the morning sky, Lord, I see that Thou art nigh").

MONETARY UNIT: The Swiss franc (SwFr) of 100 centimes, or rappen, is the national currency. There are coins of 1, 5, 10, 20, and 50 centimes and 1, 2, and 5 francs, and notes of 10, 20, 50, 100, 500, and 1,000 francs. SwFr1 = $0.1277 (or $1 = SwFr1.41).

WEIGHTS AND MEASURES: The metric system is the legal standard.

HOLIDAYS: New Year, 1–2 January; Labor Day, 1 May; Christmas, 25–26 December. Movable religious holidays include Good Friday, Easter Monday, Ascension, and Whitmonday.

TIME: 1 PM = noon GMT.

¹LOCATION, SIZE, AND EXTENT

A landlocked country in west-central Europe, Switzerland has an area of 41,290 sq km (15,942 sq mi), extending 348 km (216 mi) E–W and 220 km (137 mi) N–S. Comparatively, the area occupied by Switzerland is slightly more than twice the size of New Jersey. Bounded on the N by the Federal Republic of Germany (FRG), on the E by Liechtenstein and Austria, on the SE and S by Italy, and on the W and NW by France, Switzerland has a total boundary length of 1,852 km (1,151 mi).

Switzerland's capital city, Bern, is located in the western part of the country.

²TOPOGRAPHY

Switzerland is divided into three natural topographical regions: (1) the Jura Mountains in the northwest, rising between Switzerland and eastern France; (2) the Alps in the south, covering three-fifths of the country's total area; and (3) the central Swiss plateau, or Mittelland, consisting of fertile plains and rolling hills that run between the Jura and the Alps. The Mittelland, with a mean altitude of 580 m (1,900 ft), covers about 30% of Switzerland and is the heartland of Swiss farming and industry; Zürich, Bern, Lausanne, and Geneva (Genève) are on the plateau. The central portion of the Alps, around the St. Gotthard Pass, is a major watershed and the source of the Rhine, which drains into the North Sea; of the Aare, a tributary of the Rhine; of the Rhône, which flows into the Mediterranean; and of the Ticino, a tributary of the Po, and of the Inn, a tributary of the Danube, which flow into the Adriatic and the Black seas, respectively. The highest point in Switzerland is the Dufourspitze of Monte Rosa at 4,634 m (15,203 ft); the lowest is the shore of Lake Maggiore at less than 195 m (640 ft). The second-highest and most celebrated of the Swiss Alps is the Matterhorn (4,478 m/14,692 ft), long a challenge to mountaineers and first scaled in 1865.

Switzerland has 1,484 lakes, more than 12,900 smaller bodies of water, and many waterfalls. Lake Geneva (Léman), with an area of 581 sq km (224 sq mi), is considered the largest Swiss lake, though its southern shore is in France. Lake Neuchâtel, the largest lake totally within Switzerland, has an area of 218 sq km (84 sq mi). Switzerland also contains more than 1,000 glaciers, many the relics of Pleistocene glaciation. The largest area of permanent ice is in the Valais.

³CLIMATE

The climate of Switzerland north of the Alps is temperate but varies with altitude, wind exposure, and other factors; the average annual temperature is 9°C (48°F). The average rainfall varies from 53 cm (21 in) in the Rhône Valley to 170 cm (67 in) in Lugano. Generally, the areas to the west and north of the Alps have a cool, rainy climate, with winter averages near or below freezing and summer temperatures seldom above 21°C (70°F). South of the Alps, the canton of Ticino has a warm, moist, Mediterranean climate, and frost is almost unknown. The climate of the Alps and of the Jura uplands is mostly raw, rainy, or snowy, with frost occurring above 1,830 m (6,000 ft).

⁴FLORA AND FAUNA

Variation in climate and altitude produces a varied flora and fauna. In the lowest zone (below 550 m/1,800 ft), chestnut, walnut, cypress, and palm trees grow, as well as figs, oranges, and almonds; up to 1,200 m (3,940 ft), forests of beech, maple, and oak; around 1,680 m (5,500 ft), fir and pine; around 2,130 m (7,000 ft), rhododendron, larches, dwarf and cembra pine, and whortleberries; and above the snow line, more than 100 species of flowering plants, including the edelweiss. Wild animals include the chamois, boar, deer, otter, and fox. There are large birds of prey, as well as snipe, heath cock, and cuckoo. Lakes and rivers teem with fish.

⁵ENVIRONMENT

The Swiss have long been aware of the need to protect their natural resources. Switzerland's federal forestry law of 1876 is among the world's earliest pieces of environmental legislation. In 1986, however, the Swiss Federal Office of Forestry issued a report stating that 36% of the country's forests have been killed or damaged by acid rain and other types of air pollution. Since 1953, provisions for environmental protection have been incorporated in the federal constitution. A measure creating a federal role in town and rural planning by allowing the central government to set the ground rules for the cantonal master plans took effect in January 1980. Air pollution is a major environmental concern in Switzerland; automobiles and other transportation vehicles are the main contributors. The nation produces 23.1 tons of particulate emissions and 335 tons of hydrocarbon emissions yearly and contributes 0.2% of the world's total gas emissions. Strict standards for exhaust emissions were imposed on new passenger cars manufactured after October 1987. Water pollution is also a problem due to the presence of phosphates, fertilizers, and pesticides in the water supply. The nation has 10.2 cubic miles of water of which 4% is used for farming and 73% for industrial purposes. The country's cities produce 3.1 million tons of solid waste annually. The same pollutants that affect the water also affect the soil. Chemical contaminants and erosion damage the nation's soil and limit productivity.

Important environmental groups include the Swiss League for the Protection of Nature, founded in 1909; the Swiss Foundation for the Protection and Care of the Landscape, 1970; and the Swiss Society for the Protection of the Environment. The principal federal agency is the Department of Environment.

The bear and wolf were exterminated by the end of the 19th century, but the lynx, once extinct in Switzerland, has been reestablished. In 1994, 2 of Switzerland's mammal species and 15 bird species were endangered, and 18 types of plants were endangered. As of 1987, the northern bald ibis and the Italian spadefoot toad were extinct; several classes of the large blue butterfly were endangered.

On 1 November, 1986, as a result of a fire in a chemical warehouse near Basel, in northern Switzerland, some 30 tons of toxic waste flowed into the Rhine River, killing an estimated 500,000 fish and eels. Despite a Swiss report in January 1987 that damage to the river had not been so great as was first thought, most environmentalists considered the chemical spill a major disaster.

6 POPULATION

As of the census of 4 December 1990, the population of Switzerland was 6,873,700, with a density of 166 per sq km (431 per sq mi). By the year 2000, according to UN projections, the population is expected to rise to about 7,156,000, assuming an estimated birthrate of 12.5, a death rate of 9.6, and a net natural increase of 2.9 during the 1995–2000 period. In 1992 there were 12.6 registered births per 1,000 population and 9.1 registered deaths, for a natural increase of 3.5 per 1,000. The largest cities at the end of 1991, according to estimates, were as follows: Zürich, 343,106; Basel, 172,768; Geneva, 167,697; Bern, 134,393; and Lausanne, 123,149. During 1992, 16 towns of more than 30,000 inhabitants held 21% of the nation's population.

7 MIGRATION

Total emigration of both Swiss and foreigners in 1992 was 117,034; immigration totaled 157,190, for a net gain of 40,156. Foreigners resident in Switzerland numbered 1,190,991 (over 17% of the population) at the end of 1991. Nearly a third of all resident foreigners were of Italian nationality, former Yugoslavia, Spain, Portugal, Germany and Turkey were the next-leading countries of origin. There were 61,691 recognized refugees in 1991. In April 1987, Swiss voters approved a government plan to tighten rules on immigration and political asylum.

Internal migration came to 371,332 in 1992. There was a tendency to move from urban to rural areas and from north to south.

8 ETHNIC GROUPS

The four ethnolinguistic groups (Germanic, French, Italian, and Rhaeto-Romansh) that make up the native Swiss population have retained their specific characteristics. Originally, the country was inhabited by Celtic tribes in the west and south and by Rhaetians in the east. With the collapse of Roman rule, Germanic tribes poured in, among them the Alemanni and Burgundians. The Alemanni ultimately became the dominant group, and the present Alemannic vernacular (Schwyzertütsch, or Schweizerdeutsch) is spoken by nearly two-thirds of the total population as their principal language.

9 LANGUAGES

Switzerland is a multilingual state with four national languages—German, French, Italian, and Rhaeto-Romansh. As of the 1990 census, 63.6% of the resident population spoke as their principal language German, predominantly in northern, central, and western Switzerland; 19.2% French, mainly in the west and southwest; 7.6% Italian, primarily in the southern region closest to Italy; and 0.6% Rhaeto-Romansh, used widely only in the southeastern canton of Graubünden (Grisons). The remaining 9% spoke various other languages. There are numerous local dialects.

10 RELIGIONS

Religious freedom is guaranteed. Of Switzerland's 19 predominantly German-speaking cantons (including the half-cantons), 10 are mostly Protestant and 9 are mostly Roman Catholic. Of the 6 predominantly French-speaking cantons, 2 have Protestant and 4 have Roman Catholic majorities. The Italian-speaking canton of Ticino is mainly Roman Catholic. As of the 1980 census, 50.4% of all residents were Protestant (52.7% in 1960); 43.6% were Roman Catholic (45.6% in 1960); and 8.1% belonged to other faiths. There were some 15,000 Jews in 1990.

All cantons have one or more established churches, but there is no state church. Cantonal religious establishments are supported by voluntary contributions, as well as by taxes levied by cantonal authorities on all cantonal citizens regardless of denomination. Nonestablished churches are maintained solely by voluntary contributions. The Swiss Evangelical Church League acts as national coordinator for most of the Protestant churches. The Conference of Swiss Bishops is the representative body of the Roman Catholic Church.

11 TRANSPORTATION

Swiss railroads, 57% of which are state owned, extended 5,174 km (3,215 mi). Nearly all of the railway system is electrified. Because of its geographical position, Switzerland is an international railway center, with traffic moving from France, the FRG, Austria, and northern Europe through the Simplon, Lötschberg, and St. Gotthard tunnels to Italy and southern Europe. Construction of the new "Rail 2000" a high-speed railway network, is under way.

The Swiss road network covered 72,000 km (44,740 mi) in 1991. Vehicles included 3,065,812 passenger cars, and 311,017 commercial vehicles. The longest road tunnel in the world, the 17-km (10.6-mi) St. Gotthard, in the Ticino, opened in September 1980.

Inland waterway traffic is an important component of Swiss transportation. Basel, the only river port, has direct connections to Strasbourg, the German Rhineland, the Ruhr, Rotterdam, and Antwerp. The Rhine-Rhône canal provides an alternative link between Basel and Strasbourg. During World War II, the Swiss organized a merchant marine to carry Swiss imports and exports on the high seas; in 1991, 22 ships totaling 360,000 GRT were in operation. Switzerland's merchant fleet is larger than that of any other landlocked nation.

Swissair, partially owned by the federal and local governments, is the flag line of Switzerland. It has flights from the principal

SWITZERLAND

0   25   50 Miles

0   25   50 Kilometers

GERMANY

Schaffhausen • Konstanz

Bodensee

Rhein • Winterthur

Basel • Baden

St. Gallen

Delémont • Aarau • Uster

Besançon • Zürich LIECHTENSTEIN

Aare *Zürichsee* Vaduz AUSTRIA

La Chaux-de-Fonds • Biel *Walensee* Mels

Bieler See • Burgdorf • Zug

• Neuchâtel Luzern • Schwyz

★ Bern *Vierwaldstätter See* • Altdorf

FRANCE *Aare* *Lac de Neuchâtel* • Fribourg Chur

Yverdon *Scherhorn 10,807 ft. 3294 m.* ▲ Davos

Thun • Brienz *Rhein*

Thuner See *Brienzer See* JURA MOUNTAINS

Lausanne BERNER ALPEN RHAETIAN ALPS

Lac Léman LEPONTINE ALPS *Inn*

A St. Moritz

L *Splügen Pass* *Ticino* *Bernina Pass*

P

Rhône S

Geneva • Sion

(Genéve) PENNINE ALPS Bellinzona

Matterhorn 14,692 ft. 4478 m. *Maggiorè* Lugano

Monte Rosa 15,203 ft. 4634 m.

• Aosta

N

W   E

S

ITALY

• Milano

Switzerland

LOCATION: 5°57'24" to 10°29'36"E; 45°49'8" to 47°48'35"N. **BOUNDARY LENGTHS:** FRG, 363 km (226 mi); Liechtenstein, 41 km (25 mi); Austria, 165 km (103 mi); Italy, 741 km (460 mi); France, 572 km (355 mi).

international airports at Zürich, Geneva, and Basel to major European cities, North and South America, the Middle East, Asia, and West Africa. In 1992, Swissair had 7,433,000 paying passengers and performed 1,056.1 million freight ton-km of service.

12 HISTORY

The Helvetii, a Celtic tribe conquered by Julius Caesar in 58 BC, were the first inhabitants of Switzerland (Helvetia) known by name. A Roman province for 200 years, Switzerland was a prosperous land with large cities (Avenches was the capital) and a flourishing trade. In AD 250, however, Switzerland was occupied by the Alemanni, a Germanic tribe, and in 433 by the Burgundians. The Franks, who defeated the Alemanni in 496 and the Burgundians about 534, incorporated the country into the Frankish Empire. Under Frankish rule, new cities were founded; others, such as Zürich and Lausanne, were rebuilt; and Christianity was introduced.

In 1032, some 200 years after the death of Charlemagne, king of the Franks, and the defeat of his weak successors, Switzerland became part of the Holy Roman Empire. In the 13th century, it was placed under the House of Habsburg. Harsh domination resulted in the rebellion of several cities and the formation on 1 August 1291 of the "eternal alliance" between the three forest cantons of Schwyz, Uri, and Unterwalden, the first step toward the Swiss Confederation. The Habsburgs invaded the three provinces, but with their defeat at Morgarten Pass on 15 November 1315, the Swiss secured their independence. By 1353, five other cantons, Luzern (1332), Zürich (1351), Glarus and Zug (1352), and Bern (1353), had joined the confederacy. All these allies were called Swiss (Schwyzer), after the largest canton. Four victories over Austria (1386, 1388, 1476, and 1499) confirmed the confederation. The Swiss also defeated Charles of Burgundy, whose ambitions threatened their independence until his death in 1477. Complete independence was secured by the Treaty of Basel

(1499) with the Holy Roman Empire. Switzerland thereafter remained unmolested by foreign troops until the French Revolution of 1789. Such legendary or real heroes as William Tell, Arnold von Winkelried, and Nikolaus von der Flüe symbolized Swiss bravery and love of freedom. The Helvetian Confederation (Eidgenossenschaft) continued to grow with the inclusion of Aargau (1415), Thurgau (1460), Fribourg and Solothurn (1481), Basel and Schaffhausen (1501), and Appenzell (1513). As of 1513, there were 13 cantons and several affiliated cities and regions. Swiss sovereignty reached south of the crest of the Alps into the Ticino. The Swiss also controlled many of the vital mountain passes linking southern and northern Europe.

The power of the Confederation was, however, undermined by conflicts stemming from the Reformation, led by Ulrich Zwingli in Zürich and John Calvin in Geneva. Seven cantons resisted the Reformation, and a prolonged conflict resulted. In its first round, Zwingli was killed in action (1531). The Catholic cantons later allied with Savoy and Spain. The struggle with the Protestant cantons centered during the Thirty Years' War (1618–48) on control of the Valtelline pass. The Treaty of Westphalia ending that war granted the Swiss Confederation formal recognition of independence by all European powers.

In the following centuries, the Catholic-Protestant conflict continued with varying success for each side. Apart from this struggle, a number of abortive uprisings against oligarchic control occurred in such places as Geneva and the canton of Vaud. The oligarchs were still in power in most cantons when the French Revolution broke out. With the progress of the revolution, radical groups gained the upper hand in several cities. In 1798, the Helvetic Republic was proclaimed, under French tutelage, and during the Napoleonic imperial era Switzerland was governed as an appendage of France. Boundaries were partly redrawn, and six new cantons were added to the original 13.

In 1815, the Congress of Vienna reconstituted the independent Swiss Confederation with three additional cantons (for a total of 22) and recognized its perpetual neutrality. Switzerland, however, did not remain untouched by the great conflict between liberalism and conservatism that affected all Europe in the first half of the 19th century. Many revolutionaries found temporary refuge in Switzerland and influenced some of its citizens. Under their goading, several cantons introduced more progressive governments and liberalized their old constitutions.

In 1848, a new federal constitution, quite similar to that of the US, was promulgated. Meanwhile, the struggle between Protestants and Catholics had culminated in the Secession (Sonderbund) War of 1847, in which the Protestant cantons quickly overcame the secessionist movement of the seven Catholic cantons. As a result of the war, federal authority was greatly strengthened.

In 1874, the constitution was again revised to enlarge federal authority, especially in fiscal and military affairs. Since the last quarter of the 19th century, Switzerland has been concerned primarily with domestic matters, such as social legislation, communications, and industrialization. In foreign affairs, it remained rigidly neutral through both world wars, resolutely determined to protect its independence with its highly reputed militia. In 1978, Switzerland's 23d sovereign canton, Jura, was established by nationwide vote. In 1991, Switzerland celebrated the 700th anniversary of Confederation.

Despite its neutrality, Switzerland has cooperated wholeheartedly in various international organizations, offering home and hospitality to such diverse bodies as the League of Nations, the Red Cross, and the UPU. Switzerland has long resisted joining the UN, however, partly on the grounds that imposition of sanctions, as entailed in various UN resolutions, is contrary to a policy of strict neutrality. In a March 1986 referendum, a proposal for UN membership, approved by the Federal Assembly, was rejected by Swiss voters. Switzerland is a member of most specialized UN agencies and is a party to the Statute of the International Court of Justice.

The Swiss have also expressed ambivalence toward Europe. In December 1992, the Swiss rejected participation in the two major European organizations—the European Economic Area (EEA) of the European Union (EU) and the European Free Trade Association (EFTA). Fearing adverse effects from non-participation, the Swiss government has taken steps to bring the country's laws and economy into harmony with the EEA.

13GOVERNMENT

The Swiss Confederation is a federal union governed under the constitution of 1874, which vested supreme authority in the Federal Assembly, the legislative body, and executive power in the Federal Council.

The Federal Assembly consists of two chambers: the National Council (Nationalrat) of 200 members, elected by direct ballot for four-year terms by citizens 18 years of age or older, and the Council of States (Ständerat) of 46 members, 2 appointed by each of the 20 cantons and 1 from each of the 6 half-cantons, and paid by the cantons; deputies are elected according to the laws of the cantons. Legislation must be approved by both houses.

The Federal Council of seven members is elected for four-year terms by joint session of the Federal Assembly. The president and vice-president of the Federal Council and of the Confederation are elected by the assembly for one-year terms and cannot be reelected to the same office until after the expiration of another year. The seven members of the Federal Council, which has no veto power, are the respective heads of the main departments of the federal government.

The cantons are sovereign in all matters not delegated to the federal government by the constitution and may force federal law to a plebiscite by the right of referendum. In addition, by popular initiative, 50,000 citizens may demand a direct popular vote on any legislation or regulation proposed by the federal government, and 100,000 citizens may demand a referendum on a constitutional revision. Any proposed amendments to the constitution must be submitted for public approval.

In 1971, Swiss women were granted the right to vote in federal elections. In November 1990, the Federal Court ruled in favor of female suffrage in the half-canton of Appenzell-Inner Rhoden, the last area with male-only suffrage.

14POLITICAL PARTIES

Swiss politics are generally stable, and the strengths of the chief political parties have varied little over the past several decades. The conduct of national-level politics is generally calm and is marked by mutual esteem and cooperation. On the cantonal and municipal levels, however, the give-and-take of political life is more lively and unrestrained, as well as more partisan. The three strongest parties are the Social Democratic Party, similar to the British Labourites and the Scandinavian Social Democrats, which advocates wider state participation in industry and strong social legislation; the Radical Democratic Party, a progressive middle-class party, which favors increased social welfare, strengthening of national defense, and a democratic federally structured government; and the Christian Democrats (formerly the Christian Social-Conservatives), a clerical federalist party, which opposes centralization of power. The Center Democratic Union (Swiss People's Party) was formed in 1971 by a union of the Farmers, Traders, and Citizens Party, which favored agrarian reform, protective tariffs, and a stronger national defense, and the Democratic Party, a leftist middle-class group. Other parties include the League of Independents, a progressive, middle-class consumers' group; the Communist-inclined Workers Party, with some strength in Zürich, Basel, and Geneva; the Liberal Party; and the

Independent and Evangelical Party, which is Protestant, federalist, and conservative. In 1985, two small right-wing parties were formed: the National Socialist Party and the Conservative and Liberal Movement.

After the October 1991 elections the Radical Democratic Party held 44 seats, Social Democrats 42 seats, Christian Democrats 37 seats, Swiss Peoples Party 25 seats, Greens 14 seats, Liberals 10 seats, and minor parties, 28 seats. The next election is scheduled for 1995.

In the Council of States, the 46 seats were distributed as follows in 1991: Radical Democratic Party 18 seats, Christian Democrats 16 seats, Social Democrats 4 seats, Liberals 3 seats, Independents 1 seat, and Ticino League 1 seat.

[15]LOCAL GOVERNMENT

The Swiss Confederation consists of 23 sovereign cantons, 3 of which are divided into half-cantons (i.e., 20 cantons and 6 half-cantons). The most recent of these, Jura, was formed from six French-speaking districts in the German-speaking area of Bern Canton in 1978. In 1993, the German-speaking Laufental district of Beru joined the canton of Basel-Land. This was the first time a political unit in Switzerland left one canton to join another. Swiss cantons are responsible for their own public works, education, care of the poor, justice, and police forces. Local forms of government vary, but each canton has a legislative council (called Grand Conseil, Grosser Rat, Kantonsrat, or Gran Consiglio), which appoints a chief executive. In a few of the small cantons, the general assembly of all voting citizens, or Landesgemeinde, decides on major matters by voice vote; in the majority of the cantons, this ancient institution has been replaced by referendum. Communes, numbering over 3,000, are the basic units of local government. For the most part, Swiss districts (Bezirke), constituting a middle level of organization between the cantons and communes, are little more than judicial circuits.

[16]JUDICIAL SYSTEM

The Federal Court of Justice in Lausanne, composed of 30 permanent members appointed for six-year terms by the Federal Assembly, has both original and final jurisdiction in the majority of cases where a canton or the federal government is involved, and is the highest appeals court for many types of cases. Each canton has its own cantonal courts. District courts have three to five members and try lesser criminal and civil cases. Each canton has an appeals court and a court of cassation, the jurisdiction of which is limited to reviewing judicial procedures. Capital punishment was abolished in 1942. Minor cases are tried by a single judge, difficult cases by a panel of judges, and murder and other serious crimes by a public jury.

The judiciary is independent and free from interference by other branches of government.

[17]ARMED FORCES

The Swiss army is a well-trained citizen's militia, composed of three field army corps and one alpine field corps. Although in 1993 the standing armed forces had only 1,600 regulars and 18,500 conscript trainees, Switzerland can mobilize 625,000 trained militia within 48 hours. The air force has 242 combat aircraft, maintained by civilians. The country has universal compulsory military service for males at age 19–20, followed by varied annual training requirements until age 42 (55 for officers), with exemption only for physical disability. Service in the women's auxiliary force is voluntary, but it can be made compulsory under present law. Initial basic training of 17 weeks is followed by regular short training periods, gradually diminishing in the number of days per year for the older age groups. By tradition, the highest-ranking officers hold the rank of brigadier; only in time of war does the Federal Assembly appoint generals.

Swiss fighting men are world famous, and from the 16th to the 19th century some 2 million Swiss served as mercenaries in foreign armies. The modern Swiss citizen-soldier is trained only for territorial defense in prepared mountain positions, which is his only mission. A continuing legacy of Swiss mercenary service is the ceremonial Vatican Swiss Guard. Switzerland's civil defense program, begun in the early 1970s, has the capacity to shelter 90% of the population. Switzerland is a significant seller of arms, having exported more than $2.6 billion in armaments between 1981 and 1991. Swiss volunteers serve in four overseas peace-keeping operations. Switzerland spends $4.6 billion (1990) for defense or 2 % of gross domestic product.

[18]INTERNATIONAL COOPERATION

Although it was a member of and served as the site for the League of Nations and is today the headquarters of many UN committees, Switzerland is not a member of the UN, partly from a fear of compromising traditional Swiss neutrality. The country does participate in ECE and in all the nonregional specialized agencies except IBRD, IDA, IFC, and IMF; has actively participated in the CSCE; and has long played host to international organizations, such as ILO, UPU, and the International Red Cross. The nation is also a member of the Asian Development Bank, Council of Europe, EFTA, IDB, and OECD; holds permanent observer status in the OAS; and is a signatory to GATT and the Law of the Sea, but it is not a member of ECSC, EC, or EURATOM, again partly because of its neutralist posture. Switzerland is also the repository of the Geneva Convention, governing treatment of civilians, prisoners, and the wounded in wartime.

[19]ECONOMY

Because of the paucity of its minerals and other raw materials and its limited agricultural production, Switzerland depends upon imports of food and fodder and of industrial raw materials, which it finances with exports of manufactured goods. Agriculture is important, though limited by a scarcity of level and fertile land, but manufacturing engages more than five times as many workers as farming. Swiss manufacturers excel in quality of workmanship rather than quantity of output. Other important branches of the economy include international banking, insurance, tourism, and transportation. Switzerland was less affected than most other nations by the worldwide recession of the early 1980s and experienced a strong recovery beginning in 1983. However, between 1986 and 1992, GNP grew by an annual average of only 0.7% and it fell in 1991, 1992, and 1993. From 1990 to 1992, the annual inflation rate averaged 5.1%. Swiss unemployment has remained consistently low in comparison with other countries, although it reached an unusually high 4.5% in 1993. Meanwhile, the Swiss GDP per capita—$33,819 in 1991— has continued to be the highest among the OECD nations and remains among the highest in the world. Although actual purchasing power was lower than this dollar figure would indicate, it still represented 98% of the US GDP per capita.

[20]INCOME

In 1992, Switzerland's GNP was $248,688 million at current prices, or $36,230 per capita. For the period 1985–92 the average inflation rate was 4.0%, resulting in a real growth rate in per capita GNP of 1.1%.

In 1992 the GDP was $152.3 billion in the equivalent purchasing power of the US dollar. It is estimated that in 1985 agriculture, hunting, forestry, and fishing contributed 4% to GDP; mining and quarrying, less than 1%; manufacturing, 26%; electricity, gas, and water, 2%; construction, 8%; wholesale and retail trade, 19%; transport, storage, and communication, 6%; finance, insurance, real estate, and business services, 16%; community, social, and personal services, 8%; and other sources, 11%.

21LABOR

In 1992, total civilian employment numbered approximately 3,481,000, of whom about 33.9% were employed in the industrial sector; 5.6% in agriculture, forestry, and fishing; and 60.5% in services and other occupations. Another 9.2% worked in construction. In June 1992, the unemployment rate was 2.7%, the highest recorded figure since 1938 but still remained remarkably low in comparison with those of most other non-Communist countries. Foreign workers account for about 30% of the work force, and 40% of the total unemployed; they now have long-term residence rights which entitle them to the same unemployment benefits as jobless Swiss workers.

Trade union membership dropped in 1991 by 1,500 members (0.3%) to 442,000. About 87% of the union members were men and 13% were women. Only 29% of the labor force was unionized in 1991. Swiss law provides for and regulates union organization and collective bargaining. Most labor disputes are settled on the basis of a so-called peace agreement existing since 1937 between the head organizations of employers and employees. Other collective disputes are dealt with by the various cantonal courts of conciliation.

Despite statutory requirements, women's wages often lag behind those of men on average by 14%, and in some cases up to 30%. The average non-agricultural Swiss employee worked 42 hours per week in 1992.

22AGRICULTURE

Some 30,715 sq km (11,860 sq mi), or about 75% of the country's total area, is productive. Roughly 10% of the terrain is arable, 40% pasturage, and 26% forest. Most of the cultivable land is in the Mittelland, or central plateau, and the cantons regularly producing the largest quantities of wheat are Bern, Vaud, Fribourg, Zürich, and Aargau. Soil quality is often poor, but yields have been increasing as a result of modern technology.

Agricultural production provides only about 60% of the nation's food needs. Although productivity per worker has been increasing steadily, the proportion of the total labor force engaged in agriculture has fallen from 30% in 1900 to below 6% in 1992. Between 1955 and 1985, the number of farm holdings fell from 205,997 to 119,731. Some principal crops, with their production figures for 1992, were as follows: potatoes, 737,000 tons; sugar beets, 907,000 tons; wheat, 533,000 tons; barley, 365,000 tons; maize, 192,000 tons; oats, 53,000 tons; and rye, 29,000 tons. In the same year, a total of 137,000 tons of wine were produced, and there were 13,450 hectares (33,235 acres) of vineyards.

Swiss agricultural policy is highly regulated, with fixed prices and quota restrictions maintained on several products. Domestic production is encouraged by the imposition of protective customs and duties on imported goods, and by restrictions on imports. The Federal Council has the authority to fix prices of bread grains, flour, milk, and other foodstuffs. Production costs in Switzerland, as well as international exchange rates favorable to the Swiss franc, make competition with foreign products difficult.

23ANIMAL HUSBANDRY

More than half of Switzerland's productive area is grassland exploited for hay production and/or grazing. Dairying and cattle breeding are practiced, more or less intensively, in all but the barren parts of the country and, during the summer months, even at altitudes of more than 1,200 m (4,000 ft). In 1992 there were 1,707,000 pigs, 1,783,000 head of cattle, and 415,000 sheep. Switzerland had 6,000,000 laying chickens in 1992. In 1992, Switzerland produced about 3,845,000 tons of milk and 38,000 tons of butter. Swiss cheeses are world famous. In 1992, 36,100 tons of eggs were produced.

While home production almost covers or exceeds the domestic requirements for milk and dairy products, substantial quantities of eggs and meat must be imported. Selective cattle breeding, research, and improvement of production standards are promoted by the federal government and by farmers' cooperatives.

24FISHING

Fishing is relatively unimportant but is carried on in many Swiss rivers and on lakes Constance, Neuchâtel, and Geneva. Local fish supply about 12% of domestic needs.

25FORESTRY

Forests occupy slightly more than 1 million hectares (2.5 million acres). About two-thirds of the forested land is owned by communes; most of the remainder is owned privately. Federal and cantonal governments account for about 8%. About 80% of the wood in Swiss forests is coniferous, primarily spruce; the remaining 20% is deciduous, predominantly red beech.

Forestry production in 1991 amounted to about 1,985,000 cu m of sawnwood, 1,218,000 of paper and paperboard, and 700,000 cu m of firewood. Exports of forest products are valued at less than half that of forestry imports.

26MINING

Mining, under cantonal jurisdiction, is of minor commercial importance. Minerals produced commercially include salt, lime, iron ore, sulfur, cement, and aluminum (from imported alumina and bauxite). There are small deposits of iron, nickel-cobalt, gold, and silver.

27ENERGY AND POWER

Switzerland is heavily dependent on imported petroleum, which supplied 50% of the energy consumed in 1991. Between 1970 and 1991, the share of natural gas in total energy consumption rose from 1.3% to 8.9%. Switzerland's electric power plants, which supplied 37.9% of the energy consumed in 1991, had an installed capacity of 17.7 million kw, of which hydroelectric plants accounted for about four-fifths. Electricity production totaled 57,802 million kwh; about 58% was hydroelectric. In 1991 there were five nuclear plants in operation. In 1988, the government suspended plans to build a sixth reactor at Kaiseraugst (near Basel) because of pressure from environmentalists. Two other nuclear facilities, which were in the early stages of planning, are not likely to be built in the near future. The only natural gas produced in Switzerland comes from the Finsterwald Field, in the Lucerne canton. Natural gas consumption, which totaled 1.8 billion cu m in 1992, came mostly from the Netherlands, the Norwegian sections of the North Sea, and the former USSR. Switzerland discourages the burning of coal and other hydrocarbons.

28INDUSTRY

Manufacturing industries, although declining in importance, still employ nearly 30% of the labor force (including construction). Swiss industries are chiefly engaged in the manufacture, from imported raw materials, of highly finished goods for domestic consumption and for export. Most of the industrial enterprises are located in the plains and the Swiss plateau, especially in the cantons of Zürich, Bern, Aargau, St. Gallen, Solothurn, Vaud, Basel (Baselstadt and Baselland), and Thurgau. Some industries are concentrated in certain regions: the watch and jewelry industry in the Jura Mountains; machinery in Zürich, Geneva, and Basel; the chemical industry (dyes and pharmaceuticals) in Basel; and the textile industry in northeastern Switzerland. By number of employees, the leading sectors in 1992 were machinery and vehicles, 155,200; construction, 186,800; metals and fabricated metal products, 100,000; and electric, electronic, and optical products, 119,800.

The textile industry, using wool, cotton, silk, and synthetics, is the oldest Swiss industry and remains important. The machine industry, first among Swiss industries today, produces goods ranging from heavy arms and ammunition to fine precision and optical instruments. Watches and machinery represent about 45% of the total Swiss export value. Chemicals, especially dyes and pharmaceuticals, also are important. About 10% of the world's medicines are produced by three companies in Basel. Despite agricultural problems, Switzerland has also developed a major food industry, relying in part on the country's capacity for milk production. Condensed milk was first developed in Switzerland, as were two other important processed food products: chocolate and baby food. The Swiss company Nestlé S. A., headquartered in Vevey, is one of the world's largest food companies, with 1993 sales of $38.9 billion. Because of shifts in foreign demand, some of Switzerland's major industries, such as textiles, nonmetallic minerals, and watchmaking and clockmaking, have declined in importance in recent years, while others, such as chemicals, plastics, and paper, have grown rapidly.

In 1991, industrial products included 132,000 tons of refined sugar, 4,716,090 tons of cement, 205 million cigars, 3,353,000 pairs of leather footwear; 9,800,000 sq m of woolen woven fabrics, and 115,500 tons of chocolate and chocolate products. Watchmaking remained a major industry but continued to suffer to an extent from a falloff in foreign demand.

²⁹SCIENCE AND TECHNOLOGY

The major scientific learned societies are the Swiss Academy of Sciences, founded in 1815, and the Swiss Academy of Human Science, founded in 1956. About three-quarters of the funds for Swiss research and development—a high proportion by world standards—are supplied by industry and the rest by federal and cantonal governments. The National Fund Foundation was established in 1952 to finance noncommercial research for which funds would not otherwise be available. Total expenditures on research and development in 1986 amounted to SwFr7 billion; 29,086 technicians and 22,725 scientists and engineers were engaged in research and development. The Ministry of Public Economy, the center for federal agricultural research, has seven research stations.

³⁰DOMESTIC TRADE

Zürich, the largest city, is the commercial, financial, and industrial center of Switzerland. Basel is the second most important commercial city, followed by Geneva and Lausanne. Most Swiss wholesale firms are importers as well, specializing in one commodity or a group of related commodities. Some agricultural products, such as butter, grains, and edible fats and oils, are subject to import controls, and the prices of some foodstuffs are controlled. Wholesale trade employed some 167,900 Swiss workers in 1992; retail trade, 338,900.

Usual business hours are from 8 AM to noon and, except on Saturdays, from 2 to 6 PM. Shops are normally open from 8 AM to 12:15 PM and from 1:30 to 6:30 PM on weekdays but only to 4 PM on Saturdays; some shops stay open at lunchtime but close on Monday mornings. Banks are open to the public from 8:30 AM to 4:30 PM Monday–Friday. The five-day workweek is becoming popular; the extent to which weekday working hours are lengthened depends on whether offices are closed every Saturday or only on alternate Saturdays.

Advertising, mostly entrusted to firms of specialists, uses as media billboards, movie theaters, television, local transportation facilities, railroads, newspapers, and magazines.

³¹FOREIGN TRADE

Switzerland's annual trade balance is habitually in arrears, owing to the economy's reliance on large quantities of imported raw materials for industry. Imports of food and raw materials and exports of manufactured products are the characteristic features of Swiss foreign trade. Iron, minerals, and machinery have been the primary imports since 1954, while leading exports have been machinery and watches, pharmaceuticals, precision tools, and textiles; Swiss cheese and chocolate are noted commodities on the international market. From 1991 to 1992, Switzerland's exports increased 4.8%, from SwFr87,946.5 million to SwFr92,141.8 million. Imports fell from SwFr95,031.8 million to SwFr92,330.4 million (2.8%).

In 1992, EC countries accounted for 58.9% of Swiss exports and provided 72.2% of the imports. Principal trading partners in 1992 (in millions of Swiss francs) were as follows:

	EXPORTS	IMPORTS	BALANCE
Germany	21,592.7	30,879.9	−9,287.2
France	8,726.2	9,987.4	−1,261.2
Italy	8,058.4	9,247.7	−1,189.3
U.S.	7,786.5	5,865.9	1,920.6
UK	6,063.0	5,335.6	727.4
Japan	3,449.1	3,982.3	−533.2
Austria	3,364.5	3,608.1	−243.6
Netherlands	2,524.5	4,114.8	−1,590.3
Belgium-Luxembourg	2,514.7	3,563.5	−1,048.8
Other countries	28,062.2	15,745.2	12,317
TOTALS	92,141.8	92,330.4	−188.6

³²BALANCE OF PAYMENTS

Switzerland generally has a foreign trade deficit. In most years, however, this imbalance is more than compensated for by income from services, investments, insurance, and tourism. After extensive stagnation in 1986 and 1987, Swiss foreign trade has made a good recovery since 1988. In 1992 merchandise exports totaled $78,642 million and imports $78,893 million. The merchandise trade balance was $−251 million. The following table summarizes Switzerland's balance of payments for 1991 and 1992 (in millions of US dollars):

	1991	1992
CURRENT ACCOUNT		
Goods, services, and income	12,946	16,396
Unrequited transfers	−2,622	2,977
TOTALS	10,324	13,419
CAPITAL ACCOUNT		
Direct investment	−3,363	−3,864
Portfolio investment	−11,978	−2,936
Other long-term capital	−1,094	−2,375
Other short-term capital	4,758	487
Other liabilities	22	−23
Reserves	−857	−4,397
TOTALS	−12,512	−13,108
Errors and omissions	2,187	−311
Total change in reserves	151	−4,293

³³BANKING AND SECURITIES

In 1989, Switzerland had 631 banking institutions and finance companies. These included 5 major banks, 29 cantonal banks, 130 foreign-owned banks, 210 savings banks, and 209 other banks and finance companies. The bank balance-sheet total per capita in Switzerland is higher than that of any other nation in the world. Moreover, the number of banking and financial offices—more than 4,000 in 1991—offers the Swiss, on average, the greatest access to banking services of all the world's nations.

The government-supervised Swiss National Bank, the sole bank of issue, is a semiprivate institution owned by the cantons, by former banks of issue, and by the public. The National Bank acts as a central clearinghouse and participates in many foreign and domestic banking operations. In December 1993, the foreign assets of the Swiss National Bank totaled SwFr60.94 billion and 83.3 million troy ounces of gold.

The transactions of private and foreign banks doing business in Switzerland traditionally play a significant role in both Swiss and foreign capital markets; however, precise accounting of assets and liabilities in this sector are not usually made available as public information. Switzerland's strong financial position and its tradition (protected by the penal code since 1934) of preserving the secrecy of individual bank depositors have made it a favorite depository with persons throughout the world. (However, Swiss secrecy provisions are not absolute and have been lifted to provide information in criminal investigations.) The Swiss Office for Compensation executes clearing traffic with foreign countries.

Stock exchanges operate in Geneva (founded 1850), Basel (1875), and Zürich (1876). The Zürich exchange is the most important in the country.

34INSURANCE
Switzerland is one of the world's largest insurance centers, both for direct operations and for reinsurance, and all insurance firms are government regulated. Total exemption from federal taxation for life, accident, and inland marine insurance came into effect in 1974. There were 129 insurance companies in 1989.

In 1990, premiums totaled US$2,926.6 or 8% of the GDP.

Switzerland controls an estimated one-third of the world's reinsurance, and insurance income represents a major item in the Swiss balance of payments. Insurance investments are represented heavily in the Swiss capital market, and Swiss insurance firms have invested widely in foreign real estate. About half the domestic insurance business is in the hands of the state. The Swiss Reinsurance Co. in Zürich is the largest of its kind in the world.

35PUBLIC FINANCE
Central government accounts have shown small but recurrent annual deficits since 1971. National defense has perennially accounted for the largest central government outlay, although social welfare expenditures have been growing rapidly in recent years. The budgeted share of both total public expenditures and revenues is only about 35%; the cantons and communities are largely independent of federal policy. Increased government spending and declining tax revenues have led to a deterioration in the public sector budget situation. In 1991, the federal government incurred a budget deficit of over SwFr1.5 billion, the first one in seven years. Cantonal budgets also were in deficit. Switzerland is likely to face budget deficits at all levels well until the mid-1990s. As an international creditor, debt management policies are not relevant to Switzerland, which participates in the Paris Club debt reschedulings and is an active member of the OECD.

36TAXATION
The Swiss Confederation, the cantons, and the communes all levy taxes on income or profits. Periodic federal, cantonal, and communal taxes also are charged against capital values belonging to corporations and other corporate entities. The cantons all levy wealth taxes based on individual net assets, stamp duties, taxes on entertainment or admissions, and special charges for educational, social, and sanitary services. Most cantons also levy a tax surcharge on members of certain major churches for the support of those religions. Localities may impose taxes on land, rents, and entertainment, as well as a head tax and a dog tax.

Federal tax is levied on income or profits and on capital values or corporations. For married couples, this tax is progressive on net incomes between SwFr21,300 and SwFr595,200, above which it is a flat 11.5%. Various deductions and personal allowances are granted according to circumstances. Those between the ages of 20 and 50 who do not fulfill their military obligation are liable for an additional tax. The federal tax on corporate profits is charged at a basic rate of 3.63%, with surtaxes for profits above certain levels. The maximum effective rate, however, cannot exceed 9.8% of taxable net profits. The federal tax on corporate capital plus reserves is levied at a flat rate of 0.0825%. There are also miscellaneous federal taxes, such as stamp duties, turnover or sales taxes, and excise taxes.

37CUSTOMS AND DUTIES
Switzerland joined EFTA in 1960 and became a full member of the GATT group in 1966. In 1973, Switzerland entered into an industrial free-trade agreement with the EC; duties on industrial imports from the EC were eliminated by 1977. Although it generally favors free trade, Switzerland protects domestic agriculture for national defense reasons, and its customs tariff, established in 1921, is primarily a revenue-raising instrument. Specific duties—low for raw materials, moderate for semifinished goods, and high for manufactured goods—are levied by weight of import. Switzerland gives preferential treatment to imports from developing nations.

38FOREIGN INVESTMENT
There are no restrictions on foreign investment except in real estate. Federal grants are offered for investments in depressed areas. The cantonal governments offer tax and non-tax incentives for new investments or extensions of existing investments on a case-by-case basis. US investment in Switzerland was estimated at $28.7 billion in 1992.

39ECONOMIC DEVELOPMENT
Private enterprise is the basis of Swiss economic policy. Although government intervention has traditionally been kept to a minimum (even with monopolistic formations), international monetary crises from late 1974 to mid-1975 led to imposition of various interim control measures; in 1982, with inflation rising, a constitutional amendment mandating permanent government price controls was approved by popular referendum. The Swiss National Bank has followed a general policy of limiting monetary growth. To further raise the standard of living, the government also grants subsidies for educational and research purposes, promotes professional training, and encourages exports. Although certain foreign transactions are regulated, there is free currency exchange and a guarantee to repatriate earnings of foreign corporations.

The cause of the remarkable stability of Switzerland's economy lies in the adaptability of its industries; in the soundness of its convertible currency, which is backed by gold to an extent unmatched in any other country; and in the fact that the particular pattern of Swiss democracy, where every law may be submitted to the popular vote, entails taking into account the wishes of all parties whose interests would be affected by a change in legislation.

Switzerland's development assistance program takes the form of technical cooperation, preferential customs treatment for certain third-world products, and a limited number of bilateral aid arrangements. Official development assistance was $863 million in 1991, representing 0.36% of the GNP.

40SOCIAL DEVELOPMENT
Swiss social legislation has three main components: accident insurance; sickness insurance; and old-age, survivors', and disability insurance. In addition, there are unemployment insurance, military insurance, income insurance, and the farmers' aid organization. Accident insurance, which is compulsory, is fixed at 80% of the income lost from a 50% or greater disability due to an accident. Sickness insurance is available to every Swiss citizen, is

compulsory in many cantons, and covers well over half of all workers in business, industry, and commerce. Cantonal authorities can make it compulsory for all or some of their citizens. Old-age and survivors' insurance went into effect in 1946 and in 1959 was expanded to cover invalidity. It is financed by a 4.2% payroll deduction from both employers and employees (7.8% for those self-employed). An additional 0.2% is levied for unemployment insurance, now compulsory. In 1985 there were 38,776 marriages in Switzerland, or 6 per 1,000 population, and an estimated 11,415 divorces. Of 74,684 live births, 70,517 occurred within wedlock. Popular referendums have rejected proposals to make abortion freely available; interpretation of the national law permitting abortion on medical grounds varies among the cantons. In 1981, a constitutional amendment guaranteeing equal rights to women, particularly in education, work, and the family, was passed by a vote of 797,679 to 525,950. In 1985, 54.7% of voters approved a new law giving women equal rights in marriage.

In February, 1993, the government proposed legislation to implement more effective constitutional prohibitions on discrimination against women, including provisions that would strengthen a woman's position in sexual harassment cases.

[41] HEALTH

Health standards and medical care are excellent. The pharmaceuticals industry ranks as one of the major producers of specialized pharmaceutical products.

Switzerland's 1993 population was 6.9 million, with a birth rate of 12.7 per 1,000 people, and about 71% of married women (ages 15 to 49) using contraception. There were 86,000 births in 1992. The general mortality rate was 9.9 per 1,000 population in 1993; the infant mortality rate, which had been 70.3 per 1,000 live births in 1924, was 7 in 1992. Life expectancy was averaged at 78 years in 1992.

In 1983, Switzerland had 432 hospitals with 72,605 beds. In 1990, there were 11 hospital beds per 1,000 people. In 1988, there were 11,327 practicing physicians and 3,184 dentists. In 1990, there was 1 doctor for every 630 inhabitants; in 1992, there were 1.59 doctors per 1,000 people, with a nurse to doctor ratio of 2.6. There were about 18 cases of tuberculosis per 100,000 people reported in 1990. In 1992, vaccination rates for children up to one year old were: diphtheria, pertussis, and tetanus (89%); polio (95%); and measles (83%). Total health care expenditures were $16,916 million in 1990.

[42] HOUSING

Although housing standards are comparatively high, there are shortages in certain areas; the vacancy rate was 0.79% in 1985. In 1991, a total of 37,597 new dwellings were constructed in communities of 2,000 or more inhabitants, down from 44,228 in 1985. The total housing stock in 1991 stood at 3,181,000. As of 1986, 99.5% of all dwellings had a water supply, 97% had a bath or shower, 78% had central heating, and 100% had a private toilet.

[43] EDUCATION

Primary education is free, and adult illiteracy is virtually nonexistent. Education at all levels is first and foremost the responsibility of the cantons. Thus, Switzerland has 26 different systems based on differing education laws and varied cultural and linguistic needs. The cantons decide on the types of schools, length of study, teaching materials, and teachers' salaries. Education is compulsory in most cantons for nine years, and in a few for eight. An optional tenth year has been introduced in several cantons. Church schools in some cantons are tax supported. After primary school, students complete the compulsory portion of their education in various types of secondary Grade I schools, which emphasize vocational or academic subjects to varying degrees. Secondary Grade II schools, which are not compulsory, include trade and vocational preparatory schools and gymnasiums, which prepare students for the university and lead to the matura, or higher school-leaving certificate.

Switzerland has eight cantonal universities, including four in French-speaking areas and four in German-speaking ones. The universities' expenditures are largely financed by the cantons, with a 53% contribution from the Confederation. Approximately one-third of all higher-level educational funding goes to research and development. The largest universities are those of Zürich, Geneva, and Basel; others include those of Lausanne, Bern, Fribourg, and Neuchâtel. The Federal Institute of Technology in Zürich, the Economics College at St. Gallen, and the Federal Institute of Technology in Lausanne are also important.

Switzerland has a large number of private schools attracting primarily foreign students. These schools, most of them located in the French-speaking cantons, are known for their high-quality education, of either the academic or "finishing school" variety.

[44] LIBRARIES AND MUSEUMS

The library of Basel University and the Swiss National Library in Bern, both with approximately 2.8 million volumes, are the largest in Switzerland. The federal archives, the libraries of the UN European Center and the International Labor Office in Geneva are among the most important special libraries. The nine university libraries have a combined total of over 13 million volumes.

The National Museum, a federal institution in Zürich, houses historic objects; other historical museums are located in Basel, Bern, and Geneva. Basel houses both the Museum of Ancient Art and the Basel Museum of Fine Arts, which has a fine collection of 15th- and 16th-century German masterworks, paintings by Dutch artists of the 17th and 18th centuries, and a survey from Corot to Picasso. The Museum of Fine Arts in Bern contains paintings of old masters and impressionists (Klee Foundation). The Zürich Art Museum houses modern Swiss paintings, as well as works by Dutch and Flemish masters of the 17th century. There are arts and crafts museums in most of the larger cities, and Neuchâtel has an ethnographic museum. Many fine examples of Romanesque, Gothic, and Baroque architecture are found in Switzerland.

[45] MEDIA

The postal system and the telephone, telegraph, radio, and television systems are government owned and operated. The telephone system is completely automatic, encompassing 6,050,926 telephones (90 per 100 population) in 1991. International communications, air navigation services, and the new electronic media, including data transmission and electronic mail, are the province of Radio Suisse, a public corporation of which the Confederation holds 95%. Broadcasting is controlled by the Swiss Broadcasting Corp. (SBC), an autonomous corporation under federal supervision. In 1991 there were 6 SBC radio channels and 3 television channels. A number of independent local radio stations have been operating on a trial basis since 1983. Radio programs are broadcast in German, French, Italian, and Romansh. In 1991, Switzerland had 2,701,000 licensed radios and 2,476,000 televisions.

Switzerland had the world's third highest number of newspapers per 1,000 inhabitants as of 1992. A few papers, such as the *Neue Zürcher Zeitung* and the *Journal de Genève*, are widely read even beyond the borders of Switzerland and have excellent international coverage. In 1991, Switzerland had 98 daily newspapers with a total circulation of 3,280,000. The Agence Télégraphique Suisse (Schweizerische Depeschenagentur), co-owned by some 40 newspaper publishers, is Switzerland's most important national news agency.

The *Schweizer Illustrierte* (1991 circulation 175,000) is the most popular illustrated weekly, and the *Nebelspalter* (44,900) is the best-known satirical periodical.

[46] ORGANIZATIONS

Both agricultural and consumer cooperatives are numerous. The Swiss Office for Commercial Expansion is an important foreign trade promotion organization. There are chambers of commerce in all the major cities. The headquarters of the International Red Cross are in Geneva.

[47] TOURISM, TRAVEL, AND RECREATION

Switzerland has long been one of the most famous tourist areas in the world, and Swiss hospitality and the Swiss hotel industry are justly renowned. Scenic attractions are manifold, and in the Swiss Alps and on the shores of the Swiss lakes there are features of interest for the skier, the swimmer, the hiker, the mountain climber, and the high alpinist. There are approximately 50,000 km (31,000 mi) of marked footpaths and 500 ski lifts. The hotels are among the best in the world; Switzerland pioneered in modern hotel management and in specialized training for hotel personnel. In 1991, Switzerland had 145,677 hotel rooms with 267,067 beds and a 43.9% occupancy rate.

In 1991, international tourist arrivals totaled approximately 12.6 million; of these, 7.94 million were by visitors from Europe; 1.02 million from the Americas; and 533,000 from Eastern and Southeast Asia. Tourism receipts totaled $7.06 million. Central Switzerland and the Geneva region attract the largest number of foreign tourists. Passports or national identity cards are required, but citizens of the Americas or of Western European countries may enter without a visa.

[48] FAMOUS SWISS

World-famous Swiss scientists include the physician and alchemist Philippus Aureolus Paracelsus (Theophrastus Bombastus von Hohenheim, 1493?–1541); the outstanding mathematicians Johann Bernoulli (1667–1748) and Leonhard Euler (1707–83); the geologist Louis Agassiz (Jean Louis Rodolphe Agassiz, 1807–73), who was active in the US; the physiologist, pathologist, and surgeon Emil Theodor Kocher (1841–1917), who received the Nobel Prize for medicine in 1909; Charles Édouard Guillaume (1861–1938) and the German-born Albert Einstein (1879–1955, a naturalized Swiss citizen), Nobel Prize winners in physics in 1920 and 1921, respectively; and Paul Karrer (b.Russia, 1889–1971), authority on vitamins, who shared the 1937 Nobel Prize in chemistry. Other Nobel Prize winners in the sciences include Alfred Werner (1866–1919; chemistry, 1913); Yugoslav-born Leopold Ruzicka (1887–1976; chemistry, 1939); Yugoslav-born Vladimir Prelog (b.1906; chemistry, 1975); Austrian-born Wolfgang Pauli (1900–1958; physics, 1945); Paul Hermann Müller (1899–1965), Walter Rudolf Hess (1881–1973), and Polish-born Tadeus Reichstein (b.1897), Nobel laureates for medicine in 1948, 1949, and 1950, respectively; Werner Arber (b.1929; medicine, 1978); Heinrich Rohrer (b.1933; physics, 1986); and K. Alex Müller (b.1927) and German-born J. Georg Bednorz (b.1940), for physics in 1987.

Jean-Jacques Rousseau (1712–78), a Geneva-born philosopher, musician, novelist, and diarist in France, was a great figure of the 18th century whose writings exerted a profound influence on education and political thought. Swiss-born Mme. Germaine de Staël (Anne Louise Germaine Necker, 1766–1817) was acclaimed the world over as defender of liberty against Napoleon. Other noted Swiss writers include Albrecht von Haller (1708–77), also an anatomist and physiologist; the novelists and short-story writers Johann Heinrich David Zschokke (1771–1848) and Jeremias Gotthelf (Albert Bitzius, 1797–1854), also a clergyman and poet; and the poets and novelists Gottfried Keller (1819–90), Conrad Ferdinand Meyer (1825–98), and Carl Spitteler (1845–1924), the last of whom won the Nobel Prize for literature in 1919. The diaries of the philosopher, poet, and essayist Henri-Frédéric Amiel (1821–81) are famous as the stirring confessions

of a sensitive man's aspirations and failures. Charles Ferdinand Ramuz (1878–1947) is often regarded as the most powerful Swiss writer since Rousseau. The German-born novelist and poet Hermann Hesse (1877–1962) was awarded the Nobel Prize for literature in 1946. Other recent and contemporary Swiss writers include Robert Walser (1878–1956), a highly individualistic author, and the novelists and playwrights Max Rudolf Frisch (b.1911) and Friedrich Dürrenmatt (b.1921), whose psychological dramas have been performed throughout Europe and the US.

Renowned Swiss painters include Konrad Witz (1400–1447), Henry Fuseli (Johann Heinrich Füssli, 1741–1825), Arnold Böcklin (1827–1901), Ferdinand Hodler (1853–1918), and Paul Klee (1879–1940). In sculpture and painting, artist Alberto Giacometti (1901–66) won world acclaim for his hauntingly elongated figures. Le Corbusier (Charles Édouard Jeanneret, 1887–1965) was a leading 20th-century architect.

Ludwig Senfl (1490–1543) was an outstanding Renaissance composer. The *Dodecachordon* (1547) of Henricus Glareanus (Heinrich Loris, 1488–1563) was one of the most important music treatises of the Renaissance period. Swiss-born composers of more recent times include Ernest Bloch (1880–1959), Othmar Schoeck (1886–1957), Arthur Honegger (1892–1955), Frank Martin (1890–1974), Ernst Lévy (b.1895), Conrad Beck (b.1901), and Paul Burkhard (1911–77). Ernest Ansermet (1883–1969) was a noted conductor.

Swiss religious leaders include Ulrich Zwingli (1484–1531), French-born John Calvin (Jean Chauvin, 1509–64), and Karl Barth (1886–1968). Other famous Swiss are Johann Heinrich Pestalozzi (1746–1827), an educational reformer who introduced new teaching methods; Ferdinand de Saussure (1857–1913), the founder of modern linguistics; Auguste Henri Forel (1848–1931), psychologist and entomologist; the noted art historians Jakob Burckhardt (1818–97) and Heinrich Wölfflin (1864–1945); the psychiatrists Eugen Bleuler (1857–1939), Carl Gustav Jung (1875–1961), and Hermann Rorschach (1884–1922); Jean Piaget (1896–1980), authority on child psychology; and the philosopher Karl Jaspers (1883–1969). Swiss winners of the Nobel Prize for peace are Henri Dunant (1828–1910) in 1901, founder of the Red Cross, and Elie Ducommun (1833–1906) and Charles Albert Gobat (1843–1914), both in 1902.

[49] DEPENDENCIES

Switzerland has no territories or colonies.

[50] BIBLIOGRAPHY

Gretler, Arnold, and Pierre-Emeric Mandl. *Values, Trends and Alternatives in Swiss Society.* New York: Praeger, 1973.

Hilowitz, Janet Eve (ed.). *Switzerland in Perspective.* New York: Greenwood Press, 1990.

Lloyd, William Bross, Jr. *Waging Peace: The Swiss Experience.* Washington, D.C.: Public Affairs Press, 1958.

Luck, J. Murray (ed.). *Modern Switzerland.* Palo Alto, Calif.: Society for the Promotion of Science and Scholarship, 1978.

Martin, William. *Switzerland from Roman Times to the Present.* New York: Praeger, 1971.

Meier, Heinz K. *Switzerland.* Santa Barbara, Calif.: Clio Press, 1990.

Schimel, Carol L. *Conflict and Consensus in Switzerland.* Berkeley: University of California Press, 1981.

Schwarz, Urs. *The Eye of the Hurricane: Switzerland in World War II.* Boulder, Colo.: Westview, 1980.

Soloveytchik, G. *Switzerland in Perspective.* Westport, Conn.: Greenwood, 1982.

Story, A. T. *Swiss Life in Town and Country.* New York: AMS, 1983.

Switzerland: An Inside View: Politics, Economy, Culture, Society, Nature. Zurich: Der Alltag/Scalo Verlag, 1992.

UKRAINE

Ukraina

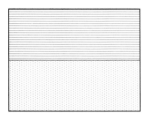

CAPITAL: Kiev (Kyyiv).

FLAG: Equal horizontal bands of azure (top) and yellow.

ANTHEM: *The National Anthem of Ukraine.*

MONETARY UNIT: The official currency, introduced in early 1993, is the hryvnia. One hundred shahy equal one hryvnia.

WEIGHTS AND MEASURES: The metric system is used.

HOLIDAYS: New Year's Day, 1–2 January; Christmas, 7 January; Women's Day, 8 March; Spring and Labour Day, 1–2 May; Victory Day, 9 May; Ukrainian Independence Day, 24 August.

TIME: 2 PM = noon GMT.

¹LOCATION, SIZE, AND EXTENT

Ukraine, the second largest country in Europe, is located in eastern Europe, bordering the Black Sea, between Poland and Russia. Comparatively, Ukraine is slightly smaller than the state of Texas with a total area of 603,700 sq km (233,090 sq mi). Ukraine shares boundaries with Belarus on the N, Russia on the E, the Black Sea on the R, Romania, Moldova, Hungary, and Slovakia on the W, and Poland on the NW. Ukraine's location is one of strategic importance at the crossroads between Europe and Asia. Its boundary length totals 4,558 km (2,851 mi). Ukraine's capital city, Kiev, is located in the north central part of the country.

²TOPOGRAPHY

The topography of Ukraine consists mainly of fertile plains (steppes) and plateaus. Mountains (Carpathians) are found only in the west and in the Crimean Peninsula in the extreme south. Fifty-six percent of the land in Ukraine is arable with approximately four percent under irrigation. The most important river in Ukraine is the Dnipro, the third longest river in Europe. It serves as a major source of hydro-electric power. Other major rivers include the Danube, Western Buh, the Tisza, the Pripyat, and the Desna.

³CLIMATE

The climate is subtropical on the Crimean Peninsula. Precipitation is disproportionately distributed, highest in the west and north, least in the east and southeast. Winters vary from cool along the Black Sea to cold farther inland. Summers are warm across the greater part of the country, except for the south where it becomes hot.

The rest of the country's climate is temperate. The mean temperature in July is 10°C (66°F). In January the mean temperature is -6°C (21°F). Northern and western Ukraine average 69 cm (27 in) of rainfall a year.

⁴FLORA AND FAUNA

The land's soil, chernozyom (black soil), is very fertile. When the Ukraine was part of the former Soviet Union it was called the country's "bread basket." European bison, fox, and rabbits can be found living on the vast steppes of the country.

⁵ENVIRONMENT

Ukraine's environmental problems include the nuclear contamination which resulted from the Chernobyl accident. One-tenth of Ukraine's land area was affected by the radiation. According to UN reports, approximately one million people were exposed to unsafe levels of radiation through the consumption of food. Three and half million hectares of agricultural land and 1.5 million hectares of forest were also contaminated.

Pollution from other sources also poses a threat to the environment. Ukraine contributes 1.8 billion cu m of polluted water, 3 million tons of heavy metal, 200,000 tons of organic compounds, and 3,000 tons of oil-related pollutants into the Black Sea annually. The water supply in some areas of the country contains toxic industrial chemicals up to 10 times the concentration considered to be within safety limits.

The pollution of the nation's water has resulted in large-scale elimination of the fish population, particularly in the Sea of Azov. Air pollution is also a significant environmental problem in the Ukraine. According to a 1992 UN report, the nation's industrial sector produces 469,000 tons of carbon monoxide and 3,072,000 tons of anhydride sulphide.

⁶POPULATION

The population of Ukraine was 51,706,742 in 1989. The estimated population in 1993 was 52,194,000. A population of 53,754,000 is projected for 2000, assuming a crude birth rate of 13.9 per 1,000 people, a death rate of 10.5, and a natural increase of 4.4 for 1995–2000. The estimated population density in 1993 was 86 per sq km (224 per sq mi). Kiev, the capital, had a population estimated at the beginning of 1990 as 2,616,000. Other big cities and their estimated populations were Kharkiv, 1,618,000; Dnipropetrovs'k, 1,187,000; Donetsk, 1,117,000; and Odesa, 1,106,000.

⁷MIGRATION

Ukraine had net immigration within the former USSR of 15,500 in 1979–88, 44,300 in 1989, and 79,300 in 1990. Emigration in 1991 came to 59,436.

There are about 12 million ethnic Ukrainians living outside of the Ukraine, but within the former Soviet Union, and an additional 4 million Ukrainians living in the United States, Canada, Australia, Western and Central Europe, and South America.

8ETHNIC GROUPS

The population was 73% Ukrainian in 1989. Russians totaled 22%, mainly in eastern Ukraine. The population of Crimea is about 70% Russian. The Crimean Tatars were deported in World War II, but some 250,000 had returned by the end of 1992. They formed about 10% of the population of the Crimean Peninsula.

9LANGUAGES

Like Russian and Belorussian, Ukrainian is an eastern Slavic language. It has several distinctive vowel and consonant sounds, however. It is written in the Cyrillic alphabet but has three extra letters. Ukrainian began to emerge as a separate language from Russian in the late 12th century.

10RELIGIONS

Ukraine was Christianized by St. Volodymyr in 988. Under Soviet rule, churches and religion were subject to suppression and political manipulation, a situation that ended with the declaration of independence in 1991. The population is 76% Orthodox, but church life has been marked by disputes between the Ukrainian Orthodox Church and the Autocephalous (independent) Ukrainian Orthodox Church. A union of the two in 1992 as the Kievan Patriarchy has apparently satisfied nationalist interests but drawn severe criticism and censure from the Patriarchy of Moscow (Russian Orthodox). Byzantine-rite Catholics account for some 15% of the population, and in 1990 there were 375,000 Jews.

11TRANSPORTATION

As of 1991, there were 23,000 km (14,295 mi) of railway, all 1.5-m-gauge. Railway traffic in 1990 totaled 75.8 billion passenger-km and 484.1 freight ton-km. Highways in 1990 totaled 273,700 km (170,100 mi), of which 86% were paved. There were some 63 passenger cars per 1,000 population in 1990.

The main marine ports are Berdyans'k, Illichivs'k, Kerch, Kherson, Mariupol', Mykolayiv, Odesa, and Sevastopol'. The merchant marine fleet includes 338 ships (1,000 GRT or over) for a total capacity of 4,117,595 GRT. The Dnipro River is the primary inland waterway, but the Danube, western Pivd Buh, Pryp'yat', and Desna are also used for import-export traffic.

Civil aviation in Ukraine performed 16.1 billion passenger-km and 100 million freight ton-km of service in 1990. The largest airports are in Kiev, Kharkiv, Donetsk, Odesa, and Simferopol'.

Important transcontinental pipelines carrying oil and gas run across Ukraine.

12HISTORY

Ukrainians, Russians, and Belarussians belong to the eastern branch of the Slavic peoples, all of which trace their origins to medieval Kievan Rus. Kievan Rus was established in the 9th century AD. St. Volodymyr the Great, one of the most celebrated rulers of Kievan Rus, adopted Christianity as the national faith in 988. Internal strife in the 12th century and the Mongol invasion in the 13th led to the ultimate destruction of Kievan Rus as a major power. Halych-Volhynia in Western Ukraine, however, became the new political center until it fell to Polish-Lithuanian rule in the 14th century. During the following centuries Ukraine found itself the object of power struggles among its more powerful neighbors.

In a protracted struggle against Poland, Ukrainian Cossacks were able to establish an independent state in the 16th and 17th centuries. To safeguard Ukrainian independence from the Poles, Ukraine concluded the Treaty of Pereyaslav in 1654 with Moscow. The nature of this agreement has generated much historical controversy: Russian historians claim that, as part of the agreement, Ukraine accepted Moscow's rule, while Ukrainians claim that Ukraine was to retain its autonomy. The ensuing war between Russia and Poland resulted in the partition of Ukraine. Most of the rest of Ukraine's territory was incorporated into the Russian Empire with the partition of Poland in 1795. Small parts of Ukrainian territory to the west were absorbed by the Hapsburg Empire.

A Ukrainian national movement arose in the 19th century. Later, the collapse of the Tsarist regime and the chaos of the Russian revolution in 1917 allowed Ukraine to assert its independence. In April 1917, the National Ukrainian Assembly met in Kiev and in November proclaimed the creation of the Ukrainian People's Republic. When the Bolsheviks formed a rival Ukrainian Communist government, the National Assembly proclaimed the independence of Ukraine on 22 January 1918.

An independent Republic of Western Ukraine was declared on 1 November 1918 after the disintegration of the Austro-Hungarian Empire. On 22 January 1919, the Ukrainian People's Republic and the Republic of Western Ukraine united and established an independent Ukrainian state, recognized by over 40 other nations.

The new government, however, could not maintain its authority in the face of civil strife and the threat of the approaching Bolshevik, pro-Tsarist, and Polish forces. By 1920, eastern Ukraine fell to the Bolsheviks and became the Ukrainian Soviet Socialist Republic while Poland occupied most of western Ukraine. Small areas of the west went to Romania, Hungary, and Czechoslovakia.

Early Soviet policy allowed for cultural autonomy and local administration by Ukrainian Communists. But Stalin changed this liberal policy in the 1930s when he initiated strict Russification and persecution of Ukrainian nationalists. This policy culminated in the Soviet-engineered famine of 1932–33 that resulted in the death of 7–10 million Ukrainians.

The 1939 Nazi-Soviet pact assigned Poland's Ukrainian territory to the Soviet sphere of influence. When Germany invaded the Soviet Union in 1941, Ukrainian nationalists in L'vin proclaimed the restoration of the Ukrainian state. The Germans arrested these nationalists and turned Ukraine into a German colony. When it became clear that the Nazis wanted to enslave them and not liberate them, a resistance movement led by nationalists fought both the Soviet and German armies. During World War II, Ukraine lost six million people through death or deportation and a total of 18,000 villages were destroyed.

The Ukrainian resistance movement continued to fight in Soviet Ukraine (the western Ukraine which had been part of Poland had been incorporated into the Ukrainian S.S.R.). It was not until the 1950s that they were completely defeated by the better equipped Soviet Red Army.

In March 1990, semi-free elections for parliament were held. On 16 July 1990, the Communist-dominated parliament declared Ukraine a sovereign state. On 24 August 1991, following the failed coup in Moscow, the parliament proclaimed the independence of Ukraine and declared that only the constitution and laws of Ukraine were valid on its territory. On 1 December 1991 the citizens of Ukraine confirmed this proclamation with a 90.3% vote in favor of independence. At the time of this referendum, Leonid Kravchuk was elected as the first president.

Ukraine joined Russia and Belarus in creating the Commonwealth of Independent States (CIS) in December 1991. This agreement was meant to facilitate coordination of policy in various fields. But despite their efforts, Ukrainian-Russian differences arose in several areas, including the command and control of nuclear weapons, the formation of a unified military command, and the character and pace of economic reform.

UKRAINE

LOCATION: 49°0′N; 32°0′E. **BOUNDARY LENGTHS:** Total boundary lengths, 4,558 km (2,851 mi); Belarus, 891 km (554 mi); Hungary, 103 km (64 mi); Moldova, 939 km (584 mi); Poland, 428 km (266 mi); Romania (southeast), 169 km (105 mi); Romania (west), 362 km (225 mi); Russia 1,576 km (980 mi); Slovakia, 90 km (56 mi).

In light of the 1986 Chernobyl nuclear power plant accident, Ukraine declared its intention to become a nuclear-free state. However, this process has been much slower than expected. The lack of fuel resources and disagreements with Russia over pricing have induced the government to keep the Chernobyl plant running. The START I agreement received the Ukrainian parliament's conditional ratification in November 1993 and unconditional ratification in February 1994, but the transfer of nuclear weapons to Russia has not occurred as smoothly as planned. On 6 May 1992 it was announced that all Ukrainian tactical nuclear weapons had been shipped to Russia for dismantling. However, Ukraine cited Russia's failure to dismantle these weapons, inadequate compensation, and security concerns as the reasons for not turning over all of its strategic arsenal.

The CIS countries agreed to a unified nuclear command, but Ukraine declared its intent to create its own national conventional military and opposed any efforts to create a unified CIS conventional force. President Kravchuk declared all conventional forces on Ukrainian territory to be the property of Ukraine. This has given rise to disputes and disagreements about the Black Sea fleet, to which Russia has also laid claim.

Since its independence, Ukraine has experienced unrest in some of the predominantly Russian areas in the east and southeast. Crimea is the most notable example, declaring independence on 6 May 1992. At the same time the Russian parliament approved a resolution that declared the 1954 Soviet grant of the Crimea to Ukraine unconstitutional and void. This resolution, however, was rejected by Russian President Boris Yeltsin. Demands for secession in Crimea have continued to complicate Ukrainian-Russian relations.

[13]GOVERNMENT

Ukraine is still governed by the 1978 Soviet-era constitution, which has been amended to allow for an elected parliament and president.

The Ukrainian parliament consists of a single chamber with 450 seats called the Rada. The prime minister and cabinet are nominated by the president and confirmed by the parliament. Ukraine's first post-independence parliamentary elections were held in two rounds on 27 March and 10 April 1994. Although many parties participated in the elections, most candidates ran as independents.

Ukraine's first post-independence presidential elections were held in two rounds on 26 June and 10 July 1994. In this election, the incumbent Leonid Kravchuk was defeated by his former Prime Minister, Leonid Kuchma.

14 POLITICAL PARTIES

There are some 30 political parties active in Ukraine. They fall roughly into four different categories: radical nationalist, democratic nationalist, liberal-centrist, and Communist-socialist.

The radical nationalist parties are fearful of Russia and advocate a strong presidency. Their commitment to democracy—particularly if regions of Ukraine seek to secede—is not firm. The democratic nationalist parties are also fearful of Russia, but also appear strongly committed to democracy, individual rights, and the protection of private property. The influential Rukh Party, which gained 20 seats in the 1994 parliamentary elections, belongs to this group. The liberal-centrist parties are particularly concerned with promoting free market economic reform. They are also committed to democracy and individual rights. The communist-socialist parties oppose privatization and seek continued state control of the economy. They generally favor close relations with Russia. The most important party in this group, the Communist Party of Ukraine, won 75 seats in the 1994 elections.

Aside from the Communists and Rukh, all other parties won 12 seats or less. Independents hold most of the seats in the Rada.

15 LOCAL GOVERNMENT

Ukraine is divided into 24 administrative regions (oblasts) plus the autonomous Republic of Crimea. In addition, the cities of Kiev, the capital of Ukraine, and Sevastopol, capital of Crimea, enjoy oblast status. The oblast is divided into districts, each of which has a representative in the Rada.

A strong secessionist movement has risen up in Crimea. In a non-binding referendum held on 27 March 1994, over 78% of the 1.3 million people who voted supported greater autonomy from Ukraine.

16 JUDICIAL SYSTEM

The court system, with a few modifications, remains that which existed under the former Soviet regime. The three levels of courts are rayon (also known as regional or people's courts), oblast (provincial) courts, and the Supreme Court. All three levels serve as courts of first instance, the choice of level varying with the severity of the crime. A case heard in first instance at the rayon level can be appealed through the next two higher stages. A case heard in first instance in the Supreme Court is not subject to appeal or review. A 1992 law added a Constitutional Court to the existing system.

The Rada (parliament) selects judges on recommendation from the Ministry of Justice based partly upon government test results. Oblast and Supreme Court judges must have five years of experience in order to be appointed and may not be members of political parties.

17 ARMED FORCES

Ukraine was able to quickly organize an impressive national army, in part because it had always been an important contributor to the Soviet armed forces. Excluding the Black Sea fleet and Strategic Rocket Forces under dual control, the armed forces numbered 230,000 in 1993. Ukraine has enacted a conscription law requiring 18 months of military training; one million Ukrainians have already served in the Soviet armed forces. Of greatest international concern is the fate of the 176 ICBMs and 41 strategic bombers on Ukrainian soil, which are supposed to return to Russia for dismantling. Although tactical nuclear weapons made the one-way trip, the ICBMs did not depart until 1993–94. The army (150,000) is organized into 19 divisions and more than 50 specialized brigades and regiments of artillery, special forces, air defense, rocket and missile, and attack helicopter units. The air

force (50,000) has 1,100 aircraft for tactical operations and 270 for air defense. The navy (30,000) is being formed from the Soviet Black Sea fleet. The Ukraine has sent one battalion to Bosnia-Herzegovina. It has a paramilitary National Guard of 6,000 for internal security missions.

18 INTERNATIONAL COOPERATION

Ukraine became a member of the UN on 24 October 1945. The country is also a member of the CSCE, IAEA, IMF, ITU, UNCTAD, UNESCO, UNIDO, UPU, WHO, WIPO, WMO, and the World Bank. It is a member of the CIS, and is applying for membership in other international organizations.. The country has established formal diplomatic relations with over 100 countries. The US has given economic and technical assistance to the country since it established formal relations in January 1992.

19 ECONOMY

Ukraine was central to the Soviet agricultural and industrial system. The rich agricultural land of this region (commonly called the "breadbasket" of the former Soviet Union) provided 46% of Soviet agricultural output in the 1980s, and also accounted for 25% of the USSR's coal production. Ukraine's economic base is dominated by industry, which accounted for over one-third of GDP in 1991. However, agriculture continues to play a major role in the economy, representing about one-fourth of GDP in the same year.

The dissolution of the Soviet Union has led to shortages of supplies for business and industry, and of consumer goods as well. In addition, the market for military goods, which had represented about 15% of total industrial production, has collapsed. Real GDP declined 3% in 1990, 11% in 1991, and an estimated 15% in 1992. Inflation in 1992 averaged nearly 1,500%.

20 INCOME

In 1992, the GNP was $87,025 million at current prices, or $1,670 per capita. For the period 1985–92 the average inflation rate was 11.5%.

21 LABOR

As of 1991, there were some 19,119,000 employees, including 6,913,000 in manufacturing, mining, and utilities, 1,639,000 in construction, and 1,699,000 in transportation, storage, and communications. Less than 0.3% of the labor force was officially reported as unemployed in September 1992, mainly because state enterprises have operated under a soft budget constraint which has enabled them to retain labor.

In November 1992, the official Soviet-era unions were renamed the Federation of Independent Trade Unions, which began then to operate independently from the government. Since 1992, many independent unions have been formed, providing an alternative to the official unions in most sectors of the economy.

The right to strike is protected, except for the military, police, and continuing process plants. Although political strikes are considered illegal, miners and transportation workers who went on strike in 1992 made political as well as economic demands.

The minimum employment age is 17, although children aged 15 to 17 can be employed by businesses with governmental permission. In 1992, a minimum wage was established, but was significantly below the cost of living by the end of the year. The maximum workweek is set at 41 hours; the law also provides for a minimum of 15 days of vacation per year.

22 AGRICULTURE

About 57% of the total land area is arable, with another 11% utilized as permanent pastureland. Agriculture accounts for one-fourth of Ukrainian GDP. Production amounts in 1992 included (in 1,000 tons): sugar beets, 28,546; potatoes, 20,427; wheat,

19,473; dry peas, 2,776; fruit, 2,351; sunflower seeds, 2,100; cabbage, 1,140; grapes, 655; wine, 290; soybeans, 140; and tobacco, 19.

Ukraine's steppe region in the south is possibly the most fertile region in the world. Furthermore, Ukraine possesses three-fifths of the world's humus-rich black soil. Ukraine typically produced over half of the sugar beets and one-fifth of all grains grown for the former USSR. In addition, two of the largest vegetable-oil research centers in the world are at Odesa and Zaporizhzhya. Agroindustry accounts for one-third of agricultural employment. To some extent, however, agroindustrial development has been hampered by the deteriorating environment as well as a shortage of investment funds due to the aftermath of the nuclear power plant disaster at Chernobyl. According to estimates, nearly 60,000 hectares (148,250 acres) of arable land in the Chernobyl vicinity are now unavailable for cultivation. Since 1989, a long-term restructuring problem in the agricultural sector has caused production levels to stagnate or even decline. The production of grain in 1991 compared to 1989 fell by 12.5 million tons, sugar beets by 15.6 million tons, potatoes by 4.7 million tons, and vegetables by 1.5 million tons. Adverse weather in 1992 exacerbated the low output levels.

23ANIMAL HUSBANDRY

Just over 10% of Ukraine's total land area is composed of permanent pastureland. As of 1992, there were 23.7 million head of cattle, 17.8 million pigs, 7.3 million sheep, 233 million chickens, and 10 million turkeys. Horses, goats, ducks, and rabbits are also bred and raised. In 1992, meat production included: beef, 1,676,000 tons; pork, 1,209,000 tons; and poultry, 605,000 tons. In 1991, sausage production totaled 849,000 tons. Ukraine supplied 25% of the former Soviet Union's meat in 1990. Milk and egg production in 1992 amounted to 19 million tons and 830,000 tons, respectively. Milk and eggs are exported to the other CIS members. In 1990, Ukrainian milk and egg productivity (kilograms produced per capita) surpassed that of Germany, France, and Italy.

24FISHING

In 1991, the total catch came to 816,000 tons. Ukrainian fish consumption per capita amounts to 12.2 kg (26.9 lb) per year—less than half that of the former Soviet Union (27.7 kg/61 lb). Fishing occurs mainly on the Black Sea.

25FORESTRY

About 13% of the total area is forest and woodland. While the radioactive contamination of forestland from the 1986 Chernobyl disaster is well-known, there is also widespread land, water, and air pollution from toxic wastes, which has also adversely affected timberlands. Forestry production in 1990 included: roundwood, 8 million cu m; sawn timber, 6 million cu m; wood pulp, 90,000 tons; paper, 353,000 tons; and cardboard, 463,000 tons.

26MINING

Ukrainian mineral production includes alumina, aluminum, antimony, coal, ferroalloys, graphite, iron ore, magnesium, manganese, mercury, nickel, potash, salt, soda ash, sulfur, talc, titanium, and uranium. Iron ore is mined in the Kryvyy Rih Basin, manganese in the Nikopol' and Tokmak basins, nickel at the Pobuz'ke deposit, potash at the Stebnik and Kalush mines, and sulfur at the Rozdol and Yavoriv deposits.

27ENERGY AND POWER

Energy production in Ukraine has steadily declined by 30% since the 1970s, but consumption has intensified by 20% during the same period. Whereas Ukraine was nearly self-sufficient in fuel in 1975, primary energy production as of 1993 supplied only 50% of domestic consumption.

Until 1992, Ukraine had been a net exporter of electricity, usually exporting about 10% of its production, which totaled 298,000 million kwh in 1990. Most electricity is generated by coal, natural gas, or oil, but nuclear power plants generated over 25% of Ukraine's electricity in 1991. Power generation fell in 1992, due to fuel shortages from declining Russian imports. In December 1992, Chernobyl's undamaged Reactor 1 was restarted, in order to provide much-needed electricity. In October 1991, the Ukrainian Parliament had decided to shut down Chernobyl entirely by the end of 1993.

Oil production peaked in 1972, at almost 300,000 barrels per day; by 1991, production had declined to less than 100,000 barrels per day, meeting only 10% of the domestic oil consumption requirement. Natural gas production exceeded 2.4 trillion cu ft (68 billion cu m) in the mid-1970s, but declined to 0.8 trillion cu ft (2 billion cu m) in 1991, when production only satisfied 20% of domestic consumption. At the end of 1992, Ukraine possessed 61.1 trillion cu ft (1.7 trillion cu m), or 1.3% of the world's total proved reserves of natural gas.

Coal, primarily from the Donets Basin, has been a traditional resource for energy production. Since 1975, however, coal production has fallen by 30%. Production costs for coal have risen as easily accessible mines have been exhausted. Many mines now are either no longer economically viable or deteriorated and hazardous.

In 1992, 45% of primary energy consumption was provided by natural gas; 30% by coal; 18% by oil; 6.6% by nuclear energy; and 0.4% by hydroelectric power.

28INDUSTRY

Ukraine is a major producer of heavy machinery and industrial equipment for sectors including mining, steelmaking, and chemicals. Significant products also include non-numerically controlled machine tools, large electrical transformers, and agricultural machinery. One-third of the former Soviet Union's steel pipes are produced in Ukraine, as are almost 17% of its oil production machinery, 25% of its computer equipment, and more than one-third of its televisions and tape recorders. Ukraine's industries are important suppliers of products—including automobiles, clothing, foodstuffs, timber, and paper—to other former Soviet republics.

29SCIENCE AND TECHNOLOGY

The Ukrainian Academy of Sciences, founded in 1919, has sections of physical engineering and mathematical sciences, and chemical engineering and biological sciences. The Ukrainian Academy of Agrarian Sciences has 14 research institutes, and the Ukrainian Academy of Medical Sciences has five research institutes. Ukraine has 93 institutes conducting scientific research. In 1989, 348,600 scientists and engineers were engaged in research and development.

30DOMESTIC TRADE

In February 1993, an affiliate of the World Bank inaugurated a program to privatize small state-owned businesses, many in retail trade and services. The first auction, in L'vin, privatized 17 shops and was considered very successful.

31FOREIGN TRADE

Ukraines's products are exported to 107 countries of the world. Raw materials and consumer goods are the main items of export. In 1988, total imports were valued at R47,400 million, and total exports at R44,500 million. Ukraine relies heavily on trade, particularly with the other former Soviet republics. Inter-republic trade accounted for 73% of its total imports in 1988, and 85% of its total exports. In 1991, imports from the other republics equaled 26% of GDP, and exports to them amounted to 25% of GDP.

In 1991/92, inter-republic trade contracted severely, partly due to a breakdown in payment mechanisms, and trade with other countries dropped as well. Much of Ukraine's foreign trade has been carried out in the context of inter-governmental agreements.

³²BALANCE OF PAYMENTS

As payment agreements between the former Soviet republics collapsed, Ukraine's trade balance contracted significantly in 1991/92, and a rising trade deficit ensued. Due to the severe shortage of foreign exchange, the convertible currency trade account went from deficit to surplus from 1991 to 1992, as imports declined faster than exports. Total exports in 1991 reportedly exceeded total imports by R327.4 million.

³³BANKING AND SECURITIES

The National Bank of Ukraine is the country's national bank. The state's commercial bank is the Ukrainian Export-Import Bank. There are nine commercial banks, including the Commercial Bank for Development and Construction Material, the Commercial Bank for Development and Light Industry, the Joint-Stock Bank, the Ukrainian Innovation Bank, and the Zepadkoopbank.

³⁴INSURANCE

Ukraine's insurance system is largely inherited from governmental institutions of the former USSR.

³⁵PUBLIC FINANCE

Ukraine's state budget, which typically had been balanced, ran a deficit equivalent to 14% of GDP in 1991. Increased subsidies and social expenditures caused spending to rise from 28% to 40% of GDP that year, which led to the deterioration. In 1992, the budget deficit increased to 18% of GDP as a result of large direct transfers to money-losing agricultural and industrial producers. However, since the Kuchma administration came to power in late 1992, soft credit to state enterprises has been terminated. In November 1992, a market-oriented reform program was announced which called for a public service wage freeze, decreased social expenditures, and the legal prohibition of financing the budget deficit by monetary creation. As of 1992, Ukraine and Russia still had not reached an agreement concerning the partition of foreign assets and liabilities inherited from the Soviet era. At the end of 1992, Ukraine's outstanding debt commitment was estimated at $1,420 million.

³⁶TAXATION

In 1992, Ukraine's corporate tax rate was reduced to 18% (15% for joint ventures with 30% or more foreign participation). There is a 15% withholding tax on dividends, interest, royalties, and other income from Ukrainian sources. Personal income taxes are levied under a 1991 law establishing progressive taxation and the taxing of foreigners living in Ukraine on the same basis as Ukrainian citizens. There is a standard value-added tax of 28%.

³⁷CUSTOMS AND DUTIES

Ad valorem duties are currently being revised. A 1992 agreement provides for reciprocal extension of most-favored nation status between Ukraine and the US.

³⁸FOREIGN INVESTMENT

In 1991, the number of joint ventures in Ukraine accelerated, rising from 76 in October 1990 to 189 in October 1991. Following the enactment in March 1992 of a favorable foreign investment law, joint ventures reached approximately 1,400 early in 1993. Most of these ventures are in industry, and few engage in foreign trade. The government's 1993 economic plan included tax incen-

tives and specific advantages for investors in areas including agroindustrial, energy, and consumer goods.

³⁹ECONOMIC DEVELOPMENT

In February 1993, Ukraine's parliament tentatively approved a new economic reform plan to stabilize the republic's economy, attract more capital from abroad, and lay the groundwork for a market economy. Measures proposed include stricter monetary and banking regulation, and demonopolization of industries. A privatization program is under way in sectors including retail trade, services, the food industry, agriculture, and housing.

⁴⁰SOCIAL DEVELOPMENT

The average family size was 3.2 in 1989, and the divorce rate was 8.7 per 1,000 women. There were 5.2 drug-related crimes and 10.2 alcohol-related deaths per 100,000 persons.

The law provides women with the same employment rights as men, although they rarely attain high-level managerial or political positions. Estimates suggest that women may account for as many as 90% of Ukraine's unemployed. In 1990, the fertility rate was 1.9.

⁴¹HEALTH

Ukraine's health care system is undergoing a complicated transition period. In 1992, there was a fixed level of expenses for health services (an estimated 10% of the national income). Total health care expenditures for 1990 (prior to independence) were $6,803 million. The deterioration of the economy and declining living standards have had a negative impact on birth and mortality rates, and women's and children's health standards need much improvement. Infant mortality was reported at 14 per 1,000 live births in 1993, with 8,400 infant deaths overall in 1992. However, a UNICEF report lists infant mortality in 1992 as 21 per 1,000 live births. Poor nutrition is another major problem in the Ukraine, and a shortage of basic supplies exacerbates the health care situation. The country has established 156 independent children's hospitals. As of 1993, there were over 400 pediatric departments functioning in central district hospitals, with 92,102 pediatric beds (84 per 10,000 children). There were 22,000 pediatricians (2 per 1,000 children) in 1993. In the same year, there were 29 regional adult hospitals; 25 regional infant hospitals; 485 central district hospitals; 1,500 rural hospitals; and specialized dispensaries and clinics. There was a total of 700,000 beds. In addition, there were 6,500 outpatient polyclinical institutions. Medical personnel in 1993 included 220,000 physicians and more than 500,000 physician's assistants. In 1991, there were 118,600 middle medical personnel and, in 1990, there were 26,744 dentists. There were 633,000 births in 1992, with a life expectancy of 70 years. The general mortality rate in 1993 was 12 per 1,000 people; the leading causes of death were cardiovascular and respiratory diseases, cancer, traumas, and accidents. In 1990, there were an estimated 50 cases of tuberculosis per 100,000 people reported. The government created 9 specialized dispensaries, 7 expert councils, and 20 medical consulting commissions to establish the incidence of disease as a result of the accident at the nuclear power plant at Chernobyl, with 15,000 people listed as of 1994. Immunization rates for 1992 for children up to one year old were: tuberculosis (93%); diphtheria, pertussis, and tetanus (88%); polio (89%); and measles (90%).

⁴²HOUSING

In 1991, average housing space per capita totaled 18 sq m. The housing and municipal services sector employed 878,000 workers in 1990.

⁴³EDUCATION

Ukraine has virtually a 100% literacy rate with nearly 15% of the adult population having completed higher education. Of the remaining 85%, 7% have completed elementary and 78% have completed secondary education.

While Ukrainian is the most commonly taught language and medium of instruction, other languages, such as Russian, Hungarian, Polish, Moldovan, or Crimean-Tater, are offered based on the ethnic composition of the particular school district. Most schools are state run. In the 21,900 general education schools, there were 7.1 million students enrolled in 1992. In the 156 institutions of higher learning, 876,200 students were enrolled.

44LIBRARIES AND MUSEUMS

There are reported to be 25,300 public libraries operating in Ukraine with an overall stock of 410,400,000 books and periodicals. It is estimated that 24.3 million people utilize these libraries annually. There are 225 museums in Ukraine. In 1991, Ukraine's publishing houses printed 5,857 books.

45MEDIA

Ukraine, which inherited part of the former USSR system, has about 7 million telephone lines, or 13.5 telephones for each 100 persons. However, as of January 1990, applications for an additional 3.56 million telephones were unfilled. The State Committee for Radio and Television controls broadcasting. There are four radio networks headquartered in Kiev, including one for foreign broadcasts and one solely for news. Ukrainian TV also broadcasts from Kiev. In 1991 there were 41,300,000 radios and 17,100,000 television sets. Among the leading daily newspapers (with 1991 circulation) are: *Silski Visti* (2,300,000); *Nezavisimost* (1,300,000); *Molod Ukrainy* (700,000); *Golos Ukrainy* (330,000); *Robitnycha Gazeta* (300,000); and *Demokratychna Ukraine* (150,000).

There are 130 theaters. The movie theater attendance is estimated at 4 million hours per year with the average attendance per citizen at 8 times per year; one of the highest in Europe.

In 1991, Ukraine's publishing houses printed 5,857 book titles.

46ORGANIZATIONS

The Ukraine Chamber of Commerce and the Congress of Business Circles of Ukraine promotes the commercial and business activities of the country to the rest of the world. Many of Ukraine's trade unions belong to the umbrella organization called the Federation of Independent Trade Unions.

47TOURISM, TRAVEL, AND RECREATION

Kiev, Ukraine's major cultural center, is known for its beautiful churches and golden-domed cathedrals, although much of its classic architecture was destroyed or obscured by Communist planners in the 1930s. The cathedral of St. Sophia, built in the 11th century, is one of the finest examples of Russo-Byzantine architecture. Another major tourist attraction is the Golden Gate, an 11th century fortification restored in 1982. Lviv (formerly Lvov) offers architectural sights ranging from late-13th-century Russian to 16th-century Gothic structures. Ukraine's tourism potential may be affected by the country's increasing serious industrial pollution problem, as well as after-effects of the 1986 Chernobyl nuclear accident.

48FAMOUS UKRAINIANS

Leonid M. Kravchuk and Vitold P. Fokin were respectively the first president and prime minister of Ukraine. Leonid Brezhnev (Dneprodzershinsk, Ukraine, 1906–82) led the Soviet Union from 1966–82. Outstanding representatives of the culture and literature of Ukraine include poet Taras Sshechenko (1814–61) and the Jewish writer Sholom Aleichem (Solomon Rabinowitz, 1859–1916).

49DEPENDENCIES

Ukraine has no territories or colonies.

50BIBLIOGRAPHY

Aslund, Anders (ed.). *Economic Transformation in Russia.* New York: St. Martin's, 1994.

Aslund, Anders, and Richard Layard (eds.). *Changing the Economic System in Russia.* New York: St. Martin's, 1993.

Bilocerkowycz, Jaroslaw. *Soviet Ukrainian Dissent: A Study of Political Alienation.* Boulder, Colo.: Westview Press, 1988.

Buckley, Mary. *Redefining Russian Society and Polity.* Boulder, Colo.: Westview Press, 1993.

Chirovsky, Nicholas L. *An Introduction to Ukrainian History.* New York: Philosophical Library, 1981.

Conquest, Robert. *The Harvest of Sorrow: Soviet Collectivization and the Terror-famine.* New York: Oxford University Press, 1986.

Dallin, Alexander (ed.). *Political Parties in Russia.* Berkeley: International and Area Studies, University of California at Berkeley, 1993.

Doing Business in Russia. Lincolnwood, Ill.: NTS Business Books, 1994.

Durgo, A.S. (ed.). *Russia Changes: The Events of August 1991 and the Russian Constitution.* Commack, N.Y.: Nova Science, 1992.

Gordon, Linda. *Cossack Rebellions: Social Turmoil in the Sixteenth-century Ukraine.* Albany: State University of New York Press, 1983.

Grimsted, Patricia Kennedy. *Archives and Manuscript Repositories in the USSR, Ukraine, and Moldavia.* Princeton, N.J.: Princeton University Press, 1988.

Hosking, Geoffrey A. (ed.). *Church, Nation and State in Russia and Ukraine.* New York: St. Martin's, 1991.

Koropeckyj, I. S. (ed.). *The Ukrainian Economy: Achievements, Problems, Challenges.* Cambridge, Mass.: Harvard University Press, 1992.

Koropeckyj, I. S. *Development in the Shadow: Studies in Ukrainian Economics.* Edmonton: University of Alberta, 1990.

Kubijovyc, Volodymyr (ed.). *Ukraine: A Concise Encyclopaedia.* Toronto: University of Toronto Press, 1963.

Marples, David R. *Stalinism in Ukraine in the 1940s.* New York: St. Martin's, 1992.

———. *Ukraine under Perestroika: Ecology, Economics and the Workers' Revolt.* New York: St. Martin's, 1991.

McFaul, Michael. *The Troubled Birth of Russian Democracy: Parties, Personalities, and Programs.* Stanford, Calif.: Hoover Institution Press, Stanford University, 1993.

Mesbahi, Mohiaddin (ed.). *Russia and the Third World in the Post-Soviet Era.* Gainesville, Fla.: University Press of Florida, 1994.

Mirchuk, I. (ed.) *Ukraine and its People.* Munich: Ukrainian Free University Press, 1949.

The Modern Encyclopedia of Russian, Soviet and Eurasian History. Gulf Breeze, Fla.: Academic International Press, 1994.

Motyl, Alexander J. *Dilemmas of Independence: Ukraine after Totalitarianism.* New York: Council on Foreign Relations Press, 1993.

Rudnytsky, Ivan L. (ed.). *Essays in Modern Ukrainian History.* Edmonton: Canadian Institute of Ukrainian Studies, 1987.

Schulz-Torge, Ulrich-Joachim (ed.). *Who's Who in Russia Today: A Biographical Dictionary of More than 2,100 Individuals from the Russian Federation Including the other Fourteen USSR Republics.* New Providence: K.G. Saur, 1994.

Sevcenko, Ihor. *Byzantine Roots of Ukrainian Christianity.* Cambridge, Mass.: Harvard University, 1984.

Shcherbitskii, V. V. *Soviet Ukraine.* Moscow: Progress Publishers, 1985.

Shevchuk, H. M. *Cultural Policy in the Ukrainian Soviet Socialist Republic*. Paris: UNESCO, 1982.

Solovev, Vladimir. *Boris Yeltsin: A Political Biography*. New York: Putnam, 1992.

Steele, Jonathan. *Eternal Russia: Yeltsin, Gorbachev and the Mirage of Democracy*. Boston: Faber, 1994.

Yeltsin, Boris Nikolayevich. *The Struggle for Russia*. New York: Times Books, 1994.

UNITED KINGDOM

United Kingdom of Great Britain and Northern Ireland

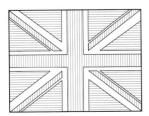

CAPITAL: London.

FLAG: The Union Jack, adopted in 1800, is a combination of the banners of England (St. George's flag: a red cross with extended horizontals on a white field), Scotland (St. Andrew's flag: a white saltire cross on a blue field), and Ireland (St. Patrick's flag: a red saltire cross on a white field). The arms of the saltire crosses do not meet at the center.

ANTHEM: *God Save the Queen.*

MONETARY UNIT: The pound sterling (£) is a paper currency of 100 pence. Before decimal coinage was introduced on 15 February 1971, the pound had been divided into 20 shillings, each shilling representing 12 pennies (p) or pence; some old-style coins are still in circulation. Under the new system, there are coins of 1, 2, 5, 10, 20, and 50 pence and 1 and 2 pounds, and notes of 5, 10, 20, and 50 pounds. £1 = $1.4822 (or $1 = £0.6747).

WEIGHTS AND MEASURES: Although the traditional imperial system of weights and measures is still in use (sample units: of weight, the stone of 14 pounds equivalent to 6.35 kilograms; of length, the yard equivalent to 0.914 meter; of capacity, a bushel equivalent to 36.37 liters), a changeover to the metric system is in progress.

HOLIDAYS: New Year's Day, 1 January; Good Friday; Easter Monday (except Scotland); Late Summer Holiday, last Monday in August or 1st in September (except Scotland); Christmas, 25 December; and Boxing Day, 1st weekday after Christmas. Also observed in Scotland are bank holidays on 2 January and on the 1st Monday in August. Northern Ireland observes St. Patrick's Day, 17 March; and Orangeman's Day, 12 July, commemorating the Battle of the Boyne in 1690.

TIME: GMT.

¹LOCATION, SIZE, AND EXTENT

The UK is situated off the northwest coast of Europe between the Atlantic Ocean on the N and NW and the North Sea on the E, separated from the Continent by the Strait of Dover and the English Channel, 34 km (21 mi) wide at its narrowest point, and from the Irish Republic by the Irish Sea and St. George's Channel. Its total area of 244,820 sq km (94,526 sq mi) consists of the island of Great Britain—formed by England, 130,439 sq km (50,363 sq mi); Wales, 20,768 sq km (8,018 sq mi); and Scotland, 78,783 sq km (30,418 sq mi)—and Northern Ireland, 14,120 sq km (5,452 sq mi), on the island of Ireland, separated from Great Britain by the North Channel. Comparatively, the area occupied by the United Kingdom is slightly smaller than the state of Oregon. There are also several island groups and hundreds of small single islands, most of them administratively part of the mainland units. The UK extends about 965 km (600 mi) N-S and about 485 km (300 mi) E-W. Its total boundary length is 12,789 km (7,947 mi). The Isle of Man, 588 sq km (227 sq mi), and the Channel Islands, comprising Jersey, Guernsey, Alderney, and Sark, with a combined area of 194 sq km (75 sq mi), are not part of the UK but are dependencies of the crown. The 0° meridian of longitude passes through the old Royal Observatory, located at Greenwich in Greater London. The United Kingdom's capital city, London, is located in the southeast part of Great Britain.

²TOPOGRAPHY

England is divided into the hill regions of the north, west, and southwest and the rolling downs and low plains of the east and southeast. Running from east to west on the extreme north Scottish border are the Cheviot Hills. The Pennine Range runs north and south from the Scottish border to Derbyshire in central England. The rest of the countryside consists mainly of rich agricultural lands, occasional moors, and plains. South of the Pennines lie the Midlands (East and West), a plains region with low, rolling hills and fertile valleys. The eastern coast is low-lying, much of it less than 5 m (15 ft) above sea level; for centuries parts of it have been protected by embankments against inundation from gales and unusually high tides. Little of the south and east rises to higher than 300 m (1,000 ft).

The highest point in England is Scafell Pike (978 m/3,210 ft) in the famed Lake District of the northwest. The longest of the rivers flowing from the central highlands to the sea are the Severn (about 340 km/210 mi) in the west and the Thames (about 320 km/200 mi) in the southeast. Other rivers include the Humber, the Tees, the Tyne, and the Tweed in the east, the Avon and Exe in the south, and the Mersey in the west.

Scotland has three distinct topographical regions: the Northern Highlands, occupying almost the entire northern half of the country and containing the highest point in the British Isles, Ben Nevis (1,343 m/4,406 ft), as well as Loch Ness, site of a fabled "monster"; the Central Lowlands, with an average elevation of about 150 m (500 ft) and containing the valleys of the Tay, Forth, and Clyde rivers, as well as Loch Lomond, Scotland's largest lake; and the Southern Uplands, rising to their peak at Merrick (843 m/2,766 ft), with moorland cut by many valleys and rivers.

Wales is largely mountainous and bleak, with much of the land suitable only for pasture. The Cambrian Mountains occupy almost the entire area and include Wales's highest point, Mt.

Snowdon (1,086 m/3,563 ft). There are narrow coastal plains in the south and west and small lowland areas in the north, including the valley of the Dee.

Northern Ireland consists mainly of low-lying plateaus and hills, generally about 150 to 180 m (500–600 ft) high. The Mourne Mountains in the southeast include Slieve Donard (852 m/2,796 ft), the highest point in Northern Ireland. In a central depression lies Lough Neagh, the largest lake in the UK.

The UK's long and rugged coastline, heavily indented, has towering cliffs and headlands and numerous bays and inlets, among them the deep and narrow lochs and the wide firths of Scotland. Many river estuaries serve as fine harbors.

³CLIMATE

Despite its northern latitude, the UK generally enjoys a temperate climate, warmed by the North Atlantic Drift, a continuation of the Gulf Stream, and by southwest winds. Mean monthly temperatures range (north to south) from 3°C to 5°C (37–41°F) in winter and from 12°C to 16°C (54–61°F) in summer. The mean annual temperature in the west near sea level ranges from 8°C (46°F) in the Hebrides to 11°C (52°F) in the far southwest of England. Rarely do temperatures rise in summer to over 32°C (90°F) or drop in winter below –10°C (14°F). Rainfall, averaging more than 100 cm (40 in) throughout the UK, is heaviest on the western and northern heights (over 380 cm/150 in), lowest along the eastern and southeastern coasts. Fairly even distribution of rain throughout the year, together with the prevalence of mists and fogs, results in scanty sunshine—averaging from half an hour to 2 hours a day in winter and from 5 to 8 hours in summer.

⁴FLORA AND FAUNA

With its mild climate and varied soils, the UK has a diverse pattern of natural vegetation. Originally, oak forests probably covered the lowland except for the fens and marsh areas, with pine forests and patches of moorland on the higher or sandy ground. Over the centuries much of the forest area, especially on the lowlands, was cleared for cultivation. Today only about 9% of the total surface is wooded. Fairly extensive forests remain in east and north Scotland and in southeast England. Oak, elm, ash, and beech are the commonest trees in England, and pine and birch in Scotland. Almost all the lowland outside the industrial centers is farmland, with a varied seminatural vegetation of grasses and flowering plants. Wild vegetation consists of the natural flora of woods, fens and marshes, cliffs, chalk downs, and mountain slopes, the most widespread being the heather, grasses, gorse, and bracken of the moorlands.

The fauna is similar to that of northwestern continental Europe, although there are fewer species. Some of the larger mammals—wolf, bear, boar, and reindeer—are extinct, but red and roe deer are protected for sport. Common smaller mammals are foxes, hares, hedgehogs, rabbits, weasels, stoats, shrews, rats, and mice; otters are found in many rivers, and seals frequently appear along the coast. There are few reptiles and amphibians. Roughly 230 species of birds reside in the UK, and another 200 are migratory. Most numerous are the chaffinch, blackbird, sparrow, and starling. The number of large birds is declining, however, except for game birds—pheasant, partridge, and red grouse—which are protected. With the reclamation of the marshlands, waterfowl are moving to the many bird sanctuaries. The rivers and lakes abound in salmon, trout, perch, pike, roach, dace, and grayling. There are more than 21,000 species of insects.

⁵ENVIRONMENT

Government officials and agencies having principal responsibility for environmental protection are the Department of the Environment, the Department of the Environment for Northern Ireland, and the secretaries of state for Scotland and Wales. The National

Trust (for Places of Historic Interest or Natural Beauty), an organization of more than 1.3 million members, has acquired some 750 km (466 mi) of coastline in England, Northern Ireland, and Wales. In addition, 127 km (79 mi) of coastline in Scotland are protected under agreement with the National Trust of Scotland. Two countryside commissions, one for England and Wales and one for Scotland, are charged with conserving the beauty and amenities of rural areas. By 1982, the former had designated 10 national parks, covering 13,600 sq km (5,250 sq mi), or 9% of the area of England and Wales—36 areas of outstanding beauty have been designated, covering 17,000 sq km (6,600 sq mi). Scotland has 40 national scenic areas, and more than 98% of all Scottish lands are under the commission's jurisdiction. Northern Ireland has eight designated areas of outstanding natural beauty, seven country parks, and one regional park. There are also seven forest parks in Great Britain and nine in Northern Ireland. England and Wales have 600,000 hectares (1,500,000 acres) of common land, much of which is open to the public. The Nature Conservancy Council manages 214 national nature reserves in Great Britain and 41 in Northern Ireland.

Air pollution is a significant environmental concern for the United Kingdom. The country produces 564.2 million tons of particulate emissions and 2,276.7 tons of hydrocarbon emissions per year and contributes 2.4% of the world's total gas emissions. In addition, its sulphur contributes to the formation of acid rain in the surrounding countries of Western Europe. Air quality abatement has improved greatly in the UK as a result of the Control of Pollution Act of 1974 and other legislation. Between 1960 and 1986, total emissions and average concentration of smoke in the air fell by an estimated 85%; the average concentration of sulfur dioxide in urban areas has fallen by more than 40% since 1970, with a further reduction of 30% expected by the end of the 1990s. London is no longer densely smog-ridden, and winter sunlight has been increasing in various industrial cities. Water pollution from agricultural sources is also a problem. The nation has 28.8 cubic miles of water of which 3% is used for farming activity and 77% for industrial purposes. The United Kingdom's cities produce 22 million tons of solid waste and 2,424.4 thousand tons of toxic waste per year. Pollution of the Thames has been reduced to one quarter of the 1950s, and more than 80% of the population is served by sewage treatment plants. A major recent environmental problem is the regulation of oil and gas development and of large-scale dumping at sea. The Food and Environment Protection Act of 1985 introduced special controls over dumping and marine incineration. In 1994, 3 of the nation's mammal species and 22 bird species were endangered, as were 24 types of birds. In 1987, the European otter was classified as endangered.

⁶POPULATION

The mid-1994 population estimate for the UK was 57,965,456, a 2.6% increase over the April 1991 census figure of 56,467,000. A population of 58,810,000 is projected for the year 2000, assuming an estimated birth rate of 13.5 and a death rate of 11, for a net natural increase of 2.5 for the 1995–2000 period. The population of England was estimated at 48,378,000 in 1992, Wales 2,899,000, Scotland 5,111,000, and Northern Ireland 1,610,000. In addition, the Isle of Jersey had a population of 84,082, Guernsey 58,867, and the Isle of Man 69,788 in 1991.

Overall population density was 237 persons per sq km (615 per sq mi) in 1991, but in England there were 371 persons per sq km (961 per sq mi), with 4,233 persons per sq km (10,968 per sq mi) in Greater London. The birthrate was 13.8 live births per 1,000 population in 1991, as compared with 20.7 in 1947, the post–World War II peak. The death rate has been falling slowly. It was 10.9 in 1991.

Nearly nine out of every ten people live in urban areas. The

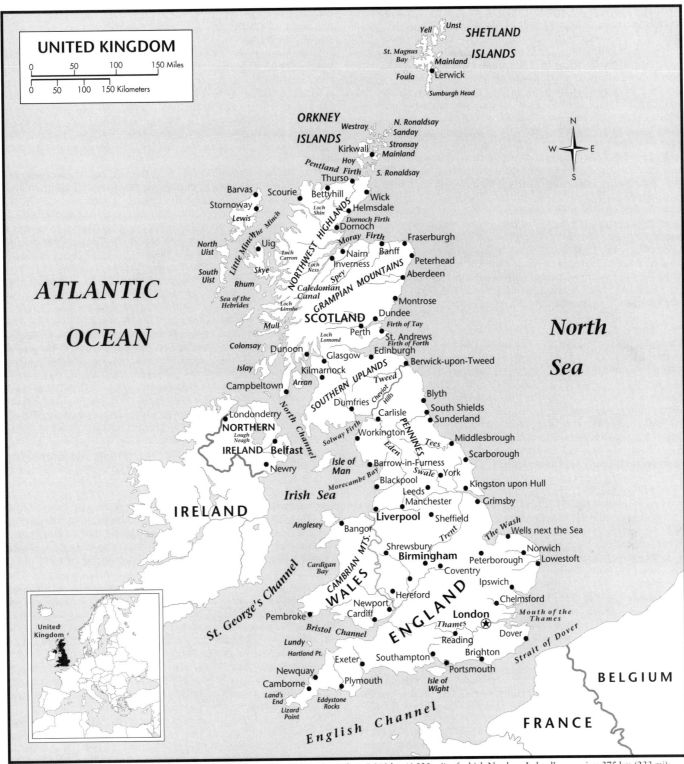

UNITED KINGDOM

LOCATION: 49°56′ to 60°50′N; 1°45′E to 8°10′W. **BOUNDARY LENGTHS:** Total coastline, 7,918 km (4,920 mi), of which Northern Ireland's comprises 375 km (233 mi); Irish Republic, 434 km (270 mi). **TERRITORIAL SEA LIMIT:** 3 mi.

major cities in England (with 1991 populations) are Greater London, 6,679,699; Birmingham, 938,000; Leeds, 677,000; Sheffield, 503,000; Liverpool, 450,000; Bradford, 451,000; Manchester, 400,000; Bristol, 372,000; and Coventry, 295,000. The major cities in Scotland, with their 1991 populations, are Glasgow, 654,000, and Edinburgh, 422,000. Belfast, the major city in Northern Ireland, had a 1991 population of 279,000; and Cardiff, in Wales, 277,000.

⁷MIGRATION

From 1815 to 1930, the balance of migration was markedly outward, and well over 20 million persons left Britain, settling mainly within the British Empire and in the US. Since 1931, however, the flow has largely been inward. From 1931 to 1940, when emigration was very low, there was extensive immigration from Europe, including a quarter of a million refugees seeking sanctuary; during the 1950s, immigration from the Commonwealth, especially from the Caribbean countries, India, and Pakistan, steadily increased. The net influx of some 388,000 people (chiefly from the Commonwealth) during 1960–62 led to the introduction of the Commonwealth Immigrants Act of 1962, giving the government power to restrict the entry of Commonwealth citizens lacking adequate prospects of employment or means of self-support. Effective 1 January 1983, a new law further restricted entry by creating three categories of citizenship, two of which—citizens of British Dependent Territories and "British overseas citizens"—entail no right to live in the UK. Those in the last category, consisting of an estimated 1.5 million members of Asian minorities who chose to retain British passports when Malaysia and Britain's East African lands became independent, may not pass their British citizenship to their children without UK government approval.

Immigration is now on a quota basis. Between 1986 and 1991, 1,334,000 persons left the UK to live abroad, and 1,461,000 came from overseas to live in the UK, resulting in a net in-migration of 127,000. In 1991 there was a net inflow of about 28,000. The total number of foreign residents in the UK was about 1,875,000 in 1990. Of these, more than a third were Irish (638,000). Indians were second (155,000) and Americans third (102,000). At the end of 1992 the UK had some 100,000 refugees.

8ETHNIC GROUPS

The present-day English, Welsh, Scots, and Irish are descended from a long succession of early peoples: Iberians, Celts, Romans, Anglo-Saxons, Danes, and Normans, the last of whom invaded and conquered England in 1066–70. In 1991, about 93% of UK residents were native-born. The principal ethnic minorities are of West Indian or Guyanese descent (499,000) or of Indian (840,000), Pakistani (475,000), or Bengali (160,000) descent. There are also sizable numbers of Africans (207,000) Americans, Australians, Chinese (157,500), Greek and Turkish Cypriots, Italians, Spaniards, and Southeast Asians.

9LANGUAGES

Spoken throughout the UK and, in 1992, by an estimated 456 million people throughout the world, English is second only to Mandarin Chinese in the number of speakers in the world. It is taught extensively as a second language and is used worldwide as a language of commerce, diplomacy, and scientific discourse. In northwestern Wales, Welsh, a form of Brythonic Celtic, is the first language of most of the inhabitants.

According to the 1991 census, 19% of those living in Wales spoke Welsh (down from 26% in 1961). Some 80,000 or so persons in western Scotland speak the Scottish form of Gaelic, and a few families in Northern Ireland speak Irish Gaelic. On the Isle of Man, the Manx variety of Celtic is used in official pronouncements; in the Channel Islands some persons still speak a Norman-French dialect. French remains the language of Jersey for official ceremonies.

10RELIGIONS

There is complete religious freedom in the UK. All churches and religious societies may own property and conduct schools. Established churches are the Church of England and the Church of Scotland. The former is uniquely related to the crown in that the sovereign must be a member and, on accession, promise to uphold the faith; it is also linked with the state through the House of Lords, where the archbishops of Canterbury and York have seats.

The archbishop of Canterbury is primate of all England. In 1990, some 1.8 million people were members of the Church of England, whose membership includes about 60% of the English population. The established Church of Scotland has a Presbyterian form of government: all ministers are of equal status and

each of the 1,758 congregations (1986) is locally governed by its minister and elected elders. In 1993, adult membership was estimated at 839,000.

Other Protestant churches, with 1991 figures, include the unestablished Anglican churches in Ireland, Scotland, and Wales; the Methodist Church (483,000 members); the Baptist Church (241,000); and the United Reformed Church (115,000), the product of the 1973 merger of the Presbyterian and Congregationalist churches, to which not all churches acceded. In 1991, the Presbyterian Church of Wales had some 58,000 members. The Salvation Army, founded in London in 1865, had 57,000 active members in the UK.

The Roman Catholic Church in the UK had some 5 million adherents in 1991. Many immigrants have established community religious centers in the UK. Christian groups include Greek, Russian, Polish, Serb-Orthodox, Estonian and Latvian Orthodox, and the Armenian Church; Lutheran churches from various parts of Europe are also represented. The Anglo-Jewish community, with an estimated 315,000 members in 1990, is the second-largest group of Jews in Western Europe. There are also sizable communities of Muslims (0.99 million in 1991), Sikhs, Hindus, and Buddhists.

11TRANSPORTATION

In Great Britain, railways, railway-owned steamships, docks, hotels, road transport, canals, and the entire London passenger transport system—the largest urban transport system in the world—were nationalized on 1 January 1948 under the control of the British Transport Commission (BTC). In 1962, the BTC was replaced by the British Railways Board, the London Transport Board, the British Transport Docks Board, and the British Waterways Board. Under the 1968 Transport Act, national transport operations were reorganized, with the creation of the National Freight Corp., the Freight Integration Council, and the National Bus Co. Organization of public transport in Northern Ireland is autonomous.

In 1991, Great Britain had 339,483 km (210,955 mi) of public highways, or 1.5 km (1 mi) for every sq km of territory; 339,483 km (210,955 mi) were paved including 2,573 km (1,599 mi) of express motorways. Northern Ireland had 23,499 km (14,602 mi) of public roads, including 592 km (368 mi) of trunk roads. Licensed motor vehicles in Great Britain at the end of 1991 numbered 26.4 million, including 22.7 million passenger cars. The Humber Bridge, the world's longest single-span suspension bridge, with a center span of 1,410 m (4,626 ft), links the city of Hull with a less developed region to the south. Eurotunnel, a British-French consortium, recently built two high-speed 50-km (31-mi) rail tunnels beneath the seabed of the English Channel. The project, referred to as the "Chunnel," links points near Folkestone, England (near Dover), and Calais, France. The Channel Tunnel is the largest privately financed construction project to date, with an estimated cost (in 1991) of $15 billion; it also has the longest tunnel system (38 km/24 mi) ever built under water.

There were 16,629 route km (10,333 mi) of standard-gauge (1.435 m) railway in Great Britain in 1991, including 4,205 km (2,613 mi) of electrified and 12,591 km (7,824 mi) of double or multiple track. Northern Ireland has about 332 km (206 mi) of 1.6-m-gauge track with 190 km (118 mi) of double track. In 1985, British Rail carried 708 million passengers and 140 million tons of freight. Underground railway systems operate in London, Glasgow, and Liverpool. In London, some 3,875 cars operate over about 408 km (254 mi) of track, 167 km (104 mi) of which is underground.

Great Britain has about 2,291 km (1,424 mi) of navigable inland waterways, mainly canals dating back to the prerailroad age. About 27% is owned by the British Waterways Board and 31% by Port Authorities. Great Britain has some 300 ports, including the Port of London, one of the largest in the world. Other major ports are Liverpool, Southampton, Hull, Clydeport (near Glasgow), the inland port of Manchester, and Bristol. The British merchant fleet, privately owned and operated, totaled 2.8 million GRT in 1991, a decline from 14.3 million GRT in 1985, a result of world recession in shipping and international competition. In an effort to curb the flagging of British merchant ships to less regulatory foreign nations, a British offshore registry program was initiated in the late 1980s. Under this program, merchant ships registered to the Isle of Man, Gilbraltar, the Cayman Islands, and the Turks and Caicos Islands are entitled to fly the Red Ensign as if under the administration of the United Kingdom. In all, British Dependent Territories have 712 merchant ships with 14.1 million GRT. The Isle of Man (separately classified) has 84 ships in its merchant fleet, with a capacity of 1.5 million GRT.

The Civil Aviation Authority was created in 1971 as an independent body responsible for national airline operations, traffic control, and air safety. The two government-owned airlines, British European Airways and British Overseas Airways Corp., were amalgamated in 1974 to form British Airways (BA). In 1984, BA was reestablished as British Airways PLC, a public limited company under government ownership, soon thereafter to be sold wholly to the public. BA carried 25.1 million passengers in 1992. The UK had 135 licensed civil airports that same year. International flights operate from London's Heathrow, which handled 40.2 million passengers in 1991; Gatwick, London's second airport (18.6 million passengers); Prestwick, in Scotland; Ringway (for Manchester); Aldergrove (for Belfast); and Elmdon (for Birmingham). There are a number of privately operated airlines, some of which operate air taxi services. British Caledonian, which maintained scheduled flights on both domestic and international routes, merged with British Airways in 1988. The Concorde, a supersonic jetliner developed jointly in the 1960s by the UK and France at a cost exceeding £1 billion, entered service between Heathrow and the US in 1976. As of the end of 1991, there were 233 aircraft in BA's fleet, which flew 601,452 hours that year.

12HISTORY

The earliest people to occupy Britain are of unknown origin. Remains of these early inhabitants include the stone circles of Avebury and Stonehenge in Wiltshire. Celtic tribes from the Continent, the first known settlers in historical times, invaded before the 6th century BC. The islands were visited in ancient times by Mediterranean traders seeking jet, gold, pearls, and tin, which was being mined in Cornwall. Julius Caesar invaded in 55 BC but soon withdrew. In the 1st century AD, the Romans occupied most of the present-day area of England, remaining until the 5th century.

With the decline of the Roman Empire and the withdrawal of Roman troops (although many Romans had become Britonized and remained on the islands), Celtic tribes fought among themselves, and Scots and Picts raided from the north and from Ireland. Early raids by Angles, Saxons, and Jutes from the Continent soon swelled into invasions, and the leaders established kingdoms in the conquered territory, while the native Celts retreated into the mountains of Wales and Cornwall. Although the Welsh were split into a northern and a southern group, they were not permanently subdued. In the 10th century, a Welsh king, Howel the Good (Hywel Dda), united Wales, codified the laws, and encouraged the Welsh bards.

Among the new English kingdoms, that of the West Saxons (Wessex) became predominant, chiefly through the leadership of Alfred the Great, who also had to fight a new wave of invasions by the Danes and other Norsemen. Alfred's successors were able to unify the country, but eventually the Danes completed their conquest, and King Canute (II) of Denmark became ruler of England by 1017. In 1042, with the expiration of the Scandinavian line, Edward the Confessor of Wessex became king. At his death in 1066, both Harold the Saxon and William, duke of Normandy, claimed the throne. William invaded England and defeated Harold in the Battle of Hastings, beginning the Norman Conquest (1066–70).

William I instituted a strong government, which lasted through the reigns of his sons William II and Henry I. The latter's death in 1135 brought a period of civil war and anarchy, which ended with the accession of Henry II (1154), who instituted notable constitutional and legal reforms. He and succeeding English kings expanded their holdings in France, touching off a long series of struggles between the two countries.

The Magna Carta

Long-standing conflict between the nobles and the kings reached a climax in the reign of King John with the victory of the barons, who at Runnymede in 1215 compelled the king to grant the Magna Carta. This marked a major advance toward the parliamentary system. Just half a century later, in 1265, Simon de Montfort, earl of Leicester, leader of the barons in their opposition to Henry III, summoned the first Parliament, with representatives not only of the rural nobility but also of the boroughs and towns. In the late 13th century, Edward I expanded the royal courts and reformed the legal system; he also began the first systematic attempts to conquer Wales and Scotland. In 1282, the last Welsh king, Llewellyn ap Gruffydd, was killed in battle, and Edward I completed the conquest of Wales. Two years later, the Statute of Rhuddlan established English rule. The spirit of resistance survived, however, and a last great uprising against England came in the early 15th century, when Owen Glendower (Owain ap Gruffydd) led a briefly successful revolt.

Scotland was inhabited in early historic times by the Picts and by roaming bands of Gaels, or Celts, from Ireland. Before the Romans left Britain in the 5th century, Scotland had been converted to Christianity by St. Ninian and his disciples. By the end of the following century, four separate kingdoms had been established in Scotland. Norsemen raided Scotland from the 8th to the 12th century, and some settled there. Most of the country was unified under Duncan I (r.1034–40). His son, Malcolm III (r.1059–93), who gained the throne after defeating Macbeth, the murderer of his father, married an English princess, Margaret (later sainted), and began to anglicize and modernize the lowlands.

Scotland United

Under David I (r.1124–53), Scotland was united, responsible government was established, walled towns (known as burghs) were developed, and foreign trade was encouraged. William the Lion (r.1165–1214) was captured by Henry II of England in 1174 and forced to accept the Treaty of Falaise, by which Scotland became an English fief. Although Scotland purchased its freedom from Richard I, the ambiguous wording of the agreement allowed later English kings to revive their claim.

When Alexander III died in 1286, Edward I of England, who claimed overlordship of Scotland, supported the claims of John Baliol, who was crowned in 1293. Edward began a war with Philip of France and demanded Scottish troops, but the Scots allied themselves with Philip, beginning the long relationship with France that distinguishes Scottish history. Edward subdued the Scots, put down an uprising led by William Wallace, executed Wallace in 1305, and established English rule. Baliol's heir was killed by Robert the Bruce, another claimant, who had himself crowned (1309), captured Edinburgh, and defeated Edward II of England decisively at Bannockburn in 1314. In 1328, Edward III signed a treaty acknowledging Scotland's freedom.

Under Edward III, the Hundred Years' War (1337–1453) with France was begun. Notable victories by Edward the Black Prince (son of Edward III), Henry IV, and Henry V led to no permanent gains for England, and ultimately the English were driven out of France. The plague, known as the Black Death, broke out in England in 1348, wiping out a third of the population; it hastened the breakdown of the feudal system and the rise of towns. The 14th century was for England a time of confusion and change. John Wycliffe led a movement of reform in religion, spreading radical ideas about the need for churchly poverty and criticizing many established doctrines and practices. A peasant rebellion led by Wat Tyler in 1381 demanded the abolition of serfdom, monopolies, and the many restrictions on buying and selling.

In 1399, after 22 years of rule, Richard II was deposed and was succeeded by Henry IV, the first king of the house of Lancaster. The war with France continued, commerce flourished, and the wool trade became important. The Wars of the Roses (1455–85), in which the houses of Lancaster and York fought for the throne, ended with the accession of Henry VII, a member of the Tudor family, marking the beginning of the modern history of England.

The Tudors

Under the Tudors, commerce was expanded, English seamen ranged far and wide, and clashes with Spain (accelerated by religious differences) intensified. Earlier English dominance had not had much effect on Wales, but the Tudors followed a policy of assimilation, anglicizing Welsh laws and practices. Finally, under Henry VIII, the Act of Union (1536) made English the legal language and abolished all Welsh laws "at variance with those of England." In 1531, Henry separated the Anglican Church from Rome and proclaimed himself its head. After his death (1547), the succession to the throne became a major issue during the reigns of Edward VI (1547–53), Mary I (1553–58), and Elizabeth I (1558–1603).

In Scotland, James I (r.1406–37) had done much to regulate Scottish law and improve foreign relations. His murder in 1437 began a century of civil conflict. James IV (r.1488–1513) married Margaret Tudor, sister of Henry VII of England, a marriage that was ultimately to unite the crowns of England and Scotland.

French influence in Scotland grew under James V (r.1513–42), who married Mary of Guise, but the Scottish people and nobility became favorably inclined toward the Reformation, championed by John Knox. After James's death, Mary ruled as regent for her daughter, Mary, Queen of Scots, who had married the dauphin of France, where she lived as dauphiness and later as queen. By the time Mary returned to Scotland (1561), after the death of her husband, most of the Scots were Protestants. A pro-English faction had the support of Queen Elizabeth I against the pro-French faction, and Mary, who claimed the throne of England, was imprisoned and executed (1587) by Elizabeth. Under Elizabeth, England in 1583 acquired its first colony, Newfoundland, and in 1588 defeated the Spanish Armada; it also experienced the beginning of a golden age of drama, literature, and music, among whose towering achievements are the plays of William Shakespeare.

Oliver Cromwell and the Commonwealth

Elizabeth was succeeded by Mary's son, James VI of Scotland, who became James I of England (r.1603–25), establishing the Stuart line. Under James and his son, Charles I (r.1625–49), the rising middle classes (mainly Puritan in religion) sought to make Parliament superior to the king. In the English Civil War, which broke out in 1642, Charles was supported by the Welsh, who had remained overwhelmingly Catholic in feeling, but most Scots opposed him. Charles was tried and executed in 1649, and Oliver Cromwell as Protector ruled the new Commonwealth until his death in 1658. Cromwell ruthlessly crushed uprisings in Ireland

and suppressed the Welsh. In 1660, Charles II, eldest son of the executed king, regained the throne. The Restoration was marked by a reaction against Puritanism, by persecution of the Scottish Covenanters (Presbyterians), by increased prosperity, and by intensified political activity; during this period, Parliament managed to maintain many of its gains. Charles II's younger brother, James II (r.1685–88), who vainly attempted to restore Roman Catholicism, was overthrown in 1688 and was succeeded by his daughter, Mary II, and her Dutch husband, William III, who were invited to rule by Parliament. By this transfer of power, known to English history as the Glorious Revolution, the final supremacy of Parliament was established. Supporters of James II (Jacobites) in Scotland and Ireland, aided by France, sought to restore the deposed Stuart line, but their insurrection was suppressed in 1690 at the Battle of the Boyne, fought on the banks of the Irish river of that name.

In Wales, after Cromwell and the Commonwealth, the people began to turn to Calvinism; dissent grew, and such ministers as Griffith Jones, a pioneer in popular education, became national leaders. Most Welsh were won to the Calvinistic Methodist Church, which played a large part in fostering a nonpolitical Welsh nationalism. A long struggle to disestablish the Church of England in Wales culminated successfully in a 1914 act of Parliament.

Colonial Expansion

English colonial expansion developed further in the 17th and 18th centuries, in competition with France and the Netherlands, while at the same time the English merchant marine gained commercial supremacy over the Dutch. The wars of the Grand Alliance (1688–97) and of the Spanish Succession (1701–14) consolidated Britain's overseas possessions. At home, to ensure Scottish allegiance to England and prevent possible alliances with inimical countries, the Act of Union of Scotland and England was voted by the two parliaments in 1707, thereby formally creating the kingdom of Great Britain under one crown and with a single Parliament composed of representatives of both countries. This union held, despite Jacobite uprisings in 1715 and 1745–46, the latter under Prince Charles (Bonnie Prince Charlie, or the Young Pretender, grandson of James II); his defeat at Culloden Moor was the last land battle fought in Great Britain. Scottish affairs eventually became the province of the secretary of state for Scotland, a member of the British cabinet. Nevertheless, a nationalist movement demanding independence for Scotland persists to this day.

The accession, in 1714, of George I of the House of Hanover (a great-grandson of James I) saw the beginning of the modern cabinet system, with the king leaving much of the governing to his ministers. The 18th century was a time of rapid colonial and mercantile expansion abroad and internal stability and literary and artistic achievement at home. Britain won control of North America and India in the Seven Years' War (ended in 1763 by the Treaty of Paris), which also established British supremacy over the seas; however, the American Revolution (1775–83) cost Britain its most important group of colonies. A few years later, British settlement of Australia and then of New Zealand became key elements in the spreading British Empire. Britain increased its power further by its leading role in the French Revolutionary Wars and in the defeat of Napoleon and French expansionist aims.

Birth of the United Kingdom

In 1800, with the Act of Union of Great Britain and Ireland, the United Kingdom formally came into being. The conquest of Ireland had never been consolidated; the Act of Union followed an Irish rebellion in 1798 after the failure of a demand for parliamentary reform. But although the act established Irish representation in Parliament, the Irish question continued to cause trouble throughout the 19th century. Absentee landlordism, particularly in the 26 southern counties, fostered poverty and hatred of the English. Moreover, there was a growing division of interest between these counties and the six counties of the north, popularly called Ulster, where, early in the 17th century, Protestant Scots and English had settled on land confiscated by the British crown after a rebellion. While the north gradually became Protestant and industrial, the rest of Ireland remained Catholic and rural. With the introduction of the first Home Rule Bill in 1886, the northern Irish, fearing domination by the southern Catholic majority, began a campaign that ended in the 1920 Government of Ireland Act, which established separate domestic legislatures for the north and south, as well as continued representation in the UK Parliament. The six northern counties accepted the act and became Northern Ireland. The 26 southern counties, however, did not accept it; in 1921, the Anglo-Irish Treaty was signed, by which these counties left the UK to become the Irish Free State (now the Irish Republic, or Éire), which was officially established in 1922.

Queen Victoria's Reign

The Industrial Revolution, beginning in the second half of the 18th century, provided the economic underpinning for British colonial and military expansion throughout the 1800s. However, the growth of the factory system and of urbanization also brought grave new social problems. The enclosure of grazing land in the Scottish highlands and the industrialization of southern Wales were accompanied by extensive population shifts and led to large-scale emigration to the US, Canada, and Australia. Reform legislation came slowly, although the spirit of reform and social justice was in the air. Slavery was abolished throughout the British Empire in 1834. The great Reform Acts of 1832, 1867, and 1884 enfranchised the new middle class and the working class. Factory acts, poor laws, and other humanitarian legislation did away with some of the worst abuses, and pressure mounted for eliminating others. The long reign of Queen Victoria (1837–1901) saw an unprecedented commercial and industrial prosperity. This was a period of great imperial expansion, especially in Africa, where at the end of the century Britain fought settlers of predominantly Dutch origin in the South African (or Boer) War. Toward the end of the century, also, the labor movement grew strong, education was developed along national lines, and a regular civil service was finally established.

The Twentieth Century

The vast economic and human losses of World War I, in which nearly 800,000 Britons were killed, brought on serious disturbances in the UK as elsewhere, and the economic depression of the 1930s resulted in the unemployment of millions of workers. In 1931, the Statute of Westminster granted the status of equality to the self-governing British dominions and created the concept of a British Commonwealth of Nations. During the late 1930s, the government of Prime Minister Neville Chamberlain sought to avoid war by appeasing Nazi Germany, but after Hitler invaded Poland, the UK declared war on Germany on 3 September 1939. Prime Minister Winston Churchill led the UK during World War II in a full mobilization of the population in the armed services, in home defense, and in war production. Although victorious, the UK suffered much destruction from massive German air attacks, and the military and civilian death toll exceeded 900,000. At war's end, a Labour government was elected; it pledged to carry out a full program of social welfare "from the cradle to the grave," coupled with the nationalization of industry. Medicine was socialized, other social services were expanded, and several industries were put under public ownership. Complete nationalization of industry, however, was halted with the return to power of the Conservatives in 1951. During Labour's subsequent terms in office, from 1964 to 1970 and from 1974 to 1979, little further nationalization was attempted.

Post-World War II Era

To a large extent, the UK's postwar history can be characterized as a prolonged effort to put the faltering economy on its feet and to cope with the economic, social, and political consequences of the disbandment of its empire. By early 1988, all that remained of what had been the largest empire in the world were 14 dependencies, many of them small islands with tiny populations and few economic resources. The UK has remained firmly within the Atlantic alliance since World War II. A founding member of NATO and EFTA, the UK overcame years of domestic qualms and French opposition when it entered the EC on 1 January 1973. After a Labour government replaced the Conservatives in March 1974, the membership terms were renegotiated, and UK voters approved continued British participation by a 67.2% majority in an unprecedented national referendum.

The principal domestic problems in the 1970s were rapid inflation, labor disputes, and the protracted conflict in Northern Ireland. Long-smoldering tensions between Protestants and Catholics erupted into open warfare after civil rights protests in 1969 by Catholics claiming discrimination and insufficient representation in the government. The Protestant reaction was violent, and the Irish Republican Army (IRA), seeking the union of Ulster with the Irish Republic, escalated the conflict by committing terrorist acts in both Northern Ireland and England. British troops, first dispatched to Belfast and Londonderry in August 1969, have remained there since.

On 30 March 1972, Northern Ireland's parliament (Stormont) was prorogued, and direct rule was imposed from London. Numerous attempts to devise a new constitution failed, as did other proposals for power sharing. In 1982, legislation establishing a new 78-member Northern Ireland Assembly was enacted. Elections were held that October, but the 19 Catholic members chosen refused to claim their seats. Meanwhile, the violence continued, one of the victims being the British war hero Earl Mountbatten of Burma, who was murdered while vacationing in Ireland on 27 August 1979. In October 1980, IRA members imprisoned in Ulster began a series of hunger strikes; by the time the strikes ended the following October, 10 men had died. In November 1985, the UK and the Irish Republic signed an agreement committing both governments to recognition of Northern Ireland as part of the UK and to cooperation between the two governments by establishing an intergovernmental conference concerned with Northern Ireland and with relations between the two parts of Ireland.

The "Downing Street Declaration" of December 1993 between British Prime Minister John Major and Irish Prime Minister Albert Reynolds over the future of Northern Ireland suggested that undisclosed contacts had been maintained for some time between the Irish Republican Army (IRA), Sinn Fein, and the British government. Violence in Northern Ireland has continued on the part of both the IRA and various loyalist paramilitary organizations. The IRA has also continued to carry out a number of attacks on the British mainland.

In 1979, a Conservative government, headed by Margaret Thatcher, came to power with a program of income tax cuts and reduced government spending. Thatcher, who won reelection in 1983 and 1987, embarked on a policy of "privatizing"—selling to the private sector—many of the UK's nationalized businesses. In foreign policy, the government's most dramatic action was sending a naval task force to the Falkland Islands following Argentina's occupation of the islands on 2 April 1982. After intense fighting, British administration was restored to the Falklands on 14 June.

Thatcher's leadership was challenged by Conservative MPs in November 1990, and she failed to win the necessary absolute majority. Thatcher withdrew and was replaced by John Major. The Conservatives were returned to power in April 1992 with a reduced majority. Major's government sought to redefine Conservative values with a renewed emphasis on law and order.

13 GOVERNMENT

The UK is a monarchy in form but a parliamentary democracy in substance. The sovereign—Elizabeth II since 1952—is head of state and as such is head of the legislature, the executive, and the judiciary, commander-in-chief of the armed forces, and temporal head of the established Church of England. In practice, however, gradually evolving restrictions have transmuted the sovereign's legal powers into instruments for effecting the popular will as expressed through Parliament. In the British formulation, the sovereign reigns but does not rule, for the sovereign is under the law and not above it, ruling only by approval of Parliament and acting only on the advice of her ministers.

The UK is governed, in the name of the sovereign, by Her Majesty's Government—a body of ministers who are the leading members of whichever political party the electorate has voted into office and who are responsible to Parliament. Parliament itself, the supreme legislative authority in the realm, consists of the sovereign, the House of Lords, and the House of Commons. Since the UK is a unitary and not a federal state, all four countries of the kingdom are represented in the Parliament at Westminster, London. Northern Ireland had its own parliament (Stormont) as well, subordinate to Westminster; however, because of civil strife in Ulster, the Stormont was prorogued on 30 March 1972, and direct rule was imposed from Westminster. After several abortive attempts over the next decade to devise a system of home-rule government acceptable to both Protestant and Catholic leaders, the 78-member Northern Ireland Assembly was established in 1982, but it was dissolved in 1986. In 1979, proposals for the establishment of elected legislatures in Wales and Scotland failed in the former and, though winning a bare plurality, fell short of the required margin for approval (40% of all eligible voters) in the latter.

The sovereign formally summons and dissolves Parliament. The House of Lords is comprised of about 1,200 peers, including hereditary peers, spiritual peers (archbishops and bishops of the Church of England), and life peers (eminent persons unwilling to accept a hereditary peerage). Over the centuries, its powers have gradually been reduced; today, its main function is to bring the wide experience of its members into the process of lawmaking. In early 1994, the House of Commons had 651 members: 524 for England, 38 for Wales, 72 for Scotland, and 17 for Northern Ireland. A general election must be held every five years but is often held sooner. All British subjects 18 years old and over may vote in national elections; women won equal franchise with men in 1922. Citizens of Ireland resident in Britain may also vote, as may British subjects abroad for a period of five years after leaving the UK.

Each Parliament may during its lifetime make or unmake any law. Parliamentary bills may be introduced by either house, unless they deal with finance or representation; these are always introduced in the Commons, which has ultimate authority for lawmaking. The House of Lords may not alter a financial measure nor delay for longer than a year any bill passed by the Commons in two successive sessions. Bills passed by both houses receive the traditional royal assent and become law as acts of Parliament; no bill has received a royal veto for more than 200 years. The Speaker of the Parliament is the chief officer of the House of Commons. The Speaker is nonpartisan and functions impartially. The first woman Speaker was elected in 1992.

Executive power is vested in the prime minister, who, though nominally appointed by the sovereign, is traditionally the leader of the majority party in Parliament. The prime minister is assisted by ministers, also nominally appointed by the sovereign, who are chosen from the majority party and mostly from the Commons, which must approve the government's general policy and the more important of its specific measures. The most senior ministers, about 20, compose the cabinet, which meets regularly to decide policy on major issues. Ministers are responsible collectively to Parliament for all cabinet decisions; individual ministers are responsible to Parliament for the work of their departments. Besides the 5 Scottish departments responsible to the secretary of state for Scotland, there are about 30 major central government departments, each staffed by members of the permanent civil service. Prior to the imposition of direct rule, separate Northern Ireland departments were responsible to the Belfast government; since 1972, they have been responsible to the secretary of state for Northern Ireland, a UK cabinet minister. There is a Welsh office responsible to the secretary of state for Wales.

The British constitution is made up of parliamentary statutes, common law, and traditional precepts and practices known as conventions, all evolved through the centuries. Largely unwritten, it has never been codified and is constantly evolving.

14 POLITICAL PARTIES

UK parliamentary government based on the party system has evolved only during the past 100 years. Although the 18th-century terms "Whig" and "Tory" indicated certain political leanings, there was no clear-cut division in Parliament and no comprehensive party organization. Not until the 19th-century Reform Acts enfranchised millions of new voters did the modern party system develop. The British party system is based on the assumption that there are at least two parties in the Commons, each with a sufficiently united following to be able to form an alternative government at any time. This assumption is recognized in the fact that the largest minority party is officially designated as Her Majesty's Opposition; its leader, who designates a "shadow government," is paid a salary from public funds.

The main political parties represented in Parliament today are the Conservative Party, the Labour Party, and the Liberal Democrats (a coalition of the Liberal and Social Democratic parties, which voted in favor of a formal merger in 1988). From time to time during the past 50 years, other parties have arisen or have splintered off from the main groups, only to disappear or to become reabsorbed. Thus, the Fascists, who were of some significance before World War II, no longer put up candidates for elections, and the British Communist Party has not elected a candidate to Parliament since 1950.

Since World War I, the Labour Party has replaced the Liberal Party, a major force during the late 19th century, as the official opposition to a Conservative government. Founded in 1900 as the political arm of the already powerful trade union movement, the Labour Party was until 1918 a federation of trade unions and socialist groups and had no individual members. Today, its constituent associations consist of affiliated organizations (such as trade unions, cooperative societies, branches of socialist societies, and trade councils), as well as individual members organized into wards. Its program calls for public ownership of the means of production, improvement of the social and economic conditions of the people, defense of human rights, cooperation with labor and socialist organizations of other countries, and peaceful adjustment of international disputes. Between the world wars, it established two short-lived Labour governments while still a minority party, and then joined Churchill's coalition government in World War II. Returned to power with a huge majority in 1945, Labour instituted a program of full employment through planned production; established social services to provide adequate medical care, old age care, nutrition, and educational opportunities for all; began the nationalization of basic industries; and started to disband the empire by granting independence to India, Pakistan, Ceylon (now Sri Lanka), and Burma.

If the rapid rise of the Labour Party has been an outstanding feature of 20th-century British politics, the continuing vitality and adaptability of the Conservative Party, successor of the 18th-century Tories, has been no less remarkable. In foreign affairs, there has been little difference between the parties since World War II. Both have generally been firm allies of the US, and both are pledged to the maintenance of NATO. The two parties have also been in general agreement about the country's social and economic needs. They differ mainly on the degree of state control to be applied to industry and commerce and on practical methods of application; Conservative emphasis is on free enterprise, individual initiative, and restraining the power of the unions. Even on these matters, however, pragmatism is the norm. In office, the Conservatives have let stand much of Labour's social program, and Labour, during Britain's economic difficulties in the late 1970s, imposed its own policy of wage restraints.

After World War II, Labour was in power during 1945–51, 1964–70, and 1974–79; the Conservatives have held office during 1951–64, 1970–74, and since 1979. Scottish National Party members were decisive in the fall of the Labour government in March 1979, after Labour was unable to enact its program for limited home rule (including elected legislatures) in Scotland and Wales. In elections of 3 May 1979, after a campaign fought mainly on economic grounds, Conservatives won 339 seats, with 43.9% of the vote, to Labour's 268 seats, with 36.9%, and Margaret Thatcher replaced James Callaghan as prime minister. Amid growing dissension, the Labour Party moved leftward in the early 1980s and broke with the Conservatives over defense policy, committing itself to the removal of all nuclear weapons from the UK and, in 1986, to the removal of US nuclear bases. The Social Democratic Party, founded in 1981 by moderate former Labour ministers, had by 30 September 1982 obtained 30 seats in Parliament, 27 of whose occupants were breakaway Labour members. In the elections of 9 June 1983, the Conservatives increased their parliamentary majority, winning 397 seats and about 42% of the vote. The Labour Party captured 209 seats and 28% of the vote, its poorest showing in more than five decades. The Alliance of Liberals and Social Democrats won 25% of the vote but only 23 seats (Liberals 17, Social Democrats 6). Minor parties took 5% of the vote and 21 seats.

In the elections of 11 June 1987, the Conservatives won 376 seats and about 42% of the vote. The Labour Party won 229 seats and 31% of the vote. The Liberal-Social Democratic Alliance won nearly 23% of the vote but only 22 seats (Liberals 17, Social Democrats 5). Minor parties took about 4% of the vote and 23 seats: Official Unionist (Northern Ireland), 9; Democratic Unionist (Northern Ireland), 3; Scottish National Party, 3; Plaid Cymru (Welsh Nationalist), 3; Social Democratic and Labour Party (Northern Ireland), 3; Sinn Fein (Northern Ireland), 1; and Popular Unionist (Northern Ireland), 1.

The general election of 9 April 1992 resulted in a continuation of Conservative government under John Major with 42% of the vote and 336 seats. Labour followed with 34% of the vote and 271 seats. The Liberal Democrats took almost 18% of the vote which netted 20 seats. Minor parties received 3% of the vote and 17 seats.

15LOCAL GOVERNMENT

The scope of local governing bodies is defined and limited by acts of Parliament, which also makes certain ministers responsible for the efficient functioning of local services. In England, local government is supervised by the Department of the Environment; in Wales, by the Welsh Office; in Scotland, by the Scottish Department of Development; and in Northern Ireland, by the Department of the Environment for Northern Ireland. The structure of local government has been the subject of several reforms and remains a controversial issue.

From 1965 to 1985, Greater London, the nation's largest metropolitan area, was subdivided into 32 London boroughs; the Greater London Council was the chief administrative authority. Under the Local Government Act of 1985, however, the Greater London Council was abolished and its functions were transferred to London borough and metropolitan district councils, excepting certain services (such as police and fire services and public transport) now administered by joint borough and council authorities. Under the Local Government Act of 1972, the county system that had prevailed throughout the rest of England and Wales was replaced by a two-tier structure of counties and districts (53 and 369, respectively, as of 1985). Below the district level are some 10,000 parishes in England and about 1,000 communities in Wales; most are governed by local councils. Scotland was divided into 9 regions by a reorganization measure effective in 1975; in addition, there are 3 island areas, Orkney, Shetland, and the Western Isles. The regions and island areas are subdivided into 53 districts, each governed by a council. Northern Ireland has a single-tier system of 26 districts, each governed by a district council. For planning and statistical (but not political) purposes, England is often divided into 8 standard regions: South East, East Anglia, South West, West Midlands, East Midlands, Yorkshire and Humberside, North West, and North.

Local councils provide numerous social, sanitary, educational, and police services. Some types of councils are responsible for levying and collecting local property taxes, called rates. Rates cover one-third of the cost of local government services; about three-fifths is met by government grants; and the rest by rents, dividends, interest, and borrowing. More than 3 million persons, including teachers and transport and building workers, were employed in local government services in 1986. The minimum voting age in local elections is 18.

16JUDICIAL SYSTEM

The UK does not have a single body of law applicable throughout the realm. Scotland has its own distinctive system and courts; in Northern Ireland, certain spheres of law differ in substance from those operating in England and Wales. A feature common to all UK legal systems, however—and one that distinguishes them from many continental systems—is the absence of a complete code, since legislation and unwritten or common law are all part of the "constitution."

The main civil courts in England and Wales are some 300 county courts for small cases and the High Court, which is divided into the chancery division, the family division, and the Queen's Bench division (including the maritime and commercial courts), for the more important cases. Appeals from the county courts may also be heard in the High Court, though the more important ones come before the Court of Appeal; a few appeals are heard before the House of Lords, which is the ultimate court of appeal for civil cases throughout the UK. In Scotland, civil cases are heard at the sheriff courts (corresponding roughly to the English county courts) and in the Outer House of the Court of Session, which is the supreme civil court in Scotland; appeals are heard by the Inner House of the Court of Session. Trial by jury in civil cases is common in Scotland but rare in the rest of the UK.

Criminal courts in England and Wales include magistrates' courts, which try less serious offenses (some 98% of all criminal cases) and consist most often of three unpaid magistrates known as justices of the peace, and some 90 centers of the Crown Court, presided over by a bench of justices or, in the most serious cases, by a High Court judge sitting alone. All contested cases receive a jury trial. Cases involving persons under 17 years of age are heard by justices of the peace in specially constituted juvenile courts. Appeals may be heard successively by the Crown Court, the High Court, the Court of Criminal Appeal, and in certain cases by the House of Lords. In Scotland, minor criminal cases are tried without jury in the sheriff courts and district courts, and more serious cases with a jury in the sheriff courts. The supreme criminal court is the High Court of Justiciary, where cases are heard by a judge sitting with a jury; this is also the ultimate appeals court.

All criminal trials are held in open court. In England, Wales, and Northern Ireland, 12-citizen juries must unanimously decide the verdict unless, with no more than two jurors dissenting, the judge directs them to return a majority verdict. Scottish juries of 15 persons are permitted to reach a majority decision and, if warranted, a verdict of "not proven." Among temporary emergency measures passed with the aim of controlling terrorism in Northern Ireland are those empowering ministers to order the search, arrest, and detention of suspected terrorists and permitting juryless trials for terrorist acts in Northern Ireland.

Central responsibility for the administration of the judicial system lies with the lord chancellor (who heads the judiciary and also serves as a cabinet minister and as speaker of the House of Lords) and the home secretary (and the secretaries of state for Scotland and for Northern Ireland). Judges are appointed by the crown, on the advice of the prime minister, lord chancellor, or the appropriate cabinet ministries.

[17]ARMED FORCES

After the general demobilization that followed World War II, compulsory national service for all eligible males over 19 years of age was introduced. Call-ups of national servicemen ceased in 1960, but those who had been trained formed part of the general reserve until June 1974, when the national service legislation expired. Reserves now form part of the long-term reserve established in 1964, composed of all men under 45 years of age who have served in the regular army since 28 February 1964, plus the highly trained units of the territorial army volunteer reserve. The regular reserves number 188,600 and the TAVR, 71,300. In 1985 a Home Service Force of 5,000 (2,900 now serving) was established to guard important installations upon mobilization.

Total active army strength in 1993 was 145,400 (including 7,800 women) and 8,700 enlisted outside the UK, mostly Gurkhas units deployed in the Falkland Islands, Germany, Cyprus (with UNFICYP), Hong Kong, Brunei, Gibraltar, Nepal, and Belize. As of 1993, 12,000 British troops were on active duty in Ulster, along with the 6,000 soldiers of the Royal Irish regiment. Naval forces totaled 62,100 (4,000 women), with units stationed on Malta and the Falkland Islands; armed strength included 13 nuclear attack submarines, 2 ballistic missile submarines, 41 surface combatants, and 3 anti-submarine aircraft carriers. Naval reserves number almost 30,000. The Fleet air arm (6,100) has 45 aircraft and 153 armed helicopters. The Royal Air Force has a strength of 86,000 (7,000 women), with units deployed in Germany, Gibraltar, Cyprus, Hong Kong, Belize, and the Falkland Islands. Combat aircraft number 466.

Basing its defense policy on NATO, the British government in the 1970s reduced its overseas commitments. The defense budget for 1992 was an estimated $42 billion or 4.3% of gross domestic product. The UK is a major seller of arms, recording estimated exports worth $22 billion during 1987–91. The UK nuclear force consists of 32 missiles in submarines. British troops man six different peacekeeping missions.

[18]INTERNATIONAL COOPERATION

The UK became a charter member of the UN on 24 October 1945; it participates in the ECE, ECLC, and ESCAP, as well as in all the nonregional specialized agencies except for UNESCO. The UK is also a member of the Council of Europe, the EC, NATO, and OECD; participates in the Asian Development Bank and IDB; belongs to many other inter-European, inter-African, inter-Commonwealth, and intergovernmental organizations; and is a signatory to GATT. The UK had refrained from signing the Law of the Sea as of September 1987. The headquarters of the IMO is in London.

The Commonwealth of Nations, an organization of 49 states, provides a means for consultation and cooperation, especially on economic matters, between the UK and its former colonies. Its main coordinating organ is the Commonwealth Secretariat, which was established in London in 1965 and is headed by a secretary-general appointed by the heads of the member governments. The heads of governments hold biennial meetings; meetings also are held by diplomatic representatives known as high commissioners and among other ministers, officials, and experts.

[19]ECONOMY

The UK, one of the most highly industrialized countries in the world, lives by manufacture and trade. Apart from coal and low-grade iron ore, some timber, building materials, hides and skins, and natural gas and North Sea oil, it has few natural resources. Agriculture provides nearly two-thirds of the food needed. The remainder of the UK's food and most raw materials for its industries have to be imported and paid for largely through exports of manufactures. The UK is in fact one of the world's largest markets for food and agricultural products and the fifth largest trading nation. Vast quantities of imported wheat, meat, butter, livestock feeds, tea, tobacco, wool, and timber have been balanced by exports of machinery, ships, locomotives, aircraft, and motor vehicles. The pattern of exports is gradually changing, however. Post World War II reduction in output of textiles—once a leading British export—due to competition from Asia, and in coal output, because of competition from oil and new mines in Europe, is being offset by industries such as electronics and chemicals. A major source of earnings is the variety of commercial services that stem from the UK's role as central banker of the sterling area. Shipping, income from overseas investment, insurance, and tourism also make up an important part of the economy.

Since the 1979–81 recession, the British economy has posted steady gains. Inflation fell from 18% in 1980 to an annual rate of 1.9% by July 1987. However, it averaged 6.3% a year during 1988–92 before falling to 1.6% in 1993. Between 1983 and 1990, real GDP increased by nearly 25%. It fell in both 1991 and 1992 but increased 1.9% in 1993. Individual productivity increased by 14% during the 1980–85 period and another 25% during 1985–90. In less than a decade, the UK went from heavy dependence on imported oil to energy self-sufficiency, but this ended in 1989, although the UK's dependence on energy imports in the early 1990s was far lower than in the past. After falling to 5.8% in 1990, the unemployment rate crept up to 10.4% in 1993.

Between 1979 and 1991, the government privatized 46 major companies, as well as a number of subsidiaries of nationalized industries and other businesses. This represented 65% of the state-owned industrial sector. Among the major companies privatized were British Telecom, British Gas, British Steel, British Airways, British Aerospace, Rolls-Royce, Austin Rover, Cable and Wireless, and ICL.

[20]INCOME

In 1992, United Kingdon's GNP was $1,024,769 million at current prices, or $17,760 per capita. For the period 1985–92 the average inflation rate was 6.0%, resulting in a real growth rate in per capita GNP of 1.5%.

In 1992 the GDP was $920 billion in purchasing power equivalent dollars. It is estimated that in 1991 agriculture, hunting, forestry, and fishing contributed 2% to GDP; mining, quarrying, and manufacturing data not reported; electricity, gas, and water, 3%; construction, 6%; wholesale and retail trade, 13%; transport, storage, and communication, 6%; finance, insurance, real estate, and business services, 21%; community, social, and personal services, 6%; and other sources, 44%.

21LABOR

The total working population of the UK in June 1991 was 28,230,000, including 12,060,000 women. The number of unemployed in the UK, only 750,000 in January 1975, reached 3,308,000 in 1986 (13.2% of the labor force), and 2,287,000 in 1991 (8.1%). During the 1990–93 recession, unemployment rose steadily, peaking at 2,990,000 (10.6%) in January 1993 before falling back to 2,910,000 (10.4%) in September 1993. It is believed that recovery will be gradual, with some 2.5 million unemployed by 1997.

Between 1983 and 1992 there was a substantial shift in employment from previously dominant manufacturing to service industries. Employment in industry, which had been 7,788,000 in 1983, was down to 6,679,000 in 1992, a loss of about 15%. Public administration, business services, trade, and commerce together accounted for 69% of all employment, with some 17,608,000 workers in 1992. In 1990, distribution, hotels, catering, and repairs accounted for 20%; transportation and communications, 6%; construction, 6%; banking, finance, and insurance, 12%; public administration, 20%; manufacturing, 21%; and other services, 12%. Agriculture, forestry, and fisheries employed 2% of all workers, and energy and water supply together with mining and quarrying accounted for 1% of employment.

About 10.2 million persons were members of trade unions in 1992. Nearly all trade unions of any size are affiliated with the Trades Union Congress (TUC), the national center of the trade union movement. Founded in 1868, the TUC was one of the prime movers in the formation of the ICFTU. The TUC is the recognized channel of consultation between government departments and the unions on general labor matters. There is a separate Scottish Trades Union Congress. The legal status of the trade unions is defined by the Trade Union and Labour Relations Act of 1974. Restrictions on the power of the trade unions are embodied in the Employment Acts of 1980 and 1982 and in the Trade Union Act of 1984.

The year-long coal miners' strike that ended in March 1985 was the longest and most bitter in British industrial history, accounting for 22,300,000 lost working days in 1984. In 1992, however, the number of working days lost due to work stoppages was only 528,000. The annual average of working days lost for 1988–92 was 11,023,000.

The standard workweek ranges between 35 and 40 hours. Besides the statutory public holidays, most employees have at least four weeks' annual vacation with pay. Equal pay for men and women doing the same work has been mandated since the end of 1975. Employers are required to contribute to the Redundancy Fund, which offers lump-sum compensation for dismissed workers with more than two years' seniority.

22AGRICULTURE

Agriculture's importance has declined in recent years; including forestry and fishing, it contributed 1.8% to the GDP, down from 2.3% in 1971. In 1992, 548,000 workers were employed in agriculture.

Just over 73% of Great Britain's land area was devoted to agriculture in 1992, some 6,600,000 hectares (16,309,000 acres) being devoted to crops and 11,180,000 hectares (27,626,000 acres) to pastures. There were about 240,000 holdings, down from 422,000 in the late 1960s. In Great Britain roughly 70% of the farms are primarily or entirely owner-occupied, but in Northern Ireland nearly all are.

Most British farms produce a variety of products. The type of farming varies with the soil and climate. The better farming land is generally in the lowlands. The eastern areas are predominantly arable, and the western predominantly for grazing. Chief crops (with estimated 1992 production in tons) were barley, 7,386,000; wheat, 14,185,000; potatoes, 7,882,000; sugar beets, 8,500,000;

oats, 523,000; and oilseed rape, 1,166,000. Mechanization and research have greatly increased agricultural productivity; between 1979 and 1992, for example, production of wheat per hectare rose almost 22%; of potatoes, 33%; and of barley, 32%. Consequently, the UK now produces nearly two-thirds of its total food requirements, whereas prior to World War II, it produced only about 33%, and in 1960, less than half. The estimated number of tractors in the UK in 1991 was 500,000, as against 55,000 in 1939; some 48,000 combines were also in use.

23ANIMAL HUSBANDRY

Livestock continues to be the largest sector of the farming industry. The UK raises some of the world's finest pedigreed livestock and is the leading exporter of pedigreed breeding animals. Most of the internationally famous breeds of cattle, sheep, hogs, and farm horses originated in the UK. In England and Wales, fattening of animals for food is the predominant activity in the southeast, the east, and the Midlands, while stock rearing is widespread in northern England and in Wales. In Scotland, dairying predominates in the southwest, cropping and fattening in the east, and sheep raising in the hilly regions. Northern Ireland's livestock industry provides 90% of its agricultural income.

In 1992 there were about 11.6 million head of cattle, 28.9 million sheep, 7.5 million hogs, and 124 million poultry. Estimated output of livestock products for 1992 included 962,000 tons of beef and veal, 355,000 tons of mutton and lamb, 970,000 tons of pork, 1,069,000 tons of poultry, 14,692,000 tons of milk, and 650,900 tons of eggs.

The most highly reputed beef breeds are Hereford and Aberdeen Angus; distinguished dairy breeds are Guernsey, Jersey, and Ayrshire. To ensure sound breeding, there is compulsory licensing of bulls.

24FISHING

Lying on the continental shelf, the British Isles are surrounded by waters mainly less than 90 m (300 ft) deep, which serve as excellent fishing grounds and breeding grounds for fish. Small fishing villages are found all along the coast, but the modern large-scale industry is concentrated at Hull, Grimsby, Fleetwood, Yarmouth, and Lowestoft in England. The major herring landings are made at numerous east coast ports of Scotland, notably Aberdeen. The fishing industry has been declining, but it remains important to Scotland, which accounts for 69% by weight and 60% by value of all fish landings in the UK.

The deep-sea fleet has declined in recent years, primarily because the adoption by most nations, including the UK, of a 200-mi fishery limit decreased the opportunity to fish in distant waters. Some of the larger vessels have, instead, turned to fishing for mackerel and herring off the west coast. Landings of all types of fish by UK fishing vessels totaled 823,225 tons in 1991.

25FORESTRY

The estimated total area of woodland in 1991 was 2.4 million hectares (5.9 million acres), or nearly 11% of Great Britain's land area. Roughly 40% of the area is in England, 49% in Scotland, and 11% in Wales. The lumber industry employs about 55,000, and supplies the UK with 13% of its timber demand. Because of the high proportion of unproductive woodland, largely a legacy of overfelling during the two world wars, major efforts have been directed toward rehabilitation. Except for the two wartime periods, home woodlands have made only a limited contribution in this century to the national requirements in wood and wood products, almost 90% of which are met by imports. In 1991, imported timber accounted for 50% of the trade deficit. The UK imports softwood lumber from Canada, hardwood lumber and softwood plywood from the US, hardwood veneer from Germany, hardwood plywood from Russia, and particleboard from Belgium.

Of Great Britain's 2,060,000 hectares (5,100,000 acres) of productive forests, 43% are managed by the Forestry Commission, a government agency that promotes development of afforestation and increased timber production. Clearance of forests for agriculture began in the Neolithic and Bronze Ages, so that by the time of the Domesday survey in 1086, only 15% of England was forested. There has been a considerable degree of reforestation in the 20th century.

26 MINING

Except for North Sea oil deposits, the UK has comparatively few mineral resources; traditionally, coal has been by far the most important. An organized coal-mining industry has been in existence for over 300 years, some 200 years longer than in any other country. The largest fields are in the North West and Yorkshire and Humberside regions, producing almost half the total output. In 1991, an estimated 97.7 million tons of coal were mined. Coal exports declined from a peak post-World War II level of 19 million tons in 1949 to an estimated 2.5 million tons in 1991. Rights to mineral fuels such as coal, petroleum, and uranium belong to the British Coal Corporation (BC), a state-owned company (which was in the process of privatization in 1991). Most other mineral rights are privately owned, except gold and silver, the rights to which are held by the royal family and are known as "Crown Rights." Since the coal strike of 1984–85, BC has become more competitive, with operating costs reduced by one-third. The total BC workforce has been reduced from 300,000 in 1980 to 74,000 in 1991; total production has been declining since 1983.

Other minerals extracted in quantity are sand and gravel, 120 million tons in 1991; limestone and dolomite, 130 million tons; crushed igneous rock, 52 million tons; clays, 22 million tons; dimensional sandstone, 200,000 tons; gypsum and anhydrite, 4 million tons; fluorspar, 75,000 tons; and chalk, 12 million tons. Lead, zinc, and tungsten are worked on a small scale. The output of iron ore dropped from 916,000 tons in 1980 to 25,000 tons in 1991. The UK is the leading world producer and exporter of ball clay, and is the largest exporter and second largest producer after the US of kaolin "China clay".

27 ENERGY AND POWER

Coal supplied 28% of the UK's primary energy consumption in 1992; oil, 40%; natural gas, 25%; nuclear energy and hydroelectricity, 7%. The share of natural gas in total energy consumption increased from 22.7% in 1981 to over 25% in 1985, but fell from 23.7% in 1988 to 21.8% in 1991.

Oil fields comparable in size to those of the Middle East were first discovered in the British sector of the North Sea in October 1970. The UK's proven oil reserves from the North Sea totaled 3.8 billion barrels at the end of 1992. Because of delays in pipeline and platform construction, the first oil was not piped ashore until October 1975. Production reached 94.2 million tons in 1992, an increase of 3.2% over 1991; the output has gradually declined since 1986. In 1992, however, the UK was still the tenth largest oil producer in the world. Natural gas was first discovered on the continental shelf in 1965, and production began in 1967. In 1992, natural gas reserves were estimated at over 500 billion cu m. Production in 1992 was 53.6 billion cu m.

Production of oil and natural gas comes from four major field systems (Brent, Ninian, Forties, Flotta) and several fields that load offshore. The UK is simultaneously a major importer and exporter of oil. Since North Sea oil is a light, high-quality oil, the UK exports this oil and imports crude oils of various qualities. Violent storms can adversely affect production; in January 1993, the production level of the Beryl field (on the Ninian system) was down by 40% from December, 1992 due to the storms.

Nationalized in 1947, the electricity supply industry, which is the largest consumer of primary fuel, is under the jurisdiction of the Ministry of Power. In England and Wales, electricity is generated and transmitted by the Central Electricity Generating Board and distributed by 12 area electricity boards under the supervision of the Electricity Council. Scotland and Northern Ireland have separate electricity authorities. A national grid of main transmission lines supplies electrical power to most of the country. The Energy Act of 1983 allowed competition from private generators of electricity. In 1991, the UK signed the European Energy Charter, which promotes cooperation and an open energy market between EC members, the US, Japan and Australia.

Most of the UK's electricity is produced by coal-fired steam generating stations. Hydroelectric generation is comparatively recent and is at present largely confined to Scotland, although there has been some waterpower development in Wales. About 22% of the public electricity supply was generated by nuclear power stations in 1991. The UK was the first country to have a nuclear power station supplying electricity to a national network (its first station was Calder Hall, in Cumberland, opened in 1956). By the end of 1991, combined nuclear generating capacity was 11,353 Mw. Total electricity generated by power stations in the UK in 1991 amounted to 322,133 kwh. Net installed capacity was 70,022 Mw in that year. The UK started 25 new wind power projects in 1991–92; by 2025, perhaps 10% of Britain's electricity needs could be satisfied by wind power, according to the government's renewable energy research program. Tidal power, passive solar design, and biofuels also show promise.

28 INDUSTRY

The UK is one of the most highly industrialized countries in the world. The industrial sector of the economy declined in relative importance after 1973, because of the worldwide economic slowdown; however, output rose in 1983 and 1984 and in 1985 was growing at an annual rate of 3%. Manufacturing accounted for 25.1% of GDP in 1985 and 22.3% in 1992. Since World War II, some traditional industries have markedly declined—e.g., cotton textiles, steel, shipbuilding, locomotives—and their place has been taken by newer industries, such as electronics, offshore oil and gas products, and synthetic fibers. In the chemicals industry, plastics and pharmaceuticals have registered the most significant growth.

The pattern of ownership, organization, and control of industry is varied; public, private, and cooperative enterprises are all important. The public sector plays a significant role; however, since 1979 the government has sold off a number of companies and most manufacturing is conducted by private enterprise. Although the average firm is still fairly small, there has been a trend in recent years toward the creation of larger enterprises.

Metals, engineering, and allied industries—including steel, nonferrous metals, vehicles, and machinery—employ nearly half of all workers in manufacturing. Steel production was 26 million ingot tons in 1968 but decreased to 12.9 million in 1980 before rising to 18.95 million in 1988. It was 16.2 million tons in 1992. The UK is one of the world's largest exporters of commercial motor vehicles, with an output of 248,453 in 1992; production of passenger cars was 1,291,880. Britain's aerospace industry is among the world's foremost. Rolls-Royce, which was privatized in 1987, is one of the principal aero-engine manufacturers in the world. British Aerospace, nationalized during 1978–80 but now privately owned again, manufactures civil aircraft, such military aircraft as the Harrier and the Hawk advanced trainer, and guided weapons, including the Rapier ground-to-air missile.

While the relative importance of the textile and clothing industries has declined considerably since World War II, the UK continues to produce high-quality woolen textiles. Certain smaller industries are noted for the quality of their craftsmanship—e.g., pottery, jewelry, goldware, and silverware. Other sectors are the cement industry (which focuses on the manufacture of Portland cement, a British invention); the rubber industry, the world's oldest; paper industries; and leather and footwear.

29 SCIENCE AND TECHNOLOGY

Great Britain, preeminent in the Industrial Revolution from the mid-18th to the mid-19th century, has a long tradition of technological ingenuity and scientific achievement. It was in the UK that the steam engine, spinning jenny, and power loom were developed and the first steam-powered passenger railway entered service. To British inventors also belongs credit for the miner's safety lamp, the friction match, the cathode ray tube, stainless steel, and the first calculating machine. One of the most famous scientific discoveries of the 20th century, the determination of the double-helix structure of the deoxyribonucleic acid (DNA) molecule, took place at the Laboratory of Molecular Biology at Cambridge University. The UK is also in the forefront of research in radio astronomy, laser holography, and superconductivity.

In 1991, the total national expenditure for R&D was £30.9 billion. In 1990, there were 790,000 scientists and engineers working in Great Britain. The leading government agency for supporting science and technology is the Ministry of Defense, which plays an important role in both the UK's national security and its role in NATO. British industry funds half of all national research and development, and government-industry cooperation in aerospace, biotechnology and electronics have opened new frontiers in science.

The largest issue facing British scientists, engineers and technicians in the 1990s is the challenge of providing new technological innovations in the global economy. In 1993, a government white paper, *Realizing our Potential*, called for the most sweeping changes in British science and technology since World War II. Among the changes called for in this white paper is the creation of a "technology forecasting program" which will allow scientists and engineers from all over Great Britain to have a more direct say in setting national science and technology priorities. It is likely that many of the recommendations from the white paper will be incorporated into national science and technology priorities, including the technology forecasting program, over time.

30 DOMESTIC TRADE

London is the leading wholesale and importing center, accounting for more than half the total wholesale turnover. Other important distribution centers are Liverpool, Manchester, Bristol, Glasgow, and Hull.

In 1991 there were 232,045 retail establishments that employed about 2,367,000 persons and had a total turnover of £132,544 million. Retail sales rose in value by about 4.8% between 1990 and 1991, but by only 0.6% in volume. Chain stores (ten or more outlets) accounted for 63% of retail turnover in 1991. At the end of 1991 there were 71 retail cooperative societies. Some 853,000 people were engaged in wholesaling in 1993.

About £6,725 million is estimated to have been spent on all forms of advertising in 1988. In 1990, 62% was spent on print media, 31% on television, 3.8% on posters, 2.2% on radio, and 0.5% on films.

Normal banking hours are 9:30 AM to 3:30 PM, Monday through Friday, except for Thursday, when the banks stay open later. Business hours in London are 9:30 AM to 5 PM, Monday through Saturday; shops in certain areas may be open to 7:30 one night a week, usually Wednesday or Thursday. Outside of London, the shops of each town or village may close for a half or full day at midweek. Sunday shopping was scheduled to be legalized in 1994.

31 FOREIGN TRADE

The UK, the world's fifth largest trading nation, is highly dependent on foreign trade. It must import almost all its copper, ferrous

metals, lead, zinc, rubber, and raw cotton; most of its tin, raw wool, hides and skins, and many other raw materials; and about one-third of its food. Its exports accounted for more than 25% of GDP in 1993.

Principal exports in 1992 (in millions of British pounds) were as follows:

Machinery (excluding transport equipment)	34,945.5
Chemicals and related products	14,976.3
Petroleum and petroleum products	6,660.6
Food, beverages, and tobacco	8,706.9
Road vehicles	8,893.6
Other transport equipment	4,834.9
Scientific instruments	3,077.2
Inedible crude materials	1,879.3
Iron and steel	3,004.4
Textiles	2,457.4
Apparel and clothing accessories	2,084.1
Other exports	16,987.3
TOTAL	108,507.5

Principal imports in 1992 (in millions of British pounds) were as follows:

Machinery (excluding transport equipment)	31,719.2
Food, beverages, and tobacco	13,426.9
Road vehicles	12,118.5
Chemicals and related products	11,618.3
Fuels and electrical current	7,014.1
Inedible crude materials	4,668.2
Textiles	3,940.5
Paper and related articles	3,801.3
Apparel and clothing accessories	4,477.9
Metal manufactures	2,598.7
Iron and steel	2,513.7
Scientific instruments	2,621.0
Other imports	25,348.5
TOTAL	125,866.8

Entry into the EC has resulted in some adjustment of UK trade patterns. The US was the UK's leading market through 1989. It was then replaced by Germany, which has been the largest supplier since 1982. In 1992, Germany accounted for 14.6% of total UK trade, and the US accounted for 11.1%. Trade with the EC increased from 43% to 54% between 1980 and 1992.

Principal trade partners in 1992 (in millions of British pounds) were as follows:

	EXPORTS	IMPORTS	BALANCE
Germany	15,212.6	19,034.3	−3,821.7
US	12,228.7	13,714.0	−1,485.3
France	11,484.7	12,223.4	−738.7
Netherlands	8,503.2	9,907.8	−1,404.6
Italy	6,146.9	6,765.7	−618.8
Belgium-Luxembourg	5,715.1	5,741.1	−26.0
Ireland	5,738.9	5,070.0	668.9
Japan	2,231.5	7,442.2	−5,210.7
Other countries	41,245.9	45,968.3	−4,722.4
TOTALS	108,507.5	125,866.8	−17,359.3

32 BALANCE OF PAYMENTS

Throughout the 1960s, revaluations of other currencies adversely affected the pound sterling. Large deficits in the balance of payments appeared in 1964 and 1967, leading to a devaluation in November 1967. Another run on sterling prompted a decision to let the pound float on 23 June 1972. The pound then declined steadily, dropping below a value of $2.00 for the first time on 9 March 1976. The oil crisis and the rise in commodity prices in

1974 were even harsher blows to the UK economy. Increasing unemployment, the worldwide recession, and a large budgetary deficit placed the government in an extremely difficult position, since replenishment of currency reserves cost more in terms of sterling, and the need to curb inflation prevented expansion in the economy. Borrowing from the oil-producing states and the EC helped finance the deficits, but a further approach to the IMF became necessary.

During the late 1970s, the UK's visible trade balance was generally negative, although surpluses on invisibles sometimes were sufficient to produce a surplus in current account. Increased North Sea oil exports helped produce substantial trade surpluses in 1980–82.

The UK has run a deficit in visible trade since 1983, reaching a peak of $47 billion in 1989, as consumer demand for imported goods ballooned. As recession took hold, imports fell, reducing the visible trade deficit dramatically in 1991. The devaluation of the pound, following the UK's late 1992 withdrawal from the EC's Exchange Rate Mechanism, increased the cost of imports at the end of 1992. The UK is a major overseas investor (especially in the US) and has an extremely important service sector, dominated by banking and insurance, which consistently generates invisible trade credits. In 1992 merchandise exports totaled $187,440 million and imports $212,058 million. The merchandise trade balance was $–24,618 million. The following table summarizes United Kingdom's balance of payments for 1991 and 1992 (in millions of US dollars):

	1991	1992
CURRENT ACCOUNT		
Goods, services, and income	–8,827	–11,696
Unrequited transfers	–2,394	–9,018
TOTALS	–11,221	–20,714
CAPITAL ACCOUNT		
Direct investment	–233	3,362
Portfolio investment	–24,307	–24,222
Other long-term capital	24,525	2,658
Other short-term capital	23,707	35,533
Exceptional financing	–43	–119
Other liabilities	–9,478	–399
Reserves	–4,997	2,603
TOTALS	9,172	19,416
Errors and omissions	14,520	–2,085
Total change in reserves	–6,021	5,347

33BANKING AND SECURITIES

The Bank of England, established in 1694 as a corporate body and nationalized in 1946, holds the main government accounts, acts as government agent for the issue and registration of government loans and other financial operations, and is the central note-issuing authority, with the sole right to issue bank notes in England and Wales (some banks in Scotland and Northern Ireland have limited note-issuing rights). It administers exchange control for the Treasury and is responsible for the application of the government's monetary policy to other banks and financial institutions. One of the main instruments for this purpose is the bank rate, the minimum rate at which it will discount approved bills of exchange. The rate has fluctuated in post-World War II years from 2% to 17%, registering 11% in January 1987. The treasury bill rate was 5.23% in 1993. Currency in circulation as of 1992 totaled £16,145 million.

The banks handling most domestic business are mainly limited liability companies. The four major commercial banking groups

are Barclays, Lloyds, Midland, and National Westminster. At the end of 1993, private sector deposits amounted to £233.6 billion. The National Savings Movement, started in 1916, encourages widespread savings investment by small depositors in trustee savings banks and the National Savings Bank (formerly known as the Post Office Savings Bank), the largest organization of its kind in the world, with about 20,000 in post offices. Merchant banks are of great importance in the financing of trade, both domestic and overseas. In addition, 275 overseas banks are directly represented in London.

In 1762, a club of securities dealers was formed in London to fix rules for market transactions, and in 1773 the first stock exchange was opened in London. In 1801, the London Stock Exchange was constructed on part of its present site; since that time, it has provided a market for the purchase and sale of securities and has played an important part in providing new capital for industry. Some 7,300 securities were quoted in 1992, with a total market value of £2,055,000 million. The Stock Exchange opened to international competition in October 1986, permitting wider ownership of member firms. Minimum rates of commission on stock sales were abolished. In April 1982, the London Gold Futures Market began operations; it is the only market in Europe making possible worldwide, round-the-clock futures dealings in the metal.

34INSURANCE

In 1989 there were 962 companies authorized to conduct insurance business in the UK, 213 life, 681 non-life, and 68 composite insurance companies. Per capita premiums totaled $1,775.2 in 1990, or 9.7% of the GDP. Life insurance in force amounted to £673,561 billion.

London is the leading international insurance center. Lloyd's, the world-famous society of private insurers, was originally established in the 17th century as a center for marine insurance but has since built up a worldwide market for other types of insurance.

35PUBLIC FINANCE

National budget deficits recurred throughout the 1970s and early and mid-1980s. Between 1987/88 and 1990/91, the public sector was in surplus, so the government repaid debt. The onset of recession in 1990 led to an increased level of public borrowing—about £14 billion in 1991/92, or 2.25% of GDP. By 1993/94, the public sector borrowing requirement had risen to £50 billion, or 8.1% of GDP. Much of the fiscal deficit is cyclical, a result of decreased tax receipts and increased benefits during the economic downturn. As the recovery continues, pressure on the deficit from these causes is expected to ease. However, a significant part of the deficit appears to be structural, a long-term inability of the tax base to support government spending commitments at the current levels. Receipts for the 1992/93 budget of £258.5 billion came primarily from income taxes (26%), value-added taxes, and social security receipts (17% each), and general government borrowing (12%). The main sources of local authority income are government grants, loans, and local taxation on property.

The fiscal year begins on April 1.

The following table shows actual revenues and expenditures for 1990 and 1991 in millions of pounds.

	1990	1991
REVENUE AND GRANTS		
Tax revenue	183,550	193,669
Non-tax revenue	18,019	18,354
Capital revenue	606	435
Grants	735	3,133
TOTAL	202,910	215,591

EXPENDITURES & LENDING MINUS REPAYMENTS	1990	1991
General public service	10,743	11,298
Defense	22,910	25,231
Public order and safety	10,932	12,983
Education	—	—
Health	27,671	30,935
Social security and welfare	62,925	73,870
Housing and community amenities	—	—
Recreation, cultural, and religious affairs	—	—
Economic affairs and services	18,746	15,255
Other expenditures	46,060	54,001
Adjustments	−2,155	−2,298
Lending minus repayments	−7,685	−7,745
TOTAL	199,964	215,643
Deficit/Surplus	2,946	−52

36TAXATION

Taxes on income include a graduated individual income tax and a corporation tax. Although personal income taxes are still high, they have been reduced several times since 1980.

Income tax is charged on all income that has its origin in Britain and on all income arising abroad of persons resident in Britain. However, the UK has entered into agreements with many countries to provide relief from double taxation. In 1993, the basic income tax rate was 25%. Taxes were lower (20%) on the first £2,000 of taxable income and higher (40%) on amounts over £23,700. Each taxpayer's marginal rate applies to capital gains in excess of £6,600.

A tax is charged on corporate profits and capital gains. In 1992, the rate of this tax was 33%, with a reduced rate of 25% for companies with profits below £250,000 annually. A value-added tax has replaced the purchase tax, bringing the UK's tax policy into harmony with the EC. In 1992, the standard rate was 17.5%. A zero rate applied to most foods, books, newspapers and periodicals, and certain other goods. Services such as insurance, health, education, and land and rents are also exempt. Other taxes are levied on petroleum products, tobacco, and alcoholic drinks. There are stamp duties, inheritance taxes, and taxes on profits from all exploration and production. Local taxes are based on property assessments, or "rates."

37CUSTOMS AND DUTIES

Import licensing and quotas were the general rule in the UK between 1939 and 1959. For specified items from specified countries or groups of countries, an individual license was required for each import. In June 1959, however, the UK began to remove important controls on virtually all raw materials and basic foodstuffs and on some machinery imported from the US. Today, imports from the non-Communist countries are, with very few exceptions, free from quantitative restrictions. With UK entry into the free-trade area of the EC, a tariff-free area has been created. In addition, the UK uses the EC's Common External Tariff for non-EC imports. The four principal types of import charges are customs duties, agricultural levies, value-added taxes, and excise duties on goods such as alcohol, tobacco, and tobacco products.

38FOREIGN INVESTMENT

Before World War I, British overseas investments were valued at more than $30,000 million (adjusted into dollars of 1960). Even in the period between the two world wars, British foreign investments remained remarkably high. After World War II, the UK, having given up many of its overseas dependencies and having incurred enormous foreign debts to wage the war, had to liquidate a large part of its overseas holdings. As its economy recovered, the UK again began to invest overseas. From 1955 to 1964, gross total private capital outflow was at an annual average of

£300 million. The abolition of exchange controls in 1979 also encouraged overseas investment. In 1985, private British investment overseas (direct and portfolio) had risen to £76,700 million. In 1993, the UK was the largest source of foreign direct investment in the US, with a total cumulative investment of $94 billion.

Overseas investment in Great Britain totaled $198 billion in 1991. Direct investment in 1992 amounted to £10,343 million and portfolio investment to £21,390 million. In that year, direct overseas investment by UK residents was £9,424 million and portfolio investment £32,818 million.

39ECONOMIC DEVELOPMENT

Like many other industrialized nations of the West, the UK has sought to combine steady economic growth with a high level of employment, increased productivity, and continuing improvement in living standards. Attainment of these basic objectives, however, has been hindered since World War II by recurrent deficits in the balance of payments and by severe inflationary pressures. As a result, economic policy has chiefly had to be directed toward correcting these two underlying weaknesses in the economy. When crises have arisen, emergency measures have often conflicted with long-term objectives. In 1967, for example, the government devalued the pound by 14% in order to improve the balance-of-payments position, but simultaneously increased taxes and reduced the growth rate of public expenditures in order to restrain home demand in both public and private sectors. Since the almost uninterrupted upward trend in prices resulted principally from the tendency for money income to rise faster than the volume of production, the government sought to institute a policy designed to align the rise in money income with increases in productivity.

Various bodies have been set up within the last 25 years to foster economic development and improve industrial efficiency, notably the National Economic Development Council, established in 1962, which is responsible for the coordination of industry. Another important body, created in 1974, the National Enterprise Board, was set up to help plan industrial investment, particularly in manufacturing and export industries. Subsequently, the Labour government began to de-emphasize increased social services and government participation in the economy and to stress increased incentives for private investment. (A notable exception was in the exploitation of North Sea oil resources.) General investment incentives included tax allowances on new buildings, plants, and machinery. The Conservative government elected in 1979 sought to reduce the role of government in the economy by improving incentives, removing controls, reducing taxes, moderating the money supply, and privatizing several large state-owned companies. This policy was continued by succeeding conservative governments into the 1990s.

The UK has long been a major source of both bilateral aid (direct loans and grants) and multilateral aid (contributions to international agencies) to developing countries. To coordinate the overall aid program and its proportions of bilateral and multilateral aid, capital aid, and technical assistance, the Ministry of Overseas Development was set up in 1962. Aid totaled £1,945 million in 1992/93 (compared with £1,463 million in 1988/89). Of the 1992/93 total, £1,036 million was in bilateral aid, including £451 million in funds for technical cooperation. Since 1958, the terms for development loans have progressively softened, and a policy of interest-free loans for the poorest developing countries was introduced in 1965. In 1992/93, about 70% of the UK's direct, official bilateral development assistance went to Commonwealth countries. That year, 40% of net bilateral aid went to the 52 poorest developing countries.

40SOCIAL DEVELOPMENT

A gradually evolved system of social security, placed in full operation in 1948, provides national insurance, industrial injuries insurance, family allowances, and national assistance throughout the UK, although the system is administered separately in Northern Ireland.

The National Insurance scheme provides benefits for sickness, unemployment, maternity, and widowhood, as well as guardian's allowances, retirement pensions, and death grants. Most of these and the industrial injury benefits are financed in part through a complex system of compulsory weekly flat-rate and graduated contributions by employees, employers, and self-employed. Sickness benefits are paid at a weekly standard rate, with additional amounts for dependents. Unemployment benefits, at the same rates, are payable continuously for up to one year. Retirement pensions cover men at 65 and women at 60. Child benefits provide weekly payments (£7.25 as of 1991) for each child, up to the age of 16 or 19, depending on when the child leaves school.

Financial assistance for the needy is provided through a scheme of supplementary benefits introduced in 1966 to replace the system administered by the former National Assistance Board since 1948. Benefits take the form of a supplementary pension for those over statutory retirement age and a supplementary allowance for others. A supplementary benefits commission guides the scheme and also provides temporary accommodation for the homeless in specially designated reception centers. For needy families in which the head of the household is in full-time employment, a family income supplement is paid.

Since 1967, abortion has been permitted, except in Northern Ireland; 141,100 legal abortions were performed in Great Britain in 1985. The UK leads the developed world in making birth control available, according to the Population Crisis Committee. In 1993, about 72% of married women (ages 15 to 49) used contraception.

Career progress by women in most sectors of the economy continues, although employed women earned about 25% less in 1993 than their male counterparts, and sexual harassment is a continuing problem in the workplace. In the same year, a divorced woman's claim to a share of her husband's pension was upheld in court. The Women's Aid Federation, a private organization, organized an advertising campaign to counter domestic violence and provide assistance to those suffering from it.

41 HEALTH

Life expectancy has increased from about 50 years at birth in 1900–1910 to about 70 years for men and 76 years for women in 1992. Rising living standards, medical advances, the growth of medical facilities and their general availability, and the smaller size of the family are some factors in the improved health of the British people. Deaths from infectious diseases have been greatly reduced, although the proportion of deaths from circulatory diseases—including heart attacks and strokes—and cancer has risen. Infant mortality has decreased from 142 per 1,000 live births in 1900–1902 to 7 in 1992 (general mortality was 11.5 per 1,000 people in 1993).

A comprehensive National Health Service (NHS), established in 1948, provides full medical care to all residents of the UK. Included are general medical, dental, pharmaceutical, and optical services; hospital and specialist services (in patients' homes when necessary) for physical and mental illnesses; and local health authority services (maternity and child welfare, vaccination, prevention of illness, health visiting, home nursing, and other services). The patient is free is choose a family doctor from any in the service, subject to the physician's acceptance. General tax revenues meet most of the cost of the NHS; the remainder is paid through National Health Insurance contributions and charges for certain items, including eyeglasses and prescription drugs. Compared with other OECD countries, the UK's per capita expenditure on health care is low ($947). Total health care expenditure in 1990 totaled $59,623 million.

All specialist and auxiliary health services in England are the direct responsibility of the secretary of state for social services. In Wales, Scotland, and Northern Ireland the corresponding services and administrative bodies are under the respective secretaries of state. All hospitals except a few, run mostly by religious orders, are also in the NHS. In 1991 the UK implemented major reforms in its health care services, including improvements in virtually all facets of the program. Areas of concern as of 1993 included incidence of coronary/stroke, cancer, accidents, mental illness, and HIV/AIDS. The NHS is currently undergoing restructuring; increased numbers of NHS hospitals are being decentralized by conversion to NHS Trust, begun in 1991. Trust hospitals are becoming the norm, and the Health Secretary estimates that 95% of hospitals will be trusts by the end of 1994. In 1990, the UK had 6.3 hospital beds per 1,000 inhabitants, 80,200 physicians, and 37,832 pharmacists. In 1989, there were 284,578 nurses and 24,801 midwives. The UK has a low ratio of doctors to population—in 1992 there were 1.4 doctors per 1,000 people, with a nurse-to-doctor ration of 2.0. Since 1982, to help control the spread of AIDS, the government has funded and implemented measures for blood testing, research, public education, and other social services relating to the disease.

42 HOUSING

In 1991 there were 22,972,000 dwellings in the UK. About 67% were owned by their occupants, about 26% were owned by public authorities, and about 7% (mainly older houses) were rented from private landlords. About 50% of families now live in a post-1945 dwelling, usually a two-story house with a garden. Most homeowners finance their purchase through a home mortgage loan from a building society, bank, insurance company, or other financial institution. The degree of overcrowding in the UK is lower than in most European countries.

New houses are built by both the public and private sectors, but most are built by the private sector for sale to owner-occupiers. The main providers of new subsidized housing are housing associations, which own, manage, and maintain over 600,000 homes in England alone and completed over 27,000 new homes for rent or shared ownership in 1991–92. Local housing authorities were in the past primarily concerned with slum clearance; however, large-scale clearance virtually ended in the mid-1980s, with emphasis shifting to modernization of substandard homes and community improvement.

43 EDUCATION

Although responsibility for education in the UK rests with the central government, schools are mainly administered by local education authorities. Expenditure on education in 1990/91 amounted to about £17,900 million by local education authorities and £4,600 million of direct central government spending.

Virtually the entire adult population is literate. Education is compulsory for all children between the ages of 5 and 16. In 1990/91, about 9 million children attended Britain's 30,500 state schools while around 600,000 attended the 2,500 private schools. Two-thirds of the state schools are wholly owned and maintained by local education authorities. The others are voluntary schools mostly run by the churches and also financed by the local authorities.

Since 1989, the government has introduced a "National School Curriculum" in England and Wales comprised of four key stages: 5 to 7 (infants); 7 to 11 (juniors); 11 to 14 (pre-GCSE); and 14 to 16 (GCSE). Similar reforms are being introduced in Scotland and Northern Ireland. The main school examination, the General Certificate of Secondary Education (GCSE) is taken in England, Wales and Northern Ireland at around the age of 16. A separate exam system exists in Scotland. Of the 2,500 registered independent schools, the largest and most important (Winchester, Eton, Harrow, and others) are known in England as "public schools." Many have centuries of tradition behind them and are world famous.

Including the Open University, a nonresidential institution whose courses are conducted by television and radio broadcasts and correspondence texts, Britain in 1990/91 had 47 universities (compared with 17 in 1945) with 334,000 full-time students and 30,000 lecturers. As a result of recent legislation, nearly all polytechnics have become universities and will award their own degrees starting in 1993. The Universities of Oxford and Cambridge date from the 12th and 13th centuries, respectively; the Scottish universities of St. Andrews, Glasgow, Aberdeen, and Edinburgh from the 15th and 16th centuries. Besides the universities, there are more than 800 other institutions of higher education, including technical, art, and commercial colleges run by local authorities. The proportion of young people entering university has risen from 1 in 8 in 1980 to 1 in 5 in 1990. Nearly 1.5 million students are taking full-time, post-secondary courses.

National policy stipulates that no person should be excluded from higher education by lack of means. More than 90% of students in higher education hold awards from public or private funds.

44LIBRARIES AND MUSEUMS

London has more than 500 libraries, among them the British Library, the largest in the UK, with about 13 million volumes. The National Library of Scotland with about 6 million items is in Edinburgh, and the National Library of Wales, with some 5 million volumes, in Aberystwyth. The Bodleian Library in Oxford has about 6 million volumes, and the Cambridge University Library has 5.2 million. Each of these five is a copyright library, entitled to receive a copy of every new book published in the UK.

Other major libraries in London include the University of London Central Library, the London Library (the largest public subscription library), the Science Museum Library, the Victoria and Albert Museum Art Library, the Public Record Office (containing such national historical treasures as the Domesday Book), and the libraries of such institutions as the Royal Institute of International Affairs, the Royal Commonwealth Society, the Royal Geographical Society, the Royal Academy of Music, and the National Library for the Blind. There are major libraries at the Universities of Edinburgh, Glasgow, and St. Andrews and at Queen's University in Belfast. Manchester has the John Rylands University Library.

Public libraries are administered by public library authorities (councils of counties, county boroughs, municipal boroughs, and urban districts), which maintain 5,270 branches and have a book stock of some 156 million. Public libraries also lend music scores, cassettes, and records. Rural areas are served by traveling vans.

Almost every city and large town has a museum of art, archaeology, and natural history. There are more than 1,000 museums and art galleries, ranging from nearly two dozen great national institutions to small collections housed in a few rooms. London has the British Museum, with its vast collections of archaeological and ethnographic material from all over the world, and the Victoria and Albert Museum, including extensive collections of works of fine and applied arts. The National Gallery, the Tate Gallery, and the National Portrait Gallery are among other prestigious London museums. The National Museum of Wales is in Cardiff, and there are six national museums and art galleries in Edinburgh. Belfast has a quasi-national museum and art gallery and is the site of the Northern Irish Folk Museum. There are important museums and art galleries in Liverpool, Manchester, Leicester, Birmingham, Bristol, Norwich, Southampton, York, Glasgow, Leeds, and other cities. Oxford and Cambridge each have many museums, and several other universities also have important collections. Private art collections in historic family mansions are open to the public at specified times.

45MEDIA

The Post Office, founded in 1635, was the first in the world to institute adhesive stamps as proof of payment for mail. It now operates nearly all postal services. As authorized by 1981 legislation, the Thatcher government relaxed postal and telecommunications monopolies in some areas. The Telecommunications Act of 1984 further promoted competition and denationalized British Telecommunications (Telecom), which encompasses a system of some 29.5 million telephone exchange lines, 111,505 telex connections, and 98,600 data transmission terminals. Some 170 countries can be dialed directly.

Radio and television broadcasting services are provided by the British Broadcasting Corp. (BBC), which was established as a public corporation in 1927, and by the Independent Television Commission (ITC) and the Radio Authority, commercial concerns whose powers are defined in the Independent Broadcasting Authority Act of 1973. The BBC broadcasts on two television channels, the Independent Television Commission on ITV and Channel Four, which began operating in 1982. BBC Radio offers five national radio networks in the medium- and long-wave bands, as well as FM programming and an overseas service in 37 languages. Both the BBC and IBA operate local radio services; the BBC has 39 local stations (including 2 for the Channel Islands), and there are 140 independent local radio stations. In September of 1992, the first national commercial radio station, Classic FM, was inaugurated, and two other similar stations are planned. There were an estimated 65,800,000 radios in use in 1991, and 25,000,000 television sets.

Although circulation totals have been decreasing, UK newspaper readership per capita was the second highest in the world in 1992. As of that year there were about 130 daily and Sunday newspapers, some 2,000 weekly papers, numerous specialized papers, and about 7,000 periodicals. Nine Sunday papers and 12 daily morning papers are "national" in the sense of circulating throughout Britain. National dailies, with their political tendencies and their average daily circulations in 1992, are the following:

	ORIENTATION	CIRCULATION
The Sun (m)	Left of center	3,588,077
Daily Mirror (m)	Independent left-wing	2,868,263
Daily Mail (m)	Independent conservative	1,688,808
Daily Express (m)	Independent conservative	1,537,726
Daily Telegraph (m)	Independent conservative	1,043,703
Daily Star (m)	Independent	808,486
The Guardian (m)	Independent	418,026
The Times (m)	Independent	390,323
Financial Times (m)	Independent	291,915
Morning Star (m)	Communist	7,000

Six of the Sunday papers have circulations in the millions. The provincial press included more than 100 daily and Sunday newspapers and some 1,600 weeklies in 1992. Two of the morning dailies (*Yorkshire Post* and *Eastern Daily Press*) have circulations of more than 83,000. Two of the Sunday papers (*Sunday Sun* and *Sunday Mercury*) have circulations of over 115,000. The weekly *Berrow's Worcester Journal,* founded in 1690, claims to be the world's oldest continuously circulating newspaper.

Wales has 1 morning daily, the *Western Mail,* with a 1992 circulation of 76,200, mostly in the southern areas. The four evening dailies with a circulation range between 32,500 and 80,900, are the *South Wales Echo* (Cardiff), the *South Wales Argus* (Newport), the *South Wales Evening Post* (Swansea), and the *Evening Leader* (Wrexham). There are about 82 local weeklies. Scotland has 6 morning, 6 evening, and 4 Sunday papers, plus the Scottish editions of the *Daily Mail* and the *Sunday Express.* The *Glasgow Herald* and *The Scotsman,* an Edinburgh paper, are the most influential. About 115 weekly papers are published in Scottish towns. Northern Ireland has 2 morning papers,

1 evening paper, and 3 Sunday papers, all published in Belfast (with circulations ranging from 20,000 to 134,000), plus 45 weeklies. The evening paper is the *Belfast Telegraph*. Britain's ethnic minorities publish over 60 newspapers and magazines, most of them weekly, fortnightly or monthly. These include the Chinese *Sing Tao* and *Wen Wei Po, the Urdu Daily Jang,* and the Arabic *Al-Arab* (the foregoing are all dailies), as well as newspapers in Gujarati, Bengali, Hindi and Punjabi. The *Weekly Journal,* aimed at Britain's black community, was begun in 1992.

The 7,000 periodicals published weekly, monthly, or quarterly cover a huge range of special interests. Leading opinion journals are *New Statesman, The Economist,* and *Spectator. The Times Literary Supplement* is highly influential in cultural affairs. The chief news agency is Reuters, a worldwide organization servicing British papers with foreign and Commonwealth news and the world press with British and foreign news.

Although there is no government censorship of news or opinion, the Official Secrets Act, stringent libel and slander laws, and restrictions governing the disclosure of court proceedings do impose limitations on press freedom. In addition, the press regulates itself through the Press Council, which adjudicates complaints about newspaper practices from local officials and the public.

46ORGANIZATIONS

A vast number of organizations in the UK carry on programs in every phase of human activity. Voluntary social service organizations number in the thousands. Social work on a national scale is carried out under religious sponsorship. Cooperation between Protestant churches is fostered by the British Council of Churches. The Council of Christians and Jews works for cooperation between these faiths. The principal coordinating body in general social service is the National Council of Social Service.

Voluntary organizations are active in adult education. The British Council promotes a wider knowledge of the UK and its people abroad and develops cultural relations with other countries. There are more than 300 learned societies. The Arts Council of Great Britain (founded in 1946) promotes the fine arts and higher artistic standards, and advises government bodies on artistic matters. The Royal Academy and the Royal Scottish Academy are other leading bodies in the arts. The National Book League, the Royal Society of Literature, the British Academy, the English Association, the Bibliographical Society, and other groups foster interest in literature, language, and scholarship.

The National Council for Voluntary Youth Services includes most of the largest youth groups. The leading political parties, major religious denominations, and some adult voluntary organizations such as the Red Cross maintain youth organizations. There is also a Scouts Association and a Girl Guides Association.

The national body representing British industry is the Confederation of British Industry, incorporated in 1965 and directly or indirectly representing about 250,000 companies. The Association of British Chambers of Commerce (founded in 1860) has 240 affiliated UK chambers. Agricultural organizations include the National Farmers' Union, agricultural cooperative societies, and other specialized associations.

47TOURISM, TRAVEL, AND RECREATION

The world's seventh most popular tourist destination in 1991, the UK is rich in natural as well as cultural attractions. Landscapes range from farmlands and gardens to sandy beaches, moors, and rocky coasts. Architectural sights include stone and thatched cottages, stately country houses, mansions, and castles. Among the many historic dwellings open to the public are the Welsh castles Cilgerran (11th century), Dolbadarn (12th century), and Conway and Caernarvon (both 13th century); 10-century-old Traquair House near Peebles, the oldest continuously inhabited house in Scotland, and the Palace of Holyroodhouse in Edinburgh; and

Warwick Castle, near Stratford-upon-Avon, the birthplace of William Shakespeare. Distinguished cathedrals include St. Paul's in London and those in Canterbury, Exeter, Norwich, Winchester, and York. At Bushmills, in Northern Ireland, the oldest distillery in the world may be visited, and some of Scotland's 100 malt whiskey distilleries also offer tours.

Among London's extraordinary attractions are Buckingham Palace, the Tower of London, and Westminster Abbey. Of the wide range of entertainment available, London is particularly noted for its theater, including the Royal Shakespeare Company. Folk music may be heard throughout the UK; traditional community gatherings for music and dancing, called ceilidhs, are held in Scotland, often in pubs, and Edinburgh is the site of one of the world's largest folk festivals, as well as an annual festival of classical music and other performing arts.

Scotland, where golf developed in the 15th century, has many superb golf courses, as does the rest of the UK; some 70 Highland Games and Gatherings take place in Scotland from May to September. Other popular sports include fishing, riding, sailing, rugby, cricket, and soccer football. Wimbledon is the site of perhaps the world's most prestigious tennis competition. England hosted and won the World Cup soccer championship in 1966.

In principle, foreigners entering the UK must have a valid passport and a visa issued by British consular authorities abroad. However, citizens of Ireland do not need a passport, and citizens of OECD, Commonwealth, and Latin American countries, among others, need no visa. Tourism yields a substantial income from overseas; in 1991, some 16.6 million foreign visitors spent $12.6 billion in the UK. The anticipated opening of the Channel Tunnel in 1994 is expected to boost travel to and from the Continent.

48FAMOUS BRITONS

Rulers and Statesmen

English rulers of renown include Alfred the Great (849–99), king of the West Saxons, who defeated and held off the Danish invaders; William I (the Conqueror, 1027–87), duke of Normandy, who conquered England (1066–70) and instituted many changes in the structure of English government and society; Henry II (1133–89), who centralized the power of the royal government, and his sons Richard I (the Lion-Hearted, 1157–99), leader of the Third Crusade, and John (1167?–1216), from whom the barons wrested the Magna Carta; Edward I (1239–1307), who subdued Wales and established the parliamentary system; Edward III (1312–77), who for a time conquered part of France, and did much to promote English commerce; Henry VIII (1491–1547), who separated the Anglican Church from the Roman Catholic Church and centralized administrative power; Elizabeth I (1533–1603), during whose reign, begun in 1558, England achieved great commercial, industrial, and political power, and the arts flourished; and Victoria (1819–1901), under whom Britain attained unprecedented prosperity and empire.

Among the statesmen distinguished in English history are Thomas à Becket (1118?–70), archbishop of Canterbury, who defended the rights of the church against the crown; Simon de Montfort, earl of Leicester (1208?–65), who in 1265 summoned the first Parliament; and Thomas Wolsey (1475?–1530), cardinal, archbishop of York, and Henry VIII's brilliant lord chancellor. Oliver Cromwell (1599–1658) established a republican and Puritan Commonwealth. Sir Robert Walpole, first earl of Oxford (1676–1745), unified cabinet government in the person of the prime minister and laid the foundations for free trade and a modern colonial policy. As England moved increasingly toward democratic government, important progress was achieved under the liberal statesmen William Pitt, first earl of Chatham (1708–78); his son William Pitt (1759–1806); and Charles James Fox (1749–1806). Outstanding statesmen of the 19th century were William

Wilberforce (1759–1833); Henry John Temple, third Viscount Palmerston (1784–1865); Sir Robert Peel (1788–1850); Benjamin Disraeli, earl of Beaconsfield (1804–81); and William Ewart Gladstone (1809–98). Twentieth-century leaders include David Lloyd George, first earl of Dwyfor (1863–1945), prime minister during World War I; and Sir Winston Leonard Spencer Churchill (1874–1965), prime minister during World War II, historian, and winner of the Nobel Prize for literature in 1953. In 1979, Margaret (Hilda Roberts) Thatcher (b.1925) became the nation's first woman prime minister. The reigning monarch since 1952 has been Queen Elizabeth II (b.1926). The heir to the throne is Charles, prince of Wales (b.1948), whose marriage on 29 July 1981 to Lady Diana Frances Spencer (b.1961; at marriage, Diana, princess of Wales) was seen by a worldwide television audience of 750 million people.

Explorers and Navigators
British explorers and navigators played an important part in charting the course of empire. Sir Martin Frobisher (1535?–94), who set sail from England in search of the Northwest Passage, reached Canada in 1576. Sir Francis Drake (1545?–96) was the first Englishman to sail around the world. John Davis (1550?–1605) explored the Arctic and Antarctic, sailed to the South Seas, and discovered the Falkland Islands. Henry Hudson (d.1611) explored the Arctic regions and North America. Sir Walter Raleigh (1552?–1618) was a historian and poet, as well as a navigator and colonizer of the New World. James Cook (1728–79) charted the coasts of Australia and New Zealand. Scottish-born David Livingstone (1813–73) explored central Africa while doing missionary work. Welsh-born Henry Morton Stanley (John Rowlands, 1841–1904) was sent by a US newspaper to find Livingstone in 1871 and, having done so, returned for further exploration of Africa. Sir Richard Francis Burton (1821–90), an Orientalist known for his translation of the *Arabian Nights,* and John Hanning Speke (1827–64) explored central Africa while searching for the source of the Nile.

Great British military figures include John Churchill, first duke of Marlborough (1650–1722), who attained many victories in the War of the Spanish Succession and in later campaigns against the French; Horatio, Viscount Nelson (1758–1805), the foremost British naval hero, whose career was climaxed by victory and death at Trafalgar; the Irish-born soldier-statesman Arthur Wellesley, first Duke of Wellington (1769–1852), whose brilliant campaigns culminated in the defeat of Napoleon at Waterloo; General Charles George Gordon (1833–85), who gained victories in China, acquiring the nickname "Chinese," and died while fighting against the Mahdi in Khartoum; Field Marshal Viscount Montgomery (Bernard Law Montgomery, 1887–1976), British military leader during World War II; Welsh-born Thomas Edward Lawrence (1888–1935), known as "Lawrence of Arabia," who led the Arabs in uprisings against the Turks during World War I; and Lord Mountbatten of Burma (Louis Mountbatten, 1900–1979), supreme Allied commander in Southeast Asia (1943–46) and last viceroy and first governor-general of India (1946–48).

Philosophers and Legal Scholars
Sir Thomas Littleton (1407?–81) wrote *Tenures,* a comprehensive work on English land law that was used as a textbook for over three centuries. Sir Edward Coke (1552–1634), a champion of the common law, wrote the *Institutes of the Laws of England,* popularly known as *Coke on Littleton.* Sir William Blackstone (1723–80) wrote *Commentaries on the Laws of England,* which became a basic text in modern legal education and strongly influenced the evolution of jurisprudence in the US as well as in Britain. The jurist-philosopher Jeremy Bentham (1748–1832) championed liberal law reform.

Roger Bacon (1214?–92), philosopher and scientist, wrote treatises ranging over the whole field of human knowledge. John Duns Scotus (1265?–1308) was a Scottish-born dialectician and theologian. William of Ockham (1300?–1349) laid the foundation of the modern theory of the separation of church and state. John Wesley (1703–91) was the founder of Methodism. Chief among modern philosophers are Thomas Hobbes (1588–1679), John Locke (1632–1704), the Irish-born bishop and idealist thinker George Berkeley (1685–1753), John Stuart Mill (1806–73), Alfred North Whitehead (1861–1947), George Edward Moore (1873–1958), Ludwig Joseph Johann Wittgenstein (b.Austria, 1889–1951), and Sir Alfred Jules Ayer (b.1910-1989). A philosopher and mathematician who widely influenced contemporary social thought was Bertrand Arthur William Russell, third Earl Russell (1872–1970).

Historians and Economists
Noted historians include Raphael Holinshed (d.1580?), Edward Gibbon (1737–94), John Emerich Edward Dalberg-Acton, first Baron Acton (1834–92), William Edward Hartpole Lecky (1836–1903), John Richard Green (1837–83), Frederic William Maitland (1850–1906), George Macaulay Trevelyan (1876–1962), Giles Lytton Strachey (1880–1932), Sir Lewis Bernstein Namier (1880–1960), Arnold Joseph Toynbee (1889–1975), and Edward Hallett Carr (1892–1982).

Thomas Robert Malthus (1766–1834) and David Ricardo (1772–1823) were among the first modern economists. Robert Owen (1771–1858) was an influential Welsh-born socialist, industrial reformer, and philanthropist. Walter Bagehot (1826–77) was a distinguished critic and social scientist. The theories of John Maynard Keynes (Baron Keynes, 1883–1946) have strongly influenced the economic practices of many governments in recent years. Sir James George Frazer (1854–1941), a Scottish-born anthropologist and author of *The Golden Bough,* was a pioneer in the fields of comparative religion and comparative mythology. Herbert Spencer (1820–1903) was an influential economic and social philosopher. Sir Arthur John Evans (1851–1941) was an archaeologist who explored the ruins of ancient Crete. Anna Freud (b.Austria, 1895–1982), daughter of Sigmund Freud, and Melanie Klein (b.Austria, 1882–1960) were psychoanalysts influential in the study of child development. Noted anthropologists include Sir Edward Burnett Tylor (1832–1917); Polish-born Bronislaw Kasper Malinowski (1884–1942); Louis Seymour Bazett Leakey (1903–72) and his wife, Mary Leakey (b.1913), who discovered important fossil remains of early hominids in Tanzania; and Ashley Montagu (b.1905).

Scientists
Present-day concepts of the universe largely derive from the theories of the astronomer and physicist Sir James Hopwood Jeans (1877–1946), the astronomers Sir Arthur Stanley Eddington (1882–1946) and Sir Fred Hoyle (b.1915), and the radio astronomers Sir Martin Ryle (1918–84) and Anthony Hewish (b.1924), who shared the Nobel Prize for physics in 1974. Other British scientists and inventors who won fame for major contributions to knowledge include William Harvey (1578–1657), physician and anatomist, who discovered the circulation of the blood; Irish-born Robert Boyle (1627–91), physicist and chemist, who investigated the properties of gases; Sir Isaac Newton (1642–1727), natural philosopher and mathematician, who discovered gravity and made important advances in calculus and optics; German-born physicist Gabriel Daniel Fahrenheit (1686–1736), who introduced the temperature scale named after him; James Watt (1736–1819), the Scottish-born engineer who invented the modern condensing steam engine; Edward Jenner (1749–1823), who discovered the principle of vaccination; the great chemists John Dalton (1766–1844), who advanced the atomic theory, and Sir Humphry

Davy (1778–1829); George Stephenson (1781–1848), inventor of the locomotive steam engine; Michael Faraday (1791–1867), a chemist and physicist noted for his experiments in electricity; Scottish-born geologist Sir Charles Lyell (1797–1875), the father of modern geology; Charles Darwin (1809–82), the great naturalist who advanced the theory of evolution; James Prescott Joule (1818–89), a physicist who studied heat and electrical energy; Thomas Henry Huxley (1825–95), a biologist who championed Darwin's theory; James Clerk Maxwell (1831–79), the Scottish-born physicist who developed the hypothesis that light and electromagnetism are fundamentally of the same nature; Sir Alexander Fleming (1881–1955), bacteriologist, who received the 1945 Nobel Prize for medicine for the discovery of penicillin in 1928; and Francis Harry Compton Crick (b.1916) and Maurice Hugh Frederick Wilkins (b.New Zealand, 1916), two of the three winners of the 1962 Nobel Prize in physiology or medicine for their research into the structure of the DNA molecule.

Literature and the Arts

Geoffrey Chaucer (1340?–1400) wrote the *Canterbury Tales* and other works that marked the height of medieval English poetry. Other major medieval poets were John Gower (1325?–1408) and William Langland (1332?–1400?). William Caxton (1422–91) was the first English printer. Sir Thomas Malory (fl.1470) derived from French and earlier English sources the English prose epic traditionally known as *Morte d'Arthur*. Two religious reformers who translated the Bible into English, making it accessible to the common people, were John Wycliffe (1320?–84), who made the first complete translation, and William Tyndale (1492?–1536), who made the first translation from the original languages instead of Latin.

During the reign of Elizabeth I, England's golden age, emerged the dramatist and poet William Shakespeare (1564–1616), a giant of English and world literature, and a galaxy of other fine poets and playwrights. Among them were Edmund Spenser (1552?–99), Irish-born author of the *Faerie Queene;* the poet and soldier Sir Philip Sidney (1554–86); and the dramatists Christopher Marlowe (1564–93) and Ben Jonson (1572–1637). Outstanding writers of the Stuart period include the philosopher, scientist, and essayist Francis Bacon (1561–1626), first Baron Verulam Viscount St. Albans; John Donne (1572–1631), the greatest of the metaphysical poets; the lyric poet Robert Herrick (1591–1674); John Milton (1608–74), author of *Paradise Lost* and other poems and political essays; John Bunyan (1628–88), who created the classic allegory *Pilgrim's Progress;* and the poet, playwright, and critic John Dryden (1631–1700). The greatest Restoration dramatists were William Wycherley (1640–1716) and William Congreve (1670–1729). Two authors of famous diaries mirroring the society of their time were John Evelyn (1620–1706) and Samuel Pepys (1633–1703).

Distinguished writers of the 18th century include the Irish-born satirist Jonathan Swift (1667–1745), author of *Gulliver's Travels;* the essayists Joseph Addison (1672–1719) and Sir Richard Steele (1672–1729), whose journals were the prototypes of modern magazines; the poets Alexander Pope (1688–1744) and Thomas Gray (1716–71); the critic, biographer, and lexicographer Samuel Johnson (1709–84); and the Irish-born playwrights Oliver Goldsmith (1730?–74), also a poet and novelist, and Richard Brinsley Sheridan (1751–1816). The poet and artist William Blake (1757–1827) worked in a unique mystical vein.

The English Romantic movement produced a group of major poets, including William Wordsworth (1770–1850); Samuel Taylor Coleridge (1772–1834); George Noel Gordon Byron, sixth Lord Byron (1788–1824); Percy Bysshe Shelley (1792–1822); and John Keats (1795–1821). Victorian poets of note included Alfred, Lord Tennyson (1809–92); Elizabeth Barrett Browning (1806–61); her husband, Robert Browning (1812–89); Dante Gabriel Rossetti (1822–82); his sister, Christina Georgina Rossetti (1830–94); Algernon Charles Swinburne (1837–1909); and Gerard Manley Hopkins (1844–89). Edward FitzGerald (1809–83) is famous for his free translations of Omar Khayyam's *Rubáiyát.* Matthew Arnold (1822–88) was a noted poet and critic. Other prominent critics and essayists include Charles Lamb (1775–1834), William Hazlitt (1778–1830), Thomas De Quincey (1785–1859), John Ruskin (1819–1900), Leslie Stephen (1832–1904), and William Morris (1834–96). Thomas Babington Macaulay (1800–1859) was a distinguished statesman, essayist, and historian. John Henry Cardinal Newman (1801–90) was an outstanding Roman Catholic theologian. Irish-born Oscar Fingal O'Flahertie Wills Wilde (1854–1900) was famous as a playwright, novelist, poet, and wit.

Major poets of the 20th century include Alfred Edward Housman (1859–1936); Walter John de la Mare (1873–1956); Dame Edith Sitwell (1887–1964); US-born Thomas Stearns Eliot (1888–1965), winner of the Nobel Prize in 1949; Wystan Hugh Auden (1907–73); Welsh-born Dylan Thomas (1914–53); Philip Larkin (1922–85); and Ted Hughes (b.1930). Prominent critics include Frank Raymond Leavis (1895–1978) and Sir William Empson (1906–84).

The English novel's distinguished history began with Daniel Defoe (1660–1731), Samuel Richardson (1689–1761), Henry Fielding (1707–54), and Laurence Sterne (1713–68). It was carried forward in the 19th century by Jane Austen (1775–1817), William Makepeace Thackeray (1811–63), Charles Dickens (1812–70), Charles Reade (1814–84), Anthony Trollope (1815–82), the Brontë Sisters—Charlotte (1816–55) and Emily (1818–48)—George Eliot (Mary Ann Evans, 1819–80), George Meredith (1828–1909), Samuel Butler (1835–1902), and Thomas Hardy (1840–1928), who was also a poet. The mathematician Lewis Carroll (Charles Lutwidge Dodgson, 1832–98) became world-famous for two children's books, *Alice in Wonderland* and *Through the Looking Glass.* Rudyard Kipling (1865–1936), author of novels, stories, and poems, received the Nobel Prize for literature in 1907. Sir Arthur Conan Doyle (1859–1930) is known throughout the world as the creator of Sherlock Holmes.

Twentieth-century fiction writers of note include the Polish-born Joseph Conrad (Teodor Józef Konrad Korzeniowski, 1857–1924); Herbert George Wells (1866–1946), who was also a popular historian and a social reformer; Arnold Bennett (1867–1931); John Galsworthy (1867–1933), also a playwright, who received the Nobel Prize in 1932; William Somerset Maugham (1874–1965), also a playwright; Edward Morgan Forster (1879–1970); Virginia Woolf (1882–1941); David Herbert Lawrence (1885–1930); Joyce Cary (1888–1957); Katherine Mansfield (b.New Zealand, 1888–1923); Dame Agatha Christie (1881–1976), also a playwright; Dame Ivy Compton-Burnett (1892–1969); Dame Rebecca West (b.Ireland, 1892–1983), also known for her political writings and as an active feminist; Aldous Huxley (1894–1963); John Boynton Priestley (1894–1984), also a playwright; Irish-born Robert Ranke Graves (1895–1985), also a poet, novelist, scholar, and critic; George Orwell (Eric Blair, 1903–50), also a journalist and essayist; Evelyn Waugh (1903–66); Graham Greene (b.1904); Anthony Dymoke Powell (b.1905); Henry Green (Henry Vincent Yorke, 1905–74); Charles Percy Snow (Baron Snow, 1905–80), also an essayist and a physicist; William Golding (b.1911), Nobel Prize winner in 1983; Lawrence George Durrell (b.India, 1912); Anthony Burgess (b.1917); Doris Lessing (b.Iran, 1919); and John Le Carré (David John Moore Cornwell, b.1931). The dominant literary figure of of the 20th century was George Bernard Shaw (1856–1950), Dublin-born playwright, essayist, critic, and wit. The playwright-composer-lyricist Sir Noel Coward (1899–1973) directed and starred in many of his sophisticated comedies. Harold Pinter (b.1930) has been a highly influential playwright.

Actors and Actresses

The British stage tradition dates back to Richard Burbage (d.1619), the greatest actor of Shakespeare's time, and Edmund Kean (1787–1833), the greatest tragedian of the Romantic era. Luminaries of the modern theater are Dame Ellen Alicia Terry (1848–1928), Dame Sybil Thorndike (1882–1976), Dame Edith Evans (1888–1976), Sir Ralph Richardson (1902–83), Sir John Gielgud (b.1904), Laurence Olivier (Baron Olivier of Brighton, b.1907-1989), Sir Michael Redgrave (1908–85), and Derek George Jacobi (b.1938). Prominent stage directors are Peter Stephen Paul Brook (b.1925) and Sir Peter Reginald Frederick Hall (b.1930). Major contributors to the cinema have included the comic actor and director Charlie (Sir Charles Spencer) Chaplin (1889–1977); the directors Sir Alexander Korda (Sandor Corda, b.Hungary, 1893–1956), Sir Alfred Hitchcock (1899–1980), Sir Carol Reed (1906–76), Sir David Lean (b.1908-1991), and Sir Richard Attenborough (b.1923); and actors Cary Grant (Archibald Alexander Leach, 1904–86), Sir Alec Guinness (b.1914), Deborah Kerr (b.1921), Welsh-born Richard Burton (1925–84), Irish-born Peter O'Toole (b.1932), Maggie Natalie Smith (b.1934), Vanessa Redgrave (b.1937), and Glenda Jackson (b.1936).

Architects

Great English architects were Inigo Jones (1573–1652) and Sir Christopher Wren (1632–1723). Famous artists include William Hogarth (1697–1764), Sir Joshua Reynolds (1723–92), Thomas Gainsborough (1727–88), Joseph Mallord William Turner (1775–1851), John Constable (1776–1837), the illustrator Aubrey Beardsley (1872–98), Graham Sutherland (1903–80), Francis Bacon (b.Ireland, 1910), and David Hockney (b.1937). Roger Eliot Fry (1866–1934) and Kenneth Mackenzie Clark (Lord Clark, 1903–83) were influential art critics. Sir Jacob Epstein (b.US, 1880–1959), Henry Moore (1898–1986), and Dame Barbara Hepworth (1903–75) are world-famous British sculptors. The most famous British potter was Josiah Wedgwood (1730–95).

Composers

English composers of note include John Dunstable (1370?–1453), whose works exerted a profound influence on continental musicians; William Byrd (1543–1623) and Orlando Gibbons (1583–1625), who were proficient in both sacred and secular music; the great lutenist and songwriter John Dowland (1563–1626); the madrigalists John Wilbye (1574–1638) and Thomas Weelkes (1575?–1623); Henry Purcell (1659?–95), a brilliant creator of vocal and chamber works; German-born George Frederick Handel (Georg Friedrich Händel, 1685–1759), a master of baroque operas, oratorios, and concerti; and Sir Arthur Seymour Sullivan (1842–1900), whose musical settings of the librettos of Sir William Schwenk Gilbert (1836–1911) are among the most popular comic operas of all time. Significant 20th-century figures include Sir Edward Elgar (1857–1934), Frederick Delius (1862–1934), Ralph Vaughan Williams (1872–1958), Sir William Walton (1902–83), Sir Michael Kemp Tippett (b.1905), Edward Benjamin Britten (Baron Britten, 1913–76), Peter Maxwell Davies (b.1934), and, in popular music, John Winston Lennon (1940–80) and James Paul McCartney (b.1942) of the Beatles. Notable performers include pianists Dame Myra Hess (1890–1965) and Sir Clifford Curzon (1907–82), violinist Sir Yehudi Menuhin (b.1916), guitarist-lutenist Julian Bream (b.1933), singers Sir Peter Pears (1910–86) and Dame Janet Baker (b.1933), and conductors Sir Thomas Beecham (1879–1961), Sir Adrian Boult (1889–1983), Sir John Barbirolli (1899–1970), Sir Georg Solti (b.Hungary, 1912), and Sir Colin Davis (b.1927).

Athletes

Notable British athletes include Sir Roger Bannister (b.1929), who on 6 May 1954 became the first person to run a mile in under four minutes; golfer Tony Jacklin (b.1944), winner of the British Open in 1969 and the US Open in 1970; three-time world champion John Young "Jackie" Stewart (b.1939), a Scottish race-car driver; and the yachtsman Sir Francis Chichester (1901–72), winner of the first single-handed transatlantic race (1970) and the first sailor to make a solo circumnavigation of the globe (1966–67).

Natives of Scotland and Wales

Duncan I (r.1034–40) was the first ruler of the historical kingdom of Scotland. Macbeth (r.1040–57), who killed Duncan and seized the throne, furnished the subject of one of Shakespeare's greatest plays. Margaret (d.1093), Duncan's daughter-in-law, reformed the Church, won fame for piety and charity, and was made a saint. William Wallace (1272?–1306) led a rebellion against the English occupation. Robert the Bruce (1274–1329), ruler of Scotland (1306–29), won its independence from England. Mary, Queen of Scots (Mary Stuart, 1542–87), a romantic historical figure, is the subject of many plays and novels. Her son James VI (1566–1625) became England's King James I.

Before the union with England, outstanding poets writing in Scottish include Robert Henryson (1425?–1500?), William Dunbar (1460?–1520?), Gavin Douglas (1474–1522), and Sir David Lindsay (1490?–1555). One of the finest Scottish poets was William Drummond (1585–1649). Sir Thomas Urquhart (1611–60) produced a noted translation of Rabelais. John Knox (1514?–72) was the founder of Presbyterianism. David Hume (1711–76) was an outstanding philosopher and historian. Economist and philosopher Adam Smith (1723–90) influenced the development of world economy and politics. James Boswell (1740–95) wrote the brilliant *Life of Samuel Johnson*. The 18th century produced several important poets, notably Allan Ramsay (1686–1758), James Thomson (1700–48), James Macpherson (1736–96), and the national poet of Scotland, Robert Burns (1759–96). A major 19th-century essayist and social critic was Thomas Carlyle (1795–1881). Scottish novelists of prominence include Tobias George Smollett (1721–71); Sir Walter Scott (1771–1832); Robert Louis Stevenson (1850–94), also a poet; John Buchan, first Lord Tweedsmuir (1875–1940); and Sir James Matthew Barrie (1860–1937), who also wrote popular plays.

Distinguished figures who were active primarily in Wales include the 6th-century monk Dewi (d.588?), who became St. David, the patron saint of Wales; Rhodri the Great (844–77), who attained rule over most of Wales and founded two great ruling houses; Howel the Good (Hywel Dda, 910–50), whose reformed legal code became the standard of Welsh law for centuries; the Lord Rhys ap Gruffydd (1155–97), ruler of southern Wales, who founded the national Eisteddfod; Dafydd ap Gwilym (fl.1340–70), a remarkable poet; and Owen Glendower (Owain ap Gruffydd, 1359?–1416), the national hero of Wales, who led a rebellion against English rule. Bishop William Morgan (1541?–1604) made a Welsh translation of the Bible which, with revisions, is still in use. Among literary figures are Ellis Wynne (1671–1734), Daniel Owen (1836–95), and Sir Owen Morgan Edwards (1858–1920).

Two natives of Northern Ireland—Betty Williams (b.1943), a Protestant, and Mairead Corrigan (b.1944), a Roman Catholic—received the Nobel Peace Prize (awarded in 1977) for their leadership of a peace movement in Ulster.

⁴⁹DEPENDENCIES

British overseas dependencies include the British Indian Ocean Territory and St. Helena (described in the *Africa* volume under UK African Dependencies); Bermuda, the British Antarctic Territory, the British Virgin Islands, the Cayman Islands, the Falkland Islands, and, in the Leeward Island group, Anguilla and Montserrat (described in the *Americas* volume under UK American

Dependencies); and Hong Kong and Pitcairn Island (described in the *Asia* volume under UK Asian and Pacific Dependencies). The Turks and Caicos Islands are discussed separately in the *Americas* volume.

Gibraltar

The colony of Gibraltar (5.83 sq km/2.25 sq mi in area), the smallest UK dependency, is a narrow peninsula connected to the southwest coast of Spain. From a low, sandy plain in the north, it rises sharply in the 430-m (1,400-ft) Rock of Gibraltar, a shrub-covered mass of limestone, with huge caves. Gibraltar has a pleasantly temperate climate, except for occasional hot summers. Average annual rainfall is 89 cm (35 in). There is a rainy season from December to May. The resident civilian population, almost entirely of European origin, was 29,651 in 1992. Gibraltar is an important port of call for cargo and passenger ships. There is a major naval base at the northeast gate of the Strait of Gibraltar and a military airfield that is used by private companies. Telegraph, radio, and television are privately operated. The telephone system is government owned.

Known as Calpe in ancient times, Gibraltar was successively occupied by Phoenicians, Carthaginians, Romans, and Visigoths. Its strategic value was recognized early. In AD 711, it was captured by Moors under Tariq, and since then it has been known as Jabal Tariq or Gibraltar. It remained in Moor hands, except for short periods, until Spain took it in 1462. In 1704, a combined English-Dutch fleet captured Gibraltar, and it was officially transferred to Britain by the Treaty of Utrecht in 1713. Since 1964, Spain has tried to negotiate the return of Gibraltar to Spanish control. However, in a referendum held in 1967, Gibraltarians voted overwhelmingly (12,138 to 44) to retain their link with Britain. Since then, Spain has continued to raise the issue at the UN and put direct pressure on the Gibraltarians by closing the land frontier between the peninsula and the Spanish mainland and suspending the ferry service between Gibraltar and Algeciras; the border was reopened to limited pedestrian traffic in December 1982 and fully reopened in February 1985.

Under the 1969 constitution, Gibraltar is governed by a House of Assembly with 15 elected members. The governor (who is also commander of the fortress) retains direct responsibility for defense and external affairs and can intervene in domestic affairs.

Gibraltar is largely dependent on British subsidies, tourist traffic, reexports (largely fuel for shipping), work provided by the former Royal Navy dockyard (which the UK closed in 1984 and which reopened as a commercial ship-repair facility), service departments, the government, and the city council. Local industries are tobacco and coffee processing. The Gibraltar pound is at par with the pound sterling. Exports in 1988 (mainly reexports of petroleum and petroleum products) totaled an estimated US$82 million, and imports US$258 million. Domestic revenue is derived chiefly from customs duties on alcoholic beverages, perfumes, gasoline, and tobacco. Government revenues were US$136 million and expenditures were US$139 million in 1988/89. There is an income tax and an estate duty.

Illiteracy is negligible. Education is compulsory between the ages of 5 and 15. There were 14 government, 2 service, and 1 private primary school in Gibraltar, with 3,585 pupils, in September 1985. There were also 1,643 secondary-level pupils. The language of the home is Spanish, but the medium of instruction in schools is English. The colony has a serious housing shortage.

50 BIBLIOGRAPHY

20th Century British History. Oxford: Oxford University Press, 1990.

Budge, Ian and David McKay (eds.). *The Developing British Political System: The 1990's.* 3rd ed. New York: Longman, 1993.

Cannon, John and Ralph Griffiths. *The Oxford Illustrated History of the British Monarchy.* New York: Oxford University Press, 1988.

The Cambridge History of English Literature. 15 vols. Cambridge: Cambridge University Press, 1964-1968.

Channon, Derek F. *The Strategy and Structure of British Enterprise.* Cambridge, Mass.: Harvard University Press, 1973.

Churchill, Sir Winston. *A History of the English-Speaking Peoples.* 4 vols. New York: Dodd, Mead, 1956–58.

Clarke, Richard. *Anglo-American Collaboration in War and Peace, 1942–1949.* New York: Oxford University Press, 1982.

The Commonwealth Yearbook. London: H. M. Stationery Office (annual).

Cook, Chris. *The Longman Handbook of Modern British History, 1714–1987.* 2d ed. New York: Longman, 1988.

Darby, H. C. (ed.). *A New Historical Geography of England After 1600.* Cambridge: Cambridge University Press, 1978.

———. *A New Historical Geography of England Before 1600.* Cambridge: Cambridge University Press, 1978.

Delderfield, Eric R. *Kings & Queens of England & Great Britain.* New York: Facts on File, 1990.

Dictionary of National Biography. 22 vols. London: Oxford University Press, 1938.

Douglas, Roy. *World Crisis and British Decline, 1929–1956.* New York: St. Martin's, 1986.

Foster, R. F. (ed.). *The Oxford History of Ireland.* New York: Oxford University Press, 1992.

Halsey, A. H. (ed.). *Trends in British Society Since 1900.* New York: St. Martin's, 1972.

———. *British Social Trends since 1900: A Guide to the Changing Social Structure of Britain.* 2d ed. Basingstoke: Macmillan, 1988.

Havighurst, Alfred E. *Britain in Transition: The Twentieth Century.* Chicago: University of Chicago Press, 1979.

———. *Modern England, 1901–1984.* 2d ed. New York: Cambridge University Press, 1987.

Jenkins, Philip. *A History of Modern Wales, 1536–1990.* New York: Longman, 1992.

Kavanagh, Dennis. *British Politics: Continuities and Change.* 2d ed. New York: Oxford University Press, 1990.

Kearney, Hugh F. *The British Isles: A History of Four Nations.* Cambridge; New York: Cambridge University Press, 1989.

Lloyd, Trevor Owen. *Empire, Welfare State, Europe: English History 1906–1992.* 4th ed. New York: Oxford University Press, 1993.

MacLean, Fitzroy. *Scotland: A Concise History Illustrations, Rev. ed.* New York: Thames and Hudson, 1993.

Mills, A. D. *A Dictionary of English Place Names.* New York: Oxford University Press, 1991.

Nolan, Peter, and Suzanne Paine (eds.). *Rethinking Socialist Economics: A New Agenda for Britain.* New York: St. Martin's, 1986.

Norton, Philip. *The British Polity.* 3rd ed. New York: Longman, 1994.

The Oxford History of Britain. New York: Oxford University Press, 1988.

Pearce, Malcolm and Geoffrey Stewart. *British Political History, 1867–1990: Democracy and Decline.* London; New York: Routledge, 1992.

Powell, David. *British Politics and the Labour Question, 1868–1990.* New York: St. Martin's, 1992.

Prescott, Andrew. *English Historical Documents.* London: British Library, 1988.

Sears, Stephen W. (ed.). *The Horizon History of the British Empire.* New York: American Heritage, 1973.

Speck, W. A. *A Concise History of Modern Britain, 1707–1975.* New York: Cambridge University Press, 1993.

VATICAN

The Holy See (State of the Vatican City)

Santa Sede (Stato della Città del Vaticano)

FLAG: The flag consists of two vertical stripes, yellow at the hoist and white at the fly. On the white field, in yellow, are the crossed keys of St. Peter, the first pope, surmounted by the papal tiara (triple crown).

ANTHEM: *Pontifical March* (no words).

MONETARY UNIT: In 1930, after a lapse of 60 years, the Vatican resumed issuance of its own coinage—the lira (L)—but it agreed to issue no more than 300 million lire in any year. There are coins of 10, 20, 50, 100, and 500 lire. Italian notes are also in use. The currencies of Italy and the Vatican are mutually convertible. L1 = $0.0006 (or $1 = L1,611.3).

WEIGHTS AND MEASURES: The metric system is in use.

HOLIDAYS: Roman Catholic religious holidays; the coronation day of the reigning pope; days when public consistory is held.

TIME: 1 PM = noon GMT.

¹LOCATION, SIZE, AND EXTENT

Located within Rome, Vatican City is the smallest state in Europe and in the world. It is a roughly triangular area of 44 hectares (108.7 acres) lying near the west bank of the Tiber River and to the west of the Castel Sant'Angelo. On the w and s it is bounded by the Leonine Wall. The Vatican area comprises the following: St. Peter's Square, enclosed by Giovanni Lorenzo Bernini's quadruple colonnade; St. Peter's Basilica, the largest Christian church in the world, to which the square serves as an entrance; a quadrangular area north of the square in which there are administrative buildings and Belvedere Park; the pontifical palaces, or the Vatican proper, lying west of Belvedere Park; and the Vatican Gardens, which occupy about half the acreage.

Outside Vatican City itself, extraterritoriality is exercised over a number of churches and palaces in Rome, notably the Lateran Basilica and Palace in the Piazza San Giovanni, the Palace of San Callisto at the foot of the Janiculum hill, and the basilicas of Santa Maria Maggiore and San Paolo fuori le Mura. Extraterritoriality outside the city of Rome extends to the papal villa and its environs (almost 40 hectares/100 acres) at Castel Gandolfo, 24 km (15 mi) SE of Rome, and to the area (about 420 hectares/1,040 acres) at Santa Maria di Galeria, some 19 km (12 mi) N of Rome, where a Vatican radio station was established in 1957.

²TOPOGRAPHY

Vatican City lies on a slight hill not far from the Tiber River.

³CLIMATE

Winters are mild, and although summer temperatures are high during the day, the evenings are cold. Temperatures in January average 7°C (45°F); in July, 24°C (75°F). There is little rain from May to September; October and November are the wettest months.

⁴FLORA AND FAUNA

The gardens are famous for their fine collection of orchids and other exotic flora. Vatican City, being entirely urban, does not have a distinctive fauna.

⁵ENVIRONMENT

The environment of Vatican City is similar to that of Rome (See Italy).

⁶POPULATION

The resident population is estimated at about 750. About 400 inhabitants have citizenship, including the pope, cardinals resident in Rome, diplomats of the Vatican, and Swiss Guards.

⁷MIGRATION

Does not apply.

⁸ETHNIC GROUPS

Although the citizenry of the Vatican includes cardinals and other clergymen from all parts of the world, most of the inhabitants are Italian. The members of the Swiss Guard are a notable exception.

⁹LANGUAGES

Italian is the official language of Vatican City, but Latin is the official language of the Holy See (the seat of jurisdiction of the pope as spiritual leader) and is employed for most papal encyclicals and other formal pronouncements. As the ordinary working language, Italian is in greater use.

¹⁰RELIGIONS

Vatican City is the center of the worldwide organization of the Roman Catholic Church and the seat of the pope. Roman Catholicism is the official religion and the primary business of the state itself.

¹¹TRANSPORTATION

Vatican City is easily reached by the public transportation system of Rome. It has its own railroad station, with 850 m (2,789 ft) of track, and a helicopter landing pad.

¹²HISTORY

Since the time of St. Peter, regarded by the Church as the first pope, Rome has been the seat of the popes, except in periods of great turbulence, when the pontiffs were forced to take refuge elsewhere, most notably in Avignon, France, from 1309 to 1377. The Roman papal residence before modern times was usually in the Lateran or Quirinal rather than in the Vatican Palace.

The Vatican City State and the places over which the Vatican now exercises jurisdiction are the sole remnants of the States of the Church, or Papal States, which at various times, beginning in 755, included large areas in Italy and, until the French Revolution, even parts of southern France. Most of the papal domain fell into the hands of King Victor Emmanuel II in 1860 in the course of the unification of Italy. By 1870, Pope Pius IX, supported by a garrison of French troops, retained rule over only the besieged city of Rome and a small territory surrounding it. Upon the withdrawal of the French garrison to take part in the Franco-Prussian War, the walls of Rome were breached by the besieging forces on 20 September, and the city fell. On 2 October, following a plebiscite, the city was annexed to the kingdom of Italy and made the national capital.

In May 1871, the Italian government promulgated a Law of Guarantees, which purported to establish the relations between the Italian kingdom and the papacy. The enactment declared the person of the pope to be inviolate, guaranteed him full liberty in his religious functions and in the conduct of diplomatic relations, awarded an annual indemnity in lieu of the income lost when the Papal States were annexed, and provided the right of extraterritoriality over the Vatican and the papal palaces. Pius IX refused to accept the law or the money allowance; he and his successors chose to become "prisoners of the Vatican." Until 1919, Roman Catholics were prohibited by the papacy from participating in the Italian government.

The so-called Roman Question was brought to an end by the conclusion on 11 February 1929 of three Lateran treaties between the Vatican and Italy. One treaty recognized the full sovereignty of the Vatican and established its territorial extent. Another treaty was a concordat establishing the Roman Catholic Church as the state church of Italy. The remaining treaty awarded the Vatican 750 million old lire in cash and 1 billion old lire in interest-bearing state bonds in lieu of all financial claims against Italy for annexing the Papal States. The constitution of the Italian Republic, adopted in 1947, substantially embodies the terms of the Lateran treaties. In 1962–65, the Vatican was the site of the Second Vatican Council, the first worldwide council in almost a century. Convened by Pope John XXIII and continued under Paul VI, the Council resulted in modernization of the Church's role in spiritual and social matters.

Ecumenism was the hallmark of the reign (1963–78) of Pope Paul VI. In a move to further Christian unity, he met with Athenagoras, the ecumenical patriarch of the Eastern Orthodox Church, in Jerusalem in 1964. In 1973, Paul VI conferred with the Coptic Orthodox patriarch of Alexandria; later in that same year, he met the exiled Dalai Lama, the first such meeting between a pope and a Buddhist leader. Steps were also taken to improve Roman Catholic-Jewish relations, including a 1965 declaration that Jews are not to be held collectively guilty of the death of Jesus. On doctrinal questions Pope Paul VI was generally conservative, reaffirming papal infallibility, disciplining dissident priests, and reiterating traditional Church opposition to all "artificial" methods of contraception, including abortion and sterilization. In September 1972, the concept of an all-male celibate priesthood was upheld. A sign of declining Vatican influence over Italian affairs was the 60% vote by the Italian electorate, in a May 1974 referendum, to retain legislation permitting divorce, which the Church does not sanction.

Pope Paul VI was succeeded by Pope John Paul I, who reigned for only 34 days. John Paul I's sudden death, on 28 September 1978, brought about the election of Polish Cardinal Karol Wojtyla as John Paul II, the first non-Italian pontiff elected in over 450 years. As pope, John Paul II has traveled widely, a practice begun by Paul VI. He has likewise established himself as a conservative in doctrinal matters, as indicated in 1982 by his elevation to the status of personal prelature of Opus Dei, an international organization of 72,000 laity and priests known for its doctrinal fidelity. Pope John Paul II urged Catholic bishops to uphold traditional moral doctrine in a papal encyclical issued in October 1993. The Pope also reaffirmed the male priesthood in 1994. On 13 May 1981, John Paul II was wounded in Vatican Square by a Turkish gunman, who is serving a life sentence. The alleged accomplices, three Bulgarians and three Turks, were acquitted of conspiracy in the assassination attempt on 29 March 1986 because of lack of evidence.

The Lateran treaties of 1929 were superseded in 1984 by a new concordat under which the pope retains temporal authority over Vatican City but Roman Catholicism is no longer Italy's state religion.

In December 1993, the Vatican and the Israeli government concluded a mutual recognition agreement.

¹³GOVERNMENT

The pope is simultaneously the absolute sovereign of the Vatican City State and the head of the Roman Catholic Church throughout the world. Since 1984, the pope has been represented by the cardinal secretary of state in the civil governance of Vatican City. In administering the government of the Vatican, the pope is assisted by the Pontifical Commission for the Vatican City State. Religious affairs are governed under the pope's direction by a number of ecclesiastical bodies known collectively as the Roman Curia.

The Pontifical Commission consists of seven cardinals and a lay special delegate, assisted since 1968 by a board of 21 lay advisers. Under the commission are the following: a central council (heading various administrative offices); the directorships of museums, technical services, economic services (including the postal and telegraph systems), and medical services; the guard; the Vatican radio system and television center; the Vatican observatory; and the directorship of the villa at Castel Gandolfo, the traditional summer residence of popes.

Much of the work of the Roman Curia is conducted by offices called sacred congregations, each headed by a cardinal appointed for a five-year period. These are the Sacred Congregation for the Doctrine of the Faith (responsible for faith and morals, including the examination and, if necessary, prohibition of books and other writings), the Sacred Congregation for Bishops (diocesan affairs), the Sacred Congregation for the Eastern Churches (relations between Eastern and Latin Rites), the Sacred Congregation for the Sacraments, the Sacred Congregation for Divine Worship, the Sacred Congregation for the Clergy, the Sacred Congregation for Religious Orders and Secular Institutes (monastic and lay communities), the Sacred Congregation for the Evangelization of Peoples (missions), the Sacred Congregation for the Causes of Saints (beatification and canonization), and the Sacred Congregation for Catholic Education (seminaries and religious schools). There are also secretariats for Christian unity, non-Christians, and nonbelievers, and there are permanent and temporary councils and commissions for various other functions.

A pope serves from his election until death. On his decease, the College of Cardinals is called into conclave to choose a successor from their number. The usual method is to vote on the succession; in this case, the cardinal who receives two-thirds plus one of the votes of those present is declared elected. Pending the election, most Vatican business is held in abeyance.

Before the reign of Pope John XXIII, the size of the College of Cardinals was limited to 70. Pope John raised the membership to 88, and his successor, Pope Paul VI, increased the number to 136. Paul VI also decreed that as of 1 January 1971, cardinals would cease to be members of departments of the Curia upon reaching the

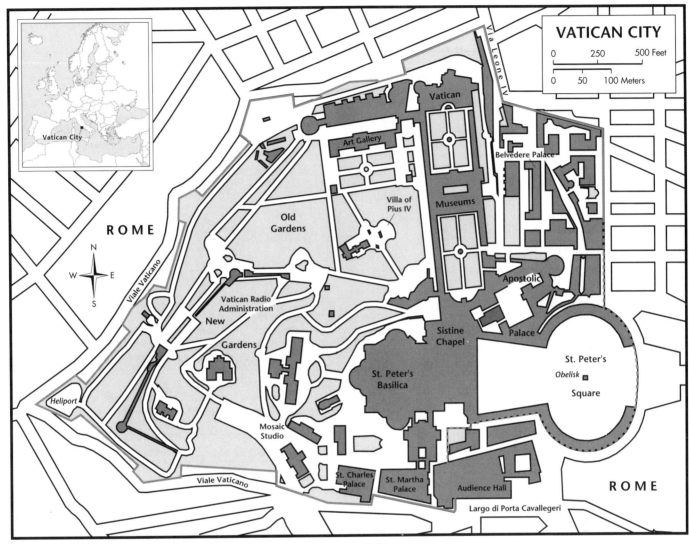

BOUNDARY LENGTHS: Italy, 3.2 km (2 mi).

age of 80 and would lose the right to participate in the election of a pope. As of 15 August 1987, the members of the College of Cardinals numbered 140, of whom 36 were over 80 years old.

¹⁴POLITICAL PARTIES
Does not apply.

¹⁵LOCAL GOVERNMENT
Does not apply.

¹⁶JUDICIAL SYSTEM
For ordinary legal matters occurring within Vatican territory, there is a tribunal of first instance. Criminal cases are tried in Italian courts. There are three tribunals at the Vatican for religious cases. The Apostolic Penitentiary determines questions of penance and absolution from sin. The Roman Rota deals principally with marital issues but is also competent to handle appeals from any decisions of lower ecclesiastical courts. In exceptional cases, the Supreme Tribunal of the Apostolic Signature hears appeals from the Rota, which ordinarily is the court of last resort.

New codes of canon law for the government of the Latin Rite churches and the administration of the Curia were promulgated in 1918 and 1983. Eastern Rite churches have their own canon law.

¹⁷ARMED FORCES
The papal patrol force now consists only of the Swiss Guard, who, sometimes armed with such ceremonial weapons as halberds, walk their posts in picturesque striped uniforms supposedly designed by Michelangelo. The force was founded in 1506 and is recruited from several Roman Catholic cantons of Switzerland. It now numbers approximately 100 members. There is also a civilian security force, responsible to the Central Office of Security, which protects Vatican personnel and property and the art treasures owned by the Church. The Vatican maintains its own jail.

¹⁸INTERNATIONAL COOPERATION
Vatican City's diplomatic relations are conducted by its secretariat of state and the Council for Public Affairs of the Church. Some 120 countries had diplomatic relations with the Vatican.

The Vatican has permanent observer status at the UN, FAO, ILO, OAS, UNESCO, UNIDO, WHO, and WTO. It is a member of IAEA, ICU, INTELSAT, ITU, UNHCR, UPU, WIPO, and WIPP.

¹⁹ECONOMY
The Vatican, being essentially an administrative center, is dependent for its support on the receipt of charitable contributions, the

fees charged those able to pay for the services of the congregations and other ecclesiastical bodies, and interest on investments. Funds are also raised from the sale of stamps, religious literature, and mementos and from museum admissions. Vatican City does not engage in economically productive work in the usual sense.

20INCOME
Income in 1992 was estimated at $92 million.

21LABOR
The labor force consists mainly of priests and other ecclesiastics, who serve as consultants or councilors; about 3,000 laborers, who live outside the Vatican; the guards; the nuns, who do the cooking, cleaning, laundering, and tapestry repair; and the cardinals, archbishops, bishops, and other higher dignitaries. Some ecclesiastical officials live outside Vatican City and commute from the secular city. The Association of Vatican Lay Workers, a trade union, has 1,800 members.

22AGRICULTURE
Does not apply.

23ANIMAL HUSBANDRY
Does not apply.

24FISHING
Does not apply.

25FORESTRY
Does not apply.

26MINING
Does not apply.

27ENERGY AND POWER
Electric power is supplied by Italy, but the Vatican's generating plant had a capacity of 5,000 kw in 1990.

28INDUSTRY
A studio in the Vatican produces mosaic work, and a sewing establishment produces uniforms. There is a large printing plant, the Vatican Polyglot Press.

29SCIENCE AND TECHNOLOGY
The Vatican promotes the study of science and mathematics through the Pontifical Academy of Sciences, which dates, in its present form, from 1936. The Pontifical Vatican Observatory was begun in the late 16th century by Pope Gregory XIII. It has modern instruments, an astrophysics laboratory, and a 33,000-volume library.

30DOMESTIC TRADE
A bakery, butcher shop, and fabric shop were phased out in the 1970s, in accordance with a decommercialization policy.

31FOREIGN TRADE
Does not apply.

32BALANCE OF PAYMENTS
Does not apply.

33BANKING AND SECURITIES
The Vatican bank, known as the Institute for Religious Works (Istituto per le Opere di Religione—IOR), was founded in 1942. It carries out fiscal operations and invests and transfers the funds of the Vatican and of Roman Catholic religious communities throughout the world. The IOR is believed to hold assets between

$3 billion and $4 billion. The Administration of the Patrimony of the Holy See manages the Vatican's capital assets.

34INSURANCE
Does not apply.

35PUBLIC FINANCE
State income is derived from fees paid by the public for visiting the art galleries and from the sale of Vatican City postage stamps, tourist mementos, and publications. The Vatican also receives income in the form of voluntary contributions (Peter's pence) from all over the world, and from interest on investments. The Prefecture for Economic Affairs coordinates Vatican finances. In 1992, the Vatican's income was estimated at $92 million, and its expenditures at $178 million. Voluntary contributions cover much of the deficit.

36TAXATION
Residents of Vatican City pay no taxes.

37CUSTOMS AND DUTIES
Vatican City imposes no customs tariffs.

38FOREIGN INVESTMENT
No recent figures are available.

39ECONOMIC DEVELOPMENT
The Vatican administers industrial, real estate, and artistic holdings valued in the hundreds of millions of dollars. Investments have been in a wide range of enterprises, with makers of contraceptives and munitions specifically excepted.

40SOCIAL DEVELOPMENT
Celibacy is required of all Roman Catholic clergy, except permanent deacons. The Church upholds the concept of family planning through such traditional methods as rhythm and abstinence but resolutely opposes such "artificial methods" as contraceptive pills and devices, as well as abortion and sterilization. Five important papal encyclicals—*Rerum Novarum* (1870), *Quadragesimo Anno* (1931), *Mater et Magistra* (1961), *Pacem in Terris* (1963), and *Laborem Exercens* (1981)—have enunciated the Church position on matters of workers' rights and social and international justice.

41HEALTH
The health services directorate, under the Pontifical Commission for the Vatican City State, is responsible for health matters.

42HOUSING
Information is not available.

43EDUCATION
The Vatican is a major center for higher Roman Catholic education, especially of the clergy being trained for important positions. Adult literacy is 100%. About 65 papal educational institutions are scattered throughout Rome; some of the more important (all prefixed by the word "Pontifical") are the Gregorian University, the Biblical Institute, the Institute of Oriental Studies, the Lateran Athenaeum, the Institute of Christian Archaeology, and the Institute of Sacred Music. There were a total of 11,681 students in 1991 with 1,584 teaching staff in all higher level institutions.

44LIBRARIES AND MUSEUMS
The Apostolic Library of the Vatican is one of the most famous in the world. Founded in 1450 by Pope Nicholas V, the collection includes more than 1,000,000 books, 65,000 manuscripts, 8,000

incunabula, 80,000 archival files, and 100,000 engravings. The Vatican Secret Archives, so called because originally they were strictly private records of the Vatican affairs, were opened to students in 1880.

Besides its 12 museums, some of which figure among the greatest in the world, Vatican City includes as part of its decoration, frescoes painted by Raphael (in the Stanze), Michelangelo (in the Sistine and Pauline Chapels), and other great Renaissance artists. Among the museums in the Vatican are the Pius Clementine, the Chiaramonti, and New Wing (exhibiting antique sculpture); the Gregorian Etruscan and the Gregorian Egyptian museums; the Pinacoteca (paintings); the Collection of Modern Religious Art; the frescoed chapels, rooms, and galleries; and the Sacred and the Profane museums, which are administered by the Vatican Library.

45MEDIA

The state maintains its own telegraph and postal facilities and has a 2,000-line automatic telephone exchange. Radio Vatican, founded in 1931, comprises two facilities, one in Vatican City proper and the other outside Rome at Santa Maria di Galeria. There are three AM and four FM stations; in addition, shortwave broadcasts can reach the entire world. Programs in 34 languages are broadcast regularly. The Vatican Television Center, founded in 1983, produces and distributes religious programs.

Vatican City is an important center for publishing. A semiofficial newspaper of wide fame, *L'Osservatore Romano,* founded in 1861, is published daily, with an estimated 1990 circulation of 70,000 copies. Since 1934, the Vatican has also published *L'Osservatore della Domenica,* an illustrated weekly. The *Acta Apostolicae Sedis (Record of the Apostolic See)* appears regularly on a monthly basis and occasionally at other times; it publishes papal encyclicals and other official papers. An annual, the *Annuario Pontificio,* is issued as a record of the Vatican and the Roman Catholic hierarchy. The international Religious Press Service (Agenzia Internazionale Fides—AIF), founded in 1927, distributes news of missionary activity and publishes *Information* (weekly, in various languages, including English), *Documentation* (irregular), and *Photographic Service* (weekly). In 1990, 47 periodicals were published, with a total circulation of 57,000. The book publishers for the Vatican are the Vatican Editions (Libreria Editrice Vaticana), the Vatican Apostolic Library (Biblioteca Apostolica Vaticana), and the Vatican Polyglot Press (Tipografia Poliglotta Vaticana). In 1991, there were 196 titles published.

46ORGANIZATIONS

The organizations at the Vatican are chiefly learned societies devoted to theology, science, archaeology, liturgy, and martyrology.

47TOURISM, TRAVEL, AND RECREATION

The Vatican is regularly visited by tourists in Rome, as well as by pilgrims attracted by the jubilees proclaimed by the pope every 25 years and by other special occasions. While there are no public accommodations in the Vatican, special inexpensive facilities are often arranged in Rome for pilgrims. No passport or identification is needed ordinarily for admission to the public parts of the Vatican.

48FAMOUS POPES

By virtue of their position of world importance, many popes are persons of fame. Among those who greatly increased the secular power of the papacy were St. Gregory I (the Great, 540?–604), pope from 590 to 604, who also was influential in matters of doctrine, liturgy, and missionary work; St. Gregory VII (Hildebrand, 1020?–1085), pope from 1073 to 1085, who engaged in conflict with Holy Roman Emperor Henry IV, forcing him to do public penance at the village of Canossa, and later was driven from Rome by him; and Alexander VI (Rodrigo Lanzol y Borja, b. Spain, 1431?–1503), pope from 1492 to 1503, who also divided colonial territories in the New World between Spain and Portugal.

The most significant 19th-century pope was Pius IX (Giovanni Maria Mastai-Ferretti, 1792–1878), pope from 1846 to 1878, who lost the Papal States to the kingdom of Italy and convened the First Vatican Council (1869–70), which established the doctrine of papal infallibility in matters of faith and morals. The first popes who reigned since the establishment of the Vatican City State in 1929 were Pius XI (Achille Damiano Ratti, 1857–1939), from 1922 to 1939, and Pius XII (Eugenio Pacelli, 1876–1958), from 1939 to 1958.

John XXIII (Angelo Giuseppe Roncalli, 1881–1963), pope from 1958 to 1963, made history by convening the Second Vatican Council (1962–65), by altering the text of the canon of the mass for the first time since the 7th century, and by strongly defining the position of the Church on problems of labor and social progress (in his encyclical *Mater et Magistra* of June 1961). His greatest achievement was generally considered to be his eighth encyclical, *Pacem in Terris* (issued on 10 April 1963), a profound plea for peace, in which he hailed the UN as a defender of human rights.

Paul VI (Giovanni Battista Montini, 1897–1978), pope from 1963 to 1978, continued Pope John's effort to attain unity of the Christian world. On 4 October 1965, he addressed the UN General Assembly, appealing for world peace and international cooperation. He presided over the concluding sessions of the Second Vatican Council and traveled to many places, including the Holy Land.

Albino Luciani (1912–78), patriarch of Venice, was elected pope on 26 August 1978 and took the name John Paul I. He died on 28 September after a reign of only 34 days. His successor, John Paul II (Karol Wojtyla, b.1920), was elevated to the papacy on 16 October 1978. This former archbishop of Cracow was not only the first Polish pope but also the first non-Italian pope since the Renaissance. Despite suffering severe wounds in a 1981 assassination attempt, John Paul II has continued to travel widely. To the dismay of Jewish and other leaders, John Paul II granted Austrian President Kurt Waldheim (b.1918) an audience in June 1987, despite accusations that Waldheim had taken part in war crimes during World War II when he was an officer in the German army.

49DEPENDENCIES

The Vatican City State has no territories or colonies.

50BIBLIOGRAPHY

Bull, George. *Inside the Vatican.* New York: St. Martin's, 1983.

Chadwick, Owen. *Britain and the Vatican during the Second World War.* New York: Cambridge University Press, 1986.

DH-TE Research Studies. *The Vatican and the Third World: Diplomacy and the Future.* St. Louis: Books International, 1975.

Flamini, Roland. *Pope, Premier President.* New York: Macmillan, 1980.

Hanson, Eric. *The Catholic Church in World Politics.* Princeton: Princeton University Press, 1987.

Jemolo, A.C. *Church and State in Italy, 1850–1950.* Oxford: Basil Blackwell, 1960.

Martin, Malachi. *Vatican.* New York: Harper & Row, 1986.

McDowell, Bart. *Inside the Vatican.* Washington, D.C.: National Geographic Society, 1991.

Nichols, Peter. *The Pope's Divisions.* New York: Holt, Rinehart & Winston, 1981.

Noel, Gerard. *Anatomy of the Catholic Church.* New York: Doubleday, 1980.

Oliveri, Mario. *The Representatives Real Nature and Function of Papal Legates.* Cross, England: Duren-Gerrards, 1980.

Packard, Jerrold M. *Peter's Kingdom: Inside the Papal City.* New York: Scribner, 1985.

Rhodes, Anthony. *The Vatican in the Age of the Dictators, 1922–1945.* New York: Holt, Rinehart & Winston, 1973.

Wynn, Wilton. *Keepers of the Keys.* New York: Random House, 1988.

INDEX TO COUNTRIES AND TERRITORIES

This alphabetical list includes countries and dependencies (colonies, protectorates, and other territories) described in the encyclopedia. Countries and territories described in their own articles are followed by the continental volume (printed in *italics*) in which each appears, along with the volume number and first page of the article. For example, Argentina, which begins on page 7 of *Americas* (Volume 3), is listed this way: Argentina—*Americas* 3:7. Dependencies are listed here with the title of the volume in which they are treated, followed by the name of the article in which they are dealt with. In a few cases, an alternative name for the same place is given in parentheses at the end of the entry. The name of the volume *Asia and Oceania* is abbreviated in this list to *Asia*.

ISBN 0-8103-9883-4

90000

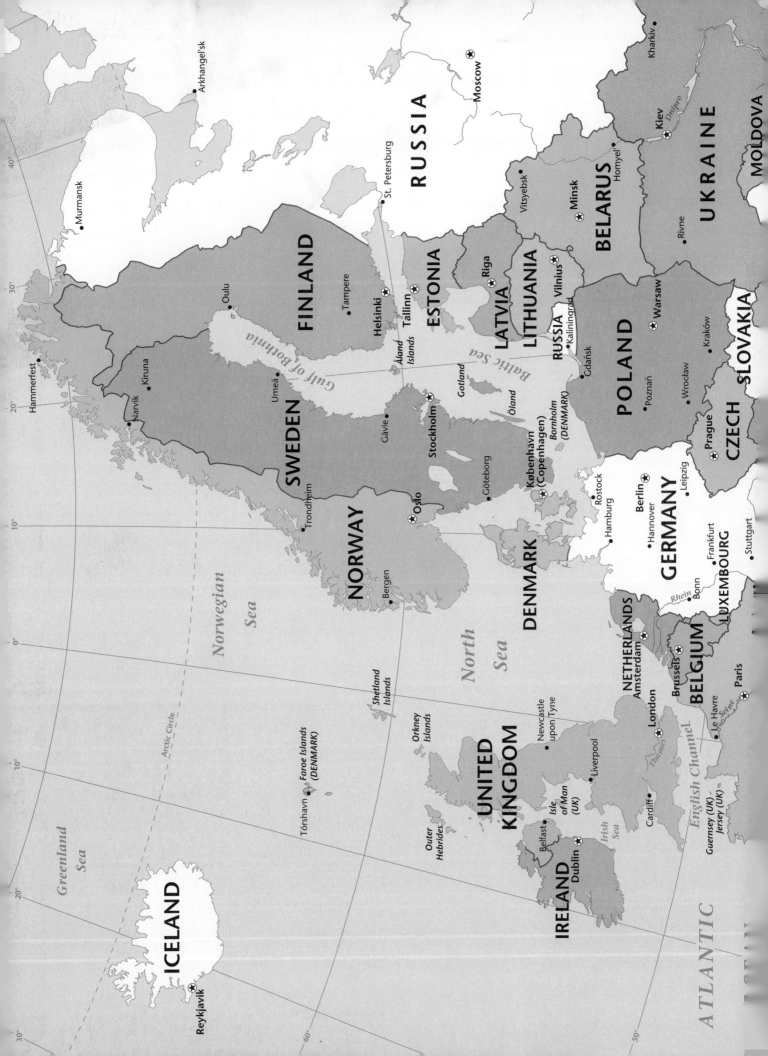